THE

COMPLETE D. D. HOME

Volume I

books written by

DANIEL DUNGLAS HOME

Incidents in My Life first series
First Published 1863

Incidents in My Life second series
First Published 1872

Lights and Shadows of Spiritualism
First Published 1877

This Combined Edition 2007

Published by
SDU PUBLICATIONS
www.sdu3.com
ISBN
1-905961-05-7
978-1-905961-05-4

Printed and bound by CPI Antony Rowe, Eastbourne

Cover picture—Tuscan Sunset
©Steven Upton
D. D. Home lived for sometime in Tuscany, Italy

PUBLISHERS FORWARD

SDU Publications' aim is to reprint books by and about some of the outstanding mediums who demonstrated their abilities during the period 1848 to 1948, the first century of Modern Spiritualism, and thereby keep their names alive.

Daniel Dunglas Home was the foremost physical medium of Modern Spiritualism. He astounded the world for over thirty years and was never shown to be fraudulent. Sometimes holding up to six and seven séances a day, an estimated fifteen hundred during his lifetime, he never once used a cabinet and all of his séances were held in the light.

He demonstrated his abilities in front of the crowned-heads of Europe, including the Emperors of Russia, Germany and France along with a staggering array of Dukes, Lords and Ladies etc. He was also tested extensively by Sir William Crookes, one of the nineteenth centuries' leading scientists. His list of friends and those who were converted to Spiritualism by his mediumship is no less impressive.

During his lifetime he wrote three books (this volume) and later his second wife wrote two more (volume II of this two volume set) about his life, his mission and his achievements. This is the first time all five books have been brought together to form a complete collection.

During the compilation of these two volumes I started listing the types of mediumship and the phenomena that were either claimed by, or attributed to D. D. Home. I know of no other medium who can lay claim to such an extensive list (see appendix at end of book).

D. D. Home's life and achievements have not only impressed me, they have inspired me. I hope they do the same for you.

MINISTER STEVEN UPTON
December 2006

INCIDENTS IN MY LIFE

By

D. D. HOME

First Edition 1863
Second Edition 1864

PREFACE

TO

THE SECOND EDITION

In issuing a Second Edition, I may say a few words to the reader to explain my present views and position, after having had the benefit of all the reviews that have been published on the first edition. These reviews have been to a number and extent unparalleled, I believe, for so simple and unpretending a book, whose only basis is plain matter of fact. My reviewers have been as various as they have been numerous, kind and unkind, truthful and false, wise and foolish, fair and unfair, daily, weekly, and quarterly, English and foreign. They have passed all kinds of verdicts upon the facts, and yet, whether acknowledging or denying, it has never occurred to me to think that what they alleged or argued had altered a single fact or circumstance stated by me. Some of these reviewers appear to believe that they can print facts out of existence, and after reading some of their articles, in which they prove so convincingly that what has happened has not happened, it has been a relief to me to find that the same things happened over again at a sitting, perhaps the same evening, in the presence of ten or half-a-dozen leading members of literary and scientific coteries. It is hard to find oneself in such a pass with reference to testimony. In my book, I have adduced a fair amount of testimony by persons who give their names, and who are so well known that it is a small thing to say of them, that they are, at least, in position and reputation, fully equal to the general run of their critics, and would be so considered at any social gathering. But, by some of the most inveterate of the critics, all their testimony goes for nothing, as not being sufficient in number, and of all that which is vouched only by initials, no account is taken, any more than if I had forged it. Those who, for sufficient or insufficient reasons, have concealed their names, have had small encouragement given them, from seeing the way in which the more courageous witnesses have been treated, and designated as dupes, impostors, credulous simpletons, and persons of no reputation. And because some fear to incur this certain torrent of abuse, and when they have happened to have their eyes open in a room where certain facts have occurred, and have afterwards written their accounts of what they have seen, under initials instead of their full names, reviewers tell us that such things never happened at all. Several of my friends have copies of my book in which all these initials are filled up with the real names; but it is not necessary to have this information, to enable us to form a judgment of such critics. I am rather disappointed at the state of the criticism of the day, which I had not thought was so low.

However, as I am once again coming before the public with this plain, unvarnished statement of some of the "Incidents of My Life," it is fitting I should say that I have nothing to retract or to alter, to extenuate or to apologise for. A wrong date for one of the incidents may pass for what it is worth, and with this exception, I can assure the reader, that each one of the facts I have stated, happened as I have described, and that those who believe the most of what I have narrated will be the nearest to the truth.

An amusing incident occurred a few months after the publication of the first edition. It appears that in addition to his other claims, Sir David Brewster sets up a claim that he alone is gifted with the power of feeling. To me he denies all feeling, and has coarsely and untruly held me up to the public as a cheat and an impostor. But when I prove by documents and independent witnesses his true character, he actually feels it, and complains. It is a pity that he has not discovered, amongst his other great discoveries, that others have feeling as well as himself. The reader shall judge how loudly this gentleman can complain when his own feelings are wounded, and how susceptible he is for himself before the public. The following letter was sent to my publishers by him.

Gentlemen,

My attention has been called to a malignant libel upon my character, published by you in a Book entitled *"Incidents of my Life."* By D. D. Home. That you were aware of this libel is evident from your *"Notes on Books for May,"* in which yon mention the contents of the *Appendix* which is the Libel itself.

It is utterly false that I ever directly or indirectly claimed to be the inventor of the Stereoscope.

It is utterly false that I ever claimed the merit of anything, either done or claimed to have been done, by Mr. Stevenson.

It is also utterly false that I ever claimed any invention made by Fresnel, or any invention made by any other person of which I was not the Author.

As the resident head of the University of Edinburgh, I need not point out to you the effect of such a libel upon my feelings and usefulness.

And having a claim, now under the consideration of the Board of Trade, (The result of the consideration by the Board of Trade of Sir

David's alleged claims has, I have since heard, been unfavourable to him.) for remuneration for my Lighthouse Inventions, and for my services in introducing them, you must have been aware, that in publishing this libel, you inflicted on me a very grave injury.

As Mr. Home is not in England, I am under the necessity of taking such steps against you as my friends may think necessary.

I am,

Gentlemen

Yours truly

(Signed)   D. BREWSTER.

Allerly, Melrose, June 27th. 1863.

To Messrs. Longman and Company.

As Sir David has provoked this discussion, which it would have been much wiser in him to have kept silence about, I will only refer the reader to the crushing account of his doings, which will be found in the 6th Vol. of Arago's complete edition of his works, recently published, where the full account may be seen of the Fresnel, Wheatstone, and other cases. Arago's exposé of Brewster is also contained in the "Annales de Chimie et de Physique," Tome 38, as well as in his complete works. The Stereoscope correspondence with Professor Wheatstone was in the Times of October 1856, and articles upon it of a highly instructive, but not complimentary nature to Brewster, are in the Edinburgh Review for Oct. 1858, and in the Westminster Review for Oct. 1856.

It is a great pity that Sir David Brewster did not bring actions to vindicate his character against the authors of some of these books, or against Dr. Carpenter, against whom he made an abortive threat, instead of attacking me, who am only one of the public forming a judgment of what these great men have written against him. I trust that before he takes "such steps as his friends may think necessary," he will lay before them the works I have here pointed out.

ROME, DECEMBER, 1863.

CONTENTS

INTRODUCTORY REMARKS

[The Introduction is written by a friend. See the note at the commencement of the last chapter.]

Mr. Home's narrative is composed of particulars so much at issue with the ordinary ideas of mankind, that his friends may well feel some apology for it to be necessary. Delicate in health, extremely sensitive in spirit, of gentle and uncombative nature, coming forward with his narration for no conceivable end but to propagate a knowledge of what he regards as important truths, it seems but right that he should be spared as much as possible of the sceptical derision which such novelties are sure in greater or less degree to evoke. Hence the present introductory remarks.

Whatever be the preconceptions of the reader regarding Mr. Home, he will scarcely fail, after reading this volume, to acknowledge that the author writes as a man thoroughly in earnest, and who has himself no doubts of the phenomena which attend him. He tells how these phenomena commenced in his childhood, how they have been with him ever since, except during a few brief intervals; how, while bringing him public notice and some valuable friendships, they have been in some respects, an inconvenience and a misfortune, and betoken conditions that do not promise length of days; all this with an unargumentative simplicity that speaks strongly of at least sincere conviction on his own part. He sustains the character of the Mystic Sensitive throughout his narration, as he has done throughout the first thirty years of his actual life, without falter or hesitation; what he was at the first he is now. It is for those who would attribute all to imposture, to show how a fictitious character can be so perfectly and so enduringly maintained.

It is also to be remarked that the facts of Mr. Home's life do not rest on his own averments alone. Their objective reality and their freedom from delusion and imposture, are certified by an immense number of persons, who are here indicated by name or otherwise. Some of these persons, and others who remain uncited, are of a character to form a strong guarantee for the truth of anything to which they might testify. It is often, indeed, remarked, as a marvel of a very suggestive kind in this our highly intellectual age, that men of knowledge and reflection, of whom so much better things might be expected, are found so weak as to be imposed upon by such transparent deception, and so foolish as to come forward and bear witness in its behalf. But of course this is not reasoning; it is only begging the question. The remark might be answered by another: it is a marvel of a highly suggestive nature, that men of critical judgment should be so far imposed upon by their self-esteem, that they can calmly set down a number of men reputedly as judicious as themselves, and whose judgment they acknowledge, as capable of seeing and hearing that which is not, and never appear to suspect that these persons have possibly some real grounds for the faith that is in them. A little modesty would evidently go a great way to solve the difficulty which the incredulous profess to feel on this point. If they would go a little farther, and so far yield to the behests of their favourite philosophy as to inquire before pronouncing, it might so chance that the position of a believer in these phenomena would become more intelligible to them. So at least it has already happened with a vast number of persons, equally positive at starting that the whole was a delusion; and we are; entitled to assume that what has been, may be again. Nay, the value of the testimony in question in a great measure arises from the very fact, that it has been extorted from the reluctant convictions of a multitude of persons, at one time wholly scornful and incredulous regarding the alleged facts.

It will be rather startling, but yet it may be very plausibly urged, that the phenomena of Mr. Home's mediumship are not opposed to the experience of mankind. On the contrary, facts of this kind have been reported as occurring in all ages; nor is it more than two centuries since they began to be doubted. Even during the two centuries of partial scepticism, they have continued to be reported as happening not less frequently than before. It may be replied, this sceptical voice has been the voice of wisdom and truth, for the first time heard in the world. Is it really so? Is it not rather a dictum expressive only of an intellectual habit—the result of the kind of studies during that time chiefly predominant? Is it not that, in an exclusive and overmastering devotion to material philosophy, men have fallen out of the habit of considering the spiritual part of the world, retaining little more than a nominal faith even in those spiritual things which their religious creed avouches? Clearly the mere fact of two centuries of partial scepticism does not go for much. But then this enlightened spirit has penetrated the mystery in so many cases, and shown it to be based in nothing but vulgar deception. Has it really done so? Has it not simply flattered itself with illusive compliments to its own penetration? One noted instance of a person professedly affected as Mr. Home has been, was Anne Parsons, a little girl living in Cock Lane, in the city of London, in 1762. If there is any case in which detection of imposture is triumphantly and unchallengedly assumed, it is that of the famous Cock Lane Ghost. Mark the facts of the detection. Knockings and scratchings were for a couple of years heard in connection with little Anne Parsons, and at length a mode of conversation with the unseen agent was hit upon. The so-called ghost averred that a woman who recently lived in Parsons' house, and was since dead, had been murdered by her quasi-husband, a Mr. Kent. It was what Mr. Home would have called a lying spirit. The girl being taken to the house of Mr. Alrich, a clergyman, a party was formed to put to the test a promise of the "ghost," that it would knock upon the coffin of the deceased in a vault of St. John's, Clerkenwell, at a certain hour in the evening. No knocks occurred—lying spirit again. Then came the grand stroke in the detection. The girl was taken into a stranger's house, put into a bed hung clear of the floor, and watched for two nights, during which no noises were heard. A result which might be owing merely to the deranged conditions, was held by the sapient committee of investigation as clear proof of imposture; but they were yet to have evidence more positive. Having become impatient with the child, they told her on the third night, that if the knockings were not heard that night, she and her parents would be taken to Newgate! Under this threat, the child took a board into bed with her, was seen to do so, (why was such a thing never seen before?) and soon sounds *admitted to be different from what happened before*, were heard. The bed was then searched, the board found, and the girl proclaimed as a proved impostor. In this clumsy, foolish, and utterly unsatisfactory manner, was the Cock Lane Ghost "detected." On no other grounds has the fallacy of the case become the proverb it now is. Now, if such be the easy terms on which scepticism assumes its greatest triumphs, what importance are we to attach to its pronouncements on this subject in instances less important, and where it has put forth, (as is the general case) less of its strength? Are they worth the air they cost to make them audible?

There is surely, after all, nothing like a serious improbability in the spiritual phenomena. We every hour of our lives have occasion to acknowledge that there is a spirit, an immortal something, in man; we equally believe that this spirit, which does such wonderful things on earth, will survive in some other sphere of existence, and not in a wholly inactive state. Is there anything *à priori* unlikely, in the idea that the spirit, which parts with so much that is dear to it here, may linger in the scenes of its earthly, pilgrimage, and desire to hold intercourse with those remaining behind? On the contrary, it seems rather likely that the "animula vagula, blandula," will hover about its old loves, and, where conditions permit or are favourable, will contrive to make itself again seen or at least heard. It may be a mere effort of the original social nature; or it may, result from a benevolent anxiety for the welfare of individuals—to inform, to guide, and protect them; or it may be a needful part of the frame of things in which humanity, is established on earth—something required to keep us in mind of that world beyond the screen, out of which we have come, and to which we are to return. It has often, indeed, been urged that the spiritual phenomena generally are of a frivolous and useless character, doing little more than show that Spiritualism is a truth. But spiritualists say, on the other hand, that experimenters generally set about their business in a frivolous spirit, and only get communications from shades of their own character. It will be found that, in the case of Mr. Home, who is a man of a religious turn of mind, pure-hearted and unworldly, the phenomena are of an elevated character, tending to heal sickness, to smooth away sorrow, and to chasten and exalt the minds of the living. There is, indeed, every reason to believe that if spiritual communications were now sought in a suitable frame of mind, results in the highest style of sanctitude, rivalling those of the most famous devotees, might be obtained. Already, Spiritualism, conducted as it usually is, has had a prodigious effect throughout America, and partly in the Old World also, in redeeming multitudes from hardened atheism and materialism, proving to them, by the positive demonstration which their cast of mind requires, that there is another world that there is a non-material form of humanity—and that many miraculous things which they have hitherto scoffed at, are true.

There remains a great stumbling-block to many, in the manner in which the communications are most frequently made. It seems below the dignity of a disembodied spirit to announce itself and speak by little pulsatory noises on a table or wainscot. It might, however, be asked if it be not a mere prejudice which leads us to expect that the spirit, on being disembodied, suddenly, and of necessity, experiences a great exaltation. Take the bulk of mankind as they are, and can we really say that there is anything derogatory to them in the supposition that, in any circumstances, they would talk by noise-signals? We must, moreover, remember that we know nothing of the conditions under which spirits can communicate. This may be the most readily available mode in most instances. Beyond doubt, in certain circumstances of difficulty, the most exalted of living persons might be glad to resort to such a mode of telegraphy. In 1823, Signor Andryane, the agent of an Italian conspiracy against Austria, was thrown into the prisons of the police at Milan. He tells us, in his very interesting Memoirs, how, being desirous of communicating with the inmate of an adjoining cell, he tapped gently on the wall, and after some time had his signal answered. "One, two, three—a pause, *a, b, c,* it was *c.* Still listening,—one, two, three, four—eight blows,—it was *h; c h.* Slowly, but distinctly, nine blows were given:

this must mean the letter *i, &c.*" After some difficulties, these two unfortunates succeeded in forming a system of communication, in the highest degree useful and consolatory to them, by raps on the wall, expressive of letters of the Italian alphabet (See "Memoirs of Alexander Andryane," translated by Ferdinando Prandi, 2 vols., 2nd Edition. Newby, London, 1848.)—being precisely the mode of communication so largely (though not exclusively) adopted by the spirits—the favourite subject of ridicule to those who are so unfortunate as to take only a superficial view of this subject, or so unfair as to select what in their ignorance they consider as the weakest point. If the disembodied find a sort of wall interposed between them and the living world with which they desire to communicate, what can be more natural than to resort to the expedient which was embraced in analogous circumstances by these two living prisoners? Short of the use of actual language written or spoken, what better possible mode of communication can be suggested?

There are two points of view in which Mr. Home's publication of his experiences appears entitled to praise as well as sympathy. Regard it simply as a curious case in pathology—for himself to describe it in detail may be considered as a useful service to mankind, just as it would be considered useful to us to obtain the self-portraiture of any other peculiar case of nervous derangement. As already stated, such cases are far from being uncommon; but the intelligence and probity required to apprehend their character truly, and describe it exactly, is rare. To the psycho-pathologist, accordingly, if he can get over the disposition to sneer and laugh, and will condescend to meet a man as honest as himself on his own grounds, this detail may serve to advance an important scientific purpose. Even more valuable is the instruction to be derived from it by the moralist and the philosophical historian. The past is full of such phenomena. Wrongly apprehended in the first place by their recipients, they have been made the bases of juggling arts; of childish mythologies; of superstitious religions; and the means of affecting individuals and multitudes to most mischievous and illogical conclusions in a thousand different ways. Even at the present day, accepted as confirmations of sundry doctrines and pretensions, they become the means of misleading a vast number of well-intending people. While philosophy refuses to see them in their true light, it can do, nothing to abate or prevent the evil in question, for the victim knows too well that the phenomena are not, as philosophy would inculcate, unreal. Let philosophy see them as they are—a part of the universal frame of things, liable like everything else to law, and having a real bearing on the good and evil fortunes of mankind and the weakest would henceforth be safe from all false conclusions to be deduced from them. To this good end the "candid reader" may find Mr. Home's autobiography a valuable contribution.

INCIDENTS IN MY LIFE

CHAPTER I

EARLY LIFE: I BECOME A MEDIUM

I was born, near Edinburgh in March 1833. When I was about a year old, I was adopted by an aunt, and accompanied her and her husband to America when I was about nine years old. I was very delicate as a child, and of a highly nervous temperament; so much so that it was not thought that I could be reared. I cannot remember when I first became subject to the curious phenomena which have now for so long attended me, but my aunt and others have told me that when I was a baby my cradle was frequently rocked, as if some kind guardian spirit was tending me in my slumbers. My aunt has also told me that when I was about four years old, I had a vision of the circumstances attending the passing from earth of a little cousin, I being at Portobello, near Edinburgh, and she at Linlithgow, all which proved to be entirely correct, though I had mentioned persons as being present about her, who it was thought could not have been there, and had noticed the absence of her father on the water, at a time when it was thought that he must be with her at home.

When about thirteen years of age, the first vision which I distinctly remember occurred. I was, from my delicate health, unable to join the sports of other boys of my own age. I had, a few months before the vision which I am about to relate, made the acquaintance of a boy two or three years my senior, and somewhat similar to myself both in character and organization. We were in the habit of reading the Bible together, and upon one occasion, in the month of April, as we had been reading it in the woods, and we were both of us silently contemplating the beauties of the springing vegetation, he turned to me and said, "Oh, I have been reading such a strange story!" and he told me a ghost story connected with the family of Lord _____, and which I have since found to be well authenticated. A portrait of the lady to whom it occurred still exists in the family, and is known as the lady with the black ribbon. The present Lord, who is of the same family, has also told me that he was born in the chamber where the spirit appeared. My friend Edwin asked me if I thought the story could be true, and I said I did not know, but that I had heard strange things of that kind. We then agreed that whichever one of us should first be called from earth, would, if God permitted it, appear to the other the third day afterwards. We read another chapter of the Bible together, and we prayed that so it might be to us. About a month from this time, I went with my family to reside at Troy in the State of New York, a distance from Norwich, where Edwin lived, of nearly three hundred miles. I had been to spend the evening at the latter end of June with some friends, and nothing had occurred during the evening to excite my imagination, or to agitate my mind; on the contrary, I was in a calm state. The family had retired to rest, and I at once went to my room, which was so completely filled with the moonlight as to render a candle unnecessary. After saying my prayers, I was seated on the bed, and about to draw the sheet over me, when a sudden darkness seemed to pervade the room. This surprised me, inasmuch as I had not seen a cloud in the sky; and on looking up I saw the moon still shining, but it was on the other side of the darkness, which still grew more dense, until through the darkness there seemed to be a gleam of light, which I cannot describe, but it was similar to those which I and many others have since seen when the room has been illuminated by spiritual presence. This light increased, and my attention was drawn to the foot of my bed, where stood my friend Edwin. He appeared as in a cloud of brightness, illumining his face with a distinctness more than mortal. His features were unchanged except in brightness, and the only difference I saw was that his hair was long, and that it fell in wavy ringlets upon his shoulders. He looked on me with a smile of ineffable sweetness, then slowly raising the right arm, he pointed, upward, and making with it three circles in the air, the hand began slowly to disappear and then the arm, and finally the whole body melted away. The natural light of the room was then again apparent. I was speechless and could not move, though I retained all my reasoning faculties. As soon as the power of movement was restored, I rang the bell, and the family, thinking I was ill, came to my room, when my first words were, "I have seen Edwin—he died three days ago at this very hour." This was found to be perfectly correct by a letter which came a few days afterwards, announcing that after only a few hours illness, he had died of malignant dysentery.

My mother was a seer throughout her life. She passed from earth in the year 1850, at the age of forty-two. She had what is known in Scotland as the second sight, and in many instances she saw things which were afterwards found to have occurred at a distance, just as she had described them. She also foresaw many events which occurred in the family, and foretold the passing away of relatives, and lastly, she foretold her own four months previously.

I was then seventeen, and was residing at Norwich, Connecticut, and my mother was living at Waterford, near New London, twelve miles distant. One day I suddenly felt a strong impulse that she wished to see me, and I walked all the way in consequence of this impression. When I got home, I felt an impression that she had something particular to communicate to me that evening. When we were alone I turned to her and said, "What have you to say to me, mother?" She looked at me with intense surprise, and then a smile came over her face, and she said, "Well, dear, it was only to tell you that four months from this time, I shall leave you." I asked incredulously how she knew, and she said, Your little sister, Mary, came to me in a vision, holding four lilies in her hand, and allowing them to slip through her fingers one after the other, till the last one had fallen, she said, 'And then you will come to me.' I asked her whether the four lilies signified years, months, weeks, or days, and she told me, 'months.'" I had been deeply impressed by this narration, when my mother added, "and I shall be quite alone when I die, and there will not be a relative near to close my eyes." This appeared to me to be "so improbable, not to say, impossible, inasmuch as the family was a large one, and we had many relatives, that I said to her, "Oh, mother, I am so delighted you have told me this, because it shows that it must be a false vision." She shook her head. Mary was a little sister who had been taken from earth under most trying circumstances about four years previously. My, mother was out for a walk, leaving the child at home, and on returning, having to cross a running stream, and whilst she was on the bridge over it, she saw what appeared to be some loose clothes floating on the water, and hastening to the side to see what it was, she drew out the body of her child.

The apparently impossible prophecy was literally fulfilled, for by a strange complication of circumstances, my mother was taken ill amongst strangers, and a telegram which they sent on the last day of the fourth month, announcing her serious illness, only reached us about half past eleven in the morning. Being myself confined to bed by illness at the house of my aunt, and she being unable to leave me, the telegram was sent on to my father. That same evening, about twilight, being alone in my room, I heard a voice near the head of my bed which I did not recognize, saying to me solemnly, *"Dan, twelve o'clock."* I turned my head, and between the window and my bed I saw what appeared to be the bust of my mother. I saw her lips move, and again I heard the same words, *"Dan, twelve o'clock."* A third time she repeated this, and disappeared from my sight. I was extremely agitated, and rang the bell hastily to summon my aunt; and when she came I said, "Aunty, mother *died today at twelve o'clock*, because I have seen her, and she told me." She said, "Nonsense, child, you are ill, and this is the effect of a fevered brain." It was, however, too true, as my father found on going to see her, that she had died at twelve o'clock, and without the presence of a relative to close her eyes.

My mother has also told me that her great uncle, Colin Urquhart, and her uncle, Mr. Mackenzie, were also seers, and gifted with the second sight.

A few months after my mother had passed from earth, one night on going to bed, I heard three loud blows on the head of my bed, as if struck by a hammer. My first impression was that some one must be concealed in my room to frighten me. They were again repeated, and as they were sounding in my ears, the impression first came on me that they were something not of earth. After a few moment's silence they were again heard, and although I spent a sleepless night, I no longer felt or heard any repetition of them. My aunt was a member of the Kirk of Scotland, and I had some two years previously, to her great disapprobation, become a member of the Wesleyan body, but her opposition was so violent that I left them to join the Congregationalists. On going down to breakfast in the morning, she noticed my wan appearance, and taunted me with having been agitated by some of my prayer meetings. I was about to seat myself at the breakfast-table, when our ears were assailed by a perfect shower of raps all over the table. I stopped almost terror-stricken to hear again such sounds coming with no visible cause; but I was soon brought back to the realities of life by my aunt's exclamation of horror, "So you've brought the devil to my house, have you." I ought here to state that there had then been some talk of the so-called Rochester knockings through the Fox family, but apart from casually hearing of them, I had paid no attention to them; I did not know even what they meant. My aunt, on the contrary, had heard of them from some of the neighbours, and considered them as some of the works of the Evil One. In her uncontrollable anger, she seized a chair and threw it at me. Knowing how entirely innocent I was of the cause of her unfortunate anger, my feelings were deeply injured by her violence, and at the same time I was strengthened in a determination to find out what might be the cause of these disturbances of our morning meal. There were in the village three ministers, one a Congregationalist, one a Baptist, and the other a Wesleyan. In the afternoon, my aunt, her anger at me having for the moment caused her to lose sight of her prejudices against these rival persuasions, sent for them to consult with her, and to pray for me, that I might be freed from such visitations. The Baptist minister, Mr. Mussey, came first, and after having questioned me as to how I had brought these things about me, and finding that I could give him no explanation, he desired that we might pray together for a cessation of them. Whilst we were thus engaged in prayer, at every mention of the Holy names of God and Jesus, there came gentle taps on his chair, and in different parts of the room; whilst at every expression of a wish for God's loving mercy to be shown to us and our fellow-creatures, there were loud rappings, as if joining in our heartfelt prayers. I was so struck, and so impressed by this, that there and then, upon my knees, I resolved to place myself entirely at God's disposal, and to follow the leadings of that which I then felt must be only good and true, else why should it have signified its joy at those special portions of the prayer? This was, in fact, the turning point of my life, and I have never had cause to regret for one instant my determination, though I have been called on for many years to suffer deeply in carrying it out. My honour has been called in question, my pride wounded, my worldly prospects blighted, and I was turned out of house and home at the age of eighteen, though still a child in body from the delicacy of my health, without a friend, and with three younger children dependent on me for support. Of the other two clergymen, the Congregationalist would not enter into the subject, saying that he saw no reason why a pure-minded boy should be persecuted for what he was not responsible to prevent or cause, and the Methodist was so unkind, attributing it to the devil, and treating me as a lost sheep, that I derived no comfort from him.

Notwithstanding the visits of these ministers, and the continued horror of my aunt, which only increased as each manifestation was developed, the rappings continued, and the furniture now began to be moved about without any visible agency. The first time this occurred I was in my room, and was brushing my hair before the looking-glass. In the glass I saw a chair that stood between me and the door, moving slowly towards me. My first feeling was one of intense fear, and I looked round to see if there were no escape; but there was the chair between me and the door, and still it moved towards me as I continued looking at it. When within about a foot of me it stopped, whereupon I jumped past it, rushed down stairs, seized my hat in the hall, and went out to ponder on this wonderful phenomenon.

After this, when sitting quietly in the room with my aunt and uncle, the table, and sometimes the chairs, and other furniture, were moved about by themselves in a singular way, to the great disgust and surprise of my relations. Upon one occasion, as the table was being thus moved about of itself, my aunt brought the family Bible, and placing it on the table, said, "There, that will soon drive the devils away;" but to her astonishment the table only moved in a more lively manner, as if pleased to bear such a burden. Seeing this, she was greatly incensed, and determining to stop it, she angrily placed her whole weight on the table, and was actually lifted up with it bodily from the floor. My only consolation at this time was from another aunt, a widow, who lived near, whose heart-felt sympathy did much to cheer and console me. At her house, when I visited her, the same phenomena occurred; and we there first began to ask questions, to which we received intelligent replies. The spirit of my mother at her house in this way communicated the following: "Daniel, fear not, my child, God is with you, and who shall be against you? Seek to do good: be truthful and truth-loving, and you will prosper, my child. Yours is a glorious mission—you will convince the infidel, cure the sick, and console the weeping." This was the first communication I ever received, and it came within the first week of these visitations. I remember it well. I have never forgotten it, and can never forget it while reason and life shall last. I have reason to remember it too, because this was the last week I passed in the house of the aunt who had adopted me, for she was unable to bear the continuance of the phenomena, which so distressed her religious convictions, and she felt it a duty that I should leave her house, and which I did.

One of the singular manifestations which occurred during this first week, was in connexion with Mrs. Force, a neighbour. I should mention that by this time the neighbours had heard of what was occurring in my presence, and were besieging the house in a way that did not tend to sooth the religious susceptibilities of my aunt. Being one evening at the house of Mrs. Force, the raps were heard, and the alphabet was used in the way that has now become familiar to many. The name of her mother was in this way given, announcing her presence, and words were spelt out, reproaching her with having so long forgotten her half-sister, who had been married some thirty years previously to a farmer, who removed to the far west, and had not since been heard of. Her mother went on by means of the alphabet and the raps, to state the name of the town where this daughter by a former husband lived, the number of their children, and each of their names. Mrs. Force wrote to the address thus given, and received a letter in reply confirming every particular; and the family was in this way again brought together, and mutual sympathies were interchanged. On visiting Mrs. Force the following year, I found that she had had one of her newly found nephews to visit her the previous autumn.

I go into these particulars not to revive or to cause painful recollections to any one, but merely to show the history of my mediumship, and the mysterious working of Providence in thus throwing me before the public. Had it not been for this chain of circumstances, these truths might have remained unknown so widely as they now are.

Although the manifestations had only lasted a week, they had become known not only to the town, but through the newspapers they were becoming public all over the New England States; and when I left my aunt's house, I went to a neighbouring town, Willimantic, and was received at the house of a friend there. Whilst I was with him, these phenomena were repeated, and those present investigated them in the most determined manner. I find the following account of what occurred stated in a newspaper of March, 1851.

"At request, the table was moved repeatedly, and in direction that we asked to have it. All the circle, the Medium included, had their hands flat upon the table, and we looked several times under the table while it was in the most rapid motion, and saw that no legs or feet had any agency in the movement. The table was a large and heavy one, without castors, and could not be moved by Mr. Hayden in the same manner by all his exertion with his hands laid open upon the table. At one time, too, the table was moved *without the Medium's hands or feet touching it at all.* At our request, *the table was turned over into our lap.* The table was moved, too, *while Mr. Hayden was trying to hold it still!* Mr. Hayden took hold of the top at first, and failing that way, he grasped the leg, and held with all his strength. The table did not move so freely as before. It would move a little way from Mr. Hayden, and then the invisible power would suddenly relax its effort, when it would spring back with the exertion of Mr. Hayden."

I was then eighteen years old, and on seeing this article which made me so public, I shrank from so prominent a position with all the earnestness of a sensitive mind; but I now found myself finally embarked without any volition of my own, and indeed, greatly against my will, upon the tempestuous sea of a public life. From this time I never had a moment to call my own. In sickness or in health, by day or night, my privacy was intruded on by all comers, some from curiosity, and some from higher motives. Men and women of all classes, and all countries; physicians and men of science, ministers of all persuasions, and men of literature and of art, all have eagerly sought for the proofs of this great and absorbing question of the possibility of spiritual causes acting on this world of nature. For myself, I have no apology to offer for the occurrence of these unwonted manifestations in my own case. As will have been seen, they came to me quite unsought, and with all the unpleasant and painful accompaniments which I have described. I have not, and never had the slightest power over them, either to bring them on, or to send them away, or to increase, or to lessen them. What may be the peculiar laws under which they have become developed in my person, I know no more than others. Whilst they occur I am not conscious of the mode by which they are produced, nor of the sort of manifestations that is about to occur. Any peculiar sensations that I may experience during certain of the manifestations, I will describe as far as I can, while mentioning the visions or external phenomena. Beyond being of a highly nervous organization, there is nothing peculiar about me that I am aware of; but I continue to have delicate health, and I firmly believe that had it not been for these phenomena, I could not have lived till now. In this belief many physicians of high standing have given their testimony to bear me out. Frequently during the most severe visitations of illness, my pains have been suddenly soothed in a mysterious way, and many times when it would have been impossible to have moved me in bed, for fear of increased hæmorrhage from the lungs, my head has been slowly lifted, and my pillow has been turned by unseen hands. This has been repeatedly witnessed by many persons. Especially, I would say, that I do not on this account or on any other, consider myself morally superior to others, nor should any one believe that these phenomena come to me, or to others, on account of moral or immoral qualities. On the contrary, with the great blessings which have been showered on me, and the ineffable proofs which I have received of God's providence and goodness to me, I feel myself only worse than others that I should have made so little progress in the path of good. I have to thank God for many kind friends, not less than for many bitter enemies, since they keep my mind in an equilibrium, and do not suffer me to feel any pride, at what is no doubt but an accident, so to speak, of my organization.

These extraordinary occurrences have, with some exceptions, continued with me ever since the time I have stated as their commencement, and they have extended their range, to my astonishment not less than to that of others, in the most striking manner. They have proved to me and to thousands of careful and able investigators, the existence of spiritual forces which are calculated to revolutionize the current ignorance both of philosophy and of theology, as men have made them. The exceptions to which I refer have been of periods during which the power has left me entirely; for instance, from the 10th of February, 1856, to the 10th of February, 1857, during which time I had external token of spirit power, though I on several occasions had visions, one of which was my seeing the manner in which a brother passed from earth. He was frozen in the Polar Seas whilst out bear-shooting, with the captain and officers of his ship. Falling into a fissure of the ice, he was not found till the following morning. I saw all this in a vision at the very time of its occurrence, and informed my family of it five months before the confirmation of the intelligence arrived. On several other occasions, the power has ceased for shorter periods, and generally I have been told before-hand, both of the times of its cessation and return. I could never detect any physical cause for such cessation, nor any difference in my general feelings or health, although the reason given for the withdrawal has commonly been on the ground of health. Upon several occasions, however, the reason given was that it was withdrawn from me as a reproof for having done that which I knew to be wrong.

CHAPTER II

BEFORE THE WORLD

I remained in Willimantic but a short time, and then I went to Lebanon, a few miles off. There I was received in the family, of an old resident. After I had been with them a few days, I saw a spirit who called himself Uncle Tilden. I asked a lady, a member of the family, if she recognized the name, but before she had time to make answer, the spirit made signs to me that he did not wish the lady to tell the name, and that he would come on another occasion to me, when he could have more perfect control. In the course of a few days he came whilst I was entranced, and signified that certain papers which his family had been seeking for years, and for which they had given up the search as hopeless, would be found in a house which he described as situate near Cleveland, Ohio. They were the title-deeds of some land which had become valuable for building purposes, and out of which a lady was entitled to her thirds, but which by reason of the loss of the deeds, were withheld from her, and she was in consequence living in very straitened circumstances. He described to them minutely through me the part of the garret, and the form of the box in which they would be found. Her son was written to with these particulars; the search was made, and the deeds were found as described.

The second week of my stay at Lebanon, I had been to pass a day or two with an English family residing about three miles off. One afternoon I suddenly became unconscious or entranced, and on awaking, the lady of the house told me that I had been speaking with some spirit, who directed me to proceed at once to the house of a Mr. B____. I had seen two brothers of this name one evening a week previously, and no interchange of visits had been made or proposed, and I felt that it would be most awkward for me to call on them, saying only that I had been sent by my unseen friends. The distance was also six miles from where I then was, and three miles of the journey I would have to walk. I knew that when I returned to my friends at Lebanon, I could have their conveyance; but still I had not any inclination to pay the visit. As soon as this was fully decided in my mind, I was again made unconscious, and on recovering, I was told that I had received strict injunctions to leave at once, though no reason was assigned why I should go. I then felt, however, that the order ought to be obeyed, and I went to my room for the purpose of dressing for the journey. While there, my reasoning faculties again assumed the ascendancy, and I thought that if I were thus sent, I ought at least to know for what purpose. However, I soon, again felt myself impelled by a force far superior to mine, and which to have even attempted to resist would have been folly. On leaving the house, all this left me, and I walked the three miles to Lebanon, wondering what could be the cause of this singular errand. On arriving, I stated to my friends there all that had occurred, and they also thought it would have been quite as well to have ascertained why I had been sent. Finding that they agreed with me in this, I now again fully determined to proceed no farther, but I was quickly made insensible, and on awaking I found that orders had been given by the family to have a horse saddled, and that I was admonished in a gentle but firm manner, for my want of Faith and overweening curiosity, whereas I ought, I was told, to have followed as a child would its teacher, or an indulgent parent.

Before I left the house to complete the journey, the sun had set, and now rain laden clouds were fast overshadowing the sky. The road was lonely, and for the month of April weather was uncommonly chill. I had agreed in my mind that my guardians had been teaching me a useful lesson, and I resolved that thenceforward I would not seek to know their purposes. In this frame of mind I reached what I knew from description must be the house of Mr. B____, and as I was about to dismount, the first rain drop fell on my ungloved hand, and with the contact came the most vivid impression that Mr. B____'s mother was dangerously ill. I rang the bell, and Mr. B____ having seen me, came himself to open the door. As he did so, I said, "Your mother is ill, and I have been sent to say what will relieve her." His look of intense surprise baffles description, as he said, "How on earth could you have known of her illness, as it is only an hour since she fell ill, and we have sent in another direction for a medical man, but I fear he will not arrive in time to save my poor mother, as she seems sinking so rapidly." On entering the house, I stood waiting to see what impression I might receive. Whilst I was standing, I was thrown suddenly into a trance, and I was told by Mr B____ that in that state I led the way to his mother's bed-room, and that after making a few passes over her with my hands, the acute pains left her, and that in a few minutes time she was in a quiet sleep. Whilst in the trance, I also mentioned simple remedies of herbs for immediate use, and others for continued use. I was then led by the unseen power into the sitting room, and there returned to my normal states greatly surprised when these things were related to me. The doctor arrived in about an hour, to find his patient quite out of danger, and on examining her, he said that from the nature and violence of the attack, it would in all probability have been fatal, had steps not been taken at once to alleviate the symptoms. A letter written a few weeks after to a friend by Mr. B____, says that his "mother has not had such health for eighteen years past, as she now enjoys; she follows implicitly all the instructions given through Daniel, and the effect is magical."

I remained in Lebanon till the month of June, having séances nearly every day, my mediumship principally consisting of visions, movements of the table and of furniture without my touching them, and of the rapping sounds through which intelligent messages were received. Whilst there, in the beginning of June, all these external manifestations ceased entirely, and I left Lebanon about the middle of June on a visit to Mr. G____ at Boonton, New Jersey. I had still visions frequently of the spirit friends of persons who were perfect strangers to me, describing their appearance; and the spirits gave me their names, and the dates of their departure from earth, with answers to other questions of a test nature which their relatives asked. These came to me whilst I was in an abnormal or trance state, and in which I was unconscious of natural surroundings, but with a facility of speech far superior, as I was told, to that of my ordinary condition, and through which I transmitted with readiness the replies of the spirits to the questions asked of them. I was so exceedingly sensitive at this time, that the playing of sacred music would frequently throw me into the trance state, in which I am always in companionship with spirit friends, and that in as perfect and palpable a manner, as in my ordinary external state I am with friends of this world. Through these means hundreds of persons became convinced of the truth of spiritual communion, and found their sceptical tenets no longer available. I then found, as I still find, that all honest, deep-rooted scepticism rather calls out than prevents the proofs of which it stands so much in need; and atheists, deists, and infidels were thus often brought to a belief in Providence and direct spirit guidance.

About the middle of July 1851, I went to Brooklyn, New York, on a visit to Mr. C____. Whilst here I had the pleasure of first meeting the learned and good George Bush, an eminent theologian and Professor of Hebrew and Oriental languages at New York. Professor Bush was quite prepared to acknowledge the possibility of such phenomena from his acquaintance with the writings of Swedenborg, and with the subject of Mesmerism, and the spiritual experiences of Jung Stilling and others. He was also a profoundly learned man, with a more open and child-like mind than often falls to the lot of those with so much worldly knowledge. He had made, moreover, the greatest sacrifices, by giving up his worldly prospects in the Church, in consequence of avowing his belief in Swedenborg's works. Professor Bush took a deep interest in observing the mental phenomena which occurred through me, though there were no external manifestations. The communications he received were of such a nature as to leave no manner of doubt on his mind, as to the real presence with us of those who had gone before. Amongst other names, he told me that I had given him that of an old school-fellow, whom he had forgotten for many years, and that this school-fellow referred to a dream which the Professor had had on the very night on which the boy had passed from earth, although he was not then aware even of the boy's illness. The spirit of the boy now told through me the whole of the Professor's dream, which was that whilst they were playing together, he suddenly saw his school-fellow taken from him, and heard his voice saying, "I leave you, George, but not for ever." A dream of forty years previously, was thus brought to his remembrance. The Professor was so strongly impressed with this, that he called an me the next day, and wished to have me reside with him for the purpose of studying for the Swedenborgian ministry. I went to his house, with the intention of so doing, but within forty-eight hours I saw in my waking state the spirit of my mother, who said to me, "My son, you must not accept this kind offer, as your mission is a more extended one than pulpit preaching." On seeing the good Professor, I told him of this spirit message. He expressed regret, but no surprise, and so I returned to my friend, Mr. C____, and remained with him till the end of August. I frequently afterwards saw Professor Bush, with whom the most kindly intercourse was interchanged. Here again in New York many were convinced.

I returned to Lebanon, but I was not able to see any on account of my very delicate health, and in the of September my young friend, the son of Mrs. E____ fell ill, and I saw the spirit of his father, whom I had not known on earth, though I had frequently seen him, and received communications from him both in the trance and waking state, on my former visit to Lebanon. He came to me whilst I was alone in my room, and standing near me, said, "Ezra will be with me within three weeks— go to him." I was then staying with a Mr. F____, about three miles from the boy. I obeyed the spirit message, and went at once, and found Ezra ill. He wished me to stay with him, but the family thought it was a passing illness, and that I might prolong my visit for a few days to Mr. F. I did not tell them what I had seen, and in about four days afterwards they sent for me to come to them, as Ezra was worse. I went, and with his sister I took care of him, till his departure, which occurred on the nineteenth day of his illness. He was about eighteen, and had become conversant with the facts of spirit intercourse through me a few months before, and had himself become a partial medium, receiving occasional communications, principally from his father, by means of the rapping and the alphabet. Soon after my first visiting him in his illness, on his sister leaving the room for a moment, he took the opportunity of telling me with perfect composure, that he knew he should not recover, as he had been told by raps on his pillow, by his father, that this was his last illness. This extraordinary composure remained with him throughout, and I had told the family ten days before of my vision, which prepared them for the coming change. About two days before his leaving us, the doctor asked me to break it to him, when I informed him that Ezra had been long aware of it. He doubted this, from seeing him so composed, and I desired him to stand at the door and hear what I would say to Ezra. I then went to his bed, and told him that the doctor had left some news for him. He laughingly said, "I suppose it is to tell me that I am going. Little does he imagine that I have already decided who my bearers are to be." The doctor now came into the room, and taking his hand, said, "My dear boy, if I had not heard this, I could not have believed it. You have everything to make life happy, and yet you are so willing to leave it." A few hours after this, a deacon of the church visited him, who was much opposed to these things, to the extent even of telling untruths and misrepresentations. He argued with the dying boy, trying to take away his happy belief, but fortunately without the slightest success. The boy told him that he willingly placed all his hope in the hands of an all wise God, and that he felt that the change would be most happy for him. The last evening of his stay on earth, several persons came to the house, and I was told by one of them that it was for the purpose of watching to see if he did not recant or turn coward at the last. I told this to Ezra, and he requested that they should be brought into his room, where I left them for a few hours' rest. At half-past one in the morning, Ezra sent for me, and I found them still there, he having been speaking with them great part of the time. In speaking to his mother, he said, "Only think, dear mother, I shan't be lame there." He had been lame since he was six months old. He asked me to look out of the window, and to tell him what kind of morning it was. I told him it was bright moonlight, and he recalled to me a conversation we had had some months previously, in which he said he should like to pass away in the moonlight, whilst I had said I should wish to go at sunset. He expressed a wish that no one should wear mourning for him. He asked me to take his hand, and whilst I held it, his face suddenly assumed a beatified expression, and he pronounced my name, as if calling me to witness some happy vision passing before his eyes, and the breathing ceased.

This is one of the many happy death-beds which I have witnessed, and such consolation given at a time like this is sufficient proof of the loving wisdom of our Heavenly Father in allowing such things to take place. Some may be surprised to find an apparent prophecy in this case given both to the boy and to me, but perhaps a larger view of spiritual insight may teach us that such is only apparent to us in this natural sphere, and that to those who have spiritual insight and perceptions, there probably was some bodily change in his organism which made clear to those in the spiritual state the mortal character of his disease. Since his departure, he has been frequently present with me, impressing me to write messages to his mother and sister. Sometimes my hand has been taken possession of apparently by him, and used in writing his own autograph. In a letter received from his sister dated the 9th of February, 1852, she says, "Ezra was with you to a certainty when you were writing, for that is his autograph and chirography; the kindness of the advice almost overwhelms me, when I think how spirits watch over and comfort us."

The following is an account taken from a newspaper of other manifestations at this time.

"After several communications had been spelled out, a request was made that the table might be moved, in order to convince some present who were sceptical. Accordingly very soon slight movements were perceptible, which soon became very rapid. A light was placed upon the floor under the table, and one remained on the table. Our hands were raised so that the ends of our fingers only touched. One end was then moved up so that it was poised on the two opposite legs upon an elevation in the floor, and in this position it remained for awhile, keeping time with music, by rocking; and in the same way questions were answered, three movements being considered an affirmative, and one a negative; and after numerous questions were given and as many satisfactory answers received, three gentle raps were heard at the door by a part of the company, and the question was asked if any one was rapping at the door? and immediately three decided movements of the table were made, and accompanying them were three more decided raps at the door.

"An emphatic call for the alphabet followed, and spelled out, Spirits—Door;' the question was asked if there were spirits at the door who wished to come in? Three raps.

"It was suggested that they were to help in moving the table, and an affirmative reply immediately followed. Then commenced larger and more decided movements—the table being slid freely about the floor, and raised alternately one side and then the other several inches; and at one time it was raised nearly to an angle of forty-five degrees, poised on two side legs, and then by oscillating movements the time was correctly kept to several tunes sung by the company.

"Several unsuccessful attempts were made to bring the table to the floor, which were relinquished for the fear of breaking the leaves. By request it was carefully let down on to one side, and in a moment raised again to its proper position. One of the company then seated himself upon the table, and it was moved about and raised up so as to render it necessary for him to hold on, and this, too, with as much ease apparently as before. Again, by request, it was slid while one was pushing against it in an opposite direction to the utmost of his strength."

I remained in Lebanon up to the end of January, 1852; the physical manifestations having spontaneously returned in October previously, and with increased power, and with the new phase of unseen hands touching me and others with whom I was sitting. We frequently were touched by them, and on some occasions a spirit hand was placed within our hands as palpably as if it were a real living hand, though invisible to us. It would remain quietly in our hands until we tried to close them upon it, and even then it was not withdrawn, but as it were melted away in our grasp.

I went to Springfield, Massachusetts, an entire stranger, but having heard of Mr. Henry Gordon, a medium there, I asked for and was directed to his house. He receive me most kindly, and said that he was about to have a séance that evening, requesting me to join them. I did so, but the contending influences prevented the occurrence of manifestations. Those who were there assembled had to leave at an early hour, and Mr. Gordon accompanied them, leaving me with five or six of his friends who had come in in the meantime. Among these were Mr. and Mrs. Elmer, the former being a believer, but Mrs. Elmer having violently opposed it. I was thrown into a trance, made to sit near her, telling her the names of her mother, father, brothers, and sisters; then of her children, all of whom were in the spirit world; and I repeated to her the last words of two of her children. Turning to an older lady in the room, I did the same and so on through all those who were present. Mr. and Mrs. Elmer have since been my friends, and at their house some most remarkable manifestations occurred. I stayed with them for some time, and great interest was excited by the accounts given by the very numerous witnesses who came to see the manifestations. Whilst here the power was very strong, and frequently I had séances six or seven times a day, at each of which as many were present as could be accommodated. Their house was besieged by visitors, and often outside in the street there was a concourse of anxious inquirers. People came from a distance, even from the extreme west and south of America, having seen the accounts given of me in the newspapers of the previous year. It was here that one of the Professors of the University of Harvard came and joined some friends in a rigid investigation of the phenomena, and after several sittings they published the following statement of the result of their investigations.

THE MODERN WONDER—A MANIFESTO

The undersigned, from a sense of justice to the parties referred to, very cordially bear testimony to the occurrence of the following facts, which we severally witnessed at the house of Rufus Elmer, in Springfield, on the evening of the 5th inst:—

1. The table was moved in every possible direction, and with great force, when we could not perceive any cause of motion.

2. It (the table) was forced against each one of us so powerfully as to move us from our positions—together with the chairs we occupied—in all, several feet.

3. Mr. Wells and Mr. Edwards took hold of the table in such a manner as to exert their strength to the best advantage, but found the invisible power, exercised in an opposite direction, to be quite equal to their utmost efforts,

4. In two instances, at least, while the hands of all the members of the circle were placed on the top of the table—and while no visible power was employed to raise the table, or otherwise to move it from its position—*it was seen to rise clear of the floor, and to float in the atmosphere for several seconds, as if sustained by some denser medium than air.*

5. Mr. Wells seated himself on the table, which was rocked for some time with great violence, and at length, it poised itself on the two legs, and remained in this position for some thirty seconds, when no other person was in contact with it.

6. Three persons, Messrs. Wells, Bliss and Edwards assumed positions on the table at the same time, and while thus seated, the table was moved in various directions.

7. Occasionally we were made conscious of the occurrence of a powerful shock, which produced a vibratory motion of the floor of the apartment in which we were seated—it seemed like the motion occasioned by distant thunder or the firing of ordnance far away—causing the table, chairs, and other inanimate objects, and all of us to tremble in such a manner that the effects were both seen and felt.

8. In the whole exhibition, which was far more diversified than the foregoing specification would indicate, we were constrained to admit

that there was an almost constant manifestation of some intelligence which seemed, at least, to be independent of the circle.

9. In conclusion, we may observe, that Mr. D. D. Home, frequently urged us to hold his hands and feet. During these occurrences the room was well lighted, the lamp was frequently placed on and under the table, and every possible opportunity was afforded us for the closest inspection, and we admit this one emphatic declaration: *We know that we were not imposed upon nor deceived.*

WM. BRYANT,
B. K. BLISS,
WM. EDWARDS,
DAVID A. WELLS.

The following account also is given in the "Shekinah" of 1852, of manifestations occurring at this time, which will show the power which they had then acquired.

"On the 28th day of February, 1852, while the undersigned were assembled at the residence of Mr. Rufus Elmer, Springfield, Mass., for the purpose of making critical experiments in the so-called spiritual manifestations, the following, among other remarkable demonstrations of power, occurred in a room thoroughly illuminated. The table, around which we were seated, was moved by an invisible and unknown agency, with such irresistible force that no one in the circle could hold it. Two men—standing on opposite sides and grasping it at the same time, and in such a manner as to have the greatest possible advantage—could not, by the utmost exercise of their powers, restrain its motion. In spite of their exertions the table was moved from one to three feet. Mr. Elmer inquired if the Spirits could disengage or relax the hold of Mr. Henry Foulds; when suddenly, and in a manner wholly unaccountable by us, Mr. Foulds was seated on the floor at a distance of several feet from the table, having been moved so gently, and yet so instantaneously, as scarcely to be conscious of the fact. It was proposed to further test this invisible power, and accordingly five men, whose united weight was *eight hundred and fifty-five pounds* stood on a table (without castors) and the table, while the men were so situated, was repeatedly moved a distance of from four to eight inches. The undersigned further say that they were not conscious of exerting any power of will at the time, or during any part of the exhibition; on the contrary they are quite sure that the exercise of the will is a serious impediment to such manifestations.

"At the close of these experiments it was perceived, on lifting one end of the table, that its weight would increase or diminish, in accordance with our request. Apprehending that the supposed difference might be justly attributable to fancy, or to some unconscious variation in the manner of applying the motive power, it was proposed to settle the question by weighing the end of the table. At the first experiment it required a force equal to nineteen pounds to raise the end of the table. This was fairly tested to the entire satisfaction of all present. The spirits were then requested to apply the invisible power. The balance was now applied in precisely the same manner as before, when the weight was found to have been suddenly increased from six to twelve pounds, varying as the mysterious force was increased and diminished, so that it now required a force of from twenty-five to thirty-one pounds to separate the legs of the table from the floor. Mr. Daniel D. Home was the medium on this occasion, and it is worthy of remark that during the performance of the last experiment, he was out of the room, and in the second story of the house, while the experiment was conducted in the back parlour below.

"The undersigned are ready and willing, if required, to make oath to the entire correctness of the foregoing statement."

The original paper was signed by John D. Lord, Rufus Elmer, and nine others, living at Springfield, Mass.

The account proceeds: "Lights are produced in dark rooms. Sometimes there appears a gradual illumination, sufficient to disclose very minute objects, and at others, a tremulous phosphorescent light gleams over the walls, and odic emanations proceed from human bodies, or shoot meteor-like through the apartment. These phenomena are of frequent occurrence, and are not accounted for by any material hypothesis, unless, indeed, they could be comprehended under the popular generalization which ascribes the whole to human fraud and delusion. I have seen these lights in all their variety. On one occasion, when a number of friends were assembled at my own house, there occurred a gradual illumination of the apartment. It appeared like the twilight half an hour after the dawn. The light continued to increase for about fifteen minutes, and then it gradually diminished.

"On the 30th of March I chanced to be one of a company convened at the house of Mr. Elmer in Springfield, Mass.—Mr. Home being present—when the room was darkened to see if the mysterious illumination would occur. Immediately the gross darkness began to be dissipated, and in a few minutes, the forms of all the persons in the room were distinctly visible. Without disclosing her purpose to any one, Mrs. Elmer mentally requested that the spirits would restore the darkness, and, almost instantly, the change was perceived by the whole company, and soon every form was lost in the deepening gloom."

This was the first appearance of these spirit lights that I had seen when others were present, though I had several times seen them when by myself, since their appearance on my first vision of Edwin as before described. Although the physical manifestations had increased, and were so continuous, yet the internal power of vision had not left me as will be seen from the following, which was published and signed by Mr. S. B. Brittan of New York, to whom occurred the fact which he describes.

"Last winter while spending a few days at the house of Mr. Rufus Elmer, Springfield, I became acquainted with Mr. Home. One evening, Mr. Home, Mr. and Mrs. Elmer, and I were engaged in general conversation, when suddenly, and most unexpectedly to us all, Mr. Home was deeply entranced. A momentary silence ensued, when the medium. said "Hannah Brittan is here!" I was surprised at the announcement, for I had not even thought of the person indicated for many days, or perhaps months, and we parted for all time when I was but a little child. I remained silent, but mentally inquired how I might be assured of her actual presence. Immediately Mr Home began to exhibit signs of the deepest anguish. Rising from his seat he walked to and fro in the apartment, wringing his hands, and exhibiting a wild and frantic manner and expression. He groaned in spirit, and audibly, and often smote his forehead and uttered incoherent words of prayer. He addressed me in terms of tenderness, and sighed and uttered bitter lamentations. Ever and anon, he gave utterance to expressions like the following: "'Oh, how dark! What dismal clouds! What a frightful chasm! Deep—down—far down!—I see the fiery flood! Hold! Stay! Save them from the pit! I'm in a terrible labyrinth! I see no way out! There's no light! How wild!—gloomy! The clouds roll in upon me! The darkness deepens! My head is whirling! Where am I!

"During this exciting scene, which lasted perhaps half an hour, I remained a silent spectator, the medium was unconscious, and the whole was inexplicable to Mr. and Mrs. Elmer. The circumstances occurred some twelve years before the birth of Mr. Home. No person in all that region knew aught of the history of Hannah Brittan, or that such a person ever existed. But to me the scene was one of peculiar and painful significance. She was highly gifted by nature, and endowed with the tenderest sensibilities. She became *insane* from believing in the doctrine of endless punishment, and when I last saw her, the terrible reality, so graphically depicted in the scene I have attempted to describe, was present, in all its mournful details, before me!

"Thirty years have scarcely dimmed the recollection, of the scene which was thus re-enacted to assure me of the actual presence of the spirit. That spirit has since informed me that her present life is calm, peaceful and beautiful, and that the burning gulf, with all its horrible imagery, existed, only in the traditions of men, and in the fitful wanderings of her distracted brain."

At Springfield, also, there were many instances of the sick being healed. I was so sensitive to any one who came near me in a diseased state, that I not only myself felt but accurately described their symptoms, and the seat and cause of the disease. One case which I remember was that of a person who had been ill for many years with no apparent cause. I brought to his mind an accident which had occurred to him some years previously, and which I was impressed to tell him was the cause of his suffering. When he applied to a surgeon and related the circumstance, the surgeon told him that I had been no doubt correct in attributing his illness to that accident. My own suffering in sympathy with other people's illness was often so great, and was indeed so frequent, that I was often warned by my spirit friends against coming in contact with sick persons.

In May, 1852, I went to New York, and was at once received by investigators of the phenomena, mediums having increased largely in number, both in public and private circles. My days and nights were fully occupied by investigators of all classes and conditions. The following account of what he witnessed is given in the words of Dr. Hallock, a physician of New York.

"Two communications, spoken through Mr. Home as a medium, were read by the Secretary. They were given on the 10th inst., at the house of Mr. Partridge. The first was preceded by physical manifestations, intended to identify the spirit about to communicate. The second embraces several topics.

"Mr. Home said, a male and female were present, who wished to commune with Mr. P.

"Directly, sounds and motions were made as of a violent storm—the roaring and whistling of the wind, the rushing of water, and the breaking of waves—sounds as if a vessel was straining at her anchor and laboring in a heavy sea, amid which she was held by her chain cables—her joints creaking, and she rolling from side to side. The picture of a shipwreck was so true, that it made the cold chills run over me. The medium spoke of a boat with machinery in it, and went through the motions of dying 'mid the raging waters and a dark storm. The Spirit making these demonstrations to identify her presence, is one whose life was lost by the wreck of the steamer Atlantic, in November, 1849. She gave the following communication:

"'But, oh! it was not death! Bright spirits were hovering around, and bore me to their happy home; but it would be no home to us, if we were not permitted to return and watch over our dear friends we have left behind.

"'To me, the storm has passed and gone, and with it went all the storms of life. From that breaking barque, I passed to one the winds could not beat. It was anchored home in the heavens, and my spirit was nearer God—more easily developed, and was amid influences more pure and holy, just what they ought to be for man's advancement.

"'Kindness never goes unrewarded; and for yours, she wishes to express her deep obligation, not thanks merely, but a deep and abiding sense of it.

"'Be upright and kind, and it will prepare you brighter spheres.

"'Be patient, as God is. Think of His forbearance, for ages past, with the blindness, the hardness, the perversity of man. If man had possessed His power, he would, in his impatience, long since have annihilated earth and all which inhabit it.

"'Think not of the grave. To us, it is past and forgotten. To you, it is but an entrance into a new and more glorious existence.

"'Oft in the silent night, when the busy toils of life are hushed and the mind is at rest from its cares, we hover around and watch over you, happy, indeed, at being able then to impress our presence upon you.'

"The question is often asked, Why have not these manifestations occurred before? Why has not God illumined ages past with these wonderful manifestations of His providence? The reason is obvious. When a little light has been from time to time thrown down, like the feeble rays of a far-off star across the gloom of night, men have shut it up in darkness! They have been enveloped in self and shrouded in scepticism! They think the age of miracles has ceased! Another cause why these things have not occurred in past ages was, the persecution of mediums—it was perceived that men would torture them. It alarmed the superstitious fears of the community. The mediums were charged with being witches, and in league with the Devil! I see them on trial, then taken to the scaffold and the stake, and I hear spirit foot-sounds accompanying them. The younger, more vigorous and more positive state of their accusers, under zeal for God and the good of his church, has made them admit themselves to be what they were not. Their defenceless, negative condition, makes them an easy prey to the will-power of their judges and accusers. Now, I perceive the sorrow of those spirits who were not sufficiently developed to foresee the catastrophe as the higher spirits did. They are comforting them in their last earthly agony and, seeing the sad results of their attempt to communicate through physical manifestations, they have suspended the effort till a more favourable epoch.

"When men are told that spirits watch over them, it is not uncommon for them to say, 'Spirits should be in better business.' The truth is, that many men are so bad that they do not want their minds inspected; they do not wish to have it known how gross they are.

"A spirit wishes to express his idea of a hell. I see a mother with her children. She is training them in the path she herself has trodden. As she was ignorant and foolish, so are they. As her path had been beset with the briars and thorns which ignorance and folly engender, so is theirs. Now, I see her leave them and pass into the Spirit-world; but, impelled by the eternal and universal law of affinity, she still watches over them. Oh, the pangs of her spirit, for the wrong she has done, for the misery she has caused! Yet she follows them through all their devious windings through darkness and through crime, and is it not hell enough? Oh, is it not hell enough!

"Again the scene changes, and I see what caused the sin of the mother: A drunken man presents himself—his children, comparatively pure and unsullied, seek associates; for all must have such; they would gladly choose the pure and the good, but they are the drunkard's children, and are spurned from the doors of the intelligent and cultivated. So they are driven back to darkness and ignorance, to glean from the great law of association the happiness for which every human being pants. They could not seek it where they *would*, they must get it where they can. Thus, with minds soured by the repulse they have met with, and their darker passions stimulated by the desire of revenge for injuries received, they plod along their devious and uncertain way—the prison their asylum—the halter their inheritance—the constable and sheriff their ministering angels. They asked society for meat; it gave them a *scorpion*—for bread; they got a *stone*. Oh, that men could see the *cause* of crime!—they would love and pity.

"If one tree is blighted so that it cannot bear wholesome fruit, should the other trees call it evil? That which is evil cannot become good, but the undeveloped may progress to development. The tree whose root is rotten cannot grow; but if it has been merely scathed, it may. So with the spirit—though a long time may elapse. The bud, placed in the sunlight, does not blossom in a day—if placed in darkness, not for weeks. A spirit, after it has left the body, will have to throw off all the perversion that remains. After that is done, progression goes on without hindrance.

"Be not wise in your own conceit. Let him that standeth in the light of truth, take heed lest he fall, through the darkness of his own wisdom."

"Dr. Hallock related some remarkable personal descriptions of spirits through Mr. Home, occurring on the same evening. One spirit was described as having been known here by the name of 'Elizabeth.' Her person was described, and her prominent traits of character as well as the disease of which she died, with such accuracy, that a gentleman present knew her at once from the description. The only inaccuracy that he could point out, being the colour of her hair, which had been described as brown, when in fact it was rather a light auburn. In explanation of which, Mr. Home said, 'When I look at the forehead, which is very white, [which was the fact,] the hair looks brown to me.'

"The gentleman (a clergyman) declared that he was not thinking of her at all, and she was brought to his recollection solely by the accuracy of the description given.

"Mr. Home then said, 'I see an old woman, and her name is Abigail; they called her 'Aunt Abby.' To the question how did she look? he commenced by compressing the lips and cheeks in such a way as to indicate a person who had lost her teeth. This at once brought to his mind is old lady of that name, called by the whole family, 'Aunt Abby,' who died in the spring of 1817, when he was some eleven years of age. The appearance assumed by the medium was that of the last impression left upon his mind. She was an old woman; had prominent features, had lost her teeth for many years, was much emaciated by her last illness, and as her body lay in its grave-clothes, the thought of his young mind, as he stood gazing upon it, was that very peculiarity first indicated by the medium. Her nose and chin nearly met, so acute was the angle formed by her attenuated gums and shrunken lips.

"Many other facts were given, going to show the identity of the two individuals in question. But one great object seemed to be to teach us, by taking persons not thought of at the time, (in the last case not thought of for many years,) that it was no psychological impression from our own minds, as some have supposed; for there was no known impression of the kind existing at the time, and the memory was only awakened by the accuracy of the pictures which the medium had presented.

"Another equally interesting and accurate description of a spirit, who said his name was William, was given. Previous to the announcement of his presence and name by Mr. Home, and while he was engaged in the other delineation, a lady of high clairvoyant powers, through whose mediumship some of the most sublime lessons of truth and wisdom have been from time to time communicated, had written and shown to a gentleman sitting by her, the following sentence: 'I am impressed that my father is here and standing by my side; I feel his presence distinctly.' When Mr. Home had said, 'there is a spirit present and his name is William,' he asked, as if to gratify his own curiosity, 'Who is William?' and then immediately said, 'O, he says, Eliza knows me.' The lady's name was Eliza, and the spirit was her father. His appearance and prominent traits of character were delineated with great accuracy.

Here at New York I made the acquaintance of Dr. Gray, one of the most eminent physicians there, and for whom I had the deepest affection and esteem. He and his kind wife have given me counsel, and befriended me at all times, and under all circumstances. From his character and attainments, he was eminently suitable as an investigator of phenomena, requiring a calm dispassionate judgment, and the testimony of such a man is, in itself, a sufficient answer to all the doubts of unthinking persons. I had also the pleasure of meeting Judge Edmonds, so well known as one of the judges of the Supreme Court. He investigated this subject in the most painstaking manner for three years, and was fully convinced, not only through the mediumship of others, but through his own and that of his daughter, a lady well known for her purity of mind and truthful nature. He was a frequent visitor to me, and saw all the phenomena which occurred in my presence. I was also acquainted with the late Professor Hare, the eminent chemist and electrician, and with Professor Mapes, so well known in agricultural chemistry, and for his acquaintance with this subject. A conference was formed at New York, which has met weekly for many years for the investigation of spiritual phenomena, and from its recorded transactions, I make the following extract:

"Friday Evening, June 18, 1852.

"Dr. Hallock related a case of physical manifestations which took place on the Friday evening previous, at the house of Mr. Partridge, after the conference had adjourned. Mr. D. D. Home was the medium, and the circle consisted of Mr. Partridge, and his wife and daughter, Mr. W. Taylor and wife, Mr. S. B. Brittan, and himself. On the table around which we were seated, were loose papers, a lead pencil, two candles and a glass of water. The table was used by the spirits in responding to our questions, and the first peculiarity we observed, was, that however violently the table was moved, everything on it retained its position. When we had duly observed this, the table, which was mahogany and perfectly smooth, was elevated to an angle of thirty degrees, and held there, with every thing remaining on it as before. It was interesting to see a lead pencil retaining a position of perfect rest, on a polished surface inclined at such an angle. It remained as if glued to the table, and so of every thing else on it. The table was repeatedly made to resume its ordinary position and then again its inclination as before, as if to fasten upon us the conviction that what we saw was no deception of the senses, but a veritable manifestation of spirit-presence and of spirit-power. They were then requested to elevate the table to the same angle as before, and to detach the pencil, retaining everything else in their stationary positions. This was complied with. The table was elevated, the pencil rolled off, and everything else remained. They were then asked to repeat the experiment, retaining the pencil and everything else upon the table stationary, except the glass tumbler, and to let that slide off. This also was assented to, with the like result. All the articles retained their positions but the tumbler, which slid off and was caught in the hands of one of the party, as it fell from the lower edge of the table. Then the table, after being restored to the natural position was moved strongly to and from Mr. Home, and to and from different individuals in the circle, as they requested.

"After this had been repeated several times, and while a corner of the table was inclined into his lap, Mr. Taylor asked if the spirits would lift it clear of the floor, while it was in that inclined position. Assent was signified, and the table after much apparent effort, was lifted clear of the floor as requested. Dr. Hallock said he was led to the conclusion that the effort was only apparent, because, while we were watching it closely, with a light upon the floor so as to see the slightest motion, the table in the meantime resting upon one castor on the floor and one corner of the leaf in Mr. Taylor's lap, was raised perhaps about one inch, after having been literally tumbled about the circle, sometimes upon one castor and sometimes upon two, the leaf resting first in one person's lap and then in another. But when the foot of the table was finally raised as described, he, to make sure that they were not mistaken in the fact, got down upon the floor to observe more closely. While looking, the foot of the table, instead of being raised a doubtful inch or so, was thrown up, clear of the floor, six or eight inches, as if all former attempts had been mere playful efforts. We then asked if they could move the table with a man on it. They replied, 'Yes, with two men on it' Mr. Partridge and I then seated ourselves back to back upon the table. Our combined weight is a little over 350 pounds; but notwithstanding, the table was moved as easily as when nothing but the candlesticks and the other things were upon it. We were rocked backward and forward, to and from Mr. Home; the table was tipped from the medium and held stationary in that position, with us upon it; and finally we said playfully, 'when you get tired of rocking us, throw us off' It was done—the table was tipped strongly and rapidly from Mr. Home, and we were thrown, on the floor."

At the end of June I received the following letter from Dr Hull:—

"Newburgh, Orange Co.
"On the Hudson.

"My dear Sir,

"I am desirous that you should make me a visit, for myself and some intimate friends, at your first leisure, or freedom from present engagements.

"I will meet all your expenses from your place, during your stay here, and for your return; and five dollars a-day for ten days, i.e. fifty dollars.

"I do sincerely trust you will answer me promptly as to the time you can make me the desired visit; and if my proposition as to terms be not satisfactory, state what your terms are. All shall be made satisfactory to yourself.

"By addressing a letter to my direction—Newburgh, N. Y., it will soon reach me.

"I regretted I did, not see more of you in New York, but I hope to have the pleasure fully made up here.

"Mr. Edward Fowler has promised to come up when you visit me.

"Very truly yours, &c,
"A. GERALD HULL."

"D. D. Home, Esq."

In reply to this, I informed him that I was not a paid medium, but that I should be happy to visit him, as he requested. I did so, and whilst with him manifestations of a very interesting character occurred to a family who had been deeply afflicted in the loss of their children. They and Dr. Hull took, a great interest in my welfare; and feeling the importance of my completing my education, which from ill health had been much neglected, and of preserving me from the wearing excitement of the life I was then leading, they kindly proposed a home for me in their midst. I could not then avail myself of their offer, having promised to visit many friends during the autumn, but in the following year as will be seen, I placed myself under their guidance.

In August, I went on a visit to Mr. Cheney, at South Manchester, Connecticut, and it was at his house that I was fit lifted in the air, a manifestation which has since frequently occurred to me both in England and France.

The following is the description of the evening, in the words of a gentleman who was present.

"On the 8th instant, in company with three gentlemen from this city, the writer paid a visit to Ward Cheney, Esq., residing in Manchester, at whose house Mr. Daniel D. Home was temporarily stopping. A circle was formed, and the well-known vibrations on the table were soon loud and distinct. One of my friends had never seen anything of the kind, and he accordingly looked under the table to make sure that no one touched it. Answers of a personal character, such as tests of identity, were given very freely. Mr. Home was then thrown into a spiritually magnetic state, discovering great rigidity of muscle, and the ordinary phenomena of the psycho-magnetic condition, including a magnetic locking of the jaws, in which an iron-like hardness of the muscles was apparent. He then spelt out (with his eyes closely bandaged) some remarkable and interesting messages to one or two of the company, the personal of which precludes their publication, but which were declared by those interested to be perfect tests. He did this by pointing, with almost incredible rapidity, to the different letters of an alphabet arranged on a seven by nine card, and thus spelling out the necessary words, A rapid writer had difficulty in keeping up with him, and when a word or a sentence was partially finished, a suggestion from any of the company as to what was intended to be spelt, would, if correct, be answered by eager and vehement rappings in various parts of the table. Among others, (all remarkable), came a message from two sailors lost at sea, relatives of one of the company—a stranger to most of those present. These spirits announced themselves, somewhat unexpectedly, by canting over the solid and ponderous table, and rolling it in the manner of a vessel in a violent tempest. Accompanying this demonstration came a violent creaking as of the cables of a ship when strained in a gale; then came the loud sound of a prolonged wailing, shrieking blast of wind, precisely such a noise as the wind makes in the rigging of a ship in a storm at sea—and the creaking of the timbers and masts as the vessel surged to one side or the other was distinctly heard by all. Next came the regular, sullen shocks of the waves as they struck the bows of the doomed vessel. All this time the table kept up the rocking motion. And now the large table was capsized on the floor! All this was done with no one touching the table, as a close and constant scrutiny was kept up by two, at least, of our party. These two sailors (whose names and ages were given) it seems lost their lives by the capsizing of a vessel as represented, although this fact, I have the best of reasons for knowing, could not previously be known to Mr. Home or to any of the company excepting myself.

"Demonstrations now increased in force and number. Several *tunes* were rocked out by the table when no one touched it, the circle being seated a couple of feet, at least, from it. The swing or motion of the table was full three feet from the floor at each elevation, and the tune was kept with singular accuracy. A simultaneous expression from all the members of the circle attested their recognition of the several tunes as they were thus performed for our satisfaction.

"The table was actually lifted up from the floor, without the application of a human hand or foot! A table weighting, I should judge, one hundred pounds, was lifted up a foot from the floor, the legs touching nothing. I jumped upon it, and it came up again! It then commenced rocking, without, however, allowing me to slide off, although it canted at least to an angle of forty-five degrees! Finally, an almost perpendicular inclination slid me off, and another of the company tried it with the same results. These things all happened in a room which was light enough to allow of our seeing under and over, and all around the table, which was touched by no one except the two persons who respectively got upon it to keep it down!

"We went into a darkened room to see the spiritual flashes of light said to have been vouchsafed to some investigators. Instead of this we were greeted with *tremendous rappings* all about us. Some of the blows on the walls, floor, and tables, within three inches of myself, were *astounding*. I could hardly produce such violent demonstrations with my fist, though I were to strike with all my might. The very walls shook. Answers to questions were given by concussions of varying force and intonation, according to the character of the spirits communicating. A favourite little daughter of one of the gentlemen present, a stranger from a remote State, who had left the earth almost in infancy, announced her presence by a thick-pattering *rain* of eager and joyful little raps; and in answer to an inward request of her father, she laid her baby hand upon his forehead! This was a man who was *not* a believer in these things—he had never before seen them,—but he could not mistake the thrilling feeling of that spirit touch. I also had a similar manifestation, in the character of which I am not deceived.

Suddenly, and without any expectation on the part of the company, Mr. Home, was taken up in the air! I, had hold of his hand at the time, and I and others felt his feet—they were lifted a foot from the floor! He palpitated from head to foot apparently with the contending emotions of joy and fear which choked his utterance. Again and again he was taken from the floor, and the third time he was carried to the lofty ceiling of the apartment, with which his hand and head came in gentle contact.

"I omitted to state that these latter demonstrations were made in response to a request of mine that the spirits would give us something that would satisfy everyone in the room of their presence. The medium was much astonished, and more alarmed than any of the rest, who, I may add, took the matter calmly, though they were intensely interested."

During these elevations, or levitations, I usually experience in my body no particular sensations than what I can only describe as an electrical fullness about the feet. I feel no hands supporting me, and since the first time, above described, I have never felt fear, though should I have fallen from the ceiling of some rooms in which I have been raised, I could not have escaped serious injury. I am generally lifted up perpendicularly; my arms frequently become rigid and drawn above my head, as if I were grasping the unseen power which slowly raises me from the floor. At times when I reach the ceiling, my feet are brought on a level with my face, and I am as it were in a reclining position. I have frequently been kept so suspended four or five minutes, an instance of which will be seen in an account which is given of occurrences in the year 1857, at a Château near Bordeaux, I have been lifted in the light of day upon only one occasion, and that was in America. I have been lifted in a room in Sloane Street, London, with four gas-lights brightly burning, with five gentlemen present, who are willing to testify to what they saw, if need be, beyond the many testimonies which I shall hereafter adduce. On some occasions the rigidity of my arms relaxes, and I have with a pencil made letters and signs on the ceiling, some of which now exist in London.

During this autumn and winter, I visited private families with whom I had become acquainted, and never a day passed without some manifestations occurring. These are for the greater part of a private nature, appealing to the sympathies of relatives and friends, and could not properly be given to the world. They are to me, however, as to them a dear reminiscence of the loving guidance of departed friends, who find their highest, happiness in ministering to and consoling those who remain to fulfil their pilgrimage here. They ever say that God in His loving-kindness allows this, and that as He is an everywhere present God, and can bear with our shortcomings, they having been mortals like ourselves, can the more readily understand the weaknesses of our human nature. During the time I have already spoken of as my public life, I have met with thousands, many of whom disbelieved even the existence of the soul after death; and some who denied the existence of a God. Amongst these were even clergymen, who told me that though they had preached the Gospel, they themselves had never been fully convinced of existence in an after life. From the letters of a friend, an Episcopal bishop, I make the following extract. "You have the pleasant assurance of having been the instrument of conveying incalculable joy and comfort to the hearts of many people; in the case of sorrow you have changed the whole aspect of their existence, and you have made dwelling places light, that were dark before."

I went from Hartford to Springfield, to spend a few days with Mr. Elmer, and although at this time I did not hold séances, still the power was constantly with me in some form or other, as will be seen from the following.

"While Mr. Alderson was at my house, Mr. Home called to see us, having been absent a long time. Soon after he arrived, he was taken with severe sickness, from which A. attempted relief by bathing his head. During. the process, Mr. Home was thrown into the spiritual condition, and described Mr. A's father and sister; spoke their names and that of his mother; and the spirit of the father, while addressing his son, called him correctly by his Christian name, which Mr. Home had no means of knowing, neither did he know the names of Mr. A.'s parents, which, he assured us, were known only to himself, as he had not mentioned them this side of Baltimore!"

On going to Boston my power returned, and with it the more impressive manifestations of music, without any earthly instrument. At night, when I was asleep, my room would, be filled as it were, with sounds of harmony, and these gradually grew louder, till persons in other parts of the house could hear them distinctly. If by chance I awakened, the music would instantaneously cease.

CHAPTER III

FURTHER MANIFESTATIONS IN AMERICA

The year 1853 was spent under the guidance of three friends, and during the summer months I resided at Newburgh on the Hudson river, where my time was passed in the completion of my studies. I was at the Theological Institute, but only as a boarder, and in no way included in the theological classes. While here, I had an extraordinary vision, which is still so vivid, that I remember it in all its details.

The institute was built on an eminence, commanding a view of peculiar beauty; below lay the city; on the right, the river was lost in its windings among the rocky hills surrounding West Point; on the left, it lay in expanse, and could be traced for a distance of many miles; behind, spread out the country, with its pretty little farm-houses dotted here and there. I have sat for hours of an evening, watching the feeble flickering lights, and endeavouring to picture in my imagination the life-emotions which must from time to time have crossed those thresholds. Now, fancy pictured to me a young girl, on whose form time and care had passed but as an evening breeze; and a little further off it was, perchance, a mother whose little one was suffering, and every beat of whose feeble pulse she had counted, with that hope which only a mother may know, as she prays God to spare the pure, gentle, and loving little one, whom He has given her. Anon, it was one bowed down with age and sorrow; all that he had loved had gone to their rest, and he was alone in the world. Bright pictures of his youth flitted before him, but these only augmented his loneliness, for the light of the past had brought out in deeper contrast the shadows of the present.

These and similar trains of thought often occupied my idle hours; and, at times, these fancied scenes became as it were real, and furnished ample resource to a mind, naturally inclined to dwell on subjects beyond the little narrow circle of every-day life.

One evening I had been pondering deeply on that change which the world calls death, and on the eternity that lies beyond, until wearied I found relief in prayer, and then in sleep. My last waking consciousness had been that of perfect trust in God, and a sense of gratitude to Him for the enjoyment I received from contemplating the beauties of the material creation. It might have been that my mind was led to this by the fact of my having watched a beautiful star as it shone and twinkled in the profound stillness of the night. Be this as it may, it appeared to me that, as I closed my eyes to earthly things, an inner perception was quickened within me, till at last reason was as active as when I was awake. I, with vivid distinctness, remember asking myself the question, whether I was asleep or no? when, to my amazement, I heard a voice which seemed so natural, that my heart bounded with joy as I recognised it as the voice of one, who while on earth was far too pure for such a world as ours, and who, in passing to that brighter home had promised to watch over and protect me. And, although I well knew she would do so, it was the first time I had heard her voice, with that nearness and natural tone. She said, "Fear not, Daniel, I am near you; the vision you are about to have is that of death, yet you will not die. Your spirit must again return to the body in a few hours. Trust in God and his good angels: all will be well" Here the voice became lost, and I felt as one who at noonday is struck blind; as he would cling even to the last memories of the sunlight, so I would? fain have clung to material, existence—not that I felt any dread of passing away, nor that I doubted for an instant the words of my guardian angel; but I feared I had been over presumptuous in desiring knowledge, the very memory of which might disturb my future life. This was but momentary, for almost instantaneously came rushing with a fearful rapidity memories of the past; my thoughts bore the semblance of realities, and every action appeared as an eternity of existence. During the whole time I was aware of a benumbing and chilling sensation which stole over my body, but the more inactive my nervous system became, the more active was my mind, till at length I felt as if I had fallen from the brink of some fearful precipice, and as I fell, all became obscure, and my whole body became one dizzy mass, only kept alive by a feeling of terror, until sensation and thought simultaneously ceased, and I knew no more. How long I had lain thus I know not, but soon I felt that I was about to awaken in a most dense obscurity; terror had now given place to a pleasurable feeling, accompanied by a certitude of some one dearly loved being near me, yet invisible: it then occurred to me that the light of the spheres must necessarily be more effulgent than our own, and I pondered whether or not the sudden change from darkness to light might not prove painful, for instinctively I realized that beyond the surrounding obscurity lay an ocean of silver-toned light. I was at this instant brought to a consciousness of light, by seeing the whole of my nervous system, as it were, composed of thousands of electrical scintillations, which here and there, as in the created nerve, took the form of currents, darting their rayons over the whole body in a manner most marvellous; still this was but a cold electrical light and besides, it was external. Gradually, however, I saw that the extremities were less luminous, and the finer membranes surrounding the brain became as it were glowing, and I felt that thought and action were no longer connected with the earthly tenement, but that they were in a spirit-body in every respect similar to the body which I knew to have been mine, and which I now saw lying motionless before me on the bed. The only link which held the two forms together seemed to be a silvery-like light, which proceeded from the brain; and, as if it were a response to my earlier waking thoughts, the same voice, only that it was now more musical than before, said, "Death is but a second birth, corresponding is every respect to the natural birth, and should the uniting link now be severed, you could never again enter the body. As I told you, however, this will not be. You did wrong to doubt, even for an instant, for this was the cause of your having suffered, and this very want of faith is the source of every evil on your earth. God is love; and still His children ever doubt Him. Has He not said, Knock, and it shall be opened unto you: seek, and ye shall find?' His words must be taken as they were spoken. It is not for men to give any interpretation they may believe or desire to believe, to what God has said. Be very calm, for in a few moments you will see us all, but do not touch us, be guided by the one who is appointed to go with you, for I must remain near your body."

It now appeared to me that I was waking from a dream of darkness to a sense of light; but such a glorious light. Never did earthly sun shed such rays, strong in beauty, soft in love, warm in life-giving glow, and as my last idea of earthly light had been the reflex of my own body, so now this heavenly light came from those I saw standing about me. Yet the light was not of their creating, but was shed on them from a higher and purer source, which only seemed the more adorably beautiful in the invisibility of its holy love and mercy,—thus to shower every blessing on the creatures of its creation; and now I was bathed in light, and about me were those for whom I had sorrowed, for although I well knew that they existed, and loved and cared for me, nevertheless, their earthly presence was not visible. One that I had never known on earth then drew near and said, 'You will come with me, Daniel.' I could only reply, that it was impossible to move, inasmuch as I could not feel that my nature had a power over my new spirit-body. To this he replied, 'Desire and you will accomplish your desires which are not sinful, desires being as prayers to the Divinity, and He answereth the every prayer of His children.'

For the first time I now looked to see what sustained my body, and I found that it was but a purple tinted cloud, and that as I desired to go onward with my guide, the cloud appeared as if disturbed by a gentle breeze, and in its movements I found I was wafted upward until I saw the earth, as a vision, far, far below us. Soon, I found that we had drawn nearer, and were just hovering over a cottage that I had never seen; and

I also saw the inmates, but had never met them in life. The walls of the cottage were not the least obstruction to my sight, they were only as if constructed of a dense body of air, yet perfectly transparent, and the same might be said of every article of furniture. I perceived that the inmates were asleep, and I saw the various spirits who were watching over the sleepers. One of these was endeavouring to impress his son where to find a lost relic of him which the son much prized, and the loss of which had greatly grieved him. And I saw that the son awoke and thought it but an idle dream, and three times this impression was repeated by the spirit; and I knew that when morning came, the young man would go, out of curiosity where he had been impressed to go, and that he would there find what he sought for. In an adjoining room I saw one who was tormented by dreams, but they were but the production of a diseased body.

I was most deeply interested in all this, when my guide said, "We must now return." When I found myself near my body, I turned to the one who had remained near my bed, and said, "Why must I return so soon, for it can be but a few moments I have been with you, and I would fain see more, and remain near you longer?" She replied, "It is now many hours since you came to us; but here we take no cognizance of time, and as you are here in spirit, you too have lost this knowledge; we would have you with us, but this must not be at present. Return to earth, love your fellow-creatures, love truth, and in so doing, you will serve the God of infinite love, who careth for and loveth all. May the Father of mercies bless you, Daniel!"

I heard no more but seemed to sink as in a swoon, until consciousness was merged into a feeling that earth with its trials lay before me—and that I, as well as every human being, must bear my cross. And when I opened my eyes to material things, I found that the little star had given way to the sun, which had been above the horizon about four hours; making in all about eleven hours that this vision had lasted. My limbs were so dead, that at least half an hour elapsed before I could reach the bell rope, to bring any one to my assistance, and it was only by continued friction that, at the end of an hour, I had sufficient force to enable me to stand upright.

I merely give these facts as they occurred; let others comment on them as they may. I have only to add, that nothing could ever convince me that this was an illusion or a delusion; and the remembrance of those hours is as fresh in my mind now, as at the moment they took place.

In the autumn I returned to New York, with the intention of beginning a course of medical studies, but a chain of untoward circumstances seemed strangely to link themselves together, and to prevent my carrying out my intention. At that time I could not well comprehend why this should be; but since then I have often had occasion to thank God that it was so ordered. The kind friends who were doing what they thought to be best, in preventing others from seeing the manifestations, did not take into consideration that the phenomena which had been a source of information and consolation to them, were God-given, and that we had no right to conceal the light from any. As what was intended for me could only be brought about by my own decision, I acted as I felt would be for the best, and so it afterwards proved to be.

Previous, however, to my taking the step, I had another vision of great distinctness. I had been with some friends to dine at the house of a mutual acquaintance, and on returning, it was necessary to cross from Brooklyn to New York in the ferry-boat. The gate-keeper allowed our carriage to enter, and we were going down the inclined plane which led to the boat, when one of the men caught the horses by the bit and stopped them, telling the coachman as he did so, that there was no room for us on the ferryboat. Not only was this so, but the chains were already down, and the boat was in the act of leaving. There we were on a steep inclined plane, with restive horses, and the deep waters within a foot of them, the only barrier being a chain not over strong. Mrs. C____ begged to alight, and I jumped from the carriage and gave her my hand to assist her. As her hand touched mine, with the instantaneous sensation of contact, as if from some change in the electrical condition, I saw with most perfect distinctness, that a little sister of mine had passed from earth. I was not aware that the child had been ill, and her illness being apparently but slight, my relatives had not thought it necessary to write to me about her. It was a strange transition; there I stood in the cold night air, and I heard the impatient pawing of the horses on the worn deal boards; I heard the waters as they broke against the side piles of the ferry; I felt a life-warm hand in mine, yet there, shielding her from the cold, beyond all fear, and where harm could not come, I saw my mother, with one of the three children she had left with me to care for on earth. The child was close pressed to her heart, and her long silky hair lay scattered in profusion over my mother's shoulder. I saw also my spirit-sister Mary, who seemed anxious to soothe the child-like wonderment of her newly arrived sister. It was but for a moment, yet I saw it all, and I knew that God had given me another guardian angel. The next day letters came to announce what I thus already knew.

January of 1854 was the beginning of severer trials, for I had been so left to myself in solitude and study the whole winter, that mind and body were alike disturbed, and I wrote to my friends saying that I could not think of continuing the life I then led; and after many letters had passed between us, I was again left to myself to decide as to my future course. I had friends in Boston, who as soon as they knew what my intentions were, generously offered to do all that my other friends had been doing, and to allow me perfect liberty to see whom I might please. My health had suffered from the nervous anxiety of my solitary life and studies, and now the medical men whom I consulted, pronounced my left lug to diseased. My spirit friends said that they were correct in their diagnosis, but that I would not yet pass from earth, as my mission was incomplete, and there was much yet for me to do.

I went from New York to Hartford, but I saw no strangers for a few weeks. From here I went again to Springfield, and Dr. Gardner of Boston, in a letter, dated March 1st, 1854, describes what he saw at this time, and which, though in some respects similar to what has been already described, will help to show the character of the manifestations at different periods of my life.

Dr. Gardner says, "I am induced to offer you the following facts, which I in company with several other persons witnessed at the house of Mr. Rufus Elmer in this city, on the evening of the 28th of February, 1854. Nine persons besides Mr. Home, were seated round a common cherry table, when the following phenomena occurred: The table commenced a trembling, vibratory motion, sounds were heard on the floor and table, some of which were very loud, then the table was rocked with great force, then raised nearly if not quite two feet from the floor, and it was held supported in mid air with a waving motion, as if floating on the agitated waters of the sea, for considerable time. This was repeated several times. Then we were directed to place the dinner-bell (weighing one lb. one oz.) under the table on the floor, where it was rung with great violence many times; questions were answered by the raps upon it, and with it each individual in the circle was touched in such a manner that there could be no mistake about it. We then requested the spirits to pass the bell from the floor, and to place it into our hands, which was done to each individual separately; and, again at our request, it was taken from our hands, and carefully deposited on the floor. Again, while we sung the hymn, 'Whilst shepherds watch,' the bell was raised from the floor, and rung in perfect time with the measure of the tune sung, after which another tune was drummed out by the bell against he under-side of the table, the sound resembling the roll of drum-sticks in the hands of a skilful performer upon a tenor drum. This was continued for several minutes.

"All the above I know was performed without human agency; the hands of each person present during the whole performance above described being on the top of the table, with the room well lighted, and in the full view of every person present; and this was also the case during the whole sitting. During the whole time of the various performances with the bell, as well as before and after it, our clothes were pulled almost constantly, two handkerchiefs were firmly knotted together while lying in the laps of the owners, we were many times touched more or less forcibly, producing a peculiar and indescribable sensation, some of us had our limbs grasped with considerable force, and distinctly felt the form of the spirit hand, a soft, delicate, elastic, yet powerful touch, which cannot be described, but must be felt to be appreciated. The reader will bear in mind that the hands of every person present were in plain view on the top of the table.

"During the evening, responses to questions asked, were made by the invisible intelligence with the bell-handle, so heavy as to leave indentations on the table which may be seen by any person who doubts. Many other manifestations were made, but the above are sufficient to convey some idea of the wonderful invisible power there manifested; and the many beautiful and sublime moral teachings there given by our heavenly visitants, through the medium while entranced, I trust will long be remembered and made a rule of life by those who heard them."

I next went to Boston, and while here the power seemed to increase in a manner, which surprised me not less than other witnesses of it. On several occasions spirits were seen distinctly by all present in the room, and more than once they kissed persons present so as to be both felt and heard. During the summer months my health gradually improved, and I once more thought that I would now be enabled to pursue a course of studies which would enable me to take my diploma as a medical man. But no! again a series of unforeseen circumstances combined to prevent me. In September, I returned to Springfield, and the letter I here insert is taken from "The Republican" and describes some phenomena witnessed by Mr. F. C. Andrue.

"On Monday last, September 25, 1854, I called after tea at the house, of my friend, Mr. Elmer, for the purpose of returning a book which I had borrowed. Unexpectedly, I met there Mr. D. D. Home, who had just arrived from Boston. After conversing an hour or two, Mr. Elmer having to leave on the morrow on business, proposed a 'circle' that evening. We accordingly sat down—Mr. Elmer's family, Mr. Home and I being the only persons present. The occurrences, though very extraordinary, were similar to those already published. We were all touched by unseen hands, the room being well lighted with gas, a large bell was passed into our hands, &c. These things were not new to me, and are not to the public. I will therefore pass them by.

"Knowing that still more extraordinary 'manifestations' at times occurred to Mr. Home during the night, I mentioned that I would like to witness some of them. They urged me to stay and spend the night, and I did so.

"After leisurely undressing, putting out the light and retiring to bed, we soon began to hear faint raps, which, rapidly increased in power and number, till the walls, floor, and bedstead fairly shook with the strokes. They came like a shower. Soon came other noises, and then the bed began to move across the floor. This seemed rather dangerous locomotion. It was the only thing that gave me any uneasiness. Having before witnessed so many wonders, I was not frightened, though Mr. Home seemed to be so, holding on to me with both hands, and begging with all his might that the bedstead should be stopped. *They* complied with his request, but only to come in a more tangible form.

Soon I began to feel some one stepping on my feet and ankles, over the bed-clothes, but with a pressure different from that produced by any hard substance. Directly after there came a hand on my head and forehead, *as much like flesh and blood* as any I ever felt, *only somewhat cold.* I began to ask questions, the fingers patting me on my forehead in answer. Several hands, touching me at the same time, claimed to be those of relatives of mine.

"A strong hand came, stated to be that of my grandfather. I asked, how am I to know that this is my grandfather? The hand moved from my forehead to my temple, over my eyebrow and eye, and then passed down over my face—the fingers patting me in the most gentle manner possible. At another time, at my request, hands patted my forehead with such force that the sound could be heard, I am confident, in any part of the room.

"I wish, before I close, to add a few words. To religious minds, (which are strangely the most sceptical in this matter) I have this to say: By what process of reasoning can you bring yourselves to disbelieve *my* testimony of what I *know* and *have seen,* and to believe the testimony of what John, Peter or Paul saw? I speak with all reverence—I doubt not their testimony; on the contrary I believe it *now* more than ever. But I know of no reason, (my veracity being unimpeached) why my testimony of what I *know* and *see* is not as good as that of any other man, living or dead. And there are thousands who know these things to be so, as well as I.

"To our wise men, whose hobby is scientific investigation, I would say: Of what use is it to those who have gone through what I have, to read Dr. Dodd's book, Dr. Rogers' theory, or to marvel over Professor Faraday's discoveries? who only proved that when he pushed, he pushed."

Early in November, I returned to New York, and resumed my medical studies. I held séances two or three times a week, at my own rooms, and was in the habit of going amongst the poorer classes for the purpose of speaking to them of this most cheering truth. I have always found them to be the most candid and thorough in their investigations; and when they were in reality convinced, they were the most thankful to God in allowing such proofs of spiritual beings and forces to exist. I have seen many a poor heartbroken mother consoled with the thought that the fair young child, given her by God as a hope-star to cheer her as she toiled for her daily bread, but who had pined and gone for ever from her sight, was still living and loving her and her God-sent ministering angel. I well remember a poor man being present one evening, and the spirit of a little girl coming with the following message. "Father, dear, your little Mary was present last Wednesday, and God gave her power to prevent you from doing what you wished. If you were ever to do that, you could not come where your own Mary and her mother are. Promise me you will never think of such an awful thing again." We all looked astonished, but could not understand to what, she alluded. Still it was evident the poor father knew too well, for throwing himself on his knees, he said, as the tears rolled down his cheeks, "Indeed, it is but too true, that on Wednesday last I decided to cut my throat; but as I took the razor to do it, I felt that had my child been alive, she would have shrunk from me with horror, and this very thought was the saving of me."

My frequent séances were attended by persons who were introduced to me by friends, and I met at this time many hundreds. One of these séances is spoken of in the "New York Conference," of December 26, 1854, and may serve to give an idea of my mediumship at this time.

"A gentleman present related the facts of a circle which met on Wednesday evening last. Mr. Home was the medium. When seated, the first thing noticed was an undulating motion of the table, which was followed by its being lifted entirely clear off the floor. This was repeated several times. Once or twice it was raised as high as the chins of the party sitting at it, the hands of every person in the room being upon the table. A guitar in its case standing in one corner of the room was heard to move, and on examination, the end resting upon the floor was found to have moved several inches. Loud raps were heard in its vicinity while this was being done, and a closet door opening upon the room in which they were seated, was shut with considerable force. The circle during these occurrences remained seated at the table, and some six or eight feet from where they took place. The guitar case was then unlocked, and the instrument placed under the table. In this position it was played upon repeatedly, not, to be sure, in the highest grade of the art, but with very fair average skill. The hands of the party during this performance were all upon the table in plain sight of every one. There was no chance for trick, the room being sufficiently light for all to see the exact position of every person and thing in the room. The guitar was then placed in the lap of each member of the circle in rotation. Each one took hold of the end presented, and held on until the instrument was removed by the invisible agency. The table, the chair, in which they were seated, and the floor of the room itself, were made each in turn to exhibit a tremulous motion sensible to all. The large rocking-chair in which Mr. Home was seated, was next rocked forcibly. Then, by direction through the alphabet, the whole party of ten persons, in rotation took the same chair, and were rocked in the same way. The application of the power was as though a person had hold of the upper part of the back of the chair with one hand, and the other on its arm. The application of the force at these points could be felt distinctly at every vibration; and the force necessary to produce them may be appreciated by stating that the feet of the sitter were held out straight, and were frequently made to strike the under side of the top of the table. Every one was touched in turn as by human hands, some large and some small. A lady present who had been touched with what purported to be the hands of her little daughter, asked if she could take the handkerchief out of her lap? Very soon it was seen to move slowly from her lap, and disappear beneath the table. In a few minutes, raps indicating the alphabet were heard, and this sentence was received: "Mother, now look and see what we have done." On looking, the handkerchief was found knotted and twisted into the form of a doll-baby, not very symmetrical, but sufficiently like to show the evident design, as well as ingenuity and power to execute. Several other interesting facts occurred during the evening.

"Dr. Hallock said he was present when the facts just narrated occurred. The point which he particularly wished to illustrate, was the open character, so to speak, of these manifestations. Then an important fact is stated, accompanied with the explanation that it occurred in a dark room, it naturally raises the question of deception in the mind of the hearer, which the most elaborate statement of particulars cannot eradicate. From beginning to end, these manifestations were free from that objection. Every person in the circle, Mr. Home included, was in full view. When the guitar was played, all our hands were seen to be on the table. A man could not have touched the strings of that instrument with the toe of his boot even, much less with his hand; without detection. So of all the other facts of the evening. In one instance, after several unsuccessful attempts to retain a sheet of paper upon the smooth surface of the table when elevated to a considerable angle, the table with the sheet of paper on it was turned so as to rest on its edge, the top being vertical, and the paper still retaining its position, until it was suffered to fall at the request of one of the gentlemen present. The exhibition of power and intelligence manifested on that evening, were done *for us*, and not *by us*—if ten pairs of eyes, with the remaining complement of senses, are to be taken as evidence."

In January, 1851, the weather was more than usually cold and severe, and my cough had so increased, with other symptoms of a more alarming nature, that all idea of completing my medical studies had to be abandoned entirely. The medical men whom I consulted, all coincided in saying that my only hope of having my life prolonged, was to visit Europe. This was to me a hard struggle, in being thus separated from those who would have tended me with every affection, and to be thrown as it were a stranger in what was now to me a strange land. My family had by this time all been residents of America for some time, and I knew no one friend in all England. I would not have heeded the advice of my medical men, and I should have remained where I was to pass from earth; but my spirit friends told me that I must go, and their counsels could not be unheeded. I accordingly went to pay a series of farewell visits to those friends who had been so kind to me; they as well as I feeling that in all probability it was the last time we should meet "in the flesh." While at Hartford in March, on one of these visits the séance here alluded to took place.

"The following occurrences transpired in this city, on the evening of the 14th ultimo. A small party were seated with Mr. D. D. Home, who is probably the most remarkable of modern mediums for spirit-manifestations of a physical or tangible order. It was intimated that if we would procure a tablecloth and place it upon the table, the unseen presences would manifest themselves by lifting up the cloth. The cover was accordingly procured, when we placed it upon the table, put the lamp upon it, and drew back far enough to prevent the possibility of any one of the party touching it, unless by stretching forward; and the slightest movement of the kind by any one present would have been instantly detected. In a moment more the table-cloth was plainly *lifted up*, on the side opposite to the medium, and in the full light of the lamp. It presented the appearance of something under it, for it *moved about* under the cloth, going first to one side of the table and then to the other. Presently it *reached out*, lifting the sides of the cloth, *towards each one present*, in succession. In this manner the force, or substance, (for it was a substantial thing, resembling a hand,) reached out and *shook hands* with the company. It felt, through the cloth, like a hand; but on retaining it for a closer inspection, it seemed to *evaporate or dissolve*, and was rapidly lost. In its nature and composition it resembled, apparently, the hand and arm seen on a previous occasion by a party of six, and described in a former article.

"Soon after this, the thing, (whatever it was) again lifted up the table-cloth, moving apparently all about the table, and raising the cloth as it moved. In a moment more it reached forward and *touched* one of the party; then drew back and again reached out and touched another. Different parts of the person were thus touched; and presently the hand—if it was a hand, *left* its protection of the table-cloth, and commenced *touching* the party in succession, some in one place, and others in another. But nothing could be *seen!* If requested to touch, for instance, the right shoulder, the hand would unexpectedly respond by touching the *left*; or if asked to touch the leg, perhaps the breast or hand of the one asking would be touched—seemingly with a view to indicate in the clearest manner that the power and the intelligence was separate from the mind of the party. The invisible agency thus operating touched the writer at first on the knee, and, gradually advancing upwards, finally took him by the hand; but, although this was in a pretty good light, (a little below the edge of the table), no traces of the hand that was palpably touching mine could be seen.

"A guitar, of a size and weight somewhat unusual, had been placed beneath the table, in the hope of getting some music from the spirits. I placed also a quire of letter paper and a pencil upon the instrument, that they might, if able and so disposed, give us a sample of writing without mortal hands. (Both of these performances have been witnessed at circles in New York, and elsewhere). As soon as we were again seated and quiet, the guitar was sounded, and then played upon, evidently by real, substantial fingers, for the touches on the strings were strong and distinct. Presently the quire of paper was thrown from the instrument upon the floor, a distance of some three or four feet, and the music was again produced, louder than before. Next, the guitar, large and heavy as it was, was dragged out from its place, and carried away to a door, a distance of five feet from the table, and there the music recommenced, stronger and clearer than ever. This had all been done while the party sat quietly at the table. At this juncture, in order to see the performance going on at that distance, the writer leaned forward towards it, and in so doing, accidentally extinguished the lamp on the table; but as a good light was reflected upon all of us from a grate of glowing coals directly in front of the party, it was decided not to break the circle to relight the lamp, and the manifestations went on.

"While we sat thus, *the guitar, at a distance of five or six feet from the party, was played upon exquisitely,* and for several minutes, by some power other than that of any one bodily present. The instrument was partially in shadow, and the hand that swept its strings could not be seen; but the music was surpassingly beautiful. It was of a character entirely new to those who listened, and was sweeter, softer, and more harmonious than anything I have ever heard. Portions of it were filled with a certain soft and wild melody that seemed to be the echo of other music far away, and for the exquisite sweetness of which there are no words. It was of that

> "'Music that softer falls
> Than petals from blown roses on the grass,
> Or night dews on still waters between walls
> Of shadowy granite in a gleaming pass.'

Anon it changed, and rose to a 'full orb' of strong, tempestuous melody, filling the house with its sounds. It was heard, by a lady residing in another part of the house, who inquired about it the next day, thus proving the strength and the *reality* of this immortal music.

"It was asked by one of the circle," Can you strike on all the chords at once? *Ans.* (by responses on the strings)—'Yes,' and this was actually done.

"The guitar was then removed to a corner of the room, still farther off; and as soon as all were seated, it was again played upon, at that distance, for some time; then it was brought back by invisible means and placed near the table. Mr. Home remarked that all this transcended anything of the kind in his previous experience, and he proposed to 'see what they could do,' taking the guitar to the most distant corner of the room. It was suggested to him by us that this would be useless, as they could do nothing at that distance from himself; but upon his taking his seat again, the spirits began playing the instrument in that farthest corner!—aft a distance (as ascertained by subsequent measurement); of nearly *eleven feet* from the circle or the medium! Then the guitar was moved from its place by the spirits and brought towards the circle; but, encountering a heavy mahogany chair on the way, *the instrument was laid down and the chair dragged several feet* out of the way; after which the guitar was taken up and carried all around the circle by the invisibles, and at length deposited in the *opposite* corner! In a few moments more the writer saw it poised in the air, top upwards, and nearly over his head! The remark was made, "Well, if I did not see this myself, I wouldn't believe it on other testimony"—whereupon the instrument *reached forward and playfully tapped the speaker three times upon the shoulder.* Then it was passed across the table (over his head) towards Mr. Home, whom it lightly touched several times upon the head! Being close to it during this performance, I watched it narrowly by the aid of the fire-light. The bottom end of the instrument was very near my face, while the opposite end was thus being used; it was not, in fact, six inches above my head, and just in front of me. *The indistinct outline of a human hand could be seen grasping the instrument just below its centre.*

" Reaching up, I grasped the instrument firmly in both hands and held it above my head, requesting at the same time that the one who had been performing would *now* play it if possible. *Immediately the strings were touched* as if by human fingers, though now invisible, and the guitar was played as well while thus held in the air as it had been while on the floor!

"The *quire of paper* before spoken of was *taken from the floor, slowly lifted up, and placed upon the table,* as I can affirm, without the aid of a human hand. Sitting at that end of the table where this was done, I was enabled to see the whole of this proceeding. The quire of paper was placed upon the edge of the table, and so near my hand as to touch it. This was done slowly and deliberately, and this time at least I was permitted to see plainly and clearly *the hand that had hold of it.* It was evidently a *lady's hand*—very thin, very pale, and remarkably attenuated. The *conformation* of this hand was peculiar. The fingers were of an almost preternatural *length,* and seemed to be set wide apart. The extreme *pallor* of the entire hand was also remarkable. But perhaps the most noticeable thing about it was the shape of the fingers, which, in addition to their length and thinness, were unusually *pointed* at the ends; they tapered rapidly and evenly toward the tips (The writer has since been shown a daguerreotype taken from a picture of the lady whose name was written as above described, and whose disease was consumption. The portrait was taken just before her death, and the hands and fingers in the daguerreotype, although rather indistinct, bear a most close and remarkable resemblance to the hand described above.) The hand also narrowed from the lower knuckles to the wrist, *where it ended.* All this could be seen by such light as was in the room, while the hand was for a few moments holding the paper upon the edge of the table. It suddenly disappeared, and in a moment the pencil was thrown from some quarter, and fell upon the table, where the hand again appeared, took it, and *began to write*. This was in plain sight, being only, shaded by one of the circle who was sitting between the paper on the table and the fire. The hands of each one present were upon the table, in full view, so that it could not have been one of the party who was thus writing. Being the nearest one to the hand, I bent down close to it as it wrote, to see the whole of it. It extended no farther than, *the wrist*. With a feeling of curiosity natural under the circumstances, I brought my face close to it in the endeavour to see exactly what it was, and, in so doing, probably destroyed the electric or magnetic influence by which it was working; for the pencil dropped and the hand vanished. The writing was afterwards examined, and proved to be the name, in her own proper handwriting, of a relative and intimate lady friend of one in the circle, who passed away some years since. Other marks were also made, and the word 'Dear' had been written just as the pencil dropped. This writing has been preserved, and remains as an evidence of the reality of the fact. That it was produced by no hand of any one bodily in that room I know and affirm.

"The hand afterwards came and shook hands with each one present. I felt it minutely. It was tolerably well and symmetrically made, though not perfect; and it was soft and slightly *warm*. IT ENDED AT THE WRIST."

CHAPTER IV

IN ENGLAND

On the 31st of March, 1855, I sailed from Boston for England in the 'Africa,' the late Captain Harrison being the captain of the ship. On the ninth day of our voyage we neared England, and the signal cannon was fired. I never can forget my feelings as I looked around me, and saw only joy beaming on the faces of my fellow-passengers; some there were who were about to reach their home, and the thought of kind friends waiting to welcome them brought the smile of joy on their countenances. Others were travellers who saw the Old World with all her art treasures spread before them, and the monotony of a sea-voyage so near its termination. I stood there alone; with not one friend to welcome me, broken down in health, and my hopes and fairest dreams of youth, all, as I thought, for ever fled. The only prospect I had was that of a few month's suffering and then to pass from earth. I had this strange power also, which made a few look with pity on me as a poor deluded being, only devil-sent to lure souls to destruction, while others were not chary in treating me as base impostor. I stood there on the ship's deck amongst the crowd of passengers, and a sense of utter loneliness crept over me, until my very heart seemed too heavy for me to bear up against it. I sought my cabin, and prayed to God to vouchsafe one ray of hope to cheer me. In a few moments I felt a sense of joy come over me and when I rose, I was as happy as the happiest of the throng.

I reached Cox's Hotel in Jermyn Street on the evening of the 9th of April; and as soon as Mr. Cox knew who I was, he welcomed me more as a father would welcome a son, than as a stranger whom he had never seen, and from that time to this he has been to me the most sincere and generous friend.

It soon became known that I was in England, and in less than a month I had more engagements than I could well fulfil While at Cox's Hotel, Lord Brougham expressed a desire to see me for the purpose of investigating the phenomena, and as his lordship's evenings were fully occupied, I appointed an early afternoon. Accordingly his Lordship came accompanied by Sir David Brewster, with whom and Mr. Cox I had a séance, which shortly afterwards, in consequence of the misrepresentations and evasions of Sir David Brewster, became of considerable public interest, inasmuch as it was made the means of a general discussion in the newspapers on the subject of the spiritual phenomena. There are few matters in which Sir David Brewster has come before the public which have brought more shame upon him, than his conduct and assertions on this occasion, in which he manifested not only a disregard for truth, but also a disloyalty to scientific observation, and to the use of his own eyesight and natural faculties. In order that Lord Brougham might not be compelled to deny Sir David's statements, he found it necessary that he should be silent, and I have some reason to complain that his Lordship preferred sacrificing me to his desire not to immolate his friend, since his silence was by many misconstrued to my disadvantage. The correspondence which ensued was so interesting and characteristic, and is moreover so useful as being the first great occasion on which one of the pretended magnates of science has come forward on the subject of these phenomena, that I have thought it well to give the substance of it, with some pertinent remarks on Sir David Brewster's conduct in an Appendix. It will be a means whereby his character may be the better known, not only for his untruthful dealing with this subject, but also in his own domain of science in which the same unfaithfulness to truth will be seen to be the characteristic of his mind.

The immediate effect, however, of this ventilation of the subject was, as I have invariably found it, to excite only the greater interest in the phenomena, and it was thereby the means of convincing numbers of all classes who visited me. My time was fully occupied, notwithstanding my delicate health, in giving séances to anxious inquirers of all ranks and classes, from the peer to the artizan, and including men of all the professions high in art, science, and literature, who were both more competent and truthful than I found Sir David Brewster to be to form a correct conclusion.

After some time in Jermyn Street, I went to stay with a friend at Ealing, who was deeply interested in the subject, and his house was, during the greater part of my stay, almost besieged by persons wishing to witness the phenomena. Hundreds had their wishes gratified, and saw what has proved enough to be the turning point of their lives, and what rendered no longer possible those materialistic and sceptical notions, which are still unhappily so rife amongst the most highly educated classes at this day. Many interesting incidents occurred during my stay at Ealing, and the hands and once or twice the head of the spirit form were repeatedly seen by many, who publicly testified to the fact. But although I was apparently wearing out my life by the fatigue and excitement which these constant séances caused to me, I was not allowed to become proud of my position, for the good clergyman of Ealing found it his duty to publicly preach against me, and to attribute the manifestations to the devil. The position which is taken up by many of the clergy, is to me, in itself, an extraordinary manifestation, for certainly these phenomena, whether from God or from the devil, have in ten years caused more converts to the great truths of immortality and angel communion, with all that flows from these great facts, than all the sects in Christendom have made during the same period. Indeed, whilst the churches are losing them adherents, the belief in spiritual laws caused by these external manifestations, is becoming widely spread through the sceptical masses. It is not at all improbable that in pursuing their new studies, these last may be the means in their turn of converting the clergy to a belief in spiritual laws.

Whilst I was at Ealing, a distinguished novelist, accompanied by his son attended a séance, at which some very remarkable manifestations occurred, and which were chiefly directed to him. The, rappings on the table suddenly became unusually firm and loud. He asked "what spirit is present?" the alphabet was called over, and the response was, "I am the spirit who influenced you to write Z____!" "Indeed," said he, "I wish you would give me some tangible proof of your presence." "What proof? will you take my hand?" "Yes," and putting his hand beneath the surface of the table, it was immediately seized by a powerful grasp, which made him start to his feet in evident trepidation, exhibiting a momentary suspicion that a trick had been played upon him; seeing, however, that all the persons around him were sitting with their hands quietly reposing on the table, he recovered his composure, and offering an apology for the uncontrollable excitement caused by such an unexpected demonstration, he resumed his seat.

The following words were then spelt out, "We wish you to believe in the _____" and then stopped. It was asked of the spirit: "In what am I to believe? in the medium?" "No." "In the manifestations?" "No." At that moment he was gently tapped upon the knee, and putting his hand down, a cross was placed there by the spirit, which thus significantly finished the sentence.

The crow was made of card-board, and had been lying on a small table with other ornamental articles in a distant part of the large room in which the party were seated. The investigator, apparently much impressed with the incident, turned to Mrs. Rymer, and asked permission to retain the cross as a souvenir, to which she assented, saying that its only value to her was that it had been made by her boy, then recently deceased, but she could have no objection to him keeping it, if he would remember the injunction. He bowed his assent, and placing the souvenir in his breast pocket, carried the cross away with him.

On another occasion the children had been playing in the garden with some fresh-gathered flowers, out of which they had formed a wreath. A séance was proposed. It was a calm summer's evening, with the full moon just rising. A large circular-shaped table was selected in the drawing-room, which room was on a level with the garden lawn, the French windows extending to the ground, and the moonlight-twilight shone through them sufficiently to make everything in the room visible.

The party seated themselves around the half circle of the table, leaving the other half nearest to the garden window vacant. After several minor incidents had occurred, the table rose slowly from the ground, and ascended to the ceiling of the room, out of the reach of all but Mr. Coleman, who was tall enough to just touch its rim. It then descended steadily and settled on the floor with no more sound than if it had been a feather's weight.

Having taken their seats again a beautifully-formed feminine hand became distinctly visible to all the party present. It came up from the vacant side of the table, and made an unavailing effort, at first, to reach a small hand-bell which had been placed there. In a short time, the fleshy and delicately-formed arm became visible up to the elbow, and was enveloped in what appeared to be a gauze sleeve, through which it was transparently seen. The fingers then took up the bell, held it suspended for a moment, rung it, and slowly carried it, ringing, beneath the table. Mr. Coleman finding the bell jingling against his knee, put down his hand, received it, and placed it on the table. He then asked if he might feel the hand, which was neither warm nor cold, but of velvety softness, and it was placed with a gentle pressure in his.

When the hand first appeared, all in the circle had hold of each other's hand, I having, at Mr. Coleman's request, placed both my hands in Mr. Coleman's grasp.

Whilst seated in this position, the wreath of flowers, which had been made by the children, was seen by all to be lifted from my head, where it had been playfully placed a short time previously. No hand was visible. The wreath then descended to within an inch of the surface of the table. It then slowly traversed round the circle and back again to Mr. Coleman who took it, and retained it at home until the flowers withered.

At another sitting, each person in the circle who wore a ring had it gently removed by a spirit hand, the hand being seen afterwards with all the rings on its fingers, and after displaying itself by turning about, showing the back and palm two or three times, inverted itself, and cast the rings upon the table.

One evening at Ealing, Sir David Brewster, Mrs. Trollope the authoress, and her son Mr. Thomas Trollope, and several others were present. The table at which. the party sat was a long telescopic dining table, having two legs at each end and none in the centre. One end of it was occupied by Mr. Trollope, Sir David Brewster, and a lady. I sat about the centre of one side, having Mrs. Trollope on my left; the others present occupying the remainder of the table. There was no cloth or drapery of any kind. Sir David was invited to look under the table and make every investigation, and he did most properly avail himself of the opportunity afforded him by carefully looking under the table, both before sounds were heard and during the time they were being made. On this occasion Sir David tried to lift the table, sometimes he could not, at other times he could or, as Sir David said, "the table was made *light and heavy at command*."

An accordion was called for: hymns and tunes were played, and without any visible agency. After the party broke up, Sir David, in the course of conversation, said, "I should have liked if we had been all standing when the table lifted." Sir David, Mr. Trollope, and Mr. Rymer then sat down to see if it were possible to move the table or to raise it by their feet, but it could not be moved by the united efforts of the feet of all three. Sir David was invited to come the next evening for the purpose of complying with his request of standing at the table, but he could not come, having a pre-engagement.

This table, which was twelve feet long, has been sometimes completely turned over, replaced, and again turned over, all our hands being on the surface. Occasionally it has been moved while we were all standing, without any one touching it, even with their hands.

Mr. Trollope came on the following evening, we sat round the same table as on the previous evening; the alphabet was called for, and three of us were told to go into another room, to get a smaller table, and stand. We were not to sit, but to stand. We did so—and a heavy card table, on pillar and claws, and which was brought from, another room, and at which we had never sat before, was repeatedly lifted off the ground at least twenty inches.

One evening a gentleman was present when it was intimated to him through the alphabet by knocks on the table that his aunt Dorothy was present; he was surprised, and assured us that could not be so, for he never had an aunt; be afterwards wrote to his sister, who was residing in the north of England, and this was her reply:—

"I never heard of our father having a sister, there were four sons, and their father died when they were all very young; but I expect to see my elder sister who knows more of our family, and I till ask her.

"P.S.—She has just come, and I find *our father had a sister*—our grandfather was twice married; by his first wife he had one daughter whose name was *Dorothy*, and who died an infant, and who, of course, was our aunt."

One evening as Mr. Rymer was passing through the room he stood for a few moments at the end of the table. His attention was arrested by the sounds, and it was stated to be his little boy, who had passed away some years before. He asked if he recollected how pleased he was when on earth to place him a chair on his return home, the chair was immediately moved round the corner of the table, by no visible agency. It was placed behind him, and he sat down upon it.

This was in the presence of five persons, one of whom was the editor of a well-known work on the "Occult Sciences." All at the table saw the chair moved to where the father was standing. The hands of all were on the table; no one knew that he intended to ask for a chair, and until that instant, he said, that he did not know it himself.

Another evening we were told through the alphabet that the same little boy was present in spirit. It was asked if he could write as on earth, and he answered that he would try. A sheet of note paper, clean, and without any writing on it of any description was taken, and placed on the cloth. The brass fastenings of the table were then displaced one by one, and fell to the ground; the table was opened or pulled out by no human agency; every one in the room was seated at the table and had their hands on its surface. It was then asked if the paper and pencil should be placed on the table near the opening under the cloth; three sounds, "Yes." Immediately the form of a small hand was seen under the cloth. It was felt by some who placed their hands upon it. The paper and pencil were then removed, the form of the hand disappearing at the same time. In a few minutes the same form of hand was again seen replacing the paper and pencil, the alphabet was called for: "*Dear papa, I have really done my best.*" The father removed the paper and pencil and on that paper was written, "Dear papa, dear mamma," and, signed "Wat." Watty was the name of the child. No one was previously aware that it was intended to ask for this to be done.

At Sandgate in Kent, where I stayed for some time, at a séance, we numbered thirteen. The table was elevated at least two feet, and the accordion was played. The tune was not known to any of us. We asked the name, and were told that it was the "Song of the Sea." A hand and arm in white drapery appeared, it was seen by all at the table on several occasions during the evening, and they had every opportunity of carefully examining it.

A few evenings afterwards the table was near the window. It was twilight. Sounds were heard on the accordion. The tune was new to us, and we were told that it was the "Song of the Angels to the Mourners." It was followed by a hymn which had been frequently played before. It was spelt out by sounds on the table, *some will show you their hands to-night.* The table was gently raised and lifted up several times, a hand appeared above the table and took from the dress of one of the party a miniature brooch, and handed it to several at the table. *Hands and arms were then distinctly seen by all at the table of different forms and sizes:* sometimes crossed as in *prayer,* and at other times *pointing upwards:* on another occasion sounds were heard, communications were made, and *hands and arms in white drapery were again seen.* A spirit hand took up a Bible which was on the table, and opened it. This was seen by all, and a leaf was *folded down,* the *hand took* a pencil and marked the two verses sixteen and seventeen of the thirteenth chapter of St. Matthew: "But blessed are your eyes, for they see: and your ears, for they hear. For verily I say unto you, that many prophets and righteous men have desired to see things which ye see, and have not seen them; and to hear these things which ye hear, and have not heard them."

At this time hands and arms were frequently seen, and they were repeatedly felt by all at the table as distinctly as though they were the hands and arms of living mortals, and frequently they shook hands with them as really and substantially as one man shakes hands with another.

Of all the accounts which have been given of the phenomena there has been none so good as that of Dr. J. J. G. Wilkinson, who towards the close of the Brewster controversy, wrote a letter to the "Morning Advertiser," under the signature of Verax. He had been frequently present at séances, and was eminently qualified not only for the investigation, but for a philosophical expression of their results and consequences, and I need offer no apology for giving at length his eloquent narration which was entitled "Evenings with Mr. Home and the Spirits."

"The 'Great Wizard of the North' has roused attention to the subject of spiritual manifestations in such a manner, that everybody is talking about them; and, moreover, the country papers are the battle-ground of letters *pro* and *con.*, which debate the subject with some warmth; and, wherever a name can be got at, with a little personality. But, hitherto, I have seen no statement of the experience of any of the writers in regard to these manifestations. This is to be regretted, perhaps, because by bringing forward experiences and explanations, the subject might have been divested of some of that heat which is so bad a scientific medium.

I will now endeavour, with your permission, to tell what I saw and felt on three separate evenings, stating them in their order.

"It was late in the spring of this year that I was invited by a friend, well known in the literary world, to pay a visit to the lodgings of Mr. Daniel Dunglas Home, then recently arrived from America, for the purpose of witnessing certain remarkable phenomena alleged to be from supernatural causes. Many feelings prompted me to accept the invitation; as, also, did the knowledge that Mr. Home was familiarly, known, as a plain honest man, to Dr. Gray, the first homœopathic physician in New York, and for whose character I have the highest esteem.

"I went to his house in Jermyn Street, and introduced myself on the appointed evening to Mr. Home, who, I found, was a modest, intelligent youth of about twenty, in ill-health; and, indeed, as he himself informed me, and as, on inspection, I found to be the case, with the marks of consumption legible upon his frame. My wife accompanied me, and I met in Mr. H's rooms three friends, all of them men of talent and integrity. Bent upon narrative, and not upon defence or hostility, I will omit nothing; and so I here observe that we were, all of us, believers, beforehand, in the possibility of spiritual manifestations.

"Before sitting down in 'the circle,' I asked Mr. Home for some account of his antecedents. To the best of my recollection he gave the following particulars. He was born in Scotland, and was taken to America when a child. Very early in life he used to surprise those with whom he was, by spontaneously narrating, as scenes passing before his eyes, distant events, such as the death of friends and relatives; and these instances of second sight were found to be true telegraphy. It was not his fault—he could not help seeing them. Later on in his career, various noises were heard in the room beside him. This was about the time when the spiritual 'rapping' became known in America.

"He lived with an aunt, who was greatly scandalised at these circumstances. A member of the Presbyterian Church, these knockings even accompanied him to Divine worship; and, coming to the knowledge of his ecclesiastical overmen, he was adjudged to be the victim of satanic influences, and either excommunicated, or otherwise banished from the congregation. Afterwards he became a medical student; but ill-health forced him to abandon the idea of pursuing medicine as a calling. Such were the heads of what he told us, in answer to our enquiries, about himself.

"We were in a large upper room, rather bare of furniture; a sofa, a large round table, and a little buffet, together with a few chairs, were the fittings up. One of the party had brought with him a hand-bell and an accordion. We sat around the table, with the hands resting upon it. In a few minutes the table vibrated, or shuddered, as though actuated from within; it then became still, and instantly every one of us shook in his chair, not violently, but intimately, and like a jelly, so that objects 'dothered' before us. This effect ceased; and now the heavy table, with all our hands upon it, raised itself high up on its side, and rocked up and down; the raising proceeding from all different quarters, Mr. Home and all the rest of us (excepting our hands and arms, which were necessarily moved,) sitting death-still. The lamp on the table seemed as if it must tumble off; but he assured us there was no danger of *that*—that it was held safely in its place. The hand-bell had been placed upon the wooden rim round the pedestal of the table, and it now began to ring, apparently under different parts of the circle. Mr. Home said that the spirits were carrying it to one of the party, and suggested myself. I was sitting nearly opposite to him, at about three feet distance. I put my hand down under the margin of the table, and in perhaps a minute's time, I felt the lip of the bell poked up gently against the tips of my fingers, as if to say, 'I am here, take me.' This palpitation of the bell continued until I moved my fingers up its side to grasp it. When I came to the handle, I slid my fingers on rapidly, and now, every hand but my own being on the table, I distinctly felt the fingers, up to the palm, of a hand holding the bell. It was a soft, warm, fleshy, substantial hand, such as I should be glad to feel at the extremity of the friendship of my best friends. But I had no sooner grasped it momentarily, than it melted away, leaving my hand void, with the bell only, in it. I now held the bell lightly, with the clapper downwards, and while it remained perfectly still, I could plainly feel fingers ringing it by the clapper. As a point of observation I will remark that I should feel no more difficulty in swearing that the member I felt was a human hand of extraordinary life, and not Mr. Home's foot, than that the nose of the Apollo Belvidere is not a horse's ear. I dwell chiefly, because I can speak surely, on what happened to myself, though every one round the table had somewhat similar experiences. The bell was carried under the table to each, and rung in the hand of each. The accordion was now placed beneath the table, and presently we heard it moving along. Mr. Home put down his hand to the margin, and the instrument was given to him. With one hand upon the table, and with the other grasping the white wood at the bottom of the accordion, he held it bottom upwards, the keys hanging down over, and the instrument resting for support on his right knee. It played 'Home, sweet home,' and 'God save the Queen,' with a delicacy, of tone which struck every one present: I never heard silence threaded with such silver lines. Afterwards, in the same way, we were favoured with 'The Last Rose of Summer.' The accordion was then taken to each member of the party in succession; we could hear it rustling on its way between our knees and the pedestal of the table, and in the hand of each person, a few notes, but no whole tunes, were played. When in my own hand; I particularly noticed the great amount of force which was exerted by the player. It was difficult to hold the instrument from the strong downward pull, and had I not been somewhat prepared for this, the accordion would have fallen upon the floor. In the course of the evening we all felt either a finger, fingers, or a whole hand, placed upon our knees, always with a pleasant impression at the time. A white cambric handkerchief was drawn slowly under the table, and in the course of a few minutes handed to another person, tied in two knots, and put as a bouquet into the bell. And this experiment also was repeated for nearly all present. While these things were going on, rappings were heard in all parts of the room, in the table, in the floor, and the ceiling; and sometimes they were so loud, that the medium requested the spirits to remember that he was only a lodger, and that these noises might disturb the people in the rooms above and below. They were very unlike the 'Great Wizard's' raps, and occurred indifferently, as I said before, in all places and corners of the chamber. Towards the end of the séance, five distinct raps were heard under the table, which number, Mr. Home said, was a call for the alphabet. Accordingly, an alphabet was made; and on Mr. Home asking if any spirit was present who wished to speak to one of the party, the following sentence was given by the alphabetic telegraph:— 'My dear E____, Immortality is a great truth. Oh! how I wish my dear wife could have been present.—D.C.' It purported to be a near relation of one of those present, who died last year. The spelling 'immortality,' surprised me at first; but I recollected that the deceased; whom I knew well, was constantly versed in black letter writing, which makes elisions in that way. This ended, the medium fell into an apparently mesmeric trance, from which he addressed some good words of exhortation to each of us; and told one of the party in particular, several details about deceased members of the family, which were not known in the circle at the time, but verified to the letter afterwards. These, I forbear to mention, because they were of a strictly private nature. In his address, Mr. Home spoke, not as from himself, but as from the spirit assembly which was present; and he ended with a courteous 'Good night,' from them.

"Considering that it requires a large apparatus of preparation for the greatest of wizards to effect the smallest part of what we saw on this evening, namely, a few raps, one might have expected that Mr. Home would have had rather bulging pockets, to do what I have related, but I can assure your readers; that he was as meagre and unencumbered as the scantiest dresser need be: he had no assistants, and no screens. When, during the evening, I asked if the jugglers did their tricks by means similar to the agencies there present, the raps said 'No:' but in a pronounced manner they said 'Yes,' when the same question was put with regard to the 'Indian Jugglers.' We also asked Mr. Home why the effects generally took place *under* the table, and not upon it. He said that in habituated circles the results were easily obtained above board, visibly to all, but that at a first sitting it was not so. That scepticism was almost universal in men's intellects, and marred the forces at work; that the spirits accomplish what they do through our life-sphere, or atmosphere, which was permeated by our wills; and if the will was contrary the sphere was unfit for being operated upon.

"It was perhaps a fortnight after this that Mr. Home came by invitation, to my own house, to sit in the circle of my family. 'He was brought to the door in a carriage by some friends, with whom he was staying, without any paraphernalia which would characterize a wizard's art I watched him walk up the garden, and can aver that he had no magic wand up his trouser leg, nor any hunch in his dress that could betoken machinery or apparatus of any kind whatever. Arrived in the drawing-room, the 'raps' immediately commenced in all parts of it, and were also heard in the back drawing-room, which opens into the front by folding doors. The party assembled to constitute the 'circle' consisted of Mr. Home, my wife, my four children, and myself, and two domestics. We sat round a large and heavy loo table, which occupied the centre of the room. In a minute or two the same inward thrill went through the table as I have described in the first séance; and the chairs also, as before, thrilled under us so vividly, that my youngest daughter jumped up from hers, exclaiming, 'Oh! Papa, there's a heart in my chair,' which we all felt to be a correct expression of the sensation conveyed. From time to time the table manifested considerable movements, and after cracking, and apparently undulating in its place, with all our hands upon it, it suddenly rose from its place bodily some eight inches into the air, and floated wavering in the atmosphere, maintaining its position above the ground for half a minute, or while we slowly counted twenty-nine. Its oscillations during this time were very beautiful, reminding us all of a flat disc of deal on an agitated surface of water. It then descended as rapidly as it rose, and so nicely was the descent managed, that it met the floor with no noise, and as though it would scarcely have broken an egg in its contact. Three times did it leave the floor of the room, and poise itself in mid air, always in the same manner. During these intervals the medium was in a state of the completest muscular repose; nor, indeed, had he had the toe of Hercules for a lever could he have managed this effect, for he and all of us stood up each time, to follow the mounting table, and he stood with as complete absence of strain as the rest of us. It requires two strong men to lift the table to that height; one person might throw it over, but could by no means raise it from the floor.

"The travelling of the hand-bell under the table was also repeated for every one present, and this time they all felt the hand, or hands, either upon their knees, or other portions of their limbs. I put my hand down as previously, and was regularly stroked on the back of it by a soft palpable hand as before. Nay, I distinctly felt the whole arm against mine, and once grasped the hand, but it melted as on the first occasion; and immediately a call was made for the alphabet, there being something to communicate. The 'spirits' now spelt out through Mr. Home, who had known nothing of what I had done under the table, 'Do not grasp our hands.' I asked why, and Mr. Home said that they had great difficulty in presenting, and thus rapidly incarnating these hands out of the vital atmospheres of those present, and that their work was spoilt, and had to be recommenced, when they were interfered with, perhaps as a thought is sometimes broken in twain, and cannot easily be resumed on the irruption of a stranger. During the séance I had the border of a white cambric handkerchief just appearing out of the side pocket of my paletot, which was open; and though I could see no agency, I felt something twitching at the handkerchief, and very gradually drawing it from my pocket. Simultaneously with this, my eldest daughter, who sat opposite to me, exclaimed, 'Oh! I see phosphoric fingers at papa's pocket!' and, now visibly to all, the handkerchief was slowly pulled out, and drawn under the table; whilst, at the same time, I felt an arm that was doing it, but which was invisible to me. At this time I was at least three feet from Mr. Home, with a person between us, and he was absolutely passive. The feeling I had was of nudges, as distinct as ever I felt from a mortal limb, and that on my breast and arm, which were above the table; and yet, though the operation of abstracting my handkerchief was going on visibly to all, the rest of the circle, as well as myself (all except my eldest daughter), could see nothing. I can swear that there was no machinery, unless the skin, bone, muscle, and tendons of an unseen hand, forearm and elbow deserve the name.

"While this was going on, and for about ten minutes, more or less, my wife felt the sleeve of her dress pulled frequently, and as she was sitting with her finger ends clasped and hands open, with palms semiprone upon the table, she suddenly, laughed involuntarily, and said, 'Oh! see, there is a little hand lying between mine; and, now, a larger hand has come beside it. The little hand is smaller than any baby's, and exquisitely perfect' Our domestics, and two of the children, as well as my wife, all saw these hands, and watched them for between one and two minutes, when they disappeared. I now held my watch at the table side, the key in my hand, the chain and watch dangling from it, and I felt the weight of the watch gradually taken off, the chain being raised horizontally to my hand, and then the key, which I retained, was pulled laterally, and I let it go. It was taken under the table to my youngest daughter, and put on her knee. Whenever objects were thus removed from the hand, they were taken with a degree of physical power sufficient to suggest that the agent was capable of holding the object without letting it fall. An hour and three-quarters were occupied in these and similar manifestations, of which I have mentioned only the most striking, or those personal to myself; and now Mr. Home passed into the trance state, spoke of the spirit life, and the coming knowledge of it on earth, and said a few words apposite to each person present; dwelling also, upon the spiritual attendants who were standing beside each. When he came to my wife be lifted up his hands in an ecstasy, and described a spirit with her, most tiny, but beautiful. He said it was a little sister who had gone away a long time. 'But,' she said, 'I never had such a sister.' 'Yes, you had, though she had no name on earth.' On inquiry in the family, an event, such as he alluded to, had happened. This is the chief part of what struck me in Séance No. 2.

"At 10 p.m., Mr. Home went away on his own legs, so limber that I never so much as thought of any explanation of pasteboard arms or electric batteries concealed about his person.

"The next séance which I shall describe took place about the third week in July, at the house of a valued friend in Ealing, who had become convinced of the genuineness of the phenomena which accompanied Mr. Home, and with whom that gentleman was now staying. The party sat down to the table with Mr. Home, in the dusk of a fine evening, and were nine or ten in number. Here again I am forced to chronicle chiefly what befell myself, in order that I may be no second-hand witness. The first thing I remarked was a gentle tremulous flash of light through the room, but what was the cause of it I am unable to determine. When we had sat a few minutes I felt a decided but gentle grasp of a large man's hand upon my right knee, and I said to Mr. H., 'There is a man's hand upon my knee.' 'Who is it?' he said. 'How should I know?' was my reply. 'Ask,' said he. 'But how shall I ask?' 'Think of somebody,' was his answer. I thought involuntarily of an intimate friend, once a

Member of Parliament, and as much before the public as any man in his generation, and who died on the 30th of June last. And I said aloud, 'Is it _____?' Hearty affirmative slaps on the knee from the same hand, which had remained fixed till then, were the reply to my question. 'I am glad to be again in the same room with you,' said I. Again the same hearty, greeting was repeated. 'Are you better?' I inquired. A still more joyous succession of slaps, or rather, if I may coin a word, of accussions; for the hand was cupped to fit my bent knee, and gently struck me in that form. 'Have you any, message to your wife, whom I shall probably see in a few days?' Again, affirmative touches, five in number, therefore calling for the alphabet. Mr. Home now called over the alpha A B C D, and when he called T, my knee was struck; again when he said H and E, and so on, until this was spelled out: 'THE IMMORTAL LOVES.' I remember at the time thinking that this was rather a thin message; but the next time I saw Mrs. _____ I told her the circumstances, and gave her the words. Her son was sitting with her, and said, 'That is very characteristic of my father, for it was a favourite subject of speculation with him, whether or not the *affections* survive the body; of the immortality of the soul itself he never doubted; but the words, the immortal *loves,* show that he has settled the problem of his life.' Such was the import which the family of the deceased quite unexpectedly to me conferred upon the phrase. To return to Ealing, and that evening, after the last stroke of the hand had indicated the end of the sentence, I said, 'If it is really you, will you shake hands with me?' and I put my hand under the table, and now the same soft and capacious hand was placed in mine, and gave it a cordial shaking. I could not help exclaiming, 'This hand is a portrait. I know it from five years' constant intercourse, and from the daily grasp and holding of the last several months!' After this it left my knee; and when I asked if there was anything more, there was no response, and the agent appeared to be gone. But in two or three minutes more another hand, evidently also a man's, but small, thin, firm, and lively, was placed in the same position which the former had occupied; and after some preliminary questioning with Mr. Home, I said, 'Is it Mr. _____?' naming another valued friend, who, after twenty years of suffering, had departed this life almost on the same day as Mr. _____. With liveliest finger tips, the affirming hand danced up and down my leg, and upon my knee. I said, 'I am glad to find you are so much better. The playful hand beat 'yes' again. And this, in reply to renewed questions, for two or three minutes. Then I said, 'Have you any communication for your wife when I see her?' There was no response, and that agent there ceased to manifest himself. After another short pause, a totally different hand, a lady's, came to me, rested in my hand under the table, rubbed my hand, and allowed me at leisure to examine the delicate, beautiful, and warmth-raying fingers. It was signified that it was Mrs. _____, whom I had known in life, and who wished to greet me. Between and during what happened to myself, many of the rest of the circle were touched; and described their impressions much as I have described mine. Some had merely a single finger put upon their knees. Mr. Home said that the presenting spirits could often make one finger where they could not make two: and two, where they could not form an entire hand; just as they could form a hand where they could not realize a whole human figure; and he also said that this was one reason why they did not show themselves aboveboard, because they did not like imperfect members to be seen.

"These phenomena occupied less than an hour; and now the circle was broken up, and reconstituted, nine persons, to the best of my recollection, being arranged at the table. The table was placed opposite a window, and the bright moon beams streamed down upon its side. There was no candle in the apartment. The space of table which fronted the window was not occupied by sitters; but the company sat round about three-fourths of it, leaving the rest vacant. The right wing of the party was terminated by Mr. Home; the left by the son of the host. In a few minutes' time, close beside the latter gentleman, there emerged into sight above the rim of the table, in the vacant space, a delicately beautiful female hand and part of the forearm, apparently of ghostly tenuity. As I was sitting exactly opposite the vacant space; I had a fair opportunity of watching this hand as it projected against the moonlight; it was a filmy-looking woman's hand, with the fingers drooping forwards from left to right as I sat. The hand curved up over the table margin, deliberately grasped a hand-bell placed near, and carrying it partly down, let it drop upon the floor. It then rose to sight again, and took away a cambric handkerchief also placed near, which was tied in two knots under the table, and presented to one of the company, who had been strongly moved from the time that this hand was first seen. I forbear to give the further details of this hand, because they seemed to be of a private nature; suffice it to say, that it caused no little emotion to a gentleman who seemed concerned. On its disappearance, another hand, large, strong, and with the fingers extended, and pushed bolt up in the moonlight rose above the table near to Mr. Home. He cried out, 'Oh! keep me from that hand! it is so cold! Do not let it touch me!' Shortly it also vanished, and a third hand was seen at the other side of the vacant table edge: this hand was in a glove. Then presently a fourth hand ascended on the extreme left—a lady's hand, of beautiful proportions—and traversed the entire vacant space from left to right, rising, and displaying the forearm; and then, as it neared Mr. Home, the entire arm. When it reached him, the hand was level with his forehead, upon which it laid its palm, and with its fingers put his hair back, and played upon his brow for perhaps half a minute. I was sitting next but one to him, and leant forward past my intermediate neighbour, at the same time requesting that if the hand belonged to my friend Mrs. _____, it might also be laid on my forehead. This was deliberately done; and I felt its thrilling impression as the palm was laid flat upon my brow, where it remained for several seconds. It was warm and human, and made of no material but softest flesh. During the interval in which I felt it, I had abundant opportunity of examining most closely the arm and forearm. The forearm sleeve appeared to be of white cambric, plain and neat, and it shone like biscuit-porcelain in the moonlight. The sleeve of the dress up the arm was darker, but I do not remember the colour. And bending over, as I did, to the vacant rim of the table, I saw how the arm terminated— apparently in a graceful cascade of drapery; much as though an arm were put out through the peak of a snowy tent, the apex of which thus fell around the shoulder on every side. On leaving my forehead, the arm at once disappeared, and I watched it go. It was drawn into the same drapery; but so naturally that I can only liken it to a fountain falling down again, and ceasing into the bosom of the water from which it rose. And I also saw the drapery itself vanish, apparently by the same dissipative process. And now the spirits spelt out 'Good night.'

"These events occurred in the house of one of my oldest friends, whose superior in integrity I have never known, and of whose talent and sagacity I never heard a doubt entertained, until he endorsed these unpopular manifestations.

"Such is my experience. One hope I have in putting it forward is, that others who have seen Mr. Home may do the like, and thus make their contribution to the facts of the case.

"In conclusion, I will observe, that Sir David Brewster, and others almost as eminent, appear to me to make a scientific error in one respect—viz., in their estimate of the value of a man's character. They seem to think that charging a man of good antecedents, and with every appearance of a blameless life, with lying and imposture of the most systematic kind, is positively the easiest account that can be given of any rare phenomenon out of the pale of their own previous philosophy. I submit that this is not, for their own credit, the very first hypothesis of the case that ought to rush into their minds. Neither, parallel with this, is the other hypothesis that men of ability in all other things, and till then, known to be shrewd and searching, are infatuated dupes, to be commended as a proper valuation of what is rare and valuable in the human species. The rule of law, that "a man must be supposed innocent till proved guilty," is also *the* rule in such scientific explorations. This rule loves facts, and hates slander. I differ, therefore, with Sir David Brewster in his mode of exploration, and also in his valuation of presumptive honesty and human testimony, which always hitherto has been the most substantial word in the world, and a pillar which Divine Providence has not disdained to use in supporting the canopy of His Revelations.

"This rule I would especially press upon the great Sir David Brewster, a man of position, wealth, worldly repute, great talents, a name no one dare assail, and withal, responsibility to Heaven and his generation, when he is dealing, with the orphan, Home, a man apparently as blameless as himself, but with neither riches, nor health, nor station, nor any possession if not honesty, and a ruinous peculiarity of gift. It is not, I say, the easiest way out of a difficulty, to call this youth a cheat. There are cheats of our own house-hold, cheats in our own heads, sometimes called prejudices, which might be suspected *first*, without violating any rule of scientific inquest, or humane valuation.

"The experience of others in these matters has, perhaps, differed very widely from my own, and I desire to see this experience also brought forward. At other séances I have seen only a part of the phenomena which I have described as taking place on the three evenings which I have selected as being the fullest and best. And once or twice, when persons were present whom it was most desirable to convince, almost nothing occurred. This, I submit, is one of the strongest arguments in Mr. Home's favour. Were the phenomena a trick, they might always be produced to order without variation. 'The Great Wizard' never fails. But as he himself says, the spiritualists always fail in his company. Let this suggest that there is a total difference between him and them. It does not surprise me that spirits and their gifts should retire to a great gulf distance from where 'the Great Wizard' is.

"It seems probable from experience as well as reason that, granting the phenomena to be spiritual, the presence of determined scoffers at, and disbelievers in them, should in case the said persons be preponderant in their influence in the circle, render the manifestations imperfect or perhaps null. The known laws of human sympathy, and the operations of our own spirits when antipathetic persons are near us, may also be cited in proof of this. I conclude, then, that to the scoffer and the strongly prejudiced, who want no evidence, and to whom evidence has no appeal, evidence is, for the most part, not forthcoming. This simplifies the position; but what still remains is the peculiar Christian politesse of this century, viz., the necessity of good manners and the agreeing to differ. On the part of those who believe, this may be best secured by letting the other party be. Providence can convince them, too, as easily as ourselves, when the time and their function comes, but by snatching at them prematurely before they are ripe, we may evoke, on a great scale, two of the most formidable spirits of this world—WRATH and FEAR.

"As a final remark, let me caution the public against being led by Sir David Brewster, Mr. Faraday, and other men of great names in their own departments, in this matter which is obviously not within their field. We hear much of not choosing Crimean generals on old Peninsular qualifications. But, to select a Faraday or a Brewster for opinion on this case, is a far worse error; for all generals, past, present, and to come, are in the military line; but these great men are not and never were in the line upon which they have professed to decide. They are so alien to the subject, that they do not know the first condition of prosecuting it, namely, a gift of sympathy, and openness to conviction. Their very specialty of excellence in physical explorations, is against them in this new walk, which is combined spiritual and physical. The common observer with little in his mind, with no repute to support, and no case to uphold, may perchance be equipped by nature for these revolutionary sciences where the *savans* are stupid upon them. Twelve fishermen, and not the High Priests, are the everlasting resource of Providence. I therefore invite the unattached laity of all descriptions, the willing fishermen, to remember that they have no overmen in this department; that it is an untrodden field; and that by the grace of God, there is at last a freedom for us all from the pressure of big names; because 'the race is not to the swift, nor the battle to the strong.'"

The admirable narrative and reasoning of this letter leave nothing further to be said as to the manifestations during the remainder of my stay in England during the year, as I found it desirable to change the climate for that of Italy in the autumn. But I did not leave England without the satisfaction of having given opportunities to many hundreds of persons to investigate the phenomena for themselves, and through them the subject began to assume a form and importance which have made it the fear and the bugbear of those who had completed their circle of knowledge, and have no room in their philosophy for further facts. There are unfortunately many, whose minds have been in early life stereotyped in too hard and unyielding a material, to admit of either corrections or additions.

CHAPTER V

AT FLORENCE, NAPLES, ROME, AND PARIS

Early In the autumn of 1855 I went to Florence accompanied by the son of the gentleman with whom I had been residing at Ealing. I remained in Florence till the mouth of February, 1866, and although some persons there did all they could to injure me by false statements, I was only the more cherished by those who best knew me. I met there many distinguished men and women, and a Prince of one of the Royal Houses became deeply interested in what he witnessed. The manifestations while I was at Florence were very strong. I remember on one occasion while the Countess O____ was seated at one of Erard's grand action pianos, it rose and balanced itself in the air during the whole time she was playing. She also, whilst we were seated at a table in the room, took up an album which chanced to be lying there, and said, "Now if this is in reality the spirit of my dear father, I know you would wish to convince me, you can do so if you will, write your name on this page." She opened the book and placed it on her knees, and held a lead pencil in her hand. In a moment the pencil was taken out of her hand, and the name of her father, the Count O____, was written. On examination she said, "There is a slight resemblance to your writing, but I would wish it to be more distinct." She placed the open book again on her knees, and again the writing came in the same way, and also the words, "My dear daughter _____." This last writing she cut from my album, leaving in it the words first written, where they still are; and on going home she showed it to an old friend of her father's, saying, "Do you know whose writing that is?" "Of course," he said, "it is your father's." When, the Countess told him it had been written that very evening, he thought that to a certainty she had lost her senses, and on appealing to her husband, and finding that he corroborated her statement, he was equally alarmed for them both.

At the house of an English resident at Florence, I had many séances at which the power was very great, and she wrote a private account of some of the phenomena, which will show the reader the nature and extent of the manifestations at that time. I am very glad that I am able thus to give the results of the observations of others rather than my own unsupported statements. The lady says:

"The house in which I at present reside, and which, for some years past, has been my home, is a large, rambling, old-fashioned villa in the neighbourhood of Florence, whose internal architecture gives evidence of its having been built at different periods—those periods probably distant from each other.

"The oldest parts of the house, judging from the ornaments of a chapel which forms part of it, must, I should say, have been constructed in the early part of the sixteenth century. The rooms which I occupy are almost immediately above the chapel, and communicate on one side with the lower part of the house by a narrow stone staircase. On first coming to reside here we learned that the villa had, in common with many others of the same description, the reputation of being haunted. Strange lights it was said had been seen issuing from the chapel windows, and unearthly noises heard in that part of the house to which I have alluded. Some friends passed the winter with us some five or six years since, and their servant occupied a small room on an *entresol* between the chapel and my rooms, but his rest became so broken, and he described the noises he heard as so peculiar, that be requested to be allowed to sleep elsewhere. I was formerly much in the habit of dismissing my maid early, and sitting up either reading or writing until a late hour. At such times I have been suddenly seized with a strange fearfulness, a kind of nervous dread, more easily imagined than described. In fact, it would be impossible to define my sensations at those moments, further than by saying that I felt I was no longer *alone*. This feeling usually lasted from five to ten minutes, and invariably left a painful impression on my spirits. I also often heard a peculiar rustling sound in my room, and around my bed, as though some one were agitating the bed curtains, and this sound was invariably accompanied by a chilliness, as if a door had been suddenly opened, and a strong current of cold wind had rushed with violence into the room.

"These sounds and the other painful sensations which I have described; and which I was totally unable to explain, continued at intervals with greater or lesser degrees of intensity until the month of October, 1855, when much sensation was created in Florence by the arrival of Mr. Home, whose reputation as a spirit medium had rendered him celebrated. A short time after his arrival in Florence, the sounds in my room became more distinct and more frequent, and the very peculiar nervous feelings of which I have spoken, were not confined so exclusively to myself, but were frequently shared by my sister, if she remained any time in my room. My rest at length became so broken, and in consequence my health so impaired, that I had my bed removed into a room adjoining the one in which I had been in the habit of sleeping, hoping that the change would bring me quiet.

"The first night was undisturbed, but the next and succeeding nights were so painful that I frequently lay awake until morning. In the meantime, we made Mr. Home's acquaintance, and having been a witness of effects so wonderful as only to be ascribed to a supernatural cause, I determined to discover, if possible, through his agency, the real secret of my haunted rooms,

"Mr. Home having been invited to make a stay of a few days in our house, was on the first day of his arrival made acquainted with the mystery of my rooms, and he proposed that a séance should be held in them for the purpose of endeavouring to ascertain whether or not the strange sounds which disturbed me were to be attributed to supernatural agency. Accordingly about eleven o'clock on that same evening, my sister, Mr. Home and myself repaired to my room, and placed ourselves at a small round table in front of, and very near the fire-place. We were warmly covered, and the fire was blazing brightly; yet the cold that pervaded the room was intense, penetrating to the very bones. I should mention that for many previous days, I had suffered from what appeared to be a cold air, which was quite independent of the atmospheric temperature, blowing over my body, especially over the lower limbs. This feeling never left me, and all artificial means failed in destroying the sensation of chilliness. This same cold air was now felt by both my sister and Mr. Home to such a degree as to be painful to them also. I have since found that it is a frequent accompaniment of the manifestations.

"Previously to placing himself at the table, Mr. Home had descended to the chapel, where, however, all was quiet. On reascending the stairs, he heard a sound as of a muffled bell tolling in the chapel. We had scarcely sat a moment at he table, when it began slowly to move about in different directions, generally inclining towards the side on which I sat. Presently the movements became more violent, and assumed, if I may be allowed the expression, an angry appearance. We asked if a spirit were present, and the table replied by making the three usual affirmative movements.

"We then further inquired whether the spirit present were a good one, and were answered in the negative. We spoke in harsh terms, which seemed to irritate the spirit, for the demonstrations became very angry. A high backed old fashioned chair, which stood at a little distance from the table was suddenly, and without human contact, drawn close to it, as though some one, in sitting down, had so drawn it. Nothing was, however, visible. Mr. Home proposed that the should move into the next room, my bedroom, and try whether any further manifestations would be made there. We did so: but all remained quiet. We then returned to the room we had just quitted, and sat down at another table covered with a cloth. We had previously heard a rustling sound about, and under the tables, such a sound as would be made by a person moving about in a heavy garment. This noise was accompanied by a scratching on the wood of the table, as though some one were scraping it with his nails. We then distinctly saw the cloth on the side of the table next to me move up, as though a hand raised it from beneath. The hand appeared to be in a menacing attitude. Mr. Home was also often touched on the knee, and he described the touch as peculiarly strong and disagreeable.

"We then entreated the spirit to leave us, requiring it should return on the following evening, and declare its purpose in thus tormenting us. This it promised, and on being further adjured in the name of the Holy Trinity to leave us, the demonstrations ceased.

"The night was very unquiet. The sensation of cold, of which I have before spoken, accompanied me every where, and I heard a frequent scratching under my pillow, and on my bed. On the next evening we met again in my room, and were joined by two other persons, one a member of our family, the other, a gentleman known to Mr. Home, and who was then investigating this phenomenon, both men of strong nerve and dispassionate judgment. The usual cold was felt, and the table became much agitated. A small stiletto, which I use as a paper-knife, was taken from the table as by an invisible hand, and drawn from the sheath. The table was then lifted from the ground, and was violently pushed across the room. It stopped opposite a door leading to the staircase, and we resumed our places.

"A small hand-bell was taken from off the table, and violently rung in different directions. The dagger was thrown about under the table, and rubbed against Mr. Home's knees. My elbow was violently grasped by a hand, the fingers of which I distinctly saw—they were long, yellow and shining. Other persons present, who felt its grasp, described its touch as clammy and horrible. I spoke gently to the spirit, who, in answer to my questions, said he was unhappy, and that perhaps I might be of some use to him. He promised to return and speak farther on the following evening, and after lifting the table several times high above our heads, he left us.

"The whole of the next day I was more or less tormented by the cold air, which blew over my face and limbs, especially in the evening, a short time before the hour appointed for the séance. This wind then became very strong, and again a hand raised the cloth of the table on which I was leaning, and touched my arm as if to remind me of my engagement. We repaired to my room, one member only of my family being present, my sister having suffered too much from alarm on the previous evening to join us.

"The demonstrations of the table immediately began, but in a quieter manner than on former occasions. I immediately spoke (I should say that Italian was the only language used (Here the writer omits a rather curious circumstance. The Italian, she observed, was incorrectly spelled; but, on afterwards comparing it with the state of the language in the sixteenth century, it was found to be correct.)), in a soothing manner. In reply to many questions the spirit told me he was unhappy, and had wandered about the house for many many years, that his name was Giannana, that he had been a monk, and had died in the room which I then occupied. I desired to know whether I should have masses said for the peace of his soul. He answered in the negative, but requested that I should pray that it might find some repose. I further begged him to tell me why on the previous evening he had made so much use of the little dagger, and he answered that in life he had but too well known how to employ it. He then promised me never again to return to my rooms; and since that evening those painful sensations and strange noises, of which I have spoken so much, have left me, and never have returned. Frequent séances, where good and loving spirits have given us comforting communications, have been since held by their own especial request in my room. The dagger has by them been drawn from its sheath, and the bell rung, as though the touch of holy hands were needful in order to destroy any painful recollections in my mind connected with these articles, or any reluctance I might feel to again make use of them. In fact my rooms seem to have undergone a complete *purification*, and I feel that whatever painful influence did once exist there, it has disappeared wholly, and I trust for ever."

The above was written shortly after the strange event it records. On the 3rd of April, 1860, being then in London, I received a letter from the same lady, dated Florence, 27th March, of which the following is an extract

"I believe I told you that the noises at the Villa are worse than ever, and the new proprietor is dreadfully disturbed by them. The house has been exorcised, but without effect. My own rooms are the most disturbed."

On the 5th of December, 1855, whilst I was returning to my rooms late at night in Florence, the streets being deserted, I observed a man stepping from the doorway of the adjoining house. I was on the step leading to my own door, and was looking up at the window to see if the servant was still up, when I received a violent blow on my left side, the force of which and the emotion caused by it, threw me forward breathless in the corner of the doorway. The blow was again repeated on my stomach, and then another blow on the same place, and the attempted assassin cried out, "Dio mio, Dio mio," and turning with his arm outstretched, he ran. I distinctly saw the gleam of his poignard, and as he turned, the light of the lamp also fell full on his face, but I did not recognise his features. I was perfectly powerless, and could not cry out or make any alarm, and I stood thus for at least two minutes after which I groped my way along the wall to the door of a neighbour, where I was admitted. I thought I must have received some serious injury, but on examining myself I found that the first blow had struck the door key, which I happened to have in my breast pocket, immediately over the region of my heart, I wore a fur coat, and this had chanced to be twice doubled in front. The second blow had gone through the four folds of it, through a corner of my dress coat, my waistcoat, and the hand of my trousers, without inflicting any wound. The third blow had penetrated the four folds of my coat, and also my trousers and linen, and made a slight incision, which bled, but not freely.

I had that morning received from a dear friend, who had in his house a clairvoyant of remarkable powers, a letter begging me not to go out that evening, as she had received a warning of impending danger, but to this I paid no attention. I never discovered the perpetrator, nor the cause of my life being attacked. Many reasons were assigned, amongst them robbery, mistaken identity, and religious intolerance.

In the month of January, Signor Landucci, then Minister of the Interior to the Grand Duke of Tuscany, sent to me to request that I would not walk about the house at night between the lights and the window, or go out in the streets in the day time, giving as a reason that some of my enemies had been playing upon the superstitions of the peasantry, and telling them that it was my practice to administer the seven sacraments of the Catholic church to toads, in order by spells and incantations to raise the dead. This had so enraged and excited them that they were fully bent on taking my life, and for that purpose were concealed about the neighbourhood with fire arms.

I met at this time a Polish nobleman, who with his family was about to visit Naples and Rome, and who most kindly pressed me to accompany them. I was left in Florence without money, and my friends in England having their credulity imposed upon by some scandalmongers, and thinking me to be leading a most dissolute life, refused to send me even money of my own which had been entrusted to their care. I told the Count B____ that I would travel with him, and the very day I gave this assent, the spirits told me that my power would leave me for a year. This was on the evening of the 10th of February, 1856. Feeling that the Count and his family must have felt an interest in me, arising only from the singular phenomena which they had witnessed in my presence, and that this cause being removed, their interest in me would have diminished, I wrote the following morning to inform them of what I was told, and to say that I could no longer entertain the idea of joining them. They at once told me that it was for myself, even more than for the strange gift I possessed, that they had become interested in me. I went to them, and in a day or two we left Florence for Naples. While here, although my powers had left me, still my presence seemed to develop the power in others; for I met, at his own residence, the Hon. Robert Dale Owen, who was the American Minister to the Court of Naples, and it was in the presence of one of the Royal Princes of that family, himself a medium, that he was first convinced. Mr. Owen has since written a most able and carefully arranged book of authentic facts, entitled, "Footfalls on the Boundaries of another World," in which he has brought together both the facts and the philosophy of this great subject. We remained in Naples nearly six weeks, and then proceeded to Rome. Here in the absence of the power, my mind sought in the natural world for that consolation which it had hitherto found in the spiritual, and now this being withdrawn, life seemed to me a blank. I read with intense eagerness all the books I could find relating to the doctrines of the Romish church, and finding them expressive of so many facts which I had found coincident in my own experience, I thought that all contending and contradictory beliefs would be for ever set at rest, could I but be received as a member of that body. My experiences of life and its falsity had already left an indelible a mark on my soul, from my recent experiences of it at Florence, that I wished to shun every thing which pertained to this world, and I determined to enter a monastery.

After two or three weeks of serious deliberations on the part of the authorities, it was decided that I should be received as a member of the church, and I was confirmed. The Princess O____ was my godmother, and the Count B____ my godfather on the occasion. I was most kindly received by the Pope, who questioned me much regarding my past life. He pointed to a crucifix which stood near to us, and said, "child, it is upon what is on that table that we place our faith." He also gave me a large silver medal, which it has since been my misfortune to lose.

It has since been frequently said of me that at this interview with the Pope, I had promised him that I would not have any more manifestations; but it is hardly necessary, after what I have narrated, to say that I could not have made any such promise, nor did he ask any such promise to be made.

In June, 1856, I went to Paris, and as I had been advised to do by the Pope, I sought the counsel of the Père de Ravignan, one of the most learned and excellent men of the day. The purpose of my remaining in France was to acquire a facility in the language. During the winter I again fell ill, and Dr. Louis, one of the most celebrated physicians in France for consumptive cases, decided on auscultation that my left lung was diseased, and advised a more genial climate. This could not, however, be accomplished, and for some time I was confined to my bed. The time was fast drawing nigh when the year would expire, during which my power was to be suspended. The Père de Ravignan always assured me that as I was now a member of the Catholic church it would not return to me. For myself I had no opinion on the subject, as I was quite without data except his assurance on the point.

On the night of the 10th of February, 1857, as the clock struck twelve, I was in bed, to which I had been confined, when there came loud rappings in my room, a hand was placed gently upon my brow, and a voice said, "Be of good cheer, Daniel, you will soon be well." But a few minutes had elapsed before I sank into a quiet sleep, and I awakened in the morning feeling more refreshed than I had done for a long timer. I wrote to the Père de Ravignan, telling him what had occurred, and the same afternoon he came to see me. During the conversation loud rappings were heard on the coating and on the floor, and as he was about to give me his benediction before leaving, loud raps came on the bedstead. He left me without expressing any opinion whatever on the subject of the phenomena.

The following day I had sufficiently recovered to take a drive, and on Friday the 13th, I was presented to their Majesties at the Tuileries, where manifestations of an extraordinary nature occurred. The following morning, I called on the Père de Ravignan to inform him of this. He expressed great dissatisfaction at my being the subject of such visitations, and said that he would not give me absolution unless I should at once return to my room, shut myself up there, and not listen to any rappings, or pay the slightest attention to whatever phenomena might occur in my presence. I wished to reason with him, and to explain that I could not prevent myself from hearing and seeing, for that God having blessed me with the two faculties, it was not in my power to ignore them. As for shutting myself up, I did not think, from my having before tried the experiment, that it was consistent with my nervous temperament, and that the strain on my system would be too great if I were thus isolated. He would not listen to me, and told me I had no right to reason, "Do as I bid you, otherwise bear the consequences." I left him in great distress of mind. I wished not to be disobedient, and yet I felt that God is greater than man, and that He having bestowed the power of reason on me, I could not see why I should be thus deprived of it. On reaching my room, I found there a very dear and valued friend, the Count de K____. He observed my agitation, and questioned me as to the cause. I told him all, and he said, "There is but one thing to do, come home with me, and we will send for the Abbé de C____, and consult him." The Abbé came, and after hearing my story, he said, "That they might as well put me in my grave alive, as to carry out what had been ordered," adding, "I would like very much to witness some of these wonderful things." Most fortunately my emotion had not destroyed the power, as is usually the case when I am agitated, for while we were together several interesting phenomena occurred. His words were, "Let this power be what it will, it is in no way of your making." He recommended me to seek another spiritual adviser, and added, "I myself would gladly be your adviser, but as it would be known, I should only be persecuted." He gave me the name of one of the most eloquent preachers of the day, and I introduced myself to him, and remained under his guidance during the few weeks of my stay in Paris previous to my going to America to bring back my sister. During my absence, the curiosity had become very great to find out who was my confessor, and the Countess L____, having heard that he was a distinguished man, called upon several of the most noted in Paris, and after a short conversation, she abruptly said to each, "So you are Mr. Home's confessor." Most naturally on one such occasion, she chanced to find the right one, and his look of surprise betrayed him. His surprise was that I should have revealed his name, and this he expressed to the Countess, who told him that I had not betrayed him, but that she had used that artifice to ascertain the fact. This was the cause of my not continuing with him longer as my confessor.

The extract I here give is one from the recently published life of the great confessor, the Père de Ravignan, who had been recommended to me by the Pope, and I can only regret he is no longer here to contradict, with his own pen, the false statements concerning me, made by his biographer, the Jesuit Father A. de Ponlevoy. At the termination of Chapter XXIV, this person says, "We could not close this chapter without making mention of that famous American medium, who had the sad talent of turning other things than the tables, and invoking the dead to amuse the living. A great deal has been said, even in the papers, of his acquaintance, religiously and intimately, with Father de Ravignan, and they have seemed to wish, under the passport of a creditable name, to introduce and establish in France these fine discoveries of the New World. Here is the fact in all its simplicity. It is very true, that the young foreigner, after his conversion in Italy, was recommended from Rome to the Father de Ravignan, but at that period, in abjuring Protestantism, he also repudiated magic, and he was received with that interest that a priest owes to every soul ransomed by the blood of Jesus Christ, and more, perhaps, to a soul which has been converted, and brought to the bosom of the church. On his arrival in Paris, all his old practices were again absolutely forbidden. The Father de Ravignan, according to all the principles of the faith, which forbids superstition, forbade under the most severe penalties he could inflict, that he should be an actor in, or even witness of these dangerous scenes, which are sometimes criminal. One day the unhappy medium, tempted by I know not what, man or demon, violated his promise; he was retaken with a rigour which overwhelmed him. Coming in then by chance I saw him rolling on the ground, and drawing himself like a worm to the feet of the priest who was in saintly anger. The Father, however, touched by his convulsive repentance, lifted him up, forgave him, and sent him away, after having exacted, by writing this time, a promise under oath. But soon there was backsliding which made much noise (*rechute éclatante*), and the servant of God, breaking off with this slave of the spirits, had him told never again to appear in his presence."

If, the rest of the book be no more truthful than this statement, it is certainly not worth reading. The good Father de Ravignan well knew that I was not an American, and that this power had began with me before I ever saw America, for I had told him all my history. He also knew that I never invoked the spirits. No good name is, or ever will be, required to introduce, or accredit a God-given truth, and I knew far too well the power of facts to think that they required the passport of even Father Ravignan's name. His biographer must have had a limited education too, both religious and historical, to write of these things as being the "fine discoveries" of the New World, for they are to be readily traced in every age and country of the world of which we have any record or history preserved to us. It is perfectly untrue that I ever abjured any magical, or other processes, for I never knew anything of such, and therefore I could not abjure them.

The Father de Ravignan used to say to me, when I told him that the spirits had said they would return to me on the 10th of February, 1857, "There is no fear of that, my child, so long as you go on as you are now doing, observing carefully all the sacraments of our holy church; they will not be allowed to return." I followed out his injunctions most conscientiously; but on the very day promised, they came as I have described, and told me they were glad to find me in so pure a state of mind, as it greatly facilitated their approach. I never yet violated any promise to my knowledge, and as to the biographer coming in and finding me rolling on the ground, and crawling like a worm, it is an entire falsehood. But had it even been true, it would not have been the place of a priest to make such a thing public. If I took an oath, and wrote it down as alleged, that writing will have been kept. Let it be forthcoming to save the character of this Father A. de Ponlevoy, that he may prove the truth of the statement he makes. In the meantime, I say that it is without even any foundation of truth. The last time I saw the good 'Father de Ravignan, I would only reason with him, for as I then said to him, no man had a right to forbid that which God gave. I left him without confessing even, so I had not been on my knees at all, much less crawling like a worm.

As I have said, when the Abbé C____ came to see me, the conversation I had with him only tended to strengthen me in my opinion of what was right, for when priests are not agreed as touching such a matter, whom or what are we to rail on, if not on the reason God has given us. The Father Ravignan never had me informed that he would not see me again. On the contrary, it was I who said I would not go to him till he would reason with me. I have letters of his to me in my possession, which will show the kind feeling he ever had for me previous to this period, and I am well assured in my own mind, that he never said aught against me, even when I no longer saw him. He was so good, so pure, and so high minded, that I would that he had had a more truthful and honest chronicler to write his life.

The Countess L____ was herself a firm believer in the manifestations which she had frequently witnessed in my presence, and she was also present when I had a vision which is described in one of the Paris papers in the following words:

"The recent failure of Mr. Thurneyssen recalls to us a strange fact that signalized the sojourn of Mr. Home in Paris during the last winter. The Countess _____ had a dozen years ago a strange hallucination. One evening being busy with some embroidery, alone with her brother, he was reading to her one of the most irreligious books of the eighteenth century. As she listened mechanically to his reading, she raised her head, and looking at her brother she was struck with terror at the sight of the strange expression of his face. He was ordinarily a most gentle, benevolent, and sympathetic young man, with calm, quiet features, but at that moment they were frightfully contracted, the eyebrows singularly convulsed, the eyes wide open, the corners of the mouth distorted by a bitter and despairing smile, and altogether he had the peculiar expression which painters would give to a fallen angel. The frightened Countess had immediately, as it were a thought revealed to her, (for she never previously dreamed of the possibility of such a thing), she was convinced that her brother was possessed by a demon. Frequently afterwards she saw the same infernal expression on the face of her brother, even when he was most calm and happy; but the idea was so horrible to her that she never mentioned the circumstance. Last winter Mr. Home was introduced to the Countess. Being at her house one evening, and in his usual quiet frame of mind, his attention was drawn to a beautiful marble bust. He was not aware of its being that of the brother of the Countess, but immediately his whole visage changed, and he became in a state of most violent agitation. The Countess much alarmed inquired why he was so affected, when Mr. Home replied, 'Madame, the man whose bust this is, is possessed with a demon.' One may judge of the astonishment of the Countess on hearing Mr. Home say what she had thought twelve years before. She pressed him with questions, and he, recovering from his emotion, rose and went to examine the bust more closely, then turning to the Countess he said, 'In a short time your brother will have a great misfortune, and this misfortune will deliver him from his enemies.'

"And so it has occurred; the Count de P____ has lost in the bankruptcy of M. Thurneyssen a considerable part of his fortune. The prophecy came four months previous to the failure. Could it have been that the spirits saw the dishonesty of Thurneyssen? if so this might account why certain persons are so ready to oppose all communication with the other world, preferring the darkness to the light."

The day previous to my leaving Paris, a wonderful case of healing occurred through me in the manner which I will now relate.

On the 19th of March, 1857, when I was residing at 13, Rue des Champs Elysées, I received a letter from a stranger to me, Madame A. Mavoisin de Cardonne, of 233, Rue St. Dominique, St. Germain, stating that she had had a dream, in which she had seen her own mother and mine, and that the latter had told her to seek me at once, in order that her son, who had been deaf for four years from the effects of typhoid fever, might be cured. This was so strongly impressed upon her mind, that she wrote to me to say that she would call upon me with her son, the following morning at ten.

Accordingly the next morning she presented herself with her son at my rooms, there being present the Princess de B____ and Miss E____, who were with me, previous to my leaving Paris that very day, to proceed on my voyage to America. I had been so overwhelmed by persons wishing to see me that I had uniformly refused such visits; but on this occasion I had been so much pre-occupied by my engagements in preparing for my voyage, that I had not been able to acknowledge her letter, or to write to her either in the affirmative or negative. I therefore received her with considerable embarrassment, which was fully reciprocated on her part. It was indeed an embarrassing meeting for both of us, the mother yearning for her son's recovery, and I, not knowing how I was expected to be instrumental in healing this long total deafness; the more so that operations had been performed on the boy, as I afterwards found, by eminent surgeons of Paris, who had said that it was impossible he should ever be restored to hearing.

She sat down on a chair near a sofa, I taking a seat on the sofa, and beckoning the son to be seated on my left. The son was in his fifteenth year, tall for his age, of a delicate complexion, with large dreamy blue eyes that looked as if they would supply the place of hearing, with their deep, thoughtful, enquiring gaze. The mother began her description of the boy's illness, commencing with the attack of the fever, and ending in the entire loss of hearing. During the recital, told with all the warmth and tenderness of a mother's heart, and describing the various surgical operations to which he had been subjected, my sympathies were deeply moved, and I had unwittingly thrown my left arm about the boy and drawn him towards me, so that the boy's head rested upon my shoulder. Whilst in this position, and Madame de Cardonne was telling some of the most painful particulars, I passed my hand caressingly over the boy's head, upon which he, partly lifting his head, suddenly exclaimed in a voice trembling with emotion, *"Maman, je t'entends!"* (Mamma, I hear you!) The mother fixed on him a look of astonishment, and said, "Emile," the boy's name, and he at once replied, *"Quoi?"* (What?) She then, seeing that the child had heard her question, fainted with emotion, and on her recovery the scene was a most thrilling one—the poor mother asking continually questions for the mere pleasure of hearing her child reply. The boy, was able to resume his studies; and has continued to hear perfectly up to the present time.

Chapter VI

In America. The Pressgang

On reaching America, I found that the American press had been publishing some ridiculous paragraphs about me, one of which was of a practical joke said to have been perpetrated by General Baraguay d'Hilliers and others in the presence of the Emperor, and that I myself had become greatly alarmed, and finally very angry on discovering the trick. The whole was a fabrication, as will be seen, for at that time I had never even seen either of the three gentlemen who were said to be actors in it. The following paragraph was, also, of the same character, as I had not then met M. Dumas.

"Home, the table-turner and magnetiser, who has of late caused such attention in Paris, has predicted to M. Alexander Dumas that he would live to the age of 113 years, and be killed in a duel."

The following is another specimen of a similar kind.

"Mr. Home, the medium who has made such a sensation in Paris, is on his way to this country, to visit his sister. He has been offered marriage by a lady of immense wealth, but has refused her."

The "New York Herald," a paper better known for its untruthfulness than otherwise, published letters from its special correspondents at Paris, stating "from the most reliable sources," that I had stolen £30,000, and was now for ever banished from France. I had at that very moment my return ticket in my pocket, and knew that an Imperial Prince, then on a visit to the Emperor was awaiting my return. Indeed, if the public judged of my life from what the newspapers said of me, they must have been greatly, puzzled by the statements and contradictions which successively appeared. I was quite content to leave both without notice, and I have never been at the pains to set them right. The following notice is of the same class as the preceding.

"The 'Indépendance Belge' states that Napoleon sent away Mr. Home, the American spirit-rapper, because the Empress was so much affected that the Emperor dreaded the continuance of the diabolical scenes. The ladies of honour were equally excited and could talk of nothing else. It is said that Home was quartered in the royal household, and was paid at the rate of £40,000 pounds per year."

The "Hartford Courant," states:

"The 'Times' says that Daniel Dunglas Home, the famous medium, whose performances are so peculiar as to utterly baffle the most acute and sagacious minds, and who is a gentleman of education and character quite out of the range of the common mediums, was in this city last Saturday. We regard him as the most remarkable man living; and no man who has not witnessed what is done in Home's presence, can claim a right to give an opinion on Spiritualism. Mr. Home says the jokes of the newspaper correspondents about him are entirely untrue. He had some *sittings* at the Tuileries, but declined conversation on that subject."

Another paper, "The Springfield Republican," noticed my presence in America as follows:

"Home, the distinguished spiritual medium, who has recently been raising spirits in the presence of the Emperor Napoleon, is in Springfield on a brief visit. He will return to France shortly, where his services are in great request among the savans."

A New York paper gave the following account, correcting some of the misstatements about me:

"What terrible gossippers some of our letter writers are. The New York Editor of the 'London Letter,' in the last 'Sunday Times,' has the following paragraph: 'It is whispered, in Paris, that Home, the American spirit-rapper, was producing so much mischief in the Court that he was ordered off by the alarmed Emperor; and the fellow who, though playing the part of a personage with £40,000 a year, was really penniless, has left for the country of the rappers.'

"Possibly it may interest some of our readers to know something of Mr. Home, who has lately afforded a prolific subject to paragraph makers. We have nothing to say as to his 'spiritual' belongings here, but simply speak of the lad—for he is scarcely more, being but twenty-two years old now—in reference to such reports as the above. Home, the 'American,' is of an old Scottish family of standing, and was born in Scotland, but brought very young to this country. Quiet and unobtrusive in his manners, he never has thrust himself forward, nor specially sought nor avoided the notoriety which attends him; *never has exhibited himself as a public medium*, as many suppose, but has simply suffered events to take their course with him.

"As to the above story of his quitting Paris, which has gone the rounds, in various shapes, we have only to say, that some two Sundays since, while reading from the English papers an account of his doings in Paris, and supposing him snugly ensconced in the Tuileries, the door opened, and to our astonishment, in walked Mr. Home, to take dinner 'at home'—it being under our own roof that, some six years since, at the age of sixteen, he found his first shelter in New York (Brooklyn), a temporary refuge from horror-stricken relatives, who had turned the I 'rapper' adrift as being 'possessed of a devil;' thus starting him as a young martyr at least; whether deservedly so or not.

"He told us of his arriving a day or two before, at Philadelphia, and stated what he had come for, and when he was going back. He has accomplished his errand—part of which was to obtain his sister, with whom he sailed from Boston, a few days since, on his return to Paris.

"So much for the 'mischief' and the 'alarmed Emperor,' who 'ordered him off,' a story made of the same bit of cloth as the Socrates joke by Baraguay d'Hilliers and others."

Whilst on the subject of these newspaper inventions, I may as well allude to a curious series of them which occurred in 1858. I had then left Paris for Rome, on account of my health, and on the 13th of March, the following telegraphic dispatch reached me there from a friend in Paris, "Tell me immediately if you are still at Rome. I have a request to make." I replied that I was still at Rome, and in course of post I received a letter of the 14th March, as follows:

"Dear Friend.—I sent you yesterday a telegraphic dispatch that you might write to me at once if you were at Rome. I made pretext of having a commission to ask you to do; but it was in reality only to have a letter from you as soon as possible. Scandal says you have been arrested, and the Hague papers say that you are in prison at Mazas. Monsieur B____, whose son is a medium, has sent to know the truth, and I have authorized him to publish that I have a letter from you, bearing date of Rome the 7th of March. I have also sent to inform 'La Patrie,' that a stop may be put to these base calumnies. I trust you will approve of what I have done."

The Parisian papers took up the report, and it was confirmed by them that I was truly in prison at Mazas. Persons even in official positions told my friends *that they had seen and spoken to me in that prison,* and one, an officer, went so far as to state that he had accompanied me there in the carriage.

Being at Rome, and altogether unaware of all this scandal which was passing about me, I had felt forcibly impressed, I knew not why, to write to M. Henri Delage, the well known mystic writer of Paris. I did so, and it will be observed by the following paragraph introducing my letter, how very opportunely my impression had been given, and how well I had acted in following it out.

Paris correspondent of "Le Nord."

"Paris, 17th March.

"Allow me to begin by a good action; it is to free an honourable man from calumnies, arising from what source I know not, but which for the past few days have been rapidly spreading. I speak of Mr. Home, who is, for the moment, in Italy, whereas it is whispered both secretly and openly that he is in the prison of Mazas, for we know not what crimes. The letter here given, dated Rome, 7th of March, was received yesterday by M. Henri Delage, an intimate friend of Mr. Home. The letter is there before me with the postal mark, and I will give you his literal words:

"'Rome, March 7th, 1858.

"'Dear M. Delage,—You were without doubt much surprised to hear of my departure for Italy; but the truth is I was very ill. I had an impoverishment of the blood, so what could I do. My power had quite left me. The dear spirits thought me too ill to see strangers. Here in Rome I go but little into society, a complete rest being necessary. Write to me soon, and will you kindly remember me to M. H____, you know I like him very much.

Yours faithfully,
"'D. D. HOME.'

"I beg of you to give the publicity of your well known journal to this letter of Mr. Home. It being the best reply which can be given to those base calumnies which attack his honour."

I well know the origin and cause, of this intrigue and I have in my possession a friendly letter, bearing date the 18th July, 1858, from the Bureau du Ministre de l'Intérieur, which is a sufficient refutation of the wicked calumny. His Highness the Prince Murat also made it the occasion of proving to me not only the Christian principles which actuated him, but also the true nobleness of his heart, in doing for a comparative stranger, that which a father alone could be expected to do for a son. He, at his own expense, sent persons to Germany, to Italy, and to England, to ascertain the foundation of such a libel, and generously gave me his public and private testimony to its entire untruth.

I have now to present the following letter, and the enclosed programme, which I also received while at Rome, and which disclose a case of personation, which is by no means either the first or the last of that kind which I could give. It is, however, an amusing specimen of them.

"Paris, April 7th.

"Dear friend,—I send you a programme taken from one of the Lyons papers, that was sent to M. Allen Kardec. What a shame to think such an imposition should be allowed in your name. I would advise you to write at once to the Prefect of Lyons, or to the police, that the villain should be unmasked as soon as possible, not only for the wrong he does to your name, but also to the cause of spiritualism. Do not allow a moment to pass, and we on our side will do all we can. Only think of the audacity in daring to say that he had been received by the Emperor.

"I am, &c., &c.

"P.S.—I have this moment heard that the imposture was at once discovered, and he has fled from Lyons."

I give the original programme, with an English translation.

"Salle du Grand Théatre. Jeudi, Avril 1, 1858, à huit heures. Soirée Américaine ou Séance de Spiritualisme de M. Home.

"'Je ne me guide jamais d'après la science, mais d'après ma conscience; je crois donc fortement aux faits magnétiques, je crois quo la force magnétique augmente prodigieusement la force de vision de l'homme; je crois que ces faits sent constatés par un certain nombre d'hommes trèsssincères et très-chrétiens.'—L'ABBÉ LACORDAIRE.

"Programme: Expérience de vision par M. Home et l'Ange miraculeux.—Obéissance à l'ordre du public.—Séance de spiritualisme par la sensitive Mme. de Cabanyes.

"Production des visions demandées par les spectateurs: Frémissement, Joie, Colère, Idiotisme, Piété, Multiplication des sens, Augmentation et diminution des forces.

"Reproduction de plusieurs de ces phénomènes sur des jeunes gens que le public est prié de présenter.

"M. Home, qui a eu l'honneur de faire ses expériences devant Sa Majesté l'empereur, invite MM. les médecins, docteurs, chirurgiens, etc., etc., à monter près de lui sur la scène, afin de contrôler la véracité des phénomènes curieux qu'il a l'honneur d'offrir au Public. Des siéges seront disposés à cet effet.

"Prix des places: Premières loges, fauteuils et stalles, 6 fr. (sans augmentation pour la location à l'avance);—premières galeries, 5 fr.;—secondes, 3 fr.;—parterre, 2 fr. 50 c.;—troisièmes, 1 fr. 50 c.;—quatrièmes, 1 fr."

"At the Great Theatre, Thursday, 1st of April, 1858, commencing at eight o'clock, American Soirée or Séance of Spiritualism, by Mr. Home.

"'I never allow myself to be guided by science, but by my conscience. I therefore believe firmly in the facts of magnetism. I believe that the magnetic force augments prodigiously the power of man's vision. I believe that these facts are certified by a certain number of men very sincere and very Christian.'—THE ABBÉ LACORDAIRE.

"Programme: The vision experience of Mr. Home, and the miraculous angel.—Obedience to the order of the public.—Spiritual séance by the sensitive Mme. de Cabanyes.

"Production of visions asked for by the spectators: Tremblings, Joy, Anger, Idiocy, Religion, Piety, Multiplication of the senses, Augmentation and diminution of strength.

"Reproduction of several of those phenomena on young persons, whom the public are requested to introduce.

"Mr. Home, who has had the honour to go through his experiences before His Majesty, the Emperor, invites the Doctors of Philosophy and others, also Surgeons, &c., &c. to sit near him on the stage to satisfy themselves as to the truth of the curious phenomena which he has the honour to present to the public. Chairs will be arranged for that purpose.

"Price of places: First boxes, fauteuils and stalls, 6 frs, (no extra charge for booking); first gallery, 5 frs.; second, 3 frs.; pit, 2 frs. 50 c.: third places, 1 fr. 50 c.; fourth, 1 fr.,'

This was contradicted by the Paris papers, which gave only as a reason that I was in Turin, whilst at the time it happened that I was really at Naples.

But it would be wrong to confine these falsehoods to the press of America or France, when the English press vied with them in fabricating and dispensing equally false statements about me. The Socrates story, was from the forge of the "Court Journal" and was disseminated through a great part of the English press. No wonder that with such teaching there should be misconception about me, and about the phenomena. I can only say that the whole of the following statements, names, dates, circumstances and persons are false from beginning to end.

Extraordinary Spirit Affair in Paris. Singular and Successful Hoax on the Spiritualists

"Mr. Hume, the all-hearing, all-seeing spirit-rapper, is gone suddenly, without warning. Many stories are afloat respecting the cause of this abrupt departure amid such striking success, when Paris was just filled with his renown, and even from the pulpit had threats and warnings been launched forth against those who dared to frequent his company, or believe in his incantations. Some newspapers have declared that he is gone to America in search of his sister, whom he pronounces a more powerful medium than himself; others that, in consequence of some of his tricks having assumed the character of *tours de passe-passe*, he had been forbidden to practise his deceptive arts upon the high personages whom he had chosen, on pain of *procès-verbal*: and that the metamorphosis of the Princess Mathilde's, pocket-handkerchief into a living scarabeus—after which exploit the practitioner had fallen into catalepsy, and remained senseless for five hours—had awakened certain scruples and suspicions in the minds of those who had witnessed the feat, which had caused his exclusion from that circle of society. Nothing of all this is the case, and your readers may be assured of the truth of what we are about to relate, and of the adventure being the whole and sole cause of the abrupt departure of the discomfited wizard.

"A few nights ago a grand séance had been prepared for him at the house of one of the principal officials about the Court, who had witnessed the divers experiments made at the Tuileries, and which, although failing to convince him entirely, had yet not left him wholly incredulous. The company was limited, and of the first water. The names had all been submitted to the practitioner—those of Eugène Guinot, the *feuilletoniste*: General Baraguay d'Hilliers; and Nadaud, the composer; all of them atrocious unbelievers, wretched infidels, and scoffers, wholly devoid of all sensibility or imagination. Numerous were the experiments tried, and all, as usual, eminently successful. The accordion glided, as usual, from knee to knee, all round the circle, and played the tunes most loved by the inquirers; the bell wandered round the ceiling, and rang its merry peal or tolled its doleful note, according to the will of any member of the company who chose to command it. But the wizard had promised that night to evoke the spirits and render them visible to the sight, and every preliminary experiment was attended to with impatience, so great was the hurry to witness the crowning masterpiece of the performance. At length the lights were all extinguished but one, a solitary wax taper on the mantel-piece, behind the figure of the practitioner, which cast its long, gigantic shadow on the walls and ceiling of the room. The silence was complete; some of the ladies crouched behind their neighbours, and resisted the temptation to faint only by reason of their curiosity; others stared around, hoping, yet dreading, to see something awful and terrific, that they would be driven to hysterics. The voice of the wizard was heard, amid the silence, demanding whose spirit should be summoned to appear. A faint whisper, from a distant corner, thrilled through the room—"Let it be Socrates, the greatest of philosophers!" A pause ensued—no objection or opposition being manifested, the wizard raised his arm, and waving it towards the door, solemnly bade the spirit of Socrates appear and stand before him. Again the silence was resumed, and the wizard remained, with extended arm and muttering lips, gazing towards the door. It slowly opened; and, amid the utmost terror, the company beheld the entrance of a figure, enveloped in a kind of floating drapery, something like a winding-sheet, which advanced with noiseless tread over the carpet, and stood before the conjuror. The white and flowing beard, the bald head and crushed nose were unmistakable—Socrates stood, as in life, in the very midst of that gay and frivolous circle, evoked from his slumber of centuries to furnish sport for a Parisian *salon!* The awe and terror of the company was at its highest, and the figure glided back in silence while yet the effect produced was at its culminating point. When it had disappeared, compliments, of course, poured in upon the operator, who, shaken to the very fingers ends, could not help expressing his surprise at the unusual promptitude with which the summons had been answered, and, full of the excitement of unlooked for success, yielded to the entreaties of the same voice which had spoken before, and which now implored the evocation of Frederick the Great. The wizard again stretched forth his hand towards the door, although doubtful if his electric current would be strong enough to accomplish two evocations so rapidly one after the other. He was observed, however, even in the dim light of the apartment, to turn deadly pale as the door again opened at his summons, when be called aloud for Frederick the Great, King of Prussia, to appear before him. The moment's pause was truly awful. By degrees, amid the shadows of the room could be seen gliding through the door-way, a short figure, wrapped, like the one which had preceded it, in a kind of winding-sheet clinging to its limbs, and held around the waist by the grasp of the hands. The face, however, was undeniably that of the great hero, and the head surmounted by the little traditional cocked hat which makes every Prussian heart beat with gratitude and loyalty even to this day. The figure advanced as that of Socrates had done before, close up to the magician, and there stood still and motionless within a few paces of the chimney. Presently, the excitement of the magician became intense, the perspiration rolled in huge drops from his forehead, and the teeth chattered. "Enough, enough—begone, depart!" said he, in a hoarse whisper, as the eyes of the figure glared upon him with a fierce and menacing expression. "Begone I say!" repeated he, in a hollow tone, as the figure still stood motionless in spite of the command. In another moment, however, the spell was broken. Rousing himself by an effort which, considering the circumstances in which he was placed, may be regarded as sublime, he suddenly exclaimed, "I have been made the dupe of some mystification," and stepped close to the figure, which had still retained its menacing attitude until that moment, when a loud and uncontrollable laugh burst from its lips, and it exclaimed: "What! don't you know me? I am Nadaud, and here is my friend, Socrates, otherwise Marshal Baraguay d'Hilliers, ready to appear again whenever you choose, and close at hand is my comrade, Eugene Guinot in life, and Alcibiades in death, waiting to be summoned after me, as he would most assuredly have been, had I been able to follow up the joke." You can just imagine the effect produced by the discovery of the mystification. Mr. Home was struck powerless and dumb; when he recovered, he begged it to be remembered that he had been the first to find out the deception, and asserted that the spirit summoned would have appeared, for that he does possess the facility of raising them. In a few moments, however, he disappeared, and the next day we heard, without astonishment, of his sudden departure from Paris. It seems that the three *mauvais plaisans* who had been excluded from the company had been determined to revenge themselves; and, with the assistance of a *confrère*, aided likewise by the false white beard of Socrates and the cocked hat of Frederick the Great, had almost succeeded in duping the operator, had it not been for the uncontrollable laughter of Nadaud which betrayed the whole conspiracy.

"This is the story told of the sudden desertion of the camp by Mr. Home. Time will show us if it be truth, for he has promised to return; and should we not behold him according to his promise in the space of three months, we shall know what to believe and what to doubt of his mysterious power."

I could tell much more of a similar kind, but what I have already given is sufficient to show the reckless invention of those who assume to enlighten the public through the press. I found it the easiest to let them have their own way, for if I had begun to contradict all the falsehoods told about me, my time would have been fully occupied in vain attempts to stop a torrent which seems as if it would never cease to flow.

Chapter VII

1857-8—France, Italy, and Russia—Marriage

I returned from America to Paris in May, 1857, and I remained there till July, having séances every day. The power was very great at that time, and the phenomena were witnessed and investigated by many hundreds of all classes. The spirit hands were frequently visible, and were seen by many to take pen or pencil and write in the autograph of the person whose spirit was represented to be present.

One morning the concierge came to me saying, "Please, Sir, there is an old gentleman here, and I think you must see him, he seems so anxious and careworn." I must mention that I had been so overrun by visitors, that I had been obliged to refuse to see any strangers, as all my time was taken up by engagements with my friends. I acceded to his request, and he announced the Count de X____. At the first moment of looking at him, I saw none of the signs of anxiety and care which had struck the concierge, nor did he seem to me so very old. He advanced to where I stood, and taking me kindly by the hand, he said to me, "I have been sent to you, and you will yet know the reason why, though you do not even know who I am. I live at No. 4, Rue _____, and you will be obliged to come to me." I shook my head at this incredulously, and told him that my time was so taken up, that I had scarcely time even to call on my friends. He smiled, and said: "You will see, you will see." The conversation then changed, and he left me after having written his address. I was to dine that evening with the Baroness de M____, and previous to leaving the house to go to her, I heard a spirit voice saying distinctly to me, "You will go to see my father, won't you?" The voice did not seem as if it required an answer, for it was said so affirmatively, and I made no reply. On reaching the Hotel de M____, and entering the drawing-room I saw a young man standing there. I was surprised at this, expecting to have met no stranger. With his eyes fixed upon me, he said, "I am glad you have come, for we will go together to see my father," and he then suddenly disappeared. I had thought till then that he was a guest, so real was the vision. The Baroness was in the room, and saw that I was agitated, and asked me what had occurred, but I did not enter into any explanation. When about to take my seat at the dinner table, again I heard the same voice, saying, "You will go to my father, won't you?" This so unnerved me that I told the Baroness the circumstance, and she kindly advised my going. The evening passed on, and after two hours I had nearly forgotten the occurrence, and had returned to the drawing-room, when, suddenly I saw by my side the same young man. His face now wore a pained expression, and I was horrified to see blood on his breast. He said to me, "My father is waiting for you; he has had much sorrow; it is your mission to console—go to him." I told him I would on the following day, but he replied that I must go then, that very night. He disappeared, and I told the Baroness of what he said, and she allowed me to leave. On reaching No. 4, Rue _____, I was directed to the rooms of the Count, and his valet told me that his master was preparing to retire, and in all probability could not see me. Again the voice told me to announce myself, and at that very moment a door was opened, and the Count came towards me, and said, "I have been waiting for you, I knew you would come." I described to him the young man I had seen, and all that had happened, and he at once recognised him as his son who had been murdered. He showed me a portrait of him, which exactly corresponded with my visions of him, and I have since seen him often. He has told me, that on his appearance that first day, he showed the blood upon his breast, merely to impress me the more deeply with the necessity of going to his father. His father told me that he had been himself for long a partial medium, and that he had been told to seek me for the purpose of having his mediumship increased, in order that his son might be able the more easily to impress him with his presence. It has since been a great comfort and relief to his mind to have the certainty of his son being with him to console him in his affliction.

About this time my guardian spirits told me that it seemed necessary that I should go to Turkey, as a way was opening by which I might be the means of bringing light there. I accordingly made all preparations for the journey, and my power left me. I had received letters of introduction to persons holding high positions at Constantinople. My trunks were packed, my passport sent for *visé*. I was making a farewell call, on the Duchess de A____, and while in conversation with her, the drawing-room seemed filed with rappings, the alphabet was called for, and I was told that my journey must be postponed, as some political troubles were just about to occur. Instead, therefore, of going to Turkey, I went to Baden-Baden. My power while there was not great, as my health was again failing, but I met the King of Wurtemburg, and the then Prince, now King of Prussia, both of whom investigated the phenomena.

My guardian spirits continually told me at this time that there was trouble in store for me, but that from the darkness light would come, and that whatever might seem to be a loss, would in the end prove to be a gain, and in all this they were correct.

I left Baden-Baden sooner than I had expected, and went to Biarritz. Here I was told that the first darkening of the cloud would come, and that those who might have understood me better, would be led to think ill of me by those about them, who, to serve a purpose, would fabricate a statement, the very absurdity of which ought to have been its refutation. The pre-knowledge of what was to occur to me, combined with nervous debility, made me more than usually agitated, and whilst at a séance, where almost the only manifestation was the taking of a bracelet from the lady sitting on my left, and the carrying of it to a lady opposite me, the gentleman on my right hand declared it to have been transported by my feet. If my legs were eight feet long it would have still been a miracle, but in such wonderful occurrences as these we must not be surprised at any absurdity that may be invented, however painful it may be to be charged with dishonesty and imposture.

Some instances of the manner in which it is said the phenomena are produced are sufficiently amusing to be repeated. A very popular idea in Paris was that I carried in my pocket a tame monkey trained to assist me. Another is that my legs are so formed as to be capable of elongation, and that my feet are like those of a baboon. Many people suppose that when I go to a strange house, my tables have to be sent first, and that, like Sir David Brewster's "conjectural" table, they are always copiously draped, and that I take with me wax hands and arms to show at the proper moment. Some suppose that I magnetize or biologize my audience, and that they only imagine they see what they see. Some that I carry with me lazy tongs and a magic lantern, and others have stated that when I am said to rise in the air, it is only a balloon filled with gas in the shape of a man. Others again will have it that is done by a magic lantern, whilst some doctors declare that I administer "a thimbleful of chloroform to each of the sitters." Sir David Brewster must have had his thimbleful when he could only say that the table "appeared to rise," and that "spirits were the last things he would give into." Some have enough spiritual belief to say that I have the devil at command. Others that I raise spirits by forms and incantations. Then we have involuntary muscular motion to account for the phenomena by the learned Professor Faraday. Dr. Carpenter speaks of their being produced by unconscious cerebration, and Mr. Morell, the philosopher, tells us that they are caused by "the reflex action of the mind." A common explanation is ventriloquism. Electricity is another, and it is said that I have an electric battery concealed about my person. Then there are the od force and fluid action, and the nervous principle, and collusion, illusion and delusion. Mechanical contrivances attached to the lower extremities are also suggested by Sir David Brewster, but without specifying their particular nature. But the most scientific and learned explanation, leaving no room for conjectures, was given by an old woman in America, who when asked if she could account for what she had seen, replied, "Lor, Sirs, it's easy enough, he only rubs himself all over with a gold pencil." The rappings are produced in many ways, each philosopher having his own theory, beginning low down with the snapping of the toe-joints, others getting up to the ankle, whilst some maintain it to be in the knees, or thigh bones. Professor Huxley has his own "spirit-rapping toe" with which he amuses his friends. It has even been attributed to a strong beating of my pulse. Some say I rub my boots together, others my thumb nails, and that springs are concealed in the table and about the room. It has been said that I have an electrical quality which I can throw off at the command of my will. A general belief is that I bribe the servants at whatever house I visit, that they may aid me in concealing my machinery. The intelligence displayed in obtaining names, dates, and other circumstances, is previously communicated to me either by my own inquiry, from servants or by visiting the tombstones of the relatives, or even by a body of secret police who are in my pay. Others know that I am clairvoyant, and that I read the thoughts of those present. I am an accomplished juggler according to others, and have always refused to be seen by any others of the craft, although the fact is quite the contrary, and the greatest juggler of France has stated that he could not at all account for what he witnessed by any of the principles of his art.

However flattering all this might be to my vanity, in conferring upon me such astounding qualities and scientific acquirements which I do not possess, it has been to me a source chiefly of amusement and wonder, to see how learned persons could so widely and absurdly disagree among themselves, and strain at gnats, though swallowing camels with such surprising greediness. I have wandered from my narrative to give my readers these attempted explanations of mediumship, hoping, however, that they will never try any of the experiments suggested by the learned in the presence of persons of average understanding. The excellent establishment at Earlswood, at the head of which is the good Dr. Conolly, would be more likely to furnish the sort of audience suited for these explanations of the men of science.

My good friends the Count and Countess De B____ left Biarritz with me on a visit to the Château of a mutual friend, near Bordeaux; and here there were several instances of direct spirit writing on paper placed before us on the table in full view. Whilst we were sitting one evening, hands appeared distinctly above the table, and we saw them successively take up a pencil and write. One of these hands was a small one, apparently of a child, another appeared to be that of a full grown man. The hand of the child wrote a little message to her mother who was present, and signed it with her Christian name. There was a striking peculiarity in this, as the child had always left out the last letter of her name, which then, instead of being a female name, became a male one. Her name was Denise, but she wrote it "Denis." Her mother had often spoken to her of this, and yet the child had not corrected herself of the habit during her life, and now to prove her identity, the final letter was again left out. This was of course unknown to me, and to all except her father and mother both of whom were there. The larger hand wrote several communications in our presence, some for his wife, who was at the table, and others to persons who were not there present. This handwriting was in his peculiar autograph.

The lady of the house turned to me and said abruptly, "Why you are sitting in the air;" and on looking we found that the chair remained in its place, but that I was elevated two or three inches above it, and my feet not touching the floor. This may show how utterly unconscious I am at times to the sensation of levitation. As is usual when I have not got above the level of the heads of those about me, and when they change their position much, as they frequently do in looking wistfully at such a phenomenon, I came down again, but not till I had remained so raised about half a minute from the time of its being first seen. I was now impressed to leave the table and was soon carried to the lofty ceiling. The Count de B____ left his place at the table, and coming under where I was, said, "Now, young Home, come and let me touch your feet." I told him I had no volition in the matter, but perhaps the spirits would kindly allow me to come down to him. They did so, by floating me down to him, and my feet were soon in his outstretched hands. He seized my boots, and now I was again elevated, he holding tightly, and pulling at my feet till the boots I wore, which had elastic sides, came off, and remained in his hands. The Count has all his life been well known, holding an important public position, and as truthful as his heart is good. To him and his dear wife, who has recently passed from earth, I owe a deep debt of gratitude, they having been my firm and fast friends ever since I made their acquaintance, six years ago. This was, I believe, the first time of my being raised in the air in France, and it has been of very seldom occurrence there, though it happened so frequently afterwards in England, as will be seen in future pages. Since I wrote the narrative of this séance, I have applied to the Count for his verification of it, and I have his letter stating its correctness.

Another incident occurred in the presence of the Count de B____. The Countess X____ was present for the first time at a séance, when a spirit manifested himself, purporting to be that of her son. The accordion was being played, and she asked if he could remember a piece of music which had particularly struck them both whilst they were travelling together for his health in Germany. It had escaped her mind she said, but it could be easily recalled to her if he would play it. Upon this the accordion played some intricate passages from the opera of Norma, which she at once recognized.

I now returned to Paris, and went to reside with my friend the Count de K____, and whilst there I had sittings almost every day. I also went on a visit to the Château de R____, to the family of the Marquis de _____. The second evening of my stay, as we were about to take tea, a table standing at the further end of the large saloon where we were, came up to us with extreme violence. We were all rather startled, as we were not expecting any manifestations, and for the next two hours they were unceasing. The elder son of the family, the Count L____ came to my room, when I had wished the family good night, and these proofs of a spirit presence were again made most evident. Amongst others there were the sound of heavy footsteps which shook the room. I also saw the distinct form of a boy, and described his appearance to L____, adding that I could recognize him if I could see his portrait. On meeting the family at breakfast the following morning the Marquis said, "What time did L____ leave you last night, and what were you both doing jumping about the room?" We told him that we had both of us our slippers on, and that he must have heard the noises made by the spirits. The Château, being one of the very oldest in France, has the walls in some places nearly twenty feet thick, indeed dressing-rooms have been made in them, and they are quite spacious. There is solidity to every floor. In order, therefore, to have been heard in the room beneath, the manifestations must have been of very great force. After breakfast the Marchioness asked me if I would not like to go over the Château, and on my assenting, she said we will begin with my boudoir. We went there, and on reaching the centre of the room I looked round and there I saw the very face I had seen the night previous. For a moment I could not bring myself to believe it to be other than the spirit himself, but it was only a portrait. My emotion was such that I caught hold of L____, who stood near me, and said, "There, that is the boy I saw last night." I was so overcome that I had to leave the room, and they then told me that L____ having related what had occurred to his mother, they had arranged to put me to the test, and not having even told me of the existence of the portrait, they wished to see if I could recognize it.

In an hotel situate on the Boulevard des Italiens in Paris, I was introduced to a family, consisting of Mr. H____, his wife, and their two sons, both of whom were at that time in the English army, and had just returned from the Crimean campaign. The father, a cool-headed, truthful minded man, was a countryman of mine, and our conversation soon turned upon the wonders of second sight and ghost seeing. Presently, whilst we were talking together, we were startled at hearing loud sounds coming from a distant part of the room, and slowly approaching us. I at once suggested to them that some spirit desired to communicate with us. The unseen one assented to this by making the sounds for the alphabet, and the name of "Gregoire" was spelt out, with the additional information that he had passed from earth, giving the time of his departure. This the two young officers at once and strongly contradicted, for they recognized in the name a very intimate friend, an officer in the French army in the Crimea, whom they had only just left there suffering under a slight wound, but so slight that it gave no apprehensions of an unfavourable kind. He, however, now gave them other proofs of his identity, and during the whole of the remaining hours of the afternoon and evening he continued to make his presence manifest. Several times things were brought from parts of the room distant from us, and there were frequent raps, and his friends felt touches. Sounds resembling the firing of musketry were heard, and indeed so indisputable were some of the signs given that no one could fail to have been convinced of spirit power and presence, though having seen him so lately, and having since heard nothing to make them think his death probable, they could hardly realize the likelihood of it.

I left the family late in the evening, bidding them goodbye, as they were to leave for England the following day. From a member of the family who resides in Paris, I ascertained shortly afterwards that they had written to ascertain the truth as to what had been communicated to them by the spirit calling himself Gregoire, and that in every detail, they were informed, the spirit had been correct. I ought here to state, however, that the eldest son, previous to this corroborative testimony reaching his family, had been sent with his regiment to Canada, and he was sitting in his tent when a letter reached him from his father, relating the results. of their inquiries from the Crimea. While he was reading his father's letter, informing him the details of his friend Gregoire's departure from earth, he was startled by hearing a rustling sound amongst some loose papers and pens, which were carelessly strewn on his table. Fearing lest his imagination might be taking advantage of his reason, he called for his servant to come in and look at the table, and, to their mutual astonishment, they saw a pen move itself into an erect position and deliberately write the name of Gregoire on some blank paper. This fact was told me by the father of the young man, and I see no reason to disbelieve it. What object could tempt the young man to tell so deliberate and wilful an untruth, if it were one, on such a subjects? Other strange occurrences continued with other members of this family after their return to England, for many months, and then left them in as sudden and unexpected a manner as they had made their appearance.

In January, 1858, I went to Holland, accompanied by Mr. T____, and was presented to the Queen. The manifestations at the Hague were in some instances very strong, and again sometimes I had séances at which nothing would occur, and this although in the presence of persons who were most desirous of witnessing them.

I went to Amsterdam, for the purpose of meeting the proprietors of and writers for a magazine of infidel tendencies. I well remember it. We were staying at a large old-fashioned hotel, the cheerless cold of the rooms with their bleak walls and their beam-bare ceilings, as I sat before the fire, which was but the ghost of such as we are accustomed to in England, when these eight or ten gentlemen were announced. None of them were known to me or to my friend, and I desired them at once to sit down, and see if any manifestations would occur. They appeared clever, shrewd persons, deeply read and thinking men. Cold reason had wrapped her chill mantle about their minds, and all that was not tangible could have no truth in it for them. The first tremulous sensation in the table and floor, which often precedes other manifestations, was felt. They delegated two of their number to sit under the table to watch me and my movements. Faint rappings were heard, and the table legs were examined to see that I had no springs concealed there. These manifestations increased in force, and they, after the most close and strict scrutiny, were obliged to acknowledge that they had witnessed that which they could in no wise account for. The alphabet was called for, and intelligent communications were received. This was a step in advance of their philosophy, and to them most singular, and soon the manifestations ceased, but not until they had each expressed their conviction that there was no imposture. I have since been informed, by letters from Amsterdam, that one of them became a medium, and that their general disbelief in spiritual causation was greatly modified. I remember as my friend and I sat together after the party had left, we expressed a wish that they had seen more, and we spoke of ourselves as being sorry prophets for such a mission. This idea pursued me after I had gone to bed, and the spirit of my mother came and comforted me by saying that sufficient had been given; and that "the wind most be tempered to the shorn lamb."

We returned to the Hague, and a deputation of young gentlemen from the University of Leyden called to ask me to visit Leyden. My engagements, however, were such as to necessitate my departure, and we left the following day for Brussels. There the power left me, and I was told by the spirits that it would be sometime before it would return, and that many things of the utmost importance to me would occur in the meantime. I had taken a severe cold while in Holland, but had intended to have remained sometime in Brussels to have séances with my young friends there, and when I found that my power had gone, I considered it better to return to Paris to consult my medical adviser there, I accordingly went there, and he pronounced my disease to be impoverishment of the blood and great nervous depression, and advised my going to Italy. I strongly objected to this, inasmuch as every time I leave Paris some silly stories are put in circulation, such as my being ordered away by the Emperor, or that I go to fly from the law. I remained, therefore, growing daily worse for two or three weeks, when I left, intending to stay at Turin with my friends there. On reaching Turin in February, I found the snow covering the ground to a considerable depth, and the cold more intense than it had been in Paris, and so I left the same evening for Pisa, to join some friends there. I found Pisa very cold, and was advised to proceed to Rome.

I reached Rome in March, and refused nearly all invitations out, wishing to be quiet to regain my health. A friend mentioned one afternoon, whilst we were walking together to the Pynchon, the name of a Russian family of distinction then in Rome, and added that they were anxious to make my acquaintance. I excused myself on the ground of my health. At this moment a carriage was passing us and stopped, and my friend before I was aware of what he was doing, introduced me to the Countess de Koucheleff, who asked me to come and sup with them that evening, adding that they kept very late hours.

I went about ten in the evening, and found a large party assembled. At twelve as we entered the supper-room she introduced to me a young lady, whom I then observed for the first time, as her sister. A strange impression came over me at once, and I knew she was to be my wife. When we were seated at table the young lady turned to me and laughingly said, "Mr. Home, you will be married before the year is ended." I asked her why she said so, and she replied, that there was such a superstition in Russia when a person was at table between two sisters. I made no reply. It was true. In twelve days we were partially engaged, and waiting only the consent of her mother. The evening of the day of our engagement a small party had assembled, and were dancing. I was seated on a sofa by my *fiancée*, when she turned to me and abruptly said, "Do tell me all about spirit-rapping, for you know I don't believe in it." I said to her, "Mademoiselle, I trust you will ever bear in mind that I have a mission entrusted to me. It is a great and a holy one. I cannot speak with you about a thing which you have not seen, and therefore cannot understand. I can only say that it is a great truth." The tears came welling into her eyes, and laying her hand in mine she said, "If your mission can bring comfort to those less happy than ourselves, or be in any way a consolation to mankind, you will ever find me ready and willing to do all I can to aid you in it." She was true to this noble sentiment to the last moment of her short life, and she is still my great comfort and sustainer since we have separated in this earthly sphere. She was my own true, loving wife for, oh! too short a period for my happiness here, but for hers I was content to lose her for a time, till it shall please God that I too pass away to join her!

Shortly after our engagement the family went to Naples, and I with them, and we remained there six weeks. Then the family left for Florence, and my *fiancée* was entrusted to the care of a Russian family about to return by Paris to Russia, that she might join her mother, and get ready the necessary papers, that the marriage might take place as soon as the family returned to St. Petersburgh. I accompanied them to Paris, and after they had left I went to Scotland for my certificate of birth, the parish clerk having sent me one with my name written Hume instead of Home. Knowing this to be incorrect I was obliged to make a journey to have it rectified, and then I returned to Paris, and joined the family who had arrived there from Italy.

We left for St. Petersburgh in June, accompanied by M. Alexandre Dumas, who was to officiate as godfather at my marriage. An amusing account of our journey may be read in Dumas' book entitled "De Paris à Astrachan." On reaching St. Petersburgh I was honoured by a most kind invitation to be received by the Emperor, but which I was obliged to decline not being in power at the time, and his Majesty most graciously sent to me to say that under any circumstances he would be pleased to see me. I excused myself on the ground of having so much to attend to previous to my marriage. A month after this, certain difficulties having arisen, and the papers which were necessary not being forthcoming, the marriage seemed on the point of being postponed. I had had no manifestations for several months, but on this evening I was told by the spirit of my mother to inform the Emperor the next day that my power had returned. I did so, and was received by his Majesty at the Palace of Peterhof, where I spent a week, and all the obstacles in the way of my marriage were removed by his most gracious Majesty, who upon this, as upon every occasion, has shown to me the greatest kindness. I have the highest veneration for him, not only as a monarch, but as a man of the most kind and generous feelings.

We were married on Sunday the 1st of August, 1858, or according to the old style, on the 20th July, first in the private chapel at the country house of my brother-in-law, according to the rites of the Greek church, and afterwards at the Church of St. Catherine, according to the rites of the Romish church. A short time after our marriage, my wife being in a sound quiet sleep, I saw the spirit of my mother come into the room, followed by one, who though I had never known him on earth, I knew to be my wife's father. My impression was one of relief that my wife was asleep, and thus that she would not see what I feared would frighten her. My surprise was therefore very great on hearing her say, "Daniel, there is some one in the room with us. It is your mother, and near her stands my father. She is very beautiful, and I am not, afraid." Her actions, however, betrayed a certain shrinking, for she turned to the side of the bed where I lay, trembling violently. The spirits now disappeared, but loud rappings were heard in and about the room, and our questions were answered. This was my wife's first introduction to anything of the kind.

CHAPTER VIII

RUSSIA, PARIS AND ENGLAND

In two weeks after our marriage we left to visit some of my brother-in-law's estates, some of which were situate on the Crimean coast, and others in the interior of Russia. The journey lasted about six weeks, and we then returned to a country house of his in the neighbourhood of Moscow. At the end of November, 1858, we were at St. Petersburgh, in the house of my brother-in-law, the Count Gregoire Koucheleff Besborodko, from whom and the Countess I have ever met with the readiest sympathy and brotherly welcome, and to whom I owe, and ever shall owe, a debt of the deepest gratitude. Here from time to time my power returned, but generally only faintly. Still a great deal of good was done. As an instance, I may mention that a young officer, who having been convinced of the truths of immortality by what he saw in my presence, gave a supper to his friends, at which he publicly announced that in place of laughing at religion as he had done, he had seen in these phenomena what convinced him of the reality of a future life, and that thenceforward he should lead a different life.

In the middle of January, 1859, I fell ill with severe internal inflammation. This lasted some time, and was increasing to an alarming extent, and beyond the power of the physician who attended me, and the dangerous symptoms were greatly increased by my usual nervous debility. Friction was recommended, but the extreme pain which it caused precluded its use. I was in this state when one evening my wife and a friend, the Baron de M____, were present, and my hands were suddenly seized by spirit influence, and I was made to beat them with extreme violence upon the part which was so extremely sensitive and tender. My wife was frightened, and would have endeavoured to hold my hands, but my friend who had had sufficient knowledge of spirit manifestations prevented her. I felt no pain, though the violence of the blows which I continued giving to myself made the bed and the whole room shake. In five minutes time the swelling had visibly decreased, and the movements of the hand began to be more gentle. In an hour I was in a quiet sleep, and on awaking the next morning I found the disease had left me, and only a weakness remained. The expression of the doctor's face baffles my description when he visited me early that morning, expecting to have found me worse, and felt my pulse and saw that a great change must have occurred beyond his skill to account for.

On the 26th April, old style, or 8th May, according to our style, at seven in the evening, and as the snow was fast falling, our little boy was born at the town house, situate on the Gagarines Quay, in St. Petersburgh, where we were still staying. A few hours after his birth, his mother, the nurse and I heard for several hours the warbling of a bird as if singing over him. Also that night, and for two or three nights afterwards, a bright star like light, which was clearly visible from the partial darkness of the room, in which there was only a night lamp burning, appeared several times directly over its head, where it remained for some moments, and then slowly moved in the direction of the door, where it disappeared. This was also seen by each of us at the same time. The light was more condensed than those which have been so often seen in my presence upon previous and subsequent occasions. It was brighter and more distinctly globular. I do not believe that it came through my mediumship, but rather through that of the child, who has manifested on several occasions the present of the gift. I do not like to allude to such a matter, but as there are more strange things in Heaven and earth than are dreamt of, even in my philosophy, I do not feel myself at liberty to omit stating, that during the latter part of my wife's pregnancy, we thought it better that she should not join in séances, because it was found that whenever the rappings occurred in the room, a simultaneous movement of the child was distinctly felt, perfectly in unison with the sounds. When there were three sounds, three movements were felt, and so on, and when five sounds were heard, which is generally the call for the alphabet, she felt the five internal movements, and she would frequently, when we were mistaken in the letter, correct us from what the child indicated.

Our boy was christened a fortnight after his birth, his godfather being the Marquis de Château Reynard, at present Minister of France at Hesse Cassel, and his godmother his aunt, the Countess Luba. His second godfather was his uncle, the Count Gregoire, and his second godmother was his relative Sophie.

A week after the christening, we went to the residence of the Count in the immediate environs of St. Petersburgh. Whilst here, there were many striking manifestations which were witnessed by many, who investigated as others had done before, and with the same results. One evening I remember, one of my friends was converted from his previous unbelief by seeing a female hand, which was visible to all of us in the room, slowly forming in the air a few inches above the table, until it assumed all the apparent materiality of a real hand. The hand took up a pencil which was on the table, and wrote with it a communication which deeply affected my friend, who recognised it as being from his mother. The general belief is, that the spirit hands always appear from beneath the table, and already formed, but this is incorrect, for on many occasions in the presence of several persons at a time, they are seen to be formed in full sight of all, in the manner I have just described, and to melt away, as it were, in the same way.Often too, they have been seen to form themselves high above our heads, and from thence to descend upon the table, and then disappear.

The anniversary of our wedding-day found us on the steamer 'Baltic' bound for Dunkerque, from whence we went to Ostend on a visit to my mother-in-law, who was there for her health. On seeing her, at the moment of our embracing one another, I had another of those singular impressions which so often come to me at the moment of external contact. It has seemed to me as if they were caused by the disturbing element of a physical substance which causes some secret chord of the soul to vibrate and awaken what I may call a memory of the Future, or that a flower of the springtime has been shadowed forth among the chill blasts of autumn, as a token of the never ceasing care of God, our loving father, for His children whether in the Past, Present or Future, all being alike known to Him. My sensations are so peculiar at the time when such foreshadowings are granted me, that words can but feebly express them. I distinctly saw at the first moment of touching my mother-in-law, that after I should leave Ostend, we should meet no more on earth. This impressional prediction, did, as has ever been the case with those which have come to me in this way, prove correct.

We arrived in Paris in August 1859, and whilst there, I paid a short visit to a friend then in Switzerland, and there we had one or two sittings. On returning to Paris, a friend had kindly offered us the use of the Château de C____, where we remained about two months, at the expiration of which time we came to England. This was in October. My power had left me for some weeks. One evening in November while I was absent, my wife being in the room with the child and his nurse, loud raps were heard upon the ceiling. They both supposed that the sounds proceeded from some one walking overhead, when they changed their position, and were heard upon the wall of the room, and in a few moments they came on the table. My wife asked who was the medium upon the occasion, and the reply was given that it was the sleeping child. It was further said, that they had power to manifest through him, but that they would not, "as the atmosphere which they made use of was necessary for his physical development in the natural world." From this time we have but once had any external evidence of any spirit presence through him, though he has given up many indications of his being a seer.

In the latter part of November we were in England, and the power returned, and I began to hold séances as usual, and continued to do so until the 24th of July in the following year. During this time, the manifestations were seen and investigated by persons of all ranks and classes, from statesmen down to those in humble life, and to them again I would rather refer for the accounts of what they witnessed, than to give my own descriptions. I select, therefore, portions of their writings, a few of which have already been published in "The Spiritual Magazine" and other Journals, and the others now appear for the first time. These will give the reader an idea of the nature and extent of my mediumship during this period.

The subjoined is a portion of a letter from Mr. Pears, who was accompanied by my friends Mr. and Mrs. Cox. He now saw the manifestations for the first time. "Almost immediately the table tilted towards Mr. Home, who, raising his hands from the table, which still retained its inclined position, invited me to look under it, to see that no material means were used to produce this result. I did look, and saw none. On resuming my seat, the table returned to its position, and then it passed into an undulatory movement, as if it were in motion on waves; it seemed, indeed, almost as if the top of the table were flexible: then from this movement it passed into a perfectly horizontal state, so that a vessel filled to the brim, would not, I think, have spilled a drop, and it rose from eighteen to twenty-four inches clear from the floor, all hands at the same time continuing on the top of the table; and finally with perfect evenness it gradually descending to its place.

"Raps were then heard on the table, in the vicinity of Mrs. Cox, which, by reference to the alphabet, purported to be produced by a deceased child of hers. Then faint deliberate raps came near to Mrs. P., purporting—by the same mode—to come from Phoebe, our deceased little daughter to whom I referred before.

"Raps were then heard under my own hands, and at the same time the depending cloth covering the table seemed to be moved up by something under it, and was made thus to strike against my wrist. I called my wife's attention to this, and she confirmed the fact, that it really did seem as if some one's hand was under the cloth, trying to touch my wrist. I said, half laughing, which you might expect from my scepticism, that I should not wonder if there were not some one for me also. Immediately there were raps under the same hand, strong enough to shake the table.

"Perhaps I looked dubiously at a phenomenon so unexpected, for Mr. Home said, 'I should like Mr. Pears to be convinced that we do not make these sounds; perhaps he would get under the table and observe.' I did so; and while I saw that they were not produced by any visible agency beneath, they were sounding as vigorously as ever; Mrs. P. being witness to their not being produced by the hands, or any other visible means above board.

"When I found that the raps under my hand purported to come from my grandfather's 'spirit,' I asked if he could take the large bell from me if I held it. It had already been taken out of Mr. Home's hand and rung under the table. The response to my question was given by strong knocks. I held it under the table, being careful to hold it in the direction of my wife, whose hands were on the table, and I felt it tugged with strength out of my hand; it was rung, and then deposited on the floor.

"Many little things which struck me at the time, occurred during our séance, which lasted between two and three hours. But there was one part of the séance which forcibly struck me, and which I must relate. Mr. Home, soon after I had assumed the presence of my grandfather's spirit, passed into a singular state—half unconscious as it were—and said, 'Here's a tall, old, upright, Quaker-like man, yet not a Quaker;' then he seemed to take on the manner and gesture, as closely as a young man can, of those of an old one—held out his hand to me, and grasped it in a way that further reminded me of my grandfather, and addressed me in words somewhat characteristic of him, and went on to speak of one whom he had held very dear, but from whom he had been long separated to his great grief, but that they had happily met in the other world and were reconciled. All upon this point was said in a broken way, but with gestures and allusions which were intelligible solely to myself, as the person and events so alluded to touched closely upon my grandfather's history in conjunction with my own. My astonishment was increased, when, from Mr. H.'s lips, fell the name of her to whom the allusion had been made—my grandfather's daughter! both dead when Mr. Home must have been a boy in America! Long as I have known you, friend Dixon, I think I never told you that my grandfather was of a Quaker family, which was the case.

"I was by this incident, astonished beyond expression, and acknowledged to Mr. Cox, that the history which had been sketched, and the reflections upon it, were just what I should have expected might have been made by my grand-father.

"I have not yet found a place in my system for these phenomena, but that they are genuine phenomena, is settled in my mind."

Another account is given by Mr. J. G. Crawford, a gentleman who had for years resisted all belief in such phenomena as being impossible and absurd. It happened that a friend of his from Liverpool was coming to meet me at the house of Mr. Coleman, in Bayswater, and he induced him to accompany him. He shall tell the story in his own frank and truthful words:

"Mr. Home laid his left hand on the table and with his right lifted an accordion, which he held under the table. My friend and I were asked to look below, when we distinctly saw it move up and down, apparently held and touched by one hand only.

"We continued to sit round the table. The room was made so dark that we could not see each other. The table gave a violent stamp upon the floor; still we kept our hands upon it. Then it rose in a mass, twelve or fifteen inches quite off the floor, so far as I could judge.

"Mr. Home now said that he held the accordion under the table by one hand only, when it played our beautiful English tune, 'Home, sweet Home!' in a most finished style.

"Shortly after this occurred, a very curious affair took place, in explanation of which I cannot hazard a conjecture. Mr. Home remarked, 'I feel as if I am going to rise.' The room was quite dark. He said, 'I am getting up,' and as I was only a few feet from him, I put out my hand to him; I indubitably felt the soles of both his boots, some three feet above the level of the floor. On my doing so, he said, Don't touch me, or I shall come down; of course I instantly desisted, but down he came. In less than five minutes after this, he remarked, 'I am again ascending,' and from the sound of his voice, we could not but infer that he was actually rising towards the ceiling of the ante-room.

"He then appeared to float under the archway, then to rise to the cornice of the room we were sitting in, and we heard him quite distinctly make three cross marks on the ceiling, besides doing some other writing. Then he came softly down, and lay stretched out with his back upon the table, in which position we found him when the gas was lighted, and when we distinctly saw the marks on the ceiling, which we had heard him make.

"I am well aware there is a ready answer by many well-disposed persons to what I have written—that it is all done by collusion and trick. In many countries at the present time, and in our own not a century back, all phenomena of a then *extra*-ordinary kind, were quickly put down to the account of the devil. He prompted Galileo to the adopted system of astronomy; Harvey to the circulation of the blood; he was the cause of witchcraft in Scotland, and had much to do with the wonders of chemistry, before it attained its present scientific certainty and value to the arts and agriculture. But the testimony of thousands of excellent witnesses cannot be set aside by any such plea. Not many years ago it was fashionable to deny the facts and uses of chloroform, homœpathy, hydropathy, magnetism, mesmerism, &c.; now the curative powers of these agents are commonly received amongst us as 'household words.' There appears to be a law of progressive development in the universe. Should the supposed facts of Spiritualism be found to be real, after oft-repeated experiments, we cannot doubt but they also will have a permanent place with recent discoveries. No one, now-a-days, who thinks at all, can be so bold and unwise as to deny that 'there are more things in heaven and earth than are dreamt of in our philosophy.'

"In the simple statement I have given, of what my friend and I were satisfied occurred on the evening of our visit to _____ Villas, I have avoided colouring the events, and for the sake of greater definiteness, have given figures of sizes, which, however, must be taken merely, as a near approximation to the actual measurements."

J. G. CRAWFORD.

Mr. Crawford mentions the circumstance of my immediately coming to the ground again on his touching my feet. I have observed that this is invariably the case when I am touched, or even anxiously gazed at, until I have risen above the heads of those who are in the room, but after I have attained that height, their looking at me, or touching me, has no effect upon me. What the cause may be I cannot explain; but it may perhaps be some break in the magnetism which is caused in the former case, and which does not occur in the latter.

On the 3rd of April, 1860, I had been with some friends to a lecture given in St. John's Wood, by M. Louis Blanc, "On the Mysterious persons and agencies in France towards the end of the eighteenth century." His lecture was a good deal occupied with Cagliostro, and during the time he was speaking, I had the strongest impression of the presence of Cagliostro, and the lady who was sitting next me, was also aware of some strong spirit presence by having her dress pulled, and by other manifestations.

On returning home, I found that my wife had retired earlier than usual in consequence of a severe headache. In the course of conversation together, she having asked how I had liked the lecture, I said, "I have been haunted all the evening by Cagliostro," on which she exclaimed, "Pray do not use that word haunted, it sounds so weird-like, and quite frightens me." I had by this time extinguished the light, and was now in bed, when to my amazement the room became as light as if the sun had for an instant shone fully in at the window. Thinking that this effect might have been only on my spiritual perception, I said, "Sacha, did you see anything?" Her reply was, "No, nor could I, for my face was quite buried in my pillow, the pain in my head is so intense." I asked her to observe, and I then mentally asked that if the light had been external, it might be reproduced. Almost simultaneously with the thought, came the light again, so distinct, and with such brilliancy, that no noon-day was ever brighter. My wife asked if this was the spirit of Cagliostro, and the affirmative reply was instantly given by three flashes of light, so vivid as almost to be blinding and painful to the sight. Answers were given to various questions in the same wonderful manner, and then in answer to a question asked, came a musical tinkle, as if a silver bell had been touched directly over our heads. In this way our farther answers were now given, and we then heard a footstep on the floor, falling so gently as if it feared to disturb us by its approach. My wife asked that it should come nearer, and it approached us till we felt a form leaning over the bed. In doing this, it pressed upon the bed-clothes just as an actual material presence would have done. We asked him if he had been a medium when on earth, and a distinct voice, audible to both of us, said in answer, "My power. was that of a mesmerist, but all-misunderstood by those about me, my biographers have even done me injustice, but I care not for the untruths of earth." Both my wife and myself were by this time so impressed by such startling and almost terribly real evidence of the presence of one who was in no way related to us, that for a few moments all power of utterance seemed to have left us. We were, however, soon recalled to ourselves by a hand being placed on our heads, and she, seizing my hands in hers, held them up, saying, "Dear spirit, will you be one of my guardian angels—watch over me with my father, teach me what you would have me do, and make me thankful to God for all his mercies?" Our hands were clasped by a hand, and her left hand was gently separated from mine, and a ring, which was the signet-ring of my father-in-law, was placed on her third finger. This ring was previously in the room, but at a distance of at least twelve feet from where the bed stood. "Good night, dear ones, and God bless you," was then audibly spoken; and simultaneously with the sound came three wafts of perfume, so delicious that we both exclaimed, "How truly wonderful!"

Her headache was perfectly cured, and although our nerves had been greatly agitated, we slept soundly. The following day, and indeed for several days afterwards, my wife had occasional proofs of the presence of this spirit, and he remained with her up to the time of her passing from earth, and during the last months of our stay in England she frequently saw him.

About the middle of May, 1860, my mother-in-law wrote to us from St. Petersburgh, as follows:—

"Dear children,—You may not be aware that to-morrow I am to undergo a surgical operation. I have seen my confessor; I have taken the sacrament, and I now feel quite happy. Do not be alarmed, but do as I do—trust in God."

On the morning of Monday, the 29th May, my wife being then engaged at a bazaar held at the Crystal Palace, Sydenham, I proposed to visit with a friend the establishment of Messrs. Barclay and Perkins. We drove there, and had gone over nearly all the establishment, when in the barrelling-room one of the workmen proposed our tasting the porter. My friend was tasting it, and the attendant brought me a pot. I put out my hand to take it, and as my fingers came in contact with the metal, a deep shudder convulsed my frame, and I suddenly knew that my dear mother-in-law, who had been for many years a patient sufferer, had been released from her earthly troubles. I refused the porter, and requested my friend to accompany me home. He wished to remain with me, but I begged to be alone. In an hour's time I was calm, and I reasoned with myself how I could best conceal the painful intelligence from my wife. That evening at a séance she asked how her mother was. The reply given was, "It is well with her now." All present but herself understood well to what this alluded, and a friend on my left did all she could to conceal her tears.

On the Thursday afterwards I heard my wife running up to my room. As she opened the door, and before she had time to speak, and indeed before I had seen her, I said, "Why, Sacha, I knew it last Monday." She came to my bedside, and gave me a letter addressed to me from my sister-in-law containing a telegraphic dispatch, announcing that my mother-in-law had passed from earth on the Monday, and this letter my wife had opened. Two nights after this, at a séance where the Count T____ and an atheist friend of his were present, her dear spirit came, and her hands were made visible, resting on her daughter's head, and afterwards on mine. She wrote in her own peculiar handwriting, "You will love her always, won't you?" and she signed it "Nathalie." He who came an atheist, was one no longer.

I take the following account of some new manifestations from the "Spiritual Magazine." It is called "Two Evenings with Mr. Home," and is introduced by the editor, who says:—

"We have received from two correspondents, well known to us, the following account of manifestations on the evening of the 1st and 9th of May last, each evening in the presence of nine persons, whose names have been furnished to us, and which we are permitted to supply privately to any inquirer who feels that the knowledge of the names is necessary for his belief. In the meantime we can vouch publicly for the perfect confidence which the narratives inspire us with, having heard the whole account from the lips of the narrators, previous to receiving the MS. from them.

"May 1st, 1860.

"The party was composed of Mr. and Mrs. Home and seven other ladies and gentlemen. We sat at the round table in the large drawing-room. Mr. Home's hand was moved to write:— 'The spirit of John is one who was kind to your father during the voyage to America.' No one understood this; but Mr. _____ entering the room a minute afterwards, expressed his conviction that it was intended for him, as his father had been to America. Three loud raps gave assent to what he said. The table then moved away from us, and we enquired if they wished us to draw it to the window. It was answered, 'Yes.' We accordingly did so, leaving a vacant space against the window, unclosing the shutters, and by their directions extinguishing the candles. The fire burned brightly. It was spelled out, "There is a little too much light." Mr. _____ and _____ screened the fire as much as possible, and the moon and gaslight from the street then alone lighted up the table; but did so completely as the moon was very bright. The spirit of Albert then took the accordion, and played a beautiful air of unearthly harmony. Mr. Home and I held the accordion together under the table, for the power was very strong, and the music loud; and the instrument at times was nearly carried away from us.

"After a short time there rose slowly in the space made by the window a most lovely hand of a female—we saw also part of the beautiful arm as it held it up aloft for some time—we were all greatly amazed. This hand was so transparent and luminous, and so unearthly and angelic, that our hearts were filled with gratitude towards the Creator for permitting so wonderful a manifestation. The hand was visible to us more from the internal light which seemed to stream as it were out of it, than from the external light of the moon. As soon as it slowly vanished, Mdlle. _____, who sat next to the open space, saw another hand forming itself close to her; and a man's hand was raised and placed on the table, far more earthly and life-like in appearance, and one that I thought I recognized, (we were subsequently told that I was right in conjecture). Then came a dear baby-hand: then the baby (Mrs. L____'s adopted child) showed its head; and finally, spirit-hands held up the little child, so that all nine of us saw her shoulders and waist. After this, a hand and arm rose luminous and beautiful, covered with a white transparent drapery; and this hand remained visible to us all for at least five minutes, and made us courteous and graceful gestures.

"Then spirit-hands held up to us an exquisite wreath of white flowers. I never saw any wreath made by human hands so perfect in form and design; and calling for the alphabet said, 'The spirit emblem of William's mother.' Then we were told they would show us 'The emblem of superstition;' and a black shrivelled hand arose. On some of us remarking that we could not see it well, the curtains were at once moved aside, and the blind drawn away from the top of the window. It was beyond the reach of any of us; and they then showed us the hand again, so that we all could see it. The 'emblem of truth' was then shown. This was more beautiful than all the rest—a fairy-like fountain of apparently clear sparkling water which threw up showers of silvery rays, vanishing from our sight like mist, and dwelling on the memory as perfection. After this it was rapped out, 'We can do no more.'

"Mr. Home was put into a trance, and as he fell back in his chair a gleam of the most vivid light fell upon me. This light fell over my shoulders, and gleamed on my right hand, and came from a direction whence no earthly light could have come. It came from a part of the room where the spirit of one who was a friend of mine when on earth has often stood before, and from whence he has communicated to us. This light was seen by no one but myself; but as I turned round in hope of seeing the spirit, Mr. Home said to me, 'Yes, he is there;' and added a communication from him. He then told us that the first hand that we, saw had been that of his own mother; the second was my father's, as I had silently expected; and the hand and arm in drapery that remained so long, came for Prudence, and was the same that she had seen one night when alone, several years ago, at Paris, before she had ever heard of spirit-manifestations. He also gave us the full name of the 'spirit John,' who had gone to America with Mr. A____'s father; and added some private information, which Mr. A____ confirmed as true.

"The events of this evening having been so wonderful, I have begged my friends present on the occasion to read over this account, and to sign it as witnesses to the truth of what I have stated."

"May 9th, 1860.

"Mingling with those interested in witnessing evidences of spirit power, I gladly accepted an invitation to meet a few friends on Monday the 9th of May, 1860, at a house at the West-end. At a quarter after eight o'clock, we went into the adjoining back drawing-room, and sat down to a loo table. There were nine of us, Mr. Home being one of the number. Immediately the table commenced vibrating and gently lifting itself off the floor, I say lifting *itself,* because no human beings in human clay were the actors. Nothing occurred for a few minutes, during which conversation was kept up, and then the table gradually rose up, *off the floor* about four feet, or rather more than a foot beyond our out-stretched arms, the hands of which had rested gently on the table before its ascent. It then descended. Mr. Home took the accordion in his right hand, by the rim at the bottom of the instrument, leaving his left hand on the table, and then were played some beautiful voluntaries, exquisitely, attenuated, yet clear and melodious. They then came out gradually fuller, and yet more full, till the room seemed filled with the volume of sound like a pealing organ, and still no false note. A friend, sitting next to me, forgetting himself, exclaimed, 'My God, how wonderful!' and after a breath, asked 'if they would give us some air we knew?' and having asked for 'God save the Queen,' it was played at once.

"A lady present, whose little boy had recently died, had indications of her son being in the room; and the accordion suddenly commenced playing a well-known air, which on earth the little boy was very fond of, as tallying with his mamma's name. Reader, was not there a truth of *life* and of *love* in the incident? The mother thought so, and her tears betrayed her thoughts.

"The detonations on the table, and sometimes under my hands, were as sharp, and as clear, and as loud, as if struck vigorously with the edge of a penny-piece.

"It was then rapped out by the sounds—'Go to the window;' we rose, and moved the loo table to about eighteen inches from the window. We sat down again, but more closely, so as to allow a vacant space at the side of the table, opposite the window. The sounds then gave out, 'Put out the lights,' which was done. We found that though the room was dark, yet the light from the window was sufficient for us to faintly see each other. The window-blind then commenced moving up and down—no one near it—evidently to tone the light; and while we were remarking the singularity of the phenomenon, and how high it went, all looking at it—suddenly it sprung up to the top, and then came gently down to its original position. Mr. Home felt something on his head, and found it was a leaf. Suddenly the leaf of a geranium was taken and dropped into the lap of a lady sitting at the table. We heard the snap as if breaking off the stem of a flower, and immediately came down past the left ear of my friend, and on to his knee, a sprig of geranium; while he held it up for us to see, I expressed a wish to have one, when a sprig came past my right ear on to my knee. I picked it up, and while showing it, another came past my face as if from the ceiling. The geranium plant was in the room several feet from any of us, and the sprigs came down both on the right and left of me.

"After a pause, Mr. Home said he felt as he were about to be lifted up; he moved from the table, and shortly he said, 'I am rising'—but we could not see him—'they have put me on my back.' I asked, will you kindly bring him, as much as possible, towards the window, so that we may see him; and at once he was floated with his feet horizontally into the light of the window, so that we all saw his feet and a part of his legs resting or floating on the air like a feather, about six feet from the ground, and three feet above the height of the table. He was then floated into the dark; and he exclaimed: 'They have turned me round, and I am coming towards you. I saw his head and face, the same height as before, and as if floating on air instead of water. He then floated back, and came down and walked up to, and sat on the edge of the table we were at, when the table began to rise with him on it. Mr. Home was then taken behind to the settee next to me, and while there, we heard sounds several times as of some one giving utterance to a monosyllable in the middle of the room. Feeling a pressure against my chair, I looked, and saw that the ottoman had been brought along the floor about six feet, no one touching it, and close to Mr. Home. He said, 'I suppose it is for me to rest on,'—he lay down, and the ottoman went back to its original position—'Oh! I am getting excited, let some one come and sit with me.' I went, and sat beside him; he took my hand; and in about a minute, and without any muscular action, he gently floated away from me, and was lost in the darkness. He kept talking to let us know where he was. We heard his voice in various parts of the further end of the room, as if near the ceiling. He then cried out, 'Oh! they have brought me a cushion to sit upon—I am sitting on it—they are taking it away.' Just then the tassel of the cushion of another ottoman in the room struck me on my hair and forehead as if coming from the ceiling, and the cushion was deposited at my feet on the floor, falling as if a snow flake. I next saw the shadow of his body on the mirror as he floated along near the ceiling. He said, 'I wish I had a pencil to make a mark on the ceiling. I have made a cross with my nail.' He came down near the door, and after a pause, he was again taken up; but I did not see him, but heard his voice as if near the ceiling. Again he came down, and shortly returned to the table we were at; and the sounds on the table bade us Good night.'"

This is an account of "Another evening with Mr: Home." It is given us in the words of the lady at whose house the manifestations occurred.

I have not, for good reasons, the liberty to give her name, but I can answer for her position and character, and for the perfect truthfulness of the narrative. I have, in addition, the names of the nine persons who were present.

"May the 3rd, 1860.—The table was moved away from the remaining seven of us, and we followed it; suddenly it rose in the air, and without any help from us was placed on a large sofa that stood before the window. The spirits told us to move this sofa away, which we immediately did, and the table then moved of its own accord up to the window where the hands had appeared to us on former occasions. The shutters were opened and the candles extinguished by their desire. Mr. Home sat next to the window, and I sat neat to him with, Miss H. on my other side. After sitting a minutes quietly I felt a form glide behind me: it touched my chair, placed two hands on my shoulders, and then drew the heavy silk curtain from a window behind me (we sat in a bow formed by three windows) and folded the drapery round me like a cloak. The hands and arms which enfolded me felt as palpable as human arms would feel. On one of the party guessing the name of the spirit, it was answered in the affirmative by three startling raps, which shook the table, and felt as if produced by a bar of iron—no human hand could have knocked with such force. As I was intently listening to catch any sound, and straining my eyes to see any form that could make itself visible, my comb was taken out of my hair by a spirit hand, and laid on the table at a distance from me. By tiny gentle raps my darling spirit child told me that he had taken it. Then a hand rose under the window, and pulled down the blind. We distinctly saw the fingers clutch the string—this is a green transparent blind, through which the light can flow softly. The hand then made graceful gestures and pointed upwards, and when it disappeared it was followed by another, and then by a child's hand. Suddenly I was touched on the shoulder, as if by some one standing behind me and wishing to draw my attention. I thought it was my daughter, and turned to speak to her, but I found no one. I had hardly turned round, when my left shoulder was more strongly touched, and on turning my head a spirit-hand held out to me a box taken from a table at the other end of the room. I received it with emotion, and as a precious gift; and the sweet hand that gave it was placed on my shoulder with a loving pressure. The spirit of A____ G____ then showed his hand, touched his sister with it, and played on the accordion, which by degrees was moved up in Mr. Home's hand over his head, the knocks at the same time beating measure, like a drum, very loudly on the table. The accordion was finally taken entirely away by the spirits, who played on it at a distance from us, the drumming continuing all the time on the table; whilst another drum accompanied it from the other side of the room. As soon as this ceased the table rose up in the air, and floated away from us high above our heads, passing over sofas and chairs in its way. We were naturally greatly interested at this wonderful manifestation, and followed it into the darker part of the room, and here arose a scene of indescribable confusion, but still producing feelings in no way unpleasant, though we knew not when we touched each other, who were spirits, and who were fleshy human beings. The four cushions of the ottoman were virtually hurled in the air at once, and flew to the other side of the room. In answer to a remark made, a hand came down on my head, as from a spirit floating above me, and pressed my forehead and stroked my hair. As we gathered round the table nine or ten chairs flew up like lightning, one behind each of us; the chair next to me was empty (to the sight), but when I tried to move it I could not do so, it appeared as if nailed to the ground, and by raps we were told that L____ sat there. The united strength of several could not move this chair. The heavy sofa on which G____ sat was moved suddenly to the other end of the room, and the spirit of her brother placed his hand in her's, and held it for several minutes. Before leaving her he gave a most touching manifestation. He blessed her by making the sign of the cross on her forehead. He then came to me and did the same. During these manifestations almost every article of furniture in the room was moved out of its place."

My dearly valued friend, Mr. Wason, who after twenty-nine years of outer scepticism, takes pride in dating his new birth to the belief of a spiritual life and a spiritual philosophy, from his observations of the phenomena which he witnessed in my presence, wrote at this time the interesting letter which I now give.

"In July, 1860, I was at a séance at the mansion of a person of distinction, in Hyde Park Terrace, London.

"Two baronets—one an M.P., and the other the heir and representative of a deceased M.P. of eminent ability; the wife of a distinguished living M.P.; and others, including Mr. Home, making eight in number present. The hour was a little after nine, p.m. Neither of the three first-named parties had ever seen any spirit manifestations, and were evidently sceptics: the rest of the party were mediums of greater or less power, and seemed as much interested in watching the effects of the spirit manifestations on the three new comers, as in the manifestations themselves. We all made a circle round a heavy loo table, capable of seating nine persons comfortably (crinoline included).

It was covered with an ordinary damask cloth, (a powerful non-conductor of electricity, completely negativing the theory that spirit manifestations were brought about by electricity); and we were desired by Mr. Home to chat and talk as naturally and cheerfully as we could, and not to be too eager or expectant of spirit manifestation, which he stated had a strong tendency to defeat the object. There were six lights burning in the room. The floor (a first floor) shook and trembled in a manner that all thought resembled the vibrations or tremulous motion on a small steamer's deck when the paddles are in full work: some said it more nearly resembled the tremulous motion on a screw steamer's deck, in which I concurred. This tremulous motion ceased at intervals and was renewed, and this seemed to strike the new comers very forcibly; it was amusing to notice their startled looks, though they said but little beyond concurring in the observations as to the tremulous movements. The walls also shook at times with a tremulous motion. The table, which was a very large, and heavy one, was frequently lifted a few inches from the ground, and at last it rose from the ground at least three feet, and remained thus suspended 'twist heaven and earth, like Mahomet's coffin, for a minute or thereabouts, probably more than less. The gentlemen were invited by Mr. Home to ascertain if any machinery was underneath, and the two gentlemen who were new comers swept with their legs under the suspended table, to catch any prop or other machinery that might be applied to raise the table, and they confessed that no such machinery or prop was present.

"This séance, wonderful as it will appear—'stranger than fiction'—was not considered to be an entirely successful one; and the lady of the house, with characteristic kindness, after speaking of the meagreness of the manifestations, invited me to another séance on the following evening, an invitation I most gladly accepted, although it kept me in London an extra day, and overthrew my previously arranged movements. At this second séance we met rather earlier, a little after eight o'clock, p.m., in the same first-floor room. The séance consisted of a barrister of eminence and standing at the bar, and well known to the public, a literary man—an author of established reputation, and others to the number of eight; all on this occasion being believers, except the author.

"The same tremulous motion of the floor and walls as on the preceding evening, took place; and the table was tilted and turned with even greater power than before, and rose perpendicularly from the floor, from three to four feet, and remained in this position suspended (Mahomet's coffin fashion) for about a minute, and then descended to its original place as softly and gently as the fall of a snowflake. An accordion was played by an unseen hand, whilst it was held by one of the party present, and afterwards by myself. I held it over the back of the chair on which I was sitting; using the back of the chair as a rest to my arm, the accordion hanging over the back of the chair. I sat on the opposite side of the table to Mr. Home and the lady of the house. The accordion was also played whilst lying on the floor, and also on the table, and was lifted without visible means from the floor on to the table. The music was of a solemn and impressive character.

"A small spirit-hand, warm and soft like that of a child, touched my hand, and placed in it a small hand-bell, and, at my request, took the bell from my hand underneath the table to its mother, who was the lady of the house. She seemed perfectly satisfied that it was the spirit-hand of her little boy, who died three or four years since, aged about eight years, and she received repeated responses, spelt out through the alphabet, such as might be expected from the spirit of a deceased child to its mother.

"The bell was carried to several of the parties present and placed in their hands; and lastly, was elevated above our heads, and rung in mid-air, revolving round and touching our heads (my own included). I could see the bell when it passed round my head opposite the window. I could see the bell occasionally as it passed between me and the window, the blinds of which had been drawn down by invisible agency. Pieces of mignonette and geranium flowers were placed in my hands by spirit hands, and inside my waistcoat. I saw one of the hands distinctly, which, as it came between me and the window was distinctly visible, as the blinds did not altogether exclude the light of a summer evening and of the gas lights in the street.

"The curtains at last were drawn by invisible means, and then Mr. Home stated he was being lifted up in the air, and he crossed the table over the heads of the parties sitting around it. I asked him to make a mark with his pencil on the ceiling. He said he had no pencil. I rose up and said I would lend him mine, and by standing and stretching upwards I was enabled to reach his hand, about seven feet distant from the floor, and I placed therein a pencil, and laying hold and keeping hold of his hand, I moved along with him five or six paces as he floated above me in the air, and I only let go his hand when I stumbled against a stool. Mr. Home, as he floated along, kept ringing the small hand-bell to indicate his locality in the room, which was probably forty by thirty feet, and I saw his body eclipse two lines of light issuing from between the top of a door and its architrave—such door leading into an adjoining room that was brilliantly lighted. Mr. Home was replaced, as he stated, with the greatest care and gentleness in the chair from which he rose, but this I could not see.

"Previously to Mr. Home's being raised up, the spirit-hands of two of the barrister's deceased children touched him. He did not doubt that the hands were the spirit-hands of his children.

"Questions were asked, and rational answers given by means of the alphabet, in one of the ordinary ways of communicating with spirits. It is right that I should say, that this séance (as in the preceding evening) was commenced with prayer, which I understood was the usual course.

"I make no comments on the above, and advance no theory or hypothesis. I have confined myself simply to facts, which I can substantiate by legal evidence in a court of justice; and I add my name, address, and profession, and have only one desire, and that is—that truth may prevail.

"I am, Sir, your obedient Servant,

"JAMES WASON, Solicitor.

"Wason Buildings, Liverpool."

CHAPTER IX

THE "CORNHILL" AND OTHER NARRATIVES

It was at this time that the manifestations occurred which are described with such accuracy and intelligence by the eminent literary friend who wrote his account of what he saw in the "Cornhill Magazine," under the title of "Stranger than Fiction." This paper travels over nearly the whole ground of the physical manifestations, and is written with such masterly observation, and ability of description that I feel it will be a boon to the reader to have some few extracts from it. He commences by quoting:

"The reply of Dr. Treviranus to inquiries put to him by Coleridge as to the reality of certain magnetic phenomena which that distinguished savant was reported to have witnessed. 'I have seen what I would not have believed on your testimony, and what I cannot, therefore, expect you to believe upon mine.'"

For the information of Professor Faraday and other such persons who believe in his foolish theory of involuntary muscular motion as being the cause of the phenomena, he says: "While we were seated at the table, we barely touched it with the tips of our fingers. I was anxious to satisfy myself with respect to the involuntary pressure which has been attributed to the imposition of hands. In this case there was none. My friends kindly gratified my request to avoid resting the slightest weight on the table; and we held our hands pointing downwards, with merely the nails touching the wood. Not only was this light contact inadequate to produce the violent evolutions that took place, but the evolutions were so irregular and perplexing, that we could not have produced them by premeditation. Presently, however, we had conclusive proofs that the vivacity of the table did not require any help from us.

"Turning suddenly over on one side, it sunk to the floor. In this horizontal position it glided slowly towards a table which stood close to a large ottoman in the centre of the room. We had much trouble in following it, the apartment being crowded with furniture, and our difficulty was considerably increased by being obliged to keep up with it in a stooping attitude. Part of the journey it performed alone, and we were never able to reach it at any time together. Using the leg of the large table as a fulcrum, it directed its claws towards the ottoman, which it attempted to ascend, by inserting one claw in the side, then turning half way round to make good another step, and so on. It slipped down at the first attempt, but again quietly resumed its task. It was exactly like a child trying to climb up a height. All this time we hardly touched it, being afraid of interfering with its movements, and, above all things, determined not to assist them. At last, by careful and persevering efforts, it accomplished the top of the ottoman, and stood on the summit of the column in the centre, from whence in a few minutes it descended to the floor by a similar process."

The writer makes the following pertinent reflection on what he has just described. "It is not to be expected that any person who is a stranger to these phenomena, should read such a story as this with complacency. Yet here is a fact which undoubtedly took place, and which cannot be referred to any known physical or mechanical forces. It is not a satisfactory answer to those who have seen such things, to say that they are impossible: *since, in such cases, it is evident that the impossibility of a thing does not prevent it happening.*

Upon many subsequent occasions the writer says that he has witnessed phenomena of a similar nature, and others of a much more startling character. He tells us for instance, "When I saw a table, at which two ladies were seated, moving towards me without any adequate impulse being imparted to it by visible means, I thought the fact sufficiently extraordinary; but my wonder abated when, on subsequent occasions, I saw tables move apparently of their own volition, there being no persons near them; large sofas advance from the walls against which they stood; and chairs, sometimes occupied, and sometimes empty, shift their places for the distance of a foot or a yard, in some cases easily, and in others with a slow, laborious movement."

As to the peculiar trembling of the table and room, he says, "On the first occasion when I experienced the effect I am about to describe, there were five persons in the room. In other places, where it occurred subsequently; there were seven or more. The architecture of the houses in each case was wholly dissimilar, both as to the area and height of the apartments, and the age, size, and strength of the buildings. We were seated at a table A which some singular phenomena, accompanied by loud knocks on the walls and floor, had just occurred, when we became conscious of a strange vibration that palpitated through the entire room. We listened and watched attentively. The vibration grew stronger and stronger. It was palpably under our feet. Our chairs shook, and the floor trembled violently. The effect was exactly like the throbbing. and heaving which might be supposed to take place in a house in the tropics during the moment immediately preceding an earthquake. This violent motion continued for two or three minutes, then gradually subsided and ceased. Every person present was equally affected by it on each occasion when it occurred. To produce such a result by machinery might be possible if the introduction of the machinery itself were possible. But the supposition involves a difficulty somewhat similar to that of Mr. Knickerbocker's theory of the earth standing on the back of a tortoise, which might be an excellent theory if we could only ascertain what the tortoise stood upon."

He now speaks of the raising of the table altogether from the floor, which he repeatedly witnessed. "Presently the table rises with a slight jerk, and steadily mounts till it attains such a height as to render it necessary for the company to stand up, in order still to be able to keep their hands with ease in contact with the surface, although that is not absolutely necessary. As there are some present who have not witnessed this movement before, a desire is expressed to examine the floor, and a gentleman goes under the table for the purpose. The whole space, open to the view of the entire party, is clear. From the carpet to the foot of the table there is a blank interval of perhaps two feet, perhaps three,— for nobody has thought of providing a means of measuring it, and we must take it by guess. The carpet is examined, and the legs and under surface of the table are explored, but without result. There is no trace of any connection between the floor and the table; nor can it be conceived how there could be any, as the table had shifted to this spot from the place where it originally stood only a few minutes before. The inspection is hurried and brief, but comprehensive enough to satisfy us that the table has not been raised by mechanical means from below; and such means could not be applied from above without the means of immediate detection. In its ascent, the table has swung out of its orbit, but it readjusts itself before it begins to descend, and, resuming its vertical position, it comes down on the spot from whence it rose. The downward motion is slow, and, if I may use the expression, graceful; and the table reaches the ground with a dreamy softness that renders its touch almost imperceptible.

"Of a somewhat similar character is another movement, in some respects more curious, and certainly opening a stranger field for speculation. The table rears itself up on one side, until the surface forms an inclined plane, at an angle of about 45°. In this attitude it stops. According to ordinary experience everything on the table must slide off, or topple over; but nothing stirs. The vase of flowers, the books, the little ornaments are as motionless as if they were fixed in their places. We agree to take away our hands, to throw up the ends of the cover, so as to leave the entire round pillar and claws exposed, and to remove our chairs to a little distance, that we may have a more complete command of a phenomenon, which, in its marvellous development at least, is, I believe, new to us all. Our withdrawal makes no difference whatever; and now we see distinctly on all sides the precise pose of the table, which looks, like the Tower of Pisa, as if it must inevitably tumble over. With a view to urge the investigation as far as it can be carried, a wish is whispered for a still more conclusive display of the power by which this extraordinary result has been accomplished. The desire is at once complied with. The table leans more and more out of the perpendicular; two of the three claws are high above the ground; and finally, the whole structure stands on the extreme tip of a single claw, fearfully overbalanced, but maintaining itself as steadily as if it were all one solid mass, instead of being freighted with a number of loose articles, and as if the position had been planned in strict accordance with the laws of equilibrium and attraction, instead of involving an inexplicable violation of both."

Of the music from an accordion playing by itself on the floor, he says:— "Apart from the wonderful consideration of its being played without hands—no less wonderful was the fact of its being played in a narrow space which would not admit of its being drawn out with the requisite freedom to its full extent. We listened with suspended breath. The air was wild, and full of strange transitions; with a wail of the most pathetic sweetness running through it. The execution was no less remarkable for its delicacy than its power. When the notes swelled in some of the bold passages, the sound rolled through the room with an astounding reverberation; then, gently subsiding, sank into a strain of divine tenderness. But it was the close that touched the hearts, and drew the tears of the listeners. Milton dreamt of this wondrous termination when he wrote of 'linked sweetness long drawn out.' By what art the accordion was made to yield that dying note, let practical musicians determine. Our ears, that heard it, had never before been visited by a 'sound so fine.' It continued diminishing and diminishing, and stretching far away into distance and darkness, until the attenuated thread of sound became so exquisite that it was impossible at last to fix the moment when it ceased."

The writer disposes of all question of fraud or mechanical contrivance, by telling us:— "We need not speculate on what might be done by skilful contrivances, since the question is removed out of the region of conjecture by the fact that, upon holding up the instrument myself in one hand, in the open room, with the full light upon it, similar strains were emitted, the regular action of the accordion going on without any visible agency. And I should add that, during the loud and vehement passages. it became so difficult to hold, in consequence of the extraordinary power with which it was played from below, that I was obliged to grasp the top with both hands. This experience was not a solitary one. I witnessed the same result on different occasions, when the instrument was held by others."

He also several times was present when, I was raised from the ground; and he gives the following description of what he observed:— "Mr. Home was seated next to the window. Through the semi-darkness his head was dimly visible against the curtains, and his hands might be seen in a faint white heap before him. Presently, he said, in a quiet voice, "My chair is moving—I am off the ground—don't notice me—talk of something else,' or words to that effect. It was very difficult to restrain the curiosity, not unmixed with a more serious feeling, which these few words awakened; but we talked, incoherently enough, upon some indifferent topic. I was sitting nearly opposite to Mr. Home, and I saw his hands disappear from the table, and his head vanish into the deep shadow beyond. In a moment or two more he spoke again. This time his voice was in the air above our heads. He had risen from his chair to a height of four or five feet from the ground. As he ascended higher he described his position, as at first perpendicular, and afterwards horizontal. He said he felt as if be had been turned in the gentlest manner, as a child is turned in the arms of a nurse. In a moment or two more, he told us that he was going to pass across the window, against the gray, silvery light of which he would be visible. We watched in profound stillness, and saw his figure pass from one side of the window to the other, feet foremost, lying horizontally in the air. He spoke to us as he passed, and told us that he would turn the reverse way, and recross the window; which he did. His own tranquil confidence in the safety of what seemed from below a situation of the most novel peril, gave confidence to everybody else; but, with the strongest nerves, it was impossible not to be conscious of a certain sensation of fear or awe. He hovered round the circle for several minutes, and passed, this time perpendicularly, over our heads. I heard his voice behind me in the air, and felt something lightly brush my chair. It was his foot, which he gave me leave to touch. Turning to the spot where it was on the top of the chair, I placed my hand gently upon it, when he uttered a cry of pain, and the foot was withdrawn quickly, with a palpable shudder. It was evidently not resting on the chair, but floating; and it sprang from the touch as a bird would. He now passed over to the farthest extremity of the room, and we could judge by his voice of the altitude and distance he had attained. He had reached the ceiling, upon which he made a slight mark, and soon afterwards descended and resumed his place at the table. An incident which occurred during this aerial passage, and imparted a strange solemnity to it, was that the accordion, which we supposed to be on the ground under the window close to us, played a strain of wild pathos in the air from the most distant corner in the room."

A most able, quiet, and philosophical description of these and others of the phenomena which he witnessed, is closed by some remarks which it is too much to hope that many will profit from. There is so much unreasoning opposition to the facts, that an appeal to reason in favour of them is almost out of place. He says:— "To say that certain phenomena are incredible, is merely to say that they are inconsistent with the present state of our knowledge; but knowing how imperfect our knowledge is, we are not, therefore, justified in asserting that they are impossible. The 'failures' which have occurred at séances are urged as proofs that the whole thing is a cheat. If such an argument be worth noticing, it is sufficient to say that ten thousand failures do not disprove a single fact. But it must be evident that as we do not know the conditions of 'success,' we cannot draw any argument from 'failures.' We often hear people say that they might believe such a thing, if such another thing were to happen; making assent to a particular fact, by an odd sort of logic, depend upon the occurrence of something else. 'I will believe,' for example, says a philosopher, of this stamp, 'that a table has risen from the ground, when I see the lamp-posts dancing quadrilles. Then, tables? Why do these things happen to tables?' Why, that is one of the very matters which it is desirable to investigate, but which we shall never know anything about so long as we ignore inquiry. And, above all, of what use are these wonderful manifestations? What do they prove? What benefit have they conferred on the world? Sir John Herschel has answered these questions with a weight of authority which is final. 'The question, *Cui bono?* to what practical end and advantages do your researches tend?—is one which the speculative philosopher, who loves knowledge for its own sake, and enjoys, as a rational being should enjoy, the mere contemplation of harmonious and mutually dependent truths, can seldom hear without a sense of humiliation. He feels that there is a lofty and disinterested pleasure in his speculations, which ought to exempt them from such questioning. 'But,' adds Sir John, 'if he can bring himself to descend from this high but fair ground, and justify himself, his pursuits, and his pleasures in the eyes of those around him, be has only to point to the history of all science, where speculations, apparently the most unprofitable, have almost invariably been those from which the greatest practical applications have emanated.' (Preliminary Discourse on the Study of Natural Philosophy, p.10.)

"The first thing to be done is to collect and verify facts. But this can never be done if we insist upon refusing to receive any facts, except such as shall appear to us likely to be true, according to the measure of our intelligence and knowledge."

This article was received by the public in the only way which was likely, from the novelty to so many of the subject of the phenomena; and though those who were acquainted personally with the marvellous occurrences so well described in the Magazine, well knew their truth, yet the writer and the Editor of the "Cornhill" were severely blamed by many for allowing the appearance of what they designated as such absurdity. As the article was anonymous, the facts stated in it were deliberately denied by the press, and to stem the torrent of abuse and unbelief, a gentleman, who has since become my very esteemed friend, wrote, giving his name, the following letter, which is introduced by some prefatory remarks, in the "Spiritual Magazine." The letter of Dr. Gully, of Malvern, first appeared in the "Morning Star," which of all the London papers has been the most fair and candid in dealing with the facts of Spiritualism:—

" Sir,—In Mr. Coleman's letter of the 11th inst., he gives his opinion that the gentlemen who were present at the meetings recorded in the 'Cornhill Magazine,' under the head of 'Stranger than Fiction,' should confirm or confute the statements made in that article. I was one of the persons present at the evening meeting. The other gentlemen were a solicitor in extensive practice, and two well-known writers of solid instructive works—not writers of fiction—who, by-the-bye, appear to be so used to inventing that they cannot believe that any one can possibly be employed in stating facts. It will be seen that the joke about 'fools of fashion' does not apply to the gentlemen alluded to, but that we were all workers in callings in which matters of fact, and not of fancy, especially come under observation. Further, it may be useful to some persons to know that we were neither asleep, nor intoxicated, nor even excited. We were complete masters of our senses; and I submit that their evidence is worth a thousand conjectures and explanations made by those who were not present. Scores of times I have been much more agitated and excited in investigating a patient's case, than I was in observing what occurred at the evening meeting in question.

"With this state of senses at the time, and revolving the occurrences in my mind again and again, since that time, I can state with the greatest positiveness that the record made in the article, 'Stranger than Fiction,' is, in every particular, correct; that the phenomena therein related actually took place in the evening meeting; and, moreover, that no trick, machinery, sleight-of-hand, or other artistic contrivance produced what we heard and beheld. I am quite as convinced of this last as I am of the facts themselves.

"Only consider that here is a man, between ten and eleven stone in weight, floating about the room for many minutes—in the tomb-like silence which prevailed, broken only by his voice coming from different quarters of the room; according to his then position—is it probable, is it possible, that any machinery could be devised—not to speak of its being set up and previously made ready in a room, which was fixed upon as the place of meeting only five minutes before we entered it—capable of carrying such a weight about without the slightest sound of any description? Or suppose, as has been suggested, that he bestrode an inflated balloon, could a balloon have been introduced inflated large enough to hold in mid-air such a weight? Or could it have been inflated with hydrogen gas without being detected by ears, eyes, or nose?

"It seems to me a much stronger sign of credulity to believe either of these suggestions, with our present knowledge, than to adopt the wildest statements or dreams of what is called Spiritualism. Let it be remembered, moreover, that the room was, for a good part of the evening, in a blaze of light, in which no balloon or other machine sufficient for the supposed purpose could be introduced; or, if already introduced, could remain unobserved; and that, even when the room was comparatively darkened, light streamed through the window from a distant gas-lamp outside, between which gas-lamp and our eyes Mr. Home's form passed, so that we distinctly perceived its trunk and limbs; and most assuredly there was no balloon near him, nor any machinery attached to him. His foot once touched my head when be was floating above.

Then the accordion music. I distinctly saw the instrument moving, and heard it playing when held only at one end, again and again. I held it myself for a short time, and had good reason to know that it was vehemently pulled at the other end, and not by Mr. Home's toes, as has been wisely surmised, unless that gentleman has legs three yards long, with toes at the end of them quite as marvellous as any legion of spirits. For, be it stated, that such music as we heard was no ordinary strain; it was grand at times, at others pathetic, at others distant and long-drawn, to a degree which no one can imagine who has not heard it. I have heard Blagrove repeatedly, but it is no libel on that master of the instrument to say that he never did produce such exquisite distant and echo notes as those which delighted our ears. The instrument played, too, at distant parts of the room, many yards away from Mr. Home, and from all of us. I believe I am stating a fact when I say that not one person in that room could play the accordion at all. Mr. Home cannot play a note upon it.

"To one whose external senses have witnessed these things, it is hard to increase the insufficiency of those attempted explanations which assert the use of tricks and machinery. As I said before, it requires much more credulity to believe such explanations than to swallow all the ghost stories that ever were related. I may add that the writer in the 'Cornhill Magazine' omits to mention several curious phenomena which were witnessed that evening. Here is one of them. A distinguished *litterateur*, who was present, asked the supposed spirit of his father, whether he would play his favourite ballad for us, and, addressing us, he added—'The accordion was not invented at the time of my father's death, so I cannot conceive how it will be effected; but if his favourite air is not played, I pledge myself to tell you so.' Almost immediately the flute notes of the accordion (which was upon the floor) played through 'Ye banks and braes of Bonnie Doon,' which the gentleman alluded to assured us was his father's favourite air, whilst the flute was his father's favourite instrument. He then asked for another favourite air of his father's, 'which was not Scotch,' and 'The Last Rose of Summer' was played in the same note. This, the gentleman told us, was the air to which he had alluded.

"I have thus borne testimony to the truthfulness of the facts related by the writer in the 'Cornhill Magazine,' whom I recognise as having been my neighbour during the meeting. And I have endeavoured to show that, as regards the principal and most wonderful phenomena, there could have been no contrivance by trick or machinery adequate to produce or account for their existence. How, then, were they produced? I know not; and I believe that we are very—very far from having accumulated facts enough upon which to frame any laws or build any theory regarding the agent at work in their production. Intelligent phenomena, such as the music played at request, point to intelligent agents; and spiritual bodies that have quitted fleshly bodies may be at work. I, for one, wish that it were proved to be so; for a more solemn discovery than that of a means of communication between embodied and disembodied sentient beings cannot be imagined. It giddies the brain to think of the possible result of such a discovery. But, whilst I obstinately stand up for the integrity of my senses during my observation of the wonders above related, my inner senses cannot but observe many gaps that must be filled up before the bridge between the spiritual body's life here in the flesh, and its life elsewhere out of the flesh, can be finished. Meantime the facts must be patiently and honestly accumulated, and enthusiasm must be banished from the minds of the enquirers. And as regards the denials, and abuses, and jests of the non-enquirers, let it be remembered that scurillity and laughter. never discovered or disproved anything in the world's history.

"Respecting the purely physical phenomena, such as the raising of weights whether of human bodies or tables, it may be that we are on the verge of discovering some physical force hitherto undreamed of; who shall say that we know all the powers of nature? Here, too, dispassionate inquiry must go on, regardless of the noise outside; regardless, too, of the ignorant and malicious prejudice which would blast the reputation of those who enquire in a direction opposite to that prejudice.

"Enquirers, unlike routine people, must be prepared to rough it among their fellow-creatures. And I suppose that I, for having asserted that I have five senses as yet unimpaired, and for having testified to what the majority disbelieve, shall come in for my share of pity or abuse. Let it be so, if it helps on a truthful search.

"I am, Sir,

"Yours faithfully,

"J. M. GULLY, M.D.

"Malvern, Oct. 14."

CHAPTER X

MIRACULOUS PRESERVATION
FRANCE AND ENGLAND

We left London the 24th of July, 1860, for the Château de C____, near Paris. One of the most remarkable interpositions of Providence which have ever happened to me occurred at this place. Many doubt the possibility of such interpositions, but I have not been allowed to doubt them, and I have to thank our Heavenly Father that I have so often been made aware of His ministering care and kind Providence. I do not suppose for a moment because of this, that His Providence is more over me than over all His children, and I believe that in looking back over our past lives, there are none of us who can fail to recognise the finger of God directing and protecting them, often in some remarkable and even almost physical way, though generally, perhaps, through means apparently more remote than those which saved my life on the 16th September, 1860.

I had just returned from Naples, whither I had been to visit a friend—but who had passed from earth before I had arrived—and I found my health, affected by fatigue of travelling and mental depression. Being recommended to take much out-door exercise, during my stay at the Château de C____, I used to take with me my gun—more that it might be said I was out shooting than for any great attraction the sport has for me. The Château de C____, distant half-an-hour by railway from Paris, stands in a beautiful old park. Some of the trees are of very great height; one of the largest, a northern poplar, stands a quarter of a mile from the Château at an angle of the park, where it is separated from the outer grounds by a hedge. To this spot, when there is much shooting going on in the neighbourhood, the game used to come for shelter; and I, who am but an indifferent marksman, could get easy shots by planting myself by the hedge.

On the day mentioned, I had been walking with my friend, Mons. T____, and on his leaving me, I bent my steps to this favourite corner, wishing to take home a partridge. As I neared the hedge, I stooped and advanced cautiously. When close up to it, I was raising my head to look for my game, when on my right I heard some one call out, "Here, here!", My only feeling was surprise at being thus suddenly addressed in English. The desire to have a good look out for my game, overruled my curiosity as to whom the exclamation had come from; and I was continuing to raise my head to the level of the hedge, when suddenly I was seized by the collar of my coat and vest, and lifted off the ground.

At the same instant I heard a crashing sound, and then all was quiet. I felt neither fear nor wonder. My first thought was that by some accident my gun had exploded, and that I was in the spirit-land; but, looking about, I saw that I was still in the material world, and there was the gun still in my hands. My attention was then drawn to what appeared to be a tree immediately before me, where no tree had been. On examination, this proved to be the fallen limb of the high tree under which I was standing. I then saw that I had been drawn aside from this fallen limb a distance of six or seven feet. I ran, in my excitement, as fast as I could to the Château. My friends, seeing me running, hastened to the window to learn the cause of my disturbance. As soon as I recovered my power of speech, I told them how God, by his good angels, had saved my life, and they returned with me to the scene of what I must call my miraculous escape.

I will not attempt to portray the feelings of those present, but if ever heartfelt prayer of thankfulness ascended to God's holy throne, it was then and there, from us all, even to the servants, who broke off twigs to keep as mementos of the mercy shown me.

The limb which had thus fallen, measured sixteen yards and a half in length, and where it had broken from the trunk, it was one yard in circumference. It fell from a height of forty-five feet. The part of the limb, which struck the very spot where I had been standing, measured twenty-four inches in circumference, and penetrated the earth at least a foot. The next day a friend made a sketch of the tree and branch. We now speculated as to how it could have happened. The tree is not a dead one; nor was the branch at all decayed, and there was scarcely wind enough to stir the leaves. he branch was so cleanly reft from the trunk that one might at first think it had been sawn off, and the bark was not in the least torn about it. I have been informed since that such accidents are not uncommon with trees of this species of poplar, and that there are trees of a similar quality in Australia, under which settlers will not remain for fear of such sudden breakages.

A day or two after, Dr. Höefer, one of the most learned men in France, and for whom I have the highest esteem and regard, as a sincere truth-seeker, and a friend deserving every confidence, came at about noon and requested a séance. We had one, and a very good one it was. Answers were given to questions of the utmost importance. All at once, it was spelled out, "Go, see the branch." Dr. Höefer, impressed as it were, withdrew from the table, saying, "Perhaps they are going there." I went to the drawing-room, and asked the ladies if they would join us, but the day being damp and the walking bad, they declined.

I ought to have said, that the thick end of the branch rested, at a height of eight feet from the ground, firmly against the trunk of the tree, so much so that the possibility of its coming down had never for an instant occurred to us, but rather that the strength of several horses should be required to move it. Our surprise, then, may be imagined when we now found that it had been moved three or four inches laterally from its original point of support. Dr. Höefer said, "I firmly believe that the branch will be pushed down before us." I replied, "That seems almost an impossibility." At the same time, I took in my hand one of the smaller twigs and mentally said, "Dear spirits, will you push this branch down?" I then distinctly felt as if some one gently touched the twig which I held; this was repeated, and at the third touch, as it felt to me, the branch fell to the ground.

Four persons witnessed this, and are ready to testify to what I here relate.

I had afterwards a piece of the thickest part of the fallen tree sawn off, and sent to me in London, where it still is, and with it on many occasions, some of which will be afterwards mentioned, some very marvellous manifestations took place.

One evening, at the Château, as we were seated at the table, the spirits having requested that the candles should be extinguished, the table drawn to the window, and the curtains opened to admit the moonlight, there had been some striking manifestations, and the time had been passing almost imperceptibly to us all, when a gentleman who was present, said that he felt very much exhausted, and he asked for a glass of brandy and water. It was brought, and he took it in his hand, and was about raising it to his mouth, when a spirit hand suddenly appeared, took hold of the lower part of the glass, and disappeared with it under the table. We laughingly said that our unseen friends surely did not believe in the use of stimulants. To this they assented by emphatic raps, and at the same moment the glass slowly rose again before him empty. The windows being closed, we supposed the water had been thrown upon the floor, and we arose to see where it was. We could discover no trace of it. About two minutes had elapsed, when the same glass which was standing empty before him, was seen without any visible cause, gradually to approach the edge of the table, and to disappear beneath it. I do not believe that above two seconds could have elapsed, before it again appeared with the brandy and water in it, apparently not less in quantity than when first brought in, though the quality had certainly undergone some chemical change, as it had now lost much of its brown colour. By the raps, a warning was given to all of us against such indulgence.

In September we left the Château to spend a month in Paris; and we paid a short visit to our relatives at Biarritz, returning to England at the end of November, 1861. My wife's health being delicate, the medical men having discovered an internal disease, which, though of a serious nature, might yet last for many years, we did not during this winter see so many friends, but I had séances as often as I could.

From an esteemed friend, who had been rescued from scepticism by the manifestations of spirit power which he had so often witnessed, I find a letter describing what he saw in London at this time.

"Seven of us were present in a large drawing-room, lighted by a good fire and three gas-burners. The accordion was taken by one of our friends who had never been present at any manifestations, and in his hands it was forcibly pulled, and several chords played—in my hand also the same was done; but the weight of the instrument made the holding of it painful to me. We then began to be touched; and I felt a soft body passing across my knees. A gentleman and I wishing our hands to be grasped by a spirit, placed our handkerchiefs over our hands, in a single fold. Shortly, the handkerchief was taken off by what seemed to me like air fingers—so gentle, so soft. It was carried to the gentleman opposite, and by him received and handed to me; the other was restored to the owner tied into a curious knot. All other hands were on the table during the whole of the time. Two of the three gas-lights were now put out— and the fire burning brightly, gave a subdued light in the room. Mr. Home then became cataleptic in his hands and arms he was raised from his seat till he stood upright, and then he rose vertically till he was a foot above the floor—his head level with the chandelier—this was repeated twice, but he did not rise higher. On sitting down again, the table-cloth was several times raised up in different parts of the table, and, I with others, placed my hand on the substance which so raised it, and to my sense of feeling, it was as if a plastic hand and fingers touched mine, yielding to my pressure. During our conversations, approval or disapproval of some things said were given by energetic concussions. The loudest affirmatives were when it was said these manifestations were by God's permission, to prove to us the continued existence of our relatives, and of our immortality; also that we could not be alone, as there were ever about us unseen active intelligences, who saw our actions, heard our words, and discerned our thoughts.

"The lady who was with me had laughed and wondered at my foolishness for these several years past for believing in spirit-power manifestations; but now, wonder, joyousness, and belief took possession of her, and the candid avowal of her conviction, and the consequences to certain materialistic members of her family, seemed to be producing a powerful effect upon her mind.

"What is the use of spirits descending to the level of our educational obtuseness, and producing the class of phenomena detailed in this rough sketch? The question is answered by my giving a portion of a letter received on the 6th of this month from one of our literary celebrities, whose name has not yet been prominently before the public in connection with spirit manifestations. Having sent to the editors of the daily and weekly newspapers and magazines a printed letter on spirit manifestations, I had a reply from one of the editors, who says:—

"'I *know* all you have stated, and more—I have seen and felt all you have stated, and more. I believe I am no 'fool'—I am sure I am no 'rogue.' To me the belief has been an unspeakable comfort, thoroughly taking me away from that materialism into which I had crept; and I believe that to be the main purpose of spiritual teaching, and the reason why the great principle is developed in our time.'

"I have had the same testimony given to me by many others.

"JOHN JONES.

"Basinghall Street, 14th January, 1861."

The important testimony of my friend Mr. James Hutchinson, for many years the chairman of the Stock Exchange, is one to which I would draw attention, as it appears from his well-known character and sagacity, to be just such as ought to be received as conclusive evidence of what he relates. Mr. Hutchinson says:—

"I have for some time past felt an interest in the subject of Spiritual Manifestations. Like most persons I had great difficulty in realising the statements made to me of the wonders which were daily witnessed by others, but the evidence of friends satisfied me that there must be something worthy of serious investigation, and I therefore determined to take every opportunity of looking into it for myself. I have now done so, and I feel it a duty to openly bear my testimony to the *facts*, leaving others to *theorise* on the causes and tendency of these remarkable phenomena.

"Recently introduced by a friend to Mr. D. D. Home, a séance was arranged for the 23rd instant, and together with Mr. and Mrs. Coleman, Mr. G. S. Clarke, Mr. T. Clarke, Mr. Gilbert Davidson, and another lady and gentleman unknown to me, we formed a party of nine. Shortly after sitting down, we all felt a tremulous motion in our chairs, and in the table, which was a very heavy circular drawing-room table. This movement of the table increased in power, and at the suggestion of Mr. Coleman, it imitated the exact action and sound of a stroke of a powerful marine engine acting on and vibrating the timbers of a weak-framed vessel.

"The rapping sounds on the table and floor were constant; the heavy table was raised up repeatedly—and these manifestations were continued whilst my friend, Mr. Clarke, and another were seated, at the request of Mr. Home, under the table.

"Two hand-bells, one weighing at least a pound and a half, were passed from one to another of the party by the unseen agencies. All of us in turn felt the touch and pressure of a soft and fleshy life-like hand. I saw the full formed hand as it rested on my knee. The accordion, whilst held by Mr. Home in one hand, discoursed most eloquent music, and then to our great astonishment it was taken from him, and whilst both his hands and those of all of the party were visibly imposed on the surface of the table—the accordion, suspended from the centre of the table, gave out an exquisite air, no human hand touching it!

"These and many other incidents of a seriously impressive but private character, of which I do not hesitate to speak among my friends, occupied about four hours of what I must admit to be one of the most interesting evenings I have ever spent. I place the facts as we witnessed them at your disposal for publicity, if you please, merely adding, that contrary to the assertions so constantly made that the manifestations are always in the dark, the whole of the phenomena of which I have spoken were manifested in a room lighted with gas, and a bright fire burning.

"yours, &c.,

"JAS. HUTCHINSON.

"January 26th, 1861."

The following editorial remarks, introducing the letter of "A Plain Man," appeared in the 'Sunday Times,' of the 17th February. The "Plain Man" is well-known to me, and I can personally vouch for his high character and intelligence, but he is in a position, which makes it a matter of prudence that it should not be known publicly that he has seen what he has seen. If science and religion are satisfied with this uncharitable state of things, I confess that I am not, and that I sigh for the days when every man and woman will be able to tell the truth without being robbed of their bread by the calumnies of those who are simply uninformed as to the facts which are observed. The editor of the 'Sunday Times,' says:—

"In accordance with the pledge we made at the time when we inserted a notice of Mr. Novra's lecture, we hasten to give publicity to a letter which we have received, accompanied by the name and address of the writer. From the high position which that gentleman holds, and the widely-admitted truthfulness of his assertions, we cannot do other wise than believe that he personally saw all that he relates, and thus we are again thrown back on the sea of doubt anxious to arrive at the truth, yet unable to do so. Fortunately, it is not our duty to decide, or even to give our opinion on such matters; we, therefore, publish the letter hoping that if a certain enlightening spirit is granted, which may clear up the truth, that it may be shed upon us, or that if the whole thing is fictitious and imaginary, the delusion may soon be dissipated. Too much credulity on the one hand is contemptible. A blind obstinacy has often nearly marred the best revelations which Providence has vouchsafed to science.

"To the Editor of the 'Sunday Times'

"Sir,—For some time I have been waiting for a favourable opportunity to address you, and to state certain facts connected with Spiritualism, which clearly demonstrate the existence of what many persons seem determined to deny. Such sceptics, by their arguments, so far from doing any injury to the cause, have been the means of inducing many to enquire into the phenomena, who otherwise, in all probability, would never have thought of doing so, and as a consequence, have converted them into thorough believers. Nine such cases have occurred at my own house. Again, throughout all the books and articles I have read, I never have found advanced one single argument against the *possibility* of a communication with the spiritual world, but merely expositions of the tricks practised by some interested persons, thus confirming those who were only half convinced, and enabling all who are fortunate enough to be present at a *bona fide* séance, more easily to distinguish between reality and deceit. Clearly, such persons deserve the thanks of us all. The columns of a newspaper could not admit, nor have I the time to write, the many reasons to be adduced in favour of the probability of spiritual manifestations; all I ask of you is to insert a plain statement, from a plain man, of certain facts so striking, extraordinary, and convincing, that those who have seen them cannot fail to believe, and by which not only are the ideas of a man's lifetime upset, but the very laws of nature and gravitation as hitherto understood, appear to be scattered to the winds.

"A few nights since, a party of seven, including Mr. Home and two ladies, assembled, *en séance*, round a heavy large circular table. For a short time nothing extraordinary took place, but at length a convulsive throbbing was felt in the table, which shortly began to move, undulating with an easy, graceful movement, and raising itself at times about a foot off the ground. At the same time there were knocks in quick succession under the table, on the floor, ceiling, and round the room, a gentleman being under the table at the time, at Mr. Home's request, to guard against the possibility of collusion. After some trivial communications, a small hand-bell was held by me under the table, and in a few minutes I perceived, on looking down, a small white hand (every other hand belonging to the party assembled, being on the table), which commenced caressing and playing with mine. After ringing the bell once or twice (in my hand), I asked that it should be conveyed to a gentleman opposite, and no sooner was my wish expressed than I felt it pulled from my hand, and deposited in that of the gentleman I had indicated. This was done several times. The hand was smooth and white as a child's, and was quite visible, there being two gas jets burning in the room. An accordion was held at the side of the table by Mr. Home, when the most lovely, plaintive, and melodious music was played, and no sooner had I expressed a wish to hear the 'Last Rose of Summer,' than that tune was played, at which moment the accordion was resting on my feet, without a hand of earthly description near it, it having been taken out of Mr. Home's hand and deposited there. Several hands now appeared in quick succession moving different articles of furniture; and one, a particularly powerful one, having touched Mr. Home, he exclaimed that enormous strength had been given him. It certainly had, and he proceeded at once to exercise it. A block of wood, from the large arm of the tree of great weight, from the falling of which he was so wonderfully preserved, was taken up by Mr. Home as if it were a straw, carried round the room under his arm, and finally deposited near the table. It seemed of no weight to him, and yet, when two gentlemen, each of them apparently much more powerful than Mr. Home, essayed, they could hardly move it. A singular circumstance connected with Mr. Home's receiving such extraordinary strength it is necessary to mention. One of the gentlemen present had lost a very dear friend in the late war in the Crimea, and who, prior to leaving this country, gave him his photograph. It was the only one he ever sat for, and after his decease the family asked for it to get it copied, but they had not returned it. On several occasions the spirit has manifested himself, and has constantly reproached this gentleman for having parted with it. On this evening a similar message was received, when he mentally asked for such a manifestation as would fully identify him with the departed friend. When in the world, he was a most powerful muscular man; and to convince this gentlemen it was he, who enabled Mr. Home, through himself to lift this mass of timber, which at another time he could not have moved. The last words spelt out were, 'Get back a copy at least.'

"Another hand now appeared; and on Mr. Home being touched by it, he exclaimed, 'They are raising me; do not look at me till I am above the level of the table, as it might have the effect of bringing me down.' Almost at the same moment Mr. Home was raised up and floated in the air at the height of about five feet, touching one gentleman on the head slightly as he passed, but on approaching the window he came again gently to the ground. He remarked, 'Their strength is hardly great enough yet, but I feel that it will be soon.' The table which for some time had remained passive, now began to heave and throb most violently, and finished by moving towards a sofa at the end of the room, obliging all sitting round to follow it. We had scarcely, resumed our seats, when our attention was attracted by seeing a small table move across the room; and finally, after much difficulty, raise itself, and stand in the centre of the large table round which we were sitting. 'Less earthly light' was now spelt out, and the two gas-lights were turned down, leaving merely a bright blazing fire, which clearly illuminated the whole room. This was scarcely done, when a small baby's hand was seen creeping up a gentleman's arm, and almost at the same time he perceived between Mr. Home and himself the form of an infant in white. Being naturally very fond of children, he thought nothing of it, merely imagining that his inclinations were known; but on his wife's asking if it was not the spirit of her little child now passed away, a timid answer in the affirmative was given—a bright light appearing close to the sofa at the same moment, which, by degrees, faded, and at last disappeared. The small table, which it must be remembered was still upon the large one, now began to move, and at the same moment the same hand that before imparted such supernatural strength to Mr. Home was again seen grasping him. His arms were raised above his head, he was again lifted about two feet off the ground and carried towards the window, and when there, he was raised to within about eighteen inches of the ceiling. After remaining floating for about two minutes he descended; but on coming near his chair, he was again elevated, and placed in a standing position in the centre of the table, together with the small one. His weight not resting on it, it had no effect, nor was there even a creak heard. In about a minute both Mr. Home and the small table were elevated for a fourth time in the air, about a foot off the surface of the large table, and, after remaining in that position for about a minute, he descended and resumed his seat.

"Such is a short account of this most remarkable and satisfactory séance. I need scarcely add that of necessity I have been compelled to omit many small details which, although interesting in themselves, sink into insignificance by the side of the wonderful manifestations above described.

"I remain, Sir,

"Your obedient servant,

"A PLAIN MAN."

By this time the health of my wife was failing, and she was sometimes confined to bed. One night the spirit of her mother came to us, and after making three crosses upon Sacha's brow, the hand being invisible but still perfectly tangible, my wife said to me, "Oh, mama is blessing me, and I feel such a strange thrill of joy." I now felt the hand laid upon my brow, and again the present was obliterated from my mind, and I saw the being so dear to me as passing from earth. It was so terrible a reality that I would have given worlds to have felt that there could be every the slightest possibility of my having been deceived. Her mother told me that the disease which would cause her to pass from earth was not the one we had so dreaded, but would be, in fact, consumption. From that moment, every time our kind-hearted and experienced doctor came, I urged him to see whether or no he could detect the slightest change, as indicating disease of the lungs; but he said, that though great weakness existed, still active disease was not going on, and he thought it might be avoided. As soon as the dear one could undertake the journey, we went to Bournemouth, where our friend, Mrs. P____ joined us, and we there found the symptoms of lung-disease to have increased. Accordingly, a medical man was called in, who, with one of his colleagues, pronounced the left lung to be unsound. I was alone when they told me this; and when I entered my wife's room, she wished to know what the result of their diagnosis had been. We had, when first married, promised to each other that if ever one knew the other to be seriously ill, we would not attempt to conceal it. Still I had never had the courage to tell her what her mother had revealed to me; for to one so young, and whose life had everything to make it desirable, it seemed hard to think that a new existence so soon awaited her. I felt, however, that I must be true to my promise, and I told her what the doctors had said. She smiled, and said, "Do you think I can remain on earth ten days?" I told her that not only ten days, but that in reality she might live ten years, but that still all was uncertain. She took my hand in hers, and said, "Do you remember, Daniel, when my mother blessed me a month ago, and I told you what a thrill of joy I felt? Well, I feel that she is here now, and I feel a continuation of the self-same thrill. I am going to her, but God will not separate us. I will ever watch over Gricha and you." She asked me for her writing desk, and then wrote letters, which she sealed and addressed, adding the words, "To be opened after I am gone." Just as she was about to finish the last letter our child ran into the room, and sitting on her knee, he caressingly stroked her cheek, saying, "Mama is too good to be ill." This so affected her, that she burst into tears, and these were the only tears she ever shed at the thought of leaving the body. Distinct musical sounds were now heard every night in our room, and on more than one occasion the singing of a bird was heard for more than an hour over her bed.

We remained at Bournemouth about three weeks, and finding the climate very unsuitable, we went to the country house of our kind friend, Mr. Cox, in Hampshire, where we remained a month. My wife now frequently saw both her father and mother, and also a little boy whom she did not recognise, and her mother told her that he was her brother who had passed from earth when only a few hours old. Here occurred some curious phenomena which are described in the letter of my friend, Mr. Cox, of Jermyn Street:—

"The late Robert Owen, a short time previous to his passing from earth, had given me a writing desk which had belonged to his wife, and which contained amongst other things a box of paints. As I had other things of his as remembrances, I felt it more just after his departure, that some member of his family should possess the desk, which had belonged to their mother; and I therefore gave it to his son, Mr. Robert Dale Owen, in order that he might take it with him to America. I felt, however, at the time an almost irresistible impulse to retain the desk, but the feeling of right overcame it. The fact had almost escaped my memory, when at nearly the first séance I had with Mr. Home after his return from Russia, the spirit of my old and valued friend, Mr. Owen, came and said, 'You must tell Robert to return you that writing desk; and why did you give it to him, for I did all I could to impress you not to part with it.' I wrote this to Mr. Robert Dale Owen, and in due time the desk was returned to me. We were then at my house in the country, and Mr. and Mrs. Home came to spend a short time with us. My little boy was then, and had been for some time previously, indisposed, and medical advice had been called in, but to little purpose. The spirits had previously prescribed for him, and now they said they would magnetize some pure spring water, which would benefit him. For this purpose a decanter was procured, and placed on the middle of the table at which we were sitting. I placed it there myself, and had taken every precaution that no one should touch it. The water in the decanter became agitated after a few moments without any visible cause, and a powerful aroma came from the bottle. We tasted the water, and found it was strongly impregnated with something which gave it a decided flavour, but what it was we knew not: it was not like anything we had tasted before. Mr. Home was then thrown into the trance state, and taking the decanter in his right hand, he walked a few feet from the table, holding it in full view all the time, when, to my astonishment, I saw another decanter, apparently precisely similar to the other, in his left hand. Thus, in each of his hands I saw a decanter; and so real was the second, that I could not have told which of them was the material one. Even if a trick had been intended, here was no opportunity for it, and as the decanter was a large one, another one could not have been concealed up Mr. Home's coat-sleeve, or about his person. A little later, Mr. Owen's spirit came and desired his wife's writing desk to be placed on the table; and now the room was darkened to see if we could distinguish spirit lights, which were then seen by three of us. Presently we heard the writing desk opened, and a hand was placed in mine, another in my wife's, and a third in Mr. Home's, each hand differing in size from the others. The alphabet was called for, and 'I fear I may have spoilt your Claude,' was spelt out. We could not understand this; but when the lamp was relighted, we found that some paint had been taken from the box from inside the desk, and had been freely used on one of my paintings which hung several feet from where we were sitting.

"WM. COX."

We now returned to London; and the first day of our arrival our valued friend, Dr. H____, called on us still hoping that the medical men had made a mistake in pronouncing the lung to be diseased; and as he was sounding the chest, my dear wife looked up at him laughingly, and said, "You see how very different it is now to what it used to be. I myself can distinguish the difference in the sound." He sorrowfully shook his head, and said, "It is but too true, and with your belief I would not attempt to conceal it from you." Many times did he reiterate these words during her illness, adding, "With my other patients I have to give them hopes that they are going to stay, and you are ever asking me for hopes that you are to go."

During our stay in London I had a séance almost every night, my wife feeling that they did her good both physically and spiritually. The character of the manifestations occurring at this time will be seen in the accounts which are given by my two friends. That of Mr. W. M. Wilkinson is an follows:—

My First Séance with Mr. Home

"Though I have been on terms of intimacy with Mr. Home for some years, and have heard and read of all the wonderful things which occur in his presence, yet this 19th June, 1861, is the first time I have come to see them for myself. It has not been because I either disbelieved them, or thought them of no importance, for I quite believed them, and thought them of very great importance. Having been, however, in the habit of hearing from friends of all that was occurring, I was fully satisfied with their accounts, and did not think that they were so much beneath me in observation, that it was necessary for my own eyes to convince me. I take no credit to myself for this, for it is mainly a consequence of my own experience. I remember about twenty-five years ago, when I first heard of mesmerism, and of its psychological wonders, I committed the folly of saying that I did not believe a word of it, and since I had on that occasion to surrender at discretion on seeing for myself, I have made much fewer similar mistakes. Since that time, I have pursued this and kindred subjects, and I may fairly say that I can now readily believe in much more than I once thought possible. I have found this, at all events, convenient, for I have not had so often to find myself at variance with facts, which is always a painful position to be in; and, besides, it has opened up to me a new world of spiritual forces, which, though generally ignored, I have found to account for many of the strangest, and otherwise incomprehensible chapters of human history.

"I had on two or three occasions, through Mr. Squire and other mediums, seen phenomena as wonderful as those which I now witnessed in the presence of Mr. Home. I had seen nearly all the wonderful things so admirably described in the 'Cornhill Magazine,' and in the letter of Dr. Gully; I had also been present when others of even a more powerful kind were done, and which were ably described by Dr. Blank, at page 161 of the 1st volume of the 'Spiritual Magazine.' I had several times seen, both in London and Paris, direct writing by invisible power, on paper placed beyond mortal contact, and I was well convinced also of the alleged power of mediums to float in the air, by having had one come down on my chest, as well as having on other occasions had hold of his hand, whilst he was floating about in the room. I did not, therefore, on this evening care to disturb myself and others by taking those precautions which would have been necessary if I were the President of the Royal Society, and were about to make a conclusive report to that illustrious body of inquirers into physics. I did not doubt, but I sat, and saw, and heard, and felt, and made notes.

There were eight of us, all well known to me, and some of them known wherever the English language is spoken. We were in the drawing-room of a house in Cornwall Terrace, Regent's Park, and we sat round a large loo table, and commenced talking. Curiously enough, one having said that Professor Faraday was coming on the following Monday to a séance, and speculating as to his guardian spirit not allowing him to be easily convinced, there were at once very loud knocks on the table in affirmation of that proposition. I was sitting next to my wife on her right hand, and immediately afterwards I felt my left leg gently touched, in a position where it was impossible for Mr. Home to have reached it. Then there began a gentle but deep vibration of the table, chairs, and floor, till all the room was shaking violently, during which the table rose about ten inches, the trembling continuing all the time. The table began to rise on the opposite side to where Mr. Home was sitting, and it was clearly out of his power to have so raised it. Mr. Home's chair was quietly moved back, away from the table, about three feet, and whilst there the dresses of my wife and of the lady next to her were both pulled, and so strongly that I could see them dragging down. I also felt my wife's dress whilst being so pulled, and there was a powerful force expended in the act resisting my hand. At this time Mr. Home was fully six feet off, and both from distance, and from his being in full view, I could see that it was done by no force of his. Mr. Home now held the accordion in his right hand beside his chair, and it at once began to play. He held it by the bottom, the keys being on the top, and they were therefore out of his reach. It was impossible that he could touch them. I carefully examined the instrument, opening the slide beneath the keys, and I found it to be a common instrument, with only the usual mechanism of the keys. There was nothing inside it. I looked steadily at it, and at the hand and fingers with which he held it. There it was, being pulled up and down, and discoursing sweet sounds, whilst his hand was stationary, and his fingers motionless. I could see above and beneath the instrument, but there was no visible cause for its motion, nor for the opening and shutting of the keys which caused the music. When it ceased, my wife asked if it could not be played in her hand, and immediately the instrument emitted three sounds, which we took to mean that it would have much pleasure in trying. It was accordingly given to her, and whilst she was holding it, she said she felt one of her fingers being touched. Immediately afterwards the table was raised about a foot steadily from the floor. As there was no sound from the accordion in her hands, she returned it to Mr. Home, but it was taken from his hand immediately, and given back to her, and whilst in her right hand it began to play. She felt it distinctly lifted up and drawn forcibly down, and she did not and could not touch the keys, which, however, must necessarily have been touched and opened to make the sounds. In Mr. Home's hands a beautiful tune was now played, during which we heard what has been so often described, the full notes gradually decreasing till they died away into the thinnest streaks of sound. By three quickly repeated notes it was promised that the instruments should play the tune of the other evening, representing 'The Two Lives,' the one in this world, the other in that which follows. The first, or this world's life, was represented by discords grating painfully on the ear, and which I thought did but scant justice to a world which, though capable of improvement, still has some rich harmonies within its depths. In mercy to our ears, the first life did not last long, and was then succeeded by the second, which was made up of beautiful soft angel music, such as I had never heard. It played for several minutes, swelling into rich sounds, of which the sweetness was enchanting to the ear, and gradually changed into the dear old tune of 'Home, sweet Home.'

What more appropriate and happy view of the second life could be given in musical sounds than this of its being home; and what a sweet sermon on the relative values of the two lives! I believe it was received more solemnly, and yet more thankfully by all who were present, from our knowing the sickness 'even unto death' of one of the party, the youngest and the happiest in her bright longings for this second life. It would be almost blasphemy to ask in her presence what is the good of Spiritualism. Such a question would not occur to a good man, and could not be asked by a wise one. The mere man of science who measures human souls by mathematics, would be out of place in such a scene, and had I not been too happily engaged with my own thoughts, I should have felt glad that we were troubled with none such. I did not during this last performance scrutinize the instrument further than to see that it was held, bottom upwards, in Mr. Home's right hand, his other hand being upon the table, as were the hands of all the other persons present, and I am not aware of any natural means by which an accordion can be played under such conditions. I do not doubt for another reason, however, having once had an accordion play in my own hands, when I know that I did not do it. I also know that Lord Lyndhurst, and many other public men whom I could name, have had a similar experience.

"But now the table rises again a clear foot from the floor, and there stands, not quietly, but strongly undulating, still so that I was able to make the following note on my paper resting on the table, whilst it was at its full height above the ground:—'Table rose a foot. Count 10. I wrote this whilst up and undulating.' It then gently descended to the floor again. We now changed places according to directions, and a gentleman became my right hand neighbour, who, in a minute after, said that he saw a hand which he believed to be his son's. I did not see it, nor did I see three fingers which my wife shortly after saw; but in answer to a question, I had three taps on my knee as from a hand, still with no such distinctness as to make me sure what it was. At this time, several at once said they saw a light cloudy appearance dart across the room, but, being behind me, I saw nothing of it.

"In one corner of the room, near where we were sitting, was a shrine with several Indian idols of bronze. Suddenly, there was a commotion amongst them, and a crash, and a large one was thrown down, and brought with some violence and noise under the table. There it appeared as if it was in the hands of some vigorous power, and presently we found a jingling of some metallic substance against it, which afterwards proved to be a metal ornamental canopy, which had been unscrewed from the back of the idol, and with which questions were now answered by knocking them together. In like manner, loud knocks were made in answer to questions, by rattling the idol against the floor. A remark was made as to the want of respect thus indicated, and at once a number of jubilant raps were produced by again knocking the two parts of the idol together. Two or three times the idol appeared, pushing up inside of the table cloth, and twice it made its appearance naked above the table, and gently reached the ground again. Some flowers were brought from the shrine, and placed in the hand of each person present. Our present consisted of a rose and several pinks. I felt the rose placed in my hand under the table, all other hands being visible and on the table.

"Several times during the evening we all perceived a cool air pervading the table, and which it was impossible not to notice. The accordion was now placed on the floor, and all hands on the table, when it was heard to sound clearly several times, but no tune was played. It then tried to get from the floor to the table, but was not able to accomplish the whole journey, and fell gently back to the floor. The table was now again raised clear from the ground, both my feet being on its pediment, and pressing heavily downwards the whole time. The resistance and upward steady movement of the table were strangely curious, as was its careful quiet descent, my feet still pressing on it, and yet it reached the ground without noise. There was now a general rattle among the idols, and several very loud knocks, and then came an end of a very interesting evening, during which I have seen and heard what was sufficient to convince me that those are wrong who deny the possibility of the phenomena. How they are to be accounted for is another matter, which may be discussed with many honest differences of opinion; but that they exist is not a matter of doubt, but of certainty. There are some well-meaning persons who say that they are done by the devil; but I saw no signs on this evening of any wickedness, either in the work, or in the persons who looked on. For myself, I took up much the same attitude I should do at a scientific lecture, illustrated with experiments and diagrams, and I perceived no special influence but that of a strong desire to observe the facts.

"As to the facts being impossible, because they do not square with the ideas of spirit and of matter which are current in the Royal Society, that is not my affair, for I did not make either the facts, or the opinions which find them so inconvenient. I do but state that which I have seen, and if I have done so clearly, that is my only wish. Facts will always take care of themselves, and those are the most wise to whom they administer no reproof. There is another reason why I hope to have enlarged the circle of observers, by my description of this evening's phenomena. It is impossible for many that they should see what I have seen, and so far as they can believe my testimony, the necessity for their personal seeing is avoided. Many things must be taken on the evidence of others. 'Non cuivis contingit adire Corinthum.' It does not, happen to every one to go to Corinth, and so they who can't go themselves, must take the account of those who have been there. A certain few of a peculiar turn of mind, common to all ages, cannot accept the testimony of others, and they are best left alone, till an opportunity offers of convincing them by a mode suitable to their peculiar weakness. It is not yet fashionable to believe in these impossible things, and as some one must begin and put up with the necessary ridicule, I willingly submit my name for as much as can be made to stick to it.

"W. M. WILKINSON.

"Hampstead."

Mr. William Howitt, who has made such deep researches into this subject, and has in his great work now ready for the press, brought together the testimonies, ancient and modern, to the supernatural in all ages, was present on several occasions to observe and investigate the phenomena, and in an eloquent and forcible letter which he wrote to Mr. Barkas of Newcastle, he gives an account of some part of what he witnessed.

"I wish some of your negatives could have seen what I and Mrs. Howitt, and several others saw at the house of a lady in Regent's Park, about three months ago, and the like of which some of our most distinguished nobility have seen there repeatedly of late. There were, besides us, Mr. and Mrs. Home, and a Russian Count Steinbock, and several others. We had beautiful music played on the accordion when held in one hand by Mr. Home, who cannot play a note, and the same when held by a lady. We had the clearest and most prompt communications on different subjects through the alphabet, and flower's were taken from a bouquet on a cheffonier at a distance, and brought and handed to each of us. Mrs. Howitt had a sprig of geranium handed to her by an invisible hand, which we have planted, and it is growing; so that it is no delusion, no fairy money turned into dross or leaves. I saw a spirit hand as distinctly as I ever saw my own. I touched one several times, once when it was handing me the flower. My wife's silk dress was pulled so strongly that she thought it would tear out the gathers, and was rustled so loudly, that it was not only heard by all of us, but might have been heard in another room. My wife's handkerchief was taken from her knee, and brought and whisked against my hand at the opposite side of the table; I thought, with the intention of my taking it, but the spirit would not allow that, but withdrew it a little, then whisked my hand with it anew, and then flung it into the middle of the room. The dress and the handkerchief were perfectly visible during these operations, but the motive power was invisible.

"Then the spirits went to a shrine of bronze idols, belonging to the lady of the house, who bought them in India. Some of these are very heavy. They pitched them down on the floor, and with such violence that the clash might have been heard all over the house. The larger of these idols—perhaps all—of that I am not certain—unscrew, and the screws work exactly the opposite way to our screws; but the spirits unscrewed them, and pummelled their heads lustily on the floor, saying, through the alphabet, "You must all do your best to destroy idolatry, both in India and in England, where it prevails in numerous ways. Idolatry of rank, idolatry of wealth, idolatry of self, idolatry of mere intellect and learning," &c., &c. The different parts were thrown under the table, that you might tread them under foot, and two parts of the idol Mahadeo, of heavy bronze, were placed on the table by a visible hand. The head of the idol felt to me to weigh four or five pounds.

"Mr. Home was lifted about a foot from the ground, but did not float, as he frequently does, in the strongest light. The table, a very heavy loo table, was also several times lifted a foot or more from the ground, and we were invited to look under it and see that there was no visible cause. To us, who have seen so much of these things, and to whom they are as familiar as the sight of a bird flying, and far more familiar than the present comet, this was not necessary.

"A few evenings afterwards a lady desiring that the 'Last Rose of Summer' might be played by a spirit on the accordion, the wish was complied with, but in so wretched a style that the company, begged that it might be discontinued. This was done; but soon after, evidently by another spirit, the accordion was carried and suspended over the lady's head, and there, without any visible support or action on the instrument, the air was played through most admirably, in the view and hearing of all."

CHAPTER XI

A DIARY AND LETTER

Nearly the whole range of the phenomena occurred during our residence with our friend Mrs. P____ in the Regent's Park, and she has been a frequent visitor at other séances, and has kept a diary of every evening, which she has kindly placed at my disposal. I propose therefore to make extracts from it of some of the more striking phenomena both of this and of subsequent dates.

Short Extracts from a Diary, 1860-61-62

December 15, 1860.—My mental questions were answered by raps upon my dress. I put my right hand suddenly upon my lap, and tried to take hold of whatever it was that was touching my dress, but could seize nothing. Mr. Home desired me to put a handkerchief over my hand. I did so, and immediately on putting it down, a hand grasped mine, and I suddenly withdrew it. Determined to conquer the nervous feelings that overcame me, again I put my hand down, and it was taken by another hand, and kisses were imprinted on it from the tips of the fingers all over the palm. An accordion, held in Mr. Home's right hand, played the most exquisite music, swelling forth in full harmonious tones, and dying away in notes of tenderness, and of exquisite and unearthly music. His left hand was all the time on the table.

A number of manifestations took place, and to mental questions I received intelligent answers, and I returned home from this my first séance with Mr. Home, convinced of the truth of our being permitted to hold intercourse with those who have passed to the spirit-land

December 24th.—The accordion played in Mr. Home's hand, then five raps asked for the alphabet, and "Christmas Hymn" was spelled out; again five raps, and "less earthly light;" we lowered the flame of the four gas jets that were burning over the table, and "The Manger, the Life, arid the passing away," was spelled out. The accordion played a sweet air appropriate to *childhood.* "The Life" was represented by the most harmonious strains intermingled with discords at times, as if it were thorny, and painful, and the *passing away* died on the air with exquisite tenderness.

January 29th.—A séance of eight persons. We had amused ourselves during the time with the article, "Spirit-rapping made easy," in the magazine 'Once a Week,' which we left on the chiffonier. I saw something pass from the side of the room with great velocity, which vanished under the table. A curious noise was heard like the crumpling of paper, a spirit hand arose, appeared, and placed in the medium's hand a sheet of 'Once a Week,' crumpled up and torn. The spirits were at work destroying the magazine they rubbed it strongly over Mr. Home's shoe, and then placed his foot upon it. The spirits gave each person a bit of the mangled magazine, and the remainder was raised up by a large spirit hand, and placed on a vacant chair, which by invisible power had a short time before been moved from a distance to the table. The table was violently moved up to the centre window, before which stood a piece of the bough of the northern poplar which had been sent from the Château de C____, and which was a part of that, from the fall of which Mr. Home so miraculously escaped. The height of the bough was three feet eight inches, and the circumference three feet. Luminous hands were now and then visible, the table rose gently, and tipped many times against the bough; the spirits threw bits of the torn magazine about it, and placed one piece under it. I asked in Hindostanee, "Are you making Mr. Novra do *pooja* to the branch?" To which they loudly rapped "Yes." The gas lights from the streets were streaming in, the spirits closed the shutters, and we heard a curious tearing noise, a spirit hand came across my hands, and placed upon them a bit of the bark torn from the poplar, the noise recommenced, and to every one of the circle a bit was given. Invisible power opened the shutters, the trunk of the tree rocked and waved backwards and forwards, and after a time it was lifted up by invisible power and laid upon the table. At this time, "Oft in the stilly night" was played by the accordion which lay on the floor, untouched by mortal hands. Mr. Home's arms were raised, and he walked to the end of the room, where he was lifted off the ground, and raised until his feet were on a level with the top of the chiffonier, between four and five feet from the ground. I distinctly saw his body carried along erect in the air, it then returned to its former place, where it remained some time—at length it floated forward in the air, passed behind the gas chandelier which was suspended in the centre of the apartment, and he descended gently upon the floor, close to the chair in which a lady was sitting. She said that when she saw him, he was about four feet from the ground. When he had descended his arms were paralized, but in a short time they returned to their natural state.

March 13th.—The trunk of the tree that stood in the window was shaken, the roll of drums was heard on the table, and it was lifted as before. The tree shook again, and the accordion which was on the ground, played untouched by mortal hand. Mr. Home took it afterwards in his right hand, and held it upside down—it was played upon in the most masterly style, the harmony was beautiful. A small chess table from a distance, came up of its own accord, and pushing up to the edge of the loo table, rose and stood upright upon it. Luminous hands often appeared. A beautiful little hand arose between the trunk of the tree and the curtain, the fingers distinctly plain; it rose higher, until it skewed the arm up to the shoulder, and the little fingers bending over the top of the tree, played with the broken points of the wood, the upright splinters, and then after we had seen it for some time it vanished. Mr. Home was pushed back in his chair a foot or so, and a luminous head came up from his right side, stopped in front of his knees, and then coming towards me, as I sat on his left hand, it disappeared.

March 19th.—*En séance* five persons at Mr. Home's. He fell immediately into the trance, and after a time he awoke. I had in my pocket a musket ball, which in battle had broken the leg of a beloved relative. My dress was pulled, and a spirit hand rapped several times on my knee—it was his spirit. I took the bullet in my right hand, and put my handkerchief over it, spirit fingers turned the handkerchief over the bullet, and took it away. Soon after, my dress was again pulled, and the hand put the bullet which had been tied up in a handkerchief into my, hand. Keeping perfectly quiet, I said, "Beloved spirit, will you kiss my hand?" and immediately my fingers were kissed four times. The spirit told me that the bullet now possessed talismanic power, not in cases of sickness, but in those of accidents. Natural flowers were taken off the table, and given to each person present. Mr. Home was now led to the end of the room, which was very dark; he was raised from the ground, a beautiful star was visible, and also one like a small comet. He said a star was on his forehead, and one on each hand; we saw the three very bright, and many others glancing about. He was fixed against the wall. The luminous appearance was so distinct as to render the papering on the wall perfectly distinct; and then he floated along the room and was placed on his knees on the sofa; again he was carried up, and the star on his forehead showed where he was—as he floated along the room, it floated above his head, and when he descended the star was quenched. Whilst he was at the table, a spirit hand raised the accordion from the floor above the table, and when he was borne into the air, the accordion floated above his head, playing beautifully all the time, and crossed from one end of the room to the other.

March 28th.—*En séance* nine persons at Mr. Home's house. I had a gilt whistle in my hand, Mr. Home took it in his left hand, and put it under the table-cloth; in his right hand was the accordion. "Oh!" he exclaimed, "it is so strange—what are they doing with the whistle? the spirit has turned it round in my hand, and I feel a mouth against my fingers!" The whistle was immediately sounded several times. This was quits a new manifestation. The spirit then took the whistle from him, the accordion began to play, and the air was accompanied by the whistle, which I then heard drop upon the floor.

March 31st.—*En séance* seven persons. I put down my hand, and held it motionless, it was kissed by two spirits, and when the table-cloth was lifted off the bracelet, I felt fingers trying to pull it off my arm, but it would not pass over my hand, then the fingers turned the bracelet round until they got hold of the clasp which it appeared they found difficult to unfasten. At length having succeeded in so doing, they carried the bracelet away. Shortly afterwards a hand arose near a gentleman opposite, and threw the bracelet gently on the centre of the table.

June 2nd.—A séance of five persons. As twilight came on, a pleasant dimness fell over the room, and a lady said, "Is the light the spirits love, like the odylic?" to which raps answered, "More refined." The spirits moved the table with violence up to the window, near the Hindoo shrine, and the accordion (no human hand touching it), played in the most charming manner, exquisitely and with great power. There was much noise at the Hindoo shrine, the image of Vishnu and the Holy Bull were brought and put on the top of the table, then a large hand, which appeared dark, being between us and the light, put up the accordion entirely above the top of the table, a second hand on the other side, took it down again, another hand took a bell off the table and rang it. Mr. Home was raised from his chair erect into the air, and descended on a foot-stool. Then he was drawn to the other end of the room, and raised in the air until his hand was on the top of the door; thence he floated horizontally forward, and descended. I saw a bright star constantly flashing forth, the raps died away in the distance, and the séance ended.

June 3rd.—A séance of nine persons. I placed a large bouquet of natural flowers on the shoulder of the great marble idol Ganesh. The accordion in Mr. Home's right hand playing most beautifully, harmonized the circle, and the spirit hands touched almost every one present. A rustling sound was heard about the idol, and something passed under the table. The spirits rapped, "They are not so beautiful as those you will find with us," and immediately the bouquet was placed in Mrs. Home's hands. Mr. Home, untying the bouquet, returned the flowers to Mrs. Home, who asked the spirit to give them a talismanic power, and take one to each of us. The first flower, a rosebud, was carried to a lady, and the spirits rapped, "From one who is a mortal, but will ere long be with us—emblem of Sacha." This announcement drew tears from us all; we were deeply affected, and Mr. Home sank back overcome with emotion. A narcissus was given to me, and a flower to every one present, also some for those who were absent, but who were loved by Mrs. Home. She spoke for a length of time consolations for those whom she was about to quit; her voice was very weak, and I lost the greater part of what she said. She shook hands with us all, a farewell we wept, but not a word was uttered.

June 5th.—A séance of four persons. Mr. Home immediately went into the trance, and after many communications said, "If you could only see the mass of spirits near Sacha! A veiled female is near her—when Sacha goes to the spirit-land, there she will be, her veil off, she will place it on Sacha's brow, heavy with its own stars, shimmering, shimmering down. Beautiful features, long flowing hair, her hands crossed thus—looks upward—upward—no sorrow, no pain! prayer is carried up by loving hands and placed before God's holy throne—they bear His blessings down to earth. A staff is placed in their hands; a cloud to shade the heart from the sunbeams—by the side is suspended the bread of life—the Hope star high in the heavens to lead them from earth, and to trust only in God."

June 11th.—*En séance* seven persons. The spirits played beautiful music, and brought to us sprigs which they tore off a sweet-scented verbena which was in the room. They brought the *Deir*, a brass idol holding a mirror, from the shrine, and put it under the table. Mr. Home saw a spirit at the shrine; then they rapped, "Faith in God, and the change of world will be most glorious, all other —" (the idols which they had placed under the table were rattled violently) "Gods" were rapped out; again they rapped the idols violently, and beat them against one another with great noise and force, and spelled "must;" they raised the great idol Mahadeo, and put it on the table. It is the large brass idol overshadowed by the expanded hood of the *cobra di capella*. Then they rapped "be brought." They took the idol off the table, and pitched it down violently with a clang and noise, then rapped "down low before him." In this manner they elucidated the words they rapped out, "Faith in God and the change of world will be most glorious; all other Gods must be brought down low before Him."

June 12th.—A verbena plant in a flower-pot stood by the shrine. A hand touched Mrs. Home, and the verbena plant, with the little sticks that supported it, having been broken off at the roots, was thrown by the spirits upon the table. Then they rapped, "we regret, but in taking the flower we have also taken the earth with it." They shook Mrs. Home's dress violently, earth was thrown on Mr. Home's shoulder, and over it on the table. He saw a spirit hand which was full of earth, and then the remainder which had come out of the flower-pot in a mass, was placed in his hand; not a bit of the living flower remained in it. The spirits rapped—"Life-giving—and the casket that remains only fit to be broken." Immediately they broke the empty flower-pot to pieces, as it lay on the ground by the window, emblematic of drawing the soul from its earthly tenement.

June 13th.—Mr. Home went into the trance, and said, "There are more spirits around Sacha, and the veiled spirit is coming nearer and nearer." Mysterious sounds which we had before heard in the chamber above were repeated. When asked, "How do you feel when you go into the trance?" be said, "At first a heaviness in my feet comes on, I feel as if fainting away on the brink of a precipice—there is a moment of suffering, and then all is agreeable."

June 22nd.—*En séance* seven persons. A spirit hand arose and came to Mrs. Home; it moved about; she was anxious to touch it; a long finger pointed to and motioned her to be quiet. A hand and arm were distinctly seen, and a spirit hand closed the shutters. Flowers were given to some, and were placed on the heads of other persons. My head was twice touched, and twice an arm waved over the table; three times an open hand was strongly pressed on my forehead. A spring-bell from the shutters, used as an alarum, was rung above our heads, and we saw the hand which held it. Mr. Home went into the trance, and said, "Where the eye ought to be are placed two crosses; the Christian faith will put the eye out. I do not understand what they mean, the spirit is doing it! Hark! hark! don't write." I ceased writing; we listened, and heard a noise like scratching on the shrine. Mr. Home woke from the trance, and the séance ended. On going to the shrine, we saw on the forehead of the great white marble image of Ganesh, two crosses made in pencil by the spirits, just over the centre triple eye of the idol, which denotes its having all-seeing power. This was the noise alluded to by Mr. Home in the trance.

June 24.—Seven persons *en séance*. A scientific gentleman, who had written to disprove spiritual manifestations, was to have joined the party; however, he requested to have a programme! which he said is due to him as a scientific man, and to his position! It being impossible to give a programme, he declined joining the séance.

June 25th.—*En séance* eight persons. The accordion playing of itself, was raised above the table; then it was shown a second time. The spirits rapped to a lady whose child had passed away—"She only went to God, she did not die." At the word God the most peculiar sounds were made, as if to impress us with solemnity.

June 27.—A séance of eight persons. Numerous manifestations took place. Flowers were given, the accordion played, and an American cane chair, which was at the other side of the room, was moved by unseen power up to the table. A hand touched our foreheads, and an arm waved in the air over the table several times. Mr. Home was drawn back in his chair, and an arm, the hand holding the alarm-bell, waved over the table; it rang in the air, and by my shoulder, which it touched, and then fell to the ground. The accordion, now in the air, untouched by mortal hand, played beautifully as it floated round the table, and touched each person present.

June 28.–A séance of eight persons. Mr. Home was raised' from his chair, and carried up a little in an erect posture, and then put down again. Music was heard in the air, and then strange sounds—we marvelled what it might be. "Is it a spirit?" "Yes." Then the spirit spoke many times; but the words were unintelligible. Mrs. Home was afraid, and begged them not to speak; and Mr. Home said, "It is their difficulty to make the material sounds of speech." It reminded me of Bournemouth, where in Mr. Home's room I had heard music, the chirping of a bird, and spirit voice very distinctly.

June 30.–A séance of three persons. The table trembled and tipped so much, we were surprised the decanters did not fall off. Then it was shaken so violently that froth was produced, and the wine in the decanters splashed up their long necks, whilst the water was scarcely affected. The spirits rapped out their dislike to wine. The table was made excessively heavy; four of us stood up and tried to lift it with all our power; it would not stir, neither could we turn it round. Soon after, it was lifted by the spirits a foot or more from the ground, with all the things upon it, and then it gently descended. One person could now lift it, and it was rendered heavy several times.

July 3rd. *En séance* seven persons. The table was shaken, and rose and undulated in the air, whilst I counted sixty-two aloud. Mr. Home was lifted up a little in his chair, and went into the trance. His arms were then raised, and he ascended about a foot from the ground, descended, and rose again a couple of feet. He leaned over until he touched Mrs. Home, and then he was carried up, his body being bent forward in a circular form, until his head was above the centre pane in the large window; he ascended some feet, and came down again. It was quite light in the window, and we were close to it. He then went to the end of the room into the darkness, and we could not see him ascend, but three bright stars were shown which denoted where he was. He descended, returned to the table quite stiffened, awoke soon afterwards, and came out of the trance.

July 7th.—We, four persons, were sitting at the centre window in the front drawing-room, talking together, when the spirits began to rap on the floor. Mr. Home brought up a small table, and we had many manifestations, in the midst of which a sofa-table at the end of the room, on which was a large lamp and two flower-pots containing fine lemon scented verbenas. One of them rolled up, untouched by any one and placed itself between Mr. and Mrs. Home. It was a fine summer evening, and the room was perfectly light. Mr. Home fell back in his chair, and went into the deep sleep for some time; then he walked about the room, led apparently by a spirit, a very large bright star shone on his forehead, several clustered on his hair, and on the tips of his fingers. He made passes over the verbena plant, but did not touch it. Immediately the air was filled with the scent which he wafted to each of us, and it remained most powerfully on his hands. Making more passes, still in the trance, he said, "Thus we extract the essence from the flower; in the same manner the soul is taken from the body; to-morrow you will see the lower leaves are withered, and the plant will die in a few days." Which fact occurred as he had said, yet no apparent cause could be assigned why it should have died. We then went into the dining-room below; and after refreshments our guests quitted, leaving only Mr. Home, who was seated in an easy chair by the fire-side, Mrs. Home sleeping on the sofa, and I sitting by the table reading by lamp-light. Suddenly, loud raps were heard on the large heavy dinner-table; it trembled, rose, and balanced in the air. Mr. Home was led about the room, the shutters were closed, I put out the gas-lights, and we were in darkness. A spirit touched my fingers as they lay on the table, voices were heard in the air, and Mr. Home said, "The spirits are trying to talk." "Yes," then a voice said,—"we are trying to come." I heard two voices of very different tone, and asked, "Who are you, dear spirit?" The name was given and repeated several times. Mr. Home was led about the room, showing stars on his forehead and fingers as he held his hands up. A cross of stars was seen by him and Mrs. Home. I only saw the cross-bar of stars, not the uprights. He was led up to the shutters, and he opened the lower part; immediately spirit power closed the lower and opened the upper part. Mr. Home was now led to the further end of the room, and passed in front of a very large mirror—a sea of glass. I saw a form leading him, over the head of which was thrown a tinted robe flowing to the ground, marking the shape of the head and shoulders. He followed close upon it; I saw them both in the mirror, his features, face, and hair, perfectly distinct, but the features of the form that led him were not visible beneath the dark blue tinted robe that covered them. They passed from before the glass, and then we all saw a female figure with a white veil thrown over her head, which fell to the ground; at the same time, but rather higher, was the form of a man in oriental costume. The startling vision faded away, and the great mirror remained with only the light from the window, which streamed in upon it.

July 12th.—*En séance* six persons. Stars appeared above Mrs. Home's head, and a light was seen, with fingers passing over it as it floated above our heads. It was the VEILED SPIRIT. I saw the hand which held the veil, which was spangled with stars, and the fingers moved distinctly as it floated just in front of us. A star was seen on Mr. Home, and flowers were given. Mrs. Home's mother made the sign of the cross on her brow, and then on Mr. Home's. Two fingers touched my forehead, and one all wet made the sign of the cross. The tearing of paper was now heard, and soon after a spirit hand took hold of my left hand as it lay on the table, and put a piece of paper into it. Other pieces of paper were torn off, and then a pencil was thrown to the other end of the room. A bell was rung in the air, the accordion floating above our heads played the most joyful and martial music, and Mrs. Home saw her spirit-father. "God bless you all, good night," was now rapped. On looking at the paper that had been put into my hand, I found the initials of a beloved spirit, beautifully written in pencil, a facsimile of his writing when on earth. A paper had been given to Mrs. Home by her father, and on it was a cross surmounted by a crown, to show us that we must bear the cross to wear the crown.

February 18, 1862.—A séance of six persons. After various manifestations, Mr. Home went into the trance, and addressing a person present said, "You ask what good are such trivial manifestations, such as rapping, table-moving, &c.? God is a better judge than we are what is fitted for humanity, immense results may spring from trivial things. The steam from a kettle is a small thing, but look at the locomotive! The electric spark from the back of a cat is a small thing, but see the wonders of electricity! The raps are small things, but their results will lead you to the Spirit World and to eternity! Why should great results spring from such small causes? Christ was born in a manger, he was not born a King. When you tell me why he was born in a manger, I will tell you why these manifestations, so trivial, so undignified as they appear to you, have been appointed to convince the world of the truth of spiritualism."

The foregoing extracts will be read with interest by those persons who were present, and perhaps by a larger circle. I give no names, but merely the facts as they occurred, because it is impossible for any one to give credit to such marvels, until by investigation they are forced to believe the truth.   F. C. P.

In this diary there are several remarkable manifestations, and amongst them that of the presence of the veiled spirit, who thenceforth was frequently seen by my wife and by me, as will be read in the beautiful memoir of my wife, written by that most estimable type of womanhood, Mrs. Mary Howitt. The veil of that spirit kept gradually being raised through the successive stages of my dear wife's painful illness, and became almost an index of the insidious advances of her disease.

There is one phenomenon, however, which has happened to me only on the occasion described in the diary. I allude to the wonderful case of the verbena plant, and the drawing of its scent, and of its very life out of it, by a few passes of my hand, wafting its whole perfume in the faces of the sitters, and leaving the tree to die for want of the vital principle which had been thus extracted from it. I have heard before of experiments tried in mesmerism upon plants with some apparent results, but never of any so marked as this, of the verbena. It is not wise to judge of isolated cases, but probably there may occur, or may be found, other instances of a similar kind, which may throw light upon the power of the human will, over the lower forms of life.

I am sorry that in so many instances I am obliged to conceal the names of my friends who have witnessed wonderful things; but if the reader is disposed to complain of this, let him remember the reason, and take the greater part of the blame on himself. No sooner is the name of some honest and courageous person given in obedience to the call for testimony, than it becomes a target for all the ridicule, jests, and abuse of the unscrupulous, the sceptical, the orthodox, and the scientific; in fact, of all who are not wise enough to think, and observe, and weigh, and judge, before they decide. There is small encouragement for men, and still less for ladies, to come forward, and stand in front of all this obloquy. If an example be needed of the truth of this, if it be not an obvious fact already in this uncharitable day, let my adventurous friends watch the extent to which I shall be abused, and called bad names, and given to the devil, for simply and truthfully writing in this little book a few of the incidents of my life, with the production of which I have had nothing to do. It has been my good fortune never to have cared much for bad opinions of me, which have been formed in utter and acknowledged ignorance; and my silence hitherto when the most gross and foolish statements have been made to my prejudice, and when a word from me would have corrected them, is a sufficient proof of my indifference to such attacks. I am sorry, however, for the want of kindness and the folly which so many exhibit, for their own sakes, more than for my own. I do not expect that they will behave differently now in regard to what they see in my book, for in the present state of their minds, the truth cannot be received. The facts become to them impossible, while to me, and to many of my friends who have been in the habit of seeing them, and watching them, and studying them and their consequences for so many years, their strangeness even has well nigh disappeared. We ought certainly to make some allowance for those ignorant persons who sit quietly at home, saying that such things are impossible, without having ever taken the trouble to try to witness them, or to get together even the first elements for forming a judgment upon them. These are not so unjust and dishonest as that other class, of which Sir David Brewster is the type, who, in the interests of what they consider their position in the scientific world, have no scruple in telling falsehoods, and in denying what they have seen, and in deceiving still further the former class of merely ignorant persons.

I hope, therefore, that both I and my friends may be in some measure excused for giving their narratives without their names. If I were at liberty to make them public, they would add greatly to the value of the narrative, and the public would have the opportunity of being greatly surprised at finding out who are the persons who have investigated the subject, and vouch for these remarkable facts. In society they are well known to many; and, perhaps, nothing is more strange than the entire belief with which these facts are spoken of and received in large mixed companies, when compared with the expression of entire disbelief with which they are accompanied in nearly all notices in the press. Of those who will openly condemn this narrative in their journals, hardly one does not reckon amongst his intimate and valued friends, or relatives, or co-contributors, several who are with good reason entire believers. It would be curious to contrast the language he holds to such persons with that he uses in describing my book to the ignorant masses, who, he meanly knows expect such abuse at his hands and will be pleased to hear it. If it were necessary, I could give some names which would amply justify what I have said of these poor leaders of the blind.

The testimony which I will now give is that of a lady, whose word and powers of observation are entitled to the most unreserved acceptance, and I am sorry that I can only give her initial, and call her Mrs. S____. She had become a widow not long before I had the pleasure of making her acquaintance.

"I first attended a séance at Mr. Home's in the summer of 1861, when I was in very deep affliction. I had never seen anything of Spiritualism before, but had heard a good deal of it from a dear old friend who introduced me to Mr. Home. My own experiences that night were far more wonderful than anything I had ever heard or read of, and were to me most convincing. After many raps, movements of the table, &c., my handkerchief was drawn from my hand, the knocks given for the alphabet, and the words 'Shed no more tears' were spelled out, and my handkerchief *came up of itself* at the opposite side of the table, raised itself half a yard above the table, moved gently across, and settled itself on the table in front of me; this I saw without a possibility of mistake or doubt. After this, Mr. Home fell into a trance, and described my dear husband most accurately, said how noble he was in mind and body, and how he should have loved him had he known him in life, and then said, 'But who is that Mary standing by his side? What a noble woman, and how she loves him, and how happy they are together, and how they both love you; you were his star in life. But what was that misery about his watch? you forgot to wind his watch, and how miserable it made you." Now this was a fact known to no living being but myself. I had wound the watch the night I lost my husband, and resolved never to let it go down again; but more than a month afterwards, when I returned to our old home, I forgot to wind it one night, and my agony was great when I discovered it in the morning, but I never mentioned it even to my husband's sister, who was in the house with me. A great deal more took place at the séance interesting both to myself and others.

"A month later I attended a second séance. Some remarkable things were told by Mr. Home, who was in a state of trance, to a lady present of her departed friend. He then went to the opposite end of the room, and she remarked to me, in a low voice, 'How very wonderful, he has been dead these thirty years,' when Mr. Home, whom I thought much too distant to hear, called out, in a loud thrilling voice, 'Do not say dead; he is not dead, but gone before; nothing kills but sin, sin kills through the devil, but those who live in Christ will never die.' Mr. Home came soon afterwards to me, and said that my dear husband and his mother (the Mary spoken of before) were behind my chair, and that both longed to comfort me. He gave me the following message:— 'My own Adelaide, all your prayers are heard, your pure thoughts seen, your patience and loving hope. We are not, nor shall we be separated, we are one in CHRIST.'

"He then went on to say that I had had a conversation with my husband eight months before, and that he blessed me for that conversation now; that we were sitting in our drawing-room at home, he his arm-chair and I in mine, with the little round table between us, that I had just been reading a chapter in the New Testament, and that on that night the angel of the Lord had laid his hand upon my husband's brow, and he had faded from that time. I remember perfectly the conversation alluded to, and it was a very remarkable one. I had been reading prayers to the servants, and we were sitting in the manner described, and talked for more than an hour before going to bed. These are facts for which I can vouch, and though my name is not given here, Mr. Home will give it to any one wishing to be convinced. To me the comfort has been unspeakable; but did I believe Spiritualism to be sinful or forbidden by our Lord, NOTHING would induce me to have anything to say to it, but I believe the reverse is the case. I have felt more at peace, more perfect trust—utter childlike trust—in my God and Saviour, than I have ever done before. Mr. Home told me that my dear husband was always with me when I prayed, and I feel that he is so, through Christ."

We spent July, August, and September, 1861, at Folkestone. My power had left me, but my wife continued to see spirits daily. We went to Brighton, where we remained till the month of December. Late in the evening of one day in November, my wife being in bed, I was in the drawing-room with a friend, when a strange chill air seemed to surround us, and creaking noises were heard. In fact, a feeling of great discomfort came upon us both, when we heard my wife knocking on the floor, this being her signal of requiring my presence. I ran up stairs, and she said, "Daniel, do not leave me; there is a spirit-presence in my room which is strange and unpleasant to me. I feel as if something had occurred, or was about to happen." I remained with her, but we no longer felt or heard anything of the kind. In the morning on the breakfast-table was a letter from a much loved friend, announcing the departure of a son under most painful circumstances. It was evident that it was his spirit who had been with us during the previous evening.

We came back to town in December; and in January, 1862, the power returned in me, but far from strongly. On one occasion whilst we were seated, the strange trembling so often noticed was felt in the table, and almost simultaneously with it I heard the nursery-bell ring. I heard the servant go upstairs, the nursery being on the third floor, and soon she came with a message from the nurse requesting my presence. I went, and found the child sitting in his bed, and a look of alarm on his face. He said to me, "Oh, papa, I don't like to have my bed rocking." I thought that he might have a headache, or some slight indisposition, which might have caused a giddiness, but he said he was very well. I remained a short time with him, and then joined my friends in the drawing-room. In about half an hour the trembling was repeated, and again the nursery-bell rang. I had to go to him, and I found that the rocking had been more violent than before, and he begged me to lay down with him till he got to sleep. I did so, and in about ten minutes he was fast asleep. The spirits then told us that they had "accidentally caused his bed to shake."

Another instance of this trembling being felt outside the room has occurred within ten days previous to my writing this. A deaf and dumb maid living in a house where I was, and knowing nothing either of my presence, or of spiritual manifestations, said to the young lady, her mistress, on her going upstairs to her, "How you must have been dancing, all of you, for the whole house has been shaking so that I have been made quite dizzy." We were upon the ground floor, and the principal manifestation that evening was the strong vibration of the room. She was upon the third floor, and the house is a large well-built one in one of the best parts of Kensington.

CHAPTER VII

IN MEMORIAM

On the 20th of February, 1862, we left England for the Château Laroche, near Perigueux, the residence in the south of France of my brother-in-law. I need not to go through again the scenes of those last days on earth of the dear one whom it has pleased God to take away, in the spring time of her life, to the bright morning land, It is well with her there, and she is only more than ever my hope, and my beaming guiding-star. My good guardian angel, watching over her dear child, and me, her husband—separated, but not lost—in spirit more than ever present. In God's loving mercy we shall meet again, and find our lasting habitation in the eternal inner world.

Let me have the pleasure of adding the sweet tribute to her memory of Mrs. Howitt, which gives such few facts as may be made public of one who amongst her friends required no written words to be embalmed in their hearts' best memories. To those who knew her not, these words will serve to show the effect of spiritual communion during the long stages of disease, and the placid contemplation of the passing onward, by one to whom the bright spirit-world has become a calm reality, from her frequent intercourse with the good angels who had gone before.

In Memoriam.

Madame Alexandrina Home, the wife of Mr. Daniel Dunglas Home, passed from earth on the 3rd July last, at the Château Laroche, Dordogne, France, the residence of her sister, the Countess Luboff Koucheleff Besborodka, in the twenty-second year of her age.

"Mrs. Home was the youngest daughter of the General Count de Kroll, of Russia, and she was the god-daughter of the late Emperor Nicholas. She was educated at the Institute of St. Catherine at the same time as the present Countess de Morny, of Paris. Mr. Home, who had been at several of the Courts of Europe, where he was received with much distinction, and where the marvellous phenomena which occur in his presence excited deep attention, was at Rome in the spring of 1858 for the benefit of his health, and there first saw the lady who became his wife on the 1st of August of that year. The marriage took place at St. Petersburgh, and was celebrated in the presence of M. Alexandre Dumas, who went from Paris on purpose to be present, and to officiate as godfather to Mr. Home, according to the custom of the Romish Church. The Emperor Alexander also was represented there by two of his aides-de-camp whom he sent as groomsmen, and the Emperor presented to Mr. Home on the happy occasion a magnificent diamond ring of great value. On the birth of the only child of the marriage, a son, the Emperor evinced his continued interest in Mr. and Mrs. Home by presenting to them as a memento of his friendship a ring of emeralds and diamonds. Mr. and Mrs. Home thus commenced their married life with all the outward accessories of station and wealth, together with hosts of friends, as a matter of course, whilst the measure of their happiness was completed by that calm domestic bliss, which is the purest source of earthly enjoyment, and to which her kindly and tender nature contributed its full share. They could not but be happy, for their affection was pure as it was sincere, and when their union was blessed by the birth of their little son, there was no more to hope for, but to bring him up worthily to be a partaker in their happiness.

"In the midst, however, of these bright human hopes and anticipations, the decree went forth that her days were numbered. About eighteen months before her departure, the physician who was called in on the occasion of some trifling illness, as it was supposed, detected, to the surprise and grief of all who loved her, such undoubted signs of consumption in her constitution that in all human probability her life could not be of long duration. Such tidings to a young and happy woman, surrounded by everything that can make outward existence attractive, would, in ordinary circumstances, have come as the direst calamity; but it was not so in the case of Mrs. Home. Though at that time only in her twenty-first year, she received the announcement with entire calmness. God's will be done, was the cheerful law of her life, and He who had hitherto made that life so rich would not fail, she knew, to continue His love and mercy to her in that higher life to which He was calling her. Nothing but the deepest religious conviction of the Supreme Wisdom and Love can bring the human soul into a state of submissive obedience to His otherwise apparently severe and mysterious decrees. Let us now see how the Divine Father had led and schooled His young disciple into that highest, that profoundest of all knowledge, the firm possession of which makes obedience and submission easy, and keeps the soul calm and even joyful under the most startling and adverse circumstances. We shall then in part, if not fully understand whence came the strange, and apparently almost unnatural, willingness to depart from the earthly life amidst its most attractive circumstances. *She was a deeply-believing Spiritualist.* God's love had made known to her the reality of the spiritual world; she had been permitted to solve the great, mysterious, and perplexing riddle of the Hereafter, and so loyal was she to the knowledge which had thus been given her, that she was ready to attest it in life or in death. Like all experienced Spiritualists she knew that the outward life, be its term longer or shorter, is but a school in which God wills to train the immortal being to a higher knowledge—is but a pilgrimage, or passage by which He is willing to conduct it to another and a still happier home. She knew that in that other state of existence, though unclothed by the body, and apparently separated from the beloved on earth, she might yet be permitted to watch over and love them as their guardian angel, and to be in the close companionship of those who had gone before—of those living and glorified spirits who should lead her to the throne of grace and love ineffable. If it be the highest heroism to meet death with unflinching courage, this amiable, gentle, young woman, this child of affluence and fortune, displayed an almost unequalled degree of this noble quality of mind, and so doing, proved how strong and all-sustaining in life's extremity is the faith of the Christian Spiritualist.

"The first startling intelligence that her disease was mortal came to a mind so prepared with wholly abated force. The sting was already taken from death; nor through the whole after-trials and sufferings of her physical frame did she lose her equanimity or firm confidence in the future. This calmness, indeed, became the most striking feature of her long and painful illness. It was so profound and marked as to be almost phenomenal, and was noticed as such by the eminent physicians who attended her in London, and subsequently in France, as well as by the Bishop of Perigueux, who frequently visited her during the latter part of her earthly life. The last sacraments were administered to her by the Bishop, who wept like a child, and, who remarked that 'though he had been present at many a death-bed for Heaven, he had never seen one equal to hers.'

"Whilst residing in London the remarkable spiritual gifts and manifestations exhibited through Mr. Home, and the many attractive qualities of his young and lovely wife had naturally gathered around them a large circle of friends to whom the singular exhibition of her calmness, her meekness, her playful, winning ways, even in the midst of suffering, and the joyfulness with which she anticipated her removal, were, if possible, a greater anomaly, and almost, for the time, cast into the shade the wonderful gifts and powers of her husband. If Addison called to his death-bed his infidel son-in-law that, witnessing his composure, he might learn with how much calmness a Christian could die, so here disbelievers in Spiritualism looking on this gifted young woman, saw with wonder not only how calmly, but how joyously the Christian Spiritualist could face death. Another equally anomalous feature to the Protestant Christian was not to find in her the self-depreciation of the guilt-awakened sinner; not to hear on her lips the usual phraseology of the dying but suffering saint; no mention made of the atonement; of the works of grace on her soul, of the sufferings of a crucified Saviour for her sake. Nevertheless, with the simplicity of a little child who accepted the Divine love as his natural gift, she loved the Saviour and rejoiced in Him, responding to His unspeakable goodness with the whole allegiance of her soul, but Gethsemane and the bloody hill of the crucifixion were not present to her mind; the agony and woe had no place in her experience. She was, it must be remembered, the embodiment of her own Greek church; of that church in which she was educated, the most ancient faith of which has ever recognized the Saviour less as the Crucified than the Arisen, the triumphant over suffering, sin, and death, as the Victor not the Victim, as the Lord who said to his chosen ones; 'Rejoice that your names are written in heaven!' Such, it appears to me, who frequently saw her during this portion of her short stay on earth, was the fact which made her relationship to the Saviour so joyous, whilst her own single-heartedness left her free from all established phraseology or any wish to produce effect, and these happily combined with her actual knowledge of spiritual existence, strengthened that remarkable state of calmness and cheerfulness with which she waited the close of her outward life. Her Saviour had indeed risen for her, and with the unquestioning, unreasoning faith of a loving, obedient child-like nature, she was not only willing to go when He called her, but cheerfully to give up all at His bidding, knowing that a more enlarged, a more glorious sphere of usefulness and angel ministration would be unfolded to Her through His love, and that thus she should be enabled more tenderly and more effectually to watch over and become a blessing to the beloved ones whom she left behind.

"During that short but interesting time of her declining health in London, her remarkable unselfishness became another endearing characteristic to all her friends. She made, even amidst her increasing sufferings, constant exertions to see them, and séances were held frequently at the house where she and her husband were then residing, in which she took a glad part. On these occasions many wonderful and touchingly beautiful incidents occurred, and few, if any, who thus met her, but retain with tender and affectionate regard some tender flower or fragrant spray—an emblem of herself which was presented to her by spirit-hands, as a little memento for each.

"In the earlier stages of her disease her spiritual perception began to open, and she commenced, and throughout her illness continued to see and converse with the denizens of the spiritual world. Her most frequent visitants were her mother and her father, and the mother of her husband. From them she received the most loving messages of endearment, and the most cheering words of welcome to her spirit home. She was also constantly attended by a veiled female spirit, whom she did not know, but whose very presence, gave her great comfort, though she never spoke, nor raised her veil. Mr. Home was told that this kind guardian spirit would continue veiled until the last, when the veil would be thrown over her own new-born spirit, to keep her from the sight of the tears and mourning around the bed where her body would be lying. Through the six months previous to her passing away, the veil was slowly and gradually gathered from the feet of the guardian spirit towards the head, until two days before her release, when for the last time she saw the spirit with the veil gathered in the form of a crown about her head, but with one part, as a festoon, still concealing her face.

"On one occasion several persons, who were in the room with Mrs. Home, saw the hand and arm of the spirit to the shoulder, the appearance being that of a luminous body, most beautifully perfect in form, and covered as if with a veil of light.

"The eminent composer, M. Magnus, of Paris, came to the Château Laroche to visit Mrs. Home during the last three weeks of her earthly stay, and almost daily she asked him to play for her, and whilst lying placidly listening to his music, her face, assumed an almost beautiful expression whilst she kept time to the music with her hands. On one occasion she said, when he had finished playing, 'Those strains are very beautiful, but I shall soon hear more beautiful still.'

"Frequently also, during the first three months and the last two months of her illness, not only she, but all those about her, heard delicious strains of spirit music, sounding like a perfect harmony of vocal sounds. During the last month, also, the words were most distinctly heard, and were recognized as the chants for the dying used in the Russian Church.

"She departed on Thursday, the 3rd of July, and on the Saturday morning following, her little boy, of three years old, said to his nurse on awakening, 'I have seen mama, and she is quite well now. She is with God, and she told me that my uncle Gregoire, and my aunt Luba are my godfather and godmother, and that they would be very good to me, and I must love them.'

"At her funeral, the service at which was performed by the vicar-general of the diocese, four of the men-servants of her sister asked each to lead a horse of the hearse to the burial-ground, saying that they could not allow hired persons to be near the dear body of her who had ever had a kind word and a loving look for all. The peasantry, instead of, as is customary; throwing earth upon the coffin, first covered it with flowers—fittest for her last garment, and fittest for the expression of their love.

"Such is a brief memorial of a short but lovely life on earth. But short as it was, rarely has the oldest and most experienced orthodox Christian attained to a higher degree of religious consciousness, clearness and trust in God, than did this young and attractive woman, by those very means and teachings which the religious world as yet so much ignores and questions.

"Blessed, however, be God the Saviour for every fresh revelation and manifestation of his Divine life, and for every renewed teaching of his Holy Spirit.

"MARY HOWITT."

To another esteemed friend, Mrs. S. C. Hall, also well-known for her true woman's heart, and for her power, of expressing the best feelings of the soul, I am indebted for her written impressions of my dear wife, and in which she embraces a most interesting account of her observations of the phenomena:

"It pleased God to remove from this life, only a few months since, a much beloved lady, who during her brief residence among us, entwined herself closely round the hearts of her and her husband's many friends—I speak of one, dear to us as "Sacha," the wife of Mr. Daniel Home.

"Educated as befitted a Russian lady of rank, she was still more richly endowed by grace, feeling, a peculiar beauty, which I may term loveliness, and a sweet simplicity of nature, that rendered her transparent and pure as crystal; she was also gifted with a rare appreciation of the beautiful. Her interest in, and admiration of whatever was excellent in art, was the result of innate perception, not often met with where observation has not been matured by age; with a refinement on the natural quickness of her sex—she felt while others reasoned—indeed, all her perceptions were vivid, and she was entirely feminine.

"When first I knew her, she was radiant with life and joy—a playful girl numbering just twenty years, and yet in the full tide of her sweet joy—loving her husband, her child, her friends! and feeling keenly how much she was beloved. If something touched her quick sympathies, her eyes in a moment grew deep and dark, her sweet lips quivered, and the girl became at once the deep-hearted, tender, earnest, woman. Wise too she was, and in her wildest moods something would come of wisdom, a sentence or even a single word, so full and suggestive.

"Soon, however, it became certain to us, that this sweet happy life was not to remain here, and to none was this so evident as to herself; not for a moment did she doubt that she had received her warning for the 'better land.' She would talk with her husband, and with all of us, her friends, of her passing away, believing—nay, knowing—that she would be permitted still to watch over her child, to companion her husband, to communicate with her friends; and this in calm, unconstrained cheerfulness, surrounded by the happy realities of a loving life, and loving, as he deserved, her devoted husband. It was almost impossible to hear the full sweet tones of her voice, to feel the affectionate pressure of her little hands, observe the life-full expression of her face, and realise her approaching change, when the mortal shall have put on immortality.

"How bitterly hard it is to feel, however we may repeat the words, 'Thy will be done!' As the spring advanced each time I saw her, I perceived some change, and yet the change could not be defined, it was more in her spirit than her person. Suffering, wearied the young fragile form, and she longed to be away, she desired freedom from the body's pain, from the perpetual endurance of restlessness—she craved to be out of the body that she might be in the spirit. She talked about this change as invalids talk of change of air, and with hope in her beaming face. I confess that I do not comprehend this phase of mind—I look forward with joy to meet those I have loved and lost from earth, and I look to the time when those I leave behind will, trusting in the same Mediator, bend before the clear Redeemer, and join in His presence, "the spirits of just men made perfect," so that we all shall be one in Christ—but this young creature's certainty that she should return and watch over her husband, child, and all she held in her expanding heart, was to me incomprehensible, it was as if she thought that after death heaven would descend with her to earth. Her faith in her future happiness was fine; but death, like life, was to her a poem, and all her thoughts and actions were poetic—with all her suffering, hers was the poetry of daily life. She enjoyed beyond description a séance with those she loved. One of her pleasures was tying up little bouquets of flowers with one of her long dark hairs, flinging a bouquet under or on the table, or into the room, and expressing a wish that a spirit would give it to one of other of her friends. This was invariably done, and I preserve these flowers as tokens of her sweet love, and shall do so while I live. These little tender acts of kindness were mingled with promises of coming to us, when she should have no mortal body—suffer no pain. She never doubted that this would be permitted, and she loved to dwell upon the delight it would be to her to be with us. There was in her no taint or tone of sadness. I never saw a more joyful, a more perpetual belief in the soul's immortality. We could not avoid observing at times an occasional abstraction, her eyes illuminated by a bright light—wandering round the room, her whole face smiling as if recognizing some spirit friend. Daily—daily was the end, as regarded her earthly tenement advancing, and still nearer came the angels!

"At times, her patience under the accumulated sufferings she was doomed to endure was marvellous, and when at last she longed to anticipate our summer, so tardy that year in arriving; and when I bade her adieu, she pressed her tiny hand into mine, "Feel it—feel it well," she said in her pretty English, no longer broken but accented—"feel it, for when I come to you, you must remember it." Some months passed, and then at last came the news, early in last July, she was called home.

"I had several times the full conviction (as I have at this moment) that she was with me, but I have no medium power, and beyond the cool breeze that passes across my hand or brow, 'the air of the angel's wing,' I receive no sign of such presence—nor do I need it.

"Mr. Home returned to England, and after our first meeting (those who loved her could not call it 'sad,' for he was assured of her happiness) we arranged an evening séance in the drawing-room, which was lit as usual: only five persons present—five who had known and loved Sacha!

"Before what the world calls death, she had asked her husband to give me a little lace cap, the embroidery by her own hands, and I had asked him for a braid of her hair; he brought both, tied in one of her white handkerchiefs, and placed them on the table. More than the usual manifestations came that night, not only the table but our chairs, and the very room shook, and the 'raps' were everywhere around us. A lady, whose consolation through spiritualism has been indeed blessed, received several messages in answer to her thoughts; and a very eminent sculptor, whose engagements on public works are unceasing, had been rising before day to finish a bust of Sacha, which he desired to present to her husband—*this fact was not even known in his own household*—he received a message thus: 'Thanks for your early morning labour, I have been often near you.' While the message was 'rapped' out, he felt her 'little hand' repeatedly on his, in loving confirmation of her thanks. This was the first time he had ever felt the touch of the 'spirit hand,' and it affected him deeply. Mr. Home then placed the embroidery and the hair under the table. 'Sacha,' he said, 'wishes to give them to you herself.' Presently my dress was pulled. I put down my hand, and the cap was not only placed in it, but my fingers closed over it, *by her hand,* I could not be mistaken, I knew that hand so well! My dress was again pulled, and I laid my hand in my lap, then I felt her hand more distinctly, it was placed entirely in mine, and after a pressure, left me the lock of hair!

"Again the alphabet was demanded, and the passage spelt out, 'Give me the handkerchief, I want to give it to Mrs. S____. Oh, I thank her for her beautiful flowers,' (flowers she was in the habit of sending her during her illness). Mr. Home threw the handkerchief that had contained the hair and embroidery down. It was rolled up and knotted, and given into Mrs. S____'s hand. There was much more that evening, the revealings were all continued evidence of spiritual power, and spirit-presence, such as come to us with healing messages on their wings, making us thankful that to us Spiritualism has been the hand-maid of Christianity.

"BUT DEAR SACHA is far from being the only one of my beloved friends, departed, or rather removed, from whom I have received sweet, and consoling, and comforting messages. One whom I love and reverence beyond all who are gone before, has given me by unmistakeable proof, the blessed certainty of the interest she is permitted to take in our spiritual welfare, and has, by her precepts, and apt quotations of holy writ, strengthened our armour of faith, and if it be possible, brightened the hope of the glory that shall be revealed hereafter. Is not this comforting? I do not prolong this brief record of happy memories, but I could do so. SPIRITUALISM has been to me a blessing, for which I cannot be enough thankful, less for my own sake, than for the sake of others, who are very dear to me; for though it brought me more sunshine, it has given me no new light. I testify here of spiritualism, as it is known and believed by me and mine; I say KNOWN, for nearly five years we have had abundant proofs of its reality. I will briefly say how this is. I thank God that I never had a doubt as to the divine truths of Christianity, neither did I receive them as cold facts. My dear mother was of pure Huguenot descent, and would, at any period of her life, have gone calmly to the stake sooner than have even seemed to abate one jot of her belief in the Existence, Mission, and Miracles of CHRIST-GOD. I drank at the fountain of this faith from my earliest years, and every night the accustomed 'chapter' was read, prayed over and discussed, thus religious faith grew to be my enjoyment, and my triumph, as well as my hope and trust. Moreover, she held the belief that the spirits of those we knew, loved, and reverenced, were permitted to watch over us, and it might be to communicate with us, but how such communication was to take place, was a mystery as much to the parent as the child. She believed that our holiest thoughts and actions were suggested to us, under Divine permission, by ministering angels; and that perseverance in prayer would protect us from the evil influences that were ever on the watch to whisper, or even to inculcate, what was contrary to Gods law.

"This was, and is pure Spiritualism—pure Christen Spiritualism!—yet having believed this all my life long, believing also that the supernatural was often permitted as one of the missionaries of Christianity, I laughed at what was called 'Table-turning.' I had never seen spiritual manifestations, but that did not hinder my laughing at the idea of a spirit giving a message by raps on a table; all my belief in the 'Cloud of Witnesses' did not prevent my catching at what seemed the absurdity of such a means of communication, and instead of investigating, I laughed. I did worse, I became angry. I said I had believed all my life in *supernatural presences*, I believed that, if necessary, CHRIST-GOD would give one of His 'Cloud of Witnesses' permission to communicate with me, but what had that to do with raps? I never called to mind that at this moment the world is filled with 'Thomases,' who will not (if they can avoid it) believe except on the testimony of their senses. Because I believed in Gospel truths, I thought that others ought to believe as I did, from the testimony which had sufficed to me and mine. I did not want to see the Saviour's wounds, I believed in them, that was enough for me. I did not think of those 'stiff-necked and stubborn,' who require, as Thomas did, a 'sign;' and we must remember (which I did not) that the MASTER *did not refuse him that sign—no, He called him to examine those marks of His suffering.* HE not only permitted the unbeliever to examine for himself, but He *called* upon him to do so.

"At length, we were prevailed on to meet a young lady-medium, one in all respects above suspicion; we we're a mixed party of twelve or fourteen at that dinner-table: and while questioning myself how it was possible that educated and intelligent men could receive as testimony of spiritual presence the 'raps' and 'tilts,' which though I could not account for, I did not believe in, my attention was wakened by the young lady's saying that a spirit was present, who desired to communicate with me. She described a presence which I recognised, and then gave me a message, a portion of which could only be intelligible to us two—the spirit who gave it, and I who received it. This was so positive and conclusive to me, that believing as I always did that such a power existed, I was *forced* to believe that there was truth in mediumship, and that *here* was the means used for communicating from the spirits of those gone before to those who still lingered in the flesh.

"This was the confirmation of a blessed reality to me, but to others, particularly to one other at that table, it was thrice blessed; his past had been clouded with doubts as to the existence of spirit-life, he had refused to believe what he could not understand; his lamp of reason, trimmed with ever so much care, only made the darkness, so to say, more visible. Faith was to him a dead letter. His heart ached to believe, but, like Thomas, he wanted 'a sign.' The first 'sign' was given him that, night, and since then directed invariably to THE BOOK which leads to life eternal, he goes on his way rejoicing.

"Only those who have stumbled amid the doubts and uncertainties of a sadly unsatisfying materialism, can comprehend the inspiration which the assurance of future existence, amended, enlightened, purified, gives. I am frequently asked, what is the use of Spiritualism? My answer invariably is, that I believe it is permitted to check the growth of materialism. No one, however sceptical, can receive messages from the spirit-world, *knowing their truth*, and disbelieve in spirit-life, in a hereafter, in immortality! This is the key-stone to a belief, in the Holy Scriptures. Scores, hundreds, thousands, at this day say as I did, 'Why don't people believe? They have Moses and the prophets.' I believed on Bible testimony. Yes, but those thousands do not believe in Bible testimony; they ask for a *sign*. Will they not seek 'the sign,' and investigate its truth? Would not they give all they possess for a 'sign' proving immortality? Do they not desire intercourse which, sanctified by prayer, will (I have often seen it done) direct them to particular passages in Holy Writ, which for the first time they comprehended, and which became sanctified to them? And again, there are many who receive Spiritualism as a fact; well-minded, timid persons, who fear that Spiritualism is dangerous. I have seen quite enough to convince me that carnal-minded people bring their evil angels with them into many a circle; and they suggest what is evil more palpably, than in those silent whispers that lead as surely astray. 'By their fruits ye shall know them.' We know that 'lying spirits' endeavour to distil their poison into the purest hearts; and be sure they are on the watch around the circle assembled for manifestations, and can only be 'sent behind' by faithful prayer; but every Christian knows that he is perpetually beset by such like.

"Spiritualism, as we know it, commences each séance with prayer; and usually (though not invariably) has reason to finish with praise. I would not join a circle where this was neglected. I could name many who have been lifted out of the slough of materialism by, in the first instance, seeing the marvellous manifestations that arise from Mr. Home's mediumship, and the mediumship of the young lady I have already mentioned. Ridicule on the one aide, and asseverations on the other, cannot alter facts. There must be a *coin* to create a *counterfeit*, and, doubtless, charlatanism has found its way into 'circles,' whence it has been driven as soon as discovered.

"MEDIUMSHIP is a mystery we cannot fathom, nor understand why the power should be delegated to one more than to another. We have the highest authority for the belief that there are 'diversities of gifts' all from 'the same spirit;' and amongst them is specified, 'To some the discerning of spirits' Why should one have 'the gift of healing,' and *not* that of 'divers kind of tongues,' or 'the seeing of spirits.' That is one of those marvels we shall comprehend when we no longer see through a glass darkly. I can only add, with no large amount of humility, that 'mediumship' is not the only thing I do not understand.

"But I must cease here. I do not attempt to give any further description of the 'manifestations' I have witnessed, the wonders I have seen, and examined, and *questioned*, and after my examinations and questionings, could not doubt their being permitted for the ONE purpose, which I again repeat, is the mission of high and holy Spiritualism.

"I do not feel called upon to write in defence of Spiritualism, nor to quote from the volume of facts by which that defence is to be sustained, and its truth proved. I have no talent for argument or controversy; there are others who have, and are willing, as well as able, to be its defenders. I believe it to be sanctioned by GOD, and that therefore it must be for a good purpose; and I content myself, as I must content those who may read what I have written, with expressing my conviction that Spiritualism is TRUTH"

CHAPTER XIII

CONCLUSION

I came to England from Perigueux, and have been since engaged, as much as my time and my health would permit, in having séances, at which most of the manifestations recorded in the previous pages of my work have been repeated. I have been several times lifted a short distance from the ground, but not so high as to float above the heads of the persons in he room. Many persons have seen and been convinced of the occurrence of what they previously deemed impossible, and have had their faith in immortality renewed and strengthened when all other means had failed in making them believe. On the 20th January, 1863, I went to Paris for a short visit to my friend, Count de K____, and there also the same phenomena have occurred in the presence of great numbers of persons. I have also been frequently received by their Majesties at the Tuileries, and by the Imperial Princes and the nobility of France, who have shown a great interest in investigating the manifestations; but enough has been given of the facts to enable the reader to form an opinion of them, and there is no need to go into further details. I have already told the main incidents, and must now leave them to be judged and analyzed by the various classes of persons who may devote their thoughts to the subject.

It would be hard if I were held answerable for facts which occur in connection with my physical organization, and towards which I am in mind and intent, wholly passive, even if there were any harm in them. As there is no harm in them beyond their disturbing certain prepossessions, on the contrary, some likelihood of good; and as they are independent of all moral action on my part; I trust that with the candid and enlightened I shall be held; as I am, innocent.

It will have been observed that they began with me when I was an infant in my cradle, and that they have since, with few exceptions, formed a part of my daily life. Their range includes nearly all the phenomena which are known under the incorrect name of Modern Spiritualism. I say the name is incorrect, because there is not one of them which is new, and which may not be traced in every age of which we have any record preserved to us. The great difference, however, is, that during the last two centuries a great change has come over the belief of the world, and by a kind of re-action, men have reversed the belief which previously existed as to the supernatural. Up to two centuries ago, it was not considered a point of wisdom to disbelieve in such manifestations and actings from the inner world, but on the contrary, such disbelief was reprehended as unscriptural and wrong.

I am, however, fortunately relieved from the necessity of showing at great length the prevalence of spiritual action and phenomena in the past ages of the world, by the publication of the elaborate and almost exhaustive work of Mr. W. Howitt,("The History of the Supernatural in all Ages and Nations, in all Churches, Christian and Pagan, demonstrating a Universal Faith." By William Howitt, Author of "Colonization and Christianity." London, Longman and Co.) to which I refer my readers, in the full confidence that in his pages they will find not only the facts but the arguments necessary to show that the spiritual has been ever present, and that nothing has occurred to me but what has been frequently observed before. I trust that this work will be extensively read, in order that much of the present ignorance on the subject may be dispelled, and that the minds of men may be led to inquire more deeply into this great subject. As a brief summary of the same subject, I may likewise point to an article in the Appendix which has been framed by a friend from a series of historical notes, gathered by a literary gentleman, who has, with great kindness, placed them at my friend's disposal.

It will be readily admitted that such facts as those I have described, are calculated to throw great light upon the hitherto neglected science of pneumatology; and that it is in the direction pointed out by such facts, that further search is to be made into the hidden questions of the soul, and its relations with the body and external things. For such a study, no facts, however small or apparently trivial, can be dispensed with.

Of those which are of a physical kind, such as the moving of furniture, the raps, the raising into the air, or levitation, and similar classes of phenomena, they are to be investigated, and their uses ascertained by the man of science and the philosopher. At present such persons have fixed *à priori* that such things have never occurred, and are impossible and absurd, and for this very reason, if for no other, it will be admitted that they are of the highest use in order to correct such notions of the relations between spiritual forces and natural things. There is no study which could be of such value to philosophers, as that of facts now known to thousands, but which their present philosophy deems impossible. For their philosophy must be radically defective when that which they say is impossible, is nevertheless of daily occurrence. The physical side, therefore, of these phenomena is to be studied by students of experimental science in order to enlarge their views of material forces, and if this can be effected, as it has been in so many instances, by the movement of tables, and by the rapping sounds, and by the raising of bodies into the air, without touch or contact, they will no longer complain of the triviality of such phenomena. Indeed, already so little are they trivial or unimportant, that the noted men of science, such as the Faradays and Brewsters, have gone out of their way to inveigh against their possibility, and to bestow the name of credulous dupes upon those who have publicly stated what they have seen and heard. The very denial of these things by these men, and by the mass of the public, shows that they are not trivial to them, but that they are really of the utmost importance. For why are they denied by the men of science, but that they contradict all their previous knowledge of the laws of nature, upsetting "the philosophy of a lifetime," and are therefore impossible to them, until they enlarge the present boundaries of their knowledge, and find out those higher laws under which these become not only facts, but possible facts.

There is of course no religious revelation, properly so called, in such phenomena, any more than there is in the phenomena of gravitation, electricity, or magnetism, but that has not latterly been a reason why such laws should be repudiated. At the institution of the present Royal Society, there was a great outcry on the part of the religious persons of that day, against the formation of such a society, on the ground that it was blasphemous and wicked to attempt to inquire into what were called God's mysteries; and it was said that men already had their bibles, and knew enough, and ought not to seek to know more. Such is not the general opinion now-a-days, and the time is not far distant, I hope, when the manner in which this subject has been received, will in the same way be brought forward to prove the same great truth, that all knowledge is to be pursued, and that we need not fear that we shall ever have too much of it. God is able to preserve His own mysteries, and whatever is possible for us, it is our right and duty to search into and fathom, and to bring forward as a part of the general stock of human intelligence. I anticipate, therefore, that when the real men of science find these facts not to be impossible, they will by their aid, be led into a knowledge of higher laws, which at present they conceal from themselves; and that a greater discovery awaits their research than that which has adorned the name of Newton, who did not find it a trivial fact when an apple fell before his eyes.

As to the other great division of these phenomena, into such as are of a mental kind, and betoken intelligence, a much larger question is raised.

The former class of manifestations we could, only commend to the scientific investigator; but so soon as we are assured of the fact of manifestations directed by intelligence, we are put upon an inquiry of another kind. We are not aware of any other being but man, who is endowed with the kind and amount of intelligence which is disclosed in many of the manifestations, and we are at once brought to the inevitable conclusion that such intelligence is exhibited by human beings, either in the body, or out of the body. Neither the od force, nor electricity, nor magnetism, nor any of the imponderable forces, has ever yet been detected in betraying intelligence, or in carrying on a conversation between themselves, or in taking part in one with others, and though they are largely engaged in their proper offices throughout nature, and in that epitome of it which is contained in a man, yet there is nothing human nor intelligent about them in the true sense of the words.

We feel instinctively, therefore, when we meet with this intelligence, that we are dealing with a man either embodied or disembodied. The wonders of clairvoyance and internal perception (if we are to consider these as faculties inherent in the living, independent of spiritual aid,) may account for some of the phenomena; but there are others which my reader will not have failed to note, which infallibly point to the intelligence being that of disembodied human beings. The intelligence declares itself to be a human being, and gives information known to it alone. It says that it is a spirit, and in the spiritual world. It is seen as a spirit, and recognised as that of one loved on earth. It says that its office is to be our guardian, and helper, and comforter. It tells us of things that have passed, of things that are happening in distant parts, of things that are to come. Can this be ourselves, who unknowingly counterfeit such a presentment, and tell this false intelligence to ourselves? No such quality or power has hitherto been recognized or known to exist in the mind of man. No such quality has been recognized or known to exist in the od force, nor in electricity, nor in magnetism, as the ability to tell either truth or falsehood. Whence is it then? Is the question so entirely a new one as to the existence of spirits and their power to communicate with man, as that we can ignore it or deny its possibility? Are we inevitably thrown upon finding some natural hypothesis to account for such facts? and are we as Christians, to say like Sir David Brewster, that "Spirit is the last thing I'll give in to." I thank God that I have been taught otherwise, and I refer to the bible, and to the spiritual books, and authorities, and beliefs of all ages and of all churches, in support of my belief. Let us then say, at once that there are spirits and a spirit world, and see what difficulties are thrown in their way by the men of science, who deny them all power of communicating with this world.

It would indeed be a very difficult matter to conceive by what possible means a spirit could satisfy some minds of its actual presence. "Suppose," says the Rev. Charles Beecher, "a departed spirit, the wife of Oberlin, for example, were permitted to attempt to converse with her husband not to establish a new revelation, not to display divine power, but merely to exercise such potentiality as might pertain to a disembodied spirit, for her own and her husband's edification and satisfaction. How could she do it in the face of the apneumatic theories. She speaks to him, moves his furniture, touches his dress, his person;— all automatic action of some brain *en rapport* with that locality. She sings, plays the guitar or piano, takes a pencil and writes, and he sees the pencil in free space tracing his wife's autograph—automatic still. She shows him a cloudy hand, nay a luminous form, and smiles and speaks as when in life—that is an optical illusion, or hallucination, or a particle exhaled from her body has impinged on his sensitive brain, and created a subjective vision. She communicates facts past, present, and future; beyond the scope of his knowledge;—that might be clairvoyance or cerebral sensing. Alas, then, what could she do more? She must retire baffled, and complaining that; he had become so scientific that all communication with him was *impossible*."

It is, therefore, very difficult to influence some minds by any proof that could be brought forward, for want of their having any point which such proof can penetrate; but assuredly such proofs as I have given in my book, of the existence of spirits, and of their ability to communicate with us, are of the kind most likely to be useful to them.

It is to be observed also, that such persons, to be consistent, must, and too many of them do, apply the same argument to all analogous facts in the past, as well as to those occurring at this day. On this all-important point the Rev. W. Beecher says truly, "Whatever physiological law accounts for these phenomena in all ages, will in the end inevitably carry itself through the whole bible, where it deals with the phenomena of soul and body as mutually related, acting and re-acting. A large portion of the bible, its prophecies, ecstasies, visions, trances, theophanies, angelophanies, are more or less tinged with odic characteristics. The physiology, the anthropology of the bible is highly odic, and must be studied as such. As such it will be found to harmonize with the general principles of human experience in such matters in all ages. If a theory be adopted everywhere else but in the bible, excluding spiritual intervention *in toto*, and accounting for everything physically, then will the covers of the bible prove but pasteboard barriers. Such a theory will sweep its way through the bible and its authority; and its inspiration will be annihilated. On the other hand, if the theory of spiritual intervention be accepted in the bible, it cannot be shut up there, but must sweep its way through the wide domain of 'popular superstitions,' as they are called, separating the element of truth on which those superstitions are based, and asserting its own authoritative supremacy."

It is on such grounds as these amongst many others, that I have found as a fact that these manifestations have a religious tendency, and bearing on the subject of religion of the most important kind. I do not claim for them the character of a new revelation, but that they are a recurrence in our day of some of the phenomena of a very old one; and that it is not a small matter to be able to convince many who stand in need of such knowledge and conviction, of the immortality of the soul, of its immediate and continued existence in the spiritual world, and of its power of communion and communication with us who are left behind. These are not new doctrines, but old facts, and whatever spirits may tell us, we must judge of, as we judge the other affairs of life, by its own intrinsic evidence, and not rely on the infallibility of what comes from the other side merely because of its spiritual origin. For instance, suppose that if any one of the sceptics of the day should go to swell the numbers of the spiritual world, and should come to me in vision, or through any of the numerous modes which I have narrated in the previous pages, and should tell me that there are no spiritual laws, and no spiritual world, and no spiritual beings, and that the many phenomena I have experienced throughout my life did not occur to me, and that such never occurred to others, and were in fact impossible, I should not believe what he said, merely because of its spiritual origin, for the reason that it would be opposed to the experience and knowledge of myself, and of many others in the present and former ages of the world. I should, as I do, on the contrary, recognize in the very fact of his being able to come and give me this false information, matter of the utmost importance to religious truth, directed to a point which of all others in this materialistic age, the most requires assurance and confirmation.

The fact, therefore, of any intelligence whether true or false, coming from the inner world, is one from which conclusions must be deduced, the value of which it is impossible to over estimate. The real and intimate communion of saints may be difficult to realize, on account of our own state being too low for such holy communion, but we need not abandon to scepticism the whole spiritual world, and deny the possibility of one of the most glorious tenets of Christendom.

APPENDIX

Sir David Brewster

I have alluded to the first sitting which I had with Sir David Brewster, and to his disingenuous statements when he afterwards wrote on the subject in the "Morning Advertiser." To those who only know Sir David Brewster by general report as one of the noted scientific men of the day, it may be useful to say, that his reputation is not of the highest order amongst persons of his own class, and especially amongst those with whom he has been brought into closer contact, and, who have more accurately gauged the calibre of his mind. It would be no disgrace to him that he is not the most learned and scientific man of his age, if he did not pretend to be so, and back up his claims by means which more honourable, and really first-rate men, would not descend to.

So far as Spiritualism is concerned, I should be very glad for my own sake if he were really what he wishes the public to believe him to be, for then I should have the satisfaction of knowing that the world's best man had been discomfited and put to the rout in his attack upon the possibility of these phenomena. I cannot in fairness claim so important a victory. Sir David Brewster is really not a man over whom victory is any honour, for his whole conduct subsequent to the sittings was not only dishonest, but childish, and altogether unworthy of such reputation as he has acquired. The correspondence is amusing, as showing the shifts to which he was ultimately driven, when the great man, or wind-bag, as Carlyle would more properly call him, could only say for himself, that "the table actually rose, as appeared to me, from the ground." It is clear that if the subject is to be further investigated from the scientific side, it must be done by a very different man from Sir David Brewster.

As I have said, the sitting was asked for by Lord Brougham; and it was only after I had made an appointment with his Lordship, that he requested to be allowed to bring Sir David Brewster, to which I assented. On that day, and for a few days previously, my cough had been most troublesome, and, indeed, it had deprived me of sleep during nearly the whole of the previous night. When Lord Brougham and Sir David were announced, I was lying down on my bed, and, hastily dressing, I went to meet them. At my request, Mr. Cox was present during the séance; and I requested, as I always do, that Lord Brougham and Sir David should make search for any machinery which might be concealed on my person or about the table. This they would not do, but expressed rather a wish to see whatever might occur. We sat at a common card-table, Lord Brougham being on my left, Mr. Cox on my right, and Sir David Brewster opposite. Rappings were heard on the table, and also on the floor; and I several times, as is my constant practice with those who are present for the first time, requested both Sir David and Lord Brougham to look under the table, and to make every examination which they could.

We had been seated nearly half an hour, and various phenomena of the usual kind had occurred, when I was seized with a violent fit of coughing, and my mouth, as I thought, filled with blood, as occurred frequently to me about that time. On searching my pockets, I found that my handkerchief must have been left in my bed-room, and I hastily quitted the company and ran up stairs, found my handkerchief, and saw that it was not blood, but only the usual tubercular expectoration of persons in a decline. I do not think more than three minutes could have elapsed from the time of my leaving the room till my return. The reader will see what use this simple circumstance was put to afterwards by Sir D. Brewster. I proposed, when I came back, to see if anything more would occur, and asked pardon for my abrupt withdrawal, without mentioning the cause of it. It was *Sir David himself* who *requested* that we should try a circular dining-table which stood in the room, and I assented, only too pleased to see that he really wished to investigate. There were several other manifestations, but nothing that to me was at all uncommon, though it was enough to astonish extremely both Lord Brougham and Sir David, who, on leaving, thanked me for what they had seen, and expressed to me in the most earnest way their great astonishment. I must now let Sir David's letter, as first published that autumn in the "Morning Advertiser," while I was in Florence, speak for itself. I would not reply at that time to his misrepresentations, as I have always kept aloof from controversy, knowing that my good friends who had satisfied themselves of the truth of the phenomena would most likely say all that was necessary, and if they did not I was quite content. However, Sir David and his "conjectures" met with a hearty and truthful response from them.

A somewhat incorrect account of what had occurred at this séance was published in an American paper, and was copied into the "Morning Advertiser," and this was the occasion of Sir David Brewster writing his first letter, which was preceded by some remarks of the editor. In this letter Sir David had got over his previous astonishment, and was only anxious to save his reputation from the thought of having been ever a believer in what he had solemnly said to Mr. Cox, upset the philosophy of fifty years. It was unfortunately for him a small matter that in doing this he had to distort and deny the facts which had occurred, and to call me publicly an impostor.

The newspaper says:

"We publish the following letter from Sir David Brewster relative to the article which we lately quoted from an American paper, in which Lord Brougham and Sir David were represented as believing in spirit manifestations. This alleged belief was illustrated by certain things which were said of the two distinguished individuals in connexion with a display of 'spiritual' agency in July last, at Ealing. In giving insertion to the letter of Sir David Brewster, we deem it due to Lord Brougham, with whom Sir David's name was associated in the 'New York Spiritualist,' to say, that we have received a private letter from his Lordship, written in the most courteous terms, in which he repudiates the idea of his being a believer, *in the sense ascribed to him*, in spiritual manifestations. The Noble Lord, in proof of this, mentions that he had written something on the subject, and that he hoped to be able to procure a copy of the production from his residence in Grafton street, in which case he would transmit it to us. At present his Lordship is residing at Brougham Hall, in Westmoreland. We are anxious, and that anxiety will be shared by the public, to see the more ample exposition of his views on the subject, which he promises to send us:—

To the Editor of the Morning Advertiser.

"Sir,—I beg to thank you for the copy of the paper which you have been so good as to send me. In consequence of being from home I have not seen it; but I presume it is either the 'Spiritual Telegraph,' or the 'Christian Spiritualist,' which you have forwarded to me, and which I had previously seen.

"It is quite true, as stated by Mr. Home in these papers, that I wrote an article (not in the 'Edinburgh,' but in the 'North British Review'), in which I have denounced table moving and spirit-rapping in the strongest terms, and it is also true that I saw at Cox's Hotel, in company with Lord Brougham, and at Ealing, in company with Mrs. Trollope, several mechanical effects which I was usable to explain. But though I could not account for all these effects, I never thought of ascribing them to spirits stalking beneath the drapery of the table; and I saw enough to satisfy myself that they could all be produced by human hands and feet, and to prove to others that some of them, at least, had such an origin.

"Were Mr. Home to assume the character of the Wizard of the West, I would enjoy his exhibition as much as that of other conjurors; but when he pretends to possess the power of introducing among the feet of his audience the spirits of the dead, of bringing them into physical communication with their dearest relatives, and of revealing the secretes of the grave, he insults religion and common sense, and tampers with the most sacred feelings of his victims.

"I am, Sir, ever most truly yours,

"D. BREWSTER.

"Carnock House, Sept. 29, 1855."

I will show afterwards that in his denial of the power of spirits to communicate with those on earth, Sir David has not always been consistent, and that he has even, when it suited his purpose, threatened those with whom he has had scientific differences, with the visits of the spirits of those who have lost their lives, because Sir David's alleged inventions have not been adopted. I should not give so much prominence to the false position taken up by Sir David on this subject, were it not that it excited a great deal of attention at the time, and that he was the first person who publicly attacked me in England, and that he did so by misstatements and falsehoods of the gravest kind. It has been no uncommon thing with Sir David to have his personal statements proved false, and in this case he was severely handled and brought to book by several of the correspondents who gave their testimony against him in the newspapers. If Sir David Brewster's character for veracity suffered severely by the investigation that ensued, that is his affair, and not mine. It has frequently been said by reputed men of science, that these phenomena could only be accurately examined and analyzed by persons of high scientific attainments. I believe that this is not so, and that the nature of their minds disqualifies them rather than otherwise for the investigation, because the facts of Spiritualism are out of the region of Physics; but the reader will agree with me that if scientific men only are competent persons for the task of investigation, they require a further faculty, namely the honesty which is requisite in accurately stating what they see, whether or not it should upset the philosophy of a lifetime. In this last faculty Sir David Brewster has repeatedly been proved to be badly deficient, and, moreover, as will be afterwards seen, he made no respectable figure in this matter, even as a man of science, for in place of giving accurately observed facts, he could, after taking a week for consideration, bring out nothing but "conjectures," and the crudest disbelief even of his own eyesight.

I should have mentioned that, after the first sitting at Cox's Hotel, Sir David came to Ealing where I was then residing, and again saw in the company of Mr. and Mrs. Trollops, and of several other persons, some more manifestations of spirit power, but it was not true, as stated by the

Editor of the "Advertiser," that Lord Brougham was with him there. On his visit to Ealing, Sir David again expressed himself as perfectly satisfied with what he saw, and shook me warmly by the hand, saying that he was "proud of being a countryman of mine," and he left all the company in the opinion that he was thoroughly convinced by what he had seen. The document which Lord Brougham said would be forthcoming from Grafton Street, has never made its appearance, and I am informed that it was kept back at the request of Sir David, on account of its not being at all in agreement with the statements which he was successively driven to publish, in order to extricate himself from the dilemma in which he so incautiously placed himself. I think that in justice to me, Lord Brougham ought to have published it, even at the price of covering his friend Sir David with confusion.

Sir David Brewster's letter brought an immediate answer from Mr. Cox, who had been present during the whole of the investigation, and who was able to remind Sir David of the inaccuracies and misrepresentations of his letter.

"Sir David,—I have read with much surprise your letter to the 'Morning Advertiser.'

"You say, 'you saw enough to satisfy you that the effects could all be produced by human hands and feet, and to prove to others that some of them at least had such as origin.' The subject is one of deep interest, and having seen these phenomena under various circumstances, and being much startled by the reality of all I saw, I was glad of the opportunity of bringing two master minds to the investigation of it.

"Without unnecessarily alluding to what I understand you saw at the house of an equally disinterested investigator—for be it remembered that all who have received Mr. Home in this country, are above suspicion, and desire to arrive only at the truth—I beg to recall to your memory what took place at my house when Lord Brougham and you did me the favour to accept my invitation, and I will appeal to your fairness and candour to say whether there was a possibility—even if you could do me the injustice to suppose that I was in collusion with Mr. Home—of the various acts being *effected by the hands or feet of any one present.*

"I have a distinct recollection of the astonishment which both Lord Brougham and yourself expressed, and your remarkable and emphatic exclamation to me:— *'Sir, this upsets the philosophy of fifty years.'*

"I think I am justified in asking whether you have had any opportunity since of further investigation, and if not, how you can reconcile the tenor of your letter with the facts I have stated?

"If the subject be beyond your powers of reasonable explanation, leave it to others; for it is not just or generous to raise the cry of imposture in a matter you cannot explain, taking advantage of your character to place humbler men in a false position, by allowing the world to think they were, by ignorance or design, parties to so gross and impudent a fraud.

"I am, Sir David,

"Your obedient servant,

"WILLIAM COX.

"Cox's Hotel, Jermyn Street, Oct. 4, 1855."

Mr: Coleman also wrote to Sir David reminding him of what he had said in his presence, and which materially differed from what Sir David stated in his letter.

To the Editor of the Morning Advertiser.

"Sir,—Sir David Brewster has addressed a letter to you attributing the phenomena which he recently witnessed in private, in the presence of Mr, Home, to mechanical agency. Spiritual manifestations, as they are called, are therefore, in his opinion, a mere trick and imposition on the credulous.

"Sir David, though he had at least two interviews, and was invited to further investigation—one with his friend Lord Brougham in the open day—failed to discover the mechanism by which these marvels were produced.

"This does not say much for his sagacity; and it will not be wondered at that humbler individuals, not committed to a life of false philosophy, should be ready to accept the evidence of their senses, when, by the exercise of their ordinary faculties, they can give no *reasonable* explanation of the marvellous facts which are brought before them.

"I am one of a hundred who has recently witnessed these manifestations, at the house of my friend and neighbour, and I am sure that they were neither effected by trick, nor were we under a delusion. Sir David Brewster is of another opinion.

"I was as much astonished at what I saw, felt, and heard in the presence of Mr. Home, as any man; and when I found that Sir David Brewster had been a witness of similar phenomena at the house of my friend, I called upon Sir David, accompanied by my neighbour, and in the course of conversation, Sir David said, that what he and Lord Brougham saw 'was marvellous—quite unaccountable.'

"I then asked him, 'Do you, Sir David, think these things were produced by trick?'

"'No, certainly not,' was his reply.

"'Is it delusion,— think you?'

"'No, that is out of the question'

"'Then what is it?'

"To which he replied, 'I don't know; *but spirit is the last thing I will give in to.*'

"I added, 'I can well understand the difficulty which a man like you would have in pronouncing an opinion on a subject which, if it be what it appears, would upset in a moment the philosophy of your life.'

"Sir David then told me what he and Lord Brougham had witnessed. 'The table—a large dinner-table, I believe—moved about in the most extraordinary manner; and among other things, a large accordion was conveyed by an invisible agency to my hand, and then to Lord Brougham's, in which, held by his Lordship's right hand, apart from any person, it *played an air throughout.*

"Is it reasonable—astounding as the fact may be—is it, I ask, reasonable to attribute such a performance to mechanical agency, beyond detection, or that it should have been effected by Mr. Home's foot?

"No, Sir; a better explanation must be found to entitle Sir David Brewster's present opinion to the slightest respect. I say present opinion, for it certainly was not Sir David's opinion when I spoke to him; and I do not suppose he has seen anything of the subject since.

"Sir David's letter, and his sneer at the Wizard of the West, are, in my opinion, only worthy of his countryman, the Wizard of the North.

"I enclose my card, which of course you are at liberty to hand to Sir David Brewster.

"I am, Sir, yours, &c.

"A LOVER OF TRUTH, THOUGH NO PHILOSOPHER.

"October 3, 1855."

To this letter Sir David sent the following answer, which is so remarkable as coming from one of the much vaunted men of science, who alone are said to be competent to investigate and come to exact conclusions on the subject, that I am glad of the opportunity of reproducing all the important part of what he intended in the interests of his fifty years of so-called philosophy, to be an elaborate refutation of all spiritual action in this world of matter. After alluding to the conversation with Mr. Coleman at the Athenæum Club, he says:—

"I may once for all admit that both Lord Brougham and myself freely acknowledged that *we were puzzled with Mr. Home's performances, and could not account for them.* Neither of us pretend to be expounders of conundrums, whether verbal or mechanical; but *if we had been permitted to take a peep* beneath the drapery of Mr. Cox's table, we should have been spared the mortification of this confession. I come now to the facts of the case.

"1. It is not true, as stated by you, that a large dinner-table was moved about at Mr. Cox's in the most extraordinary manner.

"2. It is not true, as you state, that a large accordion was conveyed by an invisible, or any other, agency into my hand.' I took it up myself, and it would not utter a sound.

"3. It is not true that the accordion was conveyed into Lord Brougham's hand. It was placed in it.

"4. It is not true that the accordion *played an air throughout*, in Lord Brougham's hands. It merely squeaked.

"5. It is not true, as stated in an article referred to by Mr. Home, that Lord Brougham's 'watch was taken out of his pocket, and found in the hands of some other person in the room.' No such experiment was tried.

"6. It is not true, as stated by Mr. Cox, that I said that Mr. Home's experiments 'upset the philosophy of fifty years.' These are the words of Mr. Coleman, used, as he alleges, by himself, and very untruly put into my mouth by Mr. Cox.

"Although I have not appealed to Lord Brougham's memory in reference to these statements, I have no doubt that his Lordship would confirm, were it necessary, all that I have said.

"In reply to Mr. Cox, I may take this opportunity to answer his request, by telling him what I have seen, and what I think of it. At Mr. Cox's house, Mr. Home, Lord Brougham, and myself, sat down to a small table, Mr. Home having previously requested us to examine if there was any machinery about his person, an examination, however, which we declined to make. *When all our hands were upon the table noises were heard—rappings in abundance; and, finally, when we rose up the table actually rose, as appeared to me, from the ground. This result I do not pretend to explain,* but rather than believe that spirits made the noise, I *will conjecture* that the raps were produced by Mr. Home's toes, which, as will be seen, were active on another occasion; or, as Dr. Schiff has shown, 'by the repeated displacement of the tendon of the *peroneus longus* muscle in the sheath in which it slides behind the external *mallelous*,' and rather than believe that spirits raised the table, I will conjecture that it was done by the agency of Mr. Home's feet, which were always below it.

"Some time after this experiment, *Mr. Home left the room and returned: probably to equip himself for the feats which were to be performed by the spirits beneath a large round table covered with copious drapery, beneath which nobody was allowed to look.*

"The spirits are powerless above board. Besides the experiments with the accordion, already mentioned, a small hand-bell, to be rung by the spirits, was placed on the ground, near my feet. I placed my feet round it in the form of an angle, to catch any intrusive apparatus. The bell did not ring; but when taken to a place near Mr. Home's feet, *it speedily came across, and placed its handle in my hand. This was amusing.*

"It did the same thing, bunglingly, to Lord Brougham, by knocking itself against his Lordship's knuckles, and, after a jingle, it fell. How these effects were produced neither Lord Brougham nor I could say, *but I conjecture that they may be produced by machinery attached to the lower extremities of Mr. Home.*

"The séance was more curious at Ealing, where I was a more watchful and a more successful observer. I will not repeat the revelations made to Mrs. Trollope, who was there, lest I should wound the feelings, of one so accomplished and sensitive. I remember them with unmingled pain. The spirits were here very active, prolific in raps of various intonations, making long tables heavy or light at command; tickling knees, male and female, but always on the side next the medium; tying knots in handkerchiefs drawn down from the table, and afterwards tossed upon it; and prompting Mr. Home, when he had thrown himself into a trance, to a miserable paraphrase on the Lord's Prayer. During these experiments I made some observations worthy of notice. On one occasion the spirit gave a strong affirmative answer to a question by *three raps,* unusually loud. They proceeded from a part of the table exactly within reach of Mr. Home's foot, and I distinctly saw three movements in his loins, perfectly simultaneously with the three raps. In these experiments all hands are supposed to be upon the table. One of the earliest experiments was with an accordion, held below the table, in Mr. Home's right hand. It played, very imperfectly, two tunes asked for by the company. During the succeeding experiment, Mr. Home continued to hold the accordion; as we thought, but he might have placed it on the ground, and had his right hand free for any sub-tabular purpose. A handkerchief had been previously taken down to be knotted, and the fact had been forgotten, amid the interest of other experiments; a knot could not be tied by feet, nor, we think, by the one hand of Mr. Home, below the table. The handkerchief, however, was, to our great surprise, after half an hour's absence, tossed upon the table with five knots, dexterously executed. How were those knots tied, unless by spirits? During the half hour's absence of the handkerchief,

Mr. Home, three or four times, gave a start, and looked wildly at the company, baying, 'Dear me, how the spirits are troubling me,' and at the same time putting down his left hand as if to push away his tormentors; or soothe the limb round which they had been clustering. He had, therefore, both his hands beneath the table for a sufficient time to tie the five marvellous knots.

"I offer these facts for the spiritual instruction of yourself and Mr. Cox, and for the information of the public. Mr. Faraday had the merit of driving the spirits from *above the table* to a more suitable place *below it.* I hope I have done something to extricate them from a locality which has hitherto been the lair of a more jovial race.

"I am, Sir, yours, &c.,

"D. BREWSTER.

"St. Leonard's College, St. Andrew's, Oct. 9, 1855."

Mr. Coleman at once answered Sir David by writing to the Editor as follows:—

To the Editor of the Morning Advertiser.

"Sir,—If the letter which Sir David Brewster has addressed to me through your columns, had not contained grave imputations on my veracity, I should have left so disingenuous and contradictory a document to be dealt with by the gentlemen who are more especially concerned.

"Sir David, it will be recollected, first wrote a letter on the subject of these manifestations, so glaringly opposed to his recent expressions, that I could not resist reminding him of the contradiction.

"Sir David says I have completely misstated, the conversation, and though most reluctant to be placed in a position of direct antagonism with a man of Sir David's position, I am bound in self-defence to reassert that my statements in your journal of the 4th inst., are true, word for word, as nearly as one can record from memory, and fortunately for me, I have a witness in the person of a gentleman whose character stands at least as high as Sir David Brewster's, and he fully confirms me:

"Sir David says:— 'I may once for all admit that both Lord Brougham and myself freely acknowledge that we were puzzled with Mr. Home's performances, and could not account for them. But if we had been permitted to take a peep beneath the drapery of Mr. Cox's table, we should have been spared the mortification of this confession.'

"Sir David, in his former letter, *does* attempt to account for them by mechanical agency, and by human hands and feet—he saw enough 'to prove to others that some of them, at least, had such an origin.' Sir David altogether omits to name that, at Mr. Rymer's house, on a subsequent occasion, he did 'take a peep beneath' the table, putting his head under for some little time. *No drapery was there*: it wag a large uncovered and very ponderous dinner-table, which was actively moved up and down, and was also, as he himself says, 'made heavy or light at command.' Is not the omission of this fact, and his imputation on Mr. Cox, most unfair and disingenuous?

"Sir David admits that, when all their hands were on the table at Mr. Cox's, rappings were heard in abundance, 'and when we rose up, the table actually rose, as appeared to me, from the ground.'

"'This result I do not attempt to explain,' &c., &c.

"*Appeared* to rise from the ground. Did it rise? Why make a question of so plain a fact? Did the table rise from the ground when all around it were standing with their hands upon it? If it did, can Sir David seriously impose upon himself the belief, for he certainly will not impose upon any thinking man, that this effect was produced by mechanical contrivance beyond detection, or by the foot of Mr. Home?

"There is yet another point in Sir David's conduct which will have its weight, and at which, I doubt not, every English gentleman will feel surprised, and that is, that he should be so wanting in honest candour as never to have breathed a suspicion to either of the two disinterested searchers after truth who had paid him the compliment of specially inviting him to their houses to investigate these phenomena, of their being duped, nor to have explained to them how it was all done.

"To Mrs. Trollope, in particular, for whom Sir David expresses so much consideration, and who, I suppose, is not, even in his opinion, a party to the fraud, he should, in common courtesy, have whispered, 'This is an insult to religion and common sense.' See the consequence. By locking in his secret breast so much important information, he allows this accomplished and sensitive lady to come, as she did, expressly from Florence to London, to see the wonders which a friend told her she should witness in this young man's presence; and after staying at Mr. Rymer's house for several days to investigate the subject, she actually left England in the full belief of the reality of all she saw, and she is at this moment entertaining this arch-impostor as her guest at Florence. Sir David may get the majority of the world to applaud him for his present manly exposure of things 'he cannot explain,' but they will not forgive him for allowing this accomplished lady to be so shamefully cheated.

"I forbear to follow Sir David further in his tortuous treatment of this subject. It is evident that the harder he is pressed, the further he will recede: I therefore most willingly leave him and the subject of spirit manifestations in the hands of your able correspondent, 'VERAX,' whose remarkable letter appearing in your columns at the same moment, will serve to heal the wounds so unscrupulously inflicted by Sir David Brewster.

"Trusting that I have not in your opinion forfeited the right, I beg still to describe myself,

"A LOVER OF TRUTH, THOUGH NO PHILOSOPHER.

Mr. Cox further impugned Sir David's veracity in the following letter.

"Sir,—I trouble you with a brief reply to Sir David Brewster's denial of the expression used on the occasion of his visit to my house, in company with Lord Brougham, for the purpose of investigating the remarkable phenomena exhibited in the presence of Mr. Home.

"I assert that both Sir David and Lord Brougham were astonished at what they heard, saw, and felt. I assert that Sir David, in the fullness of his astonishment, made use of the exact expression 'This upsets the philosophy of fifty years.' I assert that no hindrance existed to Sir David looking under the drapery of the table; on the contrary, he was so frequently invited to do so by Mr. Home, that I felt annoyed at Mr. Home's supposing that either he or I could be suspected of any imposition. I assert that Lord Brougham was so much interested that he begged me to arrange for him another sitting, and said he would put off every engagement for the purpose of further investigation.

"Sir David may not have the moral courage to express publicly his real opinions upon a subject in which he knows the world is not prepared to believe; but it is unpardonable in him to deny the facts as they occurred; to descend at the same time to banter and ridicule, and to impugn the integrity of men whose characters are as dear to them as Sir David's public reputation is to him; for in this correspondence it is his own public reputation alone, that he seems anxious to protect.

"I am, Sir, yours, &c.,

"W. COX.

"Jermyn-street, Oct. 15, 1855."

Mr. Trollope also wrote to the newspaper as follows:—

"Florence, Oct. 23, 1855."

"My dear Sir,—I have read with much regret the letters from Sir David Brewster, printed in the 'Morning Advertiser,' to which you have called my attention. And although it is extremely painful for me to come out from my tranquil obscurity into the noise and wholly inconclusive bickerings of paper warfare, it is impossible for me, when called on, to refuse my testimony to facts, of which I was a witness.

"If I had the presumption to enter into an argument with Sir David Brewster on the subject matter of his letters, I might adduce a long series of observations, and be led into an extended discussion of inferences, and balancing of probabilities. But I deem it more useful to the cause of truth, that I should confine myself to such facts, as I can affirm with accuracy, and perfect certainty, but which yet seem incompatible with some statements of Sir David Brewster's letters.

"Sir David writes, that when he was present together with Lord Brougham and Mr. Cox, at Cox's Hotel, for the purpose of witnessing the phenomena produced or caused by Mr. Home, it was 'not true that a large dining-table was moved about in the most extraordinary, manner.' Further on, he states, with reference to some other appearances, that the table 'was covered with copious drapery, *beneath which nobody was allowed to look.'*—(These italics are Sir David's.)

"Now, I can say nothing respecting things which took place on that occasion. But it is evident that these statements should not have been made, or, in any case, not made unaccompanied by further particulars, if Sir David had present to his mind the facts, to which I am about to testify.

"I declare that at your house at Ealing, on an evening subsequent to Sir David Brewster's meeting with Mr. Home at Cox's Hotel, in the presence of Sir David, of myself, and of other persons, a large and very heavy, dining-table *was moved about in a most extraordinary manner*; that Sir David was urged, both by Mr. Home and by yourself to look under the cloth and under the table; that be did look under it; and that while he was so looking, the table was much moved; and that while he was looking, and while the table was moving, he avowed that he saw the movement.

"Sir David Brewster further writes, that on this same evening the spirits were very active, prolific of raps of various intonations, making tables heavy or light at command, tickling knees male and female, but always on the side next the medium. I was repeatedly touched on *either* knee, and on the lower leg; but I experienced no sensation at all akin to tickling. Neither did any of those present, who were similarly touched, say that they were, or give any token of having been tickled. Moreover, I affirm that Sir David Brewster, who sat in the circle next to me, declared to me at the time of being touched, that he was touched on *both knees*; on the side farthest from the medium therefore, as well as on the side next him. Nor did he then speak of being *tickled*.

"Indeed the phraseology of this part of his letter is matter of the greatest astonishment to me. For it should seem wholly impossible that a man of Sir David Brewster's character, standing, and social position, in the grave and public examination of a question, on which a young man's honour and character depend, if no yet higher interests are concerned, should intentionally seek to prejudice the issue in the minds of his readers by a vulgar jest, puerile to those earnest inquirers who disbelieve the spiritual origin of these phenomena, inexpressibly revolting to those who believe therein, and which, falling from less respected lips, would by all be termed mere ribaldry.

"I must add one more remark on two other pages of Sir David's letter. The party present at Mr. Cox's, he writes, 'sat down to a small table, Mr. Home having previously requested us to examine if there was any machinery about his person; an examination, however, which we declined to make.' A few lines further on he writes, with reference to the phenomena which then occurred, 'I conjecture that they may be produced by machinery attached to the lower extremities of Mr. Home.' Now, I submit that these two statements should not stand together. It appears to me both morally unjust, and philosophically unsound in the examination of evidence, first to decline the proffered means of ascertaining the absence of machinery, and then to assume its presence.

"I should not, my dear Sir, do all that duty, I think, requires of me in this case, were I to conclude without stating very solemnly, that after very many opportunities of witnessing and investigating the phenomena caused by, or happening to Mr. Home, I am wholly convinced, that be what may their origin, and cause, and nature, they are not produced by any fraud, machinery, juggling, illusion, or trickery, on his part.

"I am, my, dear Sir,
"Always most faithfully yours,
"T. ADOLPHUS TROLLOPE.
"John Snaith Rymer, Esq., Ealing."

My personal testimony, under such circumstances, can hardly be needed to convict Sir David of untruthfulness, for the subject has since that time made such progress as to carry it far beyond the criticism of Sir David's "conjectures;" and not only he, but Professor Faraday, have had time and ample leisure to regret that they should have so foolishly pledged themselves and their "philosophy of fifty years" to the absolute impossibility of spiritual phenomena. That such things should be impossible to them, is conclusive proof that their philosophy is based on a radically false foundation, for it obliges them to protest against facts and forces which are the correlatives and basis of all true philosophy and religion. It is not saying much for science, when it will not bear facts, and when such a man as Sir David Brewster is obliged to deny them, simply because they upset the philosophy of fifty years. I myself distinctly remember his remarkable words to this effect, and which he found it convenient afterwards to deny; and I am quite sure that at the time he used them, he felt their full force, for with all his fancied science, it is evident that he has no theory upon which the spiritual phenomena either of the Bible or of modern days could possibly be true.

The occurrences, indeed, were so extraordinary, that Sir David, the philosopher, whom we are taught to look up to as a man of science, mistrusted the evidence of his own senses, and chose, as has been said of him by the learned and Rev. Dr. Maitland, "to place himself before the public as a person who really could not tell whether a table, under his nose, did or did not rise from the ground." The same learned divine contemptuously asks the very pertinent question, "Is it on men so grossly and avowedly incompetent to judge of plain matter-of-fact submitted to their senses, that we are to pin our faith in matters of physical science?"

I have been a guest at several of the first European Courts; I have visited noblemen and gentlemen of every country, and have resided in many instances for months in their houses; and if Mr. Cox allowed me to conceal machinery under the drapery of his table, they also must have allowed me to do the same thing, and for the idle, base, and blasphemous purpose of deceiving themselves and others on a subject which gives rise to the holiest thoughts, and exhibits powers which prove to demonstration the possibility of spiritual action. I may add, that I have for years met, and still meet every day, with men of the highest attainments in the arts and sciences, who have carefully examined all these wonderful phenomena, and who have not rested satisfied with "conjectures" either as to the table, or as to machinery alleged to be concealed about my person.

But the untruths of Sir David's letter, to which he was obliged to resort in order to save his philosophy, are what I have now to deal with; and I appeal with confidence not only to the published testimony of Mr. Cox, Mr. Coleman, and Mr. Trollope, but also to Lord Brougham, to convict Sir David of mis-statement and concealment of facts on the following points, which I take in the order stated in his letter.

1st. *It is true* that a large table was moved about at Mr. Cox's.

2nd. *It is true* that an accordion was placed under the table near Sir David, and that he "placed his feet round it in the form of an angle," and that *from thence* it was *taken* by invisible agency, and falling near me. I gave it to Lord Brougham to hold.

3rd. Is essentially correct as stated, but Sir David forgets the fact of no one taking it from between his feet, unless it was so taken by his "conjectures."

4th. The accordion was not said to have played an air throughout in Lord Brougham's hand, but it is not true that it only squeaked, for the instrument gave a good sound of full harmony.

5th. I never referred to the article alluded to as being true, as I knew too well the incorrectness of newspaper reports of such matters.

6th. *It is true*, as stated by Mr. Cox, that Sir David said, "Sir, this upsets the philosophy of fifty years."

Sir David says, "When all our hands were upon the table noises were heard—rappings in abundance; and, finally, when we rose up, the table actually rose, as appeared to me, from the ground." And he then goes on to state, "rather than believe that spirits raised the table I will conjecture that it was done by the agency of Mr. Home's feet, which were always below it" If this conjecture were true, I must have nearly as many feet as Sir David has "conjectures."

The shabby conjecture that when I left the room for my handkerchief under the circumstances I have stated, it was to equip myself for the feats which I was to palm on him as spiritual phenomena, is on a par with the statement that no one was allowed to look under the table, which is no other than a wilfull perversion of the truth. Sir David again "conjectures" that the bell was placed in Lord Brougham's hand, and afterwards in his own, by machinery attached to my lower extremities. This is neither a scientific nor a charitable conjecture; for only picture to yourself, a large room in Jermyn Street, with three front windows, in broad daylight, and three sane men sitting in it, allowing me to enter and walk about with such hitherto unknown machinery "attached to my lower extremities," as would reach several feet, and play an accordion, take up and ring a hand-bell, and perform all the other phenomena. As to the music, it has been my good fortune to be on intimate terms with some of the first composers of the day, and more than one of them has said of such as they have heard, that "it is such music as only angels could make and no man could write it."

However, I cannot better account for and illustrate the whole investigation of the subject by Sir David Brewster, and his subsequent conduct in the correspondence, than by giving prominence to his leading idea and foregone conclusion expressed in his own forcible language, "Spirit is the last thing I will give in to." More unphilosophical words have never been uttered; and such a frame of scepticism is unworthy both of science and religion; such crude ideas have been the cause of all the errors persisted in by mankind, who will not accept facts, when they make against their prejudices. Facts should always be accepted on their own evidence, and not according to any fancied order of priority, and still less should they be ungenerously or untruthfully put before the world. If the silly question of *cui bono* should ever be raised again, let it be enough to remember that Sir David Brewster has pledged himself as a philosopher against the *possibility* of the phenomena of Spiritualism, and so likewise have Professor Faraday and others of like attainments. The *cui bono* is, therefore, to show such men of science that they are utterly wrong in their notions of the ultimate forces of the world, and really, therefore, to upset their "philosophy of fifty years." I am sorry to find, however, that Sir David Brewster's testimony to any fact ought not, after what is known of him, to be taken without corroboration, for on several remarkable occasions he has been convicted of such conduct in scientific circles, as makes his statement of matters of fact of little value.

The attempted appropriation by him, to the prejudice of Professor Wheatstone, of the main credit of the stereoscope, is sufficiently notorious to add to his name a character altogether unworthy of a man of science. It appears to have become a habit with David Brewster, when another person has perfected any great invention on any branch of science on which Sir David had previously written, or experimented, at once to set up his own claim as the discoverer of the perfected invention; and having had the command of the pages of the "North British Review," he has, when doubts have been thrown on his universal genius, backed up his claims by a skilful anonymous article from his own pen. In this way, when Professor Wheatstone invented the stereoscope, Sir David, after writing in 1843, that "it is impossible to over-estimate the importance of his paper," thought in 1852 that the time had come when he might appropriate the honour to himself, and he wrote one of his anonymous articles in his favourite review, the ostensible purpose of which was, as the learned Dr. Carpenter says in his exhaustive lecture on this subject delivered in 1862, "to exalt its author, Sir D. Brewster, at the expense of Mr. Wheatstone, *the assertion being then for the first time put forward*, that Mr. Wheatstone could claim no more than the merit of contriving a clumsy method of carrying into operation the essential principle which had been enunciated by others." The exposure which Sir David meets at the hands of Dr. Carpenter is crushing and complete.(see—and it is well worth seeing—"On Binocular Vision and the Stereoscope," a Lecture delivered at the London Institution, March 19, 1862, by W. B.

Carpenter, M.D., F.R.S., F.L.S., F.G.S., Registrar of the University of London. Liverpool, Grenwell, 1862.)

A precisely similar attempt respecting the invention of the polyzonal lens or dioptric lights, upon which the success of our present light-house system mainly depends, is so recent and remarkable, that I will put it also shortly before the reader.

When this great invention, which was really first indicated in France by Buffon and Fresnel, began to be applied some years afterwards in Scotland by the late Mr. Stevenson, the eminent light-house engineer, Sir David appears to have coveted the main honour, not less than the profit to be derived from it, and to have actually attempted by a Memorial to the Treasury to obtain a pecuniary grant for his alleged discovery. Sir David again made use of his usual organ the "North British Review" anonymously, in an elaborate article written by himself, in which he gives, as from an impartial tribunal, judgment in favour of his own claims to the invention, as having been made many years previously. Curiously enough, as if anticipating his inquiry into spiritual phenomena, and to show that it was not always that Spirits were "the last things he would give into" he brings them forward in this review of himself to help to back up his alleged merits, by saying, "that the hundreds of lives which were lost on the Scottish coast from the imperfections of its light-houses during the ten years that the engineer refused to listen to Sir David Brewster's recommendation of the lens apparatus, lie at the conscience-door of the engineer, and that during the following nine years that the Scottish Commissioners refused to surrender to science their ignorance and their prejudices, *the souls of the men shipwrecked from the same causes may yet rise up in judgment against them.*" How does Sir David know that it was not the spirits of some of these poor sailors who came to him in Jermyn Street and at Ealing, to show him that, although they had this power, yet that they knew the baselessness of his claims too well to trouble the Commissioners or the engineer on the subject. Suffice it to say, that the Messrs. Stevenson, in a reply ("Reply to Sir David Brewster's Memorial to the Commissioners of the Treasury on the New System of Dioptric Lights." By D. and F. Stevenson, Engineers to the Commissions of the Northern Light-houses. Blackwood &.Sons, Edinburgh, &c., &c.) which this review called forth from them to protect the memory of their father, have conclusively shown the groundless nature of Brewster's claims, and placed him in a position which humbler men would altogether sink under.

Curiously enough, however apt Sir David may be as an inventor in physics, he has only one mode of action in reference to the inventions of others, for his course with Mr. Stevenson is the exact counterpart of that played off on Professor Wheatstone. He first applauded both inventions and then a few years afterwards tried to claim the principle merit connected with them for himself.

I trust that I have said enough to show that my character for truthfulness and honesty ought not to receive much injury from Sir David Brewster; and that if Spiritualism is to be further investigated by men of science, there is no reason to fear, that such as Sir David Brewster will be allowed to be amongst those who will settle the question.

Connection of Mr. Home's Experiences With Those of Former Times

[The materials of the following chapter have been contributed by a literary friend. It may be added that the Introductory Remarks and this chapter have been prepared, under editorial care, in the absence of Mr. Home in France; so that he cannot be considered as responsible for them.]

Obviously, on various considerations, the gifts attending upon Mr. Home would be less entitled to public attention if they appeared as unique or exclusive to himself. It is hardly necessary to make the remark, that they are shared by many living persons in America, and by some in our own country. More important it is to observe that such extraordinary peculiarities have been occasionally reported throughout all ages, as well as in all countries, though modern scepticism has learned to look upon them all as compositions of imposture and delusion. On the present occasion it is only proposed to adduce a few cases in which mysterious noises and other phenomena, resembling those connected with the organism of Mr. Home, have attracted a certain degree of attention, during the last two or three centuries.

A girl of thirteen, named Angélique Cottin, was brought from her home in the department of the Finisterre, to Paris, in 1843, in consequence of some mysterious physical peculiarities connected with her, which had been observed while she was employed as a winder in a thread glove manufactory. It was alleged that heavy articles moved at her approach, or contact, and that in her presence a tub rose into the air with a man seated on it. Messrs. Arago, Mathieu, Langier, and Goujon visited her at the Observatory, and witnessed a series of experiments thus described in the newspapers of the day:

"A piece of paper, placed upon the edge of a table, was immediately attracted by the left hand of the girl. She then, holding her apron in her hand, approached a guéridon, which was pushed back although the apron scarcely touched it. The next experiment was to place her in a chair with her feet on the ground. The chair was projected with violence against the wall, while the girl was thrown the other way. This experiment was repeated several times, and with the same results. M. Arago laid his hand upon the chair to prevent its moving; but the force was too great for his resistance, and M. Goujon, having seated himself on a part of the chair, was thrown off as soon as Angélique had also taken her seat. Such, said M. Arago, were the facts witnessed, and he had seen nothing to justify an opinion that any deception had been practised. Since then, other experiments have been performed by Dr. Tauchon. This gentleman had the chair in which Angélique was seated held by two powerful men. In this instance it was not driven away, but broke in their hands. A table, a guéridon (a small round table), and a heavy sofa were projected by the mere contact of the girl's clothes."

M. Arago, then occupying, it need scarcely be said, the highest place in France as a cultivator of physical science, was so much impressed by what he witnessed in Angélique's presence, that he moved the appointment of a Committee in the Academy of Sciences, for the investigation of the phenomena attending her. In the report which he subsequently presented, he stated that on two visits of the Committee to the girl, at the Jardin des Plantes, none of the experiments were successful; her friend, M. Chollet, explaining that intermittences in her power often took place; but two members of the committee who had been at her hotel, affirmed that from seven till nine in the evening, the alleged phenomena were "manifested in all their force;" and he repeated his conviction that in the repulsions between the girl and her chair, her hands were unconcerned. In consequence of other visits by the Committee being fruitless of results, M. Arago joined in a subsequent report, to the effect that former communications on the subject to the Academy should be "regarded as if they had never been received." It is evident, however, that M. Arago had witnessed effects for which he could assign no ordinary mechanical cause; and it may fairly be said that no amount of negative evidence would suffice to obliterate that which he gave as positive, unless he could explain away his positive evidence, which we are not aware he ever did. Obviously, to explain how a little girl could overcome the force of two powerful men, and that with an exertion which wholly escaped the observation of both these men and other bystanders, could not be much less difficult than to expound the nature of the alleged phenomena on the basis of their assumed verity. It is also admitted by M. Arago himself, that while the Academy's Committee could get no manifestations, multitudes of other people were favoured with them. From what on the whole appears in this case, a simple denial of the alleged phenomena is inadmissible.

The "Standard" Newspaper in June, 1841, contained several articles regarding some remarkable disturbances which then took place in a house called Want's Cottage, situated at Clewer, about a mile from Windsor, being the residence of a respectable couple retired from business, Mr. and Mrs. Wright, and their two daughters, besides one female domestic. Noises, as produced by the knuckles of a human being, were heard by day and night on a door leading from the kitchen to a water-closet. Sometimes they were loud enough to be heard by the inmates of the houses four or five hundred yards off. The disturbance went on at intervals for several weeks, to the serious discomposure of the family, and even of their neighbours, and the most active and diligent efforts to discover any ordinary mechanical cause proved vain. We are told of a group of magistrates, composed of Mr. W. F. Riley, Forest Hill, Mr. W. B. Harcourt, St. Leonard's Hill, Major-General Lord Clement Hill, Mr. Edmund Foster, Clewer House, the Rev. Mr. Gould, of Clewer, &c.; being assembled to search into the matter, in the hope of "detecting the trick," but without the least success. Mr. Riley and Lord Clement Hill stationed themselves in the hall, within three yards of the door, and as soon as the knocking commenced, rushed to the spot, but found no person near it. The water-closet was wholly broken up, and the ground beneath excavated, but with equally little effect. Mr. Wright's son, arriving from Newbury, fastened the door with a piece of wire, and after a knocking, this wire was found broken, and the door forced inwards. After this troubling had lasted several days, the landlady of the house came, and took various expedients, such as removing the floor and digging below, to discover its cause; all in vain. A scientific gentleman came from London, examined a drain, and analysed the water of a neighbouring ditch, (!) but could throw no light upon the subject. At length the family, tired out with the disturbance, deserted the house with their furniture, and from that time the noises ceased. (The newspaper accounts of this affair are extracted into Major Moor's volume on the "Bealing Bells," Woodbridge, 1841, p. 99-110.)

The conclusion arrived at from this last fact, was that trickery on the part of some member of the family was at the bottom of the mystery; but no vestige of such trickery had been detected by any of the multitudes who flocked to the house—we do not hear of even a surmise as to the means employed—and the ceasing of the noises with the departure of the family, might be supposed to have been simply because of a connection between the condition of the organism of some one of the inmates, and these mysterious phenomena.

It was in 1841 that Dr. Reid Clanny, a physician at Sunderland, published an authoritative report of the singular illness which had recently affected his patient, Mary Jobson, a girl of about thirteen, the child of parents in humble life, but of good character. This child was, in November 1839, seized with fits which lasted for several weeks, and during this time an unaccountable knocking frequently took place near her bed, and a voice was heard speaking of facts unknown at the time, but which were subsequently found to be true. Sweet music was likewise heard, as also footsteps where there was no visible human being; and occasionally locked doors were unaccountably opened. Individuals unconnected with the Jobsons, were sometimes accosted in their own homes by this voice, and told to go to see her. One Elizabeth Gauntlett, obeyed the command, and arriving at the door of Jobson's house, was told by the voice to go up. On several occasions, when visiting Mary, she heard the most exquisite music. Many persons, visiting the sick girl, heard preachings of a holy character from the voice; and some who came there were ordered to depart, as if they had been considered unworthy to be present.

The voice on one occasion said, "Look up, and you will see the sun and moon on the ceiling;" and immediately there did appear a representation of these objects in the situation indicated. To the surprise of all, these pictures remained permanent. The father, who was then only annoyed at the unaccountable circumstances attending his child, and a disbeliever in their extra-natural character, ordered the ceiling to be whitewashed; but the figures still continued partially visible.

For several months in 1840, these singular phenomena proceeded with little interruption, the child being all the time a bed-rid invalid. The voice was often heard. It told them on one occasion that Mary's own spirit had left her body, and a new one had taken possession, making her frame a mere instrument, or as it were a speaking-trumpet. Many things told by the spirit were found to be true. Frequently there were songs in parts, apparently sung in the air. The figure of a lamb was seen by one visitor, entering the room of Mary's father, who, however, did not see it himself. One manifestation of a very remarkable character in the form of a sprinkling of water, was frequently given, professedly for the curing of unbelief, in Jobson and his visitors. (This phenomenon has often happened among the American spiritualists.) At length, on the 22nd of June, Mary Jobson was suddenly raised from her extreme illness to perfect health. The voice, which had promised a miraculous care, told them to lay out the girl's clothes, and leave the room, all but the infant of two and a half years old. After a quarter of an hour's absence, the voice called to them, "Come in;" and when they entered, they found Mary sitting up dressed, and perfectly well, with the infant upon her knee. Nor from that time did her illness recur.

There were, of course, the usual suspicions of imposture in this case; but the particulars were observed by multitudes, who never detected any trick, and the whole matter is attested by Dr. Reid Clanny, and others, who not only had no interest in verifying such extraordinary facts, but in doing so risked considerable loss of reputation.

Going back into the last century, we find the noted case of Anne Parsons (adverted to in the Introductory Remarks), which is remarkable for the advances made to that system of converse with the invisible powers, now so extensively developed in America. That Anne Parsons was simply a medium, or sensitive of the same class with Mr. Home, is not to be doubted by any one conversant with spiritualism. It would be very curious to learn what became of the child in her subsequent years. (It will probably be heard with some surprise, that the illustrious Jenner, in his boyish days, appears to have had a partial experience of the mediumistic or sensitive state. Through weakness, as we are told, induced by the process of inoculation, he lost the habit of regular sleep, and was "constantly haunted by imaginary noises."—*Fosbroke's Berkeley Manuscripts.* 4to., 1821, p. 222.)

Two cases stated in the newspapers in the latter part of 1732, have features in strong parallelism with those of Anne Parsons.

"We hear from Waltham, in Leicestershire, near Melton Mowbray, that a mason's daughter, aged 11, is possessed with an evil spirit, which throws her out of bed into fits, and pinches bits out of her flesh, and has twice put her collar-bone out. In her frequent fits, she lies as one dead, and at the same time there is such a knocking and thundering noise (sometimes at the door, but mostly by and about the child) as is terrible to see about her; and if the spirit is bid knock any number of times, or to any tune, it certainly does so. The Lord Howe, the clergy, &c., thereabouts, have had the girl with them, and have all proved it to be no fallacy or imposition. All the account she gives when she comes out of her fits is, that she is carried into a wood, and tormented by three persons."—*London Newspapers*, October, 1732.

"They write from Tholouse that a young woman, now of that city, (born in the village Grand Mall in that diocese), is haunted by an invisible man, that has almost frightened her out of her wits. She is aged 25, daughter of an attorney. Her uncle, (also an attorney) has often questioned this spirit, but got no answer. At last the girl herself was prevailed on to speak to it, and ask its name, and whether it was a gentleman? At which it answered with a knock under the table. She asked again whether it was a marquis, a count, a baron, or a knight? At the word knight, it knocked again. Vast numbers flock to see this young woman, and return well satisfied with the politeness and good breeding of this spirit, who now answers in words to all the woman asks, but is dumb to everybody else."—*London Newspapers*, Dec. 1732.

The case usually spoken of as that of the St. Maur spirit has all the appearance of being one of simple mediumship, though an intelligent tracing of the connection with personality is unfortunately wanting. The external facts are detailed in an anonymous narrative, transferred into Calmet's *Phantom World*, and were as follows:

"Monsieur de S____," says the narrator, "is a young man, short in stature, well-made for his height, between four and five-and-twenty years of age. Being in bed, he heard several loud knocks at his door, without the maid servant, who ran thither directly, finding any one; and then the curtains of his bed were drawn, although there was only himself in the room. The 22nd of last March, being, about eleven o'clock at night, busy looking over some lists of works in his study, with three lads who are his domestics, they all heard distinctly a rustling of the papers on the table; the cat was suspected of this performance, but M. de S____, having taken a light and looked diligently about, found nothing.

"A little after this he went to bed, and sent to bed also those who had been with him in his kitchen, which is next to his sleeping-room; he again heard the same noise in his study or closet; he rose to see what it was, and not having found any thing more than he did the first time, he was going to shut the door, but he felt some resistance to his doing so; he then went in to see what this obstacle might be, and at the same time heard a noise above his head towards the corner of the room, like a great blow on the wall; at this he cried out, and his people ran to him; he tried to reassure them, though alarmed himself; and having found nothing he went to bed again and fell asleep. Hardly had these lads extinguished the light, when M. de S____ was suddenly awakened by a shake, like that of a boat striking against the arch of a bridge; he was so much alarmed at it that he called his domestics, and when they had brought the light, he was strangely surprised to find his bed at least four feet out of its place, and he was then aware that the shock he had felt was when his bedstead ran against the wall. His people having replaced the bed saw, with as much astonishment as alarm, all the bed-curtains open at the same moment, and the bedstead set off running towards the fire-place. M. de S____ immediately got up, and sat up the rest of the night by the fire-side. About six in the morning, having made another attempt to sleep, he was no sooner in bed, than the bedstead made the same movement again, twice, in the presence of his servants, who held the bed-posts to prevent it from displacing itself. At last, being obliged to give up the game, he went out to walk till dinner time; after which, having tried to take some rest, and his bed having twice changed its place, he sent for a man who lodged in the same house, as much to reassure himself in his company, as to render him a witness of so surprising a circumstance. But the shock which took place before this man was so violent, that the left foot at the upper part of the bedstead was broken; which had such an effect upon him, that in reply to the offers that were made to him to stay and see a second, he replied, that what he had seen, with the frightful noise he had heard all night, were quite sufficient to convince him of the fact.

"It was thus that the affair, which till then had remained between M. de S____ and his domestics, became public; and the report of it being immediately spread, and reaching the ears of a great prince who had just arrived at St. Maur, his highness was desirous of enlightening himself upon the matter, and took the trouble to examine carefully into the circumstances which were related to him. As this adventure became the subject of every conversation, very soon nothing was heard but stories of ghosts, related by the credulous, and laughed at and joked upon by the free thinkers. However, M. de S____ tried to reassure himself, and go the following night into his bed, and become worthy of conversing with the spirit, which he doubted not had something to disclose to him. He slept till nine o'clock the next morning, without having felt any thing but slight shakes, as if the mattresses were raised up, which only served to rock him and promote sleep. The next day passed off pretty quietly; but on the 26th, the spirit, who seemed to have become well-behaved, resumed its fantastic humour, and began the morning by making a great noise in the kitchen; they would have forgiven it for this sport if it had stopped there, but it was much worse in the afternoon. M. de S____, who owns that he felt himself particularly attracted towards his study, though he felt a repugnance to enter it, having gone into it about six o'clock, went to the end of the room, and returning towards the door to go into his bedroom again, was much surprised to see it shut of itself and barricade itself with the two bolts. At the same time, the two doors of a large press opened behind him, and rather darkened his study, because the window, which was open, was behind these doors.

"At this sight, the fright of M. de S____ is more easy to imagine than to describe; however, he had sufficient calmness left, to hear at his left ear a distinct voice, which came from a corner of the closet, and seemed to him to be about a foot above his head. This voice spoke to him in very good terms during the space of half a *miserere*; and ordered him, *theeing* and *thouing* him, to do some one particular thing, which he was recommended to keep secret. What he has made public is, that the voice allowed him a fortnight to accomplish it in; and ordered him to go to a place, where he would find some persons who would inform him what he had to do; and that it would come back and torment him if he failed to obey. The conversation ended by an adieu.

"After that, M. de S____ remembers that he fainted and fell down on the edge of a box, which caused him a pain in his side. The loud noise and the cries which he afterwards uttered, brought several people in haste to the door, and after useless efforts to open it, they were going to force it open with a hatchet, when they heard M. de S____ dragging himself towards the door, which he with much difficulty opened. Disordered as he was, and unable to speak, they first of all carried him to the fire, and then they laid him on his bed, where he received all the compassion of the great prince, of whom I have already spoken, who hastened to the house the moment this event was noised abroad. His highness, having caused all the recesses and corners of the house to be inspected, and no one being found therein, wished that M. de S____ should be bled; but his surgeon finding he had a very feeble pulsation, thought he could not do so without danger.

"When he recovered from his swoon, his highness, who wished to discover the truth, questioned him concerning his adventure; but he only heard the circumstances I have mentioned— M. de S____ having protested to him that he could not, without risk to his life, tell him more.

"The spirit was heard of no more for a fortnight; but when that term was expired—whether his orders had not been faithfully executed, or that he was glad to come and thank M. de S____ for being so exact as he was, during the night, lying in a little bed near the window of his bedroom, his mother in the great bed, and one of his friends in an arm-chair near the fire, they all three heard some one rap several times against the wall, and such a blow against the window, that they thought all the panes were broken. M. de S____ got up that moment, and went into his closet to see if this troublesome spirit had something else to say to him; but when there, he could neither find nor hear any thing. And thus ended this adventure, which has made so much noise and drawn so many inquisitive persons to St. Maur." (The translation in Christmas's Edition of Calmet, is here used, after collation with the reprint in *Recueil de Dissertations sur les Apparitions, les Visions, et les Songes.* 4 vols. Paris, 1751.

The two cases of the boy of Shepton-Mallet and Patrick Sandilands, though divided in both apace and time, may be placed together on account of their remarkable similarity. It was in 1657, that Henry Jones, a boy of twelve years of age, residing at the above mentioned village, was found to be liable to fits, and thought to be, bewitched by a woman named Jane Brooks, who suffered for her supposed fault next year. Jones fell into trances, during which it was averred, he would be carried by invisible means from one room to another, and sometimes wholly lifted up, so that his body hung in the air, with only the flat of his hands placed against the ceiling. One afternoon, being at the house of one Richard Isles, he went out into the garden, and there, in sight of Isles's wife, was raised up into the air, and transported over the garden wall for about thirty yards, falling at length as one dead at the door of a neighbouring house. Patrick Sandilands, a younger son of Lord Torphichen, at Calder, in Scotland, was, in 1720, believed to be bewitched, and it was by a narrow chance that a couple of suspected witches escaped burning on his account. In his physical condition there were some peculiarities well calculated to excite alarm; but what chiefly drew attention was his tendency to rise entranced into the air, which was so great that his sisters had to watch him, and sometimes only could keep him down by hanging to his skirts. In time the disease for so it appeared to be—passed away, and the young man going to sea, rose to the command of an East Indiaman.

Bodin, in his "Demonomanie," 1593, gives an account of a gentleman known to him—supposed to have been himself who seems to have enjoyed the mediumistic power of spirit communication to a degree very nearly approaching to that of Mr. Home. The narrative is curious, and has that self-consistency which we associate with truth. It is here presented in the translation of Dr. Henry More, (More's "Antidote against Atheism." London, 1655.) after collation with the original.

"This party, a holy and pious man, as it should seem, and an acquaintance of Bodinus's, freely told him how that he had a certain spirit that did perpetually accompany him, which he was first aware of when he had attained to about thirty-seven years of age. This spirit discovered himself to him after he had for a whole year together earnestly prayed to God to send a good angel to him, to be the guide and governor of his life and actions; adding, also, that before, and after prayer, he used to spend two or three hours in meditation and reading the Scriptures, diligently inquiring with himself, what religion amongst those many that are controverted in the world, might be best, beseeching God that be would be pleased to direct him to it. . . . While he was thus busy with himself in matters of religion, he light[ed] on a passage in Philo Judaeus, in his book 'De Sacrificiis,' where he writes 'that a good and holy man can offer no greater or more acceptable sacrifice to God than the oblation of himself;' and, following Philo's counsel, he offered his soul to God. After that, among many other divine dreams and visions, he once in his sleep seemed to hear the voice of God saying to him, 'I will save thy soul, I am he that before appeared unto thee.' Afterwards the spirit every day would knock at the door about three or four o'clock in the morning, though he rising and opening the door could see nobody; but the spirit persisted in this course, and unless he did rise, would thus rouse him up.

"This trouble and boisterousness made him begin to conceit that it was some evil spirit that thus haunted him, and therefore he daily prayed earnestly unto God, that he would be pleased to send a good angel to him; and often also sang psalms, learning the most of them by heart. Wherefore, the spirit afterward knocked more gently at the door; and one day discovered himself to him waking, which was the first time that he was assured by his senses that it was he; for he often touched and stirred a drinking glass that stood in his chamber, which did not a little amaze him.

"Two days after, when he entertained at supper a certain friend of his, Secretary to the King, that this friend of his was much abashed while he heard the spirit thumping on the bench hard by him, and was strucken with fear; but he bid him be of good cheer, there was no hurt towards; and the better to assure him of it, told him the truth of the whole matter.

"Wherefore, from that time, saith Bodinus, he did affirm that this spirit was always with him, and by some sensible sign, did ever advertise him of things; as by striking his right ear if he did anything amiss; if otherwise, his left. If anybody came to circumvent him, that his right ear was struck, but his left ear if a good man and to good ends accosted him. If he was about to eat or drink anything that would hurt him, or intended or purposed with himself to do anything that would prove ill, that he was inhibited by a sign, and if he delayed to follow his business, that he was quickened by a sign given him.

"When he began to praise God in psalms, and to declare his marvellous acts, he was presently raised and strengthened with a spiritual and supernatural power.

"That he daily begged of God that he would teach him his will, his law, and his truth; and that he set one day of the week apart for reading the Scripture, and meditation, with singing of psalms, and that he did not stir out of his house all that day. But that in his ordinary conversation he was sufficiently merry and of a cheerful mind, and he cited that saying for it, '*Vidi facies sanctorum lœtas.*' But in his conversing with others, if he had talked vainly and indiscreetly, or had some days together neglected his devotions, he was forthwith admonished thereof by a dream. He was also admonished to rise betimes in the morning; and about four of the clock, a voice would come to him while he was asleep, saying, 'Who gets up first to pray?'

"He told Bodinus also, how he was often admonished to give alms, and that the more charity he bestowed, the more prosperous he was. And on a time when his enemies sought after his life, and knew that he was to go by water, his father in a dream brought two horses to him, the one white, and the other bay; and therefore he bid his servant hire him two horses, and though he told him nothing of the colours, yet he brought him a white one and a bay one.

"That in all difficulties, journeyings, and what other enterprises soever, he used to ask counsel of God, and that one night when he had begged his blessing, while he slept he saw a vision, wherein his father seemed to bless him.

"At another time, when he was in very great danger, and was newly gone to bed, he said that the spirit would not let him alone till he had raised him again; wherefore he watched and prayed all that night. The day after, he escaped the hands of his persecutors in a wonderful manner; which being done, in his next sleep, he heard a voice saying, 'now sing, *Qui sedet in latibulo Altissimi.*'

"A great many other passages this party told Bodinus; so many, indeed, that he thought it an endless labour to recite them all. But what remains of those he has recited, I will not stick to take the pains of transcribing them.

"Bodinus asked him why he would not speak to the spirit, for the gaining of more plain and familiar converse with it. He answered that he once attempted it, but the spirit instantly struck the door with that vehemency, as if he had knocked upon it with a hammer; whereby he gathered his dislike to the matter.

"But though the spirit would not talk with him, yet he would make use of his judgment, in the reading of books, and moderating his studies. For if he took an ill book into his hands, and fell a reading, the spirit would strike it, that he might lay it down, and would also sundry times, be the books what he would, hinder him from reading and writing overmuch, that his mind might rest, and silently meditate with itself. He added also, that very often when he was awake, a small, subtile, inarticulate sound would come into his ears.

"Bodinus further inquiring whether he ever saw the shape and form of the spirit, he told him that, while he was awake, he never could see anything but a certain light very bright and clear, and of a round compass and figure; but that once, being in great jeopardy of his life, and having heartily prayed to God that he would be pleased to provide for his safety, about break of day, amidst his slumberings and wakings, he espied on his bed where he lay, a young boy clad in a white garment, tinctured somewhat with a touch of purple, and of a visage admirably lovely and beautiful to behold. This he confidently affirmed to Bodinus for a certain truth."

Dr. John Dee was one of the ablest and most learned men of the sixteenth century. As is well known, he took into association with himself a man named Edward Kelley; who professed to have the power of seeing visions in a piece of polished jet, and who received communications from mysterious voices. It has always been matter of surprise that a man of such attainments should have so surrendered himself to one who appears as only an under-educated man and an impostor. But the details of Dee's experience present Kelley as simply a sensitive of the same character as Mr. Home; and those who see valuable truth to be derivable through the channel of spiritualism, will not wonder that Dee employed him and listened to him. It is true that the great mathematician to some extent misunderstood the phenomena, and was unfortunately led to trust too much to Kelley's communications, so as to bewilder himself with alchemical researches, and to do many other things which are to be deplored. But the fact of mystic communications is independent of errors and falsehoods which these communications may involve. Dee and Kelley viewed the whole matter with a religious awe characteristic of their age, and were unprepared to "try" the spirits. Of their good faith, as viewed under the light of modern spiritualism, there is no occasion to doubt.

It would only weary the reader to trace history farther back for examples of sensitiveism like that of Mr. Home. Let us rather give some of the space which remains to detached instances of the phenomena.

As to the *knockings*, odd and whimsical as this kind of manifestation may appear, it is one of which we hear much in old books of demonology. John Aubrey has a distinct chapter on the subject. He tells us that, three or four days before his father died, he had a premonition of the event by "three distinct knocks on the bed-head, as if it had been with a ruler or ferula," he lying at the time perfectly awake. (Miscellanies, &c., collected by John Aubrey, F.R.S. Second Edition. 1721, p. 122.) Richard Baxter, in his *Certainty of the World of Spirits*, treats the same subject very gravely. A man of quality, known to him, had of late years fallen into drunken habits. After a debauch, he was haunted with knockings at his bed-head, which others heard as well as himself, nor did a removal of the bed do anything to banish them. (Baxter's "Certainty of the World of Spirits," 1691, p. 60.)

Major John Morgan, of Wells, lying in bed one day with Mr. Barlow, son of the Dean of Wells, they heard three knocks on their bed, and Barlow died soon after. It is curious to contrast these cases from forgotten English books of the seventeenth century, with a modern French one, detailed by Morin. It states that "a French soldier, a revolutionary hero, previously sceptical, was at five different times of his life, and always before a catastrophe in his family, warned of it by three distinct blows on the head of his bed." (Morin, "Comment l'Esprit vient aux Tables.") Or take a recent English case. On the 5th of July 1858, a woman named Smith, gave evidence regarding the murder of a policeman, named Clark, which had happened at Dagenham fourteen years before; stating that her first husband William Page had been concerned in it. She had seen the spirit of Page several times in broad day, and while taking her meals she had often heard the devil *tapping the bottom of her chair.* The identity of these experiences occurring in such different places, and amongst such different people, is very striking.

The case of Luther in the castle of Wurtzburg, hearing what he thought the devil cracking nuts in his chamber, does not seem very different from that of Mrs. Smith, *quondam* Page. It appears to be an experience incidental to an excited or reduced condition of the nervous system.

"Rushton Hall, near Kettering, in Northamptonshire, was long the residence of the ancient and distinguished family of the Treshams. In the reign of Queen Elizabeth, the mansion was occupied by Sir Thomas Tresham, who was a pedant and a fanatic, but who was an important character of his time, by reason of his great wealth and powerful connections. There is a lodge at Rushton, situate about half a mile from the old hall, now in ruins, but covered all over, within and without, with emblems of the Trinity. This lodge is known to have been built by Sir Thomas Tresham; but his precise motive for selecting this mode of illustrating his favourite doctrine was unknown until it appeared from a letter written by himself about the year 1584, and discovered in a bundle of books and papers enclosed since 1605 in a wall in the old mansion; and brought to light about twenty years ago. The following relation is extracted from this letter:

"If it be demanded why I labour so much in the Trinity and Passion of Christ, to depaint in this chamber, this is the principal instance thereof; that at my last being hither committed, and I having usually my servants allowed me to read nightly an hour to me after supper, it fortuned that Fulcis, my then servant, reading in the *Christian*

Revelation, in the treatise of *Proof that there is a God, &c.,* there was upon a wainscot table at that instant three loud knocks (as if it had been with an iron hammer) given; to the great amazing of me and my two servants. Fulcis and Nilkton."—D. JARDINE, *in Notes and Queries,* Nov. 26, 1853.

Dr. Robert Plot, in his two several books on the Natural History of Oxfordshire and Staffordshire, published in the latter part of the seventeenth century, takes care to particularize the warnings which several families of those counties were accustomed to have before a death occurred in one of them. There was "a knocking before the death of any of the family of Captain Basil Wood, of Brize-Norton, Captain in the late wars for the King. The first knocking that was heard, or at least observed, was about a year after the Restoration, in the afternoon, a little before night, at or upon the door, it being then open, as it was apprehended by Mrs. Elenor Wood, mother to Captain Basil Wood, who only heard it, none being then by or about the house but herself; at which she was very much disturbed, thinking it boded some ill to her or hers. And within fourteen nights after, she had news of the death of her son-in-law, Mr. George Smith, who died in London.

"About three years after that, there were three great knocks given very audibly to all that were then in the house, viz., to Mrs. Elenor Wood, Mr. Basil Wood, and his wife, Mrs. Hester, and some servants; which knocks were so remarkable, that one of the maids came from the well, which was about twenty yards from the place, to see what was the matter. And Mrs. Elenor Wood, and another maid that was within the house, saw three great pans of curd shake and totter so upon a shelf in the milk-house, that they were like to fall down. Upon this violent knocking, Mr. Basil Wood and his wife being then in the hall, came present into the milk-house to their mother, where, finding her somewhat disturbed, and inquiring the reason, she replied God Almighty only knew the matter—she could tell nothing, but she heard the knocking; which, being within doors, Mr. Basil Wood concluded must be for some of the family at home, that upon the door being for a friend abroad; which accordingly fell out, three of the family, according to the number of the knocks, dying within little more than half a year after; viz., Mrs. Nester Wood, a child of Mrs. Wood's sister, and Mrs. Elenor Wood.

About August, 1674, Mr. Basil Wood junior, son of Basil, living at Exeter, heard the same kind of knocking, at which being disturbed, he wrote to his father at Bampton in Oxfordshire, that one Sunday, he and his wife, and her sister, and his brother, did distinctly hear upon a table in their chamber, as they stood by it, two several knocks struck as it were with a cudgel, one of them before, and the other after morning prayer, a little before dinner. Which letter was shown by Wood senior, to several neighbouring gentlemen. After which, within about fourteen days, Mrs. Hester Wood, second wife of Mr. Basil Wood, senior, and about a quarter of a year after, her father, Mr. Richard Lisset, died, both at Bampton; since which time they have heard nothing more as yet." (Plot's "Oxfordshire," fol. edit. 1705, p. 209.)

Dr. Plot, in his book on Staffordshire, mentions that "The like signal was given before the death of Captain Basil Wood himself." He goes on to speak of other Staffordshire families, who enjoyed this unpleasant distinction. Before the decease of any of the family of Cumberford of Cumberford, three knocks were always heard at Cumberford Hall, though the party dying "be at never so great a distance. "Thus," says Dr. Plot, "I was also told at Ammington, by the worshipful Sebright Repington, Esq., that a noise somewhat like a drum was heard about eight or nine o'clock at night for six or eight weeks together, in a stack of chimneys on his house, at the death of his first lady; which, they say, was always heard upon the departure of any of the family of Burdett, whence that lady came. And thus I was informed concerning another family in this county, there is a noise of bees heard in one of the farms belonging to it, before the death of any of them, of which 'tis common for the tenants to give them notice, when perhaps there is noise of the family ill, yet in a little time some of them certainly die; as those of the family of Oxenham, in the county of Devon, likewise infallibly do, upon the appearance of a bird with a white breast fluttering about their beds." (Plot's "Staffordshire," 1686, p. 329.)

We may for the meantime discount the connected facts of the deaths in the family; but certainly it is remarkable that in so many detached and straggling instances, knocks or knockings on furniture should have been heard and reported.

Of all the phenomena connected with Mr. Home, there is none which makes a greater demand on the faith of those who have not been eye-witnesses of it, than the elevation of his person into the air. Yet we see that two of the sensitives adduced from the two past centuries, are reported as occasionally exemplifying the same mysterious process. In the annals of both hagiology and demonology, a lifting of the body by invisible means is frequently averred. The life of St. Francis d'Assisi (born 1182) has been related from immediate and direct observation by those amongst whom he lived; and it is one of the most serious statements of his secretary Leo, that the saint would sometimes, when ravished with divine meditation, be raised into the air, so that he (the secretary) could only reach his feet, to water them with his tears. The biographers of the celebrated female Spanish saint of the sixteenth century, St. Theresa, assure us with all solemnity, that in her hours of extreme devotion she was frequently lifted into the air. In the sight of all the sisterhood she was, on one occasion, floated over the grate of the convent door. Of St. Peter d'Alcantara, who starved himself till he became transparent, it is related that he was often enveloped in a lustrous light, and elevated into the air. In Wierus's celebrated book on demonology, there is an account of a nun named Magdalena Crucia, of Corduba in Spain, who was sometimes lifted several cubits off the ground. Another fact in her case, recalling one in the early life of Mr. Home, was that at the celebration of the Eucharist, one of the wafers would be conveyed to her mouth without human agency.

Glanvil tells a strange story of a gentleman's butler in Ireland, who was thought to be haunted by spirits, that threatened to carry him away, and who was actually one day raised from the ground in the presence of several persons, including Mr. Valentine Greatrakes, the celebrated "Stroker." Mr. Greatrakes and another lusty man clapped their arms over his shoulders, one before, and the other behind, and weighed him down with all their strength; but he was forcibly taken up from them, and they were too weak to keep their hold, and for a considerable time he was carried in the air to and fro over their heads, several of the company, still running under him, to prevent his receiving hurt if he should fall. At length he fell, and was caught before he came to the ground, and had by that means no hurt.

Mr. E. Fowler, Lord Orrery, and Mr. Greatrakes were the informants of Dr. Henry More and Mr. Glanvil in this case, Dr. More "heard Mr. Greatrakes tell the story, at my Lord Conway's, at Ragley, and particularly inquired about the man's being carried up into the air above men's heads in the room, and he [Mr. Greatrakes] *did expressly affirm that he was an eye-witness thereof.*"

Levitation of the body was one of the peculiarities popularly ascribed to witches. One of the tests for that kind of criminality was to weigh the accused against the parish bible; another, to bind her and cast her into a pool, to ascertain whether she could float or not. Probably these tests took their rise in some instances of actual sensitives, who, like Mr. Home, were sometimes lifted off the ground. It is also not unworthy of notice, that the people of the Hebrides to this day try to cure madness by throwing the patient into the sea with a rope round his body, and are generally under the belief that mad people have a floating power much above that of ordinary mortals.

That feature of Mr. Home's mediumship (not, however, confined to him) which consists in the appearance of a hand—a hand which touches the individuals of a company, transports little articles, or performs on musical instruments, appears a very peculiar kind of demonstration. Why so often a hand alone? Why should the remainder of a spiritual figure be so seldom seen? We may ask such questions, with little chance of a satisfactory answer; but meanwhile, it is important to observe that the appearance and the visible operations of a detached spirit-hand are amongst the most common of the special demonstrations in old times.

Aubrey relates an interesting story of the reign of King James I, in which a visionary hand performs a part. The second wife of Sir Walter Long of Draycot, had succeeded in inducing her husband to disinherit his son by the first marriage. At the assizes at Bath, her brother, Sir Egrimond Thynne, an eminent sergeant-at-law, drew up the proper document's, and his clerk had to engross them at night. "As he was writing, he perceived a shadow on the parchment from the candle; he looked up and there appeared a *hand*, which immediately vanished. He was startled by it, but thought it might be only his fancy, being sleepy; so he wrote on. By and bye, a *fine white hand* interposed between the writing and the candle (he could discern it was a woman's hand), but [it] vanished as before. With that, the clerk threw down his pen and would engross no more." (Aubrey's "Miscellanies," p. 75.) In Aubrey we also find that, when a Highland seer attempted to tell how the power of second sight came to him, he was sure to be rebuked by *strokes from an invisible hand.*' (Aubrey's "Miscellanies," p. 191.)

In the case of a house supposed to be haunted by what the Germans call a *poltergheist*, related by Mather as happening at Newberry in New England, in the year 1679, a man was "discernibly beaten by a fist, and a hand got hold of his wrist, which he saw, but could not catch." In another case, related by the same author, at Portsmouth in New England, the family "saw the appearance of a hand put forth at the hall window, throwing stones." (Mather's "Remarkable Providences," edit. 1856, pp. 104, 115.) According to Henry More, "near Elton, a village half a mile distant from Embrica in the dukedom of Cleve, there was a thing had its haunt, they called it Eckerken; there appeared never more than the shape of *a hand*; but it would beat travellers, pull them off their horses, and overturn carriages." ("Antidote against Atheism," p. 184.)

In Baxter's *Certainty of the World of Spirits*, is a letter written to the author by the famous Earl (afterwards Duke) of Lauderdale, in March 1659, his lordship being then a prisoner in Windsor Castle. Lord Lauderdale tells of a house named Powdean, in Annandale, which had been haunted for fifty or sixty years, and where a party of English soldiers quartering had been beaten by invisible means. "Within the last fortnight," pursues his lordship, "Mr. James Sharpe [afterwards the archbishop of unhappy memory] was with me. He tells me that spirit now speaks, and appears frequently *in the shape of a naked arm.*" In the like case of the Rerrick spirit—a poltergheist in 1695—the minister declared he saw a detached hand and arm. In Ezekiel, "the Lord put forth the form of a hand, and took me by a lock of mine head," &c. "A hand with a book" was sent to the same prophet. "Behold an hand touched me," says Daniel, at the conclusion of his narrative of his vision.

As a modern instance, the life of Caroline, Queen of Naples, (sister of Marie Antoinette, Queen of France,) "was closed by an uneasy death. To the Principessa di _____, who was with her in her last days at Vienna, and continued her attendance to her last moment, she said that she was troubled by visions of the past, and by loud voices speaking to her in her sleep; that she heard all night long many angry voices calling upon her to follow; and that even by daylight, she saw many *hands beckoning through the curtains of her bed*, while invisible voices whispered" Hist! hist! Caroline, hist!'"—C. *Macfarlane, Note to Pictorial History of England.*

The warbling of an invisible bird over Mr. Home's infant, becomes a remarkable incident in connection with other facts of spiritualism, in which the feathered creation performs a part. A gentleman, signing himself W. C., and dating from Brunswick Square, communicates, in the 'Spiritual Magazine' for January, 1863, an account of a recent illness he had had, during which, for many months, he was almost continually regaled with the music of birds, forming the most exquisite harmony. Sometimes a canary seemed the leader, sometimes a lark, and every time he awoke the tune was changed.

At the Conference (of Spiritualists) held in the Lyceum, New York, on the evening of the 10th of September, 1858, Mr. Taylor stated, that at the large circles held at his house, the chirping of an invisible bird was heard by all present, and Mr. Harris had been able to see it. Dr. Orton related a little incident which he said had occurred to him that morning. On the previous evening, he had had some conversation with a spirit friend, a female, who told him that she was about to make him a tangible present. In the morning (the door of the chamber being locked, and the windows, though open for air, having the shutters to) the sound of wings was heard, and a dove was seen flying towards the window. A small packet, which it dropped on the floor, was found to contain the words in delicate pencilling, "Have I not redeemed my promise?" In the course of the day, it was intimated to Dr. Orton that the dove was charged with the spirit of his friend; that the billet had been written through an entranced medium, a lady of New York; and she (the spirit) had influenced the bird to contract itself so as to pass through the lattice, which it had done in the middle of the night. ('Spiritual Age,' September, 1858.) Capron states in his work, 'Modern Spiritualism,' (p. 229), that in the house of Mrs. Anne Wilbur, of Providence, Rhode Island, a spiritual circle, experimenting in 1850, had this among other demonstrations: "we heard a sound resembling the flapping of a small bird's wings upon the white counterpane of the bed;"

Mr. J. Arbouin, a friend of Flaxman, relates a curious anecdote connected with the great sculptor in the *Intellectual Repository* for April 1814.

A nobleman applied to Mr. Flaxman with directions for a monument for his departed wife; and in communicating his instructions, said, "There must be a dove on the top." Mr. Flaxman observed, "My lord, this is not your crest." "No," said his lordship; "but I have a particular reason for it;" and was going away; but, willing to satisfy the evident curiosity of Mr. Flaxman, he returned, and communicated the following circumstance:

"A few days before the death of my wife, I was reading by her bedside. All on a sudden she appeared inattentive to my reading, with her eyes fixed towards the window, and, her lips moving as in tacit conversation. I waited till this ceased, and said, 'My dear, you have not attended to my reading.' 'No,' said she, 'I have been conversing with _____ (mentioning a female departed friend): did you not see her at the window? She has been talking to me with a dove on her finger, and says she shall call for me next Friday.'" On the Friday the wife died."

In the obituary of the Gentleman's Magazine for October, 1786, occurs the following notice: "Died 17th October, at Cranbrook, Kent, Mr. Zachariah Pearce, aged 21.

"The following remarkable occurrences can be attested by many persons in Cranbrook. Mr. W. Pearce, his father, died of a frenzy, 30th November, 1785. Some time before he died, a small bird of the dish-water kind (*sic*) came often every day, and pecked hard against the chamber-window where Mr. Pearce lay sick. The window was set open to try if the bird would enter the room, but it did not, and means were used to catch it, but in vain. The bird continued to come and do the same until Mr. Pearce died and was buried, and then it ceased to return. Since the above Zachariah Pearce was taken ill, the same bird, or one of the like kind, frequented his chamber-window, and continued to do so occasionally until the time of his death.

"A similar circumstance occurred in the same parish about two and a half years ago. These are real facts. Something not unsimilar to this is related in one of Howell's letters."

The story told in Howell's Letters has fortunately been given in a more authentic work, Lysons's "Devonshire," from a curious and rare contemporary pamphlet. It hence appears that a family named Oxenham, at Zeal Monachorum, in that county, had a bird apparition connected with it. At the death of John Oxenham, aged 21, in September, 1635, the bird was seen hovering over him for two days before. At the nearly contemporaneous deaths of Thomasine and Rebecca Oxenham, the same appearance took place, such also was the case at the demise of Grace, the grand-mother of John Oxenham, in 1618. A monument was put up, stating these facts, and this monument Howell says he saw preparing in a stone-cutter's yard in Fleet Street. It is, however, no longer in existence.

In the Gentleman's Magazine 1862, is a critical article on the Oxenham bird legend, from which it appears that the apparition was believed to continue attached to the family upwards of a century after any of the above dates. The writer quotes a letter from "J. Short, Middle Temple," dated December 24, 1741; as follows: "I have received an answer from the county in relation to the strange bird which appeared to Mr. Oxenham just before his death, and the account which Dr. Bertie gave to Lord Abingdon of it is certainly true. It first was seen outside the window, and soon afterwards by Mrs. Oxenham in the room, which she mentioned to Mr. Oxenham, and asked him if he knew what bird it was. 'Yes,' says he, 'it has been upon my face and head, and is recorded in history as always appearing to our family before their deaths; but I shall cheat the bird.' Nothing more was said about it, nor was the bird taken notice of from that time; but he died soon afterwards. However odd this affair may appear, it is certainly true; for the account was given of it by Mrs. Oxenham herself but she never mentions it to any one unless particularly asked about it; and as it was seen by several persons at the same time, I can't attribute it to imagination, but must leave it is a phenomenon not yet accounted for."

The ancient Romans had no observance more prominent in their public life than the system of augury, or vaticination from the flight of birds. Might it not have arisen—did it not most probably arise—from some actual instances of warning given by spirits in bird form? There are many such curious enquiries suggested by the facts of modern spiritualism, and individuals possessing ability and taste for historico-philosophical speculation, if they could overcome their unfortunate prejudice on this subject, would find it fruitful and interesting beyond any other now claiming their attention. Instead of being a superstition itself, as they may be disposed to think it, they would find it the explanation and the extinguisher of all superstition.

THE END

INCIDENTS IN MY LIFE

By

D. D. HOME

"Instead of being a superstition itself, as they may
be disposed to think it, they would find it the
explanation and the extinguisher of all
superstition."—Dr. R. Chambers.

SECOND SERIES

First Edition 1872

CONTENTS

PREFACE

About nine years since I presented to the public a volume entitled "Incidents of my Life," the first edition of which was speedily exhausted, and a second was issued in 1863. During the years that have since elapsed, although many attacks have been made upon me, and upon the truths of Spiritualism, its opponents have not succeeded in producing one word of evidence to discredit the truth of my statements, which have remained uucontradicted. Meantime the truths of Spiritualism have become more widely known, and the subject has been forced upon public attention in a remarkable manner. This was especially the case in the years 1867, 1868, in consequence of the suit "Lyon v. Home," which most probably was the indirect cause of the examination into Spiritualism by the Committee of the Dialectical Society, whose report has recently been published. Coincident with and subsequent to their examination, a series of investigations was carried on in my presence, by Lord Adare, now Earl of Dunraven, an account of which has been privately printed; an examination, especially scientific in its character, was also conducted by Professor Crookes, who has published his conclusions in the "Journal of Science."

I now present the public with the second volume of "Incidents of my Life," which continues my narrative to the period of the commencement of the Chancery suit. In the third volume, which I expect to issue in June next, I purpose to complete the account of the suit and give the subsequent investigations above alluded to.

D. D. H.

London, November, 1871.

INTRODUCTION

The following introductory remarks which I here republish, were written for my first volume, by the late Dr. Robert Chambers, of Edinburgh, who also contributed to it the last chapter of the appendix.

Mr. Home's narrative is composed of particulars so much at issue with the ordinary ideas of mankind, that his friends may well feel some apology for it to be necessary. Delicate in health, extremely, sensitive in spirit, of gentle and uncombative nature, coming forward with his narration for no conceivable end but to propagate a knowledge of what he regards as important truths, it seems but right that he should be spared as much as possible of the sceptical derision which such novelties are sure in greater or less degree to evoke. Hence the present introductory remarks.

Whatever be the preconceptions of the reader regarding Mr. Home, he will scarcely fail, after reading this volume, to acknowledge that the author writes as a man thoroughly in earnest, and who has himself no doubts of the phenomena which attend him. He tells how these phenomena commenced in his childhood, how they have been with him ever since, except during a few brief intervals; how, while bringing him public notice and some valuable friendships, they have been in some respects an inconvenience and a misfortune, and betoken conditions that do not promise length of days; all this with an unargumentative simplicity that speaks strongly of at least sincere conviction on his own part. He sustains the character of the Mystic Sensitive throughout his narration, as he has done throughout the first thirty years of his actual life, without falter or hesitation; what he was at the first he is now. It is for those who would attribute all to imposture, to show how a fictitious character can be so perfectly and so enduringly maintained.

It is also to be remarked that the facts of Mr. Home's life do not rest on his own averments alone. Their objective reality and their freedom from delusion and imposture, are certified by an immense number of persons, who are here indicated by name or otherwise. Some of these persons, and others who remain uncited, are of a character to form a strong guarantee for the truth of anything to which they might testify. It is often, indeed, remarked, as a marvel of a very suggestive kind in this our highly intellectual age, that men of knowledge and reflection, of whom so much better things might be expected, are found so weak as to be imposed upon by such transparent deception, and so foolish as to come forward and bear witness in its behalf. But of course this is not reasoning; it is only begging the question. The remark might be answered by another: it is a marvel of a highly suggestive nature, that men of critical judgment should be so far imposed upon by their self-esteem, that they can calmly set down a number of men reputedly as judicious as themselves, and whose judgment they acknowledge, as capable of seeing and hearing that which is not, and never appear to suspect that these persons have possibly some real grounds for the faith that is in them. A little modesty would evidently go a great way to solve the difficulty which the incredulous profess to feel on this point. If they would go a little farther, and so far yield to the behests of their favourite philosophy as to inquire before pronouncing, it might so chance that the position of a believer in these phenomena would become more intelligible to them. So at least it has already happened with a vast number of persons, equally positive at starting that the whole was a delusion; and we are entitled to assume that what has been, may be again. Nay, the value of the testimony in question in a great measure arises from the very fact, that it has been extorted from the reluctant convictions of a multitude of persons, at one time wholly scornful and incredulous regarding the alleged facts.

It will be rather startling, but yet it may be very plausibly urged, that the phenomena of Mr. Home's mediumship are not opposed to the experience of mankind. On the contrary, facts of this kind have been reported as occurring in all ages; nor is it more than two centuries since they began to be doubted. Even during the two centuries of partial scepticism, they have continued to be reported as happening not less frequently than before. It may be replied, this sceptical voice has been the voice of wisdom and truth, for the first time heard in the world. Is it really so? Is it not rather a dictum expressive only of an intellectual habit—the result of the kind of studies during that time chiefly predominant? Is it not that, in an exclusive and overmastering devotion to material philosophy, men have fallen out of the habit of considering the spiritual part of the world, retaining little more than a nominal faith even in those spiritual things which their religious creed avouches? Clearly the mere fact of two centuries of partial scepticism does not go for much. But then this enlightened spirit has penetrated the mystery in so many cases, and shown it to be based in nothing but vulgar deception. Has it really done so? Has it not simply flattered itself with illusive compliments to its own penetration? One noted instance of a person professedly affected as Mr. Home has been, was Anne Parsons, a little girl living in Cock Lane, in the City of London, in 1762. If there is any case in which detection of imposture is triumphantly and unchallengedly assumed, it is that of the famous Cock Lane Ghost. Mark the facts of the detection. Knockings and scratchings were for a couple of years heard in connection with little Anne Parsons, and at length a mode of conversation with the unseen agent was hit upon. The so-called ghost averred that a woman who recently lived in Parsons' house, and was since dead, had been murdered by her quasi-husband, a Mr. Kent. It was what Mr. Home would have called a lying spirit. The girl being taken to the house of Mr. Alrich, a clergyman, a party was formed to put to the test a promise of the "ghost" that it would knock upon the coffin of the deceased in a vault of St. John's, Clerkenwell, at a certain hour in the evening. No knocks occurred—lying spirit again. Then came the grand stroke in the detection. The girl was taken into a stranger's house, put into a bed hung clear of the floor, and watched for two nights, during which no noises were heard. A result, which might be owing merely to the deranged conditions, was held by the sapient committee of investigation as clear proof of imposture but they were yet to have evidence more positive. Having become impatient with the child, they told her on the third night, that if the knockings were not heard that night, she and her parents would be taken to Newgate! Under this threat, the child took a board into bed with her, was seen to do so, (why was such a thing never seen before?) and soon sounds admitted to be different from what happened before, were heard. The bed was then searched, the board found, and the girl proclaimed as a proved impostor. In this clumsy, foolish, and utterly unsatisfactory manner, was the Cock Lane Ghost "detected." On no other grounds has the fallacy of the case become the proverb it now is. Now, if such be the easy terms on which scepticism assumes its greatest triumphs, what importance are we to attach to its pronouncements on this subject in instances less important, and where it has put forth (as is the general case) less of its strength? Are they worth the air they cost to make them audible?

There is surely, after all, nothing like a serious improbability in the spiritual phenomena. We, every hour of our lives, have occasion to acknowledge that there is a spirit, an immortal something, in man; we equally believe that this spirit, which does such wonderful things on earth, will survive in some other sphere of existence, and not in a wholly inactive state. Is there anything *à priori* unlikely in the idea that the spirit, which parts with so much that is dear to it here, may linger in the scenes of its earthly pilgrimage, and desire to hold intercourse with those remaining behind? On the contrary, it seems rather likely that the "animula vagula, blandula," will hover about its old loves, and where conditions permit or are favourable, will contrive to make itself again seen or at least heard. It may be a mere effort of the original social nature; or it may result from a benevolent anxiety for the welfare of individuals—to inform, to guide, and protect them; it may be a needful part of the frame of things in which humanity is established on earth—something required to keep us in mind of that world beyond the screen, out of which we have come, and to which we are to return. It has often, indeed, been urged that the spiritual phenomena generally are of a frivolous and useless character, doing little more than show that Spiritualism is a truth. But spiritualists say, on the other hand, that experimenters generally set about their business in a frivolous spirit, and only get communications from shades of their own character. It will be found that, in the case of Mr. Home, who is a man of a religious turn of mind, pure-hearted and unworldly, the phenomena are of an elevated character, tending to heal sickness, to smooth away sorrow, and to chasten and exalt the minds of the living. There is, indeed, every reason to believe that if spiritual communications were now sought in a suitable frame of mind, results in the highest style of sanctitude, rivalling those of the most famous devotees, might be obtained. Already, Spiritualism, conducted as it usually is, has had a prodigious effect throughout America, and partly in the Old World also, in redeeming multitudes from hardened atheism and materialism, proving to them, by the positive demonstration which their cast of mind requires, that there is another world—that there is a non-arterial form of humanity—and that many miraculous things which they have hitherto scoffed at, are true.

There remains a great stumbling-block to many, in the manner in which the communications are most frequently made. It seems below the dignity of a disembodied spirit to announce itself and speak by little pulsatory noises on a table or wainscot. It might, however, be asked if it be not a mere prejudice which leads us to expect that the spirit, on being disembodied, suddenly, and of necessity, experiences a great exaltation. Take the bulk of mankind as they are, and can we really say that there is anything derogatory to them in the supposition that, in any circumstances, they would talk by noise-signals? We must, moreover, remember that we know nothing of the conditions under which spirits can communicate. This may be the most readily available mode in most instances. Beyond doubt, in certain circumstances of difficulty, the most exalted of living persons might be glad to resort to such a mode of telegraphy. In 1823, Signor Andryane, the agent of an Italian conspiracy against Austria, was thrown into the prisons of the police at Milan. He tells us, in his very interesting Memoirs, how, being desirous of communicating with the inmate of an adjoining cell, he tapped gently on the wall, and after some time had his signal answered. "One, two, three—a pause, a, b, c,—it was c. Still listening,—one, two, three, four,—

eight blows,—it was h; c. h. Slowly, but distinctly, nine blows were given: this must mean the letter i, &c." After some difficulties, these two unfortunates succeeded in forming a system of communication, in the highest degree useful and consolatory to them, by raps on the wall, expressive of letters of the Italian alphabet (See, "Memoirs of Alexander Andryane," translated by Ferdinando Prandi, 2 vols. Second Edition. Newby. London, 1848.) being precisely the mode of communication so largely (though not exclusively) adopted by the spirits—the favourite subject of ridicule to those who are so unfortunate as to take only a superficial view of this subject, or so unfair as to select what, in their ignorance, they consider as the weakest point. If the disembodied find a sort of wall interposed between them and the living world with which they desire to communicate, what can be more natural than to resort to the expedient which was embraced in analogous circumstances by these two living prisoners? Short of the use of actual language written or spoken, what better possible mode of communication can be suggested?

There are two points of view in which Mr. Home's publication of his experiences appears entitled to praise as well as sympathy. Regard it simply as a curious case in pathology—for himself to describe it in detail may be considered as a useful service to mankind, just as it would be considered useful to us to obtain the self-portraiture of any other peculiar case of nervous derangement. As already stated, such cases are far from being uncommon; but the intelligence and probity required to apprehend their character truly, and describe it exactly, is rare. To the psycho-pathologist, accordingly, if he can get over the disposition to sneer and laugh, and will condescend to meet a man as honest as himself on his own grounds, this detail may serve to advance an important scientific purpose. Even more valuable is the instruction to be derived from it by the moralist and the philosophical historian. The past is full of such phenomena. Wrongly apprehended in the first place by their recipients, they have been made the bases of juggling arts; of childish mythologies; of superstitious religions; and the means of affecting individuals and multitudes to most mischievous and illogical conclusions in a thousand different ways. Even at the present day, accepted as confirmations of sundry doctrines and pretensions, they become the means of misleading a vast number of well-intending people. While philosophy refuses to see them in their true light, it can do nothing to abate or prevent the evil in question, for the victim knows too well that the phenomena are not, as philosophy would inculcate, unreal. Let philosophy see them as they are—a part of the universal frame of things, liable like everything else to law, and having a real bearing on the good and evil fortunes of mankind and the weakest would henceforth be safe from all false conclusions to be deduced from them. To this good end the "candid reader" may find Mr. Home's autobiography a valuable contribution.

As an evidence of the attention of Mr. R. Chambers having been turned to this subject at an early period, I insert the following note written by him in 1855, which shows that it was not upon a short or slight acquaintance with me that he wrote the above introduction.

"Edinburgh, July 30, 1855.

"DEAR MRS. DE MORGAN,

"I return my warmest thanks for your truly obliging attention in sending me these additional notices. I have delayed writing on the subject for two or three days, that I might be able to say your wish regarding at least Professor Gregory, had been fulfilled. I have seen him this evening, and read your letter to him and Mrs. Gregory. It is scarcely necessary to say that they feel deeply interested by your notes, forming as they do such satisfactory proofs.

"Professor and Mrs. Gregory had not as yet heard of Mr. Hume and his singular phenomena, and they are much interested about him. As they are to set out on Thursday for a German spa (on account of Mrs. Gregory's health), I have recommended them to try to see Hume as they pass through London. They are willing, but do not know how to proceed. At my suggestion, they are inclined to wait upon you on Friday at 12 o'clock, to see if you can give them any information on the subject, and also to converse with you about your own domestic marvels. I have no doubt you will be glad to see this most amiable and worthy professor and his lady, if it be at all convenient to you. I believe they will stay at the Euston Square Hotel; so, if you be engaged, you may give them a few lines to say so.

"There is only one other person in Scotland to whom I care to communicate these singular phenomena—a Miss Douglas, niece of the late General Sir Neil Douglas, our commander-in-chief. With ordinary people, I scarcely can open my mouth on such subjects.

"I beg to be kindly remembered to Mr. de Morgan, and am,
        "Dear Mrs. de Morgan,
                "Yours very respectfully,
                        "R. CHAMBERS.
"This letter requires no reply."

The following, which was written to me with respect to materials for my book, speaks for itself, as well as that which follows.

'1, Doune Terrace, Edinburgh.
Dec. 22, 1859.

"MY DEAR SIR,

"I have duly received your letter of Monday, and after some little pottering, have found a book in my library which gives the writings of Aubrey, of Martin, and of Theophilus Nisalenus, on second sight, all in one—a great conveniency; so I dispatch it to you to-day by post. Thus, with Fraser's treatise formerly sent, you are now pretty complete as to Scottish materials for your proposed book. I may remark that this volume is one of a set now scarce, and therefore I hope you will excuse me asking you to take unusual care of it.

"It is interesting to hear of your interview with the venerable Lyndhurst. I hope you will be able this winter to give a few sittings to such persons and others, without injury to your health. What I have had to tell to Miss Douglas, Miss Catherine Sinclair, and Mrs. Gregory, since I came home, has interested them deeply, and they all hope that you will be in Edinburgh next year.

"Mrs. C. is much gratified to receive the kind message from your wife, and desires me to send her kind regards in return. With all good wishes, I am,

"My dear Sir,
"Yours very faithfully,
"R. CHAMBERS.

"My compliments to Mr. Cox, if you please."

"August 1, 1860.

"DEAR MR. HUME,

"The appearance of the article 'Stranger than Fiction,' in the 'Cornhill Magazine,' tempted me to trouble you with a few lines, merely to congratulate you on the good effect that may be anticipated in behalf of your personal reputation in this country. I was, I must own, scarcely prepared for so strong a demonstration from a high class periodical in favour of the subject that is stranger than fiction. So I am the more pleased to see it, and the more gratified on your account.

"I was very unlucky in the detention of my dear and valued friend, Mr. Owen, (Mr. Robert Dale Owen, author of "Footfalls on the Boundary of another World.") till after I had left town: but he is promising to be here about the 4th of this month, and Miss Douglas and I are looking forward with great pleasure to his visit. What of your proposed visit to Scotland?

"I am in expectation of being in London for some time after the autumn, when I may hope to see you and Mrs. Hume. Please, my kind compliments to her, and believe me, with all good wishes,

"Yours very sincerely,

"R. CHAMBERS.

"My ordinary address continues to be 1, Doune Terrace."

A letter from Dr. R. Chambers, to Mrs. S. C. Hall, dated Nov. 1, 1866, contains the following passage in speaking of an apparent kindness that had been bestowed on me. "Such is my opinion of him that not only do I think him deserving of it, but that he will make a good use of it. We may, I think, trust to see him propagating spiritualism from the independent point he has reached, with power only bounded by the needful regard to his health."

I append here extracts from a little brochure, by Miss Douglas, the lady who is referred to in each of the foregoing letters, with reference to which Dr. R. Chambers wrote—"These twenty-four pages, in my opinion, contain the germ of the greatest discovery, and the greatest revolution of human thought that any age of the world has witnessed."

It may indeed be conceded that on the inquiry into a future state of existence no science has yet thrown the smallest light—that natural theology has made little advance since the dawn of civilization; but it may be asked whether the time which has elapsed since that period be not too brief to compel us to despair of ultimately attaining to any knowledge of our future destinies, too brief to warrant the conclusion of the inapplicability to man's highest quests of those methods which have guided him to truth in other paths of inquiry. The idea is now arising that the cause of the undiminished darkness overhanging all that relates to a state of existence after this life, may be that the right track has never yet been entered on, that the facts really affording in this direction materials for induction have hitherto been disregarded, that they nevertheless abound, that a higher enlightenment will cause attention to be turned to them and reveal their profound significance. From sedulous observation of the spiritual phenomena in their multiform aspects, from study of the more subtle and recondite physical laws brought to bear on those phenomena, will, there is reason to believe, emerge proof of the existence within the order of nature of forces forming a link and means of intercourse between this sphere of existence and the one immediately above, through which proof may be established of the immortality of the soul. From that very quarter now most hostile to the doctrine of spiritualism may thus come demonstration of its truth: all unconsciously Science herself, it may be, has led the way to the confines of another world; ere long, we may hope, will she unbar the portals through which light from that world has hitherto struggled with fitful and refracted rays.

As to those minds disposed to make light of the religious sentiment, minds which, despite the enormous influence it has ever exercised over human affairs, despite the enduring institutions to which it has given birth, despite its universality, the outward signs of which in every land so forcibly strike the eye, from the dome which is the boast of the Eternal City, from the glittering minarets of Stamboul, from the fallen temples of a bygone world, to the village spire and to the rude altar of uncivilized man, still see in that sentiment but a weakness of human nature—to those minds proof may be afforded that it is an essential element of man's mental constitution, often indeed misled, but tending still towards truth, having its real, its fit, its correlative objects beyond this world; and thus may the general result be that conflicting sects and schools of religious opinion, guided by one common and ever-increasing light, may by degrees lay aside their differences, and unite in one harmonious and progressive movement.

Those to whom such views may appear visionary are entreated to examine the grounds on which they rest: investigation seriously and perseveringly conducted can hardly fail to convince reflecting minds of at all events the *reality* of the phenomena called spiritual, to prove to them (in the words of a distinguished mathematician) "that they are things which cannot be taken by a rational being to be capable of explanation by imposture, coincidence, or mistake."

Among the new mysteries into which enquiry has been made, the researches of Baron Reichenbach cannot fail to strike the student of spiritual phenomena; his experiments on the psycho—physico action of crystals—of the force, that is to say, emanating from them, termed Odyle, on sensitive persons, have suggested the idea that the proneness to second sight or spontaneous clairvoyance in certain regions, in the western Highlands of Scotland for instance, may be owing to the highly crystalline formation there prevailing of the rocks, from which consequently unusually large quantities of the odylic force must be emitted.

One cause of incredulity as to manifestations from another world, is the view (generally however much misrepresented) to which they lead of the future state; such revelations concerning it as we have from that source are no doubt at variance with received ideas, indicating as they do, a state similar in kind to this present life, and only a step higher in an ascending series of existences, one into which we carry our human nature, and in which progress is but gradual. This view, however little in accordance with the general conception of life hereafter, derives nevertheless support from analogy, harmonising as it does with those views of physical progress opened up by geology, and by the study of organic forms from primeval times. It is agreed, as well by those who maintain that progress to be the result of distinct acts of Omnipotence, as by those who believe in a progressive principle imparted *ab origine* to the works of creation, that where in their series breaks were once supposed to occur, closer inspection has discovered links, carrying on the chain by minute degrees, to borrow the fine imagery of a distinguished naturalist "we learn from the past history of our globe that Nature has advanced with slow and stately steps, guided by the archetypal light, amidst the wreck of worlds, from the first embodiment of the vertebrate idea under its old ichthyic vestment, until it became arrayed in the glorious garb of the form of man."

The law of gradual progress thus poetically set forth by Professor Owen, and which we behold stamped through every part of this visible sphere, may well be extended to the invisible, may well exist for the individual as for the species nor would it be less in accordance with analogy to infer that the beginning only of such progress would be slow, that the further the advance, the more ethereal the surroundings the more facile and accelerated it would become.

The common-place character of a large portion of the spirit-communications, the extravagant and turgid character of some, cease to perplex when we come to view them as proceeding from beings lately ordinary dwellers upon earth, and retaining still their earthly dispositions and ideas. True, the difficulty remains as to why some small portion at least of these communications should not bear the impress of transcendent wisdom and genius the absence from them of anything equalling, far less surpassing the highest products of the human mind, argues, it must be admitted, some hindrance to intercourse with spiritual beings of an exalted order; may we not hope to overcome it? Meantime, as a necessary consequence of the unprogressed condition of the beings from whom a large portion of the communications proceeds, many of these do but confirm the members of each sect in their own views, while some have given rise to doctrines (such as in France, that of re-incarnation) from which Spiritualists as a body recoil. We must not indeed shrink from the admission that intercourse with the invisible world has been the origin of all superstitions, and all erroneous theologies; that to it even may be due their persistence for a while after they cease to harmonise with the general spirit of the society over which they once held dominion.

To the reader familiar with spiritual phenomena it is evident even from the sneering narrative of Gibbon, that the apostacy of Julian, and his intense enthusiasm in the cause of the fallen faith, was in truth due to communication with the invisible world; spirits of departed pagans still clinging to their earthly creed, seem to have impressed him powerfully, visiting him, and conversing with him in the forms of the Olympian Gods; "we may learn," says Gibbon, "from his faithful friend the orator Libanius, that he lived in a perpetual intercourse with the gods and goddesses, that they descended upon earth to enjoy the conversation of their favourite hero, that they gently interrupted his slumbers by touching his hand or his hair, that they warned him of every impending danger, and conducted him by their infallible wisdom in every action of his life."

That so much that is erroneous should have been allowed to proceed from spiritual sources on the subject of the highest import, is indeed an enigma; is it however more than one among the enigmas which in our present state of knowledge appear as insolvable as they are painful, when we survey the system in which we have our being?

The claim to be set off against the admissions which have been made, is that every doctrine which has emanated from the spirit world, and has been accepted by any considerable portion of mankind, has either established a moral code where none had previously existed, or has been an improvement on the one it superseded.

If we must not shut our eyes to the dangers of communication with another sphere, on the other hand we may feel confident that with the progress of knowledge they will pass away; the amount of light which has already been thrown on the nature of spiritual communications precludes their being received henceforth with unquestioning faith, precludes therefore the risk of their giving rise to new forms of religious error; the general characteristic moreover of the higher spiritual communications of the present day is the absence of dogmatic teaching, and the assertion that it is only as we advance in virtue and in the deeper paths of knowledge that we can attain to further light in the science of things divine—to any criterion as to truth in the interpretation of revealed doctrine.

If the idea of a future life only gradually progressive, and of which the first phase will be similar in kind to life here below, does not give rise to the same emotions which in rapt moments may fill the soul in anticipation of perfect rest and felicity after the ills of earth; on the other hand it is a view more fitted perhaps to give steady every-day support, to afford until the last hour an incentive to exertion, to divest that hour of all its terrors.

That "the better world," should in general excite so little ardour of aspiration, and be so unwillingly drawn near to, even in advanced years, seems a strange contradiction in human nature; may not the cause lie to one extent in the nature of the pictures usually, so far as they go, presented of that world? The little relating to it that falls from the pulpit, is but shadowy and chill, based upon some few indefinite scriptural expressions, and reflecting generally the views of that class of minds in which earthly aims and joys, if not more or less associated with sin, are at all events considered incompatible with the dignity and purity of life beyond the grave.

Then again, how full of gloom is the language commonly used with respect to death; such expressions as the narrow home, the long sleep, implying as they do an intermediate state of indefinite duration, of nothingness, offer the very reverse of the picture which presents itself to the disciple of the new doctrine in connection with departure from this world; like the traveller bound to some fair region yet unknown, and

"Full of wonder, full of hope as he,"

he looks forward to the new scene as one immediately to be entered into, as one adapted to his present nature—a higher phase of the eternal life begun on earth; for there, he believes, do all human faculties find wider scope in a system purer, more refined, more plastic to progressive force, more in harmony with the ideal; there, he believes, does the Spirit of Truth guide her followers with a brighter torch, the Spirit of Beauty mould all things nearer to the archetypal forms; there shall we taste in higher perfection all that here fires or charms the mind; there the tender ties and sweet affections of our nature, not losing their special character will become only deeper and more intense; there from the supreme source will a more radiant light stream down.

The frame of mind to which Spiritualism leads is well fitted to enable us to remain calm under the attacks of its opponents; to smile patiently while sensible people, in entire ignorance of the subject, pronounce it imposture, while religious people condemn it as impious, and likewise while some silver-tongued sciolist utters to a tittering and applauding audience ridicule of nature's deepest and most wondrous laws.

Again we are supported when we remember that the new doctrine is but undergoing what every great new idea, what every great discovery, has had to undergo ere it triumphed—scorn, derision, misrepresentation; error is persistive, prejudice hard to be overcome, the boast of Caesar has never been for Truth.

The non-arbitrary character of the spiritual phenomena, their subjection to law, have in these pages been much urged; and it may indeed be affirmed that independently of spiritual declarations there is no uncertain ground for the inference that they are part of the order of Nature, for as all scientific research concurs in proving the accidental or anomalous to have no existence in the visible universe, so, guided by analogy, may we conclude that the same principle of order is extended to that more mysterious region whence these phenomena proceed; and intimately connected as they obviously are with subtle physical and physiological conditions belonging to this sphere, of a nature not more apparently insolvable than other problems which have received solution, argument still strictly inductive warrants also the conclusion that they are not beyond the boundary of investigation, and that their laws will be ultimately disclosed.

In a striking passage of his Essays the late Mr. Baden Powell seems to glance at the spiritual manifestations then just beginning to attract attention. In the present state of science, he remarks, "of all subjects that on which we know least is perhaps the connexion of our bodily and mental nature, the action of the one on the other, and all the vast range of sensations, sympathies, and influences, in which those affections are displayed, and of which we have sometimes such extraordinary manifestations in peculiar states of excited cerebral or nervous action, somnambulism, spectral impressions, the phenomena of suspended animation, double consciousness, and the like. In such cases science has not yet advanced to any generalisations; results only are presented which have not as yet been traced to laws; yet no inductive inquirer for a moment doubts that these classes of phenomena are all really connected by some great principle of order."

"If, then, *some peculiar manifestations* should appear of a more extraordinary character, still less apparently reducible to any known principles, it could not be doubted by any philosophic mind that they were in reality harmonious and conspiring parts of some higher series of causes as yet undiscovered. The most formidable outstanding apparent anomalies will, at some future time, undoubtedly be found to merge in great and harmonious laws, the connexion will be fully made out, and the claims of order, continuity, and analogy, eventually vindicated." (Essay on the Spirit of the Inductive Philosophy, p. 109.) As to the reality of the data on which these speculations rest, each must examine, and judge for himself.

CHAPTER I

On the appearance of incidents of my life, I had no reason to complain of the neglect of the press, for several journals fell foul of me with commendable speed. I had been thoroughly prepared for abuse from the press generally, and in several instances was by no means disappointed. I have however to thank some of those who reviewed my book, for the fair and candid tone in which they treated the subject. "The Spectator," "The Times," and the "Morning Herald" call for special mention in this respect.

I here give extracts from several of these reviews:—

The following is extracted from a review in the "Parthenon."

"The stereotyped form of beginning these narratives seems to run thus (we quote from Mr. Home's book):— 'One evening, as we were seated at the table, the spirits requested that the candles should be extinguished,' or, 'The spirits then gave out, Put out the lights,' which being done, the incantations begin. Suspicious, too, are the circumstances that there is (*sic*) almost invariably a hand-bell and an accordion concerned, the spirits seemingly being very partial to jingle one and sound the other, or rather, as we believe, such portable instruments being easily manipulated by Mr. Home. Now if the spirit-mediums would make the big bell of St. Paul's ring out, or play the large organ beneath the dome, we should believe in them; but a small hand-bell tinkled and an accordion played upon will not convert us. It is indeed most clear that Mr. Home and his spirit-medium fraternity are in the most favourable possible conditions to deceive their audience. To the question why the effects are not easily obtained above board (meaning the table) at a first sitting, whereas they are most easily obtained when habituated circles are present, Mr. Home answers, 'that scepticism mars the forces at work, that the spirits accomplish what they do through our life-sphere or atmosphere which is permeated by our wills, and if the will be contrary, the sphere is unfit for being operated upon.' Precisely so; the habituated are those who feel that—

> 'The pleasure surely is as great
> Of being cheated as to cheat,'

and are thus easily imposed upon; so easily, indeed, that we question much whether the dark room even is necessary. Now we would ask in the name of common sense, what there is in these manifestations one whit more extraordinary than the performance of famous jugglers, who, by the way, juggle in broad daylight, and tell you frankly that they intend to cheat your senses, and do so despite all your power to find out their tricks. We observe that Mr. Home is very angry with Lord Brougham and Sir David Brewster, because, after certain performances by Mr. Home at Cox's Hotel in Jermyn Street, both his Lordship and Sir David were sceptical. Sir David declares that neither he nor Lord Brougham were allowed to look under the table at which they were seated; to which Mr. Home illogically replies, 'If Mr. Cox allowed me to conceal machinery under the drapery of his table, noblemen and gentlemen whom I have visited in every country must have allowed me to do the same thing.'"

To this last remark I reply that the reviewer stops short in his quotation, for I go on to say that "I have for years met, and still meet every day with men of the highest attainments in the arts and sciences who have carefully examined, and have not rested satisfied with conjectures either as to the table, or the machinery alleged to be concealed about my person." I also challenge the writer of the review to point out in my book the passage which he marks as a quotation beginning "that scepticism mars," &c. or to produce any evidence that I ever made each an answer to account for the absence of manifestations. Many remarkable phenomena have been witnessed in my presence by sceptics, and at their "first sitting."

The "Saturday Review," March 21, 1863, dwelt principally on the small number of witnesses, and in mentioning the *séance* at which Lord Brougham and Sir David Brewster were present, said "Lord Brougham has preserved inflexible silence on the subject. Sir David Brewster has openly charged fraud on the whole affair. Mr. Trollope's testimony is only to his belief in Mr. Home's good faith." The "Saturday Review" omits to notice Mr. Trollope's testimony to the facts not only that a large table was moved about in an extraordinary manner, but that while it was being moved about, Sir David looked under it and saw it moving. After endeavouring to destroy the credibility of all the other witnesses, the "Saturday Review" thus sums up, determined to accept no testimony but that of eleven members of one or other of the three learned professions.

"What is wanted, in such a case as that of Mr. Home's alleged prodigies, is the testimony of unprejudiced or adverse witnesses. It is of the first importance in testing any prodigy that the persons by whom, the witnesses before whom, and the circumstances under which, the extraordinary events occurred, should be beyond suspicion. Mr. Home is, according to his own account and from the testimony of his own book, a weak, credulous, half-educated, fanatical person, born, bred, and educated in wonderful stories, who has lived from his earliest years in a whole atmosphere and mirage of dreaming. The witnesses, few in number and almost entirely unknown, are much in the same condition. Mystics, Theosophists, Mesmerists, Swedenborgians—fanatics of one sort or other, educated and living in an excited and unnatural state of the spiritual faculties—they are representatives of a class coeval with the existence of the human mind, in which a certain part of the mental constitution is in a diseased state, and of which "spiritualism in all ages," that is, the Stellings, the Böhmes, the Paracelsuses, the Guyons, the Hauffes, the Swedenborgs, are the natural result. And as to the circumstances under which the phenomena occurred, we must say that an event is not likely to receive credence when its witnesses are for the most part anonymous writers in magazines, when it is done in a chamber with extinguished lights, and under circumstances purposely arranged to disturb the judgment, and only in the presence of favourable witnesses. The alleged facts have not as yet been sufficiently examined and tested. When the spiritualists are able to produce the testimony of eleven men of high reputation and clear judgment—say of eleven Judges, or eleven Q. C.'s, or eleven Fellows of the College of Physicians, or even of eleven Bishops—pronouncing, after a full and fair investigation, conducted openly and in broad daylight, that they have seen Mr. Home suspended in mid-air, 'a man between ten and eleven stone in weight floating about the room for many minutes,' to use Dr. Gully's explicit language, we should have something else to say. At present—with all due respect to Dr. Gully and to the other ten witnesses, and without charging him or Mr. Home either, with conscious fraud, imposture, or trickery of any sort, and also not denying that such imposture may exist—we must say that whatever the testimony hitherto produced is worth, it is palpably insufficient. The evidence, such as it is, is deficient in quality and quantity; and it comes before us with an antecedent taint. It does not meet the recognised tests of even a common, still less of an exceptional, fact. We do not charge Mr. Home with imposture. This is not our argument. But we do say that alleged miracles, such as many of those of Pagan origin, of the mediaeval church, and of the Abbé Paris—to take a very familiar case—are better authenticated than those of Mr. Home, or at least are as well authenticated, though they are now known to be fictitious, partly arising from delusion, partly from conscious imposture. The spiritualists seem to be aware of the stress of this argument, and they answer it by an attempt to show—which, if anything, is the result of Mr. Howitt's book— that all these transactions are true; and their adoption of the Cock Lane Ghost is a remarkable instance of the difficulty which they feel. But does not this line of argument prove rather too much? To hint that there has never been a false miracle is at least as monstrous as Home's doctrine that any miracle is impossible."

This cool way of characterizing Mr. Cox, Mr. Coleman, Dr. Wilkinson, Mr. Pears, Mr. Crawford, Mr. Mason, Dr. Gully, Mr. Jones, Mr. Hutchison, and Mr. and Mrs. Howitt as "fanatics of one sort or other," on no other evidence than that of their believing in the reality of the manifestations is peculiarly characteristic of the "Saturday Review." I cannot be surprised at their objecting to my having in so many cases yielded to the desire of the witnesses to remain incognito, by giving only their initials. Their full names have been in general made known to all who have made private inquiries, and the veil under which they remain in my book is transparent to most of those who take such interest in the subject as to investigate. The Reviewer, moreover, wholly ignores several names which were given in full in the book.

Complaining of "anonymous witnesses," "The Saturday Review" gives an example of the initials made use of:—

"Dr. J. J. G. Wilkinson also testifies, both in this volume and in the 'Spiritual Magazine,' to a vast array of manifestations. But as to what occurred in England at Mr. Home's first visit to this country, these three names viz. Mr. Cox, Mr. Coleman, and Dr. Wilkinson, and these alone—are produced by Mr. Home. At Florence we admit that Countess O____ is said by Mr. Home to have seen some very marvellous things; but with Countess O____, or any other anonymous witness, we have no concern. We dismiss Count B____, and Count de K____, and Abbé C____, Countess L____, Princess de B____, and Miss E____, and all the other initials and anonymous witnesses. Testimony like this is simply an insult to the court.

"After another visit to the Continent, in November 1861, Mr. Home returned to England, and his manifestations are attested by 'an esteemed friend' Mr. Jones, of Basinghall Street, Mr. Hutchinson, of the Stock Exchange, 'a Plain Man,' Mr. Cox, and Mr. Wilkinson, Mr. and Mrs. Howitt, 'Mrs. P____ in the Regent's Park,' and Mrs. S____.'— And these are all. It comes then to this—that 'the immense number of persons indicated by name or otherwise,' who bear personal testimony to the spirit manifestations in England, are in almost every case anonymous, or indicated only by initials.

I have much pleasure in giving the names in full, and can assure my worthy critic, that it was only from a feeling of delicacy I refrained from giving the names at once. 'The Countess O____ is the Countess Antoinette Orsini, nee Countess Orloff. The Count B____, is the Count de Beaumont, of No. 12, Rue Royale. The Count de K____, there are in fact two Counts de K., being the Counts Alexander and Waldimir de Komar. The Abbé C____, is the Abbé Deguery of the Madeleine, who was murdered by the Communists this year. The Princess de B____ is the Princess de Beaurean, *née* Countess de Komar. Miss E____, is Miss Ellice. Mrs. P____ is Mrs. Cranford Parks, of No. 7, Cornwall Terrace, Regent's Park. Mrs. S____, is Mrs. Henry Senior, sister-in-law of the late Nassau Senior.

The writer says: "Possibly Mr. Home may deny the possibility of a miracle, but this in quite another sense from another famous Mr. Hume, or Home, who also denied the possibility of miracles. The present Mr. Home may say that all this is in accordance with natural laws, if we only knew the whole extent of nature and nature's laws. It is only a natural power co-ordinate with that of gravitation, which, in his case, suspends the law of gravitation. That is to say, there is no miracle in the case, because it is equally a law of nature that heavy bodies should, and should not, fall to the ground. But this is, of course, mere trifling. For all practical purposes, the events accredited by the testimony of the eleven witnesses are miracles. They are things contrary to all known, and firm, and unaltered experience, and the very nature of the facts, whether we choose to call them miracles or not, is such that the usual criteria of miracles may be applied to them. We admit with the opponents of Hume—the Scotch Hume, not the present American Home."

No one could, surely, in the face of this, deny that the writer in the "Saturday Review," at least has the power of miracle-working. I am changed by his magic and truthful pen into an "American." The first line of the first chapter of my book begins thus: "I was born near Edinburgh." I then proceed to state that I went to America when I was about nine years old. It might perhaps be well to tell the "Saturday Review," that Edinburgh is a goodly sized city of Scotland, and that I am a Scotchman.

The "Athenæum," March 14th, 1863, commenced by attacking the anonymous character of the preface as follows:

"This impudent and foolish book criticises itself. An introduction, professing to be 'written by a friend,' presents Mr. Home as 'delicate in health, extremely sensitive in spirit, coming forward with his narration for no conceivable end but to propagate a knowledge of what he regards as important truths; . . . . a man of a religious turn of mind, pure-hearted and unworldly'—in fact, as a person who is no fit object for the jests of railing Rabshakehs! Mr. Home throughout his book endorses this sweet and saintly character of himself and of his proceedings very much after the fashion of Wandering Willie in Scott's

'Redgauntlet,' who modestly capped the panegyrics of the notorious little knave Benjie by adding, 'All is true that the little boy says'! But we do not know the name of the mystic's 'little boy.' He is only Mr. Home's friend. Mr. Home answers for him, and he answers for Mr. Home: that is all we learn."

This attack I have now answered by reprinting this preface, with the name of its author, the late gifted Dr. Robert Chambers. The Reviewer thus disposes summarily of the evidence:

"Three points may be stated as necessary to be taken in conjunction, even by those disposed to admit the existence of a class of supernatural mediators, and who may wish to judge how far Mr. Home is a sincere and self-deluded member of such priesthood, how far the reverse. First, it has been again and again urged that persons who trafficked in awful mysteries like these, being commissioned from on high, were at once vulgarized, deteriorated, handed over to the counsels of evil spirits, if they spoke to the dead, or made the dead speak, or called them or any part of them into visible presence for lucre. When one wretched charlatan after another has been unmasked, the pure have stood sorrowfully aloof, and repudiated all fellowship with one who tampered with his birthright for a mess of pottage. 'Medium' after 'medium,' detected in imposture, has been anathematized or excused as having handed himself over to the devil by the base act of sale and barter of his gift. Now Mr. Home, as Mr. Howitt, indeed, has already told us, has gained a competence by his ghastly shows. Rings, purses (not empty) other presents more solid than praise have been showered on him as thickly as the slippers with which devout ladies glorify their dear favourite clergyman. Secondly, the Romish Church has always held practices such as those by which Mr. Home has thriven to be sinful, heretical, and tending to damnation. Those who remember this canon are invited to consider how Mr. Home, after being converted from Congregationalism to Roman Catholicism, quarrelled with the sincere and stern Père Ravignan, who insisted on his desisting from such unauthorized practices; also how he gave up his next confessor, who, it was hoped, might be more lenient to one who was driving so brisk and profitable a trade, and amusing so many great people, and crowned heads. So that Mr. Home floats strangely, not in the air alone, but between the two stools of authority and private judgment. Thirdly, the witnesses brought by him into the box who answer to their names are few. A great person has testified to his marvellous power and unimpeachable integrity; a sovereign has been as much impressed for his soul's good as the Emperor of Russia was by William Allen the Quaker, but we do not learn who the great person and the sovereign were. The godfathers and godmothers who appear in these pages to accredit these proceedings are Mr. Wilkinson (a spiritualist before he saw Mr. Home), Mr. J. G. Crawford, 'a gentleman who had for years resisted all belief in such phenomena,' Mr. T. A. Trollope, Mr. James Wason, solicitor, Dr. Gully of Malvern, Mr. John Jones of Basinghall Street, Mr. James Hutchinson of the Stock Exchange, Mr. Cox of the hotel in Jermyn Street, Mr. Coleman of Bayswater, Mr. and Mrs. Howitt, and Mrs. S. C. Hall—which last witness deposes to having received the present of a lace cap from the deceased Mrs. Home, laid by supernatural hands on her knee!"

The Reviewer thus shows how carelessly he has glanced at the book:—

"In the course of his foreign wanderings, Mr. Home fell in with the sister of Count Gregoire Koucheleff Besborodko. The lady was an ardent spiritualist and medium, like himself. They were married."

If I were ever so much a miracle worker, I would hide my diminished head in the presence of my critics. I stated in page 126 of my first volume that my wife was a sister of the Countess but here she must needs be changed into a Koucheleff Besborodko—nay, more, I now discover that she "was an ardent spiritualist and medium"; while on page 127 I give as a quotation her conversation with me when we were already engaged to be married—the following:

"Do tell me all about spirit-rapping, for you know I don't believe in it." I would most earnestly request my critics to do me the honour of reading my book, as Truth will stand when Fiction will fail.

After giving some extracts from the book, the writer thus concludes:—

"Here is enough, and more than enough, some readers will say, of Mr. Home's revelations, and of the testimonies of his disciples. From first to last there is not a statement in the book so presented as to warrant a sensible man in paying attention to it. To exhibit such a volume is to expose it; and we shall only repeat our first remark—the book contains its own criticism."

The 'Morning Herald," April 4th, 1863, approached the subject in a spirit of fairness, commencing with one of the narratives in the early part of the book, and continuing as follows:—

"The general character of the circumstances related in this volume is probably already well known to most of our readers. At certain meetings, usually in the evening, almost always in partial darkness, knocks are heard, furniture is moved about, spirit-hands grasp the feet or knees of the investigators, accordions are played without human agency, handkerchiefs thrown under the table are returned knotted, the medium is sometimes raised into the air, and floats above the heads of the other persons present, by rapping at the mention of the letters of the alphabet the tables answer questions put to them, sometimes the investigators receive messages from deceased friends written in a hand-writing they recognise. These are the ordinary manifestations which Mr. Home describes, and he asserts that they have been often repeated in the presence of many witnesses. How are we to deal with these assertions? It is obvious that the easiest way would be to treat Mr. Home as an impostor or a lunatic, and to make fun of the undignified tricks by which the spirits are said to reveal their presence. But though this course would be easy, we cannot think it wise. In the first place, this spiritualism is to its believers a sort of religious faith, and faith is strengthened, not hurt, by ridicule. But, besides this, the matter has grown too great for laughter. If it be false, then the impostor who has tampered with the highest hopes and feelings of humanity, and has driven scores, perhaps hundreds, into madness, is a villain to be denounced, not laughed at; while the imposture itself would be a matter for tears rather than mirth. But if these things be true, we dare not bring our jester's tinkling cap into the presence of the awful mysteries of the unseen world. No; spiritualism is too grave a subject in itself, and it has taken too firm a hold upon men's minds for it to be laughed out of the world. It is a matter for serious investigation, and the appearance of these volumes gives us a good opportunity for looking closely into it.

"We need hardly repeat the strong *à priori* arguments against its truth. It is improbable that any communication should be established between the living and the spirits of the dead; still more improbable that such communications should take place at times which presented no special reason for it, and to persons so placed in life that the revelation produces the least good to others and the greatest evil to themselves. And it seems most improbable that the departed spirits should establish the communication by knocking on tables, by playing 'Home! sweet home' on an accordion, or by tying knots in a pocket-handkerchief. Any man who enters on the investigation of spiritualism is bound, we think, to keep these arguments constantly in mind, that he may not believe too easily. But if the recorded phenomena seem absurd, we cannot say that they are impossible. Certainly in ordinary phrase men would say that it was 'impossible' for a table to move without being pushed, or to rise without being lifted by human agency. But the more a man learns the more wary he is as to this word 'impossible.' Mr. Grove shows us in his book on the 'Correlation of Forces' how little we know as to physical laws; on the relations of matter and spirit we know hardly anything. All we can say is, that these manifestations appear to be to us in the highest degree improbable. But here we are met by evidence that, improbable or not, they have taken place. Mr. Home is our first witness, and we are bound to say that we cannot see in this book any marks of insanity or deceit. To think him merely insane would not be enough to refute his statements, for he tells us that the manifestations have been seen by numbers of people in different countries; and it is plain that if they have believed also, either they must all have been insane, or he must be an impostor, or the thing must be true. If, like Robert Barclay or Pastor Oberlin, or many others mentioned in Mr. Howitt's book, he spoke only of visions which he himself had, we might suppose him insane; but when he declares, and makes a dozen other persons believe, that an accordion is played without hands, unless we suppose that all the witnesses were mad too, and that the instrument did not play at all, we are narrowed to this alternative, that either Mr. Home is an impostor, or that spiritualism is true.

"Now as to imposture. Assuredly Mr. Home is very different from the ordinary type of an impostor. When only eighteen years old he began his career of mediumship, by doing, or appearing to do, things so difficult as to involve almost a certainty of the early detection of any sort of deceit. In 1852 Mr. Bryant, the American poet, joined with three others in a declaration that at a *séance*, when the room was well lighted, the table rose clear of the floor, and floated in the atmosphere for several seconds; that Mr. Home frequently urged them to hold his hands and feet, and that every possible opportunity was afforded them for the closest inspection. They closed the declaration by saying, 'We know that we were not imposed upon nor deceived.' Again, we cannot but remark that the manifestations are not more elaborate now than they were twelve years ago. We might expect a successful impostor to use his advantages of experience and wealth to produce new and stronger effects; but this has not been the case with Mr. Home. The spirit hands (by far the most difficult manifestation for an impostor to produce) are said to have been seen at a very early period of his mediumship. Again, an impostor always tries to weave his deceptions into a system; generally, to form some sort of sect. Now, Mr. Home, with every temptation to do this in that he has persuaded so many of the truth of the manifestations, not only does not try to establish any great position for himself as the high priest of spiritualism, but he constantly denies that he has any power in the matter. After twelve years of mediumship he does not propound any system; and he speaks of himself as merely a helpless instrument. Thus speaking of the ridicule and obloquy which are cast upon those who confess their belief in spiritualism, he says:— 'If an example be needed of the truth of this, if it be not an obvious fact already in this uncharitable day, let my adventurous friends watch the extent to which I shall be abused, and called bad names, and given to the devil, for simply and truthfully writing in this little book a few of the incidents of my life, *with the production of which I have had nothing to do.'* In fact, Mr. Home speaks of his book as a collection of facts, which are worthy of investigation, and may be found useful in revealing some of the yet hidden laws of creation. 'It would be hard,' he says in another place, 'if I were bold answerable for facts which occur in connection with my physical organization, and towards which I am, in mind and intent, wholly passive, even if there were any harm in them.' We must note also the strangeness of the fact that Mr. Home has never been detected, if, indeed, he is an impostor. To move heavy tables, to raise himself to a horizontal position near the ceiling, to play tunes upon guitars; &c., these would require elaborate machinery. But these things have been done in palaces, and in private houses, in every part of Europe. If we believe Mr. Home to be an impostor, we shall have to suppose that a number of noblemen and gentlemen have knowingly aided the deceit. But, turning to more positive evidence, we will give a list of persons whom Mr. Home calls as witnesses. We omit the American names, which are numerous. Mrs. Trollope and her sister; Mr. T. Adolphus Trollope; Mrs. S. C. Hall; Mr. and Mrs. William: Howitt; Dr. J. M. Gully, of Malvern; Mr. James Hutchinson, many years chairman of the Stock Exchange; Mr. W. M. Wilkinson, of Hampstead; Mr. James Wason, solicitor, of Wason Buildings, Liverpool; Dr. Hoofer, 'one of the most learned men in France;' Mr. John Jones, of Basinghall Street; Mr. J. G. Crawford; Mr. Gilbert Davidson; Mr. Cox, of Jermyn Street; Mr. Benjamin Coleman, of Bayswater; Dr. J. J. Wilkinson; Madame de Cardonne of 233, Rue St. Dominique, St. Germain; Mr. T. S. Clarke. Mr. Home has been received by the Emperor of the French, the Czar of Russia the present King of Prussia, the King of Wurtemburg, and the Queen of Holland.

"Mr. W. M. Wilkinson asserts that Lord Lyndhurst has witnessed manifestations. Mr. Wason states that the *séance* at which he was present was at the mansion of a person of distinction, in Hyde-park Terrace, and that the other investigators were two baronets, one an M.P., and the other the heir and representative of a deceased M.P. of eminent ability; the wife of a distinguished living M.P., and three others, besides Mr. Home.

"Dr. Gully was present at the *séance* described in the famous article called 'Stranger than Fiction,' which appeared in the 'Cornhill Magazine' for August, 1860. He fully corroborates the assertions made in that article, and says that the other gentlemen present were a solicitor in large practice, and two well-known writers of solid instructive works. Mrs. S. C. Hall tells of a meeting which she attended, where a young lady was the medium, and says, 'I was forced to believe that there was truth in mediumship, and that *here* was the means used for communicating from the spirits of those gone before to those who still lingered in the flesh.' At page 63 of this volume, a remarkable account is given of certain spirit communications said to have been made at a *séance* at Ealing, to a distinguished novelist, whom the reader will have no hesitation in recognising as Sir Edward Bulwer Lytton. Now, if Mr. Home be an impostor, the publication of this book is an act of the greatest folly. Not only are all those we have named pledged witnesses to the truth of spiritualism; but if any man of all the hundreds of Englishmen who have seen Mr. Home has ever discovered any sort of machinery or trick by which these wonderful results have been obtained, he is bound to speak out. However loth he may be to come forward into public discussions, longer silence will be criminal. The testimony of the persons named by Mr. Home will, of course, have more weight with their personal friends than with the general public; instead of extracting their narratives, we may perhaps repeat a story which we have heard from a friend on whose judgment and truthfulness we can rely, a clergyman of the Church of England, who has for many years been engaged in teaching. He tells us that his wife was a very sensitive medium. One night, when only his brother was with them, the three agreed to have a *séance*. The wife sat at the table; he in a corner of the room asked questions by writing them on a slate. The questions and answers were as follow:— 'Is there a spirit in the room?' 'Yes.'— 'Whose?' 'A____ B____' (a name was mentioned which no one present recognised).—'Did you see me in life?' 'Yes.'—'Where?' 'At R____.'—'What was I doing?' 'Preaching.' The party were startled at this, for our friend had only once in his life visited the place named, and then he took the Sunday service. One more question was put. 'What was my text?' A passage of Scripture was named in answer; the clergyman had forgotten, in the lapse of several years, what text he really had taken, but he went to his sermon case and found the answer was correct. Until he told us this story, we could not have supposed it possible that we should doubt his word. Even on this testimony we cannot fully believe. He says, as said the writer in the 'Cornhill Magazine,' 'I would not myself have believed it on any one's assertion, I cannot expect you to believe it on mine.' We will not admit that we are believers in spiritualism, but we are compelled to own that the evidence is too strong to be ridiculed or disregarded. We should much like to meet Mr. Home, and in company with other gentlemen who have never been witnesses of these manifestations, and with the one desire of obtaining truth, to thoroughly investigate the subject. Until then our strongly-rooted opinions on the one hand, and the weight of evidence on the other, oblige us to hold our judgment in suspense. We have only space to add one or two hints upon the general subject. We would strongly urge that it should not be discussed with children, or with persons subject to any of the nervous disorders which sometimes lead to insanity. We can think of nothing more likely to drive one mad, than the belief that the barrier between the living and the dead is broken down, and that those whom we have known and lost may touch us and speak to us, telling us messages of truth or *falsehood*. In this last word is an awful thought. Mr. Home and Mr. Howitt both believe that we may have communication with evil spirits as well as with good; and that the former may tell men lies to deceive them to their destruction. It is a terrible belief. If a man were once persuaded that it was a supernatural voice which spoke to him, he would be at the mercy of every word that voice might say. Where are those—are there, indeed, any—whose faith in the God whom the Bible reveals to us would be strong enough to put aside with disbelief a message which was known to come from the world of spirits? Our clergy should look to it, it is no trifling matter. If this thing be true, it is a great blessing to the world that it has not been linked to false doctrines. There is a text which speaks of wonders which, 'if it were possible should deceive the very elect;' if spiritualism be true, may it not be sent to prepare the world for those lying prophets, working real miracles to support false doctrines, who are to be the last trial of the Church's faith?"

The "Literary Times," March 21, 1863, said: "In conclusion, we have but to state that, should 'The Incidents in My Life, be a true and honest book, it is one of the most important works ever presented to the world. But should the opposite be the case, then Mr. Home is the greatest impostor that ever deluded mankind. It is intolerable that he and his friends should occupy their present equivocal position. Why cannot society rouse itself, and determine to turn out these men as false prophets, or acknowledge them as the apostles of a new faith, however worthless that faith may be to the world?"

I do not consider "The Incidents in My Life" as "one of the most important works ever presented to the world," but I know it to be a "true and honest book." It may be intolerable to the writer of the review that with my friends I should enjoy any position whatever. I fear his power of toleration must be further tested, inasmuch as my present position is a great improvement on what it was when he wrote, and I only ask "society to rouse itself" in the form of honest unprejudiced investigation.

The reviewer in "The Critic," April, 1863, after criticising (?) Mr. Howitt's "History of the Supernatural," goes on thus: "We now turn to Mr. D. D. Home's 'Incidents in My life,' and we must frankly confess that after the perusal of it, we felt a great deal of that Christian charity and disposition to hearken which Mr. Howitt had awakened in our bosom evaporate before the unparalleled impudence of this 'medium.' . . . With him (Mr. Howitt) we may be perfectly sure that his faith is genuine. . . He is actuated by no other motive than a sincere desire to have the truth known. Can we say the same of Mr. Home?. . . But it is not by any means to the spiritual element in the book that we take exception, so much as to the bad taste exhibited throughout." The writer then takes me to task for what he is pleased to term my "impudent treatment of Sir David Brewster, and proceeds to show that, not only has his "bosom" been bereft of "Christian charity," but of truth, for he gives an anecdote (?), invented apparently on the spur of the moment. I allude to it in my letter to "The Times" of April 16th.

The "Spectator," March 14, 1863, which noticed the work as by David Douglas Home, said—"This is a very embarrassing book to review," and proceeded in a strain, which from an unbelieving point of view was very fair, to say—"Nor do the marvels related to us rest by any means entirely on Mr. Home's own testimony. If that gentleman be a deliberate deceiver, it would still be very difficult to regard the stories here related as affecting his veracity alone, though, of course, we cannot tell how far the imagination of secondary actors might aid in the work of delusion. The facts of the book, whether false or not, all drive at one conclusion, that the gates between the world of the living and the departed are always open, and that the conditions are by no means very rare which enable us to receive proof that they are thus open, and to profit by the supernatural experience of those who have passed away. These phenomena are the a b c of life with Mr. Home, if we may believe him to be sincere; and yet, of course, if we could accept them as genuine, they ought almost to absorb the attention of the higher science, of the deepest faith, and of the truest human affections. . .

"Without, therefore, any predisposition to accuse Mr. Home of dishonesty, which, if it be dishonesty, would seem to be shared by one, witness, at least, in the honour of whose personal character we have good reason to believe, Dr. Wilkinson, the well known biographer of Swedenborg—we cannot help approaching this book in the attitude of simple incredulity. . .

"On the stories connected with Mrs. Home's death, related partly by her husband, and partly by her friends Mrs. Hewitt and Mrs. S. C. Hall, we have no wish to comment. Almost more marvellous than the rest, it is still written with so much feeling that it would be brutal to ridicule, and yet is quite impossible to believe. We should add, however, that the absurd character of the phenomena once granted, Mr. Home's book is throughout written with more simplicity, and less affectation of any kind than any other book of its class. . .

"This article is not criticism—for the only true criticism on the book is one of three practical verdicts, 'Sincere, but insane,' 'sane, but mendacious,' or 'both sane and sincere.' We see no sort of indication at all that Mr. Home is insane, and if he is, he must have made so many other people insane also that the first verdict would be irrational. Now we have no right to give the second, and no power to give the third. Without personal knowledge of a man, it is unjust to decide against his veracity especially when backed by men who, if enthusiastic, are at least known to us to be honourable."

The" Spectator" further noticed an historical error, with regard to a circumstance related in the book at page 123, and the same was noticed by the "Times." This I replied to in my letter to the "Times," which will be found further on. In the next chapter I also give from the review in the "Spectator" an extract which refers to the controversy with Sir David Brewster.

The review in the "Times" commenced with the remark:— "This volume in which Mr. Home recounts the incidents of his life, or rather of his communion with the world of spirits, is a very odd production in this materialistic age." After an analysis of the book, by no means unfair, and extending to nearly three columns, the article concludes with an anecdote of Doctor Johnson, terminating with the remark, "The story wants congruity." As wit has been defined to be "The apt association of incongruous ideas," this remark may be witty, but I have no need to quarrel with it as it contains no argument against what I had published. At the time the review appeared I was in France, but on its being forwarded to me, I wrote at once to the "Times" the following letter, which appeared in that paper on April 16, 1863:—

Sir,—Allow me to thank you for the generous criticism of my book which appeared in your columns on the 9th of April. I do not censure any one for a want of belief in the strange phenomena which occur in my presence; but I do consider it unfair when the critics write to condemn a book which they have not even taken the trouble to read. One writer kills my child, another, my father, and a third calls me an

American. The "Spectator," as you justly say, discovers a mistake in the dates as I gave them. I at once wrote to the editor, giving him the name and address of the gentleman to whom the incident occurred, that he might ascertain how the mistake had arisen. I then wrote to say that I had seen the gentleman, who had just returned from the continent, and was ill, but at the same time explained the error as being entirely mine, inasmuch as the fact alluded to actually transpired in the autumn of 1856, and was all the more singular, as coming at a time when the strange power had left me. This also I explained by saying that the young officer alluded to as "Gregoire" became a medium, and this singular faculty remained with him many months. I enclose you also the name and address of the gentleman, and only request that they may not be published. Still I know Mr. _____ will favour you with any information you may require, and that he will willingly testify to, not only the entire truthfulness of what I related, but will say that I did not make the story nearly as wonderful as it was in reality.

As regards the other story "which requires explanation," I am in the very same position as yourself, and will be only too pleased that it should be "verified or explained." I have heard the same story told in so many different forms, and still always related as having occurred to Mr. Monckton Milnes, that I would fain know where such wilful misrepresentations could commence. The incident was a very simple one to begin with. Mr. Monckton Milnes was present at a *séance* where there were seven or eight ladies and gentlemen. I was seated, furthest from him at the table, and during a part of the *séance*, which was in a darkened room, I felt something tangibly material pass over my face. I put up my hand to retain whatever it might be, but it eluded my grasp. This I told to those who were present, and, on some one saying, "I, have just been touched also," I replied, "Well, why did you not do as I did, sir, and try to retain it?" Mr. Monckton Milnes then said, "I have been touched several times, and now I have taken whatever it was. Oh, it is a pocket handkerchief!" The question then became general as to whose it might be, there being two or three on the laps of the ladies, or else on the table; but we could not then ascertain to whom the handkerchief belonged. The *séance* continued at least half-an-hour after this, and when the light came the handkerchief chanced to be mine. Now, I would like to have it explained how, by any possibility, I could have stretched out my arms sufficiently to enable me to touch Mr. Monckton Milnes, he being, as I before said, furthest from me at the table; and, even if I did, why could I not as well have taken one of the handkerchiefs which were on the table; instead of taking my own? The simple fact of the handkerchief being mine, proves nothing to my way of thinking. How did it get over his head when the slightest movement I made would not have failed to be observed by those seated next to me? It has not been my lot either to have to deal with fools or mad people, and if after thirteen years of public life, the greater part of which time I have spent with those who watched my every action suspiciously, anxiously hoping to discover some material means whereby all these things could be accomplished,—if, after all this, any persons will come forward and state an instance where they, and those present with them, proved me to be an impostor, I will abide by their decision. It must not be any one person, for the simple reason that my experience has been peculiar in this respect." I have found people who, to sustain a pre-conceived idea, would not hesitate at the most gross untruths in vindication of their ideas. To prove this, I have only to allude to a story told in the "Critic" of this month, where it is related of me as arguing that a purported message from a spirit, could not be otherwise than true, as it was my father's spirit who was speaking. My father is alive and well, and the whole story is without even a syllable of truth. Why does not the "gentleman" (?) who relates that story to the "Critic" come out and give us his name?

These things are too serious to be treated otherwise than with candour. The mere fact of calling a man hard names does not prove him to be deserving of them. Let every man prove his position, and, if five hundred names of men of rank, men of good sound judgment, and men well-known for their truthfulness,—I say if these can be taken, then is my position proved, at least as being guiltless of ever having deceived them. There must be no "conjectural" imposition, for these conjectures carry men too far from simple truth. The newspaper reports of my having made a large fortune by my powers are simple fabrications or "conjectures."

The only good I have ever derived from "the gift" is the knowledge that many who had never believed in a future existence are now happy in the certitude of "life to come."

I have the honour to be, air, yours most obediently,

D. D. HOME.

"Chateau Laroche, par St. Astier, Derdogne,
"France, April 13.

CHAPTER II

SIR DAVID BREWSTER, LORD BROUGHAM, LETTERS AND TESTIMONY, DR. ELLIOTTSON, PROPHETIC INCIDENTS.

As the controversy with the late Sir David Brewster was discussed at some length in the Appendix to my former volume, it had been my intention to have let the matter rest, and not to allude to it further. But the subject has been revived by Brewster's daughter in the "Home Life" of her father, and I am compelled to notice her statements, which were alluded to by Mr. Coleman, in the "Spiritual Magazine" for May, 1870, in an article from which I extract some passages as follows:—

"The conduct of the late Sir David Brewster in his relations with the celebrated medium, Mr. Daniel D. Home, and the controversy which arose in the year 1855, form a prominent episode in the history of English Spiritualism.

"That 'dead men tell no tales' is an adage which spiritualists cannot admit. We *know* that the so-called dead do in many instances, and under certain conditions, return and tell us many tales.

"But we who have had much experience are cautious in accepting all that is revealed to us in this way, and were I now dealing with a message purporting to have come from the spirit of the departed philosopher through the ordinary channels of mediumship, I should hesitate before venturing to make a public announcement of the fact. There are, however, other means by which the voices of the dead speak to us— namely, by the records of their public and private acts when living. I have just found one, which coming as it does through the mediumship of Sir David Brewster's own daughter, will not be disputed; and as it tends to justify the statements made by those who stood forward in 1857 to defend Mr. Home and the genuine character of the manifestations witnessed by Sir David Brewster and Lord Brougham, it may, I think with propriety, find a place in the pages of this journal.

"The late Mr. William Cox, of Jermyn Street, with whom Mr. Home was residing in 1854-5, invited Lord Brougham and Sir David Brewster (A slight inaccuracy, see note on page 51.) to a private *séance;* and Mr. Cox, who was an intelligent and much respected gentleman, told me the following day how profoundly impressed both of his visitors had been with what they had witnessed, and he described minutely to me the several incidents which took place, of which I made notes at the time. This information was corroborated in a short conversation which I subsequently had with Lord Brougham, and again in a lengthy discussion with Sir David at the Athenæum Club; when he fully admitted the facts and said that he could neither attribute them to trickery nor delusion of the senses. 'But, he very emphatically added, slapping his knee, 'spirit is the last thing I will give in to!'

"It will be seen that when Sir David Brewster was publicly making the most ungenerous and unfounded imputations upon Mr. Home, and denying in the most unqualified manner the statements made by me in October, 1855, he had privately recorded, in the month of June previously, a complete refutation of his own words; added to which it is now shown that Sir David was himself A MEDIUM! a SEER in fact, with his own special experiences. His daughter's statement upon this point is sufficiently distinct and conclusive: her account of what she calls his "dual nature," and his ultimate convictions upon Spiritualism are curious and instructive. Mrs. Cordon says:—

"'Brewster's character was peculiarly liable to misconstruction from its distinctly dual nature; it was made up of opposites, and his peculiarly impulsive temperament and expressions laid him open to the charge of inconsistency, although he never recognized it in himself, conscious that he spoke what was consistent with the point of view whence he took his observations at the time. Accustomed to look at every subject with the critical investigation of the man of science, he yet united the feelings of the man of impulse, and he spoke as moved by either habit. Nothing could show this better than his views and feelings with regard to clairvoyance and spirit-rapping. Like many Scotchmen of genius and intellect he had had a strong leaning to the superstitions from the days of the steeple-vault and the cottage under the apple tree, balanced, however, by a scientific mind which required proof and demonstration for whatever came before it. His own quaint confession that he was 'afraid of ghosts, though he did not believe in them,' was as near the truth as possible. Living in an old house, haunted it was said, by the learned shade of George Buchanan, in which certainly the strangest and most unaccountable noises were frequently heard, his footsteps used sometimes to perform the transit from his study to his bedroom in the dead of night in double-quick time; and in the morning he used to confess that sitting up alone had made him feel quite eerie. On one of these occasions when the flight had been more than usually rapid, he recounted having distinctly seen the form of the late Rev. Charles Lyon, then Episcopal Clergyman of St. Andrew's, and an attached friend of his own, rising up pale and grey like a marble bust. He often mentioned his relief when he found that nothing had occurred to his friend, and pointed out what a good ghost story had thus been spoiled. A certain pleasurable excitement was combined with this *eeriness,* and many will recollect the charm of his ghost stories, recounted with so much simplicity and earnestness and *vraisemblance* of belief, as on one occasion to be rewarded by the perplexing compliment of a fair young listener at Ramornie fainting dead away.

"'On the other hand he was equally fond of giving natural and scientific explanations of ghostly marvels, and used to dwell with great interest upon the difficulties of evidence in everything connected with the supernatural, pointing out the unconscious deviations from exact testimony given by persons of undoubted rectitude under the influence of prepossession. Much of this mingled feeling he carried with him into his investigations of clairvoyance and its kindred marvels.

"'He really wished to believe in many wonders to which his constitution of mind utterly refused credence; and this feeling combined with a characteristic courtesy and wish to please, often misled those into whose pretensions he was most critically examining.

"'On one occasion, when the exhibition of a lady clairvoyante moved his companion to an expression of indignant unbelief, which was declared to be the cause of failure, his gentleness and courtesy, smoothing away difficulties, apologising for the mistakes of supernatural powers, and giving every facility for greater success, prevented the dim-sighted clairvoyance from recognising the equal but far more philosophical unbelief which was brought to bear upon her case. He always affirmed that, of the many cases which had thus come within his ken, he had never seen anything so wonderful that he could say it could have no natural explanation, though, of a few he said frankly that he could neither see nor understand the solution. He latterly took even deeper views of this school of wonders, searching the scriptures minutely for passages describing the spirits that 'peeped and muttered' of old, or those whose 'lying wonders' are yet to come, and giving it as his belief that, if modern spiritualism with its manifestations be a truth, it may be a fulfilment of the prophesied work of the Evil One and his agents.'"

Mrs. Gordon also says:— 'Although his timidity had the dual element, displayed long before in the Grammar School and playground of Jedburgh—of never fearing the face of man; he exhibited much of it in connection with the lower creation." And she might have added that there is a wide distinction between the physical courage which stimulates a man to do battle with his fists, and the moral courage requisite to declare truth boldly, no matter how much danger there may be that his reputation will suffer from his so doing.

In order to show the dual character of Sir David, which I have marked by similar figures in each letter, I here republish his letter to Mr. Coleman in October, so far as relates to the *séance* at Cox's Hotel, beside that which he had written to his daughter in June.

In October he wrote:

"I may once for all admit that both Lord Brougham and myself freely acknowledged that we were puzzled with Mr. Home's performances, and could not account for them. Neither of us pretend to be expounders of conundrums, whether verbal or mechanical; but if we had been permitted to take a peep (1.) beneath the drapery of Mr. Cox's table, we should have been spared the mortification of this confession. I come now to the facts of the case:

"1. It is not true, as stated by you, that a large dinner-table was moved about at Mr. Cox's in the most extraordinary manner. (2.)

"2. It is not true, as you state, that a large accordion 'was conveyed by an invisible, or any other, agency into my hand.' I took it up myself, and it would not utter a sound.

"3. It is not true that the accordion was conveyed into Lord Brougham's hand. It was placed in it.

"4. It is not true that the accordion *played an air throughout*, in Lord Brougham's hands. It merely squeaked.

"5. It is not true, as stated in an article referred to by Mr. Home, that Lord Brougham's 'watch was taken out of his pocket, and found in the hands of some other person in the, room.' No such experiment was tried.

"6. It is not true, as stated by Mr. Cox, that I said that Mr. Home's experiments 'upset the philosophy of fifty years.' These are the words of Mr. Coleman, used, as he alleges, by himself, and very untruly put into my mouth by Mr. Cox.

"Although I have not appealed to Lord Brougham's memory in reference to these statements, I have no doubt that his Lordship would confirm, were it necessary, all that I have said.

"In reply to Mr. Cox, I may take this opportunity to answer his request, by telling him what I have seen, and what I think of it. At Mr. Cox's house, Mr. Home, Lord Brougham, and myself, sat down to a small table, Mr. Home having previously requested us to examine if there was any machinery about his person, an examination, however, which we declined to make. When all our hands were upon the table, noises were heard—rappings in abundance; and, finally, when we rose up the table actually rose, as appeared to me, from the ground. This result I do not pretend to explain; but rather than believe that spirits made the noise, I will conjecture that the raps were produced by Mr. Home's toes, which, as will be seen, were active on another occasion; or, as Dr. Schiff has shown, 'by the repeated displacement of the tendon of the *peroneus longus* muscle in the sheath in which it slides behind the external *mallelous*;' and rather than believe that spirits raised the table, I will conjecture that it was done by the agency of Mr. Home's feet, which were always below it.

"Some time after this experiment, Mr. Home left the room and returned: probably to equip himself for the feats which were to be performed by the spirits beneath a large round table covered with copious drapery, beneath which nobody was allowed to look.

"The spirits are powerless above board. Besides the experiments with the accordion, already mentioned, a small hand-bell to be rung by the spirits, was placed on the ground, near my feet. I placed my feet round it in the form of an angle, to catch any intrusive apparatus. The bell did not ring (3.); but when taken to a place near Mr. Home's feet, it speedily came across, and placed its handle in my hand. This was amusing.

"It did the same thing bunglingly, to Lord Brougham, by knocking itself against his Lordship's knuckles, and, after a jingle, it fell. How these effects were produced neither Lord Brougham nor I could say, but I conjecture that they may be produced by machinery attached to the lower extremities of Mr. Home. (4.)

The following appears in the "Home Life," under the date of June, 1855.

Last of all I went with Lord Brougham to a *séance* of the new spirit-rapper, Mr. Home, a lad of twenty, the son of a brother of the late Earl of Home. (I do not think Sir David had any intention of prevaricating in this letter to Mrs. Gordon, and I can only suppose that on this point he had been misinformed. My father is a natural son of Alexander, tenth Earl of Home. Mrs. Gordon seems to have inherited the dual nature of her father, for the present Earl of Home having written to her to ascertain on what grounds the claim of my being a son of a brother of the late Earl was made out, she replied that they were my own, and that I had put them forth even in the Chancery suit of Lyon v. Home. Lord Home wrote to a mutual friend to ascertain the truth of this, at the same time stating he had no remembrance of such a thing as my having made such a claim. I wrote a letter for his lordship to see, in which I stated that I had no desire to establish any such claim, and stating what my connection with the family was.) He went to America at the age of seven, and though a naturalized American, is actually a Scotchman. Mr. Home lives in Coxe's hotel, Jermyn Street; and Mr. Coxe, who knows Lord Brougham, wished him to have a *séance*, and his lordship invited me to accompany him in order to assist in finding out the trick. We four sat down at a moderately-sized table, the structure of which we were invited to examine. (1.) In a short time the table shuddered, and a tremulous motion ran up all our arms; at our bidding these motions ceased and returned. The most unaccountable rappings were produced in various parts of the table; and the table actually rose from the ground when no hand was upon it. A larger table was produced, and exhibited similar movements. (2.) An accordion was held in Lord Brougham's hand, and gave out a single note; but the experiment was a failure; it would not play either in his hand or mine. A small hand-bell was then laid down with its mouth on the carpet; and after lying for some time, it actually rang, when nothing could have touched it. (3.) The bell was then placed on the other side, still upon the carpet, and it came over to me and placed itself in my hand. It did the same to Lord Brougham.

These were the principal experiments. We could give no explanation of them, and could not conjecture how they could be produced by any kind of mechanism. (4.)

Hands are sometimes seen and felt; the hand often grasps another, and melts away, as it were, under the grasp. The object of asking Lord Brougham and me seems to have been to get our favourable opinion of the exhibition; but though neither of us can explain what we saw, we do not believe that it was the work of idle spirits."

NOTE.

A further evidence of the duality of Sir David Brewster is displayed in the course of this single short letter to his daughter, for in the commencement he says, "Lord Brougham invited me to accompany him," and at the end he speaks of the object of asking Lord Brougham and me." The fact being that Lord Brougham had been invited, and about two hours before the *séance* sent word that he wished to bring Sir David Brewster. As I am not in the habit of giving exhibitions, no favourable opinion was sought for from either visitor.

The public and mendacious denials of Sir David Brewster in the "Morning Advertiser," elicited no confirmation from Lord Brougham, though such confirmation, could he have obtained it, would have been most acceptable to Sir David. Lord Brougham's final views on spiritualism are indicated by himself in the following passage which concludes his Lordship's preface to a work entitled "The Book of Nature," by Mr. Charles O. Groom Napier, F.C.S., published in 1870:— "There is but one question I would ask the author: Is the spiritualism of this work foreign to our materialistic, manufacturing age?—No; for amidst the varieties of mind which divers circumstances produce, are found those who cultivate man's highest faculties;—these the author addresses himself. But even in the most cloudless skies of scepticism I see a rain-cloud,—if it be no bigger than a man's hand, it is Modern Spiritualism."

I hope that the Editor of Lord Brougham's memoirs will fairly give to the world his Lordship's letters containing the account of the *séance* at Cox's Hotel. Although Lord Brougham, at the special request of Sir David Brewster, conveyed by telegraph, abstained from publishing these letters, he was not capable of yielding to his further request to come forward with a confirmation of Sir David's mendacious letter of October, 1855.

I also desire to add to Mr. Coleman's remark that Mr. Cox was an intelligent and much respected gentleman, my own grateful tribute to the memory of a kind friend, and a steadfast and undaunted defender of the truth. Such have I ever found the late Mr. Cox, not only in his relations towards myself, but towards all others so far as came within the range of my own observation.

The "Spectator" says, on the correspondence with Sir David, printed in the appendix to my former volume:—

"Next we must say that the correspondence with Sir David Brewster is not decisive on either side, but that, as far as we can see, there is a certain amount of disingenuousness in Sir David's letters. It seems established by the clearest evidence that he felt and expressed, at and immediately after his *séances* with Mr. Home, a wonder and almost awe, which he afterwards wished to explain away; and the suppression of Lord Brougham's half-promised testimony as to the first *séance* in question, though challenged by Mr. Home, is on the whole unfavourable to Sir David, as it might be presumed that Lord Brougham would support his friend's testimony as far as possible. Nor does the passage-at-arms between Sir David Brewster and Mr T. A. Trollope concerning the subsequent *séance* at Ealing, seem to us quite creditable to Sir David. If we may trust Mr. Trollope (uncontradicted by Sir David Brewster) there also Sir David had testified to facts which on reconsideration, he modified to square with a theory subsequently elaborated. We say this, though disbelieving entirely the genuineness of all phenomena of this sort, simply on the evidence of Sir David Brewster's' own letters and that of the other witnesses of two *séances* which he criticised. The controversy is not of any great importance one way or the other; still justice to this celebrated medium obliges us to admit that on the face of published correspondence, the hero of science does not acquit himself as we could wish or expect."

I am now also enabled to produce another independent witness in this case, namely, the late Earl of Dunraven; who has given me the following:—

"I was so struck with what Sir David Brewster—with whom I was well acquainted—had himself told me, that it materially, influenced me in determining to examine thoroughly into the reality of the phenomena. I met him one day on the steps of the Athenæum; we got upon the subject of table-turning, &c.; he spoke most earnestly, stating that the impression left on his mind from what he had seen, was, that the manifestations were to him quite inexplicable by fraud, or by any physical laws with which we were acquainted, and that they ought to be fully and carefully examined into."

The following letter which was received by Mr. J. S. Rymer, shows the effect produced by Sir David Brewster's account at first.

SIR,

"In consequence of a very remarkable account given by Sir David Brewster of the extraordinary powers of Mr. Home, together with two or three friends, I am anxious to have an interview with him. If he can make it convenient to come to my house, No. 80, Eaton Square, on Thursday or Saturday next, at 2 o'clock, I should be glad to make an appointment for either of those days. I am given to understand that although Mr. Home does not exhibit his powers for money, that he does not refuse to accept a moderate gratuity from those who have the opportunity of witnessing his powers; (An error; no sitting followed this note.) this of course I and my friends shall be happy to present to him, and we shall be much obliged to you to inform us what amount we may offer him, and in what way we may do so without doing violence to his feelings,

I remain, Sir,

"80, Eaton Sq.   Your obedient servant,
"July 2, 1855."   "EDWARD BULLER."

As Father A. de Ponlevoy, in his biography of the Père de Ravignan, has denied my having been on intimate terms with the good father, and as, notwithstanding my challenge to him to produce evidence, he has never in any way justified his attack on me by the production of a single document, or of a solitary witness to the truth of his assertions, I might have left his attack now untouched; but as he continues to maintain his unsupported assertions, I think it advisable to print the following letters from the excellent Père de Ravignan, which fully testify to the cordial relations that existed between us:—

"Mon bien cher Enfant, Etes vous malade? Faites le moi savoir. J'irai près de vous; car il y a trop longtemps que je ne vous ai vu.

Aujourd'hui, toute la journée, demain Jeudi, et apres demain jusqu' à midi, vous me trouveriez sûrement.

"Vous savez que je vous aime tendrement en N. S.,

"X. DE RAVIGNAN, S. J.

"Paris, Mercredi, 28 Janvier, 1857.

"Ne sortez-pas si vous êtes souffrant."

"Mon cher Enfant, Je vous esperais hier matin. Etes vous plus souffrant? Aujourd'hui venez. Vous savez combien je vous aime en N. S.

Peut-être sortirai-je pour un malade, du 11h a midi.

"X. DE RAVIGNAN, S. J.

"Mercredi."

"Jeudi.

"Mon bien cher Enfant, J'envoie savoir de vos nonvelles; j'espere qu'elles seront bonnes. Demain Vendredi venez, si vous pouvez sortir, me voir avant 11h du Matin. Si non je vous attendrai Samedi.

"Je vous benis: soyez fidèle et soumis a l'église; vivez de la foi, et de la grace de N. S. Tout le reste, oubliez le—adieu. Tout à vous,

"X. de R."

In the letters from Dr. Robert Chambers, allusion is made to the late Miss Catherine Sinclair, sister of the venerable Archdeacon Sinclair, a lady with whom it was a privilege to be acquainted. She was one of the early witnesses of the phenomena of spiritualism, and the following letters, addressed to me at different times, show what interest she felt in the subject:—

"Saturday.

"DEAR SIR,

"In my haste last night, I left a much-valued acquisition, which will long and often be seen in my possession hereafter. Pray give the bearer that admirable photograph, which you so very kindly presented to me. The message of last night was most marvellous! The tempest - tossed ship and the beautiful expression of thankfulness that the storms of life are over—what consolation! I live with those who have heard, from my near relative, Mrs. Hope Johnstone, a very detailed account of her experience, and also Mr. Grant's, of the "Advertiser"; but people cannot long resist conviction, seconded by manifestations so pleasing and elevating as those of last night. I merely relate what I have myself witnessed, and all become at once desirous to share in such revelations. Our circle last night, *when diminished*, was very effective! I ought to have told you beforehand about Mr. Howitt, but had no mention of trespassing on your kindness by bringing him, as I believe he had sailed in Lord Yarborough's yacht to Madeira, but he returned unexpectedly for a day. He is engaged to my niece, who accompanied me, the daughter of Sir George Sinclair, and she entreated me to take him. I had therefore no time to write and ask permission, he came so unexpectedly. I never would intrude any friend on you without special leave, seeing how persecuted you must be for admissions. With kind regards to Mrs. Home, Yours truly,

"C. SINCLAIR."

"DEAR SIR,

"It is several years since I saw Dr. Bell, and then only for one short consultation; therefore if he has quoted me as his friend, it must be on very slight evidence. I described one day to a young lady who is very ill, much that I had seen at Mrs. Milner Gibson's, and expressed my interest in it. Having told her that I had been prevented accepting your kind invitation for Tuesday, she may probably have mentioned it to Dr. Bell, who is her medical attendant. If I had wished to present him to you, I should certainly have written first to ask your permission; and should such an imposition be again attempted by any one, do not sanction it without my hand and seal. With best regards to Mrs. Home,

"Yours very truly,

"CATHERINE SINCLAIR."

"20th June."

"DEAR SIR,

"This being Sunday, I walked from The Vicarage, Kensington, leaving my young charge better, and greatly do I long to bring him some day to see you. I am greatly embarrassed, however, by the opposition of my clerical brothers, and other relations, against all those marvellous manifestations which will one day force themselves on universal conviction. All my family are behind the age on that mysterious subject, but I am glad to know that many talented men are become candid inquirers. As I have been long engaged to attend the marriage of Mr. Sandwith, the hero of Kars, next Tuesday, I must arrange to leave my patient; and that being your day for receiving visitors, I hope to call on Mrs. Home and you early, before I go to the wedding. My niece, Mrs. Hope Johnstone, who takes a deep interest in your investigations, will accompany me. I enclose a note from Colonel Knight Erskine, and if you can assist him—he has remained in London on purpose to see you.

I often think gratefully of the kind interest you take in my young nephew. With kind regards, yours truly,

"C. SINCLAIR."

"27th May."

"DEAR SIR,

"The kind and truly generous interest you felt in my young nephew's sudden calamity induces me to mention that his symptoms are already somewhat alleviated, though his three physicians think it may still be some time before the final result be certain. I sit for long hours beside him, and would have greatly wished to try mesmeric influence, but he is in the house of a clerical uncle, so strongly opposed to progress in these respects, that the subject cannot even be mentioned. People's minds are gradually opening, however; and a friend of mine, deep in the science of spiritualism, is extremely desirous to communicate with you. He is a landed proprietor in Scotland, and is in command of a regiment.

"I think you will find very few men more talented and agreeable than Major Knight Erskine, and I shall desire him, if you do not forbid him, to call on you next Tuesday about one, in hopes of conferring a mutual pleasure and benefit by making you acquainted. I return every night to town, but go early to my invalid again, as he has two medical nurses who never leave him. One of the doctors says the complaint is *delirium tremens*, from smoking cigars!

With best compliments to Mrs. Home,

"Yours very truly,

"C. SINCLAIR."

"Thursday."

"8, Chesham Place, Belgrave Sq.
"13th July.

"DEAR SIR,

"Allow me to express my most sorrowful and cordial sympathy in the loss of your amiable and accomplished, and much-loved wife, so young, so good, and so suited to render you happy. I hope hereafter to hear from you that your own health has not suffered by your long and anxious attendance, as I witnessed your grief while here, in the apprehension of that sad event, which has now so mournfully terminated all your hopes and cares.

"Pray offer my sincere and respectful condolences to the distinguished relatives of my lamented young friend, Mrs. Home.

"With kindest regards,

"Yours very truly;

"CATHERINE SINCLAIR."

Another of the early inquirers, also alluded to by the late Dr. Robert Chambers was the late Professor De Morgan, concerning whom the following correspondence appeared in the "Spiritual Magazine" for January, 1869, which completely destroys all doubt as to his belief in the reality of the Phenomena.

"To the Editor of the 'Spiritual Magazine.'

SIR,—As I am not in the habit of taking anything for granted, without what appear to me to be adequate reasons for so doing;—and, as I was not satisfied with the bare assertion that Professor De Morgan, the eminent living mathematician, had really lent the sanction of his great name to these so-called delusions (of modern spiritualism), I some months back wrote him a letter on the subject of the book 'From Matter to Spirit,' published anonymously in 1863, and received from him the following reply;—

"'91, Adelaide Road, N. W.
'April 3rd, 1868.

"'A. B. TIETKINS, Esq.

"'SIR,—It never has been any secret that the book 'From Matter to Spirit' was written by *my wife*, and the *preface by myself*.

"'For the last two years, I think, Longman has advertized our names. I vouch, of course, for the facts mentioned in detail at the end of the preface; but there are some in the book of the truth of which my knowledge is personal. And of nearly all I can testify that I heard them long before they were printed, and that they did not grow.

"'Yours faithfully,
"'A. DE MORGAN.'

"So then here we have a living philosopher who tells us, after fifteen years of investigation of these phenomena, and patient consideration of their bearing, 'I am perfectly convinced that I have both seen and heard in a manner, which should make unbelief impossible, things called spiritual, which cannot be taken by a rational being to be capable of explanation by imposture, coincidence, or mistake. So far I feel the ground firm under me.'

"Such evidence as this, in connection with that of Mr. Varley, Mr. Wallace, and a host of other scientific witnesses, is very significant of the fact that although Professor De Morgan's did not grow in the telling, spiritualism is growing apace.

"A. B. TIETKENS."

The following items of evidence in my favour may also be given here as they appeared in the "Spiritual r Magazine."

"The War Correspondent of the 'Daily Telegraph' (Mr. Kingston) in a letter to that Journal of October 31st, 1870, writing from Versailles, says:— 'Among our party was Mr. Daniel Home, the celebrated Spiritualist, whom the King promptly recognized, and addressed very kindly—reminding him of the wonders that he (Mr. Home) had been the means of imparting to him, and inquiring about 'the spirits' in by no means a sceptical tone. We may add that the King said to Mr. Home that 'he had told many of his friends of the wonderful manifestations he had seen in Mr. Home's presence: his friends did not believe him; but the facts were true for all that.'"

Mr. J. M. Peebles, the United States Consul, in a lecture on his recent travels in Europe, delivered at Buttle Breek, near Chicago, and reported in the "Present Age" of September 3rd, 1870, makes the following statement:—

"While in England I dined with John Bright, when transpired quite an earnest conversation upon the subject of spiritualism. He said he had witnessed some of D. D. Home's manifestations. They were wonderful. He could attribute them to no cause except it be the one alleged, that of intelligent, disembodied spirits. 'But,' he added, with due caution, 'I do not say that this is so, but if it be true, it is the strongest tangible proof we have of immortality."

In the autumn of 1863, while at Dieppe, I met my friend, Mrs. Milner Gibson, one afternoon on the parade there. In the course of conversation she said, "Do you know that Dr. Elliottson is in Dieppe at present?" "Is he?" I replied, "I should like to be introduced to him." Mrs. Milner Gibson expressed surprise, but undertook to introduce me, and a few minutes afterwards we observed him on a seat. I was introduced to him, and said, "Dr. Elliottson, you have said and written very hard things of me. Now don't you think it was very wrong for an old man like you to make such accusations as you have done against me, and to call a man an impostor, of whom you knew nothing whatever? If you like to know something of me, and to investigate the subject of spiritualism I shall be happy to see you at Mrs. Milner Gibson's this evening, and to give you every opportunity of testing what you see." He came, and saw so much that he was convinced of the truth of spiritualism. On the next day he called on me, and said, "What I witnessed last evening was wonderful and convincing, but it is too much for me to change suddenly the convictions of seventy years. I must ask you to let me come again, and bring a young friend with me." I agreed readily, and that evening he came accompanied by the two young

Messrs. Symes. The fullest use was made by the gentlemen of their powers of observing and testing what they witnessed, and the result was that Dr. Elliottson was perfectly convinced. On his decease in the year 1868, a short memoir appeared in the "Morning Post," from which I give the following:—

"We have to record the decease, a day or two since, of one of the most remarkable scientific men of the century, who attained to the highest rank of the medical profession, and who was held in the greatest esteem for the daring and successful character of his innovations, and yet who, after living down and conquering aspersions cast on him, has lived long enough to be almost forgotten in the busy round of life. Dr. Elliottson was born somewhere about the year 1785, and studied at St. Thomas's and Guy's Hospitals. He was one of the first physicians to adopt the stethoscope in the diagnosis of lung and heart diseases. In the course of his practice at University College Hospital certain phenomena developed themselves in the cases of two young girls named Okey, and Elliottson was thus led to investigate mesmerism, and with his characteristic boldness and love of truth he published the results fearlessly. He was at this time enjoying as large a practice at the West End as had ever been the lot of any physician. The result of his bold utterance of the truth was that his learned brethren persecuted him, and his practice fell off to the extent of £5,000 per annum, and in 1838, he was obliged to resign his professorship. His practice, however, rose in time till it was larger than before, and he became noted for his mesmeric knowledge, which he cultivated assiduously. He continued through good and evil report to publish the results of his experiments, and established the 'Zoist,' which he maintained for twelve years, the volumes of which form a history of this branch of science. He was founder and president of the Phrenological Society, and was president of the Royal Medical and Chirurgical Society of London. In 1849 he founded the Mesmeric Hospital, which has been a great blessing to many. During the greater part of his life he was an unbeliever, and while investigating mesmerism sneered at the accounts which he heard of spiritualistic phenomena, and denounced all mediums as impostors. He also wrote an elaborate treatise denying the existence of an immortal soul, and arguing that the Hebrew word 'nephesh,' translated 'soul,' had no other meaning than, 'life.' In the year 1863, he was at Dieppe, and was introduced to Mr. D. D. Home, who told him he had acted wrongly in calling him an impostor when he really knew nothing of him. He then spent some time in investigating the phenomena of Spiritualism aided by the sons of his friend Dr. Symes. The result was that he expressed his conviction of the truth of the phenomena, and became a sincere Christian, whose handbook henceforth was his Bible. Sometime after this he said he had been living all his life in darkness, and had thought there was nothing in existence but the material; but he now had a firm hope which he trusted he would hold while on earth."

The "Spiritual Magazine" says:— "We may add to the foregoing notice, that not only was Dr. Elliottson for the greater part of his life— until he became a Spiritualist—an unbeliever in revelation, but a Materialist of the most uncompromising and determined type,—the acknowledged head of that school of Physiology of which Lawrence and Engledue were the champions—which regards man as a merely corporeal being,—the faculties of the mind as synonymous with functions of the brain, and in what is usually regarded as evidence of his spiritual nature sees only the results of cerebral action. These views he set forth with great force in his elaborate work on "Human Physiology;' and they were eagerly caught up by the atheistic secular party in this country, and reproduced in lectures, articles, and tracts; and his name (which since he became a spiritualist they appear to have almost forgotten) was constantly in their mouths as that of an eminent authority on the subject. When modern spiritualism was introduced into this country, Dr. Elliottson was one of the sturdiest and most scornful of its opponents. Not only did he denounce it in the "Zoist," but he gave a series of wood-cuts in that journal to accompany the text, showing how the 'rappings' were effected. On this question of spiritualism, he joined issue with, and separated himself from his old friend and colleague in mesmerism, and in the establishment and management of the "Zoist"— Dr. Ashburner; to whom it must have been a source of great satisfaction after years of estrangement, that Dr. Elliottson's conviction of the truth of spiritualism was the means of re-establishing their former intimacy and friendship.

Spiritualism was not with Dr. Elliottson a conviction barren of results. It revolutionized the philosophy of a lifetime, as he was always ready to avow, bitterly lamenting the misdirected efforts he had made, however conscientiously, in the promulgation of materialistic principles. He became a thoroughly changed man, and changed in all respects for the better. Humbled by the recollection of past errors, his nature became softened, his demeanour more gentle, and he bore his losses and sufferings with patience and fortitude.

"Some of our correspondents have expressed doubts of the efficacy of prayer. Dr. Elliottson affirmed that he could no longer entertain any question of it, as he had personal and constant evidence of the efficacy of prayer in his own experience.

"To those who question as to the strength of evidence which spiritualism presents to the scientific investigator, or as to its origin and effects, this brief record may be useful. Let the tree be judged by its fruits."

The following letter appeared in "Human Nature," November 1, 1870:—

"Sir,—I have been informed that doubt has been expressed as to Dr. Elliottson ever having become a believer in spiritualism; and, as I happen to be acquainted with certain circumstances connected with his being so, I trespass on your space in order to remove that doubt.

"I was happy in seeing much of Dr. Elliottson from the commencement of and during his brave combat in defence of the genuineness of the phenomena of animal magnetism—(I always regretted his adoption of the term, mesmerism, thinking the original one so much more expressive of their nature)—and I am quite aware of his utter inability to receive the truth of the manifestations which he witnessed when Mrs. Hayden was in this country, and which he tried to account for by one of the many absurd hypotheses, rife then, but now completely exploded. He consequently became violently opposed to all those who admitted the genuineness of them, and avowed their belief in communication with the spirits of the departed. So strong was his honest disbelief on this subject that, when his friend, Dr. Ashburner, became one of the staunchest advocates of its truth, he broke off all intercourse with him, nor did he hesitate to write and speak of it and him in severe terms, and on the worse than folly of uniting in such a gross imposition on the gullibility of mankind. This continued for some years, until being at Dieppe, Mrs. Milner Gibson induced him to join in a *séance* with Mr. Home, I believe in more than one, the result being that he was firmly convinced, not only of the existence of the spiritual world, but of the power to communicate with the spirits of departed friends therein; and, with the perfect courageous honesty of his nature, promised to make his convictions known on his return to London. This he did; and I well remember a conversation with him, in which he said, 'What shall I do with my books?' admitting that many of them were of a kind which would promote a disbelief in the truth he had so happily attained to.

"When he returned to London, one of the first things he did was to see a mutual friend of his and Dr. Ashburner's, and to express his regret that 'he should have treated such a man in such a manner,' asking if the friend thought Dr. A. I would ever forgive him.'

"On the same morning Dr. Ashburner happened to call on the friend, and, learning the above, immediately went to 37, Conduit Street, and, in Dr. Elliottson's absence, left his card. He had not been long at home when Dr. Elliottson entered his room, with his hands before his face, saying, 'Can you forgive me?'

"This was followed, as those who knew the man may well imagine, by a perfect reconciliation, honourable in the highest degree to both.

"In one of my latest interviews with him, he expressed the great happiness his later convictions had brought him, and looked forward to the life hereafter with calm confidence. The leading characteristic of his mind, in addition to his high intellectual development, was the perfectly honest search after truth. This, when it is perfect, is sure to be rewarded by success, sooner or later.

"In his case, on this subject, it was late. May all those, who are equally honest searchers, find it, even if as late as he did.—Yours, &c.

H. C."

A remarkable prophetic incident came to my knowledge in 1863, by the following letters, which I leave to tell their own story:—

"Boston, May 17, 1863.

"MY DEAR DANIEL,—I can most fully sympathize with you in your sorrow, having recently met with a great bereavement myself. My daughter Mary (Mrs. Higginson) was taken with bleeding from the lungs, and in eight weeks she passed from earth-life to the inner world. She died of rapid consumption. While John has been ill for three years, he is still with us, awaiting humbly and patiently his summons and release. He looks like an angel, and is like one for his goodness.

"Mary was my youngest daughter, and she had a gentle, lovely temper and disposition, that twined her close round my heart. She was to me all that a daughter could be, and my loss is very great, but I shall not have very long to stay away from her. During your last visit to us, at one of our *séances*, you asked me for paper and pencil. I gave them to you, and you then asked for wafers to seal up your writing. The paper was sealed up very carefully, handed to me, and you told me to keep it till the spirits made it known that it was to be opened. I kept it thus seven years or more, and then having a good opportunity, I inquired if I might, open it. The answer was that I had better not, as the contents were not what I might like. After a while I asked again, and was told that if I were so desirous I might open it. I therefore broke the seals, and found the following words:— 'Mary will be the *first* to leave earth. Grieve not. All will be well with her. It may be years.'

"You may judge of my feelings at this announcement, and when she was taken with the haemorrhage I felt that she would be the first, although for weeks we had almost been daily feeling that John would leave us. We laid her body away last Tuesday, just five days ago, and John breathes yet. Yours, &c.,

"D. D. Home, Esq.

A. S. JARVES."

"Boston, July 5th.

"DEAR DANIEL,—I have postponed writing you since John passed away. His spirit was released from the body on the 21st of May, just eleven days after Mary had left us. Strange to say John did not ask to see his sister as we did not tell him what a surprise was awaiting him there. George (his spirit brother) told us that he had impressed John not to think of Mary, and now John tells us that when he met his sister he thought it must only be a vision. Yours, &c.,

"D. D. Home, Esq.

A. S. JARVES."

An equally remarkable prophetic incident occurred to me in the autumn of 1863, while at Dieppe. A Russian gentleman asked me if I ever saw a vision in a crystal, to which I replied no. He said, Look in this, and tell me if you see anything. I took it up; and on looking at it, to my astonishment, I saw a crowd, and in the crowd a man who was assassinated, in the act of falling forward from his chair. I said, "That is Abraham Lincoln, and within the year he will be assassinated."

I do not attempt to explain these things, I can only give the facts.

The following incidents in my experience, I related at a conference in London some time since, and I give them as reported in the "Spiritual Magazine:"—

"At one of the London Conferences on Spiritualism, Mr. D. D. Home narrated the following experiences:— Some eighteen years ago, when quite a boy, he was travelling in a railway carriage, when a gentleman, son of Professor Wayland, of Brown University, asked if he was Mr. Home; on replying that he was, the gentleman said he owed him an apology; on asking why, he said he had called Home an impostor, and owed him an apology for doing so. The gentleman said he had occasion once to call on a friend, when he found Home in his office in a trance and blindfolded. As he hesitated about entering, Home pointing to the door said, 'That is Frank, tell him to come, his sister Caroline is here.' He told them he never had a sister Caroline, and that it was all humbug. He went home and said to his father that he would be sorry to hear 'Mr. _____ had taken up with spiritualism, and had that fellow Home in his office blindfolded; and, only fancy! he told me I had had a sister Caroline.' His father said, 'And don't you really know you had a sister of that name?' 'No,' he replied, 'of course not.' 'Then' returned his father, 'you had; she was born just before yourself, but only lived a few hours, and during that time was christened Caroline; so Home was right. Mr. Home said that everybody had their own ideas of dignity, and sometimes the plain truth is withheld for the sake of upholding it. An old maiden lady once entered the house where he was staying, while he was in a trance; she was persuaded to remain, and during the *séance* she asked Home whilst in the trance what were the last words her mother had said on her death-bed; if he could tell her that she would believe. Home replied, 'Puss, puss, poor pussy.' The lady started, turned pale, and said he was right; those were the very last words used, but she thought them so undignified, that she had never told anybody of them."

While at Dieppe I made some essays in the art of sculpture which led to my removing to Rome, where one of the remarkable events of my life occurred. This was related in the "Spiritual Magazine," with the following introduction:—

"Another curious 'incident of his life' has just happened to Mr. Home, and is related by the *Times* in a letter from 'our own correspondent' at Rome, where Mr. Home has now been for some time studying as a sculptor. During his late visit to Dieppe, he had suddenly shown considerable talent as a sculptor. His first effort was highly approved, and he was advised to devote himself to the art, and for that purpose he went to Rome in the month of October last, and has since been actively working there as a student. It is now decided that he has great talent, and he is making rapid progress, with the intention of shortly commencing the practice of his new profession at Paris, where he intends establishing a studio. We give the narrative of the little episode which happened to him in the Eternal City, as it appeared in the 'Times' of the 12th of January. It is quite a *bijou* in its way, and an instance of the way in which affairs go on under the guidance of 'God's vicegerent upon earth,' and the precious gentleman who holds the keys of St. Peter.

(From our own Correspondent.)

"Rome, Jan. 6.

"Perhaps the most exciting incident of the week is that Mr. Home, of spiritualism notoriety, has been ordered to leave Rome in three days; and that I may not err in my statement of the fact which has occasioned great sensation, I give you a report of the proceedings in his own words."

I give in lieu of the "Times" report, the full extract from my diary.

I arrived at Rome on the 15th November, 1863, for the purpose of studying sculpture.

On the 2nd of January, 1864, I received, at five o'clock in the evening, a letter requiring my attendance at the office of the chief Police Station. Feeling sure that this summons could be connected with nothing but spiritualism, I could not help thinking how sad it was that men who ought to be more enlightened should treat as a crime a matter that the Church ought rather to encourage and support. In order, however, to avoid, any disturbance, I determined to do as was required of me and so, with a companion who kindly consented to accompany me, at half-past eleven on January 3rd I presented myself at the Palazzo-Citerio. We were shown into an ante-room, where there were some straw chairs, but no fire, and as the roof was covered with snow we found it very cold. After waiting for more than half-an-hour, I began to get a little impatient, and, calling a servant, I asked him if it was the custom to treat in this manner people who had been summoned; and told him to warn those who had desired my presence that I would wait no longer. After a short absence he returned with excuses for my detention, and saying that M. Pasqualonni was ready to receive me. We were shown into a large room, where that gentleman was seated at an office table with drawers. The apartment was scantily furnished—a few chairs, a plaster-of-paris bust of the Pope; an engraving of the Holy Virgin was suspended behind M. Pasqualonni, in the frame of which some visiting cards were placed.

Upon my entrance Mons. P. bowed to me, and motioned me to seat myself opposite to him; the friend who accompanied me sat at the end of the table, on the left of Mons. P., who commenced his remarks with—

Q. You are Mr. D. Dunglas Home?—A. Yes, sir, and here is my passport.

Q. (Without taking it) Very well, I must ask you some questions.—A. For my part, sir, I am ready to answer you.

Q. Were you born in Scotland?—A. Yes, sir.

Q. Are you thirty-seven years old?—A. No, sir, I am only thirty years old.

Q. But, sir, you are thirty-seven. A. No, sir; I was born in 1833; next March I shall be in my thirty-first year.

Q. (Taking a paper from a drawer, and looking at it) According to my notes you ought to be thirty-seven.—A. I am sorry that I am unable to corroborate your information; but I am only thirty years old.

Q. Your father's name?—A. William.

Q. Your mother's?—A. Elizabeth.

Q. Her maiden name?—A. McNeil. (Here I interrupted him with a request that I might be furnished with pencil and paper.)

Q. For what purpose?—A. To write.

Q. To write what?—A. I am a free man, and should wish to preserve questions and answers of such great importance.

Q. (Handing me a sheet of paper and a red pencil.) How many times have you been in Rome?—A. This is my third visit.

Q. When and of what duration were the other visits?—A. In 1856, I remained here two months, then it was that I became a Roman

Catholic; in 1858, I passed three weeks here; and upon this occasion I have been here since the 15th November.

Q. Nay, you have been here since the 1st of November?—A. Here is my passport, which will show you that I have been here only since the 15th.

Q. Is it your intention to remain a long time here?—A. No, sir, I propose in April to return to Paris.

Q. Have you a house there?—A. No, sir.

Q. What was your object in coming to Rome?—A. For my health and to study sculpture.

Q. What was your religion before 1856?—A. Protestant.

Q. Have you published any works—how many—and under what titles?—A. "Incidents in My Life."

Q. Was the book published in Paris by Dentu?—A. It was.

Q. You say that you are a medium, that you become entranced, and that you see spirits?—A. Yes, sir, I have said so, and it is true.

Q. And you hold communications with spirits?—A. When they think proper.

Q. How do you summon them?—A. I do not summon them, they manifest themselves of their own accord.

Q. How do they manifest themselves?

I was about to answer, "Sometimes in one way, sometimes in another," when raps were made upon the table close to him and far from me; he asked me in a tone of great astonishment the cause of these noises. My companion answered him by saying: "These are the spirits, and it must be evident to you that Mr. Home has no volition in the matter." "Spirits!" replied M. Pasqualonni, looking all about the table more and more astonished: then he said, "Let us continue our examination. Proceed."

Q. So you consider your gift as a gift of nature?—A. No, I consider it a gift of God.

Q. Since the year 1856 have you never exercised your power?—A. Neither before nor since, seeing that I am passive in these manifestations, which are spontaneous.

Q. In your opinion what is the object of these manifestations?—A. To assure sceptics of the immortality of the soul, and to afford heavenly consolation.

Q. You relate in your work on miracles performed by you, amongst others, cases of cure?—A. These cures are truly miracles.

Q. How did you accomplish them?—A. I know nothing about it. I am but an instrument.

Q. You have given *séances* in France, England, and Russia?—A. At friendly assemblies met for the purpose, manifestations sometimes occur. But why do you ask me all this? My book answers this question in the affirmative; all persons therein named are prepared to corroborate what I have printed, and I will maintain, even at the risk of my life, the truth of what my book asserts.

My friend, considering me a little fatigued, requested M. Pasqualonni to postpone the examination to another day, but I replied that I preferred finishing it then.

Q. You say in your work that articles of furniture move; why does not this table start off for a walk? Do you see spirits when you are awake or asleep?—A. In both states. With regard to the cases of locomotion you speak of, they occur sometimes, but not by any will of mine own. (As I said, this, a cracking noise was heard on the table which moved slightly. M. Pasqualonni looking about, said in a troubled voice, "Let us continue.")

Q. Did you not say in your book that your mother was a medium?—A. Yes, sir, and my son is also.

Q. What is the age of your son?—A. Four years and a half.

Q. Where is be?—A. At Malvern.

Q. Where is Malvern?—A. In England.

Q. Has be a nurse?—A. Yes, sir.

Q. Is she a Catholic?—A. No, sir, she belongs to the Greek Church.

Q. With whom is your son?—A. With Dr. Gully, one of my friends.

Q. Is Dr. Gully a Catholic?—A. No, sir.

At this point my friend began speaking in a low voice with M. Pasqualonni, and I learned that the subject of their conversation was my expulsion from Rome. Then I demanded that the order for it should be made in writing, which was done, and I was told that within three days I must leave Rome.

Q. Do you consent to do so?—A. (Rising up.) Certainly not, for, having infringed no law, my consenting to go would look as if I had committed something of which I was ashamed. I expect to find this the cause of much scandal before I go. I warn you beforehand, and upon my leaving you I shall at once seek advice from my consul. Then he said to me, "I hope, Mr. Home, that you will not refuse me your hand." I gave him my hand, at the same time saying, that I was sorry to see him the instrument of authority such as this. I went to my consul and told him what had happened; it being Sunday, nothing could be done, but the next day he promised to see the governor of Rome. I then betook myself to a person of considerable importance, who was kind enough to go immediately to Monseigneur Matteuci, which cardinal, in a long conversation, told my friend that he had nothing to say against me except on the matter of sorcery.

The next day, at twelve o'clock, the English consul went to see the Monseigneur, who said to him that if I was willing to sign an engagement, in which I would promise not to give any *séances*, I might remain in Rome. I lost no time in writing the following declaration:—

"I give my word as a gentleman that, during my stay in Rome, I will have no *séance*, and that I will avoid, as much as possible, all conversations upon spiritualism.

"DANIEL DUNGLAS HOME.

"Palazzi-Paoli, 4 January, 1864."

My consul, not satisfied with this, wished me to make known why I had come to Rome and why I was anxious to remain, then I wrote on the same paper:—

"I have only come to Rome for my health and to study art, therefore I should wish to be left alone.

"D. D. HOME."

This document was despatched to Monseigneur Matteuci, and for the remainder of the week I heard no more on the subject, until Saturday afternoon, at 5.30, when I received the following letter:—

"M. Daniel Dunglas Home will have the great kindness to present himself at the passport office between six and eight o'clock, provided with his passport."

I begged of my friend, who had accompanied me on the previous occasion, to perform once more the like service, and we both of us went to the Palazzo-Citerio at a quarter before six. I went to the office of M. Pegallo, who, after having taken and looked at my passport, said to me:— "But, sir, you ought first to have visited your consul." "For what purpose!" was my reply. "That he might *viser* your passport, as you intend to go." I answered that I had no intention of leaving. Then he said, looking at the passport, "In that case your passport is quite correct: with such a passport you can remain a whole year." I bowed and thanked him. The next morning, at a quarter before ten, one of the sons of the mistress of the house where I lodged entered my studio in a state of alarm, and said:— "Sir, there is a policeman awaiting you at your house." I replied that he might make himself quite comfortable at my place, for I had no intention of returning home just yet; and that if he wished to see me be must come to my studio. Ten minutes afterwards the man came and said that he was obliged to seek me in consequence of my not having the preceding day appeared at the passport office, where I had been summoned. I replied that not only had I been there, but that I had been accompanied by a friend. He then said, "Your friend had been, but you had not." Upon this, with difficulty keeping my temper, I answered, "Come along, the same person will accompany me again:" which he did. Going to the same apartment, I went to the same desk, and gave my passport to M. Pegallo, who said, "I was waiting for you till eight o'clock yesterday, and you did not come." I answered him that I had come at a quarter before six, and that having to come twice I did not find it particularly gratifying.

Q. But you did, not come?—A. I tell you I did come; you took my passport, and told me that I might remain a year. Now, say no more on that subject, don't lie unless your position requires that you should do so.

He said, "At three o'clock to-day you must leave Rome." "Very well. I have no intention, however, of going, and I do not mean to go." He replied, "You must by three o'clock be outside of the gates of Rome." I then said, "Do your duty; sign my passport." He signed it, gave it me back, and I went out to find my consul, who received me with feelings of suppressed rage, saying, "Why do you make promises to break them immediately after?" I asked him what he meant; he replied, that I had been playing the fool with M. Pasqualonni. I cried out angrily, "M. Severn, I have come to you as an English subject, and not to speak to you either as to my belief or the phenomena which happen through me, and if you had examined the matter you would know that they are independent of my will. I only require of you to do your duty as consul; any other advice is out of place, the more so that since my promise no manifestation has taken place, although in undertaking not to give *séances* I am unable to promise that no manifestations shall occur." He went to see the Governor of Rome, who told him that since I was unable to avoid having manifestations, I must not be allowed to remain longer in Rome. One of my friends called upon Monseigneur Matteuci (where I presented myself between four and five o'clock, without being received). He obtained permission for me to remain till Wednesday following. Learning that I resolved to depart on Monday, a great number of friends conducted me to the railway as a token of their sympathy.

"Such," says the "Times" correspondent, "is the report of a procedure which is eminently characteristic of the Pontifical Government. On Monday morning the British Consul saw Monseigneur Matteucci, the Governor of Rome, and complained that any British subject should be interfered with in consequence of his opinions. He stated that Mr. Home had conducted himself during his residence in Rome in a strictly legal and gentlemanly manner, and demanded that the obnoxious order should be rescinded. Monseigneur spoke of dangerous powers of fascination, of the prohibition by the Government of all the practices of the black art, and finally assented to Mr. Home's remaining, on condition of his entering into an engagement, through Mr. Severn, that he would desist from all communications with the spiritual world during his stay in Rome. An agreement to that effect was drawn up and signed by Mr. Home, who will henceforward abstain from all communication with the upper or lower world, as the case may be, during his residence in Rome. Less fortunate than Mr. Home has been a Dominican priest, who has been deprived of his curacy, I hear, for having read Mr. Home's book."

The " Spiritual Magazine" adds:— "If it were not for the refreshing and business-like style of the narrative, one could not imagine that such a scene could be enacted in this new year of our Lord, 1864, in any part of Europe. Probably, perhaps excepting Spain, there is no country, excepting that governed by the infallible and holy father, where such a lunatic act could be perpetrated. What a laugh the holy father's patron, Napoleon, and Mr. Home will have over the old gentleman when next they meet! No wonder that French soldiers are required to prop up such an old fellow on both sides, to keep him out of the clutches of his loving subjects. The Pope's own recollections of having to escape from his own palace dressed up as a flunkey, behind one of his own carriages, seem to be quite lost upon him, and we wonder that all the Jeameses do not hold an indignation meeting, to protest against his having disgraced their cloth on that memorable occasion.

The most amusing part of the business is the rescinding of the order, on condition of Mr. Home entering into an engagement, that he would desist from all communications with the spiritual world during his stay in Rome! This reminds us of what occurred during the time that the miracles of healing were being carried out at St. Medard, in Paris, upon the multitudes who flocked to the tomb of the good Abbé François Paris. When the numbers became so great that the thoroughfare was stopped by them, some wag wrote upon the wall:

"De par le roi, defense à Dieu
De faire miracles en ce lieu!"

What was suggested as a witty piece of blasphemy, has now been done by the Pope, the Holy Father, of the true Faith, the infallible head of the Church, and the lineal descendant of the Apostles, who preached and practised the spiritual religion which is based upon that super-naturalism, many instances of which have been marvellously elucidated and proved to a sceptical age, by the phenomena which occur in the presence of Mr. Home. At Rome then it is of all places in the world, where *De par le pape, defense à Dieu, de faire miracles en ce lieu*, but perhaps it is the place of all others now least likely for any spiritual developments. The scandalous frauds, and immoralities, impostures, cruelties, child snatchings, and bigotry of this poor priest-ridden place, make it little likely that any true spiritual developments could find favour within its walls. It is a country where superstition is made a trade to bring pence to its mendicant priests, and where a small proportion of true spiritual phenomena has been eked out by nine-tenths of impostures, in the shape of winking Madonnas, bleeding pictures, and chapels of our Lady of Loretto, with the Pope himself sitting in the veritable chair of St. Peter, which an exploring Englishman, on removing a part of its covering, found to be of ivory covered with Moorish characters. When a case of common mediumship happens among them, they are so ignorant of its nature, that if a young girl in a trance or magnetic state sees the Virgin Mary, straightway Europe is canvassed for money to raise a chapel on the spot. Truly the days are past for spiritual manifestations in Rome, when all the great and good saints, as they call them, are disowned by a Pope who forbids God to perform again the miracles which were common to all of them. Mr. Home is raised in the air, so were St. Francis, and St. Ignatius Loyola, and so was St. Theresa in the great square of St. Peter's in the presence of the Pope and assembled Rome. There is not one of the manifestations common to Mr. Home, but are to be seen fifty times repeated in the lives accredited by the church, of nearly all of its greatest saints, but now the Pope forbids that God should longer do miracles at Rome. If the Pope were other than a lunatic, he would have made Mr. Home a cardinal, and have retained him to have sittings twice a week at the Vatican, that by means of his manifestations, the belief in the possibility of the Romish miracles, might have some chance of being a little re-established, and rescued from the mass of fraud in which the true ones are justly lost. If Protestantism, which practically denies all spirituality in religion and in nature, had issued such an order as that of the Pope, we should not have been surprised. Our men of science and literature such as Brewster and the members of the Royal Society, will hardly be proud of their new coadjutor. They would not agree on the reasons, but only in the conclusion of the venerable Father.

"We cannot but be thankful that such an event has occurred, as it will excite increased interest in the subject, and very great contempt for Popish incapacity and bigotry."

The following is from the "Spiritual Magazine" for February 1, 1864:—

"We have just received information from Mr. Home, that, notwithstanding the permission to remain in Rome on condition of having 'no connection with any other world,' this unwonted leniency was more than the authorities could bear, and a few days after, Mr. Home was definitely informed that he must quit the Holy City, on the ground of his being a sorcerer. After his first examination by the police, which was shortly reported in the 'Times,' the indignation of the upper classes in Rome was aroused, and many called upon him to express their sympathy; and now, when he received an order to quit Rome at once, his friends rallied round him, and with expressions of detestation of the Government proceeded with him to the railway station by which he left for Naples. Amongst those who so accompanied him was His Royal Highness the Count de Trani. His quitting was quite an ovation, and a public protest against the ignorant and pitiable barbarity of the spiritual head of the only true church.

"The Governor of Rome, upon being remonstrated with, and asked if there was anything against his character, replied that there was nothing, and that 'during the two months Mr. Home has been in Rome, *we have had him watched*, and we believe that his character is without blemish. We have also information from elsewhere to the same effect; but he *is a sorcerer* and cannot be permitted in Rome, and he must go.' For four weeks previous to his departure, the Roman Government kept back all his letters, and even yet they have not been delivered to him.

"Mr. Home is now therefore at Naples, where he has been received with great distinction. His arrival has been announced in the newspapers, and he has been elected an honorary member of the highest club there, and feted by the residents, both English and native."

As bearing on this event I may be permitted to quote the following letter, which speaks for itself.

"Circular letter and ordinance of Monseigneur the Bishop of Algiers on the superstition called spiritualism.

"ARTICLE I.—The practice of spiritualism, or the evocation of the dead, is interdicted to all and every one in the diocese of Algiers.

"ARTICLE II.—The confessors shall refuse absolution to every one who does not renounce all participation, whether as a medium, as an adept, or as a simple witness, at *séances*, private or public, in short, at any operation whatever of spiritualism.

"ARTICLE III.—In all the towns and all the rural parishes of Algiers, where spiritualism has been introduced with some *éclat*, Messieurs the curés shall read publicly this letter from the pulpit the first Sunday after its reception. Besides this, they shall communicate everywhere in particular, according to the necessity,

"Done at Algiers, the 18th of August, 1863.

"+ Louis Antoine-Augustine, Bishop of Algiers.

"By command of Monseigneur:

"A. ANCELIN, Canon, Vicar-General."

After my return to England I wrote the following letter to Lord Palmerston:—

"MY LORD,

"Some months since I took up my residence in Rome for the purpose of pursuing my studies as a sculptor.

"Without having in any way infringed the laws of the place, I was expelled the territory at a very short notice, on the pretext that I was a sorcerer, and that I had published a book in London.

"Having been put to great expense as well as inconvenience by my expulsion, I beg to submit the facts to your Lordship's notice, as the best means of obtaining redress.

"I have, &c., &c.,

"DANIEL DUNGLASS HOME.'

"To the Right Honorable

"Viscount Palmerston, K.G., &c., &c., &c.

"Treasury.'

Being referred to the Foreign Secretary, further correspondence ensued, which was terminated by the following letter:—

"Foreign Office,
"April 16, 1864.

SIR,

"I am directed by Earl Russell to acknowledge the receipt of your letter of the 9th instant, complaining of your expulsion from the Roman Territory; and I am to state to you, in reply, that his lordship is not prepared to make any representation to the Roman Government on the subject.

"I am, Sir,

"Your most obedient humble Servant,   "A. H. LAYARD.
"D. D. Home, Esq.
"Cox's Hotel, Jermyn Street."

In reference to this affair I received a letter from Monsieur A. Gautier, Consul for Greece in Rome, of which the following is a translation.

"Your departure hence has been the subject of many comments, which I have carefully traced, and I think you will be pleased to have an account of them; they will afford you amusement.

"Some have given out that you were a secret agent of England, others of the Emperor of the French, and some of Russia, but others have asserted that you were the familiar spy of the Ex-king of Naples, and gave as proof your relations with Count de Trani, and M. Della Rocca. Hence you were held to mix in society only as an unavowed diplomatist, a dangerous man, having intimate understanding with so many courts; and you became properly suspected by the governments.

"But as this did not content all those moral minds who held that every one had a right to become in society an agent for this or that government, without deserving to be expelled for his opinions, a version of a different character has sprung up; and it has been said that you were compelled to leave for moral reasons. The book, the true cause, has been swamped beneath all these products of imagination.

"It is asserted that the advocate who questioned you was sensible of raps given while the interrogatory was proceeding, and that when he was told of this, he replied, 'Imagination, excitement; he had thought he heard them.'"

After a quotation from the "Memorial Diplomatique" of Paris, the letter concludes:—

"It may be presumed that all these rumours and repetitions will not end here, but that the apostle of truth will one day speak or write concerning the facts which relate to him, and in such case he is hereby authorised and recommended to make known, even by means of his pen, the name of the official interpreter who was present at this very occurrence, and who like himself professes reverence for truth. This is a right appertaining to the victim, and which could not be denied to him, any more than truth could be falsified.

Having been recommended to follow up my application to the Foreign Secretary by having my case brought before the House of

Commons, Mr. J. A. Roebuck kindly undertook to ask a question on the subject. I wrote to him as follows:—

"64, Jermyn St.
"St. James.

"DEAR SIR,

"I do indeed much regret all the trouble I am giving you: but at the same time I feel assured that your own high sense of justice and right is such that you will, I am sure, be patient with me. I submit the documents connected with my expulsion from Rome, and you will see that there is question of naught but my book and my belief as a spiritualist.

"The Papal party are now, as I am aware, doing all they can to have it said, that there were other grounds for my expulsion, but not one of them dares to come forward and, like a man, make the charge. There is, to my way of thinking, nothing so base as a dastardly attack on a man's moral character. I can well comprehend that they should feel heartily ashamed of what they term an infallible church having to expel from its states a man whose whole life is well known, and against whom naught could be said. But then it is a sad pity that they should have to resort to falsehood and calumny, to endeavour to palliate the ill usage already received. Some of them say that I did give *séances* in Rome. You will find in the letter marked No. 4, which is written to me by my old landlady with whom I lodged all the time I was in Rome, that she was not even aware of the singular powers I possess. In all common fairness I should consider this a fair refutation of the charge. Another charge is, that I was expelled as not an innocent character. I am willing to have every act of my life, not only during my stay in Rome, but elsewhere brought before the public, and will stand by their candid decision. Letter No. 1 is my first intimation to appear before them to be questioned. In No. 2 are the questions written by the gentleman who accompanied me, and you will see that there is not even an allusion to aught in my personal character. In No. 2, B., are the questions and answers prepared for print as a preface to the third edition of my book in France. No. 3 is a letter received from the gentleman who was with me during my examination. This letter was received during my stay in Paris. No. 4 is the letter before alluded to. And now, dear sir, I can assure you that I feel very grateful for the trouble you have already taken. I only ask justice. I must add to all this, that Mr. Severn was, instead of being an aid to me, quite the contrary, and it is a wonder to me that an intelligent government could ever have placed any one in so important a position who is so little qualified to fill it. Mr. Severn knows nothing of international law, and is but too apt to speak of matters which do not in the least enter into his position. He, in the presence of Mr. Wreford the 'Times Correspondent,' said that several letters had been read to him by Monsignor Mattenci the contents of which he refused to divulge, but that the purports were such that he must refuse to do anything more for me. I then, in the presence of these two gentlemen, demanded to know if there was aught in the letters which would prevent his taking my hand as an Englishman and a gentleman. To this he at once said, No. Two hours after that I was told what the letters did contain, and it was only the same absurd story which is told every time I leave Paris, i.e. that I am sent away by command of the Emperor. Such tittle tattle as this ought to be avoided by an English consul.

"Any information you may require I will be only too happy to give. Again thanking you,

"Believe me, my dear Sir,

"Your most obedient,

"D. D. HOME."

May 24, 1864."

"The Spiritual Magazine" for July, 1864, contains the following account of the discussion in the House:— "As the readers of this journal will doubtless have seen that Mr. Home's expulsion from Rome has been made the subject of complaint and enquiry in the British House of Commons, it will not be out of place to make a record here of so interesting an episode in the history of modern spiritualism. I extract the report as published in the 'Morning Star,' of the 31st of May last:

"'Mr. Roebuck rose to ask the Under-Secretary of State for Foreign Affairs whether any steps had been taken to obtain from the Papal Government redress for the injuries done to Mr. Home by that Government. The hon. gentleman said Mr. Home believed he had the power to call spirits, and he was what was publicly called a 'Spiritualist,' although he (Mr. Roebuck) did not exactly know what that meant. He did not believe in it, but that had nothing to do with the present case. Mr. Home he believed to be a man of perfectly good behaviour, and the question was whether he was to receive protection from the Government of England. The facts of the case were these. Mr. Home went to Rome to study his art, and he incurred considerable expense to carry out this object. Some time after he arrived there he received a notice from the head of the police requiring him to attend at the police-office. Mr. Home did so, when a number of questions was asked him. In the first place, the police official asked him his age, and Mr. Home gave a reply, and he was naturally a person that ought to know his own age. The official told him he was eight or ten years older, which Mr. Home denied. The signor or then said, 'You have published a book in France and in England saying that certain spirits waited upon you.' Mr. Home admitted that he had done this. The signor said, 'Will you undertake that no spirits shall come to you while you are in Rome?' (Laughter.) Mr. Home said, 'No, I cannot do that; the spirits come to me of their own accord. I cannot answer for them; but this I will promise, that I will hold no *séance*, and I will do nothing to solicit their coming to me; and further, I will do nothing contrary to the laws of the city of Rome.' Upon this the signor gave him to understand that he should not be interrupted. Some time after this, the second in command of the police sent for Mr. Home. Mr. Home went in company with the French Consul, but he found nobody at the police-office. When he got home, there came a peremptory note calling upon him to be at the police-office. Mr. Home went the second time, when the official said, 'You were not here yesterday at the hour at which you were required.' Mr. Home said, 'Yes, I was.' 'Well,' said the official, 'you must leave Rome in forty-eight hours.' Now this was the whole of the matter. (Hear, hear.) He (Mr. Roebuck) wished to know whether the Government would protect a British subject who had been treated in this way. Whatever might be the wonderful and mysterious power of Mr. Home, he ought to be protected as a British citizen. He observed the President of the Board of Trade in his place—(much laughter) but he (Mr. Roebuck) had no feeling for Mr. Home's profession, further than having a contempt for the whole thing; but still Mr. Home, being a British citizen, should be protected. He had great respect for the old gentleman at the head of the Papal Government (a laugh)—and he wished that he might long live to enjoy himself; but England must protect her subjects. Mr. Home had been ignominiously expelled from Rome, after having incurred considerable expenses there, and when Earl Russell was asked what he would do, he said 'I will do nothing.' (Much laughter, caused by Mr. Roebuck imitating the voice and manner of the noble lord.) 'He asked the noble lord at the head of the Government to protect this unfortunate gentleman against the tyranny of the Roman Government.'

"'Mr. Layard regretted that Mr. Home should have placed himself in a position to lead the Papal Government to call upon him to leave Rome, but he appeared to have infringed on their rules. ['No, no,' from Mr. Roebuck.] Well, the Roman Government thought that he carried on intercourse with spirits, and they called upon him to leave Rome in consequence. He (Mr. Layard) gave no opinion as to whether or not

Mr. Home had intercourse with spirits, nor did he seek to palliate the conduct of the Roman authorities; but such was the law of Rome, and he did not think that the Government could interfere. The Roman authorities feared that these spirits would communicate with Mr. Home whether he wished it or not, and they objected to their making Rome their dwelling place. (Laughter.) All this might be very foolish, but he did not see that there was any cause for the interference of the British Government.

"'Mr. Hennessy pointed out that the stringent laws in England against fortune-telling and witchcraft were founded on the same principle as the laws of Rome. He had always heard from English visitors at Rome that they received the greatest attention from the Papal Government'

"'Mr. V. Scully did not see that either the Roman Government or Mr. Home were to blame. The real parties against whom to bring the complaint were those unseen spirits who visited Mr. Home whether he wished it or not. He complained that the hon. member for Sheffield should have spoken of the Pope as 'the old gentleman' at the head of the Papal Government. In regard to Mr. Home's revelations, he did not believe in any spirit, except the case of the Witch of Endor—(a laugh)— but as they had been discussing 'spirits' all night he hoped they would have no more on the subject at present.

"'The subject then dropped.'

"As I have a great respect for Mr. Roebuck, whom I believe to be a bold and honest politician, I regret that he felt it necessary to qualify his remarks by stooping to meet the prejudices of his compeers in expressing his contempt for the wonderful and mysterious power of Mr. Home. If the power be, as Mr. Roebuck admits, 'wonderful and mysterious,' it is illogical and irrational to contemn that which he does not understand.

"It is more than ten years since I first spoke to Mr. Roebuck on the subject of spiritualism, and described to him the 'wonderful and mysterious' character of the phenomena which I had then witnessed. My statements were corroborated by two or three other persons present, and as Mr. Roebuck exhibited a total unbelief in these statements, I asked him, as a lawyer, what amount of human testimony it required in his opinion to establish a fact; because I could, if testimony were of any value, obtain any reasonable number of witnesses. He did not answer that question, but ended the conversation with a significant shrug and smile, implying very plainly that he pitied me, and doubtless had he been presiding as a Master in Lunacy at an investigation into my mental condition, he would not have hesitated to pronounce me incapable of the management of my own affairs.

"Mr. Roebuck, since that period, must be aware that thousands of men and women in this country, his equals in character and intelligence, have been confirmed in 'the delusion' under which he supposed I was then labouring; and therefore I repeat that it is with feelings of surprise and regret that I find one who has been in advance of the age on most subjects, venturing to sneer at a subject upon which, if he be closely questioned, he would be forced to admit that he is profoundly ignorant.

"The two Roman Catholic members, Mr. Pope Hennessy and Mr. Vincent Scully, had better have refrained from making observations which lead us to suppose, contrary to the feeling of every enlightened man in this country, that they approve and justify the bigoted fanaticism which led to the expulsion of Mr. Home from the Papal dominions. In particular Mr. V. Scully did not show his docility as a Roman Catholic in avowing his disbelief in all spirits excepting that of the Witch of Endor. Did he mean thus publicly to brand all the spirits of the Romish Church, and its Ladies of Salette as spurious and fraudulent concoctions of the Pope and the priests? I happen to know that if Mr. V. Scully will ask the opinion of the prince of his church, Cardinal Wiseman, he will find a very different measure of belief. It is only a few weeks ago that Cardinal Wiseman, in speaking of the modern spirit manifestations to one of his flock who is an occasional contributor to these pages, said that he entirely believed in them, and that he could not be a Catholic without doing so.

"If what is said of the Pope by his own people be true, Mr. Home has good reason to be thankful that his Holiness did not give him his blessing instead of giving him his *congé*. From a most interesting work, treating of persons and things in Rome, I make the following pertinent extract:—

"Even the Pope himself has the reputation of possessing the Evil Eye to some extent. Ask a Roman how this is, and he will answer you as one did me the other day, 'They say so; and as for me, really it seems to me true. If he have not the *jettatura*, it is very odd that everything he blesses makes *fiasco*. We all did very well in the campaign of '48 against the Austrians. We were winning battle after battle, and all was gaiety and hope, when suddenly he blesses the cause, and everything goes to the devil at once. Nothing succeeds with anybody or anything when he wishes well to them. See, here the other day he went to Santa Agnese to have a great festival, and down goes the floor, and the people are all smashed together. Then he visits the column to the Madonna in the

Piazza di Spagna, and blesses it and the workmen, and, of course, one falls from the scaffolding the same day and is killed. A week or two ago he arranged to meet the King of Naples at Porto d'Anzo, and up comes a violent storm and gale that lasts a week; then another arrangement is made, and then comes the fracas about the ex-Queen of Spain. Then, again, here was Lord C_____ came in the other day from Albano, being rather unwell; so the Pope sends him his special blessing, when pop! He dies right off in a twinkling. There is nothing so fatal as his blessing. For my part I don't wonder that the workmen at the column refused to work the other day in raising it, unless the Pope stayed away.'

"In Mr. Home's autobiography he recounts several instances, I believe, but certainly one in particular, where his life was saved by the interposition of Providence, through the recognized agency of spirits. As he is himself of the Roman Catholic faith, I assume that he would have been happy at any time to have secured the Pope's blessing; and, therefore, he may, on calm reflection, be, disposed to think that by a special Providence, be has been miraculously saved from the possible consequences of such a calamity. [We are sorry to say that Mr. Home already labours under the infliction of the Pope's special blessing. We have seen the original document, signed by his Holiness.—Ed.]

The "Spiritual Magazine," April 1, 1864, thus remarked upon this affair:—

"The remarks which we recently made on the violent expulsion by the Pope of Mr. Home from Rome, have been seriously reprobated by several of our Roman Catholic friends, who complain of them as being highly unjust towards the Holy Father, and as showing an unreasoning hostility towards Catholicism. We have every desire to be just to Catholicism, as to all classes of religious thought, and we are sorry to give offence to any by too severe criticisms, but we should be more sorry if we were to sacrifice freedom of discussion to the natural tenderness which offenders have for their own feelings. When we find that our Catholic friends are so sensitive themselves, it does not seem to be out of place to remind them that others too have feelings, which may be outraged by offences which may be said to shock humanity, and the very genius of the time. We should have thought much better of our friends if, in such a case, they had submitted in silence and in sorrow, to the shame which their spiritual head had brought upon all that is good in their religion; and if, instead of complaining of our remarks, they had remonstrated against his conduct. We have heard nothing of this, but only the laments of children who do not like the punishment which they deserve. Even in Rome, and amongst Romanists, the barbarous act of the infallible head of the only true Church was protested against, by means of the principal residents and visitors, both royal and loyal; but to hear Englishmen in England refrain from condemning and contemning such doings is to us the saddest spectacle of all, for it shows us how necessary it is to prevent such a class from ever obtaining temporal power. One flimsy excuse for the Pope is, that what he did was not in the exercise of his spiritual power, in which alone he is infallible, but of his temporal power, which even his adherents cannot stand up for on all occasions. We believe, that what he calls the patrimony of St. Peter, has been his greatest curse, but there is no part of his alleged possessions to which he clings more pertinaciously; and if he will be a temporal ruler we shall take the liberty of blaming him when he makes such an abuse of his temporal power. Another friend complains of us for hinting a disbelief of the House of our Lady of Loretto having been removed bodily from Bethlehem to Loretto, making a temporary sojourn in Dalmatia by the way; and he informs us, on the testimony of a person who has carefully analysed the evidence, and who went purposely to Bethlehem, to Dalmatia, and to Loretto to examine the remains at the two former places, and the building itself, that there is every reason to believe that the chapel was really so removed. But surely if Mr. Home's manifestations are sorcery for merely moving a table, or for being himself lifted in the air, this moving of a house bodily from the Holy Land to Italy must have been sorcery on a much larger scale. Of course all the world believes that this Popish miracle is a gross imposture, and that, because it is so monstrously opposed to natural laws; but if the Pope could have Mr. Home raised in the air at a solemn gathering in the Great Square of St. Peter's, like St. Theresa, it might give an air of possibility at all events to the floating of the House of our Lady. Taking levitation or the elevation of Mr. Home in the air as a special and crowning instance of his sorcery, what do we find? The same sorcery is practised by the great shining lights, the very saints of the Romish Church; and there are much fewer instances of it, unfortunately, to be found in modern spiritualism than in the authorized records of Romanism. To say nothing of the instances of it given in the, Bible, it is proved beyond a doubt in the cases of St. Theresa, St. Catherine, St. Philip Neri, Richard Abbot of St. Vanne de Verdun, Ignatius Loyola, Savonarola, St. Dominick, St. Dunstan, St. Francis of Assissium, St. Cajetan, St. Bernard Ptolœmæi, St. Catherine of Ricci, St. Cupertin, and others whom we could name if this list is not long enough; but to crown the question of the act of stupidity performed on the 2nd of January last, it is only necessary to state that, according to the requirements of the Church of Rome, the working of miracles, as they call them, is a condition absolutely necessary in the canonization of saints—it being regarded as the only assured proof of their final perseverance in those holy dispositions, which entitle them to that high honour. Hence the taking cognizance of miracles for this end has always been the province of the chief pastors of the Romish Church as requiring the greatest circumspection. It was said of the Bourbons, that after all their troubles they had learnt nothing and forgotten nothing. Neither time, nor country, nor civilization, nor progress, nor humanity, nor liberty, nor even gentlemanliness seem to have any power in moderating the bigotry and the savage fanaticism of the successor of St. Peter, and the vicegerent of God. Let our Catholic friends join us in expressing their disapproval of such disgraceful modes of thumb-screwing thought, and of heretic-hunting, and we shall then be able to separate them from, the general condemnation, which otherwise will be properly applied to the body as well as to the head of their section of religious opinions."

CHAPTER IV

Although in the gross attack on spiritualism contained in "Mr. Sludge the medium," by Mr. Robert Browning, there is indeed nothing whatever to connect his portrait of Sludge with myself, for no person who was even slightly acquainted with me could discover one point of resemblance, nevertheless, I have been asked whether such scenes as he describes in that effusion had ever occurred, and the press treated of the "poem" as meant for me. In consequence of these circumstances, as well as of the whole production being offensively coarse attack upon spiritualism in general and upon all mediums without exception; and feeling it to be moreover, though probably unobserved by himself, an insult to the memory of his deceased wife, whose intellect was far above his own, and who lived and died a believer in spiritualism, I find myself compelled to notice this remarkable poem of Mr. Robert Browning. Accepting the old and recognised definition of the word *poem* as from ποιεω *facio,* these lines constitute a poem, for they were made by Mr. Browning, but what other characteristic of poetry they possess, I must admit that I, in common with many of my friends, have been unable to discover. Some of the lines are equal to the productions of the poet Close, others suggest the licentiousness of Don Juan divorced from its poetic imagery; as an example of the first I may quote the two first lines of Sludge's confession:—

> "Fol-lol-the-rido-liddle-iddle-ol!
> You see, sir, it's your own fault more than mine."

The following passage, while giving some evidence also of writing like that of the Poet Close, is an example of the latter:—

> "I got up from my gorge
> On offal in the gutter, and preferred
> Your canvass backs: I took their carver's size,
> Measured his modicum of intelligence,
> Tickled him on the cockles of his heart
> With a raven feather, and next week found myself
> Sweet and clean, dining daintily, dizen'd smart,
> Set on a stool buttress'd by ladies' knees,
> Every soft smiler calling me her pet,
> Encouraging my story to uncoil
> And creep out from its hole, inch after inch,

> 'How last night, I no sooner snug in bed,
> *Tuck'd up, just as they left me,*—than came raps!'"

The delicacy and good taste of the following also is beyond comment:—

> "Curse your superior, superintending sort,
> Who, since you hate smoke, send up boys that climb
> To cure a chimney, bid a 'medium' lie
> To sweep your truth down! curse your women too,
> Your insolent wives and daughters, that fire up
> Or faint away if a male hand squeeze theirs;
> Yet, to encourage Sludge, may play with Sludge
> As only a 'medium,' only the kind of thing
> They must humour, fondle, . . Oh, to misconceive
> Were too preposterous! But I've paid them out!
> They've had their wish—calf d for the naked truth,
> And in she tripp'd, sat down and bade them stare;
> They had to blush a little and forgive!"

And again:—

> "Miss Stokes turns—Rabab—nor a bad exchange,"

Is followed further on by:—

> "To hear your outcries, one would think I caught
> Miss Stokes by the scuff o' the neck, and pitch'd her flat,
> Foolish face foremost!"

I have no intention of criticising writing which is, like not a little of Mr. Browning's work, either above or below criticism, as the author or the reader may think, but I must allude to one point which displays utter ignorance on the subject of spiritualism. Mr. Sludge is supposed to have been led into his confession by an over-dose of champagne, and to be sustained during its continuance by potations of egg nogg, aided by the soothing influence of the Virginian weed; near the close he becomes maudling drunk and breaks out—

> "And I've lost you, lost myself,
> Lost all, l-l-l. . . ."

He is relieved by the substantial comfort of a goodly number of five-dollar notes, poetically named V. notes, and after concluding his speech with—

"Bl-l-less you, sir!"

he breaks out—it may be supposed when outside the door with—

"R-r-r, you brute beast and blackguard! cowardly scamp!
I only wish I dared burn down the house
And spoil your sniggering!"

Which beautiful poetry continues for fourteen lines, and is followed by some regrets ending in the consoling reflection:—

"Begin elsewhere anew!
Boston's a hole, the herring pond is wide,
V-notes are something, liberty, still more
Beside, is he the only fool in the world?"

Had Mr. Browning known anything practically of spiritualism, he would have been aware that indulgence in intoxicating drink has a strong tendency to destroy medium power; but this kind of attack gives me reason to believe that Mr. Browning did intend his fancy portrait of Mr. Sludge to represent me; for I happen to know that he once remarked of me that I was in the habit of being assisted home drunk by the police nightly. The idea is worthy of his creative genius, as if there be any pleasure in the sensation of being drunk, I am as yet ignorant of it, or of its effects, for I never have been sensibly affected by intoxicating drink of any kind in the course of my life, and am, as all my friends well know, exceedingly abstemious.

With respect to this production Mrs. Sarah Helen Whitman, the well known American authoress, characterized it as a disgrace to Mr. Robert Browning, and in a letter to the editor of an American journal, said, "If you will, moreover, take the trouble to read the poem of Mr. Browning to which I have referred, you will understand why it is regarded by some of Mr. Browning's warmest admirers as 'a blot on the 'scutcheon.'"

On the appearance of Mr. Browning's book the "Spiritual Magazine," on July, 1864, gave the following article under the title of "Mr. Robert Browning on Spiritualism."—"The press is quite alert and looking up again on the subject of spiritualism, and is loud in the praises of Mr. Robert Browning's latest effort in poetry, of which sixty-eight pages are taken up with a violent explosion of his feelings, under the title of 'Mr. Sludge, the Medium.' It has not been often, nor from any great number of the critics that Mr. Browning has found hitherto any strong sympathy for his poetry, nor has he taken it much to heart that his readers and admirers were so few. It has rather fed his vanity the fuller, and has the more convinced him of his one idea that he was a poet before his time. He has been *Forstered* into this feeling by a few earnest friends of the press, who have never ceased to show their friendship for the man, by writing up the poet, and assuring him that his metal had the true ring in it. He has never wavered in this belief himself, and he is so sensitive in his vanity, that if he could have doubted it he would have collapsed at once as poor Keats did, under an adverse review. His overweening vanity, however, aided by his few devoted friends, has saved him to us, and he is happy to add still to his posthumous fame by occasional essays of his genius. We can only sit, after vain attempts to follow his ideas, in wonderment at the awful vastness of the human mind, which can complacently give birth to such red-hot words about something that we cannot understand, and of which we are rather glad than otherwise, that we are not the posterity that will have to decipher the meaning. A high priest of nature is he, ministering in the temple alone, and on a pedestal which he, happy man, never feels to be unsteady beneath him. What a striking wonder is this faculty which some men have of self-satisfaction, and of living in an atmosphere which they fancy to be of serenest ether.

"We knew him well years ago, when he was making his first soaring flights, and were almost frightened for him when the coarse critics dealt with his sensitive nature. Then it was, however, that he conquered them for ever by determining them to be fools, and wrapping himself in the mantle of posterity. This was his happiest hit of all, and to give him its full benefit, he only wanted the assistance of a few friends, who were in his eyes endued with the heaven-born quality of understanding him. Nothing after this could touch him more, or penetrate his armour; and the more the critics have raved at him, the more he has despised and contemned them with words more rancorous and violent than their own, for daring to criticize the prince of poets—the man who was before his age.

"It is necessary to go through this little outline, in order to have some idea of the mind of the man who is just now condescending to give us the overflow of his genius on the subject of spiritualism. None but one of such a nature, and only after he had received a special wound, could have got up the holy fire to such a pitch, as Mr. Browning warms himself by, in attacking Mr. Sludge the medium. What can poor Sludge have done to the poet, for beyond the rancour which he feels towards mankind in general, the poet must surely have some personal injury to resent? It is not quite easy to see that Mr. Home is intended to be the victim, but whether it be he or not, the press has at once taken it as meant for him, and has charged him upon the facts or fancies mentioned in the poem. An intimate friend, too, of Mr. Browning's has been so far taken in by the statements, as to find it necessary to inquire if such scenes ever happened as are described, and Mr. Home has had to say in answer that the whole is mere invention. It would therefore be better to take the bull by the horns at once, and to treat the poem as a violent, rancorous attack upon Mr. Home and his private character, intending to lead or allow the public to believe that the scene depicted is taken from life, and that the poet has only dressed it up in verse according to his fancy, filling up the interspaces with the usual spasms which characterize Mr. Browning's effusions.

"Even poetry, where such personal allusions and charges are made, should preserve its basis of truth as the apple of its eye. The imaginative element should not be applied to facts, or the versifier degenerates into a slanderer. A kind friend of ours, when our children tell fibs, says they are only poets, but we think he mistakes the word. We have therefore thought it best to reduce Mr. Browning's poem, so far as his facts and narrative are concerned, into plain prose, and thus to lay bare what was in his mind when he began to write. As to the rest of the poem, there are some good things in it which we could see a glimmering of, and all these we are content to leave to that posterity which is the last refuge of the author, as patriotism is said to be the last refuge of the scoundrel.

"To do this fairly, and to raise the issue between Mr. Browning and his probable victim, Mr. Home, we have very carefully gone through his sixty-eight pages, and we will afterwards give the key to the rancour and virulence which are observable throughout. It is not often that we can hope, from personal knowledge of both parties, to get to the very pith of the affair, and to show the secret springs of action, while the poet for long years is nursing his wrath to keep it warm.

"The poem, then, of 'Mr. Sludge, the Medium,' opens with the heaven-born poet's knuckles in the medium's windpipe, consequent on his having just caught him cheating the poet by giving some bogus revelation from his mother. Mr. Sludge at once owns to the cheat, and, on the ground of its being his first offence, he begs him to remove his knuckles, and not to expose him as an impostor. He protests that it was the poet's champagne that put the folly in his head. The poet, however, is relentless, and Mr. Sludge, not being able to rid himself of the knuckles, offers to tell him all about the tricks—he makes a clean breast of it, and confesses that the whole is imposture, and that he will change his trade and cheat no more.

"Mr. Sludge commences by saying that it is the fault of the curious gentlefolk more than his. He hears them talk of ghosts, and breaks in with the words 'I saw a ghost;' at once finds sympathy, and gets into their society. Once there, it is necessary to keep alive the means by which he mounted. He continues the fraud, satisfies one and then another, till he has many friends; and when a sceptic comes, they all set at him, till he, too, must succumb. At this comparatively early stage, while Sludge's conscience is yet tender and he has some qualms, is it to be expected that he will spoil all his good fortune by confessing. Having made the first step, would you thus retrace it? No! You would go on deeper and deeper, like Sludge. It is too late—he must go on. Now he makes raps, shows stars, and succeeds in producing an audible voice. The spirits now are at his command, and his delighted friends crowd round him. As he receives them at his own house, as his guests, the poet asks how guests can be critical; but if one out of a dozen should say a word all the eleven pounce on him, and Sludge waves his hat in triumph.

"Visions no longer suffice and the friends want something external. It is but a step more. He jogs the table about and learns his other tricks and sleight-of-hand turns, shoves, and tilts the table, cracks his joints, manages his feet, works wires that twitch the curtains, plays the glove at the end of his slipper, puts out the lights, and then—every one is delighted and satisfied. There are sentences given by raps—a message from a dear child to its mother. Is that a time for the mother to be critical? Oh, no, poor thing; she is an easy dupe. It gives a test answer that it was six years old and rode a rocking-horse. How could Sludge have known these facts? Oh! he makes it his business to pick up these little particulars that your uncle was a tailor and your wife thought to have married Miggs but missed him and hit you. Then with those who have been duped, how are they to be undeceived again? They won't believe it was possible to cheat them, and say that even if Sludge admitted that he cheated them they wouldn't believe him. They prefer to believe in a lie, and urge on poor Sludge to play the spirit medium for a livelihood, rather than to take him as he is and keep him fat. So he excuses himself, and says that he helps religion by his tricks, and lays the Atheist sprawling on his back, and props up St. Paul or Swedenborg at least. It is just the proper way to baulk the sceptics, and no use in being squeamish as to the means you use.

"Another excuse which Sludge gives is, that beyond all this there is in human nature a real love of a lie which liars find ready made for the lies they make, as hand for glove, or tongue for sugar plum. It is for them he cheated when he could, rapped with his toe joints, set sham hands at work, wrote down names weak in sympathetic ink, rubbed odic lights with ends of phosphor match, and all the rest.

"The admitting of the supernatural element in the Bible, which comes to us from our mothers, prepares us, or some of us, to see instances of it still in the world, and to accept omens, prodigies, and special providences. If Sludge sees Charles's Wain at twelve at night, it warns him to have his hair cut without a day's delay; and he spies a providence in the fire's going out, or the kettle's boiling; he has presentiments, his dreams come true, and he itches at the elbow when at whist he ought to trump.

"After all these his confessions are done, he is foolish enough to ask the poet to shake hands with him and finds it hard that he refuses. The poem closes with a hearty curse from Sludge upon the poet.

"This is not much to get out of nearly seventy pages, but it pretends to describe a scene which so far as it relates to Mr. Home has no foundation in fact, and Mr. Browning has further made the story the vehicle of a distinct allegation that the manifestations of spiritualism are nothing but gross imposture from beginning to end, at all times and under all circumstances. This is what it comes to, and it is unfortunately only in accordance with the general turn of Mr. Browning's mind to deny not only these things, but others related to them of much more importance to his own soul. There are many indeed who bear him sad company in this denial of all supernatural power and providence, and he is particularly unfortunate in this respect among his intimate friends; but it is almost painful, if he be a poet, either for us or for our posterity, that he should try to infect his readers with the disease which so maddens him. Especially, however, do we lament that the man who merged the name of Miss Barrett in that of Browning, should come forward now after her departure to deny what was the very soul and essence of one of the best and truest English-women who have ever lived; and of the greatest poetess, it has been said, of this or any other age. It is a shocking libel on his wife and on her dearest beliefs. There are many coarse jesters, and hard men of science to whom it is allowed to deny all spiritual action in the affairs of men; but for the husband of Mrs. Barrett Browning it was not permitted to desecrate her memory and her sweet muse by this ribald nonsense.

"With a man of his vanity, however, and that wounded, as will presently be seen, by Mr. Home, in years gone by, but not forgotten, everything must give way to his contemptuous rancour against the man, and against a spiritual world, the existence of which he looks down upon from his throne, as a personal affront to himself and to his poetic majesty.

"This is, perhaps, not the place to say all that we should wish, to show our sense of Mrs. Barrett Browning's sweet character, and of that depth and innocence of her soul which brought her at once and by sympathy into communion with the spiritual. This was the secret of her power, however, as a woman and as a poet. Every one loved her, for the love that was in her towards all, and which made an atmosphere about her that it was so enchanting and pleasant to dwell in. Happy was it for Mr. Browning to have the right to call her wife, for it gave him the best chance he could have in this world of becoming alive to the spiritual beauties of the vast inner world, which he still denied. But if he lost this golden opportunity, he gained in more earthly advantages, though again at the cost of increasing his vanity, for after his marriage with Mrs. Barrett Browning, he became invested, as her husband, with much of the respect and admiration which her qualities willingly drew from the world, and his critics became more friendly still to him, out of their love to her. Even the griffins of the press could not find heart to abuse the husband of so dear a friend. So everything we see has tended to blow him up still larger, and no one can tell yet what will be the end of it. Should he finally burst, 'The Examiner' and others of his friends will have much to answer for.

"As we wish to make this little story complete in itself, and not to have again to add to it, we will now give an exact account, for the truth of which we can vouch, of the only two interviews which Mr. Browning and Mr. Home ever had. It is given in the shape of a narrative by Mr. Home, and the reader will see how the wine turned to vinegar on the poet's stomach, when his vanity was touched, first by the wrong direction of the poet's crown and by being asked to leave the room, and next by being refused another *séance* when he asked for one: *Tantœne animis cœlestibus irœ?*

"'I have never seen Mr. Browning but twice. The first time was at the house of Mr. Rymer, at Ealing, at a *séance* there. Mr. Browning was then married to Mrs. Barrett Browning, whom I had known by repute, and through intimate mutual friends, for several years, and I thus became aware of her deep interest and belief in spiritualism, which continued up to the time of her death. Mr. and Mrs. Rymer and their family were present at the *séance*, which began by several of the ordinary manifestations. Mr. Browning was requested to investigate everything as it occurred, and he availed himself freely of the invitation. Several times during the evening be voluntarily and earnestly declared that anything like imposture was out of the question. Previously to the arrival of Mr. and Mrs. Browning some of the children had been gathering flowers in the garden, and Miss Rymer and I had made a wreath of clematis. This wreath was lying on a table, at a little distance from that at which we were sitting. The wreath was afterwards put on the table at which we were sitting, but whether naturally or by spirit hands I do not remember. During the *séance* this wreath was raised from the table by supernatural power in the presence of us all, and whilst we were watching it, Mr. Browning, who was seated at the opposite side of the table, left his place and came and stood behind his wife, towards whom the wreath was being slowly carried, and upon whose head it was placed, in full sight of us all, and whilst he was standing close behind her. He expressed no disbelief; as, indeed, it was impossible for any one to have any of what was passing under his eyes, whilst Mrs. Browning was much moved, and she not only then but ever since expressed her entire belief and pleasure in what then occurred. It was the remark of all the Rymer family, that Mr. Browning seemed much disappointed that the wreath was not put upon his own head instead of his wife's, and that his placing himself in the way of where it was being carried, was for the purpose of giving it an opportunity of being placed upon his own brow.

"'Shortly after this a communication was made, requesting that all would leave the room, excepting Mr. Rymer and me, as something was to be told of an important matter private to Mr. Rymer. During Mr. Browning's absence with the rest of the family, I was afterwards told by them that he seemed quite hurt at being sent out of the room, and said be was not aware that spirits could have secrets. Still he indicated no doubt of anything he had seen. On returning to the room he appeared to be very much out of temper, but I paid no attention to him, as Mrs. Browning was so kind and attentive to me. All that was done was in the presence of eight persons, besides Mr. and Mrs. Browning, all of whom are still living, and are ready to testify to the truth of every word here written if it should be gainsaid by Mr. Browning.

"'Two days afterwards Mr. Browning wrote to Mrs. Rymer requesting that he might be allowed another *séance*, and to bring with him his friend, Miss Helen Faucit. Mrs. Rymer replied that owing to my ill health, and her engagements, and the arrangements previous to our going to the seaside, it would not be possible to receive him again before we left town. A few days subsequently I came to town with Mrs. Rymer and her eldest son, to make some farewell calls, the first of which was to Mr. and Mrs. Browning. We were shown into the drawing-room, and he, advancing to meet us, shook hands with Mrs. Rymer; then, passing by me shook hands with her son. As he was repassing me I held out my hand, when, with a tragic air, he threw his hand on his left shoulder, and stalked away. My attention was now drawn to Mrs. Browning, who was standing nearly in the centre of the room, and looked very pale and agitated. I approached and she placed both her hands in mine, and said, in a voice of emotion, 'Oh, dear Mr. Home, do not, do not blame me. I am so sorry, but I am not to blame.' I was wonder-struck, not knowing in the least what the curious scene meant—indeed, it would have been comical, but for the deep emotion from which Mrs. Browning was suffering. For a moment all was confusion, but at last we were seated, I scarce know how, when Mr. Browning began in an excited manner, saying, 'Mrs. Rymer, I beg to inform you that I was exceedingly dissatisfied with everything I saw at your house the other night, and I should like to know why you refused to receive me again with my friend.' I replied to this, 'Mr. Browning, that was the time and place for you to have made objections regarding the manifestations, and not now. I gave you every possible opportunity, and you availed yourself of it, and expressed yourself satisfied.' He said, 'I am not addressing myself to you, sir.' I said, 'No; but it is of me you are speaking, and it would only be fair and gentleman-like to allow me to reply.' Mrs. Rymer said, 'Mr. Home is quite right, and as regards not being able to receive you and your friend, we could not do so on account of our engagements.' Mr. Browning's face was pallid with rage, and his movements, as he swayed backwards and forwards on his chair, were like those of a maniac. At this moment I rose to leave the room, and, passing him, shook hands with Mrs. Browning, who was nearly ready to faint. As she shook hands with me she said, 'Dear Mr. Home, I am not to blame. Oh, dear! oh, dear!"

"In conclusion we have only to say that, as this is a matter of fact and not of opinion, we shall be quite willing to give insertion to any reply, in prose, from Mr. Browning, if he will write it so as to be intelligible to the present generation of men who compose our readers, and we shall be all the more pleased that he should have this opportunity of explaining himself, as it is a pity he should be knocking his head against this hard subject, just at the time when his contemporaries of the first rank are one by one publicly declaring their full belief and knowledge of its truth."

In her "Notes on England and Italy," Mrs. Hawthorne says, in an account of an evening at Casa Guidi:— "Mr. Browning introduced the subject of spiritism, and there was an animated talk. Mr. Browning cannot believe, and Mrs. Browning cannot help believing."

Mr. Robert Browning, however, is by no means alone in his capacity of invention, for several paragraphs have appeared from time to time testifying to all who were in the slightest degree acquainted with me, that the writers had drawn upon their fertile imaginations for every detail, whether of character or personal appearance. I here reproduce a few which may serve to amuse those who know me. The following which appeared in "Echoes from the Clubs," for April 29, 1868, is inimitably absurd; it is headed:— "A Home Thrust.—Some two years ago a young gentleman possessing that pleasing and ingenuous expression of countenance which the late Mr. Thackeray loved to ascribe to his heroes, was seated in the halls of the—let us say, *Généralife*. To him addressed himself a dark-complexioned stranger with quiet, shifting eyes, curly and oily-looking black hair, and a nose which seemed to vouch for a purely Caucasian descent. A brisk conversation ensued. The dark-haired stranger was a man who had evidently seen the world; he had sat at the tables of the great princes, kings, and even emperors, were on familiar terms with him. "This," said he, extending a hand on which sparkled two splendid rings, and indicating a magnificent diamond, "was the gift of Louis Napoleon, for a service I rendered him." The recollection of Mr. Wyndham Flitter and his turquoise caused a smile to flit across his companion's face as he continued, "and this sapphire was a present from the Czar." The smile was now so palpable that the stranger observed in a reproachful tone, "I suppose then that you think I am a humbug." "Think," was the cutting reply, "I don't think it; I know you're one." The stranger departed incontinently, and it was not till many months after that he was pointed out to his unappreciative companion as the celebrated Mr. Home."

My friends must have wondered how they had not seen me on any occasion when my naturally dry light hair had become a head of "curly and oily-looking black hair." As to the "nose which seemed to vouch for a purely Caucasian descent," this, of course, might have been managed by a well adapted false feature, and it is needless for me to say that the remainder of the paragraph is as probable as that these miraculous changes in my personal appearances had occurred.

In the "Mask," of June, 1868, an article was devoted to me, from which I extract the following:—

"We do not deny for a moment that Mr. Home may produce marvels in his own rooms in the Sloane Athenæum, or anywhere else where he may have frequent access; but we challenge him to produce supernatural effects on any piece of furniture we chose, (sic) time and place indicated by us, and before a select few chosen by ourselves.

"We don't pretend to explain Mr. Home's performances, for we have never seen them, though we have met that modern Cagliostro several times under not very successful circumstances. Of course, we have heard him relate his connection with the court of Russia (who has not?), and seen him show his diamond ring; but on one occasion when we were present he showed it, with much pomposity, to his neighbour, who possessed and had on his finger at the time a brilliant of nearly double the size, which, on production, eclipsed the czar's gift, and chagrined considerably the great spiritualist. That he has sharp eyes, a cunning wit, and quick, long fingers, there is no denying—so has a fox. That he never receives money for his gifts, the present action will entirely disprove. And, after all, diamonds seldom fall in value. Besides, a man of the world, who has made weak man his study, knows well the effect of refusing. Anyone with a belief in Mr. Home would feel that he ought not to employ his supernatural powers for nothing but another's amusement or instruction, and at the same time would be touched by the noble magnanimity which was poor but honest. Ten guineas refused would probably be altered either to twenty guineas, forwarded anonymously, or take the form of a diamond worth five-and-twenty pounds. The dupe would be always ready to swear that money was refused, and yet would know that he had amply repaid his benefactor, which would be, in other words, *le généreux battu et Home content.*"

This sneering attack is as transparently imaginative as the former one; and though altogether ridiculous, I may ask the writer gravely, where and when he has heard and seen what he so impudently declares he has witnessed? His acquaintance with specialities in nature is highly valuable, for he seems to be familiar with long-fingered foxes, some of which he ought to present to the Zoological Society, as they are as yet unknown to students of natural history.

Shortly after I last left America paragraphs appeared in the papers then, stating that "Home, the Medium," or "*David S. Hume,*" the celebrated "Medium," had sailed for Europe to be married to a rich Scotch widow; and some time later it was announced in the English papers, that I was about to lead to the hymeneal altar no less a personage than Madame Möet, whose name is well known in connection with her wine.

The following paragraph, which I cut from a newspaper, is also thoroughly absurd to all who know anything of spiritualism; it appeared some few years since:—

"Mr. Home, the spiritualist, is said to have challenged the medium *malgré lui* to compete with him in flying through the air a distance of two miles, the winner to give the stakes to any charity he thinks fit. Mr. Addison has accepted the challenge for an early date, and the present odds are three to two in his favour."

From Naples I went to Nice, and concerning my stay there I find the following notice in the "Spiritual Magazine," giving as full an account as is needful.

"After Mr. Home's expulsion from Rome he spent several weeks at Nice, where the phenomena were examined and scrutinised by a great many of the winter residents, and many were convinced of the facts of spiritual power. We hear that these new converts are now returning with the spring to England, and a correspondent writes us that amongst his own friends he numbers half-a-dozen of them, and that they are wonderfully impressed with what they have seen. It appears that the manifestations were not confined to Mr. Home, for that after he had left Nice, a party of ladies and gentlemen formed a circle to see what could be done without him. They soon obtained very striking results. The medium was found to be a Russian lady staying at Nice with her family, and who, a month ago, was unconscious of her power. She speaks only a word or two of English, but under her influence a heavy oval table gives answers in English and German. She is also a writing medium, and her hand writes, without any play of the fingers, intelligible messages. A great progress has been made by these occurrences amongst the visitors.

From Nice I proceeded to Paris, where I remained for some weeks, after which I returned to England, and then crossed the Atlantic, to revisit my old friends in America. Here I decided on giving public readings, in which I succeeded fairly. On one occasion, after having given a reading in Norwich, Connecticut, I gave a second for the benefit of the Soldiers' Aid Society, the announcement of which led to the appearance in the local journal of the following letter from a clergyman:—

"MESSRS. EDITORS:— I crave permission, as a Christian man, to say a word to Christians in Norwich concerning the lecture this evening. I was greatly surprised to hear that the audience at the first of Mr. Home's readings was larger than had been seen at any lecture in Breed Hall this winter. But I supposed that the fact might be explained by the natural curiosity of our citizens to hear and see a man who has so *distinguished* himself as has the gentleman in question.

"I must confess, however, that I was not only surprised, but grieved, to see the announcement that Mr. Home had consented to the request of our Soldiers' Aid Society, that he should give another reading for the benefit of that institution. It was very kind and courteous of Mr. Home, and I have no doubt he is sincere in his spiritualistic belief. I have no quarrel with him. But are the Christian men and women of Norwich, who support our Soldiers' Aid Society, reduced to such extremities that they must resort to a representative and exponent of spiritualism for aid in their Christian and patriotic work? Is it seemly that Christians should patronize such an entertainment? Most of them believe one of two things in regard to spiritualism—either that it is an arrant imposition and delusion, or that it is ascribable to Satanic agency. Probably no Christian worthy of the name believes that it is what it professes to be, a system of communication with and revelation from the souls of the departed. Whoever believes this must in honesty become a spiritualist, and be guided by spiritualistic revelations. I care not which of the two theories named be adopted, it seems to me equally indecorous for Christians to have anything to do directly or indirectly with spiritualism. If it be said that Mr. Home does not bring forward his peculiar notions in these readings, I may answer that even admitting the statement to be true, it is undeniable that the crowd goes to hear him not because he has a fine voice and is an excellent reader, but because he is a spiritualist, a representative man, a famous man in that art or science or delusion, whichever it may be. And for the public publicly to patronize him is to endorse, or, at least, to patronize and countenance his principles.

"But I deny the statement. It was publicly announced in your paper after Mr. Home's reading that at least one loud rap was heard on the stage, and two faces, one quite distinct, and the other more shadowy, were seen hovering about the speaker. It seems, therefore, that Mr. Home cannot or will not leave his spiritualism behind him, and probably, every candid person who reads this communication, will confess to himself that he is vastly more attracted to the Reading to-night, by the hope of seeing or hearing something spiritualistic in the course of the evening, than by the charms of Mr. Home's voice, and skill as an elocutionist.

"I hope, therefore, that for the credit of Norwich and her churches, the Soldiers' Aid Society will receive a severe rebuke to-night in the absence of the Christian people of Norwich from that Reading. Mr. Home will doubtless understand that I have no personal feeling against him; so far as I know, he is a most estimable gentleman in private life, and his private character has my respect. But there are thousands of republicans in this city, who would not go to hear Gov. Seymour out of principle, though he spoke no politics; and many a democrat who would not listen to Wendell Phillips, though he talked poetry and literature—lest their act should seem to endorse the wed principles of the man. Shall Christians be less strict than politicians? Shall they denounce and fight against spiritualism, and turn about to countenance and publicly abet the system in the person of its most prominent exponent? I hope not.

"JOHN V. LEWIS."

To this letter I replied, and a somewhat lengthened correspondence resulted. One result of Mr. Lewis's letter, I may mention, was to attract public attention to the subject: in so far as concerned the reading for the Soldiers' Aid Society, he contributed largely to advertise it, and the room was crowded, I am happy to say, to the substantial benefit of the fund.

I sailed from New York in May, 1865, for England, and on my return to London, found letters waiting for me which rendered it necessary that I should go to Paris. The following is from a letter I wrote at the time:—

"The Empress was Regente, and I may say that I was much pleased to note how very general the satisfaction was to find that instead of her being a woman whose only thought was dress or frivolity, she was a true-hearted, great willed woman, capable not only of giving orders, but of seeing that they are executed. Deep and true in her feelings, pure and unselfish in her actions, she is a noble lady, an ornament to her sex; long May she live! When in Paris I had the honour of meeting and dining with His Highness Mustapha Pasha, the brother of the Viceroy of Egypt, and heir to the throne. I could only remain in Paris three weeks, for I had letters necessitating my presence in Russia. On leaving Paris I went to Germany on a short visit to Her Highness the Princess of the Mingrelia, and then I left for Russia.

"I have here to relate a singular incident in connection with my arrival at St. Petersburg. I sent a telegram to my friend the Baron Meyendorff, from Vergehalova on the Russian frontier, telling him the hour at which I would arrive at St. Petersburg. The Baron is an officer in the Emperor's Horse Guards, and was then on duty at Peterhoff, where the Emperor was. His father, who is an old and favourite General and Master of the Imperial Horses, sent him my telegram. He had just time to take the train and come to meet me, so that no one knew of my arrival. I reached St. Petersburg at seven o'clock P.M., and went at once to the Baron Meyendorff's, where I wrote a note to my brother-in-law the Count Koucheleff Besborodka, to tell him I was in the city, but would not have time to see him for a day or two, having to leave early the following morning for Peterhoff. Great was my surprise when there came a note from one of my dearest friends, the Count

Tolstoï, who is an aide-de-camp of the Emperor, and was my groomsman when I was married. His letter only said:—

"Dear Daniel, I am so glad you are here. Come at any moment, day or night. You know how glad we are to see you.

Yours,

'ALEXIS'

The last letter I had received from him was three months previously, and from one of his places in the very interior of Russia—at which far locality I supposed he still was; and that same afternoon, as we were nearing St. Petersburg, I was thinking of those I would fain have seen, and he was more especially of the number; but I thought him far distant. I at once went to his hotel, and his wife said,—

"'Well, Daniel, I would not have thought it possible for you not to have come at once and spoken to me.'

"I replied, 'Well, I rather think I am the one who ought to make the reproach. But where on earth did you see me?'

"'Why, at the Arcade, to be sure.'

"I, thinking the Countess meant the station, replied, 'Well, you must have seen that I was weary with the journey and in a hurry to get my luggage. But at what hour, pray, did you see me?'

"'At four o'clock. But what do you mean by your luggage? You were in the Arcade!'

"I told her I had arrived that evening at seven. She then told me she and her niece had seen me at four, and that she had come home and told Alexis, 'Only imagine! We have seen Daniel! and he did not seem to know us. Do at once send him a note, to the Count Koucheleff's.'

"Her niece confirmed this statement, declaring positively that she, too, had seen me.

"The count had accordingly sent the note to me, so positive were the ladies that they had met me; and the servant took it to a house in town—and there the servants told him that I had not been in Russia for years, and was not expected. Nothing daunted by this, the countess sent to the country seat, and the servant who took my note heard the other one ask for me, and so brought me the note.

"To say the least it is a singular incident, and it seems to add another to the list of those mysterious cases of 'double' appearance which the German writers call *doppelganger*. If the spirit of man can thus, by the mere force of friendship and attraction, leave the body while still hampered by the conditions of its visible and grosser connections, why, should we wonder that such marvellous manifestations of spirit-power are exhibited by those who have for ever cast off their perishing robes of flesh, and entered upon the freer and truer life of the disembodied soul?

"The singularity of the occurrence led to remark, and the other evening the emperor asked me 'if that was true?'

"I have been staying at the 'English Palace' in Peterhoff, and have often seen the emperor. We have had some very beautiful and interesting *séances*. I cannot tell even you, my dear _____ what manifestations occurred, for you know I never relate what transpires where there are crowned heads.

"I spent eight evenings at the place of the Grand Duke and Grand Duchess Constantine, at Strelna. The Grand Duke is now absent, but will return before I leave Russia. I had so many visits to make and receive, that at last it began to tell on my nervous system, and one of my friends prevailed on me to accompany him to the great fair Nijni-Norgorod, from which point I write to you. I will remain here in all probability three weeks, and then return to St. Petersburg to take leave of the emperor."

I returned from St. Petersburg direct to London, and it was shortly after my return that I was at a *séance*, at which a peculiar manifestation occurred, of which the following account has been printed:—

"I proceed to narrate briefly a few events which occurred at a *séance*, on the 30th January, 1866, given by Mrs. Macdougall Gregory, where Mr. Home was present, and where all the circle, if I mistake not, accepted spiritualism as a reality. One gentleman, however, while he did so, had serious doubts as to the source of the phenomena, and as to the propriety of courting these developments.

"We had not been long sitting at a large table in the front drawing-room, when the usual manifestations began, which increased with such force that the whole room was literally shaken. While the table palpitated violently by the power, the words, 'Take six with you into the other room,' were addressed by raps to Mr. Home, and caused those who were selected by the spirits to adjourn into the back drawing-room, where they sat down at a table, having removed the lamp and opened the window, as desired by the spirit message. One of the six happened to be a lady whose daughter had been lately taken to the spirit-land, a girl who had been known on earth as 'Motie,' the Hindostani name for pearl. To this lady the following message was spelled out, 'Mother—Symbol is under mother's hand for' _____. She immediately told us that she felt something like a large bead under her hand, and when the light was brought in it was found to be an unattached pearl, which had never been bored, and that had been brought to our circle by no earthly hand. After another message respecting the future disposition of the pearl, they returned to the other room and rejoined the rest of the party. A large accordion was played with more than common skill while Mr. Home held it with one hand; once or twice we distinctly perceived that two hands were touching the keys, and an air which the young girl had formerly played upon the harp, was now played with variations upon the accordion. Answers were also given by the instrument instead of by raps.

"In the midst of our conversation Mr. Home fell into a trance; this was, perhaps, the most salient feature of the *séance*, for while in this state, which must have lasted about an hour, he appeared to be influenced or possessed by the spirit friends who surrounded us, personating in manner those whom he had never seen, but who had been known by the several members of our circle. This was most remarkable in the case of one whom we will call by the name designated to her by Mr. Home, namely, that of Margaret, although she had only been known by that of Christy, as a servant in the family of one of the gentlemen present, and had been drowned forty years ago. Mr. Home went through the action of drowning, and gave such proofs of the identity of 'Christy,' that the son of her former master, who was the gentleman present, was fain to accept them as unmistakable. While entranced, Mr. Home also explained to us the difficulty that the spirits had experienced in bringing the pearl: it had passed through no less than three orders of spirits."

"'Margaret' had not come without an object to our *séance*; as there appeared to have been a slight suspicion of foul play in the manner in which she met her end, her aim was obviously to clear the character of a fellow-servant who had since joined her in the spirit-land.

"L. M. GREGORY."

The following is an account of a *séance*, on Easter Eve, Saturday, March 31, 1866, written by one of those present:

"Five persons assembled for a *séance* at Mr. S. C. Hall's house at Campden Hill: Mr. and Mrs. S. C. Hall, Lady Dunsany, Mrs. Henry Senior, and Mr. D. D. Home. When he arrived he was pale and worn, and we feared that we should have few manifestations. He sat down to the piano and played and sang for some time; and on his beginning a little Russian air, a favourite of his late wife's, a chair which was at some distance from the piano, slid up and placed itself beside him. I was sitting close to the piano on the other side, and I first saw the chair move. The others gathered round, and he went on playing some time, though his hands became perfectly rigid, and it was evident that they were not moved by his own volition. After some time his hands were withdrawn from the piano and he became entranced, knelt down, and poured forth a beautiful prayer: then he came out of his trance, refreshed and happy. In a few minutes we sat round the table, which at once began to vibrate and tremble, and was raised off the floor to a considerable height. *Very* loud and *heavy* knocks were heard on the table, the floor, and the furniture round the room; presently the accordion was touched; the alphabet was asked for, and it was spelt out— 'We will play the earth-life of One who was not of earth.'

"First we had simple, sweet, soft music for some minutes, then it became intensely sad, then the tramp, tramp, as of a body of men marching mingled with the music, and I exclaimed, 'The march to Calvary!' Then three times the tap-tapping sound of a hammer on a nail (like two metals meeting). A *crash* and a burst of wailing which seemed to fill the room followed, then there came a burst of glorious triumphal music more grand than any of us had ever listened to, and we exclaimed, 'The Resurrection!' It thrilled to all our hearts.

"Nothing more was done for some time, and we decided upon putting out the lights in the rooms so as only to have that from the outside which came through the conservatory. When this was done the muslin curtains were draped round Mr. Home, a large portfolio stand having first been removed from the window by the spirits. It was moved some distance towards the door of the conservatory, and then laid down on the floor. Mr. Home was then raised from the ground enveloped in the curtains. We saw him through them—between us and the window; then it was spelled out 'See what earth does,' and the silk curtains were all drawn close over the windows and round Mr. Home, and all was dark and black as night. After a short time they were drawn back again, and Mr. Home was let down and came back to the table. Soon after this we observed the face of the master of the house, shining as if covered with silver light; after we had all remarked it, and commented upon it, the words were spelled out, 'He who giveth shall receive light.' The accordion was carried round the circle playing beautifully 'The Last Rose of Summer,' and several other airs; it rested on the head of our host, then on my shoulder, and went on to our hostess next to me, and played on her head. After this several pieces of martial music were played.

"The spirit of a child next came, whose mother had sent flowers to our hostess that morning. She gave us each a flower, and told Mr. Home to go and see her mother. Mr. Home was then raised up to the ceiling, which he touched, and regretted not having a pencil to make a mark there. When he came down, our host gave him one, hoping that he might be again raised, and in five minutes after he was so, and left a cross on the ceiling; but just before this took place, we saw his whole face and chest covered with the same silver light which we had observed on our host's face. We had been sitting all this time at the table, and soon after our hands were touched and patted by other hands, and our brows touched by loved hands whose touch we know. Shortly afterwards we heard the knocks and sounds die away in the distance out of doors, and *we felt* that it was all over. We had been sitting more than two hours. Our host and hostess had said repeatedly to each other during the evening, 'We never have had anything like this before;' and they certainly have seen more wonders in spiritualism than most people.

"That burst of music was still thrilling on our hearts. Nothing of mortal composition could equal it, and its sound was that of a fine organ. We greatly regretted that no one in the room could take down the notes. The wondrous effect of the sound of feet, and the sound of the hammer and nails running like a thread through the music, it is impossible that those who have not listened to it could understand; in the music itself also there was a mixture of tones out of my power to describe."

CHAPTER VI

On the 15th February, 1866, I delivered a lecture, in Willis's Rooms, upon Spiritualism, in which I referred to the occurrence of various phenomena as traceable through all past history, and in speaking of the present time said:—

The question is often asked me, Why do not men of science take up the subject? To tell you the candid truth I have little faith in electrical experiments conducted by a Professor of Greek, and I think a Professor of Chemistry would smile at the mathematical Professor's endeavours to go through some intricate analysis. Every man in his place. I do not know why I should be called upon to pin my faith on what Mr. So-and-So may say of the soul, for the simple reason that he has made a discovery or two in the laws of nature.

It is, however, maintained by some that these wonders may all be accounted for by electricity. I will mention the name of one well known to every scientific scholar in England as well as in America, the late Professor Hare of Philadelphia, who had devoted more than half-a-century to scientific investigation, and who was perhaps the most distinguished electrician on the American continent.

He began a series of experiments with a view to corroborate Faraday's explanations: to this end he constructed apparatus of the most ingenious kind, of which in his book he has given diagrams, but he soon found that no mechanical or electrical theory could explain the facts; and that besides the merely physical manifestations an intelligence demonstrated itself beyond that of the medium and circle.

The result of Professor Hare's investigation was, that from having been all his life a materialist, he became a believer in God, in a spiritual world, in the future life of man, and, before his death, he openly proclaimed himself a Christian.

Another distinguished investigator was the Hon. John W. Edmonds, Judge of the Supreme Court of Appeal in the United States, one of the highest legal functionaries of the State; a man of acute intellect, cultivated by long and extensive legal and judicial practice. It would take too long to detail the course of patient and laborious investigation pursued by the Judge, aided by the circle of scientific and shrewd educated men, whom he associated with him in his inquiries. Suffice it to say that the examination was thoroughly exhaustive, and ended in the Judge becoming an entire convert. At all risks to his own popularity and position, he at once boldly proclaimed his conviction to the world, and on various occasions has given his experience, and defended with marked ability the truth of spiritualism.

I gave some descriptions of the various forms of medium development, continuing as follows:—

It was soon found that with certain persons spirits could so control the hand as to write by it without the intervention of the mind of the medium. In other cases, the hand is used to draw forms sometimes of things in the natural world, at others of things affirmed to be in the spiritual world. Again, drawings are executed conveying some lesson by symbol and correspondence. These drawings are frequently done by the hands of persons ignorant drawing, and in their normal state incapable of executing them. Spirit-drawing and writing have even been obtained without the intervention of mortal agency. Some instances of this are given by Baron Goldenstubbe, of Paris, in his work on "The Reality of Spirits, and the Marvellous Phenomena of their Direct Writings Demonstrated," in which he has furnished incontestable evidence that by this direct spirit-writing messages in Greek, Latin, Esthonian, German, Italian, English, and other languages, ancient and modern, have been obtained.

In his book sixty-seven facsimile copies of these spirit-writings are given. Other persons again have, by no visible agency, been thrown into an unconscious or trance state, in which they have personated departed persons, frequently unknown to them, but in a way so striking as to be at once recognized by friends or relatives present.

More frequently persons in this unconscious condition of trance are impelled to respond to inquiries or to deliver unpremeditated discourses, sometimes on abstruse subjects, beyond the knowledge or normal capacity of the medium, who may be, and sometimes is, illiterate and uneducated; at other times languages are spoken of which the medium knows nothing.

In urging a calm and deliberate investigation, I said of Spiritualism, There is in it ample room and verge for all, a wide field of profitable research, if only it is conducted in the true spirit of inquiry—the spirit that is willing to study and learn of facts, however strange they may seem, however counter to the prejudices of philosophy; for philosophy, as well as ignorance, has its prejudices, and sometimes those of philosophy are the most inveterate.

To an investigation then of the laws and principles as well as of the phenomena of spiritualism, I earnestly invite your serious attention, and ask that it be conducted in the spirit I have indicated. A vast ocean of truth, comparatively unexplored, lies before you.

I also said, I would not have you think for a moment that I am not aware of the many abuses which may arise from this contact with the spirit world. But God gives to every man the power of reason, and this it is in no way the province of spiritualism to supersede. So if a spirit were to give advice which our reason told us should not be followed, why should we pay any more attention to him, now that he is freed from the body, than we should if he were still moving among us on earth as formerly? All spirits are not perfect, and the moment we give up our reason either to men or spirits, that moment we wrong ourselves and insult our loving Father. I have known those who have taken up spiritualism, simply that they might be spoken of; and others that they might use it as a stepping-stone into society. I have known of the most gross impostures carried on, and in every case have exposed them; and God being my helper, ever will do so. Of course, in cases like these, I have much to contend with, even from my best friends: they say, "It is not your place; let others do it." I feel it to be my place, and when I see the pure and glorious truths I advocate drawn down, and made a mockery of by the mob, I will lift up my voice, and say, "This is not spiritualism;" and if they will prove it to be so, then I wish to have nothing to do with it, for it is a dark and damning error, and the sooner pure truth-seekers leave it the better. There is no doctrine which is without its abuses, and which is not abused by outsiders. Slander is of earth, and will die; truth is of God, and will live.

It has been argued that insanity is a natural result of the belief. I have been as much and more in a position to deny this statement than any man living. I have had repeated *séances* with various crowned heads. I have been with the peasant in his cabin, with the peer in his palace. I have travelled over a fair part of Russia, Germany, Italy, France, and Switzerland. My everyday life has been with believers and investigators, and I stand before you this evening, and solemnly declare that I never have seen any person insane from its effects. At the end of the year 1853, and the beginning of 1854, I was on a visit in Hartford, Connecticut, to a clergyman who is now a bishop. The state statistics gave as inmates of the Hartford Insane Retreat, thirty-seven from being spiritualists. On the very afternoon in which we first saw this statement, my friend was to read prayers at the asylum. I accompanied him, and asked the superintendent how many patients were there who had been rendered insane by spiritualism. Without a moment's hesitation he replied, "Not one." This little fact is, to my way of thinking, rather significant, showing to what base ends the opponents of spiritualism may resort to make their story good.

I have no wish to make my lecture a ludicrous one, which if I were to enter into some of the raciest forms of explaining, "how it's all done," it would most assuredly be. One or two of the last will suffice. When in Russia this autumn, on a visit to his majesty, it was told for a fact, that I had a great number of cats to sleep with me, and by this means became so charged with electricity, that the rappings were heard in my presence. Another, that I held my feet a long time in ice water, and then ran and sat by the Emperor, putting my feet in his hands, and so he thought he touched a corpse-like hand. It is currently reported that my feet are like monkey's feet, and that I can do as I please with them. Some of my friends have even asked to see my feet without shoes or stockings, that they might contradict this. Again, that it is a mental fluid, consisting of emanations from the person which take on the physical and mental characteristics of the individual automatic cerebration, acting upon the odic force of the medium and circle. These and many other fantastic, far-fetched, and inadequate explanations, which in turn need explaining, have been from time to time put forth; each new hypothesis unkindly exploding its predecessors, and being in its turn exploded by a new one.

One thing however is worth pointing out—that while various able and distinguished men have written volumes to account for the phenomena by causes of purely mundane origin, *all* admit the reality of the facts. Those tyros who, with little or no knowledge of the subject, think themselves justified in denouncing the whole thing as imposture, ought surely (if not wholly deficient in modesty and common sense) to be arrested by the circumstance that scientific and learned men, sceptical as themselves, as to the super-mundane origin of the facts, have yet, after the fullest investigation, been constrained to concede their reality and genuineness.

I trust no one present will be led to misunderstand my having referred to the Bible to prove the truths of my belief. I have done so in all sincerity and with respect. I can find nowhere in Scripture that God's arm is shortened, nowhere that he has left man to his own devices, and the spiritualism I have seen points to Him the source of all, as the means of salvation. Why, if God be an everywhere present God, should not those who have loved us, and been mortals like ourselves, continue to watch over and care for us. Think again, that if God, who is all purity, can be near us, why should not they?

I believe in my heart, that this power is being spread more and more every day to draw us nearer to God. You ask if it makes us purer? My only answer is that we are but mortals, and as such liable to err; but it does teach, that the pure in heart shall see God. It teaches us that He is love, and that there is no death. To the aged it comes as a solace, when the storms of life are nearly over and rest cometh. To the young it speaks of the duty we owe to each other, and that as we sow, so shall we reap. To all it teaches resignation. It comes to roll away the clouds of error, and bring the bright morning of a never-ending day.

A writer in the "Evening Star" described this lecture under the title of "An Evening with the Spiritualists," in which he sketched my portrait from his own special mirror as appears by the following extract:—

"On the platform were a table and desk, with a candle on each side; and in front of the platform were two rows of specially reserved seats, in which sat, among others, several ladies and gentlemen well, and deservedly well known in the literary and dramatic worlds. I am told they gave a convincing proof of their belief in spiritualism—they paid for their entrance tickets. Shortly after eight o'clock a slim, lithe gentleman, with pale face, light hair, and small dark eyes, stepped upon the platform, and we knew that before us was. Mr. D. D. Home, the expounder and oftentimes the subject of the elevating influences of spiritualism. With dainty white fingers he spread out before him certain pages of manuscript, displaying as he did so the neatest of wristbands, while on his left hand sparkled a lustrous diamond every time he lifted his pocket-handkerchief. The spirits could find no fault with the perfectly respectable appearance of their professional advocate."

As the article, though written, as might be expected, from a sceptical point of view, was not unfair, and contained no other misrepresentation, I am willing to believe the gentleman who wrote it to be short-sighted, and to have had some mist on his spectacles when he imagined he saw my "small dark eyes," and I have to thank him, on the whole, for the fairness of his account. His narration contrasts strongly with a disgraceful article that appeared in "All the Year Round" for March 3rd, 1866, entitled "At Home with the Spirits." The writer in "All the Year Round" says:—

"Mr. Home did not depart from England until he had appointed a band of apostles to preach the gospel which he came to found and proclaim. I trust I am not uncharitable in suspecting that, in his selection of persons, he aimed at a sort of parody of the original constitution of the Christian Mission. His chosen disciples were humble folks, flower-makers, and menders of shoes. These disciples, with the aid of converts in a higher sphere, have written his Testament in the pages of two periodicals devoted to spiritualism. In these journals we are presented with a record of Home's miracles, and those of his disciples. When Mr. Home took leave of his disciples, he was lifted up to the ceiling in their presence. Is this also a parody of a certain event in sacred history? When I come to notice the lecture which Mr. Home delivered the other evening at Willis's Rooms, the reader will be able to answer the question for himself.

"When Mr. Addison, who was said by the spiritualists to be a medium in spite of himself, offered Mr. Home fifty pounds, if he could float in the air in his presence, Mr. Home escaped from the dilemma, by declining the challenge; but the Davenports, too confident of their skill, submitted to a test and were found out. The complete exposure of this last form of spiritualism has worked a great change in the tactics of the apostles. Finding it no longer possible to cope with the band of detectors, who have made it their mission to meet and expose them on all occasions, they have dropped miracle working, and now confine themselves to preaching spiritualism as a new faith.

"On Thursday, the fifteenth of February, I attended Willis's Rooms to hear the apostle preach; but before I could bring myself under the influence of the new gospel, I was called upon to pay ten shillings and sixpence. Are there no five-shilling seats?' I asked. The answer was 'No; they are all gone; only a few half-guinea seats left.' I paid my half-guinea and entered the room, and found that there were plenty of five-shilling seats vacant, but only a few half-guinea ones. On coming out I accused the man at the door of having (to use the mildest term) *deceived* me. He did not deny it; but said in excuse, that it was not his fault; he had been told to say there were no five-shilling seats.

"I will relate briefly what I heard and saw, and what was the impression left upon my mind.

"As Mr. Home takes credit for being a medium, with extraordinary powers of body and mind, he can scarcely object to a description of his person. He is a tall, thin man, with broad, square shoulders, suggestive of a suit of clothes hung upon an iron cross. His hair is long and yellow; his teeth are large, glittering, and sharp; his eyes are a pale grey, with a redness about the eyelids, which comes and goes in a ghostly manner as he talks. When he shows his glittering, sharp teeth, and that red rim comes round his slowly-rolling eyes, he is not a pleasant sight to look upon. His hands were long, white and bony, and you knew, without touching them, that they were icy cold. He stooped over his paper, and rarely looked up, except to turn his eyes towards heaven in an appeal to the Deity. The first part of the lecture was very dull and heavy, being all about the indestructibility of matter. Before this "head" was exhausted I counted fifteen members of the congregation who were fast asleep. After my experience at the pay-place it was rather startling to hear Mr. Home disclaiming all mercenary motives, and declaring that he had never received, and never would receive, money for his work. In a private circular to his friends he says, 'I need not tell you how important it is to me to have the support of my friends, not only as a comfort and encouragement to me, but as essentially aiding the cause in which they and I are deeply interested. Much, indeed, of *my own fortune* must depend on the issue of this experiment.' I leave the reader to reconcile this appeal with his disavowal of mercenary motives how he or she can.

"It was a contradiction to deny the truth of spirit rapping, when every Sunday in church we declared our belief in the communion of saints. Such was the argument.

"When Mr. Home was in the middle of his statistics, Professor Anderson, the conjuror, rose from a back seat and said, 'That is wrong.' Said Mr. Home, 'When I have finished my lecture, I will hear what you have to say.' Accordingly, when the lecture was finished, the Professor walked up the room, ascended the platform, and began deliberately to take off his coat. Mr. Home, not liking the look of this proceeding, immediately hopped down from the platform and began distributing bills among his friends. But the conjuror had no intention of challenging Mr. Home to fisticuffs. He had merely taken off his great coat to give fuller play to his lungs in a meditated effort of oratory. But the congregation declined to listen to him. His first word was drowned in hisses and cries of 'Off, off.' He tried again and again to obtain a hearing, but in vain; and shouting at the top of his voice, 'Swindle! humbug! blasphemy!' &c., the conjuror was obliged to resume his coat and descend. He had not one friend in the room.

"Now what is the doctrine which Mr. Home propounds, and all these people subscribe to as a new article of faith? Boldly, this—that spiritualism, founded upon table-rapping, rope-tying, and banjo-playing in a cupboard, is *a means of man's salvation!* These are Mr. Home's own words."

From these extracts my readers can judge how much the writer related of "what he heard and saw," and how much of "the impression left on his mind." It is quite clear that by far the greater part of what he says consists of the impression left on his mind, no doubt, but which had existed there long previous to the lecture. Of this I should not complain, were it not that the "impression," whatever it may have been, has led him to make assertions, which, unfortunately, I must set down as impressions of falsehood. Perhaps this maybe accounted for on the supposition that the writer is a well-known writer of fiction, who naturally finds it not easy to adhere to mere facts, and this is very evident from the imaginative portrait which he has presented to his readers as my likeness, as I neither rejoice in the possession of yellow hair, pointed teeth, grey eyes, nor icy cold hands.

Can anything be more false than to say that my own words are "that spiritualism founded upon table-rapping, rope-tying, and banjo-playing in a cupboard, is a means 'of man's salvation.'" I never spoke such a sentence; I have never had anything to do with 'rope-tying and banjo-playing in a cupboard,' be these the tricks of spirits or others, and least of all have I ever said that spiritualism was founded on such manifestations. I maintain that the communion of the spirits who have departed this life, with those who still remain in their earthly bodies, is a most important means of man's salvation, and an agent of the Bible Society might as fairly be accused of stating that Mother Hubbard and the House that Jack built were on a par with Holy Writ because they were issued from the printing press, as I have been accused of the assertion above quoted.

With regard to Professor Anderson the writer says, "His first word was drowned in hisses and cries of 'Off, off'" This is totally untrue, for the 'Professor' was not interrupted until he had uttered a tolerably long tirade of abuse, unaccompanied by a word of argument or a statement of fact. It was not until it became painfully evident to all present that the 'Professor' was in a condition which rendered him unfit to stand before a public meeting that steps were taken to put an end to his speech, for which he appeared to have been preparing by leaving my lecture from time to time and resorting to a fountain of inspiration from which he constantly returned, with a flush on his countenance probably arising from anticipations of coming victory over me.

The following letter, of which no notice whatever was taken, was written to the editor of "All the Year Round," with reference to this mendacious article:—

"MY DEAR MR. WILLS,

"Will you let me enter my protest against a very false and scandalous libel which appears in "All the Year Round," and express my regret that you should be a party to its publication—you who know that such men as Robert Chambers, William Howitt, Professor De Morgan, myself, and a host of others, quite as intelligent and upright, are firm believers in phenomena called 'spiritualism.'

"No doubt you are fully free to cry such men down, however much you may respect and regard them—however much confidence you may have in their integrity and intellectual faculties—their capacity for judging, and their honesty in arriving at conclusions, but you are not free to let any contributor in your columns state that which he knows to be false, as does the writer of the article on Mr. D. D. Home.

"It is a mass of deliberate falsehood, and you ought to know it is so. I will not trouble you by going through it in proof; I will merely point to two assertions:— one, that he— 'distributed bills' after the lecture—the other, that his circular declared 'that much of his own fortune must depend on the issue of this experiment'

"In reference to the first of these two falsehoods I can only give you now my own assurance; that Home distributed no bills, having none to distribute. In regard to the second falsehood, I send you a copy of the only circular he issued. You will see for yourself how dishonourable and disgraceful has been the change of a word to give a totally different meaning to the sentence. The writer of that article, be he who he may, is a dishonest man, to say the least. He may have a right to criticise that of which he knows nothing, but he has no right to describe as dupes of an impostor, men, who I am very sure, many of them, are in all ways his betters, and far more fitted than he is to examine and judge.

"What pretence to fight can such, a man have who describes a person—much respected, at all events by many who are themselves respected—as 'seeking his daily bread by professions which he knows to be false, wicked and blasphemous.'

"Of course you have shot the arrow, and will let the barb stick; you will not show the other side. Most probably you will not even correct the scandalous misstatements to which I have drawn your attention—one of which is palpable, for here is the proof in this circular.

"You will not, I trust, be angry with me for writing you. Your contributor may, if he likes, think me a fool or a rogue, whichever he pleases; but I rim sure you do not consider me one or the other.

"Ever faithfully yours,

"S. C. HALL."

The following passages are taken from a review of this article, which appeared in the "Spiritual Times," March 17, 1866:—

"'All the Year Round,' March 3, contains an article, 'At Home with the Spirits,' written in a free style, that is, with a latitude which gives the reins to fancy with a reckless disregard of fact. The writer commences by telling us that he is disposed to 'regard the apostles of startling and incredible" doctrine rather as fools than rogues,' and takes credit to himself for impartiality, and assumes to have given all who have 'promulgated startling aid incredible doctrine' a fair hearing, and never 'scoffed.' But now he is out of patience, evidently, for he doesn't scoff, but only calls us 'fools.' How we are to receive 'fair' treatment at his hands, being prejudged by him as 'fools,' we are at a loss to understand! We next come to a humorous anecdote, detailed, no doubt, in all its *minutiæ*, with exactitude, in which we are introduced to a Scotch shoemaker and his man, who took to phrenology and electro-biology, and forsook the lapstone. The shoemaker gets the credit of having been honest, but his man whom he took about with him as a subject is credited with imposture. This anecdote is introduced to serve a double purpose—spin out the article, and clear the way for a stronger assault on spiritualism. But how can it affect electro-biology, which any ordinary person may prove a truth for himself?

"It is no discredit to a shoemaker to study mental science, and employ himself in its service; but it is discreditable for him to fabricate falsehood, or do anything that degrades his moral nature. We trust sincerely the writer in 'All the Year Round' has not consciously been guilty of this. That he has fabricated falsehood in dealing with spiritualism we shall, we think, be able to show. Let those who laugh with him help him out of it if they can. The 'fools,' we beg pardon, spiritualists, are 'tricksters,' but mostly 'credulous persons' who unwittingly help to practise the trick upon others.'

"Thus this moderate and exemplary writer deals with us as a body. But be is principally interested in Mr. Home and his late lecture at Willis's Rooms. The electro-biology 'trick' was found to be too mundane, and it became an 'object' to introduce 'a supra-mundane element.' Thus the writer in 'All the Year Round' persuades himself and his readers that a system of concerted humbug, commencing with electro-biology and ending with spiritualism was and is at work; and yet he admits 'the believers were chiefly persons moving in the upper circles of society, some of them distinguished for their high intellectual attainments.' Yet still these are, in the majority of instances, 'fools;' and what a miracle that such men as the Scotch shoemaker, who was made the dupe of his man—who practised a hoax to get rid of the stubborn necessity of lapstoning leather—could perform a work ending in making believers 'distinguished for their high literary attainments!' It is really surprising that men can write such twaddle. If a few charlatans, too lazy to 'stick to the last' can be credited with the whole spiritualist 'delusion,' which numbers its adherents by millions, many of whom are among the upper and literary classes, it would appear that men of 'intellectual and literary attainments' are easily duped.

"Another anecdote is given of an author who was in the habit of consulting the spirits, but who, like many another author, went to his account early in life. Of course, it is hinted that his death was hurried through the excitement of 'spirit-rapping *séances.*' Authors are not generally long-lived; many of them indulge too much in evening parties—some of them smoke and drink excessively, almost all of them live a life of excitement of some kind. Much of the excitement attendant upon authorship is unavoidable. If the author mentioned *did* indulge too much in 'spirit-rapping *séances*,' his fate should be a warning to the intemperate. Over-indulgence in eating, drinking, or thinking is to be condemned and must be expiated; but it by no means proves that eating, drinking, and thinking are in themselves evil.

"Mr. Home is charged with appearing amongst us and choosing disciples, after the manner of Christ, from persons of very humble origin; and he is further said to have taken leave of his disciples by being lifted to the ceiling in their presence. This may be fine writing, and very grateful to the majority of the readers of 'All the Year Round,' but it is not altogether true. Mr. Home never chose a disciple; he had something else to do. He was lifted to the ceiling in presence of people of 'exalted position and high literary attainments,' and no flower-makers and vendors of shoes that we know of ever saw him float. 'When Mr. Addison offered Mr. Home fifty pounds if he could float in the air in his presence,' says this truth-loving writer," Mr. Home escaped from the dilemma by declining the challenge.' This offer, we are authorised to state, was never made known to Mr. Home; in fact, Mr. Home knows nothing whatever of Mr. Addison. Besides, had the offer been made, Mr. Home would have acted wisely in 'declining the challenge.' It is one of the most convincing proofs of the spiritual agencies at work in the process of levitation, that he is only raised in the air occasionally, and never at his own dictation.

"The writer is not at all particular in his manner of maltreating Mr. Home and the spiritualists. He presents a word-portrait of some imaginary monstrosity, which he desires his readers to accept for Mr. Home. He tells us that he was *deceived,* on entering Willis's Rooms, by being told that there were no five-shilling seats left when there were several. This affair of the manager he mildly charges upon Mr. Home. (We have taken the trouble to enquire of the manager about this matter, and we learn that all the five-shilling tickets were sold, and that those seats which the writer saw vacant were half-guinea seats. And we are assured that a seat would have been offered him gratis, with the other reporters, had he only shown his card, and stated that he was one of the press.) We can now understand the motive of the animus which has set his pen to work on this subject. To give a specimen of his regard for the truth, he declares that before the first part of Mr. Home's discourse was finished, he 'counted fifteen members of the congregation who were fast asleep.' Is there another person besides this writer who will state this? We think not. The audience, according to the writer's own admissions, consisted almost entirely of Mr. Home's friends. Is it likely they would fall asleep in the middle of his lecture?

"With a view to make Mr. Home appear mercenary—although he stated at the commencement of his lecture that he had never exercised, and he never would exercise, his medium powers for money—the discomfited writer, violating the common rules of privacy, misquotes Mr. Home's circular to his friends by putting the word *fortune* for *future*. 'Much, indeed, of my own *future* must depend on the issue of this experiment.' 'All the Year Round,' in italics says, '*My own fortune.*' If fifteen of the congregation were not asleep, surely this writer was nearly so, or he must have purposely made this alteration.

"A lady is said to have gone up to Mr. Home, and asked him to 'settle' with her; was this meant for 'sit'? Professor Anderson next appears on the scene, and when he is described as mounting the platform and pulling off his coat, Mr. Home is described as hopping off the platform, and distributing bills amongst the audience. Surely the writer must have been very nearly asleep. Mr. Home had no bills to distribute, and he did not leave the platform until he had listened to a *tirade* of abuse from the Professor. Such is a very rapid glance at the article in 'All the Year Round.' When the writer next takes up his pen to deal with spiritualism, we trust he will recollect the words, 'A lying lip is an abomination to the Lord.'

"Rarely has an article been written against spiritualism which contained so many glaring falsehoods as this:—

"'Now, what is the doctrine which Mr. Home propounds, and all these people subscribe to as a new article of faith? Boldly this—that spiritualism, founded upon table-rappings, rope-tying, and banjo-playing in a cupboard, is a *means of man's salvation*—those are Mr. Home's own words.' The writer must have been nearly deaf as well as nearly asleep. Mr. Home said nothing of the kind. He did say that a knowledge of the reality of spirit phenomena leads the atheist and materialist to the higher knowledge of immortal life, or something of the kind.

"Fancy this writer being consistent, and saying of the Christian church—baptismal fonts, communion tables, surplices, and ceremonials, are means of man's salvation, leaving out altogether the Spirit of Christ. This would be doing by orthodoxy what he does by spiritualism.

CHAPTER VII

In the latter part of 1866, a number of gentlemen interested in spiritualism decided upon the formation of a limited society, relating to which the following circular was printed:—

"Many spiritualists and friends of spiritualism, considering that a place in London is greatly needed where they may frequently meet, have resolved to establish a society under the name of The Spiritual Athenæum, at No. 22, Sloane Street, Knightsbridge. At present, many persons who have been largely gifted with 'spiritual gifts' are without the power to make them known for the general good; while it is certain that several distinguished foreigners, thus gifted, have visited and left London without making the acquaintance of a single spiritualist.

"The society proposes to meet the difficulties that impede the progress of spiritualism, by the establishment to which they draw your attention,—where subscribers will have the advantage of intercourse with mediums who may either be found, or who visit England from America, France, and other countries; where books and periodical works in various languages may be received and circulated; where occasional lectures shall be given (written papers being sometimes printed, perhaps quarterly, as 'Transactions'); where a system of useful correspondence may he carried out; where 'experiences' may be communicated and recorded; where, in brief, there shall be a rallying point for spiritualists and their friends for the interchange of information and for consultation; and where 'sittings,' under judicious arrangements, shall be regularly held with Mr. Home and other mediums.

"It is proposed to appoint Mr. D. D. Home as resident Secretary at the Institution. He will act under the guidance and direction of a council and an executive committee, one of whom will act as honorary treasurer.

"We believe that Mr. Home's mediumship (free of all conflicting influences) may thus be made wider and more practical in its beneficial effects. We believe, also, that other mediums may be thus enabled essentially to elucidate and advance spiritualism, and that, hence, investigations into the subject may lead to convictions of its truth.

"It will be a leading duty of the executive committee, acting with the council, to make such arrangements as shall secure facilities for healthy, useful, and instructive communion to those who seek, as well as those who are willing to give, information 'concerning spiritual gifts;' while promoting social intercourse, aiming at loftier and holier objects, checking the spread of materialism, upholding the truths and extending the influence of Christianity, and bringing closer the bonds of peace and love among mankind, inculcating by another power—acting in accordance with Holy Writ, and co-operating with the Christian teacher—duty to God and to our neighbour.

"We therefore ask you to give effect to our plan, by agreeing to subscribe £5. 5s. annually, so long as it shall be satisfactory to you to do so, in order to establish the Spiritual Athenæum. No other responsibility of any kind will be incurred by subscribers. We wish to limit the number of subscribers to one hundred, but we believe that eighty will be sufficient to meet all requirements—such as rent of rooms, the supply of a library, moderate refreshments at *conversazioni*, and the expenses of the secretary.

"The following gentlemen have consented to act as the council; those who are thus indicated (*) forming the executive committee. It will be observed that several of the members are practical men of business, and therefore, that a wise superintendence will be exercised over the proceedings of the society. With the council several ladies of position and influence will be associated.

"PRESENT LIST OF COUNCIL.
(To which additions will be made.)

G. Brocklebank, Esq., Lombard Street, and Greenwich.

Dr. Elliotson, Davies Street, Berkeley Square.

Capt. Drayson, R.A., Woolwich.

Count P. de Gendre, 68, Westbourne Terrace.

H. G. Gibson, Esq., 33, Mark Lane, and Mecklenburg Square.

John Hampden Gledstanes, Esq., London and Paris.

J. M. Gully, Esq., M.D., Malvern.

*S. C. Hall, Esq., F.S.A., Barrister-at-Law, 8, Essex Villas, Kensington.

Henry T. Humphreys, Esq., 1, Clifford's Inn.

*H. G. Jencken, Esq., (Honorary Treasurer), Barrister-at-Law, Kilmorey House, Norwood.

Ion Perdicaris, Esq., Gloucester Terrace, Campden Hill.

*H. Rudall, Esq., 9, Great Tower Street, and the Grove, Camberwell.

*H. W. Spratt, Esq., Walbrook Buildings, and South Villas, Greenwich.

*E. C. Sterling, Esq., 104, Sloane Street.

The Rev. J. G. Wood, M.A., Belvedere, Kent.

22, Sloane Street, Knightsbridge.

During the perfecting of arrangements connected with the "Spiritual Athenæum," some of the members of the council met, from time to time, in Sloane Street, and at times some interesting manifestations occurred. Although each of these possessed its special interest for them who witnessed it, few of them call for any notice. I shall however briefly relate the circumstances connected with one which occurred at a preliminary meeting of the council.

On this occasion Mr. S. C. Hall, Mr. Jencken, Mr. Perdicaris, and Mr. Humphreys, with myself, had met, and, after some time, while they were discussing matters of business, I saw a spirit who gave me her name, and said she was the daughter of Dr. Robert Chambers. Mr. S. C. Hall, who was acquainted with the family, did not believe that Dr. Robert Chambers had had a daughter of that name. I said that we might be certain that he had, and as I said so three raps sounded on the floor. As the object of communication was that Mr. Hall should write to Dr. R. Chambers concerning certain matters, he undertook to do so, though rather unwillingly, and it was not till several weeks later that he ascertained that the name was correct. Even then Dr. R. Chambers was not communicated with, and at a *séance* at Mr. S. C. Hall's, at Essex Villas, Campden Hill, this spirit came to the circle and expressed to me her regret that Mr. S. C. Hall had not written to her father, as requested. She detailed the fresh position of affairs with respect to what she desired to have done, and was accompanied by the spirit of a sister who had left earth at an early age, and gave the words "Pa, love." Dr. Robert Chambers was written to, and in reply wrote: "The whole of the communications accord with actual facts. The words, 'Pa, love,' were the last words she pronounced in life." In a letter to myself, written also about this time, Dr. R. Chambers says, after relating an event which confirmed a message sent him, "So you see Mary was right about the imminence of that step, of which I knew nothing."

The formal opening of the Spiritual Athenaeum took place on the 4th January, 1867, and the following notice concerning it appeared in "The Spiritual Magazine":—

OPENING OF THE SPIRITUAL ATHENAEUM.— The opening meeting of the Spiritual Athenæum took place on Friday evening, January 4. Mr. S. C. Hall, F.S.A., opened the meeting by an excellent introductory address. A brief paper by Dr. Gully was read; and Mr. D. D. Home - Lyon lectured on, and described 'Spiritual Drawings,' a number of which, by various persons, were laid on the tables. The remainder of the evening was occupied by conversation concerning the prospects and progress of spiritualism. The meeting was well attended, and highly gratifying to all who took part in it.

One result of the establishment of the Spiritual Athenæum was to attract the attention of spiritualists in various parts of the kingdom, and I received letters from several quarters relating the progress which spiritualism was making, and giving accounts of numbers of circles organised for the purpose of investigating the subject. My own loss of health in 1867, together with other circumstances, fully explained in connection with the Lyon lawsuit, led to the Athenæum being closed.

The whole history of my acquaintance with Mrs. Lyon being fully detailed in the account of the lawsuit which commences in a subsequent chapter, I pass it by for the moment and proceed here to give accounts of a few *séances* which occurred in 1867.

The following account of the appearance of "Guardians of Strength" is worthy of being recorded, the manifestation of such spirits being of rare occurrence; it appeared in "The Spiritual Magazine" for March, 1867, from the pen of Dr. Gully, Malvern.

"About the 28th of last November, my friend Mr. Home, being in a trance, was examining my body with a view of ascertaining the state of health in which it was. All who have seen Mr. Home in this state of trance, are aware how clearly he sees and communicates with spirits that have passed from the body. And marvellous and marvellously beautiful have been the communications made by them, through him, which it has been my fortune to hear. The gestures, the most trivial actions of bodily life, the mode of walking and speaking, the voice, the infirmities of persons who have passed away long before he was born, and concerning whose peculiarities in all these particulars Mr. Home had not the least possible means of obtaining any knowledge, are all repeated by him when in this state with an accuracy of detail which leaves no doubt, either that he is at the moment possessed by the spirit whose earthly characteristics he is delineating, or that he is receiving from them or from other spirits impressive communications which enable him to reproduce them. On the occasion referred to, Mr. Home stated that the spirits were saying that there was something wrong in the electrical state of my body, and he added, 'They seem to say that glass cups under your bed would be of use. These cups were procured the very next day by those who were anxious about my health; they were, in fact, very thick glass saltcellars, with a cup-like depression in the centre, just sufficient to receive the end of each post of the bedstead; the circle round this depression was certainly one inch and a quarter thick. The object of this apparently trivial detail will appear afterwards. The glasses were placed one under each post of the bedstead on the 30th of November last.

"On the evening of that day Mr. Home, who was my visitor, had a *séance* at which five of us were present. After some defective physical phenomena about the table, the alphabet was called for, and we were told, 'We are not able to manifest our love to-night. Come to-morrow night at half-past nine.' We therefore broke up the *séance*. The real and striking manifestations were destined to be made in my bed-room that same night. (I should say that Mr. Home's bed-room was next to mine and separated by a wall of only slight thickness.)

"I went to bed at twelve o'clock, having been writing up to that time. As I passed along the corridor of the bedrooms I had the most distinct intimations of the presence of spiritual beings, and at one moment felt as if I were jostled by a distinct bodily agent. Something of the kind is frequently experienced whilst Home is staying with me by more than one member of my household. I went to bed; but I had just laid my head on the pillow when numerous and loud raps began to be heard in different parts of the room, but especially on the right side of the head of the bed, where hung the portraits of several of those whom I loved and have lost. I have often had trifling manifestations of the kind in my room when Home was asleep in the adjoining room; but these came with a rapidity, strength and multiplication far greater than I had ever experienced. Still they did not discompose me: I knew the raps (all but one) perfectly well; they were those of my father, brother and child; and they gave me a feeling of happiness rather than of agitation. Under this influence I was sinking off into sleep, when all at once I was horribly roused by the noise of two *tremendous blows* administered in rapid succession on the *left* hand post of the head of the bedstead. They were not raps; they were such blows, and produced such noise as if an iron poker had been wielded by some brawny arms and made to descend with all their force upon a large table or on the sides of a large tub. They shook the bedstead violently; and, as in all my experiences of spiritual phenomena I had never heard anything which had the smallest approach to this exhibition of power, they shook my nerves also, rousing me moreover, as they did suddenly, from drowsy quietude. I started up in bed, and shouted to Home, in the next room, to come and be witness of what was going on. After four loud calls, he answered; then hurriedly dressed, and came into my room, which was in profound darkness. In a few words I told him what had happened, and begged him to lie down outside the bed, and remain to see what further might happen. He had not done so longer than five minutes when two more blows, exactly similar to the former in force and noise, were given upon the *right* hand post of the head of the bed. Upon hearing these, Home was, like myself, agitated; but he told me that he had no doubt that the spirit was one of those protectors of man called 'Guardians of Strength;' that every man had such a guardian; that their office was to shield the body from destructive agents, especially from disease; that they were spirits of a very elevated order, and never manifested themselves save on occasions when something threatened the life of the body which they protected; that they never communicated messages, and that they had never been known to give more than five raps or blows. Further, he said that in all his experiences of spiritualism he had only met with this kind of spirit on four occasions. When he had told me all this, all the spirits present gave affirmative raps. I asked, 'Does that mean that what Home has told me is correct?' Again affirmative raps from all. I asked my father's spirit, 'Who is this powerful spirit?' Answer with the alphabet, 'It is your Guardian of Strength.' No sooner had this reply been given, than the *fifth* blow was administered as before to the *left* head-post of the bedstead, making the *third* blow at that point, and two at the right aide. I confess to having felt very great agitation on the occasion of this last blow; my legs became cold up to the hips, and my head hot and throbbing. Home also was not a little dismayed, and became presently still more so when, after a few minutes of silence, he said to me, 'My dear friend, I don't like these occurrences at all; my wife's spirit has just said to me, "There is danger." I immediately said to my father, 'Tell me what danger there is.' The reply was, 'Danger to you. I asked, 'To body or soul?' 'To your body.' Whilst all this was going on, we heard the spirits moving articles about the room, and rustling the curtains of the canopy, and the silk of the duvet which covered the bed. In the thick darkness also, we *both* plainly saw, as it were, a wall of luminous matter all along the right side of the bedstead, and I asked, 'Are those spirits standing around the bed?' Answer from all, 'Yes.' 'Are you looking upon us?' 'Yes, as you are looking upon us.' They all gave me their names; but, as I have said, there was one whose raps I did not recognize, and these were very sharp, quick, and merry. I asked this one specially to give me his name; the answer was given, 'M. L____,' and at the same time a large framed medallion cast of a woman's profile, which for many a year has hung near the head of my bed, was rapped quickly upon the wall. Astonished, I said, 'What? is that Margaret L____?' Answer, 'Yes: I love you always.' 'All these thirty-nine years?' 'Yes; and I must come *now*.' 'Because I am in danger?' 'Yes.' Now, it is necessary that I should let the reader into a private episode of my life. The Margaret L____ here spoken of was my first boyish love: like most loves, ours 'did not run smooth.' We were both eighteen years old when she was taken ill, and I went for the first time to the University. At her urgent entreaty I was permitted to go to her bedside to say 'good-bye' on leaving. I never saw her again: a simple illness became complicated, and she passed away six weeks after my last sight of her. I have never forgotten the love and the distress of that time. Years afterwards I visited her tomb, and found a very accurate profile likeness of her in a marble medallion on it: I had a cast taken from this, and it has been in my bedroom ever since. It is thirty-nine years since she passed away; and, in my experiences of spiritualism during the last ten years, I have often wondered that she did not manifest herself to me; probably her spirit is in higher spheres, and only became manifested to me like that of my Guardian of Strength, on an urgent occasion. To return. I have said that the spirits in the room were moving about. After the fifth blow of the Guardian of Strength, they became still more restless; they pressed our arms and legs, and my child stroked my face lovingly. Yet the air seemed to be charged with magnetic fluid; we could scarcely breathe; as I have said, my head was full and hot, and my lower extremities cold. When the whole physical condition seemed to have become no longer tolerable, the Guardian of Strength came upon the bed, and I felt him, as palpably and certainly as I ever felt a flesh hand, handle my legs from hips to feet, pressing them firmly but equally all down,—a sort of shampooing, in fact. He continued to do this for nearly a quarter of an hour (I feeling his general form on the bed just as assuredly as I felt his hand on my lower extremities), until the limbs became hot, and suddenly burst into a profuse warm perspiration, which immediately relieved my head. He then passed across the bed, drew the silken duvet after him, and we heard it rustle as it fell to the ground on the left hand side of the bed. Home then said to me, 'If it be really your Guardian of Strength, and if he will touch us you will find that his touch is icy cold they always are cold.' The operations of this spirit had completely restored my physical and mental comfort, so that I directly said, 'If you be my Guardian of Strength, will you touch Home and myself?' In a flash of time Home called out to me, 'Oh, his hand is on my forehead like a plat of ice—how cold?' I said, 'I hope that you will touch me too.' Immediately the points of his fingers were pressed upon the crown of my head, which was covered with a cotton nightcap. I observed, 'I don't find it so cold,' whereupon the spirit placed the whole inner side of his hand along the top of my head, so that the finger ends rested on my bare forehead, and certainly no ice could be colder. He rested his hand so, but also patted my head in the most kindly manner repeatedly. Upon this I said, 'You don't mean me any harm, do you?' The answer 'No' was given by pulling the tassel of my cap once. I then said, 'I dare say you mean me good?' Reply—'Yes,' by pulling the tassel three times. After the third pull he drew the cap off my head altogether, though my head was resting heavily on the pillow, and threw it on Home's face, from whence he immediately withdrew it, to throw it at mine. I dare say he thought us very stupid not to understand his meaning hitherto, and in all these manifestations; but it is certain that neither of us had the slightest idea what the danger was, or whence it was to come. I may add that after I had been assured by my father that the danger was not to my soul, I ceased to speculate much about it. At the above point the spirit pushed my left shoulder strongly, so as to make me say to Home, 'He is driving me towards you for some purpose or other,' whereupon Home exclaimed, 'and he is pulling me out of bed by the right shoulder;' and sure enough, when I took hold of Home I felt that something was pulling him away from me. These manifestations caused me to say, 'It is plain now that we are to get off the bed altogether, in which case I will light the candle,' which was done, and it discovered the towel horse moved out of its place, the towels thrown about, the medallion on the wall all awry, slippers and boots scattered about the room, and the *duvet* lying on the floor; giving abundant explanation of the bustling sounds which we had heard in the darkness.

"Still, where was the danger? We tried the canopy of the bed, but it was firm enough in its place. At length in looking around and around, Home spied the glass cups underneath the bedposts, and asked what they were there for, having no remembrance of course, of what he had said in his trance two days before. Explaining to him that he had himself suggested them, he asked the spirits present, 'Are these glass cups wrong?' Loud affirmative raps from four or five quarters. 'Shall we remove them?' The same raps as before. We proceeded to remove them, lifting the bedstead with some exertion, but it was readily done for the two lowest posts and the *right* upper one. The two glasses of the lower posts were complete, but the glass under the *right* upper post, which had received *two* out of the *five* strong blows, was found broken into three pieces. We passed to the *left* upper post, which had received *three* blows, but in consequence of a heavy chest of drawers, whose proximity left only a space of five or six inches between it and the bedstead, it was impossible to do more than touch the glass under that post, and quite impossible to lift the bedstead therefrom. As we approached this side of the bed, I holding a lighted candle, we both simultaneously exclaimed, 'There is a large luminous mass in the corner—that must be the Guardian Spirit.' I saw it as plainly and undoubtedly as I see the hand that is writing these words. That some powerful agent was there became evident from what followed. Home said, 'We can't get near enough to this glass to lift the bed and remove it,' when immediately, without our touching the bed at all, the whole mass was raised without any touch of his or mine, and Home withdrew the glass, which had received *three* blows, and which we found to be in four pieces, one of which was almost in a state of powder, so thoroughly had it been broken. This done, we beard and saw no more of the Guardian of Strength; and when, on lying on the bed again to wait for what might happen, we asked about him, the spirits told us that he had gone away. And certainly we might have guessed that some potent agency had left the room, for the atmosphere, from being exciting and stilling (like the air just before a thunder-storm), calmed down, and our physical sensations were totally changed from tension to placidity. After which my father said, 'Good night; I must go.' 'Are you all going?' 'No; Dan' (my brother) 'and Fanny' (my child) 'will remain with you.' And so, after a little more talk about these strange occurrences, Home went to his own room again, having been in mine upwards of an hour and a half. When he had gone, I picked up the silk duvet and spread it over the bed, into which I got, with the hope of sound sleep, after such tumult. It was not yet to be. During an hour and a quarter I was dozing off repeatedly; but each time I was roused by two or three, or four loud raps on the floor of the room. At length, between three and four A.M., worried and feverish with this frequent awakening, I impatiently threw the duvet off the bed. The act was followed by a shower of approving raps. Then, for the first time, I perceived what these awakenings meant; and I said, 'Was I to throw the duvet off the bed?' Answer, 'Yes,' and with the alphabet, 'Good night' In a quarter of an hour I was asleep.

"In subsequent communication with spirits of my own family, 'I was informed that had I on that night gone to sleep with the electricity of my body isolated by the glass cups underneath the bedstead, and the silk duvet above me. I should have had a seizure in the head, and most probably have passed away in it: and that the emergency was very pressing, so as to render the presence and aid of the Guardian of Strength necessary. In answer to questions they also told me that these guardians always had strong sympathy with those over whom they watched that it was not simply because they were sympathetic that they became guardians; but that they are specially chosen by God for each individual. Further, I was informed that in a serious illness through which I had passed on a former occasion, this same guardian had been much occupied with me.

"The question arises, How came spirits to recommend these glass cups, when subsequently it became necessary to rescue me from them?

I never got any decided answer to this; but one night, some time afterwards, my friend Home, in a trance, exclaimed, 'Oh, you remember the glass cups and that night? They say that the whole was contrived for your good, and to impress upon you.' And most assuredly it did impress upon me; it is impossible to experience anything more real, palpable, visible, audible, than the facts of that night! it is impossible, without the denial of all sense, external and internal, to refuse belief in the intelligent, extra-corporeal agency at work on that occasion. Of the existence of such agency I had long ceased to have any real doubt; but I may have speculated and spun theories to account for spiritual manifestations in some other way, and it may have been to put a stop to these that this marvellous night was contrived for strongly impressing me with the reality of the interference.

"Regarding the existence, attributes, and duties of these Guardians of Strength, I have been unable to find any account in any works on spiritualism to which I have access. M. Kardec has a chapter on Guardian Spirits, but nothing is said of the special act of guardianship over the bodily health by a specially appointed spirit."

The following instance of direct spirit mesmerism will also be interesting; it appeared in "Human Nature," for September, 1867.

"SIR,—The following is an account of some remarkable phenomena of Direct Spirit Mesmerism, witnessed by myself and others at my house early in the evening of the 8th of August, and I should be glad if you could give publicity to my letter—copy of which I have forwarded to the 'Spiritual Magazine' with a similar request.

"It is necessary to premise that Mr. D. D. Home, the medium present, had been staying with me for some short time, and that owing to the state of health of Mrs. Jencken, who had been seized with paralysis, I had determined not to allow any *séances* to be held. On the evening in question, however, I yielded at the request of my mother, and we sat round a small square table in front of the sofa, Mrs. Hennings, our neighbour, making up the party of four.

"We had not been seated many minutes when raps were heard in different parts of the room, the table was tilted and raised straight off the ground; numerous raps were then heard under the table, in the drawer—which was pulled out and replaced; a cold current of air then passed over our hands,—spirit hands touched several of us on our hands and knees,—a hand appeared between myself and Mr. D. D. Home, but only for a moment. We then observed the form of a hand under the shawl Mrs. Jencken had drawn across her knees. A pause then ensued followed by the phenomenon of "Direct Spirit Mesmerism," and to record which is the special object of my present communication.

"At first we heard the rustling of Mrs. Jencken's dress as though a hand was rudely moved over it; we then noticed a hand making mesmeric passes down the right side of Mrs. Jencken; her knee was then grasped, and we distinctly heard the tapping, kneading sound of shampooing a patient. Mrs. Jencken, who remained perfectly calm and composed throughout the process, described her sensation with great precision, observing that she felt as if a powerful hand were making passes down her paralysed side, almost causing pain. Her hand was then seized by, as she described it, a soft, warm hand, rubbed and stretched out with sufficient force to leave a red mark on her hand and wrist. She farther said, that she felt as if an electric stream had passed through her, causing every limb to glow. The whole process lasted about eight to ten minutes, and resulted in the restoration of the use of the paralysed limb and side of Mrs. Jencken, who all but immediately called our attention to the fact of her being able to move her right arm and hand, hitherto perfectly paralysed. On essaying to rise from her chair, she found to her great joy that she could walk, and ever since her convalescence has steadily progressed.

"Fortunately during the *séance*, Mr. Jones of Enmore Park, joined our circle, at which I was much pleased, as I felt it desirable that a farther witness should be present to testify to the truth of the statement I am recording.

"Other and very marked phenomena were produced that evening. Mrs. Hennings' hand was repeatedly touched and grasped; her chair seized and drawn back and half turned round. Mr. Jones was also touched by a hand. A voice was distinctly heard to pass through the room, the note being not unlike the wail of a female voice. But I will not burden you with an account of these phenomena; my object being to confine myself to the description of the phenomenon of Direct Spirit Mesmerism.

"I may, however, add that Mr. D. D. Home is in full power, and that during his stay at my house very remarkable phenomenon occurred.

"Mrs. Jencken is now occupied in writing a statement of what took place, anxious that a document should be placed on record to prove at some future time the possibility of Direct Spirit Mesmerism.

"H. D. JENCKEN."

"Kilmorey House, 15th August, 1867."

CHAPTER VIII

NEW MANIFESTATIONS—ELONGATION—VOICES—PERFUMES.

During the latter part of 1867, several novel manifestations occurred in my presence, accounts of which appeared from time to time in the "Spiritual Magazine," "Human Nature," &c. I here give some of these with the names of those present, and those of the writers of the accounts. The first of these which I give occurred in Great Malvern, at Dr. Gully's, and is recorded in a letter from Mr. H. D. Jencken to "Human Nature," for November, 1867, as follows:—

"The party present had only incidentally met, and owing to a prohibition being laid upon Mr. Home by his medical man, against trying his strength, no *séance* was attempted. I name this as characteristic. Spiritual presence, however, soon made itself heard, by raps in different parts of the room, and the movement of the furniture told of the presence of the invisibles. The library in which the party had met communicated with the hall, and the door having been left half open, a broad stream of light from the burners of the gas lamp lit up the room. At the suggestion of one of the party, the candles were removed. The rapping which had till then been heard in different parts of the room, suddenly made a pause, and then the unusual phenomenon of the appearance of spirit forms manifested itself. The opening of the half-closed door was suddenly darkened by an invisible agency, the room becoming pitch dark. Then the wall opposite became illumined, the library being now lit up by a luminous element, for it cannot be described otherwise. Between those present and the opposite and now illumined wall two spirit forms were seen, their shadowy outline on the wall well-defined. The forms moved to and fro, and they made an effort to speak. The articulation, however, was too imperfect to permit of the meaning of the words being understood. The darkening which had obscured the half-closed door was then removed, and the broad light from the hall lamp re-appeared looking quite dim in comparison with the luminous brilliancy of the light that had passed away. Again the room became darkened, then illumined, and a colossal head and shoulders appeared to rise from the floor, visible only by the shadow it cast upon the illumined wall. What added to the interest, was the apparent darkening and lighting up of the room at will, and that repeatedly, the library door remaining half open all the while. The time occupied by these phenomena was perhaps five to ten minutes, the manifestations terminating quite abruptly."

Another remarkable *séance* took place in Mr. S. C. Hall's house, Essex Villas, Campden Hill, at about the same period, and I give it from the notes of Mr. H. T. Humphreys, who was present, as follows:—

"Hearing from Mr. S. C. Hall that Mr. Home was at his house for a day or two and wished to see me, I went out to Essex Villas in the evening, and after having had some conversation with him and others who had also called, the other visitors left. We were shortly afterwards— that is to say, Mr. and Mrs. S. C. Hall, Mr. Home, and myself—standing in the recess leading to the conservatory, when Mrs. Hall remarked that it was a long time since they had had a *séance*. Mr. Home at once replied that he was unwell, and had been talking about matters which excited him, and could not sit. He then sat down to the piano, and was about to open it when a shower of little raps were heard inside the instrument. 'Do you hear the raps?' he said. 'Come, we will have a sitting.' We four then sat down, Mr. and Mrs. S. C. Hall being seated opposite each other, and I opposite to Mr. Home, round a small kettle-drum octagon table covered with velvet, the legs being screwed into the top. After a short pause raps were heard on the table, which was tilted and raised straight up in the air, next rolled into the lap of Mrs. S. C. Hall, then into my lap; after which it was placed on my foot, and balanced to and fro whilst in that position; it finally turned itself upside down, the top being at about the height of our heads, and the legs in the air above. Raps were then heard, and a sentence was spelt out, to the effect that this was the present condition of spiritualism, but that it would soon come—at this word the table was again placed on its legs in our midst, thus signifying the word—'right,' and a guess as to this meaning was answered by affirmative raps. Mr. Home then rose from his chair, impelled he said to do so, and walked to and fro. Then followed the extraordinary phenomenon of the lengthening out and shortening of the medium's body; a phenomenon not unknown to those who have followed this inquiry, but nevertheless very remarkable, and equally unaccountable. Mr. Home said he felt as if his hair was being pulled, but without causing pain; on the contrary, he described the sensation as pleasant. At his request, I placed my feet on his up to the instep, to be satisfied that he did not stand upon his toes; and at the same time placed my right hand on his body horizontally, partly on his waistcoat and partly on his trousers; the upper part of his body then rose to such an extent that my hand was in a few moments resting on his shirt, with, I should say, about an inch of space between it and the trousers below, and a similar space between it and the vest above. After remaining for a few moments at the stature of at the least seven feet, Mr. Home sank quietly down to his normal size, and then appeared to be pressed down till less than five feet in height. This remarkable manifestation was repeated three or four times, and we were given to understand that it would have a curative effect.

"On Mr. Home resuming his seat, raps were heard in different parts of the room. The octagon kettle-drum table was again seized by an invisible power, raised straight up into the air and placed inverted upon the head of Mr. Home. It is necessary to name that Mr. Home remained perfectly motionless whilst the table was being held and balanced on his head. Words were again spelt out, significant of the meaning of this droll procedure, such as, '*It is hard to bear, but it is a crown.*' The table was then replaced in the centre of the circle, and again taken suddenly from our midst and thrown down on the floor at about a distance of six feet. We sat quietly for a time, and as I held both my hands down between my knees, I felt something touch my knuckles. I opened my hand and took hold of the leg of the octagon table, which, it now appeared, had been screwed off, and brought to me. Sentences were then spelt out, 'Let it represent the weapon of truth;' 'Truth is strength;' 'We will give you strength where you most need it' After holding the leg of the table for sometime I felt that something had begun to pull it away from me. I resisted for some time, but at length it was dragged from me with a considerable amount of force, and was immediately stuck into Mr. Home's back, sticking up from his collar. While in this condition, messages, somewhat similar to what have been given above, were given by tipping the leg against my hand which I held up to it. It was then worked about Mr. Home's back, and finally slid down it beneath his coat and vanished. I had my hand on the end of it as it was sliding down, but failed in feeling it underneath the coat, though I at once left my seat and went round to feel for it. On my return to my seat I found this leg of the table laid on it, resting on the seat and the middle bar of the back of the chair. During this process Mr. Home described his sensations as if under the influence of shocks from an electric battery. The octagon table now with its two legs, was replaced by the invisibles, in the centre of the circle. While here, and apparently unsustained by any of us, messages were given, and at length I asked what was to be done with the leg of the table? At the moment the leg rose from its position on my chair beside me, upright in the air, bent towards me and gently touched me on the eye, next bent towards and touched Mrs. Hall, saluted Mr. S. C. Hall in the same manner, and then rapidly darted across the table and down to the floor. We then heard the sound of screwing it into its place, and I put my hand under the table to touch it. This stopped the work, but on my taking away my hand, it was resumed, and when completed, the table was jumped upon this leg as if to show that it had been firmly replaced, raps were heard all over the room, and sounds like the laugh of a child resounded in the air. A large sofa which stood by the wall at about seven feet from us was drawn quietly up so as to touch the chair on which Mr. S. C. Hall was seated. This occurred while we all remained seated. Two large photograph albums were also removed from a shelf behind the sofa.

"After these manifestations, the final and culminating phenomenon was manifested, which in itself constitutes quite an epoch in the history of spiritual phenomena, replete as the records of spiritual manifestations are with what, under ordinary circumstances, would be regarded as impossible. After a short pause, a luminous coronet of star-like light points settled upon the head of Mr. S. C. Hall, and remained stationary, resting on his head for several minutes. Then a semi-luminous appearance was manifested, which assumed the outline of a face with two star-like eyes. Mr. Hall said he felt as if this item was pressing against him. Mr. Home then rose from his chair, and was walked to and fro complaining of pressure on the head. Suddenly he said he felt a weight on his head. It was then noticed that a crown shaped like a Greek patera, the base fitting on like a skull-cap, had been placed on his head. Tendrils and outlines of leaves were plainly visible, the leaves being vine-shaped, appearing to hang from the edges of the broad patera. Mr. Home appeared greatly agitated, and repeated, 'I am crowned;' 'I am free from pain;' 'I am receiving a new mission;' 'The pain in my head is gone.' He then walked up and down the room, the excitement all but overpowering him. Finally, the crown was removed from his head, while sweet-toned notes were distinctly heard proceeding from it; after which it was gently carried towards those present, as though for their inspection, and then removed into the angle of the door, where it remained luminously visible for four or five minutes—visible as though it were from its own intrinsic light. The brilliancy of its star-like form had so deeply impressed all present, that after its disappearance they continued to gaze at the place where the beautiful luminous crown had once stood, unable to realise its disappearance. These notes are necessarily very imperfect; but I have been very careful to set down nothing save what I can most clearly and distinctly depose to."

This *séance* was to myself remarkable, as I had been very ill and weak previous to it, and on that evening was restored to perfect health. It was therefore an instance of direct spirit mesmerism.

Mr Jencken also gives the following account in "Human Nature," for November, 1867:—

"In this instance the *séance* was held by appointment at Dr. Gully's, Great Malvern. Our object being that of investigation, we limited the number to three, and I must add, used every precaution we could think of, to preclude the possibility of self-deception; we likewise guarded against any possible preparatory arrangement. Accordingly we changed from the library to the dining-room. We were soon seated at a heavy square table. Twenty minutes passed without any manifestations; then came gentle raps, followed by the table being lifted, tilted, and gently vibrated. Then simultaneously raps were heard in different and opposite parts of the room. At my suggestion the lamp was partly turned down; when a cold current of air was felt to pass over our hands and faces, and a pause ensued. The dining-room table leaf-stand in the corner of the room commenced to vibrate, and one of the leaves being taken from the stand was passed between Mr. Home and the table at which we were seated. It was then raised straight up, and passing vertically over my friend, gently touched him; in passing over me it struck me on the crown of my head, so gently that I could hardly realise it to be the heavy leaf of the dining-room table; the touch nevertheless caused the leaf to vibrate all but sonorously. I name this to prove how delicately balanced and suspended in the air the leaf of the table must have been to have produced the sonorous vibration. It then passed to the right, touching my shoulder, and finally was placed upon the table at which we were seated. The distance the leaf was carried I compute at nearly twelve yards (allowing for the circuit made) and at an elevation of six feet. A small round table was then moved from the corner of the room, and placed next to my friend, and in reply to his question who it was, he received the answer, audible to us all, *'Pa'—'Pa dear'—'darling Pa.'* An arm chair behind my friend, and at a distance of three yards, was raised up straight into the air, carried over our heads, and placed upon the dining-room table to my left—a voice clearly and loudly repeating the words, 'Papa's chair.' We then observed the wooden box of the accordion being carried from the extreme corner of the room, up to my friend. In passing my right hand, I passed my hand under and over the box, as it travelled suspended in the air to my front. I did this to make sure of the fact of its being moved by an invisible agency, and not by means of mechanical aid. The box was finally deposited on the table in front of my friend. Mr. Home had in the meantime taken the accordion in his right hand, giving me his left hand. Words were spelt out that the spirits would play his life, from his early infancy to the final drama, 'Daniel in the Lion's Den,' evidently in allusion to his suit with Mrs. Lyon. The accordion immediately commenced playing, and continued so for fifteen minutes. What added to the interest was the accompaniment by voices imitating the clock in the hall, the rush of the waves, and when the 'Lion's Den' was played, loud roars in imitation of lions were heard. I counted three or four voices. The accordion was then taken from Mr. Home, carried about in the room and played. Voices were distinctly heard, a low whispering, and voices imitating the break of a wave on a shore. Finally the accordion placed itself upon the table we were seated at, and two luminous hands were distinctly seen resting on the keys of the instrument. They remained luminously viable for twenty to thirty seconds, melting away. I had in the meantime, and at the request of my friend, taken hold of the accordion; whilst so held by me, an invisible hand laid hold of the instrument and played for two or three minutes what appeared to me to be sacred music. Voices were then heard, a kind of murmuring or low whistling and breathing; at times in imitation of the murmur of the waves of the sea, at other times more plaintively melodious. The accordion was then for a second time taken by an invisible power, carried over our heads, and a small piece of sacred music played—then a hymn—voices in deep sonorous notes singing the hallelujah. I thought I could make out three voices, but my friend said he could speak to four. A jet of light then crossed the room, after which a star or brilliantly luminous disk, followed by the appearance of a softly luminous column of light, which moved up between me and my friend. I cannot say that I could discern any distinct outline. The luminous column appeared to me to be about five to six feet high, the subdued soft light mounting from it half illumining the room. The column or luminous appearance then passed to my right; and a chair was moved and placed next to me. I distinctly heard the rustling of a silk dress. Instinctively I put my hand forward to ascertain the presence of the guest, when a soft hand seized my hand and wrist. I then felt that the skirt of a dress had covered my knees. I grasped it; it felt like thick silk, and melted away as I firmly clenched my hand on it. By this time I admit I shuddered. A heavy footstep then passed to my right, the floor vibrating to the footfall; the spirit form now walked up to the fireplace clapping its hands as it passed me. I then felt something press against the back of my chair. The weight was so great that as the form leaned on my shoulder I had to lean forward under the pressure. Two hands gently pressed my forehead. I noticed a luminous appearance at my right. I was kissed, and what to me at the time made my very frame thrill again, spoken to in a sweet, low, melodious voice. The words uttered by the spirit were distinctly heard by all present. As the spirit-form passed away, it repeated the words, 'I kissed you, I kissed you,' and I felt three taps on each shoulder, audible to all present, as if though in parting to re-impress me with the reality of its presence. I shuddered again, and in spite of all my heroism, felt very 'uncanny.' My friend now called our attention to his being patted by a soft hand on his head. I heard a kiss, and then the words, 'Papa,' 'Dear Papa.' He said his left hand was being kissed, and that a soft child-like hand was caressing him. A cloud of light appeared to be standing at his left.

"Direct spirit-writing, which has so often been questioned, was also manifested that evening in my presence. The writing I have preserved, but cannot, for serious reasons, give its contents, startling and unusual as they are. A sheet of paper which had been placed before me at the commencement of the *séance* was rolled up into the shape of a speaking trumpet, the edge having been torn off and placed in a wooden box, which the spirits had placed in front of my friend. Voices, raps, soft breathing, music, were heard, and finally, after the hallelujah had been sung, words were spelt out telling us 'they could do no more.'

"Were it not that I feared I had already trespassed too largely on your valuable space, I would have given my narrative in greater detail, but I know there is a limit to your space. So suffice it to say, that every precaution was taken to prevent mistakes or self-deception. I do not use the word collusion, for from my intimate knowledge of Mr. Home, I unhesitatingly aver his utter incapability of practising deception; but we used more than ordinary precaution—first, because we had met with the express object of thoroughly investigating these interesting phenomena; and also, should occasion need, to be able to answer to any doubt which might be raised. This much for a statement of facts. I use the word facts advisedly. The manifestations I have given a record of have been witnessed by men, all of whom are, strange enough to say, and without exception, literary, scientific, or professional, and who would, if called upon, unhesitatingly testify to the truth of that which they have seen."

The following is from the pen of Mr. H. D. Jencken, and appeared in "Human Nature" for December, 1867:

"I have again to record some interesting facts in connection with the subject of spiritual manifestations, and which have occurred since I last addressed you. The *séances* to which I now allude were held at my house; and I need hardly add that deception, or even self-delusion, are quite out of all question. At the first of the *séances*, and at which, as well as at those subsequently held, Mr. D. D. Home was present, I had invited a friend of mine to attend, who had to be more than ordinarily satisfied of the truth of the manifestations, owing to his scepticism. The manifestations commenced. Whilst we were seated at the tea table in the dining room, the table was unexpectedly moved, and this was followed by loud, sonorous raps. The fire-screen behind Mr. Home's chair was removed, laid on the floor, and glided towards Mrs. _____. The sceptical guest had in the meantime arrived, and we soon found ourselves seated round a square table in the drawing-room. Raps and tilting of the table soon manifested themselves. Sentences were spelt out—the names of near relatives of one of those present. Mr. Home had now gone off into a trance state. Whilst in this condition, he said he saw a spirit form standing next to a gentleman present. The form, character, and past history were so accurately detailed, that the identity was unmistakably established—much to the surprise of the gentleman, whose departed friend had been quite unknown to Mr, Home. A few sentences were spelt out, and the manifestations thereafter ceased.

"At a subsequent *séance*, the physical demonstrations of spirit power were very marked. On this occasion six in all sat down to a *séance*. Raps, very gentle at first, but gradually increasing in strength, were heard; then the table tilted. After a while the curtains began to be moved, as though by a hand from the window, pushing them into the room. This phenomenon was repeated several times. The semi-grand now showed signs of movement. On three or four occasions this heavy piano was bodily raised quite an inch off the ground, and carried from the wall two to three feet into the room. Raps were then heard in and on the semi-grand. The table next to Mrs. _____ (not the one we were seated at) was now gently and elegantly raised, and suspended in the air from eighteen inches to two feet off the ground, as far as I could judge. It remained in this position for one or two minutes,—time enough to allow one of the party to lie down under the table, and make certain that no mechanical means had been used. This manifestation was repeated three or four times. The accordion was now taken by Mr. Home; and whilst held by him with one hand, a very beautiful hymn was played, and some pieces of sacred music. I noticed distinctly the movement of the keys of the accordion, which, as the instrument was now horizontally suspended in the air, with the fingerboard end towards the lights, I was enabled to see. The keys were moved regularly, as though pressed by the fingers of a hand. In answer to a question how many spirits were present, the table tilted twelve times. This was repeated for several minutes, the twelfth tilt being marked by a loud rap or knock. Finally, the sentence was spelt out that they could do no more—that they had no more power: the word 'power' being spelt by movement of the end of the semi-grand.

"SPIRIT-SEEING—SPIRIT VISIONS.

"I have also to record several very characteristic instances of spirit visions of Mr. D. D. Home's. On the occasion I am now narrating the friends present had only occasionally met, and had seated themselves round the drawing-room table. Suddenly Mr. Home, who had all the while been engaged in conversing with the ladies, changed the expression of his face, rose, and having played a few chords on the piano, returned to resume his seat; but now in a state of trance, his face rigid, hands cold, and the fingers extended. He steadfastly looked across to where Mrs. _____ was seated, and said, 'L____ S____ is standing between you and Mr. _____. I see her as she was in life—mark, not as she is, but as she was when on earth. Mr. Home accurately described the person of the spirit. So marked and clear were the traits he delineated, that no doubt as to identity was possible. He sad that a child, which had passed away in early infancy, was standing next to L____ S____, adding that L____ S____ was much pleased, and anxious to communicate with Mrs. _____, whom she had loved on earth; and, to prove identity, recalled a conversation that had taken place years ago between the two friends. He then said that L____ S____ wished to say that, since passing away, her views had much changed—that she had first to unlearn in order to learn. The spirit then impressed Mr. Home to remind Mrs. _____ of a conversation she had recently held with her husband. I may state that Mr. Home was a perfect stranger to the deceased person, whose name be had never even heard. We have here, then, a proof of the presence of spirits of the departed; for we have name, description of person, and marked incidents in past life all given, establishing an identity beyond dispute or cavil.

"Visions of spirit forms I have become tolerably familiar with since I followed the inquiry of spiritual phenomena; and what has added to the deep interest in this subject, is the conviction, confirmed by proof, that the departed again visit us to solace, soothe, warn, as we travel onward to the boundary line of the unknown world. I could render other instances that have come under my notice of spirit visions; but, for this time I will not ask for more space in your columns. Possibly, in my next, I may be able to give you some further account of the extraordinary phenomena we are constantly witnessing. The suit now pending in the Courts of Chancery so completely occupies Mr. Home, that, except at friends' houses, he is rarely to be seen. This suit, one of the most interesting that has for the last century been before the public, is now rapidly coming on for a hearing. The history, incidents, the course of the proceedings, are all of an unusual character; and will form, when on record and allowed to be published, one of the most interesting phases in the history of Spiritualism. That all who have investigated the question of spiritual manifestations look forward to this trial with the utmost interest, I need hardly tell you. We feel that the day has arrived for vigorously testing the truth of what we know to be the fact, and applying the inexorable logic of actual observation. Testified to in a court of law, I reject the word "belief," for it is not an acceptance of the existence of the unseen, but the admission of the seen, and heard, and evidence to our external sensibility of an objective fact, that we contend for. No severer test can be applied than that brought in by judicial inquiry, when every statement will have to be proved and substantiated. I repeat that the suit now to be heard will indeed prove, of a high order of interest. The mistake the public makes is that of mixing up some crotchet of a belief with the inquiry as inseparable from spiritualism. Now nothing is more erroneous. All that is contended for is, that the fact of certain physical phenomena is true, and that neither deceit nor self-deception have aught to do with it. I had intended to add some few remarks of my own, but space will not allow my doing so this time. When next I address you, and you will grant me space, I will endeavour to render my theory of the cause of some of the phenomena I have been recording, more especially in reference to the vision power of mediums."

The following, which appeared in January, is also by Mr. H. D. Jencken:—

"I have again to address you, and would hesitate, but for the very exceptional circumstances of having Mr. Home staying with me for some weeks, which has given me the amplest opportunity of investigating the truly remarkable phenomena constantly occurring at my house. What adds to the interest of these manifestations is their varied character, not one *séance* resembling another. It is from this fact that I am enabled to single out instances from the many we have witnessed, which present the more marked phases of spiritual manifestations. The *séances* which I here render an account of are given in their order of date. On the first of these evenings eight of us met, two of whom were hard-to-be-convinced sceptics. We had not been seated many minutes when raps were heard, the table vibrated and tilted, and pieces of furniture at distant parts of the room moved; a pause ensued, followed by the simultaneous movement of two small side tables. One of these held a work-box and a flower-stand; the other a fern plant. The table with the fern plant was raised ten to fifteen inches off the ground, and carried several feet at an inclined plane of thirty degrees to Mrs. _____; and what added to the interest, was the fact of the fern plant remaining firmly fixed on the table during the whole of the time. Whilst thus suspended in the air, the table vibrated, raps were heard in and on the table, and the fern-plant leaves pressed themselves against those whom it was intended to greet in the most affectionate manner, quite overshadowing their faces. One of the sceptic friends had in the meantime lain down on the floor to make sure that no deception was being practised, and had placed her hands under the pedestal of the table whilst it was suspended in the air. Passing Mr. Home, the small side-table crossed over to Mrs. _____, and the bowing, vibrating, and pressing of the fern leaves into her face repeated themselves. Simultaneously, the other small side-table was raised up into the air four to six inches high, and carried up to Mrs. _____. These movements took place under circumstances rendering deception impossible; the room was well lighted, and the tables were moved simultaneously on both sides at some short distance from Mr. Home, and that quite independently of each other, being closely watched by those present. After these manifestations had ceased, the table we were seated at was raised straight up into the air eighteen to twenty-four inches high, and whilst so suspended, answered by an up-and-down movement to any mental questions. The charm of this latter manifestation consists in the elegance of the balance and the softness of movement, the table appearing to be resting on an electric wave. Cold currents of air were passed over our hands and faces. Voices were heard, a low kind of whistling, and breathing. The accordion was then moved and glided up to Mr. Home. Whilst held by him in one hand, the finger-board end was carried out horizontally into the room, and a short piece of sacred music was played; then the following sentences were spelt out:—

"'We would fain do more to show our love.'

"'The emblems of God's love we bring for you.'

"And, finally, the ordinary message, 'We can do no more,' warned us that our evening had ended.

"A few days later, we were quietly sealed round our dining-room table, reading and writing, when raps were heard, first on the side-board, then on the table. As these grew louder and more marked, we paused in our occupations to observe what might occur. The flower-stand behind me moved and vibrated; I heard a snap, as if a leaf or flower had been broken off; the table then moved and trembled. By this time two of our neighbours, whom I had sent for, arrived. Almost as soon as they were seated, raps, trembling of the floor and room occurred, the strong vibratory motion quite unlike any ordinary movement, and of power enough to make the house shake, so that the servants in the upper rooms distinctly felt the tremor. Mr. Home then said he felt a hand touching him, and then his neighbour said she was being touched, and her dress pulled finally, a flower, one of the fuschia flowers from the stand behind me, was placed in her hand. As you may imagine, we all grouped round to examine the gift, and raps in different parts of the room, and tilting of the table told us who the donors were. Mr. Home had now passed into a trance state. His appearance was singularly strange, and around his head I noticed a luminous halo. Whilst in this condition he recalled scenes of the past life of departed friends so graphically, so touchingly true, that it was hard, indeed, to repress emotional utterance; finally, raising his hands towards heaven, he repeated the words, 'Light, glory—glory be to our Father in heaven.'

"The trance state had now passed away, and Mr. Home resumed his seat. The accordion which I had placed near him moved and pushed itself up to Mr. Home. He laid hold of it, and a few chords were played. The instrument was then taken from him, carried to the opposite side of the table, and, raising itself about two feet off the ground, not touched by, nor near to any one present, played, resting horizontally in the air, a very sweet-toned piece of music. To me this independent action, unaided by any human hand, was very interesting, and to make certain of the fact, I asked the lady next to me to stoop down and carefully observe the movements of the instrument. The accordion then travelled back to Mr. Home, and a piece of music was played, followed by the melody, 'The last rose of summer." At first only three or four notes were struck, but, on our remarking that the performer could not do more, loud raps were heard, and the whole piece was performed, though not altogether without some imperfections. When this was finished, Mrs. _____ was tapped three times on the knee, as if to say, 'I have done it.' The instrument then spelt out 'Goodnight,' and the *séance* ended.

"On another occasion, Mr. Home had gone off into a slumber on the sofa in my drawing-room. Mrs. _____, who was sitting next to him, suddenly observed a black object glide along the floor towards her. On examination, it proved to be the footstool which had of its own accord moved across the room placing itself at her feet. The oval-shaped drawing-table now moved into the centre of the room, and the arm chair at the farther corner came wheeling up to Mrs. _____, balancing its broad back into her lap. My arrival interrupted these manifestations—the displacement of the furniture only remaining to prove what had occurred.

"At a sitting some few days later on, after the raps, trembling, and lifting of the table which usually prelude a *séance*, several very impressive messages were spelt out—some of these by the raising of the table, at which we were seated, off the ground, and other sentences were given by the accordion. I will render some few, that you may judge of their character and bearing:—

"'There is but one God, the Father of us all.'

"'God is tolerant: he bears with our shortcomings.'

"'Love and Charity; God gives the one, and expects the other.'

"The latter sentence was particularly pertinent, as we had been speaking, perhaps not unkindly, but reproachfully, of some of our neighbours, whose derision at our assent to the belief of these phenomena had pained us. The accordion had in the meantime placed itself in Mr. Home's hand and played a very fine piece of solemn music. I noticed the keys as they spontaneously moved, the instrument being extended horizontally into the room; it then, extending itself across the table, played in sweet, soft toned notes. This lasted quite three or four minutes.

"A sentence was then spelt out—'You are quite right, it was A____ who touched the keys.'

"Mr. Home's left hand had by this time become luminously white, and to me it appeared to have changed its form, assuming that of a lady's. Whilst thus luminously visible, it wafted the scent from the flowers on the adjoining stand over our faces, and into the room. Flowers were now given to every one of those present; a lady seated near to me had a flower placed under her pocket-handkerchief, and the words were then spelt out:—

"'We have done as we promised; look under the handkerchief.'

"We all expressed our satisfaction at the gifts, thanking our donors, but were reminded by the sentence:—

"'Our thanks are to God, to Him praise is due; Him we must praise.' Following this, came a perfect outburst of very solemn sacred music terminating our evening. One more *séance*, and I shall have finished.

"The remarkable part of this last evening was the trance state of Mr. D. D. Home, and the elongation of his body, already noticed in previous letters. Whilst in his trance he established the identity of two persons; and in commenting upon the future of a friend, who was about leaving for the seat of war, Mr. Home said—'The spirit who is to guard you is as tall as this.' Then occurred the extraordinary phenomenon of elongation, Mr. Home attaining a height of quite six feet six inches. As I stood next to him, I only reached to his shoulder. His feet were firmly planted on the ground, and my friend placed his hand upon them to make certain that no levitation was taking place. Twice Mr. Home lengthened out to nearly seven feet in height, and the separation of his clothing at the waist showed the extension. Whatever may be the cause of this extraordinary phenomenon, I cannot venture to say; I merely give the fact as I witnessed it, adding that this is the fourth time that this phenomenon has occurred. Mr. Home then mesmerised my friend, and, returning to his seat, awoke from his trance. I have not given you the sublime prayer he uttered whilst in his trance: your space will not allow of this. We now, at Mr. Home's request, went for a few minutes into the drawing-room. Whilst there, spirit lights manifested themselves, like stars or luminous disks of the size of the palm of the hand. The semi-grand was raised, remaining horizontal the whole time, two feet off the ground; and to verify the levitation, I placed my hand under the castors of the piano! Very remarkable was the resting of the leg on my hand, for several seconds, and this without causing severe pressure. I fear being considered prolix while detailing how I satisfied myself as to the truth of what was passing, but the unusual character of the phenomena will warrant my repetition of the mode of proof. Spirit voices were heard, and the strings of the piano vibrated not unlike an Æolian harp.

CHAPTER IX

ELONGATION AND COMPRESSION—HANDLING OF FIRE.

In February, 1868, Mr. Jencken says:—

"For brevity's sake, I will avoid repeating attendant circumstances, as well as the minuter description of how those present were placed, and the mode employed to verify the phenomena. Suffice it to say that the phenomena were all carefully examined and tested, not because we doubted Mr. Home, but because the wish to be in a position to affirm positively as to what we were witnessing has become quite a creed with us who have followed this enquiry.

"The first evening of the series of *séances* I am about to narrate commenced after some thirty minutes' pause, with the well-known raps, tremblings, and movement of the table. Then voices were heard to repeat the words 'Holy, holy, holy;' and then was spelt out, 'We will play heavenly music.'

"The accordion, which had in the meantime been taken hold of by Mr. Home, played a very beautiful piece of sacred music; at times the instrument was carried horizontally out into the room, then taken from Mr. Home, suspended in the air, and played. The words, 'This is earthly music' having been spelt out, discords were sounded in rapid succession, followed by breaks of fine harmonies. At one time the accordion was carried underneath the table to Mr. _____, and, whilst thus separated from Mr. Home, the instrument played a very soft, sweet, toned piece of music. Mr. Home now rose, and, seating himself at the piano, performed with wonderful execution; then rising from the piano he walked three or four times round our circle, mesmerising each in turn. Here the extraordinary manifestation of elongation and shortening occurred. The height he attained must have been quite six feet nine inches: as he lengthened out, his clothing at the waist separated fully six inches; and again, as he became shorter and shorter, the waistcoat descended quite down to his hips—Mrs. _____ holding the end of his waistcoat to make certain of the elongation. The trance state in which Mr. Home had been up to this time now ceased, and we were reminded by a 'Good night' that the evening had ended.

"The next day at dinner, whilst the servants were in the room waiting upon my guests, a chair moved spontaneously from the corner of the room right up to Mr. Home, then another chair, then the dining-room table tilted and moved, and trembled violently. Mr. _____, who was seated next to me, said he was being touched and pulled—at the same time, a hand was observed to lift the table-cloth. I need not assure you how greatly the servants were startled; and even those who were more

- 355 -

habituated to these phenomena could not refrain from expressions of surprise. Later in the evening, nine in all had assembled in the drawing-room; raps, movements of the table, the lifting of the semi-grand bodily off the ground, and the spontaneous moving of a small side table up to where we were seated, forewarned a very interesting *séance*. Several very beautiful sentences were then spelt out. I will transcribe some few as characteristic. We had been speaking of the late Professor Faraday, and his strong disbelief of these phenomena, when the table tilted, and the following was spelt out:— 'He now knows that our God is all-powerful in very truth, and that his ways are not for man to criticise.'

"As the word 'God' was spelt out, every letter was given in the most solemn, emphatic manner; each letter was differently spelt—that is, the letter 'G' by the lifting of the table; the letter 'O' by the movement of the semi-grand; 'D,' by loud raps at a distant part of the room. This I have remarked on many occasions; also that the table is generally bodily raised into the air, not tilted, and I have seen instances where the table remained suspended in the air three to four minutes. Then followed the sentence—'Thoughts are a part of the divine; when thoughts are pure, the soul is nearer God.'

"The invisibles then addressed a lady present—'Trust, there is a morning star: it will surely rise.' Another sentence, and I must proceed with my narrative. A lady present had been repeating the following verse, 'And all save the spirit of man is divine.' The invisibles at once responded, 'He too is divine when he forgets himself and follows God.' We were so much pleased at this taking part in our conversation, that we expressed our thanks, and asked if they, the invisibles, really sympathised with us: to which the reply at once came, spelt out by the movement of an adjoining table, to which no one was even near—'Why not? we were as you are—we sought for light; the morning came; the day is everlasting.'

"Mr. Home had by this time passed into a trance. After making several circuits and mesmerising us, he placed himself behind Mrs. _____, whom he mesmerised. I have not space to describe the whole of the proceedings, though I have kept, for my own satisfaction, accurate notes of what passed. Remarkable was the breathing of Mr. Home upon Mrs. _____'s spine, causing alternately a feeling of cold and then of intense heat. Mr. Home said, "I am now going to grow taller;" and then the remarkable phenomenon of elongation was witnessed. The elongation repeated itself three times. The first time Mr. Home lengthened to about 6 ft. 9 in.; and then he shortened down below his normal height to about five feet. He then asked me to hold his feet, which I did by planting my foot on his instep, whilst Mr. _____ held his head, his left hand being placed on his left shoulder. We carefully measured the extent of elongation against the wall; it showed eight inches. Mr. _____, who had been watching the extension at the waist, measured six inches elongation!—Mr. _____, who stood behind Mr. Home, barely reaching up to his shoulders, though himself six feet high. Mr. Home had now seated himself. Again he said, 'I am going to be elongated. Daniel will be elongated thirty times during his life: this is the sixth time" (?) Mrs. _____ who sat next to Mr. Home, placed her hand on his head, and her feet on his feet. Thus held, the elongation nevertheless proceeded, measuring six inches. I repeat, Mr. Home was seated all the time, and held by those present, anxious to verify this truly unaccountable phenomenon. By this time Mr. Home had awakened from his trance. Shadows on the wall were seen, voices heard, and finally, 'Good night,' spelt out, terminating the evening.

"During the night, the manifestations continued in Mr. Home's bed-room. Mr. _____, who slept in the same room with Mr. Home, said he repeatedly saw spirit forms cross the room. A spirit hand rolled up the blankets of his bed, and a form was felt to walk across his mattress, the pressure of the foot, as it stepped across, quite indenting the bed-clothes.

"MORE FACTS.—At this *séance*, after some considerable lapse of time, three of those present went into the adjoining room. The shutter bell was taken from underneath the sofa, carried across to those present—the spring-band resting for a time on the arm of Mrs. _____, who noticed a clear, brilliant luminosity under the table. The bell first went under Mr. Home's chair and rang, and then raised itself on to his knee, winding the steel-spring round his arm; then it carried itself on to the lap of Mrs. _____, and the spring suspended itself by the curve on her aim quite firmly, and, disengaging itself went under the table to Mrs. _____, the luminosity increasing in intensity Mr. _____ had now joined the party. The steel spring had again attached itself to Mr. Home's arms. What added to the interest, was that the end of the steel band answered by taps to the questions put.

"The four friends had now rejoined us. Movements of the table and loud raps at once occurred—Mr. Home falling off into a trance almost immediately. In his trance state, he delivered a very beautiful address, too long to be copied; then, passing up to the hearth, placed his hands and then his face in the flames, and on the burning coals. This fire test I have witnessed several times, and particularly call attention to it, as its interest is increased if we but look back to the records of religious persecutions of past ages. On this evening, I had the amplest opportunity of watching the exact movements, and quite satisfied myself of the fact that Mr. Home touched the burning coals. A lady present, unable to resist her expressions of alarm as his face neared and closed upon the flames, was reproved—Mr. Home extending toward her his right hand, which had now become white and luminous, in reproachful warning, saying. 'Have you no faith, no faith? Daniel will take no harm.'

"The accordion was now laid hold of by Mr. Home, who had seated himself at the semi-grand; he attempted to play both instruments, but the notes would not tune to accord. He then seated himself at the harmonium, and played a very beautiful piece of sacred music on both instruments—the accordion being carried horizontally into the room whilst held by him with one hand, the harmonium being played by his right hand. What added to the interest, was that both instruments were in perfect accordance—a choir of voices accompanying the instruments, and giving fullness to the performance. Suddenly the music ceased, and the dying voices of the choir appeared to melt away into space. The evening terminated most pleasantly, the spirits literally taking part in our conversation. I will only instance one or two of the sentences they spelt out in reply to our questions. We had been speaking of Swedenborg's dyspeptic ideas of a future state, and his hell torments, when loud raps made us understand how wrong he had been in his descriptions. Again, we spoke of the demi-obscurity of our churches, and the magic of this sombreness. The sentences were spelt out by loud raps at the extreme end of the room—'The partial obscurity is typical of earth.' 'The soul longs to seek the milder light.' *God is light; God is love.'* Requesting us to sit on a given evening, our spirit friends departed—the words 'Christmas Eve' being uttered and clearly articulated three or four times."

In the March number of "Human Nature" Mr. Jencken thus describes what he had witnessed:—

"Sir,—According to promise, I now give you an account of the interesting *séances* alluded to in my last letter. These evenings were chiefly occupied by the delivery of some very remarkable addresses, during a trance state—one of which lasted two hours. I can only mention these in barest outline; to give them in full would occupy too much space in your journal. Suffice it, if I select from the several one as a specimen. Mr. Home, who was in a trance the whole of the time, after commenting upon the great difficulty experienced by spiritual beings in communicating with us on earth, continued to say, 'that the spirits were watching their opportunity; that the day would come at which a general outburst of spiritual manifestations would occur; that the most favourable time for such an inroad would be Christmas, as then family circles had gathered home, and the human race become more fit for intercommunication.' Then followed a very learned and philosophical discourse; the address terminating with exhortations and moral teachings.

At the subsequent *séance* a party of us had assembled in the drawing-room, when raps told us that the invisibles were present. We were soon seated round a square table, when the sentence was spelt out:— 'The spirit of healing wishes you to extinguish the lights, and place a bottle of water on the table. In five minutes let Lord Adare have half, and in ten minutes let him have the other half.' I accordingly extinguished the lights, and placed a decanter of water on the table; the bright clear fire on the hearth illumining the room enabled me to watch every movement.

"The decanter of water was now laid hold of by Mr. Home, and whirled about, inverted; no water however flowed from the open mouth of the bottle. A star-like luminous disc was now seen in the bottle, and after a short time the water became aromatic, filling the room with perfume.

"Mr. Home, who had by this time passed into a trance, asked me to bring in another decanter, but empty, and pour off half the water from the full bottle. This I did. He then ordered me to bring in another decanter filled. Seizing hold of the full and half-full decanters, Mr. Home whirled the bottles about, then, inverting them, shook them violently. I again observed the luminous star-like point. Strange enough, though both bottles had no neck-stoppers, yet the water did not flow out; and on replacing the two decanters on the table, one was found to be empty. How emptied I cannot pretend to explain—I merely give the fact. Mr. Home again having laid hold of one of the decanters walked up to the fireplace and deliberately poured some few drops of water upon his finger-points. They literally hissed, and jets of steam arose. I noticed several jets of electric light, not unlike those Reichenbach describes emanating from the fingers of sensitives.

"As some of us present had not closely watched this manifestation, Mr. Home repeated it three times. The perfumes that filled the room, Mr. Home appeared to be able to vary at will. At times a powerful aroma of otto of roses, then a perfume of millefleurs, then that of lavender water was wafted across the room.

"The water in the decanters was now noticed to have become strongly perfumed; and Mr. Home, now addressing us, said, 'That all the phenomena we were witnessing were not produced by supernatural means; that, for instance, the perfume that filled the room had been abstracted from scents in the house; that they (the spirits) only possessed greater knowledge of chemical agencies, and could eliminate the volatile substances from the fluids which contained them.' And then continuing to address us, said, 'The cures we perform are only effected by our knowledge of the diseases. We do not raise the dead; we merely watch our opportunity to reawaken life. We do not perform miracles.'

"Mr. Home then continued, 'We have gladly shown you our power over fluids, we will now show you our powers over solids.' He then knelt down before the hearth, and deliberately breaking up a glowing piece of coal in the fire-place, took up a largish lump of incandescent coal, and placing the same in his left hand, proceeded to explain that the caloric had been extracted by a process known to them (the spirits), and that the heat could in part be returned. This he proved by alternately cooling and heating the coal; and, to convince us of the fact, allowed us to handle the coal, which had become cool, then suddenly resumed its heat sufficient to burn one, as I again touched it. I examined Mr. Home's hand, and quite satisfied myself that no artificial means had been employed to protect the skin, which did not even retain the smell of smoke. Mr. Home then reseated himself, and having described how the waters in the decanters were to be used, awoke from his trance quite pale and exhausted.

"I have not detailed the usual accompaniments of a *séance*—raps and vibrations, movements of the furniture—which also occurred during the evening. The semi-grand was lifted massively off the ground; voices were heard; several of us had our hands pressed by spirit-hands; and the lady next to me was moved several feet away from the table, chair and all.

"At a subsequent *séance*, which was held without any preconcertment, those present having only casually met, a lateral upward movement of the semi-grand warned us that the invisibles were in power. We had no sooner seated ourselves, than a gentleman present fell into a trance. This was to me the more interesting, as my friend, a professional man of some note, was quite sceptical, and had only yielded a courteous tolerance to our operations. I examined his arms and hands, which were as rigid as iron. Whilst in this state, he spoke of departed friends, accurately describing them; and conversed with the invisibles. Mr. Home had likewise fallen into a trance and the conversation of our two clairvoyants, with one another and the invisibles, was truly remarkable. After awakening, my friend complained of pain in his back and limbs, and begged not to be made to join our circle again."

"Human Nature" for April, 1868, has the following from Mr. H. D. Jencken:— "I have again to record spiritual manifestations presenting another phase of the truly remarkable phenomena, and which I have had the opportunity of investigating. On the first evening we met, the tilting of the table, vibrating of the floor, and raps in different parts of the room soon occurred, and a few sentences were spelt out, followed by cold currents of air passing from time to time over our hands and faces. The table we were seated at was raised off the ground twelve or fifteen inches, and the accordion, which Mr. Home had taken into his lap, was laid hold of by an invisible hand, and swung about and over Mr. Home's head, a few chords being played. Mr. Home now took his watch and chain from his pocket, and swung them over his head and to and fro, his arm and hand perfectly cataleptic. The ring of the watch handle appeared to be attracted to his finger ends, and several times we noticed that a short space, about half an inch, intervened between the watch and the finger-points; then, seating himself, the watch was taken from his hand, and carried across and under the table to each of us in turn, and finally placed in my hand. The lady next to me said she felt a hand press her own, describing the sensation as from a velvet glove. Mr. Home's hands were during the whole time on the table, and cataleptically rigid.

"The trance state, which I have noticed in former letters, now supervened, and Mr. Home, quite unconscious of his movements; walked to and fro, then approached a gentleman present, who, by this time, had also fallen into a trance. The evident struggle of my friend to resist the influence was extremely interesting and satisfactory, as far as the fact of an independent agency was concerned. Both the trance mediums then repeated a most beautiful prayer, in alternate cadence and response. I will select a few lines from the prayer and the concluding sentence, as illustrative of the character of the same:—

"'Blessed are those that forgive; for in them is a gleam of the divine.'

"'How comforting is the presence of the departed!'

"And, in conclusion—

"'We magnify thee, O Lord, for thy deeds; for thy glory is never ending.'

"Mr. Home now took a guitar, and, placing it in the hands of my entranced friend, requested him to play. At first the guitar fell from my friend's hand, whose rigid, cataleptic arms and hands were not yet released from the spiritual mesmeric influence; no sooner had the rigidity passed, than he played two very sweet, full-toned pieces of music, representing, as Mr. Home told us, 'doubt and hope.' Both the gentlemen now awoke—my friend somewhat bewildered, and perfectly unconscious of what had passed. The table now moved and tilted, and finally turned upside down. My friend's right arm was, then influenced, and made to seize hold of the leg of the table, and aid in setting it up again. This manifestation so far interested me as proving the presence of a power capable of acting upon a person whilst in his waking state, and controlling his corporeal action. Greetings and kind touches from spirit-hands terminated the evening.

"The manifestations I have next to give an account of are of a very interesting character, as they occurred at the passing away of an old and faithful attendant of our household. On the morning of the patient's decease, who had been suffering from phthisis, the nurse in attendance was startled by a chant of sweet, solemn music passing through the room which the patient occupied. Raps were heard over and near the bed; and, at the request of the sufferer, Mr. Home, who was sleeping in an upper room, was sent for. On his entering the sickroom, the music again, in mournful cadences, swept through the air—in all, the music lasted thirty minutes. Spiritual raps on the bed, over head, all round the dying woman, spoke in unmistakable language of the presence of kind attendant spiritual beings. At two o'clock in the afternoon the soul left the body. We, who had witnessed the last moments of a kind friend, sat silent and sorrowful in my dining-room, when, to our surprise, spiritual manifestations came, in raps, gentle movements of the furniture, and soft, kind touches, all warning us that friends do not leave us, though death may sever for a awhile by changing our physical condition. I cannot describe how the presence of spiritual beings, so manifested as was their communion, cheered and solaced us.

"A few hours later in the day, we entered the bedroom, and, to our surprise, found the room perfumed. The perfume appeared to enter through the open window. I cannot describe it otherwise than like the finest incense, or the scent of dried flowers, such as violets. The perfume passed through the house, not in a steadily-conducted current, but, as it were, capriciously, in limited bounds, as though restricted to the movements of an electric undulation. Fortunately, a friend called in upon us in the course of the evening, and being experienced, from his scientific pursuits, in investigating physical facts, I asked him to examine this extraordinary phenomenon with care. This he did, and fully established the following facts:—

"1st. That the perfume did not arise from any substance in the room, but appeared to be carried in from the outer atmosphere.

"2ndly. That the perfume was restricted to some unknown but independent current, for, contrary to all laws of diffusion of scents, the strong draught of an open door and window did not carry the perfume into the landing, six inches of space absolutely intercepting the aroma.

"3rdly. Contrary to known laws, the aroma descended to the rooms below, and even entered the drawing-room of my neighbour's house.

"4thly. The room felt dry, magnetic, warm. The following day, the medical gentleman who had attended the patient noticed this phenomenon of the wonderfully sweet perfume pervading the room, remarking that it made the impression upon him of something 'holy.'

"But I must revert to the manifestations on the day the patient passed away. During the whole of the afternoon, Mr. Home had been passing from one trance into another. In one of these states he proceeded to the room of the deceased. Returning with her Bible, he opened it at the 12th chapter of 1st Corinthians, and pointed to verses 1 and 10. The language of the Bible being in Esthonian, made the selection of this passage so far more remarkable, as Mr. Home does not understand a word of this little known language—even admitting he could have read with his eyeballs turned up, and the lids drawn spasmodically down and closed. As I tried to understand which verses were intended, gentle raps at the far end of the room guided me.

"In the evening, Mr. Home again fell into a trance, and then stated 'that M____ had lived a pure life, and that her body had been purified by spiritual agency; and the miracle known to have occurred with some of the saints of the Catholic church had been repeated this day, not as a miracle, but in proof of the power of spiritual influence and presence.' Impressive beyond language was the manifestation of gentle, sonorous raps on every side as we stood grouped around the departed, wondering why this strange phenomenon of holy perfume should be allowed—the spiritual beings appearing to converse with us by the agency of the simple telegraphy of raps, answering to our prayerful questions in quick response, 'Yes, yes, yes, we are present.'

"Two evenings later, Mr. Home was seated quietly at the fireside, when raps came close to me, and a sentence was spelt out, that we, three of us, should proceed to the room where the body had now been laid out, but not to enter, only stand at the door. This we did, and, on opening the door, a strong current of perfume passed over us, this time filling the landing, and hall, and house. The phenomenon of perfume entering my house, continued to the day of the funeral—at times being, despite of open windows, quite overpowering. Manifestations of spiritual presence during the whole of the time were constantly occurring, and, even in my bedroom, I was awakened by trembling of the floor, and raps against the wall and bed; and a friend who was staying with me said he had mental questions answered by raps at the foot of his bed, which moved and vibrated."

Mr. Jencken in "Human Nature," May, 1868, gives the following account:— "We had, as usual, seated ourselves round a table in the drawing-room, and after the lapse of a considerable time, the trembling of the floor, movement of the table, and vibration of the semi-grand commenced. Mr. Simpson, whose scientific training had given him the aptitude for experiment, suggested the placing of a large flat music-book on rollers on the table, and then for us to rest our fingers on the edge of the book; the object being to check any involuntary movements. Much to my satisfaction, the table moved more violently than before, and Mr. Simpson, who had lain down on the floor to observe the movement of the table more closely, quite satisfied himself of the independent motion. We next suggested trying the alternating weight and lightness of the table, a manifestation occasionally produced. Mr. Simpson re-examined the table to satisfy himself that no disturbing cause could interfere; this done, we made the request to have the table 'heavy.' On attempting to raise it, we could not possibly manage to lift it. Then we requested that the table should be made 'light,' and the table only just before heavy and immovable could now be raised upon the slightest effort. Mr. Simpson, satisfied with this test, suggested repeating the experiment with the music-book, which had been placed on rollers on the table. I at first quite doubted the result, but on trying to raise the edge of the book it felt as if cleaved to the table, and then on changing to, 'Let it be light,' the book became as light as a feather. Again and again we repeated the experiment, and finally satisfied ourselves of the reality of the important fact of an independent agency, guided by intelligence, and of the presence of an invisible being, possessing the power of reading our thoughts, and of producing at will the phenomenon of alternately making the book heavy or light. You will think me tedious for dwelling at such length upon so comparatively insignificant a phenomenon, but the very simplicity of the manifestation gives interest. The phenomenon was, so to speak, quite within grasp; and I like, above all things, to have a manageable fact before me. The law is the same; the raising of a single pound weight, or of a ton, does not affect the principle: and here I had all I could desire,—a strong clear light; our own home for our theatre of operation; our own friends with us; a scientific man at my elbow, ready to catch at a shadow of a doubt, and whom we allowed to arrange at will, and place himself in any position he chose; and Mr. Home, the medium—good-tempered in the extreme—actuated only by a sincere desire to aid the investigation: all gave additional interest to our evening. I am now in a position safely to assert that I have proved, beyond a doubt, by this simple experiment, the operation of an unseen power, guided by intelligence.

"Later in the evening, the accordion, which had been placed on the table, spontaneously moved six to eight inches from one side of the table towards the other—not a hand, not a finger touching it. The semi-grand was raised off the ground, and moved a foot from the wall into the room, no one touching the piano at the time. An adjoining oval walnut-wood table trembled, raised itself first on one leg, then on the other, and glided up to our table. Mr. _____, at my request, placed himself on the floor, to watch the movement, and, after a rigorous examination, satisfied himself that the motions were produced by an unseen, independent agency.

"We had now reseated ourselves, when we noticed the curtains being pushed into the room; first, the curtains behind Mr. Home, then those of the farther window. They were then drawn aside, and I noticed a hand—for a moment only—between the curtain and the table. As if to give us a final proof of independent action, the water decanter and wine decanter, on the tray with refreshments, which we had placed on the adjoining table, moved, tilted, the water bottle placing itself at the edge of the tray. Of course my friend was on the alert, re-examined curtain, table, and tray, and pronounced the coast clear of magnets or other appliances.

"Another test: I am certain you will bear with me. It is so satisfactory to have done our utmost to convince ourselves, we quite long to communicate the result of our inquiry to others. Raps having been heard under the leaf of the table we were seated at, it was suggested to pin a sheet of paper underneath the table, which would effectually intercept the action of any instrument—such as the point of a stick or finger point—that might be used to produce the sound. The sheet of paper, after some slight difficulty, was pinned on, and then we waited for the result. After a pause, raps came, again and again; some appeared to vibrate against the table, and inside of the paper, others sounded sonorous and clear. The fact was established, that the placing of the paper did not interfere with the raps. But enough of physical tests; now as to identity.

"Mr. Home had laid hold of the accordion in one hand, and after waiting a few minutes, some chords were played by an invisible hand, followed by an air, which was repeated three or four times. I cannot say I quite followed the tune; it appeared to me broken, and changed from its original melody. 'What does it mean?' was asked. The name 'John' was spelt out, and the tune repeated. Again we asked, 'To whom does this apply?' No answer; and so the matter was passed over. A few days afterwards, I received a letter from a gentleman who had been present, explaining that the air that had been played was meant for him; that at the time, anxious not to disturb the mind of the medium, and to shut the door even upon thought-reading, he had kept his counsel; that the tune played was one he had himself altered, to suit his voice; that only two persons alive knew the notes he had changed, the third who knew it was beyond the grave. He writes—'It is an air my wife particularly liked, and always asked me, if alone with her, to play. The words are by Mrs. Hemans, and the two last lines are—

"'Yet would I buy with life again
That one dear dream of thee.'

My friend continues to say—'These are simple facts; I give them as such.' The accordion, as it played the air or melody, moved horizontally towards Mr. Simpson, who narrowly kept observing it all the time, and to his praise, be it said, remained calm and watchful throughout, anxious only for the truth. Next to actual speech, to the actual visible presence of a spirit form, this test of identity appears to me most satisfactory and conclusive.

"The other instance of identity is of a totally different character. Mr. Home had spontaneously, whilst seated at the fire-side in my drawing-room, passed into a trance state. We were alone, only Mrs. _____ being present. I noticed the clairvoyant-expression of face which characterises the trance medium. After a pause, Mr. Home addressed us, and gave an account of the passing away of one we all had known in life. He said the spirits embalmed the body of Miss A____, and the perfume that filled the room after her passing away was created by. them. Then suddenly changing his discourse, he said, 'Who is Louisa? she loves your son, cared for him like a mother;' and then accurately described the person and peculiarities of character of a kind friend who had passed away from earth many years ago. What added to the interest was, that none present had even in thought named the person alluded to, so that thought-reading was not possible. I carefully watched Home's movements; he evidently appeared to be seeing an object, and the remarks he made were spoken as if prompted by an external agency.

"I admit the great difficulty presented by visions, their subjective character rendering proof, if not impossible, at all events very difficult; and the only mode of ascertaining the truth is to compare the accounts of visions of trance mediums with one another, group the experiences together, and then to generalize.

"At a subsequent *séance*, Mr. Home fell into the trance state almost as soon as the circle had been arranged; then blindfolding himself, he drew an alphabet, and having finished this, commenced spelling out sentences. The first spelt out was—'I am not convinced even now, but can see that I have much to learn.—DAVID BREWSTER.'

"Sentences followed explanatory of his passing away; then—'The earthly and spiritual are two distinct existences. It is not to be inferred because we say we were present, that we took cognizance of his earthly surroundings. We are in no way connected. We have our share of curiosity, and we desire to know many things which are forbidden. We know, for instance, that 'Speke' is not in spirit life; Doctor S., his brother, knows it; the traveller knows it' Then followed the words, 'At lunch—Gibson.'

"I had not intended to publish these communications, but for the extreme interest the public have taken in Rev. Mr. Speke's strange freak of hiding himself. The *séance* took place nine days before the news of his discovery was made known, and this fact may add interest to my account of the spirit communications I have recorded. I render this strictly as it occurred, without even hazarding a comment."

Between JANE LYON .... Plaintiff

and

DANIEL DUNGLASS HOME
and WILLIAM MARTIN WILKINSON .... Defendants.

AFFIDAVIT FILED ON THE PART OF THE PLAINTIFF, BY MESSRS. DRUCE SONS & JACKSON OF 10 BILLITER SQUARE HER SOLICITORS.

Filed 27th June 1867.

I JANE LYON of No 17A Albert Terrace Albert Gate Hyde Park in the county of Middlesex widow the above-named Plaintiff make oath and say as follows:—

1. Referring to the third paragraph of the bill filed by me in this cause I say that I sought and obtained an interview with the above-named Defendant Daniel Dunglass Home as therein stated under the following circumstances My late husband Charles Lyon Esquire of Wooth Grange Bridport Dorset died in the month of August 1859 and he told me shortly before his death that he believed that a change would take place in seven years after his death and that we should meet and I had in consequence an impression that I should not survive him for a longer period than seven years. In or about the month of July in last year I called upon Mrs. Sims a photographer in Westbourne Grove to have a photograph taken of a portrait of my husband and saw her several times upon the subject of such photograph and in course of conversation with her I mentioned the above circumstance in connection with my husband's death and the impression which I had formed in consequence and she told me that it was not necessary that I should *die* in order to meet my husband again but that if I were to become a "Spiritualist" *he* would come to *me*. I had never before heard of Spiritualism Mrs. Sims afterwards lent me several books upon the subject which I read and after some little time she told me that the head Spiritualist Mr Home (being in fact the said Defendant Daniel Dunglass Home) had opened an "Athenæum" at 22 Sloane Street Hyde Park and she suggested that I should write to him to send me a prospectus and particulars of it as I wished after what she had told me to become a subscriber. Accordingly on the 30th of September last I wrote to the said Defendant that I was anxious to become a subscriber and asking for a prospectus and particulars and inquiring when and to whom the money was to be paid. Not having received any reply from the said Defendant I called on the 3rd October last at No. 22 Sloane Street aforesaid and asked to see him and I was shown upstairs to the first

- 368 -

floor where I was received by him in the room which he calls the "Athenæum." I had never before seen the said Defendant nor had I ever even heard of him until his name was mentioned to me by Mrs. Sims as aforesaid and he is not related to or connected with me or my family or the family of my late husband by birth marriage or otherwise nor did my said late husband in his lifetime know the said Defendant or to the best of my knowledge information and belief ever hear of him.

2. The said Defendant (who was alone) then entered into conversation with me respecting the Athenæum and my aforesaid letter to him and my wish to become a subscriber and the terms of subscription and he then asked me to go with him to see the rooms upstairs where as I afterwards found he lived. I went with him accordingly into his sitting room (on the second floor) in which was a table with writing materials and an accordion upon it. No one besides the said Defendant and myself was present. We sat down at the table and raps came to the table almost immediately. The said Defendant then said "That is a call for the alphabet" or words to that effect, I was not at that time aware of the mode in which the so-called "spiritual *séances*" are conducted but I have from subsequent experience learnt that the presence of a so-called "medium" is considered necessary in order to evoke what are believed to be the spirits of the deceased and that the supposed spirits on being summoned signify their presence by rapping and on questions being put respond to them either by three raps (for the affirmative) two (for doubtful) one (for the negative or by five raps which are supposed to signify, that the alphabet is required. In the latter case the letters of the alphabet are either repeated by the medium or some one else present or a printed or written alphabet is produced and the letters are pointed at by the medium or some one else present and on the letter desired to be indicated by the supposed spirit being repeated or pointed at raps are or a rap is given to signify that such is the letter intended and so on until a complete word or sentence as the case may be is spelt out. On the occasion of my first interview with the said Defendant as aforesaid no printed or written alphabet was used but he repeated the letters of the alphabet from time to time a rap being given as he arrived each time at the letter intended to be indicated. In this way the supposed spirit on that occasion spelt out "My own beloved Jane I am Charles your own beloved husband I live to bless you my own precious darling I am with you always I *love, love, love* you as I always did" or words to that effect and as nearly as I can remember those very words. I was induced by the said Defendant to believe and I really believed at the time that the spirit of my late husband was in reality speaking to me to the effect hereinbefore

mentioned. Nothing further material to this suit passed on that occasion and the supposed spirit spelt out in the same manner as before "I have no further power at present to speak but I will not leave you my own darling" or words to that effect and as nearly as I can remember those very words. I was very much gratified at what I then believed to be a real manifestation of the spirit of my husband to me and not having my cheque book then with me I asked the said Defendant to call upon me at No 18 Westbourne Place Hyde Park where I was then living in apartments and told him I would give him a cheque for £10 for my subscription to the Athenæum.

3. On the following day viz. the 4th October last the said Defendant called upon me at No. 18 Westbourne Place aforesaid where I received him alone in my sitting-room and almost immediately raps came indicative as he induced me to believe and as I in fact believed of the presence of my husband's spirit and the following words were as nearly as I can remember then spelt out in the manner before referred to the said Defendant repeating as before the alphabetical letters "My own beloved Jane—I am your own Charles and I am indeed constantly with you I am so happy to be with you. I *love, love, love* you. Be very calm I will touch you." I was then repeatedly touched as I believed by the spirit of my late husband and the said Defendant was at that time seated close to me at the table. I then being much gratified drew out and gave to the said Defendant a cheque on my bankers for £30 (instead of £10 as promised) as my subscription to the Athenæum. At this time I became much impressed with what I believed to be the power of the said Defendant to evoke the spirit of my husband and he soon acquired a great ascendancy over my mind.

4. On or about the 6th of October last the said Defendant again called upon me in Westbourne Place aforesaid and I again received him alone in my sitting-room and he commenced talking to me on the subject of his marriage with his deceased wife and told me how happy he had been with her and he stated his intention of marrying again but said that he should not marry a young lady as he did not like young ladies but was anxious to marry an elderly lady and that he should make a very loving and affectionate husband and from those remarks! and others which followed on the same subject I then inferred and now verily believe that he intended to make to me proposals of marriage but I told him that the subject was distasteful to me and I silenced him upon it at once. Almost immediately afterwards raps came again indicating as the said Defendant induced me to believe and as I in fact believed the presence of my husband's spirit and the following word or words as nearly as possible to the following effect were (with other

words) then spelt out in the manner before referred to (the said Defendant repeating rapidly the letters of the alphabet and stopping from time to time as raps came indicating the letters to be used)—"My own darling Jane— * * * * * I love Daniel" (meaning as I understood the said Defendant) "he is to be our son he is my son therefore yours. Do you remember before I passed I said a change would take place in seven years? That change has taken place." The table was then thrown up from the floor and the words "I am happy, happy, happy" were spelt out in the same manner as before. I then said to the supposed spirit "Do you remember I said at the time to you. Shall we then meet?'" and the answer spelt out in the same manner as before was in the following words or to the following effect—"In a little time I will make myself visible to you" and the supposed spirit continued. "Do not my own darling say the light of other days is gone the light is with you Charles lives your own Charles lives and loves you and is near you constantly my own darling Jane I will have power to come to you entirely I will be so happy and so will you my wife beloved of God. Now beloved I will speak to you as often as I can I will come for your health and Daniel's" It was also spelt out in manner aforesaid that be the supposed spirit of my husband wished to make Daniel (meaning as I understood the said Defendant) independent as he was to be our son and that he the supposed spirit would speak of the manner in which it was to be done another time. I then drew out a cheque on my bankers for £50 and gave it to the said Defendant as be was to be (as I then believed according to the directions of the spirit of my husband) our son that he might not be without the means of living.

5. Referring to the three last paragraphs hereof I say that the sentences spelt out as aforesaid were written down by me from memory shortly after the happening of the events hereinbefore mentioned in a book now in my possession from which they are respectively hereinbefore quoted and I say positively that whether the words so quoted were the exact words spelt out as aforesaid or not words to the same effect as those so quoted were spelt out as aforesaid.

6. The said Defendant then commenced paying repeated visits to me and on or about the 8th day of October last and certainly either on that day or the day next preceding or the day next following such 8th day of October he called upon me in Westbourne Place aforesaid and on that occasion also raps came indicating (as I was induced by the said Defendant to believe and did believe) the presence of the spirit of my said late husband and it was spelt out in manner before mentioned (the said Defendant repeating the alphabetical letters as before) It was then spelt out in the manner before mentioned and as I was induced to

believe and did believe by the spirit of my late husband that the said Defendant was to be our adopted son and that I was to make over to him a sufficient sum from my funded property to bring him in £700 a year.

7. On several of the occasions referred to in this my affidavit when sentences were being spelt out as I was induced by the said Defendant to believe and did believe by the spirit of my late husband I remonstrated with the said Defendant telling him while he was hurriedly repeating the letters of the alphabet that he was "going too fast" and he frequently answered that it was not so as he well knew beforehand what was coming.

8. On or about the 10th October last and certainly within a day or two after the meeting referred to in the 6th paragraph hereof the said Defendant Daniel Dunglass Home called upon me in Westbourne Place aforesaid and took me to the City in a cab to carry out the aforesaid transaction as to the £24,000. While we were on the road constant raps were heard in and about the cab which the Defendant told me showed that the spirits approved of what I was about to do. We drove straight to the office of Messrs. Fox Taylor & Company stockbrokers employed by the said Defendant and of whom I knew nothing the said Defendant having previously told me that the transaction must not be effected through the brokers employed by my bankers Messrs. Williams Deacon & Co. as I had wished. I then went to the Bank of England with the said Defendant and one of the said firm of Fox Taylor & Co. (at whose request I was identified by one of the clerks employed by Messrs. Williams Deacon & Co.) and signed a book at the said Bank of England transferring as I understood a sufficient amount of stock to represent in value £24,000 sterling but whether to the said Defendant or to a purchaser I did not know and no account receipt or other paper in connection with the transaction was given to me on that occasion or subsequently but to the best of my knowledge information and belief such stock was sold and the proceeds thereof were paid to the said Defendant Daniel Dunglass Home. I was then allowed by the said Defendant to return to Westbourne Place by myself and he went either on that or on or about the following day to Brighton and thence to Malvern where he remained as I believe some few weeks and where I sent to him in accordance with his request on or about the 28th day of October last a cheque for £20 for his own use. I also on other occasions paid other small sums to him or on his account by his request. The said Defendant on or about the 5th day of November 1866 as appears by a stock receipt (left by him accidentally as I believe in my possession) invested £23,913 17s. 3d. cash being as I

verily believe part of the aforesaid sum of £24,000 so acquired by him as aforesaid in the purchase in his own name of the sum of £26,756 15s. 5d. Consolidated Bank Annuities.

8. In or about the beginning of November last the said Defendant again called upon me in Westbourne Place aforesaid when I was alone and he then became as he induced me to believe and as I did believe entranced and represented in trance the spirit of my said late husband which he induced me to believe then spoke through him the said Defendant and told me to lay some sheets of note paper on the table with pens and ink and I was to write what he was about to dictate. He then dictated to me word for word instructions for a will giving all my property to him absolutely and directing him to take the name and arms of Lyon and at his dictation I addressed an envelope to the Defendant William Martin Wilkinson (who was as I afterwards found out the intimate friend and solicitor of the said Defendant Daniel Dunglass Home but of whom I then knew nothing) and enclosed the said instructions therein with a note to the said Defendant William Martin Wilkinson which I also wrote at the dictation of the said Defendant Daniel Dunglass Home requesting the said William Martin Wilkinson to prepare a Will for me in accordance with the aforesaid instructions and bring it for signature on a certain evening therein appointed I also wrote at the dictation of the said Defendant Daniel Dunglass Home letters to Dr. Hawksley and Mr. Rudall (who as I afterwards found out were also intimate friends of the said last-named Defendant but of whom I knew nothing) requesting them to call without fail at No. 18 Westbourne Place aforesaid on the evening appointed as aforesaid. On the evening so appointed which was to the best of my belief the 12th of November last the said last-named Defendant and also the said Dr. Hawksley and Mr. Rudall came as arranged and the said Defendant William Martin Wilkinson also came bringing with him the will prepared by him in accordance with the aforesaid instructions in duplicate. The said Defendant Daniel Dunglass Home then left me alone with the said Defendant William Martin Wilkinson the said Dr. Hawksley and the said Mr. Rudall and the said William Martin Wilkinson then read over the will to me and questioned me as to whether I had fully considered the terms of the will and understood its effect to which I replied that I had fully considered the matter and understood the effect of the will and was ready to sign it. I then signed it in duplicate in the presence of all the said three persons each of whom attested it and the said Defendant William Martin Wilkinson then took away the original and duplicate one of which I have since obtained from him being the paper writing marked A produced and shown to me at

the time of swearing this my affidavit but my signature at the foot thereof has since been obliterated by me and the note at the foot referring to revocation has been since added by me. Before the said will so prepared as aforesaid was brought by the said William Martin Wilkinson as aforesaid the said Defendant Daniel Dunglass Home informed me that as a matter of form he the said William Martin Wilkinson would question me as aforesaid as evidence of his having done so might be called for hereafter in case the will should be disputed and the matter should come into court after my death and that therefore every means must be taken to show that I was making the will of my own free will and not under the dictation of the spirit of my husband and that all letters from the said Defendant William Martin Wilkinson to me would be written cautiously in the same view so that I was quite prepared for the questions put to me by him. I however signed the said will under the full conviction and belief that it was dictated by the spirit of my late husband and that I was in signing it complying with his wishes.

10. Very shortly after and to the best of my recollection on the day after I had signed the said will as aforesaid the said Defendant Daniel Dunglass Home alias Daniel Home Lyon again called on me and when we were alone together became as he induced me to believe and as I did believe entranced and represented in trance the spirit of my said late husband which he induced me to believe then spoke to me through him the said Defendant and told me to bring out my will (made previously to that signed on or about the 12th day of November last as hereinbefore appears) in duplicate and burn it which I accordingly did in the belief that in doing so I was complying with the wishes of my said late husband. On a subsequent occasion when the said Defendant called upon me (though I am unable to recollect the date of his visit) he told me that my late husband's spirit had told him that all communications from him the said supposed spirit on the subject of business transactions between the said Defendant and myself were to be burnt and he the said Defendant thereupon looked out and placed on the table all papers of that description in my possession and burnt them.

11. In or shortly prior to the month of December last at another interview which I had at my rooms with the said Defendant Daniel Dunglass Home alone I was induced by him to believe and I did believe that the spirit of my said late husband was again present and was speaking to me by raps as aforesaid and it was then spelt out by the supposed spirit in the manner hereinbefore referred to that I was to give to the said Defendant as a present for his birthday a sum of £6,000

more to make up with the aforesaid sum of £24,000 the aggregate sum of £30,000. Accordingly I went on or about the 10th day of December 1866 (in the full conviction and belief that I was obeying the orders of my said late husband) with the said Defendant alone to the Bank of England and transferred into his name as Daniel Dunglass Home the sum of £6,798 17s. 4d. Consolidated Bank Annuities belonging to me such sum being then equivalent in value to the sum of £6,000 sterling or thereabouts. The said Messrs. Fox Taylor & Co. were the brokers employed on that occasion and the instructions for such transfer were as I verily believe given to them by the said Defendant.

12. Referring to the eleventh paragraph of the bill filed by me in this cause I say that since filing my affidavit in this cause on the 15th day of June instant my attention has been more particularly drawn to the date of the deed poll referred to in such eleventh paragraph and that to the best of my recollection such deed was not nor was any deed relating to the subject matter of this suit executed by me on the said 12th day of December or at any time other than the occasion upon which I executed the deeds in connection with the security for £30,000 in the said bill mentioned as hereinafter more particularly referred to but I believe that on such last-mentioned occasion a deed of or to the purport or effect mentioned in such eleventh paragraph was executed by me with the other deeds then executed by me as hereinafter appears while my mind was under the influence and control gained over it by the said Defendant in manner aforesaid and I say that the said last-mentioned deed poll was to the best of my belief prepared by the said Defendant William Martin Wilkinson under instructions given to him by his said co-Defendant and not under any instructions given by me or by my order and without the intervention of any solicitor or independent person on my behalf.

13. At the interview referred to in the eleventh paragraph of this my affidavit or at another interview held by me with the said Defendant Daniel Dunglas Home just about that time and when I was alone with the said Defendant and when he had induced me to believe that the spirit of my said late husband was again present and speaking to me it was spelt out in manner aforesaid by the said supposed spirit that the said Defendant William Martin Wilkinson was to procure a mortgage for £30,000 to be advanced out of my money which mortgage was to be taken in the name of the said Defendant Daniel Dunglass Home and I was to have the interest for my life and the principal was to go to the said Defendant at my death. The mortgage for £30,000 referred to in the indenture of 19th January 1867 mentioned in the thirteenth paragraph of the said bill was accordingly obtained by or through the

said Defendant William Martin Wilkinson with my sanction in the belief and conviction on my part that in giving such sanction it was fulfilling the wishes of my said late husband's spirit but I ultimately refused to consent to the mortgage being taken in the name of the said Defendant Daniel Dunglass Home and suggested that the arrangement eventually carried into effect by the said indenture of the 19th day of January 1867 should be made. The said last-mentioned indenture and also the indenture of transfer of even date therein recited were accordingly prepared by the said Defendant William Martin Wilkinson and both deeds and as I believe the said deed poll of the 12th day of December 1866 were on or about the same 19th day of January 1867 brought to me from his office by his son and a clerk (Mr. Hartley by name) for signature. The deeds were read over to me and the said Daniel Dunglass Home was then present and sitting close to me at the time and he kept touching me and persuading me to sign and I accordingly then signed the said indentures of the 19th day of January 1867 and as I believe the said deed poll of the 12th day of December 1866 while my mind was under the control gained over it by the said last-named Defendant by the means aforesaid and without the intervention of any independent solicitor or other person on my behalf. And I say that the suggestion hereinbefore referred to as to the arrangement for carrying out which the said indentures of the 19th day of January 1867 were prepared was made by me while under such control and influence as aforesaid.

14. Another mortgage for £30,000 was afterwards obtained for me by the said Defendant William Martin Wilkinson at my request and on or about the 13th day of February last. I sold out for the purposes of such mortgage a sum of stock which produced to the best of my information and belief £26,596 13s. 8d. net cash leaving a deficiency of £3,403 6s. 4d. to make up the principal to be advanced and the said last-mentioned sum was at the request of the said Defendant William Martin Wilkinson provided by the said Defendant Daniel Dunglass Home by sale of part of the stock which he had acquired in manner hereinbefore appearing.

15. The said Defendant William Martin Wilkinson at that time or shortly afterwards told me that I had still a sum of £2,290 9s. 5d. Consolidated Bank Annuities standing in my name of which I was not aware and it occurred to me that I should towards replacement of the stock so sold out by his said co-Defendant as last aforesaid transfer to him the said Defendant Daniel Dunglass Home the said remaining stock so standing in my name and I accordingly on or about the 21st day of February last transferred such last-mentioned sum into the name

of the said Defendant Daniel Dunglass Home and I say that the last-mentioned transfer was made by me while I was still under the control and influence acquired over my mind by the said last-named Defendant by the means aforesaid.

16. On or about the 13th day of March 1867 (as appears by an account of the sale rendered to the said Defendant Daniel Dunglass Home by the said Messrs. Fox Taylor & Co. which is in my possession it having been accidentally left with me by the said Defendant he the said Defendant sold out the sum of £21,947 17s. 6d. Consolidated Bank Annuities part as I verily believe of the aggregate sum of like annuities so acquired by him as hereinbefore appears and the net proceeds of such sale amounting to the sum of £20,000 sterling were as I have been informed by the said Defendant and as I verily believe lent and advanced by him through the said Defendant William Martin Wilkinson as mentioned in the sixteenth paragraph of the said bill and the securities for the same sum of Twenty thousand pounds have as I am informed by my solicitors and believe been deposited together with the securities for the firstly hereinbefore mentioned principal sum of Thirty thousand pounds with the Clerk of Records and Writs in pursuance of the order made in this cause on the 18th day of June instant.

17. Having regard to the sales of stock hereinbefore mentioned to have been made by the said Defendant Daniel Dunglass Home I say that to the best of my belief there is a sum of £3 per Cent. Consolidated Bank Annuities exceeding £9,000 (Stock) still standing in the name of the said Defendant in the books of the Governor and Company of the Bank of England and a distringas has been placed by my solicitors on my behalf upon the sum of £9,000 like annuities part of the larger sum of like annuities so standing as I believe in his name as aforesaid.

18. I have lately upon reflection become convinced that I have in the several transactions matters and things hereinbefore referred to been altogether imposed upon by and made the dupe of the said Defendant Daniel Dunglass Home and that the several directions which at the time I believed to have been given as aforesaid by the spirit of my said late husband were not in reality so given but that they without exception emanated entirely from the said Defendant and not otherwise and I say that apart from his supposed power of putting my said late husband's spirit into communication with me I had no affection or even respect for the said Defendant but that the said Defendant by the means aforesaid worked upon my belief in his supposed power until he acquired almost unlimited control and influence over my mind during the continuance of which control and influence (which I felt utterly

powerless to resist) the several transactions hereinbefore referred to took place.

19. The book now produced to me and marked with the letter B contains entries written by the said Defendant of sentences spelt out as I was induced by him to believe and as I did believe by the spirit of my said late husband in manner aforesaid on various occasions and of circumstances in connection therewith and I refer particularly to the following passages written by the said Defendant on the 7th and 16th pages of such book and spelt out as I was induced by the said Defendant to believe and did believe by the said supposed spirit on the 22nd January 1867 and on another date which I am unable to recollect viz.: "My darling Jane—it would not be pleasing to me to have you sit with any medium but our son (meaning the said Defendant) at present I have good reasons for this. I will tell you when I wish another medium than our son" (meaning the said Defendant) "It stands to reason Daniel is the best medium on earth we have chosen him for you what we have to say and what we have to do we can say and do thro' him" which words are confirmatory of my present conviction and belief that the several directions supposed as hereinbefore set forth to be given by the spirit of my late husband emanated entirely from the said Defendant and for his own purposes.

20. The several paper writings marked respectively C and D now produced and shown to me contain sentences written by the said Defendant Daniel Dunglass Home himself and spelt out on two different occasions by (as he induced me to believe and as I did believe) the spirit of my said late husband while the said Defendant was alone with me the first of such paper writings (written entirely by the said Defendant) on to the best of my recollection the 26th of February last being as follows:— "26th February—Daniel is correct and if you remember darling I made sounds on the floor that Sunday as you were going to bed. Not that Tuesday but the following Monday. And well in your senses but *we made you think this to be so.* You longed for communications yet your very anxiety prevented our approach. *We had to get control of your mind.*" And in explanation of such last-mentioned paper writing I say that I had on or previously to the said 26th day of February last in conversation with the said Defendant alluded to the first and original manifestations of the spirit of my said late husband (as I believed them to be) particulars of which are set forth in the second and following paragraphs of this my affidavit and that the said Defendant then denied that there had been any such manifestations during the first seven days of my aforesaid acquaintance with him and in corroboration of his statement appealed as he induced

me to believe and as I believed to the spirit of my said late husband while he the said Defendant was alone with me as aforesaid and that the words last above quoted or words to precisely the same effect were spelt out as he induced me to believe and as I did believe by the said supposed spirit in manner aforesaid in answer to such appeal.

21. I also refer to the following sentence written by the said Defendant as aforesaid on the second occasion above referred to the date of which I am unable to recollect and comprised in the other of such paper writings viz. "Only remember Daniel is our medium all communications I have to give will be thro' him." And with reference to the sentences quoted in this and the preceding paragraph I say that they are corroborative of my full conviction and belief that I have in the several aforesaid transactions with the said Defendant Daniel Dunglass Home been the victim of gross and wilful imposition.

22. On or about the 16th day of June instant I received from the said Defendant Daniel Dunglass Home a letter written by him to me and dated June 17th 1867 which letter is now produced and shown to me and is marked with the letter E in which letter the said Defendant offers to come to an arrangement with me with reference to the subject matter of this suit but to which letter I have not replied nor do I intend to come to any arrangement whatever with him short of getting back all the property which he has acquired from me in manner hereinbefore appearing.

23. I depose to the several facts and circumstances hereinbefore set forth from my own personal knowledge except where it is hereinbefore otherwise stated.

Sworn at my Office No. 33 Mark Lane in the City of London on the 26th day of June 1867

JANE LYON .... Before me Richd. Cattarns

A London Commissioner to administer oaths in Chancery.

This Affidavit on behalf of the Plaintiff is filed by DRUCE, SONS, & JACKSON, Solicitors, 10, *Billiter Square, in the City of London.*

Between JANE LYON, Widow...Plaintiff

and

DANIEL DUNGLASS HOME,

and WILLIAM MARTIN WILKINSON......................Defendants.

THE ANSWER of DANIEL DUNGLASS HOME, otherwise (at the Plaintiff's request) DANIEL HOME LYON, one of the above-named Defendants to the Bill of Complaint of the above-named Plaintiff.

IN ANSWER to the said Bill, I, DANIEL DUNGLASS HOME, otherwise DANIEL HOME LYON, say as follows:—

1. I was born in Scotland on the 20th March 1833 and from my earliest childhood I have been subject to the occasional happening of singular physical phenomena in my presence which are most certainly not produced by me or by any other person in connection with me I have no control over them whatever they occur irregularly and even when I am asleep. Sometimes I am many months and once I have been a year without them. They will not happen when I wish and my will has nothing to do with them. I cannot account for them further than by supposing them to be effected by intelligent beings or spirits. Similar phenomena occur to many other persons. In the United States of America I believe about eleven millions of rational people as well as a very great number in every country in Europe believe as I do that spiritual beings of every grade good and bad can and do at times manifest their presence to us. I invariably caution people against being misled by any apparent communications from them. These phenomena occurring in my presence have been witnessed by thousands of intelligent and respectable persons including men of business, science and literature under circumstances which would have rendered even if I desired it all trickery impossible. They have been witnessed repeatedly and in their own private apartments where any contrivance of mine must have been detected by their Majesties the Emperor and Empress of the French, their Majesties the Emperor Empress and late Empress Dowager of Russia, their Imperial Highnesses the Grand Duke and Duchess Constantine of Russia and the members of their august family their Majesties the King of Prussia, the late King of Bavaria the present and late King of Wurtemberg, the Queen of Holland and the members of the Royal family of Holland and many of these august personages have honoured and I believe still honour me with their esteem and good will as I have resided in some of their palaces as a gentleman and their guest not as a paid or professional person. They have had ample opportunities which they

have used of investigating these phenomena and of enquiring into my character. I have resided in America, England, France, Italy, Germany and Russia and in every country I have been received as a guest and friend by persons in the highest position in society who were quite competent to discover and expose as they ought to have done anything like contrivance on my part to produce these phenomena. I do not seek and never have sought the acquaintance of any of these exalted personages. They have sought me and I have thus had a certain notoriety thrust upon me. I do not take money and never have taken it although it has been repeatedly offered me for or in respect of these phenomena or the communications which sometimes appear to be made by them I am not in the habit of receiving those who are strangers to me and I never force the subject of Spiritualism on any one's attention. I trust that I am a sincere Christian I conscientiously believe as all the early Christians did that man is continually surrounded and protected or tempted by good and evil spirits. I have in my circle of friends many who were not only infidels but atheists until they became convinced by the study of these phenomena of the truths of immortality and their lives have been greatly improved in consequence. Some of the phenomena in question are noble and elevated others appear to be grotesque and undignified. For this I am not responsible any more than I am for the many grotesque and undignified things which are undoubtedly permitted to exist in the material world. I solemnly swear that I do not produce the phenomena aforesaid or in any way whatever aid in producing them. In 1858 I married a Russian lady of noble family who was a god-daughter of the late Emperor Nicholas and educated by him. She died in 1862 and by her I have one son christened "Gregoire" but alluded to in the conversations and letters hereinafter set forth by the pet name of "Sacha." The present Emperor of Russia has graciously consented to be his godfather and the Grand Duchess Constantine his godmother on the occasion of his being baptised into the Greek Church which is to take place.

2. Having met with considerable success as a public reader in America in the year 1865 I determined last year to go on the stage but my health which has been feeble for a long time proved unequal to the task and some of my friends who were desirous of investigating the phenomena aforesaid formed a society with the title of the Spiritual Athenæum taking rooms at No. 22 Sloane street London and at their request I accepted the position of resident secretary with a salary which post at the Plaintiffs desire I have since resigned. The members of the said society are without exception persons of character and position

who could gain nothing by aiding in or abetting fraud or deception. The following extract is taken from their circular printed for distribution:—

"It will be a leading duty of the Executive Committee acting with the Council to make such arrangements as shall secure facilities for healthy useful and instructive communion to those who seek as well as those who are willing to give information 'concerning Spiritual gifts,' while promoting social intercourse aiming at loftier and holier objects, checking the spread of Materialism, upholding the truths and extending the influence of Christianity and bringing closer the bonds of Peace and Love among mankind, inculcating by another Power acting in accordance with Holy Writ and co-operating with the Christian teacher—duty to God and to Neighbour."

3. Under the circumstances hereinbefore mentioned and not otherwise I believe I am what is called a spiritual medium but I do not gain a living by it or make money by it. I had some private means of my own. I made some money in America by public readings unconnected with the phenomena aforesaid. I twice only read a public lecture on Spiritualism which is still in my possession and I was for a short time such secretary as aforesaid. Otherwise I do not to use the language of the Plaintiff's Interrogatory gain a living. I do not profess and never did profess to have the power of evoking the spirits of deceased persons or of putting other persons in communication with them. I have hereinbefore truly stated what occurs to me without any volition whatever of my own and I have never made any other profession whatever I am and have been for a long time as the Plaintiff well knows in feeble health. Yet as the Plaintiff has thought fit to prefer against me charges of fraud and imposture of the basest character which are utterly untrue I desire the public cross-examination of myself and the Plaintiff as well as of all or such of the witnesses on both sides as the Court may think fit to allow.

4. On. Monday the 1st October 1866 I received a letter signed Jane Lyon of whom I had never heard before requesting to be furnished with the terms of admission to the said Spiritual Athenæum. According to the laws of the said society no one could be admitted as a member except by the "unanimous vote of the executive committee." I laid her letter before one of the members of the executive committee. On the next day namely Tuesday the 2nd October 1866 Mrs. Jane Lyon the Plaintiff called upon me and stated that she was the writer of the letter before mentioned and entered into conversation with me respecting my book entitled "Incidents in my Life" which she said she had read with much interest and she also said she had been making enquiries about me. She told me she had been a believer from her childhood in the

occurrence of such phenomena as are therein mentioned though she did not know them by the name of Spiritualism. She also said she was a much more wonderful medium than I was. She appeared to me however to dwell much less upon Spiritualism than on the fact of my knowing "them high folks" as she termed the royal and aristocratic personages mentioned in my book and she asked me if they were still my friends to which I answered that having done nothing to forfeit their esteem I believed they were. She avowed her disbelief in the Bible at which I expressed my regret and I told her (as the fact is) that there are very many Christians of all denominations and clergymen also who are Spiritualists. In fact with many thousands of persons the Bible is the foundation of their belief in Spiritualism while Spiritualism on the other hand strengthens their belief in the Bible as opposed to the prevailing Materialism of the day. She asked to see my private rooms and looked at various pictures which I had there. She was much struck by a family group of the Grand Duchess Constantine of Russia and her family and asked how it came into my possession. I told her as the fact was that Her Imperial Highness had presented it to me when I was last in Russia staying at the palace of the Grand Duke. She said "Did she really give it to you with her own hand?" I told her as the fact was that such was the case and not only so but that Her Highness had even had the kindness to send to Warsaw on purpose for it. The Plaintiff seemed much astonished and said "Well you are a celebrity" Then she asked me if I had ever stayed at the palace of the Emperor. I told her as the fact was that I had done so. "Well" she said "you are indeed a celebrity and it is only a pity you should be poor." I told her that it was well to be poor and that I wanted for nothing and also that I should be in a very comfortable position as soon as my affairs in Russia were settled. She said "You may be comfortable even before that." I told her I was comfortable even now and had no desire ungratified. She then asked me about my circle of friends in London and whether it included many "great folk." I told her as the fact was that I was exceedingly fortunate in my circle of friends. She then enquired the terms of subscription to the Athenaeum and I told her it was a large sum namely five guineas. She made no reply but ticked me to call on her on the following day to talk it over. I told her I could not do so until Thursday the 4th instant I was rather pleased with her homely kindness and as I had occasion to call in Westbourne Terrace which was near her I thought I would gratify my curiosity by going to see her at home. She enquired if she might call on me again in the interval but I told her it would be better to wait till the time fixed. On leaving she said "Well I had expected to find you proud and stuck up from knowing so many great folks but I like you very much and I hope you will like me I think of going to Paris next year to the Exhibition would you like to go with me?" I laughed and said "Yes." She said "I hope we shall see a great deal of each other." She said she had one request to make namely that I would give her my portrait saying she would prize it very highly. I gave her one and thus ended my first interview with her. She was an utter stranger to me I never having heard of her except from her said letter and from her dress and manner and the apparent relish she had for my aristocratic connexion. I thought she might be a kind-hearted housekeeper but it never crossed my mind that she could be rich. No allusion whatever was made to her late husband Charles Lyon and no spiritual manifestations whatever took place. The Plaintiff did not as she now says offer to pay £10 nor any other sum to the Athenæum.

5. On Thursday the 4th October 1866 I called on the Plaintiff as requested by her and found her living in indifferent lodgings over a stationer's shop. She asked me many questions about myself and told me she wondered at my accepting a salary as secretary to the Athenæum being such a celebrity that I ought to be rich and should be and with these words she handed me a cheque for £30 which I immediately declined. She then said "Oh this is nothing to me I am very rich I might live in great style but I prefer to live as I do. I like you and will be your friend." I told her I was not in the habit of taking presents from any one. Finding I would not take her money she told me it was for the society of which I was secretary and not for myself. She then questioned me again about my past life and enquired whether if I were to marry again my wife would be received by the great people I knew. I told her I had not the slightest intention of ever marrying again and that I certainly should marry no one whom I could not present to my friends. She then asked me what I would say to being adopted by herself for she had been thinking for some time of adopting a son who could take care of her. She added "I will settle a very handsome fortune on you. We will take a house and your son (whose name had been mentioned) will live with us and have his tutor. This will be an amusement to me. You will have a handsome house to entertain your friends and we will travel abroad together when we like." I laughed at the scheme as a mere romance and asked what her relatives would say. She said "Now I will tell you a little of my story and you will see how free and independent I am." And then she told me as the fact is that she was the illegitimate daughter of a tradesman in Newcastle who afterwards became a farmer. That she could have no legal relations and that she did not know any of her father's family. That her late husband was of good family and his family always held aloof from herself and

husband and there were other reasons why she and her husband took a dislike to them and that he made over all his property which was very considerable to her before his death so that the probate of his Will cost only £50 and that not one of his relatives were mentioned in his Will. She then went onto say that previous to her late husband's death he told her a change would come over her in seven years and that she thought it meant her death but that now she thought the event to occur was that she was to meet and adopt me. I said that in that case I should not only have an adopted mother but that I would call her husband my spiritual adopted father inasmuch as he had foretold such a thing. I said this in a laughing mood so much so that the Plaintiff seemed displeased and said that I seemed to take the whole thing as a joke. I told her I certainly did and not a very good one either for I could not conceive how any one could talk thus to a man who was a perfect stranger to her. She then said she had not finished her story and that she had lived such an isolated life since the death of her husband and that during the five years she had been in London her husband's family had shown her so little attention that the previous winter she had spent in Yarmouth and some of them lived not far off yet she saw none of them and wished to see none of them. The men she said are parsons and my husband used to call them black coats and when he received letters from them particularly from his nephew Charles who writes with a great flourish he used to throw the letter from him and say it was enough to make one hate one's own name "Now" she added "I have lived five years in London in one lodging-house not this one and I only know an old woman who sells mixed sweets and with whom I used to sit and chat a great deal and a lodging-house keeper a Mrs. Pepper who is a bad one and a Mrs. Sims whom I have just picked up as a photographer and who has been a source of great comfort to me for I have been trying to live with a niece of my husband's but I could not do it and my comfort has been to get out and have a talk with Mrs. Sims. Now you will introduce me to your friends and two people will be made happy one of them myself the other you." The doubt crossed me whether she was sober and in her right mind. I said to her "Why I may be a scoundrel or an impostor for anything you know." "Oh dear no" she said "you're a public man and if you had done anything wrong the public would have been too glad to seize on it and show you up." Her reasons were so much to the point and her manner was so very earnest and affectionate that I thought she must be in her right senses and that she had well calculated the step she was urging on me to take but I told her it was all too hastily done. I said "I fear you seek me for the strange gift I possess and as that is not at my control I might lose it." She said

"Have I ever alluded to that it is true that will bring people about you and that is what I want. I always select my lodgings in a place where there is bustle and confusion for I like it so. I shall like to see your friends and nothing will spite my husband's family more than to see me amongst great folks. I always swore I would be even with them some day and now I will." I told her that this was not the way I liked to look on the proceeding for I wished to harm no one or stand in no one's way. She said "Oh I'll tell that Mrs. Fellows such a story about it all that I shall allow you a thousand a year it will be such fun." I told her again that I could not like such an idea that I had gone thus far through life and no one could say ought against me or that I had ever sought to injure any one. She rose and threw her arms about me and kissed me saying "it shall be just as you like darling." I did certainly think this rather violent but her age and the conversation we had just held seemed to be a justification of her conduct. She requested me as yet to say nothing about her to my friends further than that she had given £30 to the Athenæum.

6. There were no spiritual manifestations whatever at this interview. I wrote to several of my friends at the time saying that a lady had given thirty pounds to the Athenæum simply from having read my work. I determined not to see her for a day or two alone that she might in the meanwhile ask about me if her intention really was to do as she said for this reason I did not again see her till the 7th October 1866.

7. During this interview of the 4th October the Plaintiff said it was not for nothing that she was the daughter of a tradesman for it had made her a "capital woman of business" and that she liked to have everything well and legally done and wished me to consult a lawyer to know whether or no being adopted by her and taking her name gave me a legal right as heir to her property and "how the job was to be done."

8. From her statements to me I believe the Plaintiff to be a widow and that she has no child. She has varied in the mention of her age to me sometimes saying that she was fifty-two at other times different ages so that I cannot answer her Interrogatory as to her age further than that she is extremely robust and vigorous both in body and mind and she is in the habit of boasting that she has never been confined to her bed by illness. I believe that exclusive of her gifts to me her income is about £5,000 a year arising from consols and mortgage securities. She has told me but I have no independent knowledge on the subject that she was originally possessed of some property of her own. She has also told me and I believe and charge it to be the fact that her influence over her husband the late Charles Lyon was so great that she prevailed upon him

to make over the bulk of his property from time to time to her during his life and that he bequeathed the residue which was of trifling amount to her by his Will. During the period of my intimacy with the Plaintiff she has told me that she used to quarrel with her late husband at times but yet I think she was attached though I cannot say whether greatly attached to him. From her statements to me I believe that he was greatly attached to her and completely under her power and control.

9. Save as hereinbefore mentioned I cannot set forth as to my belief or otherwise whether she had heard she could be placed in communication with his spirit through the agency of a spiritual medium or how otherwise. Under the circumstances hereinbefore appearing and not otherwise she did seek for and obtain an interview with me on the 2nd and not on the 3rd October 1866 at Sloane Street in the said Bill mentioned and she did on the 2nd and not on the 3rd October 1866 see me at Sloane Street and not elsewhere and I deny that I did by any means whatever induce her to believe nor to the best of my knowledge and belief did she believe that a manifestation of the spirit of her deceased husband took or was taking place as nothing of the sort occurred whether through my instrumentality or any otherwise howsoever. And in answer to the Plaintiff's further Interrogatory I deny that I did on that occasion induce the Plaintiff to believe nor to the best of my knowledge and belief did she believe that the spirit of her deceased husband was in communication with her nor that certain expressions of endearment or any other expressions on the part of the spirit of which there were in fact none were conveyed through the medium of me to her and I make out the contrary in manner hereinbefore appearing. The Plaintiff was not much or in fact gratified thereby because nothing of the sort happened but she did under the circumstances hereinbefore stated and not otherwise desire me to call upon her on the following day but she did not promise to give me £10 or any other sum. Under the circumstances hereinbefore stated and not otherwise I did in fact call upon the Plaintiff at her lodgings in Westbourne Place but not at her present lodgings in the said Bill mentioned on the 4th October 1866 and not on the day following the previous day and I deny that I did again or at all induce the Plaintiff to believe or that she did or could believe that the spirit of her deceased husband was manifested to her through my instrumentality or that she did thereupon though I admit that she did under the circumstances hereinbefore stated and not otherwise in fact give me the sum of £30.

10. On the 7th October 1866 I called upon the Plaintiff and she greeted me most warmly and affectionately and said she had now made up her mind to adopt me and asked me if I had seen a lawyer about it. I

said I had not and that I did not like her to act thus hastily in a matter of such importance. She told me she had resolved to pay to my account £24,000 on the 11th of the month that she had at first intended the sum to be £30,000 but had now decided I should have only £700 a year to begin with to see how we got on together and that if she found me all she expected me to be she would give me much more afterwards. She also told me she had watched with much interest the trial which had been going on relative to Bishop Colenso and that it had been her intention had he been deprived of his income to have given him a fortune adding "it is lucky for you I did not." She told me that her income was more than five thousand a year and that her husband saw none of his family and that she had no feelings but that of distaste to them all with the exception of Mrs. Clutterbuck who was rich. I felt like one in a dream at this strange conversation which I could not credit and rising from where I was seated myself at the piano. The Plaintiff gave an exclamation of surprise and said "Turn your side face again that I may see your profile." I did so and the Plaintiff came where I was seated and said "Why I have seen you in visions these many years and the only difference was that your hair was lighter more of a golden yellow than it now is many, many years ago even before you could have been born." She went on to say "Why even my father before he died told me I should adopt a son and I will have no one but you and whether you will or no I shall settle a fortune on you and you will be obliged to accept it." I told her it was cruel to talk thus to a man who was poor and she said "It is the only means I have of binding you to me I am alone. I have and can have no relatives I had a fortune of my own of £30,000 so surely I can do with that as I please. My husband's relatives look down on me because I am the natural daughter of a Newcastle tradesman. So much the worse for them for I will prove to them that I may sit up if I please and pitch my money pound after pound out of the window and they and indeed no one has a right to interfere. You are a gentleman and have friends in the best society. I will show them all that I can be received as well as they when the fancy takes me for I shall go out with you and your friends will come to us and my old age will become a joy instead of a burthen." I said "Well I promise you I shall love you as a mother and shall even call you mother if you like for there are plenty of old ladies whom I address and write to as mother." She replied in a very hasty manner "Thank you but the less of that kind of love the better I shall love your son with a mother's love he will be our darling." She asked if I would not like to have her see some of my friends or even a legal man to talk it over with them and I told her I would. She said "Very well I will go with you to-morrow to call on any one you please or you may come here with any one." I told her that for the moment I thought of no one but that there was plenty of time. She made a singular remark which impressed me even at the time for she said "I am apt to change my mind so you had better catch me while you can." I told her I had no desire to catch her and that the very thing I feared was that having taken me up so suddenly without cause she would put me down just the same. She only replied to this "O dear no I shall never tire of you." At this moment she was standing near me and she went and sat down saying "I always have had my own way and unless you will promise to do as I wish you to you will only make me dislike you." She seemed to think for a moment and then said "Now I know what I shall do I shall give a fortune to your son and have him take my name I will take a house and have a tutor for him in fact I will adopt him and then you will have to see him and you would not dare to refuse anything for his good." She then asked me the day of the month and I told her it was the 7th. She went to a tin box and brought out her cheque book and turning it came to a blank on which was written "Mrs. J. Fellowes" and to the best of my belief £5 but underneath was written "the last to her for ever" while I was looking at it she kissed me on the brow and said "Now for the first to you from your adopted mother who is this day a happy woman" she said "I asked for the day of the month because a "Sunday's date is not legal." She then wrote out and handed me a cheque and on looking at it I found it to be for £50. When she saw my surprise she came and kissed me on the brow and said "That is only a drop in the ocean." I placed the cheque on the table and told her I must refuse it for though I was poor I was also proud and had always refused thus to accept money. I told her I was sensitive (as the fact is) that though people wished to pay me for the strange gift I possessed that I felt I had no right to obtain money from such a source. She said "Why you foolish fellow I've seen nothing of your strange gift as you call it and though it is through your being celebrated for that that I first heard of you now that I know you I love you for yourself and should not care if you never had anything singular occur to you again." She then took up the cheque and folded it with the printed side out saying as she did so "You must always fold bank notes and cheques with the printed side out else you might throw them away as waste paper." I took the cheque and put it into my pocket. Up to this time no phenomena known as spiritual manifestations had taken place at any interview between the Plaintiff and myself but as I rose to go there came sounds known as rapping. A call for the alphabet was made and the following sentence or words nearly similar spelled out "Do not my darling Jane say alas the light of other days for ever fled the light is with you Charles lives and loves you." Whether these sounds were produced by the Plaintiff who pretends to be a medium I cannot say but I solemnly swear that they were not produced by me. I was not near the table when they occurred. The Plaintiff alone was seated near the table. She left her place in the most quiet manner and went into her bed room and I heard her unlock a box and she then brought and showed to me a very badly executed water colour drawing of a house and on the back of the picture was written in the Plaintiff's handwriting "Alas the light of other days for ever fled" or words precisely similar and underneath "Binchester." She then said this was a very favourite place of her husband's but from family difficulties which she explained it was sold by an Order of Chancery and she also told me that she had told her husband previous to its being sold that she had seen in a vision it would be sold. She also told me that it was in the library of that very house she had first seen me in vision. I was much surprised at the perfect calmness of the Plaintiff. I solemnly swear that I did not seek to influence her in any way whatever except only against her own impulse and desire to force upon me a position of wealth also that I did not induce her to believe she was having communication with the spirit of her husband. I did not know and could have had no means of knowing the name of his former estate of Binchester or of the words the Plaintiff had written on the picture as she had not mentioned Binchester or the picture to me before this. I had made no inquiries as to who she was and as she told me on the Thursday she was only intimate with the wife of a photographer and an old woman who sells mixed sweets in Knightsbridge and a lodging-house keeper and as these persons were not in my circle of acquaintance I would not and did not see them. I did not induce the Plaintiff to believe but then and repeatedly afterwards told her that the identity of all spiritual communications was most uncertain and that we must always use our own reason in judging them. I have not been interrogated as to the above manifestations which I have related but I mention them because I have no wish to conceal the truth.

11. There were no other manifestations at this interview than those above stated. The statements of the Plaintiff contained in the 2nd, 3rd and 4th paragraphs of her affidavit filed in this suit on the 27th June 1867 as to the events therein alleged to have taken place are untrue and I believe and charge that the book to which she refers as though she had written down what occurred in it shortly after the events was not commenced until a much later period and after she turned against me as hereinafter mentioned and had planned to undo her gifts to me.

12. I deny that the Plaintiff did on the day mentioned in the Plaintiff's Interrogatory as the following day or on any other day under the belief that the spirit of her deceased husband had again or in fact at all through my agency been brought into communication with her but I assert that she did for the totally different reason hereinbefore mentioned give me the further sum of £50.

13. I deny that I did by the means in the said Bill mentioned or by any other means acquire a great or any ascendancy over the mind of the Plaintiff and I did not by the exercise of what the Plaintiff now calls my alleged spiritual powers or in fact induce her to believe that what I represented to be communications from the spirit of her deceased husband to her were real communications as I never represented anything of the sort. And I shall make out the contrary by proving from independent testimony that her charge of my exercising undue influence or in fact having any influence over her is wholly untrue. I shall prove that it was I who was the victim and the sufferer that under the influence of gratitude for her unsought generosity to me and her many acts of real and unaffected kindness I put up with much that I felt to be galling and degrading that I made many efforts to return her gifts and sever the connection between us but that enfeebled as I was from severe and exhausting attacks of illness I had not the energy to throw off the dominion exercised over me by her strong will and her affectionate expressions of regret as well as the position I was placed in by the publicity that had been given to my change of fortune.

14. I called again on the Plaintiff on the Monday the 8th October 1866 a little after eleven a. m. and putting down the cheque for £50 said I could not and would not accept it. The Plaintiff burst into tears and said she had thought a new and joyous life was opening to her for she had no friends and that it was cruel of me to treat her thus for she had been making so many plans for our future and as my health was delicate she wished she had not sold a cottage she had once possessed near the sea called Sea View but that she had done so and now she would buy me a place near the sea where we might go together.

15. She then said that not only was her mind made up to adopt me and have me take her name but that it was to be done so surely that nothing could undo it and that she would make a new Will and that if she should by any chance die suddenly that I had her fortune contingent on taking her name for she was not in the habit of being influenced by any one but did as she pleased and that was why she did not and would not live with Mrs. Fellowes. She again entered into detail concerning the whole family which would be injurious to them so I omit them. She requested me to go to the bank myself to get the

cheque cashed and said that she would be at my rooms at two o'clock precisely. There were no spiritual manifestations whatever at this interview nor was any mention whatever made of spiritualism.

16. I would not go to the bank alone but asked my friend Mr. Rudall to accompany me. I told him that the same lady who had given the £30 to the Society had now given me £50 to myself and as she lived in such poor lodgings and dressed so wretchedly I thought there must be something wrong about it and that perhaps it was all a myth and that the bankers would laugh at me. It would not have surprised me in the least if they had told me they knew no such person. They however cashed the cheque.

17. The Plaintiff was awaiting my return in the shop below my rooms and she went first to my bedroom and looked about. I showed her a service of silver which belonged to my late wife and she said she did not like the form of the forks and that I had better sell them and put all my money in the funds where I should have plenty besides very soon. I told her they were precious to me as a souvenir. She again repeated her firm intention to adopt me and neither spirits nor spiritualism were alluded to. She said she could not love me more if she had been my mother and adopt me she would. "No, no" she said "we will live together and have a nice house we will make the money fly and nothing will spite my husband's family more. There is no one I care about but Mrs. Clutterbuck and she is old and sickly as well as rich. No I will enjoy the days I have to live." I told her that as I was a well-known man it would be much talked about. "So much the better" she said "all your friends will be able to come and see you and you will be able to entertain them." I told her I must first see some of my friends as she first suggested to talk the matter over with them and begged she would not come to see me the next day and that on my side I would not visit her and that she might give the subject very serious consideration. She again asked me who of my friends "a clever business man" could see her that she might talk it over with him for she added "I know no one in London." I told her that the only person whose name occurred to me at that moment was my old friend Mr. S. C. Hall who is an author of distinction and I said that he was sure to call on me the following day and I would ask him to see her.

18. It was not spelt out as the Plaintiff now says by the spirits that Mr. S. C. Hall was to go to her but the Plaintiff wrote or made me write his name down that she might remember it when he called and be sure to see him. She afterwards at a much later period when as I now believe she was bent on creating a case against me made me write his name in a book as far as I can remember as if it came in a spiritual

communication as she used often to dictate her pretended revelations for me to write and I did so at her request and under the influence and control she had acquired over me by her munificent kindness.

19. It was not spelt out as the Plaintiff now says on this occasion or on any other occasion that the Plaintiff was to adopt me.

20. It was now late and I had to dine out. I again told her we must not see each other the next day and that I would ask Mr. Hall to see her. She said "I see you wear a very beautiful ring. Is that a present from some grand person." I told her as the fact was that His Majesty the Emperor of Russia had given it to me on the occasion of my marriage. "Oh yes" she said "I read of that in your book and he gave you another jewel when your child was born." I told her that that had been for my wife and she asked me if I had it and I told her I had. I brought my small jewel case and showed her the brooch which is of great beauty being a large emerald surrounded by sixteen large diamonds. I also showed her a beautiful large diamond in a ring and told her this was one she had not read about inasmuch as the Emperor had given it to me on my last visit to him when he had graciously consented to become my boy's god-father my wife having been the god-daughter of His late Majesty the Emperor Nicholas and that I did not consider it to be mine but rather the boy's from his god-father. She said "Now as I am your mother I shall take care of these things for you" and she accordingly took with her on this the fourth time I had ever seen her in my life these two jewels worth several hundred pounds and at this moment she still has them. And in November she took three most valuable bracelets and all the rich and valuable Indian and lace shawls and other laces and under clothing belonging to my late wife and she still retains possession of them. She has repeatedly worn and displayed these ornaments in the society of my friends to whom I introduced her and others I submit that she should at least offer to return them as they in fact belong to my boy when she comes into a Court of Equity to demand the restitution of her gifts to me. She said before leaving that although I had presents from crowned heads I would find that an old lady was the best friend for she would give me a present which would put me at ease for the rest of my life and that I might "snap my fingers" at my Russian law suit for I would not require it now. She also asked me at once to attend to what was necessary about changing my name legally and that it was to be Daniel Dunglass Home Lyon as she liked this best.

21. The details of all the circumstances are stamped in my memory from their peculiarity and from having had to repeat them so very often to my friends both in the presence and absence of the Plaintiff and on

many occasions when she was present she always assented and would herself add little details which I had omitted to complete the narrative.

22. In answer to the Plaintiff's Interrogatory I deny that I did at such meeting or at any meeting whatever with the Plaintiff allege or represent to her or induce her to believe that the spirit of her deceased husband required her to adopt me as her son or to place me in a position of independence suitable to my rank and position in life as her adopted son. My rank and position in life were infinitely superior to hers at the time for she had not maintained the rank and position to which her husband's station and her wealth might have entitled her. It was I who gave her rank and position of which she was entirely destitute. She gave me wealth and left me no freedom in its use. Before I knew her I could and did give much more to charitable objects than she would allow me to do afterwards. And save as aforesaid I made no allegation to the Plaintiff on that occasion nor did I at the same time or at any time allege or represent to the Plaintiff or induce her to believe nor to the best of my knowledge and belief did she believe that the spirit of her deceased husband desired that Mr. Hall (in the said Bill named) should be sent for nor did I make any other allegation or representation to the Plaintiff respecting the said Mr. Hall than is hereinbefore mentioned.

23. On the next day Tuesday the 9th October 1866 the said Mr. S. C. Hall called on me and I related the simple outline of the case saying it was an old lady without any children or relations who had taken a liking to me and wished to adopt me as her son. Mr. Hall in the most decided manner refused to go near her and said "Either you are insane and telling me a falsehood or she is one of the two and I will in no way have my name mixed up with the affair." I recalled to him that he had known me some years and that he had known my wife and reproached him with a want of friendly feeling in thus refusing to see one who wished to assist me and after nearly an hour's persuading he said "As she wants to be a member of the Athenæum write me a letter of introduction and I will call and speak to her on that subject but unless she herself broaches this adoption I will not allude to it."

24. He was absent more than an hour and was much agitated on returning. He said "Why it is the most wonderful thing I ever heard of. She tells me she is worth some hundreds of thousands and asked me what I thought she should settle on you at once which she could have the power of adding to but not of taking away from." I told her that two or three hundred a-year if you lived with her would suffice to which she said "Oh that's not enough." He said that she wouldn't speak or let him speak about spiritualism and he brought back the letter of introduction in his pocket without having presented it. Finding from Mr. Hall's

conversation that he thought her not only sane and in her right mind but a very sharp business woman who gave efficient reasons for what she had contemplated doing I decided to accept what she offered me.

25. I did not see the Plaintiff all this day but as she had told Mr. Hall that she wished him to meet me the next day at twelve. I went on Wednesday the 10th October 1866 at half-past eleven again to beg that she would at least delay for a time what she wished to do. I told her as the fact was and as she knew that I was ill and that a week or two's absence would do me good. She said I know that and you shall go just as soon as the "job is done." She then said that she had written to me for the last time in my name of Home and it was a most important letter for she had so fully decided on giving £700 a-year that nothing would stop her and the letter was to prove why she did so. "For" she added "I am a capital woman of business and as my Will now stands if anything should happen to me before I can carry out a deed of gift the family would be sure to be down on you and I would rather see the money in the fire than they should have it I only wish I had not given my husband's (your father as you are to call him) gun away for I wish you had it." Mr. Hall came at this juncture and she at once went to her box and produced a bundle of stock receipts. Mr. Hall did not to the best of my belief touch one of the papers. The Plaintiff herself picked out the papers with the largest sums and put a pin through them and handed them to me. It was not spelled out as she now says that I was to be her adopted son or anything about her funded property or that she was to hand over the stock receipts to the said S. C. Hall or that he was to hand them over to me or anything to that or the like effect whatsoever to the best of my remembrance and belief.

26. I never caused any spiritual manifestations or communications to be made to the Plaintiff. Whatever communications were at any time apparently given were caused by the Plaintiff herself if they were caused by anybody and were at her request written by me in a book narrating everything that occurred between us which was read over in the presence of the Plaintiff and no paper or papers were burnt by me as the Plaintiff untruly states. I do not remember what the apparent communications were but when I see the book which I wrote I can easily ascertain whether it has been altered since and if not I shall be able to state accurately all the circumstances that happened. This book was afterwards read through to Mr. Shorter in the presence of the Plaintiff and she then assented to its containing a true and complete narrative of the adoption as was the fact. The Plaintiff took away the book and kept it and I have never seen it since. It is still in her

possession unless she has destroyed it. It is not the book marked B referred to in her said affidavit filed on the 27th June 1867.

27. When the Plaintiff said as she did on this occasion that she would give me £24,000 Mr. Hall said "Do my good lady take time and think this well over. Do not act so hastily." And I joined with him in saying so but she only said "What is £24,000 to me in comparison with having a son that I can love and who will be kind to me." It is untruly stated by Plaintiff that on this occasion a gold snuff box was given to Mr. S. C. Hall. She gave it to him about a month later namely in November 1866. It is worth about £3 or £4 and she has lately recalled it. She also gave him at the same time namely in November 1866 a silver pencil case which Mr. Hall of his own accord returned when she demanded a restitution of her other gift to him. Mr. Hall gave her from time to time many valuable books which she has not thought necessary or becoming in her to return. Mr. Hall did not and could not have said as the Plaintiff now swears that it was too late to go to the bank for it was then not more than one o'clock. The Plaintiff wished to know the name of a stockbroker who could sell out for her and said it was usual for her own bankers to transact all such business but that "till the job was done she did not care about them knowing it." I then left her and having ascertained the name of the firm of stockbrokers Fog, Taylor and Backhouse, Tokenhouse Yard. I returned to Mrs. Lyon the same day with their names she wrote them a letter and requested me to take it to them in the City myself alleging that as the sum was a large one and they did not know her they might think it a hoax. I took the letter she had written to the brokers in my hand and said to her "You have not yet known me ten days and this is not the tenth time you have seen me and you are making me a rich man. Oh do for heaven's sake think well of what you are doing." She caught me in her arms and kissed me saying "This is only a drop in the ocean." There were no manifestations whatever and no mention made of the subject of spiritualism on this occasion.

28. I took the letter to Messieurs Fox, Taylor and Backhouse and the same day I received by post the following letter which must have been written and sent before the interview between Mr. Hall myself and the Plaintiff on the same morning I swear that I was not near Mrs. Lyon when it was written and not even in the house and in nowise influenced her to write it and except for her allusion to it as aforesaid knew nothing of it or its contents before I received it. It was her own free action and was but a part of the business tact which she has ever displayed throughout the whole of her proceedings with me.

"18, Westbourne Place, Hyde Park,
"10th October, 1866.

"My dear Mr. Home,—I have a desire to render you *independent* of the world and having ample means for the purpose without abstracting from any needs or *comforts* of my own I have the greatest satisfaction in now presenting you with and as an *entirely* FREE GIFT from me the sum of £24,000 & am

"My dear Sir, yours very truly & *respectfully*,
"JANE LYON.

The underlineations (Now printed in italics and small capitals.) in this and her other letters herein set forth were made by herself.

29. Either on the evening of the 10th or the morning of the 11th October I received another letter from the Plaintiff beginning "My dear Daniel, I want you to take a nice mutton chop for your breakfast before you come. I write knowing your timidity to come and be made a rich man" or words to that effect and signed "Yours affectionately Jane, Lyon." The Plaintiff as I believe after she began to fabricate her case against me abstracted this last mentioned letter from amongst my papers as herein after appears. The other letter set forth above escaped her by happening not to be amongst my other papers.

30. On the following day namely Thursday the 11th October 1866 I called at her request and we went into the City in a cab. There were no manifestations in the house before leaving and none in the cab while going into the City the Plaintiff sat very near me with my hands in hers under her shawl all the way to the City and when we were going down Holborn Hill she turned and said "This my darling boy is one of the happy days in my life and I never expected to be so happy again. The feeling that I had money and a parcel of people for whom I cared nothing might think I had made a Will in their favour and so be looking out for my death has ever worried me for I know they all speak of me as 'the old woman.' I don't know how many Wills I have made. Let's see one just a month or so after any husband died I left all to one of his sisters and then I have in others distributed it about. That horrid Mrs. Pepper's daughter was in one and when I was making another Will after her death Mrs. Pepper had the impudence to ask me to put in Joe her son because he was Louisa's favourite brother but I told her I should do nothing of the sort." The Plaintiff has in fact at different times made at least five Wills that she has told me of. In one she told me she had largely benefited her adopted daughter Fanny Hemming. We drove straight to her bankers and not straight to the brokers as the Plaintiff untruly states and I left her alone with them while I fetched the

broker to see her identified. We then went to Tokenhouse Yard and the Plaintiff began asking if the Backhouse of the firm was in any way related to Jonathan Backhouse of Darlington (I should mention that the day before she had said the same thing to me and hoped they were for then they would know her name as Mr. Lyon had transacted business with Jonathan Backhouse). To the best of my remembrance she told them that she had adopted me and she did the same to Mr. Young at the bank of Williams, Deacon and Company in Birchin Lane who proved her identity. We then went to the Bank of England and the sale was made. I did not see the cheque or money for it. But the Plaintiff directed the brokers to lay it out in the New Three per Cent. Annuities which was immediately done and the brokers bought and sold notes and the stock receipts were handed to her and she took them away with her. On returning to the office in Tokenhouse Yard she wanted to pay the broker's bill and not having her cheque book sent me to the bank to buy her one. I did so leaving her alone with the brokers and I have been informed by them and believe that she then told them truly the story of her adoption of me.

31. In answer to the Plaintiff's interrogatories I say that the said Mr. Hall was and is a friend of mine and save and except as hereinbefore truly appears I deny that the said Mr. Hall was accordingly or in fact sent for or that any other meeting at this time than is hereinbefore mentioned took place between him the Plaintiff and myself. And I deny that I or the said Mr. Hall or either of us at such meeting or at any other meeting alleged or represented to the Plaintiff or induced her to believe or to the best of my knowledge and belief that she did believe that the spirit of her deceased husband required her do produce her stock receipts or any of them or to go to the Bank of England or to transfer stock equivalent in value to £24,000 sterling or to any other amount to me or to sell the same and give me the proceeds as a provision by the Plaintiff for me as her adopted son. I deny that there was any allegation or representation then made by me and the said Mr. Hall or by either of us to the Plaintiff. And I deny that the Plaintiff accordingly or in fact in the full conviction and belief that she was fulfilling the wishes of her deceased husband communicated to her through the medium of me or so far as I know for any other reason than is hereinbefore stated went on or about the 10th October 1866 or at any other time to the Bank of England with me or any other persons or person and I did not know that she signed a book there but I have since been informed and believe that it would have been necessary for her to do so and therefore I presume she did on the occasion of the hereinbefore mentioned sale and purchase and under the

circumstances hereinbefore stated and not otherwise. I admit that a large sum of Bank £3 per Cent. Consolidated Annuities belonging to the Plaintiff and representing in value £24,000 or thereabouts was sold and not transferred and save and except that the proceeds thereof were as hereinbefore stated invested for my benefit in the purchase of £3 per Cent. Reduced Annuities and the papers relating to the same given to the Plaintiff. I deny that the proceeds of such sale or of any part thereof amounting to £24,000 sterling or to any other sum were received by me and I make out the contrary in manner aforesaid.

32. I deny that the whole or any part of the said sum of £24,000 was obtained by me from the Plaintiff through the alleged ascendancy or power which the Plaintiff falsely alleges I had acquired over her mind by the means in the said Bill mentioned and I make out the contrary in manner herein appearing.

33. I went to Brighton for my health as had been previously arranged with the Plaintiff on the following day namely the 12th October 1866 and I solemnly swear that during the whole of the day when we went in the cab together as aforesaid both before and during the completion of the said gift no mention was made of spiritualism or of any matter connected with it save in the office of the said brokers when the Plaintiff mentioned me to be the celebrated Mr. Home but that I was now to take her name. I wrote to the Plaintiff from Brighton and begged she would undo what she had done. She said that she would only write to me as Daniel Dunglass Home Lyon and by so doing people would see that the celebrated Daniel Dunglass Home was now in reality a Lyon.

34. Much correspondence passed between us during my absence as I wrote every day to her. I have not kept copies of my letters to her and I saw them in her possession in the month of March 1867 and she has them still unless she has destroyed them. They were both affectionate and grateful and I told her (speaking relatively) that all I had in the world belonged to her and that she could take back what she had given and I thanked God and all good angels for sending me so kind a mother. There was but little mention made by either of us of spiritualism and scarcely any allusion to her late husband. All her letters to me are addressed to "D. D. Home Lyon Esq."

35. On the 13th October 1866 she wrote and sent me the following letter addressed to Brighton:—

"18 Westbourne Place, Hyde Park,
"Octr. 13/66

"My dear Son,—I have just received a letter from you this morning from Brighton. I like the G. Hotel tho' I had never lived in it, but have been shown it all over. I do not know if it is the same manager he was marked with the small pox, but he was most attentive to me and quite a gentleman, also the inspectress a lady Miss Jessie Thomas she went up in the lift with me and showed me the bedrooms and baths, she has left I *believe* now, they were the manager 2 years ago, I was then at Gladding's the silversmith's King's Road at Yarmouth last year I spent several months Kimberley Terrace, Esplanade; now, my son, I must first begin to get angry with you, how could you *possibly* take a *cold* bath, which is I am sure the worst thing you could do in your state, now I request you immediately to go and consult a doctor and have an English prescription for me to see. I am half a doctor myself and am sure you have *inflammation* of a serious description let your health be *permanently established* is the first object for you to consider if you wish to add to my comforts, you must excuse me if I tell you at our first acquaintance I rather felt a repugnance towards you when you said 'Mother I shall so love you' I said and drew away from you, 'The less of that the better I shall love your child,' now I am quite altered, I feel so anxious on your account and afraid you should *be ill* or anything should happen to you that I am sure it is a mother's maternal love towards her beloved child so now if you *value* my comfort, my dear son take *care* of *yourself* and attend to what the doctor says and prescribes for you, do not be tempted with wine it is to stimulating, I shall seal this letter with your father's seal *previous* to his *marriage* the next after his marriage the next with my own seal ladies have no motto or crests the letter of your friend I could not well make out and perhaps you cannot make out mine I had a bad day yesterday my cold was worse to-day it is better thanks to our *Great God.* Your friend knew a Jane Lyon. My husband's aunt Lady Jane Lyon was, the sister of John 9th Earl of Strathmore and aunt to Thomas the 10th, 11th Earl of Strathmore sister to Lady Ann Syman the mother of Lady Ravensworth she was a dear good creature very dark and shortest of the family she promised me an amber cabinet the notorious Sir John Dean Paul was her trustee and executor and all her valuables disappeared, her property was divided amongst her nieces and nephews that was secured on the Glamis and Strathmore Estates one of her sisters Lady Susan Lyon married General Lambton father of the first Lord Durham. Now say dear Daniel I fear I have tired you with this stuff be sure you attend to the instructions I have given you respecting your health that is the *greatest consequence* to me I have written to our darling in answer to one from him and expect him here to-morrow if fine but not to come if it rains to take another opportunity with his friend I have bought him a pretty book suitable for his age *full of pictures* the lady you mentioned coming yesterday never came and I was glad for I was ill and not quite well now but a great deal better. When you *want* money you know we *can coin* it soda not be afraid but act cautiously attend to your health and doctor's advice it is not by acting for the *good of an hotel that will do you good*—I must conclude, for the post is closing,

> "Your affectionate mother,
> "JANE LYON."

"P.S.—The post has gone so I open my letter to tell you I have read your letter again and find I have in my hurry made a mistake it is a warm bath you have taken instead of a cold bath and I am so glad for that will do you good. Excuse me for being so stupid keep yourself calm and know that the great God is working for you.

> "From loving mother,
> "JANE LYON."

I did not at the time understand her statement about having felt repugnance to me at first which was entirely contrary to her previous statements to me and to others or why she should have alluded to loving my child whom she had not yet seen but I did not trouble myself about it.

36.—On the 11th October she had unknown to me written and sent the following letter to my little boy:—

> "18, Westbourne Place, Hyde Park,
> "11th October, 1866.

"My dear Sacha,—You tell me your father came to you last night and woke you out of a sound sleep, did you not think, that very naughty 'No,' you say 'I was so very glad to see him that I never thought of sleep or Bedfordshire.' He comes my child in joy to tell you that the *great God* had found him a mother who would be kind to him and you his boy. You must be good and the great God will bless and love you for ever God is so kind and loving to all good people like *your father* and I have heard you are so good and gentle that I am sure I shall like you, and if it is a fine day on Sunday next I shall be glad to see you but if it rains I shall see you with pleasure and your friend Mr. Perdicaris another time. I hope your dear father will receive benefit at Brighton he is not very well you will pray for him will you not and God will bless you.

> "My dear Sacha, your affectionate Grandmother,
> "JANE LYON."

37. On the 15th October while I was still at Brighton she wrote and sent me the following letter:—

18, Westbourne Place,
"Hyde Park, 15th Octr. /66.

"My dearest Son,—I have just time before the post goes, to write a few words, our dear little Sacha and his friend Mr. Perdicaris was here yesterday, he is a dear boy I love him, and kissed him many times, I like your friend *very much indeed* he brought an umbrella with him which a friend of yours who last accompanied you to Henley left behind, will you darling tell me who is the gentleman or his address that it may be sent to him. I enclose you the papers of *your fund* security you will be sure not to lose it and when you have shown it to your friend Dr. Gully, some other time when you return I can have it to take care of for you. I am glad you are going to Malvern to your friend who will care for you, but how will you get oysters there they are strengthening and good you can take a little barrel with you and get strong and well as soon as you can avoid everything hurtful I think the sea air too strong for you. My cold is not better but progressing. I fear you cannot make this out in such haste,

"I am, my darling Son,
"Your affectionate Mother,
"JANE LYON."

38. The papers of my fund security which the Plaintiff enclosed as she said in the last letter were the stock receipt and broker's note relating to the transfer of stock representing £24,000 mentioned in the 8th paragraph of her affidavit filed in this suit on the 27th June 1867 in which she swears that "No account receipt or other paper in connection with the transaction was given to her on that occasion or subsequently."

39. On the 16th October 1866 the Plaintiff wrote and sent me the following letter to Malvern where I had gone for my health:—

"Tuesday night.

"My dear Daniel,—I am glad you feel better you are amongst your dear friends at Malvern that you love so well I trust your health will improve. I sent a letter to you yesterday which you ought to have had by 1 o'clock enclosing your security fund papers I thought you would like it with you. I hope they will forward it to you. I am now quite annoyed I should have sent it as I fear it is lost, there is two stamps on the letter. Pray write immediately you get and pray *write* to the managers to forward into you I shall be quite uncomfortable until I hear you have got it you ought to have had it about. I have no time to say more.

"God bless you, dear son,

"And believe me, your affectionate mother,

"JANE LYON."

40. On the 17th October 1866 she wrote and sent me the following letter:—

"18, Westbourne Place, Hyde Park,
"17th Octr. /66.

"My dear Daniel,—I am glad you got my letter with enclosure I was afraid it was entirely lost however all well that ends well present my very kind love to your dear friend & Miss Gully for her very kind letter to me with their polite invitation to the Priory. I will with pleasure avail myself of it another time. I have sent her 2 photographs of myself in lieu of three pretty views she has sent thanks for them I have been at Malvern many years ago previous to my marriage with the best of men your spiritual father Charles Lyon. I went along with my father who took me to see England and North Wales and Cumberland.

"My dear Son,—I am really very much pleased to hear you are a little better but it will take time to reinstate you in good health I hope Dr. Gully with God's assistance will do so in the meantime you must not think of returning to London until you are quite better in 2 or 3 weeks you may be so then drop me a line to say you are but I should not agree that you should come until I receive a note from Dr. Gully with his sanction and approval for giving up the treatment you will be subject to under his care. He saved your life 5 years ago and I think you are in just such a state at death's door, therefore do not flatter yourself before your time comes for you to throw up your hat and say thank God for health and wealth and a good kind doctor. You do not mention your friend's umbrella, what is his name, where does he live, and I will send it to him. Dear little Sacha behaved very well be was pleased with his book. I gave him a guinea he gave it to his uncle saying he would lose it he is very fond of rowing a boat and fishing. I hope they will soon come to London for I should so like to see the spiritual painting, how very wonderful. With kind love to yourself and all your dear kind friends in haste.

"My dear Daniel, your affectionate mother,

"JANE LYON."

She here alludes to what I had said that her husband would be my spiritual father as she was my mother. The person mentioned as the uncle of my boy is not his uncle but a friend. We are rather in the habit of calling our fiends relatives as an affectionate mode of expression.

41. I had been desirous she should leave London with me but she refused. Dr. Gully desired me to ask her to visit him and his sister wrote as well as myself requesting it. She refused to come then so little was my influence over her even at this time.

42. In this letter she speaks of me as "at death's door" and in another letter written to me on the 24th October she fears I am on the edge of a precipice and the least pitch will send me headlong. I was indeed and had been for some time very ill.

43. About the middle or end of October 1866 I was having a miniature of her late husband taken from a photograph she had given me painted by Mr. Egley as a surprise for her. I had it beautifully mounted as a brooch set in diamonds of mine of great value and afterwards gave it to her. I wrote to her to ask the colour of the late Mr. Lyon's eyes to which she replied in a letter wrongly dated the 9th October. In that letter she speaks of Mr. S. C. Hall whom she now calumniates in her said affidavit "The kind friends the Halls are going to Brighton to-morrow." And she says to me "If you are well enough to come up the same time and not by any means before I shall be most glad now recollect not before if you do my dear son I will not see you" and she gives me medical advice.

44. On Thursday the 18th October 1866 I came to see Mrs. Lyon hoping to induce her to return to Malvern with me but I could not persuade her to do so.

45. On the 19th October 1866 she wrote and sent me the following letter to Malvern:—

"18, Westbourne Place, Hyde Park,
"Friday morning, October, 1866.

My dear Son,—I hope you got safe to the priory without catching any cold so miserable a night it was. I was so very vexed at myself for giving you your father's empty purse. I should have put some money in it but you were in such a hurry. It quite escaped my memory although I intended to have offered you some before you left. Now let me know how I can send you some a check is of no use but I could send a post office order you must enquire at the post office and let me know the particulars what I am to do and the sum you want. I hope you found dear little Sacha well. Did he get his little book? Did you see the spiritual painting? Please to tell Dr. Gully with my respects that I am ½ a doctor and felt your pulse and found it very wiry and hard which proves to me that there is some serious *inflammation* somewhere about you that must be cured or otherwise all your *baths* will be of no *avail*. I am certain in your present state all stimulants are poison though given and taken with the best motives but we must not kill with kindness which is often done with those we best love, and *best love us.* Will the baths you take *cure* inflammation without any other mode? I fear not without internal means however I trust all will be well. Pray let me know the postage rules for Malvern, viz. what time letters should be posted here for Malvern.

"I am with every kind wish for your health and *comfort,*
"Your affectionate mother,
"JANE LYON."

Not only, did she urge this purse on my acceptance but also the watch of her husband though I had my own watch and told her I had no less than two others. She so urged the acceptance of it that I took it. She said she wished me to have something with the family crest on it. The watch was out of repair and in December I had it repaired. Two days after it was repaired Mrs. Lyon asked me to return it to her I did so with all the pleasure imaginable for I had never wished to have it.

46. From her urgent way of forcing things on me this being only the seventh or eighth time I had seen her in my life my estimate of her character was that if I did not accept I should give offence. As she again alluded to money I wrote and asked her for twenty pounds though I did not require it for I still had a greater part of the fifty pounds she had given me on the 7th October. In the 8th paragraph of her said affidavit she suppresses all mention of her having pressed me to accept money as appears by the lastly-stated letter and says only "I sent to him in accordance with his request on or about the 28th October last a cheque for £20 for his own use."

47. In a letter which she wrote and sent to me on the 21st October 1866 addressed to Malvern where I was staying after giving me much medical advice and wishing to get rid of the inflammation that she says is consuming me she says "There is a great work for you to do I am gifted with a knowledge you have not. I wish you to be a living worker not a dead one." Hundreds of times has she said these words to me "I am gifted with a knowledge *you have not*" and would then make me write her ideas or impressions. In the same later she also says "Dr. Hawksley called but I did not see him. Mr. Hall said he wished I had but he did not cure your wife. He would not cure you." In the 9th paragraph of her affidavit filed in this suit the Plaintiff swears that at some period subsequent to the 9th November 1866 she found out that the said Dr. Hawksley was an intimate friend of mine but of whom she knew nothing. I had told her that he was my medical adviser and friend

and that he as well as my other friends would call upon her in my absence and introduce themselves to her as she particularly desired. And as they in fact did. The said Dr. Hawksley is one of the leading physicians and is on the staff of the Margaret Street Hospital for consumption.

48. She wrote and sent to me on the 24th October 1866 the following undated letter addressed to Malvern:—

> "18, Westbourne Place, Hyde Park, London,
> "October.

"My dear Daniel,—You say do not worry about my health I cannot help it God has given me a son and I much fear he is on the edge of a precipice the least pitch will send him headlong. You say to me you are better to Mr. Hall *not so well* which shall I believe I am anxious to think the best. I like you to sleep your nature requires rest it is almost worn out by anxious thoughtful care. I well know my dear boy what you must have suffered which has added tenfold to your malady now you have the brightest of prospects before you repelling those of darkness look forward with joy to the bright union of glory resplendent with happiness God your Father I trust will assist you and impart a healthy influence over your frame and enable you to throw off the seeds of sickness and disease which has so long had dominion over you. Do not think of returning until you are better the air will be good for you rest and kind friends I trust will reinstate you. My cold is much better thank you. Lemon juice and sugar is good for me also for you it will not turn acid on the stomach but act as a stimulant. I have written you a long letter to little purpose and heartily tired I conclude with my best wishes for your health and happiness and am,

"My dear Son, your affectionate mother,

> "JANE LYON."

And again on the 28th October 1866 she wrote and sent to me the following letter:—

> "18, Westbourne Place, Hyde Park,
> "28th October, 1866.

My dear Daniel,—I herewith enclose you a cheque for Twenty pounds the sum required by you. You say you feel so much better that you are *almost* sure the Doctor will let you come to London on Thursday. Now I beg you will not come unless the Dr. considers you strong enough and not likely to get any better by *remaining longer* where you are. Does he think if you were to go to *Torbay* or *Torquay* it would be more beneficial. You believe you are consumptive and all here think the same. What does the Dr. say is *your complaint* and what the cure. The painting is over and smell also. I shall be glad to see Miss Ellen Gully when in Town or any friend of yours and yourself when well which I trust in the great God will soon be is the sincere wish of your Mother Jane Lyon. Now dear Daniel do not come on Thursday if you are not well enough and the Doctor does not approve of it. You will be sure to let me know what be says.

"J. LYON.

"D. D. Home Lyon, Esq.,
"Priory, Malvern."

49. Again in a letter dated the 29th October 1866 which she wrote and sent to my little boy to whom she had given a story book with pictures in it she hopes he will learn to be clever and good and grow to be a great and good man that is what his father requires him to be and so does his grandmother and yet notwithstanding the expressions in these letters the Plaintiff in the 18th paragraph of her said affidavit swears that apart from my supposed power of putting her said late husband's spirit into communication with her she had no affection or even respect for me. Again in the 9th paragraph of her affidavit filed on the 18th July 1867 she repeats that she did not care at all for me personally and that I was nothing to her.

50. In another letter which she wrote and sent to me about this time she said she would have loved me just as much if I had not been a medium and that she was only too thankful to have done for me as she did having made two people happy one of the two being herself. This letter I fully believe she has also abstracted from amongst my papers which she frequently examined during my absence but I have the envelope still.

51. I returned from Malvern the 1st of November 1866 and found the Plaintiff most delighted to see me. She told me that I must at once attend to having my change of name made a "legal job" for the family were up in arms and had been sending her all the newspaper notices of her having given me money. She showed me a letter which she had had from Mrs. Clutterbuck enclosing a notice from the "Athenæum Newspaper" where it was said the sum given was ten thousand pounds and she wished me to write to the editor and rectify the mistake and to say that it was twenty-four. "And would soon be fifty thousand" again alleging that this would spite the family and increase my celebrity. On both grounds I refused. At this very moment the servant announced the arrival of two of my friends and I went to the door to meet them. She told me she had been thinking a deed of gift necessary and that when I

publicly took her name she would make one out. I am so little of a business man that I did not know what she meant. I told her there was time enough about the name. At six o'clock my friend Mr. Rudall came and after spending the evening went away with me. This is the gentleman of whom the Plaintiff in the 9th paragraph of her said affidavit filed on the 27th June 1867 swears that she found out at some period subsequent to the 9th November 1866 he was an intimate friend of mine but of whom she knew nothing. There were no spiritual manifestations whatever but upon this occasion she brought out a roll of papers and laughingly showed them to me saying she either had shown or would show them to people as real communications and she thought them so good that she wished me to write them in a book for her in form of a dialogue purporting to be from her husband to herself. I told her I could only treat them as fictions. In fact they had little meaning in them.

52. She made me take the papers with me to my rooms that I might copy them there and show them to my friends. She also called my attention to the fact that there was a certain similarity in our hand-writing which in pencil writing is perhaps slightly the case. I took the papers with me. I never destroyed any papers relating to any business transactions with the Plaintiff or any real or supposed spiritual communications as she untruly states in her said affidavit.

53. On 1st November, 1866, she wrote and sent me the following letter:—

"1st Novr., /66.

"My dear Daniel,—Can you contrive to bring me your receipts to look at I fancy there is a mistake in your funds papers you know the sum in my papers was £28,000 and in your fund papers they only make £27,566 8s. 3d. I wish you had had consols like what my husband your father and myself always had I do not like annuities. I wish my Bankers had done the business the same as mine bring the papers with you to copy I have got a book. Take a nice mutton chop for breakfast. Do you like chocolate I think it is more nutritious than tea for you I hope you went to bed soon but I fear you *did not* as you had your friend. And I am my dear Daniel,

"Your affectionate mother,

"JANE LYON."

The above letter illustrates her rapid changes of mind.

54. I had on returning from Malvern given to the Plaintiff the fund papers and kept the broker's note she had sent me I did so because in

her letter she had said "You will give them to me to take care of for you" on going to see her on the 2nd I took the paper as desired and she told me she did not like "annuities" I did not know to what she alluded and she pointed out on the heading of the paper £3 per Cent. Annuities As she always kept my papers with her own I cast by chance my eyes on one of her papers and drew her attention to the fact that annuities were also written thereon. She read it but still she would not acknowledge she could be in the wrong and so told me I must put mine in the same funds as hers were. She made me there and then write to the brokers to sell out at once and make the change into consols no delay allowed. The following letter which she wrote and sent to me on the 2nd November 1866 will show the haste and determination of her character. She does not even wish to see me unless all is as she wishes:—

"2nd Novr.

"My dear Daniel,—Do not dear come over to-night unless you have got the funds settled. Come to-morrow about 12 or, 1 o'clock.

"Your affectionate mother,

"Jane Lyon."

55. The Plaintiff in the 8th paragraph of the said affidavit filed on the 27th June 1867 alludes to this transaction thus "The said Defendant on or about the 5th Novr. 1866 as appears by a stock receipt (left by him accidentally as I believe in my possession) invested £23,913 17s. 3d. cash being as I verily believe part of the aforesaid sum of £24,000 so acquired by him as aforesaid in the purchase in his own name of the sum of £26,756 15s. 5d. Consolidated Bank Annuities." The Plaintiff told me and I believe that another reason for her wishing this change was that the dividends might be payable on the same days as hers were. Under the circumstances hereinbefore appearing and at the Plaintiff's request and not otherwise I did on or about the 5th November 1866 invest the sum of £23,913 17s. 3d. as far as I can remember but the Plaintiff had the papers connected with the transaction aforesaid delivered to her immediately after it and has retained them ever since I never having seen them subsequently such sum being the whole of the purchase money arising from the sale of the Reduced Annuities aforesaid in which the said sum of £24,000 had been invested. But I deny that such sum or any part thereof was obtained from the Plaintiff as in the said Bill mentioned. Such new investment was in my own name and was in the sum of £26,756 15s. 5d. £3 per Cent. Consolidated Bank Annuities. I do not know to what she alluded in the last letter but one in saying I wish my bankers had done the business for

it was her own wish they should not and she did not even like the thought of having to go to be identified by them "till the job was done." She had not informed her banker Mr. Goode of Bridport and there was a good deal of difficulty when her dividends were due and Mr. Goode wrote to her saying he hoped she would inform him when she made any change in relation to her funds and that he would transact even for nothing the business for her rather than get into confusion in his accounts with her affairs. The papers she alludes to are the communications she pretended she had received I took them to her and copied them in her presence in the book she had which I have before mentioned as containing the history of my adoption. She read it and liked it and said it read so well particularly the part she had made up that it must be printed some day.

56. The Plaintiff now came almost daily to my rooms and I dined or breakfasted with her frequently I was most wonderfully disappointed in her general character I found a most fearful want of truth combined with a revengeful spirit and before I had known her a week I regretted having accepted her gift. It was this alone which prevented me from taking publicly her name which she now daily urged me to do but she had changed her mind as to what it was to be and resolved that it was to be Daniel Lyon. To this I objected in the most decided manner and told her it would look as if I were ashamed of my own name. She said "Oh very well just as you please but the day will come when I shall have my say about it." She was as resolute in this as in everything she desired and I had so little influence over her that I even had to ask my friends to intercede with her for me on the point which they accordingly did as I shall prove. At that time there were no spiritual communications given regarding any change of name or any business and indeed we but rarely had any spiritual manifestations certainly not more than two or three times when we were alone together. The witnesses who were present on the other occasions will prove that if there was any fraud whatever practised it was the Plaintiff alone who practised it. I do not allege that on any occasion a manifestation of the spirit of the Plaintiff's deceased husband took place or that his or any spirit was placed in communication with the Plaintiff I make no allegation on the subject and I am willing to give the Plaintiff to the best of my power the names descriptions and addresses of all and every persons and person present at any interview between the Plaintiff and myself if she will specify the occasion.

57. She used to say she had visions and extraordinary manifestations and I used to credit her. With all her peculiarities she was sometimes so kind and thoughtful to me personally and expressed such regret

occasionally for her temper that I at last decided I would sacrifice my life to her and what finally decided my so doing was the interest she took in my family. She arranged the sums I was to allow them yearly including my sister who had been living under the gracious protection of the Empress of the French for the last nine years. About a week after I had written to my family at her request she suggested I should not give quite so much although in fact it was my own property I was thus disposing of no part of the allowance being to come from her.

58. About a week after my return from Malvern and I think on the 8th November 1866 the Plaintiff said to me "Who is your legal man?" I told her as the fact was that I had no legal man as I had no law business to transact and that the only legal man I knew well was Mr. William Martin Wilkinson. She asked me if he was an honest man and I told her truly that I had never heard any one question his honesty. She asked me for his address and I gave it her.

59. She then asked me the address of my friend who had been introduced to her by me the day I returned from Malvern namely the 1st November and I gave her the address of Mr. Rudall. She wrote these addresses down on a slip of paper and took them to a side table and taking up a card came back and wrote on the same bit of paper what was on the card I asked why she was copying a card and she said "This is the address of your friend Dr. Hawksley and I am going to transact some important business and I want the three addresses handy when I write I want most particularly a medical man for I wish in case of necessity he should be able to swear to not only my sanity but general business habits and clear judgment and memory." She then asked me the names of my father and mother I gave her all then and as I was leaving her that evening she said "Now to-morrow I am going to be very much occupied in the morning so do not come to see me. She said I think to-morrow is the 9th you had better go and see the Lord Mayor's Show and tell me all about it any way do not come here till the evening." I did not then know for what purpose she had asked these names and addresses nor had any spiritual communication been given nor had I sought to influence her in any way.

60. On the morning of the 9th I went to Dr. Hawksley and be found it necessary to have me submit to an operation of no great importance but causing inconvenience and pain I did not to the best of my belief mention to him that he would hear from Mrs. Lyon but on Monday the 12th when I had to see him again professionally he mentioned having heard from her. On leaving Dr. Hawksley on the 9th though I was in pain yet as I had promised the Plaintiff to tell her about the Show I went to Charing Cross but was so faint and ill I could not stay so I went

to Mr. Wilkinson's office and gave orders my old Will should be destroyed.

61. Mr. Wilkinson did not mention having heard from Mrs. Lyon I did not tell him she was about to make a Will I could not have done so for I did not know it myself. I did not on that or any other occasion give any instructions whatever to the said Defendant William Martin Wilkinson concerning the Plaintiff or her business or even allude to it. In fact I knew nothing about it as she always kept her business matters secret from me and even derided my ignorance of business. He never told me nor did I suggest to him on that or on any other occasion that he should ask her certain questions or that she must be prepared to answer nor did I then or at any time say so to the Plaintiff or say that Mr. Wilkinson's letters to her would be written cautiously or anything whatever about his letters to her or hers to him. The Plaintiff's allegation to that effect in the ninth paragraph of her said affidavit is like the rest of it infamously false as will be proved.

62. The Plaintiff was exceedingly pleased with Mr. Wilkinson and said he had put her so much on her guard that one would think he was more her friend than mine. I crave leave to refer to the whole of the Answer of the Defendant Wilkinson filed in this cause filed on the 20th July 1867.

63. The only thing I have any remembrance of ever hearing Mr. Wilkinson say to me on the subject was that it was a pity the Plaintiff would not do something for her husband's family or be more generous to public charities not showering all her munificence on me and to this I have replied as I have to all my friends that I had no influence to stop her in anything she undertook and that I myself intended as I in fact did in case her property came to me to share it with her husband's relatives for I ever thought and said both to her and to others that it was most unjust that a part of the property at least should not go back to where it came from though I felt and said that I had as good a right to it as the comparative strangers to whom she had left it in some of her Wills.

64. On the evening of the 9th November 1866 I saw her for a very short time I remember it because she gave me on going in a fruit of prickly pear saying however that it was very dear sixpence I think. She told me she had written some most important letters concerning myself but that she must not tell me the contents I was in great pain and left very early that evening. The accusation that I dictated to her the instructions for a Will as she alleges is her said affidavit or the letters of invitation to these gentlemen is wholly without a shadow if truth. I was not in the house when the letters were written nor did I know their contents till this suit was begun nor was any spiritual communication

whatever given on the subject nor did I seek to influence her in any way whatever nor had I any power over her.

65. I never dictated or wrote or gave instructions for or suggested to her in any way whatever any one of the business letters written by her to the Defendant Wilkinson set forth in his Answer and to which I crave leave to refer nor did I know the contents of any one of them until after this suit was commenced. I am not a man of business knowledge as my friends will prove and I do not believe I could have written such letters had I wished to do so. In fact I do not understand the meaning of some of them.

66. The Will itself which is set forth in the 3rd paragraph of the Defendant Wilkinson's Answer and to which I crave leave to refer bears internal evidence that I did not dictate it as the Plaintiff untruthfully swears. In the first place she is determined to make me drop the name of Home which I had always objected to do and in the next place I knew she had no right to armorial bearings without a bar sinister.

67. Save and except as hereinbefore appears the Plaintiff did not to the best of my remembrance and belief shortly after the said sum of £24,000 was given to me by her in manner aforesaid for I deny that it had been obtained by me from the Plaintiff by the means or under the circumstances in her Bill alleged in fact have another meeting or interview with me. I deny that I did at such meeting or interview allege or represent to the Plaintiff or induce her to believe or to the best of my knowledge and belief that she did believe that she was required by the sprit of her deceased husband to destroy the Will she had then made or to make another Will in favour of me or that I then made any allegation or representation to the Plaintiff on the subject or that I represented to the Plaintiff or induced her to believe or that she did as far as I know believe that the spirit of her said husband dictated the terms of such new Will under which I was to be the universal legatee of all the Plaintiff's property or that Dr. Hawksley and Mr. Rudall or either of them (in the said Bill respectively named) were to be sent for to attest the execution of such new Will or that the spirit of the Plaintiff's said late husband dictated the terms of the letters to be written to the said Dr. Hawksley and Mr. Rudall or either of them asking them to attest the said Will or that I made any allegations or representations then to the Plaintiff on the subject. The said Dr. Hawksley and Mr. Rudall were and are friends of mine. I deny that a Will purporting to be the Will of the Plaintiff was accordingly or in fact prepared by or for me. The Plaintiff did as she afterwards informed me cause a Will to be prepared by the Defendant Wilkinson without any knowledge or

suggestion of mine under which but not under such a Will as is referred to in the Plaintiff's Interrogatories as having been prepared for me I was named as the universal legatee of all the Plaintiff's property and such Will as I have alleged was as she afterwards informed me executed by the Plaintiff on or about the 12th of November 1866 in the presence of and attested by the said Dr. Thomas Hawksley of 70 Brook Street Hanover Square an eminent physician Mr. Henry Alexander Rudall of 8 and 9 Great Tower Street London a merchant of good standing and the Defendant William Martin Wilkinson all three being as I fully believe men of irreproachable character I deny that the said Will was in fact executed by the Plaintiff at my instigation suggestion or desire or was so executed while as the Plaintiff now pretends she was under the influence of the ascendancy and power which she alleges I had acquired over her mind by the means and under the circumstances in her said Bill stated and I shall make out the contrary by proving that I never had any such influence ascendancy or power over her.

68. I had told her that my presence might be required in Russia relative to my law suit. This and the idea that I should ever marry again were now the two reigning ones in her mind for she used to say "you would neglect the old woman for the young one." Then she used to talk to me and to my friends about our future arrangements. The house was to be taken in my name and I was to pay the rent out of my income. We were to have two carriages I was to keep my own servant we were to have a house at the sea-side she was to pay for the servants. One of the carriages was to be a landau and for her sole use. The sea-side house was where we were to go with some literary friends or some persons of note to enjoy their society.

69. On the 12th of November in the afternoon the Plaintiff went into her bedroom and brought out what seemed to be a document of some kind and said "Do you see this? Well look well at it for it will soon be smoke and ashes. It is my Will and I have made many of them but I shall make no more" and she then burnt it. I say that I neither used any inducement or control over nor made any representation whatever to the Plaintiff on the subject nor induced her to believe that the spirit of the late Charles Lyon requested or desired the Plaintiff to destroy the former Will or make and substitute another in its place nor did I ever see her new Will nor in fact have I ever known its contents before the commencement of this suit further than that she had told me generally it was in my favour.

70. I made no effort or attempt whatever to keep her from her husband's relatives or any friends or connections that she might have but on the contrary desired her to see them which she did and often in

my absence as I arranged and wished it to be. On the 18th November 1866 the day after the signing of the Will she wrote and sent me the following note:—

"½-past 12 o'clock.

"My dear Daniel,—I have this moment received a note from my niece to tell me she has been prevented coming to see us this morning but will come to-morrow afternoon so I shall expect you dear as usual.
"Your affectionate mother,

"JANE LYON."

The niece mentioned in this note was Mrs. Tom Fellowes one of her husband's relatives. Mrs. Lyon used after this to tell me "That horrid Plessy" (meaning the said Mrs. Tom Fellowes) "tries all she can to put me against you and yet she will not succeed. Why she even said it would make people talk if we were to live in the same house together. To which I replied evil to them that evil think and they must be bad-minded people to think of such a thing."

71. One evening while we were at dinner she said she felt a spirit by her chair. This was in the presence of the said Mrs. Tom Fellowes and as soon as she was gone she laughed and told me it was all made up on her part to astonish her niece.

72. On Mrs. Fellowes leaving London the Plaintiff told me that she had given £50 to her and since then I have never seen her open her cheque book but what she would say "I wish I had it back again."

73: One morning about the 10th November 1866 the Plaintiff showed me the photograph of a little boy and asked me if I did not think it like my son. I told her that I could not see that it was in the least. She said Mrs. Sims had brought it saying that the spirits must have made the photograph for she—Mrs. Sims—did not know such a child. I said I had no belief in any such thing and that if the spirits had sent it they might have made it less vulgar looking. A day or two after this Mrs. Tom Fellowes asked me for the portrait of my child and Mrs. Lyon jumped up and said "Oh I have one of him I will give it you." I was too much under obligations to her to expose her untruthfulness and therefore did not contradict it and Mrs. Fellowes took the said portrait and so far as I know has it now. I give these details in order that I may be contradicted if my statements are false.

74. A similar act of duplicity on her part took place in the month of January 1867. An American lady gave me what is known as a Ferotype of herself. Mrs. Lyon said the upper part of the head was like hers and she put ink on the lower part of the face and showed it as a spiritual

production and even dictated to me a communication to give an air of fact to the same.

76. The Plaintiff now used to come to my rooms at any hour and she came nearly every day. On Wednesday the 21st November 1866 she wrote and sent to me the following letter:—

> "Wednesday Morn.
>
> "My dear Daniel,—I shall expect you at seven this evening as usual. I am going to be engaged to-day therefore do not expect me. I write in haste that you may get this in time not to keep you in the house and am
> "Your affectionate mother,
>
> "J. LYON."

I introduced her to my friends and took her into their society and went with her to dine and spend the evening with them and she was very proud of being introduced to them.

77. When she wished to leave Westbourne Place a step which I had long requested her to take for I wished her to have such rooms as I could bring my friends to she one day took me to look at some inferior apartments where she had lodged five years. This was 17A, Albert Terrace a house kept by the said Mrs. Pepper hereinbefore mentioned as one of her friends notwithstanding her being as she said "a bad woman who had driven her daughter to all sorts of extremities and when she married a valet would not see her and when on her death-bed she sent to see her mother the answer returned by Mrs. Pepper was that she would see her in her coffin.'" I did all I could to persuade her not to reside with such a woman whose apartments were even worse than the others. But so little was my influence over her that she actually took the said apartments and used to say that she liked to be able when "she and Mrs. Pepper had their tiffs to throw Louisa in her teeth." She has from that time continued to reside in the said apartments for which she pays 30s. a-week out of the season and two guineas during the season.

78. One morning in November and shortly after the Plaintiff had been to look at her old apartments in Albert Terrace the said Mrs. Pepper came to see me in my rooms in Sloane Street professing a great interest in me and wishing to know if the old lady had done in a legal way what she had done for she said "If it is not so done in a short time she will change her mind. Why she is always changing her Will. Once she told me when my daughter was alive that she had put her in her Will so once when she was dead and Mrs. Lyon was changing her Will I went to her and said Joe (that's my son air) was his sister's favourite brother and as she is dead why could not you put him in your Will but

law sir she was in such a rage with me. Oh she is a hard-headed and as hardhearted an old one." I expressed my displeasure at a lodging house keeper or indeed any one speaking thus of a person who was kind to me. She then said "Oh you are not the first person she has adopted there is such a fine young woman named Fanny Hemming whom Mrs. Lyon adopted even as a baby and she just took her up and put her down as suited her fancy. When she came to me she decided to take her to live with her but she would not go to the expense to have an extra room and so wished the young woman to sleep with her. Mrs. Hemming refused to give her daughter up to Mrs. Lyon and told her that if the father did give his child to her the father was dead and she would not allow her daughter to live with such a woman.

79. The Plaintiff afterwards told me that excepting the abuse of herself the whole of the above statement of Mrs. Pepper was true and the Plaintiff also told me she had ascertained that Miss Hemming had been to her friend who sells mixed sweets and said that she Mrs. Lyon was a bad woman who did not believe in God. The Plaintiff also told me and I charge it to be the fact that she had adopted other children but grew weary of them but she said she would not do so of me.

80. A few mornings after this I had a call from Mrs. Pepper before I was out of bed requesting me to lend her £200. I could not do it and told her so. She came many times about it and each time for a less sum till it was £15. I told her (as the fact was) that the Plaintiff had made me promise not to sell out the stock she had given me without first informing her of it and getting her consent and that she (Mrs. Pepper) had better show the Plaintiff the letter which she exhibited to me from a man connected with Tattersall's threatening to post her son and then I would use all the influence I had to get it for her. Mrs. Pepper came into the Plaintiff's room that morning to clear away the breakfast things and bursting into tears said "Oh Mrs. Lyon you might have saved Louisa but you did not and have regretted it save her brother now." She left the letter and the Plaintiff gave me a good scolding because I said a few words in favour of the young man observing that she never allowed anyone not even her father nor her husband to interfere with her in matters of business which she always arranged for both of them.

81. The Plaintiff refused to give or allow me to give the required assistance and from that day Mrs. Pepper became my enemy and the Plaintiff who is rather fond of going to the kitchen used to come up foaming with rage and saying "That beast Pepper will call you Home though I always tell her it is Lyon."

82. To the best of my belief it was Saturday the 24th of November the Plaintiff went to reside at Albert Terrace Miss Peel had the first floor and the Plaintiff the second.

83. I have during the months I was with the Plaintiff never known her to keep to the one idea so long as to the change of my name. And at last for she was again determined it should only be Daniel Lyon I had my friends write to me and I showed her the letters requesting me to keep the name of Home at least. I had three card plates engraved to please her for she changed so often. One was D. D. Home Lyon one D. D. H. Lyon and the last D. H. Lyon. At last she said we must ask the spirits on this occasion I said I not only did not wish so to do but would not do it. The Plaintiff said my friends would think her so whimsical about my name that we must do something to avoid this.

84. One evening while we were seated together she bade me take paper and pencil and write and she would dictate. The Plaintiff then dictated as if it were a message from some spirit who was related to me that the name of Home should be retained. The Plaintiff said "This will look all right and your friends will not think me a whimsical old woman." The name of Home was accordingly retained and that of Lyon added to it.

85. Just previous to her leaving Westbourne Place one afternoon the servant brought up the card of a "Mrs. Bailey." The name was unknown to me and the Plaintiff said it was to her also but she asked her to be shown up then she recognized a lady whom she had known and to whom she introduced me as her adopted son. I went away soon afterwards leaving her alone with the lady. In the evening she told me that the said Mrs. Bailey was the wife of a lawyer in Sloane Street. I asked her why she had not employed him instead of Mr. Wilkinson but she said she knew nothing of him further than that he had married this lady. I on one or two occasions after this asked her why she did not employ Mr. Bailey but her usual answer was that Mr. Wilkinson was as true as steel and she wished for no other. I swear that this was her expression and not mine. I called with her on Mrs. Bailey I also called on Mrs. Sims and was very glad at all times to have the Plaintiff do what and see whom she pleased. She was very angry because I would not go with her to see her friend named Prior who sells mixed sweets at number 2 Park Side opposite Wilton Place but I did not see the necessity of so doing.

86. On the last day of November 1866 Mr. Wilkinson made a draft of the deed poll for my change of name and the Plaintiff saw and approved of it. I executed it on the 3rd of December 1866. It bore date on that day and I executed it at the Plaintiff's request and at her request

it was afterwards enrolled as of record in Her Majesty's Court of Chancery and I did thereby declare as the Plaintiff well knew that I had taken the name of Lyon in lieu of and in addition to that of Home and that in future I intended to be called and known as Daniel Home Lyon. A true copy of such deed is set forth in the 6th paragraph of the Defendant Wilkinson's Answer to which I crave leave to refer. On the evening of the same day the 3rd December 1866 the Plaintiff and I dined at the house of a friend of mine named Mr. Griffin of number 1 Palace Gardens Bayswater when we met several people to whom the Plaintiff announced that I had that day signed my name for the last time as Home. I advertised my change of name and that I intended thereafter to call myself Daniel Home Lyon in the "Times" "Morning Post" and other papers at the Plaintiff's request.

87. On Sunday the 2nd December 1866 we called at the house of a friend of mine named Jencken residing at Kilmory House, Thicket Road, Norwood, a gentleman who was formerly called to the bar but is not now practising as I had told the Plaintiff. When there she gave him in my presence the true narrative of her adoption of me as I have hereinbefore stated and afterwards asked him to go with her into another room alleging that she had some business to transact with him and then as I have since learnt and charge enquired of him how she could best settle the sum she had given me with any additions she might please to make in such a way that her husband's family could not after her death upset it or that even she herself could have no power over it and he then asked her if spiritualism had anything to do with it or if I had in any way influenced her all which she then and there indignantly and emphatically denied but said she had wished for a son and that in him (meaning myself) she had found all she required and her only dread was lest he (meaning myself) should marry again. He then advised her to see a medical man that the fact of her being in her right mind might not be disputed. She told him that she had already had a physician as witness to her Will that in case of necessity he might not only prove that she was sane but a clever woman of business Mr. Jencken then advised her to execute a deed confirming the gift.

88. On Tuesday the 4th December 1866 Dr. Robert Chambers the Editor of Chambers' Edinburgh Journal called on me and I took him to call on the Plaintiff who was very proud of this as she was of being introduced to my other friends of distinction literary or otherwise. And she has told many of them in my absence the story of my adoption as I have given it. I allude particularly to Mrs. Nicholls whom she told on the 10th January 1867 as the fact was that she had to urge me to take her money and that spiritualism had nothing whatever to do with it. She

told Mr. Gerald Massey the Poet in January her delight at seeing my astonishment when she made her proposals her gifts being so unsought and unexpected. She spoke to Mrs. Ritchie to the same effect in November 1866 and she told Mr. Perdicaris as early as the 14th October 1866 that she "would have done the same for me if I had not been a medium" and that she would "Rather see her money in the fire than that any of her relatives should have it" and "That what she had done for him" (this Defendant) "was not all that she intended doing." On or about the 13th October 1866 she told Mrs. S. C. Hall that he had given me this Defendant £24,000 which though she could add to she could not diminish as she wished me this Defendant to feel perfectly independent of herself. On the 11th December 1866 she gave Miss Houghton the true narrative of my adoption as I have given it above and said to her that she the Plaintiff had not given me this Defendant the sums of £24,000 and £6,000 "As a Spiritualist or in consideration of his" (this Defendant's) "medium powers but because she loved him" In February 1867 she told Mr. Dyne (as the fact was) that she had to urge me to take the money and she spoke to others to the like effect. All the above statements with one exception were made by the Plaintiff in my absence and without my privity and many of them whilst I was away from her in the country.

89. On the afternoon of the 7th December 1866 I was unwell and went to my rooms before dinner I remember it because we were going to the house of a friend of mine the Right Hon. Elizabeth Lady Dunsany. In the evening on my return to the Plaintiff she seemed elated at something and said "Such a singular thing has occurred in your absence" I asked her to what she alluded but she only said "It's a great secret and you are not to know." I knew the best way with her was to seem perfectly indifferent and she would tell me. In the evening on our way out she said "You would be astonished if you knew what occurred to-day when you were out." Still she did not tell me that evening.

90. The following morning the 8th December 1866 at breakfast for I lived entirely with the Plaintiff and only slept at my rooms she said "Now Dan I dislike uneven sums." I fully expected the Plaintiff was going to request me to return to her four thousand pounds which I should then most certainly have done without any hesitation when to my astonishment she said "I am going to have a deed of gift made out and I am going to add six thousand to the sum already given." I told her I had already more than enough and did not wish for more. In fact I had so often seriously thought of returning what I had that I did not relish the new obligation.

91. She said it would be burdened however with the condition that I should defray out of the dividends or interest derivable from the same the outgoings we might incur in wines sweets and fruits and travelling expenses.

92. I have since learnt for I knew nothing about it at the time and I charge that the Plaintiff on the 7th December 1866 wrote and sent to the Defendant Wilkinson the letter bearing that date set forth in the 8th paragraph of his Answer to which I crave leave to refer in which she says "On the occasion of my adopted son taking the name of Lyon I wish to give him a little surprise" and requests him to prepare a deed thoroughly legal and that she also wrote unknown to me on the same day a letter to the said stock brokers Messieurs Fox, Taylor and Company which is as follows:—

17A, Albert Terrace,
"Albert Gate, Hyde Park,
"7th December, 1866.

"Gentlemen,—You will have the goodness to transfer consols standing in my name Jane Lyon of Bridport Dorset Widow to the amount of Six thousand pounds cash to the account of my adopted son D. D. Home or Daniel Home Lyon as is now his legal name. I will call on Monday at One o'clock to sign the transfer.

"I am, Gentlemen, your most obedt.,

"JANE LYON."

93. On the 10th December 1866 I at the Plaintiff's request accompanied her to the Bank when she in order to carry out her said intention voluntarily and against my desire transferred to me the farther sum of (I believe) £6,798 17s. 4d. £3 per Cent. Consolidated Bank Annuities into my old name of Daniel Dunglass Home that being the name in which her original gift was then standing. On this occasion she discussed with the brokers I taking no part in the conversation whether the transfer should be made in my new or original name. They decided in favour of the latter. The Plaintiff took the papers relating to the said new gift away with her and I have never seen them. It is a new invention of hers and entirely false that anything whatever with respect to this new gift was rapped out or that she thought the spirit of her husband induced her to do such a thing as to give me the money as a birthday present my birthday being in fact on the 20th March.

94. In answer to the Plaintiff's Interrogatory I deny that the Plaintiff on the 10th December 1866 or at any other time was at my request or suggestion or while under the alleged influence of the ascendancy and

power which the Plaintiff now alleges that I had by the means in the said Bill mentioned or in fact acquired over her mind or by any other means induced by me to go again or in fact with me to the Bank of England or to transfer the sum of £6,798 17s. 4d. or any other sum of £3 per Cent. Consolidated Bank Annuities in my name as Daniel Dunglass Home and I make out the contrary in manner hereinbefore appearing I believe that the sum of bank annuities voluntarily transferred into my name by the Plaintiff as I have hereinbefore truly stated and not otherwise was equivalent in value to a sum of £6,000 sterling.

95. On the 11th December 1866 I was in the house when the draft of the deed of gift came to the Plaintiff and she opened it and began reading it to herself. She had not done so more than a few minutes when she called out in a very angry tone "Daniel bring me pen and ink at once I wonder if Wilkinson is a fool or if he thinks me one." I handed her pen and ink as she desired and she drew her pen across some words and then wrote something in the margin. She said "Look at this line. 'And all my husband's family and connexions are well provided for.' Why they may bring in some street-sweeper and say he was a connexion. Even Mrs. James Fellowes could claim under that clause for her boys are not well provided for" (She gave reasons why they were not well provided for but as they are most injurious to the family I omit them). She showed me what she had written on the margin "Jane Lyon I have drawn my pen over this I do not approve of such." I said "Well mother I only wish you did not feel as you do against the family." She drew me towards her in a way which made me angry saying "You are my family." I left the room. She ran after me bidding me to send her Mr. Phillips my secretary. I did so and later in the day he told me as the fact was that Mrs. Lyon had sent him with some documents and a letter to Mr. Wilkinson. I only saw the Plaintiff in the afternoon in the presence of my friends at my own rooms and no allusion was made to the deed or anything else. And I did not know what was in her said letter of the 11th December 1866 which is set forth in the 10th paragraph of the Defendant Wilkinson's Answer.

96. The next evening the 12th of December I came in with my little boy and found Mr. Wilkinson with the Plaintiff. She said she had not terminated her business with Mr. Wilkinson and sent me and my boy into her bed room. When we returned she showed my boy the parchment she had executed being the deed of gift and he remembers it well for she kissed him and told him that "There was his fortune when his father died." No influence of mine was used to cause such deed to be made or executed nor was any spiritual communication

given with respect to it nor did the Plaintiff think that the spirit of her husband dictated it. It was to suit her own purposes and nought else. She spoke to all my friends about it immediately afterwards in the most triumphant manner and her only surprise was that it was not in the papers. The Plaintiff's deliberate assertion in the 12th paragraph of her said affidavit filed in this suit on the 27th June 1867 still more deliberately repeated in the 8th paragraph of her further affidavit filed on the 18th July 1867 that she did not execute this deed of gift on the 12th December nor till the time when she executed the mortgage deed of the 19th January 1867 is utterly untrue and will be as completely disproved as the rest of her assertions.

97. Under the circumstances hereinbefore appearing and not otherwise I believe that such deed poll or instrument in writing as in the said Bill is mentioned to bear date the 12th December 1866 and therein stated to be of or to the purport and effect in the 11th paragraph of the said Bill set forth (so far as the same is therein set forth) was duly executed by the Plaintiff.

98. The said deed poll was prepared by the Defendant William Martin Wilkinson but not as the Solicitor for and on my behalf but as the Solicitor employed by and acting for and on behalf of the Plaintiff. I gave no instructions or suggestions whatever to the said Defendant Wilkinson on the subject of the said deed poll. I have been informed and believe that the costs for the same have lately been paid by the Plaintiff without prejudice. It is untrue that such deed poll or any other deed or instrument whatever was executed by the Plaintiff at my request or instigation suggestion or desire or while under the alleged influence of the ascendancy and power which the Plaintiff now pretends I had acquired over her as in the said Bill mentioned and I make out the contrary in manner herein appearing. I have been informed by the said Defendant Wilkinson and I believe that the Plaintiff was repeatedly requested by him to employ some other Solicitor and that she persistently refused to do so and I crave leave to refer to the correspondence between the said Defendant and the Plaintiff set forth in the said Defendant's Answer. And save her aforesaid application to Mr. Jencken unknown to me and his advice I am unable to set forth as to my belief or otherwise whether such deed was executed by the Plaintiff without the intervention of any or if any what other independent or other Solicitor or person for or on her behalf. Both said Defendant Wilkinson and the said Mr. Jencken acted entirely independently of me and of each other in the transaction aforesaid.

99. The Plaintiff had told me some weeks previous to the 12th December 1866 that she wished Mr. Wilkinson to find a mortgage for

Thirty thousand pounds for she said "I shall put out Sixty thousand at 5 per cent. and that will make my income quite as good as it was" I did as she requested and heard no more of the affair till about Christmas time when I saw her receive a letter which I knew to be in Mr. Wilkinson's handwriting. I asked her what it was about and she said "it was none of my business but that I should know when the time came."

100. On the 30th of December 1866 we spent the day and evening at the house of Mrs. Henning a friend of mine residing at Sunninghill House Thicket Road Norwood and so absurdly affectionate was the Plaintiff towards me and so much did she talk of her great fear that I should marry and leave her that this lady has since told me as the fact was that she determined never to ask her again to her house inasmuch as even the servants had made remarks upon her conduct.

101. This was the day of the burning of the Crystal Palace and the Plaintiff was for a long time in a room without any fire in it watching the conflagration and she took a most severe cold from which she did not recover all the winter. From the fact that the Plaintiff had taken cold and was feverish and ill I remember distinctly the 31st of December and I also remember her sending me to post a letter for Mr. Wilkinson the contents of which I was entirely ignorant of.

102. The Plaintiff was feverish and ill and for the only time since I had known her she was on the sofa almost all the evening of the 31st December. I sat by her and she then told me that she was about to transact or had transacted some very important business which greatly concerned me. She told me that the letter I had posted for Mr. Wilkinson was respecting a mortgage for me. As she had for some time been speaking of my putting my money out on mortgage for she never considered me capable of transacting business I thought she referred to my own money being placed out on mortgage and that she had found a good investment for me through Mr. Wilkinson so I thanked her and begged she would not worry herself about it at least while she was ill. She then told me that it was a mortgage of her own money which she had decided to have in my name reserving only a life interest for herself and that her husband had made over his property to her during his life. I told her I did not see the necessity of such a step but she silenced me by saying "My first deed of gift might at a push perhaps be upset for my love for you was such a sudden thing that people may say I acted without due judgment but this is an affair of more mature consideration" and she added "my letters to you will prove the affection I have and all your friends will testify to my solicitude for your welfare. You have taken my name I am happy with you and it is no one's

business what I do with my money." Under such circumstances I could but be quiet and allow her to do as she wished.

103. I did not see one of the letters written by her at this time nor did I know their contents till this suit began. It was through no belief in the spirit of her husband or any other spirit that she acted. She was determined to have her own way in everything.

104. She was very angry with me in the early pert of January because I had asked her why she would live in so wretched away doing no good to any one. She said it was ungrateful in me to talk as I did. I told her it was for her own present and future happiness. I reminded her as the fact was that I had obeyed her in everything. That she had at the first exacted a promise from me that I would never sell out any stock without first informing her and she had promised to pay some small debts I had. And not only did she now refuse to pay these but placed me in a false position in not allowing me to sell out the two or three hundred pounds which would have done it and that she would not allow me to be kind to the poor. That in short I was a more toy for her and was heartily ashamed of myself. She declared she would not sign the trust deed. I told her I was glad of it for I felt my own degradation more and more every day. She was ill and she began to cry. I told her what I had said had not been meant in anger but that my illness made me irritable and Dr. Gully on the 10th January had found me so ill that he wondered I did not go abroad. And I would not do so without her for I felt I had no right to be enjoying myself while she was ill and alone. There was nothing more said at the time about the trust deed but a few days later she changed her mind apparently for she told me she was going to give me another surprise and that after due consideration she had resolved to carry out her first intention and that all was arranged.

105. On the 19th January 1867 I was with her as usual and Mr. W. J. Wilkinson and Mr. Hartley clerks of Mr. Wilkinson came having with them the deeds and copies. I rose to leave the room knowing that the Plaintiff did not like to have me know anything about heir business. She called me back and I resumed my seat by the fire but she afterwards called me to her and kicking a footstool from under the table pointed for me to kneel there I did so close to her and she put her left arm round my neck and fondled my cheek while they were reading the parchments. I was mortified at her so doing and when they were so reading the parchments I tried to draw away but the Plaintiff held me there. She followed the reading of the deeds with great caution and stopped them once or twice to make such remarks as "A most clever deed" "Quite right." I neither urged her nor did I touch her as she now

swears otherwise than the nearness with which she made me kneel would necessitate. Under the circumstances hereinbefore appearing the Plaintiff was not in the month of January 1867 or at any other time induced by me to execute though she did in fact execute a deed purporting to be an indenture bearing date the 19th January 1867 and made between the parties and of or to the purport and effect in the 13th paragraph of the said Bill set forth (so far as the same is therein set forth) and she was not induced by me to execute any other indenture of such or any other date or made between the same or any other parties or of or to such or the like or any other purport or effect than is hereinbefore stated. The indenture of the 19th January 1867 which is hereinbefore stated to have been executed by the Plaintiff on that day was prepared by the Defendant William Martin Wilkinson as the solicitor for and on behalf of the Plaintiff and not of me this Defendant and I have been informed and believe that the costs for the preparation of the same have lately been paid by the Plaintiff without prejudice. The said Defendant William Martin Wilkinson acted in that transaction and throughout all his transactions concerning the Plaintiff's business in entire independence of me. And save as aforesaid I am unable to set forth whether the said indenture was seen or approved of by any other independent or other solicitor or person for or on behalf of the Plaintiff. The Plaintiff also executed the indenture of even date recited in the said last-mentioned indenture whereby she assigned the principal sum of £30,000 and interest and the securities for the same to the said Defendant William Martin Wilkinson and I believe that such indenture of even date was prepared by the Defendant William Martin Wilkinson as the solicitor for and on behalf of the Plaintiff and not me this Defendant. And the said Defendant William Martin Wilkinson acted independently of me as hereinbefore mentioned. And save as aforesaid I am unable to set forth whether the same indenture was seen or approved of by any and if any what other independent or other solicitor or person for or on behalf of the Plaintiff. And I deny that the Plaintiff executed the said two last-mentioned indentures or either of them at my request or instigation or while she was under the alleged influence of the ascendancy and power over her mind which the Plaintiff now pretends that I had acquired by the means and under the circumstances in the said Bill mentioned and I make out the contrary in manner hereinbefore appearing. The said two last-mentioned deeds were executed by the Plaintiff on the 19th January 1867 in the afternoon at her own lodgings 17A Albert, Terrace Knightsbridge in the presence of Mr. William J. Wilkinson, Mr. Hartley and myself and they were the only deeds then executed by her.

106. A day or two after this I was so much worse that Dr. Hawkesley wished me to try change of air and as I did not dare to ask such a favour my friend Mr. Rudall asked the Plaintiffs permission for me and she consented. I wished her to go with me urging her bad cold but she would not do so and would not see a medical man.

107. I went to Hastings about the 26th January 1867 apart from the Plaintiff who remained in London and I did not return to town till the 13th February 1867. Up to the time I left London the only sources of difference between the Plaintiff and myself so far as I know were her parsimonious habits and her embarrassing display of affection towards me both when alone and when in the presence of my friends who made remarks upon it. I had introduced her to most of my friends including many persons of rank and distinction who treated her with much attention as my adopted mother. After I left town in January as aforesaid the majority of them discontinued their visits to her. There was however one great exception. I had introduced to her in November Mr. Henry Gould Gibson of No. 33 Mark Lane wine merchant. He begin from the very first to pay marked attention to the Plaintiff. Even before I left, town he used to bring her frequent presents of such as Hungarian bread, sardines, vinegar and so forth. After I went away he visited her almost daily to the best of my information and belief. And on at least one such occasion as will be proved he was heard to suggest to the Plaintiff that it was a pity she had adopted me. He also as I am informed and believe was with the Plaintiff present at a *séance* of a true or pretended medium named Miss Nicholls held at the Plaintiffs lodgings early in February 1867. The said Mr. Henry Gould Gibson as I am also informed and believe has continued on very intimate terms with the Plaintiff ever since and has been and is still in the habit of attending *séances* of other true or pretended mediums with the Plaintiff notwithstanding that she now pretends to have renounced her belief in Spiritualism. I am further informed and believe that the said Mr. Henry Gould Gibson has been mainly instrumental in the institution of this suit. After my departure for Hastings the Plaintiff's illness and comparative solitude and her resentment at my having discouraged her advances enabled Mrs. Pepper to gratify her feelings of revenge and envy towards me by irritating the Plaintiff against my little boy and myself. She persuaded the Plaintiff that my son was taught to look forward to her death which was entirely untrue. And she suggested to the Plaintiff that it was a pity she should have tied herself to a dying man. The said Mrs. Pepper also advised the Plaintiff to re-adopt instead of me the said Fanny Hemming whom she had cast off. The said Mrs. Pepper was also as I am informed and believe present at the aforesaid

séance held in February 1867 and has also together with the said Mr. Henry Gould Gibson incited the Plaintiff to take these proceedings in Chancery against me.

108. Several letters passed between the Plaintiff and myself during my said absence. I have not kept copies of mine but the originals are in the Plaintiff's possession unless she has destroyed them.

109. In a letter which she wrote and sent to me on the 28th January 1867 she says—"Enquire of the spirits *if you can* who's is the face they have given me now to look at instead of yours. I will not describe it let the *spirits* do so if *they can*. When I was looking at it they touched me on the leg it was a most *extraordinary face* like no one I *ever saw*. I first saw your profile then it vanished and the full face of another looked at me. Would it be _____?

110. On the 5th February 1867 she wrote and sent me a letter wrongly dated the 5th January 1867 in which the following passage occurred—"Poor Mr. Hall is very ill he has got erysephelas in his head if he does not get soon well it is most dreadful it will fly all over his body. I trust he will shortly get well poor dear fellow and poor Mrs. Hall has also been ill but she has now got pretty well again. Mr. Gibson dined with me yesterday off the turkey which kept quite well." The turkey aforesaid was one of the said Mr. Henry Gould Gibson's presents to the Plaintiff.

111. On Monday the 11th February 1862 she wrote and sent to me at Hastings the following letter:—

"17A, Albert Terrace, Albert Gate,
"11th Feb., 1867.

MY DEAR DANIEL,—I am much gratified to find you are much better. I have just had Mr. Wilkinson here and he says he would be glad if you would stay till next Saturday. He will be with you on Thursday for a couple of days and then you can come up together and it will also do you good to stay till Saturday.

"I had Sacha here yesterday he came last Saturday. I was not at home. I think there is no occasion for Mrs. Richie to send him here not knowing whether I require him to come. You know little boys are no amusement to me a little girl is different and they are only in the way when not required and am

"Dear Dan, your affectionate mother,
"JANE LYON."

This was the first intimation I had of a dislike taken to my child. From this day she never even asked me or the friends with whom he was staying how he was and in April the last and only time she ever saw him afterwards she did not even kiss him. After this she told me that Mrs. Pepper did so hate the child and that she had told the Plaintiff undoubtedly he was looking forward to her death that he might be rich.

112. I returned unexpectedly in the afternoon of Wednesday the 13th February 1867 and found the Plaintiff at my rooms in Sloane Street. She had just returned from the stockbrokers and the Bank of England where she had been with Mr. Wilkinson to sell out stock belonging to her and partly to me in order to complete another mortgage transaction for £30,000 of which I knew nothing except only that she had asked me before I left town to lend her the amount requisite to make the sum even as she knew she had not enough of her own and to this I had gladly consented. On going up to shake hands with her I saw her give a sly push to some papers which were near her on the table and she seemed confused but I could not tell why. I saw that they were her previous letters to me and as after her departure I for the first time missed it. I believe that she took away with her at least one on that occasion and then or on some other occasion another and that these missing letters were those mentioned in the 29th and 50th paragraphs of this my Answer.

113. The evening I arrived from Hastings namely the 13th February 1867 Mrs. Pepper came up and shook hands with me. When she left the room the Plaintiff said "Well that is the most wonderful woman." She then told me that Mrs. Pepper had brought the said Fanny Hemming to see her and she added "I know well enough what it was for only to get her into your place I shall tell the old beast that I have had a communication from Fanny's father telling me I am not to take her." I implored of her not to do so. The Plaintiff went on to say "Mrs. Pepper has been up here every day during your absence trying to put me against you and here she shakes hands with you."

114. I found the Plaintiff much changed. She seemed to watch my every movement and I distinctly remember the following incident. The Plaintiff used to keep her watch on a stand on her mantelpiece. The girl had only just left the room and I by chance looked at the watch and saw it was a quarter past twelve. Almost immediately afterwards the Plaintiff said "Are you awake dear." I said I was and asked her what she meant. She said "Oh you have just been in a long trance and you have told me all about yourself." I said "Indeed and how long have I been in a trance. She said "At least half an hour." I looked at the watch and saw it was just seventeen minutes past twelve and besides I had none of the peculiar faint and cold feelings which I have after having been in a trance. I asked her what I had said. She told me that I had

acknowledged that I had no property or claims to any in Russia at all. This was so absurdly false and irritating that I told her once more I should then and there cease to have anything more to do with her and that I had already for too long a time sold my soul to such a woman as she was. She answered with a look of the fiercest anger "I *will take* it back when the time comes, I have ever warned you not to turn my love to hate for I will hunt you to the death and there is no insult I will not heap upon you. You forget you are but a medium and I will say it was all by undue influence you got what you have from me. I can pay those I please to give evidence for me and you and your brat may go to the devil. When the woman who gave me birth lay on her death-bed and her husband came to say she wished to see me I said she might die like a dog by the way side and I would not move a finger to save her. So beware." I was so horror stricken at this outburst that my mouth filled with blood, as I am subject to internal haemorrhage and I was too ill even to go to my rooms. I must have fainted for when I recovered consciousness the Plaintiff was sitting near me and seemed much alarmed. She kissed me and begged me with the tears streaming down her cheeks to forgive her. She told me that Mrs. Pepper had put her up to it and also that she had been much annoyed by Henry Gibson having been bothering her for money but that I must not think anything more about what had passed.

115. After this she was "inspired" as she said "very frequently" and I now believe and charge that her so called inspirations which she dictated to me and made me write were artfully designed by her for the purpose of having me in her power I was so ill and weak at the time that for the sake of peace and quiet I used to write just what she wished.

116. From this time I grew afraid of the Plaintiff and shrank from being alone with her for she would taunt me one moment and be too loving the next and once or twice just before I left for Torquay she told me she had been going over and dating her inspirations and pretended communications.

117. On one occasion she said she would like to learn French and she requested me to write in French "Would you like to be President of the United States." I did so and was about to throw it in the fire when she had read it but to my surprise she put it into her pocket. This is but one of the many scraps of paper she had in her possession of that kind.

118. I had as hereinbefore mentioned advanced and lent to the Plaintiff the sum requisite to make up the second sum of £30,000 of her own which she had put out on mortgage. This had been done in the following manner. I had when at Hastings in February executed a power of attorney to the brokers to sell out of my stock so much as

would produce the sum of cash which she required as well as the further sum of £400 which I required for my own purposes. The brokers accordingly as I have been informed and believe raised £3,403 6s. 4d. cash by the sale of £3,755 7s. 8d. consols standing in my name which was advanced to the Plaintiff and £400 cash by the sale of £441 7s. 7d. consols also standing in my name which was for myself. She referred to this in her letter of the 13th February 1867 set forth in the 39th paragraph of the Defendant Wilkinson's Answer to which I crave leave to refer wherein she says "If you have sold out from Daniel's let me have that paper of exact amount also. If you have not I would sell out the remainder of my stock as part and not have so much of his. J. L."

119. On the 21st February 1867 the Plaintiff took me with her to the said stockbrokers and to the Bank of England where she of her own accord and without even a request from me transferred the sum of £2,290 9s. 5d. Bank £3 per Cent. Consolidated Annuities which the brokers had told her were still standing in her name into my name as Daniel Dunglass Home that being the name in which the other consols were standing. And this she did in part repayment of the sum of £3,755 7s. 8d. consols which she had borrowed of me as aforesaid leaving her still indebted to me in the sum of £1,464 18s. 3d. Bank £3 per Cent. Consolidated Annuities. The Plaintiff took away with her and kept the papers relating to this sum of £2,290 9s. 5d. consols along with my other papers and I never saw them. The Plaintiff charges in the 15th paragraph of her Bill of Complaint that she was induced by me to accompany me to the Bank of England and to transfer this sum of £2,290 9s. 5d. Bank £3 per Cent. Consolidated Annuities into my name as Daniel Dunglass Home. And that this last mentioned transfer was also made by the Plaintiff while under the influence of the ascendancy and power which she alleges I had acquired over her and was then exercising by the means in the said Bill mentioned. And she suppresses all mention of her having borrowed the said sum and more from me or from my stock a few days previously as aforesaid.

120. I deny that the Plaintiff was on the 21st February 1867 or at any other time again or in fact induced by me to accompany me to the Bank of England and transfer the sum of £2,290 9s. 5d. or some other and what sum of Bank £3 per Cent. Consolidated Annuities into my name as Daniel Dunglass Home and I make out the contrary in manner aforesaid and I deny that the last mentioned transfer was also or in fact made by the Plaintiff while under the alleged influence of the ascendancy and power which the Plaintiff now pretends that I had by the means in the said Bill mentioned or in fact acquired or was then

exercising over her mind and I shall make out the contrary by showing that this charge is as utterly without foundation as the rest of her case.

121. I had been home but a few days from Hastings when the Plaintiff told me that Mrs. Pepper had got it out of her about making over the last mortgage deed to me and that Mrs. Pepper was in a great rage about it and had said fearful things about me and wondered she was not afraid I would kill her. I again tried as I often had done to tell her that this intimacy with such a woman as she well knew Mrs. Pepper to be was unseemly but the Plaintiff used not only to have Mrs. Pepper sit with her during my absence but after I returned I used often to find the Plaintiff coming up from the kitchen. She had taken a dislike to some of my friends and used to say most horrible things of them. In short my life was a misery. I could do nothing to please her. She used to swear at me when I was so ill I scarcely knew what I was doing or where I was but I felt that I was bound to her and I had not then the moral courage to free myself. I became so ill that again she seemed to pity me and before I left for Torquay which I did on or about the 10th March 1867 she was quite herself again. She was most unfeeling at times and one evening when I was ill she said "She had made a pretty bargain in tying herself to a living corpse" and that she had been a fool in not doing as Mrs. Pepper advised "to adopt her son Joe."

122. The Plaintiff had in the months of January and February repeatedly desired me to invest £20,000 or £25,000 upon some mortgage security so as to increase my income which however she would never let me spend. I was too ill to trouble myself about it and she herself spoke to Mr. Wilkinson and desired him to get a good mortgage security for me. He accordingly procured a mortgage and while I was ill at Torquay namely on the 13th March 1867 the brokers sold out for me a sum of £21,947 17s. 6d. Bank £3 per Cent. Consolidated Annuities part of the said sum of £26,756 15s. 5d. like annuities and £6,798 17s. 4d. like annuities less the sums of £3,756 7s. 8d. and £441 7s. 7d. like annuities so sold out as aforesaid but adding the sum of £2,290 9s. 5d. like annuities replaced as aforesaid. The said Mr. Wilkinson received the proceeds of such sale amounting to £20,000 cash and on my behalf and in my name lent and advanced such last mentioned sum upon mortgage of property in Yorkshire and such sum of £20,000 has ever since been and is now invested on the security of the said mortgage. The said security has since been and is now deposited in this Court where the Plaintiff can inspect it. No part of the said sum so lent and advanced has been repaid.

123. I believe that a sum of £9,701 9s. 6d. and not a sum of £13,898 4s. 8d. Bank £3 per Cent. Consolidated Annuities being the residue or

balance of the said three sums of £26,756 15s. 5d. £6,798 17s. 4d. and £2,290 9s. 5d. like annuities after deducting from the aggregate amount thereof the said sums of £3,755 7s. 8d. like annuities lent and advanced to the Plaintiff as aforesaid and £441 7s. 7d. like annuities sold as aforesaid and also the further sum of £21,947 17s. 6d. sold out as aforesaid is still standing in my name as Daniel Dunglass Home in the books of the Governor and Company of the Bank of England. I do not threaten but I intend to sell and dispose thereof or deal therewith when this suit is terminated as it in fact belongs to me.

124. During my absence from London several letters passed between us. I have not kept copies of mine but the originals are still in the Plaintiff's possession unless she has destroyed them.

125. In a letter which she wrote and sent to me on the 17th March 1867 she says "I have had a letter from dear cousin Lady Shelley. She has been so very ill and has had rheumatic fevers and her adopted daughter Flossie has been extremely ill. She says tell Dan how very sorry we are not to have seen him in London. Do pray write to her in a *few days* she says. She never knew so very trying a winter." And further on "I am glad you like Torquay and have met with friends you like and that you enjoyed yourself yesterday in the sunshine. I hope you will enjoy many such days when you are stronger and the weather finer. Go to the Land's End and all the pretty places it will do you good to go about and make yourself acquainted with the beauties of the finest counties we have. It is an excellent chance you have now and believe me my dear Daniel your affectionate mother

"JANE LYON."

I had known Lady Shelley since 1860 and in the latter part of November 1866 I introduced her to the Plaintiff when in the course of conversation it was discovered that their fathers were second or third cousins and that Lady Shelley had the same name as the Plaintiff and comparing notes they stated that they had both been from their childhood very wonderful mediums. The Flossie alluded to is also a very wonderful medium. In the month of February 1867 the Plaintiff told me when angry with me on one occasion that she intended to make a new Will in favour of her new found relatives Lady Shelley and her family. To this I answered that she was quite welcome to do so as far as I was concerned but that as her money came principally from her husband I thought it would be just to give his relatives some of it. This only increased her anger and she said "Not one farthing." In further proof of her spite against her husband's relatives and desire to display to them "her high folks" I insert an extract from a letter written by the Plaintiff to Mrs. Tom Fellowes on the 5th December 1866

"5th December.

My dear Mrs. Fellowes,—Many thanks for your kind letters I am very well. The indisposition you allude to was very short indeed. I send by this post 'The Spiritual Magazine.' The article called 'The freed soul' was written by me and copied by my husband in 1826. You will see by this that I have not in the least changed my belief. My health is very good and I go out to dine quite often. I have been delighted to find Sir Percy Shelley's wife my cousin. He is the only son of the poet and I shall hope to see a good deal of her. Her name was Jane Gibson we were named after the same woman. She is very desirous we should pay them a long visit in January and if we can so arrange it we will."

The Plaintiff had in fact I believe composed the article alluded to in the above letter in or before the year 1826 and in the month of November or December 1866 she without consulting me caused this article to be inserted in the "Spiritual Magazine" and was afterwards much vexed "that she had neglected to publish that the authoress was the mother of the celebrated D. D. Home,"

126. On the 19th March 1867 she wrote and sent to me the following letter addressed to Torquay:—

"19th March, 1867.

"My dear Daniel,—You say your birth-day is the 20th *i.e.* to-morrow. May you see many of them and may they be *happy* days *full* of *health* and *joy.* Look forward to see my *words verified* for I write with the thought and pen of *inspiration.* Your health will flourish like the *young bay tree* full of *life* and *sap.* I will never see those far days but you will *remember* my *prophetic* prognostications herein. I am glad you sleep well and your cough is much better. You will all be well together *very soon think of that only.* The weather here is most thoroughly miserable snowing one hour sleeting the next cold and comfortless we never see the colour of the sky it is so black. My cold no better no getting out no change for me the sooner I am off to the sunshine land *if such* be better. You say that 60 miles from here the ground is covered with snow 2 and 3 feet thick but you do not say whether *east* or *west.* This you will say in your next. God bless and protect and restore you to *perfect health* and may your birthday of /68 be more auspicious and am my dear Daniel your very affectionate mother

"JANE LYON."

This is the last letter in which she signs herself mother. In the 11th paragraph of her said affidavit filed on the 27th June 1867 the Plaintiff swears that in December 1866 I induced her to believe that the spirit of her deceased husband directed or wished her to give me a birthday present of £6,000 and that she accordingly did so on the 10th December 1866 in the manner therein mentioned although she had in a letter written to the Defendant Wilkinson on the 7th December 1866 without my privity or knowledge said "On the occasion of my adopted son taking the name of Lyon I wish to give him a little surprise I intend to add six thousand pounds to the twenty-four I have already given him making a sum total of thirty thousand."

127. During my absence at Torquay the Plaintiff notwithstanding the kind expressions in her letters towards me was endeavouring to fabricate evidence against me and she attempted to bribe amongst others as I shall prove Eliza Clymow the servant in Mrs. Pepper's lodgings to swear contrary to the truth that she had never posted any letters for the Plaintiff to Mr. Wilkinson and that she had heard me this Defendant dictate letters for the Plaintiff to write. Finding that this poor girl's honesty was proof against her efforts the Plaintiff began to abuse her in her letters to me and on Tuesday the 2nd April 1867 the Plaintiff wrote and sent to me the following letter addressed to Plymouth:—

"Tuesday, 2nd April, /67.

"My dear Daniel,—I hope you like Plymouth and the Royal Hotel. You must not come to London so soon as you say. You must remain for two or three weeks longer and go to Penzance they say it is equal to the South of France and no doubt it will do you good the change of air and you are so far on your road I wish you much to see it. Miss Peal is there and this is some inducement for you to go I want to hear all about it and the beauties of Cornwall. I think as your cough is a good deal better you may venture in a few days or a week's time and either stay there or return to Plymouth if you like it. I do not wish you to come to this house as I am going to quit. I have been to No. 1 where you called once a Mrs. Loudon told me you said it was for a lady but you did not say who or she would have agreed to take me and she is very sorry she did not. However she will take me as soon as I can leave I have said I would not stay if Eliza remained she is a very *bad slut* and *story teller* I think her most dangerous. She is not any friend of yours or of mine but I do not mind that she can do us no harm and it will do you good to remain in the west until towards the latter end of this month and take great *care* of *yourself* and you will soon be WELL. J. Fellowes is in the Royal Engineers but I do not wish you to court his acquaintance his mother and Charlotte Dennison was here I did not see them I did not wish to. The latter is to be bridesmaid the marriage is to take place on the 7th of May. Charlotte is on a visit to the intended at Plymouth Miss Hodges. I mean to have my boxes away shortly but I hate to go to the house of Mrs. J. Fellowes to have them away but I will shortly. I am quite well and to-day I have began to alter some clothes and things required and am

"Yours most affectionately,

"JANE LYON."

128. Although I have kept no copies of my letters to the Plaintiff I distinctly remember writing to her about this time and mentioning that I had heard there was a skeleton hand in the Roman Catholic Chapel belonging to the Gerrards near Warrington in Lancashire which was reputed to possess miraculous powers of healing and that I thought of trying it. She tried to take advantage of this in the following letters to entrap me into some sort of admission that we ought to follow implicitly whatever spirits may dictate. I believe that she was incited to do this by the said Mr. Henry Gould Gibson who at this time visited her almost daily and he wrote at least one letter to make inquiries about me unknown to myself. The said Mr. Henry Gould Gibson also wrote a letter to me dated 1st April 1867 in which he asked me to give him permission to ask the Plaintiff to lend him £500 at £10 per cent. interest wishing me to "drop a line" to Mrs. Lyon to inform her that he would do so. I now believe and charge it to be the fact that the said Mr, Henry Gould Gibson of number 33 Mark Lane in the City of London wine merchant wrote this letter with the full knowledge and connivance of the Plaintiff for the purpose of inveigling me into some sort of implied admission that I had great influence over the Plaintiff, and that she could not manage her own business affairs without me whereas in truth and in fact I should not have dared to write nor accordingly did I write any such request to the Plaintiff.

129. On the 4th April 1867 the Plaintiff wrote and sent me the following letter:—

"Thursday, 4th April, /67.

"My dear Daniel,—You would have a letter from me when you got to Plymouth. You wish to know where James Fellowes is quartered it is at *Picklecombe Fort Devonport.* I send you his photograph. I do not dislike him I think him a very good young fellow I know nothing against him WHATEVER I *wish him well with all my heart.* It is his mother I dislike she is a d____l out and out. You astonish me respecting the hand. If the spirits think it will do you good go in God's name if not stay where you are or go to Penzance. Do the spirits communicate with you? For my part I shall let them go to sleep I never think of them or them of me. Mr. Gibson was here to-day is just left me. He said he would write to you not to come to the amateur performance and am in haste yours affectionately,

"JANE LYON."

130. Again on the 7th April 1867 the Plaintiff wrote and sent me the following letter:—

"Sunday, 7th April, /67.

"My dear Daniel,—I hope you feel better for the change you have had so like a weathercock E. W. N. South. You mean to try the spirit-hand no doubt. I am still in the same quarters for a week or two longer but have had a quantum suf although I do not blame so much Mrs. Pepper as the good for nothing servant. Would it not be better for you to go at once to France as you can now cross the Channel? No doubt it would do you good the change of air suits you. I shall not quit London for some time yet and you would return in a month or two and pack up your things at the Athenæum for I do not think it will be carried on *much* longer. Then probably I might go but 'tis quite uncertain as I think it will be better to leave well alone but I shall as usual go to the sea-side. Mr. Harrison Green sent yesterday a lot of new laid eggs for you but they would not pay for the carriage to Liverpool. I have a person working for me in my room and if you come to London soon to pack up your things previous to your going to Paris you can breakfast and dine at your lodgings or at Michell's and come to me at six o'clock. You will then have the *day to yourself* and so shall I with my workwoman. She goes at six o'clock you can then if you chose have tea a chop or steak with me. Mr. Bernard the lame gentleman lives here and creates a great deal of additional work. I wish I were out of it I fear poor Jencken is very ill. I hope you are very *much better* although you may not be *quite* well. I *sincerely believe* you *will* after you have been in France a time. Then you may say I have been to France and I *am so well* that now I have learnt to dance. I understand the private theatricals went off well and *your boy Sacha* performed *wonders* that is a piece of good news for you viz. that your boy will be a star. May you live to see him shine and am my dear Daniel your affectionately

"JANE LYON."

131. Again in another letter which she wrote to me about this time but which is merely dated Sunday night she says:—"Mr. Gibson was here last night."

132. Feeling at this time very unwell and depressed in spirits with an indistinct foreshadowing of the evil which was impending over me I wrote to her to that effect. She answered it in a mode which from her reference to my boy whom I know she by this time hated was meant to be sarcastic.

"Thursday.

"My dear Daniel,—I am very sorry to hear that you feel yourself sometimes so depressed in thought. You have no reason to be so. Look forward to brighter days when you will as I told you in a former letter be quite well it will be so. Look forward to see your son an ornament a shining star as I told you he will in all probability be. He is your son the image of yourself in every way temper and disposition. You must be proud of your son. Take care of yourself for his sake that you may live to see him grow up."

133. On the 13th April 1867 the Plaintiff wrote and sent me the following letter:—

"17A Albert Terrace, Albert Gate,
"Hyde Park, 13th April, /67.
"Saturday.

"My dear Daniel,—I am indeed very sorry that you do not seem to get much better for the excursion and change of air. You say that you are going to try the wonderful hand. I do not think you will derive benefit therefrom. I fear it is an imposture like many others. However there is no proof like trial so you might regret you did not make that when you quit Liverpool so if you get no good I trust in God you will get no harm but I think you should ask the spirits for their advice in the matter but that is too late and by this time you will know all about it. They say the spirits are not to be relied upon at all times. I wish you had gone to Penzance as I think Liverpool is far too cold for you however you should keep up your spirits. There are better days in store for you as I know by TRUE inspiration that you will get better of this and be *quite* well it may be a *little* time first but you must be looking forward until that *good* time arrives patience and resignation. A word to the wise you know may do a little good. The weather here is very changeable it is to-day rainy cold and comfortless enough to drive one into the dolefuls. I wonder if the spirit-land is any better if worse. God help them that is there. It is all to prove if we shall be able to do so. If I had been the Great Giver of all good I think I should have given *all good* not one particle of evil no *pain* no *sickness* no *sorrow* no *death* no *dark gloomy* weather all *sunshine* and joy no *storms* at sea no shipwrecks all *calm* and beautiful all spiritual no mortality no flesh no decay the earth always beautiful growing spontaneously whatever we desire delicate fruits and ever shining flowers of exquisite beauty birds of the most splendid beauty ever singing *chattering* and amusing you in fact angels themselves no labour but that of tuning your instruments and cultivating your exquisite flowers and transporting yourself to ever varying endless scenes of beauty and variety music and angelic musicians ever varying their tunes sitting on banks of flowers. Oh! could we be assured of that the sooner we are off the better Heigh for the spirit-land lay down the flesh and be off to the spirit-land lay down your bones and be off to the spirit-land. I have no time to say more.

In haste my dear Daniel yours affectionately

"JANE LYON."

134. I think this is the last letter I received before I returned to London which I did on the 22nd April 1867 and spent the evening with her. I had written to Mr Rudall to spend the evening with us for by this time I had a nervous dread of being alone with the Plaintiff who knew that for private reasons I had a horror of insanity which she took advantage of to awe me and have me still more under her control. She used to feign in her conversation as she afterwards did in her letters a singularity of manners which had been up to this time or at any rate before February quite foreign to her.

135. On my return Mrs. Lyon openly evinced her dislike to me and her hatred of my child whom she would never even see. She used also when we were alone to tell me she had me in her power and if I did not take care would make me feel it. I was still in a feeble state of health and her manner so preyed upon my mind that I was soon much worse than when I returned and Dr. Gully told the Plaintiff that I was in a very dangerous way. Then all of a sudden her former affection and kindness for a moment returned and one morning she came up saying "Oh that horrid Mrs. Pepper how she does hate you I dare say it is because you would not lend her the money she wanted. She has just been saying hat Mr. Verra had told her that I (the Plaintiff) was a fool to have given my money to a swindler like you but I told her that I had made so good an investment." I left town on the 1st or 2nd May for Malvern

136. Much correspondence passed again between us during my absence. I have not kept copies of my letters but the originals are in the Plaintiff's possession unless she has destroyed them. In the first letter which she wrote to me after my departure she said "Mr. Gibson was here last night enquiring after you. I hope you will write two or three times a week just to let me know how you progress two or three times

will suffice unless you have any subject to communicate to me as I do not always expect a *long* letter like the last but there is one thing do not forget to put day of month and residence."

137. On the 4th May 1867 she wrote me as follows:—

"Saturday, 4th May.

"My dear Daniel,—Please to return my blank cheques by *return* of *post*. You have put me to great inconvenience by taking my cheque book instead of your own which is of *no use to me* whatever. You know you got the last in my book to change. I particularly wanted to make out a cheque to-day and found I *could not* as you had taken my book and left yours. Be sure you at once return mine or as many as you have and I will immediately enclose yours in a *letter*. *Take* off *the back*. I will do the same by yours. I cannot make a cheque until I get them. In haste,

"Yours &c.

"JANE LYON."

"I hope you do feel better let me know. Perhaps it will be as well to send three or four complete with the memorandum part. I will do the same by yours. *Do not use any more of mine* which are orders. You recollect yours are blue—by bearer—and in no way proper for me. Therefore use no more of them."

I had not even seen her cheque book and by this time would not have touched it for the world. The cheque which she mentions my having cashed was for herself.

138. On the 7th May 1867 she wrote me as follows:—

"7th May, 1867.

"My dear Daniel,—I am sorry I wrote to you in such a pet respecting the cheque book I certainly was greatly annoyed to find I could not make out when I wanted one so very particularly. I thought you had taken away mine instead of your own. However I have been to the Bank to-day and had it changed for one as I usually have. I know I wrote savagely. I do not recollect what I said. Destroy it. You say you are getting stronger I am glad to hear it but you know you are to get better the spirit that you rely on says so therefore that is proof. Your sister-in-law has as you state gone to live again with her husband after a trial to divorce her. He must be a poor wretch to live with her after knowing her so well but I suppose they are both alike *pot* and *kettle*. But do not imagine you will ever get money from him to found promises upon an impossibility which you will never succeed to obtain until the moon is made of cheese and comes down upon earth to be eaten by men therefore be at *no expense* on that business for sooner will you get wings yourself and fly to him and *bite of his nose*. This is quite as likely altho' they say cows may fly but very unlikely. Mr. Hall called yesterday he and his wife goes to Paris Monday fortnight. I expect company to spend the day to-morrow therefore I wrote to put off Mrs. Riche and your boy until you come home and he will like it quite as *well* and *better* I know. Please present my regards to Dr. Gully and his sister Ellen your dear respected friend her sister if at home and believe me yours affectionately

"Jane Lyon."

139. On the 13th May 1867, she wrote and sent to me a letter addressed to Malvern where I then was in which she says:— "I am heartily glad to hear you are so much better but have little doubt of your ultimate recovery or what would the spirits' word go for? We must bid good-by to them as they have always said you had a great work to perform on earth before you departed. I wonder what it is. Are you going to bring down the moon to earth to let us see what it is made of? Then we shall see what we shall see as the showman says. With regard to the Russian money I am glad you are so sure of it. All I can say I wish you may get it" and further on "My hopes are in *eternity*. The spirits say I shall be blessed in this state. They are not to be relied upon. By the spirits I have been told many things that are far from being correct as yet."

140. Again on the 21st May 1867 she wrote and sent me the following letter:—

"Tuesday, 21st May.

"My dear Daniel,—By yours of this morning I am happy to find you are no worse also by a nice letter from your dear friend Miss E. Gully I had yesterday she gives me great hopes that you will soon be well again so to prove they spirits *true* who always say you will get quite well therefore do look forward and never dispond. You are under the care of God and excellent good friends. You are a most fortunate fellow you have been born under a fortunate planet. You were in a bad way when you left London pale and sickly when you return you will not be rosey for that does not belong to you but health will I have no doubt be depicted on your countenance and many years duration thereof."

She herself in her letter to me of the 19th March wherein she laid claim to inspiration had predicted that I would get quite well.

141. I had written to tell her that the doctors said I would be able to go to town in ten days and on the 27th May 1867 she wrote to me as follows:—

"Monday, 27 May, /67.

"My dear Daniel,—I am rather surprised to find that you are as you state viz. 'I am about *as I was'* that is to say the same as when I left London. I am indeed very sorry for that you were much better. However I still believe there is a time for all things that you will eventually get better probably never quite well but very different from what you are at present and the spirits say that you will be strong in ten days that will soon be up and then you will prove their power and veracity although I think they have not such powers. The time is not come for them to display it however the great God's will must be done we all must succumb to that sooner or later and as the world goes there is not much worth living for and if we have not health there is nothing if robbed of life's great blessing we but drag on our weary way with pain distaste and sorrow but let us look forward into that mystery of mysteries another and a better state *another world.* Oh had some power the giftie gie us to see that world as spirits see it then would our minds be set at rest I hope with sights to *make us blest.* You astonished me with the paper houses and paper boats. I wonder what next flying. I hope I shall see that before I fly off and be no more seen paper wings and paper houses to carry on our backs and set them down where we please. Oh would not that be fine. 'Over the water and over the sea and over the water to Charlie.' 'Oh for the happy days of good Queen Bess.' Mr. Rimel sent the enclosed. When you send a cheque for your subscription please put one *pound* for me as I promised him to give. Keep up your *heart.* Better days coming for you. All love to all kind friends. Yours affectionately

"JANE LYON."

142. From the 6th May 1867 the Plaintiff had in fact been taking final measures to prepare for the Chancery suit against me which by this time at latest she had resolved on. And had been in consultation with the said W. Bailey of Sloane Street for that purpose. Notwithstanding which she still wrote affectionately to me. She been exceedingly angry with me before I left town because I had been on the Committee for the French Hospital to which her enclosure in the last letter had reference and because I had subscribed ten guineas and she then said I was very lavish "with other people's money."

143. On the 30th May 1867 the plaintiff had an interview with, the said Mr. Jencken to whom she had written for the purpose. And she consulted him how she should recover from me and the Defendant Wilkinson the trust deed and mortgage security for the £30,000 which she had settled upon me as aforesaid after her decease. And she told

him that she did not wish to disturb the gifts of £24,000 and £6,000 to me but thought that she had been too lavish in bestowing on me the subsequent gift. Still she had not asked me to restore it or expressed a wish to that effect and I knew nothing of her secret design to recover it.

144. On the following day namely the 31st May 1867 she wrote and sent to me at Malvern the following letter:—

"Thursday, 31st May.

"My dear Daniel,—I am glad to hear you are better than I thought from the wording of your letter although I think you are not sufficiently well to quit the locality of your friends at Malvern from whence you will obtain if it is to be got your permanent recovery therefore I say stay where you are until your throat is better. You remember I told you to when you left do not return until you are quite well you are not required here by anyone that I am aware of therefore stay where you are required to perfect your recovery. Mr. Starling wishes he had remained longer saying it would have been better for him then I said return again. 'Ah' said he 'But now I am in London' therefore do not repent *when in London* wishing you had remained for further improvement. Get all the benefit you can from your good friends and I am sure the spirits wish you to. I saw Mr. Jencken yesterday just returned from Paris. With kind regards to your friends at Malvern yours affectionately,

"JANE LYON."

And on the 6th June 1867 she wrote and sent me the following letter:—

"17A, Albert Terrace, Albert Gate,
"Hyde Park, 6th June, /67,
"Thursday.

"My dear Daniel,—You say I will be delighted to hear you have got a frightful cold I do not see that a frightful cold will in the least benefit your disease and you said in your last 'A bad beginning makes a good end.' I think the reverse. I am sorry you have got a bad cold and am sorry you had a bad beginning for I have always been told that makes a worse end. You have not been well since I knew you. More is *the pity* for you I do PITY YOU. The spirits instead of doing you good does the reverse therefore I would *cut them* in *toto* wash your hands of them as I mean to do. They are not to be *relied* upon. I had a book sent to me last week which has made some impression on my mind. *I will not* at present make any comment or observation thereon but at a future time I will tell you what I think of it. May you GET WELL and be *happy* without spirits or spiritual power. It tends to no good. Rather the reverse. Mrs. Pepper has desired me often to request you to enclose her street-door key in a letter to me but I have *always* forgot to name it. Will you please to send it me in *your next letter?* Then I shall be done with her bother *about it.* I wish you had not taken it with you. However do send it at once. She is afraid you have lost it. Then she must she says have a new lock to her door. I have had a letter from Mrs. Senior who writes from her bed. I have answered her letter. I like her much. I do not see Mr. Starling but hope he will go to Malvern. My best regards to Dr. and Miss Gully and am yours affectionately,

"JANE LYON."

145. The book referred to in the last letter was as the Plaintiff herself afterwards informed me a book written upon spiritualism by a Frenchman named Chevalier. He advertised in this work that he had been a member of the Spiritual Athenæum hereinbefore mentioned which was untrue. And although he stated that the phenomena of spiritualism could not be and were not produced by fraud or contrivance yet he attributed them to the Evil One. He has lately I believe with the Plaintiff's permission added a printed slip or notice to the book to the effect that it was in consequence of having read this book that the present proceedings in Chancery were commenced which is also untrue as hereinbefore appears.

148. I have been informed and believe and I charge that immediately before and subsequently to writing the above letter the Plaintiff was having *séances* with true or pretended spiritual mediums.

147. On the 8th June 1867 she wrote and sent to me the following letter also addressed to Malvern where I was:—

"Saturday.

"My dear Daniel,—I am sorry you have not sent the key as I am sure I could not write stronger on that point. Now I *request again* that I may have the key on *Monday* morning it is particularly required by Mrs. Pepper as I told you in my last she requires it for a gentleman who sleeps in the house. They are she says obliged to sit up to let him in therefore *send it at once* and do not come here on Wednesday you will not see or be sufficiently well remain until you *are quite well.* Do not come on my account for I mean *carefully to avoid* any more manifestations they are *not good* and do not tend thereto. I was happier before I had any of them and am

"Yours affectionately,

"JANE LYON."

148. As I had used the latch key of her lodgings to which she referred to let myself in throughout the winter and I knew as the fact was that the latch key was not really required by any one else and observing the angry and impatient tone of her letters I concluded I had better at once return. I did so on Sunday the 9th June 1867. And at half-past eleven o'clock on the following morning (Monday the 10th June) I went to call on her. I found the outer door locked instead of being on the latch as usual and when the servant had opened the door I went to the Plaintiff's sitting-room. She appeared very glad to see me and was extremely demonstrative in her affection. She expressed sorrow that I was not looking better. I said that I was sorry that my ill health had kept me away from her. She said "Yes poor fellow they may say what they like against you but they can't deny but that you are ill and a great sufferer." She rang the bell and told the servant to bring another cup that I might have some tea. She then sat down opposite to me and looking fixedly at me said "Even if you like. Now I have not gone so far but what it can be undone." Or words to that effect. I said "What do you mean?" She answered "Oh you know well enough what I mean." I was irritated with her and remained silent and I did not know what she was offering to undo. She then said in a sneering manner that she had been seeing a great deal of Mrs. Berry and had been having a great many wonderful *séances* with her niece Emma Berry whom Mrs. Berry as she said had been urging her to adopt and that she would do so only Mrs. Berry rather stipulated that the girl should have a French governess. She also said "I have been seeing a great deal of Fred Kent lately. He is a *darling* boy. Poor fellow he has but twenty-three shillings a-week where he is but never mind I shall do something very handsome for him. He is *very fond* of me. "She then went on to say she had also seen a great deal lately of her friend Mrs. Sims the photographer and had been having *séances* with her adding "I have found out why Mrs, Sims hated you all the winter. Because you did nothing for her." I asked why I should do so. She answered that Mrs. Simms claimed to have introduced me this Defendant to the Plaintiff. I said that was not so as the Plaintiff well knew that she had herself made enquiries about me of Mrs. Burns and had then introduced herself to me. She ordered me not to come again to the house till she sent for me. I told her I hoped she would do so the next day for breakfast and that then perhaps she would be able to tell me what on earth I had done to irritate her. For in truth I could not accuse myself of having been wanting in gratitude or kindness towards her. The said Mrs. Berry who lets furnished houses herself told me on the 17th June 1867 that she had urged the Plaintiff to go into Chancery and that I this Defendant had

better run away to America. The said Mrs. Berry claims to be a wonderful medium.

149. Not hearing from the Plaintiff and not having any unkind feelings towards her I wrote and sent the following letter to her the next morning:—

"22, Sloane Street,
"June 11th, 1867.

"My darling Mother,—I am sorry not to have heard from you this morning I was in hopes your better judgment would not allow you to be influenced by those about you. A few months ago it would not have been so. I console myself with the idea that it is but a momentary thing. I will not attempt to influence you in the least I never have done so and will not now. I am packing up as the Dr. intends to send me abroad to some of the German baths. I wish you would go with me I will pay all expenses. It would be such a deep pleasure to have you with me. My health is so delicate that ere long there must be a change for the worse or better. And if I should pass from the earth I know you would be sorry to think that any want of kindness from you did me harm. I will not disguise from you or from any one that such would be the case. It is not the simple fact of being so generous and noble in action to me as you have been that constitutes true kindness. It is more fully shown in every-day life. I took your name because I could in no other way show my esteem and respect for you. I felt that I was taking upon myself a solemn undertaking in the sight of God and man when I called you by the sacred name of mother. My feelings are all unchanged and I have done my duty as well as my feeble health would allow. I have been out of London more than I wished but I have ever asked you to join me. More I could not do Praying God to bless and His good angels to guard you.

"Believe me ever your affectionate Son,
"D. H. LYON."

150. On the same day she wrote and sent me the following letter in answer:—

"17A, Albert Terrace, Hyde, Park,
"11th June, /67.

"My dear Daniel,—I have this instant got a letter from you viz. that you are packing up to go away I perfectly approve of your determination I think it will do you good and be assured I wish you every enjoyment and that of health in particular for without that you cannot enjoy anything and I hope with the blessing of God you will perfectly recover your health and strength. I should be glad to see you ere you go. Will you appoint this evening at 8 o'clock or to-morrow at 12 o'clock I shall be at home and am my dear Dan

"Yours affectionately,

"JANE LYON."

"D. H. Lyon, Esq."

151. I wrote a few hurried words to say I would be with her at eight o'clock and went accordingly I found her very pale and she did not shake hands with me as I went in. She said "Are you going abroad at once?" I told her I was not as I could not do so before packing up all my pictures and things and that would require some time even after I heard from the doctor who had not yet given me his permission. She then said "Now Daniel I wish you to return me that trust deed as I wish to have it." I said "Certainly mother and you know I never asked you for it." She said "It is just as well for you to do so quietly for I have made up my mind to expose the whole swindle. You first sought me and then surrounded me with a set of people whom I now find to be a pack of well-known swindlers but I intend to expose the whole thing. I have written for Wilkinson to bring that deed and I will burn it before his eyes. You may come with him if you like and I will tell you both what I think of you. And you may bring all your friends and I will tell them the same. Mrs Pepper has been right to caution me and to keep the door locked lest I should be killed in my bed." I sat dumb with astonishment. She then told me that Mrs. Parks was her friend and had seen her almost every day and did so pity her for being forced to make her Will. I said "How could that be when I was not in the house when you wrote the letter concerning it." She said "She had been told to go into Chancery and take everything from me and give it to the others who were more deserving and that Fred gent' was an angel in comparison to a sickly man like me." I said "Now listen to me. Vituperation is quite unnecessary. I would willingly have given you all you asked me as you gave it me of your own free will and accord but you have closed my hands by making these vile charges against me and my friends." The Plaintiff became still more abusive in her language and I left her.

152. As she had on previous occasions repented of her ebullitions of ungovernable temper towards me. I wrote and sent her the following letter of which I kept a copy:—

"June 12th.

"My darling Mother,—I hope you are quite well is morning. I have not yet heard from Dr. Gully to know what I am to do about going abroad. I do wish my health could have been stronger. I am very sorry to have been away from you so much I hope the days of sunshine will come soon.

"Your affectionate Son,

"D. H. LYON.

"I am so ill that I shall go into the country for a few days. My address will be:

"Stockton House,
"Fleetpond, near Winchfield,
"Hants."

153. To this I received no reply and I wrote and sent her the following letter of which I have kept a copy on the 16th June 1867 and she received it on the same day although by mistake it was dated the 17th June. I should most certainly not have done so had I known that she was really meditating hostile proceedings.

"22 Sloan Street,
"June 17th, 1867.

"My dear Mother,—When I left you on Tuesday last I told you I should consult with my friends before I took any steps. I have now done so and they one and all declare I should do no such thing as give up a deed which had been signed by you and could be proved to have been done when you were in a sane mind and uninfluenced by any one. Now dear mother comes for me to have my say in the matter. You gave me the deed of your own free will. The letters you wrote to Mr. Wilkinson were with one or two exceptions written when I was not in the house as I can prove by the servant who took them to the post. It was then your own goodwill and kindly feeling which prompted all this. Your mind is changed and you wish it back. Nothing in the world more natural. Unknown to anyone I have decided and now write to say that I will give it you on the acceptation of the following conditions:—

"1stly—You will write me a kind letter as you have ever done in which you will acknowledge my personal honesty and that of the friends who have been introduced to you since I knew you. This is but fair to me and my friends both ladies and gentlemen.

"2nd—You will give me your written permission to resume my name of Home without that of Lyon.

"3rdly—You will return to me all my valuable jewels laces &c. with the exception of the two brooches I had made for you. On my part I will return to you the two rings you gave me and anything else I may have of that kind.

"4thly—You will leave me and mine in undisputed possession of the thirty thousand pounds you in your noble generosity and kindness of heart gave me. I would like to have you refund the sum you borrowed last winter but will leave that quite for you to decide. I have between thirty and forty letters of your writing to me at different intervals all of them breathing a spirit of perfect kindness and good feeling and most decided in character. In some of them you call me your 'darling boy' and sign yourself 'your affectionate mother.' I have also a list of thirty ladies and gentlemen of high position both by birth and breeding who will come forward as they already declare their willingness to do who will prove that you were perfectly sane and also the affectionate manner you ever spoke of me to them as indeed you had no occasion to do otherwise. I write this letter at the instigation of no one. I know indeed my kind friends would rather prevent me from sending it. In all human probability I shall not have long to remain on earth and I wish to have no unkind feelings towards any one and to you I would not have an unkind thought yet I must act with decision in a case like this. My name in every country where I have been stands high for honesty and I could not allow a taint of that kind to attach itself to me now when God knows I deserve it so little.

"I will if agreeable to you see your lawyer on Tuesday at 12 o'clock at my rooms 22 Sloane Street when I will remit to him the trinkets you gave me if the conditions herein named are accepted. Hoping you are well and praying God to bless and His good angels to guard you.

"Believe me ever affectionately and gratefully yours,

D. H. LYON.

151. I was wholly ignorant at the time when I sent her the above letter that she had filed her Bill in Chancery making charges against me and my friends. I was in very feeble health at the time and required rest and freedom from anxiety. I had no ill-feeling towards the Plaintiff and I wrote the above letter without taking advice of any one and for the sake of peace and quiet. Had I been aware of such Bill having been filed I most certainly would have scorned to make or accept any offer of compromise unaccompanied by a complete withdrawal of every one of such charges.

152. On the 13th June 1867 as I have since been informed and believe the said Mr. Henry Gould Gibson introduced the Plaintiff to

her present solicitors. On the 15th June the Plaintiff filed her Bill and on the 17th obtained on an ex parte application a writ of Ne exeat regno against me. This was granted to her upon two affidavits of hers the one filed on the 15th June 1867 and the other on the 17th June 1867. In the first of these she says "I am informed by the said Defendant in private letters which he has written to me during the last three or four days that he has been recommended by his physician Dr. Gully to go at once to the German Baths for the benefit of his (the said Defendant's) health and in one of these letters (written to me on the 11th day of June instant) he says that he is 'packing up' and I verily believe that he intends forthwith to go abroad in accordance with such advice as aforesaid." And in the other of the said affidavits that was filed on the 17th June 1867 she says "Referring to the statements contained in the Bill filed by me in this cause I say that the sum of £20,000 obtained by the Defendant Daniel Dunglass Home alias Daniel Home Lyon under the circumstances in the said Bill stated is now justly due and owing in equity from the said Defendant to me and is as I verily believe in danger of being lost to me by reason of the intention of the said Defendant to go abroad out of the jurisdiction of this Honorable Court of which intention the said Defendant has informed me in his private letters as stated in the affidavit already made by me in this cause. And I say that if the said Defendant is allowed to get out of the country I verily believe I shall lose the whole of the said debt."

153. In her said affidavits she suppressed all mention of my having in the letter from which she quoted desired her to accompany me. She suppressed all mention of her said letter to me of the 11th June 1867 in which she had approved of my determination to go. She suppressed all mention of our conversation at our last interview on the same day in which I had told her that it would take some time for me to pack up my pictures and things after I had heard from the doctor who had not yet given me his permission. She suppressed all mention of my said letter of the 12th June 1867 wherein I told her that I had not yet heard from Dr. Gully what I was to do about going abroad and gave her my country address. And finally she also suppressed all mention of my letter received by her on the 16th June as she has since stated in the 22nd paragraph of her said affidavit in this suit filed on the 27th June 1867 in which letter I had told her that I was ready to meet her lawyer at my rooms in Sloane Street on the Tuesday which would be the 18th June 1867. And upon the writ of Ne exeat regno so obtained upon such suppressions and misstatement as aforesaid I dangerously ill as the Plaintiff knew me to be was ignominiously arrested at the house of a friend on the 18th June 1867 and thrown into Whitecross Street Prison

whence I was liberated the following day on my depositing in Court the deeds in my possession. The shock to my system was so great that I became delirious for four days and I have found it necessary to consult with five physicians. And my state of health was such that for nearly three months my reason was tottering and I was wholly unable to give proper or in fact any instructions to my legal advisers. And when I applied for time to answer I had to bear the further indignity at the Plaintiff's instigation of being examined in the presence of a lawyer's clerk by a strange doctor who condescended to insult me in his certificate.

154. I charge that the Plaintiff in order to have me as she fancied more completely in her power has from time to time since the month of February 1867 in the conversations and some of the correspondence with me feigned insanity. And that on the 17th June 1867 she told Mr. Perdicaris that she had been induced by spiritual communications given through the said Mrs. Berry her niece Emma Berry, Fred Kent and Mrs. Sims at the House of the said Mrs. Berry to believe that she had been deceived by the familiar spirit of me this Defendant and that she had been advised at Mrs. Berry's to go to law at once and endeavour to recover the money she had given me. And she said to him that she hated my child and that she would rather be locked up in a lunatic asylum than have any of her money go to the child. She also complained of her disappointment to me this Defendant on account of my ill health and frequent absences and asked him whether it was not outrageous that she should be tied to a dying man. And she asked him further whether I this Defendant was willing to compromise the affair and if so upon what terms. He told her as the fact was that he was not in a position to answer those questions and that it was as her friend and not mine that he had called. She never mentioned to the said Mr. Perdicaris that she had already filed a Bill and obtained a writ for my arrest. The said Mr. Perdicaris had much difficulty in seeing the Plaintiff as the said Mrs. Pepper the landlady falsely told him and all those who called upon the Plaintiff at the time to ask the meaning of her sudden change against me that the Plaintiff could not or would not see them.

155. If the Plaintiff intends to allege or pretend or insinuate at the hearing that she is now really mad or of weak or of unsound mind let it he plainly stated in her Bill as well as the time when she became so in order that I may be prepared with evidence on the subject. In that event it must be explained how the infamous charges contained in her said affidavits against Mr. S. C. Hall, Mr. Wilkinson and myself came to be

deliberately inserted and repeated upon the mere assertion of a woman alleged to be mad or of weak or of unsound mind.

156. Since the institution of this suit the Plaintiff has attended *séances* of real or pretended mediums and has tried to convert others to spiritualism. And yet the Plaintiff speaks in her Bill and affidavits as if she treated the whole of spiritualism as an imposture.

157. I have been informed and I believe and charge it to be the fact that the Plaintiff in connivance with the said Mrs. Berry has caused Emma Berry the niece to leave the country in order to prevent her being examined upon the matters mentioned in this Answer.

158. On the 23rd June, 1867 after the institution of this suit and my arrest under the circumstances hereinbefore described the Plaintiff received from the artist and still retains a miniature of herself wearing a lace shawl of my late wife which she had in January ordered him to paint as a present for me. And on the 24th June she acknowledged the receipt of it and lest she should be called upon to pay for it described it as "the miniature ordered by Daniel." This observation she interpolated in her letter as an after thought. And the Bill for the picture was accordingly sent in to me on the 3rd July 1867.

159. I submit my case with confidence to the righteous judgment of the Court of Equity being fully persuaded that here at least no prejudices will be allowed to obstruct me in the vindication of my own character and of the honour of my friends who have been so wickedly and wantonly assailed.

F. Kelly.

Sworn at No. 32, Lincoln's Inn-fields, in the County of Middlesex, this fourth day of November, 1867,

Before me,

Wm. Williams,

A London Commissioner to administer Oaths in Chancery.

D. D. Home.

Between JANE LYON, Widow.. Plaintiff.

AND

DANIEL DUNGLASS HOME and WILLIAM MARTIN WILKINSON.

Defendants.

THE ANSWER of WILLIAM MARTIN WILKINSON, one of the above-named Defendants, to the Bill of Complaint of the above-named Plaintiff.

IN ANSWER to the said Bill, I, WILLIAM MARTIN WILKINSON, say as follows:—

1. I have read with great surprise the Bill filed by the Plaintiff and her two first affidavits in this suit. I have throughout my connection with her business acted with such care and anxious endeavours to protect her against injuring herself by giving away her property without the fullest determination on her part and I have remonstrated so fully with her on many occasions and have put before her so clearly the legal and other consequences of what she was doing that I thought it impossible for her to make any charge against me whatever change might come over her own mind as to the propriety of the gifts she made from time to time to the other Defendant. The other Defendant has a perfect right to the name Home-Lyon having taken that name at the request of the Plaintiff but after the Plaintiff's studiously offensive conduct towards him I prefer to describe him by the name of Home.

The first communication I had with her was on the 9th November 1866 when I received from her a letter of that date. She had at that time on the 11th October previously given to the Defendant Home £24,000. I received the letter from her by post of which the following is a copy:—

Strictly private.

"Dear Sir,—I wish you to draw up a Will, in the name of Jane Lyon, widow of Charles Lyon, of Wooth Grange, Bridport, Dorset, making sole heir, my adopted son, Daniel Dunglass Home son of William Home and Elizabeth Macneil his wife, the said Daniel Dunglass Home who will take the name of Daniel Lyon and the arms of Lyon, quartered with the Gibsons of Northumberland, being my own armorial bearings, the said Daniel Lyon my adopted son, to be as I before said, sole heir, residuary legatee, of all such estates, property real, and personal, I may or may become possessed, you will have the kindness, dear sir, to make this my last Will and testament, so binding, and precise, in all its legal formalities, that there cannot be any possibility of disputing the claims of my adopted son, as sole heir and executor; on Monday next, at half-past four, Monday being the twelfth of November, you will bring me the Will, when after reading, I will be prepared, to sign it in the presence of Witnesses.

"I am, dear Sir, yours very faithfully,

"JANE LYON."

"18, Westbourne Place,
"November 9th, 1866."

2. On the same day I wrote her a letter and received an answer in her handwriting of which the following are copies:—

"44, Lincoln's Inn Fields, London, W. C.
"9th Novr., 1866.

"Dear Madam,—I beg to acknowledge the receipt of your letter giving me instructions for your Will, and I will have it prepared, and ready to submit to you for your approval on Monday at ½ past 4 as you request.

"I should have been glad to have seen you before completing the Will, in order that I might have enquired of you the amount of benefit you are giving by the Will, and also whether there are not any relatives to whom you might think it right to give legacies.

"The Will however can at any time be revoked or added to by a Codicil.

"I am, dear Madam, yours faithfy.,

"W. M. WILKINSON."

"Mrs. Lyon,
"18, Westbourne Place, W."

————

"18, Westbourne Place,
"10th November, '66.

"Dear Sir,—I beg to say as my husband did not mention any of his relations in his Will, I can see no plausible reason why I should do so. Please to leave no blanks in the Will you make, it is not requisite.

"And am, yours faithfully,

"JANE LYON."

3. Upon this I had the Will prepared as follows as appears by my draft:—

WILL OF MRS. JANE LYON.

This is the last Will and testament of me Jane Lyon of 18 Westbourne Place in the county of Middlesex widow of the late Charles Lyon of Wooth Grange Bridport Dorset esquire. I devise and bequeath all the real and personal estate to which I shall be entitled at the time of my decease or over which I shall at the time of my decease have a general power of appointment or disposition by Will unto my adopted son Daniel Dunglass Home of 22 Sloane Street Chelsea esquire his heirs executors administrators and assigns respectively for his and their own absolute use and benefit nevertheless as to estates vested in me upon trusts or by way of mortgage subject to the trusts and equities affecting the same respectively and I hereby declare it to be my wish that the said Daniel Dunglass Home shall take upon himself and be called by the surname of Lyon [only] and shall thenceforth style and write himself in all letters deeds and instruments and upon all occasions whatsoever by that surname and shall also use and bear the arms of Lyon [only] quartered as the same are now quartered with the arms of the Gibsons of Northumberland as the same are now used and borne by me. I appoint the said Daniel Dunglass Home sole executor of this my Will and thereby revoke all other testamentary writings,

In witness &c. November 12th 1866.

Attested by Thos. HAWKESLEY, M.D.,

H. A. RUDALL,

W. M. WILKINSON.

4. On the 12th November I called on her with the Will intending fully to satisfy myself as to her competency in the first place to make a Will at all as I considered her extraordinary wish to benefit largely a person who was so recently unknown to her required me to act with the greatest caution. I accordingly began the conversation with general subjects connected with Northumberland and Durham and the families there. I found her memory excellent and her whole manner and conversation giving evidence of a very strong-minded woman. She asked me to show her the Will which I did and read over to her one copy whilst she read the other. I asked her about her family and whether or not they were dependent upon her and she informed me they were well provided for that her late husband's sister Mrs. Clutterbuck was of considerable age and an invalid and was wealthy and that all her husband's relatives were well off and did not require her assistance and that moreover neither she nor her late husband had ever cared much for any of them excepting his said sister. I asked her if she had already made any Will and she said she had, but she did not say to

whom she had left her money nor how much she had but she said it was considerable. I said to her "Well you must before have been satisfied to leave your property to some one or more of your family and now that you have so suddenly become acquainted with Mr. Home who was a stranger to you a month ago it does not seem right to give him all and them nothing they will be sure to be greatly disappointed and it is a pity to leave it so." She repeated that she did not now intend to leave them anything as she had determined to adopt Mr. Home and it was the happiest thing that had ever happened to her and that she had been living so much by herself with no one to care for her that she now found the greatest comfort in thinking that she could have him as her son and have him always with her. I reminded her of what she had already done for him which was so much more than enough and that she might be disappointed with him or he with her and that as the property had come from her husband it would not be proper to give it away from his relatives. She would hardly let me argue the case with her and said she was quite able to do as she liked and she was determined to leave it to him especially as she had no injunctions from her husband as to the way she should deal with her property. I asked her in the most pointed way if what she was doing was in consequence of any spiritual control or orders and she said it was not but was her own unbiased wish and determination. I mentioned to her that I was bound to ask her all these questions and to satisfy myself that she was under no control or improper influence. She told me that she had been a believer in spiritualism all her life and that she could not remember a time when she did not have wonderful things happen to herself of that kind and that the subject was therefore not new to her. I told her that if she were to act upon any such reasons in making her Will in Mr. Home's favour she would be doing a great injustice for that the truth and identity of spiritual communications could never be depended on. She assured me in the most positive manner that in what she was doing she was not influenced by any such reasons but that she had taken the greatest liking to Mr. Home and found him all that she could wish and it was a delight to her to find that she could make such a good use of her money. I asked her if she would not wait but she said she had that afternoon destroyed her former Will and pointing to the fire she said "It is nothing but ashes now and I must make my Will now as I wish." I told her that as I was a friend of the other Defendant it would be much more satisfactory to me if she would advise with some other Solicitor but she said she was perfectly satisfied with me and would not go to any one else and that I had cautioned her in every way that any one else could and she quite understood what she was about and was a good woman of business. I said everything I could think of to her to put her on her guard and prevent her from making the Will at all in his favour till she knew more of him and to employ another Solicitor but she was so energetic and determined that I could make no impression on her. Shortly after Dr. Hawkesley and Mr. Rudall came and I repeated the same in their presence omitting only the particulars as to the Will she was making. Ultimately she said there was nothing more to prevent her signing the Will and it was done in duplicate. The other Defendant was not in the room at any part of the time and only came in after the Will had been signed and put away. Before I left I asked her what she would do with the Wills and suggested that she might keep one and leave the other at her bankers. She hesitated a moment and said "No please to take them both yourself and keep them safely." I said "I had better take only the copy at all events and you keep the other." But she refused and put both copies into my hand and I brought them away with me. The next morning I made a memorandum which is as follows:—

"13th Nov. 1866, 10 a. m.

MRS. LYON'S WILL.—Yesterday at ¼ p. 4 I called on Mrs. Lyon at 18 Westbourne Place and had a quarter of an hour's conversation with her on indifferent subjects principally as to her acquaintance with Northumberland and Durham. Then she told me that Dr. Hawkesley and another gentleman were coming shortly, and I had better read over her Will. I then produced the Will in duplicate and read one copy. She said she feared the words would not include property she might afterwards acquire which might be considerable. She desired me to strike out the word "only" twice, so that Mr. Home might be Daniel Home Lyon. I asked her again if there were no relatives or friends whom she would like to benefit, she said no. I pressed her 5 or 6 times on this point, and she refused. She said her husband had told her that he would not indicate any mode of dealing with the property he was leaving her and that he wished it to be entirely her own to do with as she pleased. I reminded her that she had known Mr. Home a very short time and that she was giving him a very large benefit, and that certainly there were some of her connexions who would be disappointed. She said, "Yes, they will, but this is the way in which I choose to leave it."

Dr. Hawkesley shortly after came, and soon Mr. Rudall. In the presence of both I repeated the substance of the above excepting that I did not indicate what was done for Mr. Home, but asked if she did not wish to include any others than were mentioned. I also asked if she had any Solicitor whom she would consult as well as me. She said she had none, and there was no occasion for any but me. The Will then executed and attested.

W. M. W.

5. A few days afterwards the Defendant Home desired me to prepare a deed announcing his change of name. I had ascertained at the Herald's College that it could not be done by Royal Warrant I sent him a draft of the deed which the Plaintiff informed me she had read over and approved of and wished it to be carried but at once.

6, The following is a copy of the deed:—

DEED POLL.

To all to whom these presents may come I Daniel Dunglas Home of 22 Sloane Street in the county of Middlesex esquire send greeting whereas Mrs Jane Lyon the widow of the late Charles Lyon esquire of Wooth Grange Bridport in the county of Dorset has adopted me as her son and has desired that I should take and use the name of *Lyon* as my last and principal surname in lieu of or in addition to the name of *Home* and to omit the name of *Dunglas.* Now therefore know ye that I the said Daniel Dunglas Home do hereby for myself and my heirs publicly adopt assume and take for me and them for ever hereafter the name of Lyon as a surname in lieu of and in addition to that of Home and I do declare that my name from henceforth will be and is DANIEL HOME LYON and that all and every acts deeds and assurances done and executed by me in the name of *Lyon* shall be as valid and effectual against or for me as if the same had been done and executed in the name of Daniel Dunglas Home.

IN WITNESS whereof I the said Daniel Dunglas Home have hereunto set my hand and seal this third day of December A.D. 1866.

D. D. HOME.

Signed sealed and delivered by the above named Daniel Dunglas Home in the presence of

W. J. WILKINSON,
44, Lincoln's Inn Fields.

7. Mrs. Lyon had without any previous communication with me on the subject sent me a message through the Defendant Home soon after the date of her Will that she would be glad if I could find a mortgage security for her for £30,000. She had resided many years in the north of England and I heard of a security in the neighbourhood she had lived in and where the family of the principal persons in the firm were known to her. She wanted to have £5 per cent. for the money. Having been

applied to for £25,000. I wrote her the following letter omitting the parties' names and particulars which might be injurious to the borrowers.

> "44, Lincoln's Inn Fields, London, W. C.
> "4th December, 1860.

"Dear Mrs. Lyon,—I have now been applied to for a sum of £25,000 on mortgage, upon a security which although not of the usual marketable description, is yet one which for safety, could not, I believe, be improved.

"It consists of 20 acres of land valued at £1,000 an acre at _____ in Yorkshire, upon which furnaces and works have been erected, and only one year in operation, at a cost of £75,000; so that the value of the whole is about £100,000.

In addition to this there is the security of the gentleman to whom the property belongs, and whose security alone would be more than ten times sufficient—

"The interest to be paid half yearly to the bankers of the lender.

"If you merely look to the security for the repayment of the money, and the punctual payment of interest in the meantime, I believe this would be certain, and I could confidently recommend it, so far as I have been informed at present, and if on the necessary investigation, it should turn out in all respects as represented I shall be glad to know what you think of it and remain,

> "Dear Mrs. Lyon,
> Yours very truly,
> "W. M. WILKINSON."

"Mrs. Lyon,
    "17A, Albert Terrace, Knightsbridge."

8. The next day the 6th December she called on me to speak about the mortgage and I told her all I could about it and she determined to have it if the title and value were satisfactory but said that if it was good for £30,000 she would much prefer that sum to a smaller. On the 8th December I received from her the following letter which was the first intimation I had received of the intention therein expressed:—

> "17A, Albert Terrace, Albert Gate, Hyde Park,
> "7th December, 1866.

"My dear Mr. Wilkinson,—On the occasion of my adopted son taking the name of Lyon I wish to give him a little surprise. I intend to add Six thousand pounds to the Twenty-four I have already given him, making a sum total of Thirty thousand; will you kindly prepare a deed thoroughly legal in every respect and let the previous sum which I gave him on the 11th October be included so that there can be no after difficulty about the whole proceeding.

"I am, dear Mr. Wilkinson, yours very truly.
"Jane Lyon."

9. The same day I wrote and sent her the following letter:—

"44, Lincoln's Inn Fields, London, W. C.
"8th December, 1866.

"Dear Mrs. Lyon,—In carrying out your wishes as expressed in your letter of yesterday, I shall be glad to know if it is your desire to make a transfer of Consols of the value of £6,000 cash, or in what other way do you wish it to be carried out. If you wish to make a transfer, it will only be necessary to give directions to the brokers when it will be convenient to you to go to the bank, and I can prepare a deed expressing your intention of giving him the money, and include it in the former sum also.

"I remain, dear Mrs. Lyon, yours faithfully,
"W. M. Wilkinson."

"Mrs. Lyon."
"17A, Albert Terrace, Albert Gate, S. W."

I received from her the following letter which I proceeded to act upon by having the deed prepared:—

"17A, Albert Terrace, Albert Gate, Hyde Park,
"9th December, 1866.

"Dear Sir,—It is my intention to make a transfer of Consols to the value of £6,000 *cash*, and you can if you please, prepare a *Legal* deed, expressing my intention, of giving him *Daniel Home Lyon*, the money above, including the former sum of £24,000 was transferred of the 11 October, and the £6,000 will be transferred to-morrow, 10th December, 1866.

"I am, dear Sir, yours very truly,
"Jane Lyon."

"W. M. Wilkinson, Esq."

10. I wrote to her on the 11th December with the draft of the deed the following letter:—

"44, Lincoln's Inn Fields, London, W C.
"11th December, 1866.

"Dear Mrs. Lyon,—I have now made a draft of the intended deed in favour of Mr. A. H. Lyon according to the directions contained in your letter, and I send it to you that you may look it over, and see that it is according to your wishes.

"I wish to bring clearly before you that in making the gifts of £30,000, which you have done, you have given it to him absolutely, and without power of revocation, and as I have known Mr. Lyon so long and so intimately, I shall best do my duty to you by suggesting that you should have some other legal advice in carrying out the business, if you think it necessary.

"I remain, dear— Mrs. Lyon, yours very truly,

"W. M. WILKINSON."

"Mrs. Lyon."

On the same day she returned the draft to me approved and sent me the following letter:—

"17A, Albert Terrace, Albert pate, Hyde Park,
"11th December, 1866.

"Dear Mr. Wilkinson,—I am perfectly *satisfied* with legal advice, and wish for *no other* adviser in respect to the transfer deed of £30,000 which I give *permanently* to my adopted son, D. H. Lyon, Esq.

"And am, &c., &c., &c.,

"JANE LYON."

After the word "children" at the end of the 9th line of the deed I had inserted in the draft the words "And all my husband's family and connections are well provided for." These words she struck out and put in the margin "I, Jane Lyon, have drawn my pen over this; I do not approve of such insertion." She afterwards told me that she had struck out the words because she did not know but what some one of them might appear and say he was poor enough to have some of her money.

11. On the 12th of December I wrote to her a letter of which the following is a copy:—

"44, Lincoln's Inn Fields, London, W. C.
"12th Decr. 1866.

Dear Mrs. Lyon,—I will call on you if possible this afternoon about ¼ p. 4, with the deed for your signature.

Yours faithfully,

"W. M. WILKINSON."

"Mrs. Lyon,
        "17A, Albert Terrace."

I went to her according to this appointment and on my reaching the house she said she was very glad to see me alone as she wished to have some important conversation with me. I produced the deed of gift and read the whole over to her she looking at the deed and I reading from the draft and she then executed and I attested it. Then she commenced by saying that the more she saw of Daniel the more she liked him and it was the greatest happiness to her to have him about her—that there was no chance of her making any alteration in her Will and that she was desirous of doing as her husband had done towards her all she could to save the duty in case of her death. She asked me what the duty would be and I told her £10 per cent. She said that her husband had transferred all his mortgages to her so that there was hardly any probate duty to pay and she had determined to give him the further sum of £30,000 and to have the mortgage deed made out in his name. I told her that the mere question of saving legacy duty was not to be considered against the all important question of divesting herself of her property and that it was impossible to say that she might not afterwards regret giving so large a sum to one whom she had known so short a time. I repeated also what I had before said about her relatives having the first claim on her and she said she was determined to give nothing to them adding that neither she nor her husband had ever liked them in consequence of some old family quarrel which compelled him to sell an estate to which he was much attached and that she had no sympathy with them except Mrs. Clutterbuck.

I also urged upon her that she had already given the Defendant Home so large a sum and placed him in such a position as was only to be equalled in novels and romances and that a man like him with £30,000 had as much as he could possibly make a good use of. That I saw no occasion but the contrary for increasing it and that I would rather give money to hospitals than to make such a gift after what she had already done for him. She said she would do it and desired me to have the mortgage deed made out in his name. I asked her if she were desirous of doing this in consequence of any spirit communications for that if so I could have nothing to do with it on any such ground. She said that she was not influenced by anything but the intention of placing him in an independent position and saving the legacy duty as she was satisfied she should never change her mind. I told her that the legacy duty was not worth thinking of. That she ought to act entirely and independently on her own judgment and that it was never wise to give away much during one's life and she had already given an unheard of sum which was more than enough for all the Defendant's wants. She said she had considered it in every way and wished it to be done and that I was very right to give her the warnings I had done but she would take the consequences. I then told her there was no occasion to come to a conclusion now as the deed would not be ready for some time and she must consider it in the meantime. Soon afterwards the Defendant came in and nothing more was said about it. We dined and spent the evening together.

12. The following is a copy of the deed which she executed on that day in my presence and I attested her execution of it:—

DECLARATION

As to Gift of £24,000 Cash and the transfer of £6,798 17s. 4d. Consols.

To all to whom these presents shall come I Jane Lyon of No. 17A Albert Terrace Albert Gate Hyde Park in the County of Middlesex the widow and relict of Charles Lyon late of Wooth Grange Bridport in the County of Dorset Esquire deceased. Send greeting whereas under and by virtue of the last Will and testament of my said late husband Charles Lyon Esquire deceased I am entitled to a large fortune in money and securities for my own absolute use and benefit free from any trust or condition imposed thereon by his add Will or otherwise howsoever. And whereas I have no children and whereas I have been minded and desirous to take and adopt Daniel Dunglas Home of 22 Sloane Street Hyde Park aforesaid as my son. And whereas with my sanction and at my desire and request the said Daniel Dunglas Home has executed a deed poll or instrument in writing bearing date the third day of December instant and the same is intended to be enrolled as of record in Her Majesty's High Court of Chancery whereby the said Daniel Dunglas Home declared that he had taken the surname of "Lyon" in lieu and instead of "Home" and that in future he intended to be called and known as "Daniel Home Lyon." And whereas I the said Jane Lyon being desirous of placing him in a position of independence suitable to his rank and position in life as my adopted son and with a view to that end on the eleventh day of October last I gave to the said Daniel Home Lyon the sum of twenty-four thousand pounds cash. And whereas in further pursuance of such desire and on the occasion of his having publicly taken my name on the tenth day of December instant I caused to be transferred from my own name in the books of the Governor and Company of the Bank of England into the old names of Daniel Home

Lyon the sum of £6,798 17s. 4d. Three Pounds per Cent. Consolidated Bank Annuities equivalent to the further sum of six thousand pounds cash. And whereas it was my intention in making the said respective gift and transfer as aforesaid and it is my present wish and intention absolutely and irrevocably to vest in the said Daniel Home Lyon for himself his executors administrators and assigns the absolute use and enjoyment of the moneys thereby respectively given and transferred as aforesaid. Now know ye that in further evidence of such my desire and intention and to remove all doubts suspicions and controversies in that behalf. I the said Jane Lyon do hereby for myself my heirs executors and administrators freely absolutely and irrevocably declare that I have made the said gift and transfer of my own will and pleasure only and without any influence control or interference of the said Daniel Home Lyon or of any other person and that the said Daniel Home Lyon his executors administrators and assigns shall stand possessed of and be entitled to the said sums of Twenty-four thousand pounds and the said Three pounds per Cent. Consolidated Bank Annuities so representing the sum of six thousand pounds by me transferred as aforesaid for his and their own absolute use benefit and enjoyment without any reservation condition trust or purpose whatsoever. As witness my hand and seal this twelfth day of December One thousand eight hundred and sixty-six.

JANE LYON.

Signed, sealed, and delivered by the above-named Jane Lyon, in the presence of W. M. Wilkinson, Solicitor, 44, Lincoln's Inn fields.'

13. On the 21st December 1866 I wrote to her as follows:—

"44, Lincoln's Inn Fields, London, W. C.
"21 December, 1866.

"My dear Mrs. Lyon,—I have now had the examination of the title to the property at _____ together with the plans, &c., and I find all to be satisfactory. I have also placed the plans and statement of the property to be mortgaged in the hands of Mr. May, of Great George Street, Westminster, who is I believe the most competent person as a valuer, and I have his preliminary valuation at above £75,000, so that I consider the value is quite sufficient for a loan of £30,000, which you told me you would much prefer to a less sum.

"I am also preparing the mortgage deed to you, and I am making arrangements to complete the business on the 3rd or 4th of January. I shall be glad to know if that time will be convenient to you to sell out the stock.

"Be Kind enough to let me hear from you here as to your wishes.

"Yours very truly,

"W. M. WILKINSON.

"Mrs. Lyon."

14. The Plaintiff in answer wrote me as follows:—

"17A, Albert Terrace, Albert Gate, Hyde Park,

"21st December, '66.

"Dear Mr. Wilkinson,—I am glad you find the examination to the title of the _____ Property in question satisfactory, and that the value is sufficient for the advance of £30,000 by me as a mortgage thereon, and should you have the deed ready for completion by the time you mention I have no doubt the cash will be *comatable*. Of course I must approve first, by a meeting to be arranged here, by you, there must be a legal deed, also respecting the interest to be paid to me, and to be kept in my deed box, in the Bank, Birchin Lane, and am, dear Sir, with great confidence all will be correct.

"Yours very truly,

"JANE LYON."

15. I then went out of town for ten days and the following correspondence took place between us in the interval:—

"44, Lincoln's Inn Fields, London W. C.

"23rd December, 1866,

"Dear Mrs. Lyon,—I have got the intended mortgage deed drawn by Counsel, and as you have given me no instructions in writing to make it out in any other name than yours, your name is inserted in it as the lender of the £30,000.

"As the sum is so large, and the gift of it so beyond experience, after what you have so munificently given to Mr. Home Lyon, I ought in justice both to you and to myself to have your definite and well considered instructions before I act upon them. You have already placed him not only beyond want, but in a position of affluence, and so that with whatever affection you may regard him, there is no reason why you should not consider any claims of your connections to whatever extent you may think desirable. I ought also to bring forcibly to your notice, that if you give Mr. H. Lyon this farther sum of £30,000, by allowing his name to be inserted in the mortgage deed instead of your own, you are making him an irrevocable gift which whatever may occur, you cannot recall. If however you wish to do this, and with full knowledge of its consequences, I shall be obliged by your giving me definite instructions, to strike out your own name from the draft and to insert him as the lender.

"In that case I shall have no difficulty in securing you by a proper deed to be executed by him the payment of the annual interest on the mortgage for your life which is what you mentioned to me to be your wish to reserve for yourself, giving him the absolute property in the principal.

"I remain, dear Mrs. Lyon, yours faithfully,

"W. M. WILKINSON.

"I write this from the Country, but please address me here as usual.
"Mrs. Lyon."

16.
"17A, Albert Terrace, Albert Gate,
"Hyde Park,
"26th December, '66.

"Dear Mr. Wilkinson,—In reply to your favour, carrying truth, reason, and best advice, we cannot surely foresee what time may bring forth and it is best to be on the safe side. Daniel is at *present*, all that the most fastidious can wish for, but there is no knowing what time and an entire independence may do; he may consider me *a bore*, and cut me altogether, which may probably be anything but agreeable *to me*; otherwise he may inherit all I have, as I have little love for any of my husband relations, except his favourite sister, Mrs. Clutterbuck, and she is not *likely* to outlive me. I wish you to make out the mortgage deed without inserting either Daniel's name or mine, until you *bring* it here for approval. I also wish you to make a *strong* legal deed, *at my expense*, as to the interest being paid me, without any *interference* or *control* thereof by Daniel, as I do not like, or *intend* to be, *in any* way, an *annuitant*, or have the *appearance* of such. If such a legal deed can be made, I should prefer it, and not *otherwise* as I pay for it, *whichever* way it turns.

"In all my mortgages, I have a power of receiver, in case of the interest not being paid, within 6 months after due, and a limited time of 21 days, for the interest to be paid half-yearly. If not paid then, int. to be 6 pr. ct. Mine is at 5 pr. ct. Also a power of sale, without impeachment, but this is all irrelevant, you knowing much better than me, and remain,

"Dear Sir, yours very respectfully,

"JANE LYON."

----

17. "Dawlish, Devon,
"29th December, 1866.

"Dear Mrs. Lyon,—Your letter has been forwarded to me here, and in answering it I can only repeat what I said in my former letter, that if you make the gift of this additional large sum it will be irrevocable, as much as is that which you have already given to Mr. Lyon.

"You can alter your Will whenever you please, but not such a matter as this. It is my duty to place this before you in the clearest way, in order that you may exercise your judgment upon it, and after having done this, I have only to carry out your determination.

"If you determine to keep the control over the mortgage-money I have only to leave the deed as it is drawn, but if you choose to give him the principal, you might reserve the interest to be paid direct to yourself so long as the mortgage lasts during your life, and if it should be paid off then Mr. Lyon should enter into a deed for you to keep, engaging that in whatever it is invested, the interest shall be reserved to you.

"The only inconvenience to this is that it will disclose to the borrowers on the face of the deed the nature of the transaction, but there is no practical objection in this which should at all weigh against the security it would be to you to have the interest paid direct to yourself.

"I shall provide in the deed for the interest to be 6 per cent. but to be reduced to 5 if paid punctually.

"With such a security as furnaces &c. it would be of no use to have a receiver, but I have done what is better by making the borrowers tenants at a rent to cover the interest so that you will have power of distress and in addition a power of sale of the fullest kind.

"If you will kindly write me to Lincoln's Inn-fields your well-considered decision I can have the deed completed and it can be going on during my absence but if you wish to see me before you decide I will come up at once and bring the draft with me for your approval.

"Yours very truly,
"W. M. WILKINSON.

"Mrs. Lyon"

18. "17A, Albert Terrace, Albert Gate,
"Hyde Park,
"29th Decr. 1866.

"Dear Mr. Wilkinson,—In reply to yours of this date, I can only repeat, what I did in my last, 1st, that I *wish* for Daniel to have the principal at my *demise*; that the only difficulty is the interest, payable to me, during my life. Daniel *may* consider the principal so much as *his own*, that he may *in time* pay it with a grudge, and as I said before, think me in the way. I am sure I shall *never wish* to leave the principal past him; I am *decided* upon that point, very *certainly*; so now you know the difficulty, and I *now leave the matter* to you *altogether*, I have the *fullest* confidence in your integrity, and your clear and *disinterested* management. I shall keep your letters, with the deed, for me to keep, feeling sure you will do the best for me in the concern, and am, dear Sir, yours very truly, with the compliments of the season to yourself and Mrs. Wilkinson,"

"JANE LYON,"

———

19,

"Dawlish, Devon,
"30th December, 1866.

"Dear Mrs. Lyon,—As there is so little time to get the mortgage completed before you leave town, and there ought to be no haste in deciding upon so extremely important a matter as whether you should or not give up £30,000, I would suggest that it will be better that your name shall be retained in the mortgage deed, and you can at any time afterwards, by a short deed, transfer the principal, if you should wish to do so, retaining the interest for your life. I think that this would be better than doing it in the mortgage deed itself; and if you approve, and will kindly write me at once to Lincoln's Inn-fields, I can have the deed made ready to send into the country on Tuesday for execution, and settle in London on the 4th. I shall be back on Tuesday and at the office on Wednesday.

"Yours very truly,

"W. M. WILKINSON."

"Mrs. Lyon."

20.

"17A, Albert Terrace. Albert Gate, Hyde Park,
"31st December, 1866.

"Dear Mr. Wilkinson,—I wish you to make out a mortgage deed for Thirty thousand pounds in the name of my adopted son Daniel Home Lyon and he must make out a deed giving me a life interest in the Thirty thousand pounds reserving none of it for himself viz. the interest thereof simply giving me a life interest in it, and the power to receive *all* interest accruing *from* the said Thirty thousand pounds. We are not going out of town on the fifth, therefore it can remain until you come to town.

"And am, dear Mr. Wilkinson, yours most truly,

"JANE LYON."

"P.S.—I consider the sooner the business is done the better, so that it is well done, and it is only you can do it so!"

_____

21.   "44, Lincoln's Inn Fields, London, W. C.
"2 Jany., 1867.

"Dear Mrs. Lyon,—I got back last night, and in coming here this morning, I have had a fall and sprained my ancle, so that I fear I shall not be able to get out for 2 or 3 days, I intend therefore to stay with my friend Mr. _____ at 44, Russell Square, so as to be near here, and ready for business.

"I got your letter last night, but as it would very much complicate the mortgage to set out in it the private arrangement for giving the principal to Mr. Lyon and reserving the interest to you, I have found it far better to take the mortgage to yourself in the usual way, and with all the necessary powers.

"You can as soon as it is signed and completed, by a separate deed assign the principal as you wish to retain the interest, so that it shall be paid direct to yourself without any interference.

"I dare say that the mortgage deed will be signed by all the parties by Friday, and therefore if the weather should allow your going to the City to sell out the £30,000 on or before that day, it can be completed then.

"Will you write me here as usual and I shall get your letter.

"Yours very truly,

"W. M. WILKINSON."

"Mrs. Lyon."

_____

22.   "17A, Albert Terrace, Albert Gate, Hyde Park,
"2nd January, 1867.

"Dear Mr. Wilkinson,—There is one other circumstance in my letter I forgot, viz., that in my letters I do not mention that it is my wish *that I do appoint you at all times my Solicitor* over the Thirty thousand pounds *as long as* I *do live*, and to receive my interest *at all times* from the *parties* holding the said principal of Thirty thousand pounds. My receipt to you is to be sufficient guarantee for the interest arising therefrom. This will *add to the strength* of the deed for me to keep.

"And am, dear Sir,

"Yours respectfully,

"JANE LYON."

"P. S.—Should the present mortgage be paid off, I must have full power to invest again through you, in accordance to my wish at all times for my life. If I have not this power, he *might* call it in and invest it, God knows where or how, this must not be, he must not have that power, while I live, and *reserve the interest*, I must have sole control over the principal.—JANE LYON.

"N.B.—Will you please bring this letter when you come. There is no haste, we are not going from home.—J. L.

––––––

23. "17A, Albert Terrace, Albert Gate, Hyde Park,
"2nd Jany. 1867.

"Dear Mr. Wilkinson,—I certainly did think, that my letter on the subject, was very clear, viz., that I by a strong legal deed, give Thirty thousand pounds to Daniel *reserving* to myself, all interest thereof, for the whole term of my natural life. Daniel by strong legal deed, gives me all interest thereof, taking none of it for himself, so long as I live; this is I think the purport of my last letter to you, and this mode will obviate any difficulty which might arise, as to *any other* mortgage. *Should* this be *paid* off, there will be no occasion to make out another deed. I think, you will see this, but I know you are *scrupulously* honest, and wish me to be secure, for which I thank you, but I can as I have said place the *greatest confidence* in your proceedings in this business, viz., make out the mortgage deed *entirely* in Daniel's name. I have nothing to do with, except the interest in it, only the Thirty thousand pounds, viz., the interest thereof, and whichever way it is invested, without having reference to *this mortgage* or any other; it is simply the interest upon the principal, for which the *Legal* deed must be made by *Daniel* which I know now, you must perfectly understand.

"I am, dear Sir, yours very faithfully,
"JANE LYON."

"W. M. Wilkinson, Esq."

––––––

24. "17A, Albert Terrace Albert Gate,
Mid January, 1867,

"Dear Mr. Wilkinson,—Since I sent off the letter to you, I have thought of the *best* way to obviate *all difficulties*, viz., by appointing you *my trustee over the* Thirty thousand pounds, and by your inserting your name *with Daniel's* in the mortgage, without *reference* to the trust, the interest to be paid to yourself, and my receipt to you to be sufficient during my life for the interest. I think *this is the best plan yet* thought of, and then I shall be *perfectly* satisfied with you as trustee and receiver, the interest going direct to you from the parties holding the principal, and Daniel having no power over any of the property during my life, neither to *call in* or invest, *probably in America.* The trust deed must be made strong and legal, giving *myself, through you,* my trustee and receiver, all power.

"And am, dear Sir,

"Yours faithfully,

"JANE LYON."

————

25.   "44, Lincoln's Inn Fields, London, W. C.
"4th January, 1867.

"Dear Mrs. Lyon,—I got your letter of the 2nd last evening and can only say that whatever be your wishes I will carry them out in the best way I can for your security.

"Your suggestion is a perfectly practicable one, and can be substantially carried out by a legal deed. But it would be very inexpedient to make all these private arrangements on the face of the mortgage deed itself to which so many strangers are parties, and I would recommend for your consideration whether it would not be best to do what you want by a separate deed with which the borrowers will have nothing to do.

"It is in fact only another, and in my opinion a better, mode of carrying out the same thing; and if you approve of this, I will in a few days after the completion of the mortgage submit to you the draft of the intended deed.

"I hope that I may by that time be sufficiently recovered to call upon you.

"Yours very truly,

"W. M. WILKINSON."

"Mrs. Lyon."

————

26.   "17A, Albert Terrace, Albert Gate, "Hyde Park,
"5 Jan. 1867.

"Dear Mr. Wilkinson,—I perfectly agree with you that it would be highly injudicious, to endeavour to carry out my wishes in a mortgage deed, open to the inspection of so many persons.

"You can I have no doubt do it more effectually, carrying out my views in a *separate* legal deed; therefore, you perceive, I highly approve of your making a draft of such, for my approval. I trust you will be sufficiently well soon to see the completion of the mortgage. Do pray take great care of yourself, and have the *best* advice; an honest man in the law is worth *far more* than his *weight in gold.*

"And am, yours faithfully,

"JANE LYON."

"W. M. Wilkinson, Esq., 44, Lincoln's Inn Fields."

27. On Monday the 7th day of January, I saw her and had a long conversation with her respecting the completion of the mortgage and also as to her intended gift of it to the Defendant Home. She expressed the greatest affection for him and said she was determined to carry it out in the way proposed. I reiterated to her all the old arguments and in addition I told her that it would not now even be the means of saving the duty inasmuch as there would be succession duty now chargeable. I again warned her against being in any way influenced by any spirit communications or by anything but her unbiased reason and she assured me she was not. On this occasion she told me that she had received the same advice from Lady D. who had told her not to be guided in any worldly mattes by any communications and she did not intend to be. She said whatever happened she had more money than she could want and she was only too glad to make Daniel independent after all the obloquy he had suffered.

28. The following correspondence then took place between us:—

"44, Lincoln's Inn Fields, London, W. C.
"9 January, 1867.

"My dear Mrs. Lyon,—I am happy to inform you that I have to-day completed the mortgage for £30,000 to you and have paid over the money.

"I will bring the deed for your signature in a day or two.

"I will also now prepare for your approval the draft of the deed in favour of Mr. Lyon according to your instructions in your letter, and in the conversation I had with you on Monday last.

"I hope in a day or two to be able to lay before you the proposal for another mortgage security.

"Yours faithfully,

W. M. WILKINSON."

"Mrs. Lyon."

29.   "44, Lincoln's Inn Fields, London, W. C.
"11th January, 1867.

"My dear Mrs. Lyon,—I am still so lame that I have great difficulty in getting about, but I hope in a day or two to be better and see you.

"I have now got the particulars of another mortgage security, and which I believe to be as good and safe as the one just completed, and that either the property to be mortgaged, by itself, or the personal security of the borrowers, by itself, would be perfectly ample; but of course you would have the security of both in the mortgage, should you be willing to take it.

"The parties wish to borrow £26,000 on 12 acres of freehold land valued at £1,000 an acre. They have recently had to pay £12,000 for an additional acre, and this land there are five first-rate furnaces and extensive foundries, the whole being valued at over £80,000.

"The borrowers are several of them the same as in the last mortgage, but this business is quite distinct from the other, and the works about one mile off.

"The names are:—

I shall be glad if you will consider the question, and let me have your opinion upon it.

"Yours very truly,

"W. M. WILKINSON."

"Mrs. Lyon."

---

30.   "17A, Albert Terrace, Albert Gate, Hyde Park,
"11th Jany. '67.

"Dear Sir,—I have always had, an authenticated, examd. copy, of the mortgage deed. This is *essential*. My husband was very particular, on this point, he examined it with the *deed itself*, and saw that it corresponded in every point, before he signed it, therefore please when you come to bring them *both* with you, it is at the borrowers' expense. Please to drop me a line previous. I hope your ancle is now *quite well*.

"Yours faithfully,

"JANE LYON."

"W. M. Wilkinson, Esq."

31.   "17A, Albert Terrace, Albert Gate, Hyde Park,
                                        "13 Jany. 1867.

"Dear Mr. Wilkinson,—I am sorry to hear that you are still lame, you surely take the best advice, there may be some small bone or leader injured, some clever person may detect ere it is too late. The *"present time"* you know. The mortgage you mention viz., the 12 acres of freehold land, the security must depend upon the erections thereon, whether they are of sufficient value, and the permanency of their present use, and whether they would be available for any other purpose equally profitable. Then with the joint security of the company you mention and their bond, there can be no doubt of their respectability. I think it would be an eligible security, and you will please to give it your attention, on my account and strictest enquiry.

                    "And am, dear Sir, yours respectfully,
                                        "JANE LYON."
"W. M. Wilkinson, Esq."

"You will be here to-morrow Daniel tells me; we dine at ½ past 5. I hope you will come to meet Dr. Mary Walker."

32. On Monday the 14th January, I went to dine with the Plaintiff and I took with me the draft assignment of the mortgage and the declaration of trust I left them with her for her approval I was there a quarter of an hour before any one else and we had the same sort of conversation as before and she said she would go through the drafts by herself and thought they might be deferred as she saw no reason for doing them at once. I strongly advised her to do nothing further in it but to leave things as they were. We had no further conversation on the subject that evening as I left early before the others had gone.

33. On the same day I wrote to the Plaintiff as follows:—

                    "44, Lincoln's Inn Fields, London, W. C.
                                        "14th Jany. 1867.

"My dear Mrs. Lyon,—The land and the premises and other erections upon it are valued at £80,000, which I believe could not be so reduced as not to make a loan of £25,000 perfectly safe, without taking into account the personal security of the borrowers, upon their covenant jointly and severally to pay the whole of the mortgage money.

"I consider that the security therefore is ample; and if the title to the property should on investigation prove to be equally good, I do not think you will run any risk, whilst you will be materially increasing your income.

"When you have fully considered the matter, I shall be glad to have your directions,

"Yours faithfully,

"W. M. WILKINSON."

"Mrs. Lyon,
"17A, Albert Terrace."

34. On the date of the following letter it was brought to me by the Defendant Home who said that the Plaintiff wished to see me.

"17A, Albert Terrace, Albert Gate, Hyde Park,
"17 Jany. 1867.

Dear Mr. Wilkinson,—Will you be so good as to call in my principal of £31,000 from the estate of the late Frederick Drew, Esq.?

"Yours very truly,

"JANE LYON.

"W. M. Wilkinson, Esq."

On the afternoon of that day I called on her and she produced the draft deeds I had left with her on the 14th and which she desired me to read over to her. I did so and she approved of them and said she had determined now to carry out the gift. I once more went through the arguments I had before addressed to her but she said she was determined now to do it, and desired me to have them ready for her to sign on Saturday.

The next morning I received from her, the following letter:—

"17A, Albert Terrace, Albert Gate,
"Hyde Park,
"17th Jany. 1867.

"Dear Mr. Wilkinson,—I have examined the copy trust deed, to you, relating to the mortgage of £30,000; and also, the reservation gift deed copy, to Daniel, at my demise, and approve of both.

"And am, &c., &c.,

"JANE LYON."

The assignment of the mortgage to me as drawn and approved by her was absolute on the face of it and I had it re-ingrossed with the alteration referring to the declaration of trust so that my character of trustee should appear. Two of my clerks my son and Mr. Hartley called on her on the Saturday to see her sign the deeds and I afterwards signed in their presence I was not there myself and did not execute the deed till the Monday following.

35. The following is a copy of the deed:—

"DECLARATION OF TRUST.

"This Indenture made the 19th day of January One thousand eight hundred and sixty-seven between Jane Lyon of No. 17A Albert Terrace Albert Gate Hyde Park in the County of Middlesex widow of the one part and William Martin Wilkinson of 44 Lincoln's Inn Fields in the County of Middlesex gentleman of the other part. Whereas by a deed poll or instrument in writing under the hand and seal of the said Jane Lyon bearing date the 12th day of December 1866. After reciting that under the last Will and testament of her late husband Charles Lyon Esquire the said Jane Lyon was entitled to a large fortune in money and securities for her own use free from any trusts or reservations imposed thereon by the said Will or otherwise. And reciting that the said Jane Lyon had no children and had been minded and desirous to take and adopt Daniel Dunglas Home of 22 Sloane Street Hyde Park aforesaid as her son. And reciting that with her sanction and at her request the said Daniel Dunglas Home had exerted a deed poll bearing date the 3rd day of December then instant and the same was intended to be enrolled as of record in Her Majesty's High Court of Chancery whereby the said Daniel Dunglas Home declared that he had taken the surname of "Lyon" in lieu of and instead of "Home" and that in future he intended to be called and known as "Daniel Home Lyon" And reciting that the said Jane Lyon being desirous of placing him in a position of independence suitable to his rank and position an life as her adopted son and with a view to that end on the 10th day of October then last gave to the said Daniel Home Lyon the sum of £24,000 cash and reciting that in further pursuance of such desire and on the occasion of his publicly taking her name on the 10th day of December then instant the said Jane Lyon had caused to be transferred from her own name in the books of the Governor and Company of the Bank of England into the old name of Daniel Home Lyon the sum of £6,798 17s. 4d. £3 per Cent. Consolidated Bank Annuities equivalent to a further sum of £6,000 cash and reciting that it was the intention of the said Jane Lyon in making the said respective gift and transfer as aforesaid and it was her wish and intention absolutely and irrevocably to vest in the said Daniel Home Lyon for himself his executors administrators and assigns the absolute use and enjoyment of the moneys thereby respectively given and transferred. The said Jane Lyon in further evidence of such her desire and intention and to remove all doubts suspicions and controversies in that behalf did by the deed poll now in recital for herself her heirs executors and administrators absolutely and irrevocably declare that she had made the said gift and transfer of her own will and pleasure and without any influence control or interference of the said Daniel Home Lyon or of any other person and that the said Daniel Home Lyon his executors administrators and assigns do stand possessed of and be entitled to the said sums of £24,000 and the said £3 per Cent. Consolidated Bank Annuities so representing the sum of £6,000 by her transferred as thereinbefore mentioned for his and their own absolute use and benefit without any reservation condition trust or purpose whatsoever. And whereas the said Jane Lyon is entitled (among other property) to a sum of £30,000 secured on mortgage of certain leasehold land buildings machinery and hereditaments situate at _____ in the county of York made by an indenture dated the 9th day of January 1867 and expressed to be made between _____ of the one part and the said Jane Lyon of the other part. And whereas the said Jane Lyon being minded and desirous to make a further provision for her said adopted son the said Daniel Home Lyon is addition to the said sums of £24,000 cash and £6,798 17s. 4d. £3 per Cent. Consolidated Bank Annuities so respectively paid and transferred to him as aforesaid has of her own free will and pleasure only and without any influence control or interference of the said Daniel Home Lyon or of any other person determined absolutely and irrevocably to settle the said sum of £30,000 secured on mortgage as aforesaid for the benefit of her adopted son the said Daniel Home Lyon reserving only to herself the interest of the same during her life with full power to her of calling in and varying the investments of the said sum. And whereas for effectuating and in part performance of the said will and determination the said Jane Lyon has by an indenture bearing even date with but executed before these presents and expressed to be made between the said Jane Lyon of the one part and the said William Martin Wilkinson of the other part assigned the said principal sum of £30,000 and interest and the securities for the same to the said William Martin Wilkinson his executors administrators and assigns to the intent that he and they may stand possessed thereof respectively upon the trusts and with and subject to the powers and provisoes thereinafter declared. Now this indenture witnesseth that for effectually carrying out the said determination and intent and in consideration of the premises it is hereby agreed and declared by and between the said parties hereto and in particular the said Jane Lyon doth hereby for herself her heirs executors and administrators absolutely and irrevocably declare that the said William Martin Wilkinson his executors administrators and assigns shall from the date of these presents stand possessed of and interested in the said sum of £30,000 and all interest now due or hereafter to accrue due for the same and the securities for the same. Upon trust that he the said William Martin Wilkinson his executors administrators and assigns shall either continue the said sum of £30,000 in its present state of investment if the said Jane Lyon shall so desire or at her request shall call in and compel payment of the same sum or any part thereof and shall invest the moneys so called in as aforesaid in the names or name or under the legal control of him the said William Martin Wilkinson his executors administrators or assigns in any of the public stocks or funds or Government securities of the United Kingdom or freehold copyhold leasehold or chattel real securities or in the purchase of real or leasehold estate or in any other mode or form which the said Jane Lyon shall by writing under her hand from time to time direct and appoint it being the intent and meaning of the said Jane Lyon in making such assignment and settlement as aforesaid to retain to herself the exclusive control of the future investments of the said sum of £30,000 and every part thereof and that the said William Martin Wilkinson his executors administrators or assigns shall pay the interest dividends and annual income of the said sum of £30,000 and of the stocks funds and securities in or upon which the same sum or any part thereof may for the time being be invested and the rents and profits of the real estate which may be purchased therewith or with any part thereof unto the said Jane Lyon during her life and subject thereto shall stand possessed of and interested in the said sum of £30,000 and the stocks funds shares and securities in or upon which the same or any part thereof may from time to time be invested and the real estate which may be purchased with the said sum or any part thereof and the interest dividends and annual income rents and profits thereof and of every part thereof. In trust for the said Daniel Home Lyon his heirs executors administrators and assigns according to the nature and tenure of the said property. And it is hereby agreed and declared that the power of appointing a new trustee or new trustees who shall die or desire to be discharged or refuse or become unfit or incapable to act shall be exercisable by the said Jane Lyon during her life and upon every or any such appointment the number of trustees may be augmented or reduced and in addition to the ordinary indemnity and right to reimbursement by law given to trustees the trustee or trustees for the time being of these presents shall not be answerable for any loss which may be occasioned to the said trust fund by investing the same in any manner which the said Jane Lyon may in her absolute discretion think fit to direct. Provided also and the said Jane Lyon doth hereby expressly declare that the settlement hereinbefore expressed to be hereby made by her is absolute and irrevocable and shall in no wise be disputed or controverted by her heirs executors or administrators and that the sum of £30,000 therein and stocks funds securities and estate that may be purchased with the said sum or any part thereof are (subject as aforesaid) freely and absolutely given to the said Daniel Home Lyon for his own use and benefit without any reservation condition or trust whatsoever and are intended by the said Jane Lyon to be in addition to and not in lieu of or substitution for the said sums of £24,000 and £6,798 17s. 4d. £3 per Cent. Consolidated Bank Annuities so respectively given paid and transferred to her said adopted son the said Daniel Home Lyon as aforesaid. In witness whereof the said parties to these presents have hereunto set their hands and seals the day and year first above written.

"JANE LYON.   W. M. WILKINSON.

Signed sealed and delivered by
the within named Jane Lyon and
William Martin Wilkinson in
the presence of

WM. J. WILKINSON
WM. HARTLEY,
Clerks to W. M. WILKINSON.

36. Copies of the two deeds were sent to her with the following letter:—

"44, Lincoln's Inn Fields, London, W. C.
"21 January 1867.
"Dear Madam,—My father desires me to send you the accompanying copies of the documents you required on Saturday. I hope you will find them all right.
"Yours faithfully,
"W. J. WILKINSON."

37. On the 24th January 1867 I directed the following letter to be written and sent to the Plaintiff:—

"44, Lincoln's Inn Fields, London, W. C.
"24 January 1867.
"Dear Madam,—My father desires me to say that he is afraid his imposition will prevent him accepting your kind invitation for Friday next.

"I return you the papers relating to the Wootton Estate which you sent me according to your request.

"Yours faithfully,

"Wm. J. Wilkinson

38. At her request I called on her on the 25th January with one of the duplicates of her Will and left it with her. I was with her only a few minutes and do not remember what passed. On the 13th February I went with her to the stockbrokers and to the Bank to sell out stock for the second mortgage of £30,000. She thought that she had only enough stock to produce about £26,500 and she had arranged that the Defendant Home should sell out of his stock and lend to her what was necessary. I had accordingly got a power of attorney from him to the brokers to sell out and was done by them and they raised £3,403 6s. 4d. cash by the sale of £3,755 7s. 8d. Consols which was advanced to her and £400 cash by sale of £441 7s. 7d. Consols for Mr. Home himself. When at the Bank we discovered through the brokers that the Plaintiff had a further sum left in her own name of about £2,300 and she told me ongoing home that she would at once transfer it to the Defendant Home in reduction of what she had borrowed and which I believe she afterwards did.

39. The following are copies of further letters which have passed between myself and the Plaintiff:—

"17A, Albert Terrace, Albert Gate, S. W.
"13th Febry. '67.

"Dear Mr. Wilkinson,—Will you please let me know by return, *when* I shall receive the deeds of my new mortgage, being usual with my husband to receive the deeds when he paid the money, which I have done, and I wish to go to the bank, to deposit some other documents, which I mentioned to you, at the same time I deposit them. Will you please also, to send the papers of the *exact* amount I sold out of the funds, with price, &c. This is usual, we always had it from, the bank, will you please procure it from Taylor and Fog.

"I hope you are much better, and am,
"Yours very truly,

"JANE LYON."

"W. M. Wilkinson, Esq."

"Daniel came home this afternoon quite well."

"P. S.—Also, if you have sold out from Daniel's, let me have that paper of exact amount also, if you have not, I would sell out the remainder of my stock as part, and not have so much of his.—J. L."

40.   "44, Lincoln's Inn Fields London, W. C.
                                                    "14 February, 1867.

"Dear Mrs Lyon,—The mortgage deed requires to be registered at Northallerton, and immediately on its return, which will be about a week, I will bring it to you. I shall have a copy made for you I hope by Saturday.

"The amount of stock you sold yesterday was £29,348 2s. 9d., which produced £26,596 13s. 8d., for which sum I received the broker's cheque yesterday.

"Mr. D. H. Lyon's stock was sold yesterday to make up the sum of £30,000, which I also received.

"I will get the broker's note of the amount for you, and you can when convenient replace his stock, and pay him the dividend of July next, in case it should not be earlier replaced.

"It will thus be simply a loan of stock for a short time.

"I am much better to-day.
                                        "Yours faithfy.,

                                                    "W. M. WILKINSON."

"Mrs. Lyon."

———

41.   "44, Lincoln's Inn Fields, London, W. C.
                                                    "21 February, 1867.

"My Dear Mrs. Lyon,—I send you the last mortgage deed for £30,000, and also an examined copy, which I hope you will find correct.
                                        "Yours faithfully,

                                                    "W. M. WILKINSON,
                                                    "per W. J. W."

"Mrs. Lyon,
    "Albert Gate."

42. The manner in which the Plaintiff had disposed of her property had always been an uneasy thought for me and I determined to bring the question again before her and accordingly wrote her the following letter:—

44, Lincoln's Inn Fields, London, W. C.

"6 May, 1867.

"My dear Mrs. Lyon,—I am just beginning to get here again a little after my long illness, and am sorry that I have been so long without being able to call on you.

"I have for some time been intending to remind you of the terms of your Will, which has now been made for some time, and you have had an opportunity in the interim of fully considering whether you would not wish to benefit some of your own or your late husband's relatives by making an alteration in their favour.

"I have no right of course to do more than bring the matter to your notice, for of course the decision must rest with you alone, and I will therefore say no more than that I can now attend to any directions you may give me on the subject.

"Yours very faithfy,

"W. M. WILKINSON."

"Mrs. Lyon,
"17A, Albert Terrace, Hyde Park."

43. The following is a copy of her answer:—

"17A, Albert Terrace, Albert Gate,
"6th May, '67.

"My dear Mr. Wilkinson,—I most sincerely congratulate you upon, I hope, your restoration to permanent health, and a good long life to enjoy it, and your dear good wife; I also wish her much joy upon that anticipation. May you both together reap the benefits of that happy change, for health is most assuredly the greatest blessing this world can grant. Have you heard any thing from the Wootton Mortgage? Will you please give me a copy of your notice for them to pay in the money? I hope it will answer the purpose. Have you got a security for it *good* to pay 5 pr. ct.? Mr. Jencken mentioned one that Spratt mentioned to Daniel, probably he named it to you, paying 6 pr. ct., that was for twenty thousand. I hope you will find another good one, equal to the last, or *better*. I should like to see you, when you can; if you please, bring the copy notice with you, and am, with best wishes for your health,

"Yours very truly,

"JANE LYON."

"Will you please give me some intimation when you will be here, as I wish to be in the house; and this fine weather I might be out after one o'clock, or if not convenient to call please write. I have had a letter from poor Dan., and think he is rather better, not so much pain: he is now taking wine. I think there is hopes of his recovery.

J. LYON."

44. I afterwards received from the Plaintiff a letter of which the following is a copy:—

"17A, Albert Terrace, Albert Gate, Hyde Park,
"10th May, 1867.

"Dear Sir,—Not having heard from you, in answer to my last, *requesting* the copy of the notice you sent respecting the Wootton Mortgage, (it has always been usual with my husband and self to *have* each copy notice). I have requested Daniel to desire you to send or give it to him for me, but I suppose he forgot it. As the payment of the interest was a *private* transaction, probably a different notice may have to be given. If yours is not in conformity with the deeds, this must be done at once, *May* and *October* were the months the interest was paid usually; *not* January and July, as last entered upon.

"And am yours truly,

"JANE LYON."

"W. M. Wilkinson, Esq."

45. On Saturday the 11th May I called on her to speak to her about her Will and the calling in of the Wootton Mortgage &c. I found her alone and after speaking a little on the other matters I opened the question of her Will and told her that as Mr. Home had now had such a benefit from her I wished to bring very seriously before her that she should not exclude her relations by her Will. She said that she was just as well satisfied with him as ever and that nothing could surpass his kindness to her. All that she feared was that he would not live long and if he died she would alter her Will for she did not wish that any more of her money should go to his little boy whom she did not like "Indeed," she said, "I am sorry that I gave him more than a life contingency in the second £30,000 for I think the first £30,000 quite enough to go to the boy." I said "Well, I am sorry if you have changed your mind, for I did all I could to make you hesitate, and I am sorry that you ever gave him the second gift at all. But now," I said to her "why don't you make your Will in favour of your relations? If Mrs. Clutterbuck does not want it, there is Mrs. Denison, who, with her husband incapacitated, and her large family really wants it. Besides you have given Daniel more than he can ever want." She thought for a moment and said "No, I don't care for them, and neither did my husband, and I will not alter it as long as Daniel lives; but if he die, I will alter it, for I don't wish his son to have

any more. And why should I change? I am perfectly satisfied so long as he lives." I again pressed her to leave a part to her husband's relatives and if not to some hospitals as it was absurd to leave so much to one person and I said "I wish you would do it, for I think it is only just." She positively refused and said her mind was made up. I said to her "Well, I only wish your relatives could have been within hearing of all I have said to you, that they might know how earnestly I have pleaded for them, and I am sorry to say how unsuccessfully." We parted on the best terms and I made the following memorandum of the interview.

"Saturday, 11 May, 1867.

MRS. LYON,—Attending you as to altering your Will, which you determined not to do, or to take anything away during Mr. Lyon's life; but should he predecease you, you would at once make a fresh will.

46. The following correspondence then took place:—

"17A, Albert Terrace, Albert Gate,
"27th May, '67.

"Dear Mr. Wilkinson, You promised, when here, to write respecting the notice, and when they would be ready, to pay the mortgage off, and drop me a line as soon as you received an answer. Will you please let me know the reply.

"And am, dear Sir, yours truly,
"JANE LYON."

———

47.   "44, Lincoln's Inn Fields, London, W. C.
"28th May, 1867.

"My dear Mrs. Lyon,—I wrote to the Solicitors, Messrs. Warden and Ponsford the day after I saw you, and not having received any answer from them, I wrote them again yesterday urging them to let me know if they could promise the money on the day as you were about making arrangements for its investment.

"I have not yet received any answer, but the moment I do so, I will let you know.

"I should have called on you long before this, but I have been again unwell, and obliged to save myself as much exertion as possible.

"I shall hope to see you in a day or two.
"Yours very truly,
"W. M. WILKINSON."

"Mrs. Lyon."

48. "My dear Sir,—I am sorry to find by yours that you have been ill again, I think you require change of air. I am much surprised you do not hear from Ward and Ponsford; I fear I am going to have some trouble in that quarter, I have all the deeds belonging the estate at the bank; will you please, when you come here, to bring me the deeds belonging to the last mortgage, I have only the *mortgage deed* to me, and cannot take it to the bank until I have the deeds of the property in mortgage as it is usual to have, it is not complete without. In a 2nd mortgage, they have copies of them. I have neither. I have had a good account of Daniel.

"And am yours respectfully,

"JANE LYON."

"W. M. Wilkinson, Esq.
   "44, Lincoln's Inn Fields, W. C.
     "Wednesday, 29th May, '67."

---

49.   "44, Lincoln's Inn Fields, London, W. C.
                        "7th June, 1867.

"My dear Mrs. Lyon,—I have now heard from Messrs. Warden and Ponsford in answer to my letters, and they say that they have not yet obtained the money to pay you off, but they are still trying to get it.

"There is no doubt they find it a more difficult task than they anticipated.

"I will bring with me the first day I can call, the other deeds relating to your mortgage in the North.

"I have been worse again in health lately, or I would have brought them before now.

"Yours very truly,

"W. M. WILKINSON."

"Mrs. Lyon."

---

50.   "17A, Albert Terrace, Albert Gate, Hyde Park,
                        "11th June 1867.

"Dear Sir,—I am sorry to hear that you have been ill again, but hope now you are quite well, when you come with the deeds you name, will you also please to bring my Mortgage deed and Trust to Dan. I wish to see them again compared with my copies; I fear I shall have some difficulty with the Wootton Estate Mortgage, I wrote to Mr. Good, he thinks they will get the money, but not so soon as anticipated, will you please appoint Thursday first, to bring the above deed, mentioned, or a day probably more convenient to you, say Friday.

"And am, dear Sir, yours truly,

"Jane Lyon."

"W. M. Wilkinson, Esq."

"44, Lincoln's Inn Fields, London, W. C.
"14th June, 1867.

"My dear Mrs. Lyon,—I shall try to call on you at 2 o'clock to-morrow (Thursday) or the same hour on Friday, if not inconvenient to you.

"Yours very truly,

"W. M. Wilkinson."

"Mrs. Lyon."

51. The next and last time I saw the Plaintiff was on the 13th June when I found her in a very excited state. She said I ought to have advised her to have another solicitor and to put off giving away the mortgage and when I told her I had done so she denied it and said she should try to get the mortgage deed back. I told her I was sorry she had ever given it at all and it was quite against my wishes and advice and if Mr. Home had deceived her as she said she had most effectually concealed it from me and that I could not believe she had been acting a part with me for so many months for no reason at all. The following is the memorandum I made immediately on my return.

"13th June, 1867.

"I called on Mrs. Lyon with the deeds belonging to her, and she complained that I had not brought the trust deed to compare with her copy. I informed her that hers was an examined copy. She said she was determined to have it back, as she had been defrauded of it by Mr. Lyon and had not had proper advice from me. That I ought to have asked her to have another Solicitor or to have insisted on her delaying for 6 months. I referred to my having written to her repeatedly and also spoken to her against doing it at all, and that I could not prevent her doing what she did. She said she had done it under the influence of Mr. Home in everything, and I said that if so she had concealed it from me. She said she was determined to set aside the deed, and was saying she would go into Chancery with it, when a gentleman and lady called, and she said that the interview had better terminate.

52. The neat day I resigned my trusteeship in the following letter:—

"44, Lincoln's Inn Fields, London, W. C.
"14th June, 1867.

"Mr. Wilkinson presents his compliments to Mrs. Lyon, and begs to say that as Mrs. Lyon named him as trustee of the £30,000 mortgage, and she is now dissatisfied with what she did, he is desirous of retiring altogether from the trusteeship.

"Mrs. Lyon has the power of nominating another trustee.

"Mr. Wilkinson throughout considered the further gift unnecessary, and has always been sorry that Mrs. Lyon persisted in making it."

53. I have since deposited in Court the mortgage and the assignment and declaration of trust and the deeds relating to the mortgage and also the mortgage for £20,000 to Mr. Home so that I have no further interest therein and I am willing to assign the first-mentioned mortgage to a trustee to be appointed and I submit I ought to be discharged from the suit I have not been paid either by the Plaintiff or the other Defendant for any of the business I have transacted for them.

54. I have now gone through the only letters and papers which have passed on the subject and I have given as nearly as I could a true account of the material parts of my interviews with the Plaintiff. She was always till the last occasion very kind to me and I had a respect and liking for her and a determination to do all I could to protect her more against her own absurdly generous impulses than against Mr. Home for she assured me repeatedly that she was not influenced in any way by spirit communications but only by her liking for him and that if he were not a medium at all she should have the same affection for him. If it were otherwise she is alone to blame for concealing it from me and constantly denying it but I spoke to her so often against being led away by communications that the subject got quite threadbare between us and she from the first told me that she was well acquainted with all that I could say on that subject and she afterwards told me on several occasions she had received the same caution from others. She was principally anxious to have all she did for Mr. Home done in such a manner as that her husband's relatives could not dispute it after her death and she informed me she could have no next of kin of her own and that her property "would go the Crown" if she did not make a Will and her only anxiety was as to Mr. Home's health and the fear lest he might marry and leave her. The first evening I saw her she said in the presence of Mr. Rudall after Dr. Hawkesley had left that Mr. Home had told her he must go to Russia to look after a law suit he had

pending there respecting his late wife's fortune and she said that now she had given him so much there would be no occasion for him to go away and he need not care whether he got the money in Russia or not as he had now enough of his own and she had plenty more.

55. On one occasion she showed me a letter from a lady in which it was said that her husband's relatives were gathering evidence on which to prove her insane and she expressed great indignation against them. She also told me she had left her last lodgings in Westbourne Street because she suspected Mrs. Fellowes and others of being in league with the landlady Mrs. Keys to get evidence of her insanity.

56. I have reason to complain of such allegations being made against me as that I did not advise her to employ another solicitor nor fully cautioned her against giving away her money as they are contrary to the fact and are expressly contradicted in her own handwriting which I suppose she has forgotten. I did both to the best of my ability and almost if possible beyond my duty by my persistence against her repeated declarations of her intention. Her own statements that she acted on her own judgment only and not on any communications and that her determination was to do as she said were if they were not true her fault and not mine for I quite believed what she told me. I have given her the same advice both when by ourselves and in the presence of the Defendant Home and on such occasions he has always said the same to her. I could have done nothing more than I did except refusing altogether to carry out her strict orders and had I done so and she had gone to another solicitor and had told him the same as she told me he would have had no alternative but to act on her instructions.

57. The Plaintiff has repeatedly told me that she acted altogether on her own judgment in what she was doing and that it was the greatest pleasure to her to have made such an use of her money and to have found one who was such a comfort to her.

58. The foregoing 57 paragraphs have been repeated with a few slight alterations from my affidavit filed in this snit on the 8th July 1867. After my said affidavit up to this place was prepared and printed I was furnished with the copy of the Plaintiff's further affidavit sworn the 26th June and filed the following day.

So far as it relates to matters within my own knowledge it is almost wholly untrue and is at variance with the facts or with her own previous and repeated statements to me and what there is true in it is so mixed up with what is not so as to give an entirely false colouring to her statements. From my conversations with her during the nine or ten occasions on which I had interviews with her of a business or a friendly nature I always considered her to have an excellent memory and good business habits and knowledge beyond those of most women but from this affidavit not only must her memory be most defective but her imagination must be very great if she herself really believes what she has said in it.

59. I was the friend of the Defendant Home though I seldom saw him but I was scarcely his solicitor for he had no law business on which to employ a solicitor and though I had made a short will for him I made no charge for it. I have always found him a person of honour and integrity and when I heard that he had been adopted by the Plaintiff and that she had given him £24,000 I was glad of it as a compensation for the unmerited abuse to which he has been subjected. When however that munificent gift had been made to him I thought it was enough for all purposes and any further gifts I considered quite unnecessary. This made me very independent in advising her and very determined that she should do nothing more for him upon my advice. I never told Mr. Home or any other person what I intended to do in the way of questioning her when I took her Will but I questioned her in the strictest way and received the most determined answers from her expressing her satisfaction and her determination to make her Will in his favour and for the reasons which she gave me for so doing as I have above set out. There was no halting or hesitation on her part in her answers to awaken my suspicions or make me think she was not speaking the truth. I knew nothing of the circumstances she now alleges under which she first wrote to me and made her first gift to the Defendant and if she had at the time she signed her Will the conviction that she was influenced by any spiritual cause she not only concealed it from me but resolutely denied it and gave as her reason that she did it out of her liking for Mr. Home and to make him independent.

60. It is incorrect also that she destroyed her former Will after making that of the 12th of November last for she told me pointing to the fire that she had destroyed it that afternoon shortly before I came.

61. It is also entirely incorrect what she now alleges in paragraph 11 of her lastly-mentioned affidavit as to the gift of £6,000 and the circumstances under which she made it as appears by the correspondence and documents in the preceding 8th, 9th, 10th, 11th and 12th paragraphs of this Answer. She herself originated the correspondence with me respecting it and says in her first letter that she makes the gift "as a little surprise" to the Defendant on the occasion of the Defendant taking her name which he did publicly and advertised it in the "Times" "Post" and other papers and she told me at the time of her having got the papers containing the announcement. It is also untrue that any but the Plaintiff herself gave the instructions to the

brokers. The letter to them is in the Plaintiff's own hand. The Defendant's birthday is not in December but on the 20th March. The following is a copy of a letter in the handwriting of the Plaintiff addressed and sent by her to the Defendant Home the day before his birthday:—

19th March, 1867.

"My dear Daniel,—You say your birthday is the 20th, *i.e., to-morrow*, may you see *many* of them, and may they be *happy* days, *full* of *health* and *joy*; look forward to see my *words verified*, for I write with thought and pen of *inspiration*: your *health* will flourish like the *young bay tree*, full of *life* and sap. I will never see those far days, but you will *remember* my *prophetic* prognostication herein. I am glad you sleep well, and your cough is much better, you will all be well together *very soon, think of that only*. The weather here is most thoroughly miserable, snowing one hour, sleeting the next; cold and comfortless; we never see the colours of the sky, it is so black. My cold no better, no getting out, no change for me, the sooner I am off to the sunshine land, *if such*, the better. You say that 50 miles from here the ground is covered with snow 2 and 3 feet thick, but you do not say whether east or west, this you will say in your next,

"God bless and protect and restore you to *perfect* health, and may your birth day of '68 be more auspicious.

"And am, my dear Daniel,

"Your very affectionate mother,

"JANE LYON."

62. What she says in paragraph 12 of her lastly-mentioned Affidavit is also incorrect as to the time when the deed poll as to the two gifts of £24,000 and £6,000 was executed. The correspondence with her and my account of my interviews with her in the preceding 8th to the 12th paragraphs of this Answer clearly prove the time of its execution and the circumstances under which it was prepared and it is untrue that I received any instructions excepting from her. It is also untrue if she then spoke the truth to me that she made the gifts or executed the deed under any spiritual or improper fancies or influence and although she had no other Solicitor but me on that occasion her letter shows that it was because she refused to act on my advice to employ one. I submit that she should have been more cautious before making such statements so derogatory to my character as that I had taken instructions for such a deed from any one but herself and had given it a

false date whilst acting as the Solicitor of the Defendant instead of her who was really my client.

63. The circumstances erroneously stated in the 13th paragraph of the Plaintiff's lastly-mentioned affidavit relative to the first mortgage for £30,000 and her gift of it to the Defendant are sufficiently explained and many of them distinctly refuted by the correspondence and documents I have already given and they are directly at variance with the facts in several important particulars as the correspondence and documents prove. If she executed the gift of the mortgage under the influence she mentions she falsely stated the contrary to me at the time and acted in defiance of my warnings.

64. It is incorrect that the deficiency to make up the second mortgage was advanced by the Defendant Home at my request. The mortgage was to have been for £25,000 only for which she had money enough of her own ready and I strongly advised her not to lend more as it would be a pity to leave herself without any capital sum but she so insisted that she disliked uneven sums and would prefer £30,000 if the security were sufficient that afterwards on the parties applying that the larger sum might be advanced she asked Mr. Home herself in my presence to let her have the balance out of his stock which he did.

65. The circumstances relating to the sale of the Defendant's stock to provide for the £20,000 mortgage to him are also incorrectly stated so far as they give the impression that she only knew of that mortgage by accident. The first idea of it was given by herself to me and she was throughout not only aware of it but desired it to be lent and she inquired the nature of the security and knew of its being accepted and so far from her discovering it from the sale note being left accidentally with her not only that sale note but the notes of the previous transactions in the stock by the Defendant, and the coupons of the stock were in her own possession and she kept them in the same bundle as her own. She has several times shown them to me along with her own when I was with her assisting her to calculate what she had in the funds and she told me that she kept them as Mr. Home did not understand such matters as well as she did. I find that in a letter from the plaintiff to the other Defendant of the 15th October last she says "I enclose you the papers of your fund security. You will be sure not to lose it and when you have shown it to your friend Dr. Gully some other time when you return I can have to take care of for you." Her property amounted to about £140,000 before she gave part of it to the Defendant.

66. If it be true as the Plaintiff states that she had no affection or even respect for the Defendant apart from the peculiar phenomena

which occur in his presence she has repeatedly and consistently assured me to the exact contrary and she has also written to the contrary in the above correspondence. And I prefer to believe and do believe what she then told me and my own observation of her affectionate conduct to him to what she now says. The Defendant whose health is very delicate left London for Brighton and Malvern on the 12th October and returned on the 1st of November. He again left London the end of January for Hastings and stayed there till the 13th February. He left London again for Torquay about the 10th March and stayed there till the 22nd of April and he left London for Malvern on the 1st of May and stayed there till the 9th of June last.

67. I believe that the Plaintiff is a widow lady. Except as I am informed by her affidavit filed in this suit on the 15th June 1867 and from her correspondence and behaviour as hereinbefore appearing I cannot set forth as to my belief or otherwise whether she is between sixty and seventy years or of what age she is. She has apparently not outlived the caprices of her sex. She informed me and I believe that she has about £140,000 invested in the funds and upon mortgages.

68. The Defendant Home is a person of very delicate constitution and extremely nervous sensibility. He has been I believe all his life subject to the occasional occurrence of peculiar phenomena in his presence. Such phenomena have been carefully observed by several of the most powerful sovereigns of Europe and by persons of eminence in the leading professions and in literature and science and by practical men of business under conditions when anything like fraud or contrivance were impossible. Various theories have been suggested by way of explanation connected with the abstrusest problems in biology and metaphysics. My own views on this subject are probably unimportant but as charges and insinuations are made against me and the subject of Spiritualism is so misunderstood by the public I have the right to say that having had my attention drawn to certain remarkable occurrences about eighteen years ago in the house of a relative and which continued for nearly twelve years I have since that time occupied a portion of my leisure in inquiring into the subject and in arranging the various phenomena and comparing them with historical statements of similar occurrences. I have very seldom been at any *séances* and that not for many years having entirely satisfied myself years ago of the truth of most of the phenomena that is of their actual happening and I have at the same time and for many years formed and constantly expressed the opinion that it was wrong to believe in or act upon what might appear to be communications from the unseen on their own evidence merely I have invariably inculcated that no such communication should

be received as of so much value as if it were told by a friend in this world inasmuch as you know something of your friend here and cannot know the identity or origin of the communicant. I have frequently referred to the passage in the Old Testament in which it is said that God sent a lying spirit and to the directions given us in the New Testament to try or test the spirits. I have pursued the enquiry under great misrepresentations and obloquy and I intend to continue it as long as I can and I believe that the subjects of spiritual visions trances ecstasies prophecies angelic protection and diabolic possession anciently recorded have already had light thrown upon them and will have much more. I submit that I have a right to pursue an enquiry into psychological laws without being subjected to ridicule or abuse and that the proof of supernatural occurrences is valuable in both a scientific and religious point of view. The mere physical phenomena which the public erroneously fancies to be the whole of Spiritualism and which of course afford room for spurious imitation and fraud are in my belief the most unimportant part of the subject and have not for years engaged my attention. In this inquiry are also many persons of all the professions and of the highest literary and scientific attainments.

69. The Plaintiff told me that she was and I am informed and believe that she still is greatly interested in this enquiry although it appears she has conceived a dislike to the Defendant Home and has been as I am informed and believe induced by others to charge him with imposition in order to get back the money. The Plaintiff told me that she was subject to supernatural occurrences herself and she told me some most interesting anecdotes of what had happened to her.

70. The Defendant Home has I believe always stated and I believe that he has no control over such phenomena that he is perfectly passive when they occur and does not consciously exercise any volition. He has I believe and so far as I know always repudiated the notion that he possessed any power whatever of evoking the spirits of deceased persons or of putting other persons in communication with them.

71. The said Defendant connects some of the phenomena which I have mentioned with such communications as aforesaid and in so far as such phenomena or communications occur to him more often and in more marked degree than to the majority of persons as I believe from his bodily organization but not further or otherwise he describes himself as a spiritual medium.

72. I have been informed and believe that the said Defendant is entitled to considerable property in Russia being the fortune of his late wife and has some small private means besides and that he does not practise any profession or business. And save as aforesaid and his being

a highly accomplished gentleman I cannot say what if anything he calls himself or by what means if any he gains his living.

73. I am unable to set forth as to my belief or otherwise whether or not the Plaintiff was greatly attached to her late husband or how otherwise or whether or not she heard that she could be placed in communication with his spirit through the agency of a spiritual medium or how otherwise have been informed and believe that of her own motion she did seek for and obtain an interview with the Defendant Home on or about the 2nd October 1866 at Sloane Street in the said Bill mentioned.

74. The Plaintiff has always repeatedly and invariably assured me that in her adoption of the said Defendant and the presents which she has made him she was in nowise influenced by any spiritual communications whatever but acted spontaneously as she wished and the said other Defendant denies the charge made in the Plaintiff's Bill of Complaint and save as aforesaid I am unable to set forth as to my belief or otherwise whether or not the Defendant Home by any or what means induced her to believe or whether she did believe that a "manifestation" of the spirit of her deceased husband took or was taking place or whether or not through the instrumentality of the said Defendant or how otherwise or whether or not the said Defendant on that occasion induced the Plaintiff to believe or whether or not she did believe that the spirit of her deceased husband was in communication with her or whether or not that certain expressions of endearment or some other or what expressions on the part of the spirit were conveyed through the medium of the Defendant Home to her or how otherwise or whether or not the Plaintiff was much or in fact gratified thereby or whether or not she desired the said Defendant to call upon her or whether or not on the following day or whether or not she promised to give him £10 or some other or what sum or how otherwise or whether or not the said Defendant accordingly or in fact called upon the Plaintiff or whether or not at her residence is the said Bill mentioned or at some other or what place on the following or on some other or what day or whether or not he did or whether or not again induce the Plaintiff to believe or whether or not she did believe that the spirit of her deceased husband was manifested to her through the instrumentality of the said Defendant or how otherwise or whether or not she thereupon or in fact gave the said Defendant the sum of £30 or some other or what sum or how otherwise whether or not the Plaintiff on the following day or on some other or what day or whether or not under the belief that the spirit of her deceased husband had or whether or not again through the agency of the said Defendant been brought into communication with

her or for some other or what reason give the said Defendant the further sum of £50 or some other or what sum or how otherwise.

75. From the statements made to me by the Plaintiff from time to time as hereinbefore mentioned I believe that the Defendant Home did not by the means in the said Bill mentioned or by any other means acquire a great or any ascendancy over the mind of the Plaintiff who has a strong will of her own and is not likely to yield such an ascendancy over her to any one and I believe that the said Defendant did not by the exercise of his alleged spiritual powers or in fact induce her to believe that what the Plaintiff now alleges he represented to be communications from the spirit of her deceased husband to her were real communications. But on the contrary she always assured me that she was attached to the said Defendant for his own sake as she might well be wholly apart from any such phenomena or communications.

76. From the Plaintiff's own statement I believe that she has no child.

77. I am unable to set forth as to my belief or otherwise whether a meeting or another meeting took place between the Plaintiff and the Defendant Home a day or two after the last alleged meeting or in fact or save as appears from her own statements to the contrary and the other Defendant's denial of her present statements whether or not the said Defendant at such alleged or any meeting alleged or represented to the Plaintiff or induced her to believe or she did believe that the spirit of her deceased husband required her to adopt the said Defendant as her son or to place him in a position of independence suitable to his rank and position in life as her adopted son nor can I set forth as to my belief or otherwise what was the allegation. And representation if any made by the said Defendant to the Plaintiff on that alleged occasion or whether or not the said Defendant at the same time alleged or whether or not represented to the Plaintiff or whether or not induced her to believe or whether or not she did believe that the spirit of her deceased husband desired that Mr. Hall (in the said Bill named) should be sent for or what allegation or representation if any was then made by the said Defendant to the Plaintiff respecting the said Mr. Hall.

78. I believe that the said Mr. Hall was a friend of the Defendant Home. The Plaintiff has informed me and therefore I believe that she sent for the said Mr. Hall because she wanted some friend of the said Defendant's to talk with her about her adoption of him as her son and whether the mere adoption of him would confer legal rights to property and so forth and that the said Mr. Hall was accordingly but not otherwise sent for and that a meeting took place between him and the Plaintiff the Defendant Home not being present.

79. Save from the Plaintiff's denial as aforesaid of her having been under any spiritual influence and the Defendant's denial of her present statements I am unable as to my belief or otherwise to set forth whether the said last named Defendant and the said Mr. Hall or one or which of them at such meeting or at some other or what meeting alleged or whether or not represented to the Plaintiff or whether or not induced her to believe or whether or not she did believe that the spirit of her deceased husband required her to produce her stock receipts or some or one or which of them or whether or not to go to the Bank of England or whether or not transfer stock equivalent in value to £24,000 sterling or to some other or what amount to the said Defendant or whether or not to sell the same and give him the proceeds or whether or not as a provision by the Plaintiff for him or whether or not as her adopted son or what was the allegation or representation if any then made by the said Defendant and the said Mr. Hall or by one or which of them to the Plaintiff or whether or not the Plaintiff or whether or not accordingly or whether or not in the full conviction and belief that she was fulfilling the wishes of her deceased husband communicated to her through the medium of the Defendant Home or for some other or what reason went on or about the 10th October 1866 to the Bank of England or whether or not with the said Defendant or same other or what persons or person or whether or not the Plaintiff signed a book there or how otherwise or whether or not a large or some or what sum of Bank £3 per Cent. Consolidated Annuities or whether or not belonging to the Plaintiff was sold or transferred or whether or not the proceeds thereof or of any or what part thereof or whether or not amounting to £24,000 sterling or to some other or what sum were received by the said Defendant. The Plaintiff informed me and I believed that she spontaneously gave the said Defendant a sum of £24,000 sterling because she wished to make him independent and to prevent his having to go to Russia to look after his property there but she never mentioned a word about her husband but always assured me she acted entirely of her own accord and of her own will and judgment and that she had never laid out any money which gave so much pleasure and happiness and that whatever happened the sum was unimportant to her. The following is a copy of her letter written to the other Defendant on the occasion:—

"18, Westbourne Place, Hyde Park,
"10th October, 1866.

"My dear Mr. Home,—I have a desire to render you *independent* of the world, and having *ample* means for the purpose without abstracting from any needs or *comforts* of my own, I have the greatest satisfaction in now presenting you with it as an *entirely* FREE GIFT from me, the sum of £24,000, and am,

> "My dear Sir,
>> "Yours very truly & respectfully,
>>> "JANE LYON."

> "To D. D. Home, Esq.
> 22, Sloane Street."

80. Save as aforesaid I am unable to set forth as to my belief or otherwise whether or not the whole or any part of the said sum of £24,000 was obtained by the Defendant Home from the Plaintiff through the alleged ascendancy or power which the Plaintiff now alleges he had acquired over her mind by the means in the said Bill mentioned.

81. Save as aforesaid I am unable to set forth as to my belief or otherwise whether the Plaintiff or whether or not shortly after the said sums of £24,000 had been given by the Plaintiff to the Defendant Home or as the Plaintiff now alleges had been obtained by the said Defendant from the Plaintiff by the means and under the circumstances in her said Bill stated or in fact had a meeting or another meeting or interview with the said last named Defendant or how otherwise or whether or not the said Defendant at such meeting or interview alleged or represented to the Plaintiff or whether or not induced her to believe or whether or not she did believe that she was required by the spirit of her late husband to destroy the Will she had then made or whether or not to make another Will in favour of the said Defendant or what was the allegation or representation if any then made by the said Defendant to the Plaintiff or whether or not the said last named Defendant represented to the Plaintiff or whether or not induced her to believe or whether or not she did believe that the spirit of her said husband dictated the terms of such new Will under which he the said Defendant was to be universal legatee of all the Plaintiff's property or whether or not also that Dr. Hawksley and Mr. Rudall in the said Bill respectively named were to be sent for to attest the execution of such new Will or whether or not that the spirit of the Plaintiff's said late husband also dictated the terms of the letters to be written to the said Dr. Hawksley and Mr. Rudall asking them to attest the said Will or what were the allegations or representations if any then made by the said Defendant to the Plaintiff. Both the said Dr. Hawksley and Mr. Rudall were friends of the Defendant Home.

82. A Will purporting to be the Will of the Plaintiff was prepared by me for the Plaintiff at her request in the manner and under the circumstances hereinbefore mentioned and not otherwise. I had nothing to do with Defendant Home in the matter nor would I have accepted any instructions from him. The said Defendant was under such Will named as the universal legatee of all the Plaintiff's property and such Will was executed by the Plaintiff on the 12th of November 1866 in the presence of and attested by the said Dr. Hawksley, Mr. Rudall and myself. Neither the Defendant Home nor any one else was present on the occasion except the Plaintiff. The descriptions of the attesting witnesses are given in their affidavits already filed in this suit. The said Thomas Hawksley is a doctor of medicine residing at number 70 Brook Street Hanover Square in the county of Middlesex and the said Henry Alexander Rudall is a merchant carrying on business at numbers 8 and 9 Great Tower Street in the city of London. Save from the Plaintiff's and the other Defendant's statements to the contrary I am unable to set forth as to my belief or otherwise whether the said Will was in fact executed by the Plaintiff at the instigation suggestion or desire of the Defendant Home or was so executed while the Plaintiff was under the influence of the ascendancy and power which the Plaintiff now alleges he had acquired over her mind by the means and tinder the circumstances in the said Bill stated.

83. I have been informed and believe that the Defendant Home did on or about the 5th November 1866 at the Plaintiff's request invest the sum of £23,913 17s. 3d. or thereabouts being the said sum of £24,000 less brokerage which the Plaintiff now alleges was obtained from the Plaintiff as in the said Bill mentioned in the purchase in his then name of Daniel Dunglass Home in the sum of £26,756 15s. 5d or thereabouts of £3 per Cent. Consolidated Bank Annuities.

84. The Defendant Home did on or about the 3rd December 1866 and at the Plaintiff's request execute a deed poll of that date. Such deed has since been at the Plaintiff's request and in fact enrolled as of record in Her Majesty's Court of Chancery and the said defendant thereby declared that he had taken the name of Lyon in lieu of and instead of Home and that in future he intended to be called and known as Daniel Home Lyon and she ordered a frame in which to have it hung up in her room.

85. I have hereinbefore and especially in the 8th to the 12th paragraphs both inclusive of this my Answer and in the 61st and 62nd paragraphs set forth all the facts and correspondence with which I am acquainted relating to the gift of £6,000 cash from the Plaintiff to the said Defendant and save as herein appears and from the Plaintiff's

former denial as aforesaid and the Defendant's denial of her present statements I am unable to set forth as to my belief or otherwise whether the Plaintiff on the 10th of December 1866 or at some other or what time or whether or not at the request or suggestion of the Defendant Home or whether or not while under the influence of the alleged ascendancy and power which the Plaintiff now alleges he had by the means in the said Bill mentioned or in fact acquired over her mind or by some other or what means induced by the said Defendant to go again with him to the Bank of England or whether or not to transfer the sum of £6,798 17s. 4d. or some other or what sum of £3 per Cent. Consolidated Bank Annuities into the name of the said Defendant as Daniel Dunglass Home that being the name in which the aforesaid sum of £26,756 15s. 3d. like annuities was then standing having been invested as aforesaid prior to his change of name. I believe that such sum of £6,798 17s. 4d. Bank Annuities was then equivalent in value to a sum of £6,000 sterling or thereabouts.

86. Such deed poll or instrument in writing as in the said Bill is mentioned to bear date the 12th December 1866 and is therein stated to be of or to the purport and effect in the 11th paragraph of the said Bill set forth so far as the same is therein set forth being the same instrument as is set forth verbatim in the 12th paragraph of this my Answer was in fact duly and under the circumstances hereinbefore mentioned executed by the Plaintiff.

87. The said deed poll was prepared by me as the Solicitor for and at the request of the Plaintiff alone as hereinbefore appears but not in any respect as the Solicitor for or on behalf of the Defendant Home. The costs for the same were at the time debited to the Plaintiff alone in my bill but they have not yet been paid. Save as appears from the Plaintiff's statements and letters to the contrary and the Defendant's denial of her present allegations I am unable to set forth as to my belief or otherwise whether the said deed was executed by the Plaintiff at the request or instigation or suggestion or desire of the said Defendant Home or whether or not while if she was in fact ever under the influence of the ascendancy or power which the Plaintiff now alleges he had acquired over her as in the said Bill mentioned and I refer to the circumstances hereinbefore related in the 8th to the 12th paragraphs both inclusive and the 61st and 62nd paragraphs of this my answer. I repeatedly and strongly urged her to employ another Solicitor which she refused to do as hereinbefore truly appears. And under the circumstances hereinbefore appearing and not otherwise it is the fact that she executed the said deed without the intervention of any other Solicitor or person as far as I know on her behalf. I acted as her

Solicitor and with entire independence of the Defendant Home from whom I neither did receive nor would I have received any instructions whatever on the subject.

88. I have hereinbefore and respectively, in paragraphs 7 to 41 both inclusive and paragraphs 63 and 64 of this my Answer truthfully set forth the facts and correspondence relating to the indenture of the 19th January 1867 in the Plaintiff's Bill mentioned and save as hereinbefore appears and from the Plaintiff's former denial as aforesaid and the other Defendants denial of her present statements I am unable to set forth as to my belief or otherwise whether or not the Plaintiff in the month of January 1867 or at some other or what time was induced by the Defendant Home to execute a deed or whether or not purporting to be an indenture bearing date the 19th January 1867 or made between the parties or of or to the purport and effect in the 13th paragraph of the said Bill set forth so far as the same is therein set forth or some other or what indenture of such or some other or what date or made between the same or some other or what parties or of or to such or the like or some other or what purport or effect or how otherwise.

89. Under the circumstances hereinbefore appearing and not otherwise the said indenture of the 19th January 1867 was prepared by me as the Solicitor for and on behalf of the Plaintiff and in no respect as the Solicitor for or on behalf of the Defendant Home. The costs for preparing the same were at the time duly debited to the Plaintiff alone in my bill but such costs have not yet been paid. I repeatedly and strongly urged her to employ another Solicitor which she refused to do as hereinbefore truly appears and under the circumstances herein appearing and not otherwise it is the fact that the said deed was not as far as I know seen or approved of by any other Solicitor or person for or on behalf of the Plaintiff. I acted as her Solicitor and with entire independence of the Defendant Home as hereinbefore truly appears and I did not receive nor would I have received any instructions from him in the matter. The Plaintiff also executed the indenture of even date recited in the said last-mentioned indenture whereby she assigned the principal sum of £30,000 and interest and the securities for the same to me. Such indenture of even date was prepared by me as the Solicitor for and on behalf of the Plaintiff alone and in no respect as the Solicitor for or on behalf of the Defendant Home and under the circumstances hereinbefore appearing and not otherwise. The same indenture was not as far as I know seen or approved of by any other Solicitor or person for or on behalf of the Plaintiff. I acted as her Solicitor and with entire independence of the Defendant Home as hereinbefore truly appears and I did not receive nor would I have

received any instructions from him in the matter. And save from the Plaintiff's former denial as aforesaid and from the other Defendant's denial of her present statements I am unable to set forth as to my belief or otherwise whether the Plaintiff executed the two last mentioned indentures at the request or instigation of the Defendant Home or whether or not while she was if she in fact was under the influence of the ascendancy or power over her mind which the Plaintiff now alleges the said last named Defendant had acquired by means or under the circumstances in the said Bill mentioned. The said two last mentioned deeds were executed by the Plaintiff on Saturday the 19th January 1867 at her own house in the presence of my son and Mr. Hartley two of my clerks who attended with the deeds for the purpose. I was not there being ill at home and I afterwards executed the deed myself at my office in the presence of the same witnesses.

90. I have hereinbefore in paragraphs 38, 39, 40 and 64 of this my Answer truthfully set forth the circumstances relating to the transfer of £2,290 9s. 5d. or thereabouts Bank X3 per Cent. Consolidated Annuities. And save as therein appears and save from the Plaintiff's former denials as aforesaid and from the other Defendant's denial of her present statements I am unable to set forth as to my belief or otherwise whether the Plaintiff on the 21st February 1867 or at any other or what time was or whether or not again induced by the Defendant Home to accompany him to the Bank of England or whether or not to transfer the sum of £2,290 9s. 5d. or some other or what sum of Bank £3 per Cent. Consolidated Annuities into his name as Daniel Dunglass Home though I believe that was the name in which the large sums of like annuities was standing the first and largest sums having been invested prior to his change of name or whether or not the last mentioned transfer was or whether or not also made by the Plaintiff while under if she ever was under the influence of the ascendancy or power which the Plaintiff now alleges the said Defendant had by the means in the said Bill mentioned or in fact so acquired or was then exercising over her mind or how otherwise.

91. The Defendant Home did on or about the 13th March 1867 sell out a sum of £21,947 17s. 6d. Bank £3 per Cent. Consolidated Annuities which was I believe part of the said sum of £26,756 15s. 5d. like annuities and of the said sum of £6,798 17s. 4d. and £2,290 9s. 5d. like annuities. On behalf of the said Defendant and at his request he being then ill at Hastings I received the proceeds of such sale amounting to the sum of £20,000 cash from the brokers and the Defendant Home on or about the date last aforesaid lent and advanced the said sum of £20,000 through me upon mortgage of property in

Yorkshire and such sum of £20,000 has ever since been and is now invested on the security of the said mortgage. The said security has since been and is now deposited in this Court where the Plaintiff can inspect it. No part of the said sum so lent and advanced has been repaid. As regards the said advance of £20,000 upon mortgage I refer to the 65th paragraph of this my Answer.

92. I am unable to set forth as to my belief or otherwise whether a sum of £13,898 4s. 8d. Bank £3 per Cent. Consolidated Annuities or any other or what sum of such annuities but I believe that the residue of the balance of the said three sums of £26,756 15s. 5d. £6,798 17s. 4d. and £2,290 9s. 5d. like annuities after deducting from the aggregate amount thereof the said sum of £21,947 17s. 6d. sold out as hereinbefore mentioned is still standing in the name of the Defendant as Daniel Dunglass Home the first and largest amount having been paid into that name before the said Defendant changed his name at the request of the Plaintiff and the subsequent additions having been made to the same account in the Books of the Governor and Company of the Bank of England. I am unable to set forth whether the said last-named Defendant threatens but I believe that he intends to sell and dispose thereof or deal therewith as and when he thinks proper as belonging to him.

93. I refer to the 52nd and 53rd paragraph of this my Answer and I am ready and willing to do in the premises whatever this Honourable Court shall think proper to direct upon having my reasonable costs paid and satisfied I claim a lien on all deeds and documents in my possession or which I have deposited in this Court for the purposes of this suit or otherwise which may belong to the Plaintiff or in which she is interested for all costs due to me as her solicitor.

94. After my Answer was prepared and printed to this point I have received and read the print of the Plaintiff's Affidavit sworn and filed on the 18th duly instant. It is entirely untrue as stated in the 6th paragraph of that Affidavit that the Plaintiff ever informed me that she was obeying the dictates of her husband's spirit. Had she said so or had I known of it I should at once have refused to proceed with the business. It is also untrue as stated in the 7th paragraph that I was ever present when any instructions were received from her husband's spirit with reference to the said deeds. The only occasion on which I saw any phenomena in her presence was one evening after I had taken my hat to leave she asked me to remain a few minutes which I did and there were some movements of the table and rapping but there were no directions nor instructions relating to the said deeds. It is untrue that the deed of the 12th of December last was signed on any other day than that of its date.

It was seen the next day executed by the Plaintiff by several of my clerks. It is also untrue as stated in the 9th paragraph of her Affidavit that she told me on the occasion therein referred to that she did not care for the Defendant Home personally nor that she was obeying the orders of her husband's spirit in what she had done or wished to do. I was very unwell on that day and have no distinct memory of her conversation had she told me so I would have had nothing further to do with the business. She always expressed to me her great affection for the Defendant Home. I find the following paragraph in one of her letters to him bearing out this under her own hand one of which is as follows "I feel so anxious on your account and afraid you should be ill, or anything should happen to you, that I am sure it is a mother's maternal love towards her beloved child, so if you value my comfort my dear son take care of yourself." She several times told me that her only fear was that the Defendant Home would marry and that she would lose his society. It would be doing the greatest injustice to the Plaintiff could I believe that she is now expressing the truth in stating that she did not love the Defendant.

END OF VOL. II.

LIGHTS AND SHADOWS

OF

SPIRITUALISM

By

D. D. HOME

"Light—more Light!"—GOETHE

First Edition 1877

TO MY WIFE,

Whose loving sympathy and constant care have soothed me in many hours of trial and pain, and whose superior counsels have aided me in composing a work, the end and aim of which is to place a much-insulted Truth on a plane where honest lovers of such Truth would not have cause to blush in avowing themselves to be what she is, a Christian and a Spiritualist,

I, IN AFFECTION AND ESTEEM,

Dedicate

THIS BOOK.

CONTENTS

PART I

ANCIENT SPIRITUALISM

CHAPTER I

PART II

SPIRITUALISM IN THE JEWISH AND CHRISTIAN ERAS

CHAPTER I

PART III

MODERN SPIRITUALISM

CHAPTER I

CHAPTER II

Delusions.

CHAPTER III

Delusions *(continued)*.

CHAPTER IV

CHAPTER V

People from the other world.

CHAPTER VI

Sceptics and tests.

LIGHTS AND SHADOWS OF SPIRITUALISM

PART I

ANCIENT SPIRITUALISM

CHAPTER I

THE FAITHS OF ANCIENT PEOPLES

There descend to us, among the fragmentary records which, with shattered temples and decaying cities, form the only remaining proofs that such nations as the Assyrian and the Egyptian were once great upon the earth, many evidences of the vividness with which light from another world broke in upon man during the earlier ages of our own. Every spiritual phenomenon which has in the present day startled the Christians of the West was, centuries ago, familiar to the Pagans of the East. On the common foundation of a belief that spirit visits were neither few nor far between every mythology of those far-back times was based. The most superhuman virtues, and abominable crimes, of Chaldean, Phoenician, Egyptian, Hebrew, Greek, and Roman; are traceable to a spiritual source. For then, as since, the good of the truth that man cannot "die, to live again," but, living once, lives eternally, was at times largely perverted to evil. Side by side with noble natures, made yet higher and purer by communion with high and pure minds that no longer tenanted the flesh, were demons doing the behests of demons— evil creatures of both sexes, and all ages and conditions, who, instigated by spirits still fouler, worked ceaselessly to fill the earth with bloodshed and uncleanness. By intercourse with spirits the cheerful assurance of immortality was perpetuated through all times and nations, and the dark vestibule of the grave brightened with a glory from beyond. Through intercourse with spirits also the awful rite of human sacrifice—men seeking to appease imaginary deities by the murder of their brethren— had birth. It was natural that when, at the touch of the departed, the clouds that veil our hereafter shrank away, man, gazing on the newly revealed morning-land, should imagine he saw gods walking there. Thus the power of the spirits for good and evil became immeasurable. The valiant phalanx of the Greeks rushing down upon the Persian multitude at Marathon, every breast thrilling with the thought that around thronged the spirits of their ancestors, and the deities of their nation, inspiring and encouraging them to the combat, supplies an example of the best phase of spiritual influence. The same Greeks, solemnly hewing in pieces or burying alive unhappy captives, whose torments would, they supposed, win them favour in the sight of evil beings erringly exalted into deities, may stand as an instance of the worst.

But the dark and the bright phases alike witness to the intensity of faith which primæval man had in the invisible. Even when we know little else of a nation we know generally that the corner-stone of its mythology was a belief in the return of the departed. Heroes and sages were not, when death snatched them, lamented as having for ever passed away. Their spirits hovered still above the land they had loved and served: at times visibly appearing to the posterity by whom they were adored, counselling them in the moment of danger, or leading on their hosts to victory. If a spirit were frequent in his appearances and mighty in the services he rendered, he speedily became worshipped as a god. Again, when it was discovered that only in the presence of certain persons could spirits manifest themselves, these mediums were set apart, and priesthood had its origin. Immortal man is immortally ambitious—peculiarly liable also to mislead and be misled. The priest speedily aspired to be the founder of a sect—the builder up of some system of theology or government. He walked among men as one with them but not of them; clothed with distinctive garments; hedged round by the sanctity of mysterious rites. From among the invisibles who surrounded him he selected as his peculiar guardians and guides those whose counsels were agreeable to his soul. It leaves a dubious impression of the majority of spirits and mediums in ancient days, that in every land of which we have knowledge we find altars dripping with human blood; prisoners of war butchered ruthlessly, as acceptable offerings to the gods; temples polluted with licentiousness; the most unblushing vice; the most systematic cruelty. These things all sprang from the abuses of communion between world and world; abuses for which spirits alike with men were blamable. Were the beings anciently worshipped as gods in reality devils? If by devils we understand human beings depraved to the lowest pitch, then many probably might be accounted so. It is not to be doubted that then, as now, the messengers of God—high, holy, and pure spirits—constantly watched over and communicated with the better children of earth. But to that end mediums were necessary, and the mediums were usually ambitious and often depraved. Loth to be but the servants of the spirits, they foolishly and uselessly aspired to govern them. The entreaties and admonitions of their good angels were neglected and contemned, until these in grief held aloof, and seemed to have forsaken the earth. The dangerous beings who counselled pleasant things, and, while seeming pliant to the slightest wish, held their victims firmly to the service of evil, reigned almost unchecked. Dwellers in darkness, they desired, with the malignity of unrepentant wretchedness, that souls yet on earth should enter the spirit-realm tainted with a leprosy deep as their own. Through their fancied masters and real tools, the priests, nation after nation was led away from faith in the One God to worship his creatures. What these deities were, the records that have descended to us irrefragably prove. Resembling men, they are depicted as possessing the passions and attributes of fiends. In every mythology it was a cardinal point that to avert their wrath blood was necessary. Fearful penalties were denounced against such as offended these pseudo-gods. Among the light lively peoples of the South of Europe the idea of punishment after death took the shape of confinement in silence and eternal night; with sterner nations it was a vision of unhappy faces looking up from a burning tomb. The infamous doctrines that have disgraced our own age—doctrines which seek to sap the very foundations of society, and, taking from love all that is beautiful and endearing, leave only its filthy and debasing mockery—were inculcated by these deities; enforced in their temples by precept and example, and disseminated through nations with the effects of a pestilence. What society was two thousand years ago history witnesses but too well. Good, and good spirits, seemed almost to have fled from the earth. The servants of evil were everywhere. All temples of all deities had become offences to the eye of heaven—plague-spots of bloodshed and licentiousness. The many accepted, as they have in all ages done, the deities offered to them, and, obedient to their behests, cultivated the evil of man's nature and carefully repressed the good. The intelligent and gifted perceived that, living or fabled, the beings to whom the nations erected temples were assuredly not gods, and the creators of the universe; but either monsters of the imagination, or creatures of a scale somewhat beneath that on which they themselves moved. They sought refuge accordingly in epicurean negation, and attention to the things of this life. At length the evil grew to an unendurable height. That period when the Roman power had attained its zenith, was the nadir of the morality and happiness of man. Then the forces of good in the invisible world began once more to stir. Upon an earth enervated with wickedness and convulsed with strife; upon nations where the most hideous vices stalked the land openly and unashamed; upon nations where the stake, the cross, and the scourge were in hourly use, and where man plotted how to be most inhuman to his fellowman; upon the century of Tiberius, Caligula, and Nero, of Messalina, Agrippina, and Locusts,—the great awakening of the Christian gospel dawned. Founded in miracle, attested by prodigy, spread by apostles whose touch healed the sick, whose words caused the maimed to become whole, and the cripple to arise and walk, and to whose eyes was revealed the whole radiance of the Unseen, it conquered rapidly region after region, setting at defiance the possible and the common, and discovering by burning proofs that the ladder which Jacob beheld was but faintly typical of that immortal one stretching from earth to heaven by which multitudes of the departed have in all ages continually ascended and descended.

I have said that since the founding of our world communion with another has existed, and that in every fragmentary history of an ancient nation its tokens peep through. Among the very few legends that Time has floated down to us respecting the mysterious Etruscans is one which ascribes to them devotion to magic, and the power of raising the dead. Their cognate race, the almost equally mysterious Phoenicians, had in the highest degree the belief both in evil and beneficent spirits; and in their evocation by means of wild and complicated rites. Other nations, of whose mythologies but the most slender scraps have been handed down—the Scythians for example, the Gauls, the Teutons and the Sarmatians—appear also to have cherished this universal faith. In France and our own isles the Druids were acquainted with the phenomena of clairvoyance and animal magnetism; they cultivated the trance, and through visions sought for an insight into futurity. The histories of Egypt, Assyria, Chaldea and Persia, of Greece and Rome, of India and China, are steeped in spiritualism. In a later portion of this work I shall dwell upon the Hebrew annals. It will be sufficient that at present I, under the head of ancient spiritualism, devote my attention to the countries already named; that I bring from the storehouse of history the best-attested incidents illustrating the communion of men and spirits, and make clear their relation to the phenomena witnessed in our own age. I confess that it is impossible to construct from the imperfect relics of ancient chroniclers narratives of such weight and authenticity as are available from the rich materials of more modern times; but enough remains to amply illustrate and verify whatever I have already asserted in this introduction to my task. I shall seek to show that the occurrences received with stubborn incredulity in the nineteenth century were familiar to the first, and perhaps equally familiar to centuries long anterior to the Christian era. I shall point to the belief in the supermundane entertained by the mightiest minds of these ancient ages, and rank as spiritual believers such giants as Homer, Hesiod and Pindar; as Alexander and Cæsar; as Virgil and Tacitus; as Cicero, Seneca, Pliny, Plutarch, and a hundred more. Finally, having pointed out the vivid resemblance which the spiritual phenomena of the past bear to the spiritual phenomena of to-day, I shall call attention to the fact that the outbreaks of evil which of old convulsed the earth, were heralded by just such clouds as, at first no bigger than a man's hand, have rapidly come to overcast the present spiritual horizon.

CHAPTER II

ASSYRIA, CHALDEA, EGYPT, AND PERSIA

The uncountable years that have elapsed since Ninus shared his sceptre with Semiramis, and the first sage watched on the summit of the Tower of Bolus, have all but whirled away with them into oblivion the history of the Assyrian realm—the mightiest of the ancient world. From the scanty fragments of Berosus, and the more copious remains of Herodotus, together with the Hebrew scriptures, do we chiefly glean what is known to us of this remarkable people; unless we dare trust the Greek historian who recounts that Semiramis invaded India with an army of two millions of men. The researches of Layard and Smith, indeed, have of late greatly added to our knowledge of this antique race. From disinterred Nineveh come to us the pictures, the picture writings, and the sculptures of the mighty Assyrian warriors—the scourges of all neighbouring nations. We have by their own hands portraits of the men who devastated Egypt, and carried the Ten Tribes of the Hebrews into captivity. And, formidable as was the Assyrian soldiery, the priests wielded a yet more terrible power over their fellow men. Of the most ancient among them we know little; save that they were devoted soothsayers, and respected by all men for their gift of looking into the future. With the period of the division of the Assyrian empire our information begins to increase. Pre-eminent is that awful instance of spiritual power recorded in the Hebrew annals, and apparently confirmed by late researches—the passing above the Assyrian camp of an angel who destroyed silently, and in a single night, Sennacherib's army of a hundred and eighty thousand men.

We know from Herodotus and others that when the Babylonian empire was in the glory of its power, the influence of the Chaldean sages had also attained its zenith. Every secret of nature which man had unveiled, the whole knowledge then acquired respecting the visible and the invisible, was locked in the bosoms of these famous philosophers. They held in the Babylonian commonwealth a station equally dignified with that held in a neighbouring country by the powerful magicians of Egypt. They guided the footsteps of the young just entering upon this present life—they smoothed the passage of the old just departing to another. Futurity was their especial study, and, by diligent comparing and interpreting of dreams and prodigies, they had established what they believed to be a complete system of divination. Especially were they famous for their watchings of the stars. The astronomers of the eighteenth and nineteenth, and the astrologers of the sixteenth and seventeenth centuries A.D., alike recognise predecessors in those inquiring spirits, who from the summit of the Tower of Belus nightly searched the Assyrian heavens. Even when the Babylonian empire fell before the shafts of the Mede the magi survived. They flourished in Babylon in unchecked power, from the era of Cyrus to that of the Darius whom Alexander subdued, and they made one of their most remarkable prophecies to the Macedonian hero himself.

At the distance of three hundred furlongs from the great city Alexander was encountered by a deputation of the most famous magi. These warned him that he should on no account presume to enter Babylon, as the gods had decreed that once within the walls he must assuredly die. So deeply was the conqueror of Asia moved by this prediction that, while sending his chief friends into Babylon, he himself encamped at a distance of two hundred furlongs from the walls. But the Grecian philosophers who accompanied him, the doubting disciples of Anaxagoras and others, went into the King's presence, and by their lively ridicule temporarily effaced from his mind all respect for the wisdom of the Chaldeans. Alexander entered Babylon, and in a few months was gathered to his fathers. Various other omens had foreboded the disappearance of this royal meteor from the earth which he astonished. Shortly after the magnificent obsequies of his favourite Hephæstion, a Babylonian who had been placed in confinement was found by the King dressed in the royal robes and seated on the throne Alexander, amazed, demanded of the man who had advised him to this act. The intruder answered simply that, "he knew not how he found himself there." By the advice of the soothsayers he was put to death; but the omen sank deeply into the conqueror's mind.

Not long afterwards he sailed forth, accompanied by a small flotilla, to view the harbour of Babylon. A storm arose, and Alexander's vessel was parted from the rest. After tossing on the waters for several days refuge was found in a narrow creek choked with overhanging shrubs. The King's diadem was plucked from his head by a projecting bough, and flung into the waves. A sailor swimming from the vessel recovered the crown, and placed it on his own brow the more speedily to reach the ship. Both by Alexander and the Chaldeans this second prognostic was considered ominous, and he was counselled to offer sacrifices to the gods. At the feast which accompanied the proposed rites the great conqueror quaffed at a draught a huge goblet of wine, sighed, appeared smitten with an overwhelming sickness, and was assisted forth to his deathbed. Two days before, Calanus, an Indian philosopher, had, on ascending his funeral pyre, announced to Alexander that the latter must prepare to speedily follow him to the Shades.

The philosophy of Egypt divides with that of Chaldea the honour of being the most ancient of which we moderns have knowledge. So many centuries have been numbered with the past since even the decay of either of these civilisations, that it almost ranks with the impossible to decide on which nation the light of learning first dawned. The preponderance of evidence, such as that evidence is, inclines to the side of Egypt. Zonaras, indeed, asserts that the Egyptians derived their mythology from the Chaldeans, but this modern researches contradict. It is, in any case, incontestable that the Egyptian priesthood was the wisest and the most magnificent of the ancient earth. In dignity they were equal to their brethren of Chaldea, in wisdom they even surpassed them. What their temples were, the awful ruins of Karnac, the city of shrines, even now witness. The avenues of sphynxes extend for miles; the desert is crested with columns whose massiveness no other nation can equal. In these stupendous recesses was once hived that wisdom a few fragments of which, despite the sleepless jealousy of its guardians, Greek sages bore back to their own land, and embodied in Greece's sublimest philosophy. The splendour of the little that remains causes us the more to regret that mass of knowledge which, by the erring system of the Egyptians, is irrecoverably lost. For here, as in each of the great empires of the East, the few enlightened ones in whose keeping was the wisdom and the science of the age, far from striving to disseminate the seeds of knowledge among the great body of the people, jealously restricted that knowledge to themselves and their descendants, leaving the outer world in hopeless darkness. The mass of the nation were estimated as cattle, the puppets of the nobles and the magi, fit only for contemptuous abandonment to the worship of apes and beetles. In the temples, on the contrary, the utmost striving after discovery was apparent—an intellectual activity that never ceased. The paintings which Denis and Montfaucon have copied from their walls make manifest that mesmerism and clairvoyance were familiar things with the magicians of Egypt; that through these or other means they obtained communication with the world of spirits, and practised with spirit-aid the art of healing. In the temples were placed representations of the more miraculous cures. These seem to have been chiefly procured by aid of the trance or mesmeric sleep, in which, without doubt, spirits no less than men usually operated. To induce this sleep incense was used. Its influence was assisted by the soft music of lyres. Elevated thus above its material prison, the soul for a space held free communion with the spiritual world. King Rhampsitimus, the magi of Egypt asserted to Herodotus, descended by such means to the mansions of the dead, held converse with the gods, and returned after awhile to the upper day.

Into Egypt went Pythagoras, to increase from the greater stores of that country the wisdom which he had acquired in Greece. But so rigidly did the magi restrict all learning to their own caste, that not until he had passed from temple to temple, and had undergone disciplinary initiations more and more severe, was the philosopher, after twenty-two years of patience, admitted to the inner mysteries. Returning to Greece, he became the martyr of the spiritual truths with which he astonished his countrymen. Delos, Sparta, Elis, and Crete, in turn cast him out. Everywhere derided as a madman, he passed over into Italy and wandered through the magnificent colony of Magna Græcia, teaching and working miracles in Crotona, Rhegium, and Metapontus. The fate of the prophets of all ages pursued him. At Crotona the mob burned down his school, and forty neophytes perished in the flames. Hunted by enemies thirsty for his life, he immured himself in the Temple of the Muses at Metapontus, and was there suffered to die of want. But his doctrines, the fruits of the painful years passed in Egypt, endured after him—the error with the truth. From the Egyptians he had acquired the theory of transmigration, as inculcated in the sacred books of Hermes Trismegistus. At death, according to these strange metaphysics, the soul of man passed into another body. Sometimes the spirit reappeared as a human being—sometimes as an animal. The nature of the new receptacle was determined by the purity or wickedness of the former life. Three thousand years were passed in this manner, and if then sufficiently purified, the spirit ascended to the immortal gods. During the latter centuries of this curious species of purgatory, the soul was supposed to reside in those animals which the Egyptians held peculiarly sacred. Thus a cat represented a being particularly close to eternal felicity: a beetle was perhaps still nearer. A modification of this marvellous religion was taught by Pythagoras, exaggerated after his departure by his disciples, and finally extinguished in the grossness of its own absurdities. Our own century, strange to say, has witnessed the resurrection of this ancient folly. I shall take occasion in a later portion of this work to treat of the belief of those apers of antiquity who, discarding the animals, have unearthed from their dusty receptacle the remaining relics of the Pythagorean system, and, clothing these with the fantasies of their own imaginations, have submitted to the notice of a bewildered world the identity-confounding chimæra of re-incarnation.

Our information respecting the Egyptian oracles, falls far short of the ample knowledge accorded to us of the Grecian. The most famous— can it, however, be held an oracle of Egypt?—was that renowned temple buried in the solitudes of the Libyan Desert, and consecrated to Jupiter Ammon. Alexander of Macedon, in the plentitude of his power, visited it to interrogate the deity on some subject near to his heart. Question and answer were alike kept secret; but the magnificence of the conqueror's offerings intimated that he was satisfied with the response accorded him. A very few predictions of less celebrated oracles have been preserved by the Greek historians. Among such, two singularly-fulfilled prophecies deserve notice.

Whilst Sethon, formerly a priest of Vulcan, held the Egyptian sceptre, he was dismayed by the approach of that Sennacherib whose invasion of Judæa heaven so terribly frustrated. Deserted by the warrior tribe, he betook himself to the temple of Vulcan, and implored against the Assyrians the aid of the deity whom he had served. As he stood before the image a vision came upon him. Vulcan, he dreamed, spoke, and bade him be of good cheer, for that he himself would fight in his worshipper's behalf. Hereupon Sethon, gathering courage, marched to encounter Sennacherib. He was followed only by a rabble of tradespeople and mechanics; at sight of whom the Assyrian laughed, accounting himself certain of victory. On the morning of the battle, however, Sennacherib found that he was overthrown before the strife commenced. During the night myriads of field-mice had entered the Assyrian camp, and devouring the bowstrings and quivers of the warriors, had left them almost defenceless. The victory of the Egyptians was easy and complete.

Herodotus tells us that after the death of this Sethon twelve kings reigned in the different provinces of Egypt. An oracle announced that he who, in the temple of Vulcan, poured a libation from a brazen vessel, should expel his fellows and reign as sole monarch. On the occasion of a certain sacrifice, Psammeticus, one of the twelve, having found himself without the accustomed golden cup, filled a brazen helmet with wine and made his libation. On this the remaining kings banished him to the marshes of the coast. Burning with indignation, he consulted the oracle as to how he might best avenge the injury. It was replied that vengeance would be accorded him when brazen men arose from the deep. The answer was naturally held by Psammeticus a mockery. Shortly afterwards, however, certain pirates clad in brass armour appeared in Egypt from Ionia and Caria. These strangers Psammeticus took into his pay, and having, by their aid, become sole ruler of the Egyptians, the oracle's prediction was most curiously accomplished.

From the dim magnificences of the race who reared the pyramids we pass to Persia and Zoroaster. Even before the time of that mighty iconoclast the history of his country bears interesting traces of intercourse with another sphere. Cyrus, the subduer of Asia, was heralded and attended by prophecy, both in Persia and among the Jews. Astyages, his grandfather, saw in vision a vine proceed from his daughter Mandane, by which the whole of Asia was overshadowed. The soothsayers explained this to mean that Mandane would be delivered of a son who should conquer all the kingdoms of the East. Fearing lest he himself might be among the rulers deposed, the jealous monarch wedded his daughter, not, as was the usage, to a prince of the Medes, but to Cambyses, a native of the subject kingdom of Persia. He again dreamed of the vine that overshadowed Asia, and again received the explanation of its pointing to the coming of a conqueror who should tread all nations under foot. On this the King determined to destroy the fruit of the marriage the instant that it saw the light. The fruit was Cyrus, whom Astyages commanded Harpalus, his chief captain, to take with him and put to death. Harpalus, reluctant to execute the foul mandate, sent the babe to be reared far from the court, in the rude Highlands of Persia. Arrived at manhood, Cyrus speedily approved the truth of the prophecy, and, deposing Astyages, reigned over Persia and Media in his stead. He conquered Crœsus of Lydia, and, overthrowing the Babylonian empire, permitted the captive Jews to return to Palestine. According to Josephus this favour was won by the Jews at Babylon displaying to Cyrus the prophecy wherein Isaiah alludes to him by name. The forty-fifth chapter of the prophet thus opens:— "Thus saith the Lord to his anointed, to Cyrus, whose right hand I have holden, to subdue nations before him; and I will loose the loins of kings to open before him the two-leaved gates; and the gates shall not be shut; I will go before thee, and make the crooked paths straight: I will break in pieces the gates of brass, and cut in sunder the bars of iron: And I will give thee the treasures of darkness, and hidden riches of secret places, that thou mayest know that I, the Lord, which call thee by thy name, am the God of Israel. For Jacob my servant's sake, and Israel mine elect, I have even called thee by thy name, though thou hast not known me."

Cyrus, continues Josephus, on being shown this prediction, and the equally remarkable one contained in the twenty-eighth verse of the preceding chapter, acknowledged that the Jehovah of the Hebrews was indeed the God of nations, and that from Him he received the sceptre of the world.

Nor was the close of the mighty conqueror's career unaccompanied by prodigy. Invading Scythia, he dreamed that Darius, the son of Hystaspes, stood before him with wings springing from his shoulders; of which the one overshadowed Europe, the other Asia. Believing that the gods had thus warned him of a plot against his throne, he sent Hystaspes back to Persia, to watch over Darius until he should himself return. But, although the son of Hystaspes was in reality destined as his successor, no conspiracy had been implied. The vision given to Cyrus was an admonition of his own approaching death. He was vanquished and slain in a battle with Tomyris, queen of the Massagetæ; and the sceptre of Persia descended to Cambyses, his son. On the death of that monarch anarchy distracted the empire, and Darius Hystaspes, inspired by various omens, stood forth as a competitor for the throne. Overpowering his rival Smerdis, he assumed that imperial purple to which he had not been born, and began a reign of prosperity almost unequalled in his country's annals.

In the time of this Darius, Zeréthoschtro, the "Golden Star" of Persia, dawned upon the world. His name, softened into Zoroaster, is familiar to us as that of the mightiest religious reformer of the ancient East. By both lines of ancestry, as well through his mother Dogdo, as his father Poroschasp, could he boast of descent from the remote kings of Persia. Poroschasp, says tradition, was descended from that Djemschid, the fabulous embellisher of Istakhar, whom Ormuzd gifted with creative powers; and who was, according to Persian legends, fifth in line from Noah. Of omens vouchsafed immediately before and after the birth of Zoroaster, the Easterns have many most marvellous tales. His mother, being pregnant, saw in vision a being glorious as Djemschid, who assailed the djins or devs—the Persian evil spirits—with a sacred writing, before which they fled in terror. The interpretation of the magian to whom she applied, was that she should be favoured among women by bearing a son to whom Ormuzd would make known his laws; and who should spread them through all the East. Against this son every power of evil would be in arms. Tried by afflictions and perils innumerable, the prophet would ultimately drive his foes before him like chaff, and receive even in his own country the utmost honour. A king should be raised up who would accept his sacred writings as the word of truth, and make them the law of Persia: everywhere the new religion would prevail: Zoroaster would ascend to the side of Ormuzd in the highest heaven, and his foes sink to Ahriman and hell.

Alarmed lest the prophet whose advent was thus heralded should prove the destroyer of their order, certain among the magi conspired to slay him immediately upon his birth. Darius, whose ear they had gained, becoming possessed with an evil spirit, rode off in search of the babe. Less fortunate than Herod, he discovered the object of his hatred, and, on lifting his sword to hew in pieces the infant Zoroaster, the arm that grasped the weapon was withered to the shoulder, and the

King fled convulsed with terror and agony. Disappointed in their opening plot, the magi speedily took heart a second time to attempt murder. On this occasion they were themselves the agents of their evil wishes. A fire having been kindled, the embryo reformer was stolen from his mother's dwelling, and cast into the flames. Dogdo, seeking on all sides for her son, found him at length lying peacefully on his fiery couch, as if in a cradle, and carried him home uninjured. As he grew to manhood numerous other efforts were made to compass his death. He was placed in the way of savage bulls, was cast to wolves, and fed with victuals in which poison had been mingled. Through all this the spirits to whose service Zoroaster had been consecrated supported him unhurt. At thirty years of age his mission began. Quitting his native place he journeyed towards the court of Iran; but being warned in a vision of an attack which the magi and devs combined waited to make upon him, he turned aside into the mountains of the Albordi. There the things which "eye had never seen" were revealed to his gaze. He was lifted up to the highest heaven, and beheld Ormuzd in his glory, encircled by the hosts of the angels. Food sweet as honey was given to him, on eating which his eyes were opened to all that passed in the heavens and the earth. The darkness of the future was made to him as day. He learned the inmost secrets of nature; the revolutions of worlds; the influences of the stars; the greatness of the six chief angels of God; the felicity of the beatified; the terrible condition of the sinful. He went down into hell and there looked on the evil one face to face. Finally, having received from Ormuzd the Divine gospel which should illumine the East, he was bidden to return to earth, and teach it to all conditions of mankind. Celestial fire was given to him, to be kept burning as a symbol of the glory of God in every city where his teachings were received. Placed again upon the mountains of Albordi or the Balkan, Zoroaster reared in a cavern an altar to the Creator, and kindled upon it the first sparkles of the sacred flame. As he resumed his journey a host of furious devs and magi beset him, and sought to destroy the Zendavesta—the gospel which Ormuzd had committed to his care. These the prophet put to flight by pronouncing some verses from the sacred book. He continued his course to Balkh, and, being denied admittance to the King, cleft the roof of the palace, and descended into the midst of the court. All save the monarch himself fled in terror. The King caused them to re-assemble, and Zoroaster, encircled by a ring of courtiers and magi, expounded with vehement eloquence the doctrines he had been sent upon earth to spread. The magicians present then endeavoured to confound him with the learning of which their minds were the repositories; but the prophet solved with the utmost ease the most abstruse problems of their science, and broke through every mental net that could be spread. Hereupon the monarch declared himself a convert to the new religion, and was followed by others of his court. Many Persians, however, including the whole body of the magi, were stirred to rage by the thought that a single daring and successful reformer should succeed in subverting beliefs which had endured from an antiquity almost immemorial. For years the prophet's history is that of attempts on the part of enemies to destroy his life and credit, and of the miracles by which he put their rage at defiance. At length the good cause triumphed. Opposition was beaten down, and Zoroaster became to the Persians whatever, at a yet more ancient date, Moses had been to Israel.

His law, like that of the Hebrew prophet, was at once theological and civil. The portion remaining to us of the Zendavesta, or Living Word, has three grand divisions: the Izeschne, the Visfered, and the Vendidad. These again are parted into sections too numerous to be here mentioned. A Litany, a Liturgy, and a general code of laws, are among the matters included. Prayers are drawn up for even the most trifling occasions. On cutting hair or nails; before making pastry; after sneezing; on seeing a leprous person, mountains, a cemetery, a city, the sea; on killing cattle; on killing vermin; and at a thousand other times, verbose petitions are to be reiterated by the devout.

The theology of Zoroaster is far more tolerant than that of the Calvinistic section of Christendom. The eternal hell to which all but the elect are to be consigned, makes no appearance in his religion. Even Ahriman and his devils are in the end to be pardoned and restored. The Creator, he teaches, formed together with the world Ormuzd and Ahriman, the good and the evil principle. These, with their respective hosts, shall contend on the battle ground of the universe for a space of twelve thousand years. At the end of this period comes a conflict like the Christian Armageddon, in which Ahriman and his subordinates are utterly overthrown. The evil one hereon repents, and, in presence of the Eternal, enters into a solemn league of amity with Ormuzd. Hell itself is purged, and through all creation sin and sorrow are annihilated. I may mention that Zoroaster condemns all men, even the best, for a space to his inferno; but none are to be chastised beyond their deserts, and not even the vilest eternally.

Such a revelation was of a truth spiritual and sublime. Zoroaster's place is high above that of Mahommed in the ranks of the founders of faiths. The disciples of the Koran did, indeed, vanquish and subvert to a newer creed the disciples of the Zendavesta, but the event was no miracle. When, in, the seventh century after Christ, this conquest took place, the Zoroastrian system had endured for near twelve hundred years. As shaped by the founder its moral teachings were pure and beautiful, and its idea of the Divine One high and just. But with the passing of centuries abuses began, like foul parasites, to cling to and mar the noble structure. As with all other systems of the ancient world, the evil portion of the unseen beings around us, having undermined with malignant patience, at length succeeded in overthrowing the work of the good. Aided by the unworthy servants to be found before all altars, they defaced with vice after vice the temples where constantly burned the sacred fire. Sensual indulgence, against which Zoroaster had launched his, sternest anathemas, made foul the lives of his descendants. The adoration given at first to the unseen Creator, was lavished in process of time on the visible objects He had created. The sun, the stars and the sacred fire were the gods of this new idolatry. Thus the great decay went on. The evil influences without worked mightily and with success. Licentiousness desecrated the temples; human sacrifices began to make foul the altars. At last, when hypocrisy had replaced piety, and sensuality and sloth stood in the place of spiritual zeal, there poured down on Persia that ardent multitude of fanatics whom Mahommed's intolerant enthusiasm had inflamed. The choice was the Koran or the sword. Sapped already at all points by internal corruption, the edifice Zoroaster had reared hasted to its fall. The few who refused to abjure their religion fled from Persia for ever, or, remaining, were relentlessly put to death. At the present day the numerous Parsees scattered through Hindostan and other countries of the far East are the dispersed relics which remain of that once mighty and united brotherhood which revered the teachings of the "Golden Star."

CHAPTER III

INDIA AND CHINA

"I have seen," says Apollonius of Tyana, "the Brahmins of India dwelling on the earth, and not on the earth, living fortified without fortifications, possessing nothing, and yet everything." The "dwelling on the earth, and not on the earth" alludes to their being frequently levitated. Apollonius had journeyed into Hindostan to seek admittance to the treasury of Indian wisdom. The supermundane attainments of the Brahmins were displayed to him immediately that the object of his mission became known. He was brought into the presence of the chief sage of the caste, who addressed him in the following words:— "It is the custom of others to inquire of those who visit them who they are, and for what purpose they come; but with us the first evidence of wisdom is that we are not ignorant of those who come to us." Thereupon this clairvoyant recounted to Apollonius the most notable events of his life; named the families both of his father and of his mother; related what, the philosopher had done at Ægae; described by what means Damis had become the companion of his journey, and repeated all that they had heard and talked of by the way. Awed and humbled by knowledge so unearthly, the astonished Greek earnestly besought to be admitted to its secrets. After the usual length of waiting he became duly illuminated, and returning, astonished Europe with his piercing clairvoyance and wondrous powers of healing. Lecturing at Ephesus the words suddenly died upon his tongue. He bent forward amazedly, and, gazing into space, exclaimed, "Strike! strike the tyrant!" Then, turning to the bewildered audience, he continued, "Domitian is no more; the world is delivered from its bitterest oppressor." In the very day and hour when Apollonius beheld this vision at Ephesus was the despot assassinated at Rome.

If a stranger acquired such gifts chiefly from a sojourn in the temples of the Brahmins, what must have been the spiritual wealth of those Brahmins themselves? The aim of their religion was to lift the soul, above the thraldom of the senses and place it in unity with God. Like the Platonists, they judged that the spirit is enveloped by a form of luminous ether—as the Vedas have it, "sûkshonasarira," a finer body. A multitude of sensations perplex us, and these "buddhi," or reason, was created to command. Sent into earthly life, the soul migrates from body to body in a most marvellous and truly Pythagorean manner. These incarnations ended, the spirit appears before Yamas, the Minos of the Brahminical theology. As its actions have been righteous or unjust, so is it translated to the paradise of Indra, or condemned to various of the purifying hells. Final beatitude, according to the ideas of both Brahmin and Buddhist, consists in absorption into the Divine nature and eternal union with God. By Europeans this creed is commonly regarded as betokening a species of annihilation; but although violent pains and pleasures would seem to be immortally banished from these Eastern "just spirits made perfect," the individuality of each is unchangeably preserved. To the heavenly felicity of "Nirvana" but one path conducts—unceasing mortification of the spirit and the body. The laws of Manu minutely prescribe the inflictions which the devotee must endure. To scorch in summer before the hottest fires; to shiver naked in running streams in the depth of winter; to pass hours buried in ant-nests, or writhing on couches studded with numerous spikes; to be clad in the bark of trees, and have for food leaves and roots, and for drink impure water; to deny the tongue its use; to swing suspended by hooks passed through the flesh of the back: these are some of the torments in which from immemorial antiquity Hindoo existences have been spent. In the day of Alexander of Macedon such penances flourished in full rigour, and they have continued unremittingly popular down to the present time.

Brahmins and Buddhists alike teach that the Deity has repeatedly descended in human shape to purify the world. The Brahmins, however, decline to recognise Buddha as one amongst these avatars. They describe the deity whom the Buddhists worship as a species of demon permitted, at a time when the earth was filled with evil, to arise and lead the wicked astray. Thus an irreconcilable enmity exists between the followers of the two great creeds. "By their fruits ye shall know them." Despite the holy horror of the Brahmins, the faith of the Buddhists is vastly more spiritual and elevated than their own. If a demon inspired it he had undeniably forgotten his condition, and was for the nonce masquerading as an angel of light. His teaching Christians cannot but recognise as wise and pure. The wasting of life in sacrifice is strictly forbidden, and even the blood of animals may not, on any pretext, be spilt. The faithful are earnestly entreated to live at peace with their fellow-men, and to keep themselves in the words of St. James, "pure and unspotted from the world." The eating of flesh is prohibited, and the doing injury to even the smallest creature which God's hand has formed held a sin. The Vedas and Puranas of the Brahmins Buddha altogether rejects, and reprobates these writings for their unholy advocacy of living sacrifices. By so stern a denunciation of the darker among its doctrines the more ancient sect of the Brahmins was moved to fury. They drove the converts of the new heresy from Hindostan Proper, and relentlessly persecuted all who dared re-enter that peninsula. But beyond the Ganges, and east and north of the Himalayas, Buddhism waxed mightily. Overspreading, and becoming the state religion of Nepaul, Thibet, and Affghanistan, of Burmah China, Mongolia, and Japan, it stands at the present day foremost, as regards the number of devotees, among the great religions of the earth. That this splendid fabric is more imposingly vast than solidly real; that in various of these lands—China and Burmah in especial—systems of unblushing foulness and hideous cruelty usurp the pure name of Buddhism, are incontrovertible facts. But a faith that has had so unequalled an influence on the destinies of the East well deserves notice, and the space can hardly be wasted that is accorded to a brief *résumé* of the beliefs prevalent among this mighty family of spiritualists.

An article of faith constantly iterated in the Buddhist writings is that departed souls have in all ages returned to our world. Like Milton in his thousand times quoted avowal, these scriptures say that

> "Millions of spiritual beings walk the earth
> Unseen, both when we wake and when we sleep."

Countless numbers are continually ascending and descending on the missions of the gods. Some are the guardians of cities, others of individuals; others again haunt by night caverns, forests, and all solitary spots. In describing these unseen beings every resource of the glowing imagination of the East is expended. They pass to and fro among men wrapped with an ethereal veil, and thus conceal from earthly eyes their forms, a thousand times more beautiful than those of mortals. They are crowned with unfading flowers, and brilliant with all the glories of Paradise. The brightest of the stars are less clear and radiant than their eyes, and the white garments in which they are robed emit the most delicious perfumes. Some are kindly, others fierce; but all wield the mightiest influence over the destinies of mankind.

As was natural in the case of beings so attractively depicted, and whose presence it is probable that spiritual tokens were continually making manifest, the mass of the people have in process of time come to adore them as divinities. At this day there are probably some hundreds of millions of deities set up in the niches of the Buddhist Pantheon. By the kindred sect of Brahma three hundred and thirty millions of these false gods are computed to be adored.

We find in Thibet, where Buddhism flourishes in the fullest vigour, a startling copy of the ritual and ceremonies of the Roman Church. The priests are tonsured. The faithful have their rosaries for prayer, and tell the beads as zealously as any Spaniard. Monasteries have multiplied to such a degree that monks and priests are held to be in number almost a moiety of the population. The priesthood, magnificently robed, sometimes in yellow, sometimes in purple and gold, pass on festival days to the temples, attended by bursts of barbaric music, canopied with banners, and surrounded by censers heavy with incense; the faithful as the procession moves by prostrating themselves in the dust. Holy water is abundant throughout the temples, baptisms continually occur, and relics of saints are to be found everywhere. The priests are permitted housekeepers, "around whom," says Mr. Howitt in his "History of the Supernatural" "families unaccountably spring up, and are styled nephews and nieces." Indeed, so parallel are the customs, social and ecclesiastical, to those of the Catholic Church, that, when first her emissaries obtained entrance to Thibet, two of their number, Fathers Grüber and Maffie, indignantly wrote home to accuse the devil of having "set up in that far land a most blasphemous mockery of the rites and paraphernalia of the true faith."

In China of old the worship of a single Supreme Being seems to have obtained. Gradually falling from this original Theism, the adoration of the visible objects of creation, and of a host of invisible powers, became in process of ages the theological taints of the Celestials. Spirits presiding over the elements were recognised, and temples erected to each. Ancestors, too, were deified, and annual festivals instituted at which the progenitors of the reigning monarch received the homage of that mighty empire which in former days their sceptres had swayed.

With the increase of idolatry abuses of every kind grew and multiplied, until, in the seventh century before Christ, China was eaten up with all imaginable error and corruption. In the latter years of that century the reformer Lao-tse appeared. Spiritual faith had been almost extinguished, and this present world was the only one of which the Chinese took heed. Lao-tse drew around him the few inquirers into the problems of futurity who still remained, and strove with their aid to awaken a longing after spiritual things in the bosoms of his countrymen. Persecuted vehemently, as all prophets of all eras and kingdoms have been, he fell into a disgust with his mission, and, shaking the dust of cities from his feet, retired to pass the remainder of his life in religious calm. Yet, although the labourer had turned back from the sowing of the seed, the harvest of such efforts as he had already made was in no long time reaped. A religious awakening took place, and the sceptical and vicious public mind was stirred to its inmost depths. Then appeared Confucius, the great purifier of the morals of the empire, as Lao-tse had been of its metaphysics. He inculcated the necessity of honouring parents, of being truthful in every business of life, of actively fulfilling all social and natural duties, of keeping faith with others, and of rendering obedience to the laws of man and God. In his writings the most striking of the ancient Chinese legends are transmitted to modern times. These traditions speak like the Hebrew Scriptures of the fall of man, and the hurling down into misery and darkness of an angelic host who had rebelled against the Supreme.

Lao-tse and Confucius are alike in their deep belief in the nearness of the spiritual world. All truth respecting the future state, says the former, has been brought down to man by the messengers of God. Prayer and self-denial are the charms which open the eyes of the mind to the spiritual beings around us. Apparitions have occurred since the creation of the globe. Invisible to the dim eyes of the flesh, spirits, evil and good, constantly hover above the earth, checking or aiding the advancement of man. The limitless universe constitutes but one family; earth, heaven, the spirits yet in the flesh, the spirits of the dead, form a single empire ordered by the eternal reason of Schang-ti. The beings ever near man watch constantly his deeds. Do we give way to evil, the evil spirits enter, and become strong within us, by reason of their affinity to the darkness of our souls. If, despising temptation, we drive from us these demons, ministering angels constantly attend us, and cherish within our bosoms a light that gleams brighter and brighter unto the perfect day.

Such were the high and wise teachings of the two chief prophets of the Celestial Empire. They so far succeeded in their mission as to implant in Chinese bosoms a faith in the supermundane which, if anything, has grown stronger with the lapse of ages. Intercourse with the world of spirits is daily sought after in every temple of the greatest empire of the East. But, whatever the state of spiritual health may have been when the teachings of Lao-tse and Confucius had yet the eloquence of novelty, the present degradation of this unfortunate race appears almost irremediable. Guardian angels seem for a space to have abandoned the Chinese, and the whispers of demons tempting to evil are the only messages from the invisible listened to to-day. In China itself opportunities of observation are almost denied to Europeans, and the corruptions of the empire, though known to be extreme, are in great measure hidden. But in the cities of the Pacific seaboard of America—inundated of late years by uncountable thousands of the race I at present treat of—the whole measure of their gigantic wickednesses and dwarfish virtues may be observed. The most rapidly enlarging portion of San Francisco consists of a rookery of wretched dwellings styled the Chinese Quarter. There the vices which chroniclers shudder to name, and which among even the most fallen of European races, lurk but by stealth in the darkest and foulest dens, walk abroad openly and unashamed. Murder is too common to excite more than the attention of a moment. Truth in man, and chastity in woman, are virtues equally unknown. The filth of the dwellings is such that hogs or pole cats could scarcely be at ease within them. Children die in frightful numbers, or are placidly put out of the way should the parents find them inconvenient to keep. And with all this the Chinaman is frugal, gentle, industrious, and prepossessing in appearance and manners. But beneath the varnished outside crust a sink of iniquity is concealed. The refuse of Europe and America has been drawn to California and Utah by the thirst of gold, yet the veriest wretches among the white men stand amazed at the depths of iniquity to which their yellow rivals can, without compunction, descend.

CHAPTER IV

GREECE AND ROME

I pass now from Asia to Europe, and from the faint grandeur of the traditions preserved respecting the empires which were the mistresses of the ancient East to the fuller and more reliable information possessed respecting those civilizations of the West enthroned by the Egean and upon the Tiber. The "glory that was Greece" is indeed irrecoverably extinct, and the "grandeur that was Rome," fallen into an almost hopeless decay. Empires have been founded, have flourished, and have perished, since the last of the Delphian Pythonesses drew a last response from the spirits whom she was appointed to serve. It was centuries anterior to the birth of Mahommed that the last public reading of the books of the Cumæan Sibyl took place in the temples of Rome. But the array of mighty spirits who shone with so immortal a lustre on the City of the Violet Crown, the City of the Seven Hills, and other cities and commonwealths of the Grecian and Roman dominions, have bequeathed to us works in whose undying pages the actions and the thoughts, the worship and beliefs of the Italians of two thousand and the Greeks of almost three thousand years ago, are as undyingly preserved. These great writers were with few exceptions believers in the return of the departed. Scarcely a poet or philosopher amongst them but, whilst busied with the things of this present world, had as active a faith in, and was as anxiously inquisitive respecting, the things of the life to come. And the great historians of Greek times—Herodotus and Xenophon in especial—when giving account of apparitions or marvellously fulfilled prophecies, do not present them as paradoxes which are to, be received with wonder and distrust; but rather relate them as truisms known and accepted from time immemorial by the race for whom they wrote. Let me, in support of the views I have advanced, select some proofs of the extent to which belief in the presence of an eternal and invisible order of things side by side with this temporal and visible creation, prevailed amongst the Greeks. I shall open with the poets: in all nations the voices of the popular faith.

"The gods," says Homer, "like strangers from some foreign land, assuming different forms, wander through cities, watching the injustice and justice of men. There are avenging demons and furies who haunt the ill-disposed, as there are gods who are the protectors of the poor."— (Odyssey, xvii. 475). Says Hesiod:—

"Invisible the gods are ever nigh,
Pass through the mist, and bend the all-seeing eye.

The men who grind the poor, who wrest the right
Aweless of heaven's revenge, stand naked to their sight;
For thrice ten thousand holy demons rove
This breathing world, the delegates of Jove;
Guardians of man, their glance alike surveys
The upright judgments and the unrighteous ways."

Works and Days. Elton's Translation, p. 32.

It is Sophocles who supplies me with the following beautiful passage:— "I fondly thought of happier days, whilst it denoted nothing else than my death. To the dead there are no toils. They drink purer draughts and continually ascend higher."

Can we term this aught but the spiritual teaching of the nineteenth century anticipated. And hearken to Pindar:— "But the good, enjoying eternal sunshine night and day, pass a life free from labour; never stirring the earth by strength of hand, nor yet the crystal waters of the sea in that blessed abode, but with the honoured of the gods all such as lived true lives, and took pleasure in keeping their faith, spend in the heavens a tearless existence."

"Spirits," says Pythagoras, "announce to man secret things, and foretell the future." The doctrine of Socrates was the same. "Socrates thought that the gods knew all things—both what is said, what is done, and what is meditated in silence—are everywhere present, and give warnings to men of everything."—*Mentorab.* i. 1.

The fragments that remain to us of Æschylus are throughout instinct with the mysteries of another world. Strange and appalling beings—the Titans and the Furies—move in shadowy procession across his pages. He loves to contemplate the supermundane; but it is the supermundane in its gloomiest guise: "a land of darkness, as darkness itself, and where the light is as darkness." From the grim sublimity of such tragedies as the Prometheus, it is pleasant to turn to the more truly Greek beliefs preserved in the plays and poetry of Sophocles, Euripides, and Homer, and in the philosophy of Plato. Homer and Sophocles have been already called as witnesses to the intensity of the Greek conviction of the nearness of spiritual things, and I shall content myself with describing, by the aid of these, and other great brethren of the guild of poets, the faiths which they represent as having prevailed in their age and land.

The Greeks, then, saw gods everywhere. The eternal snows of Parnassus; the marble temples of Athens glistening in the rays of a Southern sun; the thousand isles nestling in the blue waters of the Egean; the fragrant groves where philosophers disputed; the fountains shadowed by plane-trees; the solemn fields of Platæa and Marathon:

each and all of these had their attendant sprites. A thousand deities received homage in a thousand temples. Yet amidst this error the form of that One God, the Untreated and the Supreme, whom Christianity adores, was by the higher minds of the nation perceived "as in a glass, darkly." Socrates taught that a single deity governed the universe. "To the Unknown God," said the inscription which Paul found at Athens. The people, it is true, were not disposed to receive such a doctrine. To the light, lively Greek a pantheon of divinities was a mental necessity. From the picture of a single mighty spirit controlling the destinies of creation; everywhere present, yet everywhere unseen; knowing all, yet known of none; eternal, invisible, and incomprehensible,—the multitude shrank in disgust. Gods who mingled visibly in the actions of man; who clothed themselves with material forms to lead on to victory the hosts of the countries they cherished; who shared the passions of humanity and sympathised with its infirmities; who, while controlling the present, gave omens of the future of nations and individuals: these were the beings to whom, in love or fear, the Greek bowed down. His poets represented one god as appearing angrily in the clouds, and hurling down thunderbolts into the midst of armies contending on the earth; another as wandering in the shape of a beardless youth from city to city, and challenging men to contend with him on the lyre which he loved: this goddess as snatching from out the midst of the battle an endangered warrior, of whose stately form she had become enamoured; that, as urging her celestial steeds from capital to capital to stir up the surrounding nations against a commonwealth that was the object of her hate. And the legends of these gods, which with the vulgar were objects of devout credit, were by the philosopher made the vehicles of a higher purpose allegories for the delicate shadowing forth of spiritual things. The sage had been struck by the thought that the soul perhaps came from an existence in some distant and different world to be incarnated here, and he hid his idea in the lovely myth of the love and union of Cupid and Psyche. He saw that the great benefactors of mankind—the increasers of the world's stock of mental or physical power—were uniformly tormented by that world in life, and worshipped by it after death. Thus the legend of Prometheus and his theft of fire from heaven for the benefit of man; of his torture on Mount Caucasus, and unconquerable defiance of the deity who oppressed him; of his ultimate deliverance and triumph, arose. So with all the fables of the Greeks. Through this beautiful mythology constantly breaks the radiance of the spiritual world; even as the eyes of Athenian actors gleamed through the openings of their masks. We learn from a hundred master-pieces of the intellect how untiring was that spirit of restless inquiry with which every people of Hellas searched into the secrets of the unseen. No city was founded; no army marched forth to battle; no vessels laden with emigrants set sail for Italy or Asia Minor without consulting the oracles of the gods. The fiery imagination, and the intellect at once subtle and vigorous of the Greeks, peculiarly fitted them for the reception of impressions from the invisible world. To the profounder realities of such intercourse, indeed, they seem never to have penetrated. The secrets hived in those imperishable temples where were celebrated the rites of the mystic Isis, entered not into the philosophy of Hellas, or entered only through such men as Pythagoras, who, scoffed at and persecuted in life, were revered and imitated by their countrymen after death. But, although the more startling of spiritual phenomena were not among the Greeks things of daily occurrence, no race more generally impressionable to spiritual influence existed in the ancient world. It is through the Grecian nature that the Grecian name has become immortal. Knowledge was not here, as in the great Asiatic empires, regarded as a lamp of inestimable rarity, to be carefully reserved for guiding the footsteps of a few, while the mass of their fellows wandered in darkness. Like the rain, it fell everywhere. The philosopher or poet, inspired consciously or unconsciously by the whispers of attendant spirits, hastened to publish to all men the ideas which fermented in his brain. Inspired by the whispers of attendant spirits? Are not poets, philosophers, and indeed all geniuses, knowingly or unknowingly the subjects of inspiration from another world? To what but the promptings of numerous spirits influencing a single mighty imagination can be ascribed the marvellous creations which glow in the dramas of Shakespeare? From whence but the sphere of all light could proceed the Divine gleams that crossed the brain of a Raphael? And the citizen of Attics was in respect of supremely gifted countrymen peculiarly fortunate. For him the inspirations of a hundred minds had taken imperishable shape. "He saw," says Lord Macaulay, "the plays of Sophocles and Aristophanes; he walked amidst the friezes of Phidias and the paintings of Zeuxis; he knew by heart the choruses of Æschylus; he heard the rhapsodist at the corner of the street reciting the shield of Achilles or the death of Argus." And Homer, Æschylus, and Zeuxis—Phidias and Sophocles, alike inculcated with all the strength of their magnificent genius the constant interference of spirits in the affairs of men! Had the Greeks missed being a nation of spiritualists it had indeed been a miracle. But, save with such philosophers as those of the Atomic school, the belief in the immortality of the soul and the return of departed spirits to watch over those yet on earth was, as I have endeavoured to show, deep and universal. Every nature fitted to be the instrument of the spirits was secluded with jealous care from influences prejudicial to such a mission, and consecrated as the life-long servant of a shrine of more or less renown. The majority of such media were of the fairest portion of the fairer sex. A succession of virgins presided over the most renowned oracle of Greece, that of the Delphic god, and received from another world the messages of prophetic import destined, now for commonwealths, now for individuals. And besides that of Delphos a hundred oracles of lesser fame were scattered through Hellas. Even the smallest of these shrines blazed with jewels and gold; the gifts of crowds of anxious devotees. This ceaseless hunger for communion with the unseen, and constant exposure to spiritual influence, had, as in all lands and ages, its dark no less than its glorious side. Human sacrifices sometimes made horrible Grecian altars; departed spirits were frequently elevated into imaginary gods. But the corruption of the Greeks was not as the corruption of Nineveh, Babylon, and Memphis. Brilliant virtues redeemed it: magnificent acts of heroism were inspired by this intercourse with the unseen. "Tonight," said Leonidas to the three hundred of Thermopylæ, "we shall sup with the immortal gods." "On, sons of the Greeks!" was the battle-cry of Marathon, "above you the spirits of your fathers watch the blows which, to preserve their tombs from desecration, you strike to-day."

Hundreds of well-attested instances have been handed down to us of the manner in which the oracles of Hellas were fulfilled. From these I shall select such as are not only most striking in themselves, but best supported by outward evidence. As has been already mentioned, the Delphic oracle far outstripped all competitors in the importance and truthfulness of its prophecies. Says Plutarch:— "It would be impossible to enumerate all the instances in which the Pythia proved her power of foretelling events; and the facts of themselves are so well and so generally known, that it would be useless to bring forth new evidences. Her answers, though submitted to the severest scrutiny, have never proved false or incorrect." And he relates, amongst other proofs of his assertions, that she predicted the eruption of lava and ashes with which Vesuvius overwhelmed the cities of Pompeii and Herculaneum.

To Delphi sent Crœsus of Lydia, when uneasy at the rapid growth of the Persian power. He had previously despatched ambassadors to the most renowned shrines of the age; bidding them demand of the oracles on a certain day in what work the King was at the moment employed. The replies from other temples are unknown, but that from the Delphic god ran as follows:—

"See! I number the sands; I fathom the depths of the ocean;
Hear even the dumb; comprehend, too, the thoughts of the silent.
Now perceive I an odour, an odour it seemeth of lamb's flesh;
As boiling it seetheth; commixed with the flesh of a tortoise;
Brass is beneath, and with brass is it covered over."

The divination was in all respects complete. At the appointed hour Crœsus had retired alone into an inner apartment of his palace; and there had, indeed, cut to pieces a lamb and a tortoise; afterwards cooking the flesh in a vessel of brass. Awed by the proof of superhuman knowledge which the Delphic oracle vouchsafed, he sought by magnificent gifts to obtain the favour of the god. The embassy which bore his second question had in charge three thousand oxen, numerous gold and silver vessels, a golden lion, a hundred and seventy ingots of the same metal, and a statue also in gold, and adorned with girdle and necklace of incredible value. Depositing these before the shrine of the god, the ambassadors of Crœsus demanded whether it were well that he should march against the Persians. The oracle's response ran thus:—

"If Crœsus pass the Halys he shall destroy a great empire." Unconscious that the empire indicated was his own, Crœsus already exulted in the thought of subjugating Persia, and at once prepared for war. A third and yet more magnificent embassy, bore from him a gift to every inhabitant of Delphi, and a demand whether his rule should long continue. The oracle replied, "When a mule becomes the ruler of the Persian people, then, O tender-footed Lydian, flee to the rocky banks of the Hermos; make no halt, and care not to blush for rocky cowardice."

Crœsus smiled at a pleasantry which appeared to him to confirm the impossibility of any interruption to that success which had attended the earlier actions of his life. At the head of a vast host he crossed the Halys, and, encountering the Persians under Cyrus, was made captive, his army annihilated, and his kingdom reduced to the condition of a province of the Persian empire. In despair he reproached the Delphic god for luring him to ruin by predictions utterly false. But the oracle replied that, through his own carelessness in not seeking the name of the empire over which destruction impended, was he brought low; and that, with regard to the last of its responses, Cyrus, the son of a Median princess and a Persian of humble condition, was the ruler prefigured under the type of a mule.

Xerxes, the monarch whom the combined fleets of Greece vanquished at Salamis, crossed the Hellespont at the head of the mightiest host Europe had ever seen. Dismayed by the myriads who marched under the orders of the Persian king, the Athenians sent to beg counsel from the chief oracle of Hellas. The Delphic god replied:— "Unfortunates, wherefore seat yourselves? Fly to the verge of the earth: forsake your houses and the lofty crags of your wheel-shaped city. For neither does the head abide firm; nor does the body, nor the lowest feet, nor therefore the hands, nor aught of the middle remain—all is ruined. For fire and guiding Mars, driving the Syriac car, overturn her, and destroy many other towering cities, not yours alone; and to the devouring flame deliver many temples of the immortals, which even now stand dripping with sweat; shaken with fear. Down from the topmost roof trickles black blood: token of woe unavoidable. Begone then from the shrine, and pour the balm of courage into the wound of calamity."

This prediction, and the counsels which accompanied it, reduced the Athenians to despair. No city, ancient or modern, was ever more beloved by its inhabitants than that of the Violet Crown. To die, sword in hand, in its defence, seemed a doom far preferable to a flight, the citizens knew not whither. They sent a second embassy; humbly beseeching that the immortal gods would not command them to leave to destruction and desecration their hearths, and the tombs of their fathers. But the Pythoness replied that Heaven knew not how to change its purpose, and that the decrees of the deities were as adamant. Yet for the comfort of the suppliants she was inspired to add: "When all is taken that Cecrops' hill in itself contains, and the fastnesses of sacred Cithæron, wide-knowing Jove gives unto the goddess Triton-born a wooden wall alone to abide inexpugnable; this shall save you and your children. Await not quietly the throng of horse and foot that invades your land; but turn your backs and withdraw; the time shall be when you too will stand against the foe. Godly Salamis! thou shalt see the sons of women fall, whether Ceres be scattered or collected."

Never was prediction more exactly fulfilled. The mighty host of the Persians, having disembarked from their ships at the nearest point available for an attack, marched against Athens. As the heads of the enemy's columns came in sight the Greek galleys put to sea. The city was deserted, save by a few desperate patriots who, knowing that the Acropolis had once been encircled by a hedge, and vainly imagining that this might be the wooden wall of which the god had spoken, determined to defend that portion of Athens to the last. They fell to a man; fighting with the valour common to the Hellenes of the age. Athens was entered by the Persians, and, after having been plundered, destroyed by fire. Then the invading host returned through Attica; burning and pillaging whatever lay in the way. Expeditions were despatched for the sacking of distant towns; and finally the Asiatics returned to their ships. Off Salamis, in accordance with the prophecy of the oracle, the combined navies of Greece encountered them; and, by reason chiefly of the burning valour which animated the Athenian portion of the fleet, and the skill with which Themistocles, the Athenian admiral, manœuvred his ships, a complete victory was obtained, and the freedom of Greece achieved. An oracle of Bœotia had, we learn, predicted this event in equally clear terms with that of Delphi.

I have mentioned that expeditions were despatched by Xerxes for the destroying of towns distant from the line of march adopted by the main body of his army. Amongst other squadrons, one of four thousand men marched to pillage the shrine of Delphi, and bring into the treasury of the Persian King the vast riches collected there. Unprepared for any effectual defence, the alarmed priesthood demanded of the oracle whether they should flee with the treasures of the temple to some more secure spot, or bury those treasures in the precincts of the shrine itself. The deity replied that he would himself preserve his property, and forbade even the least of the offerings consecrated to him to be moved. On this all, save the Pythoness, and a few of the boldest dwellers in Delphi, departed to seek refuge in the mountains. Speedily the Persian legion came in sight, and pressed forward exultingly to the pillage of the wealthiest fane of the ancient world. The temple at first remained silent as the grave. When, however, the barbarians sought to ascend the crag on which it stood, clouds suddenly gathered overhead, from which unceasing flashes of lightning broke forth, accompanied by deafening thunders. Then a superhuman voice was heard to proceed from the shrine, and huge rocks, loosened from the summits of Parnassus, crashed through the ranks of the invaders, and levelled them like grass. Appalled, the remnant turned and fled. On this the Delphians gathered heart, and hastily snatching weapons, descended from their hiding-places, and pursued the fugitives for miles. Such was the slaughter occasioned in the Persian ranks by lightnings, falling crags, and the spears of the Greeks, that of the whole four thousand scarcely a man escaped.

The foregoing instances are gathered from Herodotus. I have chosen them because, occurring (save in the case of Crœsus, the narrative of whose intercourse with the Delphian oracle other historians confirm) at no great distance from his own time, the Father of History was well qualified to judge of the truth or falsehood of these portions of his work. And, when not deceived by evidence merely hearsay, no ancient author adhered more rigidly to facts. Says Professor Gaisford, his translator:— "It can hardly be doubted that one who took such pains to ascertain the truth would be equally scrupulous in offering nothing but the truth to his reader; and, indeed, strange as it may sound to those who have been in the habit of hearing Herodotus stigmatised as a liar by persons who ought to know better, there is probably no author, ancient or modern, the inspired writers excepted, who deserves to be placed before him in the scale of truth and accuracy."—(Introduction, p. xxxi.)

Pausanias, Plutarch, and a somewhat less trustworthy writer, Diodorus Sieulus, are equally full of the supermundane, and equally emphatic is asserting the veracity of the narratives they give. In the Laconies of Pausanias is to be found one of the weirdest and most picturesque stories of pagan times: that of his namesake the King of Sparta, who commanded the Greeks at the battle of Platæa, and Cleonice the Byzantine maid. Cleonice, slain unknowingly by the monarch who had enslaved her, was thenceforward the haunter of his life; appearing when any great evil menaced Pausanias, and predicting the woe that was about to happen. Plutarch also has the tale. In modern times it has furnished the groundwork for one of the noblest passages of Byron's "Manfred:"

> "The Spartan monarch drew
> From the Byzantine maid's unsleeping spirit
> An answer, and his destiny. He slew
> That which he loved, unknowing what he slew,
> And died unpardoned—though he called in aid
> The Phyxian Jove, and in Phigalia roused
> The Arcadian evocators to compel
> The indignant shadow to depose her wrath,
> Or fix her term of vengeance: she replied
> In words, of dubious import, but fulfilled.

The prediction to which the poet refers was that in which Cleonice indicated the ghastly manner of her slayer's death. Pausanias, after rendering many eminent services to the state, was detected in a conspiracy against it, and fled to a temple for sanctuary. In Lacedæmon the kings were merely elective magistrates, such as in more modern times have been the doges of Venice. The oligarchy of Sparta assembled, and, having deposed and outlawed their monarch, caused every opening of the temple in which he had taken refuge, to be hermetically closed. Thus entombed alive, the unhappy Pausanias perished of want.

Space forbids that I should quote more than a very few of the instances to be gathered from Plutarch and Diodorus. The remarkable narrative which succeeds is given by the former writer.

" Pan is Dead."

In the reign of Tiberius certain mariners had set sail from an Asiatic port for one in Italy. As they lay becalmed off the Echinades, an unearthly voice was heard thrice to call upon one Thamus, an Egyptian of the company, and, after the third time, to bid him that as the ship passed Palodes, he should declare loudly that "the great Pan was dead." Thamus, having consulted with his fellows, resolved that, should a steady gale be blowing when the vessel reached Palodes, he would journey on silently; but that if becalmed there, he would speak that which the voice had commanded. As the mariners gained the charmed spot the wind again died away, and the bark lay idly on a smooth sea. Then Thamus, looking forth towards Palodes, cried with a loud voice "The great Pan is dead." This he had no sooner done than there broke forth the sound of many voices, uttering mighty lamentations, intermingled however, as it seemed, with shouts of triumph. Then a breeze sprang up, and the sails of the vessel filling, Thamus and his companions were borne rapidly away. The date assigned to this occurrence is that of Our Saviour's death.

Tiberius, says Plutarch, was extremely concerned to discover the truth or falsehood of this narrative, and, having made searching inquiries, fully satisfied himself that these events had taken place exactly as described.

According to Diodorus, Althæmenes, the son of a king of Crete, was warned by the oracle that he would unknowingly slay Catreus his father. Dreading the fulfilment of the prophecy, he quitted his country, and settling at Rhodes, hoped to escape so horrible a fate. In course of time, his father became extremely old, and longing to see his son once again before he died, set sail for the place of his exile. Having landed during the night, a fray commenced between his attendants and some persons of the town. The unhappy Althæmenes, coming angrily forth to end the riot, slew one of the strangers in the heat of passion, and looking on the face of the dead man perceived his father.

From the same writer we learn that Philip of Macedon, when he consulted an oracle respecting his ambitious design of attacking Persia, was bidden to remember that the ox being crowned and garlanded implied his end to be at hand, and that men stood prepared to sacrifice him. This enigma Philip's wish made father to the thought that he should seize and slay the monarch of the Persians. He began, therefore, mighty preparations for war. But the death foreshadowed was in, reality his own. As, clothed with more than royal magnificence, and having his image borne before him in company with the statues of the gods, he entered the theatre at Ægea, Pausanias, an esquire of his body-guard, suddenly drew a dagger, and struck him to the heart.

I cannot better close this portion of my subject than with a reference to the spiritual guidance vouchsafed to the noblest mind of all pagan antiquity. Socrates, as every one in the slightest degree acquainted with Grecian history must be aware, was from his earliest youth the object of unearthly monitions. A "Divine voice" (as he himself terms it) attended him, not to urge to good, but to restrain from evil. It was equally busy in the most momentous and the most trifling actions of life. At Athens, at Corinth; when he lifted a spear against the enemies of his country when he bore with meekness the revilings of the shrewish Xantippe; when in the height of his success he stood surrounded by Plato, Alcibiades, and others of the noblest youth of Greece; when old, feeble, and persecuted, he calmly prepared himself to die—the voice was ever with him. It did not advise respecting the conduct of any action in which he was engaged, but it uniformly warned him against taking any step which might have proved prejudicial or evil. This has been made the ground for interpreting the history of the unearthly monitor as nothing more than an allegorical representation of conscience. But the conscience of Socrates was unlikely to warn him of unknown dangers awaiting himself or his friends, nor, when any of those friends meditated a crime, was it probable that it would perceive and endeavour to prevent it. Yet Xenophon testifies that Socrates obtained from the voice and imparted to his intimates many foreshadowings of perils which awaited them, and was never convicted of error. Yet Plato relates that Timarchus, a noble Athenian, being at a feast in company with Socrates, and rising to depart, was peremptorily bidden by the latter to reseat himself. "For," said he, "the spirit has just given me the accustomed sign that some danger menaces you." Some little time after Timarchus offered again to be gone, and was again stayed by Socrates, who had heard the warning repeated. Taking advantage, at length, of a moment when the philosopher was absorbed in earnest discourse, Timarchus stole off unobserved, and a few minutes afterwards committed a murder, for which being carried to execution, his last words were, "that he had come to that untimely end by not obeying the spirit of Socrates."

As the *Quarterly Review* once remarked, it is impossible to avoid being struck by the extreme similarity between certain points of the careers of Socrates and Joan of Arc. The Greek sage and the French heroine were alike accustomed from early childhood to be controlled by heavenly voices, which none but themselves could hear. Both rendered to those counsellors the most implicit obedience. In either case the voices approved their unearthly origin by undeniable tokens.

The subject of such monitions saw at times in vision the radiant beings by whom he or she was guided. Each demonstrated by a noble and blameless life the heavenly nature of those beings, and the purity of their teachings. Both were warned by the invisibles who guarded them that their careers would close in the reception of the crown of martyrdom. Both, amid the execrations of the mob, passed by roads terrible to travel from a world that was not worthy of them. Here the parallel ends. How immeasurably beneath the Greece of two thousand three hundred years ago was the Europe of the fifteenth century after Christ! Socrates, though execrated as the attempted overturner of his country's religion, was suffered to pass away in the gentlest manner consistent with a sudden end. Indeed the death he died can hardly be described as a violent one, or bitter to be endured. Surrounded by attached friends, he took from a weeping executioner the cup of poison, and draining it, departed calmly, and almost painlessly, to be with the immortals. Joan—reviled, tormented, and immodestly used— endured for months deeper than the bitterness of any death, and in death the utmost agony of which the human frame is capable. Lied to and abased; mocked by enemies with false hopes of life, and by pretended friends with false hopes of succour, her torment of suspense was only ended by that other agony of the stake of which even to think is to sicken with horror. From the fate of Socrates no less than that of the French heroine may we reap the lesson of the blindness of man in all ages to spiritual light! But no other, narrative in the world's repertory reveals so mournfully and awfully as that of the saintly maiden of Domremy the unrelieved darkness of those depths to which, when it misconceives the origin of that light, humanity can descend.

In Rome we find reproduced the spiritual beliefs prevalent among the Greeks, but darkened and made more severe, to accord with the darker and severer natures of the masters of the ancient world. The poets, like the poets of Greece, crowd their pages with portraits of the dwellers in the invisible. Virgil is as rich in the spiritual as Homer; Ovid, Horace, and Lucan deal throughout in miracle. As in Hellas, the gods descend among men, and are described as displaying passions akin to the passions of man. But love—which was in Greece the chief motive for the visits of these deities, who, like their brethren described in Genesis, "saw the daughters of men that they were fair,"—was in Rome altogether absent. To wreak their wrath on nations which had offended them; to lead on to conquest peoples that stood high in their favour; to enjoy the tumult and carnage of the battle-field—these are the motives by which the Italian poets represent the truly national among their gods as invariably actuated in their descents to earth. The lust of pleasure is supplanted by the lust of blood. It is such a difference as exists between the good-natured amorous Zeus worshipped by the Greeks, and the stern majesty of the Jupiter of the Roman people.

Yet from Greece came the whole of the philosophy and arts of Rome. The oracles of Greece were revered in Italy, and up to the very time of their becoming finally silent did emperors and senates send to consult them. As Horace tells us:— "Capta ferum victorem cepit." Greece, enslaved by the swords of the Romans, ruled yet by supremacy of mind.

Nor should we forget the peculiar connection between the civilisation of Italy and that far more ancient one whose almost immutable relics slowly moulder by the Nile. The metaphysics of Rome were those of Egypt, brightened by a sojourn in Greece. The mesmeric treatment of the sick practised in Roman temples was but an apish reflex of that deep knowledge of magnetic and spiritual phenomena possessed by Egyptian priests. Nay, the most celebrated of all Roman miracles, the extraordinary cure by the Emperor Vespasian of a blind man and a paralytic, was wrought on Egyptian ground. This event, which two great contemporary historians—Pliny, and the sceptical Tacitus—have described from the narratives of eye-witnesses, and which David Hume, in his "Essay on Miracles," declares the best attested instance of the supermundane in all history, took place in that magnificent Egyptian city named after Alexander the Great. I quote the story:—

"Vespasian spent some months at Alexandria. During his residence in that city a number of incidents out of the ordinary course of nature seemed to mark him as the particular favourite of the gods. A man of mean condition, born at Alexandria, had lost his sight by a defluxion on his eye. He presented himself before Vespasian, and falling prostrate on the ground, implored the Emperor to administer a cure for his blindness. He came, he said, by the admonition of Serapis, the god whom the superstition of the Egyptians holds in the highest veneration. The request was that the Emperor with his spittle would condescend to moisten the poor man's face and the balls of his eyes. Another who had lost the use of his hand, inspired by the same god, begged that he would tread on the part affected. Vespasian smiled at a request so absurd and wild. The wretched objects persisted to implore his aid. He dreaded the ridicule of a vain attempt; but the importunity of the men, and the crown of flatterers, prevailed upon the prince not entirely to disregard their petition.

"He ordered the physicians to consider whether the blindness of the one, and the paralytic affection of the other, were within the reach of human assistance. The result of the consultation was, that the organs of sight were not so injured but that, by removing the film or cataract, the patient might recover. As to the disabled limb, by proper applications and invigorating medicines, it was not impossible to restore it to its former tone. The god, perhaps, intended a special remedy, and chose Vespasian as the instrument of their dispensations. If a cure took place the glory of it would add new lustre to the name of Caesar, if otherwise, the poor men would bear the jests and raillery of the people. Vespasian, in the tide of his affairs, began to think that there was nothing so great and wonderful, nothing so improbable or even incredible, which his good fortune could not accomplish. In the presence of a prodigious multitude, all erect with expectation, he advanced with an air of severity, and hazarded the experiment. The paralytic hand recovered in functions, and the blind man saw the light of the sun. By living witnesses who were actually on the spot both events are confirmed at this hour, when deceit and flattery can hope for no reward."

The hour alluded to was that at which Tacitus wrote. Vespasian was dead, and the imperial tiara had passed for ever from his family.

Nothing remained to impede the exposure of deception, if deception there had been; nothing could make those witnesses with whom the historian conferred fear to speak the truth, or hope to profit by a lie. It deserves to be mentioned that Strabo and Suetonius, as well as Pliny, confirm this narrative of the greatest of the Roman annalists.

A species of apparition of which I have myself been made the subject occurred to this same Emperor. He saw in a temple at Alexandria the double of one Basilides, then living, and known to have been at a considerable distance from the place. Here is the tale as Tacitus relates it:—

"Vespasian was now determined to visit the sanctuary of Serapis, in order to consult the god about the future fortune of the empire. Having given orders to remove all intruders, he entered the temple. While he adored the deity of the place he perceived, in the midst of his devotions, a man of principal note amongst the Egyptians advancing behind him. The name of this person was Basilides, who, at that moment, was known to be detained by illness at the distance of many miles. Vespasian inquired of the priests whether they had seen Basilides that day in the temple. He asked a number of others whether they had met him in any part of the city. At length, from messengers whom he despatched on horseback, he received certain intelligence that Basilides was not less than fourteen miles distant from Alexandria. He therefore concluded that the gods had favoured him with the preternatural vision, and from the import of the word Basilides (royal), he inferred an interpretation of the decrees of heaven in favour of his future reign."

Pliny the Younger has preserved to us numerous accounts of apparitions, among which stories that respecting the philosopher Athenodorus is the most remarkable. Athenodorus, having occasion on his arrival at Athens to purchase a house, a large and fair one was shown to him. The lowness of the terms demanded being out of all proportion with the size and beauty of the mansion, he perceived that there was some mystery in the case. He inquired, and received the history of the events which had driven all former tenants from the house. At midnight a noise was heard, and the ghastly figure of a skeleton passed through the various apartments, dragging with it a rusty chain. Athenodorus, undaunted by the story, philosophically bought the mansion, and installed himself therein. As, at midnight, he sat writing, the spectre appeared, and clanking its irons, motioned that he should follow. The philosopher calmly signed to it to wait, and proceeded with his task. At length, when the entreaty had been several times repeated, he rose, and intimated himself ready to follow where it desired. On this the spirit preceded him to an inner court of the mansion, and there vanished. Athenodorus laid some leaves and grass to mark the spot, and returned to his studies. The next morning he sought the magistrates of the city. A search was instituted, and a skeleton loaded with rusty chains discovered beneath the place marked. This having been interred in a proper spot, the philosopher placidly pursued his labours in the house he had purchased, unvisited for the future by such grisly guests.

Trajan, says Macrobius, previous to his invasion of Parthia, was invited to consult the oracle of Heliopolis, where the method of inquiry was by sealed packets. Incredulous as to the power of the deity, he forwarded a packet and desired a sealed reply. This arriving, and being opened, a blank paper only was found. The courtiers expressed amazement, but the Emperor confessed that, being sceptical as to the wisdom of the oracle, he had placed nothing in his own packet but a blank sheet. The response was therefore apt, and Trajan now confessed his curiosity and mystification by sending ambassadors to demand whether from his war in Parthia he should return safely to Rome. A vine cut in pieces and wrapped in a linen cloth was sent him, as symbolising the manner of his return. He died in the East, and even so were his remains brought back to Italy.

I shall cite now some instances of phenomena strikingly similar to the phenomena occurring in our own day. The handling of live coals without injury—a manifestation which has frequently occurred to myself—was witnessed also in these ancient times. Strabo and Pliny unite in assuring us that in the reign of Augustus the priests of a temple at the foot of Mount Soracte dedicated to the goddess Feronia, had been known to walk bare-footed over great quantities of glowing embers. The same ordeal, says Strabo, was practised by the priestesses of the goddess Asta Bala in Cappadocia.

That a mode of conversing with spirits by means of the alphabet was known and used in Roman times, the historian Ammianus Marcellinus proves by the following narrative:—

"In the days of the Emperor Valens, A.D. 371, some Greek cultivators of theurgy, who in those days usurped the name of philosophers, were brought to trial for having attempted to ascertain the successor to the throne by means of magical arts. The small table or tripod which they had used for this purpose was produced in court, and on being submitted to the torture, they gave the following account of their proceedings:—

"'We constructed, most venerable judges, this small ill-omened table which you behold, after the likeness of the Delphian tripod, with wood of laurel, and with solemn auspices. Having duly consecrated it by muttering over it secret spells, and by many and protracted manipulations, we succeeded at last in making it move. Now, whenever we consulted it about secrets, the process for making it move was as follows. It was placed in the centre of a house which had been purified by Arabian incense on every side; a round dish composed of various metallic substances, being, with the needful purifications, set upon it. On the circular rim of this dish the four-and-twenty characters of the alphabet were cut with much art, and placed at equal intervals, which had been measured with perfect exactness. A person clad in linen garments, in slippers also made of linen, with a light turban wreathed about his head, and carrying branches of the sacred laurel in his hand, having propitiated the deity who gives the responses, in certain prescribed forms of invocation, according to the rules of ceremonial science, sets this dish upon the tripod, balancing over it a suspended ring attached to the end of a very fine linen thread, which also had previously undergone a mystic initiation. This ring, darting out, and striking at distant intervals the particular letters that attract it, makes out heroic verses, in accordance with the questions put, as complete in mode and measure as those uttered by the Pythoness or the oracles of the Branchidæ.

"'As we were, then and there, inquiring who should succeed the present Emperor, since it was declared that he would be a finished character in every respect, the ring, darting out, had touched the syllables ØEO, with the final addition of the letter Δ (making Theod), some one present exclaimed that Theodorus was announced as appointed by fate. Nor did we pursue our inquiries any further into the matter, for we were all satisfied that Theodorus was the person w e were asking for.'"

It is amusing to note the pedantic minuteness with which these ancient theurgists detail the rites and invocations through which their intercourse with another world was, as they supposed, obtained. Of the fact that their intense desire for communion with spirits alone attracted spirits to them they seem to have been blissfully ignorant.

It is quite within the limits of probability that genuine messages from the spirit world would be obtained by a circle which should repeat with the same solemn faith the "derry down" chorus of the Druids, the nursery rhyme of "Mother Hubbard," or the theosophical nonsense of the present day.

The story has a tragical and remarkable sequel. The tyrant Valens, fearing for his throne, caused Theodorus, though a man eminent for his virtues and attainments, to be at once put to death. Nor was his jealous alarm satisfied with a single victim. The pagan philosophers were also judicially murdered, and as many whose names commenced with the letters "Theod" as the emperor could get into his power. Yet the prediction was, in spite of all, fulfilled. Theodosius, whose name was similar to the letters of the answer so far as that answer had been suffered to proceed, succeeded Valens upon the throne of the West.

The story of Marcellinus, I may add, is confirmed by the early Church historians—Socrates, Scholasticus, Sozomen, &c.

In view of that similarity of phenomena, as an instance of which the foregoing narrative is given, a passage to be found in Tertullian is very striking. The Christian father thus reproaches the pagans of his age: "Do not your magicians call ghosts and departed souls from the shades below, and by their infernal charms represent an infinite number of delusions? And how do they perform all this, but by the assistance of evil angels and spirits, by which they are able *to make stools and tables prophesy!*" The object of Tertullian's book, like that of his whole life, being to destroy paganism, it was natural that he should represent these things as the work of fiends. Whether evil spirits or good were concerned, the fact that fifteen centuries ago séances were held with tables remains a most remarkable one.

Space fails me to describe the omens that attended Caesar's death; and how the apparition of that Caesar was beheld by Brutus at Philippi; how Caracalla was foreshown his assassination in a dream; and Sylla, the night before he died, saw in a vision the manner of his end. These, moreover, are things that have a thousand times been described. Nor can I find room to tell of the spiritual in the lives of Scipio, Marius, Cicero, Antony, Augustus, and other famous Romans. I have now depicted intercourse with another world as it existed in the various ancient nations, and have given the principal and best-authenticated instances to be found in the history of each people; but, were the whole of the supermundane occurrences that old historians relate to be collected and commented upon, we might suppose with the apostle that the world itself could hardly contain the books which should be written. With some remarks on Roman spiritualism in its relation to the social condition of the people, I shall therefore close.

The worst and most frightful time of heathen misgovernment, was that of the twelve Cæsars. During the whole of this period the foulest vices and the most hideous cruelties stalked abroad: arm-in-arm. Nothing in the nineteen centuries of the Christian era—neither the Italy of Alexander VI., nor the England of Charles II., nor the France of the Regent Philip—has yet been found to equal the Rome of Nero and Tiberius. The hard, systematic, unblushing vices and ferocities of the Italians of that age remain unapproachable. As the Christian revelation is the highest of all gospels; so the time of the dawning of that light was the darkest in the history of the world. And why had earth fallen so low? An impartial student of history will answer, as I answer, Because of the corruptions of those who served as instruments for intercourse with spiritual beings. "Ye are of your father the devil, and do his works," said Christ to the Judæan priesthood of His day. The same reproach might be applied to the priesthood of imperial Rome, and more or less, as I have already endeavoured to show, to every hierarchy of the ancient world. Only spirits yet more evil than themselves could manifest through beings so corrupted as these consecrated mediums gradually became. Every wickedness that can be committed by beings merely human, was on the head of the wretched *sacerdos* of the Roman Empire. It had been found in a long course of ages that the true spiritual phenomena were exhaustive, infrequent, and difficult to obtain. Attention was therefore directed to simulating them by falsehood, and priest after priest toiled with a misdirected ingenuity to invent or perfect the machinery of imposture. By the time of Augustus this system of deceit, was in full flow. It continued so for centuries, decaying only with the decay of the Roman power itself. Exposures, doubtless, were less frequent than in our own age. The medium power of the ancient world was chiefly to be found in the ranks of the priesthood; it is chiefly to be found outside those ranks at present. Thus the whole weight of sacredness and authority might of old be allied with fraud. But, although fewer and further between, exposures did come, and their effect was exceedingly great. The lives and teachings of the priests, too, were causes of endless scandal and demoralisation. What were the intelligent to think of a man whose life was one long career of hypocrisy and vice, interrupted only when he was asleep or drunk; whose temple was filled with contrivances for palming off the vilest impostures on a credulous public; and who, from a succession of false pretences to medial powers, had come at last almost to disbelieve in their existence? What were they to think of the deities whom these priests were appointed to serve: deities who cried constantly for human sacrifices; who saw their temples made receptacles for the foulest vice, and smiled approvingly; who gave teachings inciting to every form of immorality and bloodshed? The intelligent stigmatised the priests as utterly worthless impostors, whose deities were the hideous creatures of their own foul minds. They cried, as so many in our own day have done, that religion was from first to last a lie; that there was no God, neither any immortality for man. Suddenly, from out this chaos rose the foundations of the first Christian Church. It was founded, as in the succeeding part of this work I shall seek to show, by men to whom spiritual signs and wonders were as their daily bread, and whose pure minds held communion only with the beneficent portion of the dwellers in another world. To the spiritualism of the Christian era will my next chapters be devoted. It suffices to say, in concluding this description of communion with another sphere as practised in pagan times, that the corruptions, through which the pretensions to mediumship of the Roman and other priesthoods ultimately came to be received with such derision, are rampant among the mediums of our own age. How often do we see men—ay, and women—who, although possessed of medial powers, have degraded themselves and the noble cause to which they should be devoted, by the vilest and most unblushing fraud! How often, too, do we perceive a still lower class of impostors who, destitute of the slightest pretensions to mediumship, earn a shameful livelihood by the simulation of certain forms of spiritual phenomena! And what among the lives and teachings of the flamens who consented to deify Nero, could surpass in foulness the antic filthinesses of a few creatures of our own age, who have introduced themselves like ghouls into the spiritual ranks, disgusting and repelling the pure-minded and the thoughtful? Is modern spiritualism a Divine revelation given for the elevating and brightening of the world? Then how are we to estimate the impostors mentioned above, whether they mingle medial gifts with their deceit, or confine themselves to falsehood unrelieved by any gleam of truth? How are we to regard the vile and foolish teachings which have of late years been produced in such plenty, through these and their kindred harpies? Above all, in what manner may we regard the weak-minded enthusiasts by whom these evils are encouraged and perpetuated; who accept the most absurd and vicious doctrines with a kind of inspired idiocy of belief, which, if not able to remove, can at least gulp down, mountains; who, as regards spiritual phenomena, display a folly almost unparalleled in ancient or modern times; whom any boy can delude with imposture, and any madman with absurdity; and who, whether that boy or madman were willing or unwilling, would exalt him to the rank of a prophet, and revere him as a spiritual guide? It is these who will accept "explanations" of whose supreme ridiculousness an Australian savage might be ashamed, rather than admit that a medium can deceive. It is these who reject the admonition to "try the spirits" as a needless insult, and thus bar the door at once on scientific research. Finally it is from these and the knaves whom they encourage that modern spiritualism emphatically requires to be delivered.

PART II

SPIRITUALISM IN THE JEWISH AND CHRISTIAN ERAS

CHAPTER I

THE SPIRITUALISM OF THE BIBLE

I have separated the Hebrews from the peoples dealt with in the former portion of this work because it has appeared to me that the spiritualism of the Testaments, Old and New, would best be treated of as one great whole. The signs and wonders recorded by the prophets and apostles of Israel, from Moses to St. John, are indubitably the mightiest and most famous which the Creator has vouchsafed to mankind.

I do not, however, propose to devote to them any very great proportion of these pages, and my reasons will, I trust, be held sufficient. Ninety-nine out of every hundred of my readers are as familiarly acquainted with the histories of the signs accorded to Abraham, and the miracles wrought through Moses, as with any of the chief events of their own earthly lives. The commentaries on the prophecies of Isaiah, Jeremiah, Ezekiel, Daniel, and others would require a lifetime to number. The sermons preached on the miraculous events recorded in the lives of Christ and his apostles might, if collected and printed, fill a hundred libraries as large as the Alexandrian. Were I to quote the chief wonders of Hebrew times, as recorded in our own noble version of the Scriptures, I should be simply deluging the reader with histories, magnificent indeed, but the tritest of the trite.

Were I to attempt in my own language a description of these occurrences, how poor would such efforts seem beside those of the inspired writers I shall confine myself to the citation of certain remarkable instances, and to an inquiry into their influence, and the circumstances of their origin. The few incidents dwelt upon at any length will be found incidents bearing more or less upon the phenomena of to-day.

We find the foundation stone of the Biblical writings to be everywhere miracle. The assumption which, since the mighty discoveries of Newton, has been constantly becoming more rooted among scientific men, that the physical laws of the universe are eternal and immutable, here has no place. Such an assumption indeed, if admitted, reduces the Hebrew Scriptures to a collection of fables,—and not even "fables cunningly devised." The present condition of the scientific world affords a striking example of its effects. In no other age has research into the mysteries of creation been so diligently pursued. In no other age has the disposition to set up the "laws of nature" as a species of idol, appeared so strong. The natural consequence has been that our scientific men have progressed from a disbelief in miracle in general to a disbelief in the particular miracles recorded in the Bible, and from a disbelief in the Bible appear rapidly progressing to a disbelief in God. In 1874 we had Professor Tyndall's Belfast address. It appears likely that in a very few years this minute and studied oration will be openly received by the school which the Professor represents, as an able exposition of their articles of faith. I search it in vain for any indication of a belief in a Personal God. The deities to whom this scientist would appear in secret to bow down, are known to him and his fellow-adorers by the awe-inspiring titles of Atom and Molecule. Not yet, however, are the penetralia of the temple to be unveiled to the outer world. Such a casting of pearls unto swine would utterly misbecome a man of the Professor's acumen. For the uninitiated he has a kind of convenient shadow known as "Nature," which he interposes between their gaze and the inmost secrets of his philosophy, and respecting which he discourses in a most excessively mystic jargon. Nature appears to serve him as she served the Arbaces of Lord Lytton's novel. On her shoulders may be laid the burden of all that does not accord with the philosopher's idea of the fitness of things. It would be unjust to say that the whole of the scientific men of the age are at one with Professor Tyndall in his peculiar theology. But, although the law of the physical sciences is progress, the law governing the ideas of devotees to those sciences respecting religion, both natural and revealed, would seem to be as undoubtedly retrogression. The deity whom even the most religious of such men worship is nothing more than an imitation of the Zeus of the Greeks; as limited in power as that Zeus, and governed like him by an inexorable Fate. The Omnipotent God of Christianity they totally reject. That this is so, quotations from a hundred authorities would prove. I shall content myself with citing part of a critique directed, in the early years of the spiritual movement, against certain phenomena occurring at Ealing, I being the medium through whom they occurred:—

"These are strong facts, and it is allowing a great deal to say that we think Mr. Rymer to be in earnest in stating his belief in them. For ourselves we entirely disbelieve them, and shall gladly give anyone the opportunity of convincing us.

"In the meanwhile we venture to recommend to Mr. Rymer's attentive study an old-fashioned college text-book, which we suspect he has never opened: Pratt's 'Mechanical Philosophy.' He will there learn of those immutable laws which the unchanging God has impressed once and for ever on creation; and, reading of the wondrous harmony and order which reign by their operation throughout the wide bounds of creation, he may perhaps come to share our doubt and disbelief of those imaginings which tell us of their violation in moving tables and shaking lamps and dancing chairs, and he may, perchance, should his study prosper, catch also a sense of the pitying scorn with which those nurtured on the strong meat of the inductive philosophy within the very courts and halls that a Newton trod, view these sickly spiritualist dreamers, thus drunk with the new wine of folly and credulity."

Such is a fair specimen of the mode in which these Sir Oracles discourse on subjects not in accordance with their own systems of philosophy. I may answer them through the mouths of their own gods. It is tolerably certain that, nigh two hundred years ago, Newton was to Descartes and others of the renowned scientists of the age "a sickly dreamer drunk with the new wine of folly and credulity." It is still more certain that Francis Bacon was, by many philosophers of the time of James I., allotted a place in that "Ship of Fools" to which this admirer of Bacon's inductive philosophy so calmly consigns the spiritualists of the era of Victoria.

As regards any and every system of Christianity, is not the friendship of such men more dangerous than their hostility? They diligently search for and remove from between the covers of the Bible whatever the scientific mind cannot grasp. They gravely assure us that the laws of the universe are not to be altered or superseded even by the Deity who instituted them—thus at once depriving that Deity of his attribute of Omnipotence, and reducing the Creator to be subject to the created. Did Elisha cause iron to float on water? Was the shadow of the sun turned back on the dial of Hezekiah? Was Aaron's rod, on his throwing it down, changed into a serpent? The worshippers of "the laws of Nature" would consider themselves besotted did they credit any such absurdities. They are not as the early Christians were. They are assuredly not followers of the Christ who, taught that "with God all things are possible." The theory that there are everywhere throughout the universe wheels within wheels; laws by which that of gravity may be modified or temporarily set aside; invisible forces which exert power over matter: such a theory is to the scientific Christian what the creed he professes was to the Greeks of the first century—foolishness. He calmly assumes that the whole of the ways of God in the governing of the worlds which He has made are now known to man, and he stops his ears against any evidence to the contrary. He dismisses, as I have said, from that Bible which he professes to reverence as the Word of God, whatever may be considered as savouring of miracle. To what extents this demolition proceeds I shall now endeavour to show. Christianity, deprived of all but what may be explained by the known laws of creation, and exposed in such a condition to the assaults of sceptics, resembles a vessel which, having been carefully denuded of rudder, masts, and compass, and pierced with innumerable holes, is sent to sea to encounter a storm.

We are told frequently in the Old Testament of God appearing visibly to man, and speaking with him face to face. Yet we read in Exodus that, when Moses desired to behold the Lord in all His glory, He replied, "Thou canst not see my face; for there shall no man see me and live." How are the apparent contradictions to be reconciled? Spiritualists reconcile them by their knowledge of the countless ministering spirits which constantly watch over earth, and ceaselessly pass to and fro on the errands of the Master of spirits. Such, clothed in a material form, may have executed God's commands regarding Adam. Such wrestled with Jacob, and were seen by him, in trance, ascending and descending between heaven and earth. Such appeared to Abraham as towards evening, he sat in the door of his tent. Such delivered Lot from the destruction which impended over the Cities of the Plain. Such carried the commands of God to his servant Moses, guided that Moses to the presence of the Egyptian King, and wrought, by means of the powers accorded to them, the whole of the wonders related in the Pentateuch. By spirits like these was Gideon prompted to his mission of deliverance. By such spirits was the mighty host of Sennacherib destroyed. To the beholding of these spirits were the eyes of Elisha's servant made equal when the Syrians sought the life of his master. "And when the servant of the man of God was risen early, and gone forth, behold, a host encompassed the city both with horses and chariots. And his servant said unto him, Alas, my master! how shall we do? And he answered, Fear not: for they that be with us are more than they that be with them. And Elisha prayed, and said, Lord I pray thee open his eyes that he may see. And the Lord opened the eyes of the young man; and he saw: and, behold, the mountain was full of horses and chariots of fire round about Elisha."

We have here a striking proof that the human eye can be made to perceive spirits. I see no room for sceptical cavilling, or explaining away. The prophet prayed that his servant's eyes might be opened, and God opened them, so that this Israelite saw the glories of the spiritual beings around. "Clairvoyant" he would have been termed in our own day, and as such, ridiculed by the scientific men with whom that word is another term for dreamer. But the particular story I have quoted is from writings all European Churches hold to be sacred. It requires to be accepted or rejected in its entirety. Professing Christians must admit that the eye of man can occasionally behold spiritual beings, or condemn the Hebrew chronicler as the narrator of a circumstantial lie.

That spirits can, in the present day, operate upon matter with powers similar to those possessed by human beings still in the flesh is an assertion received with derisive incredulity by myriads who profess every sabbath their belief that such occurrences were common from two to four thousand years ago. The tens of thousands of clergymen who have preached against such facts of modern spiritualism as the moving of material objects without visible agency, and the millions of listeners who have agreed with their sermons, would doubtless be indignant were it asserted that they disbelieved in the loosing by an angel of the chains of Peter, or the rolling away by another angel of the stone which secured the sepulchre of Christ. With what intense scorn, too, are the testimonies regarding that levitation by spirit power of which I and others have in modern times been the subjects, received by Christians of Europe and America who may read on one page of their Bibles how the apostle Philip was suddenly snatched up from out the sight of the eunuch whom he had baptized, and conveyed from Gaza to Azotus, a distance of thirty miles; in another place the verses in which Ezekiel tells how the hand of the Lord lifted him, and carried him into the midst of the valley which was full of bones. Again, the appearances of spirit forms and hands which have so frequently occurred in the present age, are heard of with absolute incredulity, and the vouchings of witnesses of the highest standing, intellectual and social, calmly set aside. Yet one of the most picturesque chapters of the Old Testament is that wherein Daniel recounts how the "fingers of a man's hand," at the impious feast of Belshazzar, were seen by the monarch himself and a thousand of his satraps, to write in fiery characters upon the wall of the palace an intimation of the approaching doom of Babylon. And Ezekiel recounts how he beheld a spirit-hand, and the roll of a book therein, and that, when the hand spread out the book before him, it was written within and without. As to the human body being made insusceptible to the action of fire, have we not Daniel's history of the three Jewish youths who walked unhurt in the midst of the flaming furnace? If such mighty works were done two thousand five hundred years ago, why should not lesser wonders be witnessed in our own time? Is the arm of God grown less mighty? The question has often been asked, but never responded to. Science cannot, and religion dare not answer in the negative.

How science treats spiritual phenomena in general, I have already endeavoured to show. How she behaves with regard to the particular phenomena of which I have just spoken was instanced in the *Quarterly Review*, of October, 1871. The article on spiritualism contained therein has been praised as logical and able. Yet the argument it was written to enforce is simply this:—B, the author of the essay, has never witnessed certain phenomena which have occurred in the presence of A, and to whose occurrence A has testified. It is highly improbable that such phenomena should occur. The premise that such events are unlikely to happen, and the premise that B has never known them to happen, when put together produce the inference that their occurrence in the presence of A is an utter impossibility, and his narrative therefore worthless. And has the inductive philosophy come to this! Were such arguments to be advanced by a man of science on the opposite side, would not his hostile brethren have re-discovered that "many dogs can arrive at more logical conclusions?"

I return to the examination of miracle as contained in the Bible. The first passage on which I light (1 Chron. xxviii. 19) is a remarkable illustration of the inspirational writing and drawing of the present day. David had given to Solomon his son the patterns of the temple, and all with which it was to be furnished. "These things," said he, "the Lord made me understand in writing, by His hand upon me, even all the works of this pattern."

It would seem that a species of divination practised in the East to this very day was known of old among the Hebrews. How are we to understand Gen. xliv. 15—"Is not this it by which my Lord drinketh, and whereby, indeed, He divineth"—unless as an intimation that the obtaining of visions by looking steadfastly into a cup filled with wine or other liquor, was a species of clairvoyance practised in the days of Joseph?

Had I space, and did the patience of the reader permit, I might proceed to minutely analyse the prophecies contained in the writings of Isaiah, Jeremiah, Ezekiel, Daniel, and the lesser seers. The chief of these prophecies related to the coming of Christ, and all who have ever searched the Scriptures know how exact were the forebodings of his advent. Of lesser interest are those mystical predictions given by Daniel and others, on which the ingenuity of theologians of all nations and ages has been fruitlessly expended. Perhaps the terrible attractiveness with which the prophecies relating to the last siege of Jerusalem are invested, may excuse my lingering over them for a moment. The most awful is that description given by Moses of the calamities which should befall the Hebrews when they had utterly forsaken the God of their fathers, and space for repentance was no longer allowed. This denunciation, the bitterest ever spoken by a prophet, occurs in the twenty-eighth chapter of the book of Deuteronomy. Before Jerusalem was taken by Titus every item of its horrors had come to pass. And the words of Christ, though they shock us with no such literal presentment of the miseries to be endured by the doomed race, are solemnly significant of the wrath to come. "When ye shall see the abomination of desolation, spoken of by Daniel, stand in the holy place, then let them which be in Judea flee unto the mountains. . . . And woe unto them who are with child, and who give suck in those days. . . . For then shall be great tribulation, such as was not from the beginning of the world to this time, no, nor ever shall be" (Matt. xxiv.). Again, "And when ye shall see Jerusalem compassed by armies, then know that the desolation thereof is nigh. . . . For these be the days of vengeance, that all things which are written may be fulfilled. . . . And they shall fall by the edge of the sword, and shall be led away captive into all nations; and Jerusalem shall be trodden down by the Gentiles, until the times of the Gentiles shall be fulfilled" (Luke xxi.).

Seventy years after the Crucifixion came this great woe. The legions of Titus marched into Palestine. Rome still reigned as mistress of the world; indeed, her power had scarcely attained its zenith. The conquests of Trajan lay yet in the womb of the future, when those of the son of Vespasian were made. Yet the Jews for long deemed themselves secure of triumph. Their city was the strongest of all cities; and false prophets were not wanting to delude them. Thus encouraged, they fiercely defied the power of the Empire, and vowed to recover that independence which the Maccabees had died, to preserve, or like those heroes fall fighting to the last. Did not the whole Christian world regard the miseries of Jerusalem as chastisements sent of God, how frequently would the superhuman endurance of her children be quoted to instance what can be borne by nations striving to be free! In no other siege was the valour displayed so frantic. In no other siege did the attacked seem so completely to have triumphed over death. The Romans were at first disposed to make captives of such as fell into their power. But these, in nearly all cases, preferred death in defence of the Holy City to a life of ignominious servitude, and fought desperately to the last. And what they so stoically endured, they were no less ready to inflict. Such of their enemies as they captured they remorselessly put to death. Enraged by this, and the determined resistance of the besieged, the Romans proceeded to display in its most refined form, the cruelty seldom absent from their wars. All Jews who came into their hands alive were crucified in view of the city, and perished in torment, with their dying eyes fixed on home and friends. Even as their fathers had done unto Christ, was it done unto them. At length came the end. Wall after wall had been carried, until the last stronghold of the Jews was reached. Within the city no food remained save human flesh. Even mothers, as Moses had prophesied, slew and ate their children in the madness of hunger. Many Jews had frantically endeavoured to break through the Roman lines, and, being taken, were crucified in such numbers, that wood became scarce, and no more crosses could be made. Then followed the capture of the temple. As if inspired with a sudden frenzy, the Roman soldiers rushed forward, flinging in firebrands from every side. Titus, who desired the preservation of so magnificent a shrine, in vain ordered his guards to beat them off. The fabric consecrated to Jehovah was burnt to the ground, and over against what had been its eastern gate did the Roman legionaries set up their standards, and, offering sacrifices to them, hail Titus as Imperator with "acclamations of the greatest joy." The most awful siege recorded in the world's history was at an end. Eleven hundred thousand of the Jews had been slain. So many were carried into captivity that the markets became glutted, and the Roman soldiery sought in vain to find purchasers for their slaves. I think none who read of these events but must endorse the pathetic assertion of Josephus: "It appears to me that the misfortunes of all men, from the beginning of the world, if they be compared to these of the Jews, are not so considerable as they were." So fearfully had the predictions of Christ and Moses been fulfilled.

In quitting the Old Testament for the New let me say that there is to be noticed a remarkable similarity between the miracles recorded of the Jewish prophets and those afterwards performed by Christ.

The rendering inexhaustible by Elijah of the widow's cruse of oil and barrel of meal, is a parallel on a lesser scale to the miracle of the loaves and fishes. So with the means by which Elisha fed a hundred men. The restoration to life of an only child by each of these prophets recalls the raising from the dead by Jesus of that young man of Nain, "the only son of his mother, and she was a widow." Naaman, who was healed of leprosy upon having faith sufficient to obey Elisha's mandate of washing in the Jordan, reminds us of several of the miracles of Christ. And, finally, the narrative of the man whose dead body was cast into the tomb of Elisha, and sprang up revivified on touching the prophet's bones, is a marvel almost equalling anything that the New Testament contains.

One other incident in Old Testament spiritualism deserves to be noticed. Although such marvellous tokens of spiritual power were vouchsafed to the Jews, the Levitical law forbade them to seek intercourse with the spirits of the departed. The reason is not difficult to find. Jehovah feared that, like the nations around them, his people would be drawn from the worship of the One God to adore a multitude of the beings whom He had created. Nor were restrictions unnecessary. On a hundred occasions do we hear of the Jews hastening to this and far grosser forms of idolatry. As Macaulay with great justness remarks, their whole history "is the record of a continued struggle between pure theism, supported by the most terrible sanctions, and the strangely fascinating desire of having some visible and tangible object of adoration." I know that the European mind of to-day and the Hebrew mind of three thousand years back have little in common. That childish savagery which could satisfy the craving for some outward symbol of spiritual things with the image of a calf, has disappeared from among civilised men. But for a few weak minds the danger out of which all idolatry springs still exists. There are not wanting enthusiasts to say to the spirits, "Ye are gods," and revere, as something more than human, those through whom tokens of their presence are given. It was against this great evil that the Levitical law was directed. With the Jows of old almost a whole nation was at all times ready to fall into error; with the spiritualists of to-day comparatively few are led into such folly. Yet it behoves all who wish well to our cause to raise their voices earnestly against these things, and, impressing upon their weaker brethren that mediums and spirits are alike but fallible, urge that to neither should this unreasoning faith and baseless reverence be accorded.

It is from the abuse of the faculty of veneration that such things in great part spring. By minds in which that faculty was exceedingly strong, and caution and judgment correspondingly weak, the wildest extravagances of religious history have been perpetrated. The sceptical type of intellect, which can perceive nothing beyond this present world, and rejects with the greatest disdain all testimony relating to a future life, may be accepted as a character whose weakness is the antipodes of that just described. The mass of mankind hold a course equally distant from the two extremes, and are neither disposed to accept without testimony nor to reject without investigation. Yet there come periods when almost the whole world seems to be infected with one or other of these diseases. Just at present the second is rampant, and is the deadliest foe by which Christianity can be menaced. For the essence of the religion of Jesus is miracle, and signs and wonders accompanied him throughout his career. The account of His birth is the chief marvel in all history, yet it is almost matched by what occurred at and after His death. From the commencement of His mission until the final agony of the cross He continued to enforce the tidings He had come upon earth to proclaim by the mightiest works that earth had ever seen. And the power that was His He kept not to Himself. In His name the apostles whom He sent out were made to do many marvellous works. "And when He had called unto Him His twelve disciples He gave them power against unclean spirits to cast them out, and to heal all manner of sickness, and all manner of disease. . . . And He commanded them, saying: Heal the sick, cleanse the lepers, raise the dead, cast out devils; freely ye have received, freely give." Yet, as Christ prophesied, these men were hated of all the world for His name's sake; and to Himself the nation whom His mission particularly concerned gave only death. They saw Him raise the dead, and cleanse the leper; give sight to the blind, and cause the lame to walk. They received from Him teachings such as ear had never before heard, and they rewarded Him with the crown of thorns and the cross. For their condition was worse than that of the man who sat by the wayside as Christ went out from Jericho. Bartimeus, through all his darkness, could recognise his Lord; but the chiefs of the people, though spiritually blind, desired not that their eyes might be opened; and, unable to comprehend the Light of the World, they sought to extinguish it.

Had the high-priest Caiaphas, when, with his acolytes, he mocked the victim stretched upon the cross, saying: "He saved others—himself he cannot save;"—had this man been told that there should come a day when his victim would be worshipped as the Son of God in almost every country over which the Roman sceptre extended; and in yet vaster regions, of whose existence those Romans had never dreamed; that in the very city from whence then went forth the fiats of Caesar, would be set up the authority of pontiffs who deemed it their all on earth to be revered as vicegerents of this Christ; that the ancient glory of Jerusalem should be extinguished, and even the foundations of her temple almost pass from view; and that a scanty remnant of the once mighty and flourishing nation of the Jews should wander from city to city of realms possessed by the triumphant Christians, ever expecting to behold the Messiah who should deliver them from their woes, and ever disappointed: would he not have scorned the prophecy as a madman's dream? Had Lucian, when, in the reign of Trajan, he wrote with pitying wonder of that contempt of death which the Christians displayed, been informed that the statue of that very Trajan would be one day hurled from the noble column erected as its pedestal, and an effigy of a chief among these Christians take its place, with what a display of lively ridicule would he have laughed down such a tale! And could the incredulity of either have been held matter for surprise? Was it probable in the days of Caiaphas that the teachings of Christ would ever spread beyond Judæa? Was it probable in the days of Lucian that this, carpenter, and son of a carpenter, would be adored as God by all the nations of the Gentiles? How comes it then that at his name the heads of such uncountable millions bow?

The Protestant will answer that, Christ being God, the Christian religion was of God, and that, therefore He has nourished and preserved it. But how has it been nourished and preserved? By miracle, all history replies. It is an easy thing now that men should accept the faith which their fathers have from time immemorial accepted. The matter was far otherwise in the days of Nero, Trojan, and Diocletian. Then, Christianity was professed only in secret, and by a few; being held by the many an abomination or a foolishness. Its ethics were as noble as at present; but with those ethics was inseparably connected the rejection of the hundreds of deities whom Greek and Roman worshipped, and the acceptance of Christ as God; and he or she who did so accept Him, became thereby immediately exposed to inflictions such as human nature faints but to contemplate. The renunciation of the pomps and vanities of this world was then no vain form. With the embracing of the Christian religion the certainty of a life of privation and suffering was also accepted, and the peril of a death of agony dared. To encounter the constant opposition of those they loved, and provoke the hatred of their nearest and dearest; to be in continual danger of denunciation to the authorities; to meet for worship only in deserts and catacombs these were some of the things which all Christians endured.

It was well if at a meeting for praise and prayer the little congregation were not broken in upon by bands of fierce soldiery, and minister and hearers involved in one common massacre; if an assembling to celebrate the supper of the Lord did not end in those who had partaken of that love-feast being thrown to the beasts of the arena; if from the funeral rites of some brother or sister departed, the mourners were not snatched away to be smeared with pitch and set up as torches in the garden of Nero. How many Christians perished by these, and modes of death equally dreadful, in the three centuries that followed the Crucifixion, it is impossible to compute. However great the number of martyrs, their agonies were insufficient to check the progress of the new faith. Nay, these agonies were even coveted by many converts as the most glorious mode of finishing their earthly career. Numbers denounced themselves to the authorities, and passed to deaths of lingering torture with triumphant joy. The whole population of a small town in Asia, we learn from Tertullian, sought such a fate. Having heard that the emperor had issued an edict commanding all Christians to be put to death, they flocked in a body to the proconsul, and acknowledged themselves adherents of the new faith. On this the Roman deputy executed a few of the chief men, and dismissed the others to their homes. And they departed; not lamenting that their friends had come to so terrible an end, but that they themselves had been deemed unworthy to receive the solemn crown of martyrdom; not rejoiced because they had escaped dying in unutterable torture, but because a select few of their number had obtained admittance into the noble host of those whose blood was shed in the service of God. The words of St. Paul express the sentiment with which every martyr seems to have met death: "I am now ready to be offered, and the time of my departure is at hand. I have fought a good fight; I have finished my course; I have kept the faith: henceforth there is laid up for me a crown of righteousness, which the Lord, the righteous judge, shall give me at that day."

And why were the Christians of the first century so much more devoted to their creed than those of the nineteenth? How came it that, in spite of the most bloody and unsparing persecutions men had ever groaned under, the new creed spread with rapidity over the whole of the then civilised world? What was it by which zealot and atheist—the prejudices of men bigoted in favour of their old religion, and the prejudices of men bigoted in favour of their no-religion—were alike so speedily and so thoroughly conquered? Was it not in great measure by the continual working of signs and wonders?—by the impetus which the unceasing intervention of spiritual beings gave to the advancement of the Christian religion? Could a creed whose high teachings were supported by such striking miracles be likely to fail? The internal evidences, indeed, were alone sufficient to prove this faith to be of God. But those internal evidences were recommended to such men as Paul, John, and Peter, by the power which they themselves possessed of working mighty things, by the marvels which many of them had seen the great Founder of their belief accomplish, by the frequent descent upon them of the Spirit of God, by the gift of miraculously healing, by the ability of understanding many and diverse tongues. Nor was it to the apostles alone that spiritual things were brought so close. The faith of such of their successors as Polycarp, Ignatius, and Justin Martyr, as Tertullian, Cyprian, Ambrose, Augustine, and a hundred others, was strengthened by signs; and wonders almost equally great. Nor are these signs and wonders yet extinct. The noblest Christians of all ages have sought for and received them. It may be affirmed, without danger of the assertion being disapproved, that there never was a truly great man of any church—one distinguished by the intensity of his faith and the nobility of his life—but knew himself to be attended constantly by ministering spirits. Such was the faith of Savonarola, of Loyola, of Bunyan, of Fenelon, of Wesley, and of numerous others, whom I have not space to name. Nor is it probable that such men as Calvin and Torquemada were unsupplied with spiritual guides; though, doubtless, spiritual guides of an exceedingly undeveloped class. I purpose in my next chapters to point out how a constant vein of miracle runs through the history of the early Fathers, and how traces of miracle have continued down to the present day in every Church worthy the name of Christian. Not now, indeed, does faith "subdue kingdoms, stop the mouths of lions, quench the violence of fire, escape the edge of the sword." By these things were the early Christians "out of weakness made strong." Those countless thousands who in the time of the power of the Romans went to death as to a bridal, did not *believe* that the faith they professed was the truth—they *knew* it to be such. Spirits had spoken with them face to face; they had been permitted while yet on earth to catch a glimpse of the glories of the hereafter. It mattered not what men might do against the body; for the soul an incorruptible crown was laid up in heaven. Such Christians would have heard with mute amazement the assertion that death is a "bourne whence no traveller returns." By a thousand incidents of their lives were such teachings disproved. Signs that a Thomas could not have doubted were continually afforded them of the watch which those who had gone before kept over the disciples of the true faith yet on earth. Some, like Stephen, saw in the hour of death the heavens open, and the Son of Man stand at the right hand of God. Others, like Peter, were delivered from bondage and the peril of death by spiritual hands. Like Polycarp they stood in the midst of flames and were not harmed. Like Polycarp, too, voices whispered to them to be strong, and quit themselves like men. As Ammon, they were borne by spirits through the air. With Montanus, they were thrown into ecstatic trances, and delivered messages from another world. With John, they were circled at times by the glory of the inner heaven, and those that looked on them saw their faces "as the faces of angels." It was by men like these—men strong with an unshakable certainty of the truth of what they taught—that Christianity was carried to the farthest ends of the earth. It was thus that the philosophy of Greece and the pride of Rome were overthrown, that incense ceased to smoke on the altar of Jupiter, and Poseidon and Isis were laid prostrate in the dust.

I do not advance these views as theories. They are facts, as every genuine Christian will be ready to admit. But there are numbers of men, professing to be Christians, who, denying that such things have happened, will stigmatise these great truths as dreams of the most baseless kind. For Christ is now, even more than of old, uncomprehended by many who call themselves his disciples. They "understand not the sayings which He speaks unto them." It was thus, as every Evangelist proves to us, in Judæa. Upon the earth to which he came to bear tidings of peace and goodwill the Son of Man walked alone. Mary understood Him not, nor Joseph, nor they who, according to the belief of the Jews, were the sisters and brothers of this Jesus. He began his mission, and the nation to whom He preached understood him not. Even the most beloved of his disciples could but faintly comprehend and sympathize with their Master. They perceived his miracles, and "being afraid, spoke among themselves, saying, 'What manner of man is this?'" They listened to his teachings, and "wist not of what He talked." They approved their charity by forbidding others to cast devils out in the name of Christ, and the extent of their faith by failing to do so themselves. Whether Christ walked in Jerusalem or in the desert, surrounded by his disciples, or absent from all men, He was, as regards this world, equally alone. The love that He bore to man, not even John or Peter could understand. The spirit in which He taught none could perceive. When, in the garden of Gethsemane, He became "sorrowful even unto death," He withdrew to endure that mighty agony alone. The afflictions that tormented Him were not trials into which the twelve could enter. Whilst He suffered, his disciples slept. So was it before Pilate. So when passing from the judgment-seat to the cross. So when on that cross He cried: "My God, my God, why hast Thou forsaken me?" So when, having bowed his head, He said "It is finished," and, as He gave up the ghost, the earth quaked and the veil of the temple was rent in twain. And equally solitary does Christ remain unto the present day. Never have his teachings been truly understood of men. The master is still alone. "The light shineth in the darkness, and the darkness comprehendeth it not."

Had it been better comprehended how different would have been the history of the whole Christian world! Then Athanasius and Arius would not have cursed each other both for this life and the next. Then Constantine would not have been accepted as a fitting head for the Church of Christ. Then Julian would not have been driven in despair to the worn-out philosophies of pagan times. Then religion would not have been found throughout the dark ages uniformly on the side of might, and ever straying further from what was right and true. The career of Becket could never have been lived. Dominic would not have believed in burning the bodies of men to save their souls from eternal fire. Religious wars would never have desolated the world. The Inquisition would not have been established. Such natures as those of Torquemada and Calvin would have been viewed with abhorrence by men of all climes and creeds. In the pages of history we should read of no such laws as those established in the sixteenth century at Geneva; of no such reigns as those of Henry VIII. of England, and Charles IX. of

France. The touch of Borgia or of Leo would not have defiled the papal tiara. Instead of sects too numerous to be counted, there might, at this day, be seen a single Church embracing all Christendom. Instead of brethren inflamed against each other by causeless hatred there might be found that unity which the Psalmist tells us it is so pleasant to see. Instead of gigantic wars, and rumours of wars, we might be living in the midst of the reign of universal peace, the "federation of the world." Controversy would be a name forgotten, and the pens and works of polemical divines moulder in oblivion and dust. But these speculations are indeed dreams.

It is time that this chapter should conclude. I have done my best to prove how intimately miracle is bound up with each of the many books of the Bible, and how total would be the ruin effected by tearing all miracle away. I have sought also to point out the resemblance between certain phenomena of Jewish times and the phenomena of the present day. Want of space, indeed, has prevented me from doing the subject justice. Besides the instances adduced, there are numerous others scattered through every book, from Genesis to the Revelation of John. But these any searcher of the Scriptures can readily find for himself. He will also, I think, find sufficient evidence to make plain to him that the shadow of Hebrew spiritualism was the tendency which, even more than Assyrians, Egyptians, or Persians, the race chosen of God had to listen to the whispers of evil spirits, and exalt those spirits into deities: a tendency which the most terrible threats and chastisements proved insufficient to restrain. He will agree with me that solely against this tendency were the terrors of the Levitical law directed. He will also agree with me that by rejecting whatever in the Testaments, Old or New, is inexplicable by known laws, or apparently opposed to those laws, men make the prophets and chroniclers liars and the teachings of Christ of no authority. If we are to believe that so much of Scripture is false, what security have we that the rest is true? A single error admitted injures Holy Writ: what then of this mass of error? It is but cold truth to say that those who, professing to be worshippers of Christianity, would either totally deprive the Bible of miracle or accept only the miracles attributed to Christ, treat the chief of religions as of old the soldiers of Pilate treated her Founder. They deprive her of the vestments that so well become her. Having plaited a crown of thorns and shaped a sceptre from a reed, they adorn her with these. Then, bowing the knee before her, they expose her in this state to the derision of the nations.

CHAPTER II

THE SPIRITUAL IN THE EARLY CHRISTIAN CHURCH

A favourite dictum with many divines is, that miracle ceased with the apostolic age. We have no certain evidence, say they, that signs and wonders occurred after the last of the twelve had departed from earth. Learned bishops have not been ashamed to employ the whole force of their ecclesiastical eloquence in endeavouring to prove this hypothesis a certainty.

Yet the fact undeniably is that, as regards external evidence, certain miraculous occurrences recorded by Athanasius, Augustine, and others, are better supported than anything the New Testament contains. The internal evidence which in the Bible carries such weight is, of course, weaker in the case of the Fathers. Yet, conjoined with the historical testimony, it has proved sufficient to induce such men as Locke and Grotius to admit the authenticity of these narratives. The first tells us that we must allow the miracles, or, by denying that they occurred, destroy the authority of the Fathers, and even their reputation for common honesty. The second not only warmly defends the spiritual in the early Church, but avows his entire belief that such things had continued down to his own day. Milton, Cudworth, Bacon, Addison, Dr. Johnson, and a host of men equally distinguished, have held one or other of these opinions. Indeed, it is difficult to see how Christians can do otherwise. The words used by Christ are, "He that believeth on me, the works that I do shall he do also, and greater works than these shall he do." If Protestant divines deny that such works are now done, is not the inference plain? They are of opinion that men have ceased to believe in Christ.

Not such was the faith of early and fervent members of that Church. How hardy seem the expressions of Tertullian on the subject! So earnestly did he hold to the text above quoted, that men asserting themselves to be Christians, who yet could not expel a demon, were in his judgment, worthy of death. "Let some one be brought forward here at the foot of your judgment-seat, who, it is agreed, is possessed of a demon. When commanded by any Christian to speak, that spirit shall as truly declare itself a demon, as elsewhere falsely a god. In like manner let some one be brought forward of those who are believed to be acted upon by a god. . . . Unless these confess themselves to be demons, not daring to lie unto a Christian, then shed upon the spot the blood of that most impudent Christian." (Apol. 23.)

The words of St. Paul to the Corinthians are:— "Concerning spiritual gifts, brethren, I would not have you ignorant. . . . For to one is given by the Spirit the word of wisdom. . . . to another the gifts of healing by the same spirit; to another the working of miracles; to another prophecy; to another discerning of spirits; to another divers kinds of tongues." As regards the last but one of these gifts, a curious passage is to be found in the "De Anima" of the Tertullian above quoted:—

"We had a right," says the beat orator, "after what was said by St. John, to expect prophesyings; and we not only acknowledge these spiritual gifts, but we are permitted to enjoy the gifts of a prophetess. There is a sister amongst us who possesses the faculty of revelation. She commonly, during our religious service on the Sabbath, falls into a crisis or trance. She has then intercourse with the angels, sees sometimes the Lord himself, sees and hears Divine mysteries, and discovers the hearts of some persons; administers medicine to such as desire it, and, when the Scriptures are read, or psalms are being sung, or prayers are being offered up, subjects from thence are ministered to her visions. We had once some discourse touching the soul while this sister was in the spirit. When the public services were over, and most of the people gone, she acquainted us with what she had seen in her ecstasy, as the custom was; for these things are heedfully digested that they may be duly proved. Among other things, she told us that she had seen a soul in a bodily shape, and that the spirit had appeared unto her, not empty or formless and wanting a living constitution, but rather such as might be handled: delicate, and of the colour of light and air—in everything resembling the human form."

Thus, in the early Christian Church, we have an exact counterpart of the clairvoyance, the trance speaking, and the healing mediumship of the present day. It is also noteworthy that what Tertullian calls the "corporeal soul," or "soul in bodily shape," minutely coincides with the spirit-form as beheld in the visions of ancient and modern seers. Pythagoras and Plato speak of it as a "luciform etherial vehicle," St. Paul calls it the "spiritual body," Swedenborg the "spiritual man," the seeress of Prevorst the "nerve spirit," and Davis the "inner being." All genuine clairvoyants, in short, convey, under different forms of expression, the same idea.

At the age of eighty-six took place the martyrdom of Polycarp. A few nights previous, whilst praying in his bed, the aged saint had perceived his pillow wrapped in fire, without being consumed. This he knew to be an omen of approaching martyrdom. On the day of his departure a number of Christians attended to the place of execution one who had been the disciple and friend of the Apostle John. As they went a spirit voice was heard by all to cry loudly: "Be strong, O Polycarp, and quit thyself like a man." When the pile was lighted the flames refused to touch him, and curved outward on all sides from his form. A fragrant scent, as of aromatic drugs, was diffused around, and the martyr, with a glorious countenance, stood quietly in the midst of the fire, appearing to the beholders like a figure of burnished gold. In dismay, the executioner thrust him through with a sword. There died with him other believers, respecting whom the Church of Smyrna says:— "While they were under torments the Lord Jesus Christ stood by, and, conversing with them, revealed things to them inconceivable by man." Such were the experiences of the early saints.

Sozomen and Socrates, the Church historians, relate two striking instances of information obtained from the departed respecting matters which had troubled the living. Irene, the daughter of Spiridion, Bishop of Trimithon, had been entrusted by a member of her father's flock with the keeping of a large sum of money. Shortly afterwards she died; and the owner came to Spiridion for the return of the deposit. Spiridion, knowing nothing of the matter, searched in vain every spot where his daughter might have placed such a trust, and was forced to inform his visitor that the money could not be found. On this the man tore his hair, and exhibited the greatest distress. His pastor bade him be calm, and proceeding to the grave of Irene, solemnly called upon her spirit to appear. She at once responded to the summons, and informed her father that she had buried the money for greater security in a certain corner of the house. There it was found by Spiridion, and immediately restored to the rightful owner.

But the second narrative is yet more interesting. Evagrius, a Grecian philosopher, had been, with much difficulty, converted to Christianity by Synesius, Bishop of Cyrene. Even after his conversion he would appear to have felt doubts as to the certainty of a future life, and these doubts he, on his death-bed, expressed in a peculiar manner. He gave to Synesius a bag containing a very large sum in gold, which sum he requested him to apply to the benefit of the poor of the city, and desired, moreover, that the Bishop would give him an acknowledgment of the debt, and a promise that Christ would repay him in another world. Synesius willingly subscribed to these terms, and the poor were made happy with the legacy. But Evagrius had no sooner passed away than his heirs brought an action against the Bishop for the recovery of the debt, a memorandum of which they had discovered among the papers of the deceased philosopher. In vain did Synesius plead the circumstances of the case; and, proving that the gift was for the poor, relate the expectation of his creditor that Christ would repay him in another world. Judgment was about to be given for the heirs, when a visit from the spirit of the departed relieved the Bishop of their claims. At dead of night Evagrius appeared, and with a joyful voice, confessed that the Lord had satisfied the debt in full. He further bade Synesius go to his sepulchre, and told him that he would there find a quittance for the sum. Next day, the Bishop, accompanied by the heirs of Evagrius, and the authorities of the city, proceeded to the grave, and caused it to be opened. In the hand of the corpse was found a paper, subscribed as follows, in the undoubted handwriting of the departed:— "Evagrius the philosopher, to thee, most holy Sir, Bishop Synesius, greeting. I have received the debt which in this paper is written with thy hand, and am satisfied; and I have no action against thee for the gold which I gave to thee, and by thee, to Christ, our God and, Saviour." The bill upon which this appeared was the acknowledgment made by Synesius, at the time of receiving the gold. It had been placed within the tomb, as the heirs of Evagrius admitted, in accordance with their father's dying request. But they solemnly denied that the extraordinary words by which the debt was cancelled had then been present on the paper. The receipt thus remains, like the sentences interpreted by Daniel, an instance of that direct spirit-writing so much cavilled at in the present day.

Numerous other miracles occurred in the early ages of the Church which I have only space to name. Pre-eminent are those of Anthony, Martin, and Ambrose, the second of whom is reported to have raised the dead. The cross seen in the heavens by Constantine and his army, is a spiritual sign with the history of which the reader is probably familiar. So with regard to the discovery, by the Empress Helena, of the sepulchre wherein Christ had lain. Marvels equally deserving of notice are to be found scattered through the pages of Irenæus, Origen, Tertullian, Eusebius, Athanasius, Theodoret, and Evagrius. Amongst these are the narratives of miraculous incidents which occurred during the relentless persecutions of Maximian and Diocletian, and the history of those Christians of Carthage whose tongues were cut out by Hunneric the Vandal, and who yet continued to speak with all their former fluency. Regarding this last event, the testimony is as perfect as that concerning any incident in modern history. Bishop Douglas, feeling too much embarrassed by the weight of evidence to deny the occurrence of this wonder, and yet anxious to reconcile it with his pet theory of the confinement of miracle to apostolic times, had the pleasing audacity to assure his readers that nothing was more common than that men who had lost their tongues should retain their speech. The right reverend father in God was unfortunate in living a century or so too soon. His statement would have formed a fitting pendant to the theories of certain scientists of the present day.

"We might easily prove by citations from the fathers," says a writer in the "Encyclopædia Metropolitana," "that one object of the experiences to which the Christian neophyte was subjected, was his introduction to a lawful communion with the spirits of the departed." In this assertion I heartily concur. Indeed, nothing can be more amazing than the ignorance displayed by those divines who at the present day inform us that the Mosaic law forbidding men to seek communion with the departed, has, in all ages, been observed by the Christian Church. Have they the slightest acquaintance with the writings of the fathers of that Church? If so, are they not aware that, besides the instances cited from Tertullian in the opening of this chapter, a score of others might be given to prove that, while vehemently condemning spiritualism as practised by the Pagans, the early Christians were themselves devoted to spiritualistic practices? They anathematized the mediums of the heathen because they believed that the spirits manifesting through them were uniformly evil. They sought earnestly for communion with another world by means of their own mediums, because they perceived the spirits who gave token of their presence through these to be departed friends, and believed them, without exception, angelic beings: natures glorified and happy.

The outpouring of this "gift to discern spirits," was coveted by every congregation of Christians, whether Asiatic or European, of the East or of the West. Even when occurring amongst those whom the orthodox deemed heretical brethren it was not the less rejoiced in. Montanus, though the body of the Church held his teachings in the highest degree pernicious, was connived at by many on account of his spiritual gifts. Two of his female followers, the ladies Maximilla and Priscilla, were held in such esteem as prophetesses and clairvoyants, that the protection of the Papacy itself was granted them against their enemies.

The Montanists, it is true, appear to have been far worthier of reverence than the majority of those who persecuted them. The great purposes of their leader were to put down the follies and vices of the period, and to reform the discipline of the Church. Wherever a church of Montanists arose, there appeared numerous energumens, or, as we now say, mediums. In the midst of the congregation these would pass into an ecstatic state, and deliver addresses whilst entranced. Such a speaker was the sister alluded to by the most eminent disciple of Montanus, the great Tertullian.

Nothing can better express the confidence which the early Christians had in the continual protection of guardian spirits than the beautiful words of St. Augustine:—

"They watch," says the son of Monica—"they watch over and guard us with great care and diligence in all places and at all hours, assisting, providing for our necessities with solicitudes; they intervene between us and Thee, O Lord, conveying to Thee our sighs and groans, and bringing down to us the dearest blessings of Thy grace. They walk with us in all our ways; they go in and out with us, attentively observing how we converse with piety in the midst of a perverse generation, with what ardour we seek Thy kingdom and its justice, and with what fear and awe we serve Thee. They assist us in our labours; they protect us in our rest; they encourage us in battle; they crown us in victories; they rejoice in us when we rejoice in Thee; and they compassionately attend us when we suffer or are afflicted for Thee. Great is their care of us, and great is the effect of their charity for us. They love him whom Thou lovest; they guard him whom Thou beholdest with tenderness; they forsake those from whom Thou withdrawest Thyself; and they hate them that work iniquity, because they are hateful to Thee."

So living was the faith of Christians from fourteen to eighteen centuries ago! Disputes on other points of faith might distract the Church in these early ages—Homoiousians rage against Homoiousians, Gnostics anathematize Sabellians, the Arian Constantius persecute the followers of Athanasius, the Athanasian Theodosius persecute the Arians; but to one strong stay the devotees of either creed equally clung: that of the nearness of the spirit world, and the possibility of communion between those still on this side the grave and those who had known the change called death. Origen might differ from Cyril as to whether the condition of the devil were hopeless or not; but he could agree with him that multitudes of spiritual beings, benignant and malevolent, continually surrounded his brother Christian and himself. The certainty of a continual spiritual presence—the consciousness of the ceaseless watching of spiritual eyes—were common to every flock of believers, from the Pillars of Hercules to the shores of the Persian Gulf, and from the cornfields of Sicily to the forests of the Grampians. It mattered not whether their condition in this world were one of happiness or pain. In the first century or the fourth, as well in the reign of Nero as in that of Constantine, the same angelic whispers upheld the believer in life and strengthened him in the hour of death; the same Christ stood ready to bid the faithful servant welcome to the glory of his Lord. Such men could say with Paul, that neither principalities nor powers might wrest from them the great joy of their faith. To live was Christ, and to die gain. The pleasures and pains of earth they equally despised. All their hopes were concentred on the glorious mansions wherein was prepared for them a place; all their ambition was devoted to the brightness of an eternal crown. In honour or in lowliness, they saw only the mighty mark towards which they pressed. Whether surrounded by the gloom of the catacombs or the glory of the palace, they lived less in this world than in the next. Already the heavenly things which by other men were seen faintly, or not at all, were to them more real than the turmoil of that Vanity Fair wherein for a space their lot was cast. That this might be, a hundred miracles were wrought. Lest they should forget that God is mighty to save, they were snatched from the mouths of lions, and protected amidst the violence of fire. Lest their faith should wax weak, the spirits who had gone before gave to them continual tokens of their nearness and their love. When "afflicted, destitute, tormented," they wandered in a world unworthy of them, their vision was withdrawn from the things of earth, and fixed on the glories awaiting all who should hold fast to the end. Before the judges, in the arena, at the stake, voices whispered to them of the realm where God should wipe away all tears, and in the ecstasy of the mind the body's agonies were forgotten. Triumphant over death, serene amidst the extremity of pain, their radiant countenances witnessed to their enemies of how little avail against those to whom the spiritual had been brought so close was the fiercest malice of man. Upon such the splendours of the world of light could not break with a brightness altogether unconceived. Whilst yet on earth they tasted of the joys to come. Their eyes were opened to the glories of their future home. Their ears were filled with its music. Their spirits enjoyed its peace. Thus supported, they encountered victoriously all the obstacles of their pilgrimage, and, "faithful unto death," passed to enjoy the crown of life which, throughout that pilgrimage, had been ever before their gaze.

I am not sure that in a chapter respecting spiritualism in the early ages of the Christian Church the Alexandrian school of philosophy should find a place; but the inexorable limits of space forbid my devoting to Plotinus, Iamblichus, and the rest of the Neo-Platonists a full chapter, while it is certain that such men must not be passed unnoticed. Of all Pagan systems theirs most nearly approached the religion of Christ. Doctrines, indeed, which Neo-Platonism still more intimately resembles, are those of Buddha and Brahma; and it was imperative that this should be, since from India much of the philosophy of the school was confessedly drawn.

The teaching of Nirvana was held by Ammonius and his successors in its sublimest form. To the lessons drawn from the East they added the noblest portions of the wisdom of Plato, and mingled with the whole fragments both of the truth and error of Pythagoras. The philosophy thus formed flourished long in the schools of Greece, and became, by reason of the nobleness of its ethics, the grandeur of its speculations, and the extent to which spiritual gifts were possessed by its first teachers, a formidable rival to the Christian faith. It was not until the reign of Justinian, when the men who had been its chief glories had long departed, that Neo-Platonism finally fell from its high estate.

The prophet of the school was Apollonius of Tyana. As mentioned in a former chapter of this work he acquired his theurgic wisdom almost wholly in the East. He was a native of Tyana, in Asia Minor, and nearly contemporary with Christ.

Numerous miracles of the highest class are attributed to him. He cured by spiritual means the most violent diseases, and gave frequent predictions of future events. Meeting a funeral procession, where a bridegroom in an agony of despair followed the bier of his young wife, he caused the procession to stop, and succeeded in recalling the dead girl to life. At Corinth he became the hero of that legend which has formed the subject of Keats's "Lamia." Apollonius was greatly attached to a young Greek named Menippus, who persisted, contrary to the wishes of the philosopher, in marrying a rich and beautiful woman of the city. When the guests were assembled for the wedding, Apollonius, unbidden, walked into their midst, and commanded the demon which animated the body of the bride to come forth. After a fruitless struggle, it is said, the spirit complied, and confessed itself an *empuse* or vampire, whose intention was to have destroyed Menippus in his sleep.

By temperance and purity the earthly life of this sage was prolonged to almost a hundred years. "My mode of living," he wrote, "is very different to that of other people. I take very little food, and this, like a secret remedy, maintains my senses fresh and unimpaired, as it keeps everything that is dark from them, so that I can see the present and future, as it were, in a clear mirror. The sage need not wait for the vapours of the earth and the corruptions of the air to foresee plagues and fevers; he must know them later than God, but earlier than the people. The gods see the future, men the present, sages that which is coming. This mode of life produces such an acuteness of the senses, or some other power, that the greatest and most remarkable things may be performed. I am, therefore, perfectly convinced that God reveals his intentions to holy and wise men." By "acuteness of the senses or some other power" Apollonius evidently implied clairvoyance. How wonderfully this attribute was developed in him numerous events in his history prove. At Ephesus, as related in my chapter on India, he perceived and made known the assassination of Domitian in the very hour when that event occurred at Rome.

Unlike many beings less highly gifted, this philosopher never sought to assume a dictatorship over the souls of men. He was totally undesirous to become the founder of a religion. His mission was to bring nearer to man the glories of the spiritual world, and the only preparation for that world which he felt himself empowered to inculcate was purity, physical and moral. He lived revered by all Greece and Italy, and after his death was regarded with yet higher veneration. At Tyana a temple was built in his honour—a species of memorial which he could scarcely have expected or desired. The Emperor Hadrian collected his letters, and every authentic document which existed respecting his life. These, having long been carefully preserved, were finally delivered by the Empress Julia, the mother of Severus, to Philostratus, who constructed from them his life of the great theurgist—a work which all well-informed critics have agreed in regarding as authentic.

Long after the death of Apollonius arose Ammonius Sacchas, the true founder of the Neo-Platonic school. His successors, each of them more famous than Ammonius himself, were Plotinus, Porphyry, Proclus, and Iamblichus. By these men Neo-Platonism was rapidly carried to its highest development. As I have said, this school professed extreme respect for the deeds and writings of the philosopher of Tyana. He had, however, left nothing behind him which could justify his being exalted into a Messiah, and no such attempt was made. Indeed, high as was the admiration of the Neo-Platonists for Apollonius, they appear to have felt an equally high, perhaps higher, admiration for Christ. They admit his miracles, and show no trace of antagonism to his teachings. It was chiefly the fault of the Christian Church itself that it failed to absorb the Alexandrian philosophers. Even in those early ages intolerance had sprung up and become strong. Nor need we wonder at this, since, once rooted in any religion, it is a weed that attains maturity as rapidly as Jonah's gourd. Plotinus and Iamblichus were now libelled as deadly enemies to the Church of Christ. They claimed to have purified the soul so that they could perceive spirits, and, by the help of these spirits, perform miracles. The Christians, perceiving that irrefragable proof of spiritual gifts existed among the Neo-Platonists, adopted the priestly tactics of all ages and faiths. Without showing that the spirits who communed with Ammonius and his followers were evil, they denounced the mediums of Alexandria as sorcerers. Forgetting the reply of Christ to that reproach, they hurled against them the cry of the Pharisees, "Ye cast out devils by Beelzebub, the prince of the devils!" Nay, even this did not content them. At the head of a rabble of such bigots as have in all ages defiled the pure name of Christian, a Bishop of Alexandria (Cyril, if I remember aright), succeeded in seizing and murdering a beautiful and saintly maiden named Hypatia, whose teachings were esteemed throughout the city. The outrage was attended by circumstances of the foulest horror. Cyril, and his fellow-disgracers of the human form, having stripped their victim, hewed her almost in pieces, and dragged the mangled remains in triumph through the streets. No worse crime was ever perpetrated by Calvin! Yet there can be little doubt but that the ecclesiastical monster and his satellites returned thanks to God for the great work He had permitted them to accomplish, and, with the blood of the victim yet fresh on his hands, Cyril may have found matter for a very eloquent sermon in the command, "Thou shalt not suffer a witch to live." Happily, such crimes as this were rare in the early ages of the Church. Not until that Church had ceased to struggle for existence, and was become in her turn dominant, did murder assume a clearly defined position amongst the duties of her servants.

Plotinus, the successor of Ammonius Sacchas in the leadership of Neo-Platonism, was as deeply tinged with asceticism as any Christian hermit of ancient ages. He lived sparely, held fasts whose length and frequency tasked to the utmost his bodily powers, and displayed clairvoyance in its highest form. The minds of men, he repeatedly proved, were to him as open books. As recounted by Porphyry, his teachings resembled exactly those of the Indian Brahmins and Buddhists. He held God to be not only without but within us. He is present to all, yet men flee from Him. *Spirits released from the body are not divided by space, but by the difference of mental and moral qualities. If such difference cease they are immediately near to each other.* In the words I have italicised the great Neo-Platonist expresses a truth which the revelations of all modern spiritualism go to confirm. Plotinus taught, moreover, that a perfect union with God might be attained by resembling Him in quality and disposition. Withdrawn from the sensual attractions of earth the spirit became filled with light from the Source of all light. Out of that source flow increasing shapes and spirits—the *cidolen* of Heraclitus. To community with these we arrive by despising the things of earth. Such communion is obtained in ecstasy— ecstasy being almost invariably the work of spirits. Plotinus possessed this ecstatic sensitiveness, and drew from it all his theurgic power, working thus signs and wonders, predicting future events, and healing the most hopeless diseases. Like Socrates, he knew himself to be constantly attended by a guardian spirit, who warned him from evil and inspired him to good.

Porphyry, the disciple of this Plotinus, naturally clung to the doctrines of so enlightened a master. He industriously collected materials from which the life of Plotinus might be written, and compiled an account of it with the greatest care. Himself distinguished less by medial power than by intellectual gifts, he was succeeded in the direction of Alexandrian philosophy by a man the most truly spiritual of all the Neo-Platonists. This was Iamblichus, one of the greatest seers of the ancient earth. Albeit clinging still to some of the errors of Pythagoras, he lived a blameless and exalted life. So famous was he for his learning and power of healing (that, in process of time, he came to be styled the "divine." It was this Iamblichus who, according to Eunapius,

> "From out their fountain dwellings raised
> Eros and Anteros at Gadara."

Indeed, no magian of Egypt appears to have had a closer intercourse with the world of spirits. He was, above all his brethren; familiar with the phenomena of clairvoyance. Divine music frequently resounded in his ears. He endured unhurt the blows of weapons and the touch of fire. His life was passed in a total abstraction from the things of earth. He displayed in the highest perfection the three cardinal virtues, faith, hope, and charity, and his remarks on prayer are worthy of the noblest Christian. With those remarks I shall conclude the present chapter:—

"Prayer constitutes a portion of the sacred service, and confers a universal advantage on religion, by creating an unerring connection between the priests and God. It conducts us to a perfect knowledge of heavenly things. It procures us that inexpressible devotion which places its whole strength in God above, and thus imparts to our souls a blessed repose. No act prospers in the service of God, where prayer is, omitted. Daily repeated prayer nourishes the understanding, and prepares our hearts for sacred things; opens to man the Divine, and accustoms him by degrees to the glory of the Divine light. It enables us to bear our sufferings, and the weaknesses that are human; attracts our sentiments gradually upwards, and unites them with the Divine; enkindles whatever is holy within our souls. It purges away all waywardness of mind; it generates true hope and faith. In a word, it helps those to an intimate conversation with spirits who exercise it diligently and often. How effectual it is! How prayer and sacrifice mutually invigorate each other, impart the sacred power of religion and make it perfect! It becomes us not therefore to contemn prayer, or only to employ a little of it, and throw away the rest. No; wholly must we use it; and above all things must they practise it who desire to unite themselves sincerely with God."

CHAPTER III

SPIRITUALISM IN CATHOLIC AGES

I have now to deal with that portion of the world's history in which the light kindled in the early Christian Church was constantly becoming dimmer by reason of the gross vapours that surrounded it. No record is written in blacker characters than that of the seven centuries which followed the assumption of the crown of the West by Charlemagne. The demon of Intolerance, driven forth for a space by the pure teachings of Christ, seemed to have returned, bringing with him seven other devils worse than himself. Hypocrisy was there, and murder, and crimes and vices which men shudder to name. The chair of St. Peter was filled by a succession of degraded pontiffs—each more worthless than his predecessor. The profligacy of churchmen became appalling. "Viler than a priest" was one of the common expressions of Southern Europe in the twelfth century. Those who styled themselves the keepers of the Gospel sneered in secret at the teachings which that Gospel contained. Nay, they appeared, with the perverseness of profligacy, to pride themselves upon shaping their conduct in diametrical opposition to the rules laid down by Christ and the Twelve. Because the Messiah was meek and lowly, the prelates of his Church displayed themselves through a succession of ages the proudest of the proud. Because He had blessed those who hungered after righteousness, they plunged defyingly into the foulest vice. Because He had praised the merciful, these corrupted servants made their hearts hard as the nether millstone. Because Paul had said that a bishop should be blameless, just, and temperate, able with sound doctrine to exhort and convince, they made a mock of the episcopal dignity by bestowing it on children just able to speak, and men fallen beneath the brutes. Nor was this the worst. For dogmas in which they put no faith, for ethics that they did not reduce to practice, the rulers of the Church were yet ready to inflict death in its most horrible form. And in the infliction of such death they contrived to unite with the most hideous cruelty the blackest hypocrisy. Because the Christian kingdom was not of this world, they handed over to secular executioners the victim whom they had sentenced, with a jocular request that all possible tenderness might be shown. The mode of slaying was already determined. Since the Gospel forbade the shedding of blood, its ministers thought it well to substitute for a short and easy death the unendurable agony of the stake.

To such men it was impossible that beneficent spirits should manifest themselves. Accordingly, in numerous instances, the miracles of the Catholic Church were accomplished through the undeveloped beings whom the evil natures of its priests attracted, or, if such resources failed, were simulated by means of accomplished fraud. Few readers of history need to be reminded of the exposures made in our own country at the time of the Reformation. The winking Madonnas, the roods of grace, the talking heads, and bending images, were dragged into the light of day and their concealed machinery exposed to the disgust and derision of men. And the inner secrets of monasteries and convents were exposed with equal ruthlessness and found equally foul. To take one instance, and that extremely mild, in that beautiful Abbey of Furness, from which Thomas Cromwell ejected the monks by the summary process of demolishing the roof, strange things were brought to light. The magnificent pile lies low in a charming valley, nestling amidst ancient trees, and so situated as to be well shielded and hidden by rising ground. Like the architects of Newstead, its holy founders

> "Preferred a hill behind
> To shelter their devotion from the wind."

This earthly paradise, about the meridian of Henry VIII.'s. reign, was inhabited by numerous men outwardly saintly. Presumably each was as Adam during his first days in Eden, but, unlike him, cut off from all expectation of an Eve. Yet what did Cromwell and his subordinate iconoclasts discover? They learned that the society they came to disestablish had long been one of the wealthiest in England. Tired of the literal interpretation put by dull predecessors on the vows of fasting and silence, the abbots and brethren had hit on means whereby to render those vows agreeable. Fasting they found compatible with an immense expenditure on wine and provisions, and their solitude was enlivened by the introduction of the fair sex into the abbey. Nay; to such lengths had they gone that, unsatisfied with paramours, they had ventured the introduction of their necks into the forbidden noose of matrimony. Rogerus Pele, the then abbot, had two wives, although for a priest to have even one was, according to Church canons, a deadly sin. A holy subordinate, fired with the ambition of surpassing his superior, had encumbered himself with fair helpmeets to the number of no less than five. Such, in the sixteenth century, were some of the milder abuses of the Church.

I have alluded to the prevalence of mock miracle in the days when Catholic power was at its height. It was disgust at this rank growth of tares which caused the Reformers of the sixteenth century to reject the whole spiritual harvest as worthless. Yet reason might have discovered to them that with so much imposture there was assuredly mingled a certain proportion of truth. In nations destitute of a coinage the counterfeiting of money is impossible. Where a coinage exists base money is certain to be also in circulation. The more esteemed the products of the true mint, the more numerous will the spurious imitations become. It is thus with the occurrences that come under the definition of miracle. Were real miracles impossible the world would never have been vexed with false. Had not miracle been found a mighty engine for upholding a faith and extending its limits, the Romish Church would scarcely have played the cheat to such an extent. Why the counterfeit signs and wonders so greatly out-numbered the true may easily be shown. An undetected imposture was equally advantageous to the Church with a work really wrought by spiritual hands, and the imposture was the more readily obtained of the two. Rome, therefore, received under her protection a number of coiners of spiritual phenomena, and ordered that their production should pass current as genuine miracle. Such a policy, of course, proved suicidal. It was one of the broad and easy ways that in the end lead to destruction. Were a government to collect secretly the most skilful counterfeiters among its subjects, and keeping them, unknown to the rest of the community, employed in the constant manufacture of base coin, send forth large quantities of spurious money mixed with a certain proportion of genuine, how great would be the amazement of all civilised men when the deed was brought to light! The idea seems too wild for the wildest fiction. Yet such was, in spiritual matters, exactly the course which the Papacy of old adopted, and even since the Reformation has, in a modified degree, continued to follow. As was natural, a tremendous retribution followed when things had reached their worst. Laymen who perceived the chicanery that was sought to be practised on them, and priests disgusted with the chicanery they were required to practise, joined in the mighty outbreak of the sixteenth century. From all countries ripe for Protestantism the false prophets of Rome were expelled with contumely and disgust. The tools of their nefarious trade were publicly exposed and destroyed. And, as in the vehemence of reaction against such a government as I have imagined, its injured subjects might, when they had brought to condign punishment the corrupters of their coinage, resolve that, to prevent the recurrence of an event so disastrous, even the issue of genuine money should be made illegal, so Protestantism has ordered that wherever its rule extends miracle shall cease. The natural result has followed. Those whose faith demands imperatively the support of the spiritual seek that Church where the spiritual is to be found. They may know that Rome is still often guilty of fraud, but they prefer running the risk of false money to wanting money altogether. The Church which manufactures miracle is in their eyes far preferable to the Church in which no pretensions to miracle are made. Thus, while Protestantism languishes everywhere, new converts are daily flocking to that hierarchy which claims to hold unceasing intercourse with another world,—which, when better-attested phenomena fail, discovers ignorant peasant boys to whom the Virgin has revealed herself, and enthusiastic country maidens marked with the five wounds of Christ. Supported by these and nobler aids, the Church of Rome may, in the words of a great critic, "exist in undiminished vigour, when some traveller from New Zealand shall, in the midst of a vast solitude, take his stand on a broken arch of London Bridge to sketch the ruins of St. Paul's." This is not a consummation devoutly to be wished, but it is decidedly one to be feared. If Protestantism be not in its turn reformed, Protestantism is doomed. A Church cannot long make head against such scepticism as that of the present day, which, when assailed on all sides for proofs of its doctrines, answers only that those doctrines prove themselves. We see in countries like Germany and England a constantly growing inclination to separate the ethics of Christianity from its dogmas. That which men want to-day is a foundation for their faith.

Such a foundation many have had in even the darkest ages of the Roman Church. Dominic, Torquemada, and Borgia might be "damned to everlasting fame"—pilloried in the pages of history for the searing of future generations from the Catholic faith,—but coeval with these workers of iniquity, whose evil deeds have lived for centuries after them, were doers of the noblest good. Among the chief of these was St. Bernard. His life is one continual record of the marvellous. Wherever he went he approved the literal exactness of Christ's words, "He that believeth in me, the works that I do shall he do also." At his prayer the blind saw and the lame walked. A biography of this great man has been compiled by a Mr. Morison. His prejudices against the spiritual seem inveterate, but he is nevertheless staggered by the facts which, as a faithful biographer, he is bound to record.

He relates how visions of the future were granted to Bernard, and how he thus predicted with the most marvellous accuracy that which should come to pass. He describes how the saint's journey through the Rhine country was glorified by a constant exhibition of miraculous powers. In one day at Constance his prayers, and the imposition of his hands, restored sight to eleven persons totally blind, and acquired for eighteen cripples the use of their limbs. At Cologne he healed twelve lame citizens, besides causing three who were dumb to speak, and ten deaf persons to hear. Nor were these things done secretly, and in a fashion that left room for suspicion to enter. It was before mighty multitudes, and under the scrutiny of innumerable eyes, that Bernard worked. The testimony of ten of these eye-witnesses remains to what they saw. Herman, Bishop of Constance, and nine others, kept a diary of the miraculous cures accomplished before them. This account, as Mr. Morison remarks, would seem to have been drawn up with the express purpose of avoiding cavil, whilst attracting attention. The names and the condition of these witnesses are given, and they solemnly make oath that they witnessed with their own eyes the miracles recorded. They describe how the halt, the blind, the deaf, and the dumb were brought from all parts to be touched by Bernard. When the patient was presented to him he simply prayed, made the sign of the cross upon the part affected, and the cure was perfect. The following extract contains the wonders wrought in a single day:—

"In the Church of St. John, at Cambray, after the mass, a boy deaf and dumb from his mother's womb received his hearing and spoke, and the people wondered. He had sat down beside me deaf and dumb, and having been presented to Bernard, in the self-same hour he both spoke and heard. The joyful excitement was scarcely over before a lame old man was raised up and walked. But now a miracle occurred which, beyond all others, filled us with astonishment. A boy blind from his birth, whose eyes were covered with a white substance—if, indeed, those could be called eyes in which there was neither colour nor use, nor even so much as the usual cavity of an eye—this boy received his sight from the imposition of Bernard's hand. We ascertained the fact by numerous proofs, hardly believing our senses that in such eyes as his any sight could reside. In the same place a woman who had a withered hand was healed. In the town of Rosnay they brought to him in a waggon a man ill and feeble, for whom nothing seemed to remain but the grave. Before a number of the citizens and soldiery Bernard placed his hands upon him, and immediately he walked without difficulty, and, to the astonishment of all, followed on foot the vehicle in which he had just before been carried."

Next year, in France, the same marvels were wrought wherever Bernard passed. I venture to quote the narrative by an eyewitness of one among the most striking of these miracles:—

"At Toulouse, in the church of St. Saturninus, was a certain regular-canon named John. John had kept his bed for seven months, and was so reduced that his death was expected daily. His legs were so shrunken that they were scarcely larger than a child's arms. He was quite unable to rise to satisfy the wants of nature. At last his brother canons refused to tolerate his presence any longer among them, and thrust him out into the neighbouring village. When the poor creature heard of Bernard's proximity he implored to be taken to him. Six men, therefore, carrying him as he lay in bed, brought him into a room close to that in which we were lodged . . . . Bernard mentally prayed to God, 'Behold, O Lord, they seek for a sign, and our words avail nothing unless they be confirmed with signs following.' He then blessed him and left the chamber, and so did we all. In that very hour the sick man arose from his couch, and running after Bernard, kissed his feet with a devotion which cannot be imagined by any one who did not see it. One of the canons meeting him nearly fainted with fright, thinking he had seen a spectre. John and his brethren then retired to the church, and in a Te Deum gave praise to God."

I might describe many other marvellous cures which Bernard performed, but the above notable and strongly attested instances are sufficient. They will carry conviction of his spiritual gifts to any unprejudiced mind. Of later events of the kind the cure of Mademoiselle Perrier, niece to the celebrated Pascal, is a marvellous and invulnerably well-attested case. The miracles also, wrought in 1731, and subsequent years, at the tomb of the Abbé Paris, are equally well-attested, and still more marvellous. The first of these wonders occurred in 1656. Mademoiselle Perrier was, at the time, between ten and eleven years old. Since the age of three years and a half, her left eye had been consumed by a lachrymal fistula, the malignant humour of which had decayed the bone of the nose and that of the palate. So offensive was the disease, that the nuns of Port Royal, in which famous institution she had become a boarder, were forced to keep her strictly apart from the rest of their young charges. As a forlorn hope it was determined to try the actual cautery, and for this purpose the girl's father came, accompanied by a surgeon, to Port Royal. But, immediately before the time fixed for the operation, the nuns were inspired to touch the eye of the sufferer with a thorn, held in high veneration as a professed relic from the crown of Christ. To the awe and amazement of all present the decayed bones became instantly firm and sound, the effusion of humour ceased, and all trace of disease vanished in an instant. The father beheld the miracle, and wept for joy. The surgeon who had come to operate upon this apparently hopeless case, scarcely dared trust his sight. Eleven other surgeons and physicians of eminence afterwards examined Mademoiselle Perrier, and confessed, without exception, the miraculous nature of her cure. The court, though it bore to Port Royal a deadly hate, and had ordered the destruction of that seminary of Jansenism, was compelled also to admit the authenticity of the marvel. A mass in music was instituted by the parents of the young girl, to be celebrated for ever in the Cathedral of Clermont, on March 24th of each year, the anniversary of their daughter's instantaneous recovery. A picture of the event was placed in the church of Port Royal. Racine drew up a narrative of the case, which Pascal, Arnauld, and Felix attested. The Archbishop of Paris, and the doctors of the Sorbonne, investigated with the severest scrutiny of malice the whole of the circumstances, and were forced, in their sentence of October 22nd, 1656, to admit that "this cure was supernatural, and a miracle of the omnipotence of God." Benedict XIII. forever consecrated the case in Catholic eyes by quoting it in his printed Homilies as one of many proofs that miracles had not ceased. Finally, during the twenty-five years which Mademoiselle Perrier lived after being thus suddenly healed, the malady showed no signs of return.

A volume would be required to treat in detail of the miracles wrought at the grave of the Abbé Paris. Douglas, Bishop of Salisbury, employed great part of a dull work in simply seeking to weaken the credit attached to them. Destitute of facts to support his theory—that the cures were in some instances performed by ordinary means, in others merely pretended to be performed—he strove, by suppressing various authentic narratives, and mis-stating the remainder, to show how dishonest a sceptic a Christian divine may be. He employed against these particular miracles the very arguments which David Hume had previously employed against all miracles: strange weapons for a Churchman to use! The two chief axioms of his work are: 1. That we must suspect as false asserted miracles which are not published at the time when, and in the place where, they are said to have occurred. 2. That we must suspect them to be false if in the time when, and at the place where, they are said to have occurred, they might be supposed to pass without examination. Were the authority of these rules conceded they have yet absolutely no bearing on the cases the Bishop designs to attack. The miracles at the tomb of the Abbé Paris took place chiefly in 1731, and the three or four years next in sequence. They were published at the time when and in the place where they happened. The Abbé had been a Jansenist. Far therefore from allowing them to pass without examination, the mis-named Order of Jesus, with whose tyranny France was still cursed, strove by every means, allowable or iniquitous, to cover these alleged miracles with disgrace, and their upholders with confusion. Yet the solemn truth of the facts resisted the utmost efforts of calumny. If Douglas succeeded in making them doubted in England, it was by shameless perversion and suppression of testimony. The most unscrupulous of Jesuit casuists might have been proud to own the Bishop's work: the least candid of Protestant divines should have blushed to write it. It is sufficient, in the judgment of all who know the facts, to pillory the author on "infamy's high stage" forever.

Carrè de Montgeron was a dissipated courtier of the "siècle de Louis Quinze." His father had been Master of Requests under Louis XIV.; his mother was a daughter of Field-Marshal Diery. Wealthy and idle, M. de Montgeron plunged headlong into all the sensuality of the court. His conscience was the sole thing which troubled him, and this he stifled by educating himself into a determined Deist. He became a *conseiller au Parlement* whilst the final life and death struggle of the long war between the Jesuits and the Jansenists was raging. The Jansenists had right with them, but might was on the side of the Order of Jesus. Port Royal fell, and the supporters of the bad cause rejoiced. That cause had, however, received deadly wounds in the conflict, and after languishing long, succumbed to the first attack of a new foe. It does not appear that M. de Montgeron took more than a languid interest in the struggle and its issue; but he drew from it the inference that the doctrines which the Jesuits and their supporter, Pope Clement XI., condemned as heretical, were among the chief foundations of the Christian religion. Thus he became convinced that the professedly orthodox thought secretly as he did himself, and that religion was only a cloak with which hypocrites covered vice. He went on confirmed in his own immorality and infidelity until the year 1731. In that year he heard, like all Parisians, of the miracles performing at the tomb of the Abbé Paris, in the cemetery of St. Medard. At first he ridiculed them, then the mass of evidence advanced in favour of their reality troubled him with a fear lest, after all, the teachings of the Christian faith were true. He determined to visit the scene of these alleged wonders, and by calling to his aid the chief medical men of Paris, unmask completely the imposture, if an imposture were being practised. He first went to the churchyard alone. The extraordinary scenes which greeted him, the multitude of afflicted, and the fervour of their prayers, touched his heart for the first time in many years with a sentiment of religious awe. Perplexed, he fell on his knees by the edge of the tomb, and petitioned that, if there were indeed an immortality for man, light from that future world might shine in upon the darkness of his mind. Immediately, he tells us, reasons for crediting the teachings of Christ poured upon him in vivid succession with a force he had never felt before. He rose a changed man. For four hours had he remained kneeling beside the tomb, heedless of the pressure of the crowds around. Day after day, he now returned to the churchyard, and investigated the miracles there wrought. By this time all Paris was stirred with these events. The Jesuits, maddened that such works should be wrought at the tomb of a Jansenist, had recourse to the civil power. All avenues of access to the tomb were ordered to be closed. It was then, says Voltaire, that some wit inscribed on the churchyard wall:—

> "De par le Roi,—défense à Dieu
> De faire miracles en ce lieu."

The remark of the great infidel that God obeyed is contradicted by the fact that miracles still continued to be performed for a space of at least twenty years.

Meanwhile M. de Montgeron had selected from above a hundred well-authenticated cases nine in which the injuries or diseases had been of so terrible a character that the physicians had adjudged a cure hopeless, and in which the cure by means of prayer at the tomb had been widely published, and put past doubt by medical and other evidences. He sought with indefatigable industry all the attestations available on the subject. He procured the testimony of the miraculously healed sufferers themselves, of their friends, of their enemies, of celebrated physicians and surgeons, of magistrates, notaries, courtiers and priests. The whole he published in a quarto volume, dedicated to the King. He personally presented a copy of the work. It was received with apparent favour, but the same night M. de Montgeron was rewarded for his fearless advocacy of the cause of truth with a lodging in the Bastile.

I shall now attempt to give in a brief compass the history of seven of these nine cases. The first on our author's list is that of Dom Alphonse de Palacios, a young nobleman of Spain, son of Dom Joseph de Palacios, councillor of state to the Spanish King. He was in Paris to seek relief for his right eye. His left had been destroyed six years before by a fluxion succeeded by inflammation. The right had been since injured by a blow, and another cause had now made its state apparently hopeless. This was the withering up of the optic nerve of the lost eye. The nerve of the remaining eye, being in connection with it, began to wither also. Sight by rapid degrees disappeared. The famous oculist, Gendron, examined the right eye, and pronounced recovery not to be hoped for; the sufferer must submit to total blindness for the rest of his days. At this stage, according to the narrative penned by Dom Alphonse himself, the eye more resembled a crushed mulberry than an eye; a ray of light falling on it caused intolerable pain; the unhappy youth was driven to sit in darkened rooms with his eye carefully bandaged. For seven days before the miracle he was without sight.

He heard of the marvellous cures wrought in the cemetery of Saint Medard, and besought to be taken there. The fear of bringing down on his family the wrath of the Pope and the Inquisition caused his attendants and his tutor, the celebrated Rollin, to hesitate. At length his agony and unceasing prayers wrung forth a consent. He was carried to the Abbé's tomb. The journey was not made in vain. On the instant the sight of the right eye returned, and he could cast away his bandage and in full daylight give thanks to God. He went two days after to the great oculist whose fiat had doomed him to a life of darkness. On seeing his late patient Gendron desired in amazement to know what had happened. The story was told, and the surgeon declared that no man on earth could have restored Dom Palacios to sight, and that a startling miracle had been accomplished. A full statement of the facts was drawn up, and deposited with the notary public. At once the clergy began to persecute all concerned. Dom Palacios returned to Spain, and the terrors of the Inquisition were let loose on him. It was at one time asserted by the Archbishop of Paris that he had signed a statement denying the miracle. Inquiry being made, the highest Church dignitary in France appeared to have deliberately lied. To the last, in spite of menaces, imprisonment, and the ruin of his worldly prospects, the grateful young nobleman continued to avow that he had been cured by the hand of God, and that his recovery of sight was in no way owing to the skill of man. Numerous witnesses supported him. Gendron, the oculist, Rollin, Rector of the University of Paris, Sir Edward Aston, the celebrated surgeons Demanteville and Souchay, Linguet, a physician who had attended the young Spaniard, and his relation M. Linguet of the College of Navarre, publicly attested the veracity of Dom Alphonse's statements, and made depositions as to their knowledge of the case before and after the cure. Priestly power, though used with more than priestly intolerance, was as a reed against the truth.

The sixth of M. de Montgeron's cases is also one of blindness. Pierre Gaultier was a saddler's apprentice in a village of Languedoc. The small-pox had left scars on the pupil of his left eye which weakened its power of vision. Whilst busied one day with a knot in some harness, it yielded unexpectedly, and an awl which he held was plunged into the other eye. It pierced even to the retina, and left him with no vision but that of the defective eye which disease had injured. The surgeons could do nothing. By the advice of his confessor Gaultier journeyed to Paris, and visited the famous tomb. He returned with the sight of that eye which the awl had blinded perfectly restored. The two small-pox scars of the left eye still remained.

At once the priesthood was in arms. Famous oculists were consulted; who examined the eyes and declared that had the scars of the other been removed, the miracle would have been past doubt. These scars could not be obliterated by any mortal skill. Again the confessor advised Gaultier to go to Paris, and again he followed the advice. This second journey to the tomb resulted in perfect restoration; the scars totally disappeared. The sight of both eyes was fully regained.

A new method of attack was now adopted by the Jesuits. At the instance of his father, a baker to the army of Italy, the young man had gone to join him. It was reported that the disappearance of the scars was merely pretended, and that the Bishop of Montpellier, a warm defender of the miracle, had caused Gaultier to be hidden from observation lest the truth might become known. The fact was that, on hearing of the cure, the Bishop had made careful investigation, and only when perfectly satisfied of its reality had he attested it in a letter to the Archbishop of Sens. His superior now reproached him with lending himself to an imposture. The accused, a man whose noble character was esteemed throughout the South of France, caused a search to be instituted, and soon had the satisfaction of discovering Gaultier amongst the forty thousand soldiers at the time in Italy. He was brought back, and his sight was demonstrated to be perfect.

The Order of Jesus, though beaten at all points, was not to be put down. The arrest of Gaultier was procured for the crime of being healed by miracle. Once in prison, he was threatened with a dungeon for life. In terror, he consented to sign a statement that he still saw but very imperfectly. The statement was published. All his relations denied its truth. His father proved to the intendant the reality of the miracle, and obtained his son's release. The Jesuits now turned their attention to the confessor who had advised the journey to Paris. He and another priest who affirmed the miracle, were dismissed from their benefices. The plea was, that they had lent themselves to imposture. In grief, their congregations, by whom they were greatly beloved, appealed to the Bishop of Agde. He took up the case, and demonstrating the innocence of the deprived clergymen, procured their restoration. They returned amidst the exultations of their flocks. The Jesuits were now humbled effectually. Gaultier, freed from his dread of their power, publicly recanted the statement fear had wrung from him, and described by what menaces and cruelties the pretended confession had been obtained.

In the fifth of these cases the Jesuits once more demonstrated the truth of the assertion contained in M. de Montgeron's dedicatory preface, that they had used the most unscrupulous means to suppress the proofs of the miracles. The case was that of a woolcarder named Philippe Sergent. Having become paralyzed in all his limbs, he was admitted to the Hotel Dieu as incurable. His friends, hearing of the miracles, demanded his discharge from the hospital, and took him in a cart to the Abbé's grave. Instantly recovering the use of his limbs, he sprang on the tombstone unassisted, and sang a To Deum. After showing himself at the hospital he took a cellar, and recommenced his business. A stranger called on him, and offered a hundred pistoles if he would sign a declaration that he had not been cured. Sergent refused indignantly, and a persecution at once commenced. He was driven from Paris, and settled at Rheims. Still enemies were on his track. After fleeing successively to Dinant, Namur, Mons, and Liege, he returned in despair to Paris. There, finding that the priesthood were circulating lying statements respecting his case, he boldly proceeded to make a public deposition as to the miraculous circumstances of the cure. Besides this testimony the evidence of the doctors who attended him is given by Montgeron.

I have gone at such length into these three instances that I can do little more than allude to the remaining miracles. Two of the sufferers, Mesdemoiselles Thibault and Courronneau, laboured under fearful complications of paralysis and dropsy. Despite that famous physicians had pronounced their disorders incurable, they were wholly healed by visits to the tomb. The case of the eighth patient, Marie Cartin, resembled that of the Mademoiselle Perrier before alluded to; she also was pronounced incurable. Not only, however, was the disease which consumed her face eradicated, but one half of her body, after being paralysed for twelve years, recovered fully its vigour. I shall mention one more miracle; in some respects the most extraordinary of the nine.

Mademoiselle Coirin had been twelve years affected with a cancer in the left breast. The affected part was destroyed, and came away in a mass; and the disease had tainted the blood of the whole system. The effluvium was horrible. When medical science had abandoned the case as hopeless, a single visit to the tomb obtained an entire cure. Most wonderful of all, the breast and nipple were perfectly restored, and left free from even the slightest scar. The royal physician, with others of the profession, inquired into the miracle. Their testimony was decisive. They admitted that they had known the case, and had pronounced it incurable by any merely earthly skill. It was now cured, and the cure was perfect. No human hand had accomplished the marvel—it was to be ascribed to the hand of God. "The restoration of a nipple absolutely destroyed, and separated from the breast," said M. Goulard, the King's physician," is an actual *creation*, for a nipple is not merely a continuity of the vessels of the breast, but a particular body, which is of a distinct and peculiar organization."

I may here take my leave of the Abbé Paris. If the wonders wrought at his tomb are to be rejected, there is an end of all the miraculous healing in history. No such evidence supports the miracles of Scripture. In favour of the reality of these cures, we have the attestations of the sufferers themselves, the depositions unwillingly wrung from some doctors and frankly granted by others, the reluctant testimony of the clergy and the court. Against all these are set only the unscrupulous fabrications of Jesuit malice—the calumnies of an order which yet more than that of Dominic has disgraced the Catholic Church. It is on such testimony as the last that the dishonest Bishop of Salisbury would persuade us the assertors of these miracles were yet more dishonest than himself. *Credat Judæus!*

The "Lives of the Saints" are one and all ridiculed by Protestant minds. The Pharisee of England or Prussia looks with pitying contempt on the devotee who believes that St. Martin restored the dead to life, and that St. Gregory turned a lake into dry land by his prayers. It is not my business to take up the cudgels on behalf of a Church so well able to defend itself as that of Rome. I shall content myself with quoting from the work of Mr. Howitt a few of the more remarkable miracles attributed to her saints.

St. Francis Xavier raised various people from the dead. St. Winifreda healed numbers of diseases at her miraculous well. St. Gregory stayed a flood by striking his staff into the ground, which staff thereon took root and became a tree. St. Martin, like the poet Horace, was miraculously protected from the falling of a tree. Such protection, as described in the first volume of my "Incidents," I have myself been favoured with. St. Charles Borromeo was fired at whilst performing mass, but the bullet merely struck upon his rochet, and fell harmless to the ground. Dominic, the evil enthusiast who founded the Inquisition, is asserted to have by prayer restored a nobleman to life. One would think that if the prayers of such a nature were heard, it could only be by spirits equally dark. St. Hyacinth crossed the Vistula, when because of a flood no boat dared venture, by walking on the surface of the waves. St. Francis of Assissium bore in his hands, feet, and side the five wounds of Christ.

The last phenomenon has occurred in all ages of the Church, and never more strikingly than at the present day. I need only refer to Louise Lateau, the Belgian stigmatist, to mention a case which has baffled medical science. Equally celebrated in their own times were such stigmatists as Saints Catherine, Hildegarde, Brigitta of Sweden, and Pasithea. More recent cases are those of Catherine Emmerich, Maria von Morl, and Dominica Lazari. Catherine bore the mark of the crown of thorns, and was besides clairvoyant. Her attendant physician published a description of the case in the year 1815. Maria had the stigmata. Dominica also bore them, and more prominently. Her marks, says Ennemoser, bled on the Friday of every week.

It is natural that I should be deeply interested in a particular manifestation, of which abundant instances are given in the lives of Catholic saints. I refer to the being raised from the ground by spirit-power, and held, without any physical support, floating in the air. Such a phenomenon is denied and derided in our own days by persons who have had no opportunity for observation of the facts, but whose illimitable conceit prompts them to imagine that all things in heaven and earth are known to their philosophy. The most convincing evidence is dismissed as worthless. The most unimpeachable witnesses are reviled as not to be trusted. A few sneers, and the usual parrot jargon regarding "the violation of known physical laws," end the matter, and the reviewer retires amidst the plaudits of his brethren. Yet such violations of physical laws are reported as having occurred since the age of Enoch, and may have occurred for unknown thousands of years before. As I have said, they were frequent amongst those on whom the canonical honours of Rome were conferred. St. Theresa was many times the subject of such experiences. She relates that frequently during her, devotions an unseen power raised her, and held her suspended above the ground. A bishop, a Dominican, and the sisterhood of her convent attest as witnesses her rising in the air. In the year 1036, Richard, Abbot of St. Vanne do Verdun "appeared elevated from the ground as he was saying mass in presence of Duke Galizon and his sons, and a great number of his lords and soldiers. Savonarola, of whom I shall have occasion to speak in the following chapter, was beheld, a short time before his martyrdom, to rise slowly from the ground, and "remain suspended at a considerable height from the floor of his dungeon, absorbed in devotion." Mr. Madden in his life of this great man, most truly observes, "To any one conversant with the lives of the saints it will be well known that similar phenomena are recorded in numerous instances, and that the evidence on which some of them rest is as reliable as any human testimony can be." In the case of Savonarola, the evidence, as Elihu Rich points out, is peculiarly authentic. Those who recorded the phenomenon were the very men who condemned him to the flames. Was it probable that they would seek by a circumstantial lie to glorify the object of their hate?

Calmet tells us that he "knew a good monk who rose sometimes from the ground, and remained suspended without wishing or seeking it, on seeing some devotional image, or hearing some devout prayer, such as 'Gloria in excelsis Deo.'" Also he claims to have been acquainted with a nun "to whom it has happened in spite of herself to be thus raised up in the air to a certain distance from the earth;—it was neither from choice nor from any wish to distinguish herself, for truly she was confounded at it." The same thing happened in the cases of St. Philip Neri, St. Catherine Colembina, and St. Ignatius Loyola, which last was "raised up from the ground to the height of two feet, while his body shone like light." It may be remarked that this luminosity of the human form—a not uncommon manifestation of modern spiritualism—has also been noticed from extremely ancient times. Iamblichus rose frequently to the height of ten feet from the earth, and his body and dress on such occasions assumed the colour of gold. But the most striking narratives of the kind are to be found in Scripture. I need cite but few other instances of ecclesiastical levitations. St. Dunstan, a little before his death, was observed in the presence of several persons to rise from the ground, and, whilst all who witnessed the phenomenon were yet astonished at it, he spoke, and predicted his approaching end. St. Albert of Sicily, during prayer, was elevated to a height of three cubits. St. Cajetanus, St. Bernard Ptolomei, and St. Philip Benitas were also seen frequently thus to rise from the earth. To end with two cases not clerical and somewhat nearer to our own time, the celebrated Anna Maria Fleischer was beheld during the period of the Thirty Years War in Germany to be frequently lifted by invisible means "to the height of nine ells and a half, so that it appeared as if she would have flown through the windows." In days still more modern similar phenomena were reported of the Seeress of Prevorst.

It cannot be said that the whole, or even the half of the miracles claimed by the Catholic Church, are worthy the faith of reasoning men. He who pats credence in all she asserts to have occurred is equally foolish with the man who believes that all calling themselves mediums in our own times have spiritual gifts. But he who disbelieves that any "signs and wonders" can ever have come out of Rome is the very one who will denounce the spiritualism of the present day as nothing more than a gigantic imposture, and will, sometimes openly, but more often in secret, hold all miracle impossible, and look upon every record of spiritual phenomena, whether contained in Scripture or elsewhere, as untrue. To such natures historical evidence is nothing, and less than nothing. Sceptics so pronounced may indeed be at times converted to a belief in the truth by wonders occurring in their own presence; but they are far more difficult than Thomas to convince. The absurd, inference drawn in the present day is, that such men should be shunned by every good spiritualist, and zealously excluded from all séances; because they are ever on the watch for trickery in the medium, and when successful in discovering such trickery immediately set up a shout of triumph, and call the attention of the general public to the imposture they have unmasked. Would not the better course for spiritualists be to set their faces as one man against fraudulent mediums, and to send after the "reveries of Jacob Behmen" and the gospel according to Joe Smith those wretched "explanations" of the simulation of spiritual phenomena which just now it is sought to make pass current as articles of faith? But for the discussion of such matters the concluding portion of this work will be more in place.

I shall pass now to the darkest phase of Catholic spiritualism—dark in the sense of its having left the deepest stain on the Roman Church. In ending this chapter of less tragical occurrences a most remarkable prophecy, delivered and fulfilled a little above a century ago, deserves to be given. It is recorded, says Mr. Howitt, by the Abbé Proyaid, in his "Louis XVI. détrôné avant d'être Roi," and was confirmed by an inquiry which Cardinal Maury caused to be set on foot in 1804.

Bernardino Renzi, a simple peasant girl of Valentano, predicted with much confidence, in the year 1774, the approaching death of Ganganelli, who then filled the chair of St. Peter. On hearing of the prophecy his Holiness caused its utterer to be arrested and cast into prison. With her was seized the curé of Valentano—the confessor of the girl. Neither manifested the slightest surprise or alarm when the arrest took place. Bernardino quietly remarked "Braschi will liberate me;" and the cure informed the officer who made him prisoner that this seizure had been three times predicted by the young prophetess. At the same time he delivered up some papers in which were set down not only the prophecy of the Pope's death and the date when it should occur, but the day of his own arrest, the duration of his imprisonment, and the date when he should be released. The day fixed as Ganganelli's last on earth was September 22nd, 1774; but this approached, and still the Pope felt no sickness. At ten o'clock on the morning of the 22nd of September, however, Bernardino accosted the superior of the convent of Montefiascone, in which she had been placed as a prisoner, with the words, "You may order your community to offer up prayers for the Holy Father. He is dead." By the first courier came a confirmation of these startling tidings. The Pope had died suddenly at eight in the morning, that is to say, some two hours before the girl's intimation of her prophecy having been fulfilled was delivered. And the accomplishment of her second prediction was, if possible, still worthier of notice. Cardinal Braschi, although none, when the conclave met, had dreamed of making him pontiff, was found when it parted to have been elected to the vacant seat. Yet his success seemed to hold out no hope of Bernardine's liberation. Angered by the pasquinades circulated on his owing the tiara to the influence of a village girl, Braschi determined to render her second prophecy a lying one, and prove that she would not be freed through him. He appointed as her judges men on whom he thought he could rely, and instructed them to condemn her. The case was tried, and still Bernardine triumphed. So manifest had been the fulfilment of her prediction regarding Ganganelli that even partisanship could do nothing. The girl and the confessor were both acquitted, as innocent of any evil design. Thus the second prophecy was as accurately accomplished as the first, and Braschi and his tools were driven to console themselves by pronouncing that Bernardine had been under the influence of a fiend.

To that convenient accusation of working miracles by the help of demons, we owe the blackest crimes which disgrace the annals of the Church of Rome. It was a weapon misused alike by the just and the unjust; mighty for evil, but impotent for good. Was it desired to ruin a man on whom the stigma of heresy could not be fastened? Then the charge of sorcery speedily sent him to the stake. Did a sudden outbreak of spiritual manifestations excite the inhabitants of any particular region? As the occurrences were useful or injurious to the temporal power of the Church, so did that Church act. If the phenomena could be made subservient to her purposes, she canonised the mediums as saints: if they appeared to militate against those purposes, she burnt the mediums as wizards. Nay, so entirely was her recognition of the spiritual governed by worldly policy, that the same man might be at one time extolled as inspired by the angels of God, and a little later denounced as in league with the powers of darkness. The Papacy, as I have shown, had recognised that miracle is a mighty weapon for the advancement of a faith. When she found a servant of the spirits who was also content to be her slave, she, to borrow a metaphor from the language of Scripture, clothed him with a robe of pride, and set him in a high place, proclaiming that thus should it be done to the man whom the Church delighted to honour. So that he faithfully devoted his medial powers to the advancement of the Catholic religion, it mattered not what his character in other respects might be. As arch-fiend of cruelty such as Dominic, and a nature gentle as St. Bernard's, a pure creature like St. Catherine, and a brutal wretch like Francis, were equally prized. Their names were glorified during life, and all but worshipped after death. The magnificent sepulchres that enshrined their bones witnessed daily the prayers of the faithful. But was the man who formed the link between this and the future world a high-minded and free-spirited being, disposed to become neither the serf of spirits nor of men; taking from the Catholic religion only what was good, and making manful war on the innumerable abuses which defaced it,—such a one as Savonarola in short? Then the Vatican let loose on him its terrors. He might perhaps be barely tolerated, while his line of conduct did not diverge too widely from the line of policy marked out by the Church; but on the instant that he raised his voice against her wrong-doing there were made ready for him the faggots and the stake. Another victim was added to the long list in which are enrolled such names as Savonarola and Jeanne D'Arc; and Rome took hypocritical credit to herself for having punished one more servant of the devil. Doubtless, among the millions of unhappy beings destroyed as wizards and witches, there were numbers really under the influence of evil spirits. Nothing else can explain the frantic outbreaks which so often dismayed Europe during the Middle Ages. Our fathers, having greater faith than ourselves as regards spiritual things, were both better qualified to judge of the phenomena and more ready to admit their reality. Their eyes were not carefully closed against light from another world, but anxiously strained to perceive its faintest gleams. They often, however, committed the deadly error of mistaking the origin of that light, and such mistakes were made excuses for the most frantic cruelty and intolerance. The great criminal was the Catholic Church, though as I shall have occasion to point out in a future chapter Protestant Churches also deeply burdened themselves with the crime of murder. But it is against Rome chiefly that the blood shed during the Dark Ages in torrents throughout Europe cries out for vengeance. She denounced all spiritualism outside her own pale as magic, and its adherents as workers of wonders by means of the power of Satan. Yet she had a kind of magic of her own, and that same "Satan" was the word with which she conjured. It was laid aside or brought into play, as circumstances commanded. A miracle which benefited the Church was ascribed to God. A miracle which embarrassed or injured the Church was laid to the account of the Prince of Evil. But this was not the worst: we may detest the cruelty which is founded in bigotry and misplaced zeal; but a far deeper detestation should be reserved for the cruelty which is the effect of cold worldliness and calculating hypocrisy. Such was, in perhaps the majority of instances, the cruelty of the Church of Rome. She lighted her pyres and launched her anathemas, not because she really believed burning the bodies of men to be for the advantage of their souls, but because she considered persecution a necessary means of preserving her temporal power. Her two battle-cries were "Heresy" and "Sorcery," and whenever the first failed the second was unsparingly used.

Of the demoniac fury with which the Church of Rome formerly persecuted heretics much has been written. The eloquence of Protestant authors of all sects and every age has been employed in painting such martyrdoms as those of Huss, Oldcastle, Anne Askew, and Coligni; in describing how Torquemada ruled over Spain like a subordinate fiend commissioned by the Prince of Darkness to make that fair country hideous in the sight of God and man; and how the burning of Latimer and Ridley lighted a flame in England which has never been put out. Such diatribes are praiseworthy: the effects of a revolt of the best principles contained in human nature against inhuman cruelty. It is not, in truth, easy to be too vehement in attacking the Catholic treatment of heretics. That treatment was, over and over again, such as Nero would have shuddered at. But of the yet more frightful scenes enacted under the pretence of punishing sorcery strangely little has been said. This indifference is puzzling, in view of the history of the past. It is scarcely too much to assert that the persecutions for witchcraft were to the persecutions for heresy as the Catholic Hell to the Catholic Purgatory—as a whip of scorpions to a whip of cords. Nine millions of persons are computed to have been burned, hanged, or drowned for sorcery under the auspices of the various Churches of Christ. Protestantism is responsible for some hundreds of thousands of these deaths, but immeasurably the greater number of the victims were victims of Rome. In every country of Europe witchcraft was of old the charge which committed the hugest number of sufferers to the hands of the executioner. To quote a few lines from Leckey's chapter on the subject in his "History of Rationalism," "Seven thousand victims are said to have been burnt at Treves. Decrees were passed on the subject by the parliaments of Paris, Toulouse, Bordeaux, Rheims, Rouen, Dijon, and Rennes, and they were all followed by a harvest of blood. The executions which took place in Paris were, in the emphatic words of an old writer, 'almost infinite.' In Italy a thousand persons were executed in a single year in the province of Como, and in other parts of the country, the severity of the inquisitors at last created an absolute rebellion." Multiply the instances similar to these almost to infinity, and, taking into consideration the hundreds of years for which the devilish work went on, that total of nine millions, which I have quoted from a German authority on the subject, will no longer appear difficult of credence.

It is worthy of remark that the years in which persecution for witchcraft raged most wildly were years in which Europe was distracted by great calamities. During the period of the Black Death the excesses wrought in Christendom were beyond anything heathen history contains. A single instance will suffice:— at one of the French towns— Chinon, if I remember aright—the populace rose on their usual victims, the Jews, and accused them of having caused the pestilence by magic spells. It is not to be supposed that, in proportion to their numbers, the Jews suffered less from the Black Death than the Christians; but popular fury knows nothing of logic. The whole of the doomed race within reach, to the number of two hundred, were seized. A vast trench was dug. In this trench straw, fagots, and other combustibles were heaped; fire was put to the mass, and the captives bound and brought close. Then, when the flames were at their fiercest, the unfortunates were raised one by one and cast upon the pyre. Infants and old men, mothers, husbands, and children, young men and maidens, perished together. The eloquence of Cicero could add nothing to the horrors of the bare description. "I command ye," said Christ, "that ye love one another." Thus did certain, defiling the name of Christian, execute that command.

Some may object that the persecutions for sorcery were the outcome of an unenlightened age, and that the Church, unable to arrest the movement, was forced to be content with directing it. But all history testifies that the fury of the popular mind against witchcraft was the sequence, and the inevitable sequence, of certain teachings which the Papacy had adopted and exaggerated from that Levitical law Christ came to supersede, and of other laws which she had invented for herself. "Thou shalt not suffer a witch to live," commanded Moses. "All workers of spiritual signs and wonders, save those stamped with my approbation, are wizards and witches," was the decree of Rome. She promulgated the two teachings, as requiring the obedience of all who owned her supremacy, and horrors such as earth had never before witnessed were the result.

The learning of Europe was, until the invention of printing, almost wholly confined to the cloister. The ecclesiastical power represented the brain, and the civil the arm which that brain moves. To the priesthood men of the law and men of the sword were alike subservient. Rome, therefore, had at her command the two powers which move the world, and which, in almost all ages of the world, have been found at war—brute and intellectual force. Ahriman and Ormuzd had for a space ceased their battles, and were united in common subjection to a mighty mistress. Until the printing-press of Guttenburg overturned this condition of things the Papacy was, for good or evil, omnipotent. It will scarcely be denied that, as regarded intercourse with the world of spirits, she perverted her limitless power steadily to evil. Her pontiffs and priests were, in unnumbered instances, the most detestable of mankind—creatures whom every possible crime had polluted. Their lives are inconceivable on the supposition that they put the least credence in the Scriptures committed to their charge. Heaven, Hell, and Purgatory were to them the various parts of a cunningly devised fable, invented for the purpose of bringing money into the coffers of the Church. In Satan and his subordinate fiends they put not the slightest faith; they knew that Christ nowhere expressly inculcates the dogma of a personal devil. They were aware that the devil, such as the multitude believed him, to be, was a gigantic shadow, manufactured to suit the purposes of Rome. The Prince of Darkness then, if they did not exactly, like one of Shakespeare's characters, pronounce him a gentleman, was in their eyes a useful though a rather ugly puppet, who could be made available for a variety of evil purposes. They wondered at the fear the multitude had of the figure, and jested much over that fear among themselves; but they did not hesitate to turn the awe of the vulgar to account, and in a way that has blackened their names everlastingly. Under cover of a charge of sorcery they wreaked private grudges without number. If they believed anything, it was that the making a compact with Satan was as impossible as the making a compact with the forms one sees in a dream. Yet for this impossible crime they consigned millions to the executioner. Did space permit my passing from the general to the particular, I could show, by hundreds of examples, that the Catholic law condemning sorcerers to the flames was but an engine by which the priesthood defended their temporal power from attack, stayed the reform of vile abuses and the march of intellect, and satisfied their malice on those they hated. A genius surpassing that of ordinary men had perfected some great invention which the Church thought it to its interest to suppress. "A compact with the devil" explained the matter, and inventor and invention perished in the same fire. A reformer had arisen who witnessed with indignation the evil lives of the clergy, and sought to end such scandals. His own pure life had, perhaps, brought him into a fit state for communion with the better dwellers in the spirit world. At once the Church seized on him as a wizard, and his projected reforms ended at the stake. A prelate desired pretext for robbing some wealthy layman of his property or his life—perhaps of both; what easier to contrive than a charge of sorcery? A priest had in vain endeavoured to lead astray some fair member of his flock; what more thorough revenge could disappointed lust imagine than to procure her punishment as a witch? Such infamies are not dreams. They were the every-day facts of existence three or four centuries ago. Mixed with them were other causes predisposing to the waste of life. There were the ignorant passions of the multitude, there was the furious bigotry of those who sincerely believed witchcraft a possible crime. There were continual outbreaks of strange and hideous phenomena, such as only the most degraded spirits, working through congenial media, could have produced—phenomena sufficient to fill even the most liberal of men with horror and disgust. By means of these instruments the more astute and unimpassioned persecutors worked. They dragged the worst phases of spiritualism conspicuously into the light, and in this and other ways stimulated popular fury to a more ungovernable pitch. They encouraged their brethren who persecuted from zeal, and pretended a similar zeal, if they had it not.

Europe was filled with bloodshed, from Lisbon to the confines of Muscovy, and the authors of this bloodshed contemplated their work with satisfied complacency, as a masterpiece of polity. By means of stake and halter they had tamed the spiritual. Lawful miracle was to be found only within the bounds of the Church, and under such conditions ranked among the mightiest of her weapons. Outside the Roman pale all miracle was illegal. Intercourse with the spirit-world, which, properly directed, would have speedily delivered the human mind from the thraldom of Papal error, was classed as of the works of the devil. Industriously drilled by the priesthood to that belief, the idea of a suppositious supervision constantly exercised by a suppositious Satan over mundane affairs became at last a chief article in the creed of the vulgar. To the Prince of Evil every event in the least uncommon was ascribed. If a Roger Bacon discovered gunpowder, or an old woman hit upon a method of butter-making superior to that practised by her neighbours, if a Guttenberg invented the art of printing, or a cow produced a five-legged calf, Bacon and the old dame, Guttenburg and the cow, were equally denounced as emissaries of hell. Nay, the faith in miracles from Satan would appear to have been stronger than the faith in miracles from God. The Protestant separatists rejected Rome's teaching of the continuance of celestial signs and wonders, but belief in infernal marvels was too ingrained to be destroyed. Ministering angels were repudiated by Luther and Knox, but tempting demons were solemnly recognised, and their supposed servants on earth persecuted with a fury born of antipathy and unreasoning fear. In a certain company where Luther was present, the talk fell on witches spoiling egos. "I would have no compassion on these witches," remarked the great reformer, "I would burn all of them. Yet he was one of the most enlightened Protestants of his day. The first winnowing-machine introduced into Scotland was denounced from many pulpits as a demonize invention which brought with it literally "blasts from hell." One reverend Calvinist refused the communion to all who had accepted this gift of the devil to man. And the folly of rushing to Satan for an explanation of anything unusual or miraculous, which folly it was the policy of Rome to inspire and foster, still continues. In what a number of ridiculous sermons, Protestant and Catholic, have the spiritual phenomena of the present day been attributed to the direct agency of the fallen Son of the Morning and his myrmidons! The notion that all media not clerical have given themselves over to Beelzebub is evidently still strong among peasants and priests—that is to say, with the two most unenlightened classes of mankind.

A famous tale of horror among the many accounts of trials for witchcraft which history has preserved, is the burning of the noblest virgin of the Middle Ages—Jeanne d'Arc. Joan, an angel of light, was condemned as a fiend of darkness by a mixed tribunal of soldiers and priests: the former inspired to their cruelty by hatred, the latter by policy. The reproach of England, she is at once the glory and the shame of France. Churchmen of her own country sat among the judges who decided on her murder; the king and the nobles whom she had saved, the army which she had led to victory, stirred not a step to save her. For the chieftains of England and France were equally enraged against the inspired shepherdess. Talbot, Bedford, and Burgundy were wrathful that, before this girl they, the successors to the victor of Agincourt, should have been forced to flee like sheep; Charles and Orleans chafed to think that they had approved themselves more timid soldiers, and less skilful generals, than a simple peasant girl. French and English alike knew, indeed, that she had done those things by a power not her own. They had witnessed her penetrating clairvoyance, they had beheld her every prophecy fulfilled; and when the brief and brilliant mission of the wonderful maid was accomplished; when, after advancing almost to the Mediterranean, the invaders were beaten back to the shores of the English Channel, her foes, having seized her, condemned and slew her, as in league with devils, and her false friends appeared, by their inaction and silence, to acquiesce in the truth of the verdict and the justice of the sentence. Neither party thought of recognising in the deliverance of France the hand of God. The doubtful sort of halo which hung around Joan prevented her recognition as a saint. Instead of wasting her existence in a convent she rode at the head of armies. Instead of the sable garments of a nun, she wore the glittering armour of a knight. She was no tool of the Papacy, but an instrument shaped by Heaven to accomplish the deliverance of her fatherland. It was scarcely possible that a corrupted Church could recognise in her one of the noblest of the daughters of God; and the Church held true to its traditions. At first it denounced her as a servant of the Evil One, and when the sure changes of time had rendered this policy unsound, and English and French were alike busy in "gleaning up into the golden urn of history" the ashes of her whom their forefathers slew, the Church of Rome stood sullenly aloof, and lent neither aid nor countenance to the work. A bishop of that Church had been one of the foremost among the murderers of Joan, and by Romish ecclesiastics the perjuries were sworn, and the indignities and cruelties planned and put in action, of that long agony, worse than death, which preceded the fiery ascent of the Virgin of Domremy to the place prepared for her on high. These churchmen acted after their kind. It would have been strange indeed, when so much of the infamy of persecution was to be obtained, if the priesthood had not contrived to come in for the largest share.

Joan belonged to the village of Domremy, in what is now the department of the Vosges. In early childhood unearthly voices sounded in her ears whilst she tended sheep in the fields. Soon majestic forms, which she believed to be those of St. Margaret and St. Catherine, appeared to her in all the glory of another world. They were sent to prepare the little peasant maiden for her appointed task. During the next few years Joan lived the happiest and most spiritual of lives; a life that could scarcely be considered of earth. She drank in the lessons of her guides, and gazed with reverent delight on their glorious forms. She was clasped in their arms, and felt the loving kisses and embraces of these sisters gone before. Were they absent from her, she passed the hours in an expectant longing for their presence, and kissed frequently the turf whereon they had appeared to stand. Her every thought was of her guides; her single prayer to be for ever with them in the land where there are no more tears. "When I saw my saints," said she to the tribunal which murdered her, "I wished to follow them to Paradise."

At length this happy existence ceased. Henceforth her life was to be one of action and endurance, of glory, agony, despair. A voice like a trumpet announced to her one day that the work was ready; and the hour for attempting it at hand. By her means the banner of St. Denis was to advance to victory, and that of St. George to fall from its high estate. She was appointed by Heaven the deliveress of France. Great renown would be hers, but still greater pain. Yet, in the darkest as the brightest hour, ministering spirits would be by her side, and voices, not of earth, would whisper comfort. And the example of the Man of Sorrows mast be ever in her mind. As Christ had expired in agony, mocked and insulted by all around, so a martyrdom equally terrible was appointed to be her lot. She would fall into the power of enemies; her body they might destroy, but the spirit no malice could harm. As was her cross, so hereafter would be her crown. She might be tried with agonies such as human nature shudders to conceive, but she should assuredly pass from those agonies to be one of the greatest in the kingdom of heaven.

How she accomplished her mission is written with imperishable characters in the history of the world. The importance of that mission it is difficult to over-estimate. Without Jeanne d'Arc Charles VII. would never have been crowned at Rheims, and the English Henry VI. might have reigned peacefully at Paris. In the conquest of France, England, alike with her victim, would have been ruined. All the miseries which usually attend the conquered would have fallen on the conqueror. The desire of a yet further aggrandisement would have occupied the sovereigns of the unwieldy empire which, at first that of Great Britain and France, must speedily have become that of France and Great Britain. Constantly forced to visit the continent, Henry VI., or some succeeding monarch, would have ended by fixing the seat of government there. His descendants would have become more and more alien from England, and more and more attached to France. The larger country would have been exalted at its neighbour's expense. Another war would have arisen. The English, disgusted with the injuries of their country, and ill-disposed to recognise as its princes men born and bred in a land which the valour of their fathers had conquered, would have sprung to arms. After years of desolation and bloodshed the conflict would have ended, as such conflicts must of necessity end, in the separation of the two realms. England would have been again the England of Henry IV., and, as consolation for a ruined commerce, a depopulated territory, and an empty treasury, would have had the miserable boast that statues of the victor of Agincourt had been erected within the walls of Paris, and that for a space Englishmen had trodden on the necks of their neighbours. The miseries of an unnatural and sickly union between two kingdoms intended to flourish apart from each other, and the still sharper miseries with which the violent dissolution of that union would have been attended, Joan's deeds averted. For this great benefit to the two nations she was rewarded with the stake. England burned her, and France stirred not a finger to avert her death.

With the various stages of her career every schoolboy is familiar. She made known her mission. Undaunted by threats, unimpressed by ridicule, she pressed her suit for an interview with the Dauphin until that interview was obtained. At a glance she selected him from the crowd of courtiers, amongst whom, in a dress that had about it no indication of his rank, Charles had purposely hidden himself. She proclaimed to him that through her should he be crowned at Rheims, and that by her would the city of Orleans be relieved. She declared to him a secret which he had thought known to himself alone. She spoke of her mission in a tone of lofty faith. "No one upon this earth, neither king nor duke, nor the daughter of the King of Scots, no one but myself, is appointed to recover this realm of France. Yet I could more willingly remain to spin by the side of my poor mother; for war seems no work for me. But go I must, because the Lord my Master wills it." "And who is the Lord your Master?" "The King of Heaven," Joan replied.

After long and tedious examinations, and after giving various proofs of knowledge more than mortal, the Virgin of Domremy was permitted to clothe herself in armour, to place at her side an ancient sword which spirits had directed her to take from the church where it was preserved, and to depart at the head of a brigade destined for the relief of Orleans. This city, the single stronghold of note which yet held out against the English, was at its last gasp. The besiegers had confidently announced that they would capture it by a certain day. It was the crisis of the fate of France.

Joan arrived before the walls of Orleans. She succeeded in conveying food to the beleaguered and starving garrison. At the head of a small body of troops she threw herself within the city. She purified the morals, and revived the fainting courage of the soldiery. By the evidences she gave of her inspiration from another world she gradually roused them to enthusiasm. When their minds were prepared for battle she led them against the invaders. The English were defeated, and forced to raise the siege. In that victory Joan's country was saved.

Until now the men of Agincourt had been considered invincible. When the forces of England and France met, the latter fought half-heartedly and were beaten almost before the battle began. The relief of Orleans dissolved the spell. Before a city which they had disdainfully vowed to take within a certain time, the English had met with sudden and striking disaster; they had suffered defeat at the hands of a foe inferior in strength, and had been driven to raise the siege with ignominy. Thenceforth the tide of fortune ran strongly in favour of France. Among her armies there was no more of the old panic fear. Occasional reverses might cause anxiety, but in the main things went well. Wherever Joan commanded, and her counsels were implicitly followed, England strove in vain. The skill and valour of Talbot and Bedford were turned to foolishness before a country maiden of nineteen. At length all which her guides had commanded her to promise was accomplished. The invaders were beaten back to the provinces of the extreme north. At Rheims, in the old cathedral of Notre Dame, Charles was solemnly crowned king of France, the holy maid standing by his side.

Joan threw herself at the feet of the new-made sovereign, and earnestly implored that she might be allowed to retire. Her mission, she said, was accomplished, and in token of this, the voices by which she had been guided in her career of victory had suddenly become silent. She could no longer be of use, and awful misfortunes threatened her. In violation of the duties of gratitude Charles refused the desired permission to depart. The English were still in France. It was necessary that the holy maid should drive them forth. Sadly and reluctantly, but overpowered by the warmth of her patriotism, Joan suffered herself to become pledged to the attempt. She went forth, knowing that it was to certain death. Her spirit-counsellors had left her, and with them had departed success. The worst speedily came. Deserted by her troops, she was made prisoner, and placed in confinement whilst her captors deliberated as to what should be her fate. Her treatment henceforth until death, has stamped all concerned in it as blots on the human species. Now she was threatened with the rack; now forced to assume male attire, and exposed to the brutal insults of the English and Burgundian men-at-arms. She was one day told that the morrow should see her led to the stake, the next soothed with lying oaths that her life should be spared. At length the fiends around her were weary of their sport. They determined, with one crowning deed of cruelty, to release their victim from the earth, whereon they had caused her to suffer horrors equalling anything in the Inferno of Dante, and in that deed to hold themselves up to the detestation of all posterity. A stake was fixed in the market-place of Rouen. Weeping bitterly, and clasping a crucifix to her breast, the unhappy maiden of nineteen passed to the scene of death. She was chained to the post, and brushwood heaped around her. The captains of England and Burgundy, and certain churchmen of France, looked on with the implacability of a cold and unmanly hate. The pile was kindled, and the flames rose. Speedily the dense smoke hid for ever from sight the form of the noblest, martyr of the dark ages; the most unhappy heroine of all time. The last cry heard to issue from Joan's lips was the one word "Jesus." Her ashes were collected, and thrown into the Seine.

The man or woman is little to be envied in whose breast the name of Jeanne d'Arc excites no sentiment of interest or compassion. The author has irremediably blackened his fame who stoops to assail her memory with ribald sneers, and unprincipled distortion of facts. Such a stigma attaches to Voltaire. In a lesser degree it soils even the great name of Shakespeare. The principal fault of the poet of all time was a ready pandering to the passions of the multitude. Where his audience had a strong prejudice respecting an historical character he depicted that character to suit, indifferent whether the portrait were a likeness or a caricature. In the present instance the English detested the memory of Joan as that of a strumpet and a witch; as such Shakespeare drew her. History gives the slander the lie. She was pure in every respect, and the purest of spirits ministered to her. The misdirected genius of even the prince of dramatists cannot sully her fame, far less the ribald calumnies of Voltaire. In everything she approved herself sent of Heaven. She declared that spiritual beings had commissioned her to save Orleans, and cause Charles VII. to be crowned at Rheims. She persisted in her task until the prophecy was fulfilled. She then declared that her guides had departed, warning her to return at once to her quiet village home, if she would avoid a hideous fate. The king overruled her wishes, and victory at once went and death came. Whilst spirits guided her she triumphed over obstacles that according to human calculations were insurmountable. When those counsellors were gone she attempted a less difficult task, and perished. Historians have termed her an enthusiast, and have sought to account by her enthusiasm for her success. An enthusiast she truly was; but there are two species of such natures the one wonderfully useful to human progress, the other in the highest degree pernicious. There is the noble and unconquerable enthusiasm which is founded on the certainty of inspiration from another world; there is, moreover, the irrational and flighty enthusiasm which is attributable to the unstable fancies of a diseased mind. It is easy to discern that Joan's inspiration was of the former sort. Nothing of her prophecies remained unfulfilled; but the wild vaticinations of madness are not thus accomplished. A simple country girl, she led to battle the armies of France. Herself possessed of not an acre of ground, she gave to Charles VII. a kingdom. At an age when most girls are just beginning to be occupied with affairs of love, she was busied with affairs of state. At an age when such conquerors as Cæsar and Napoleon were yet obscure citizens, she had covered herself with imperishable renown. The angel of the Lord was as visibly with her as when he shone, a pillar of fire, on the night journeys of the astonished Israelites. Not less than Enoch did she walk with God. Like Moses she led a nation out from the house of bondage, and the translation of Elijah pales before the tragic grandeur of that flaming chariot in which she was whirled away to hear the words, "Well done, good and faithful servant!" and to receive the diadem of unspeakable brightness promised to all who in the cause of truth endure steadfastly unto the end.

Jerome Savonarola was born at Ferrara in the year 1452. He took orders as a Dominican friar, and became speedily the best and greatest man of that corrupt order. The time when Savonarola commenced his mission was one of those which are the reproaches of history. The priesthood with few exceptions wallowed in a sea of vice. An abnormal monster, having every vice of Belial without his graces, and the cruelty and craft of Lucifer without his courage, had foisted himself into the chair of St. Peter under the title of Alexander VI. His son, Cæsar Borgia, was astounding Italy with his genius and his crimes. Savonarola became "mad for the sight of his eyes which he saw." He stood forward to attempt a reform of discipline and morals. Spiritual counsel was not wanting. He had in great measure the gifts of mediumship, and listened constantly to voices not of earth. At first his design prospered. The citizens of Florence were awed by the eloquence of a man who denounced their sins with the energy of an Ezekiel, or one of the witnesses foretold in the Apocalypse. The most spacious buildings were too small for the crowds that listened with tears and cries of repentance when Savonarola preached. The gay Capua of the Arno seemed rapidly becoming purified from all taint of frivolity and vice. He whose eloquence had wrought these marvels contemplated them with astonishment and joy. The desire of still greater triumphs arose in his mind. He would be to Rome, her prelates and her pontiff, as Jonah had of old been to the princes of Nineveh. He would make of Italy a land pure in the sight of God. Armed with spiritual weapons, surrounded by the heavenly host, he would arrest the progress of those myriads of invaders who were descending from the Alps on the fertile plains and rich cities of Tuscany, Lombardy, and Venetia. The attempt was made. He journeyed to the camp of Charles VIII., and rebuked him with the authority of an apostle. He supported by striking predictions the warnings which he believed himself commissioned to deliver. The king was so far influenced by the speedy fulfilment of one of these prophecies as to abandon his projected siege of Florence, since Savonarola was the mastermind of that city. But his army, and the companion vultures of Spain and Switzerland, still retained their grasp on Italy, and still battled for possession of the prey on which they had pounced. Disappointed in his patriotic hopes, Savonarola turned more ardently than ever to his religious projects. He denounced the Pope, and called on all true servants of Christ to join in hurling him from the throne which he disgraced. He lashed with vehement eloquence the vices of the priests. A storm arose such as at a later day broke upon the head of Luther. Like Luther, Savonarola faced it with the most dauntless fortitude. With two of his chief disciples he was seized and imprisoned. It was impossible that against so devout a Catholic a charge of heresy could be sustained. The Church had recourse, therefore, to its other and yet more terrible weapon. There was ample proof that Savonarola held intercourse with the dwellers in another world. He had uttered prophecies and they had been fulfilled. He had a miraculous power of reading the thoughts of men. In his dungeon he had been seen to rise slowly from the ground, and remain without any support suspended in the air. Evidence not a hundredth part as strong had procured the deaths of countless thousands. Savonarola was condemned as a sorcerer, and in company with his two adherents died at the stake.

The one other martyrdom I think it necessary to quote is that of Urban Grandier. In the career of Joan of Arc we behold illustrated the apparently inadequate means with which heaven sometimes accomplishes its mightiest designs; in the fate of Savonarola the entire success that had attended the efforts of the Papacy to imbue the mind of Christendom with an unreasoning belief in the omnipotence of the devil. A monk, learned, pious, accepting fervently every doctrine of the Catholic Church, blameless in morals, and powerful throughout the north of Italy, is accused of being a wizard. The evidence on which he is condemned as a servant of the Evil One exactly resembles that on which Theresa and Loyola were pronounced saints of God. But the Church saw reason for the distinction. Ignatius and Theresa were the submissive tools of the pontiff for the time being: Savonarola attacked his vices. The Papacy decided that manifestations which in the one case were produced by angels, were in the other the work of devils. Reduced to its simplest form, the decree was that, in the matter of spiritual manifestations as in every other, the Catholic Church was infallible, and that when she pronounced white to be black it must be accepted as such. And for centuries all Europe did so accept it!

Grandier's case instances the ease with which, when ecclesiastics high in the Church desired to crush an enemy, a lying accusation of sorcery might be fastened on a man absolutely destitute of medial powers. This victim was, during the reign of Louis XIII, parish priest of Loudun, in the diocese of Poitiers. His success in the pulpit induced the jealousy of other priests, and a conspiracy was formed to ruin him. In Loudun was a convent of Ursuline nuns. These women were instructed to feign themselves possessed by devils, and to charge Grandier with having brought about the possession. The Archbishop of Bordeaux investigated the case, and acquitted the accused of all the charges. He advised him, however, to resign his benefice, and remove from the neighbourhood of his implacable enemies. Grandier obstinately refused. Another plot was formed. Some unknown wit had produced a satire on Richelieu, then the real ruler of France. It was declared that the priest of Loudun was the author. The malicious cardinal resolved on an action worthy any devil of heathen or Christian theology. Grandier was tried once more on the old charge, and, in defiance of all justice, condemned. Nothing in the least approaching evidence was offered. The martyr, after being racked repeatedly, became the victim of that infernal torture of the boot which the last and worst of the evil Stuart dynasty afterwards watched inflicted on the

Scottish Covenanters. When bones and flesh had been crushed into a mangled mass, Grandier was carried to the place of execution, and burnt alive. At the instant the pile was lighted he summoned Father Lactance, a chief amongst his murderers, to meet him in a month before the judgment-seat of the Eternal God. Lactance, perfectly well when the summons was delivered, died at the prescribed time. The nuns who had been tutored to act the possessed continued to behave as though inspired by Beelzebub himself. Of the various ecclesiastics concerned in the murder of Grandier, Richelieu alone would appear to have known neither repentance nor remorse. The cardinal's punishment was reserved for the hour when, in another world, he and his victim should again be brought face to face.

These three narratives may be accepted as striking illustrations of the crimes done by Rome under cover of the charge of sorcery. Yet the instances I have given can by no means be put forward as the worst. The blood of millions of other victims cries from the ground against the Papacy. "In whatever market-place the symbol of the cross was upreared during the Middle Ages a stake and a gallows appeared on either hand. The number of victims handed over by the priesthood to the secular arm, with a charitable prayer that all possible tenderness might be shown, would about equal the united populations of Scotland and Ireland at the present day. Demons more cruel than Richelieu may have inflicted on many of these doomed ones tortures even surpassing the tortures endured by Grandier. Natures as noble as that of Jeanne d'Arc may have perished and made no sign. We have the history of the persecution as a whole, but of particular agonies we know little. There are indeed hideous records of these ancient horrors scattered through various cities of Europe; into which records few have the wish or the opportunity to penetrate. Fortunately, the moral of history lies usually on the surface. The lessons to be deduced from what I have described as the Shadow of Catholic Spiritualism are, that the inhumanity of a priesthood surpasses that of other men as the malice of a fiend might be supposed to surpass the malice of an elf, and that never has the Church of Rome known respect for the rights of men or sympathy with their sufferings when the advancement of her power, temporal or spiritual, was to be obtained by increasing those sufferings or disregarding those rights. The Greek Church, more truly Christian, and at least equally rich in spiritual gifts, exercises, and has for centuries exercised, a tolerant and nobler policy.

CHAPTER V

THE SPIRITUALISM OF THE WALDENSES AND THE CAMISARDS

Few churches have been more evidently protected of God than that little band of brothers whose sufferings inspired Milton to the cry—

> "Avenge, O Lord! Thy slaughtered saints, whose bones
> Lie bleaching on the Alpine mountains cold!"

The Waldenses were justly designated "The Israel of the Alps." They preserved through centuries their independence and their faith, albeit surrounded on all sides by hostile nations, the weakest of whom had a hundred times their resources. Against the power and the cruelty of France and Savoy they bore up unyieldingly, supported simply by spiritual aid.

They were neither to be exterminated nor subdued. In the darkest hours of their fortunes light from another world cheered them, and when they seemed fallen to the very earth spirit-hands raised them up. As in the Hebrew scriptures, we read of a few men driving armies before them. As in Palestine, the deliverances of the oppressed were frequently so miraculous that the oppressors cried in astonishment, "This is the hand of God!"

The Vaudois, or Waldenses, are sometimes asserted to have originated in the twelfth century, and to have had for their first leader a Peter Waldo of Lyons. The truth seems to be that, far from these ancient Protestants taking their designation from Waldo, he drew his own from the Waldenses. It was during the fourth century that their schism from Rome took place. At first they disclaimed the desire of a total separation, and contented themselves with strong protests against abuses. The Church, with the lapse of time, departed yet more widely from apostolic traditions, whilst the Waldenses had become but the more strongly attached to them. The split gradually widened. At length the little Piedmontese congregation withdrew wholly from communion with Rome, and was thenceforth persecuted with unrelenting fury.

The separatists sought refuge in one of the most romantic of nature's strongholds. They peopled the higher valleys of the Piedmontese Alps, and there vowed to defend their religion to the last. We may imagine them, as Mrs. Hemans has imagined, exclaiming—

> "Thou hast placed our ark of refuge
> Where the spoiler's foot ne'er trod;
> For the strength of our hills we bless Thee,
> Our God, our fathers' God!"

For above ten centuries the attack and defence continued. Rome gave no quarter. Her desire was to extirpate these heretics—not to convert them. With all the forces of Europe at her command, the attempt failed. The Waldenses were a Church when Charlemagne sat on the throne of the West, and they were a Church when Napoleon surpassed the conquests of Charlemagne. They beheld the kindred heresy of the Albigenses arise, menace the supremacy of the Papacy, and become extinguished in the seas of blood shed by De Montfort and Dominic. They were battling for existence when Wickliffe thundered against the corruptions of Rome—when his bones were torn with ignominy from their sepulchre—when his disciples were hunted with fire and sword. Whilst Savonarola was raising his voice against Papal abuses, the Papacy was hounding on France and Savoy to lay waste the valleys where the Vaudois had so long dwelt. Whilst Luther was crying for all who truly worshipped Christ to come out from the Roman Babylon, and range themselves by his side, the devil of persecution was doing his worst among the Piedmontese Alps. Then came the Huguenot wars of France, and the fierce religious struggles in Germany. The attention of Rome was directed to a greater schism, and an immensely more imminent danger. For a space the Waldenses tilled their fields and celebrated their worship in peace. But the storm which had menaced the very existence of the Catholic Church blew over. Protestantism, after progressing to the shores of the Mediterranean, was driven back almost to the Baltic. The Papacy could turn its attention again to the little community which had been a thorn in its side for ages. The flames of persecution once more raged furiously amongst the mountains of Northern Italy. In those Eden-like recesses scenes of the wildest horror were perpetrated. The Catholic princes not actively engaged in the devilish work looked approvingly on. At length the news of maidens dishonoured; of children tossed on spears; of women ripped up, or hurled down rocks; of men slain in defence of their homes witnessing with their last glance their wives and daughters exposed to horrors worse than death; of whole families burned in their burning dwellings, reached and roused the heroic usurper who then controlled the destinies of England. Cromwell stood forth as the champion of the Vaudois. The voice of the first soldier of Europe was not one against which Rome might stop her ears. Sullenly the mandate was given that persecution should cease. As sullenly was it obeyed. The ruler of Savoy retired from the valleys which he had devastated, and, like a wolf overawed by the interference of some more lordly animal, remained watching the moment when he might with impunity rush once more on the coveted prey. In no long time the opportunity was granted. Death struck down the English Protector; his throne passed to a debauchee and a coward; his wise and magnanimous policy was abandoned. France and Rome hastened to give the signal to their tool, the Duke of Savoy. An army was once more marched into the fastnesses of Northern Piedmont. The last and most merciless of the Waldensean persecutions commenced.

Nothing in modern history, unless it be the triumphs won a few years later by the Protestants of the Cevennes, can equal the marvels which the Vaudois now accomplished. Of their former wars we have but scanty accounts. Judging by the disproportion between their strength and that of their enemies, even the first of these crusades should have ended in the extirpation of the Waldenses. Yet century after century passed by, and beheld them still resisting. We turn to the histories of that great struggle in which they were occupied during a portion of Louis XIV.'s reign, and can no longer wonder that the little Piedmontese community was enabled to defend itself so long and so well. Of these narratives, some are given by the Vaudois themselves, some by their persecutors, some by their friends. In almost every page occur traces of spiritual aid. We read how seventeen of the persecuted encountered and defeated a force of near nine hundred men. We read how the little hamlet of Rora, containing but fifty houses, was held for a while against ten thousand regular troops, and how, when its smoking ruins were no longer tenable, the gallant handful of defenders made good their retreat. It is told us that when their implacable enemies had closed with heaps of brushwood the mouths of the caverns wherein certain Vaudois had taken refuge, and had endeavoured by lighting the piles to suffocate them or burn them alive, the imprisoned mountaineers, bursting suddenly through the fiery barrier, chased before them fifty times their number of French and Savoyards, who cried, as they fled, that the heretics were aided by the powers of hell. The precipices which in the darkest night they traversed without hurt; the hardships they endured without succumbing; the miraculous way in which they were sometimes supplied with food; the fervour with which they thanked God for victory; the serene enthusiasm with which they triumphed over death,—all are there. "I have witnessed," said Arnaud, their pastor and leader, "prodigies beyond the course of nature, or the natural strength of man."

In April, 1686, came the crisis. As Savoy was unequal to the conquest single-handed, the vast resources of France were joined to hers. The allies, having united their forces, made a final swoop on the doomed race. After two days of desperate fighting the Waldenses laid down their arms. Fourteen thousand were cast into various prisons; of whom eleven thousand perished. The extremes of cold, heat, hunger and thirst, were the ills which slew these unhappy captives. Such unconquerable spirits as had disdained submission betook themselves to Switzerland or the Protestant States of Germany.

Among these last was a chosen troop of between eight and nine hundred men, headed by the great Waldensean pastor, Henri Arnaud. Three years later this band resolved to attempt a return to their Piedmont valleys. They crossed Lake Leman on the night of August 16th, 1689. It was the commencement of a march in some respects more marvellous than that of Xenophon. The little band of brothers succeeded in baffling the united forces of France, Savoy, and the Catholic cantons of Switzerland. In ten days eighteen battles were fought. The allies lost several thousand men; the Waldensean killed amounted to seventy. At the bridge of Sababertran, they forced a passage against two thousand five hundred well-entrenched troops. Of the Vaudois, fourteen were slain. The enemy's loss was at least six hundred. "Who is so dull," cries Arnaud, "as not to see that God alone could give victory to a mere parcel of men, without money, and almost without arms, against the King of France, before whom all Europe trembled?" For the heroic achievers of these marvels were a few hundreds of fainting wretches, clothed in scarcely decent rags, and sleeping usually on the earth. Their drink was water, their food roots and herbs. Against them were arrayed over twenty thousand of the finest troops of France and Northern Italy; abundantly provided with arms, ammunition, and provisions, and accompanied by mules burdened with ropes for the hanging of captured Vaudois. No balance could have been more unequal; but the sword of Heaven was cast into the lighter scale, and it sufficed for the outweighing of the other. The halters remained unused. The best soldiers of Europe fled before a handful of ill-armed starving peasants. In passes where a few men might have held thousands at bay, thousands were dislodged by a few. At length the Italian Alps were reached. With tears of joy and exulting hymns the Waldenses entered the familiar valleys. Their brethren who had been spared in the persecution eagerly welcomed them. It was expected, however, that the endeavours to crush the little congregation would speedily recommence. Fortunately the fear proved groundless. Discord arose between France and Savoy, and Duke Amadeus allied himself with the English. At the request of William III. he grudgingly conceded to his Waldensean subjects certain rights over their lives and properties. The grateful Vaudois enlisted by thousands under his banner, and did excellent service against the French. The war ended in the discomfiture of Louis. Immediately the Duke hastened to oppress his Protestant subjects once more. Three thousand persons not born in the valleys were banished. The remaining Vaudois endured the weight of numerous oppressive edicts. But the worst of the persecution was past. Catholic princes dared no longer gratify their appetite for intolerance with the murder of women and children, or the wholesale massacre of defenceless men. The Duke of Savoy might still occasionally venture on the burning of a Waldensean pastor or two, but laymen were not now robbed of their lives. By slow degrees their rights over their property came also to be recognised. The persecution which exterminates had ceased, and the persecution which irritates also in process of time drew to an end. It was not, however, until late in the present century that the government of Piedmont finally ceased from vexing that little Alpine Israel in whose behalf such great things were done of old.

In the extreme South of France lies the beautiful region of the Cevennes. Mountains green with vines, delightful valleys, a cloudless sky, and a delicious climate, combine to create one of the most charming of European paradises. From the summits of the higher peaks the magnificent expanse of the Mediterranean is visible. Roads are few, and often of the rudest character. The dwellers in this primitive region mostly hold the Protestant faith. The villages are old and picturesque. Sometimes, in the remoter recesses of the mountains, a congregation assembled in a solitary nook surprises the eye of the traveller. The pastor stands on a fragment of rock under the shadow of some ancient tree. The little flock gathered round him listen reverently to his eloquence, or join in the simple and monotonous psalmody of the district. Minister and hearers belong to some village nigh at hand that is destitute of a church. It was destroyed probably during the war of the Cevennes.

Nothing in the annals of France can interest a spiritualist more than the events of that wonderful struggle. The evidences of spiritual intervention are still more complete than those afforded by the persecution of the Vaudois. There were men among the little Camisard army of three thousand whom fire would not burn nor bullets pierce. There were clairvoyants to whom the most hidden secrets of the enemy were as an open book. Through these seers spies and ambushes were detected, the route and numbers of the royal army revealed, and the words which its leaders spoke in their tents carried to the leaders of the Protestant host. In battle the patriots seemed transfigured. They were endowed with a strength and a bravery far surpassing those of their calmer hours. Outnumbered a hundred to one, they disdained the defensive and pressed eagerly on to the attack. Yet a more incongruous rabble than the Cevennois heroes never moved the laughter of regular troops. Boys of twelve fought in their ranks side by side with men in the prime of life. The Samson of the Camisards was an under-sized slender youth of seventeen. The commander-in-chief was a vine-dresser. His associates in authority were bakers and carders of wool. There was but one leader who had previously seen anything of war. Yet in the counsels of these strange generalissimos nothing but harmony and wisdom prevailed. Before their spiritually directed movements the craft of the oldest marshals of France was turned to foolishness.

Amongst the peasants who adored and followed Rowland the vine-dresser and Cavallier the baker, the strangest diversities existed. At the beginning of the war the majority were in want of everything. A few had guns; of the remainder most were armed with swords or scythes. The others contented themselves with such weapons as David employed in doing battle with Goliath. Like David too they endowed themselves with the arms of the enemy and clothed themselves in his spoil. Every new field made more soldierly the appearance of the Camisards. Rags were replaced by coats, and staves by muskets. The chiefs adorned themselves with the broad and feathered hats and the scarlet uniforms of slain king's officers. They glittered with gold chains and rings of ruby and diamond. They charged the ranks of Montrevel and Villars mounted on magnificent chargers, the mementoes of their prowess on former fields of fight. Gaps were to some degree made in the Protestant ranks. The recruits who filled these gaps exhibited all the squalor which had characterized their brethren at the commencement of the war. Thus the motley appearance of the little army was never wholly effaced. Beside men splendid with uniforms torn from the dead captains of Louis the Great fought hungry peasants clad in little more than a tattered blouse, who mowed at the legs of the horses with weapons that had formerly served to reap their fields. And the Camisards were unquestionably less formidable when their means of defence became apparently increased, than when, naked, half-armed, and starving, they charged desperately upon the foe. Their mightiest victories were achieved by little bands of undisciplined and almost weaponless men. The power of another world went with them, and those whom a single company of dragoons might have seemed sufficient to scatter, defied successfully the whole might of France.

It is to the revocation of the Edict of Nantes that we are to look for the cause of the rebellion. The Catholic priesthood owed to the influence of Madame Maintenon that coveted increase of power, and Protestant France owed to her the expatriation or slaughter of half a million of citizens, and the letting loose of tens of thousands of soldiers on a peaceful and inoffensive race. The government chiefly directed its crusading efforts to the Cevennes. That portion of Languedoc offered an enticing field for attempts at conversion. The heretic's were numerous, and enthusiastically attached to their faith. Accordingly Louis dispatched to them missionaries in the shape of regiment after regiment of his best troops. These armed apostles showed themselves as benevolently zealous in proselytizing as their master could have desired. They quartered themselves perforce on the objects of their solicitude. They commenced industriously to furnish materials for that page of history infamous as the "Dragonnades of the Cevennes." The Inquisition might have taken lessons from them in the art of cruelty. Some of their catechumens they rolled naked over floors covered with broken glass. Some they anointed with oil, and held before fierce fires until half-roasted, in the vain hope of thus indoctrinating them in the mysteries of the Eucharist. They impressed on women the necessity of attending mass by tearing the dresses from their backs, and flogging them until their shoulders streamed with blood. Men who were mutinous they shot. Maidens who were good-looking they dishonoured.

The prisons overflowed with victims. Although the captives died by thousands; although their dungeons were hideous depths into which the sun never penetrated, choked with filth and alive with snakes and toads; although malaria, insufficient and impure food, cold, dampness, and want of light, were constantly at work destroying life, sufficient room could not be found. A happy few were placed under hatches, and shipped off to reach America, or find a grave in the depths of the ocean. The gibbet and the wheel disposed of others. The residue were condemned to the galleys or imprisonment. Some toiled for life at the oar; some were let down with ropes into the filthy pits which were to be their places of captivity; some pined in cells where they could neither lie down nor stand upright. Carrion and the garbage of cattle were flung to them for food. Their bodies swelled to an incredible extent; their skin peeled off; such as were liberated issued like living corpses from the hideous dens in which they had been caged. The features of many were unrecognisable; others had lost their hair or teeth; others again had become imbeciles or raving madmen. It seemed that even a few weeks confinement in one of these Infernos was enough to take from the immured wretch all semblance of humanity.

Yet the Cevennois remained unconquerable, and patiently endured whatever the ingenious malice of their tormentors could inflict. Imprisonment, torture, pillage, the rack, the gallows, the wheel—all were in turn tried, and all proved insufficient to tame the noble obstinacy of the oppressed race. The missionaries of Louis reported the failure of their efforts. It was owing to no lack of zeal that such a failure had to be confessed. They had destroyed villages by the score, and taken lives by the thousand. Yet, although so many heretics had perished, scarcely a convert could be shown. It was necessary that decisive measures should be authorised. The true course for a Catholic king evidently was, to treat his Protestant subjects as Israel had treated the inhabitants of Jericho and Ai: exterminate the heretics, and their places could be supplied by a colony of the faithful.

Extermination was resolved upon. Marshal Montrevel and the Intendant Lamoignon de Baville received orders to divide the doomed territory into sections, and to distribute to each its troop of soldiers, who should rase every house, lay waste every field, and slay every man, woman, and child who refused to embrace Catholicism. The diabolical work began, and the Cevennois at length rose in rebellion. A brigade of between two and three thousand men was organized, and this little army, without experience, and almost without weapons, ventured to take the field against a host of sixty thousand veteran troops, trained in the most approved discipline of the time, and seasoned by more than one war.

For ten years the struggle went on; for ten years the deeds wrought by the Cevennois continued to astonish Europe. The oppressed had cried to heaven, and the cry was heard. Every day some new spiritual manifestation occurred amongst them. Many became mediums, and thus served as channels for communications from another world. They spoke, whilst in the trance, not the ordinary patois of the district, but the purest French. They revealed the plans of the enemy; they warned their brethren of approaching battles, and named those of the Camisards who would fall. Such invariably went forth in triumph to their martyrdom, assured that death would bring to them a glorious reward. The Camisards who issued from the conflict unhurt frequently owed their preservation to miracle. Bullets were found within their shirts which had flattened against the skin. The swords of those who struck at them flew from their bodies as from a coat of mail. And, whilst the weapons of the persecutors thus failed to hold, the sword of every Camisard carved through the royal ranks like that of a destroying angel. In battle the inspired knew nothing of fatigue. The veteran soldier of France might faint beneath the heat and burden of the conflict; but his peasant adversary fought on steadily to the end. Spirits were at hand to strengthen the arm of every patriot. Often, in the fiercest of the fight, the Camisard seers looked up, and saw that the space around was filled with an, angelic host, who imparted to the onset of the oppressed a strength not of earth. The patriots, as I have said, never at any one time exceeded in number three thousand men. They slew in the ten years that the war lasted, one-third of the royal army.

Laporte was the brain of the Camisards, and Cavallier their right arm. The former was a man of forty, endowed by nature with a considerable share of intelligence, which constant intercourse with spirits brightened gradually into astonishing wisdom. Through his exertions all was orderly in the Protestant ranks, and each man had his fitting place. He exhorted continually the troops of whom he was commander-in-chief; he prayed and, prophesied in their midst. He caused magazines to be constructed in the caverns of the rocks and in the depths of the forests. Here abundant stores of provisions and clothing, of cattle, corn and wine—all taken from the enemy—were laid up. The wisdom of the precaution was speedily apparent. Before the war had lasted long, every Cevennois town and village was in ashes. Save for the store-houses, whose existence was owing to the wisdom of Laporte, the insurgents must have surrendered or starved. Nor was it only in the matter of provisions that, through, the spiritually directed genius of this extraordinary man, the persecutors were, against their will, compelled to be of service to the persecuted. The patriots, like the Christ whom they worshipped, had not where to lay their heads. Laporte gave them for abodes the castles and chateaux of their enemies. Retreats had been constructed for the wounded; but beds, surgical appliances and medicines were wanting. He forced the Catholics to furnish all. At times the royal generals sought to entrap, by means of negotiation, the patriots whom they could not crush. But to oppose to the commanding sagacity of Laporte the craft of diplomacy, was seeking to entangle an eagle by means of a cobweb. The first disdainful exertion of his strength broke through all.

Cavallier had a weaker head, but a yet stronger heart. In battle his brandished sword was the principal; standard of the Camisards. Where the chosen troops of the enemy clustered thickest round their banners, there that sword was ever seen carving for itself a terrible path. At the right hand of the young hero rode his friend Ravenel, a man of gigantic stature; at his left a boy still younger than himself, his brother Daniel. Behind came the cavalry of the Camisards, almost every man mounted on a horse that had formerly been backed by some soldier of the king. Cavallier himself rode a noble charger, which he had torn in battle from its royalist master, Colonel La Jonquière. This successful single combat was but one of many similar exploits. Whatever opponent he selected was as certainly doomed to death, as though the sword were already in his throat. The royalists whom he and his followers charged, if not above three to one, were scattered as with the shock of a thunderbolt.

As a cavalry leader Cavallier seems to have excelled both Rupert and Murat. Their exploits were achieved against foes seldom more numerous, often less disciplined, and never better armed than their own squadrons. The force that the Camisard hero led was a mob of undisciplined peasants, unskilled in the science of war, and unacquainted with the use of the weapons they wielded. To remount themselves, or equip recruits, they had only the horses which they captured from the enemy. It was a fortunate circumstance for these raw countrymen, when each patriot had opposed to him only two of the best soldiers of the age. Such was the force which, under the command of Cavallier, achieved exploits more astounding than those attributed to any fabulous hero of old romance. Out-numbered, sometimes seven to one, they yet remained masters of the field of battle. Dismounted, they, without artillery, captured fastnesses which might have withstood a regular siege. For ten years they continued to prove themselves superior to the fiercest efforts of the whole chivalry of Catholic France. It was not until disunion rose amongst them, till puffed up with success they despised the counsel of their spiritual guides, till luxury and corruption supplanted piety and abstemiousness, till their leaders proudly styled themselves dukes and counts, till Cavallier was outwitted, and Rowland Laporte suffered himself to be betrayed, that their glory departed.

And the hero under whose guidance they achieved their most terrible triumphs—he whom every foe dreaded, and every friend adored,—was not this Cavallier one in whom, if strength of body were wanting, skill in arms might to some degree explain the marvellous way in which he fought? The only verdict which a candid inquirer into his history can return, is, that never was warrior so apparently incapable of the marvels attributed to him. He was but nineteen when his career of glory ended. A peasant, and the son of a peasant, he had received not the slightest education; he knew nothing of the management of any weapon; his stature was low, his frame slender, his countenance simple and almost child-like. Save during his career in the Cevennes, he accomplished no exploit which, in the slightest degree, deserves to be termed striking. And how came it then that, whilst uneducated, and still a boy, he led armies to battle with all the skill of Clive, with more than the valour of Murat? I answer, as he himself would have answered, and as every unprejudiced student of the Camisard war must answer, because he was veritably a "heaven-born general," an instrument controlled by spirits and chosen of God. While he listened to the voices of his guides he was invincible. When he came to rely on his own strength he fell.

In common with many of his followers Cavallier was clairvoyant. Once, at a place between Nair and La Cour de Creviez, he started as from a dream, and cried that he had seen Marshal Montrevel at Allez, who gave to a messenger, to carry to Nismes, letters containing important plans against the Camisards. He described the dress and features of the courier, the colour of his horse, and the numbers and appearance of the escort which attended him. "Ride full speed," said he, "and you will encounter them at the ford of the Gardon." At once a number of Camisards sprang to the saddle, and the messenger was captured at the place indicated. His appearance and surroundings were as Cavallier had seen them in his vision. The letters found upon him contained a complete exposition of Montrevel's plans. These the Cevennois could now take steps to baffle.

But the most wondrous manifestation recorded of the Camisards is the well-attested power which some among them possessed of resisting the action of fire. I select as an instance the ordeal undergone at Serignan, by a medium named Clary, in the presence of Colonel Cavallier and many spectators, some time in August, 1708. Whilst entranced, he was commanded by his guides to place himself in the midst of a large fire. A spot was selected. Around rose a natural amphitheatre of low hills, where the crowds assembled could arrange themselves to behold the event. A large pile of dry branches having been collected, Clary placed himself upon it. The pyre was kindled; the flames speedily shot up above the head of the apparent martyr, and he stood enwrapped with fire. In this position he remained until all the wood was consumed. When the last flicker had died away, he walked forth unhurt. All rushed to congratulate him on the wonderful justification of his faith. "I was one of the first to embrace him," writes an eye-witness; "his white blouse was not in the least injured by the action of the fire. I examined his hair, and it was not singed." Having satisfied themselves that Clary was wholly unscathed, the Camisards around burst forth into a Huguenot version of the hundred and fourth Psalm:—

> "Bénis le Seigneur, O mon âme!
> Seigneur! maître des dieux, roi de l'éternité,
> Sur ton trone éclatant, ceint d'un manteau de flamme,
> Tu règnes, couronne de gloire et de beauté!"

In 1704-5, came the fall of the Camisards. Marshal Villars, some years later the antagonist of Marlborough, was dispatched to cope with Laporte and Cavallier. After the defeat of Blenheim the presence of the troops hitherto employed against the Cevennois had become imperatively necessary outside France. Fortune favoured the arts of the new royalist commander. He induced Cavallier to appoint a meeting at Nismes, and gave hostages for the safety of the young hero. The conference duly came off. The marshal exerted his utmost subtlety. In presence of the dangers menacing France, it was time that this fratricidal war should cease. The king had empowered him to offer liberty of conscience to the brave Cevennois. His majesty desired, moreover, to form of them a regiment for service against the English. Who was so fit to be the commander of this battalion as the hero Cavallier, whose sword had a hundred times led the way to victory, whose name was famous from Lisbon to Vienna? Cavallier listened and wavered. He demanded other privileges; more certain guarantees. Villars responded that, by a gentleman and loyal subject the word of a king was always accounted sufficient guarantee. Besides, his majesty's goodness was infinite. He had expressed himself willing that the Cevennois should pray in their own fashion, but not that they should rebuild their churches. Could Colonel Cavallier doubt, however, but that, when Louis the Great found his brave Protestant subjects ready to march against Marlborough and Eugene, he would accord them whatsoever privileges they desired?

Laporte and the spirit-guides of Cavallier were alike absent. The weak youth yielded. He signed the contract binding the Camisards to lay down arms, and departed to summon to other fields of glory the heroic few who had so long followed him as a deliverer sent of God. A roar of execration greeted his statement of the treaty. He announced that liberty of conscience was henceforth to be granted. At once Laporte started forward. "What liberty?" cried the indignant chief. "No! unless the Camisards have liberty to worship God, not in deserts and caverns only, but in their own churches, with all the rights and guarantees of citizens, they will live and die with arms in their hands."

The rage of the Camisards grew frantic. "Traitor!" "Betrayer!" shouted the thousands whom, until now, the voice of Cavallier had stirred like a trumpet, who had again and again followed him cheerfully to apparently certain death. He strove to explain. Fresh clamours instantly drowned his voice. Then Rowland again made himself heard. "Though we cannot agree with our deluded brother," said he, "let us not part in anger." Silently, and for the last time, he embraced his fellow-chief. The hearts of the Camisards melted. They thought of the days when to follow Cavallier was to rush on to victory; when his sword had been as the sword of Azrael, and the charges that he led had scattered armies. With sobs and tears the little host crowded round to bid adieu for ever to its beloved leader. The unfortunate Cavallier seized the moment: "Let all who love me follow me!" he cried. Forty came forth from the ranks, the rest remained with Rowland. The pity of the Camisards was with their former hero, but no longer their obedience.

Cavallier and his melancholy troop sought the camp of Villars. They were instantly sent under guard to Versailles. Thence Louis destined them to a life-long captivity in the fortress of Brisac. On the way thither they escaped, and crossed the frontier in safety.

A few words will relate the subsequent history of the Camisards. Laporte, having become proud, despised the warnings of the spirits, and did what was agreeable in his own sight. He styled himself Duke of the Cevennes, and boasted that the country was his, won by his sword. His guardian angels left him, and with them went victory. Lured into an ambush by a traitor, the unfortunate hero died, fighting to the last. Two subordinate chiefs, Ravenel and Catenat, were burnt alive at Nismes, almost within sight of the battle-field where, two years before, the Camisard patriots had triumphed over the royal forces commanded by the Comte de Broglie.

Cavallier had gone to Holland. There he collected a regiment of Huguenot refugees for service against the French in Spain. The war over, he betook himself to England, and died in 1740, governor of the island of Jersey. It is scarcely necessary to add that he never returned to the Cevennes.

With Laporte and Cavallier departed the independence of the Cevennes. The army split itself into numerous petty bands, which were overpowered and slaughtered in detail. Some Camisards quitted the country, some were made prisoners and hanged, burnt, or broken slowly on the wheel. For nearly a century the renewed martyrdom of the mountaineers continued.

At length the humanity of irreligion triumphed over the intolerance of the Church. Voltaire, Rousseau, and Diderot arose; to their efforts, and the efforts of their followers, was owing the final cessation of the long agony of the Camisards. Men who disbelieved in Christ procured for their Protestant fellow-countrymen the right of worshipping Christ in peace.

CHAPTER VI

PROTESTANT SPIRITUALISM

If there were heroes before Agamemnon, there were also reformers before Luther. I have instanced the Waldenses as among the oldest separatists from Rome; but in all ages of that Church dissent has abounded. The Manichæans, Pelagians, and Montanists came out from her in early times. In the twelfth century the heresy of the Albigenses shook the Papacy to its foundations, and was only extirpated by means of the Norman swords which Rome called to her aid. A little later arose the minor sect of the Apostolikers and the Beghards. The locale of the first was Italy. Gerhard Segarelli, whose teachings led to this schism, was burnt at a slow fire in the year 1300. His creed seems to have greatly resembled that of the Waldenses. It was founded on the gospel in its purity, and was well worthy of commendation. The doctrines of the Beghards, on the contrary, were derived from corruptions of the Scriptures worse than any indulged in by Rome herself. They accepted the assertion of St. Paul, that those who are in Christ are no longer under the law, as a license for all imaginable crime and vice. After spreading through most of the kingdoms of Germany and committing everywhere the wildest orgies, an unsparing persecution finally exterminated them. To uncontrolled license succeeded maniacal penances. Whilst the Beghards were fiercely sinning, and the Catholic Church was as fiercely persecuting them, occurred the unique pestilence of 1348; the most awful sickness which ever devastated earth. The great agony by which Europe was convulsed gave birth to the sect of the Flagellants. They proclaimed that the Almighty was wroth with the wickedness of man, and that the Black Death was the awful token of his displeasure. Only unceasing prayer, and mortifications exceeding the mortifications of an anchorite, could induce Him to arrest the hand of the destroyer. They stripped themselves to the waist, they passed from city to city lashing themselves with cords twisted with wire. Many expired under the severity of the discipline. At length the Vatican directed all its powers against the new mania. The leaders were seized and burnt, their followers were dispersed by main force. Again, however, they re-assembled, and penetrated even into Spain and Italy, despite all the severity of the Inquisition. Scourging themselves until the blood streamed down, and chanting wildly the "Dies iræ," they created everywhere an extraordinary excitement. Princes, and even prelates, were to be found in their ranks. It was not until 1481 that the Flagellant mania ended. It had lasted one hundred and thirty-two years.

In 1374 appeared the Dancers. They outdid in wildness even the actions of the Flagellants. Half-naked, and crowned with garlands, they danced madly through the great cities of Germany and the Netherlands. They considered themselves inspired by angels; the Church reviled them as under the influence of demons. Although infinite licentiousness resulted from their own orgies, the Dancers professed extreme disgust for the corruptions of the Papacy. They cried loudly for a new Church; they plundered monasteries and slew priests. Exorcism having been tried in vain, the aid of the secular power was invoked. With much slaughter the heretical mania was, about the year 1418, finally put down.

Among the noblest precursors of the Reformation were the Lollards. Their leader, Wickliffe, was assuredly infinitely superior to Calvin and Knox, and will scarcely suffer even by comparison with Luther or Zwinglius. The imperfect accounts of his career remaining to us do not permit of any very confident statements regarding his possession of spiritual gifts. That he deemed himself a prophet sent of God to rebuke the corruptions of the Church is certain. That he raised against himself a storm yet more terrible than that which sent Savonarola to the stake, is also clear. Whether he was throughout life supported in his task by communion with spirits is unknown. It may, however, be asserted with considerable confidence that sufficient evidence remains to indicate his having been on more than one occasion delivered from imminent danger by power not of earth.

The central figure of Protestantism is undoubtedly Luther. Like a lighthouse fixed unshakably on some mighty rock, the giant Saxon towers up from the troubled sea of the sixteenth century. Against that solid form the hurricane of religious fury struck in vain; solitary, but unconquerable, he continued to hold stoutly forth amid the tempest the light that had been given into his keeping. In himself the only potent enemy of that light was to be found. Sometimes it streamed brightly forth, lighting up with a radiance as of noonday the tossing waters around. Sometimes it seemed ready to expire. Prejudices dimmed it; passions caused it to dicker unsteadily to and fro; the lamp, at one time clear as a diamond, and fed with the purest oil, would a little later appear untrimmed, almost empty, and choked with murky vapours. But, in darkness or in day, Luther could not be other than great. The lighthouse, rising like a pillar of fire from the midst of the raging waves, is an object at once noble and useful. The same lighthouse left with but a feeble spark to indicate whence that blaze once issued which had directed the course of so many ships, is an object no longer serviceable, indeed, but still stately. What was a pillar of flame has become a pillar of cloud. The glory has departed, but the possibility of that glory is yet there.

Perhaps the justest comparison of Luther's character would be to a statue, magnificent indeed, but unfinished. The nobility of the features which the master's hand has carefully elaborated makes us regret the more the crudity of those parts on which the chisel seems scarcely to have been employed. We see magnificence and deformity side by side.

The Luther at one moment exalted almost to the level of Socrates, appears at another sunk to an equality with some familiar of the Inquisition. It is as though the statue I have compared him to should contain some strokes more than worthy of Phidias, and others which would disgrace the vilest bungler that ever hacked marble. Can we recognise the Reformer who declared it to be against the will of the Holy Ghost to burn heretic, in the bigot who believed that the hero Zwinglius, although he had sealed with his blood his attachment to the Protestant faith, was damned for all eternity, simply because he differed in a single point from the Wittenberg idea of Scripture? Was the Luther who "could do nothing against conscience" the Luther who, because Erasmus claimed for himself that same liberty of conscience, cried furiously, "Erasmus of Rotterdam is the vilest miscreant that ever disgraced the earth" Whenever I pray, I pray for a curse upon Erasmus"?

He believed that he was justified in rejecting the Epistle of James. In such rejection there was nothing blamable. The gentle teachings of James accorded ill with the austerity of the Lutheran scheme of salvation, and the great Reformer rejected them. "I hold," said he, "that this epistle is of none authority." As he dealt with James, so he dealt with other scriptural writers. He admitted that it is absurd to regard the Bible as altogether infallible. "These good and true teachers and searchers," says he, in speaking of the prophets, "fell sometimes upon hay and straw, sometimes on pure gold and precious stones." He took, therefore, from the Scriptures whatever accorded with his own belief, and denounced the rest as error, or hastily slurred it over. The Christ he worshipped was not the Christ of the four Gospels, but the Christ of Paul. Yet the liberty he claimed for himself he denied to others. All who agreed with him he welcomed with hearty geniality. His opponents he cursed and damned with the fury of Athanasius or Doctor Slop.

He declared it blasphemy to assert that faith without works is dead. He declared that those who do not believe Christ to be literally present in the Eucharist, who do not receive the bread as his body and the wine as his blood, deny Him, and bring upon themselves the doom, "Depart, ye cursed, into everlasting fire." He was unwilling that heretics should be burnt. He saw, however, no objection to their being banished. He denounced the policy of the Church of Rome in forbidding the exercise of private judgment. He raged with equal fury against those "who would speculate into God's works with their devilish whys and wherefores." He believed in the omnipotence of God, and in the possibility of communion with "just souls made perfect;" yet he reviled every spirit that visited him as a devil. He was just when not misled by bigotry, and liberal when no prejudice impelled him to be otherwise. In short, like other men, he was "fearfully and wonderfully made"—a whirlpool of error and truth, of good and evil, in which, however, the good decidedly predominated.

What was the secret of his wonderful success? I think it to have been that the spirits who surrounded him forced him to do their work in spite of himself. He had a warm and impressionable nature, indomitable courage, and fiery eloquence. His faults, like his virtues, were those of a high soul. He was not mean or cruel. He was simply domineering, hot tempered, and somewhat despotic and harsh. The spirits whose servant he was could not eradicate his vices; they were forced to content themselves with turning his virtues to the best account. They kindled a flame in his breast that no persecution could quench; they thrust into his hand the standard of reform, and clothed him with the armour of faith. Thus equipped, they sent him forth to do manful battle against the corrupt domination of Rome. Throughout that long conflict they were at his side. When he fainted they inspired him; when he was surrounded by dangers they raised him up friends. No wonder that his deeds were great. No wonder that his words were, as Longfellow has described them, "half-battles for the free."

He treated these spiritual guides scurvily enough. The thoughts with which they inspired him he accepted as from God. If, however, a spirit contrived to make its presence more directly manifest, it was at once objurgated as a fiend. The devil was never absent from Luther's thoughts. As a medium he could not avoid receiving constant and striking tokens of the nearness of the spirit-world. Yet he detested those tokens. He had directed all the rude energy of his rhetoric against the shams miracles of the Catholic Church. He had taught that signs and wonders were no longer permitted; how was he to reconcile this theory with their constant occurrence to himself? Luther's mode of escape was by making a scapegoat of Satan. The devil, he maintained, was, as a miracle-worker, more powerful than God. Good spirits could no longer visit earth; bad ones, however, ranged up and down it at their will. By such he supposed himself continually tormented. Whether the unearthly visitor tempted him to evil or exhorted him to good, it was equally a waif from the bottomless pit. On a certain Good Friday, whilst, he was in fervent prayer, there appeared to him in his chamber a bright vision of Christ. Luther was, at the very moment of the apparition, ecstatically dwelling, he tells us, on the inestimable benefits of the Saviour's death. Did he not welcome the spectacle vouchsafed him with tears of joy? Far from it. "At first sight," says he, "I thought it had been some celestial vision. Presently I reflected that it must needs be an illusion and juggling of the devil, wherefore I spoke to the vision thus: 'Avoid thee, confounded devil!' whereon the image vanished, clearly showing whence it came."

At Wartburg he hurled his inkstand at a demon's head, who had visited him with the view of interrupting his translation of the Scriptures. In the same castle some spirits disturbed in his chamber two bags of nuts, and made noises on the stairs when no one in the flesh could have been there. Luther vengefully set all this down to the credit side of his account with Satan. He tells us that whilst he was in bed his Satanic Majesty often visited him. He would make noises as of some one walking. He would hurl things about the room; he would strike at the Reformer as if with a human hand. These things exactly accord with the pranks of undeveloped spirits, as witnessed in our own day, but they can hardly be considered in keeping with the character of that

> "Chief,
> Who led th' embattled seraphim to war."

Yet, whist attributing to Satan such petty practical jokes, Luther had the highest respect for the vigour of his intellect. "He is not, it is true, exactly a doctor who has taken his degrees, but, for all that, he is very learned and expert. He has not been carrying on his business these thousands of years for nothing." Again, "If the devil cannot come and strangle men with his claws, he can do so, at all events, with his pressing arguments." He relates how Satan vanquished him in an argument about the Practice of celebrating mass privately. Luther had been in the habit of doing so for nearly fifteen years. One night a spirit came to him. The great Reformer at once hailed it as the Prince of Evil. An argument commenced regarding the sacrament of the Lord's Supper—a strange subject, one would think, for Satan to discuss. The spirit maintained that the wafer and wine were not really converted into the body and blood of Christ. It rebuked Luther for his foolish belief that such a change could take place; it rebuked him also for celebrating alone, and in private, a rite meant to be public, and partaken of by the whole congregation. It quoted numerous apposite passages of Scripture. Luther became convinced. He acknowledged humbly that Satan was in the right, and a sounder Christian than himself with regard to private masses. From that day he never again celebrated one. His pride was not so stubborn that he would refuse to serve God because the devil bade him. It is strange that such a mind should have been so completely the victim of a maniacal delusion regarding the omnipotence of evil. Once confronted with the question of spirit-communion, Luther's powers of reasoning deserted him. He saw nothing unlikely in Satan's seeking to do the work of God. He forgot that Christ had said, "Every tree is known by its fruits." For all spiritual phenomena he had the stereotyped verdict, "Ye are of your father, the devil."

It is, however, with regret that the mind turns from Luther to Calvin. The faults of the great Saxon were neither few nor small. He wanted courtesy, charity, and patience, and his admirers can afford to admit that he wanted them. The errors that stain his career were but those of a Titan who, after long confinement in darkness, has beaten for himself a way through the wall of his dungeon, and reels to and fro, blinded with excess of light. History, placing in the one scale his vices and mistakes, and in the other his virtues and mighty deeds, sees the former balance fly rapidly upward, and cries, "This was a man." Calvin, on the contrary, resembled an iceberg. His single virtue was consistency. He shrank from no consequence, however horrible, to which his doctrines logically led. Predestination being accepted, God becomes the author of evil. Calvin admits that He does. All sin occurs by the will of the Deity. Satan can accomplish nothing without that will. All the horrors detailed in the Old Testament were the work of God. It is absurd to pronounce Him a loving father; the human race are, with few exceptions, hated by their creator. Unborn myriads, before they have accomplished a single good or evil action, are predestined to eternal misery. Repentance for sin is useless; human righteousness is a filthy rag. The most splendid deeds of humanity are in themselves but wickedness. Unsanctified workers of good deeds merit no reward, but rather punishment. But man cannot of himself become sanctified. God has reserved Paradise for a few, who were chosen by Him before the creation of the world; all others are doomed to damnation. "There is more joy in heaven," said Christ, "over one sinner that repenteth, than over ninety-and-nine just persons that need no repentance." "Man," said Calvin, "is in his whole nature odious and abominable to God. He finds nothing in men which can incite Him to bless them. Grace delivers from the curse and wrath of God a few, but leaves the world to its destruction. I stop not to notice those fanatics who pretend that grace is offered equally to all." Could such a teacher profit earth?

He lay like an incubus on Geneva. Studying the details of his tyranny, one feels that life would have been more endurable under a Henry VIII. or a Domitian. Their cruelties reached only a few. Calvin's iron rigour pressed equally on all. His code of laws is the strangest earth ever knew; it seems sometimes inspired by Puck, sometimes by Moloch. The fantastic and the horrible are blended in a manner at once ludicrous and painful. One law was directed against sumptuousness in dress: slashed breeches were forbidden; it was made illegal to fasten nosegays with gold cord; brides were no longer to adorn themselves with gay robes and floating tresses. Wedding revelry was prohibited not more than a single course of meat could be set on the table at a marriage-dinner, and this was to be followed by, at the most, one tart. The fashion in which hair was to be cut was prescribed. A bonfire was made of all the romances and playing cards in the city. Sunday became the only holiday.

Every indiscretion was a criminal offence. A young girl received a severe whipping for singing to a psalm-tune in church the words of a song. A man was banished from the city for remarking, when an ass brayed, that "he sang a pretty psalm." But the worst remains behind. A law was passed condemning children who disobeyed or cursed their parents to the punishment of death. In 1568 a girl who had struck her mother was beheaded; at another time a boy, for merely threatening to strike a parent, received sentence of death. And this infernal legislation there are, even at the present day, partisans of Calvin left to praise! They find "great beauty in the earnestness with which parental authority was defended." Not so did the people of Geneva. As speedily as might be after his death they reversed the Reformer's laws. No reverence was paid to his memory; no statue has ever been erected in his honour; a plain stone with the letters I. C. marks his grave. In Geneva at the present day few names are more detested.

He had spiritual gifts. On December 19th, 1562, a vision occurred to him of the great battle between the Guisians and the Protestants then raging not far from Paris. Besides being clairvoyant he had the prophetic faculty, and predicted many events which duly came to pass. But a spiritualist can feel little desire to claim the murderer of Servetus as a useful ally. His name is the name of one whose nature was as adamant. We can hardly imagine Calvin ever to have smiled, unless it were when the news came that at length the author of the "Restitutio Christianismi" was in his power. I think of that little mount with the heap of green oak-wood, of the kindled fagots, of the long agony, lasting some say almost two hours, and I find the memory of the remorseless bigot through whom Servetus died, as provocative of indignation as one can well find the memory of a man who departed from earth some three hundred years since. Had his doctrines died with him how infinitely happier and better the world would be at the present day!

I could wish, did the limits of my task permit, to trace out the spiritual in the lives of other great Reformers. The scholarly Erasmus, the gentle Melancthon, Knox, the patriot and iconoclast, who knew neither the fear of man nor the courtesy due to woman, the meek Hamilton, the headlong Zisca, Zwinglius, the hero and the martyr, whom the utmost fury of Rome could not daunt, nor the churlish injustice of Luther render intolerant; from the lives of all these examples of spirit-communion might be drawn. I pause a moment to do homage to the last great man. A nobler nature than that of Zwinglius never consecrated earth. Less towering than the soul of Luther, his soul was far freer from error. There are few more beautiful aspirations than that Confession of Faith in which he anticipates "the future assembly of all the saintly, the heroic, the faithful, and the virtuous," where the patriarchs of Israel shall mingle with the sages of Greece, and the upright and holy of all creeds and every era dwell for ever in the presence of their God. Honour to the truest Christian of the sixteenth century! On the red field of Cappel died a man entitled to the reverence of every thinker who believes that the love of God is over all his children. The name of Ulrich Zwinglius may well serve for a foil to that of Calvin. As in battle his place was before the ranks of Zurich, so in liberality he was before all the theologians of his time. There are few divines, even in the present day, who have attained that elevated platform of thought which was the standpoint of the gallant Switzer.

In Britain the Reformation had its share of miracle. Certain instances may be found in McCrie's "Life of Knox." Among the most striking of these is the prophecy of the Scottish apostle Wishart. Led to the stake by the order of Cardinal Beatoun, he fixed his eyes on the turret-window from which that prelate watched the tragical scene. The fire was lighted, and the powder fastened to the martyr's body blew up. Perceiving him to be still alive, the captain of the castle drew near and bade him be of good heart. Wishart answered, "This flame hath reached to my body, yet it hath not daunted my spirit; but he who from yonder place beholdeth me with such pride shall within a few days lie in the same as ignominiously as he is now seen proudly to rest himself." A week or two later the castle was stormed by a band of Protestant conspirators, and the body of the cardinal suspended from that very window whence he had witnessed the martyrdom of Wishart.

Numerous spiritual manifestations occurred in England and Scotland during the sixteenth and seventeenth centuries. They were almost without exception attributed to the agency of the devil. The Protestantism of the two countries had adopted in their entirety Luther's ideas of the cessation of miracles from God, and the increase of miracles from Satan. Hideous laws were passed against witchcraft. The tragedies of the continent were re-enacted on a smaller scale, and for a briefer period. To the burnings and hangings of Britain and the American Colonies much of what I have written in a former chapter will apply. These Protestant persecutions essentially resembled the chief shadow of Catholic Spiritualism. On the basis of certain startling facts the wildest theories were reared. A kind of insane panic seized the nation. The various Protestant Churches, like the Catholic Church, found it politic to encourage that panic. A drivelling pedant, with whom witchcraft was as much an article of faith as the mission of Christ, and for whose folly no lie was too absurd, united the crowns of Elizabeth and Bruce. Under his patronage murder went merrily on. Christ had expelled demons by virtue of the powers which he possessed. King James determined to expel them by virtue of the tar-barrel and the stake. The result is well known. Fearful tragedies were enacted in every part of the island. To be old, frail, and attached to some domestic pet such as a cat or dog, was sufficient justification for a death warrant. Unfortunate beings who understood their situation just well enough to know that they were about to be burned alive, underwent solemn trials before the highest judicial dignitaries of the realm, and were then as solemnly conducted to execution. Students who, in Macaulay's phrase, "have the heart to go through the sickening details," will find in certain of the phenomena described at these trials a striking similarity to spiritual phenomena of the present day. There are clairvoyance, trance-speaking, the moving of heavy articles by unseen means, the levitation of human bodies, apparitions of spirit-hands and spirit-forms, raps, lights, voices, &c. With these are mingled narratives of the wildest and most incredible kind. The judicial science of the age was unable to distinguish between the one and the other, and accepted both. The custom of the present day is to carefully keep out of sight the immense weight of evidence by which certain of the occurrences were attested, and to bring prominently forward whatever is horrible or absurd. Of these latter the supply is plentiful. The senility of most of the accused, the stupid bigotry of the accusers, the prejudices of the judges, the passions of the mob, the villanies of the professed hunters for witchcraft, the detestable cruelty of the judicial murders enacted; such things furnish unequalled themes for ridicule and invective. The folly of much of the evidence may be admitted. It is also certain that some of the phenomena on which great stress was laid were attributable to what are now known as "natural causes." Yet when these and other deductions have been made there still remains a respectable residue of occurrences which a spiritualist may with confidence claim as manifestations produced by dwellers in another world.

As was natural, the clergy were the master-spirits of every cruelty perpetrated under the pretence of awarding punishment to servants of Satan. The divines of Scotland, especially, were men after Calvin's own heart. Whether Presbyterian or Episcopal, the sight of a human being dangling on the gallows or writhing at the stake was to them an exquisite delight. The next highest pleasure to the death of a witch was her torture. To bind the wretched sufferer hand and foot, and, in this condition, drag her through a mill-pond until half dead; to thrust pins up to the head in her flesh; to whip her through their parishes at the cart's tail, these were the daily amusements of their lives. With even more reluctance than their brethren south of the Tweed did they consent to abandon them. In England the slaughter of supposed sorcerers had almost ceased by the commencement of William III's reign—in Scotland it was scarcely yet at its height. Nor were the black-coated tormentors beyond the Atlantic less expert in their work. One of the most frightful episodes in the history of persecution for witchcraft was that which cast a gloom over Salem in the autumn of 1692. Numbers of supposed wizards and witches were hanged. A wretched patriarch of eighty was crushed to death by means of a board loaded with heavy stones; he lingered for two days in horrible torture before the merciful hand of death released him. And such atrocities as these Puritan divines considered deeds done to the glory of God, and complacently chronicled as worthy of imitation by succeeding ages!

A score of volumes, each larger than the present, would scarcely afford room for full treatment of the iniquities perpetrated under the name of trials for witchcraft. How Hopkins, Cotton Mather, James I., and the Westminster Sanhedrim "damned themselves to everlasting fame," how the vilest of witnesses were believed, what infamous modes of torture were resorted to, how frequently the gibbet was erected and the tar-barrel blazed,—these things it does not fall within my province to treat of. Nor can I afford to fill chapter after chapter with the instances of miraculous phenomena which have occurred in Britain since her revolt from the See of Rome. It will be sufficient that I briefly notice certain strongly attested cases, and draw attention to the Spiritual in the lives of various famous Protestants.

Few readers of Clarendon's noble history will have forgotten the account of the apparition of Buckingham's father shortly before the death of "the Wicked Duke." The spirit manifested himself to a gentleman in no way related to the Buckingham family. He desired this person to visit his son, and to inform him that, if he did not turn from his sins, his career would be cut short by a terrible fate. The selected messenger promised to act as desired, and failed to fulfil his promise. The spirit speedily returned, and upbraided him with his breach of faith. Again he consented to carry out the mission, and again broke his word. The spirit once more appeared, and spoke more angrily than before. This continued for some time; the persecuted medium could obtain no sleep; the menaces of the apparition became terrible. At length the object of its visitations could hold out no longer. He declared solemnly that, if some secret were made known to him, by revealing which he might conquer the ridicule that would probably greet his narrative, he was ready to obey the behest of his visitor. The spirit consented, and made a communication. The medium went next morning to Villiers House. He obtained an audience, and related the whole facts of the case to the duke. Buckingham was astounded, and confessed the secret which formed the credentials of the messenger to be one he had thought known only to God and himself. He exacted a promise of silence. No reform of his life followed, however, and a few months later he fell by the dagger of Felton.

Equally striking is the apparition to Doctor Donne of a double of his living wife, as related by the poet himself. This doppelganger Donne accepted for an indication of his wife's death, but he found on reaching home that his child and not his spouse was dead. There is, moreover, the famous history of Lord Tyrone's visit after death to Lady Beresford, the dame who "wore, for evermore, a covering on her wrist," rendered necessary because of the indelible marks impressed there by the grasp of the spirit. To Lord Lyttelton came, with a menacing face, the departed mother of a young girl whom he had seduced, and announced to him the day and hour of his death. His friends strove in vain to vanquish the deep melancholy which at once seized on the doomed nobleman, and at the appointed time he died. Lady Diana Rich, whilst walking in the garden of Holland House, saw an exact counterpart of herself, and passed away shortly afterwards. At Waltham in Essex a spirit announced to Sir Charles Lee's daughter her approaching death, which took place with the utmost suddenness at the hour indicated. In the reign of William III. a Catholic gentleman named Prendergast gave information to the king which led to the discovery of the Assassination Plot, and the execution of many of the conspirators, among them Sir John Friend. Years later, when Prendergast was fighting under Marlborough, Friend appeared to him, and predicted his death on a certain day. The doomed man made known what had occurred to him.

The appointed day came, and a battle was fought; at its close Prendergast still lived. "What of the ghost now?" said a brother officer. "I shall die to-day, notwithstanding," replied gravely the object of the prophecy. Even as he spoke a shot was dispatched from a French battery which the order to cease firing had not reached, and Prendergast fell dead. A host of other instances might be quoted.

One of the noblest of spiritualists was Bunyan. During his whole career he was the subject of spiritual manifestations. His life was several times miraculously preserved. He heard voices; he saw visions. The world to come was to him as real as the world he lived in. At one time, indeed, it seems to have been brought so close that he became as it were one of its inhabitants. It was then that he wrote "The Pilgrim's Progress." A captive in Bedford gaol, he could explore freely the mysteries of that region where the glory of God's countenance makes eternal day. Spirits were continually at his side. In few of his subsequent writings do we trace any resemblance to the wonderful story of the "Pilgrimage of Christian." The "Holy War," perhaps, affords some traces of the genius which beams so resplendently from every page of Bunyan's masterpiece; but how faint are those traces compared with the marvellous manner and matter of that allegory which tells how Christian hasted to set forth from the City of Destruction; how, looking from the land of Beulah on the Everlasting City, he sickened with desire to taste of its glories; how his soul fainted in the black depths of the River of Death; how, to the sound of celestial music and canopied by the wings of the Shining Ones, he passed with Hopeful through the heavenly gate, and embraced in presence of the angels that Faithful whom the fiery chariot of martyrdom had borne upward from the noise and turmoil of Vanity Fair! The "Pilgrim's Progress" is the most spiritual of works. Never did another author drink in such inspiration from the invisible world. Never again was that inspiration granted in equal measure to Bunyan. He had accomplished his task. Surrendering himself to the service of his Maker, a work had been produced which can be forgotten only when all memory of the English language shall have perished from among men.

A lesser light was George Fox. "This man, the first of the Quakers, and by trade a shoemaker, was one of those," says Carlyle, "to whom under ruder form the divine idea of the universe is pleased to manifest itself, and, across all the hulls of ignorance and earthly degradation, shine forth in unspeakable awfulness, unspeakable beauty, on their souls; who therefore are rightly accounted prophets, God-possessed." Fox's struggles towards the light resembled, in the fine language of Burns, "the blind gropings of Homer's Cyclops round the walls of his cave." It is his fortune to have been always either over-praised or unjustly depreciated. Reasons equally strong may be advanced for revering him as a prophet or reviling him as a madman. Those whose attention has been directed solely to his ignorance, his eccentricities, the strange garb which he adopted, the strange actions which he persisted in, the wild vagaries of his talk, the meaningless absurdity of much that he has written, have turned from the spectacle in disgust, or pointed at him the finger of scorn. Those who have contemplated only the fervour of his religion, the warmth of his heart, the greatness of his fortitude, have claimed for him a place among the foremost of mankind. They alone judge such a man justly who, taking into consideration both the strength and the weakness of his nature, pronounce it one in which the gigantic development of certain qualities renders more striking the dwarfish proportions of others. Fox as an example of heroic fortitude and heroic sincerity, deserves our admiration and respect. Fox as a teacher, requires to be followed with ceaseless vigilance and suspicion.

His life is one long record of communion with spirits; His visions were countless. His power of magnetic healing was great. At Twycross he healed a sick person by prayer. At Arnside he restored to a man the use of one of his arms, when it had long been impotent. At Ulverstone he was himself instantly made whole by his spirit-guardians after having been beaten almost to death by a ferocious mob. He frequently proved himself possessed of the power of prophecy. Several years before the occurrence of that great fire which consumed half London it was predicted by Fox. He warned several of his persecutors that judgments would shortly befall them, and in no case did the person so warned escape. These spiritual gifts seem to have continued in unabated vigour down to the period when, full of years, and surrounded by a circle of attached disciples, the apostle of the Quakers died peacefully in his bed.

The rappings in the parsonage of Epworth have been too often described for a detailed history of them to be necessary here. The first lengthy account of these disturbances was published by John Wesley in the *Arminian Magazine*. Had the father of the famous Methodist but thought of questioning the spirits by means of the alphabet a great spiritual movement might have convulsed England in the reign of George I. The knockings exactly resembled those of the present day. They gave the same proofs of being governed by an intelligent power. When Mrs. Wesley desired the spirit to refrain from vexing her devotions the knocks instantly ceased. At evening prayers raps were heard everywhere in the room whilst the prayer for the king was being repeated, and the loudest rap attended the "Amen." This circumstance had evident reference to an unfulfilled vow of Mr. Wesley, son. Here is the story in John Wesley's words. "The year before King William died my father observed that my mother did not say Amen to the prayer for the king. She said she could not, for she did not believe the Prince of Orange was king. He vowed he would never cohabit with her till she did. He then took his horse and rode away, nor did she hear anything of him for a twelvemonth. He then came back and lived with her as before, but I fear his vow was not forgotten before God."

Having frightened the daughters of Mr. Wesley the spirit was bidden by him "to cease vexing those children and come to him in his study, who was a man." It readily obeyed. He begged of it, if the spirit of his son Samuel, to give three raps. The knocking at once ceased. Strangely enough no other questions were put. When, however, any of the family stamped with the foot the exact number of noises was repeated. A gentle tapping at the bed-head of the children began at the same hour every night. At length the spirit grew weary of its fruitless efforts. Towards the end of its endeavours to communicate the raps and other noises were constant. Mr. Wesley was advised to quit the house. He steadily refused. Suddenly all disturbance ceased. "Old Jeffery," as the children named the invisible knocker, had discovered that the vicar's mind was not of a calibre to comprehend his system of spirit-telegraphy. He therefore retired in disgust.

Spiritual gifts were common to John Wesley and the other founders of Methodism—Whitefield, and Fletcher of Madeley. Wesley healed numerous sick persons by prayer and the imposition of hands. He records the instantaneous cure of a woman named Mary Special of cancer in both breasts. His last sermon was a defence and advocacy of Spiritualism. To those who, like many in our own day, cried, "Cui bono?" Wesley makes answer, "If but one account of the intercourse of men with spirits be admitted, their (the unbelievers') whole castle in the air falls to the ground. I know no reason, therefore, why we should suffer this weapon to be wrested out of our hands."

Here this chapter must close. I have passed in review various of the lights of the Reformation in Germany and England; the mighty Luther, the noble Zwinglius, Calvin, with his hateful inhumanity, the stern Knox, the fervent Wishart. I have shown that the spiritual phenomena so common in Catholic ages have occurred with equal frequency in Protestant times and lands. The simple difference is, that the one Church encourages and the other represses them. When Protestantism succeeds in casting out the demon of unbelief that has at present full possession of her various sects she will for the first time be able to receive and comprehend the teachings of Christ. The credulity which, two centuries ago, ascribed all spiritual phenomena to the devil, was bad. The materialism which at the present day denies that the dead can return is still worse. We may bear with equanimity the retirement of his Satanic Majesty into the background: Lucifer's deposition will cause few any deep concern. But a Church which denies the possibility of communion between the departed and those yet on earth simply prepares the way for the triumph of infidelity. The fruit of her doctrines, as the present state of the public mind in England and Germany amply testifies, is a widespread disbelief in a hereafter and an open denial of God.

Chapter VII

The Spiritualism of Certain Great Seers

"There is a small market-town in the Upper Lusatia called Old Seidenburg, distant from Gorlitz about a mile and a half, in which lived a man whose name was Jacob, and his wife's name was Ursula. People they were of the poorest sort, yet of sober and honest behaviour. In the year 1575 they had a son whom they called Jacob. This was the divinely illuminated Jacob Behmen; the Teutonic philosopher whom God raised up to show the ground of the mystery of nature and grace, and open the wonders of His wisdom."

Such is the enthusiastic language which the biographer of Behmen holds towards the object of his idolatry. If Jacob were "raised up to expound the mysteries of nature and grace," he succeeded but ill in his task. Far from casting light on the subject, he wrapped it in deeper gloom. Yet he was certainly a great man. He seems like a blind giant pressing eagerly towards some mark which his affliction of darkness forbids him to discover, and stumbling over every obstacle that lies in his path. His works are as it were the misty nebula; of that to which Swedenborg afterwards gave shape and consistence. They found anciently many admirers. Charles I. praised them; George Fox "read and commended them;" extracts from them were discovered amongst the MSS. of Isaac Newton. The Rev. William Law, author of the "Serious Call," was a zealous disciple of Behmen. But the deformed Titan has had his day. Few are to be found in the present age willing to wander in the misty region of Jacob's spiritual experience—his signs, his teachings, and his dreams.

Sixty-four years after the death of Behmen was born a truer and a greater prophet. Emanuel Swedenborg, who saw the light in 1688, prepared the way for a revolution of the popular idea regarding the future home of man which is still being silently accomplished. He was perhaps the mightiest seer of modern times. During twenty-eight years the clearness of his spiritual vision was such that he beheld constantly the scenes and the beings of another world. He astonished mankind by describing that world as having an intimate resemblance to our own. Its inhabitants he found employed in a

> "Better business
> Than loafing around the throne."

The golden harps were invisible, and the palm-branches had retired into infinite space. For beatified idleness there was spiritual industry; and for eternal stagnation, endless progress. Futurity was peopled as earth is peopled. There were still men and women, and these men and women retained the aspirations, the joys, the sorrows, the affections of humanity. The just were busy in the service of good, the wicked in the service of evil. The high, while teaching the low, continued themselves to soar into regions of a grandeur more and more supreme; and the low panted upward in their footsteps. Where yesterday was Socrates, to-day stood Aristophanes. Galileo, resting for an instant on the summit to which he had just attained, might see at the foot of the mountain some one of his ancient persecutors painfully commencing the ascent. There was nothing of the selfish strife of earth. No false prophet preached the doctrine of the "survival of the fittest." Man learned at length that his destiny was to ascend, and that eternity was given him for the accomplishment of that destiny. Sin was recognised as a disease, and suffering as the remedy of that disease. Progress was light; stagnation was darkness; every good deed accomplished, every bad passion trampled under foot, brought the soul a degree nearer to God. Those children alone knew true happiness who did constantly the work of the Father.

Such are the teachings which have by degrees become the substance of modern thought. They continue more and more to permeate society. The revelations of modern spiritualism are at one with the doctrines of Swedenborg. The influence of the Swedish seer on the mind of man is not to be judged of by the outer and more palpable tokens of that influence. It is by such things that the vulgar judge. The material portion of the world reverence only heroes as material as themselves. Had a creature of this sort been asked a hundred years ago to decide between the relative claims to greatness of Swedenborg and Frederic II. of Prussia, with what derision would he have dismissed the pretensions of the former! Was not the name of Frederic famous throughout the civilised world? Was he not the foremost soldier of his age? Had not he resisted successfully the combined efforts of France, Austria, Russia, Saxony, and Sweden? He was dreaded and admired in every court of Europe, from that of St. Petersburg to that of Lisbon. Portraits of the potentate of Berlin were to be found in a thousand towns and cities. Statues rose in his honour. The pens of eminent writers were employed to canonise or defame him. Could any name be more secure of immortality? Could any lot be more enviable?—And Swedenborg? A poor fool who saw visions and dreamed dreams.

Yet the prophet is likely to be mentioned with reverence when the conqueror is forgotten. The work of the one is ended, that of the other has but just commenced. What does earth owe to Frederic? A series of desolating wars, as causeless as dreadful. What does his history teach us? That great qualities and great vices may be found united in a single mind; that it is possible for a tyrant also to be a hero; that a crowned robber may hold so gallantly to the booty he has snatched as to render useless the efforts of half-a-dozen of his neighbours to recover it. His example is that of successful wickedness. His efforts were directed to the hindering of progress, and the making it law among men

"That they should take who have the power,
And they should keep who can."

Fortunately the confusion created by those efforts has long spent itself. Treaders in Frederic's footsteps have arisen; even as he himself trod in the footsteps of Alexander and Caesar; of Henry V. of England, and Louis XIV. of France. But of Frederic himself there remain only the name and the example. The one has lost its interest; the other we could well spare. Earth has recovered from the shock of the War of the Pragmatic Sanction, and the greater shock of the War of the Seven Years. None are left who fought at Rosbach. Every trace of the horrible carnage enacted there has vanished from the fields of Leuthen and Kunersdorf. A century ago Europe had an enthralling interest in such events. The thrones of kings, the lives of tens of thousands of their subjects, the boundaries of nations, were involved in the fate of Frederic and of Prussia. But that interest is extinguished. The volcano has spent its rage. We learn with equal indifference that at Fontenoy the French were commanded by a tactician and at Rosbach by a dunce. Even in Germany the events of the Seven Years are in themselves no longer productive of joy or grief. No Russian army threatens Berlin. No Austrian host is levying contributions. These things were the miseries of a far-past day. To the Prussian of the present age they are "the shadow of a shade."

The difference then between Frederic and Swedenborg is the difference between a body and a soul. The one is tangible, but temporal; the other intangible, but eternal. The warrior for a brief space influenced matter; the seer continues eternally to influence mind. What the multitude consider the necessary insignia of power may, indeed, be wanting in his case. No eloquent pens and tongues have celebrated his praise. No mighty sect reverences him as its founder. Such a reverence would have been repulsive to the nature of Swedenborg. His teachings were for all; not for a few. He made no attempts to collect followers. He desired no dictatorship over human minds. His mission was simply with his whole soul and strength to proclaim the truth. Having done so he left that truth to fight her own way, secure that "the eternal years of God are hers." Those, then, who base their judgment of a man solely on externals will pronounce that Swedenborg has never greatly influenced humanity, and is now almost forgotten. Those who look deeper will perceive everywhere tokens of his power. The most eloquent divines tincture their sermons with Swedenborgianism. The greatest writers, both in poetry and prose, preach it in a different fashion. He has, as Macaulay says of Bacon, "moved the minds who have moved the world." To Swedenborg is it in great measure owing that the old unnatural heaven, the old revolting hell, have, at the present day, all but vanished into air.

The favourable testimony of an enemy is always of more weight than the favourable testimony of a friend. I select therefore from the numerous narratives respecting the proofs given by Swedenborg of his spiritual powers, that of Immanuel Kant. It is in the form of a letter to a certain Fräulein von Knobloch:—

"In order, most gracious Fräulein, to give you a few evidences of what the whole living public are witnesses of, and which the gentleman who sends them to me has carefully verified on the spot, allow me to lay before you the two following incidents:

"Madame Harteville, the widow of the Dutch envoy in Stockholm, some time after the death of her husband, received a demand from the goldsmith, Croon, for payment for a silver service which her husband had ordered from him. The widow was confidently persuaded that her husband had been much too orderly to allow this debt to remain unpaid; but she could discover no receipt. In this trouble, and since the amount was considerable, she begged Baron Swedenborg to give her a call. After some apologies she ventured to say to him that if he had the extraordinary gift, as all men affirmed, of conversing with departed souls, she hoped that he would have the goodness to inquire of her husband how it stood with the demand for the silver service. Swedenborg made no difficulty in meeting her wishes. Three days after this the lady had a company of friends taking coffee with her; Baron Swedenborg entered, and in his matter-of-fact way informed her that he had spoken with her husband; that the debt had been discharged some months before his death, and that the receipt was in a certain cabinet which she would find in an upper room. The lady replied that this cabinet had been completely emptied, and amongst the whole of the papers this receipt could not be found. Swedenborg said that her husband had described to him that, if they drew forth a drawer on the left side they would see a board, which being pushed aside, they would find a concealed drawer in which was kept his secret correspondence with Holland, and there this receipt would be found. On this representation the lady betook herself, with all the company, to the upper room. The cabinet was opened; they found the secret drawer described, of which she had hitherto known nothing, and in it the required paper, to the intense amazement of all present.

"The following circumstance, however, appears to me to possess the greatest strength of evidence of all these cases, and actually takes away every conceivable issue of doubt.

"In the year 1756, as Baron Swedenborg, towards the end of the month of September, at four o'clock on a Saturday evening, landed in Gottenburg from England, Mr. William Castel invited him to his house with fifteen other persons. About six o'clock in the evening Swedenborg went out and returned shortly to the company, pale and disturbed. He said that at that moment there was a terrible conflagration raging in Stockholm, on the Südermalm, and that the fire was increasing. Gottenburg lies three hundred miles from Stockholm. He was uneasy, and frequently went out. He said that the house of one of his friends, whom he named, was already laid in ashes, and that his own house was in danger. At eight o'clock, after he had again gone out, he said joyfully, 'God be praised! the fire is extinguished, the third door from my very house.' This information occasioned the greatest excitement in the company and throughout the whole city, and the statement was carried to the Governor the same evening. Next morning he sent for Swedenborg, and asked him about the matter. Swedenborg described exactly the conflagration; how it had begun, and the time of its continuance. As the Governor had given attention to the story, it occasioned a still greater commotion throughout the city, where many were in great concern on account of their friends and their property. On Monday evening arrived in Gottenburg a courier who had been dispatched by the merchants of Stockholm during the fire. In the letters brought by him the conflagration was described exactly as Swedenborg had stated it. On the Tuesday morning a royal courier came to the Governor with the account of the fire, of the loss it had occasioned, and of the houses which it had attacked; not in the least differing from the statement made by Swedenborg at the moment of its occurrence, for the fire had been extinguished at eight o'clock.

"Now, what can any one oppose to the credibility of these occurrences? The friend who writes these things to me has not only examined into them in Stockholm, but about two months ago in Gottenburg, where he was well known to the most distinguished families, and where be could completely inform himself from a whole city, in which the short interval from 1756 left the greater part of the eye-witnesses still living. He has at the same time given me an account of the mode in which, according to the assertion of Baron Swedenborg, his ordinary intercourse with other spirits takes place, as well as the idea which he gives of the condition of departed souls."

With feelings of admiration and affection I take my leave of the great Swedish seer. I make no attempt to canonise him as an example of perfect excellence. He had many of the usual failings of humanity. His character was disfigured by strange eccentricities. But, taking him on the whole, he was a Saul who towered head and shoulders above his generation. If any readers of this work have not yet studied the life and writings of Swedenborg, I advise them to do so without delay, secure that, when the pleasurable task is accomplished, they will confess with Thomas Carlyle "that never until then did they comprehend how great a prophet had been among mankind."

The most marked characteristic of Jung-Stilling was his intense and unquenchable faith. He had the strongest confidence in the Providence of God; the most vivid conception of the nearness of another world. His career is one of the few which from the outset to the close are delightful to contemplate. "Let this be thy greatest honour in the world," said his grandfather to him, "that thy forefathers were all men who, though they had nothing under their command out of their house, were, notwithstanding, beloved and honoured by all men." Stilling never forgot the words. He lived and died beloved and honoured by all whose love and honour were worthy to be prized.

From the humbleness of a seat on a tailor's shop-board he struggled through the various grades of merchant's clerk, schoolmaster, and family tutor, till he reached the university, which he entered with the sum of one dollar in his pocket. For years he fought against the deepest poverty. His faith was veritably tried with fire, and proved itself genuine. At times marvellous occurrences sustained it. He commenced his studies, as I have said, with a single rix-dollar for capital. For the whole course a thousand dollars were necessary. Stilling knew not where to raise the fiftieth part of the sum. Yet the anxiety which tormented him did not for an instant cause his trust in God to waver. He met an acquaintance whom he terms Leibmann. "Where," said this last, "do you get money for your studies?" "From God," was Stilling's reply. "I," said Leibmann, "am one of God's stewards," and handed the penniless youth thirty-three dollars. He afterwards sent him a further remittance of three hundred. By these and similar acts of kindness, Stilling was enabled to struggle on until he had obtained his diploma. He then married, and commenced practice as a physician. His capital was five rix-dollars.

The fight was sharp. In the midst of his difficulties he contracted an intimate acquaintance with Goethe, Herder, and others of the leaders of German thought. The first and greatest of these became warmly attached to him. He urged him to write memoirs of his life. Stilling consented, and, in a period of great adversity, accomplished the task. Through the kindly offices of Goethe the work was sold for a hundred and fifteen rix-dollars. It was the turning-point of the author's career. The money lifted him out of his difficulties. The book made him famous.

He was appointed Professor of Agriculture at Rittersberg. In Elberfeld, where he had settled to practise as a physician, he owed eight hundred dollars, and knew not how to defray the debt. Certain of the chief merchants, however, hearing that he intended quitting the town, made him parting presents. He counted the sum thus obtained, and found it eight hundred dollars, neither more nor less. It sufficed exactly, therefore, to satisfy his creditors, and with an empty purse he left the place. A few years later, he became famous for the cure of cataract, and at the same time debt again pressed heavily on him. He was sent for, to perform operations in Switzerland. One thousand six hundred and fifty gulden were paid to him, exactly the amount that he owed. His whole life abounds with such instances of pressing need, and providential supply.

The most famous of his works were written under spiritual dictation. These are "Nostalgia," and "Scenes in the Invisible World." Of the latter we learn that "the state of mind which Stilling experienced whilst labouring at this work is utterly indescribable. His spirit was as if elevated into ethereal regions a feeling of serenity and peace pervaded him, and he enjoyed a felicity which words cannot express. When he began to work ideas glistened past his soul, which animated him so much that he could scarcely write so rapidly as the flow of thought required. This was also the reason why the whole work took quite another form, and the composition quite another tendency, to that which he had proposed at the commencement." Of the "Nostalgia" we are told:— "There was besides another singular phenomenon. In the state between sleeping and waking, the most beautiful and as it were heavenly imagery presented itself to his inward sense. He attempted to delineate it, but found this impossible; with the imagery there was always a feeling connected, compared with which all the joys of sense are as nothing. It was a blissful season!"

The "Nostalgia" was received with enthusiasm. The author found that certain scenes in his work, which he had supposed to be fiction, were actual fact. A great prince wrote, demanding how he had learned the particulars of a certain secret association. Stilling could only reply that the very existence of the association was unknown to him. One day a handsome young man whom he says was the celebrated _____, but leaves his readers to guess the name, entered his apartment. This visitor saluted the author of the "Nostalgia," as his secret superior. Stilling utterly disclaimed the imputed honour. "How then," said the stranger, "did you contrive so accurately to describe the great and venerable brotherhood in the East, to point out our rendezvous in Egypt, in Mount Sinai, in the monastery of Canobin, and under the temple of Jerusalem?" "All fiction," answered Stilling. "Pardon me," cried the other, "that cannot be; the matter is in truth and reality as you have described it; such a thing cannot have come by chance!" And he retired, dissatisfied.

On the 13th of July, 1799, Stilling predicted the death of Lavater. In a letter, that day, to Antistes Hess, of Zurich, he informed him that, whilst writing, he had felt suddenly a deep impression that a violent and bloody end awaited the great Switzer. He desired that this might be communicated to him. Exactly three months later the army of Massena stormed Zurich, and Lavater was shot down at his own door. Other of Stilling's presentiments proved equally unerring. Did space permit, a number of interesting cases might be adduced from his "Pneumatology." But Zschokke, Oberlin, Madame Hauffe, and others, have yet to be noticed, and I am forced to pass on. I do so, citing that noble passage from "Scenes in the Invisible World," which contains so forcible an apology for the author's spiritual faith:— "Whether we are reckoned fools and ignoramuses, or set down as mad fanatics—it is all one. Our Lord and Master himself was pronounced such. Let us go out to Him, and bear his shame."

Zschokke was by birth a German, by adoption a Swiss. He combined the almost irreconcilable attributes of a profound thinker and an energetic man of action. Devoted, during the greater part of his life, to the public service of the Helvetian Republic, his intense patriotism yet allowed him to gratify, so far as opportunity permitted, the equally intense desire which possessed him for knowledge respecting the things of another world. He was himself gifted with a peculiar phase of mediumship. The past experiences of many with whom he conversed were presented to his mind.

"It has happened to me sometimes," says he, "on my first meeting with strangers, that, as I listened silently to their discourse, their former life, or some particular scene in that life, has passed, quite involuntarily and as it were dream-like, before me. During this time I usually feel so absorbed in contemplation of the stranger life that I no longer see clearly the face of the unknown, wherein I undesignedly look; nor distinctly hear the voices of the speakers, which before served in some measure as a commentary to the text of their features. For a long time I held such visions as delusions of the fancy; the more so that they showed me even the dress and motions of the actors, the rooms, furniture, and other accessories. By way of test I once, in a familiar family circle at Kirchberg, related the secret history of a seamstress who had just left the room and the house. I had never seen her before in my life. People were astonished, and laughed; but were not to be persuaded that I did not previously know the relations of which I spoke; for what I had uttered was the *literal* truth. On my part I was no less astonished that my dream-pictures were confirmed by the reality. I became more attentive to the subject, and when propriety admitted it, I would relate to those whose life thus passed before me the subject of my vision, that I might thereby obtain confirmation or refutation of it. It was invariably ratified, not without consternation on their part. 'What demon inspires you? Must I again believe in possession?' exclaimed the spiritual Johann von Riga, when, in the first hour of our acquaintance, I related his past life to him. We speculated long on the enigma, but even his penetration could not solve it. I myself had less confidence than any one in this mental jugglery. As often as I revealed my visionary gifts to any new person I regularly expected to hear the answer, 'It was not so.' I felt a secret shudder when my auditors replied that it was true, or when their astonishment betrayed my accuracy before I asked. I will mention one example which pre-eminently astounded me. One fair day, in the City of Waldshut, I entered the Vine Inn in company with two young student foresters. We supped with a numerous company at the table d'ôte, where the guests were making very merry with the peculiarities and eccentricities of the Swiss; with Mesmer's magnetism, Lavater's physiognomy, &c. One of my companions, whose national pride was wounded by their mockery, begged me to make some reply, particularly to a handsome young man who sat opposite to me, and who allowed himself extraordinary license. This man's former life was at that moment presented to my mind. I turned to him and asked whether he would answer me candidly if I related to him some of the most secret passages of his life; I knowing as little of him personally as he did of me? That would be going, a little further, I thought, than the physiognomy of Lavater. He promised, if I were correct in my information, to admit it frankly. I then related what my vision had shown me, and the whole company were made acquainted with the private history of the young merchant, his school years, his youthful errors, and lastly, with a fault committed in reference to the strong-box of his principal. I described to him the uninhabited room with whitened walls, where to the right of the brown door, on a table, stood a black money-box, &c. A dead silence prevailed during the whole narrative, which I alone occasionally interrupted by inquiring whether I spoke the truth? The startled young man confirmed every particular, and even, what I had scarcely expected, the last mentioned. Touched by his candour, I shook hands with him over the table and said no more."

On the 22nd of February, 1862, passed from earth Dr. Justinius Kerner. Distinguished both as a physician and a poet, he interests us yet more on account of his patient, Madame Hauffe, widely known as "the Seeress of Prevorst." Kerner's account of this extraordinary case was published in 1829, and went through three editions. Pseudo-scientists, as was natural, received it with much easy derision. Observers more worthy of the name, who had taken the trouble to inquire into the facts of the case, confirmed all that the doctor had stated. Among these last were such men as Kant, Schubert, Eschenmayer, Görres, and Werner. They, without exception, pronounced Madame Hauffe a clairvoyante of the highest order, "who lived more in the spiritual world than in the physical." Her soul was retained in its casket by the frailest of threads.

She was twenty-five when she came under the care of Kerner, and twenty-eight when she passed from earth. Even while yet a child she proved herself a medium. Her sensitiveness was excessive; she shuddered at the neighbourhood of graves, and in church could not remain below, but went up to the loft. At twenty she married, and went to live at Kurnbach, a solitary and gloomy village, lying embosomed among savage mountains. Here her ill-health and her spiritual development increased together. The physicians were bewildered with her case. Several considered her illness hypochondriacal, and her visions and prophecies wilful imposture. Her relations became prejudiced against her, and treated her with the utmost harshness. As a last resource they carried her to Weinsberg, and constituted her a patient of Kerner.

This was on November 25th, 1826. The unfortunate woman reached her new abode more dead than alive. It was imperative to give her every few minutes a spoonful of soup, to prevent her swooning away. Kerner's rebukes increased her misery; he had been prejudiced against her by the reports that had reached his ears, and considered her a compound of hysteria and cunning. He now informed her, with the utmost sternness, that her pretences of clairvoyance and magnetic slumber must at once cease. He was determined to listen to nothing which she said whilst assuming to be in such a state.

His opinion speedily altered. During two and a half years he continued to observe the manifestations which occurred to Madame Hauffe, becoming every day more convinced of their spiritual origin. Like other clairvoyants she read letters laid upon her body, which were enclosed between thick sheets of paper. She made many predictions, and the predictions were always fulfilled. Numerous spirits rendered themselves visible to her, and were recognised from the descriptions which she gave. By means of communications from one of these visitors, a mystery, was cleared up which had continued to cause unpleasantness for nearly six years. Whilst in the magnetic sleep she spoke a language unknown to any about her. She executed various remarkable drawings under spirit-influence. Revelations were made through her immeasurably beyond the scope of her intellect in its normal state. She had received but the scantiest modicum of education; yet, without ever having heard of those leaders of thought, she gave teachings mystically resembling certain abstruse theories of Pythagoras, Plato, Leibnitz, and Swedenborg. Various physical manifestations attended her; articles were thrown by invisible hands about the house in which she dwelt; furniture rose and floated in the air; she was herself levitated several times. On one occasion there appeared a figure surrounded by a bluish light, which figure was visible to all present. In the face of evidence so strong it is not surprising that Kerner, from a determined sceptic, became a firm spiritualist. All who candidly examine into the facts of the case must agree with the great German's verdict regarding his patient. "She was more than half a spirit, and belonged to a world of spirits; she belonged to a world after death, and was more than half dead. In her sleep only was she truly awake; nay, so loose was the connection between soul and body that, like Swedenborg, she often went out of the body and could contemplate it separately."

Oberlin, the great pastor of Alsace, found, on commencing his evangelical labours in Steinthal, that the people had a devout belief in the return of the departed. He was intensely grieved that his parishioners should be attached to what he regarded as a pernicious and degrading superstition. He denounced their faith from the pulpit; he reproved it in private; he set himself to reason down the chimæra. Far from succeeding, the stubborn logic of facts caused him to become himself a most earnest believer in spirit-communion. His departed wife appeared to him many times; almost daily she sat conversing with him, and, describing the conditions of life in the next world, counselled him regarding his undertakings in this. Occasionally she was visible to others of the household. These visits continued for nine years; then a spirit-message reached the good pastor, informing him that his wife had passed to a higher sphere, and could return no more. Deprived of the comfort of her presence, Oberlin found a certain solace in meditation upon the events of that long communion so suddenly brought to an end. In a simple and affecting narrative he has recorded the particulars.

I might extend this chapter to an incredible length by the introduction, from the lives of other famous men, of spiritual facts highly worthy of notice. The renowned therapeutist Gassner, the gentle and philosophic Lavater, the enlightened Eschenmayer, the learned and conscientious Schubert; Görres, in youth the fiery worshipper of freedom, in age the eloquent defender of Spiritualism;—the diligent Ennemoser, the brilliant Kant, the great Schiller, the greater Goethe,—to all these the next world was brought close, and their faith in its realities made more vivid by the veil which drapes that world being at moments partially withdrawn. In our own country, in France, in Italy, in Russia, in every land of either hemisphere, spiritualists, equally distinguished, have in all ages stood forth boldly from the common run of men, and done battle for the truth. Want of space, and no want of admiration for their valour, alone forbids me doing honour to their names. The nature of the task I have taken upon myself is opposed to a frequent descent from the general to the particular. I turn, therefore, from the dim greatness of the past, casting, as I withdraw, a look of lingering regard upon that noble company amongst whom I have been busied. From the lights and shadows which exist for us but in history, I turn to the living realities of the present.

With what pleasure does the eye of the mind rest on the great believers long departed from earth! Compared with the paths in which they trod, the pilgrimage of a spiritualist of to-day is "through pleasant meadows, and by the side of refreshing waters." How many of us, if placed in the situation of these old heroes and heroines, would cast down every weapon and flee ignominiously from the fight! How few would have the heart to endure steadfastly to the end! Servants of God were they, for whom, assuredly, the Master had reserved crowns of righteousness, and to whom, as they passed into His presence, He said "Well done!" A nobler army of martyrs earth has seldom seen. They are gathered from every country and era. The wise, the pious, the gentle, the patriotic—Socrates, Polycarp, Hypatia, Savonarola—all are there. But, purest of the pure, greatest of the great, clothed with a celestial glory, radiant with an everlasting fame, towers up foremost of that indomitable host the empress of womanhood, the fear of England, the thunderbolt of France, the wonder of every age, the reproach of her own. In that mind it is scarcely a hyperbole to say that every virtue had met. High above even the high teacher of Plato rises the stately form, shine the beautiful features, of the daughter of Heaven, Jeanne d'Arc.

NOTE.—In composing the first and second parts of my work great assistance has been afforded me by Mr. W. Howitt's valuable "History of the Supernatural."

PART III

MODERN SPIRITUALISM

CHAPTER I

INTRODUCTORY

The chapters now opening are to myself, and I trust will prove to my readers, the most interesting and important of the volume. For years I have seen with pain abuse after abuse attach itself to a cause in whose service my life has been passed, and with which such foulnesses have nothing in common. So wonderfully have these parasites increased and multiplied, that, like a pearl crusted with spots of dirt, the purity and beauty of the original seem at present almost hidden; and I cannot too strongly reiterate my conviction, that between spiritualism and the majority of the abuses by which it is disgraced there is just as little in common as between a precious stone and the mud which may happen to cling to it. Perceiving this, and guided by promptings altogether apart from my own mind, I determined to write a work in which, whilst the beauty and radiance of the truth were sufficiently dwelt upon, the corruptions ever striving to darken and degrade it were, in the interests of that truth, analyzed and exposed. An experience exceedingly varied, and extending over a period of five-and-twenty years, gives me, to my own mind, and will give me to the minds of the reasoning portion of humanity, sufficient title to be heard. Pecuniary motives in publishing this work I have none. The desire to create a sensation is equally far from influencing me. As a duty I accepted the task, and as a duty I shall endeavour dispassionately and unshrinkingly to fulfil it. I shall level no attacks at individuals, but will simply, by recording facts, and making plain the philosophy of those facts, attempt to serve the truth. That all honest and intelligent lovers of that truth will be upon my side I am certain. That all the dupes and tricksters who are in any way bigoted to or concerned in upholding imposture, will join in a common chorus of fury against me, I am also conscious. Indeed, of the verity of both hypotheses I have already been afforded convincing proof. Some time back I briefly made known by an advertisement the work in which I was engaged, and asked for assistance in points where I considered that assistance might be of service. Not a single name was mentioned or even hinted at; not an allusion made which could be considered as directed against the fame of any individual in the old world or the new. Generalities were all that I dealt in, and seldom have generalities raised

- 651 -

such a storm. I was assailed, both openly and anonymously, with slander, lying charges, foul personalities, venomous abuse—in short with every weapon which the most unscrupulous partisan hatred can direct against the object of its hostility. It was what I expected, and what I had been forewarned of. If the attacks made on me have moved me at moments, the support I have received from within and without, and the consciousness of the rectitude of my intentions, have made the effect but that of a moment. The few, but of course unpleasant anonymous letters sent me, I pass over with contempt. To carry such emanations to the nearest fireplace is all that an ordinary human being can do. Of my open, and thus more respectable enemies, I need say almost equally little. All through my life the evil spoken of me by outsiders has been to me a matter of extreme indifference. I am fortunate in possessing a large circle of friends, who have in many instances known me from my childhood. Their esteem and respect I have, and I desire no more. Had that esteem been vulnerable to the assaults of calumny, it would have been shaken long ere now. I believe that there is scarcely any crime, or any mode of deception, possible or impossible, which has not been imputed to me. Some of these I might have accomplished unaided, but in by far the greater number accomplices would have been imperatively necessary. The impossibility of my, under the circumstances, having had these accomplices is a point which scandal-mongers invariably contrive to forget. I have said that when a cowardly stab is dealt me in the dark I bear it quietly; having confidence in the good sense of my friends, and caring nothing for what my enemies may think, or profess to think. I speak this simply with reference to my moral character. There I belong to myself, and conscious of their baselessness, can look with forgiving contempt on "the small whispers of the paltry few." It is far otherwise when my character as a medium is impugned. In this I am the exponent of a cause counting its adherents by millions in both the old world and the new. As the servant of a power outside of, and uncomprehended by myself, I am compelled to protect this phase of my character from misconception and misrepresentation. Where, through the malignancy of enemies, libels tending to threw suspicion on particular manifestations occurring through me have been circulated, I have uniformly, if able to trace those libels to their source, succeeded in proving them groundless. If in the case of honest inquirers doubt has arisen, I have always found my best remedy to be perfect passivity. Again and again the particular manifestation called in question would be repeated through me, and repeated under conditions utterly precluding the idea of trickery. I may add that I like, and have always liked, to meet with an intelligent and honest sceptic. The questions asked by such a one are, as a rule, pertinent and natural. His reluctance to accept untested phenomena is only the natural reluctance which all beings gifted with reason feel to commit themselves to a blind faith in the unknown, and readily vanishes when that unknown becomes the known and proved. I have never myself found the spirit-world "up in arms," when confronted with a, doubter of this class. Can there by any possibility be a more illogical cry than that vociferated everywhere at the present day? The same folly appears and re-appears under, a hundred different shapes. "Make no attempt," cries one, "to bring over sceptics." "The spirits desire no converts," adds a second. "Let us shut out all but the enthusiastic and easily duped from our *séances*," proposes a third. Such are the insane utterances which at present grieve and disgust sensible spiritualists, and which lead directly up to the frauds it is my aim to denounce and expose. I am confident of reckoning on my side all whose eyes are fairly opened to the imminence of the evils which menace our cause. The best friends of spiritualism are inimical to its present aspect. Men of science who have investigated or would desire to investigate the subject; are repelled by the attitude which certain calling themselves spiritualists assume, and by the seething mass of folly and imposture which every attempt at examination discloses. This condition of things has long been to me a wonder and a grief. After much consideration, I determined on the present work. Before commencing it, I apprised various friends of my intention, and requested their counsel and opinions. Those opinions were in the majority of instances favourable. I was pleased to find that a wide-spread conviction existed, both of the necessity of such a protest as this volume constitutes, and of my fitness for the task of uttering it. To give the whole, or even the greater part, of the letters which have encouraged me is impossible; and I content myself with returning thanks to their writers. But there are certain prominent spiritualists, old and much valued friends of mine, and names of weight in the movement, whose expressions of opinion I desire, and have obtained permission to quote. Let me submit first to the reader the sentiments of my friends, Mr. and Mrs. S. C. Hall. The former writes to me (under date 11th January, 1876):—

"MY DEAR DANIEL.

"I rejoice to know that you have been called upon to do this work: I believe it is an inspired call; that you are the only person who could do it, and that you will be aided by holy, good, and pure Christian spirits and angels sent direct by God. I shall pray fervently for help to you in your holy work.

"Spiritualism now is in a sad state of disorder, and is producing frightfully evil work. It may be—I trust and believe it will be—released and relieved from the burden of filth that weighs it down, and, I repeat, nobody living in this life can do the work so effectually as you can.

"You will pray—you have prayed—for the guidance of God and our Lord Christ, and the direct help of beatified angels. You will have all these, I am very sure.

"M. and I had much talk over this matter last night, when your letter came; and she bids me say, with her affectionate regards, that she takes exactly the same view as I do—and with me prays that God will be your guide. We are fully sure He will be.

"The excuse for trickery I now find to be that evil or deceptive spirits 'come in,' and do the tricks—for which the medium is really not responsible; that in a normal state he or she would be incapable of fraud; that the spirits do the cheating independently of them.

But surely such spirits, such *séances*, such persons, are to be avoided; each and all shunned, in private or in public circles. It is the pitch that cannot be touched without defilement.

"Ever your friend,

"S. C. HALL."

"It is clear to us, my dear Daniel," writes Mrs. Hall, "that God has speared you for the express purpose of proving pure spiritualism to be the handmaid of Christianity:— that is what I always believed it to be."

The following lines are from the pen of that eloquent defender of true spiritualism, Mr. William Howitt:—

"This, my dear Mr. Home, is what I said so much disgusted me with the spiritualists. The petty cliques, the low aims, the spites and factions of spiritualists; the lying mediums and lying spirits who speak through them, confirm everything that the outsiders say of spiritualism being from the devil. The materialists, Carpenter, G. H. Lewes, the Times, are always writing against spiritualism, but they produce no effect. The thing lives in spite of them; but, if anything can kill it, it will be the follies and contemptible meannesses of the spiritualists themselves."

"I have been informed by two or three people," Dr. Sexton tells me (June 6th, 1876), "that you have given up the idea of publishing your new book. Is that so? I hope not. The need for such a work increases day by day: in fact, if something be not done—and speedily—to put an end to the outrageous trickery that passes current under the guise of spiritualism, the whole thing will be ruined. The worst part of it is that mediums who have been caught cheating are still tolerated in the movement, and defended by men whose sole business ought to be to drive them out of our ranks. I have to suffer terribly for the course I take. What with my denunciation of the tricksters, and my advocacy of Christianity, I am avoided and shunned by great numbers, and denounced as a traitor to the cause. Still I shall go on doing what I believe to be right, and leave the issue to God."

In a previous letter he says:—

"It is really heart-breaking that a noble cause should be thus dragged in the mud. If you saw the letters that I receive on the subject from good, pious, Christian men, you would grieve more than you do, and I know that you feel it keenly as it is."

It has been again and again repeated to me that I should find no other medium in favour of my work. Let me submit a couple of extracts which would seem to disprove this assertion. In a letter dated February 17th, 1876, Mrs. K. Fox-Jencken thus expresses her sympathy with the objects I have in view:—

MY DEAR MR. HOME,

"I was very happy to hear from you, and to learn that you were writing such an important book. I am truly glad, and I think it will be one of the most valuable works ever written. Anything that I can do to aid you in bringing it forth I will do with all my heart. No one has dared to do this except yourself; I was myself contemplating it but thought I would wait. Some good spirit must have admonished you to do it.

Yours,

"K. F. JENCKEN."

"I know," writes Mrs. M. Sunderland Cooper to me, "that you are doing a work which is right and just, and I think every honest and truthful medium will give you a helping hand. And this I propose to do. I gave the first public *séance* for spiritual manifestations in New England. I was then a mere child. My father edited and published the first spiritual paper ever published in the world—Dr. Laroy Sunderland; you have no doubt heard of him. But the pioneers of spiritualism are pushed on one side, and Indian gibberish, and dark *séances* ('Punch and Judy shows,' as you call them) are all the rage now. And the mediums who have these dark circles, no matter how many times they are exposed by investigators for the truth, are allowed to go on, and upheld by some of the spiritual papers of the day."

With these quotations I may rest content. There are various persons styling themselves "mediums" whose approbation I should be very sorry to have for any work of mine, but whose opposition I consider a striking testimony to its value.

To return to pleasanter themes. Only a fortnight back there reached me, from an esteemed co-worker in the cause of truth, the accompanying expression of opinion:—

"Sept. 1st, 1876.

"'MY RESPECTED FRIEND,

"Your most unexpected, but, I must assure you, most welcome letter, came two weeks ago, but found me suffering from fever, from which I have only so far recovered as to-day for the first time to be able to sit at my desk. Had it been otherwise I should have written by return mail a Godspeed to the great and needed enterprise in which you are engaged. A book like that you propose is needed, and no one can prepare it better than you. We here are in a strange state of transition; and it seems to me the larger the camel offered by the mediums the better for the credulous mass of swallowers. The demand for marvels is insatiate—so great that, like H____, a class propose to shut their eyes to make them greater. Spiritualism will run a brief career to ruin if this tide is not at once stayed. It is a great science. It rest on *facts*, well observed and recorded, and the mass of loose observations which passes for such is of little account. In my connection as reviewer with the press, I am amazed at the mass of rubbish borne on this great tide.

Most fraternally yours,

"HUDSON TUTTLE."

Such are samples of the communications which have from time to time cheered me whilst I laboured on the present work. Every friendly opinion of my task, however, has not been so favourable. Of the dissuasive counsels tendered me, some have evidently proceeded from a misconception of my aims. Thus my friend, Mr. William Crookes, writes to me:—

"Jan. 21st, 1876.

"I am doubtful whether such a book as you propose to publish will do any real good. You know mediums have the reputation of being very jealous one of another, and consequently, any accusations which may be brought by one against another, however well supported they may be by facts, are explained away in this manner. And even when two partners quarrel, and one makes a clean breast of it, or when one medium makes a confession of fraud, and explains how it is done, very few thorough-going spiritualists will believe them, but will rather call in the agency of bad spirits, trance, &c.

"Another thing you must bear in mind—you, or I, or any other tolerably clear-headed observer may be perfectly sure that cheating is being perpetrated by some professed medium; we may even have had a full confession by the medium that the whole thing is a fraud; yet it may be so difficult as to amount practically to an impossibility to bring this fraud home to the impostor in so clear a manner as would compensate one for the vexation and trouble which would thereby be caused."

I have no intention of making charges against particular persons. I simply design to put the array of facts which I have collected in so clear and strong a light that the reasoning portion of the world may find it easy to draw conclusions from the said facts. From the unreasoning portion of humanity it is of course quite natural that such outbursts as the following should proceed. Be it remarked that the writer is of mature years, and claims the title of "a leading American spiritualist."

"March 10th, 1876.

"ASTONISHMENT! SURPRISE! MARVEL! Have the heavens fallen upon you, Mr. Home, and crushed out your humanity? . . . . Have you forgotten the golden rule of Confucius: 'Do unto others,' &c.? Have Christ's teachings, 'Love one another,' &c., been in vain? Do you believe in one of the unvarying laws of God—compensation?

"You may be 'taking the bull by the horns,' but you are certainly entering the field, as it were, of the deadly rattlesnake, that warns you, and does not strike without a warning. Your road before you is a 'broad one,' but it leads to destruction; for, as sure as there is a God, as sure as justice, sooner or later, hounds out malice and evil, so sure you will be called to account for your slander—and I write advisedly.

"I cannot think of a more ungracious, ill-repaying task than that of exposing the faults of other. 'I will repay,' says the Lord, and can you not trust to Him? Every 'exposure,' *however true and well—sustained it may be*, will only be a thorn—a sharp, a cruel thorn—in your future path. Your alliance with the Russian nobility, your high social position in England, will not shield you. You will fall like LUCIFER, and, if not with a bullet through your head,[*] I believe it will be with shame and sorrow in your heart. You will go down to your grave mourned by few but despised by many; whereas you have it in your power—no, you had it, to make the world rejoice that you had lived. . . . . You will doubtless say that you only promulgate the truth. Is the truth even to be spoken at all times? What is truth to-day may not be so to-morrow. A man or a woman may be immoral this year, and as pure as an angel the next. The thief upon the cross was forgiven at the last moment. None of these condemn thee, neither do I," was the beautiful expression of Him who loved so much, and said, 'Let him who is without sin throw the first stone.' Conversions at our many 'revivals' mean that the person was a sinner, and has now become good; and while you might have said of some of these converted ones, 'You are a vile wretch, a drunkard, a slanderer' (meaning 'you were'), yon would have done a great wrong and spoken falsely, whereas a little while before it might have been the truth.

"But really what have we to do with the faults of others? When Christ turned to the back-biters what did he say? 'Pluck the beam," &c.; and this implied more: 'Mind your own business, and let your brother alone;' and if you had done this, Mr. Home, you would have withheld a stinging shaft that will return to you, a bitter draught you will sooner or later be obliged (or your memory will) to accept. . . . . Now, Mr. Home . . . I cannot but ask God to forgive you, for 'you know not what you do.' The *interior* 'light' of which Christ spoke, I am morally certain you do not possess and I beg of you with all the earnestness I can command, with much admiration of the good you have done as a wonderful medium, to seek that light. Mosses, Plato, Jesus, Apollonius, Plotinus, Pythagoras, Porphyries; and in more modern times, Bacon, Flood, Cagliostro, the Fakirs of India, had this light, and the Fakirs have it now. It is God's divine truth; the absolute wisdom and perfect intelligence of the Buddhists.

". . . . I pray for your health and happiness.

"G. D____"

[*] Did Lucifer fall "with a bullet through his head?" If so, we need hardly be surprised at Shakespeare's assurance that those who fall, fall like Lucifer, "never to rise again."

Such is, with the exception of a few omitted sentences, a facsimile of this incomparable production. Since the writer's large charity leads him so benevolently to pray for me, I am benevolent enough in return to abstain from giving his name. To comment on his letter is, of course, almost impossible. I cannot refrain, however, from lingering a moment over that astonishing list of "possessors of the interior light." Omitting the name of Christ from such a comparison, may we not expect to bear soon that "Socrates, Solomon, Isaiah, Jeremiah, and Nebuchadnezzar in ancient times; and Sir Isaac Newton, Dr. Mesmer, Joe Smith, and

Messrs. Maskelyne and Cooke in more modern days, were prophets of God, and Maskelyne and Cooke are his prophets now"?

Unsatisfied with inflicting on me such a letter as the foregoing, the writer is hard-hearted enough to add a postscript of two closely written pages. Here are a few extracts which excellently illustrate the character of their author:—

"You say you are a great invalid. A person told me that he knew a man still paralyzed, who came by his misfortune in this wise. One day he had been abusing unmercifully a child left to his care by a deceased brother; and, as the man, or brute, passed out of the room, the deceased brother met him in the hall (so he says) and with a mighty blow felled him to the earth. He arose paralyzed, and still sits thus in his chair. 'Whom the gods wish to destroy,' &c. *God will not,* our *good loving God,* will not help you to publish your book. . . . .

"Now, Mr. Home, as a brother spiritualist, as one who wishes you well, as one who will pray for your liberation from these un-Christ-like diabolical spirits, as one who is much your senior in years, take my advice and *abandon* the idea and the practice of *exposing others,* and you will thank me, and thank God, and the *loving, forgiving* Jesus, for being led to do it. You see already how you are accused publicly of being now 'a tool of the Jesuits;' and hosts will believe it, and hate you for it.

"God enlighten you is the prayer of
Yours,

"G. D____."

Strange that a man should reduce himself to the writing of letters such as this? Let us blush once more for human nature, and pass on. To be angry with the effusion is impossible, for it seems to me sunk even beneath the level of contempt.

I might quote other letters of the kind; but, after such a jewel as the foregoing, they would pall. I content myself, therefore, with remarking that the intellectual capacity of all these correspondents appears to be of about the same calibre, and that the said calibre is not extensive.

The moral status of such people is as little satisfactory as their mental capacity. Like Sheridan's Sir Benjamin, they have a pretty turn for slander. If no falsehoods are to be had second-hand, they set themselves to coin a few. They even have the audacity to print these fabrications. Towards the close of 1876 there appeared in an American newspaper, the *Cincinnati Commercial,* an attack upon myself, purporting to be furnished by its English correspondent, a Unitarian preacher. Whether the well-known authors whose names this obscure journalist makes use of are in any way responsible for the assertions attributed to them I am unable to say authoritatively; but I should decidedly fancy that they are not. In any case, I deny the said assertions *in toto.* None of the adventures fabricated for the injury of my reputation ever occurred, whether at Florence or elsewhere; and I can only regret that the correspondent of a journal of any standing (to which class I imagine the *Commercial* to belong) should descend to the ungentlemanly behaviour of giving circulation to stories that he must surely know to be without authority or foundation. His animosity against spiritualism is no doubt great, but I can hardly be expected to admit that as an excuse.

He does not stand alone. One person writes to me that the well-known fact of the hand of Napoleon I. having been seen, during a *séance* at the Tuileries, to take up a pen and inscribe his name is an invention of mine. He adds that he placed himself in communication with the late Emperor of the French, who denied the occurrence of the manifestation in question. Possibly this person's business connections may have brought him into communication with some one in the Emperor's culinary department. I do not doubt the possibility of such a correspondence as this last; but that his Majesty should have condescended to gratify the personal dislike of the individual in question towards me by telling a falsehood I both doubt and disbelieve. My correspondent forgets that I published the account of the phenomenon in question many years before the death of Napoleon III. Had no such manifestation occurred, the assertion would not long have remained uncontradicted.

A would-be controller of both spirits and spiritualism writes me a threatening letter from America. After piling slander upon slander and falsehood on falsehood, he crowns the edifice with the promise of publishing "a complete history of the Lyon case." Does he wish to spare me trouble? I have published half the evidence in the second volume of "Incidents in My Life," and I intend that the remainder, together with the judgment of V. C. Giffard, shall appear in the third.

For there are many false opinions afloat regarding this same case. Thus, a London magistrate, when favouring the world with *his* ideas of law and justice in the case of Dr. Slade, must perforce introduce me in the doubly incorrect character of the injuring party in the suit and a "professional medium." I never was a professional medium. Against men and women who are I have nothing to say, provided that they be but honest. For myself, however, I have all through life felt an invincible repugnance to making merchandise of the gift bestowed on me. Large sums of money have been offered me for but a single *séance*, and they have been invariably refused. I make no boast of the fact; but it gives me, I think, a title to utter such a protest against the abuses of spiritualism as these chapters constitute.

And now I proceed to my task. If I am wrong, I err only through the sincere desire of doing good. My whole being is bound up in the cause as an exponent of which I was early set apart, and to advance whose mighty truths I have laboured for a quarter of a century past. An injury done to that cause, I feel like a wrong inflicted on myself. I utter my protest, then, against the follies and knaveries which at present disgrace it; and I utter that protest as a species of alarum which, I hope, may rouse all true spiritualists to action and unity. Spiritualism can well be compared to a noble corn-field. The wide plain is before us. As we sow thereon, so shall we reap. Lovers of the truth will desire that the harvest should consist solely of that truth. There are among us, however, not the one enemy of the scriptural wheat-field, but a thousand enemies, whose delight it is to be ever scattering the tares of falsehood. We, as the husbandmen, have a perfect right to uproot these. "Ill weeds grow apace," and, if left to flourish unchecked, speedily sap the life from the delicate corn. They come to a rank maturity, and flaunt everywhere their gaudily coloured flowers. Children—or those credulous and enthusiastic spiritualists whose one desire is some new marvel more incredible than the last, and who may fitly be compared to children—are attracted by the worthless plants, and, trampling down the wheat with contempt, hasten to secure the showy toys. It is ours to convince them of their error; and, while seeking to convince, destroy the causes of that error. When the last weed has been extirpated, and the golden harvest of Truth smiles in its full glory, we may point with pride to the cheering sight before us, and cry, "See that for which we have striven!"

NOTE—Among the readers of these pages will doubtless be many who have known me at various periods of my career, and who may preserve the recollection of interesting incidents which have escaped my memory. I shall consider it a personal favour if such will kindly furnish me with any details of these bygone manifestations, &c., addressed to the care of W. Crookes, Esq., F.R S., 20, Mornington Road, N.W., London, England.

CHAPTER II

DELUSIONS

One of the most delicate yet momentous portions of my work is that with which I deal in this and the following chapter. It is hard to know how best to treat of those who, themselves deluded, delude others. Such culprits against progress need not be dishonest. In many instances a latent and perhaps unsuspected insanity lurks at the bottom of the whole; in others, overweening pride, or love of rule, forms the motive power of the wild rush on to ruin. But to analyze the subtly mingled causes of the disastrous effects which have from time to time brought misery to many and astonishment to all, would be beyond the scope of a work like this. These wrecks lie scattered through the histories of all polities and religions. They are the tombstones which point out the graves where lie buried the errors of the past. We must expect to find such in spiritualism. Let us, then, turn our attention to them, not in curiosity, not in contemptuous scorn, but with a desire to shape from these landmarks of rain, beacons which may warn the future from such dangerous ground.

In every instance where a dictatorship is sought to be established in spiritual matters, it behoves lovers of the truth to join in resistance to an attempt so inimical to the dearest interests of that truth. The weaker portion of mankind have ever been but too ready to kneel in worship before such gods of clay, and the one course that their stronger brethren can take is, to demonstrate the hideousness and impotence of the idol. Had a method of searching scrutiny and prompt denunciation of unfounded claims been instituted by the undeceived portion of those to whom such claims were submitted, many movements, mistakenly termed religious, might have been checked at the outset. There are men—and women not less often than men—who hold it gross injustice that they should not have been born to mitres or crowns. In all who have striven to found sects or communities, and establish themselves as the high-priests of such, this characteristic has been dominant, conjoined usually with a certain enthusiasm, which aids in attracting minds weaker, though perhaps yet more enthusiastic, than their own. Such always render blind submission to the energy which has fascinated them, and become the blindest adorers of the pseudo-prophet or prophetess. I recall an instance in which a young man of good position, possessed of high literary gifts, and, in his earlier years, of sound judgment, was submitted to an ordeal sufficient to have utterly overwhelmed any ordinary organization. He emerged from it with his intellectual power almost unscathed, but the injury which a reason once eminently masculine had undergone was sufficiently evinced. He became the humble and unquestioning adherent of one among the pseudo-religious charlatans referred to.

It is not to be doubted that these "God-inspired" beings are at times sincere in their wild visions and impracticable theories. So are those sincere, who, being yet more advanced in their idiosyncrasies, and having them less under control, are entitled "dangerous madmen," and restrained in asylums. Yet the insanity partially swayed by reason of the one is, in reality, much more dangerous than the raging madness, into which no suspicion of reason enters, of the other. Bedlam makes no proselytes; nor, if the whole of the tenants of asylums were let loose in a body, could they do more than appal, disgust, and perhaps injure bodily, those of mankind who encountered them. But all history teems with the mischief which minds, less disordered than these, but still disordered, and accompanied with an energetic will and a restless thirst for domination, can do to natures weaker than their own. I might produce instances from every century of the Christian era, but a reference to the nineteenth will be sufficient for my purpose. Joanna Southcote and Joe Smith, to select two instances out of many, lived and worked harm in the century yet unfinished. Of all beliefs spiritualism is the one where such as choose to assume to themselves a prophetic character may most readily expect to find adherents. We are granted proofs of the continued existence of the loved and lost ones who have been released from the fetters of earth, and it is not unnatural that those through whom such proof is granted should be looked upon as gifted with some quality of soul superior to the endowments of their fellow-men. This is a sad and most fatal error. We who are mediums have in no way natures stronger than the natures of others. It is, on the contrary, unquestionable, that the supersensitiveness of our organization causes us to be but the more easily influenced and led astray. Every teaching obtained through a medium should be tried by the most searching tests, and rejected or accepted as it bears the refining fires of common sense and reason. A spirit, on manifesting, may simply describe himself as John Smith, or may assure me that he is Socrates. Naturally I regard the humbler name with the less suspicion. It is, to my experience, a more probable thing that he should be an ordinary Englishman than a great Greek. Besides, as John Smith he may, without making pretension to superior wisdom, give to Mary Smith, his mother, overwhelming proofs of identity. Here the outside world can have no pretext for interference. Should he, however, arrogate to himself the position of a teacher, others than Mary Smith must be allowed to decide respecting the validity of his claims. All fortunate enough to be convinced of the great truth that death is rather an awakening than a sleep, are interested in deciding whether spirits or mediums who teach that evil is good and folly wisdom; that man is destined to undergo transformations as numerous as those of the harlequin in a pantomime, and, returning continually to the stage of earthly life, play more parts there than Shakespeare ever dreamed of; or that doing evil that good may come is acceptable in the sight of God; or that beings in either world who appear by their actions and doctrines children of darkness are in reality angels of light; shall be permitted with impunity to poison the minds of those weak enough to listen and admire.

I know that not in our own cause solely is evil to be found. Crimes and vices of a hue often far darker than anything which has disgraced spiritualism are to be met disgracing religious denominations everywhere throughout the world, for the same rules which apply to mediums apply to the exponents of all beliefs having reference to a life to come. What fatal teachings a mass of priests, pastors, rabbis, or whatsoever these shepherds of souls choose to be termed, have inculcated in all countries and centuries, the religious strifes by which the world has at different times been convulsed sufficiently prove. To the depths of infamy in which ministers of every creed have plunged themselves, annals stained with inconceivable crimes bear witness. It is pointed out by our enemies that among spiritualists excessive disunion exists, and that men professing a common faith in the possibility of communion with spirits, regard each other, in many cases, with the deadliest hate. It is, alas, but too true! and deeply do I regret it. But what of the adherents of every orthodox faith? Has not the saying, "See how these Christians love one another," a saying which was in its origin so beautiful and so true, been, for at least a thousand years, a mockery and a by-word? Did Dominic and De Montfort preach to heretics with aught but fire and sword? Was it not the legate Arnold, to whom, when a town of thirty thousand inhabitants, part heretic part Catholic, had been taken by storm, came the captains of the Catholic host for instructions? The task of selecting from the Albigenses the sheep of the Roman fold might have perplexed Solomon. With a blasphemy unmatched in history, Arnold cut the Gordian knot. "Kill them," said the holy man, "kill them all—the Lord can choose his own."

Did not Torquemada, again, burn, in an inquisitoriate of less than the tenth part of a century, above five thousand unhappy wretches, and torture and imprison ten times the number whom he slew? Did not a pontiff of the Catholic Church decree a solemn thanksgiving because some sixty thousand heretics had been massacred in France? Did not Cranmer burn Joan Bouchier? Did not Calvin burn Servetus? Did not

Elizabeth hang, draw, and quarter every Catholic priest who fell into her hands? Have not Catholics persecuted Protestants, Calvinists persecuted Lutherans, Puritans persecuted Papists, with a fury utterly antagonistic to the teachings of Christ? And, finally, is it not altogether certain that there exist bigots in every Church who, did the greater enlightenment of their brethren permit, would plant the stake in the market-places of the present day?

None can regret more than myself the evils which degrade that spiritual movement whose welfare I have so much at heart. But what of the clergy of to-day? Are they not as liable as mediums to betray the sacred trusts confided to them? The movement known as "modern spiritualism" sprang into prominence a little more than a quarter of a century since. During that quarter of a century numerous wickednesses have unquestionably been committed by men and women really or professedly mediums. And what of clergymen within the same period? Have not murder and every imaginable crime been committed over and over again within the last twenty-five years by the shepherds of orthodox folds? Have they not, in but too many instances, forgotten the sacredness of the work to which they are devoted, and brought ruin and infamy into once happy homes? Is not their immorality a proverb in many countries? Have they not, by the greed of gold and the lust of power, been tempted to commit deeds recorded in characters of everlasting blackness? Is it not their mission to preach peace, and have they not often by every means in their power incited to the shedding of blood? Within the past fifteen years I have known clergymen nail the flag of declared war to their steeples, and, in sermons delivered within walls dedicated to the worship of a loving God, prompt his children to mutual slaughter. I have known clergymen also, who were faithful servants of Christ, good men and true, who worked earnestly below to fit themselves and others for the life to come. It is not as an attack on the Churches that I have written the paragraphs to be found above; I simply desire to point the old moral that to err is human, and, as a certain analogy exists between the position of the clergy and that of mediums, I have selected the clergy for the purposes of comparison. Similar temptations try both classes. Both are liable to seek to become masters where, in fitness, they should serve. The same duties are incumbent on the men who sway the minds of congregations that crowd to hear them expound the Divine word, and on the medium who has, in the order of nature, been set apart as a chosen instrument through whose peculiar organization is permitted the refutation of the fallacy that the things to come are "unheard, unfelt, and unseen," and through whom the realities of the next world are brought close to those who have not yet experienced the change called death, that, inspired to higher and holier actions, the "places" may be honourable ones which, according to their merits, shall be prepared for them there.

"In my Father's house are many mansions," said Christ; "I go to prepare a place for you." Christians of all denominations are too apt to lose sight of this great fundamental truth. A most perfect explanation and reconciliation of the supposed discrepancies of spiritual teachings is contained in the above heavenly and inspired words. That they were inspired, none save the peculiar class of fanatics who deny a hereafter can refuse to believe. Recall the circumstances under which they were spoken. The darkest hour in the life of Him "who had not where to lay his head" was at hand. The great crime of the Hebrews approached its consummation; already upon the Messiah fell the shadow of the cross. Yet, when earth yielded no ray of love or hope, Christ rejoiced because of his nearness to the Father's house; and, rejoicing, thought of the "many mansions" and the "places" there to be prepared. If all men be made alike at death what need of "many mansions," and why seek to "prepare a place?" Were the dogma correct, that from earth the "elect" depart to a uniform assembling point, "before the throne of God," there, arrayed in the same white robes and wearing the same golden crowns, to wave palm-branches in concert through a wearisome eternity, and that the "reprobated" as uniformly depart into a darkness lurid with unquenchable fire, the meaning of the Messiah's words would be lost. That they were not without meaning—and a mighty one—the spiritual revelations of this age have made amply manifest. We find in the world of the future a diversity of conditions endless as in our own. Everywhere good and evil are in ceaseless activity, everywhere humanity is sinking farther from or advancing nearer to its God. But the prospect, considered as a whole, is cheering. There is reaction here and there. The great progress, however, goes steadily on. Wisdom and virtue continue to expand, and with the passing of each year or period of years the cry of the majority of spirits is the triumphal one, "Nearer, O God, to Thee!" Thus in eternity as on earth, the watchword of humanity continues to be "Excelsior."

For the love of the Father is, like Himself, omnipresent. "All discord," as a great poet wisely tells us, "is harmony not understood." The jarring notes which so many of us produce from the instrument termed Life, it is the province of God to blend into accordance. The children who, whilst on earth, have misconceived his attributes, are certain of enlightenment hereafter. He waits only until they seek Him in humility to be instructed. Man must learn before he can teach, and human philosophy becomes ridiculous when it assumes to be an "intellectual all in all." To such wisdom perverted to foolishness did Christ allude when He said, "Thou hast hidden these things from the wise and prudent, and hast revealed them unto babes." Judæa was filled with men, who, too proud to obey God, thought themselves fitted to command their fellows. Doubtless places calculated to afford the lessons they so much needed were prepared, for them in a future world.

Spiritualists have had among them many such erring brethren. Discontented with equality, these pretenders aspired to lead. The majority were stopped at the outset of their career. The ridicule directed against them, or the common sense of those whom they sought to dupe, proved insurmountable obstacles. Others, however, succeeded in pushing their struggles for domination far enough to cause more or less of harm. They drew together followers, and formed sects. Utterly incompetent for the task they had taken upon themselves, these would-be builders invariably found their exertions lead to ruin. The flimsy absurdities with which they disfigured our cause did more to injure it than the fiercest attacks of enemies from without. Their conduct and "revelations" were the grief of all sincere spiritualists and the laughing-stocks of the sceptical world.

Two prominent prophets of this class arose in the year 1850. The names they condescended to be known by whilst on earth were Scott and Harris: both rejoiced in the title of "Reverend." Mr. Scott had long been a shining light among the New York Baptists, and Mr. Harris had held forth from a Universalist pulpit. Their secession to spiritualism appears to have taken place about the same time, and the events I shall now narrate led to an intimate acquaintance between the two converts.

In the town of Auburn, N.Y., a circle known as the "Apostolic" had been formed. The medium secured was a Mrs. Benedict, and the attendant spirits belonged to the most select class. A chief rule of the association forbade the receipt of communications from any born out of Judæa; or after the first year of the Christian era. The beings whose presence was desiderated appeared highly to appreciate this resolve. St. John and the prophet Daniel became the directors of the favoured circle. Communications, whose utter lack of meaning was set off by bad grammar and worse orthography, speedily showered down on happy Auburn. Nevertheless, matters prospered not; a heartless world refused to waste attention on the Apostolic Circle, behaved it never so strangely. In this emergency a fresh champion was sought, and found. By advice of "John" and "Daniel" the Auburn spiritualists summoned the Rev. J. D. Scott to put his hand to the plough.

He came, and lent himself with enthusiasm to the work. "St. Paul" was speedily added to the other guides of Mrs. Benedict; and improvements of grammar and orthography displayed themselves in the messages received. One of these messages fell into the hands of the Rev. T. L. Harris. The idea of being put in communication with such an apostle as Paul greatly excited him; and Scott and Mrs. Benedict were sent for. By the aid of these spiritual sponsors Mr. Harris became "remodelled." On their return to Auburn he went with them as the "oracle" of that Hebrew of the Hebrews who experienced such a mighty spiritual manifestation on his way to Damascus. Scott claimed to be the mouthpiece of St. John.

A periodical was at once started under the title of *Disclosures from the Interior.* The two editors, Harris and Scott, contented themselves at first with being known as "chosen vessels." Soon presumption, and the unlimited folly of their dupes, tempted them a step farther. They claimed to visit the celestial regions in trance. Whatever they spoke, wrote, or thought, was the inspiration of a chosen band of apostles and prophets directed by "the Lord Himself."

The outcry grew strong in Auburn. Sensible spiritualists were disgusted, and withdrew from all communion with the two ex-Reverends and their flock. The extravagances of Scott and Harris, however, only waxed the wilder. Threats of mobbing were made by the rougher among the unbelievers. The position of the "chosen vessels" became unsafe. Under these circumstances an exodus was resolved upon. The spirits entered warmly into the plan, and full instructions were received from them. Mountain Cove, Fayette County, Virginia, was to be the new resting-place of that ark which unworthy Auburn had cast forth. No less a person than Isaiah would guide the little band of brothers to the chosen spot; which, it appeared, was the prophet's favourite spiritual residence. All property was to be in common. The golden day of "liberty, fraternity, and equality," had at length arrived.

About one hundred persons accompanied Mr. Scott to Mountain Cove; Harris for the present held aloof. His brother "vessel" speedily soared to a height of blasphemy such as few human beings have attained before or since. Prophets and apostles were despised as human and created. Nothing would content the reverend gentleman but the Creator Himself. In his own words he "came even unto the counsels of the Most High." Full authority was delegated to him in all matters "social, religious, and financial; temporal or eternal." On the 2nd December, 1851, he called together the faithful and informed them that, in the fashion of Moses, he had conversed "face to face with God!"

Such were his words, and the ineffable idiots whom he had gathered together heard them with credulous awe.

Scott now appointed himself "medium absolute." Nothing but pure truth, he gave his followers to understand, could or would henceforth be received through him. Whoever dared to express a doubt of that truth must be cast forth as an unworthy heretic.

Notwithstanding these claims dissensions arose. A charge of licentiousness was preferred against the "man of God." He investigated it himself, and promptly decided the accused to be innocent. Still the unpleasantness continued. Money ran short. The faithful, whatever their disagreements in other matters, were unanimous in declining work. Several families left the place. A plantation which had been purchased was returned to its former owner, as the payments on it could not be met. It was necessary that Scott should have a new vision. "I must go," said he, "to New York, and seek there minds for the carrying-on of the Lord's work."

Arrived in New York he resumed his old connection with Harris. The confederates succeeded in bringing over several persons of property to the enterprise. The Mountain Cove estate was repurchased. In May, 1852, the Rev. T. L. Harris proceeded there, accompanied by his family and his dupes. A fresh gleam of worldly prosperity shone on "the Holy Mountain—the New Jerusalem," as the partakers of its joys enthusiastically termed it. The arrogance of the reunited prophets and the credulity of the faithful were stretched to the utmost. It was proclaimed that God had chosen Scott and Harris "as his mediums, through whom He might communicate with man on earth." Their minds were to become blended into spiritual unity. The utterances proceeding from their lips would "instruct and comfort the people of the Lord." Neither of the prophets could lie; and besides being infallible they were supreme;—the only children of the Truth. All other persons claiming to be mediums received their inspiration from the devil, and ranked among his servants.

I find the following sentences given as a specimen of the revelations with which the faithful were "instructed and comforted." They are from an address spoken in the "interior condition" by Scott:—

"I read, written in letters of fire, 'Dost thou believe? and what dost thou believe? Who, thinkest thou, called thee here? Who inspireth? Not an angel, for he is led; not a seraph, for he is controlled; not created existence, for that is inspired. Who, then, thinkest thou, called thee to the mountain? Who but God inspireth?' . . . . I am that I am inquireth of thee; and prepare to answer thou Me. None other than God, thy Redeemer, calleth thee. None other than He who hath the keys of Death and Hell addresseth you through one of your members.'"

Even this was mild compared with what followed. Harris declared Mountain Cove to be the gate of Heaven. The redemption of man could only be accomplished there. Whoever opposed "the two perfect prophets" was to be driven from the holy place. For such outcasts there remained no longer any hope of salvation. Not even himself or Scott could again open "the gate of Heaven" to them.

The house wherein the two prophets dwelt Harris pronounced *"the veritable house of God."* It was necessary that an estate should be added to it. Accordingly, the seers indulged in yet another vision. The Lord desired a certain piece of land to be leased to Him as his heritage. A meeting of the faithful was called. Harris and Scott pointed out that as they, and they alone, were the "chosen vessels of God," the lease must be drawn in their names. The request was too reasonable for refusal, and the worthy stewards commenced forthwith to administer the estate they had acquired in so spiritual a manner.

The crowning stroke of impiety was at hand.

Persecutions had been directed against all rebels from the domination of the "perfect mediums." Endless discord convulsed the little community. As the "New Jerusalem" seemed ready to fall to pieces, an assumption was resolved on whose boldness should awe even the most mutinous. Some time in the autumn of 1852, therefore, Harris and Scott revealed themselves to their amazed followers as the two witnesses spoken of in the eleventh chapter of Revelations. They claimed the whole of the super-mundane gifts assigned to these witnesses by St. John. Power to send fire from their mouths, and with it consume their enemies; power to shut heaven so that it rained not; power to turn the waters of earth to blood, and to smite men with plagues: all these weapons were at the command of the ex-Universalist and the ex-Baptist. They did not, indeed, design to use them except at the last extremity. If the dwellers on the "holy mountain" would but turn again into the way of righteousness, all might yet be well. *"O Lord,"* said Harris, in one of his prayerful rebukes to the chosen hundred, *"Thou knowest we do not wish to destroy man with fire from our mouths!*

Blasphemy could hardly go farther. Several listeners were disgusted; and withdrew from the brotherhood. The majority, however, accorded full credence to the claims of the reverend "witnesses." The state of mind of these believers is a thing to be contemplated with wonder and awe.

But a dissolution was inevitable. Even fanaticism has its tender points. Though there were dwellers in the "New Jerusalem" for whose utter and abject credulity no impiety was too impious and no folly too foolish, a test of faith was now insisted on which even these could not support. The Rev. Mr. Scott made an onslaught on the pockets of the faithful. "Spirits," he justly remarked, "operate from the interior; but man in clay demandeth external benefit." He called on his followers, therefore, to yield up to him the whole of their possessions, pecuniary or otherwise. "Come!" cried he, "with thy substance; give it to the Lord." The gift, of course, was to be made to heaven as manifested in its servant, Mr. Scott. How many responded to the appeal the history of the movement saith not. Mountain Cove, however, lost at once all vestiges of fraternity. The New Jerusalem became a Pandemonium. Quarrel succeeded to quarrel, and departure to departure. Various charges were made against the two prophets of the community. At length, when of the Virginian Israel scarcely any but the leaders remained, those leaders recognised the necessity of causing their light to shine elsewhere. They struck tents accordingly, and departed. Of the wealth of the faithful scarcely a farthing remained. Such was the end of one of the darkest follies of modern spiritualism.

Had a sufficient degree of opposition been organized against this movement at its outset, it could never have worked such extensive harm. Even after the settlement at Mountain Cove, the steady and unfaltering resistance of the more sensible brethren to the dictatorial claims of Scott and Harris might have done much. But such brethren were few, and they contented themselves with quitting the place in disgust. The attempts at mutiny were desultory and ill sustained, and their only effect was to incite the reverend "witnesses" to some of the most blasphemous antics that ever made spirits or spiritualists blush.

With the career of Mr. J. L. Scott I have henceforth no concern. The name of his fellow-prophet, however, continued, even after the dispersion of the Mountain Cove flock, to be intimately linked with spiritualism, both in America and England. For a few years his mediumship was at once brilliant and useful. He published in rapid succession a series of fine poems—"A Lyric of the Golden Age," "An Epic of the Starry Heavens," "The Morning Land," &c. The spirits who inspired these productions he asserted to be Byron, Shelley, Coleridge, and others of the great departed. Unequal and, in places, slightly turgid, the compositions given by Mr. Harris to the world bore the impress of high spiritual inspiration and masterly poetic power.

But so commendable a course could not long be persisted in by the restless "prophet." He cast away the pen, and, thrusting himself into that field of action for which he was so ill qualified, commenced a career of the wildest apostasy and excess.

On his return to New York from the deserted paradise of Mountain Cove he had, for a short while, figured as a lecturer. In this capacity he poured forth floods of virulent abuse against Christ and the Christian Gospel. None who listened to those attacks can have forgotten their vehemence. I was myself present on one occasion and, rising in utter disgust, left the building. "They were too strong," says Mr. C. Partridge, "even for those whom Mr. Harris now denounces as rejecting the divine authority of Scripture." For, in no long time, this human weathercock again veered round. He was determined, at any cost, to have a church, and to be to that church a dictator and a prophet. His first attempt was made with those New York spiritualists who had been edified by his diatribes against the Bible. They could not, however, be tempted. Ready to engage him as a speaker, they declined to find a master in him. One such experiment as Mountain Cove was sufficient.

Disappointed in this quarter, Mr. Harris changed his tactics. From the coarse assailant of Christianity he transformed himself once more into its devoted champion. From an ardent spiritualist he became an equally ardent denouncer of spiritualism. He first preached to a small congregation in New York. This little gathering was known as "The Sacred Family." Whilst acting as its father the prophet sent forth another epic to the world. He very reasonably styled this new production, "The Song of Satan." It contained an elaborate exposition of the devil-theory regarding spiritual manifestations. The Byron, Coleridge, &c., by whom Mr. Harris had formerly been controlled, were merely fiends masquerading in the guise of those great poets. From their snares he was now free. A select cohort of angels had come down to take charge of the "Sacred Family" and its leader. All other spirits manifesting anywhere on earth were waifs from the bottomless pit.

Soon the prophet grew weary of his New York flock. He determined to travel, and fixed on England as the country to be now illuminated. Calling the "Sacred Family" together, he informed them that he had become developed above their comprehension. The Lord had instructed him to proceed to Europe, and disseminate there the supernal wisdom which burdened his mind. He made choice of a successor "fitted for the New York plane of teaching," and set off.

Arrived in London, it speedily appeared that the "supernal wisdom" with which English spiritualists were to be favoured was comprised in a series of rancorous attacks upon their brethren in America, which attacks were usually of the most baseless nature. Having succeeded in creating much ill-feeling through these libels, Mr. Harris considered his mission satisfactorily disposed of, and, despite his being developed above American comprehension, condescended to favour the States once more with his presence. A second "Sacred Family" was inaugurated, and in its, doubtless, happy bosom the perfect medium of the Virginian New Jerusalem still remains. His converts and "spiritual children," I may remark, contain among them persons whom one would have thought little likely to bow to the yoke of an unstable and brain-sick enthusiast. No extravagance, however, of his later attempt at sect-founding has as yet approached the madnesses in which Mr. Harris indulged at Mountain Cove.

Almost contemporary with this American insanity, a movement was carried on in the city of Geneva, the freaks of whose founder equalled the blasphemies of Harris and Scott; whilst the credulity of the dupes even surpassed the confidingness of the Mountain Cove disciples. The little table through which "St. Paul" gave directions for the founding of the Virginian "New Jerusalem," was the prototype of a table, equally small, and venerated still more highly by certain dwellers in the staid city of Calvin.

Towards the close of 1853 persons could be found everywhere throughout the world who took great interest in the "turning and tipping of tables." Professor Faraday's verdict was delivered about this period. As regards spiritualism in its entirety, that verdict was an essentially foolish one, for on no better grounds than the data furnished by a few hasty observations, Faraday considered himself competent to condemn the whole subject. I am convinced, however, that as regards the particular instances of phenomena which came under his scrutiny, his theory was just. The more I have seen of the persons known as "tipping mediums," the more unable I have been to trace the movements of the table and the messages communicated through those movements to any other source than the so-called mediums themselves. Yet in at least one-half of the cases observed by me, the persons concerned were innocent of all wish or effort to deceive. They simply laboured under undue excitement of the nervous system, and every attempt to dispel their hallucinations failed.

I knew once an old lady who, before dining, invariably seated herself at small table, and commenced to tip it. The table was supposed to stand as representative for the spirit of her deceased husband. When the tipping was fairly started, interrogatories began.

"Dear Charles, may I eat fish today ?".

The table would execute affirmative motions.

"Thank you, dear Charles, I thought I might, for I felt a strong desire to have fish for dinner."

At times the response was in the negative. Then came something like the following:—

"Ah! I thought so, Charles! I felt one of my chills coming on, and fish is bad for me when I have my chills."

I never knew an instance when the answer was not in full unison with her own wishes. This delusion extended itself to every action of her life, and I had to proceed with great caution in attempting to convince her that the "dear Charles" of the table was simply a fantasy due to unconscious muscular exertion and an excited brain.

I recall another case. In 1855, I was one day dining with Lord H____. A well-known baronet was at table. Spiritualism became the subject of conversation, and Sir R____ inquired whether I could obtain manifestations at will. I told him, as is the truth, that I could not. He laughed, and remarked, "I am a better medium than you then; for I can tip the tables at pleasure." I replied that I had not the slightest doubt of his ability to do so, and continued, "Perhaps you will show us this talent after dinner." No sooner had we reached the drawing-room than he selected the species of small table known as a "what-not." He seated himself, and the tipping commenced. Nothing could have been more evident than that he accomplished it himself. "Perhaps, Sir R____," I said, "you will allow me to place a sheet of paper between your hand and the table?" He gave permission, and I spread out the sheet, so that his hands would rest on it. The table no longer tipped, but the paper moved very visibly. It was afterwards reported to me—I hope, incorrectly—that Sir R____ had said, "Oh! Home was jealous of my power as a medium."

Were it necessary, I could subjoin to these two instances hundreds equally striking. In none was the motive power traceable to spirits. Regarding "writing mediums," the same thing may be said in ninety cases of every hundred. In the early stages of my own career I was a writing medium. Little by little, I began to reason respecting the messages given through me. I found them strongly tinged with my own bias of thought; and I at once ceased seeking for such communications. Since then I have only written medially when my hand has moved altogether automatically, and my attention was so completely diverted that I could not catch the faintest inkling of what was written.

I should not, it is true, be warranted in asserting even such tippings as those of Harris and Scott's "St. Paul" to be the results of deliberate imposture; but I am perfectly satisfied that they constituted a monstrous delusion, in which disembodied spirits had not the slightest share. St. Paul as little controlled the Mountain Cove leaders as did Tom Jones. The same absence of all spiritual tokens is discernible in the wildly blasphemous attempt at spiritual dictatorship which I am now about to describe.

The method of obtaining communications was through a very small table. The medium laid his hands on the said table, and it tipped out messages by means of the alphabet. *There is not a single instance of the table having been levitated, or of a movement when no person was in contact with it.*

In the American folly, Harris and Scott never went beyond St. Paul, as a servant for tipping purposes. Their higher flights of blasphemy they reserved for their inspirational moments. Our Genevan enthusiasts took a bolder stand. They solemnly consecrated their table, and proclaimed that it was tipped by the Messiah himself. They set a chair apart at their meetings, which chair was supposed to be invisibly filled by Christ. Nay, they ventured even farther than this. On one occasion God the Father was introduced as communicating a miserable species of homily, pilfered from various portions of Scripture. The messages, whether pronounced to emanate from Raphael, from Gabriel, or from the parsons of the Trinity, were received with credulous ecstasy, preserved, arranged, and published in volume shape. I have copies of two of these precious productions. One bears the moving title-page:—

"POST TENEBRAS LUX.

ROME, GENÈVE,

ET

L'ÉGLISE DE CHRIST.

DICTÉ AU MOYEN D'UNE TABLE PAR LE FILS DE DIEU,
LE SAUVEUR DU MONDE,
SEUL MÉDIATEUR ENTRE DIEU ET LES HOMMES.
1856."

I do not print the names of the persons concerned in this movement, but they are at the service of any desirous of privately investigating the case. These unfortunates have abandoned their delusion. They are reduced from positions of comfort and even of wealth to a condition bordering in instances on absolute want. To-day, October 5th, 1876, I had an interview with the deepest sufferer of them all. At the age of seventy-two she is still young in patience and hope. As she narrated to me her losses and trials the peaceful smile that lit her face was the very gleam one might suppose to irradiate the countenance of some martyr, while, with his last accents, he breathed forgiveness to his enemies. From the notes I took whilst listening to her, I, with the help of a retentive memory, proceed to lay bare this item of Genovese history in almost my informant's own words.

"It is a sad story, sir. Perhaps it would be well to seek to forget it, but, as you truly say, it may serve to warn others. God grant that it should!

"I am unable to give you the exact date, but some time in 1853 a strange piece of news reached us. We heard that, at the house of a Mr. X____, some little girls had become developed as writing mediums, and that Mr. X____ himself had great power over a table, through which messages were given. He was a teacher of music, and a good and truly pious man. (Oh! he was honest, as we all were.) Well, out of curiosity I went to see these things, and, finding that the *séances* began with prayer, and that all the messages given were pure and good, I came home, and asked my husband to investigate the matter. How many times since then has he said, 'It was you who first led me into it.' These words were not said complainingly, for what right have any of us to complain? We all thought we were doing God's work, and even now, sir, I can only say that, if it were a delusion, I still believe God will pity us, for our object was to glorify Him. My husband was a man of great intelligence, and in proof of it I need only say that he had been Professor of Mathematics in the college here. At the time alluded to, however, he no longer taught. By a number of fortunate speculations he had acquired a large fortune, and we were living in ease and luxury. (I see you are looking round my poor little room, sir; but it must have been the will of God, and that consoles me.) Mr. X____ said his table was moved by our Saviour; but now, in looking back, I wonder how we could have been foolish enough to credit such a thing. We were told by 'the table'" (the words she used were "the Saviour," but this constant repetition of a holy name is so repulsive that, for the remainder of the narrative, I substitute "the table,") "that we must take Mr. X____, his father, mother, &c., to reside in our house, and share with them the fortune it had pleased God to give us. I said to my husband, 'Let us give them a large sum of ready money instead, and ask them to live elsewhere; for their tastes are not mine, and I could not be happy with them.' My husband answered, 'The life of the One we worship was a life of self-abnegation, and we must in all things copy Him. Overcome at once these worldly prejudices, and your sacrifice will prove your willingness to obey the Master.' Of course I consented, and seven additions were made to our household. Then began a life of utter recklessness as regards money. 'The table' ordered us to purchase another carriage and four new horses. We had nine servants in the house. Not only that, but 'the table' ordered us to buy a steamboat. Very expensive it was. Painters and decorators were set to work on the house in which we lived; and, however rich and beautiful our furniture might be, 'the table' made us replace it with newer and still more costly articles. (All this, sir, was to be done that our mansion might be worthy to receive the One whom we foolishly believed came to it.) We were told, too, by 'the table' that it was necessary everything should be made as ostentatious as possible to attract the notice of the outside world. We did as we were ordered. We kept open house. The results were what might have been expected. People came, and made a pretence of being convinced. Young men and women visited us, and 'the table' ordered them to be married. When they consented, the necessary outfits were furnished at our expense. Not only that, sir, but as often as these couples had children, the children were sent to us to be brought up, and I well remember that at one time we had eleven infants in the house. Mr. X____, too, married, and his family went on increasing itself. At last, no less than thirty of us regularly sat down at table together. This continued for three or four years, until one day we discovered that our means were nearly all gone. 'The table' told us to go to Paris, and 'He' would provide for us there. We went, and my husband was bidden to speculate on the Bourse. He did so, and lost. Still we had faith. As there were now but few in the family, we contrived to live on, Heaven only knows how. I have been for days together without other food than a crust of dry bread and a glass of water. I must not forget to tell you, sir, that whilst in Geneva we had been bidden to administer the sacrament of the Lord's Supper, and that there were sometimes from three to four hundred communicants at table. A monk from Argovie, too, left the convent of which he was Superior, and renounced the Catholic religion to join us. You see, sir, we were not alone in our blindness.

"Even during our trials in Paris our faith held firm. My husband often said that 'the table' had sent us there, and that he would not return to Geneva without 'his' permission. At last we asked for that permission, and were told we might return. Ah! it was then that we fully realised our position. We were poor, and those who had profited by our fortune whilst it lasted were the first to turn their backs upon us. I do wrong, though, sir, to tell you this, for it betokens a restless and complaining spirit, and I have no right to murmur.

"I had almost forgotten to relate that, amongst other wild fancies, 'the table' bade us buy a manufactory in France. We did so, and the undertaking proved a total failure. The place was sold for ten thousand francs, not a tenth of what it had cost us.

"You are looking at that large engraving, and wonder, no doubt, how it comes to have a place in my humble room. Well, sir, during the height of our folly, Mr. X____ was inspired with artistic ideas, but, strange to say, could not give expression to them. A professional painter was engaged, therefore, and X____ described to him his visions. That large engraving is taken from the picture which represented X____'s idea of the Crucifixion. It is at the moment when our Lord says, I thirst.' The original painting was sold at auction by our creditors, with our house, and whatever else remained to us. No, sir, we have never seen Mr. X____ from that day. He married my niece whilst we were all living together, and had four children by her. She was called by God, and X____ has married again, and, I hear, never alludes to the past. Yes, he has been in Geneva, but he did not come to see us. Why should he? he is poor like us. I will tell you one little thing which has happened within the past three or four months." (The incident not being at all to the credit of X____, I refrain from giving it. The character of the narrator is well displayed by the self-rebuking manner in which her narrative terminated.) "Indeed I am wicked, sir, to have told you such a thing as this. God forgive me! I ought to have been silent about it. Please, *please* forget that I told it. I am a sinful old woman, and I bow my head in all humility to ask heaven's pardon for speaking such harsh words. Even in his wanderings, my husband" *(the unfortunate man is insane)* "never makes allusion to the past. Oh! I am perfectly convinced, sir, that it was not our connection with this affair which deprived him of reason. He began to work with his head very young, and mathematics fatigue the brain so. It is very, very hard not to have him with me, but he is at times beyond my control. Still I wish I could be allowed to have him here, and care for him.

"It is a sad story, as you say, but we were all striving to obey the dictates of what we thought to be a high and holy power. I assure you some of the messages were very beautiful, quite superior to what Mr. X____ could have given. Well, the day of life will soon terminate for us, and then we shall read the riddle. Speaking of those messages, I fear, sir, that even when we believed ourselves most humble, there was a strong tinge of vanity in our thoughts, for we all, of course, believed ourselves the chosen of the Lord. I remember that often, on seeing a funeral move past me, with its gloomy hearse and trappings of sorrow, I have said to myself exultingly, 'Ah! how happy it is that we shall have no such ordeal to endure;' for 'the table' had told as that, as the chosen of the Lord, we should none of us see death, but be translated bodily to 'his' Father's home. Remember, sir, that neither Mr. X____ nor any others of those concerned made, or sought to make, money out of the affair. We were all of us honest in our convictions. We bear our crosses cheerfully, therefore I cannot but think that, although we may have erred, the Lord will repay us, since we erred out of love for Him."

I left that little room with a heavy heart. What an incomprehensible thing is human nature! A man seats himself before a table a foot or so in diameter, and tips out blasphemies to the laborious calling of the alphabet. This, only this, is sufficient to cast people, pious, intelligent, honest, of high social position and large fortunes, into a delirious ecstasy of credulity, from which they awake only to utter ruin! Nay, they hardly awake from it even then. We see them in the above narrative still hoping against hope that their faith may have had some foundation tending to warrant it; still blind to the character of the man through whom they have been despoiled of their all. That man seems to me one of the strange beings, half fanatic, half impostor, who abound in all ages of the world, and who, whilst deluding others, fall more and more into the habit of deluding themselves, till they may end by becoming fanatics more fervent than those who originally were their dupes. Certainly there was nothing in the proceedings of this person to warrant our supposing him possessed of much intelligence, or any capacity for weaving deeply meditated schemes. His blasphemies were of the rankest kind and his mode of operations was baldly simple.

I have just obtained some further light as to the origin of the "messages." A hard-shell Calvinist, pastor of a Genevan church, was amongst the deluded worshippers of the little table. With this old man (he is now eighty-four) I, very recently, had an interview.

"You are most welcome," said he, "to any information I can give; but I have little to tell. I took the matter up because the messages given were in perfect accord with Scripture; and I at last dropped it, because some ideas were communicated which did not harmonize with the Bible and my belief. I gained nothing by it. On the contrary, I had, at the outset of my connection with the affair, a good income, and I returned to Geneva from that Paris journey with only two hundred francs in the world. I certainly consider that the matter, and the peculiarly Biblical formation of the messages, were superior to what Mr. X____ could have given. The communications more resembled my ideas than his. My hands were usually on the table too. Do I not now think it blasphemy? Certainly not. Why should not such things be? The Bible has bidden us expect a second coming of Christ. He came to a manger before; why not to a table now? It was all very strange; and it is nonsense to talk about the messages proceeding from the mind of some one present. Why, there was not even a medium there! I am not a medium. Mr. X____ is not a medium. No! he had not an excitable nature."

The memory of the old gentleman must have played him false. I have questioned persons who knew X____ from childhood, and their testimony is uniformly the same. "A most impulsive nature, with very kind instincts, but self-deluded. He brought his friends to ruin, and himself shared their fate. His vanity was flattered, and would brook no demur. He, or his table, invariably became angry when any one rejected or desired to calmly investigate his monstrous pretensions."

The preface to the volume of "messages" confirms strongly the truth of the above description. It is supposed to be dictated by the angel Gabriel, and contains the following:— "And whosoever laughs in his heart" (at the contents of the book) "is a blasphemer, and must not remain with us."

In the volume itself Christ is introduced as uttering the following threats:— "Look at my cross; but let him who mocks it take care of himself. We are not on Calvary here. . . . . You would like to see miracles! Miracles were only done, and will only be done, for believers. When I was on earth men asked me to do miracles, and I replied, 'Generation of vipers, begone to your father, and *he* will make miracles for you. He is waiting for you in the everlasting flames which consume him and his angels.' Sinner! I did not come here to-night to ask your belief in the phenomenon you have before your eyes." (Wonderful phenomenon truly! A man, seated at a small table, with his hands placed upon it, tips it monotonously towards himself. A child ten months old might have done the same, and a theologically-inclined boy of ten years, who had mastered the Bible as interpreted by Calvin, could with ease have constructed the "messages").

Is there not a certain analogy in the above to the dark *séances* and puppet-shows of the present day? The honest sceptic who wishes to investigate is deridingly informed: "You want to see miracles, do you? Miracles are done with us only for the true believers." Had such a course been pursued at the outset of the movement, would spiritualism to-day have counted twenty adherents in any country of the old world or the new? But I must return to my old pastor.

"Mr. X____," he informed me, "was a musician, and very enthusiastic. I do not term that excitable. I think we were all calm when we sat around the table. As I have said, the messages were, at first, holy, heavenly, and perfectly in accordance with my views of the Bible. What caused me to retire was that I found the table afterwards become rather uncertain on various points. To this day, however, I am convinced that those beautiful communications could not have proceeded from the mind of Mr. X____. The affair remains a deep mystery to me."

The chief mystery it presents is the blindness of the dupes concerned to the most palpable facts. The old pastor, Mr. B____, was a thorough Biblical scholar of the school of Calvin. He made it his custom to open every *séance* with prayer. Besides this, he generally kept up a running fire of theology all through the proceedings. These scraps of Calvinism the "medium" X____ had only to treasure up, and, reproducing them through the table, behold the messages! No wonder that those messages agreed so completely with the Scriptural views of the old pastor. No wonder he was flattered to find that heaven and he were so completely at one on the questions of election, predestination, and so forth. The whole thing is simply a reproduction of the case of Allan Kardec, with the exception that Kardec's interpreters wrote down his ideas instead of spelling them out by means of a table. The delusion was honest, but, for all that, it must be pronounced a delusion. Be it remarked that in the Genevan episode not only was the personal vanity of all concerned flattered, but also their national pride, and their religious sympathies and antipathies. Geneva was to be the chosen city of the Lord, and Rome tottered on the verge of destruction. I find in the volume of which I have spoken messages describing the two as follows:—

"Rome. Behold the lamp of the demon!"
"Geneva. The Eternal hath chosen it, from whence to reveal Himself to the whole of mankind as a God, jealous and forgiving. God in his goodness lighted in Geneva a torch of Truth and Life. God gave Geneva as a retreat for the Bible. The Eternal required a new Bethlehem. He chose Geneva. And yet the new Bethlehem, though glorious, can only offer the Little Child a table for shelter. You laugh, reader. Yes, you are so highly placed that you can disdain Me. Is it not truly vulgar that the Son of God should speak through a simple table?"

Such is a fair sample of the incomparable homilies which were considered so far beyond the capacity of Mr. X____. The second of the works in my possession might also well be credited to a lunatic asylum. It has the following title page:—

"RÉVÉLATIONS DIVINE ET MYSTÉRIEUSE,

ou

COMMUNICATIONS ENTRE LE CIEL ET LA TERRE
Par le moyen d'une table.
Genève, 1855."

Various of the communications are too unpleasant to quote. In one place the angel Gabriel manifests, and informs the adorers of the table that God the Father and God the Son are about to speak through it. Then follows a dialogue between the Divine Persons so heralded.

This can never be termed spiritualism. Just as soon might the ravings of those lunatics who declare the moon to come down every night and whip them, be deemed doctrines inherent to our cause. As I study this incident of religious monomania, I discern more and more clearly that the only spirits concerned in this and kindred follies are the twin-demons of Vanity and Pride. It is so with Kardecian dreams and fallacies. The votaries of those doctrines are, almost without exception, to be found in the working and *bourgeois* classes. They console themselves for their humble position and contracted minds by the reflection that they have been before, and may be again, powerful potentates, or men of mark in the realms of action and thought.

Perhaps the strangest shadow which ever darkened spiritualism was that cast upon it by the utterly absurd incident known as "the new motive power." In this extraordinary display of human folly four persons were chiefly concerned. These were the Rev. John M. Spear, medium and Universalist minister; his friend, Mr. Hewitt, editor of the *New Era*; Mrs. A. E. N____, of Boston, and her husband, Mr. N____. If we except Mr. Hewitt, whose chief failings seem to have been gushingness and credulity, the mind of each of the above persons was marked by extraordinary idiosyncrasies.

John M. Spear's enthusiasm was of the philosophical sort. He "lived by faith; and trusted for direction and financial resources to the invisible world." His mind was occupied with confused ideas regarding the possibility of interblending matter and spirit. The result was extraordinary. To these ideas did the "holy motor machine" owe its birth.

The mother of "The Thing," as Mr. Hewitt reverentially termed it in the columns of the *Era*, was Mrs. N____. John M. Spear constructed the machine, and this lady engaged to endow it with perpetual motion. Spirits, she declared, had informed her that they "would make of her a second Mary, and she should become a distinguished mother in Israel." Although two children had already been born of her in an ordinary manner, she believed herself destined to bring a third into the world, which should owe its existence to no earthly father. This "spirit-babe" was to be the motive power of John M. Spear's machine.

Mrs. N____ became pregnant. Mr. Spear toiled industriously at the frame which was to contain the "power," and in due course finished his task. The machine was carried to High Rock, in Lynn, Mass., a place made celebrated in American spiritual annals by more than one ridiculous, and at least one tragical event. The language of the *New Era* became glowing. It was announced that an "association of Electrizers" in the spirit-spheres were about to reveal to mankind a "new motive power, God's last, best gift to man." The "Thing" once born, would "revolutionize the world."

At length the hour drew nigh. Mrs. N____ went down to High Rock. John M. Spear, the machine, and various attendants from earth and the spirit-world, awaited her there. In presence of this devoted band the mystical delivery of the wondrous babe took place; in other words, "the power was imparted to the machine." It moved slightly. John M. Spear shouted for joy. The editor of the *New Era* hastened back to his office, and indited an article, from which the following are extracts:—

"We are prepared to announce to the world:—

"First, That spirits have revealed a wholly new motive power, to take the place of all other motive powers.

"Second, That this revelation has been embodied in a model machine, by human co-operation with the powers above.

Third, That results are, thus far, satisfactory to its warmest friends.

"THE THING MOVES.

"We have the birth of a new science, a new philosophy, and a new life. The time of deliverance has come at last, and, henceforth, the career of humanity is upward and onward—a mighty, a noble, a godlike career. All the revelations of spiritualism heretofore; all the control of spirits over mortals, and the instruction and discipline they have given us, have only paved the way, as it were, for the advent of a great practical movement, such as the world little dreams of; though it has long deeply yearned for it, and agonised, and groaned away its life because it did not come sooner. And this new motive power is to lead the way in the great speedily coming salvation. It is to be the physical saviour of the race. The history of its inception, its various stages of progress, and its completion, will show the world a most beautiful and significant analogy to the advent of Jesus as the spiritual saviour of the race. . . . Hence we most confidently assert that the advent of the science of all sciences, the philosophy of all philosophies; and the art of all arts, has now fairly commenced. The child is born; not long hence he will go alone. Then he will dispute with the doctors in the temples of science, and then—!!"

Breath failed the editor, and other fanatics took up the cry. The machine was hailed as the "New Creation," the "Philosopher's Stone," the "Act of all Acts," the "Greatest Revelation of the Age." John M. Spear sat for a moment in the seventh heaven, and Mrs. N____ already felt the halo of a Madonna encircling her brow.

Alas for the "wonderful infant!" Alas for the folly of its devotees, and the money and faith they had so uselessly thrown away! The main mechanism of "The Thing" remained, as it had ever been, inert. The motion perceived at the moment of birth was confined to a few balls suspended by wires. These oscillations, as a Massachusetts spiritualist plaintively remarked, could scarcely be considered sufficient to constitute a "physical saviour." Common sense spiritualism declined to recognise the "Advent."

Several prominent spiritualists, amongst whom was Andrew Jackson Davis, visited High Rock, and inspected the machine. They agreed as to its utter uselessness. The general opinion, however, was that its construction had certainly been directed by spirits; and that John M. Spear and the other parties to the affair deserved pity rather than the blame now liberally showered upon them. With this verdict I coincide, and can endorse the following expressions of Mrs. Hardinge:— "That Mr. Spear honestly believed in a spiritual origin for the various 'missions' he undertook, and the remarkable part he played, none who have ever come into personal relations with him can question. The unwavering fidelity with which he adhered to his purposes, and the patience with which he endured reproach and odium for their execution, would attest his sincerity, were other evidence wanting." It must ever be regretted that an excellent heart should have been so often and so far led astray by the perversities of the head with which it was connected.

"Let the machine," one spiritualist wrote, "stand at High Rock as a lasting evidence of human credulity." I appreciate his feelings and echo his words. How appropriately, had the machine been left there, might the "Punch and Judy" cabinets of the present day, and the insignia of the Theosophical Society, be collected together at the same place. But it was not to be. The worshippers of the "holy infant" trusted that a change of scene would develop the power they still supposed to be latent within it. "The machine," says Mr. Spear, "was moved to Randolph, New York, that it might have the advantage of that lofty electrical position." Such advantage it did not long enjoy. Ribald paragraphs respecting the transaction had gone the round of the press. The mystifying and revolting story of a perpetual motive power born of a woman furnished space for endless invective and satire. The comments of the journals stimulated the public to fury. A large and disorderly crowd entered at night the structure which had been raised as a temporary cradle for Mr. Spear's "physical saviour." They tore the machine in pieces, trampled the shreds under foot, and scattered them to the winds. From the threats uttered, it seems that a similar fate was reserved for the constructors of the "Thing," could the furious mob have seized them. Such was the ignominious end of the metal Frankenstein destined to revolutionize the American world. The frame lay in atoms. The mysterious "motive power" was relegated to an obscurity more perplexing than ever. No new pæans gladdened the subscribers to the *Era*, and John Y. Spear turned sadly to less glowing schemes. A fond hope, however, remained to him that time would yet behold the realisation of his cherished idea. "Thank God," he wrote, "the principles which have been presented, and the philosophy which has been communicated, are beyond the reach of the mob, and cannot be harmed by the slanders of the pulpit or the misrepresentations of the press." And, consoling himself with the line.:—

"Truth crushed to earth shall rise again,"

the servant of the "Associated Electrizers" departed from the spot where was extinguished the "Greatest Revelation of the Age."

So rose, progressed, and fell, three of the wildest follies which have disgraced modern spiritualism. Other insanities of the kind have since occurred. There were in America the Kiantone movement, the "Sacred Order of Unionists," the Cincinnati "Patriarchs," and, worst of all, the "Harmonial Society." Mrs. E. Hardinge describes this last as one of the most extraordinary evidences of human folly, credulity, impudent assumption, and blasphemous pretension that the records of any movement can show."

The "Society" did not directly originate through spiritualism. On the contrary, it was simply a parasitical excrescence foisted upon that movement by interested persons. As in the case of Mountain Cove the leading spirit was an ex-Reverend. A certain T. E. Spencer, formerly pastor of a Methodist flock, planned, and, with the aid of his wife, carried out this infamous affair. A settlement styled "Harmony Springs" was formed in Benton County, Arkansas. All applications for membership Mr. Spencer submitted to his "controlling angels." These displayed a worldliness of mind hardly to be expected from such elevated beings. Rich dupes were eagerly welcomed into the Harmonial paradise; but its gates remained inexorably closed on the poor. Once admitted, the neophyte found his wealth melt with wonderful rapidity. The Spencers, like Dives, clothed themselves in fine linen, and fared sumptuously every day. Their followers were enforced to content themselves with an extremely meagre vegetarian diet; the inducement to do so being the hope of earthly immortality. For the doctrines of the "Harmonial Society" were extremely curious. Many spirits, Mr. Spencer taught, perished with the body. Others languished for a short time after the separation, and then expired. Only human beings who followed the Spencerian system could arrive at immortality, which immortality should be earthly. And an indispensable condition of the system was that its promulgator should have full control of the property of his dupes.

In a year or two the bubble burst. Dark rumours issued from Harmony Springs. It appeared certain that, whether immortal or not, Spencer and his followers, male and female, were extremely immoral. Dissension, too, was rife among the community. For a time Mrs. Spencer quieted recusants by diatribes on the annihilation which awaited them should they persist in their mutinous conduct. "Death," she remarked, "is the prying into things that are of the world, and acquisitiveness, and keeping anything to yourselves, and looking into things too much for your knowledge, and inquiring into things that the angels only hint at, and questioning what the angels say or do, and doubting much, and *fixing up separate dishes for yourselves!*"

Despite this sublime philosophy matters continued to grow worse. Several members determined to take legal measures for the recovery of their cash. On learning *this* the Spencers gathered together what was left of the spoil, and fled. They were pursued, arrested, tried, and sentenced to imprisonment. Of the large sums that had been embarked in the "Harmonial Society," scarcely a dollar remained.

In this, as in all other enterprises of the kind, ridicule, disappointment, and ruin, were the portion of the dupes. Nor can one compassionate them very highly. They appeared to have taken leave of common sense, and to be utterly destitute of reason. No claim was too absurd for credence. The extraordinary spiritual pretensions of the self-constituted prophets who domineered over them were accepted without the slightest examination. That two ex-reverends could be the witnesses foretold by John, that a machine might be endowed with life, that earthly immortality was attainable by immoral practices and spare diet, the faithful religiously believed. Nor, reviewing the long record of human credulity, need we be surprised. Two very opposite errors exist, into which, according to their bias, mankind are liable to fall. On one side we have the bigoted sceptic who disbelieves, in face of the plainest evidence, that spirits can communicate with man. The father of such an one ridiculed the notion of an electric telegraph; his grandfather laughed at Watt and Stephenson, and wrote in the *Quarterly Review*, when railway travelling was first proposed, "Twenty miles an hour! As well trust one's self to be fired off from a Congreve mortar." Others of his ancestors imprisoned Solomon de Caus in a madhouse, and all but broke the heart of Columbus. As a contrast to this species of mental deformity we have the bigoted enthusiast, who accepts the wildest dreams without examination, and feels insulted should any one speak of proof. Such enthusiasts adored Joanna Southcote as a prophetess; and such put faith in all the lies of Titus Oates. During the Middle Ages they searched for the philosopher's stone; and persecuted old dames who rode on broomsticks, and kept familiar demons in the shape of cats. In Mandeville's time they sent ambassadors to Prester John. In the era of Procopius they knew Britain to be an island inhabited only by the invisible spirits of the dead. At present one class of such persons put faith in Papal Infallibility, and another, under the name of "Reincarnationists," vamp up the worn-out follies of Brahminical India, and seek to reconstruct the exploded theories of Pythagoras.

CHAPTER III

DELUSIONS *(continued)*

I class Kardecism amongst the delusions of the world, and I have excellent reasons for the course I take. I knew well the founder, or rather the reviver, of this phase of paganism. His entire honesty of purpose I do not for a moment doubt. He was perfectly convinced that he had dug from the grave of Pythagoras a light which should illumine the world. This intensity of conviction mastered not only himself but others. His earnestness was projected on the minds of the sensitive magnetic subjects whom he termed his mediums. The thoughts thus forced into their brains, their hands committed to paper, and Kardec received his own doctrines as messages from the spirit-world. Had these teachings really emanated from the great minds which were professedly their authors, would they have taken the shape they did? How came Iamblichus to be such a master of good modern French? Through what cause had Pythagoras so completely forgotten his native Greek? If, too, these communications were really the work of disembodied spirits, by what right does "Par Allan Kardec" appear on the title page of every volume? And then the teachings promulgated. Are they truths? If so, let us have some *fact* in support of these truths; the wild dreams of believers and the revelations of clairvoyants will not suffice. I am well known to be a clairvoyant, and have the right and the power to speak with confidence regarding this particular phase of psychology. All students of the question are aware that two forms of clairvoyance exist; the one entitled "natural" the other induced by magnetism. I have never yet met with a case of magnetic clairvoyance where the subject did not reflect directly or indirectly the ideas of the magnetiser. This is most strikingly illustrated in the instance of Allan Kardec. Under the influence of his energetic will his clairvoyants were so many writing machines that gave his ideas as he desired to have them. If at times the doctrines promulgated were not exactly in accordance with his wishes, he corrected them to meet those wishes. It is, or ought to be, well known that Allan Kardec *was not himself a medium.* He simply magnetized or psychologized minds frailer and more sensitive than his own. I can testify to the fact that, before I knew, or could by any possibility have known, of his passing from earth, I received, in presence of the Earl of Dunraven, then Viscount Adare, a message; saying: "I regret to have taught the *spirite* doctrine. Allan Kardec." ("Je regrette d'avoir enseigné la doctrine spirite. Allan Kardec.") By comparison of the minute of this occurrence with the minute of his passing away, the interval between the two was found so short as utterly to preclude the idea that even a telegram could have reached me regarding his departure from earth. As, moreover, his decease was preceded by no illness, the possibility of that decease had never been for a moment present to my mind. I could not, on receiving it, at first credit the above message. It was not, I may remark, received during a *séance*, but suddenly interrupted a conversation between Lord Adare and myself.

The subjoined most remarkable communication was dictated through M. Morin, whom in earth-life Allan Kardec considered one of his best mediums, and relied on greatly. To say the least it is reasonable, and bears the impress of truth.

"All. Kardec.

" M. Morin, medium, somnambule parlant,

"Communicant chez M. Caussin, Rue St. Denis, 345,

du 6me novemb., 1869.

"All. Kardec parlant par la bouche de Morin.

Sa confession posthume.

"Dans les dernières années j'ai travaillé avec soin à éloigner toutes les intelligences, tous les hommes entourés de l'estime public et qui, travaillant à la science spirite, eussent pu accaparer pour eux une partie des bénéfices que je voulais pour moi seul.

"Cependant, plusieurs, d'entre eux, placés très haut dans les sciences et les lettres, se seraient contents en se dévouant an spiritisme de briller au second rang, mais dans mon effroi d'être éclipse, je préférai toujours rester seul à la tête du mouvement spirite; en être à la fois la tête qui pense et le bras qui agit.

"Oui, je l'avoue, c'est ma faute si le spiritisme n'a jusqu'à ce jour compté dans ses rangs aucun de ces champions princes de la parole ou de la pensée; chez moi l'homme avait dompté l'esprit"

Sur l'avenir du spiritisme, tel qu'il l'avait conçu, et sur les conséquences actuelles:

"De mon vivant, le spiritisme, tel que je le concevais, me paraissait ce que l'homme pourrait rêver de plus grand, de plus vaste; ma raison s'égarait.

"Maintenant que, débarrassé de l'enveloppe matérielle, je regarde l'immensité des mondes, je me demande comment j'ai pu me draper dans mon manteau de demi-dieu, me croire un deuxième Sauveur de l'humanité. Orgueil insensé que je déplore amèrement.

"Je vois le spiritisme tel que je l'avais conçu, si petit, si restreint, si éloigné, dans ses parties mêmes les moins imparfaites, des perfections qu'il doit atteindre.

"Considérant les résultats produits par la propagation des idées spirites, que vois-je à présent?

"Le spiritisme traîné dans les bas-fonds du ridicule, représenté par d'infimes personnalités que j'ai trop élevées moi-même.

"En voulant produire le bien j'ai motivé beaucoup d'aberration qui enfante le mal.

"Au point de vue de la philosophie, peu de résultat. Pour quelques intelligences combien d'ignorants!

"Au point de vue religieux, que de superstitieux sortis d'une superstition pour tomber dans une autre!

"Conséquences de mon égoïsme.

"Si je n'avais pas écarté les intelligences transcendentales le spiritualisme ne serait pas exclusivement représenté dans la majorité des adhérens par des adepts pris an sein des classes laborieux, les seules chez lesquelles mon éloquence et mon savoir ont pu avoir accès.

"ALLAN KARDEC."

I append a translation of the above:—

"All. Kardec.

"M. Morin, inspirational medium.

"Communication given at the house of M. Caussin,
Rue St. Denis, 345, Nov. 6th, 1869.

"Allan Kardec speaking through M. Morin.

His posthumous confession.

"During the last few years of my life, I sought with care to keep in the background all men of intelligence who merited public esteem, who were investigators of the science of *spiritisme*, and might have taken for themselves a share of the benefit which I wished for myself alone.

"Nevertheless, many of these, occupying high positions in literature and science, would have been perfectly satisfied, in devoting themselves, to *spiritisme*, to have shone in the second rank; but, in my fear of being eclipsed, I preferred to remain alone at the head of the movement, to be at once the thinking brain and the arm of action.

"Yes, I acknowledge it to be my fault if *spiritisme* to the present day has numbered in its ranks none of those champions—princes of language or of thought; with me the man (or my humanity) overcame my intelligence."

In speaking of the future of *spiritisme*, as he had understood it, and of the actual position:

"Whilst I lived *spiritisme*, as I had conceived it, seemed to me all that mankind could imagine of grandest and most vast; my reason was bewildered.

"Now that, free from the material envelope, I look on the immensity of the different worlds, I ask how I could have clothed myself in the mantle, as it were, of a demi-god; believing myself to be a second Saviour of humanity. Monstrous pride which I bitterly regret.

"I now see *spiritisme*, such as I had imagined it, so small, so contracted, so far from (even in the least imperfect of its teachings) the perfections it ought to attain.

"Taking into consideration the results produced by the propagation of the ideas *spirite*, what do I now see?

"*Spiritisme* dragged to the lowest depth of ridicule, and represented only by puny personalities, which I had striven too much to elevate. "In seeking to do good I have incited much aberration productive only of evil.

"So far as the philosophy is concerned how small the results! For the few intelligences it has reached, how many are unaware of its existence!" From a religious point of view we find the superstitious leaving one superstition only to fall into another.

"Consequences of my egotism.

"Had I not kept in the shade all superior intelligences, *spiritisme* would not be represented, as it is to the majority of its adherents, by adepts taken from amongst the working classes, the only one where my eloquence and my learning could gain access.
"ALLAN KARDEC."

Such is the message submitted to us through the instrumentality of M. Morin, and claimed to be from his former hierophant. I pass now to an examination of the philosophy, if philosophy it deserves to be termed, unfolded in "Le Livre des Esprits."

"Q.—What foundation is there for the doctrine of re-incarnation?

"A.—The justice of God and revelation.

"Q.—What is the aim of re-incarnation?

"A.—Expiation; progressive improvement of mankind. Without this aim, where would be its justice? "—*The Spirits' Book.*

Justice and Expiation are thus the key-notes of that fantasia with which Allan Kardec would have bewildered the brain of man. His scheme of creation is a plagiary from the severer schools of Christianity; but a plagiary which omits their central figure, Christ. For the Messiah he substitutes an endless dream of change. He discards the theory of Pythagoras, so far as it relates to man's entrance into the bodies of animals; but he discards this only to accept and refine upon other parts of the Pythagorean system. Like most theologians he finds in the Deity more of anger than of love. His Father is the Father of Calvin and of Knox. These, however, teach that God's wrath is pacified by the sacrifice of his Son. Kardec informs us that God pacifies his wrath by confusing the identity of his creatures. The order which reigns in the material universe finds no counterpart in spiritual things. The quiet harmony with which system wheels round system serves only to mock the confusion prevalent among the souls for whom those systems were created. It would seem that the happiness of just men made perfect is, in the Kardecian heaven, coincident on their having at last found out "who they may possibly be." The Biblical assurance that "there is no rest for the wicked," acquires a new and startling significance from the views put forward under the title of Re-incarnation. Unhappy spirits, we learn, spend a considerable portion of eternity in finding out how much "worse confounded" their confusion may become. Their constant dread is that, in forgetting the incidents of their earthly lives, they may have also forgotten the lessons of those lives, and so be sent back to learn them more perfectly. The incarnations, it seems, which spirits undergo "are always very numerous." Yet the soul "never loses its individuality." Fairly stated, the Kardecian argument would appear to be that a soul must lose its individuality in order to find it.

There is no limit to the monstrous perplexities which continued incarnations involve. It is, according to Kardec, part of the justice of God that a grandmother maybe her own granddaughter. The Nero of the first century becomes the Madame Guyon of the eighteenth. "The soul of a bad man can become the soul of a good man. If he have repented, his new incarnation is the reward of his efforts at amendment." On the question being put, "Can a spirit who has animated the body of a man, animate that of a woman in a new existence, and *vice versa?*" the reply was, "Yes."

From such propositions as these an almost infinite succession of revolting corollaries may be deduced. Some among these corollaries are of a nature which I dare hardly do more than indicate. We might, for instance, meet with such a case as the following:— Two persons marry. Children having been born to them, the parents in due course pass from earth. They are once more incarnated. In this existence, however, the man has become the woman, and the woman the man. Should they again marry, how are we to read the riddle of their relationship, and the relationship of their children?

The doctrine of re-incarnation, in fact, destroys all relationship. It takes away whatever binds society together. It crushes the holiest feelings of our nature. What is left to us when all that we love has lost its identity? The re-incarnationist deliberately cuts himself off from the hope of being once more rejoiced by—

> "The touch of a vanished hand
> And the sound of a voice that is still"

The hand has vanished from us to the clasp of somebody else, and the voice, though it may not be still, has forgotten us for ever. The same fate awaits ourselves. We, too, must pass away and forget. We, too, must spend eternity in a sort of bewildered wonder as to what will next be our lot. We are more unhappy than the old Biblical heroes who had "no abiding place on earth." They looked for an eternal dwelling-place hereafter, and crowns which should never fade away. But we, if Kardec and Kardec's "spirits" prophesy aright, possess no continuing city either on earth or in heaven. We are doomed to a ceaseless and unhappy wandering. Innocent of the crime of Cain, we share his punishment. And we are no longer men and women. We have no longer wife, husband, mother, father, sister, brother, son, or daughter. Such words have lost their meaning. Indeed, we are not even masters of our own souls. The world of the re-incarnationist is simply a stage from which puppets dance on and off as the showman pulls the strings. With each change of scene the puppets are taken to pieces and thrown into a promiscuous heap, from which new dolls are constructed as casually as the shifting figures of the kaleidoscope. Yet Kardec asserts that this doctrine is "at once eminently consolatory and strictly conformable with the most rigorous justice," and thousands of enthusiasts endorse his assertion.

It is evident, however, that even the warmest of these disciples accept the new faith with sweeping reservations. Human nature revolts from re-incarnation in its Kardecian entirety. For the logical outcome of the system is an annihilation as complete as that anticipated by the hardest Materialist, and far more painful. In a few thousand years there would remain nothing of a world conducted under re-incarnationist conditions, save an insanity of confusion. The children would have become undistinguishable from the fathers. The only thing remaining in life would be a frantic endeavour to grasp some tangible idea. Naturally, even fanaticism shrinks from this. Re-incarnationists, therefore, far from surveying their creed in its full scope, grasp only at portions which may be moulded to suit the wishes they have in view. Treated in this manner, Kardecism becomes a truly plastic faith. Even the maternal heart can find comfort in reincarnation by resolutely refusing to note the direction of the great wave, and attending only to minor eddies. Thus we hear of a French lady, whose only daughter dies while still quite a child. Another is born to her. The second girl receives the same name as the first. Surprised by the coincidence, friends naturally question the mother as to the reasons that may exist for such a re-naming. She explains that there is nothing of re-naming in the matter; the second daughter, is simply the first given back to her by God. She tells how one day, whilst she held the baby on her knee, it suddenly spoke, and said: "Mamma, do you not know who I am?" Startled by such an occurrence, she could scarcely find breath to reply, "No, my child." "I am your little *Mimi*," was the answer, "and I have come back to you. Look at me, dear mamma, and you will see that I am really your Mimi." And the mother looked, and saw that the features of the child were assuredly those of her lost daughter. Such are the fond dreams for which, even in re-incarnation, the heart of a mother will find scope.

There is a touching something in the above incident. What, however, save bewilderment, can be extracted from the narrative I now give? It appears here, as it appeared in the *Spiritualist* of September 18th, 1874:—

"As *The Spiritualist*, Vol. V., No. 8, page 85, contains Miss Kislingbury's very judicious remarks about the two contending theories in spiritualism, allow me, in my turn, to communicate to you a fact, which seems strongly to corroborate my belief in re-incarnation, and which happened to me in the summer of 1869.

"A very distinguished French writing medium, Madame C____, had come to spend some weeks at my house, at N____ W____, and we had asked our leading spirits whether it was possible or not to evoke, during the sleep of the body, the spirit of a person now alive? Soon after there fell from the ceiling, on the table where Madame C____ was writing under spiritual control, a small oval bronze medal, quite tarnished, with some dry yellow earth sticking to it, bearing on one side the likeness of Christ, on the other one that of the Virgin Mary, and seeming, by its style, to belong to the sixteenth century. We were then told that this medal had been buried a long time ago, with a person who had constantly worn it, and who had died a violent death that this person was now re-incarnated in Germany—that an object which had belonged to her formerly was necessary to establish between her and us a fluidical connection, which might enable her to come and appeal to us for assistance against a sort of painful obsession under which she was labouring—that her name began with an A— and that we were to call her *'In memory of the town of Dreux.'*

"Accordingly, on the following and some other evenings we set to work, Madame C____ (whom I had mesmerised to sleep for better control) holding the pencil: and presently the spirit wrote, in small, hasty writing:— 'I am here.'

"'*Quest.*—How is it that you are already asleep? (It was only ten o'clock.)

"'*Ans.*—I am in bed, ill of fever.'

"'*Quest.*—Can you tell us your present name?'

"'*Ans.*—Not yet. When I wore the medal I was in France; in the reign of Louis XIV. I was killed by a man who was carrying off a lady from the monastery where I was a nun.'

"'*Quest.*—Why did he kill you?'

"'*Ans.*—He did so unintentionally. I had just returned from Dreux, where I had been sent on an errand by our Abbess. I overtook them unawares, and threatened to scream; he then struck me on the head with the pommel of his sword, in order to stun me into silence, and killed me.'

"'*Quest.*—How did he manage to enter the convent?'

"'*Ans.*—By bribing the man who kept our doors, and who feigned to be asleep while they were stealing his keys. When he saw that I was dead he was frightened. He and his servant bore me off and buried me in the first place they found fit. There are now houses built all over it, but my grave exists, still unknown in a garden.'

"'*Quest.*—What place was it?'

"'*Ans.*—The Pré-aux-Clercs, Paris.'

"'*Quest.*—Was the man who killed you a nobleman?'

"'*Ans.*—Yes. He belonged to the *Lesdiguières.*'

"'*Quest.*—Who was the nun he carried off?'

"'*Ans.*—A novice of a noble family. He had led her already to a coach, which was to carry her off in another direction than the one he intended to take; they were to meet again later. So she knew nothing about my death. They fled to foreign countries. She died soon after.'

"'*Quest.*—What did your spirit do when it left your body?'

"'*Ans.*—I hastened straight to our Abbess, but she was terribly frightened when she saw me, thinking it was a nightmare. I then roamed about the chapel, always thinking myself alive still. I only understood that I was dead when those who were burying me said a prayer before covering my body with earth. A great trouble overcame me then, and I felt it a hard task to pardon them. I have great difficulty in obeying your call, because as soon as I am asleep, I am usually forced to return to Dreux and to haunt the church under my former aspect, as I used to do before my present incarnation. It is a terrible subjection, a constant hindrance to my progress, as it paralyzes all my efforts to come into contact with the good spirits who guide and comfort those who are in the flesh and asleep. Emile! You mast help me to Free myself.'

"After some words of advice and encouragement, and my promise to help her, we continued:—

"'*Quest.*—In which street at Paris was your monastery situated?'

"'*Ans.*—Rue de l'Abbaye.'

"'*Quest.*—Under the patronage of which saint?'

"'*Ans.*—Of St. Bruno; the congregation of the Ladies of the Passion.'

"'*Quest.*—Does the monastery still exist?'

"'*Ans.*—Destroyed; plundered during the revolution.'

"'*Quest.*—Is there anything now remaining of it?'

"'*Ans.*—A wall.'

"[Having, after this, written to Paris for information, the friend to whom we wrote informed us that, after many long searches, he had indeed found out, incrusted between houses, an old wall, which once, as was said, belonged to a lady's monastery.]

"'*Quest.*—Have you, in your present incarnation, any recollection of the one gone by?'

"'*Ans.*—I have a sort of apprehension, as if I were to die of a violent death—an injury to the head. It makes me very nervous at times! I see now that it is only a reflex of the past. I also dream of phantoms in monastic gowns, and of murderers rushing at them; also of a spectre in an ancient dress, who grins at me.'

"'*Quest.*—Do you live far off?'

"'*Ans.*—In Germany.'

"'*Quest.*—Is your name a German one?'

"'*Ans.*—Yes. Those questions hurt me!'

"'*Quest.*—Do I know you?'

"'*Ans.*—To be sure you do!'

"'*Quest.*—Where do you live?'

"The medium then begins to trace with great difficulty:— F . . . Fu . . . I exclaim, under sudden inspiration, *Fulda!* and at the same moment Madame C____ gives a shriek and a violent start, nearly upsetting her chair. She says she felt a commotion, as of a strong electric discharge. I understand at once that the controlling spirit is that of my cousin, the Countess *Amelie* of Y. . . who lives in Fulda (a small town about five hours' journey away by the railway), where she occupies a high charge in a Protestant Chapter of noble ladies.

"'*Quest.* (*after a long pause.*)—Why did you give the medium such a shock?'

"'Ans.—I did not want you to know yet.'

"'*Quest.*—Did your body awake?'

"'*Ans.*—No; but I was startled.'

"While we were still (Madame C____ and I) debating whether it were really my cousin or not, the medium's hand unconsciously wrote down a name which cut short all my doubts, as it referred to a secret known only to the Countess of Y____ and myself.

"'*Quest.*—How am I to ascertain your identity, and make sure that you are not a frivolous spirit, mocking us?'

"'*Aus.*—When you meet me, before long, ask whether I have any dreams, in which it seems to me as if I were killed? I shall say no, and add, that I dream sometimes of a priest murdered by ruffians. You may also show me the medal: I shall feel then as if I had known it before.'

"With this communication we closed our evocations of Amelie, which had taken us several evenings.

"A few months later I met my cousin at my sister's country seat. Amelie, as was her wont, began joking with me about my faith in spiritualism, declaring that it was all delusion and deception. I bore her merry attacks merrily, defending, however, my theories about dreams, reminiscences, spirit messages, and so on, till I came to ask, as in a joke, whether she, for example, never dreamt that she was being murdered? She answered 'No,' adding, after a slight pause, that, in fact, she had sometimes a disagreeable dream, always the same—a sort of nightmare—which made her nervous and uncomfortable for the whole day after. On my insisting upon receiving the particulars, she said at last, that she dreamt of a Catholic priest in sacerdotal dress, flying from a burning church, with armed men at his heels, who wanted to kill him. After changing the conversation, I took the medal out of my pocket and showed it to her feigning to have bought it at an antiquary's. She handled it about for some moments, and then began to examine it so long and so closely that I, at last, asked her 'What was the matter?' whereupon she answered that 'she could not understand how that object seemed as familiar as if she had possessed or seen it formerly, although she could not, for the world, recollect under what circumstances!'

"I now told her all about our evocations; and she, being very much struck by my narrative, requested to be shown the medial writing. This writing, I had thought, was not like her own. I had known hers only by her letters, in German, written with pen and ink, while the former, traced by a French medium, was written in French. When she saw it she exclaimed that it was positively *her* writing, when she used a pencil instead of a pen; and forthwith she wrote some words which I dictated, and which proved to be exactly like the original.

"She got into a great fright at the thought of her soul haunting an old church, and I advised her, in order to paralyze the attraction, to pray every evening for help to her guardian angel, and to say three times aloud, before going to bed, '*I will not go!*'

"Since she has done this, I was informed by my leading spirits that she has entirely succeeded in ridding herself of the aforesaid subjection.

"This, my dear sir, is my personal experience of a fact, interesting enough I think, to find a space in your columns; and I would be thankful for every explanation of it, given in the non-reincarnationist sense, in favour of the French proverb which says, *Du choc des opinions jaillit la vérite.*"

There is nothing in the above which can be construed as a proof of re-incarnation. The whole may be explained by the theory that the Countess of Y____ and Madame C____ being sensitives, the same spirit had contrived to impress the same ideas on the brain of each; with greater clearness in the case of the latter lady. I do not advance this supposition as the true one. I advance it, however, as at once more plausible and more reasonable than the theory which attributes such dim reminiscences to a transmigration of souls. The hypothesis I have offered covers the facts of the case at least as well. It is less far-fetched. It accords better with proved phenomena. To speak of such is useless, indeed, in the present instance. Re-incarnation remains, and always must remain, a theory whose very nature renders it incapable of proof.

Putting aside the revolting confusion to which it logically leads, how illogical are the delusions into which it betrays its votaries! It is evidently impossible that the particular qualities of mind which, nineteen centuries ago, were put together to constitute Julius Cæsar, can be reproduced through more than one man or woman at a time, even in this age of wonders. And, although a lady may be firmly convinced that, in a former incarnation, she was the consort of an emperor or king, it becomes perplexing when one encounters half-a-dozen other persons equally enthusiastic, and equally certain of their identity with the said empress or queen. The souls of famous men and women would appear to cut up into more fragments than the wood of the true cross. As I remarked once in a published letter of mine:— "I have had the pleasure of meeting at least twelve Marie Antoinettes, six or seven Marys of Scotland, a whole host of Louis and other kings, about twenty Great Alexanders, but never a plain 'John Smith.' I would indeed like to cage the latter curiosity."

M. Kardec's mesmerised mediums tell us that spirits never degenerate. "Can a man," it was asked, "descend in his new existence to a lower point than that which he has already reached?" The reply came promptly, "As regards his social position, yes, but not as regards his degree of progress as a spirit." The Alexanders and Caesars with whom we are inundated have thus advanced to a higher degree of intelligence than when they scattered the hosts of Darius, or drove Pompey from the Pharsalian plain. Why then, in the name of all that is mystifying, do they accomplish so little? Where were these heroes in the day of their country's agony, when French eagles looked down only on disaster, and a German army lay outside the walls of Paris? From all the Hannibals, the Scipios, the Charlemagnes, the Turennes, the Condos, whom France possesses, could not one warlike patriot have come forward as her saviour? Either want of patriotism is a Kardecian virtue, or greatness of mind has place among "the impurities which spirits must strip themselves of."

Perhaps, indeed, the soul becomes bewildered with its multiplicity of existences. Thus, we can well conceive that if after having figured on earth's stage as Nero, Constantine, Mahomet, Charlemagne, Friar Bacon, &c., a spirit should be incarnated as Pierre Dubois, he may find even three-score years and ten, if he be allowed so much, insufficient to determine whether he shall set fire to Paris and fiddle whilst it is burning; transfer the metropolis of France from the banks of the Seine to the shores of the Gulf of Lyons, or the Bay of Biscay; collect Catholics, Voltairians, Protestants and Positivists under the banner of a new religion; or invent some material of murder which shall be to gunpowder as gunpowder was to the spears and axes of the fourteenth century. Is it surprising if, confused by the entrance of so much genius into one small mind, the unfortunate mixture of great men spends his— or I might more appropriately say *their* time, in perplexedly trying to determine to what he had best turn his powers? And before he has settled whether there is more of the Mahomet or the Friar Bacon in him, death knocks, and the world finds that it has profited by this particular re-incarnationist as little as it profits by the philosophy of re-incarnation in general.

What miserable times must the poor nondescripts have in the spirit-world! Imagine two collections of existences meeting, and perplexedly iterating to each other:—

> "Perhaps, my friend, I'm you!
> Perhaps, my friend, you are me!
> Perhaps, we both are somebody else!
> And 'tis puzzling, you'll agree."

In this very dilemma lies the essence and the drawback of the Kardecian philosophy. But the spirits may console themselves with memories and anticipations of their greatness, past and future. For, as I have remarked, it is very, very seldom that the ordinary run of human minds are re-incarnated. Your heroes and geniuses seem to reserve to themselves "the right of re-admission to earth." How lamentable it is that their last state here should be so worthless in comparison with their first! But, no doubt, it consoles the frivolous lounger of Parisian salons to assume that he was at a far back day Conde or Molière, and that, as "spirits cannot degenerate," he must now, although he appears a dunce, be raised above the mental platform on which he stood as victor of Rocroy or author of "Le Misantrope."

What becomes of ordinary souls? Shakespeare and Sophocles must be very weary of the many parts they have to play; but the curtain never rises for the entrance of plain John Smith. He dies, and earth knows him no more. No doubt he is one of the spirits M. Kardec tells us of, "who at their origin have only an instinctive existence, and have scarcely any consciousness of themselves or their acts; it is only little by little that their intelligence is developed." But where does that intelligence become developed? The spirit cannot, surely, depart from earth a plain member of the Smith family, to return in a year or two a full-blown Alexander! Has Dame Nature, then, some far-off planetary workshop, where the raw material of a hundred butchers or bakers is kneaded into one conqueror or inventor? Or can the mass of humanity be composed of insignificant, jog-trot creatures; content to be born in an ordinary manner, to live an ordinary life, to possess the ordinary hope of immortality, and to depart from earth with the vulgar expectation of finding "a place prepared for them," according to their merits? I sincerely trust that this last supposition is the correct one. If it be, we unfortunates whom the re-incarnationist pities as suckled in the outworn creed that no individual can possess more than one soul, need hardly envy our kaleidoscopic brethren. We need not lament that we are not as Cicero-Napoleon-Jones; or if a touch of longing thrill us when contemplating his greatness, we may stifle it by reflecting that, however obscure our identity may be, that identity is peaceful and unperplexed. We are safe, moreover, from such nightmare visions as that which caused a feminine re-incarnationist to describe to the world the monstrous intertwinements of two complicated souls. These souls pass a confused series of existences in various planets. They change from sex to sex. After a series of perplexities, always absurd, and often disgusting, the soul which happens at that precise moment to be the woman is summoned to earth. In her previous existences she has sometimes been married to her fellow Tiresias, but, oftener, has dispensed with the Hymeneal knot. However, she contrives to forget her much incarnated lover, and weds with an ordinary mortal. A child is born. Confusion madder than the maddest intricacy of an insane brain ensues. The discarded lover, watching his opportunity of revenge, has appeared on earth in the form of the said child. Through the carelessness of a nurse, however, he is killed whilst still young. His mother-wife is reported to have married again, very recently, and to remain at present in an agreeable state of doubt as to whether she have not literally wedded her grandmother. Such is re-incarnationist literature. There is much more of this kind of thing than is sketched above. There are works infinitely madder and more disgusting than anything I have quoted. There are others distinguished chiefly by the; perverted ingenuity they display. A second feminine disciple of Kardec has elaborated a theory of emanations. Disincarnated beings who wait their turn of material life are made up, we learn, of numerous souls, fitting one within another like the ivory balls of China. Should one of this strange race of beings wish to communicate with mankind, he throws forth a soul, which throws forth another, which continues the emanating process until earth is reached. Then these curious links hand up and down the electric chain they have formed their own communications and those of the human beings with whom they are in sympathy. The task finished, they uncoil, and creep once more the one within the other.

These theories find accepters. The more absurd and contradictory they appear to ordinary minds, the more do they delight enthusiasts. Nor need this be wondered at. Contradictions crop up everywhere in the revelations of Kardec himself, and whosoever accepts those revelations evidently has a vigorous capacity of credulity. How puzzling must spiritualists who are not "Spiritists" consider such doctrines as the following:—

"*Q.*–Do spirits employ any time in transporting themselves through space?

"*A.*–Yes, but their motion is as rapid as that of thought.

"*Q.*–Is not thought the movement of the soul itself, a transportation of the soul to the object thought of by it?

"*A.*–Wherever the thought is there the soul is, since it is the soul that thinks. Thought is an attribute.

"*Q.*–Is the spirit, properly so called, without a covering; or is it, as some declare, surrounded by a substance of some kind?

"*A.*–The spirit is enveloped in a substance which would appear to you as mere vapour, but which, nevertheless, appears very gross to us, though it is sufficiently vaporous to allow the spirit to float in the atmosphere and transport himself through space at pleasure."

If "wherever the thought is, there the soul is," how can these spirits inform us that spirits travel? Travel implies time, and thought is instantaneous. Perhaps, indeed, they would answer that the duration of a journey is equivalent to the time occupied in the formation of a thought regarding that journey. A spirit wishes to traverse a distance of some millions of miles, and, presto! it is accomplished. The wish and the deed were one.

But, if so, why say that "the motion of spirits is as rapid as that of thought?" According to the teachers whose utterances are supposed to be given to the world by Kardec, that motion is thought. If a spirit can but form an idea of any sphere, the said spirit finds itself instantly there. Distance matters nothing. Distance *is* nothing, for to thought distance is inappreciable. To select an earthly and therefore familiar illustration, it is the same thing as regards time occupied whether a man in London thinks of Brighton or of Queensland. He forms a thought of the province fifteen thousand miles away just as rapidly as of the town from which he is only fifty miles distant. Thought, then, knows nothing of time or space.

But matter does, and the Kardecian spirits are clothed in matter. "It would appear to you mere vapour, but it, nevertheless, appears very gross to us." What then enables it to race as swiftly as thought? Even vapour must take an appreciable time to traverse a given distance, and that time increases with the increase of the distance to be traversed. But to thought the distance of the farthest star is as inappreciable as that of the nearest planet. Evidently, then, these Kardecian teachings are incongruous. The dilemma they present is the following one. If in the next world spirits are still enveloped in matter, they cannot travel with the rapidity of thought. If they travel with the rapidity of thought they cannot be enveloped in matter. One or other of these statements must necessarily be false.

I pretend not to decide which. Neither can I pretend to decide why Kardec's mesmerised clairvoyants and writers have advanced such doctrines as the following:— "All spirits are created equal, not knowing whence they come, for their free-will must have its fling. They progress more or less rapidly in intelligence as in morality. The state of the soul at its first incarnation is a state analogous to that of infancy. In proportion as spirits advance they understand what has retarded their progress. A spirit may remain stationary, but he never deteriorates."

Is the Greece of to-day more intelligent than the Greece of Homer and Socrates? Is the France of our century more moral than the France of fifteen centuries back? He will be a bold man who answers Yes. And if not, can the change be called progress? Even a Kardecist will scarcely claim it as such. Why then, if whole nations of spirits may deteriorate in particular respects, are we told that spirits *never* deteriorate?

The mistake arises evidently from the mistaken view its author took of the civilisation of to-day. He saw that the world, as a whole, has progressed. What he did not see was the true source of that progress. He accounts for it by supposing that spirits return to earth in a more enlightened state with each successive incarnation. Reasonable men will account for it by pointing out that it is the tendency of truths to accumulate; that the heritage of knowledge we leave to our children is greater than that we inherit from our fathers; in other words, that mankind progress in proportion as they laugh at the teachings of Kardec and follow those of Bacon.

The assertion that all spirits are created equal is certainly a convenient one when taken in connection with other parts of the re-incarnation theory. Homer, Socrates, Shakespeare, Galileo, Newton, and their fellow monarchs of mind, were, of course, simply incarnated beings who had reached their twentieth or thirtieth incarnation. The drunkard of the present age is no doubt a returned drinker of the days of the Caesars. The missionary who preaches to Hindoos or South Sea Islanders in the nineteenth century probably preached to Ephesian or Corinthian Pagans in the first. The different qualities and powers which the minds of men exhibit are thus dismissed as being nothing more than different stages of development, induced by the few or many incarnations which the exhibitors have passed through.

And here be it noted that M. Kardec's mediums assert the moral qualities of the parent to have no effect on the moral qualities of the child.

"*Q.* Parents often transmit physical resemblance to their children; do they also transmit to them moral resemblance?

"*A.* No; because they have different souls or spirits."

So the experience of centuries is as nothing! The millions of instances in which proof has been given that virtues and vices can be transmitted; that drunkenness in the parent induces drunkenness in the child; that fear experienced by the pregnant mother will impress timidity and nervousness on the mind of her infant; that particular talents may descend from father to son; that particular forms of insanity can be inherited: these, and countless other evidences of moral resemblance are calmly set aside by the Kardecian "Nay." I fear few who have made any study of mental pathology will be inclined to bow to the doctrine that physical resemblance is all a parent can transmit.

Of the many other contradictions which re-incarnation presents, I have space to notice but few. It is admitted, for example, in the "Spirits' Book" that "incarnated spirits lose the remembrance of the past." Yet, in another part of the same volume we find the following dogma:—

"*Q.*—Is the spirit of a child who dies in infancy as advanced as that of an adult?

"*A.*—He is sometimes much more so; for he may previously have lived longer, and acquired more experience, especially if he be a spirit who has already made considerable progress."

Such doctrines really require little more than to be stated. They refute themselves. If the incarnated spirit loses the remembrance of the past, of what value is the experience of former lives? They are as if they had never, been. How absurd then to tell us that the child who dies in infancy may be more advanced than an adult, because he may previously have lived longer and acquired more experience. The contradiction involved is of the plainest nature. Put succinctly, it is as follows:— "This child is wiser than you, because he knows something that he has forgotten!"

"*Q.*—Do the beings whom we call angels, archangels, and seraphim form a special category, of a nature different from that of other spirits?

"*A.*—No; they are spirits who have purified themselves from all imperfection, have reached the highest degree of the scale of progress, and united in themselves all species of perfection."

What is left to God when his children "reach the highest degree of the scale of progress and unite in themselves all species of perfection?" The created become equal to the Creator. Yet the authors of this doctrine tell us also that—"Spirits are the work of God, just as a machine is the work of the mechanician who made it; the machine is the man's work, but it is not the man." And since when has the work of the mechanician been estimated as highly as the maker? Since when has it been the custom of man's work to progress to an equality with man himself? Yet we are given to understand that man, here compared to a machine, can uplift himself to an equality with his maker, God!

It will be new to many that re-incarnation is the resurrection of the body which Scripture speaks of. "English spiritualists," remarks a distinguished re-incarnationist, "do not believe in re-incarnation, the *resurrection of the flesh, as it is termed in the Bible.*" And M. Kardec supports by a most astonishing argument, his opinion as to "the doctrine of the plurality of existences" being "the anchor of safety which God in his mercy has provided for mankind." "The words of Jesus Himself are explicit as to the truth of this last assertion; for we read in the third chapter of the Gospel according to St. John that Jesus, replying to Nicodemus, thus expressed Himself:— 'Verily, verily, I say unto thee, Except a man be born again he cannot see the kingdom of God.' And when Nicodemus inquired, 'How can a man be born when he is old? Can he enter again into his mother's womb, and be born a second time? 'Jesus replied, 'Except a man be born of water and of the spirit, he cannot enter the kingdom of God. That which is born of the flesh is flesh, and that which is born of the spirit is spirit. Marvel not that I said unto thee, Ye must be born again.'" And the above texts are gravely advanced as Scriptural supports to the theory of a "plurality of existences!" Truly, that theory rests on adamantine foundations!

We say to the re-incarnationist, "Give us proof—a single proof even, if it be decisive and well-attested, that the dogmas you advance are facts." He meets us with such evidence as the following:—

"When first I saw Katie, a very extraordinary and spontaneous sympathy drew us all at once to each other. I asked my leading spirits about its cause, and they told me that some hundred years ago we had intimately met in Turkey, where she was a slave named *Sulmé*, who died young, of a violent death. . . . In the letter mentioned just now, I tried, without stating anything more positive, to rouse her remembrance, in begging her earnestly to look into her past existence, and to try to recollect me, in a country far away (of which I described the principal features), asking her, at the same time, whether the name of Sulmé did not wake any echo in her mind. Here is the answer I got from her, through Al. de _____:—

"'My dear friend, I would wish very much to see you before I go. Can you come to me? I cannot remember anything about a former existence, but fancy I have known you before. Try to, recollect if we have met. The name you mentioned seems familiar to me; why cannot I remember?'"

I have known a man who was convinced that, at some misty period before that eventful one when

"Came forth the elect, the Ascidian,
From the mixture of sea and of slime,"

he had slept in the bosom of the earth as the mineral, Sulphur. To this unfortunate circumstance, and the having been subsequently incarnated as a tiger, he attributed the fiery temperament he possessed. And I have known another man who remembered having been of old a piece of steel. Perhaps I may place with these the laundry-woman who once spoke to me regarding "the faint recollection she had of having been a queen."

Does re-incarnation offer us nothing save these less than trifles in support of its gigantic assumptions, and speculations as revolting as daring? Absolutely nothing. The whole system is, indeed, but a vision, and, like all visions, the fabrics which constitute it are of the most baseless sort. I may confidently affirm that there never was an incident advanced as testimony in favour of that system which would not more easily and naturally bear an explanation other than the explanation sought to be placed on it.

The doctrine carries within itself the seeds of inevitable decay. It may, by its startling nature, captivate weak or enthusiastic minds, even as a modification of the same teachings captivated men in the far-back day of Pythagoras; but brought to the test of reason it appears miserably wanting. True philosophy launches its fiat against dogmas which, in the very spirit of medieval theology, require men to accord faith to them, but render no reason why such faith should be accorded. Upon the active life and the guided thought of the nineteenth century, re-incarnation intrudes itself as the fossilized skeleton of some schoolman who swore by Aquinas, and disputed according to the rules of Aristotle, might intrude upon a party of scientists busily working by means of the light which Bacon afforded. In its dead hand it carries a scroll proclaiming, "My mission is twofold. I take the place of Christ, and I confound the identity of man." And when the new doctrine has been expounded, and the startled listener inquires, "What proof do you offer me of all this? How can I discover whether I have lived before on earth or not? *Why does the incarnated spirit lose the remembrance of his past?* "the spectre turns over the leaves of the "Spirits' Book," and points to the page where is stereotyped the old, old formula, old as the

dogma it was first invented to support, old as Superstition herself:—
"Man cannot and may not know everything; God in his wisdom has so
ordained."

It is the dreary belief of re-incarnationists that spirits who have not
completed their appointed number of "expiations," wander hither and
thither during the years or ages which intervene between each
incarnation, wondering, with a sort of vacuous perplexity, what will
happen next. There have arisen, however, certain mighty inquirers who,
by turning the antiquated telescopes of Paracelsus and the Rosicrucians
on these unhappy beings, have made marvellous discoveries, and
arrived at marvellous conclusions. It was, indeed, the wildest of poor M.
Kardec's many delusions to suppose that these shadows had before
dwelt on earth. "They are the emanations of matter thrown off in the
efforts of Mother Nature to produce her noblest offspring—the sentient
human being. They have neither souls nor consciences, and are thus
devoid of moral restraint." Let an awe-struck world listen to these
solemn revealings of America's chief Occultist, and "in reverent silence
bow."

Having "neither souls nor consciences," it is somewhat puzzling to
imagine what elementaries can consist of. Had they been very material
substances one or more of the species would have assuredly been caged
at the numerous *séances* which, we learn, they attend. Are they too
small for the microscope to reach? Are the atoms of which they consist
too refined and too loosely-hung together for the grasp of mortal eye or
hand? Are these weird creatures illustrations of Tyndall's molecular
theory, or of the doctrine of spontaneous generation? I know not; but
this I know, that, like the genie of the Arabian Nights, whom a fisher-
man outwitted, their beginning and end is smoke.

"They second every crazy scheme propounded to them." This I
consider a libel on the species. They have not yet given any sign of
seconding the crazy scheme of a society enthusiastically constituted to
hunt down and (*literally*) bottle one of these wondrous little imps. The
said learned body, it appears, was "organized in the city of New York,
October 30th, 1875, and the inaugural address of the president of the
society delivered at Mott Memorial Hall, in the city of New York,
November 17, 1875." Never did a more astounding flourish of
trumpets sound in the form of an inaugural address. The learned and
worthy president displayed the second officer of the society as a
phenomenon, before whom Kepler would fade into nothingness and
even Galileo and Newton grow dim!

"Without claiming to be a theurgist, a mesmerist, or a spiritualist, our vice-
president promises, by simple chemical appliances, to exhibit to us, *as he has to*

others before, the races of beings which, invisible to our eyes, people the elements. Think for a moment of this astounding claim! Fancy the consequences of the practical demonstration of its truth, for which Mr. Felt is now preparing the requisite apparatus! What will the church say of a whole world of beings within her territory, but without her jurisdiction? What will the academy say of this crushing proof of an unseen universe given by the most unimaginative of its sciences? What will the positivists say, who have been prating of the impossibility of there being any entity which cannot be weighed in scales, filtered through funnels, tested with litmus, or carved with a scalpel? What will the spiritualists say, when through the column of saturated vapour flit the dreadful shapes of beings whom, in their blindness, they have in a thousand cases revered and babbled to as the returning shades of their relatives and friends? Alas! poor spiritualists—editors and correspondents—who have made themselves jocund over my impudence and apostasy! Alas! sleek scientists, overswollen with the wind of popular applause! The day of reckoning is close at hand, and the name of the Theosophical Society will, if Mr. Felt's experiments result favourably, hold its place in history as that of the body which first exhibited the 'Elementary Spirits' in this nineteenth century of conceit and infidelity, even if it be never mentioned for any other reason!"

Never mentioned for any other reason! The Theosophical Society need entertain no dread of oblivion. It is destined to occupy a niche in history between the Lagadan College of Swift and the philosopher who planned to extract gold from sunbeams. "Think of our astounding claims!" cries the president. The world has thought them over for above a year now, and still they are—claims. The high-priest swings his censer and prays anguishedly to Adon-Ai; the vice-president and his chemical appliances are there; the saturated vapour ascends, and the whole array of Theosophists kneel around; but the "elementaries?"—"The dreadful shapes" flit as yet only through the high-priest's brain. Distorted and eerie shapes they indeed are. Vainly does Mr. F____ "prepare the requisite apparatus." The "races which people the elements" refuse to people his laboratory; and the world grows impatient, and the Theosophists are in the position of the priests of Baal. They have called on the elementaries "from morning even until noon, saying, Hear us! but there was no voice, neither any that answered." The spiritualists whom they have contemned are converted into so many Elijahs, who "mock them, saying, Cry aloud, for are they not your servants? either they are talking, or pursuing, or on a journey; or they sleep and must be awaked." Will not the society carry out the parallel to the bitter end? We shall hear of them, perhaps, dancing wildly in front of their Memorial Hall, or building altars in some New York park, and hacking themselves with knives and lancets. Alas for that day of anticipated triumph, when the president, clad with a robe of Tyrian dye, should have taken his stand at the head of Broadway, crushing the "editors and correspondents" who had made themselves merry over his pretensions, by the exhibition of a stoppered phial, neatly labelled "spirits," and tenanted by that "shadow of a shade," an elementary!

The most perplexing thing of all is that the said elementaries have been previously caught and commented on. "Our vice-president promises to exhibit them to us, *as he has to others before.*" And when did this previous exhibition take place? In what corner of the earth were the unhappy "emanations" hunted down? What occultist or occultists enjoyed the privilege of "babbling over" the "dreadful shapes?" Did they test them with litmus, or carve them cunningly with scalpels, or filter them through funnels, or weigh them with scales? Possibly the elementaries were disgusted with the shabby treatment they received, and decline a second visit. In that case it is not to be wondered at if the "columns of saturated vapour," like the smoke of Baal's altar, ascend uselessly to heaven; and that, though high-priest and vice-president pray and prophesy with due fervour from morning even until the time of the evening sacrifice, there should be "neither voice, nor any to answer, nor any that regarded." The "emanations of matter" may have no souls, but they are altogether too smart for the Theosophical Society.

And the society appears to have discovered this; and, since the vice-president's promises are saturated vapour and nothing more, his chief has ordered, regardless of expense, the best thing in the way of magicians that Africa can furnish. A "newly-affiliated member" has been dispatched to those haunts of sorcerers, Tunis and Egypt. The little fiasco of the chemical apparatus and the "dreadful shapes" is ignored. The high-priest's rhodomontades are as wordily-grandiloquent as ever. "One of these African sorcerers will, for a small fee, show you images of the dead, and enable you to converse with them in audible voice. They will walk, self-levitated, in mid-air; climb poles which rest upon nothing, until they positively go out of sight" (the poles, or the conjurers?), "and, dismember themselves even to decapitation without injury.... You" (the newly-affiliated member) "have the opportunity to introduce to western scientists, under the patronage, restrictions, and guarantees of a scientific (?) society, those proofs of occult powers, for lack of which they have been drifting into materialism and infidelity."

"The Theosophical Society," remarks the *New York World,* (August 4, 1876.) "engages itself to pay for bringing the fiend over. That seems to us unnecessary. Let him levitate, and hitch Mr. S____ on behind Let them appear together hovering over New York from the eastern sky, a true sign in the heavens, a new constellation of the Gemini, whereat the multitude shall flop confounded, and confess a new faith, while the Theosophical Society, assembled on Pier No. 1, hold the president forcibly down from joining them aloft. No true philosophy can, at this day, be kept selfishly secret. Old Socrates killed this esoteric business. It will be the square thing to let the fiend float in sight of the whole people, and his time ought to be taken at both ends. We don't often get a fiend pure and simple. Let us not entreat this one so shabbily that no more will come to us."

And when will the first fiend arrive? No doubt the day after the circle has been squared, and the philosopher's stone discovered.

The single outcome of occultism is brag. The tree which Mr. Felt planted and African magicians are to water may be pretty, but it bears only an enormous crop of empty promises. Words—idle words, are the stock in trade of the society, from the president down to the youngest member. The literature of the movement, if such unproductive folly deserve to be termed a movement, is equally idle and equally empty. It consists so far of a volume termed "Art Magic." This book is made up partly of descriptions of travel, partly of stories respecting Oriental jugglers and dervishes, and partly of rubbish dug from the forgotten works of Cornelius Agrippa and his medieval compeers. The only spirit I have yet heard of as evoked by a perusal of "Art Magic" is the spirit of credulity.

A faith that promises everything and accomplishes nothing is unlikely to have much influence on the future of the world. We may look with pitying indifference, therefore, on these English-speaking fetichists who stand frantically inviting us to—

"Come and worship Mumbo Jumbo
In the mountains of the moon."

CHAPTER IV

MANIA

Since mental disease has been made the subject of careful study, the difficulty of determining where the responsibility for an action ceases has vastly increased. We reason, with reference to the characters of others, by induction; assuming from the knowledge we possess of certain of its qualities what the mind as a whole may be. But in the most logically conducted process the absence of necessary data may lead to a false conclusion, and in inquiries conducted with regard to the human mind we are peculiarly liable to go astray. No subject of inquiry has so fascinated philosophers as that of pure metaphysics, and none has ever proved so valueless. It is, in the language of Bacon, a tree with a magnificent display of leaves, but never producing fruit. The outcome of inquiries purely metaphysical, if unsupported by revelations from another world, has in all ages been endless bewilderment and strife. The inquiries conducted into the deeper subtleties of insanity seem, at the present day, to have plunged physicians into a bewilderment almost equally profound. The soul is too fearfully and wonderfully made for the dissection of even its morbid peculiarities by merely human hands. If a case be strongly marked, indeed, doctors seldom disagree. It is easy to decide that a man who requires to be restrained by force from doing meaningless injury to his fellow creatures or himself is irresponsible for what he does. The indications here are too decisive for a doubt. It is when a multitude of facts and symptoms jostle each other—some apparently irresistibly proving that reason still retains her throne; others as clearly demonstrating her overthrow—that medical men give deplorable proofs of their inability to decide whether or not they are dealing with a mind diseased.

There exist, and have existed since the creation of our species, minds in which some brilliant quality increases constantly in stature and splendour, while the rest of the faculties remain stunted or commonplace. There are other minds in which, from the first, some taint of unsoundness has place, that, constantly enlarging, usurps at last the place of reason as an adviser, and permeates every action of life. It is with regard to beings so unhappily constituted as these last that human philosophy is most frequently at fault. By every test that can be applied the person so afflicted is sane. His or her life is, to all seeming, the ordinary life of humanity. No magistrate would reject the testimony of those of whom I speak; they are competent to marry, to inherit estates, to carry on businesses, to transact all the affairs of the every-day life of the world. Even their nearest and dearest may see in them little or nothing that is peculiar. Yet the poison is there, working unseen beneath the surface, and influencing every action of existence. When, at length, the crisis of the malady has arrived, some fearful action startles those around, and a thousand tongues and pens begin busily and unavailingly to discuss the mental condition of the doer of the deed. That deed is, in most cases of such malady of the soul, a self-inflicted death.

I am not aware that in England, or on the Continent of Europe, any instances of suicide have been plainly traceable to spiritualism. Even in America the number of victims has not been large. But the subject is a dangerous one for those mentally afflicted. The spot which I have alluded to as tainting certain minds is in many instances a species of false enthusiasm which, with the lapse of years, becomes but the less regulated and the more excitable and unreflecting. In the case of communion with another world the perils to such a class of minds are peculiarly great. By their fervid imaginations that world is depicted in the brightest of hues. In every one of the countless trials and miseries which beset our earthly life they fly for refuge to the thought of the happiness to be found in another sphere. Thus the longing for the imagined joys of immortality, and the temptation to seek by suicide to attain them, become, by continual growth, irresistible. It may happen that, in process of time, the gloom of some really great affliction, some trial hard to be endured, darkens the present path of these longers for a future life. At once a mournful end invests with tragic interest the name of the man or woman whom such a sorrow has befallen. No spiritual interference is necessary. Of the suicides by professed spiritualists which have been recorded, there is not one in which the theory that death was brought about by the evil suggestions of disembodied beings can be supported by a fragment of anything deserving the name of evidence. I do not say that such tempting may not have taken place. There may be debased beings in the world of spirits who are watchful for the opportunity of doing evil, and who, having acquired influence over the minds of those yet on earth, will use it for the purpose of leading astray. By such it is possible that the more impressionable of the victims to a disgust of life, who have been found in the spiritualist ranks, may have suffered themselves, knowingly or unknowingly, to be guided. The hypothesis is, I have admitted, a possible one. But I do not think it, in general, at all probable; nor, with regard to the various cases I might lay before the reader, (They are omitted, on account of their tragic nature.) would the testimony be found to bear it out. Delirious broodings, exaggerated in a particular direction at the expense of all other attributes, until the balance of the mind had been overthrown, and the sufferer was, for every action committed under the influence of that delirium, practically irresponsible, were the tempters that hurried these victims to their sad and untimely graves. That bringing near of another world, which to so many has been the source of consolation unspeakably divine, was with them the innocent means of intensifying to a more terrible pitch the original disease of their minds. In the wild hope of thereby at once participating in the joys of the next world they rebelliously abandoned this present one, and passing into futurity by a road the most terrible of all to travel, have left their histories as melancholy examples of the mischief that ensues when a mind, weak but enthusiastic, unresistingly abandons itself to one insane and absorbing idea.

There are works purporting to be contributions to the literature of spiritualism which reflect much discredit on the writers who produced them. The one thing kept throughout in view is effect. Superficially glanced over, these compositions appear valuable. Critically examined, they prove worthless. The impression left by a book of this class on the mind of a careless reader is usually attained by the most unworthy means. Theories are palmed off as facts. Trifles favourable to the ends which the author has in view are magnified into mountains of evidence. Inconvenient truths are suppressed. Where suppression is impossible, the distortion of the truth is resorted to. The writer appears to consider him or herself engaged in the construction of an edifice in which a certain effect has, by fair means or foul, to be obtained. If the materials proper for the task seem opposed to the desired result, they are at once rejected, however sound. In their place the first rubbish forthcoming, provided that it be but showy, is pressed into the builder's service. Legends which, however attractive, bear too often in themselves the marks of their falsehood and unsubstantiality, fill the gaps caused by the casting aside of unpleasant facts. When completed, the work exactly resembles the makeshift buildings seen on the stage. Viewed at a little distance, and in a proper light, the thing is charming. But approach it more closely, and examine it by the clearness of noon: we are disenchanted at once, and for ever. What was at first sight a fairy palace, is now a miserable composition of daubed canvas and pasteboard. A single blow would suffice to lay the whole structure in ruins. So with the flimsy productions I treat of. They are, in general, exceedingly taking, when beheld by the false glare of credulity. But expose them to the sober daylight of reason, the paltry tawdriness of the decorations, and the weakness which those decorations were intended to hide, become at once apparent. Before the first assault of a competent critic the unstable fabric goes down, and utter is the ruin thereof.

The book which furnishes the subject of my present chapter may fairly take rank as one of the worst compositions of this bad class. Let me, before entering on its examination, guard myself against a supposition some readers may entertain, that I am representing such writings as peculiar to spiritualism. They are to be met with everywhere, and infest all departments of literature. In some their influence is in the highest degree pernicious—in others, comparatively harmless. At times, indeed, they are allowable. No one, for example, expects strict consistency and unswerving accuracy of statement in a novelist or a poet. It surprises us little to meet with exaggeration in the leader-writing of sensational newspapers. But in works that claim to be works of science, in records that are put forth as records of facts, we are surely entitled to demand strictness in examining evidence, caution in putting forward or endorsing statements, a careful separation of the true from the false, and the proved from the merely probable, a judicial impartiality in coming to decisions; in short, common-sense, candour, and honesty of purpose. Not one of these attributes, I regret to say, can be considered as attaching to the work before me. Had the author of "People from the Other World" put forward that volume as a romance, one might have been content with remarking that it was sometimes dull and sometimes absurd, and would have been a better book if the writer had taken more pains. But it is gravely advanced as a truthful and dispassionate narrative of certain observations of recondite phenomena, made with scientific care, and published in the interests of the world at large. It is dedicated to two English scientific men. The title page bears the words of Bacon: "We have set it down as a law to ourselves to examine things to the bottom, and not to receive upon credit, or reject upon improbabilities, until there hath passed a due examination."

In "People from the Other World" the author has observed one, and but one, of the laws here laid down by the prince of philosophers. He certainly cannot be accused of "rejecting upon improbabilities." On the contrary, his depth of credulity is absolutely fathomless. This, however, is not the condition of mind which Bacon desiderated, nor is it, I submit, one proper to scientific investigation. For the rest, the placing of such a motto on the title-page of such a book is one of the most laughable displays of folly with which I am acquainted. "I have set it down as a law to myself to examine things to the bottom." How modest this assumption on the part of a man who tells us (p. 342, "People from the Other World") that the manifestations, as a record of which he constructed his book, "were not happening under test-conditions, and hence would not satisfy the judicial mind;" who confesses (p. 347) that "Chittenden was no place for him to try philosophical experiments;" and who sums up by hoping (p. 409) that his readers "will bear him out in the statement that all his efforts have been to interest American scientists in the phenomena to such an extent that they would commence real investigations, in comparison to which these made by himself are but child's play." What, in view of such an avowal as the last, is the value of his investigation, or pseudo-investigation? On p. 414 of his work he is kind enough to answer the question. The narratives that he gives are sufficient "to arouse the greatest wonder." Could less be said of the histories of Munchausen, or the equally veritable tales of the Thousand and One Nights? Is it not too much that a man should trumpet himself forth as a devotee of science who, in reality, and by his own confession, is merely seeking to act as showman to a couple of persons, whose claims to mediumship he does nothing either to prove or to negative?

"I do not receive upon credit," says he. "There must pass a due examination." Such is the assertion made in taking the motto of Bacon as one suited to his own circumstances. He reiterates that assertion with even greater distinctness in the pages of his book. "We should take nothing for granted, and respect no man's judgment who does. We should demand from the spiritualist as broad a basis of facts for our belief as we do from Huxley before receiving his theory, or from Tyndall, if he would have us accept any of the dogmas propounded in his Belfast address. A philosophy that shrinks from crucial tests I want none of. No real investigator takes things on faith. We should flout at and cease debate with the spiritualist who assumes to set his creed above all other creeds as too sacred to be tried and tested by every appliance of reason and science. The individual preferences or fears of mediums are nothing to us, for we are in quest of the truth, and would seek it even at the bottom of a well. We should weigh the mediums and their phenomena in the balances, and reject whatsoever appears false." I agree most cordially with every word. The doctrines here repeated are doctrines which, during my whole career, I have never ceased inculcating. But what do we find in "People from the Other World" when we turn from theory to fact; from the author's magnificent sentiments to his pitiful practice? Joseph Surface's life and language were not more contradictory. One-third of the volume is devoted to stories received at second-hand, of whose truth or falsehood the writer knows nothing, and which are, therefore, utterly worthless as evidence. Internally they are equally valueless. They come exactly under the definition of "old women's tales." With just such narratives may Mrs. Sairey Gamp have enlivened over the tea-table the sullen moods of Mrs. Betsey Prig. The "investigator," indeed, to whose taste for authorship we owe "People from the Other World" would appear to have a great deal of the Gamp about him. All through his book he continues to direct rapturous apostrophes to a certain "science," conspicuous by her absence from his writings. I cannot venture to remark, as the vehement and ungrammatical Mrs. Prig remarked of Mrs. Harris, that "I don't believe there's no such person." Of this, however, I am certain, that, though the said science undoubtedly exists, the writer with whom I am dealing knows nothing at all about her.

Had his mind been of the scientific cast he would never have filled paragraph upon paragraph with records of phenomena, only to remark naively that, after all, these records are of no value. I may instance the story given on page 234. Not satisfied with narrating this affair, he accompanies his account with a *facsimile* of the truly "wretched Latin and bad English" obtained under such suspicious circumstances. The excuse offered is that it "is probably the first thing of the kind which has appeared in a newspaper." I am not aware whether the New York dailies for whom these sensational narratives were in the first instance constructed had before inflicted on their readers illustrations of such doubtful interest. Certainly, however, it is "the first thing of the kind" which has adorned the pages of any work professedly devoted to philosophical investigation. And as he has acted here, so does this writer act all through. Facing page 148 will be found what is styled "the picture of a young girl, with her head and shoulders emerging from a sort of fog or steamy vapour." I turn to the accompanying letter-press for an explanation. There I find it recorded that this engraving is a copy of one of Mumler's so-called 'spirit photographs.'" (The inverted commas are our author's). *"I have no confidence in this picture," he continues, "or, in fact, in any emanating from the same source, as directly or indirectly of spiritual origin."* Why then cause it to be engraved, and engraved in a volume which has not the slightest reference to the genuine or fraudulent nature of alleged spirit-photographs? The author seems to anticipate that such a question may be asked. He seeks, therefore, to guard against it by a maudlin dissertation on the Holmeses, Dr. Child, the Hon. Robert Dale Owen, a Chittenden spirit who, "losing power, sank into the floor up to her waist," and "certain communications" sent him from various persons, "attesting to the fact of their seeing materialized spirit-forms dissolve." It is difficult for a plain man to extract the few grains of meaning concealed in this bushel of rigmarole. Put in the clearest form, however, the drift of these paragraphs and others of a kindred nature evidently is,—"I, who now address the public, have very little to offer that is worth the offering. It is convenient that I should swell my volume to a certain size. This I accomplish by inserting a number of worthless stories picked up at second or third-hand from various people. Don't think, however, that I am weak enough to believe in these stories. The reader may do so, if he or she please; but I; myself have not the slightest faith in them." And this is a scientific investigator! This is the man who takes mottoes from Bacon, and dedicates his worthless speculations to Mr. Crookes! The dullest school-boy would blush to contradict himself thus. The most abject dunce that Satire ever pilloried would be ashamed of the company of such a philosopher. That any human being should have the folly to construct such a work is strange enough. That, after having constructed it, he should consider it a work of philosophical research, and under that designation send it forth into the world, is enough, in the words of a great essayist, "to make us ashamed of our species."

As a composition it is almost below criticism. As a display of reasoning it is altogether beneath contempt. This last proposition I shall have occasion presently to substantiate. For the present I confine myself to a few words regarding the literary demerits of the volume before me, and to a brief exposition of the motives which have led me to attempt the examination of this most worthless and most dishonest book.

It would be waste of space to discuss at any length its endless literary shortcomings. The supply of such sentences as the following is almost inexhaustible. "Poor Mrs. Eddy's *misfortunes* followed her even into the grave, as she one day told the children it would." "He hired three or four of the children out to one showman, who took them to nearly all the principal cities of the United States, and to another who took them to London." Grammatically considered, this sentence leaves us in an agreeable state of doubt as to whether one showman took the children to another, or one city of the United States took the children to London. What the writer probably meant was, that the father of the Eddys, after receiving back his olive branches from the first showman, hired them out to a second.

"I am quite aware of the fact that, as a scientific experiment, the procuring of the second set of names has no value; for no one was present when it was written, or can affirm it was not by the medium himself, so I let that pass. But what shall be said of the cards written in the light-circle before twenty people, which bear so marked a resemblance to *them?*" To what does the word "them" apply? After careful consideration, the only meaning I can arrive at in the sentence last given is, that the cards bore a marked resemblance to the twenty people! This is evidently not what the writer intended to convey, but his mind seems too contracted to have much grasp of language. But enough of so tiresome a task. I have selected these charming specimens of composition from pages which I had marked for other purposes. To wade through the whole volume in search of its thousand absurdities of grammar, &c., would be more than human nature is capable of bearing.

"Why devote space, then, to the dissection of so worthless a performance?" the reader will ask. I grant that, intrinsically, this volume has no value whatever,—that it is ten times more meaningless than the gospel of Mormon, or the speculations of Joanna Southcote. But things which are in themselves valueless often deserve attention on account of the harm they work. Weeds grow faster than the corn into which they intrude themselves, and require, therefore, to be rooted up, or they spoil the harvest. This book is emphatically a weed, and one of the worst, perhaps the very worst, of its species. Other productions of the kind infest spiritual literature; but there are few which display such an utter lack of principle; such a happy audacity in assertion, or so complete a disregard of facts. A certain cleverness in distorting occurrences to whatever form the peculiar genius of the writer considers desirable, renders the work dangerous. This capacity for making what is more than half a fabrication resemble the truth is invariably inherent in certain dispositions.

When I had succeeded in struggling through "People from the Other World" my first feeling was one of mingled amusement and pity. The lackadaisical sentimentality of the style—the maudlin feebleness of the reflections, made me set down the writer as a good, easy blue-stocking of fifty, who was concealing her identity under a masculine *nom de plume*. Very foolish she seemed to me, intensely gushing, still more credulous, and totally unfit for the position she had thrust herself into. I have since, however, discovered, and can assure my readers, that the author in question is really of the sterner sex. Besides the title of a man, he arrogates to himself that of a philosopher. How he could be guilty of such a production as "People from the Other World" is, therefore, the deepest of mysteries. He has written three letters to me since the appearance of his book, which letters I hope will be published *in extenso* in the forthcoming volume of "Incidents in My Life." Self-respect prevented me from answering the last of these communications. To adopt to this writer the language he hurls at others, he "sheds a magnetism as disagreeable as dirty water, or the perfume of the *Fetis Americanus.*"

Yet he has his ludicrous side. Could we but put out of view the more unpleasant attributes of such a mind, much amusement might be derived from its ridiculous qualities. His self-conceit is ineffable. His dearest pleasure is to pose himself in some impressive attitude. Now he is the adorer and benefactor of mediums. Now he is the lofty denouncer of "calumnious behaviour reserved for blackguards *and* mediums." (The italics are his own). At one time he is putting on his paper armour, and taking pen in hand, to do battle for the Eddys against the world. A little later we find him, according to his own confession, "waiting patiently for a grand exposure" of the same Eddys. Now he is the humble admirer of spiritualism and science; and, clinging to the coat-tails of distinguished spiritualists and scientists, pathetically implores these people to lift him into notice. Now he starts forth before the public as a sort of Pagan wet-nurse, ready to suckle grown up infants in "heathen fantasies outworn." Again, he is the smart investigator whom "the conductors of two of the great New York Dailies would not have engaged to investigate and describe the phenomena at the Eddy homestead, had they supposed him either of unsound mind, credulous, partial, dishonest, or incompetent." Now he is a spiritualist; now he is *not* a spiritualist. In short, his changes are Protean. Through all, however, he seems troubled with an uneasy consciousness of absurdity. If he be a Bottom, he at least suspects himself to possess an ass's head. For a moment the particular attitude he is taking appears to him the perfection of grace. Presently doubts arise, and he begs earnestly the opinion of bystanders as to his position and get-up. The next instant we behold him dismounted from his late pedestal, and in full career towards some new hobby-horse.

It is probable that nine-tenths of my readers are but very imperfectly acquainted, or not acquainted at all, with the Chittenden career of this literary phenomenon. That career is not one spiritualists may be proud of. I shall seek, therefore, in sketching the circumstances under which "People from the Other World" was written, to accomplish my task with the utmost brevity.

The author of the work in question was, he tells us, sent to the Eddy ghost-court in his capacity of newspaper paragraphist. The appointment was lucrative, and its holder in no hurry to terminate it. This idea has struck others besides myself. "Both Mrs. _____ and I," writes an American friend of mine, who was present at Chittenden during this pseudo-investigator's "investigations," "are convinced now that there was a *determined* resolve in his mind to see and hear nothing that lessened the chances of his lucrative position there."

He possesses a fervid imagination, and brilliant powers of invention. There are few who can see farther through a stone wall. This imagination is as powerful a talisman as any mentioned in the "Arabian Nights." The "glamour" of mediæval magic was as nothing in comparison. Not only, under its influence, do night-gowns, scarfs, and smoking-caps figure as "magnificent costumes," but incidents are described which never occurred, and portraits are given without the faces supposed to be copied in those portraits having ever been seen. And here come under notice the irremediable blemishes of the book; those which, above all, demonstrate how unblushing is the assurance of its author.

"The light has been very dim," says he, on page 163, "and I have not been able to recognise the features of a single face." On the next page I find,—"What go to constitute a likeness are a number of lines about the eyes, nose, and mouth, as thin as a knife-blade's edge; the expression of eye, shape of features, colour, and hair—these, in such a light as this, are indistinguishable." The paragraph immediately following tells us that the light is so poor, "one cannot, with untrained eye, distinguish accurately between forms varying as much as six inches in height." Similar avowals occur all through the book. Strong as they may appear, the testimony of unprejudiced observers is still stronger. The light at Chittenden was a libel on the term "darkness visible." What, in view of such a fact, can be the value of the engravings of "materialised" forms, &c., with which the volume is profusely decorated? Not one has the slightest pretension to be considered a portrait. They are, without exception, fancy sketches evolved from the inner consciousness of the artist. It is thus romances are illustrated. It is *not* thus that men truly scientific illustrate their works. But, putting this aside, *what was the value of the numerous recognitions of departed relatives and friends which we are solemnly assured occurred?* Does not every candid reasoner answer, as I answer, that they were valueless? Even had these so-called recognitions been honestly described, they would serve only to prove the insane enthusiasm of persons able to conjure up departed relatives in figures whose features they could not discern, and whose voices they did not hear. But the descriptions, as I am now about to show, are not honest.

On page 271, we learn how there appeared "an Arab, an old friend of a lady well known in magazine literature as 'Aunt Sue.'" Our author's description of the said Arab is glowing. "He was of short stature, slight and wiry build, and his very salaam to the lady, when recognised, was in marked contrast with the constrained bows of the Indians, and the more or less ungraceful salutations of the whites. *His name is Yusef.* He was dressed in a white tunic, gathered at the waist by a sash, and the skirt ornamented with three equi-distant bands of red, of the same width. On his head was the national fez, and in his sash was thrust a weapon of some kind which I could not see distinctly. A number of questions propounded to him were answered by respectful bows, and his parting obeisance was of that deferential, but, at the same time, self-respecting character, that is peculiar to the people of the Orient."

Why answer questions by respectful bows? Either this taciturn Eastern had forgotten his native tongue in another world, or had forgotten to materialise organs of speech when returning to this. But now for a "plain, unvarnished" account of what really occurred. It is furnished by the very "Aunt Sue" to whom the visit and salaams of this obsequious spirit were directed. Here is what this lady writes me:—

May 15th, 1876.

"MY DEAR DAN,

"You shall have my experience with pleasure. Mrs. C. and I read" (our author's) "glowing description of ghosts and things in the vicinity of, and at the Eddy homestead; and we said, 'Let's go: it is among the lovely hills of Vermont, and we will have a good time any way.' And we went. We were introduced to the Eddy brothers, and shown to our room. You don't want to hear about the peculiarities of the *ménage* there. Suffice it to say we went prepared to accept a gridiron for a bed, and a stove pipe for a pillow, if necessary, and to take all creature discomforts philosophically; and we took them.

"The evening came, and we all sat about—after tea—in the sitting-room (so-called because there were chairs in it, and mostly nothing else), awaiting the announcement that the Hall—the large room up-stairs over the dining-room—was ready for us. Up we went, and sat on the benches prepared for us. All on the front row joined hands 'to make a magnetic chain,' though where the magnetic current went at either end, I don't know. The man with the violin played vigorously. The light, back of us all, was turned so low that it was impossible to distinguish features two feet from us. When the curtain over the door of the cabinet was lifted, and a 'form' appeared, the violin was hushed; the 'form' was mum, until the front bench, beginning with No. 1, commenced to ask the stereotyped question 'For me?'—'For me?' until the form bowed. 'Oh! for me?' said No. 1, 2, 3, 5, 7, as the case might be. 'Is it father?'—no response. Is it uncle?'—still silent. 'Is it Charlie Myrtle?'—the form bows. Why, Charlie, I'm so glad to see you! Then it is reported that 'Charlie Myrtle' was distinctly recognised, and that is about all there was of it. What I specially noticed was, that the shawls and scarfs 'materialised' by 'Honto,' a light one and a dark one, were always, of exactly the same length; the light one about three yards long, and the dark one about two yards. The magnificent costumes' seemed to be composed of a loose, white wrapper (nightgown?); dark calico tunic, some scarfs and Indian caps (smoking ones?), which different combinations made quite a variety of costumes; but I would defy any one to describe them minutely by the dim light in which they always appeared. One evening the 'For me?'s' had been negatively answered, until it came to my turn. I asked 'For me?' and the figure bowed. 'Is it Ruloffe?' I inquired. The figure slowly nodded ascent. At the close of the *séance*" (our author) "asked me concerning 'Ruloffe.' I informed him that I had been told, mediumistically, that one of my 'spirit-guides' was an Arabian called 'Ruloffe.' He remarked that 'Ruloffe' was not an Arabian name, and Yusef would be more appropriate. I replied, smiling, that one name would answer my purpose as well as another; so it was 'Graphic'-ally announced that 'Aunt Sue' had had an interview with one 'Yusef.' And that is the true and veritable history of that little episode. I certainly shall never recognise Mr. 'Ruloffe' or 'Yusef' if I meet him on the thither shore, if the light should be ass dim there as it was at Chittenden.

AUNT SUE."

In view of such a misfortune the author of "People from the Other World" kindly supplies a no doubt correct portrait of "*Yusef*" in his work; which portrait may serve as a guide to my friend "Aunt Sue," when she encounters her spirit-visitor of Chittenden on the "thither shore."

How much credit such revelations do to the ingenuity of that philosopher whom "two of the great New York dailies" successively engaged as special correspondent to the Chittenden spirit-court! Certainly he is by no means "incompetent" as a sensational journalist. As an investigator, however, he must be pronounced "credulous, partial," and, above all, incorrect. I would beg him, therefore, to "spare himself the trouble, and the public the annoyance," of inflicting upon a much enduring world any further volume of such unattested absurdities as "People from the Other World" mainly consists of.

There was present with "Aunt Sue" at Chittenden a friend of that lady—Mrs. C____. She has kindly furnished me with notes of the "materialisations" witnessed during her stay, and the following are extracts. Mrs. C____ speaks for "Aunt Sue" and herself.

"We could *detect* no fraud, as all real opportunity for investigation had been dexterously cut off notwithstanding the clumsy expedients resorted to by" (the author of "People from the Other World") "as 'tests;' but that we were in the presence of real spirits we never for once believed. The only persons allowed to take a seat upon the platform were a Mr. Pritchard and a Mrs. Cleveland; dear old gullible souls who could be readily psychologized into believing that they were eating a piece of the moon in shape of 'green cheese.' These both touched and conversed with the *substantial* shadows which stepped cautiously from the door of the cabinet, as if making sure that some investigator were not ready to spring upon them; and occasionally went through the shuffling manoeuvres characterised by (our author) as *dancing*! while no one of the audience circle was permitted to advance near enough to distinguish their features in the distressingly subdued light of the solitary lamp, acting its part in the fraud upon a distant table.

"Every evening Mr. P____ had a visit from his aged mother—attired in a *robe de nuit,—she*, understand, was thus attired, not *he*. Every evening Mr. P____ saluted her with a 'Good evening, mother!' and she replied in a husky whisper, 'Good evening, my son!' Every evening she added, I am glad to see you, my son!' and then asked, 'Why didn't Mary come?' Every evening she was blandly assured that Mary was not in health, and could not be there; but still the question was renewed, and then the aged spirit shuffled back, and disappeared through the door of the cabinet. I asked this gentleman if he recognised his mother beyond all peradventure in this spirit. He admitted that he did *not* see much likeness as he *remembered* her; but he had not seen her for the two or three years before her death, and 'no doubt she had altered.'

"Mr. _____" (our author) "would brook no antagonism in conversation to the methods of the media; nor even lend an ear to the suggestion of any doubts of their honesty."

So unphilosophically did this pseudo-philosopher strut his hour on the Chittenden stage! The spectacle must have been at once trying and amusing to the ordinary men and women present. Some of the antics they witnessed would have drawn a smile from the Wandering Jew. Others might have ruffled the temper of Job. How our investigator assumed the chief direction of what he appropriately styles the "performances;" how he courted the wonder of the public with such programmes as "The Spinning Ghost!" "Mystery of Mysteries!" "The

Malicious Barber!" "The Smoking Squaw!" "Wonderful Feats!" "Whence comes the Power?" "Four Hundred Spirits!" &c.; how he "went for" intrusive sceptics; how he acted as the trumpeter-forth of prophecies which were never fulfilled; how he accepted any story which anybody present chose to relate to him, so that it did but go to confirm the spiritual origin of the manifestations; how he bought scales with which to weigh the spirits (this being certainly a new mode of trying them); how, when he was refused permission to use the scales himself, that "dear old soul," Mr. Pritchard called off the weights for him; and how, notwithstanding all this, he "has excluded from his case every individual phenomenon that can be explained upon the hypothesis of trickery," are not all these things written in his "Other World" chronicles? Behold him there, "standing" (in a Napoleonic attitude) "upon his dory of phenomena observed, with the confidence of one whose house is built upon a sure foundation."

I have now to notice the brilliant displays of reasoning with which this "investigator" has favoured the world, both in his book and subsequently to its publication. The reader will confess that seldom before have human minds been astonished with such utterances. For most of these absurdities I can find no place whatever in the whole system of logic. Every new "explanation" contradicts one previously tendered. Such conflicting sophisms were surely never resorted to before or since, unless by a monomaniac or a Theosophist.

"Nor will it escape the notice of the intelligent," I find, in the preface to "People from the Other World," "that the Philadelphia tests go far towards corroborating the Chittenden experiences, for, if "materialisation" can occur in one place, it may in many, and hence the supposition that real ghosts were seen at the Eddy house is made to appear only half as improbable. The cheerful alacrity shown by the Holmeses to submit themselves to crucial test conditions makes the behaviour of the Eddy boys appear in a correspondingly unfavourable light. It was alleged as an excuse at Chittenden, that the author's magnetism was so positive and repellent to the spirits as to prevent their bearing his near approach, whereas the fact appears to be that they can allow him to handle them, to gaze into their faces from a distance of six inches, and otherwise to come to closest quarters, without causing them the slightest inconvenience." If these words mean anything, they mean this:— "The Holmeses allowed certain tests. The Eddys might have allowed those tests, and ought to have allowed them. Therefore, as the Holmeses are mediums, the Eddys are mediums also." Truly, an owl of any standing would be ashamed of coming to such conclusions.

I might extract many such gems from the work before me. Will my readers believe that on p. 168 of "People from the Other World" the author laments that it was impossible for him to make his experiments at Chittenden under test conditions, and that he afterwards coolly heads p. 213, "Another Test?" What, moreover, are we to think of the investigator who, after placing in capitals over p. 307 "Abundant Tests," and entitling Chapter XXIII. "Tests continued," tells us, on p. 342, "The things I saw were not happening under test conditions." And, as he has behaved in the volume itself, so did he behave after its publication. Chapter XV. of his book is an account of what, he tells us, were "Philosophical Tests." Yet in a letter published January 1st, 1876, in the columns of the *Banner of Light*, he confesses his belief in the Eddy spirits to be "the result of intuition, not of absolute demonstration," ("No *real* investigator takes things on faith."–*People from the Other World*, p. 170.) and demands piteously, "What tests did I have that would be deemed conclusive to a scientific association?" And are not "philosophical tests" deemed conclusive by the scientific associations of either Europe or America? If the tests science employs are not philosophical what are they? Surely never before did any being capable of using a pen so completely stultify himself. When such contradictory nonsense is brought forward as "a sure foundation" on which this writer may rest his claims to be considered "an investigator in the interests of science," what can we do but treat the assumption with mingled derision and contempt?

Since the appearance of "People from the Other World" its author has favoured our own planet with displays of absurdity that reveal still more vividly the utter absence from his mind of all reasoning power. I had stated in a letter of mine that one of his friends was in a certain European city in the year 1858. He rejoined, with the fierce triumph of one who completely demolishes a calumny, that "he could tell me" the person in question was somewhere else in the years 1859 and 1860. Such is invariably his style of argument!

He thinks nothing whatever of contradicting himself point-blank. On p. 418 of "People from the Other World" he asks, "What does the reader say when I tell him that, on the evening of September 28th, I saw the spirit of a woman who was murdered on the night of Sunday, August 27th, 1865, at Williston, Vt.?" The reader will no doubt say that, if this writer saw the spirit, he saw it. Not at all! In letters published since the appearance of his book, he has burst upon the world in the attitude of a great discoverer. The discovery he has perfected is that the spirits who produce the physical phenomena at *séances* are none of them human. They are sylphs, gnomes, elementaries, and have never lived on earth. "It is these beings," he wrote to me, "who produce the phenomena of physical mediums." But "materialisation" is a physical phenomenon. Therefore, according to the rules of logic, the spirit that materialised on the evening of September 28th, 1874, had never lived on earth. Never having lived on earth it could not have been the soul of a woman murdered there, and whilst the above-quoted passage remains uncontradicted in the book before me the author is deliberately endorsing what he now knows to be incorrect.

Mark, too, what graceful compliments this nineteenth-century reviver of Paganism pays to spiritualists! Physical phenomena are not the productions of departed human beings. All the "exhibitions of tender pathos," therefore, at Chittenden, the "sobs, wails, and outbursts," the "reunion of those parted by death," the "mothers weeping with joy at the sight of their beloved ones," were simply sad mistakes, the results of mischievous frauds enacted by beings altogether alien to humanity, and who contrived to deceive certain fathers, mothers, sons, daughters, &c., by masquerading in the shapes of their departed relatives! But the author of "People from the Other World" is not satisfied with exhibiting himself as the abettor of so shameless and wicked a deed. He remembers that there are other spiritual phenomena besides those classed as "physical." He writes, therefore, a letter to the *New York Tribune* (About the end of September or beginning of October, 1875.) In this he informs the world that nine-tenths of *all genuine spirit-manifestations whatever* owe their origin to beings which "are not spirits of men or women from the earth, but something quite different, and something that does not inhabit our future world." Surely then, that poor tithe of phenomena remaining to us must be produced by human spirits of a high order! Surely, if so few of her children return to earth, those few must be earth's dearest and best! By no means. "The wise, the pure, the just, the heroic souls, who have passed on before us into the silent, land," continues the author of "People from the Other World," in his letter to the *Tribune,* "cannot, and do not, come back!"

Let me, in the name of the spiritualists of all times and countries, thank this calumniator. What! the beloved ones who have given us such glorious tokens of their presence were none of them "wise, pure,: just or heroic souls?" The few spirits really human which attend at *séances* are then the vilest of the vile, the refuse of our species? If a departed friend give such convincing proofs of identity that even the philosopher I am dealing with cannot claim this particular spirit as an "elementary," he or she must necessarily have been on earth a drunkard, a libertine, a murderer, or in someway stained with shocking vice or crime! And the author of this shameless libel on the spirit-friends so dear to us has the pleasing audacity to reproach me in print with what I "seem likely to say about mediums!" This, too, when it was impossible that he could have the faintest inkling of what I intended to say. To turn his own words against him, "is not the worst" truth I ever uttered regarding deceitful or pretended mediums (for with all honest brethren I am in perfect harmony), incomparably milder than the mildest accusation which this self-elected critic has fulminated against our spirit-guardians in his published diatribes? And the crowning wonder of all is that he loves the spirits whom he slanders! In one of his letters to me he describes spiritualism as a cause to which I merely profess to be devoted, but to which he really is devoted, heart and soul.

For he is a spiritualist of the most ardent type. "If to have long acknowledged that phenomena occur in the presence of mediums which are not the effects of legerdemain," says he, "*and to admit that they rooted fast and strong my faith in God, and my soul's immortality,* makes me "a spiritualist, then I have been one for many years." As my friend, Mr. Roberts, of Burlington, N.J., well remarks, in his caustic criticism of the *Tribune* letter, these sentiments, if honestly spoken, show their author to be a spiritualist in the only sense to which that term is applicable. In another of his letters this staunch spiritualist explains why he published an account of the manifestations at Chittenden. He "wanted to do this much for a cause that had been dear to him for more than twenty years." Moreover, "every cent paid him as copyright for his book has been donated by him to help that cause, in such ways as seemed most judicious." Surely we believers in the return of the departed have here a brother! The value of that brother may be small, but he is undoubtedly a spiritualist.

So thought the New York *World,* and classed him accordingly. At once our author was up in arms. Will it be believed that, in the very letter to the *Tribune* from which the sentence beginning, "If to have long acknowledged"—is quoted, he writes, "The *World*, reviewing my book, calls me a spiritualist, and so have other papers, *whereas nothing could be more opposed to the truth!*" What are we to think of such inconsistency? Can it be a reasoning being who, in one and the same letter, says, "It is altogether false that I am a spiritualist," and, a little further on, "I beg pardon, I am undoubtedly one?"

I have in my possession a letter from him, dated March 1st, 1876. Enraged by certain utterances of mine (which, I may remark, parenthetically, in no way concerned him), he casts about in this communication for a crushing reproach, and finds it. "Such behaviour," he tells me, "is reserved for blackguards—*and mediums.*" Yet we find him, March 8th (only a week later) writing to the *Banner of Light*, "I am the friend of mediums" (*and blackguards, of course*). "No man will go farther, or sacrifice more of time, of labour, or of money, to protect them from iconoclasts." All this for a class of people whom he esteems disgraces to humanity!

In fact, on his own showing, it is impossible that he can consider mediums as otherwise than utterly and irredeemably bad. Here is the definition he gives of such persons:— "They are slaves. While under control their own will is set aside, and their actions, their speech, and their very consciousness, are directed by that of another." And to whom are we slaves? "To spirits," says our author, "of whom nine-tenths are lying 'elementaries,' whose dearest delight is to deceive mankind; the remainder consisting of the very dregs of the human race." If such are the masters, what must the servants be? Good does not serve evil. This "friend of mediums" confesses as much. "It is," says he, in the *Spiritualist* of January 28th, 1876, "a direful calamity to yield to physical mediumship to the extent of perfect passivity. It is the same as saying to give one's self over as the helpless slave of the elementaries." There is certainly no small share of absurdity in all this. Mediums are first defined as, of necessity, slaves, and then reproached for being slaves. But, to return to our main inquiry, what use do the "elementaries" make of their victims? Our philosopher informs us: they teach mediums, it seems, "to lie, cheat, and indulge in immoral practices." Such conduct is, of course, quite natural in such beings. And, if nine-tenths of the spirits act thus, we may be sure that the other tenth, having no "wise, pure, just, or heroic souls" among them, will not be behind hand in wickedness. Yet of people who "lie, cheat, and indulge in immoral practices," this writer declares himself the friend! Were it not that his estimate of mediums is just as false as his estimate of the spirits who control them, a homely proverb, which I need not particularize, would here be in point. I remember, however, though I do not quote it, a passage written by Leigh Hunt regarding one of Wycherley's heroes.

I may turn from this part of my subject. If our Pagan friend is to be credited, the spirits "whom he loves" are nine-tenths enemies to humanity, and the other tenth disgraces to humanity. If he is to be credited, the mediums of whom, in his own language, he is "the friend, the warm and appreciative friend," are slaves to these spirits, and learn from them to lie, cheat, &c. As malignantly and wrongfully as he has judged myself in particular, does he judge all spirits and all mediums. Yet he has the exquisite impudence to write to the *Banner of Light* regarding me: "The worst thing I" (our author) "ever said against mediums is incomparably less harmful to them than the best this self-elected purist and purger seems likely to put in his book." Cool, certainly, after addressing a whole class in much such words as Christ's to the Pharisees, "Ye are of your father, the Devil."

Our author acts at present in the capacity of president to the very peculiar body known as the "Theosophical Society." (See Chapter ii., on "Delusions.") As such he has recently given one more proof of his utter disregard for consistency. The society has dispatched a member to Africa in quest of a magician. The president writes to impress this member with the importance of his mission. "You have the opportunity," he remarks magniloquently, "to introduce to western scientists those proofs of occult powers for lack of which they have been drifting into materialism and infidelity." This is equivalent to a confession that no one at present affiliated to the Theosophical Society can afford to a scientist "proofs of occult powers." Yet, in "People from the Other World" the author writes of a fellow theosophist: "Instead of being controlled by spirits to do their will, it is she who seems to control them to do her bidding. Whatever may be the secret by which this power has been attained I cannot say, but that she possesses it I have had too many proofs to permit me to doubt the fact." He afterwards found this assertion too sweeping. His third letter to me contains the following words:— "I certainly did assert that ——, instead of being controlled by spirits, controls them. This I now find to be true only in part. I failed to discriminate as to the spirits over whom occultists have control. I should have said that no one can dominate real human spirits, but only the elementaries." If this fellow theosophist can "dominate elementaries" what need of a wizard from Tunis or Egypt to "dominate" them? If such "wonders occur in her presence," why is not every scientist in America by this time a convert? Evidently facts and statements do not agree.

Indeed, what the president diplomatically terms his "blunders" are, on this subject, piteous. I subjoin a few of his statements respecting the fellow theosophist alluded to:— "This lady is one of the most remarkable mediums in the world;" "She is no medium;" "She was a medium until the age of twenty-five;" "She conquered her mediumship;" "She controls spirits to do her bidding;" "She never pretended to control human spirits;" "She is an adept in occultism;" "She never claims to possess occult powers." What is an amazed reader to think of all this? I quite accept our author's remark that on his head must fall the weight of these contradictions. "They are expressions," he wrote to me, "for which I alone am responsible."

By his own confession he knew, when he published the above statements, that certain of them were untrue. "I called her, in writing my book, 'one of the most remarkable mediums in the world,'" he says of this sister in occultism. "At that very time she denied the possession of mediumship, but, thinking I knew better, I assumed to classify her, without her consent, as I did." No doubt he is also entirely responsible for the following assertion regarding the same person, which assertion occurs in his first letter to me: It was her *spirit-controls*" (underlined by him) "who made her do the crazy things she did." Will the president enter the plea here, "Another *blunder* of mine?" It is, to say the least, curious that he should talk of the spirit-controls of a person who, he tells us, controls the spirits.

On page 355 of his book he "doubts if any circle ever witnessed a more astounding spiritual feat than that he is about to relate." Then follows a sensational account of a buckle brought by alleged spirit-power from a Russian grave. Much has since been said and printed about this occurrence. The matter is not worthy of any extended notice; but I desire to state that I still maintain the impossibility of any such manifestation having occurred. The said buckle formed part of a Russian decoration. "This," says the narrator, "with all other medals and crosses, must have been buried with the body, as is the universal custom." In Russia decorations are never buried with the dead. Until very recently, they were, without exception, returned to the government.

Not feeling very strong on this point, our author summoned to his aid another theosophist, the Baron de Palm, whom the Society a few months later were called on to gratify with pagan funeral rites. This person wrote a letter which the president caused to be published. Baron de Palm confesses that on the demise of the wearer of any order the insignia are returned to the sovereign by whom they were conferred. "But," he continues, "almost invariably the recipient has duplicate and triplicate sets of his decorations. The triplicate set is buried with the body." I have little acquaintance with the customs of the Baron's country, Bavaria, and do not feel called on to speak authoritatively of what is unknown to me. It would have been well had others imitated this carefulness. In making public Baron de Palm's letter, the author of "People from the Other World" proved strikingly how unfamiliar Russian customs are (as the Baron has it) to a class of people whom we call snobs." Nowhere in the Czar's dominions can duplicate and triplicate sets of decorations be found. The wearer has invariably but a single set. This suffices alike for "common wear, select occasions, and *grand tenue*," since Russian holders of insignia are usually able to afford the expense of servants by whom their decorations may be kept in order.

On page 452 of "People from the Other World" the author talks of "M. Aksakow, the eminent St. Petersburg publisher, former tutor to the

Czarowitch." M. Aksakow is not, and never was, a publisher, and never was tutor to the Czarowitch.

And now for a brief summing-up. In this writer's own judicial language, "Let us see how far we have gotten on our way towards the truth."

It will be perceived that his "investigations" (so-called) at Chittenden were utterly worthless. He carried them on, for the, most part, in darkness so great that the features of a face could not be distinguished at the distance of even two feet. He was not permitted to approach within five times that distance of the "spirit-forms." Except a Mr. Pritchard and a Mrs. Cleveland, none of the sitters ever mounted the platform while the "forms" were there. On these two "dear old gullible souls" our philosophical theosophist mainly depended for his "facts." He saw very little himself. He verified nothing whatever of the little that he did see. With the aid of hearsay and exaggeration he has succeeded in producing a romance—not very clever, indeed,—but which reflects more credit on his ingenuity than his candour. To style it an account of scientific observations made in the interests of the truth was the acme of absurdity. Given the same conditions as at Chittenden, a writer equally unscrupulous could produce a still more startling narrative from the feats of those very clever conjurors Maskelyne and Cooke, or from the feats of any other chiefs of the juggling fraternity. It is not in darkness like the darkness of the Eddy homestead that the facts which are the true stays of Spiritualism require to be groped for. Nor, though the author of "People from the Other World" becomes owlish enough when exposed to the clear light of truth, does he seem to have that bird's capacity for seeing when all light is wanting. On the contrary, the greater the darkness outside, the more ludicrous is the confusion of his mind. The most palpable snares are fatal to our poor philosopher.

I offer no theory as to the origin of the manifestations which he has recorded. In spite of jealously-preserved darkness and utter, want of tests the Eddys may be mediums. The conditions are suspicious; but no reasonable man will base a verdict on suspicion alone. The work before me counts as simply nothing. It presents not a single proved fact either for or against the "materialisations" of the Vermont homestead. How worthless the author of "People from the Other World" knew that book to be, one can sufficiently estimate from the fact that, not long after its publication, he wrote to the New York *Sun* (Nov. 30th, 1875) respecting the grand exposure of the Eddy spiritual manifestations which he, in common with the whole public, had been patiently waiting for."

NOTE.—There is to be found in "People from the Other World" a misstatement regarding myself which, as being a personal matter, may, I consider, be more appropriately dealt with in the, forthcoming volume of "Incidents in My Life."

CHAPTER VI

Certain spiritualists have, of late, astonished the world by informing it that the best method of proving the facts of spiritualism is to debar all possibility of proof. No tests are to be imposed at *séances*. No light is to be allowed; admittance is to be accorded only to persons whose credulity is unmistakable, and whose enthusiasm has been put past all doubt. It is from this happy class that the champions of suspicious phenomena, and more than suspected media come forth.

"I was pleased to learn," remarks one Quixote, "that the sensitive Mrs. _____ has decided not to admit any person to her *séances* whose name has not been previously handed in, submitted to her controlling band, and approved of by them. Faith that spirits return is now so widely held, that public approbation will be given to any refined, delicate, and sensitive mediums, whom a breath of suspicion or a disparaging word will agitate, agonise, and temporarily unfit for spirit control, if they bar out from access to themselves the suspicious, hypercritical, rude, and ill-mannered, and husband their peace and forces for use in the presence of none but those devoid of hostility to spirit-advent and mediumship."

The best commentary on the above is that the sensitive Mrs. _____ has since been detected in unmistakable imposture.

"It was really refreshing," writes another of the genus enthusiast, variety gushing, "to read in last week's *Banner* the two communications from Professor _____ and Mrs. _____. With the aid of such able defenders, I hope the long and sorely persecuted materializing mediums will soon feel themselves able to dispense at *séances* not only with all *testing scientific* enemies, but with what are still more cavilling, scientific and would-be *scientific* friends. Let all such be debarred the privilege of joining in spirit-circles, until they become humble enough in their minds to be willing to receive spiritual truth in crumbs apportioned by the guardian spirits of the mediums to their respective needs and capacities to swallow and digest."

Anyone desirous of doing the utmost harm possible to our cause need only write or collect a score or two of such effusions as these, and submit them to the world as principles adopted by spiritualists. The perniciousness of the doctrine is palpable to every mind whose share of sense is of the size of a mustard-seed. Spiritualism is so utterly at variance with many popular ideas, that a hundred various schools of belief which agree in nothing else agree in directing their antagonism against it. Its adherents, therefore, must build with adamant. The New Testament parable of the two houses is here applicable. Those who accept nothing as proof which leaves the tiniest loophole for the entrance of doubt; who try all mediums and all spirits by the strictest tests; who refuse to be carried away by enthusiasm or swayed by partisanship; whose search is for the truth, and nothing but the truth; these are the spiritualists of whom the spirit-world is proud. The spiritualism to whose advancement their efforts are devoted is, indeed, a "house built upon a rock."

There exist, however, other spiritualists, whose ideal would seem to be the house built upon the sand. They tell us that it is their design to advance the cause of Truth; yet their lives are devoted to inflicting injury on that truth. No material is too flimsily unreliable for builders of this class. Out of dark *séances*, and foolish reports of the same, and unreliable phenomena, and unlimited enthusiasm, they contrive to construct their house. So that the effect of the whole is glaring, it matters little how shaky the component parts may be; there is enough of the mortar of credulity to hold all together. Sensible persons turn from the sight with shame and disgust, and strive to convince of their error the enthusiasts to whom that sight is owing. Such efforts, how ever well-intended, are usually vain. More obstinate than their Scriptural compeer, the spiritualists of whom I treat are not to be convinced of their folly even when the flood has swept away the flimsy erection on which they have wasted time and pains. They industriously proceed to rear another edifice of the same kind, and, pointing to it, ask triumphantly what harm has been done.

Some, indeed, have contrived to improve even on the above process. Their house may be destroyed, but, to save the labour of rearing a new one, they quietly assure mankind that the old building is still there. By these expressions I mean that, when the theory of such an enthusiast is demolished, or his pet-medium convicted on the plainest evidence of fraud, he will find you, in half the time which it occupied Puck to put a girdle round the earth, "explanations" of the behaviour of the medium, and "reasons" tending to prove that, although his theory be demolished, it is still sound. And these are the persons who "would dispense at *séances* with scientific enemies, and still more cavilling scientific friends!" That is to say, instead of leaving imposture to enter, if at all, like a thief in the night, they would fling wide every door for its admission.

The most cowardly thing in the system of such philosophers is the method by, which they "explain" imposture. I call such "explanations" cowardly because they have the un-Saxon-like quality of attacking those who cannot defend themselves. In order to whitewash some Ethiopian of a medium they blacken the spirit-world. There is proof that imposture was committed; there is no evidence that any but incarnated men and women were concerned in it; yet spirits are accused as the criminals; are tried without being present, and condemned, though not a shadow of testimony is advanced against them. The stupidity of such conduct equals its wickedness.

Our opponents have not been slow to recognise the weakness and the folly of these theories. "Are lies told in the circle?" remarks one attacker of spiritualism. "Bad spirits! Does the 'materialized' form bear too striking a resemblance to the 'passive?' Bad spirits! Is the bull's eye turned on too quickly, revealing the medium off his seat, and endeavouring to escape from his bonds? Bad spirits! Is the sensitive being favoured by the starry hosts" a drunkard? Bad spirits, undoubtedly! So it is all through. Blind faith is the only royal road: proof you cannot have."

Happily it is by no means thus all through spiritualism. The most prominent workers for the cause resolutely refuse to accept blind faith as the only "royal road." The weighty and judicious article I proceed to give is from the eloquent pen of Hudson Tuttle, and well expresses the views entertained on the subject by every thinking spiritualist:—

"HIGH-PRIESTHOOD OF MEDIUMS.

"The *Banner* of February 26th, 1876, contains an article from T. R. H____ which is fraught with the most mischievous tendencies. What makes the matter still worse is the fact that Mr. _____ has boldly spoken what a large class of spiritualists really think, but fail to articulate. It has been repeated that spiritual phenomena were for the express purpose of convincing the sceptic. To convince, they must be given under test conditions, such as do not violate the laws of their manifestations; yet in the face of all science, Mr. _____ says:—

"'I hope that the day is not far distant when mediums, as a general rule, will acquire strength and independence sufficient to enable them to deny altogether having their divine powers tested in any way whatever.'

"This is the first intimation we have had that mediums had special *Divine power*, too holy and sacred to be gainsaid! What does this lead us to? To medium-worship! Is there to be a class set apart like the Levites of old time, who are to set themselves above the rules governing others, and are we to accept whatever they please to call spiritual without question? Why, an infallible Pope is a pigmy to such a colossus, which would bestride the judgment, bandage the eyes of reason, and make its votaries Punch and Judy figures to dance as the medium pulled the wire! If this be the end of spiritualism, to receive its greatest strength from 'untested,' 'untrammelled' mediums, its career is short, and it runs swift to ruin.

"We venture to assert that the strictly test conditions imposed by Prof. Crookes, and his accuracy of observation, have done more to impress the learned world with the claims of spiritualism than the haphazard observations and laudating letters of any number of common observers. Every spiritualist in the world points with just pride to his splendid investigations. Who quotes the wonder-tale of any one who has sat in a dark circle, when the 'conditions' were those of fraud, and no safeguard imposed to prevent deception?

"No amount of such evidence that can or may ever be produced has a feather's weight with the sceptic. Yet it is claimed that for the benefit of the sceptic the manifestations are given to the world.

"I have studied the laws of spiritual phenomena somewhat, and no one will accuse me of seeking the injury of the cause to which I have given the best hours of my life, nor of knowingly endeavouring to institute conditions contrary to the spirit-force. Because I love spiritualism, is why I would strip it of all this falsehood, and cleanse its skirts of the stain of deception.

"Prof. Crookes placed a wire cage over the musical instruments, and tunes were played upon them, by which it is proved that the spirit-force can act through such wire cages. Why not place a wire cage over the instruments, in all cases sealed to the table; and then there could be no dispute if they were played upon? Or in case of the medium disappearing, place such a cage over her, or over the paraffin in the 'Mould' experiment? Why must there be always some weak place left to excite the scepticism of those whom it is desirable to convince? Why is the honest investigator who proposes such absolute test conditions at once hailed as a Judas?

"When mediums will not comply with conditions that I know by my own experience, and the recorded experience of others, are not detrimental to the manifestations, I have no desire to confer further with them.

"Why the honest medium should rebel against such 'test conditions' I confess I do not understand. Certainly nothing can be of more value to them or the cause than thorough investigation, and the placing of every observation on absolute grounds. Because a medium has been tested once does not prove the genuineness of any other manifestation received under less stringent conditions.

"Science is the classification of accurately observed facts: Spiritualism claims to rank as a department of science, and the task of spiritualists for the present and future is to make good its claims. This can be accomplished only by making the conditions of every manifestation as strictly test as possible. After those have been established, of course others not under test conditions have a significance and value, depending, however, not on themselves, but on, those of like character which have been established.

"In opposition to this course of slowly winning our certain way by patient, honest investigation, Mr. _____, as champion of a mediumship which scorns to be trammelled and tested, arrogates 'divine' sanctity, which at once places the whole subject beyond investigation, and leaves the investigator outside bound hand and foot, privileged only to open his mouth and receive what is given by the 'spirits.'

"The constant exposures of the tricks of mediums throw obloquy and reproach on all, for when one is exposed it is thought others may be. The evil has become great, and every spiritualist should feel it his duty, while defending the true and honest, to expose imposture. The genuine medium should court rather than shun test conditions, and refuse to hold *séances* under any other. Then there would be an end to fraud, and the manifestations would have value in the records of science.

"Let no spiritualist believing with Mr. H____ accuse 'men of science' of refusing to investigate. He advises mediums to 'deny altogether having their divine power tested,' and how can anyone investigate? If we accept that, we merit the scorn of all thinking men, and will be swift in receiving it."

Side by side with the above protest must the following excellent utterances of the Boston *Spiritual Scientist* be placed:—

"HOW QUESTIONABLE MEDIUMSHIP IS SUPPORTED.

"In a recent article relating to 'Materialization' T. H____, a 'veteran' spiritualist, as none of our readers can doubt, embraces the opportunity to continue his practice of manufacturing sentiment in favour of 'conditions' that will admit of trickery on the part of the medium, either in a normal state or as the unconscious instrument of spirit-power. He says that the 'conductor of the circle on the spirit side' (?) was willing that professional sceptics should examine all the surroundings of the circle-room and cabinet provided some truthful spiritualist was with them at the time; and further, that he would permit them to be present at the *séances* if they would occupy positions outside of the circle, apart from the wire, and permit themselves, after being searched, to be securely tied, hands and feet, and placed in a strong wire cage with a rope or small chain put tightly about their necks and fastened to an iron-ring in the wall.

"Mr. H____ may have written the above in an attempt to be funny: if so, the old saying that 'many a true word is spoken in jest' is quite applicable: for it certainly express the attitude of 'questionable mediums' and their 'veteran' supporters toward a class of spiritualists who, standing between the public and those who *would* be representative mediums, labour to separate the true from the false and endeavour to discover what portion of the manifestations can be accepted as having a spiritual origin. They would also experiment to know more of the laws governing the phenomena of Spiritualism. These are intelligent investigators; but M. H____ and other 'veteran' supporters of questionable mediumship, are pleased to term them 'professional sceptics.'

"The individuals who possess this 'questionable mediumship' are usually wanting in the mental development that would enable them to appreciate the vast importance of the principles of the spiritual philosophy. They cling to spiritualism for the 'loaves and fishes'—the dollars and cents that it contributes to their pockets—and they are shrewd enough to discern what conditions are conducive to best results in this direction. First, it is necessary to secure the attendance of a few 'veteran' spiritualists; credulous wonder-seekers, who can write a fair descriptive article of what they *think* they see. The more credulous these 'veterans' are, the more they are in demand, and the more wonderful are the manifestations that they witness. They are given front seats in all circles, FREE, and from this time forth are the particular favourites of the materialized spirits; who greet them with fond caresses, permit them to cut locks of hair from their heads, examine drapery, and do other things to the end of the catalogue of wonders that have been chronicled in the columns of papers ever open to such trash. These 'veterans' form a body-guard around these mediums, and defend them from charges of fraud, and deny any person the right to test their 'divine powers.'

"The arrogant assumptions of both mediums and 'veterans' are supported by another class of 'representative' spiritualists who are in some way dependent upon spiritualism and the favour of its adherents for an easy living. These are obliged to sail with the tide; if they would win popularity they must be in advance when the public feeling is to be moulded in any particular case. The cheapest stock for an investment of ideas in case of an *extempore* speech is to give out a weak sentiment of charity for the 'world's saviours,' the 'persecuted media,' &c. *ad nauseam.*

"The opinions of the 'veterans' and the speeches of the 'representatives' find their way into print because they are best suited to the interests of those who might publish a journal 'for money—not for spiritualism.' Should the people be taught to think for themselves the wonderful stories would lose their interest, and spiritualists would donate that money to spiritualism which is now given in support of shams.

"See then what spiritualism is struggling against. See why many true spiritualists are prevented from identifying themselves with a cause they truly love. They wish to serve the bread of life, to teach the truth of truths, to preach, that all may hear, the joyful tidings of a future existence and communion between the two states proven; but their efforts are impeded by those who would control spiritualism for their own selfish advancement; opinions contrary to their expressed views are denounced; investigation is discountenanced. 'Believe everything,' they say, 'and you are accepted as one of us. Reject anything, and we and the rest of the 'veterans' will class you as a 'professional sceptic.'

"I am classed, not only as a "professional sceptic," but as "jealous of all mediums." The latter accusation is hurled at me wherever I attempt to utter a word of warning. Only a few months ago Mr. Benjamin Coleman, in writing to the *Spiritualist*, said: "The opposition which the Davenport brothers met with in this country a few years ago was stimulated by the bitter hostility of a rival medium who refused to witness their exhibition, but loudly condemned them as impostors."

Should Mr. Coleman have the intention of styling me a "rival" of the Davenports, I must beg to repudiate the proffered honour. I believe the whole statement to be simply a wild assertion on the part of the writer. If he did point it at me, I can correct his bad memory by assuring him that the Davenports gave their last "exhibition" April 8, 1865, and that I arrived from America (where I had been during the whole period of the Davenports' stay in England) towards the end of May, 1865.

Surely the nadir of folly is reached at last! It seems scarcely credible that any human being professing to be in possession of his senses should gravely enunciate such a proposition as the one regarding "professional sceptics," commented upon in the above article. So Professor Huxley is to be searched by some "truthful spiritualist," should he attend a *séance*, and Dr. Carpenter can only be permitted to attempt the verification of his "unconscious cerebration" theory under the uncomfortable conditions consequent on being "tied securely hand and foot, and placed in a strong wire cage, with a rope or small chain put tightly about his neck, and fastened to an iron ring in the wall!" The mind must be thoroughly reason-proof which considers spiritualism benefited by absurdity such as this.

A somewhat more enlightened view of the subject is contained in one of the leading articles of the *Spiritualist* for June 23rd, 1876. The soundest portions of the teachings advanced are as follows:— "Experience has proved that, so far as physical manifestations at *séances* are concerned, it is necessary to obtain them under very strict test conditions whenever it is intended to publish the facts. . . . The facts of materialization are of too much importance to rest upon doubtful evidence so far as publication is concerned; hence experienced spiritualists in, this country will never commit themselves to publicly recognising as genuine any full-form manifestations which may be witnessed on the premises of the medium, in which an ordinary room is used as a cabinet."

So far good; but the reasons which the writer submits as chiefly leading him to advocate stringent tests are, in my opinion, unsound:— "The spirits who produce materialization manifestations are, for the most part, tricky. Unprogressed spirits will sometimes fight their way in, and, by means of spirit-hands and arms, impose upon the best friends of the mediums, at one end of a room, by producing that which is not what they state it to be, and all the time the medium may be in a dead trance at the other end of the apartment. It is also a strange fact that, if a physical medium resolve to play tricks, there are spirits who will help him."

Is it a fact? It may be; but where are the proofs? The "Jedbro justice" dealt out to spirits by behaviour such as this out-Jedwoods even Jedwood. Accusation and condemnation press hard upon each other; but the evidence which should support them is never forthcoming. It is only within the last few years that these "tricky materialization spirits" have been heard of. Fifteen or twenty years back, when a trickster was detected in the act of simulating spiritual phenomena he accepted his fate resignedly; and bore in submissive silence the consequences attendant on his villany. Why need he have done so? If the frauds of late brought to light be mainly referable to the influence of bad spirits, is it not more than probable that the frauds which disfigure the earlier history of the spiritual movement are also referable to such influence? And can we believe that, if the fraudulent mediums of those earlier days had been simply unconscious instruments in the hands of evil beings, they would not have discovered and proclaimed so exonerating a fact? Or are we to suppose that they were conscious of innocence, but sacrificed their own reputations to shield the reputations of their guardians? Either theory is absurd. The simple realities of the case are that, fifteen and twenty years ago, imposture either had not discovered this method of cloaking itself, or did not suppose that there were spiritualists foolish enough to accept such libels on the spirit-world.

We hear much of "Fathers of English Spiritualism." If the paternity be genuine, I must needs be the grandfather, for they are, almost without exception, my converts; and thus, in a symbolical sense, my children. I must confess that I stand in the position of many parents; being heartily ashamed of some of my offspring. With me, their father, they were thorough in their investigations, and based conviction only on absolute certainty. Now, they have cast caution aside, and seem to experience an insane pleasure in being duped. Should I try to convince them of their folly they turn on me in fury; and, if unable to injure me otherwise, degrade themselves by inventing and circulating monstrous falsehoods, which they trust will damage my moral character. Truly, I am an unfortunate father. Happily, however, this class of my children is in a decided minority; and of the majority I may well be proud. These last, and not their self-assertive brethren, were the real founders of our cause. While pseudo-"Fathers of spiritualism" blew the trumpet of their own praise, others worked. Some of those workers have retired with sorrow and disgust from the wilderness of puppet-shows at present miscalled spiritualism. Others are rejoicing in the change which has freed them from the cares of earth. Amongst these last, let me name with affectionate remembrance my friend, Mr. William Cox, of Jermyn Street. Years before modern spiritualism had birth, he was, by thought and act, a spiritualist. Thus, when the subject arose into prominence, it came to him as a familiar, rather than a novel guest. His house was a home for mediums arriving from every country, and he the best of hosts; a man incapable of an unworthy action; the very soul of truth. At the time of the Sir David Brewster falsehood he first took up the cudgels in my defence. We owe a grateful tribute to men of his stamp, and his name should not be forgotten. But I must turn from this pleasant theme.

The first "discovery" made in the interests of mediums was, that "colouring matter might be transmitted from the materialized hand or form to the medium." Various committees had hit upon the plan of secretly placing paint on the instruments used at dark *séances*. The said instruments having been actively swung and sounded, stains of paint would be found on the "medium's" hands. For a time spiritualists no less than sceptics were content to denounce such persons as impostors. At length some veteran dupe delighted his fellow-enthusiasts with the ingenious "explanation" above mentioned. It was the first thing of the kind, and obtained a rapturous reception. Such success naturally excited emulation. There arose a race of spiritualists whose lives were devoted to the upholding of the extraordinary theory that because when fraud was committed, the mediums concerned appeared to be the guilty parties, they must needs be innocent; and because the spirits appeared to be innocent, they were assuredly guilty. And now these "explanations" fall upon us "thick as autumn leaves in Vallombrosa." Here is a sample of the class; extracted from the columns of the *Banner of Light*; (was not such a title given in jest to such a paper?)

"The use of a medium's physical organs in the performance of what is assumed to be a spirit-manifestation, though it may engender suspicions of fraud, does not of itself prove the medium fraudulent, nor does it exclude admission that some spirit produces the witnessed result. 'Come now, and let us reason together,' and do it logically.

"It is a general habit to regard all sane men and women as being actual authors of, and, therefore, responsible for whatever their tongues utter or their hands perform, and this habit is so prevalent and so active that the wisdom and justice of its promptings are usually conceded without question or consideration. What this habit exacts may be generally just toward those who are non-mediumistic, or relatively so; may be just toward all whose physical organs are never controlled by other will-power than that of their legitimate owners. But the latter class does not embrace all mortals, and consequently there may be persons whom public habit condemns unjustifiably.

"Whether a medium's hands are used in distributing flowers about a room, in procuring rag-babies, in obtaining paraffin moulds, and other acts which engender suspicions of fraud and falsehood (though made a primal question by the world's habit), has really but little, if any, pertinency in the case of a genuine and well-unfolded medium. If the limbs of one who is meanwhile entranced to absolute unconsciousness be used by a spirit, the work performed by using them is just as much that of a controlling spirit as the same would be if he performed it without the use of those limbs, and the medium's denial of any participation in or knowledge of what his limbs have been seen performing, may be made in all sincerity, honesty, and truthfulness, because the fact that the body was subject to the will of an outside intelligence involves a presumption that the owner of the body was not in condition to operate through it nor to know what was done through it."

There is just one flaw in the above delicious morsel of logic. The foundation on which this superstructure of argument has been reared with so much care is, in reality, no foundation at all. The weakness of the proposition with which our author starts is such that an attack directed against it sends the whole theory instantly to the ground.

That proposition is contained in the sentence:— "The use of a medium's physical organs," &c. The arguer knows the weakness of his position, and attempts to mask it in the following manner:— "Whether a medium's hands are used in distributing flowers about a room, in procuring rag-babies, in obtaining paraffin moulds . . . has really but little, if any, pertinency." Indeed! Suppose even that the point were conceded of mediums being sometimes "entranced to absolute unconsciousness" whilst acts of fraud are committed, our enthusiast is no nearer than before to the points he seeks to establish. Ample evidence remains to convict the mediums of conscious imposture. Whence come the flowers, the rag-babies, the paraffin moulds, the masks, the shawls, &c., which constitute the paraphernalia of fraud? Evidently and undeniably from the places where they have been concealed by the pretended medium, previous to the commencement of the *séance*. Was the impostor, at the time of concealment, in a state of "absolutely unconscious existence?" When, before a sitting, a woman laughs and talks with her intended dupes; having paraffin moulds, or shawls and veils for "materialization" concealed about her person; when a man carries newspapers in his pocket to eke out a "spirit-dress;" and has one thin fabric concealed in his neck-tie, and another arranged to appear the lining of some article of dress, is all this the work of spirits? The impostor is not in a trance. He does not even pretend to be in a trance. Yet, should a careful search be instituted at that moment, the destined apparatus of fraud is discovered hidden about the person of the "medium," or in the cabinet where he intends to "manifest." These discoveries have occurred. They will, I suppose, occur again. What, in face of such damning testimony, becomes of the "bad spirit" hypothesis? Its place is with last year's snow. And yet, should fraud be discovered at the close of a *séance*, instead of just before the commencement, spirits, and not mediums, are to be held responsible for introducing the shawls, masks, or rag-babies seized! Verily, the brains of some spiritualists are fearfully and wonderfully made. Since the charges against the other world break down so utterly, and "evidence there is none," certain persons seek to introduce to us imaginary spirits confessing imaginary sins. Thus we have (always in the *Banner of Light*) the following puerile nonsense saddled on a "controlling spirit":—

"Friends, in the lessons of to-day may you learn many of the laws of spirit-control. While you are looking with distrust on those who are giving physical manifestations, and are endeavouring to pick everything to pieces lest you should not get the truth, the whole truth, and nothing but the truth, we bid you, as we have once before bade (sic) you, be careful what you do. We warn those who, with the hammer calling itself truth, are pounding to pieces the very souls of our mediums in different parts of the country. We say to them, Step lightly, walk carefully. . . . I know this—that many times mediums are moved like automatons in their circle. Even those who may be used for bringing flowers, or for other manifestations, often move their arms or muscles in obedience to our world. . . . Hence there has been the cry of 'humbug.' Mediums have been called humbugs when they were really truthful to themselves, and could not tell why it was so. We have once before called your attention to this subject, and we would again impress it upon your minds to be cautious, to look well before you wound by the deadly shaft of slander the good name of those who are trying to do all they can for the spirit-world."

One is driven to the conclusion that, if the above really proceeded from a spirit, that spirit was the Rev. Mr. Chadband returned to cry out once more, "My friends, what is Terewth?" But I know of nothing which should lead us to attribute such folly to the spirit-world. The whole communication has a mundane, an excessively mundane air.

The same may be said of almost all the messages received in the *Banner of Light* circle-room. Ninety-nine out of every hundred spirits have the same peculiarity of speech. "I went out of the world," is the stereotyped remark, "on such and such a morning or afternoon." I may add that I knew intimately two of the persons whose spirits have been represented as communicating. Nothing could be more unlike their styles of thinking and expressing themselves than the "messages" attributed to them.

The position taken by an enthusiast who gives vent to the cry of "Bad Spirits!" is that of an accuser. He makes certain charges against the men and women who have departed this life. Now, it is a fundamental maxim of every impartial legal code that the *onus probandi* should rest with the prosecution. It is not sufficient that the, accused should be unable to make his innocence manifest. His accusers must demonstrate his guilt.

But the philosophers with whom I am dealing totally reverse this process. Nay! they do more than reverse it. Not only do they condemn those against whom no evidence is brought; but they acquit persons of whose guilt the evidence is conclusive. In every exposure which has been "explained" by some libel on the spirit-world the evidence against the inculpated medium has been such as would have ensured his or her conviction ten times over in the most impartial court of justice. Specimens of that evidence will be found in my chapters on "Trickery and its exposure." Yet these enthusiasts coolly put all such testimony aside. They would rather believe the purest dwellers in the spirit-world guilty of wicked and meaningless fraud, than admit that the lowest wretch who ever advanced pretensions to the possession of medial powers will act the hypocrite, when a hundred circumstances combine to make it to his interest to lie and cheat. And so our "loved and lost" only come down from the Beautiful City, and through the Golden Gates, to "speak lies in hypocrisy," and revel in the meanest sin! It is difficult to think calmly of such a doctrine, or to speak with patience of its professors. If, as David said, all men be liars, let us at least have the consolation that those are less prone to the vice in question who have passed from the temptations of earth. My own very varied and extended experience has always gone to prove such the case.

A peculiarly-illogical folly of vindicators of "persecuted mediums" remains to be noticed. The circumstances which lead up to it are usually as follows: Some "persecuted" being has been detected in plain and unmistakable fraud. Perhaps it was in the "paraffin mould" business—perhaps in the "materializing" line of life. The detectors of the fraud, having their senses about them, and feeling naturally indignant at the imposition sought to be practised, testify publicly to what they have seen. Should the medium, or pretended medium, concerned be of any note, indignant enthusiasts rush from all quarters to the spot. A *séance* is instantly convened; all but the faithful are excluded. Some mild test is imposed to give a certain colour to the report that "manifestations were obtained under the severest test-conditions imaginable." The evening passes merrily; the results are magnificent. Perhaps a half-dozen of "materialized forms" appear; perhaps the carpet is littered with paraffin moulds. The sitters are jubilant. The persecuted and interesting medium is uplifted to the seventh heaven, and receives the adoratory congratulations of all present. The editor of some "leading spiritual paper" rushes to his office, and prints in big type a brief and brilliant pæan like the following:—

"Yes! _____ was completely vindicated last night." How vindicated, in the name of common sense? Even if, on the evening in question, the manifestations were genuine, by what strange process of reasoning can this be considered to invalidate the fact that, fraud was detected and exposed at a previous *séance*? Yet such is precisely the manner in which nine "vindications" out of ten are accomplished.

We see then two classes of spiritualists. On one side is the searcher for truth, on the other the whitewasher of falsehood. The first says to the sceptic, "Examine, test, and then, if the evidence be sufficient, believe." The second says, "Believe, and when you have given sufficiently enthusiastic proofs of your credulity you may be permitted to examine a little, though never to test." The first says, "These phenomena should be observed under scientific conditions." The second tells us, "I hope the day is not far distant when mediums will deny having their divine powers tested in any way whatever." With which class is the victory to remain? In which host are the worthiest warriors ranked?

The first says, "I know that humanity is liable to err. Irrefutable evidence compels me to admit both that there are pretenders to mediumship who possess no medial gifts whatever; and that men and women exist who, being truly mediums, will yet stoop, when manifestations are not forthcoming, to lie and to defraud. I believe, too, that in another world we grow better and not worse. Therefore, it seems to me improbable that the goodness of God should permit spirits to return to us whose sole intent is to work evil. If this be so, prove it; I see no evidence that spirits plan and carry out the deceptions often practised at *séances*; but I see ample testimony that human beings are guilty of such frauds. I prefer, therefore, to condemn this world rather than the next."

The second tells us, "Your friends who return to you from beyond the grave are, almost without exception, liars and cheats. Their dearest delight is to deceive spiritualists, and inflict injury on mediums. Whenever, therefore, imposture is discovered at a *séance*, blame the spirits. They make masks and exhibit them. They dress up rag-babies;

they fill the pockets of the medium with flowers; they introduce paraffin moulds; they will simulate materialized forms with shawls and veils, and afterwards hide the shawls and veils carefully away; they will tie newspapers around the legs of a medium, or cover him with 'spirit-drapery,' or decorate him with false whiskers and a turban. What proof have we of all this? Oh, none! that it is a subject which requires faith rather than proof. Be assured that you had better believe all acts of imposture spirit-manifestations. Unless you do so much weakening of the foundations of spiritualism will be effected."

As one or other of these doctrines prevails so will be the future of spiritualism. If we wish the name to become a by-word and a mockery, and the cause a rank field of corruption, let us hold our *séances* only in the deepest darkness; and drive far off all enquiry and every species of test. If we wish that our belief should conquer, and its truth be made manifest, let us court examination, and do all things in the light. Where there is secrecy there will be suspicion. To have no concealments is the one effectual method of defeating fraud.

CHAPTER VII

ABSURDITIES

In dealing with spiritualism it is the custom of a certain class of minds to break loose from all restraint. "Reason being weak," and enthusiasm strong, the very thought of communion with the dwellers in another world appears to intoxicate these unfortunates almost to madness. Their vagaries are often scarcely distinguishable from those beheld in madhouses, or at the wilder kind of revival meetings. The disease manifests itself in a variety of ways. Some of the men and women attacked by it pin themselves to a particular delusion, with a fanatical tenacity which nothing can affect. Others flit tirelessly from mania to mania. One or more of the class will invariably be found at every "materialization" *séance* where the light is too poor to distinguish features. Should two of this kind of Greek meet, the "tug of war" is never far off. When the first indistinct form appears both are ready to recognise a relative in it. With equal vehemence do they

> "Swear from out the press
> They know him perfectly, and one can swear
> He is his father, upon which another
> Is sure he is his mother's sister's brother."

If we are to believe the conjurors, Maskelyne and Cooke, such visitors are frequent at the Egyptian Hall. "The 'materialized spirit' there," they tell us, "is often addressed in an imploring tone by some of the faithful amongst the audience, with 'John! John! speak to your old friend, John!'"

It is always at dark *séances* that this form of folly blossoms in the highest perfection. The "phenomena" witnessed at such gatherings are, in but too many instances, the laughing-stocks of sceptics, and the shame of every sensible spiritualist. Satirical verse has been directed at them. Our opponents remind us that—

> "Shakespeare's spirit visits earth, to tell
> How he and Washington are very well;
> And Lindley Murray, from the body free,
> Can't make his verbs and nominatives agree."

The reproach is mild. Spiritual journals have again and again published communications whose absurdity is simply sublime. These follies are usually of the same type. A great spirit has, for no conceivable reason, earthly or heavenly, descended from his high home to perform strange antics before a little circle of spiritualists. And how wofully these spirits have deteriorated! How wonderfully they are clad! The favourite costume of Oliver Cromwell when "materializing" himself consists, we learn, of a "white muslin skull-cap, black velvet suit, and yellow top-boots."

His shoemakers, however, understand their business but badly, since in giving, by particular desire, "the stamp that dissolved an English Parliament," Oliver altogether disarranged his ill-fitting "tops," and was forced to stoop and adjust them. Then the spirit shuffled with awkward dignity round the table, and after solemnly kissing the whole of the sitters, male and female, bore back his skull-cap and yellow boots to the summer-land.

Italy would seem to surpass both England and America in the number and quality of the "people from another world" who visit it. In "Notes of a Séance held at Naples" we find that, "Of the spirits who manifested three were in the flesh, and amongst the disincarnated the most noteworthy were Margherita Pusterla, Dionysius of Syracuse, Genseric, Cleopatra, Richard Cœur de Lion, *Aladdin*, Belcadel, Guerrazzi, Manin, and Vico." After these came "Abraham, Melchisedec, Jacob, Moses, David, Sennacherib, Elisha, Joachim, Judith, Jael, Samuel, Daniel, Mary Magdalene, St. Paul, St. Peter, and St. John." Even this concourse did not suffice. "The Biblical spirits," we are told, "came one after another, before the Nazarene. St. John immediately preceded him, telling us that he came to purify us before receiving the Great Master." Comment is as unnecessary as impossible.

America, it appears, rejoices in a spiritualist terming himself "the prophet and servant of God." This valuable exponent of our cause lately drew together in Philadelphia other enthusiasts as crazy as himself, and styled the astonishing assembly "A National Convention." His own part in the said convention was a truly benevolent one. Before the reformers whom he had gathered he drew from his pocket a frightened pigeon, and, tossing it up to the roof, proclaimed that the era of universal brotherhood had at last arrived, and that, in token thereof, he let loose the dove of peace.

Many years ago I had an experience with this man, which, I think, deserves to be placed on record. I was at the time very young, not being above eighteen, and was staying with friends in Hartford, Conn. One day, whilst the younger members of the family and myself were together, the servant brought word that "a strange-looking man had called, asking to see Mr. Home." I sent back a message to the effect that I was unable to come, and that one of my friends would see him, and learn his business with me. Presently I changed my mind, and went myself. In the drawing-room I found a visitor whose singular appearance somewhat surprised me. He was standing with his eyes tightly closed, and a generally-cataleptic air pervading him. However, I had not much time to study his looks. At the sound of my footsteps he moved slightly, and, without opening his eyes, ejaculated:—

"I don't want you; I have come for Daniel Home!" and motioned me away with his hand.

I regarded him quietly for a moment, and then asked, "What is your business with Daniel Home?"

"I can't tell you; let him come himself."

"Unless you tell me, he will know nothing about it; let me hear what you want."

"I am the spirit of his mother, speaking through this medium. I have come to tell Daniel that he must travel through the country with this brother in the cause, and make a charge of twenty-five cents for admission to his séances. Unless you let me speak with Daniel, the medium will shake the dust of the house from his feet, and my son will come to ruin."

The disgust and anger I experienced were such that I did not trust myself to reply. I silently left the room, and begged my friends to get the fellow out. He was sent from the house; and probably remains to this day in ignorance that, whilst he supposed himself addressing some one of the family whose guest I was, his pretended message was really delivered to the person whom it most concerned.

A few years later I met him again. Hearing, whilst in New York, that he was giving *séances* in Fourth Avenue, I determined to return his Hartford call. I found him seated before a small table, not much above a foot across; which table he caused to tip, and in this manner "spirit-messages" were given. I withheld my name, and he was thus left without the faintest conception as to the identity of his visitor. He received me graciously, and enquired whether I should like to ask the spirits if I were a medium. I signified that I should. The farce commenced.

"Will this brother be a rapping medium?"

The table tipped once. "No, dear brother, you will not be a rapping medium."

"Will he be a writing medium?"

The table gave two tips. This, as all spiritualists know, is considered to signify "doubtful." "Perhaps, dear brother, you will be a writing medium."

"But," said I, "the table always tips towards you. Will not the spirits tip it in an opposite direction?"

"Oh, certainly they will!" He commenced trying to tip as desired. As his hands were laid flat on the table, and had no purchase, they naturally slid along the top without effecting anything. He looked towards me.

"If you will put your foot against the leg of the table nearest you" (and, of course, farthest from the medium), "the spirits, my dear brother, will tip as you wish."

The coolness of the request amused me. I did as desired. My foot afforded the requisite fulcrum, and the table began to tip towards me in the liveliest manner possible. Such were my experiences with the "prophet and servant of God" who addressed the "Philadelphian Convention" of July, 1876.

The wildest imaginings of the Catholic children, who beheld "the Virgin washing her feet in a brook," have been more than paralleled amongst spiritualists. Some years ago our cause rejoiced in a "medium" of twelve years old, who was assuredly a highly-favoured boy. Angels of the most select class guarded him. The chief of the band was no less a personage than the Virgin. Herself and coadjutors possessed, it was declared, an insatiate appetite for plum-pudding and dried fruits. I have myself heard the uncle of the lad in question relate, with the gravest conviction, how at their *séances* spirit-voices would suddenly speak from out the darkness, telling the sitters, "Here we are! The Virgin Mary's coming, get out the sherry wine, and the raisins."

It would seem, indeed, that materialized spirits are rapidly developing a taste for the good things of earth. They commenced by timid sips from glasses of water. Next we hear of an angel band who had advanced so far as to "mix glasses of very nice gin and water," and who, "for several years, always had a Christmas party, at which they used to slice up, and hand round the plum-pudding to the sitters." Nor did they, it seems, forget "to partake sufficiently themselves of the good things provided." The habits of these strange beings were convivial. Champagne formed an invariable element of their Christmas feasts, and they would "carefully unwire corks, and extract them by means of the screw." This feat, we are told, acquired additional interest from being performed in total darkness. In fact, all for which the sitters could vouch was, that dinner, dessert, and wine had been duly honoured. Spirits, they were assured, had borne their part in the consumption; they believed it, and were happy.

Not always, however, is the spiritual presence left so entirely to faith. Materialization has become too solid a process to be affected by daylight, or the human eye. Thus it was that two or three enthusiasts who had gathered together in a North of England town, were treated to "phenomena," which one of the party described (*Medium*, August 18th, 1876.) in frantic terms as—

"A MOST ASTOUNDING AND PERFECT SÉANCE.

"Materialization Extraordinary in Good Daylight. The Spirit Partakes of a Substantial Repast of Well-Buttered Tea-Cakes, Tea, Milk and Sugar; with His Guests Specially Invited. He (The Spirit) Also Bountifully Extending Said Good Things to All the Sitters (Eleven in Number); Whose Names are Hereunto Attached in Solemn Attestation of the Truth of the Following Record."

After this display of capitals the chronicler proceeds to remark that he "shall offer no excuse or apology to Mr. Editor for writing and forwarding the report which follows." This, of course, is in consideration of its value. It would be difficult, indeed, to over-estimate the impression which such reports make on sceptical minds, and the immense success they have in bringing over sensible men to our cause. From the one in question I glean the following particulars respecting "this most lengthy and momentous *séance*, which extended over the long period of three hours and twenty minutes."

Speaking from the cabinet, the spirit instructed the sitters to prepare tea whilst he "materialized." All were immediately at work. "Soon the table was set near the centre opening of the curtains, with chair for our celestial host and visitor to sit on; and soon the table was adorned with table-cloth, teacups and saucers, sugar and milk vessels with contents, a fine lot of well-buttered tea-cakes, warm and ready for use, a large Britannia-metal teapot, with fragrant contents, *and spoons withal to sweeten the same.*" Strange beverage! which required to be sweetened with spoons in place of the sugar humanity ordinarily uses.

Singing, it appears, followed. "In the fluidic element of its delightful cadence, the curtains seemed to open, as if by silent magic, and there stood our celestial brother, 'John King,' dressed for the occasion. Instantly all was silence. The spirit bowed a reception, and the solemn yet joyous greeting burst forth from every heart and lip. The spirit took his chair and, adjusting it, sat down, and soon began to be talkative as well as the company at table, and invited them to begin, not forgetting to set the example. Of course, we were all guilty (more or less) of bad manners, in watching our host, to see how he partook of these substantial and earthly things. And, when we had all finished one cupful, with due complement of tea-cake, our friend the spirit seized the teapot in the usual way, and poured out to each a second cup, inviting all to proceed; then, handing round the plate of cake, which, as a matter of course, we all seemed eagerly to accept of, he did not forget himself; and then he extended the cake and the tea to all in the room, by special notice. Whilst engaged with our second cup, my right-hand friend, Mr. P____ queried, and said, 'John, do you de-materialize your tea and cake as you take it, or are you completely and fully materialized?' To which he answered, 'I am fully materialized.' Then it was observed, 'It will be dissipated when the form is de-materialized.' When the tea-party had ended, the table was soon cleared away, the spirit remaining materialized all the while. . . . When the table had been taken away, the door was still wide open. On enquiry, the spirit said he could stand the light, and he walked about in it, and said, 'Give us more light. Men say they want more light now-a-days. Let us have more light, Mr. P____.' And Mr. P____ gave all the light that could stream into the room by the door and the hall-window; and the spirit walked about in triumph." The giving, more light was certainly commendable, but there would appear to have been something of darkness in the mind of the genius who penned the foregoing account. His final impression of the *séance* was that it constituted a "pentecostal and glorious communion, in which he had been bathed with heavenly simplicity and love during the long period of three hours and twenty minutes." Exhausted by this outburst of eloquence, he hastes to conclude the report which he had "undertaken to give on behalf of the invisible and the visible brotherhood of immortal beings." "Thus," he perorates, "thus ended the most remarkable and momentous *séance* ever witnessed by any one present at the same . . . a season of truth and reality never to be forgotten so long as mortal life continues."

This writer has at least one brother spiritualist as gifted as himself.

"O tempora, O mores, mutantur!" cries the second enthusiast. "A few years ago the hour of seven on Sunday evening would have found me either with surplice on shoulder, or seated, with due solemnity, in, the old church pew. Now I find myself, by polite invitation, seated in the drawing-room of Mrs. ____. Here, in this vestry, we await the arrival of our officiating priest. No priestly robes wears he, no cowl, no shaven head . . . Service-time arrived, without the tolling of a bell, we repair by twos, like unsurpliced choristers, to the dining-room. That is to be our church for the evening. Our only visible altar, the table, around which we sit, not kneel . . . . A pause. Our host and hostess rise, withdraw to the side, and return with flowers of chastest white. With these they make their first offering of the evening to Mrs. ____, as priestess of the new communion. Not with thanks from mortal lips alone were they received . . . . Our little congregation waited on the spirit-world for directions. They came. We sang . . . The lights are lowered. . . . . Be patient. Medium, go into that corner recess called a cabinet." (O, shades of Punch and Judy!)

"We sit awhile gazing at the curtain. A face appears. It is a lovely face, all aglow with life and beauty. An angelic smile is upon the lip; the eye is alight with sweetest tenderness; the whole expression is one of universal love. Upon the forehead is a star of glistening jewels. The diamond, ruby, sapphire, chrysolite, and oriental pearl sparkle and blend, and blend and sparkle in symbolic harmony."

Truly, it was an unkind cut on the part of the spirit to "dematerialize" that star. The "glistening jewels" would, doubtless, have been an acceptable present to the circle, and especially to the writer of the sentimentality above quoted, who has given evidence on other occasions of the interest he takes in precious stones. But by what name are we to hail the wearer of the star? Our enthusiast proceeds glowingly to enlighten us. "The form retires and reappears many times, each time growing in brightness and beauty. The hand is waved in graceful salutation. The well-shaped arm is projected, with its pendant drapery. The finger is placed upon the jewelled star on the forehead. And there before us is the form of Mary, Queen of Scots!" Certainly, this revelation surprised me. I have had the honour of speaking face to face with some six or seven Marys of Scotland. Each of them, although reincarnated in a less exalted condition of life, retained a distinct recollection of the days when she feasted with her courtiers in Holyrood, or listened yieldingly to the suit of Bothwell. These "sad, discrowned queens" were of all ages and appearances, and the only thing difficult to discern amongst them was the slightest trace of anything queenly. Besides these substantial Mary Stuarts there are any number of Marys yet in spirit-land, whose presence has been manifested at a thousand different circles. Surely, however, we have at last hit upon the consort of Darnley. The reporter of the *séance* in question exhausts a whole vocabulary of amazed negatives in raptures regarding the "spirit's" charms. "No wonder that such beauty led captive the hearts of men. No, wonder that a Bothwell could intrigue to possess himself of such a form. No wonder that a Norfolk paved his own way to the scaffold to call her wife. No wonder that an ugly English queen should be jealous of such a Scotch sister. No wonder that history played out so tragical a drama in the person of one from whose every feature such gleams of other than human beauty shone forth. There she was; the Mary Stuart of what precise date I know not, but some time before A.D. 1587, back again among us in material form, after nearly three centuries of spirit life! Visibly back again! Nay, more; audibly so. She speaks to us. From those lips come words; few, it is true, but sounding to us across the ages as:— 'I, Marie Stuart, whose head was laid upon the block, and whose blood was lapped by a dog, am not dead, but alive for ever.' Is it possible? Can this be a real spirit form?" Strange doubt to intrude on such a mind! "Watch that aperture in the curtain," continues our interlocutor, authoritatively. "The invisible spirit clothes itself with a visible form before our very eyes. We trace its growth—watch yet longer." In the attitude of "watching yet longer" I leave the reporter in question. A second Truthful James, he stands exclaiming:—

> "Do I sleep?—do I dream?
> Do I wonder and doubt?
> Are things what they seem?
> Or are visions about?"

Such spiritualists and such incidents do harm chiefly by their folly. There are, however, absurdities, purporting to be the work of spirits, which appear to every sensible human being at once degrading and mischievous. They would be ludicrous were they not so disgusting. Of late they have fallen on spiritualism in a plentiful shower. I select a few which appear to me the worst.

Towards the end of 1875 a man was executed in England for a cold and cowardly murder. The execution had hardly taken place before a medium announced the coming of the estimable being in question to control her. This, however, was not enough. It seemed good that a worthy and venerable name, respected by spiritualists as that of an early and courageous supporter of our cause, should be dragged into contact with the name, of the homicide. Accordingly a self-styled Judge Edmonds was introduced as his sponsor in the spirit-world. The following edifying extract from a "spiritual" journal describes the results of the first "control":—

"I was receiving a communication from a spirit-friend, through Mrs. _____, when the utterance of the medium was impeded and her face assumed the fixed appearance of a corpse. Her companion was much alarmed, but knowing that she was in good hands I waited the result with interest. Soon the medium's hands were used to manipulate her neck and chest, and she gasped convulsively for breath. At a signal I approached the medium, and also made some passes over the region of the neck and throat. The spirit now indicated, in reply to questions, that he had met with a violent termination to physical life, and further indicated that he was '_____.' The animation now somewhat returned to the medium's face, and looking upwards the spirit said that he beheld his mother, but at such a distance from him that there was no communication between them. He complained of the intense cold and darkness of his situation. I spoke to him encouragingly, and the influence which he derived from our sphere somewhat subdued his despair and reconciled him to existence. He relinquished control with thanks for what had been done for him.

"'Judge Edmonds' now spoke in a hearty, friendly manner, stating that he had brought the spirit there, knowing that his effort to aid him would be seconded, and thanking me for the assistance I had rendered. He said '_____' was an intelligent and mediumistic spirit, and would in time become very useful in the work of human progress. His personal condition was not due to grossness, but to moral influences, from which he would rapidly emerge after that interview. . . . ."

"The conversation was at last rather abruptly terminated, as the 'Judge' stated he had exhausted so much power in bringing '_____' that he had none left whereby to enable him to express his views, but he promised further intercourse on a more suitable occasion."

Whether the farther intercourse did or did not take place I have not been able to discover. Some months later, however, a lengthy communication was published which purported to have been received from the same assassin. Looking at the various facts of the case, I think I am justified in calling it one of the most revolting things ever seen in print.

Our murderer commences by remarking that when the drop fell he "seemed to rise above the fog and smoke of London into some brighter and purer atmosphere." He goes on to tell us that many things have become plain to him which were dim and obscure before. "I would endeavour, for the instruction and benefit of my fellow-countrymen," says he, "to make known my mature conclusions and convictions as to the murder, and my own execution for it."

The first conclusion he arrives at is that he committed the deed in question. "I confess the murder. I confess that, driven to the last extreme of difficulty by the importunities of the poor girl, I was led to shoot her. This I confess—and it is with the deepest sorrow that I confess it."

Scarcely has he said this before it appears to him too sweeping. The world may be led to entertain the absurd idea that he repents. Repent, indeed! of such a trifle as deliberately taking the life of a fellow-creature. The spirit energetically hastens to prevent the notion, or dissipate it if it be already formed. "My sorrow is, in another than the ordinary sense, 'the sorrow that maketh not ashamed,' for I am educated enough, and have thought enough to see clearly that, granting the previous chain of inevitable events, *I could not have done otherwise; that I was and am, as all men are, the victim of imperious, invincible law, working on for ever towards pitiless and unseen ends.* But, though I am at one with the philosophers and deep, hard thinkers of modern times, so far—though I am relieved by this strong assurance of the imperishable necessity of things from the tumult of wild reasonless remorse which assails the thoughtless and the vulgar—though I now, speaking in a larger, clearer atmosphere than that of the Old Bailey, and before judges other than poor pompous Cockburn, and eyes other than those of the leering, jeering, heartless and brainless spectators of my trial—withdraw, to some extent, that last confused and partial confession, wrung from me by bitter mental and physical agony, and the well-meant prayers and entreaties of the chaplain and my friends, while, on the other hand, confessing my complete guilt (as the term goes) in reference to the murder, more fully than I did therein—though I feel and do all this keenly and unwaveringly, I am, notwithstanding, placed at last (as all men will one day be placed) on a platform of lucid thought sufficiently high to enable me to experience *the most heartfelt sorrow for my sad offence*, while at the same time possessing *the pure calm of an absolute certainty that that crime, in the essential nature of things, could never have been avoided, and that I was but an instrument in the rigid hands of undeviating fate.*"

One hardly knows how to deal with such mischievous nonsense. What could lead this orator to talk of "deep, hard thinkers?" There is little trace of deep thought in the tangled web of foolishness displayed above. He tells us that he was "the victim of imperious law, an instrument in the iron hands of undeviating fate." Then he expresses "the most heartfelt sorrow for his sad offence." What should lead an instrument to express sorrow? Does the gun express sorrow to its employer for the number it kills? However, his sorrow "is the sorrow that maketh not ashamed." This is equivalent to telling us, "I feel no remorse for the crime I committed." Nor does he. "I am relieved by this strong assurance of the imperishable necessity of things from the tumult of wild, reasonless remorse which assails the vulgar." It seems strange that this contradictory, illogical materialism should have been admitted to the pages of a spiritual journal.

What did he think of in the hour immediately preceding death? Was there any dim horror of meeting his victim haunting him? Listen! "I thought of" (the murdered woman) "too, but not with such marked sadness, as I expected to meet her soon, and go through many comforting explanations." Are we really requested to believe that at such a time such a man could have a thought like this?

This strange being read the various London newspapers containing accounts of his execution! "By-the-bye, it was stated in one paper that when I approached the scaffold my hair was seen to be carefully combed. This is true." And, further on, he remarks concerning "the two swift glances which the reporters told you I took towards the spectators."

It is not surprising that he should be thoroughly dissatisfied with his fate. "Capital punishment was, in my case, and is in nearly all modern cases, a profoundly barbarous and pernicious blunder. . . . . I rejoice to think that my case will be looked back upon in history as one of the crucial cases which helped materially to disclose to the nation the utter folly of the whole thing, and so for ever to put an end to it." Would to heaven one could for ever put an end to pseudo-spirit-communications such as this!

The above assassin does not stand alone in his theories and teachings. John Wilkes Booth is reported to have manifested to a certain American circle. The remorse that besets him can be sufficiently judged of from his communication. "I, and Lincoln," he remarked, "often have a cosy chat up here. We agree that it was just as well I shot him. You see, it was set down in the order of things for me to do it, and I don't see why I should be blamed for accomplishing my destiny. The world was all the better for it."

The world is not much the better for such communications as these. Were they generally accepted among spiritualists, spiritualism would be the greatest curse which could befall mankind. They are by no means, however, to be regarded as doctrines germane to our cause. Only a few crack-brained and perverse-minded enthusiasts promulgate such nauseous folly, and only a few vicious and silly listeners are attracted by it. The wickedness of the belief equals its stupidity. Picture a world from which all sense of moral responsibility has been withdrawn, and in which all crime is dismissed with the one remark, "Destiny." Such fatalism resembles that of the wild enthusiast who maintains that "once in Christ" he can sin no more. Indeed, it goes further. Maniacal Christians assert only that for the elect crime is impossible. The fanatics I am dealing with dismiss crime altogether from their idea of the universe. A man, they teach, is no more blamable for alternating good with evil than the night is blamable for succeeding the day. Humanity is simply a machine, and free-will a delusion. Contemplating such a scheme of creation as this, one is driven to remark that—

> "If it be true indeed,
> The vicious have a comfortable creed."

It is one, at least, which few ordinary men and women will envy any person the possession of. I protest, however, with my whole heart, against the saddling of such earthly trash on spirits.

A less revolting absurdity, but one equally baseless, is that which puts forward mediums as a race of inferior saviours to whom heavily-laden spirits may come, and find relief. One of these gifted beings describes in the *Spiritualist*, June 5th, 1874, "a singular experience with a spirit calling himself an Egyptian:"—

"He looked," she tells us, "a tall, dark spirit, wearing robes, his eyes glittering, his countenance sullenly serious; except when he indulged in mocking laughter, which he frequently did. I had much mental, or perhaps I might say voiceless, conversation with him, in which the attitude I bore towards him was one of considerate regard, and pity. I spoke to him reasoningly, even affectionately. No doubt my feelings were inspired. I will not dwell upon the different arguments I used, inspired by my guides, to induce him to change his manner of life, and seek to rise. But I felt after a time he was moved. He relented, drew nearer to me, and seemed to regard me with a deep interest. He seemed to search me, and at length a humbled, grateful, softened feeling appeared to be creeping over him, which he sullenly refused to yield to entirely. I knew it was the loving sphere of my dear guides, as well as the feelings they gave me towards him, which were gradually influencing him.

. . . . . "My whole soul from the first had been filled with an earnest, pitying desire to help him. Just at this moment, as if carried beyond himself, he wrote energetically, 'Dear, dear woman, I thank you much—I love you!'

"I shrank at this, but continued:—

"'I am, glad you love me, Thoth; it will do you good. But I want you to love my guide.'

"'I do love your guide.'

"'Do you know him? do you see him?'

"'I do know him; I see him.'

"'He will help you, Thoth, if you wish to rise out of your present state, and will try to do so.'

"'I will try.'

"'I am glad, Thoth. You give me great happiness. I am sure you see that I am most anxious for your good.'"

Hereon the spirit proceeds to inform the medium that he intends making a confession.

"I have been in this world," he tells her, "upwards of three thousand years of your time. I have not progressed, because I was of a dark nature by choice. I loved evil. . . . I am a stubborn one. It is not easy to change a nature that for three thousand years has grown wrong."

Yet the "dear, dear woman" accomplishes that change in about the space of three days!

"I repent," writes the spirit. "You know not what it is to wring these words from me. I mean it; it is beginning! A hell will I endure, if needful. At last the spark has been fired. The voice of love, which I have resisted all these ages, at last I have heeded. I am to become an angel then! And you have touched me in the right place. You are Thoth's saviour!"

There are persons who accept all this, but who cannot accept a belief in Christ. They denounce the claims of the Gospel. It does not, however, appear startling to them that a few minutes of such conversation as is given above should dissipate the darkness of three thousand years. The cheering belief of spiritualists is that the ministering spirits of light are eternally busied in urging to better things their suffering and erring brethren. Yet thirty centuries, and all the hosts of Heaven had made no impression on Thoth. And this medium subdued him with an hour's talk! Surely she would be invaluable as a visitress to those penal establishments whose unfortunate inmates sit fast bound in wickedness and iron. If a sinner of three thousand years' standing can be cured by her in so short a time, she would assuredly make sharp work of pickpockets of ten years' experience, or burglars of twenty.

The communications attributed to spirits are, the reader will perceive, sometimes ludicrous in their absurdity, sometimes revolting. A few "messages," however, contain teachings whose soundness is past question. Of this class is the "Essay on Wisdom," which tells us that "Wisdom is what is wise. Wisdom is not folly, and folly is not wisdom. Wisdom is not selfishness, and selfishness is not wisdom. Wisdom is not evil, and evil is not wisdom. All is not wisdom; all is not folly." The caution with which this inspired being philosophises is particularly commendable.

Some are more daring in their utterances. Thus we have, a spirit who unlooses you the Gordian knot of planetary life; "familiar as his (earthly) garter." His chosen medium gives the benefit of this scientifically-minded being's experiences in a small pamphlet of inestimable value. On Jupiter, it seems, glass is the one necessity of a comfortable existence. The dead are cased in glass, and placed as ornaments in the houses of the living. The said houses are themselves constructed of glass (stones being, presumably, never thrown in the planet). "Lemena," the spirit tells us, is the name by which these rows of Crystal Palaces are known. We hear also of a mysterious kind of sacrament which, about once in seven years, is rolled through the glass cities on a glass car. The dwellers in these cities, and partakers of the said sacrament, are from seven to eight feet high. As household pets they have a useful race of parrots, which vary in height from two to three feet. A visitor to any of the glass houses of Jupiter invariably finds "a parrot sitting behind the door, *knitting night-caps.*"

These interesting discoveries have been paralleled by other mediums and other spirits. There is a "sphere" where the elevated portion of the inhabitants feast monotonously on pork and beans. What the "vulgar herd" are enforced to content themselves with, our informant saith not. Another spirit dictates particulars respecting life in a certain planet—Mercury, if my memory serves me rightly. The production best adapted to the soil and climate of that world is, it appears, the rice-plant. It is no longer, however, a "plant." Favourable influences, and agricultural skill, have united to render it, like Wordsworth's philosopher, "a self-sufficient all-in-all." It grows, we are told, to a height exceeding that of an English oak. The *Mercurial* being who desires to enjoy in perfection *otium cum dignitate* must invest, when young, in a rice-swamp. He selects a particular individual among the gigantic stalks which have become his property. Then, like the Jack of beanstalk fame, he proceeds to exercise his climbing capabilities. Arrived at the gigantic and cauliflower-like head of the plant, he contrives to burrow out an abode for himself. There, after the fashion of a rat in a Cheshire cheese, he remains till food is exhausted, and his house seems ready to fall about his ears. His last rice-pudding duly honoured, he decides on making tracks for "fresh stalks and dinners new." Surely it is to a Hindoo spirit that we owe this remarkable dream.

These "spirit-teachings" are not always content with being simply absurd or astonishing. A fervid re-incarnationist, and devoted disciple of Allan Kardec, has given to the world a volume ("Le Flambeau du Spiritisme") whose blasphemous folly is hardly to be matched by any publication in any language. There is not a page of the work but must excite the heartiest disgust in the mind, of any ordinary person. Yet to read it without laughter is impossible. The lisping French in which it is written seems that of a child six years old. The "spirit-authors," however, are represented as being no less personages than the twelve Apostles of Christianity. We are gravely assured that at various periods they dictated this incomparable production to the person who has caused a few copies to be published. The subject is the life of Christ. The mixture of ribaldry, insanity, and absurdity is almost incredible. One of the Apostles favours us with particulars regarding the every-day doings of the Twelve. "We always took a small boy with us to clean our shoes. The Master liked as all to look well, and he was very particular that our shoes should be nicely blacked." The ordinary attire of Christ consisted of a flowing robe, and "bright blue boots." On one occasion He was reviled as an impostor. The incident is thus described:— "How can you call me an impostor?" said the Master, turning round. "Don't you see my curly yellow hair, and my nice blue boots? Would I have such things, do you think, if I were an impostor?"

An apostle gives various "facts" respecting a journey to Jerusalem. "We were very poor, and we sold little pamphlets of the life and doings of Jesus to bring us in money. We made great haste to get to Jerusalem, for fear that the newspapers should get hold of our coming, and announce it." Lest my readers should doubt their eyes, I hasten to assure them that this is an exact translation of the passage in question.

Arrived in Jerusalem, matters become even worse. The eleven other apostles are discontented that Judas should carry the bag, "as he was always a very loose sort of character." "The Master," after a supper, "joins in a round dance with his Apostles and Mary Magdalene." Various incidents follow which I dare not even hint at, and then comes the trial before Pilate. It was a very cold day. The Apostles, we are told, remonstrated with the governor for leaving. Christ to sit on the stone of the pavement, and, bringing in rushes, strewed them there. Then, turning to Pilate, they hoped he would not take offence at what had been done. Let our "spirit-author" relate the sequel: "Oh, that's all right," said the governor; "I have no objection to that. But, mind you," he continued, turning to Christ, "*none of your miracles here.*"!!

And this book was published to advance the doctrine of reincarnation! It must be confessed, indeed, that every re-incarnationist possessing a spark of sense expressed disgust on its appearance. For there are parts which it is simply impossible to quote. Such a tissue of folly and blasphemy was surely woven from the brain of a madman. And there are *three hundred pages* of the nauseous stuff.

Other works almost equally astounding have proceeded from the pens of re-incarnationists. I do not, however, design to notice them here. Let me direct the reader's attention to a pleasanter theme—the nobleness of the mission which a particular spirit is sent on earth to fulfil. His appearance is quite in keeping with the grandeur of his task, and the purity of his mind. A mediumistic beholder thus describes him:—

"A radiant figure stood in our midst directly in front of me; . . . . his face more beautiful than I had ever seen it, with a spirit delicacy and beauty unsurpassable; the regular features wearing an expression of God-like majesty, the eyes shining like stars, and the flesh almost transparently luminous. But, brighter than all, shone the cross, formed of long rays of light, brilliant as the sun; behind which John's figure, clothed in radiant white, seemed almost to disappear and be lost; although shining brightly itself, it appeared as if it would be refined away into the very brightness of life, and yet the noble face, with the long black hair and beard, and beaming eyes, was intensely vivid. The sight was ravishing, and filled me with such delight that it was some little time before I could be brought down to the more ordinary stage of writing, under control, the following explanation given by John King of the Cross of Light in A.'s picture:—

"It means the purity of my mission. I bear a cross in coming to earth, because I endure a good deal for you all, and my cross is pure and white, because my work is pure and good; and I bear my cross upon my face, as it were, because it is a Divine mission, in which I find my glory—the glory of an angel. Therefore the cross is luminous. I love my work for its good and use, and upon the cross's arms I lightly rest my upraised hands to indicate that love. It is no burden upon my shoulders, but, borne before me, becomes the insignia, or badge of my office in the spirit world, and is my support, consolation, joy, and uplifter; for by it my soul makes its progress into higher states of purity through the love of that humanity for which I work, to aid in uplifting mortal man to a knowledge of spirit life.'"

Sublime!

"How pure in heart, and sound in head,
With what divine affections bold,
Must be the man whose thoughts must hold
An hour's communion with *such* dead!"

This devoted missionary desires to be known to man by the humble *alias* of "John King." On earth he was evil and famous. Now, it is at once his duty and his pleasure to do good to his fellowmen. He is the reprover of the sinful, and the comforter of the sad. His is a divine mission, and in it he finds his glory, "the glory of an angel."

Imagine the sanctity of the atmosphere which surrounds this spirit. Imagine the reverent awe with which all present listen to the words of wisdom that he communicates. Imagine his

"Voiceless prayer,
Soft rebukes, in blessings ended,
Breathing from his lips of air."

And then imagine him throwing a sofa-cushion at the head of a sceptic. Imagine him looking beamingly on, whilst his subordinate, "Peter," pulls the noses of those present in the circle, and beats people about the head with pasteboard tubes. Imagine him rubbing a paper tube over an inquirer's cranium, and remarking, "This is hair-brushing by machinery." Imagine him, whilst in "materialized" form, presiding over a tea-party of enthusiastic old women, "seizing the tea-pot in the usual way, and pouring out to each a second cup."

Such is the "Divine mission in which he finds his glory." He enlivens it occasionally by a little of what some spiritualists consider (Heaven save the mark!) "facetiousness." "I'll tell you what," he remarked to one gentleman, "you ought is find spiritualism a jolly thing. I'm jolly enough. Look here now! "I'll sing you a song of my own composition:—

"I wish I had a bird
I would stick it on a spit" (and so on *ad nauseam*).

"Have you not," he asked on another occasion, "have you not seen the swift-running tide, Bending with violence the firm gutter-side?" Over which question, no doubt, the recipient ruminated perplexedly.

"Regular baths; and a bottle of Guinness's stout every day after dinner," John considers efficacious in bringing about a fit tone of mind for inquiring into spiritualism. His own ideas on the subject are not always so lofty as when he "loved his work for its good and use," and found it his "support, consolation, joy, and uplifter." "Look here, H____," he remarked on one occasion, "I've been put to do this work of convincing mortals for a certain number of years, to work out my own salvation, and, as I have to do it, I think it's as well to make myself jolly over it." "He then," says Mr. H____, "began to whistle in a devil-may-care kind of way." Such is the fashion in which John King "makes his progress to higher states of purity."

I have already called attention to the select nature of the spirit-band which favours Italy with its presence. The "bright, particular star" of that band has, however, departed from an ungrateful earth. Our planet is no longer illuminated with the glory of the Archangel Gabriel. Once Naples was his chosen mundane residence, but he has been forced to shake the dust of that city from his celestial shoes. The events which led to the departure of so distinguished a visitor were, some years back, narrated by the London *Echo*, as follows:—

"A. M. Valente, of Naples, has just been condemned by the Correctional Court of that city to six months' imprisonment for 'spiritistic' swindling. This Valente, formerly an officer in the service of his Bourbonic Majesty, was, says a Naples correspondent, the spiritual medium of a small but, select gathering. Valente, when in his state of ecstatic coma, was favoured by visits from no less a person than the Archangel Gabriel, a dignitary whose celestial functions do not, it seems, afford him the means of making both ends meet, for the burden of his song was still that he wanted money, and the money was always forthcoming, and delivered to Valente for transmission to the Archangel, or to be applied as he might direct. In this way Valente became by degrees the cashier of the society, and, incredible as it may appear, its richest; softest, and most fervent adept, one Agillo Braga, suffered himself to be stripped by degrees of all his worldly possessions, being, however, duly rewarded for his self-denial by the receipt of an archangelic diploma, conferring upon him the dignity of Nuntius or Grand Master of the little community. Valente had the keys of the money-chest, and when poor Braga wanted a pocket-comb or twopence to replenish his snuff box, he had to prefer his request in writing for presentation to the Archangel. But, while in the heyday of his prosperity, our Valente fell a victim to the passion that rules the court, the cottage, and the camp. In an evil hour for him a widow lady, one Geronimo Merici, in age somewhere upon the confines of gorgeous summer and mellow autumn, was admitted among the members of the society. She was a widow of recent date, and all her thoughts were set upon one object, to be put in communication with the spirit of her departed lord. The Archangel was willing to arrange the matter upon the payment of certain stipulated fees, and at last, thanks to the liberality of the widow and to the intercession of Valente, it was settled that the visitor from the spirit world should appear on a certain night in the lady s chamber, borrowing for the nonce the terrestrial semblance of Valente himself. Enthralled Valente, in this thou reckonedst without thy host! The widow hesitated, suspected, and finally declined to receive her visitor except in a purely ghostly and immaterial shape. Valente, finding her inflexible on this point, dropped upon his knees, confessed his imposture and the intensity of his passion, and offered his hand and his 'rich booty' to the charming widow, on condition of her helping him to make a clean sweep of what remained in the pockets of the spiritist community. Another and a worse mistake. The lady betrayed him to Braga, who after a severe internal struggle opened his feeble mind to conviction, and applied for a legal remedy. The trial, which occupied some days, was full of amusing incidents. The Court, in consideration of the temptation afforded to the swindler by the colossal stupidity of his dupes, took a lenient view of the case, and sent Valente to prison for six months with the addition of a fine of 51 francs."

Colossal as the stupidity of these dupes appears, we can almost equal it in England. If we have not archangels demanding money for themselves, we have inferior spirits begging jewels for their mediums. Italian spiritualists fully recognise the importance of the fact. "Where were you," an enthusiast dating from the very city where "Gabriel" dwelt, asks his opponent, "when, in the twenty-seventh year of Modern Spiritualism, in the City of London, there took place one of the most memorable *séances* since the beginning of our era?" The only memorable points about the affair in question are the false doctrines and the strange demands saddled on the spirit said to have manifested. As to the *séance* itself, it simply ranks with many hundred other assumed "materializations." There were no tests, and infinite credulity and enthusiasm.

Numerous appearances of the supposed spirit had previously occurred. This, however, was to be his final visit. About a fortnight before he had announced himself as the recipient of a call to a higher sphere. "Just the night previous we had had his most perfect embodiment, when he had appeared to us with a 'John King' lamp fully lighting up his face; moving about the room with life-like activity and ease, and conversing with us with all the freedom of one in the body, like ourselves. . . . To hear that we were never again to have such a pleasure was like another death, and fell upon our hearts desolately, like an ice-cold freezing rain, killing the tender buds of our newly-awakened hopes."

A special *séance* was arranged in order that this very material form "might bid a final adieu to his brother." The meeting came off.

"The spirit," we are told, (*Medium*, August 13th, 1875.) "materialized with unusual power and strength. He brought with him his lamp, and remained with us in continued conversation for the space of an hour, if not more. His voice was stronger than ever before, and he spoke in the most solemn and impressive manner regarding certain things he wished his brother to do for him. Kneeling before us upon one knee, with one hand held by each of us, as we leaned over to draw as near to his face as possible, after earnestly enjoining upon his brother the accomplishment of a certain duty which he wished him to undertake, he made a most startling disclosure to us.

"'I have to inform you,' he said, 'that my last life on earth was a reincarnation. In a former existence I was a Persian prince, and lived upon this earth some hundreds of years before Christ. In that life I was possessed of a quantity of beautiful and valuable jewels. Strange to say, I have become aware of the existence of some of those jewels in this very city of London. They are diamonds of the purest water and brilliancy, and, moreover, they are charmed stones, and would therefore be of inestimable value to their possessor. I wish you, my dear brother, to become the purchaser of those stones.

They are for sale in a shop in this city. I know exactly where they are, and the price—a price much beneath their value. They are five diamonds set in a hoop ring. I can give you the name of the man, the name of the street, and the price. But you must lose no time, for there is a person after them, and if you do not purchase them by eleven o'clock to-morrow you will lose them.' He then gave us the most circumstantial directions as to the situation of the shop, the name of the jeweller, the exact position of the ring in the window, even going so far as to tell me what omnibus I was to take to bring me to the spot, that his brother might have my aid in finding the ring." (Well-informed "spirit!") "Be sure,' he continued, 'that you say nothing to the man as to the value of those stones—a value beyond all earthly price, indeed, for they have been endowed with rare virtues of a spiritual kind. This ring, my dear brother, I wish you to present to our medium, as a testimonial of my gratitude to him for his services in enabling me to materialize for you. It has given me a very great pleasure to return in this way and confer with you again. You cannot estimate as we spirits can all that a medium gives up for these materializations, and I feel I cannot thank him enough for giving so unselfishly his life and strength to our service. Therefore I wish him to have the ring. It will be a talisman to protect him; it will increase his power as a medium, and with that ring he can never want for a friend; indeed, he will bear a species of charmed life. I wish you also to make a formal public presentation to him of that ring.' . . . Much more was said. Our adieux, tender and affecting, as to one we were never to see again (except clairvoyantly), were made, and again, and again were his solemn injunctions repeated. We were only permitted to kiss his hands, his head he would not allow us to touch, and our dear brother, rising to a standing position, slowly retired from us, repeating in solemn tones 'Farewell! Farewell!'"

Whatever disclosures the "spirit" may have made, there is one little point on which the earth-dwellers concerned in this affair are jealously reticent, viz., *the address of the jeweller from whom the ring was bought.* I maintain, as I have all along maintained, that, could this be procured, the "flashing gems," far from having existed in their present form for over two thousand years, would turn out to have been cut in Amsterdam, I have asked for the said address, and it has been refused to me. I can see nothing to alter, therefore, in the following letter. It first appeared in the *Medium* of August 20th, 1875:—

"MY DEAR MR. BURNS,

"Ill as I am, and unfit for letter-writing, it is my duty to make a protest against such a statement as the one by C____ W____, contained in the *Medium* of August 13th. As a spiritualist, it is a duty to say that I have never, in the whole course of my experience, met with a spirit teaching the old doctrine of Pythagoras, lately re-advocated by Allan Kardec, who, more than twenty years ago, tried to convert me to his way of thinking (I say this advisedly, for he told me it was 'by a careful study of the Pythagorean philosophy that he had been induced to believe as he did'). This absurd statement first teaches re-incarnation and then makes a present of precious stones (the which, I will wager, can be traced to having been cut in Amsterdam). If spirits, after being twice incarnated, have still nothing better to do than to give 'the exact position of the ring in the window,' and 'the omnibus' one is to take; then God help us, for it is a fearful absurdity, to say the least of it. Mrs. _____ is a most decided sensitive, and I can well account for her seeing the imagined dual presence. Let her be in a clairvoyant state away from the influences at that time surrounding her, and she will then explain the whole affair. We must use the reason God has endowed us with, and such statements are only calculated to do great harm to the cause we advocate. It is almost as bad as one case in my knowledge, where the person very solemnly declares that a spirit visits her frequently, and she gives details so disgusting that they are unfit to be heard. All this is the effect of a poor diseased brain. Spiritualism has its great and glorious uses, but this side of the question shows its abuses to the very fullest extent, and it behoves us to lift up a warning cry. I know nothing of Mr. _____, but if I were in his place I would sooner wear a serpent's poisoned fang than a ring given under such circumstances.—Yours,

"D. D. HOME."

["It is well known," adds the Editor of the *Medium*, "that Mr. Home has received from various crowned heads, as well as persons of note, most valuable presents of jewels, but they were never given or suggested by spirit-intercourse. This was the ground taken by Mrs. Lyon, but she *signally failed to prove it*, as all the Chancery records can testify.']

The ring was presented; the presumed spirit glowingly "explained" the whole business in the following speech:—

"Friends! In this work of repeated materializations of my spirit-form, which I have just completed—because, being called to a higher plane of existence, I shall never more clothe my spirit in temporary flesh at your circles—I was commissioned by a band of higher spirits. . . . One of the fields of progress opened to me was working for the good of mankind at your circles. We always raise ourselves when we try to raise others. I have to reveal to you, my friends, that I, the spirit who has (*sic*) so frequently materialized here in London, was a re-incarnation upon this planet. In my former existence I was a Prince of Persia; my name was *Hafiz Hemishpha*, and I was a descendant of *Kai Kaoos*, called *Cyaxares I.* by the Greeks, of the *Kaianian* dynasty, some six hundred or seven hundred years before Christ. I was not aware of this previous existence when first I entered the spirit-world after my last re-incarnation, but by degrees I entered into the knowledge that I had doubtless lived before. Within the last few days of your time, since, indeed, I received my call to ascend from the earth-sphere, I have lived through an eternity, and entered upon an eternity's stores of knowledge, principally by the aid of a wondrously wise Jewish spirit, or, more properly speaking, angel, who has revealed to me, and awakened within me, the recollection of former states of existence. They are mostly undeserving of being dwelt upon here; the principal one, and the one before the last, having been that of a Persian Prince. Rising from that life to a state of great happiness in the spirit-world, the desire for re-incarnation was not awakened within me for a long period. At length my soul felt its necessities; the planet had advanced to a state of higher civilisation I required new experiences of mortal life, new conquests over self and the grossness of matter. This also is too vast a subject to dwell upon this evening. Who can read the secrets of a man's life? who can judge of the unfoldments of a soul, and its necessities? Only God, and that soul itself. I descended to earth again, and was born of American parents. What I gained by that existence I know somewhat, but not yet all, for the soul of man is wonderful, and himself is revealed to himself in the slow progress of eternities. This revelation is a part of the work I was deputed to perform by the higher spirits, of whom I have spoken.

*   *   *   *   *   *

"And now, friends, I can never more materialize. It is not permitted to those who have left the earth-sphere and risen higher, unless by a particular dispensation for purposes of usefulness to mankind. Indeed it is too painful a process for the more etherealized inhabitants of our world to resume those garments of heaviness, as I have so frequently done. And now I will say, Farewell! My blessings upon you all!"

Was ever "spirit-communication" more painfully ridiculous? As taught by *Hafiz Hemishpha,* alias _____, alias _____, the doctrine of re-incarnation defines the next world to be a place where souls deteriorate. Some twenty-five hundred years ago Hafiz rose from earth "to a state of great happiness in the spirit-world." After a long period of blissful idleness he became awakened to the embarrassments of his position. Earth had got ahead of heaven. The life which we "incarnated" beings sometimes find so weary and so trying is, it seems, contemplated by the "pilgrims of eternity" with envy and reverence. To "satisfy the necessities of the soul,"—to make "new conquests over self," poor humanity must, perforce, skip backwards and forwards between this sphere and the next; like the harlequin of a pantomime through his trap-doors. Certainly, this is a cheerful creed. Not only are we to lose all trace of identity, but all prospect of happiness. What is the use of any longer singing that—

"We are going on a journey
To a bright and better land!

The "better land" is, we find, a savage desert, from which souls come back to civilise themselves; much as an Asiatic might journey to England for the instruction his native land could not afford him. The angel-spirits who guard us are lower in the scale of humanity than those whom they guard. Such are the chimæras to which this shadow, with the string of aliases, would have us bow.

I need not linger over the subordinate absurdities of his speech. Any little slips are atoned for by the fine concluding outburst:— "What I gained by that existence I know somewhat, but not yet all, for the soul of man is wonderful, and himself is revealed to himself in the slow progress of eternities." Certainly, this is at once lucid and sublime; the spirit meant, no doubt, that it takes "eternities" (whatever they may be) for a man to find out how many other persons he has been. As I entertain no hope of ever making such a discovery myself, I quite agree with him that, in the majority of cases, the "progress" of such a revelation will probably be slow.

The whole thing has a most unpleasant look. Is this bad example of enticing enthusiastic believers to bestow presents of much value on mediums the only example which "Hafiz" can set? Is the absurd doctrine of the spirit-world being a place where everybody progresses backward the only doctrine he can teach? If so, it is indeed well that he has retired for ever from among us, and can "shuffle on the garments of heaviness," in the way of "materialization," no more. Pity though that he, or his Jewish friend, cannot "clothe the spirit in temporary flesh" just once, in order to tell us *the name of the jeweller from whom the ring was bought,* and settle for ever the question as to Amsterdam.

There are rank harvests of absurdities which I have not space to notice. They crop up with the suddenness of the prophet's gourd, flourish for an hour, and as rapidly decay. It would be, however, an utter misnomer to term these wretched follies and wickednesses spiritual. They are no more part of our movement than the polype is part of the body to which it clings. Insanity sometimes snatches at spiritualism as a theatre whereon to display its antics. Needy sharpers turn their attention to it as a thing out of which money may be made. It is such lamentable occurrences that make the cause unpopular. The sacredness attaching to a communion with the departed renders even the thought of the follies and vices with which it is sought to sully that communion infinitely maddening. How painful then is it for reasoning men and women that day after day absurdity should succeed absurdity, and fraud, fraud! "Still they come." The climax of stupidity which disgusts us one week, is next week set off by its natural anti-climax of wickedness. Where there is so much of brainless enthusiasm, there are certain to be persons ready to prey on that enthusiasm. The damaging absurdities treated of in this chapter lead smoothly up to the still more damaging exposures treated of in the next. Thus spiritualism is placed between two fires. On the one side she is assailed by false friends, on the other by a hostile world. I have no fears regarding the result; but the circumstances of the battle are hard.

What, for instance, can be done with such spiritualists as a Frenchman of rank, and advanced in years, whom I will style Count Z____. During the winter of 1875 I heard that he had been boasting much of a wonderful medium just discovered by him, and that he was holding *séances* with the said "medium"—a gentleman of position and good family; but who, to my certain knowledge, even then professed atheistical doctrines. It seemed to me, therefore, that this mediumship must be pretended. I said so; and a dozen parrot-voices at once took up the old cry, *Home is jealous!* In fact, so much had I to endure regarding my jealousy, that I determined to obtain convincing proof of the true nature of the mediumship in question. Meeting Count Z____'s "medium" in the south of France, I interrogated this gentleman on the subject, and obtained from him a certificate, of which the following is a literal translation:—

<blockquote>

"9th May, 1876.

"In response to the desire of Mr. Home, I declare by the present document that I have never assumed to myself the power of mediumship. On the contrary, I have always, in those private gatherings where people *amuse themselves* with spiritualism, and where it was sought to make me pass for a medium, denied being one; and have pointed out that, as I am a materialist and atheist, it is impossible for me to believe in the doctrine of spiritualism.

"FREDERIC S____."
</blockquote>

I sincerely wish the writer of the foregoing a speedy deliverance from that atheism on which he at present appears to pride himself. Certainly, however, the "spiritualism!" in which he became mixed up was unlikely to conduce to his conversion to a belief in immortality. His own account of it ran as follows:—

"I told Count Z____ that the whole of the 'manifestations' he witnessed in my presence resulted from trickery; that I was not a medium, and had no belief in the thing. 'Yes, yes,' he replied, 'I am sure you are quite honest in thinking you do these things yourself; but I know better. It is not you, it is the dear spirits, and you are the most wonderful medium in the world.'

"When all this began in Paris, I and some ladies who stayed in the same hotel, often went into fits of laughter over the Count's credulity. Whilst sitting together, one of us would slily pat his head, or pinch his knee. 'Dear, dear spirits,' he used then to remark, 'please do that again.' Often, too, the person nearest the fireplace would watch for an opportunity of giving the sheet-iron screen a kick. Always, when this occurred, the Count would cry out in an exultant voice, 'The dear spirits are imitating thunder.'

"Not only have I told him that these things were done by ourselves for amusement, but I explained to him how they were done. 'Those flowers,' I would say, 'which were found on the table last evening I took from my pocket and placed there.' Still the only reply was, 'Yes, yes, you think so, but I know better—it was the dear spirits, and you are the most wonderful medium in the world.' Nothing could convince him otherwise."

Yet Count Z____, and such as he, are considered *supporters* of our cause!

Let me with a few words dismiss the people and the actions that remain to be noticed under the present heading. There are "spirits" who, after having been "reduced to the necessity of self-release" from earth, return there to make such communications on behalf of "materializing mediums" as the following:—

"Far be it from me to keep silence, while the belittled and belittling croakers are doing their best to disgrace and ruin a band of as true and noble workers as the age may boast of—and all for the reason that their sphere of faith, sight and action, is quite above and beyond the reach of microscopic eyes. Do these penny-a-liner journalists, and all the obscene birds for whom they cater, know, or think, what they are about? I believe not. If they did, they would see themselves murderers of the most malignant type. They foul the finest character, and then, with long faces and solemn drawl, pronounce it carrion; and they taint with their own foul breath the purest air." After this the spirit remarks that were his voice clothed with thunder, and his pen armed with lightning, he would make all these skin-deep exposers shiver in their shoes." Manner and matter continue equally beneath contempt through the whole communication. I dismiss it, therefore, and proceed. What I have given may serve as a specimen of the trash which the most degraded of spirits must blush to find attributed to them.

England, and still more, America, have numbers of such advertisements as "Madame _____, Clairvoyant on business, love, marriage, &c.;" "Professor _____, Astrologer, may be consulted daily, on the events of life;" "Madame _____, magnetic treatment, love powder, one dollar." These setters of traps for the foolish can in no sense be considered spiritualists. The only spiritualists blamable in the matter are the one or two editors who admit such announcements to their columns.

I have already shown what perplexing "people from the other world" are occasionally reported as presenting themselves at *séances*. One or two other examples deserve to be touched upon. The following extract introduces and explains itself:—

"A monthly has appeared in Boston—a novelty in the periodical world, for it professes to be edited by a disembodied essence. Nor are the spirits content with the spiritual direction, for with an eye to the loaves and fishes, one of the number acts as business manager; though the visible person, the amanuensis and publisher, is a physician. There are angels of darkness as well as angels of light, and in the *Voice* a strict impartiality is preserved, for one of the first angels who has come upon the stage is James Fisk, jun., and now we learn the secret of that speculator's life. He describes himself as having been, when in the flesh, the unconscious medium of a band of reckless spirits who manipulated him as a skilful pianist handles the keys of his instrument, and he could no more help doing what he did than could the instrument discoursing the music of the operator. The editor in chief has that spiritual penetration into the weakness of humanity which tells him that if he would interest the public he has to give voice to the bad spirits rather than to the good. People want to know what the rascal did and why he did it; and Fisk, jun., was a good subject to commence with."

Possibly those beings were members of the above band, who, at a particular *séance*, caused the instruments to play by "spirit-power" their favourite tunes; the said tunes being "Durang's Hornpipe," "Yankee

Doodle," and "The Devil's Dream." We hear, too, of a spirit whose "ordinary manifestations are working a sewing-machine, and playing upon a mouth-organ." Another celestial visitor "wrote a letter, directed the envelope, put a stamp on it, and mailed it in the iron-box at the street corner." But such stories are numberless.

They have as little of the spiritual in them as have the wild dances in which "mediums" (generally females) indulge under the influence of imaginary Indian controls. Like these, they are the products of over-heated and morbid minds. I believe that of the many and glaring absurdities upon which I have commented in this chapter, not a twentieth are attributable to spirits. It is not to drink tea and play on the fiddle, to give blasphemously-ludicrous communications regarding Christ and His Apostles, to strut about in skull-caps and yellow boots, to beat people over the head with paper tubes, to throw cushions at sceptics, to hold up murderers as respectable objects, to tell people by what omnibuses to travel, or to describe the next world as a place where humanity deteriorates, that departed spirits return to earth. Their mission is great—their opportunities are limited. What time have they then to waste in idiotisms, of which a school-boy would feel ashamed? Let us refer such to their proper sources; some to insanity, some to knavery—many to this world, few to the next. Let us recognise the height and the holiness of phenomena which show how

> "The beloved, the true-hearted,
> Revisit earth once more."

Let us put from our path all which savours of folly or of fraud, and press, steadfastly and undeviatingly, towards the truth. It is full time that the errors I have been treating of should "die among their worshippers."

"The most severe blows that spiritualism has sustained have been those aimed by unprincipled and avaricious mediums, who, when the manifestations failed to come as freely as the circumstances required, practised imposition to supply the deficiency." So wrote Mrs. Hardinge, in her "History of American Spiritualism," and every year fresh evidence testifies to the truth of her assertion. Wherever the facts of spiritualism have penetrated lying imitations of those facts may be found. The producers of such imitations are of both sexes, and every age. They may be divided into three classes. The first is made up of persons who, while really possessing medial gifts, will, when much tempted, resort to fraud. The second section consists also of mediums; but of mediums who, being utterly unprincipled, rather prefer to cheat than not, and who will, therefore, lie and deceive even when no encouragement exists to do so. It is with such that the most frequent and damaging exposures occur. They are seldom expert conjurors. The difference between the false and the genuine phenomena witnessed in their presence is too glaring to escape the notice of any person not blinded by folly and credulity. Soon, therefore, some decisive exposure crushes the faith of all but the insanely enthusiastic, and Othello, in the shape of the untrustworthy medium, finds his occupation for the present gone. It is true that he almost invariably resumes it when the storm caused by his rascality has blown over; but meanwhile our cause has received another wound, and the broad and easy way of fraudulent mediumship has been once more demonstrated to lead to destruction.

In the third class I place those charlatans who, though destitute of any real claim to the title of medium, find it profitable to impose themselves as such upon credulous spiritualists, and to imitate the phenomena by methods of more or less dexterity. This species of impostor usually varies the monotony of his frauds by showing how those frauds were accomplished, and, after disgracing the spiritualists who have received him as an exponent of truth, disgraces the unbelievers who receive him as an exposer—not of spiritualism, but of his own villainy.

The first class alone affords any very tangible hope of reformation. Mediums who have been led by temptation into ill-doing are, in general, capable of repentance and amendment. It is true that even these persons well deserve both rebuke and punishment; but their guilt is not so glaring as that of the swindler who habitually mixes genuine mediumship with fraud, or as that of the still more degraded creature who makes a lying pretence to gifts of which he possesses not the slightest share. Against these last it behoves every honest searcher for the Truth to be up in arms, and to strike with no hesitating blows.

For the evil has assumed gigantic proportions. Dishonesty, and its natural ally, darkness, are arrayed against honesty and light. It is with pleasure that I see signs of an organized attempt to abate the nuisance. Certain enlightened spiritualists, and a few (alas! a very few) select mediums who, in the consciousness of their honesty, can afford to encounter fearlessly investigation and the sun, are banding themselves against those "children of the night" who affect carefully-darkened rooms, and *séances* from which all opportunity for enquiry is excluded. To aid in this noble work of putting down imposture and destroying abuses my present volume is written. The battle in which I and other honest men are engaged will no doubt be hard. Experience has organized trickery to a high pitch, and the dupes are many. Let lovers of the truth, then, do their best to cast light upon the dark places with which spiritualism is cursed. I have acquired from various sources information regarding the fashion in which certain impositions are accomplished, and I proceed now to detail the *modus operandi* of such fraudulent manifestations. Once awakened to these cheats, investigators may with ease guard against their being practised.

The form of fraud at present most in vogue is the simulation of a spirit form or forms. To be successful such simulation usually requires the aid of a room so ill-lighted as practically not to be lighted at all, a "cabinet" into which the medium withdraws from the view of the sitters, and various other "conditions" of the sort. When the rules of such *séances* are broken, awkward discoveries occur. Sometimes the light is turned up suddenly, and the medium revealed in his or her "spirit-dress." Sometimes the "spirit-form" is grasped, and found to be none other than the medium. But should all go well, the credulous are often highly gratified. Figures appear, clad in flowing and parti-coloured robes. The display of drapery seems most extensive. Yet when the medium is searched at the conclusion of the *séance* no trace of this drapery can be found. Whence has it vanished? The believers present reply that "the spirits have de-materialized it." The sceptics probably examine the cabinet, and are astonished that they find nothing. Perhaps the evidence I have to offer may throw a little light on the concealments sometimes practised. Let me commence with the narrative of an unimpeachable witness, my friend Serjeant Cox:—

"DEAR HOME,

"I am satisfied that a large amount of fraud has been and still is practised. Some of it is, doubtless, deliberately planned and executed. But some is, I think, done while the medium is in a state of somnambulism, and therefore unconscious. As all familiar with the phenomena of somnambulism are aware, the patient acts to perfection any part suggested to his mind, but wholly without self-perception at the time, or memory afterwards. But such an explanation serves only to acquit the medium of deliberate imposture; it does not affect the fact that the apparent manifestation is not genuine.

"The great field for fraud has been offered by the production and presentation of alleged spirit-forms. All the conditions imposed are as if carefully designed to favour fraud if contemplated, and even to tempt to imposture. The curtain is guarded at either end by some friend. The light is so dim that the features cannot be distinctly seen. A white veil thrown over the body from head to foot is put on and off in a moment, and gives the necessary aspect of spirituality. A white band round head and chin at once conceals the hair, and disguises the face. A considerable interval precedes the appearance just such as would be necessary for the preparations. A like interval succeeds the retirement of the form before the cabinet is permitted to be opened for inspection. This just enables the ordinary dress to be restored. While the preparation is going on behind the curtain the company are always vehemently exhorted to sing. This would conveniently conceal any sounds of motion in the act of preparation. The spectators are made to promise not to peep behind the curtain, and not to grasp the form. They are solemnly told that if they were to seize the spirit they would kill the medium. This is an obvious contrivance to deter the onlookers from doing anything that might cause detection. It is not true. Several spirits have been grasped, and no medium has died of it; although in each case the supposed spirit was found to be the medium. That the detected medium was somewhat disturbed in health after such a public detection and exposure is not at all surprising. Every one of the five (Since this was written by Serjeant Cox the numbers have greatly increased. I doubt if there remain now five "materializing mediums" who have not been seized in the act of personating a spirit-form.) mediums who have been actually seized in the act of personating a spirit is now alive and well. There need be no fear for the consequences in putting them to the proof.

"But I have learned how the trick is done. I have seen the description of it given by a medium to another medium who desired instruction. The letter was in her own handwriting, and the whole style of it showed it to be genuine.

"She informs her friend that she comes to the *séance* prepared with a dress that is easily taken off with a little practice. She says it may be done in two or three minutes. She wears two shifts (probably for warmth). She brings a muslin veil of thin material (she gives its name, which I forget). It is carried in her drawers! It can be compressed into a small space, although when spread it covers the whole person. A pocket-handkerchief pinned round the head keeps back the hair. She states that she takes off all her clothes except the two shifts, and is covered by the veil. The gown is spread carefully upon the sofa over the pillows. In this array she comes out. She makes very merry with the spiritualists whom she thus gulls, and her language about them is anything but complimentary.

"This explains the whole business. The question so often asked before was—where the robe could be carried? It could not be contained in the bosom or in a sleeve. Nobody seems to have thought of the drawers.

"But it will be asked how we can explain the fact that some persons have been permitted to go behind the curtain when the form was before it, and have asserted that they saw or felt the medium. I am sorry to say the confession to which I have referred states without reserve that these persons knew that it was a trick, and lent themselves to it. I am, of course, reluctant to adopt such a formidable conclusion, although the so-called 'confession' was a confidential communication from one medium to another medium who had asked to be instructed how the trick was done. I prefer to adopt the more charitable conclusion that they were imposed upon, and it is easy to find how this was likely to be. The same suspicious precautions against detection were always adopted. The favoured visitor was an assured friend; one who, if detecting trickery, would shrink from proclaiming the cheat. But one was permitted to enter. A light was not allowed. There was nothing but the 'darkness visible' of the lowered gas rays struggling through the curtain. I have noted that no one of them ever was permitted to see the face of the medium. It was always 'wrapped in a shawl.' The hands felt a dress, and imagination did the rest. The revealer of the secret above referred to says that, when she took off her gown to put on the white veil, she spread it upon the sofa or chair with pillows or something under it, and this is what they felt and took for her body!

"The lesson to be learned from all this is, that no phenomena should be accepted as genuine that are not produced under strict test conditions. Investigators should be satisfied with no evidence short of the very best that the circumstances will permit. Why accept the doubtful testimony of one person groping in the dark when the question can be decided beyond dispute once and for ever by the simple process of drawing back the curtain while the alleged spirit is outside, and showing the medium inside to the eyes of all present? Where absolute tests are refused upon any pretence whatever, and where the conditions imposed are just such as are calculated to prevent detection if trickery is designed, we are bound to look with the utmost suspicion upon all that is done, and, indeed, we should refuse to take part in any such unsatisfactory experiment.

"In the investigations in which you so kindly assisted me there was nothing of this precaution and mystery. You sat with me anywhere, at any time; in my garden, and in my house; by day and by night; but always, with one memorable exception, in full light. You objected to no tests; on the contrary you invited them. I was permitted the full use of all my senses. The experiments were made in every form ingenuity could devise, and you were as desirous to learn the truth and the meaning of it as I was. You sat alone with me, and things were done which, if four confederates had been present, their united efforts could not have accomplished. Sometimes there were phenomena, sometimes there were none. When they occurred they were often such as no human hand could have produced without the machinery of the Egyptian Hall. But these were in my own drawing-room, and library, and garden, where no mechanism was possible. In this manner it was that I arrived at the conviction—opposed to all my prejudices and preconceptions—that there are forces about us of some kind, having both power and intelligence, but imperceptible to our senses, except under some imperfectly-known conditions. I did not, and with subsequent extended inquiry I cannot now arrive at the conclusion you have come to, that these invisible agents are spirits of the dead. On the contrary, the more I see of their operations the more I am satisfied that they are *not* such. The solution that most presses upon my mind is that this earth is inhabited by another race of beings, imperceptible to us in normal conditions, probably our inferiors in intelligence, by whom what we witness is done. If it be not this the agent is the spirit of the medium more or less separated from the body. But whosoever that agent may be, the medium through which it is enabled to manifest its presence, and to operate upon molecular matter is the Psychic (that is to say, the soul) force of the assembled sitters. But now that the phenomena themselves, or some of them, have received general acceptance as facts in nature, it may be hoped that many observant minds will investigate them with a view to learn their precise nature and extent, as produced under absolute tests. Then we shall be in a position to inquire what they are, whence they come, and to what they point.

"It is a great misfortune to the cause of truth that your state of health prevents you from contributing to this great work. But I hope still that your recovery may enable you to do something more to promote honest investigation into the greatest and the grandest mystery that could engage the human mind.

"Yours most truly,

"EDWARD WM. COX.

"March 8th, 1876."

The narrative above given bears a peculiar value from the circumstances attending the confession of imposture to which it refers. The exposure meets even the conditions demanded by those enthusiasts who would rather libel a hundred spirits than believe one medium guilty of trickery. "The only conclusive proof that a medium has perpetrated fraud," a philosopher of this class writes, "is proof that the physical organs of the medium acted in obedience to his or her own will and purposes at the time when the seemingly fraudulent acts were performed." This proof the "medium" in question herself affords.

But there are numerous other methods by which impostors of this class may successfully conceal the materials necessary for the deceptions they contemplate. To expose those methods the *Religio-Philosophical Journal* some months back printed an article which the *Spiritual Scientist* promptly copied. The course of these serials was in honourable contrast to that uniformly pursued in such cases by the least creditable of American spiritual publications—the miscalled *Banner of Light*.

"All the material for bogus mediums to imitate spirit manifestations can be so concealed about the person," the *Religio-Philosophical Journal* points out, "that the most rigid search may fail to find it. A common silk neck-tie tied around the neck under a paper collar, will conceal a gauze-like texture, white silk handkerchief, &c., sufficient to produce your sister, mother, or daughter, as the case may be. The expert, too, can conceal them in the lining of his pants, vest, and coat, with threads so arranged as to deceive the eye, and in a moment's time they can be taken out and replaced. Those who have never investigated this matter would be astonished at the small space required for the articles necessary to materialize a first-class spirit.

"Tissue paper also acts an important part in bogus materialization, it being used on the head and various parts of the body to complete the dress. It can be concealed in the lining of the vest, coat, or pants, and you may search for it but will not discover it easily. It is an easy matter to deceive three out of five who attend these bogus circles. . . . . Some people like to be humbugged; they take pleasure in it, as those did who attended G____'s circles in New York."

Such are the means by which pretended materializations are accomplished. The ordinary mode, it will be perceived, is to conceal the "spirit-dress" about the person. This, however, is not invariably done. A notorious trickster, whose exposure and punishment occupied some time back the attention of the spiritual press, was accustomed to operate in a different, but equally elaborate manner. On entering the *séance*-room his first request would be to see the "cabinet." "Cabinets" usually contain a chair or a couch. The "medium," after a glance round, seated himself on one or the other, and commenced a desultory conversation. Presently he rose, with some such remark as "It's growing late; we had better begin the *séance*. First," he would add, "let me retire with some of you and be searched." The retirement and the search duly took place. Nothing could be found. The medium re-entered the recess, and the circle was arranged. Presently the curtains parted, and a much-draped form appeared. Was it possible that all this could be accomplished by imposture? After various of these exhibitions had taken place, the question received an answer in the affirmative. That conversation in the cabinet had a deeper significance than might at first have been supposed. Whilst the impostor's tongue was busy his hands were by no means idle. The light talk he started was merely intended to afford him time for concealing somewhere about the couch or chair on which he sat a tight little parcel containing his "spiritual trappings." This accomplished, he was, of course, perfectly ready to be searched. The most rigid investigation of his dress was vain. Shawl, veil, &c., all of the lightest and thinnest fabric, awaited him in the cabinet.

The number of such swindlers is astonishing. The harm they do our cause is incalculable. As the *Spiritual Scientist* well remarks, in its leading article of March 16th, 1876:—

"It would be interesting information if any one could tell us of the number of darkened parlours on back streets that are the scenes of frequent *séances* for spirit-materializations. A description of the 'wonder;' that are here witnessed would be highly interesting to credulous people, but a careful investigator would ask more particularly concerning the conditions under which these manifestations are obtained. A few words tell the story. They are patterned one after the other—the original being the one that has been the longest in the business. The individual who would attend these shows is obliged to make, personal application; he is met at the door by a strong specimen of the *genus homo* who informs the humble applicant that his petition will be referred to John King. (John King is the familiar name for the manager on the spiritual (?) side of the show.) The answer of John King will be given to the applicant if he will call at some future day; and, it may be said, the success or failure of his attempt to enter the charmed circle will depend greatly on his personal appearance, and the number of ladies that are to be present on any evening he may wish to gain admittance. These shrewd managers have found that the best conditions are obtained when the ladies are in a large majority, and the number of men present does not exceed one to every two friends of the operator or medium. If an applicant should gain admittance he is assigned to a seat in the back part of the room; the front seats are reserved for the tried friends of the spirits. The sitters in the front row hold in their hands, and are held by, a stout wire bent in the form of a horseshoe; at either end sits a friend of the medium. The medium enters; she may be a small, slender, middle-aged lady, or one that is fat, fair, and forty. She takes her seat in one corner of the room or behind a pair of folding doors in a dark ante-room, or in an alcove furnished with doors opening into closets. Any of these are favourite conditions; and a correct type of several of the apartments of 'materializing mediums' in this city. A curtain now conceals the medium from view. Someone starts a discordant noise which is called singing; and the manifestations commence. The standard stock in trade consists of the materialized forms of an old woman and a sailor; these you will find at nearly all the *séances*. In addition each medium has an attendant 'materialization,' whose office corresponds to that of the *genus homo* in the circle—he keeps things in order.

"The above is no exaggeration; it is a faithful representation of the majority of the so-called materializing *séances* in Boston. Woe to the man or woman who ventures to suggest other conditions; he or she is sent to Coventry immediately, and is ever afterwards looked upon as a suspected person whose presence endangers the success of the enterprise. There are enough patrons from among the weak and credulous phenomenalists—people who will recognise in the materialized old lady the shade of their grandmother. Better make a few dollars and be safe, than endeavour to make a few more by admitting sensible people who will readily discover the imposture.

"It is a reflection upon spiritualists that test mediums who are always able to give some message, token of love or valuable information from the dwellers-in-the-spirit, should be neglected for a darkened room where forms that may be inflated masks, or something else, flit in an uncertain light at intervals for about an hour and then vanish, leaving the minds of the audience in a state of unpleasant uncertainty. It is no wonder that spiritualism languishes, and that its adherents are unable to support a single course of lectures in Boston. The causes are apparent."

(Every true spiritualist owes a debt of gratitude to E. Gerry Brown, editor of the *Spiritual Scientist* (18, Exchange Street, Boston), for an honest and manly stand against the impostures of the day. Unlike spiritual editors (so-called) who "run their papers for money," he has preferred to run his excellently conducted journal in the interests of pure spiritualism. May the success he has deserved crown his efforts.)

An article like the above is at once honourable to the writer, and cheering reading for all lovers of the truth. It contrasts well with the shameless and foolish manner in which other spiritual papers (so-called) have sometimes attempted to explain away the most glaring fraud.

"Light" was the dying cry of Goethe: "Light" should be the demand of every spiritualist; it is the single test necessary, and it is a test which can and must be given. By no other means are scientific enquirers to be convinced. Where there is darkness there is the possibility of imposture, and the certainty of suspicion. In the light no loop-hole remains at which either doubt or deception can creep in. The sceptic has opportunity for the use of all his senses. Should he refrain from applying the fullest tests, the responsibility is with himself.

In October, 1875, I wrote as follows to my friend, Dr. Sexton: "I implore you to advocate the suppression of dark *séances*. Every form of phenomena ever occurring through me at the few dark stances has been repeated over and over again in the light, and I now deeply regret ever having had other than light *séances*. What we used to term darkness consisted in extinguishing the lights in the room, and then we used to open the curtains, or, in very many instances, have the fire lit (which, if burning, was never extinguished), when we could with perfect ease distinguish the outline form of every one in the room."

Of another class are the dark *séances* at present held. Sometimes the pitchiest blackness prevails; instruments rattle discordantly; voices bellow through paste-board speaking-trumpets. Persons in various parts of the circle are touched or patted by supposed spirit-hands. Nothing is offered that can in the slightest degree be considered as approaching a test; the imposture is often of the baldest and grossest character; yet the "medium" is congratulated on the success of the *séance*, and credulous fools are happy. Perhaps the sitting is for "materialized" forms or faces; in such case the proceedings are regulated according to the character of the persons present. Should these be unknown, or regarded as possessing a fair share of common sense, nothing goes well. The circle is described as "inharmonious." The cabinet is jealously guarded. A distressingly tiny ray of light having been introduced "materialization" takes place. All that the persons present can perceive is something white; shape or features there are none. Such is a faithful portraiture of perhaps the majority of sittings for "spirit forms."

If, however, the audience consist of known and enthusiastic dupes, conditions are at once pronounced favourable. A larger share of light is admitted; the form appears, and moves about among the believers present. Their credulity rapidly mounts to fever-heat. Patched and darned shawls are discovered to be "robes of delicate texture and surpassing gorgeousness." A kerchief twisted round the head becomes an unmistakable turban; false whiskers and Indian ink produce "a manly and noble face," rouge and pearl-powder, in conjunction with a skilfully-arranged head-dress, are sufficient to send the credulous into raptures over "the vision of surpassing loveliness" presented. The familiarity of the spiritual visitors is charming; they have been known to seat themselves at the tea-table, and make a hearty meal, "enquiring jocularly whether the muffins were well buttered." They have mixed stiff glasses of grog for the sitters, and, not satisfied with mixing, have themselves partaken of them. In such little re-unions tests are never employed or mentioned. Not a dupe present but would rather perish than take a suspicious peep into the cabinet whilst the "materialized form" is out, and moving about the room. Not a hand among the party but would rather be cut off at the wrist than grasp, in detective fashion, the said form. The spirit is in every respect at home, and may walk in and out of the cabinet as he or she lists.

The darkness of the *séance* is thus proportioned to the sense of the sitters. Where scepticism is rife the most jealous precautions are adopted lest that scepticism should behold too much. To meet this condition of things various supposed tests have been devised. If they be of an inconvenient nature, the impostor, whom they are intended to unmask, usually declines them. If, on the other hand, they appear such as may be eluded by jugglery or confederacy, they are at once adopted. The most common method is to fasten the medium by some means; often painful, and, almost without exception, imperfect. Such tyings are simply useless. There is no binding submitted to by mediums to which professional conjurors have not also been submitted. The feats accomplished by Maskelyne and Cooke in the way of releasing themselves from ropes, &c., have been such as to drive certain credulous spiritualists to a most audaciously foolish expedient. These persons had again and again put forth jubilant utterances respecting the rapidity with which pet mediums of theirs were released by "the spirits" from their bonds. Maskelyne and his partner proceeded to yield to a tying at least equally severe; they released themselves with even greater rapidity. Some enthusiast, jealous for the reputation of his favourite medium, lighted on what was considered a happy idea. The amazed jugglers were gravely congratulated on the excellence of their physical mediumship; denial availed nothing. In spite of all they could say, print, or prove, rabid credulity continues to rejoice over them as "the best of living mediums for the production of strong physical manifestations." Surely spiritualism must have fallen very low, when a couple of professed conjurors are hailed by spiritualists themselves as its best exponents.

I need not dwell long on the point which at present occupies me. Almost every sensible person knows how easy it is for hands of a particular shape to release themselves from even the most complicated fastenings. The trick is seen every day in the street. The larger the wrist, and the narrower and slenderer the hand and fingers, the better suited are they for this particular form of jugglery. Other aids are also forthcoming; at times the tying may be done by a confederate. In this case the fastenings are so arranged that, whilst apparently tight, they become at once relaxed on a particular drawing-together of the body, and may be slipped off with the utmost celerity. Uneasy workings of the hands and arms are often employed to derange the operation of fastening, and may succeed to a greater or less extent. In fact the tyer and the person whom he binds are placed in a position somewhat analogous to that of armoured ships and heavy ordnance. Whatever thickness of plating the Admiralty may adopt, a gun is presently devised to pierce it. However cunning the knots employed, jugglery speedily contrives some mode of overcoming them.

Handcuffs have often been advocated; they are as useless as other forms of binding. Keys may be carried in the mouth, and cuffs opened. When, however, the hands are of the shape I have indicated they slip from such fastenings as readily as from ropes. The following extract details the result of a test of this kind. I take it from the columns of the *Religio-Philosophical Journal:—*

"After this Mrs. _____ went back into the cabinet, and closed the door; in a minute the door was opened, and we found an iron ring upon her arm (all done by spirits, without removing the cuffs, of course). At this point one of our party asked to take the handcuffs; the request was granted. A stripe of black paint was made inside each cuff (entirely unknown to the medium), and they were carefully replaced on her wrists, so that the paint was not seen by her; then the door was closed, and she proceeded to put the ring on again. When the door was opened all were able to see paint on the medium's hand, from the wrist to the ends of her fingers. This closed our investigation and the performance; all were well taken aback by the discoveries made."

Exposures, indeed, occur with great frequency. One of the most decisive was reported in the L____ *Daily Courier* of Christmas Day, 1875. After describing the "manifestations" witnessed at previous *séances* the journal; thus narrates how matters went on the evening of the catastrophe:—

"Several gentlemen had formed a very strong opinion as to the utter imposture of the whole thing. There was but one chance remaining, and that not availing the spiritualists would have achieved a great result. However, the fates were in other directions, and the spirits themselves must have played against the spirit-conjurors. The eager circle gathered together for a final manifestation. The stock-broker was there, hoping, probably, to get some augury that would help in his speculations; the master-carterish individual was also present, drinking in the wonders with great relish; there, likewise, was the dapper young gentleman who had come in his gymnasium dress, labouring, it is believed, under the delusion that the gigantic spirit was that of a noted ex-pugilist named King, with whom he was eager to have a 'set-to.'"

Near the cabinet sat "a strange man in spectacles." The occurrences of the evening were varied: "Poor Old Joe," and the "John Brown chorus," brought forth "a baby-spirit, believed by the sceptical to be nothing more than a newspaper sheet." Shortly afterwards a trifling discord marred the harmony of the circle. "Some one having tampered with the gas, manifestations were interrupted for a time, but harmony was restored, and the baby-spirit came again." The end, however, approached. "A tube of paper was handed out, presumably by a spirit, and then came the form of 'John King;' first, as if tentatively selecting his position, and eventually appearing full at the aperture in the curtains. This was the critical moment; the strange man in spectacles bounded like a panther towards the cabinet, and made a grab at the spirit. The white drapery, or whatever it might be, was seen to shrivel up, as if vanishing away. 'Gracious heavens! could it be a spirit after all?' was the question that overwhelmed for a moment the minds of the spectators. But, at the same instant, the brawny person, already described as a master-carter, sprang from his seat, and seized the medium on the left-hand side; so that the hapless impostor was thus caught in a vice. A howl of terror escaped his lips, and, as the gas was being turned on, another conspirator against the spirits made a dash at the cabinet and brought the whole arrangement to the floor. The medium was handed out, and disclosed a most ludicrous make-up. About two yards of tarlatan was arranged round his head turban-wise, and covered him in front down to the thighs. On each leg was tied loose a newspaper—both copies of the *Daily Courier*—and these served as the spirit's pantaloons; in the full blaze of the gaslight they reminded one of the top-boots of a brigand in a melodrama. When dragged into the light the terrified medium was still clutching one end of the strip of tarlatan, doubtless thinking his spirit-dress would be some protection to him against the violence of the sceptics."

It would appear that the irate meeting resorted to personal chastisement of the impostor. Such punishment was regrettable, as being wasted on a decided unworthy object. Indeed, the harm done to the few persons directly concerned was trifling compared with the harm done to a great cause. In all cases like the foregoing the press pounces on the exposure with journalistic alacrity. The newspaper happy enough to get the first grasp at the facts of the case, draws up a strong account, interspersed with sneering comments on the folly of people who are "dupes to spiritualism." This account is bandied about from one organ of public opinion to another. Persons who were on the threshold of being persuaded to investigate read the narrative, and draw back. The incredulity of sceptics is immensely strengthened. Meanwhile the enthusiasm of the more rabid among spiritualists becomes roused, and it is ten to one that some such rush into print with blatant "explanations" of imposture so palpable as to disgust all reasoning adherents to the cause. The fraudulent medium may not have a word to offer in his own behalf, but misguided admirers will assuredly utter a thousand.

I have remarked upon the readiness with which journals outside the movement call attention to flaws in the fabric of spiritualism, and the length at which they dilate on the said flaws. It would be well had the press honesty enough to be equally unreserved regarding the long array of tested facts which are the pillars of our cause, and which spiritualists can render as reasons for their belief. Perhaps it is the reluctance of adverse newspapers to publish evidence in our favour that makes various spiritual journals so slow to insert exposures of imposture. A narrative has been sent me, with the names of seven witnesses appended, which was refused publication by one of the journals in question. Yet the trickery it refers to was of the most shameless sort, and detection thorough and convincing. I quote from the letter in question the description of the catastrophe:—

"We sat as usual at eight o'clock, commencing with a hymn from the "Spiritual Lyre." 'James Lombard' was the first presentation, who, after calling several of the sitters some very objectionable names, retired to make way for the manifestation of John King. When this gentleman was announced, he beckoned the sitters one by one, and touched their hands and faces. My friend, Miss _____, having previously resolved on her course of action, requested to be touched on the hand, and was touched accordingly. She then asked the spirit (?) to be allowed to shake hands. The request was granted; but she was told not to come too near, or she would melt him. She grasped the offered hand tightly, and lifted the curtain: the light (which at all the materialization *séances* was allowed to burn dimly) was immediately turned up, and Mr. R____ stood discovered, with one hand held by Miss _____, the other engaged in taking from his head and face a pair of fake whiskers *à la* John King, and some white muslin which had served as a head-dress. Not even being entranced, he entreated the persons present not to expose him. . . . . When counselled by us to give over his nefarious practices, he replied that he should do no such thing. Did we think he was going to work while a living could be got so easily by this means?"

The above impostor, although he "had no intention of working" while a living could be obtained by trickery, appears no longer to find dishonesty a paying policy. The cheats he resorted to were so clumsy, and their exposure was so frequent, as to disgust even the most credulous of enthusiasts. It deserves to be remarked that he was the companion and pupil of the "medium" whose newspaper trappings and tarlatan turban were dragged into the light at L____.

More than one "materializing medium," indeed, has learned the tricks of his trade from the same personator of John King. Thus an ambitious teacher of—let us say—drawing, who advertised in a spiritual journal that he would give art-lessons in return for "development," was taken in hand by the person in question. The process appears to have been at once simple and easy. Eight days after its commencement the teacher of drawing burst forth on the world a full-blown "medium for materialization." His paraphernalia of "Punch and Judy box," darkened room, &c., were as excellently devised to prevent investigation as the most thorough-going enthusiast could desire. His guardian angels were numerous and select. Queens and princes, Jews and Persians, spirits a thousand years older than the advent of Christ, and others whose incarnation adorned our own century, group themselves gracefully around him. There is, however, just one perplexing peculiarity in the brilliant band. The medium has a slight defect in his speech, and every individual of the substantial "shoal of shades" who throng to his cabinet labours under identically the same defect. Strange! to say the least.

If such be the pupil, what of the master? He must be a decidedly highly favoured mortal who, from the superabundance of his spiritual gifts, can create a "fully-powered medium" in a space so short as eight days. Yet the reputation borne by this talented developer is, to put it mildly, unenviable. He appears to have been once on the point of making an engagement with a music-hall proprietor, under whose auspices he might expose, not spiritualism, but the gross frauds by which he had imposed on a portion of the adherents to that cause. It is certain that in the presence of various spiritualists he avowed the "phenomena" witnessed through him to have been the results of trickery, and it is certain, too, that he gave mock *séances* with the object of injuring one who had been most kind to him, and who is well known as an honest man, but whose mediumship this impostor wished to make appear of the same fraudulent type as his own. It is certain, finally, that the editor of a spiritual paper wrote and printed an article declaring the estimable being in question to be "according to his own confession a professional cheat, and quite willing to make a living by receiving money under false pretences." What is the value of "mediumship" developed at a source so foul? The aspirant after spiritual gifts who takes as hierophant a "professional cheat," need hardly be surprised if spiritualists acquainted with the character of the master look suspiciously on the disciple. That master has assuredly done his little utmost to injure the truth.

Perhaps he consoles himself for the more than tainting of his name by the reflection that he is but "one of a goodly company." The hardest trial which those who truly deserve the name of spiritualists are called on to endure is the constant outcome of accessions to the already long list of detected tricksters. Even as I pen these lines journals reach me with tidings of three additional "materializing" exposures; one in England, the others in the United States. All are connected with "cabinet manifestations," and all involve the personation of materialized forms by the medium. Of the first American imbroglio the *New York Times* opines as follows (August 23rd, 1876):—

"It is pleasant to note that Mr. C____, of Rochester, has finally had the good sense to begin the task of investigating the materializing business in the only rational manner. Mrs. M____, a medium of extraordinary powers, undertook to exhibit a company of select and first-class ghosts to a Rochester audience a few nights since. Mrs. M____ was assisted by Mr. M____, who acted as master of ceremonies and introduced the ghosts with brief and complimentary biographical sketches. The medium was tied with the usual ropes in the usual cabinet, and the audience sang hymns, in accordance with Mr. M____'s request, doubtless in order to prevent the ghosts from cherishing any longing to permanently return to a world where people who can't sing are always ready to try to sing. After the spirit of Daniel Webster had thrust his head out of the window of the cabinet, and made the astonishing revelation that there was 'a Mr. Smith' in the audience, and that he rather, thought he had met a Mr. Smith while in the body, the ghost of 'Sarah' walked out upon the platform, clad in white, materialized to the apparent extent of a hundred and fifty pounds. This was the moment for which Mr. C____ had waited. He leaped on the platform and seized Sarah in his arms. The ghost, regarding this as a liberty, shrieked loudly; Mr. M____ caught up a chair and knocked the investigator down, and Sarah, escaping into the cabinet, was seen no more.

"There was, of course, a tremendous uproar. Mr. M____ loudly proposed to destroy Mr. C____ on the spot, as a villain who had laid his hand on a female ghost in other than a spirit of kindness. Mr. C____ argued that his destruction was unnecessary and undesirable; and the audience was divided in opinion as to whether C____ or M____ was the person who stood in need of immediate destruction. The presence of mind of Daniel Webster happily restored order. That eminent ghost yelled out of the cabinet window that the medium would die if the audience 'didn't everlastingly sing something,' and some sympathetic spiritualist suddenly striking up that pathetic hymn beginning 'Tramp, tramp, tramp,' the audience joined in, and Mr. M____ postponed his bloody resolution.

"With the singing of the hymn the exhibition ended, Mrs. M____ was found in the cabinet still tightly bound, and with her face covered with blood, which, as Mr. M____ explained, was in some vague way the result of Sarah's hasty 'de-materialization' of herself. At any rate, no wound could be found upon her person, and though Mr. M____, with great liberality, offered to put a bullet through Mr. C____, or to provide him with an additional and obviously superfluous head, he finally decided that his first duty was to wash Mrs. M____, and to send Daniel Webster to inquire whether Sarah had sustained any serious injury"

The final scene of this eventful history I find to be "the preferring of charges against the husband of the pretended medium, his conviction, and sentence to a fine of twenty-five dollars, or three months in the county gaol."

The second materializer had much of method in his "mediumship." The town favoured with his presence was Rochester, N.Y., and his career, though short, seems to have been decidedly brilliant. Nemesis, in the shape of sceptical investigators, pursued him, however, and, at length, when ingenuity availed no longer, the affidavit of the entrapped "medium" made clear to whoever cared to read it the mystery of his shows. I extract the chief points of the document in question:—

"The first *séance* I held after it became known to the Rochester people that I was a medium," our penitent illusionist writes, "a gentleman from Chicago recognised his daughter Lizzie in me after I had covered my small moustache with a piece of flesh-coloured cloth, and reduced the size of my face with a shawl I had purposely hung up in the back of the cabinet. From this sitting my fame commenced to spread."

He procured a confederate. A secret closet was arranged in which this person could be hidden on *séance* occasions, and from which he came forth in the character of any spirit whose "materialization" the two worthies considered desirable. The entrance to this closet being undiscoverable, confederacy appeared impossible; and as the "medium" submitted to the severest tests, every "form" which glided into view of the audience was, to use his own words, "a staggerer for doubters."

In the day-time both spirit and medium rehearsed for the evening's performance. "My accomplice used false hair, wigs, beards, &c., and put flour on his hands to give a ghostly appearance. For baby faces we had a piece of black velveteen, with a small round hole cut out. This, placed over the face, gave the appearance of the tiny features of a babe."

The "medium," it would seem, sometimes did a little in the spirit way himself. "I had my accomplice paint me a couple of faces, the one a man's, the other that of a woman. I then proposed to have two apertures in the cabinet, one on each of the doors, which was done. On the night in question I entered the cabinet, and the singing and music commenced. I straightened out a piece of wire, attached one of the faces to it, rolled the mask up, poked it through the screen, and then unrolled it by turning the wire. I also had a piece of thick, dark, worsted cloth which I used as a beard for myself. . . . . So on this night two faces appeared at once, and almost threw the meeting into ecstasies."

Being at another time hard pressed (whether for time or disguises I don't know), the "spirit" merely held his coat-tails up to his chin, to form a pair of whiskers as he peered through the aperture. A presence of mind that, which, as Lord Dundreary (whose ghost was doubtless being presented) would say, "few impothtaws ewould imitwate."

But this genius no longer adorns the scene of his triumphs. "J____," says the *Spiritual Scientist*, "has left the city of Rochester, for obvious reasons." With a regret that the talents this pretended medium evidently possessed should have been wasted in such unworthy deceptions let us also pass on.

I had intended to describe at least one additional instance of detected fraud. In view of the present position of "materialization," however, this chapter is already sufficiently long. One can hardly take up a newspaper, whether English or American, without lighting on the history of some new exposure. I therefore confine myself to the notice of a point on which much misconception prevails.

Nothing can be more unjust than the often-repeated assertion that spiritualists, however honest, are, on discovering imposture, invariably disposed to hush it up; their reason being the harm which such histories, when made public, inflict on the cause. It is an indubitable fact that, of the many exposures of fraudulent materializing mediums recorded, the, most noteworthy have been accomplished or aided by prominent spiritualists. I may point as, an example to the case of Henry Gordon of New York. Let me add, however, that Gordon was assuredly, when I knew him, a genuine medium. Becoming surrounded by various of the enthusiastic *gobentouches* who care nothing for scientific investigation, but who insist on sensational phenomena, he was led to attempt the fraudulent practices which ended so fatally for him.

His exposers were spiritualists. So were the exposers of a medium (Since the above was written, at least three additional instances of discovered fraud have been put on record, where the discoverers were spiritualists.) whose malpractices came to light in that very building where, a few weeks later, the gas, on being turned up, revealed the too thoroughly materialized John King of the tarlatan turban and newspaper wraps. A noticeable feature in the case is its resemblance to that of Henry Gordon. To my knowledge the person chiefly concerned was, in past years, possessed of genuine medial powers. The same class of enthusiasts who encircled Gordon came round this medium also, and, by their folly and voracious appetite for marvels, tempted him to ruin. He commenced to hold dark *séances*; allied himself to the ranks of ropetiers and "cabinet mediums," and—behold the end!

Nothing is more astonishing to reasoning spiritualists than the gross imposture by which the credulous portion of their brethren are often deluded. Thus, we may read of a medium "still in the trance, walking about, and exhibiting the materialized spirit by the light of a candle held in his hand; calling up each one of the company in his turn, and subsequently, under the same control, and in a good light, seemingly picking up from the carpet a length of pink tarlatan, which visibly grew in his hands; materializing and de-materializing it in the open room as he advanced and receded before us; waving, twisting, and wreathing" (what a wealth of incomplete participles), "waving, twisting, and wreathing it as if in sport, and finally causing it to disappear in the air before our very eyes." And an American paper once described how "Mrs. _____ asked the spirit whether she could disappear before the visitors as she had done on former occasions. To this interrogatory she made the same reply as she had to the other, and, surprising to relate, gradually faded away into thin air before us until not a vestige of her was to be seen."

Surprising indeed! But to relate the simplicity of the means by which these wonderful results are attained will possibly be found more surprising still. The disappearance of the "spirit-form" is usually accomplished as follows:—

Behind the cabinet curtains stands the concealed form of the pretended medium. In his hand he has a length of some gossamer-like fabric, arranged to simulate a robe, and gathered at the top into something like the shape of a head, or surmounted by a mask. This puppet-like construction he cautiously advances through the opening of the cabinet until it is in view of the sitters. Let any reader attempt the process, and the completeness of the deception will amaze him. With lights down, the sitters at some distance from the cabinet, and expectation wrought to the highest pitch, this unsubstantial doll will have the closest resemblance to a human form. Should any very enthusiastic spiritualists be present, the spectator need not be surprised if two or three at once recognise a relative, and declare the form to be a materialized visitor from another world in spite of all the evidence to the contrary that can be offered them.

But we will suppose the fraudulent medium we were treating of keeps the "form" in sight for some little time. The company, at first sated by the marvel of its presence, find an appetite for new wonders growing on them. "Can the dear spirit," it is asked, "de-materialize before us?" The dim light is just sufficient to dimly reveal the dear spirit nodding assent. The figure commences to dwindle and fade. The drapery seems to dissipate into thin air. The head sinks down until it rests upon the ground. And then credulous old women tell us of "spirits who, losing power, sank into the floor up to the waist," or remark that "the head remained some time after the rest of the form was de-materialized." Let us see how such de-materialization is accomplished.

When the impostor has caused his puppet to nod assent to the request that it may fade away in sight of the company, he commences cautiously to draw towards him the lower extremity of the "spirit-robe," and at the same time lowers the upper part of the form towards the floor. His own person, it must be remembered; is wholly concealed. The figure dwindles and dwindles, and the awed company see it by degrees growing "beautifully less." At length the whole of the robe is within the cabinet. The mask, or gathered part which simulates the head, rests on the ground close to the entrance. These masks, be it observed, are constructed to inflate or shrink together, as may become necessary. Should one be employed, therefore, the "medium" has only to cause it to collapse. Should the cranium supplied to the "materialized form" consist of some gauzy fabric gathered into a bunch, he simply allows it to spread out on the floor, and then dexterously draws it towards him. In either case the deception is complete. The head appears to have suddenly crumbled into nothing. The audience are enthusiastic with delight and amazement.

"But," it will be remarked," we read often of the materialized form and the medium appearing together; and appearing where no secret ingress to the cabinet could exist, and confederacy was an impossible thing. Is not such a *séance*, however suspicious the cabinet and other surroundings may be held, a triumphant proof of the reality of materialization? Can these occurrences be explained on the theory of fraud?"

Easily enough. The medium (so-called) is perhaps seated within the cabinet. The dummy which does duty as a materialized form he holds upright by his side; or may even thrust it forward to a position outside the curtains. And such puppets any impostor can, with slight practice, cause to bow, dance, and walk a step or two, in an exceedingly lifelike manner. Even should the performance be clumsy it matters little, unless some sceptical spiritualist or investigator have place among watchers. *Gobemouches* swallow whatever is offered to them, and strain neither at camels nor at gnats. I have myself sat as spectator at a *séance* where the faces displayed were simply so many masks presented before an aperture. I called the attention of a credulous spiritualist beside me to the empty and eyeless sockets. His reply came promptly, and with a certain triumph:— "The dear spirits have not had time to materialize the eyes." Is it surprising that cheats should be found to practise on folly like this?

To return to our materializing medium and his "forms." There are still at least two methods by which "spirit" and mortal may be made to appear at the same moment. The first trick is sufficiently exposed by the letter of Serjeant Cox. In the instance yet to be described the medium stands somewhat apart from the angel visitor. Both forms bow, advance, recede; go, in short, through the usual pantomime. A curtain, however, is between the two, and this conceals the outstretched arm by which the impostor is enabling his puppet to play its part, in the deception. Such are the duplicated figures which adorn the materializing stage.

And the "tests" which are to prevent these deceptions! Truly fraudulent mediums must be astonished by the simplicity of the preventatives sometimes applied. Thus, in the case of a female, we are often informed that her dress was nailed to the floor. The usual very material forms appear. When the *séance* is announced to be at an end, the sitters enter the cabinet. Its occupant is found calmly seated in her chair. The dress is fastened as it was fastened at the commencement of the *séance*. Everybody feels secure. Should a report be issued, it concludes by stating that "whatever may be thought of the forms seen, they were not personations by the medium." Yet it is next to certain that they were. The occupant of the cabinet has simply unfastened her dress at the waist, and stepped out from it. Then the curtain rises on the usual John or Katie King.

Of ropes, handcuffs, &c., I have already given my opinion. To release himself from such bonds is part of the stock-in-trade of every third-rate conjuror.

Noise, however, is often caused during the process, and if heard might excite suspicion. The audience are therefore requested to sing. The worse the voices of those present, the more readily and loudly they comply. "Yes, we will gather at the river," makes night hideous, and effectually precludes the possibility of detection. Whilst the rest of the apartment is thus filled with a gush of most excruciating harmony, the cabinet becomes for the nonce a dressing-room. Possibly the medium is a woman. The doleful sounds without may strike on her ears, but the fair being heeds them not.

Like Jezebel she is tiring her head. A pocket-handkerchief or a simple strip of muslin bound round the face alters it so as to render recognition almost impossible in the dim light which is religiously preserved. Let the reader put this to the test. Pin together the window-curtains, and step behind them; pass around the face such a band as I have mentioned, and take care that the hair is concealed by it. A little cosmetic or rouge maybe employed to heighten the effect. Now turn up the eyes in approved "dying-duck" fashion, and expose the face to those outside. The change from its ordinary expression will be startling. Half-darkness is, of course, desirable; but impostors arrayed in the manner described, have been known to expose themselves even to a strong light without detection. (Deformed hands and feet are sometimes given to "spirit-forms" by the simple process of bending back a few fingers or toes.)

If the "spirit-form" displayed be masculine, some hair on the face is, of course, desirable; and whiskers and moustaches maybe cunningly concealed. One person confessed to me that he had carried them, fastened in the hollow under his arm. So with the other paraphernalia of "materialisation." The exceedingly fine India rubber masks employed when it is desired to exhibit a variety of faces, females may hide in the gathers of their dress, or even in their hair. Indeed, should the audience be sufficiently enthusiastic, and countenances only on the programme, those countenances may be furnished by so simple a means as a few engravings. Though the likeness held up to the cabinet-aperture be that of a Wellington, one excited beholder will recognise in it his much, loved grandmother, and another dispute the claim by pronouncing it the face of her equally venerated aunt. I have witnessed these sad exhibitions, and know, therefore, of what I speak.

The duty performed in this and the succeeding chapter is not an agreeable one. Like all duties, however, it is necessary that it should be accomplished, and accomplished thoroughly. I have put my hand to the plough, and do not intend to turn back. I know well what awaits me. All who are interested in the upholding of such practices as I here seek to expose will join in a common howl of fury. Punch-puppets of "John Kings" will be made to squeak out indignant anathemas from the depths of their jealously-guarded boxes. The mouths of *gobemouches* will open more widely, than ever to emit reproaches on my conduct; and shocked upholders of the "divine rights of mediums" will lift their hands in astonished horror. Let the storm exhaust itself. The consciousness of right is with me, and, as a medium and an honest man, I insist on being heard.

I say, then, that to the credulous enthusiasts whom I denounce do we owe the wave of imposture which at present threatens almost to obliterate the landmarks of spiritualism. I say that I will visit the kitchen of any such, and, should the scullery-maid be one degree removed from helpless idiocy, will teach her in a single hour to go through the usual repertory of dark *séance* tricks undetected by her masters. If I, however, afterwards inform those masters that the whole thing is imposture, the doors of that house will be immediately and for ever closed upon the utterer of such a calumny. The scullery-maid will be put forward by one party as an additional proof that "Home is jealous of mediums," and by the Occultists and Kardecists as conclusive testimony of my having been "bought over by the Jesuit party in the Church of Rome to injure spiritualism." I defy any one acquainted with the libels circulated respecting me in the past to pronounce the above picture overdrawn.

Let it not be thought that I pronounce what is known as spirit-materialization impossible. I firmly believe such a phenomenon to have occurred through the mediumship of others, and I know it to have occurred through my own. Through me, indeed, the first phases of this species of manifestation were witnessed. I allude to the years 1852, '53, and '54. Perhaps I may qualify this statement by saying that it is possible forms had been seen previously in the presence of the Fox girls; but I am not aware that such was the case. *In every instance when these phenomena have occurred through my own mediumship no preparations were made, and I, as medium, was seated among the other persons present.* At the house of my friend, Mr. S. C. Hall, the first materialization which can be construed as involving the use of a curtain occurred. The figure was distinctly seen to appear above the curtain in question. Speedily curtains were the rage, and they have terminated in the "Punch and Judy shows" now in use. *But there are two prominent features of the said séance which its plagiarists fail to copy; the first, that it was held in a well-lighted room: the other that I, as medium, was before the curtain, and in full sight of all present.* I need hardly point out how idly-useless in a case like this would have been the indignities of rope-tying, sewing in a sack, &c. When the materializing mediums of to-day "go and do likewise," I shall cease to denounce their *séances* as more or less cunningly-contrived vehicles of deception.

Concerning genuine materialization, I need hardly remind my readers that the carefully-conducted experiences of Mr. Crookes with Miss Cook were repaid by evidence giving undeniable certainty of the phenomenon. Other mediums might be named through whom well-attested manifestations of the kind have occurred. Why, then, should we be stunned with the foolish outcries against light, and against tests, fulminated by rabid enthusiasts who would exclude investigation and admit falsehood? Why should *séances* be converted into puppet-shows, where greedily-venal impostors install themselves as the showmen? Why should spiritualism be made more and more a mockery and a by-word, whose reproach is such that its best friends are compelled, despite themselves, to shrink sorrowfully from the subject? Why should weak-minded dupes be permitted to arouse the derision of the outer world by follies which make every reasoning spiritualist blush? Let those of us who love the truth be up and doing. When the last of dark-séance mediums has abandoned his or her vocation in order to set up as a third-rate conjuror, and the last puppet-box, alias cabinet, is demolished, or preserved in some convenient place, as a gauge by which posterity may estimate the credulity of certain of their fathers—

when this has been accomplished the golden day of our cause's triumph may be accounted at hand.

I have never yet beheld anything which could cause me to accept the asserted phenomenon of matter passing through matter. The instances witnessed by me (and they have been many), in which this was said to have occurred, could one and all be explained by less far-fetched theories. I do not say that the phenomenon is impossible. All through my life I have been cordially of the opinion of Arago, that "he who pronounces the world 'impossible' outside the domain of pure mathematics is a bold man." I simply ask, and I think the demand reasonable, that, if such feats be in very truth accomplished by spirits, the next live eels and lobsters they bring may be left imbedded in the re-integrated wall, instead of being brought through into the room where the circle is held. Then for the convincing of a sceptical world!

Or, perhaps, it would be better were the objects fetched inanimate. A block of ice imbedded in the wall, and "weeping itself away," would be a striking object. And how pleasant to find a ripened gooseberry or two coyly peeping from the plaster! Pleasanter, certainly, than to be greeted with the disenchanting discovery that the articles in question had assuredly come from the pocket of the "medium." I recall an instance in which about half a pint of the above-named fruit was thrown on a table in the dark. "There," cried the "medium," "is not that a beautiful manifestation? Don't you think it's perfectly astonishing?" A burst of indignation ensued when the two other persons present "could find nothing astonishing in it." "What," said the wonder, "you think I had the berries in my pocket, do you?" And to prove the honesty of all this wrath, the said pocket was turned inside out. Alas for the result! The "medium" had forgotten those little withered ends (the botanical name escapes me), which adhere to the gooseberry. At least a dozen of these were disentombed from the depths of that pocket. Was there no method of escape? Oh yes! Up came that ever-ready excuse, "Evil spirits must have placed them there."

Alas for the evil spirits! Surely as they do their marketing they laugh over the credulity of spiritualists. If a mother, whilst on earth, desired to bring her son eels or gooseberries from Covent Garden or a fishmonger's, she would hardly, in the first instance, steal the articles in question (though spirits are represented as doing so); and, in the second place, she certainly would not convey them to the boy in such a questionable manner that, to prevent his suspecting her of deception and falsehood, she would be driven to engage the services of some gifted Bedlamite who might bewilder the child with theories regarding "the disintegration of matter by spirit-aura," and the power another world possesses of passing rabbits, onions, &c., through the solid walls and locked doors of this.

Let me give an idea of how the bringing fruit, fish, &c., into a darkened room is often accomplished. The expectant circle, we will suppose, is seated round the table. The stream of harmony gushes forth as usual. Presently the "medium" (generally a lady—ladies' dresses offer such facilities for concealment,) feels, and announces, the presence of the "spirits." She commences to speculate as to what they will bring. "Let me see! At our last *séance* the dear spirits brought in some cabbages. Suppose they were to bring lilies of the valley (Provided always they are in season. The "spirits" never bring flowers which are out of season, or the products of distant lands.) this time, how nice that would be. Oh, dear no! We must not ask for lilies of the valley. Let us think of something else. What would any of you like?"

Naturally a voice proceeds from some one in the circle, "I would like to have lilies of the valley."

The "medium" energetically repudiates the suggestion. "Perhaps the dear spirits could not bring them. Why will you ask for such out-of-the-way things?"

"If they bring me lilies of the valley, I shall consider it a test."

The next instant a scattering sound is heard. A "spirit-voice" probably announces, "We have brought the lilies, since you wish for them so much." And, sure enough, on a light being struck the table is found strewed with the flowers in question. And the next issue of some spiritual journal describes, as a "good test," that "at Mrs. _____'s *séance* a few days ago, Mr. A____ wished for some lilies of the valley, which the spirits instantly brought." Such is a specimen of the suggestive methods by which "mediums" at times contrive to mould the wishes of the circle into accordance with theirs.

There are other ways of accomplishing the trick, and objects will even be produced after a strict investigation of the room, and the person of the asserted medium. Some years ago I knew of a person who was greatly favoured with phenomena of this kind. In more than one instance, after the most rigid scrutiny of her dress had been made, flowers, and even small branches of shrubs with the leaves attached, were brought—in total darkness, of course. A gentleman known to me arrived one evening too late for admittance to the mystic chamber where walls or windows were being de-materialized to allow of the passage of flowers and leaves. The circle terminated—the floral trophies were triumphantly exhibited—and the "dear medium" was complimented in most honeyed terms. An aunt of the gentleman I have mentioned gave him one of the little "spirit-brought" branches to examine. Just at that moment the "dear medium" turned to speak to some one. As she did so the attention of the gentleman was drawn to a leaf hanging from the lower part of the red opera-cloak she wore. It corresponded exactly with the leaves on the twig he held in his hand. He caught at it, held up the cloak, and showed to all present that the "spirit-productions" had been concealed in the lining. It was then remembered that the "medium" (no longer "dear") had, after being well searched, complained of feeling chilly, and had requested permission to put on the red opera-cloak which she had left (quite promiscuously, of course) in the hall. Her fee was paid; a cab was called; and she departed, leaving another exposure to go the rounds of society. (Confederates play a great part in these deceptions. I have even known of cases where the servants of the house were bribed into acting as accomplices.)

The dark *séances* held for the rattling of tambourines, and the antics of pasteboard tubes, are made the vehicles of a deception which investigators may with ease prevent, unless confederates be present, and have seats next the "medium." Here is this trick, as to the *dark* circle born. The impostor B is seated between A and C. His left hand grasps the right hand of A, and his right hand the left hand of C. A series of violent twitchings follow, of course on the part of the medium. These end in all four hands being brought very close. Presently B suggests that, as it is warm, or for some other reason, it will be as well not to hold his entire hand, but simply the little finger. Should A and C hard-heartedly refuse, "the spirits" speedily declare them "inharmonious," and desire that their places may be taken by other members of the circle. Should they consent, the performance proceeds as follows. B approaches the hands of A and C still nearer. Suddenly a twitch more violent than the preceding ones unexpectedly releases one of the "medium's" hands, generally the right. The sitter from whom it was withdrawn gropes for it, and encounters what he supposes to be the finger that he previously held. There is no more twitching. The instruments begin to perform in lively style. *Instead of recapturing that little finger of B's right hand which he previously held, C has been given the thumb or forefinger of the hand whose little finger A grasps.* The momentary release of one hand enabled the "medium" to effect the change. When careful watching of the hands renders this trick impossible, the teeth are often resorted to; and in Amsterdam and Paris bitten relics of such *séances* may be seen.

Variations of the particular imposture in question have lately been devised. The said variations even dare "with their darkness affront the light;" a tiny ray of light, that is. As an example of the exposure of such frauds I make the following extracts from two letters written me in the spring of 1876 by an English correspondent. The first describes the performances of the asserted mediums; the second gives proof of the trickery perpetrated.

"A green baize curtain was drawn across that corner of the room which formed the cabinet. Mr. _____ stood in front of the curtain, and opened it after each manifestation. The younger boy was considered the most mediumistic, and the greater part of the phenomena took place with him alone. His coat was taken off, his hands were placed behind his back, and his shirt-sleeves sewn together about two inches above the button, and then sewn to his trousers. The elbows of his sleeves were also sewn together, and stitched to the back of his vest. He was then put in a bag made by the lady of the house, the strings of which were drawn tightly around his neck, and fastened to the chair-back. A rope was also tied round his legs, and the legs of the chair, and he was then lifted into the cabinet. A few seconds after the closing of the curtains the bell, tambourines, &c., which had been laid on his knees, commenced to sound. Rings taken from his lap were found in his pockets, on his fingers, and in his boots; all within a few seconds. A jug of water and glasses were placed on his knee. Some of the sitters then thrust their hands between the curtains, and the glasses were given to them filled. A slate was put on the boy's knee. The sound of writing was heard, and on the slate's being examined writing was found.

"These things were repeated at each *séance*, and up to the last evening we all felt delighted. Towards the close of the *séance* in question . . . . five or six persons declare that they saw the boy's head move several times towards the wall, as though he struck it sideways with the hat" (placed on his head for the spirits to rap upon). "Of course several spoke, and wished both boys to be moved from the wall. This was done, and raps were again given; but they were totally different from those heard a few moments before, and sounded exactly as though the boy knocked his hat against that of the brother sitting by his side. I need hardly tell you that we were not satisfied, and after the boy's denial that he did or could move his head were compelled to feel suspicious, and to doubt the genuineness of the other phenomena."

One of the sitters ultimately discovered that the whole of the said phenomena might be produced with the aid of a little manual dexterity, and, after no long practice, succeeded in conclusively demonstrating this. I wrote, making inquiry regarding the methods of accomplishing the feats, and received the subjoined reply:—

"March 27th, 1876.
"DEAR SIR,
"Your favour of the 14th came safely to hand. I informed Mr. M____ of your desire to know how he performed his tricks, and was requested by him to explain to you the *modus operandi*. He was secured in the same way as the boys (see above). He is then put into a bag; the strings drawn round his neck, and the ends fastened to the chair-back against which he reclines. You can also tie cords round his legs below the knees.

"Whilst being put into the cabinet, or behind a curtain, he unbuttons one of his sleeves with the fingers of the other hand. He then lowers the arm as much as possible, and gets the sleeve and sewings above the elbow. The hand and arm can then, as you will easily see, be brought to the front, and, through the bag, take a bell or any such article from his lap, and ring it. If a tray be put in his lap, with a jug of water and glasses, he can easily pour the liquor from the jug into the glasses. With a little practice the glass may be worked by the hand up the bag as far as the mouth, and he may drink. He then lets it slide down into his lap. Rings laid in his lap are also worked up the bag by means of the fingers, until his mouth is reached. He then grasps the article between his teeth; passes his fingers through the neck of the bag; and, taking the ring from his mouth, puts it on his finger, or in his pocket. Mr. M____ did this repeatedly in *from nine to twelve seconds*. I think you will perceive from this that the feats in question, although they may appear to the uninitiated 'very wonderful,' and 'beyond human power to accomplish,' prove, like many other things, quite simple, when you comprehend *how* they are done."

Simple, indeed! And absurdly simple, too, are certain other modes of imposture sometimes resorted to in the dark *séance*. The persons to be duped are ranged in a circle. Inside this circle sits the "medium;" guitar, bells, &c., all well within reach. The extinguishing of the lights follows. The medium commences to clap his or her hands "with a steady, rhythmical beat." Guitar-strumming, bell-ringing, patting by "spirit-hands," and other performances of the kind follow. Yet the clapping of hands continues without a moment's intermission. The "test" was at first thought perfection; and the guitars, &c., "went merry as marriage-bells," until some unduped investigator lit upon the awkward fact that "*the clapping of one hand on the cheek, the forehead, or any exposed part of the body, would produce exactly the same sounds as the clapping of the palms, and leave the digits of the other hand free to 'manifest.'*"

"But oh dear no!" continues a small volume lately issued by one of the conjuring firm over whom rabid spiritualists sing pæans as "the best of living mediums for the production of strong physical manifestations." "But oh dear no! To show the impossibility of such a thing, one gentleman shall now be allowed to hold the medium's hands; still a bell shall ring, a guitar be strummed, and possibly the gentleman holding the fair one shall have his face fanned. How then can all this be accomplished? Simply thus: Miss X____ will pass a bell to a confederate's mouth (his hands being held), which bell he will shake as a terrier does a rat, the while his boot operates upon the guitar-strings and produces the thrumming; and the medium, with a fan held between her teeth, will gently wave it in the face of him who holds her hands.

"Before I quit this subject," continues our conjuror, "I must name how Miss X____'s business agent made an offer to me by letters which I have now in my possession, that for a sum of money the medium should expose the whole affair, as she was not properly supported by the spiritualists; '*complicating*'—I suppose he means "implicating"—"at least six big guns, the F.R.S. people Miss X____ is now every night materializing, and is immense; another point I will give, she is in the RING of all the best mediums in London, and gets letters every day that will be big to work upon." The managerial offer was not accepted by me.

I desire, apropos of these and other professional jugglers, to call attention to the persecution which my friend, Dr. Sexton, has of late endured. Not only have wrong-headed spiritualists attacked him, because of his manful war on pretended mediums; but his exposures of the carefully prepared tricks which conjurors pass off on their audiences as reproductions of spiritual manifestations (they resemble the genuine phenomena about as closely as an artichoke does a moss-rose) have drawn on him the wrath of the whole sleight-of-hand fraternity, on account of the injury done to their business, and consequently to that tender point of a showman, the pocket. Since these exposures, the jugglers have, with steady malignity, done their worst to injure Dr. Sexton. To me it seems that the honest part which he has had courage to play deserves to attract the sympathy and cordial support of all worthy the name of spiritualist.

And now another variation of "phenomenal" trickery. I was once asked to visit a "boy" who obtained most wonderful phenomena *in the light*. I went; and found that the degree of light permitted was jealously restricted to the outside of the theatre of operations. A species of cabinet concealed the musical instruments, &c., to be operated upon. Close to the entrance of this the boy took his seat; and any revelation of what went on inside the cabinet was prevented by a green baize curtain. The boy's arm when free could easily reach every article the recess contained. I asked to be allowed to sit next the medium; and, being a stranger to all present, save two persons who were like myself lookers-on, my request was granted. I was placed on the left of the boy, who had now taken off his jacket; and from neck to foot we were most carefully concealed from the view of the spectators by a heavy woollen shawl, the end of which was attached to that green baize curtain I have described as hanging before the entrance to the cabinet. As will be observed, the boy had only to get his right arm at liberty, to carry on a "cabinet performance" without fear of detection. Of course, however, "tests" were given, to prevent the possibility of his acting thus. He grasped my right arm with both his hands, and drawing it upon his knee, began a series of twitchings, accompanied with pinchings and pressures of the captive arm. After about five minutes of such treatment my arm was almost numbed. His own right hand continually shifted with great rapidity from my wrist to my elbow, and *vice versa*. His left hand grasped my wrist, and with the elbow of the same arm he would again and again press mine, until, at length, I could hardly distinguish whether both hands were on my arm, or whether I was not simply touched *by the elbow and one hand.* Suddenly the bell in the cabinet was heard to ring. I distinctly felt the movement of the boy's body as he rang it. Then, with great rapidity, the right hand of the "medium" was *substituted for that left elbow which had been made to press my arm during the performance.* The audience asked me where the boy's hands were? I replied, as was the truth, that they grasped my arm; and a common "Oh! how wonderful!" was heard. My poor arm endured another series of twitchings and squeezings, and then I again felt the boy's left elbow pressing it, whilst his left hand grasped me near the wrist. Had I not been giving the strictest attention I should have believed that both his hands were on my arm. His right arm was now once more at liberty, and the bell a second time rang—the banjo being also sounded on this occasion. Then the "medium's" right hand again grasped me, and silence ensued. The trick was several times repeated. At last—my quiescence having in all probability given him courage—the "manifestations" became quite prolonged. It was again asked me, "Have you his hands?" No sooner said than the right hand darted back to that position on my arm where the left elbow had been doing duty for it. "At this moment I have," said I. Something in the tone of my voice must have aroused suspicion. The manifestations totally ceased—I was voted "not harmonious;" and the *séance* closed.

Thus far dark *séances* in the various phases of their development. There exists, however, a species of imposture which, strange to say, imperatively demands for its successful accomplishment a considerable degree of light. I allude to the pretended photographs of spirit-forms showered of late years on the spiritual public. The exposures of the fraudulent nature of many of these peculiar *cartes* have been so convincing that a reasoning man can put but little faith in the unexposed few. That they may be attributable to spirits, is the most one can say.

Baron Kirkup of Florence has had much experience with these productions, and the "mediums" who produce them. Here is what he writes me on the subject, Aug. 3, 1876: "I have preserved a specimen of each sham photo. There were four different scamps who forged them. They produced 'spirit-figures' in numbers. I believe all four to have been cheats, and I am certain that two were. It is my opinion that they used double glass negatives. Moreover, I have found out who posed for the spirits.

"Your sincere friend,

"SEYMOUR KIRKUP."

Amongst the photographs of this class in my possession are two taken by the notorious Buguet. Identically the same figure does duty as the "spirit-form" in each. It serves as the near relative (in one instance the father), of two natives of different countries; men who never saw or heard of each other. How many enthusiasts besides may have recognised a relation in the same dummy, Heaven only knows.

Certain words of the said Buguet deserve to be quoted. During the legal inquiry into his swindling transactions, the magistrate reproached him with having worked upon the credulity of a "certain portion of the public,"—i.e., the spiritualists. "Monsieur," was the reply, "moi, je n'ai jamais cherché à faire rien croire à personne. Je me suis borné à flatter la manie des croyants. Au surplus, il n'y avait pas à les contredire. Une fois leurs idées arrêtées, ils n'en veulent plus démordre. Je n'avais donc qu' à dire comme eux." That is to say, "Sir, I have never tried to make any one believe anything. I have rather restrained than flattered the madness of the believers. Moreover, it was impossible to contradict them. Once their ideas were fixed nothing could make them relinquish those ideas. All that was necessary was for me to agree with whatever they said." The evident truth of the estimable photographer's words renders it wholly unnecessary to comment upon them.

From America comes the following explanation of the methods whereby "spirit-artists" contrive to extract ghosts from the camera. The author of the article is himself a professional photographer, and has evidently examined with care and keenness into the trickery which certain black sheep among his brethren employ for the deluding of the public. To give the whole of his description would occupy more space than I can well afford, but I shall omit nothing which bears at all importantly on the subject. Here are our investigator's ideas of certain "spirit-photos" which fell in his way:—

"A number of queer monstrosities and nondescripts were also exhibited to us as the work of the spirits. Among these we examined a photograph in which the sitter's face came out black and the hair white, while the rest of the figure was normal; the photograph of a gentleman without a head, a ghost having decapitated the negative, and a photograph of some person of the masculine gender, enveloped in a coil of ropes. 'Now, if it isn't spirits,' observed Mr. _____, 'I'd like to know what is it. It's contrary to all the chemical laws of photography.'

"We observed, however, that there were certain characteristics of uniformity about the whole collection of spirit pictures, which indubitably attested that their production was governed by chemical laws of some kind. A careful examination of the ghostly stock revealed the fact that the spirit figure in nine cases out of ten appeared *before* the figure of the sitter, and overlapped it; and a further examination led to the discovery that in all cases where the figure appeared to be behind the sitter and embracing him, only the arms, shoulders, and head of the spectre were visible. There was no trace of flowing raiment behind the chair, no appearance of breast or bosom;

'the Embracing Ghost' was invariably bodiless. In other cases where the figure appeared behind the sitter, but did not embrace him, it melted into air at a high altitude, never descending to the back of the chair. In one case we thought that the end of a lounge on which a ghost was lying, and which according to rules of perspective should have been at least twenty feet to the rear of the sitter, actually overlapped the figure of the latter. Indeed, in a large number of cases the perspective of these spirit pictures seemed all out of joint, so to speak—a fact which the medium would probably explain on the ground that spirits have a tendency to idiosyncrasy. We further observed that in the cases of spiritual embrace, above spoken of, the arms of the ghost were invariably either handless or shapeless; the fingers of the hands were never visible; they never clasped naturally; and where the hands should join was marked by a shadowy blur, even while the rest of the arms were strongly defined. This, if the work of a human being, would evince clumsiness or lack of shrewdness; but who can account for the whims of spirits? An examination of the photograph previously, alluded to, in which a figure appears hidden by a tangle of ropes, revealed to us the fact that the 'ropes' were simply cotton twine well photographed; and that their apparent size by comparison with the figure, was owing to the fact that the pieces of twine and the figure were photographed with different focuses. On the whole the result of our investigation convinced us—

"Firstly. That spirits have nothing to do with the spirit photograph business at _____ Street.

"Secondly. That the figures of the ghosts and those of the living sitters, although visible in the same picture, are the result of separate 'impressions.'

"Thirdly. That inasmuch as the spectre generally appears *in front* of the sitter, it is generally the last of two impressions taken separately on the plate, but developed together.

"Fourthly. That even in cases where the spirit appears to be in the rear of the sitter—embracing him, &c., it would actually appear in front of him, but for the fact that only its arms and head are ever produced.

"As a general rule, believers in spirit photography are people who know nothing of photography, although occasionally spiritualists with some inkling of the business will allow themselves to be duped by the most transparent frauds of this description. To no class of people is the old proverb: 'Convince a man against his will,' &c., more applicable; and our remarks in the present instance are rather intended for those whose ignorance of photography might lead them to believe in a very commonplace humbug. There are no more than half a dozen processes known to photographers by which spirit photographs may be manufactured—perhaps not that many; but each of these processes is capable of numerous modifications, and every professional spirit photographer has his special modifications. But there is no trick known to these tricksters which an experienced photographer could not perform for the amusement of an audience with equal success. In order to give our readers some idea of the method in which these frauds are practised, it will be necessary to describe a part of the ordinary process of photography. The most important preparation of the glass plate for the negative is termed sensitizing; and is effected as follows: The operator, holding the clean glass plate horizontally on his left hand, carefully pours upon it sufficient collodion—a preparation of gun-cotton dissolved in a mixture of ether and alcohol—to cover the whole surface, and leave thereon a thin transparent film when poured off. When this coating has settled to a gummy consistency, it is placed on an instrument called a dipper—a species of hook made of glass, porcelain or rubber—and deposited in a 'bath' containing a solution of nitrate of silver, where it is left for perhaps two minutes. The 'bath' is generally a vertical glass vessel, flat-sided like a pocket flask, but uncovered. The plate is so placed in the bath, that no portion of the colodionized surface touches the sides of the vessel. When the plate is lifted out on the dipper, its face is covered with a creamy, opaque film, and it is then fully 'sensitized,' that is, prepared to receive impressions through the camera. This preparation must be completed in the dark room; inasmuch as the plate is more or less sensitive from the moment of entering the bath, and exposure to light would ruin it. The ensuing part of the process, including the placing of the plate in the dark slide and carrying it to the camera, focusing, exposing and returning the plate to the dark room, has been witnessed by most people who have had a picture taken.

"After returning to the dark room the operator takes the plate from the slide, and pours over the surface—still covered with the white sensitive film—a solution of iron, called in photographic technicology the developer. This iron precipitates the silver; here and there the creamy white of the film fades away, black shadows come forth, and the picture grow out from the pallid surface, first in pale shadows, which ultimately develop to strong relief, of white and black, like the shadows on a wizard's mirror.

"The plate is liable to impressions from the moment of immersion in the nitrate of silver bath until the development of the picture is complete, so that at any intermediate stage of the negative-making process it is possible to produce ghosts on the picture, as we shall shortly explain. But even after the negative is made there are large opportunities for ghost manufacture during the making of the positive, which is printed from the negative on albumenized paper, rendered sensitive to light by immersion in a nitrate of silver solution. The sunlight acting through the glass negative on the sensitive paper makes the positive picture for the 'card-photograph.'

"There is considerable opportunity for humbug during the operation of 'retouching' the negative before printing. The term 'retouching' covers a multitude of means by which smoothness, clearness, transparency of shadows, strength of colour, &c., are given to prints, freckles removed, boils eliminated, scars obliterated, beauty bestowed, and the original of the portrait gracefully flattered to his heart's content. Further description of the process will not be essential to our purpose of showing that in the dark room, before exposure, in the operating room during exposure, in the dark room after exposure, in the development of the negative, in the retouching of the negative, and in printing from the negative, fraud may be successfully practised by spirit-mongers. Ghost pictures may also be taken in the ambrotype and ferrotype processes; but the medium's opportunities are less numerous and promising of success, as the ambrotype is but a thin negative, taken on glass, and the ferrotype a negative on varnished sheet iron.

"Now for the process of Ghost Manufacture. The plate upon which one negative has been made may subsequently serve for scores of other, if carefully washed; and in all photograph galleries numbers of old negatives are washed out from time to time and used afresh. The washing must be very thorough, else the old impression will come out faint and misty with the new one. It is consequently a common expression in photograph galleries, 'Wash these plates cleaner; old impressions are coming out.' Well, some Eastern photographer had at one time lying in his dark room an old negative of a picture representing a fair girl in her snowy bridal dress, fleecy veil and fresh orange flowers—at least, we will so suppose. The dust of years had noiselessly enveloped the old negative with its ashy molecules; the bridal dress had passed in fragments into the grimy bags of some great rag merchant; and the very memory of the wearer had passed away like the fragrance of her bridal flowers from the musk-haunted atmosphere of fashionable society. So there was no more use for the old negative; and they bade a boy wash it out. The glass was freed from dust and film and the shadowy presence that had dwelt there; and the sunlight sparkled through it as through crystal. And it came to pass ere long that a bearded man came to have his picture taken; and when it was developed by the strange magic of chemistry, behold the shadow presence had returned, fainter, indeed, but still lovely; and it floated in pale light by the figure of the bearded stranger. Probably the careless apprentice was scolded for his carelessness, and a new plate procured; but the strange picture, haunted by the gentle shadow, all in diaphanous robes of samite, and wreathed with ghostly flowers, was preserved by reason of its weird beauty. And one day the junior partner of the firm, while gazing upon it, suddenly slapped his thigh, and cried aloud, 'By G_d, Jim, let's go into the spirit-manufacturing business!'

"By imperfect cleansing of the plates the most eerie effects can be produced. About a year and a half ago a poor Indiana photographer created a tremendous sensation by the production of spirit photographs in this manner, his success being in great part owing to the skill of a shrewd 'retoucher' in his employ, who utilized the shadows of dead negatives in a truly admirable manner. This fellow might have made a fortune had not the trickery been exposed a little too soon. The best of spirit photographs seem to have been made by various modifications of this process, portions of the old negatives being thoroughly washed out, so as to admit of proper adjustment. The knave's dupe is deceived by being allowed to handle and examine the apparently clean plate in the first instance, and afterward, to follow it through all its peregrinations. Whenever the ghost impression is thus made the spirit figure will appear behind the sitter unless, indeed, the old impression be so strong as to affect the development of the new. In brief we may say that all ghost impressions made before exposure—that is, before the plate is exposed in the camera—will come out apparently in the rear of the living figure; and when the ghost figure is created subsequent to exposure, the spectre will seem to stand in front of the person photographed. As the spectres at _____'s lair almost invariably stand in front of the sitter, we must conclude that the ghost impression is almost invariably made subsequent to exposure. This is not rendered any more likely, however, from the fact that _____'s patrons are requested to bring their own plates with them, and mark them carefully, for we have already shown that the fraud may be practised in the dark room after sensitizing, before exposure, after exposure, or during exposure.

"By the old method above described, by which both an old and a new impression are together developed from the same plate, it is far easier to make good ghost pictures. Both the imperfectly washed-out ghost figure and the fresh impression are negative impressions, and produce good positives in printing. But the figure of a ghost impressed upon the sensitive plate by another negative, will produce a positive in development and a negative in printing; so that in the card photograph the living figure would come out as a positive and the ghost as a negative. This will account for certain ghosts with black faces and white raiment, whose acquaintance we had the good fortune to make. Taking these things into consideration we must conclude that when _____ produces ghosts subsequent to the preparation of the plate for exposure, the secret of his art lies in the manufacture of ghosts from transparent positives. Thus the ghosts become negatives in the new picture, and both figures will be printed as positives. This operation requires great judgment in focusing.

"While the plate is in the bath impressions may be made upon it, which will remain unperceived until the exposure has been made and the plate developed. A well-known photographer was not long since bothered considerably by finding that every plate dipped into a certain nitrate of silver bath in his dark room came out in developing with the letters 'P. Smith' across the face of the picture. It was finally discovered that a ray of light passing through a tiny crevice in the wall of the dark room struck the side of the glass bath on which the name of the maker was stamped in relief, and the letters were thus impressed on the face of the sensitive plate. With a glass bath and a concealed light wonderful frauds in the spirit line can be practised, and, by placing a transparent positive between the light and the plate in the bath, splendid ghosts could be made, even while the dupe is looking on in the belief that he cannot be fooled. We might dilate at great length on this use of the bath, but it will not be necessary. After exposure, the plate may be returned to the bath for a short time without fear of injuring the impression, and the ghost figure then impressed upon it.

"Another method is to hold up the sensitive plate (either before or after operating) for one or two seconds before a jet of gaslight, in the dark room, or even before the yellow-paned windows, as though to examine the coating of the plate, holding between it and the window or gaslight an old negative, transparent positive, or magic lantern transparency. Two or three seconds will suffice for the clearest of impressions; and the looker-on would probably never dream of deception, supposing that the operator was simply examining the plate, 'to see if it was all right.' According to the distance between the two plates the ghost figure will be stronger or fainter. We witnessed last Thursday, a splendid operation of this kind at the Boston Gallery, in which two seconds sufficed for the production of a ghost figure by gaslight. By a clever device the sensitive plate may be impressed with the figure of a ghost while in the dark slide, on the way to or from the operating room, or even while in the camera itself. Indeed, twenty different varieties of deceptions may be practised during exposure. A common artifice is to place a microscopic picture within the camera box, so that by means of a small magnifying lens its image may be thrown upon the plate. Spectral effects may also be produced by covering the back of a sensitive plate with pieces of cut paper, and using artifices well known to retouchers. The 'rope' picture, described in our account of the photographs, might have been produced by the adroit use of cotton twine, before or in the camera during exposure, or might have been produced by double printing. Extraordinary spectral effects, such as that of a man shaking hands with his own ghost, cutting off his own head, or followed by his own doppel ganger, may be produced by 'masking,' a process which it would take too long to describe here. There is scarcely any conceivable absurdity in portraiture which may not be accomplished by the camera; and the peculiarities of the business are so extraordinary, the opportunities for humbug so excellent, the methods and modifications of methods whereby spirit photographs may be manufactured so numerous, that it is hopeless for any person totally ignorant of photography to detect a fellow like _____ in the act of fraud. Indeed, it often takes an expert in photography to detect certain classes of deception. Were we not limited by time and space in this article we could readily fill forty columns with an account of the many artifices practised by spirit-photographers."

The length and thoroughness of the above leave neither space nor need for additions. I shall pass, therefore, to other subjects; trusting that the ray of light thus thrown upon the mystery of the "spirit-artist's" operations will not be thrown in vain.

It would seem that the substantiality of "materialized forms" while outside the curtain, and the suddenness and totality of their disappearance when once more safely esconced within the depths of their "cabinet," have tempted admirers to seek for some solid memorial of these solid yet fleeting ghosts. One of the geniuses in question, we learn, after thoughtful consideration of a paraffin candle, suddenly started, and cried, "Eureka! I have hit it." Forthwith his discovery was made public, and became popular. Mediums arose, who gave *séances*, the necessary adjuncts to which were tables with sliding leaves in the centre, pails of hot water, packets of paraffin, careful precautions against too-close scrutiny, dim light, an utter absence of tests, and, it would appear, *moulds of hands and feet, carefully packed in cotton-wool to prevent breakages.* The more than suspicious disclosures presented during such *séances* are past counting. In England "ugly green slippers" have been left on the carpet, and have turned out to be moulds taken from a foot which, if that of a spirit, was strangely enough the counterpart of the medium's. Other gatherings have resulted in paraffin moulds avowedly taken from a spirit-hand, which "spirit-hand" appeared on examination of the mould to have presented itself in shape of a plaster-cast. But the most striking story of the kind comes from America, and the events to which it has reference transpired among the spiritualists of New York.

A distinguished medium for paraffin mould effects gave a course of *séances* in that city. The first of the series was "on the whole, considered satisfactory," despite the perplexing fact that a piece of dry cotton-wool displayed itself within the mould spirits were supposed to have formed from the paraffin dissolved in boiling water, which a pail placed below the *séance* table contained.

Two days afterwards a second *séance* took place.

"About thirty people were present. (From a statement subscribed by seven leading New York spiritualists, and published in the *Spiritual Scientist* of March 30, 1876.) A small pine table was previously prepared by Mr. A____, with an opening across the centre, into which a board or leaf was so closely fitted, that, though it could be removed with one hand, it would require *both* to replace it. The pail containing the paraffin and water was sustained by one arm of a scale-beam, which was suspended from the frame of the table in such a way, that while the pail was under the table, the other arm, supporting the nicely balanced weights, was outside, and in full view of the audience, passing through a slot in the black glazed-muslin bag, which enclosed the table and its contents. The seams of the muslin bag were sewed by a lockstitch machine, and over the table were thrown blankets to exclude the light.

"Mr. A____ had some coloured paraffin which he desired to use, but it was declined. No light was allowed in the room, and only a moderate amount from an adjoining one, as the 'spirits' complained that the conditions were not favourable. Very soon a slight motion of the outside beam was increased to such a degree as to throw the weights from their place, which naturally attracted the gaze of all to this point, except that of Mr. A____ and two other gentlemen who were intent upon the fact that Mrs. _____ frequently introduced her left hand under the blanket; and finally the motion became so attractive to her, that she rose many times, and leaned over the table to observe it, but *never* failed to pass her hand under the blanket at the same time.

"The last time of this leaning over a violent motion to the outside beam indicated the same to the pail within, and on the instant a light 'thud' was heard as of some substance dropping inside upon the carpet. The left hand of Mrs. _____ was withdrawn, and the blanket, previously left rumpled, was now carelessly smoothed out, and it was soon indicated that the work was finished. Upon removing the blanket Mr. A____ found the muslin pinned differently upon the top of table from the way he had pinned it, and having, in the spot where the left hand had been hidden, a strained appearance; and the middle board was found displaced. A paraffin mould was lying upon the bottom of the bag, a little under the edge of the bowl."

However little the said paraffin mould may have been prized by the spiritualists present at its production, they did not yet consider the evidence sufficient to warrant a verdict of fraud. But testimony quickly accumulated.

"On Wednesday evening, as Mrs. A____, the medium, and her husband were coming to a *séance* at the house of Mrs. H____; the husband being quite in advance, and his wife next; Mrs. A____, who was last, saw, in crossing the street, a paraffin mould lying in the gutter, where the medium had just passed. She exclaimed, 'Why, there's a paraffin hand!' The medium, returning quickly, crushed it, and both ladies picked up pieces from the fragments. Mrs. _____ scolded her husband for being so careless 'about carrying that bag;' he 'ought to know that the top was liable to spring open; and now perhaps there would not be paraffin enough to form another mould to-night.' Mr. and Mrs. _____ had, just before leaving Mrs. A____'s house, denied that they had any paraffin moulds with them."

The evening's *séance* duly came off. "Dr. H____, who occupied a favourable position during the materializations of 'spirit-hands,' &c., declared to Mrs. H____ and Mrs. S____ that he assuredly saw *toes* three times, when the medium professed that the spirits were showing hands. Present thirty people. Lights very dim."

On the Thursday some ladies who were talking with the medium "saw the fingers of a paraffin mould protruding from beneath her dress." They informed her of what they had discovered. "She hastily concealed the mould, and declared them mistaken." The same evening a third *séance* was held. One of the sitters glanced beneath the table while "manifestations" were going on, and "saw the medium's foot manipulating the bell."

Saturday, March 18th, beheld the winding up of the series of *séances,* and the acquirement of final and conclusive evidence respecting the trickery practised. "A packet of paraffin designed for use at that evening's *séance* was received by Mr. M____. Taking it to an apothecary near by, he had it accurately weighed, and the weight, which was 11 lbs. 4 oz. avoirdupois, marked on the wrapper. Mrs. H____ and Mrs. S____ kept this packet sacredly until the evening, when it was shaved up in their presence, and before them, Mr. M____, and others, was placed in a pail, and hot water poured upon it. . . . The lights were required so low as to be of no avail in the back parlour, at the extreme rear of which sat the medium, facing her audience. No one was allowed within a semicircle of five or six feet from the table. The mould was soon declared finished, and on being quickly examined (by a novice, as it happened), another bit of dry cotton-wool was found within the orifice of the wrist; which Mr. A____ has, with the first, in his possession. Thirty-five people were present."

The paraffin in the pail was carefully collected. Mr. M____ took the package, and had it weighed on the same scales, when it balanced exactly at 11 lbs. 4 oz. avoirdupois, the same as before the *séance*. He also received the paraffin mould or glove from Mrs. H____ and Mrs. S____, and found its weight to be 21½ ozs. avoirdupois. The druggist performed the weighing in both instances.

"Mrs. A____ was unaccountably annoyed by bits of cotton-wool about her carpets, while the medium and her husband were with her.

"Upon Sunday, the 19th, Mrs. A____ saw the medium's stockings, worn the previous evening at Mrs. _____'s *séance*; at about two inches below the *toe they were cut across the sole, and left open.*

"Each can draw his inferences from the facts we state. We subscribe our names to verify what is attributed to us in this statement." (Here follow the seven names.)

How was a narrative like the above to be disposed of? The inculpated medium, or rather her husband, contemptuously swept it out of the way. "Most of the charges are too insignificant and ridiculous to claim notice!"

Into the voluminous correspondence and disputes which this matter involved, and the desperate attempts of "veteran spiritualists" to whitewash the reputation of the inculpated Mrs. _____, I think it unnecessary to enter. One demand, however, of the believers who clung to her "through glory and shame" deserves notice. "If not the work of spirits, how were the moulds produced?"

"Agreeably to promise," says the *Boston Herald,* of April 9th, 1876, "one among the signers of the so-called expose of Mrs. H____ favours the *Herald* with his theory of producing paraffin moulds. Briefly stated, he says the mould may be made before the *séance* by dipping a mortal hand into wax. This mould may be secreted in the pocket of the medium's dress. Aided by time and darkness, the medium may break the thread at the seam of the sack, and through an aperture thus formed let the mould slide to the floor, after which she may sew up the broken seam. Taking a small quantity of water from the bucket with a syringe or sponge, to account for difference of weight, completes the job. There, now, who may not be a moulding medium?" (Who, indeed?)

"If two mediums," says the *Spiritualist* of August 11th, 1876, "would sit to get letters written by sceptics, regularly carried in a few minutes between circles many miles apart, *as Baron Kirkup of Florence once did*, it would be a most useful manifestation, and a death-blow to the psychic force theory." Let us see what my friend Baron Kirkup's own opinion now is of the means by which his letters were carried. "You shall be free," he writes to me, April 29th, 1876, "to make any use you like of what I shall tell you."

The pseudo-manifestations which the *Spiritualist* values so highly were, one and all, the results of conspiracy. "My daughter," writes the Baron to me, May 4th, 1876, "married a stranger against my wishes. I took them into my house for a year, where they *performed* a correspondence, pretended to be by the direct agency of spirits; and, stealing the said correspondence, deposited my letters in the tribunate to prove me insane. . . . . I have since learned much from my wife; who for six years saw so much of the frauds of my daughter and her Italian friends, that she is not a spiritualist at all. She has explained many things to me which I thought it impossible could be trickery—the chief, and most frequent, being the responses of the table, whilst, I *supposed*, untouched. In the year 1871 I was favoured with materialization, and two 'spirits' walked through my rooms, and shook hands with us. I have since found out who the persons were that enacted this comedy. . . . . . The conspirators were all Italians. My English and American friends were taken in like myself."

The various parties to this shameless fraud, by producing the letters which spirits were supposed to have carried, succeeded so far in their object as to have a keeper appointed over the Baron for a time. They also strove persistently to obtain the control of his property, and after two lawsuits he was forced into a compromise. "I found," he writes to me, "that I had spent all my ready money in the lawsuits, and I began to feel my situation getting dangerous. I had no resource but to accept a compromise. . . . My daughter and her husband have now agreed to sell me my liberty for a ransom, like the brigands of Calabria, and I have paid a part of my small fortune to save the rest. From the day they left my house I have heard or seen no more of spirits."

Despite the persecution and the cruel deceptions he has endured Baron Kirkup is yet a spiritualist. He repudiates, not the whole phenomena of spiritualism—but the fraudulent manifestations which he was deceived into believing genuine. "Some of my friends who were interested in the subject give it up," he tells the present writer, "as a total delusion. I do not. I have witnessed prodigies enough in twenty years. I have seen much, and so have millions of competent witnesses. It is the treachery of sham mediums that has been my bane."

Under such headings as "Correspondence with Spirits," "Delusions and Dupes," &c., the New York press has lately made itself very merry over the misdeeds of a "medium" who professed, as others still do, to answer sealed letters by spirit-aid.

"He respected, without knowing it, the Horatian maxim," says the *New York World*, "and wouldn't disturb a ghost on any ordinary occasion. With much propriety and patience he submitted the sealed envelopes containing these precious inquiries to the sweet influences of a kettle-spout until the steam opened them, and then he answered them himself with neatness and despatch. Being an illiterate man, and perhaps not imaginative, though benevolent, he kept a phrase-book, or complete celestial letter-writer, full of nice things to put into the answers, such as this: 'We shall journey along together my ("brother," "sister," or "love," as the case might be), with hands joined, one on either side of the curtain that falls between yours and mine.' Or this: 'I have walked with you upon the western side of life, and will soon meet you upon this.' Some hundreds of these tidbits he had carefully written out, ready for reference and use. . . . . What ought to be done to him? It is too hard a question for us. We should rather like to leave it to his clients. . . . As we have said, there are thousands of letters. We can't print all of them; but surely in what we have given is matter for much and not wholly pleasing meditation on the world we live in."

The taste displayed in printing the names, and often the addresses, of those whose letters to the impostor had fallen into journalistic hands is certainly more than questionable. It must be confessed, though, that the letters themselves are curious. One smart Yankee addresses a deceased relative in the following business-like fashion:—

"Brother William,—We are engaged in making Nature's Hair Restorer. Will you give us your personal attention? Inform me what is the best plan to adopt to make it pay a profit very soon. What shall I do to make my wife a happy believer in spiritualism?"

Another correspondent makes bold to ask the spirit of Daniel Webster for legal advice regarding certain lawsuits against insurance companies. A third writes to his deceased wife to inquire whether he shall marry a Miss B____; if he may sell his farm, and go to Europe with his patent rails. "To all which queries," says *The World*, "the 'medium' annotates in the margin of the letter 'No.'"

Here this portion of my task must end. I might stretch this chapter to a much greater length by a few additional selections from the accounts of exposed fraud before me; but I am heartily tired of so uncongenial a task. Enough has been written and quoted in the foregoing pages to display the reality and magnitude of the evils which act as incubi to spiritualism. I have conceived it my duty to reveal their nature and to protest against their existence; but, while I wish the protest to be effective, and the revelations to the point, I would not have either cumbrous or diffuse.

Can no good thing come out of the spiritual Nazareth? Is our cause in its entirety made up of legerdemain accomplished under cover of darkness, of credulous dupes, of impostors ever on the watch to entrap such dupes; in short, of knavery and folly mixed as it pleases fate? Far from it. Let us turn from darkness into light, and, abandoning this study of the gloomy face of a cloud, cheer a little our depressed hearts in contemplating its silver lining.

CHAPTER X

THE HIGHER ASPECTS OF SPIRITUALISM

As I have in other portions of my work refrained from giving names, I shall adopt the same practice in my present chapter. There are, indeed, numerous reasons why the incidents about to be described should be veiled under partial obscurity. The persons concerned are, in most instances, opposed more or less strongly to their names being made public. It does not appear certain that such publication would answer any useful purpose. I shall therefore preserve a strict incognito regarding the actors in these interesting dramas. It is my duty to add; however, that in every case, names, dates, and other testimony, are in my possession, to be made use of as necessity shall dictate. Nothing will find place in the ensuing pages but facts to whose verity witness after witness yet living can testify. Should any doubt be cast upon the truth of these narratives, I have at my command ample means of dispelling such doubt, and of proving that in every instance reality has been strictly adhered to. A faithful record, indeed, was the one thing necessary. In spiritualism above all subjects truth is stranger than fiction. The wonderful legends which credulous enthusiasts can construct with the aid of darkened rooms and puppet-shows, are as nothing compared to the facts which from time to time the spirit-world furnishes under conditions whose perfection of evidence renders doubt impossible.

The incident I commence with occurred in Hartford, Conn., some twenty-three or twenty-four years ago. I give the story as an answer to a question often asked. "Why," it is said, "should spirits visit us, and indicate an interest in those everyday trivialities of earthly life from which the grave parts them for ever? Is it not excessively undignified that eternity should be wasted thus?"

Undignified indeed, if we are to entertain the old, old myth never taught by Christ—that death is a magician whose potent touch changes us with the rapidity of lightning from men and women to angels or fiends. What is earth to us in such a case? The golden crowns are on our foreheads—the golden lyres in our hands. And the past?—A disregarded dream. The future?—A peaceful slumber in the lap of beatified idleness—a lulling symphony of eternal song. What to us are the stumbles and the afflictions of brothers and sisters yet on earth? Let the darkness be never so deep in which they wander we have endless light. And shall we return, to cheer with whispers of affection, and assurances of brighter days, that pilgrimage which, long ago, we ourselves found so dreary and so long? Sanctified selfishness shudders at the thought. Rather let us wrap closer around us the spotless robes which mask the deformity of our minds, and, with pharisaical ostentation, call God's attention to the praises we offer Him for having made us other than the worms of earth. The fact that we were once ourselves worms may be forgotten, with whatever else it is convenient to forget.

Such is Mrs. Grandy's heaven. The good old lady can be found with due regularity every Sabbath (unless it rains), seated primly in her cushioned pew, and drinking in with orthodox rapture the words of life which a fashionable preacher has found himself commissioned, in virtue of so many hundred pounds sterling per annum, to deliver to a thirsty flock. For Mrs. Grandy never pins her faith to anything that is not strictly orthodox, and in accordance with the way of the world. She comes of a very respectable family indeed. Eighteen centuries ago her great-great-grandfather made broad his phylactery, and enlarged the borders of his garments, and was called of men Rabbi, Rabbi, and loved the chief seat in the synagogue, and the uppermost room at feasts. He it was, and no other, whose saintly indignation against the iconoclast of Nazareth found vent in the cry, "This man eateth with publicans and sinners!" His wife, the venerated ancestress of the present Mrs. Grundy, doubtless drew her skirts shudderingly together whenever Mary Magdalen passed her; and may have remarked, on hearing of a certain incident of which all the world has heard, that had she been in the temple on the memorable morning in question, she would have felt it her duty to cast a stone. To come to more modern times, I am convinced that it was a worthy, though, doubtless, erring woman of the family who, on hearing that the steep path to heaven was common to herself and her footman, and that no carriage-road had been set apart for people of quality, nobly determined to become the martyr of her respectability, and not go to heaven at all.

But we must return to the Mrs. Grundy of the present age. In her the perfections of the whole race of Grundys have centred. A more estimable woman it would be impossible to find. Her creed is as orthodox as the most rigid of divines can demand. Her practice is equally exemplary with her precepts. She renounces the pomps and vanities of the world in a dress from Worth. Her prayer to be delivered from all uncharitableness is offered up by the same tongue which a few hours before talked scandal of some dear friend. Her favourite pastor tells her that the meek are blessed; she listens, assents, and goes home to scold her maid. Since she does all these things, and many more, she feels herself perfectly respectable and pious; and she sits, as I have said, in her pew on Sundays, gorgeous with false hair, a Parisian bonnet, and just a touch of rouge; and, in the nicest of falsetto voices, informs all whom it may concern that she

> "Wants to be an angel,
> And with the angels stand;
> A crown upon her forehead,
> A palm-branch in her hand."

One day she will awake and find it all a dream. As we have sown we reap. Death may be the golden gate of a world divinely beautiful, or the black portal of "a land as darkness itself, and where the light is as darkness," but it destroys nothing of the identity of earth. Rather would the great change seem, with a revivifying touch, to brighten into fresh existence every faded character on the blotted pages of memory. Such a keeping of remembrance green may bring sorrow to some, but for the majority of earth's children it must be the source of unspeakable joy. What golden crown could glitter brightly enough to console the mother, did she find heaven a jewel-bedecked prison, in whose gates of pearl and jasper walls she must vainly search for one tiny chink through which to catch a glimpse of the loved ones left behind? Did she forget them, immortality would be a dream. Her life was in the love she bore for her offspring. Destroy that love, and her identity is destroyed. An angel may remain, fitted for white raiment and endless psalms; but all of the woman is gone.

Let as thank God that in His universe this selfish heaven of forgetfulness has no place. His love is over all His works, and He would have His children's love, like His own, eternal. None need tremble lest the darkness of oblivion shadow their dying bed. Those who pass from this temporal state to an eternal one leave only the dross of earthly life behind. The pure gold of affection is still theirs, and from that affection they weave a bright chain of communion with the loved of earth. That chain is in general invisible to our darkened vision, but when at times a few links become revealed, why should those who see them only afar off complain that they seem trivial and slight? To the persons intimately concerned in such revelation the apparent trivialities may bear a value which the outside world can never estimate. The circumstances of the communication are all in all. There are hearts to which a commonplace word may say more than would all the wisdom of Plato. Little everyday incidents may be connected with that life from which the spirit has passed, the recallment of which will do more to prove identity than would the most brilliant description of the life to come. It is in these apparent trifles that the greatest strength of spiritualism has lain. They are evidences which it is impossible to doubt—arrows which cannot fail to be barbed with conviction. Why then call that little which accomplishes so much? Why think undignified what contributes so mightily to the victory of the truth?

For many years I have scrutinised anxiously, and treasured up with care, even the most trifling incidents testifying to the continuance of identity after death. The only supports of theories are facts. I select, therefore, from among the narratives in my possession, one or two which appear to me of the greatest interest. The events to which the first has reference occurred in 1852 or the following year, and the scene of their occurrence was, as I have said, Hartford, Conn., U.S.A.

At the time in question the medium who bears a principal part in the ensuing history was staying in Springfield, Mass., confined to his bed by a severe attack of illness. His medical man had just paid his customary visit. Hardly was the door closed upon the doctor, when a spirit made known its presence to his patient, and delivered the following message:— "You will take the afternoon train to Hartford. It is important for the present and future welfare of yourself, as well as for the advancement of the cause. Ask no questions, but do as we direct." The occurrence was made known to the family, and the medical man recalled and consulted. "Let him go," said he, on finding his patient determined to act in conformance with the message received. "His death will be on his own head." And the medium left, unconscious of the import of his journey, and not knowing what its end would be. As he got out at Hartford a stranger came up to him. "I never saw you but once," said this gentleman, "and then only for a moment; but I think you are Mr. _____. The other replied that he was indeed the person in question; and added, "I have come here to Hartford, but for what reason I am perfectly ignorant." "Strange said his interlocutor," I was waiting here that I might take the next train to Springfield in quest of you." He then explained how a well-known and influential family had become desirous of investigating the subject of spiritualism, and were anxious for a visit from the very medium whose departure from Springfield had taken place under such peculiar circumstances. Here, then, was a foreshadowing of the object of the journey. What had yet to happen rested, however, in as much mystery as before.

After a pleasant drive the residence of the family alluded to came in view. The master of the house was by chance at the door just then, and thus gave the first welcome to a guest whom he had not expected before the morrow at the soonest. The medium entered the hall; and, as he did so, a sound resembling the rustling of a heavy silk dress struck on his ear. He naturally glanced round, and was surprised to see no one. Without, however, making any allusion to the incident, he passed on into one of the sitting-rooms. There he again heard the rustling of the dress, and was again unable to discover anything which might account for such a sound. It would seem that the surprise he felt was depicted in his look, for his host remarked, "You seem frightened. What has startled you?" Unwilling to make much of an affair which might, after all, prove explicable by quite ordinary means, the other replied that, having been very ill, his nervous system was undoubtedly out of order; but once reposed from the fatigue of the journey he would feel more at ease.

Hardly were the words uttered when, looking back to the hall, the medium saw standing there a bright, active-looking, little elderly lady, clad in a heavy dress of grey silk. Here then was an explanation of the apparent mystery. The visitor had heard the movements of this member of the household, but had missed catching sight of her until now.

Again the dress rustled. This time the sound was audible both to the medium and to his host. The latter inquired what such a rustling might mean. "Oh!" said his visitor, "it's caused by the dress of that elderly lady in the grey silk whom I see in the hall. Who may she be?" For the appearance was one of such perfect distinctness that he entertained not the slightest suspicion of the little old lady being other than a creature of flesh and blood.

The host made no reply to the question asked him, and the medium was diverted from any further remark on the subject by being presented to the small family circle. Dinner was announced. Once at table, it surprised the guest to see no such person as the lady in grey silk present. His curiosity became roused, and she now began seriously to occupy his thoughts.

As all were leaving the dining-room the rustling of a silk dress again made itself audible to the medium. This time nothing could be seen, but he very distinctly heard a voice utter the words, "I am displeased that a coffin should have been placed above mine. What is more, I won't have it."

This strange message was communicated to the head of the family and his wife. For a moment the pair stared at each other in mute astonishment, and then the gentleman broke silence. "The style of dress," said he, "we can perfectly identify, even to the peculiar colour, and heavy texture; but this regarding a coffin being placed on hers is at once absurd and incorrect." The perplexed medium could, of course, answer nothing. That speech on quitting the dining-room had been his first intimation as to the old lady of the grey silk having passed from earth, and he was not even aware in what relation she stood to his host.

An hour slipped by. Suddenly the self-same voice came once more, uttering precisely the same words. This time, however, it added, "What's more, S____ had no right to cut that tree down." Again the medium made known what he had heard. The master of the house seemed greatly perplexed. "Certainly," said he, "this is very strange. My brother S____ did cut down a tree which rather obstructed the view from the old homestead; and we all said at the time that the one who claims to speak to you would not have consented to his felling it had she been on earth. The rest of the message, however, is sheer nonsense."

Just before retiring the same communication was a third time given, and again the assertion as to the coffin was met by an unhesitating contradiction. The medium went to his room, feeling greatly depressed. Never before had an untrue message been received through him; and, even were the statement correct, such close attention on the part of a liberated spirit to the fact that another coffin had been placed above hers seemed ridiculously undignified. Golden crowns, spotless raiment, endless harpings, anything or everything was preferable to this. He thought of the occurrence through the whole of a sleepless night.

The morning arrived, and the medium made known to his host how deeply the affair had affected him. The other replied that he was himself just as sorry, and added, "I am now going to convince you that if it were the spirit it purports to be, it is sadly mistaken. We will go together to the family vault, and you shall see that, even had we desired to do so, it would be impossible to place another coffin above hers." Host and guest at once proceeded to the cemetery. The sexton was sent for, since he had the key of the vault in question. He came: and proceeded to open the door. As he placed the key in the lock, however, he seemed to recollect something, and, turning round, said, in a half apologetic tone, "By the way, Mr. _____, as there was just a little room above Mrs. _____'s coffin, I have placed the coffin of L____'s baby there. I suppose it's all right, but perhaps I should have asked you first about it. I only did it yesterday."

Never did that medium forget the look with which his host turned to him, and said, *"My God, it is all true!"*

The same evening the spirit once more made known her presence. "Think not," ran the message now delivered, "that I would care were a pyramid of coffins to be piled on mine. I was anxious to convince you of my identity once and for ever—to make you sure that I am a living, reasoning being, and the same E____ that I always was. For that reason alone have I acted thus."

He to whom her visit was chiefly directed has since joined her in another world. His deeds were as noble as his nature, and his whole career was purity, unspotted by any taint of wrong. Some of the best of America's sons and daughters gathered around the bier of one whose life and death it was felt added another to the many proofs that

> "The actions of the just
> Smell sweet, and blossom in the dust."

Spiritualism was to him a glory and a joy. He had tested it, and knew it to be real. Yet he was never deluded into enthusiasm or easy credence. With the whole strength of his manly intellect did he winnow the wheat from the chaff, and, casting away whatsoever was worthless, hold firmly to the good and true. Now he rejoices in the reward of the course that he ran on earth, and, having "outsoared the shadow of our night," can behold clearly things which are dim to mortal eyes. A message communicated by him shortly after his departure from our world is so characteristic that I have determined to print extracts from it here. The remaining portions relate to family affairs, of which the medium through whom the message was received could by no possibility have known anything, and which served to relatives as excellent proofs of the identity of the author.

"Well, A____, it's the same old story, and whether we tell it on earth or from the eternal home it comes to just the same thing, and has exactly the same mystery attached to it. I had hoped to solve a little more of this, but, bless you, I rather feel that it is even now further than ever from me. I am confident the knowledge will eventually be mine; but will it benefit you, and those who are still on earth? Is it not rather a natural or spiritual influx adapted only to the actual condition of the identical spirit, and hence utterly unfitted for another? I am for the moment inclined to this view of the matter. I am no longer surprised at the lack of distinctness. From my point of view it is perfectly clear; but to make it so to others is quite another question. *I am, We are;* but the why and wherefore remain still enshrouded in the haze of the great unexplored future. It is, however, a great revelation to know that we exist, for existence betokens activity, and must include the development or unfolding of wisdom. All this is an incentive to well-doing in every stage of existence. I have seen those I loved, and the recognition was mutual; no hesitancy, no shadow of doubt. I have seen no Personal God. What I may see I know not. I lift up my thoughts in prayerful praise to a great and benign Creator; for I feel assured that a creative and harmoniously-constructed power does exist; but what that may be is not as yet made clear to me. I wait to be taught; but, in being taught, I must also ascertain why undevelopment stands side by side with a higher perfection; known, as the two are, as Good and Evil. Does the same power produce both? This, and many questions of a like nature, I am asking just as I used to; only I hope now to have them made clear. If I can frame in clearly-to-be-understood language the replies I have, or rather the knowledge I gain, I will give them to you. Of one thing I am already certain; I am all unchanged."

The following narrative was written for me by my dearly-valued friend Mrs. S. C. Hall, in answer to a request I had made that she would furnish me, if possible, with some well-attested incident which might constitute an addition to the "Lights" of my work.

"Several years ago, when some persons looked on spiritualism as a myth, others considered it a jest, others a snare of the evil one, and many wise and well loved friends entreated us to have nothing to do with it, or its 'prophets'—striving to convince us it was a peril to mind and soul—we for a very long time heard, saw, and listened, and doubted! but at last meeting with Daniel Home, and also with Miss Andrews, better known as 'L. M.,' we gradually became convinced of the existence of a great truth, clear and incontrovertible as the sun at noonday: and we felt it a delightful privilege to enjoy the society of both those 'unprofessional' mediums, at intervals, when they could escape from other friends.

"Mr. Home had loving domestic duties to attend to, but 'L. M.' was more at liberty, as she was not chained by them, and was not married until some time after the incident I am about to relate.

"One afternoon when Miss Andrews was our guest, I was sitting in the sunshine in our pleasant drawing-room in Ashley Place, accompanied by the sweet and gentle little woman, who had gained great reputation as a medium. As I have said, when first we met her, we had laughed at the wonderful things we had heard of 'L. M.,' and not even her beautiful hair, her soft eyes, and gentle plaintive voice had won us to put faith in her miraculous power: still she gained upon us, and the more we knew the more we loved her, and up to this very hour we have never lost faith in the fragile delicate woman whose faith in the righteous Lord has enabled her to bear physical suffering I could not attempt to describe. In those days she was in the enjoyment of better health than she has since known; and I well remember that on that sunny morning we were recapitulating the enjoyments of the past evening, when the servant announced a gentleman of high repute in the literary world and whom we frequently met in fashionable as well as literary circles. I see no reason why I should not give his name that of Colley Grattan is well known and much esteemed. He was the author of some works of much interest and value; and had been for some time Consul both at Antwerp and Boston, U.S.A.

"After the usual salutations he inquired—his laughing eyes fixed on my *mignonnte* friend, whose pale face had become serious when he entered—'Well, mademoiselle! have you had any visitors from the spirit world lately? or have you been obliged to content yourself with us—poor miserable worldlings?—come! do not continue silent, but confess you have seen nothing; heard nothing worth recording.'

"'I see,' she said, 'a spirit standing beside you at this very moment, and her words drop from her lips apparently in letters of gold—she says her name is Emma _____.'

'L. M.' spoke slowly, but, as she always did, distinctly—and the gentleman, Colley Grattan, sprang from his seat, and repeated, 'Emma _____ Emma _____! say on.'

"He stood trembling before her. She continued—'She says she follows you to protect you often against yourself, in gratitude for the benevolence you and your wife showed her, when but for it she must have been sacrificed to the brutality of her husband—do you remember drawing her from the step of your hall door out of the rain one stormy night into your house—when she became insensible, and your wife folded her in her arms on her bosom, and you mulled the wine she poured into her lips? Do you remember how you challenged him for his brutal cowardice?' When 'L. M.' had said this, Mr. Grattan exclaimed, 'There—there—I cannot bear it—I must go, I must go. Poor Emma! poor sufferer! that man, though a member of Parliament, was the greatest brute unhung—but I can hear no more now—Miss Andrews—I will never scoff again."

"Mr. Grattan stumbled out of the room. I followed him into the corridor and found him sitting on one of the sofas almost fainting.

"'I daresay she may tell you more—but I cannot bear it; that dear creature was my wife's dearest friend,' he exclaimed, 'but that fact which occurred soon after midnight outside our hall door was known only to my wife and myself.'

When I returned to the drawing-room, 'She has followed him, for she feels it a duty,' she says, 'to help him sometimes. Will you tell him that poor Emma _____ died of cancer,' L. M. continued, 'he knows that, but he does not know that the cancer was caused by a blow inflicted by her husband!'

"Two or three days after, Mr. Grattan's visit was repeated, but then L. M.' had gone home.

"He questioned me very closely to learn what she had said after he left the room, and was greatly struck when I told him that her death was caused by a 'blow inflicted by her husband.' 'We knew,' he said, 'she died of cancer, but she never told us it was so produced.'

"'Oblige me,' he added, 'when you next see Miss Andrews, by telling her she will never again hear me scoff at spiritualism.'"

If the following incident read like a romance the reader may be assured that it was at least a romance of reality, enacted in that most prosaic of all possible cities—London. A medium—who it matters not— had found himself, on the evening when the events in question came to pass, a guest at a party given in a country house on the outskirts of the modern Babylon. Suddenly, and without the least premonition, a spirit-voice spoke to him, bidding him at once leave, and return home. He obeyed. Passing along Piccadilly, and when almost in front of Apsley House, a miserable group arrested his gaze. Crouched against a wall, and almost hidden by the night and the obscurity of the position they had selected, were two most wretched figures. Their squalor and hideousness seemed scarcely to belong to earth. Indeed, the medium of whom I speak doubts to this day whether the figures whom he saw were real flesh and blood, or a phantasmagoria which spirits had created for purposes of their own. However, he halted, and looked at them; and a young man who was passing did the same. At that instant the spirit-voice again made itself heard. "Speak to the person beside you," ran the new mandate, "and on no account suffer him to escape you." The medium could conceive no reason for such a dictate; but, by way of obeying, he turned to the stranger with the remark,—"Is it not sad that such misery as this should exist in a wealthy city like London?" The other replied that it was indeed sad, and made a motion as if to continue his route. "You are going my way, I think," said his interlocutor. "Let us walk on together." The young man seemed embarrassed, and evidently wished to evade compliance; but the other was determined to carry out the directions he had received. The two, therefore, passed on, conversing in a desultory fashion, and arrived finally before the medium's lodgings. Again the voice spoke. "Invite him in," ran this third message. The medium turned to his companion: "You are not particularly pressed for time, I suppose?" said he. "Come in, and take some supper with me." The young man to whom the words were addressed started, and appeared greatly surprised. "Why do you invite me?" he questioned.

"No matter for that. Come in."

"But *why?*"

"I will tell you afterwards. Come with me—we can talk more at our ease inside the house."

The stranger hesitated, reflected, and at last accepted the invitation given him. Once within the house, he continued anxiously to press the medium as to why he had asked him to supper. Not being as yet able to furnish any sufficient reason for having done so, the other at first evaded answering. He was speedily relieved from his perplexity, however. The spirit-voice once more spoke, and made a sufficiently strange communication. The medium addressed his companion:—

"You will go back to the city in the morning," he said. The other started from his seat.

"In heaven's name," said he, "who are you? Tell me that—who are you?"

"Never mind who I am. Go back to the city in the morning." "But, if you know so much, you must know that it is impossible for me to go back."

"Not at all. Go just as usual, and all will be arranged."

The conversation continued for some time. The young man made clear those parts of his story—a sad narrative from first to last—which the spirit-voice had not revealed. What the difficulties were in which he had become involved need not be told. He at length agreed that he would return as usual next morning to his employment in the city; and pledged his word to that effect. It was now late. The medium, therefore, offered his guest a bed on the sofa in the drawing-room for the night, which the other accepted. He left early in the morning, promising to return that evening, and take tea with his new acquaintance.

Hardly was he gone when the voice said, "He has not told you all." What the youth had kept back was then explained, and, armed with this new knowledge, the medium awaited the other's return. His guest was punctual; and the two sat down at table together. After tea the conversation ran on the subject of the other's affairs, and the host suddenly remarked, "But you have not told me all."

"Oh yes!" was the reply. "Everything."

"No," said the medium, "you did not tell me that when I spoke to you yesterday evening you were about to commit suicide."

"For a moment the other seemed too astounded to reply. "'Great heaven!' said he when he had recovered speech, 'it is true. How you have discovered it I cannot by any possibility conceive; but last evening when you met me, *I was on my way to throw myself into the Thames.*'"

As I have in a former chapter remarked, it has given me much pleasure of late to notice a growing desire to obtain phenomena in the light. With Mrs. M. Sunderland Cooper, for instance, materialised hands and other manifestations are reported as witnessed "in the warm sunlight of a cloudless day." Such mediumship is the only one worth valuing. The slightest phenomenon regarding whose occurrence the proofs are complete, outweighs, in the estimation of all reasonable men, a whole conjuror's sabbath of dark *séances*.

In *Blackwood's Magazine* for March, 1876, appeared a remarkable article entitled "Powers of the Air;" the text for which was "furnished by certain phenomena occurring in my presence, that had been described to the writer. As, however, the sketch given is decidedly incomplete, I have obtained from the lady to whom the article in question alludes an account, in her own words, of what she witnessed; and this I now design to offer to the reader, interspersing it with such extracts from *Blackwood* as may serve for commentaries and introduction.

The writer in Maga commences with an echo of the regrets to which Macaulay long ago gave utterance, regarding the small success which this world has had in piercing the mysteries of the next:—

"It is lamentable and discouraging," he or she says, 'to reflect how little progress the human intellect has been able to make towards the solution of some questions among the most important that can occupy it. One of these questions, the existence or non-existence of spirit in the universe, was disputed between the Pharisees and Sadducees in the days of the apostles, has been disputed ever since, and, in these latter days, has separated disputants more widely than when the argument was young. For although one must suppose that the extreme of materialism had been reached by the Sadducees, who denied the resurrection of the dead, and acknowledged the being of neither angel nor spirit, it is certain that until the last century no philosopher went so far in the opposite direction as to deny altogether the existence of matter, and to affirm of spirit what the materialists affirm of substance—namely, that it is alone sufficient to account for everything in nature. Idealism, or the doctrine of the non-existence of matter, has had very little success, because men can hardly be persuaded to discredit the evidence of their senses.

> "'When Bishop Berkeley said there was no matter—
> And proved it—'twas no matter what he said;
> They say his system 'tis in vain to batter,
> Too subtle for the airiest human head;
> And yet who can believe it?'

wrote one of our wittiest poets; and Materialism, or the doctrine of the non-existence of spirit or soul, also finds it difficult to make converts, because men refuse to surrender an internal conviction that they are in part immortal.

"Between idealism and materialism there have been very numerous shades of opinion—more, probably, than I ever heard of, and far more than I could presume to claim acquaintance with. I cannot write philosophically about any; but about two doctrines, which are more or less attracting attention at present, I should like to set down a few words.

"The former of these is Spiritualism. We hear constantly that the existence of innumerable spirits is easily and frequently made plain to the senses; that our atmosphere is thick with spirits who, under certain conditions, can be seen, heard and felt.

*   *   *   *   *   *

"I will mention the last striking narrative that has come in my way, not doubting that it will be found closely to resemble the majority of modern experiences in the same field.

"It happened that, a few months since, I was in a foreign city where a well-known medium was also residing. He was frequently to be seen in public; but I did not, during his stay, hear of any appointed *séance*, or any spiritual manifestation in that city. After his departure it chanced that I sojourned in the hotel where he had been staying, and where many of those who had been his fellow-guests still remained. A few days after my commencing my residence there, some other new-comer complained at dinner of noises which disturbed his rest at night. 'Noises!' echoed half-a-dozen voices; 'why, it is the quietest house in the city—notoriously so.' The stranger didn't know: he could only say he heard people constantly moving about in the night, and the oddest sounds, as of things thrown or dragged about, workmen at their work, persons shouting or laughing at a little distance, and so on. At this there was quite an excitement, the majority of the hearers, jealous for the peaceful character of the house, protesting in earnest tones that the new-comer must be mistaken. He, however, was not going to be talked out of belief in the evidence of his senses; and the contention waxed warm, and might have become angry, had not an elderly lady interposed by asking the complainant if he did not inhabit a certain number on a certain flat? When he said that those were his number and *étage*, she answered quietly, 'Yes, I thought so. Those are the apartments which were inhabited last by Mr. _____' (the medium). 'I am not surprised at your hearing noises there.' Then a general conviction lighted on all the champions of the house. 'Oh, if it's that,' said they, 'of course it's another thing: those noises are different.' Little by little, then, it came to be mentioned how the great medium had really desired perfect quiet during his stay; but the spirits would not let him rest, and were always calling his attention (This is a slight exaggeration.—D. D. H.) night and day; there used to be such curious sounds about those rooms! I ventured to observe that as the medium was now in another and a distant place, that was a reason why the spirits who were so fond of his company should not make noises in the hotel. But all the answer I got to this was, 'Yes, you would think so; but they are not quick to leave a place once they get used to it.' It certainly seemed to me that the conduct of the spirits would have been more consistent if they had not remained to make themselves disagreeable after he for whose sake they came had departed. And I thought but little more on the subject, these vulgar nocturnal disturbances not recommending spiritualism to my consideration at all.

"Some days later I and one or two more of the lately-arrived guests sat together in the *salon* conversing, when we were joined by a lady who had been resident in the house for two or three months. She happened to mention the medium, whereupon we asked whether she had known much about him while they were in the house together; and she said that she had been acquainted with him since the time of her coming thither, and that towards the end of his stay she had known him rather intimately. We asked whether she believed that the nightly noises had any connection with him, and she said she really could not tell; everything about the spiritual world was so strange that she did not know what to think. Had she ever witnessed any of these strange things? we asked. Well, yes; she had witnessed a great many strange things. Let me state in brief that she did not at first answer at all readily to our inquiries, but that she yielded by degrees to pressure, spoke after a time with less reserve, and finally became communicative. The substance of what she told was as follows:— The company in the house, knowing that, they had a person of some celebrity among them, greatly desired to witness some manifestation of his power. They besought him to hold *séances*. But this he persistently refused to do; saying that he was there for repose—repose, indeed, from those very *séances*, which had been wearing his nervous system more than he could endure. Howbeit, though this was his answer to the guests as a body, he had some few intimate acquaintances whom he invited occasionally to spend an evening with him, and to whom he would say that, although he could do nothing calculated to bring spirits to meet them, yet they must not be surprised at anything they might see, as spirits would present themselves unbidden sometimes, and be very demonstrative. The strange things which occurred at these reunions were a good deal talked about in whispers, and led the excluded portion of the guests to make strong efforts to obtain the entree to the medium's rooms. Very few, however, succeeded in this. The lady who narrated these things made no endeavour to be admitted, but rather shrank from that which so many desired; being inclined to look on spiritualism as imposture, and having a great dislike to tricks and surprises. But a friend of hers who had been greatly impressed by what she had seen on her visits (being one of the elite) induced the medium to invite her, and then importuned her until she accepted the invitation."

The above account is slightly incorrect. The real circumstances of the introduction, and the phenomena which passed at the ensuing *séances*, are described for me as follows, by the lady to whom the *Blackwood* article alludes:—

"My first experience was as striking as unexpected. I had arrived at a hotel in one of the cities of continental Europe an entire stranger. I found the absorbing topic of the drawing-room the strange phenomena witnessed at a recent private *séance* given by Mr. Home. I expressed a desire to converse with the great medium, which favour was accorded me, and eventuated in an invitation to be present at a *séance* to be held that evening.

"We were a party of seven, all strangers to myself, and all having met Mr. Home only within a few days. We sat about a large table, with the hands lying carelessly upon it, and chatted on indifferent subjects. At the end of perhaps a quarter of an hour a sensible vibration of the table was apparent, and shortly after several of the circle were startled by the sensation of being repeatedly touched where no hands were visible. Then came five distinct raps upon the table; supposed to be a call for the alphabet—whereupon, Mr. Home repeated the letters; the rappings being transferred to my knee, and in such rapid succession as to render it impossible to mark the letters indicated. There being apparently two influences, each striving for expression, Mr. Home requested that they would rap more slowly, and upon the table. All to no effect. At last he asked, 'Will you then reply upon the accordeon?' Immediately that instrument—which was lying upon the table—expanded, apparently of itself; giving out three clear, separate notes; supposed to indicate assent. The replies to questions were, for the remainder of the evening, all given by raps upon the woodwork of the instrument. With the consent of Mr. Home I put my hand under the table, requesting that it might be touched. Each finger of the open hand was touched in succession; and a hand giving the sensation of being as warm as my own was placed in the open palm. I quietly closed my fingers upon it; it remained quiescent for the space of perhaps a minute, and then—was gone—how, I cannot say. *It was not withdrawn*, nor did it appear to diminish gradually. Since then, I have, in an open and frequented thoroughfare, felt, whilst accompanied by Mr. Home, the same strange touch; the circumstances being such that he could by no contrivance, mechanical or otherwise, have succeeded in producing it.

"A request was rapped out that Mr. Home should take the accordeon. He accordingly took it in one hand, the end having the keys dropping almost to the floor; the music produced was beautiful beyond description, like the strains one sometimes hears in dreams, which can never be repeated, At Mr. Home's suggestion two lights were placed upon the floor, that we might watch the instrument, which continued to dilate and contract, and the keys to rise and fall with the music, without the intervention of any visible touch.

"When the music ceased Mr. Home withdrew his hand—the accordeon, still remaining open, moved slowly—as if by attraction to the person seated beside him; against whose knee it rested, swaying like a balloon, during the remainder of the *séance*. From first to last the room was not only lighted, but well lighted.

"*By permission I put several mental questions, each of which was promptly and correctly answered; with the full names of friends and relatives deceased, and circumstances which could not have been known to any of those present; all, as I have stated, having been previous to the past twenty-four hours strangers to me.*

"Finally, Mr. Home, passing into a trance, described the personal appearance, and narrated correctly the incidents of the illness and death, of a relative of one of the party present.

"The following evening I was present by invitation of Mr. Home at the house of an artist friend, where the phenomena were somewhat different in character. The circle numbered as before seven—to myself a new set of strangers. The first notable circumstance was that the table around which we had been seated for perhaps twenty minutes commenced slowly rising from the floor, with a swaying motion like that of a boat riding upon the waves—six pairs of hands being upon the table—Mr. Home sitting a little out of the circle, with arms folded. When about a foot from the floor the table righted itself, and moved steadily upward—our hands resting upon it till it passed out of reach. It rose till within a foot of the ceiling, and then commenced slowly descending. The lady of the house sprang nervously forward to grasp a petroleum lamp which seemed in imminent danger of sliding off the now slanting table—Mr. Home said calmly, 'Do not be alarmed; no accident will happen;'—the table came down with a bang, but not one of the numerous articles upon it was disturbed. Again it rose within a foot of the ceiling, descending this time as lightly as a feather. A third time it mounted with no visible hand upon it, making its way back so gently that one might have heard a pin drop as it touched the floor.

"Shortly after, several of the party saw hands moving along the edge of the table. I confess I could not see them, although I could distinctly feel their touch. Four successive times flowers were taken from a vase and placed in my hand—how, I cannot say, the agency was invisible. Once a hand holding a flower was placed upon my forehead; the flower being repeatedly drawn backward and forward over the face. A watch-chain worn by one of the party was repeatedly pulled with such force as to cause the wearer to bend with the movement:—on the following day the links were found so stretched apart as to have reduced the chain to pieces. All took place in full light.

"In the course of the evening an accordeon lying upon the floor began discoursing beautiful music; in the midst of which a railroad train rushed screaming by, winding up its salute with three piercing shrieks. The music ceased abruptly, the accordeon took up the long demoniac cry of the engine, with its three wild notes of warning, in such a manner that one would have declared it an actual echo; then the quiet, soothing melody was resumed, growing gradually more and more faint, yet every note distinct, till it seemed to fade away in the distance like the music of a retreating band.

"Presently the chair in which Mr. Home was seated was by an invisible force moved slowly back, a distance of perhaps two feet, placing him quite out of the circle. A moment after a hand appeared on the knee of one of the party, distant about four feet from the medium, a hand like that of a tall, powerful man; the fingers long, the joints strong and large, the finger-ends bent slightly backward, the fingers in constant motion, opening and shutting, as they lay upon the knee, like a fan. This appearance remained from three to five minutes I should say, although the time appeared to us much longer. All rose, and gathered round, watching the phenomenon, Mr. Home apparently as much interested as the others. When it disappeared no one could say how it went; it did not fade out gradually, nor did it glide away: we knew only that it was no longer there.

"Only a few of the prominent incidents of these two *séances* are here given; much that was interesting and striking was of too personal a nature to be with propriety introduced.

"One occurrence impressed me very much. Mr. Home, whilst in a trance, turned to me and said, 'There is a portrait of *his* mother.' I made no reply; but my thought was, 'There is *no* portrait of her.' Scarcely could the idea have taken form in my mind, when Mr. Home said, 'Oh yes, there is a portrait.' I was determined to give no clue, and I still said nothing; but I thought to myself, 'Strange as all the rest has been, you are mistaken in this.' 'But we are not mistaken,' said Mr. Home instantly, as though in answer to my unexpressed thought; 'there is a picture of her with an open Bible upon her knee.' I then remembered that some thirty years before there *was* a picture taken of his mother, and, at his request, with her open Bible in her lap. Had Mr. Home made use of the word picture instead of portrait in the first instance the fact might have been at once recalled; but I was classing 'portrait' more as an oil painting. The picture in question had never been in my possession, and I had not seen it for many years. These circumstances, also, may help to account for the fact of its existence having faded from memory.

"It is impossible that Mr. Home can ever have seen the daguerreotype in question. Even had he seen it, however, it would have been equally impossible that he should have discovered the small, indistinctly-copied book there represented to be a Bible."

It is much to be regretted that various of the communications, received at these *séances* were, as Mrs. _____ remarks, "of too private and personal a nature to be with propriety introduced here." This esoteric spiritualism, while furnishing the strongest of all possible proofs to those immediately concerned, remains, in general, by its circumstances and character, valueless to the outside world. There are few who have sufficient strength of mind to come forward, and, with the sure knowledge that the course they take will expose them to ridicule, misconception, and calumny, make public the evidence of man's immortality which has been granted to them. The greater honour then to that small band of noble men and women who, from a sense of duty, have gallantly dared the storm of popular prejudice, before which the sensitive and the timid recoil.

The secret nature of many communications, and the repugnance with which various persons whom these communications have convinced shrink from identifying themselves publicly with a cause so unpopular as spiritualism and defaced by so many abuses, should be held prominently in view by every critic who would deal impartially with the subject. They are points which the *Blackwood* writer seems somewhat to lose sight of in the following remarks:—

"I think it ought to be taken as proved that very many things have been, and are continually being, witnessed which are not traceable to any known terrestrial agency, yet which must proceed from rational beings. Once this is admitted, the existence of spirits will hardly be denied. This is something gained; but, against the materialist, not much. For the latter may still say: 'I don't care whether or not spirits may exist somewhere in nature; I say that there is no need of spirits to account for anything we know or experience.'

"I might here be reminded that he who believes these spiritual manifestations to be genuine, has the witness of the spirits themselves as to many of them being the souls of human beings who once lived on the earth. But I have not let slip the recollection of their testimony; I am only troubled with doubt concerning it; I think there is question of their credibility. The fondness of the spirits for darkened rooms"— (let me once more repeat that all the manifestations recorded in this and my concluding chapter took place in *full light*)—"their decidedly mysterious proceedings, their sparing and unsatisfactory communications, and the utter uselessness of many of their most startling deeds, are fatal to confidence. Thus spiritualism does not, I fear, prove that which many believers would be glad to prove; namely, that those who have preceded us on the earth certainly had soul—that there are spirits who influence and control matter—that matter is the creation of spirit."

If the occurrences which form the groundwork of the Maga article do not prove spirits to have control over matter, what can they be considered as proving? If the narrative with which my book concludes, does not show that those who preceded us on the earth certainly had souls, what hope is there of an immortality for man?

I am glad to notice, however, that the author of "Powers of the Air" is, in general, both liberal and thoughtful in his treatment of the subject. The following remarks will commend themselves to all unprejudiced minds as, on the whole, just:—

"I have read sometimes of philosophical persons attending *séances* with the intention of testing the reality of the apparitions; but they would appear to have tested the media, not the spirits. The trials were as to whether the media were or were not impostors and mere practisers upon human credulity. But these philosophical persons, though they may have damaged the reputation of some of the mediums, have not succeeded in proving spiritualism itself to be mere imposture."

*   *   *   *   *   *

"I ought to state that, although I appear to favour belief in spiritualism, I do so entirely in deference to what seems to me to be candid testimony. My natural bias did not prejudice me in its favour; and I never in my life attended a *séance*. The evidence seems strong, and has never been fairly rebutted. If we reject testimony simply because it witnesses something disagreeable to us, or something that we arbitrarily pronounce to be false because it is extraordinary, how much are we better than those opponents of Christianity who have decided to reject the miracles of Scripture 'because they are contrary to experience'? We reasonably expect that the record of eye-witnesses and contemporaries should have more weight than a philosophic idea or axiom which a man may have taken into his mind. By the same rule, if unimpeachable testimony of the existence of these spirits can be adduced, we must not put it aside except on still stronger testimony which can show the first to be mistaken."

That evidence could hardly be considered "unimpeachable" which "still stronger testimony should show to be mistaken." I dare assert, however, that "unimpeachable" is by no means too strong a word to be applied to many of the facts which modern spiritualism has placed on record. They have been tried by the most searching scrutiny, and with the severest tests, and like gold from the furnace they have come forth from the ordeal in all the brightness of sterling truth. It is to these glorious gleams of the light of another world that we may turn for consolation from the blackness which at present overcasts our cause.

CHAPTER XI

THE HIGHER ASPECTS OF SPIRITUALISM *(continued)*

In the episode which furnishes a subject for this concluding chapter of my work I am fortunately able to give every name, date, and circumstance necessary for the complete authentication of the facts recorded. Those who have formed no idea, or but an imperfect one, of what a spiritual *séance* really is, may enlighten themselves by consulting the following narrative. They will find no magnifying of trifles into confirmation 'strong as Holy Writ;' no false glare of enthusiasm, no wealth of credulity, no want of tests. A simple statement of events is made, exactly as those events occurred. That the narrator to whom the spirit-world was thus unexpectedly brought so close should have been rendered happy with complete certainty of the existence of that world and the possibility of communion between its inhabitants and ourselves, was the natural result of the perfect evidence of identity which the loved ones whom she had lost accorded her.

The lady in question, and the author of the following account, gives me full permission to publish her name and address. I thank her much for the courageous course she has taken, impelled by a high sense of duty, which I could wish were more common than popular prejudices upon the subject of spiritualism have rendered it. She is Madame la Comtesse Caterina Lugano di Panigai, Via Jacopo da Diacceto, No. 8, Florence. As her narrative has a completeness and an interest to which no words of mine would add anything, I need say no more. It is the Countess who now speaks.

"The evening of July 7th, 1874, I had the good fortune to be present at a *séance* given by Mr. D. D. Home. His celebrity is so extended, and his position and high moral worth are so thoroughly recognised by a very large circle of friends, whose standing in society renders it impossible for even a breath of suspicion to rest upon their testimony, that any attempt to portray him here would be superfluous.

"We seated ourselves towards eight P.M. around a large table, belonging to the hotel where Mr. Home was staying. The persons present were the Marchioness Bartolomei Passerini, Mrs. Webster, the Chevalier Soflietti, Mr. Monnier, Mrs. and Mr. D. D. Home, and myself.

"The table about which we grouped ourselves stood in the centre of the drawing-room. In a corner of the apartment, and quite away from the company, was a second table, small and square in shape. Two wax candles stood on the table where we were seated; and on the other and smaller one was placed a petroleum lamp. The lamp and candles together rendered the room perfectly light.

"Madame Passerini and myself were on either side of Mr. Home; she to the right, I to the left. Whilst seating ourselves, and before Mr. Home had done so, a singular tremulous motion of the table became perceptible, to which I, who had placed my hand on the surface, called attention. The motion continued to increase until it was distinctly felt by all present. Then the table rose; first one side lifting itself from the ground, and then another, until this had been done in every direction. Rappings commenced, and were in some instances very loud. They sounded, not alone on the table, but in various parts of the room; on the floor, and even on our chairs. At last five distinct but tiny raps were heard directly under my hands. Mr. Home said that this was an indication of the alphabet being required, and commenced to repeat it; whilst another of the party wrote down the letters at which the rappings came. My astonishment may be conceived, when I found the name of Stella given in this manner. I was an utter stranger to Mr. and Mrs. Home. They had been but a few days in Florence, and had heard my name for the first time when an hour or two before a friend asked permission for me to be present at the *séance*. And now was given in this strange manner a name most precious to me—that of a dearly-loved child who, at the tender age of five years and ten months, had been torn from me after a few days of cruel suffering. Time had elapsed since her passing from earth, and in my dress there was nothing to indicate the mourning of my bereaved heart. I spoke; asking whether it could be that God in his mercy allowed the angel once so entirely and fondly mine, but now for ever freed from earth and its sorrows, to be near me. A perfect shower of gladsome little raps was the instant response. I then begged that, if it were indeed my child, her age at death might be given. It was at once rapped out correctly.

"My strained attention bent itself with all the eagerness of maternal love on those sounds—sounds which brought, as it were, faint echoes of the music of heaven to cheer my sad heart. Tears, that even the presence of strangers could not restrain, coursed plentifully down my cheeks. I thought myself in a dream, and feared every instant that I would awaken, and the celestial vision vanish, leaving only an aching void.

"The rappings continued, and the alphabet was again made use of. The message this time was, 'You must not weep, dear mamma.' At the same time the handkerchief that I had taken forth to dry my tears, and which now lay before me on the table, moved slowly to the table-edge, and was then drawn underneath. Whilst this was passing the form of my darling seemed to stand beside me. I could distinctly feel, as it were, the pressure of her body, and the folds of my silk dress were disturbed, and rustled so as to be heard by all present.

"But a few seconds had elapsed from the disappearance of the handkerchief when I felt what seemed the touch of a baby hand on my right knee. Almost instinctively I placed my own hand there. To my surprise the handkerchief was at once laid in it; and a little hand grasped mine, so perfectly corresponding to the hand of the tiny form which the grave had hidden from me that I felt my precious one and no other was beside me. Would the heart of every sorrow-stricken mother could be gladdened with a ray of the deep joy mine experienced then!

"I had not expected such a touch; I had not been told that I might experience it, and therefore it could by no possibility be the phantasm of an overwrought imagination.

"Mr. Home's name was, of course, one that I had heard before. I had heard of him; but had never read any details of his *séances*. On coming, therefore, to the one in question, my supposition was that we would be enshrouded in that utter darkness which I knew to be frequently demanded by those terming themselves mediums. Had I sat under such conditions the most palpable touch would have left no other impression on my mind than the suspicion of trickery. My disappointment was pleasant. I sat in a well-lighted room, and could make full use of my eyes. Already, within the short space of half an hour, I had heard sounds which could not have been imitated by a number of electric batteries combined; I had seen movements of the table that even the confederacy of half the persons present could not under the circumstances have accomplished; and now came this thrilling touch. I may state that when the table's movements were most active, Mr. Home, placing a light on the floor, not only invited, but urgently desired us to look under. So marked was the request, that even had curiosity not prompted us, good breeding would have necessitated compliance with the evident wish of our host. One and all obeyed, and saw the table lift from the floor, but nothing which could solve the mystery.

"There came another token of my darling's presence. On my left wrist—the one farthest from Mr. Home; whose hands, as the hands of all present, rested on the table, I felt the touch of tiny fingers. I looked, but saw nothing; although my eyes were strained on the spot where the pressure still continued. One of my lace sleeves was next gently grasped. All present saw this; and one of the party exclaimed, 'The Countess's sleeve is being pulled!'

"Our attention would seem to have been over-concentrated. For the space of several minutes manifestations ceased, and all was as void of a spiritual presence as our ordinary everyday, prosaic life. We were roused by sounds proceeding from the smaller table, which I have mentioned as standing in the corner of the room. All present saw it move slowly from its place, and approach the table at which we sat.

"Again rappings made themselves heard, and a second name, also that of one very near and dear to me, was spelt out by means of the alphabet. An accordeon lay on the table. It did not belong to Mr. Home, but had been brought by one of the guests present. Mr. Home now desired me to take this instrument in one hand, that it might, be seen whether the spirits could play upon it. Hardly had I touched the accordeon when it began to move; then sweet, long-drawn sounds issued from it; and finally a military air was played, *while I held the instrument, and could see that no other person touched it.*

"The alphabet was here called for. This time, instead of the usual rappings on the table, the message was communicated through distinct movements of my dress. The words were words of consolation and love, and their reference was to an incident known only to the nearest of my relatives, and which none of my fellow-guests at the *séance* in question could by any possibility have been acquainted with.

"Just after this communication had been made, my eyes rested for a moment on a most beautiful rose worn by Madame Passerini. I said mentally, 'If you are in reality the spirit you claim to be, I ask you to take that rose from Henrietta, and bring it to me.' The thought had hardly taken shape in my mind, when a hand, visible to every one present, the large, nervous hand of a man, grasped the rose, and disengaging it, brought it to me, and placed it in my fingers. This was not done in darkness, or in a dim light. The room was well lit, the hands of every person present rested on the table, and there hovered in the air before us a hand as perfect in form as human hand can be. Not only was it perfect in form, but it had shown its capability for physical action by the unfastening of the rose from the lace to which that rose was securely attached, and the carrying it a distance of two or three feet. And further, that action indicated the presence of an intelligence able to comprehend a mental request, for I had not uttered a word. I grant most willingly that all this is strange, but I affirm most solemnly that it is true. We were in presence of beings who could even read our thoughts. The names of those long since summoned from earth were given; and the most hidden things connected with their earthly lives recapitulated. Not to me alone did these things happen, but to every one. In some instances there had even been forgetfulness on the part of the person addressed, and attendant circumstances were given that the incident might be recalled. Thus Mr. Home, passing into a trance, said to the Chevalier Soffietti, 'There is an old nurse of yours standing beside you—a negro woman.' The Chevalier could recall no such person. 'She says you ought not to forget her,' continued Mr. Home, 'for she saved your life when you were but three and a half years of age. You fell into a stream of water near a mill, and were just about to be drawn into a water-wheel when she rescued you.' Chevalier Soffietti now recalled the whole, and acknowledged the communication to be perfectly correct. He had been wholly unknown to Mr. Home till within three hours of the message being given, and not one of the remaining guests knew of the incident in question. I narrate this to show that others were like myself made happy by proofs of the continued existence of those dear to us. If, indeed, all these things be explainable by some hidden force or forces of nature, then God have pity on the shipwreck of our hopes of immortality. If they be dreams, then must our present also be a dream, and our future but that dream's continuation. Am I to believe that they were so many *ignes fatui*, leading only to destruction? Prove to me, or to any other present at that most memorable *séance*, that we were deluded, and I will prove to you that I have not written these words, and that you are not reading them.

"As I have said, Mr. Home passed into a trance. After the communication to Chevalier Soffietti he addressed himself to me, and gave facts which not only could he by no possibility have previously known, but which were in some instances unknown to any person in the world save myself. He told me he saw various members of my family. That he did in reality see them I am unable to affirm; but that he gave me their names, and most accurately described them, I do affirm. 'Stella is present,' he said, 'and she says'—The words given need not be placed on record. To me they were most touching and precious—to the world they would be unmeaning. I understood them, and greatly do I thank God that in His mercy He permitted them to be given me: for they have made the burden of life seem lighter, and I can await now more patiently the joy of endless reunion with those I love.

"I *will*, however, give the conclusion of the message. My darling thus finished what she had to say: '*And I know, mamma, that you took the last pair of boots I wore, and laid them away with my little white dress in a box that you had ordered for the purpose. You locked them in that box, and when you are quite alone you take them out, and shed such sad, sad tears over them! This must not be, for Stella is not dead. I am living, and I love you. I am to tell you that you will have a very distinct proof of my presence, and that it will be given you to-morrow. You must not again open the drawer where the box is placed which contains what you call your treasures, until you hear distinct raps on the bureau.*'

"Not even my family knew anything of this box. I had kept the contents as to me most sacred relics; showing them to no one, and never by any chance alluding to their existence. Mothers who have been afflicted like me will alone be able to appreciate the sentiment by which I was guided.

The *séance* ended. I naturally wished to thank Mr. Home for having been the means of giving me so great a joy. He refused to accept my thanks, and said that he was simply an investigator like others, and just as deeply interested in the thorough examination of the subject as I or my friends could be. The phenomena we had witnessed purported to be due to his presence; but he was, as we could all well testify, simply a passive agent; deep interest, or a strong desire for phenomena on his part, rather tending to prevent than to bring about manifestations.

Everything had been foreign to my preconceived ideas. I had expected darkness, or, at the least, very little light; and some kind of dictatorial arrangement called 'conditions.' I was most agreeably disappointed. Mr. Home showed himself even more anxious for thorough investigation than were his guests. He was a confirmed invalid, and had just undergone a course of severe treatment. He suffered from a nervous paralysis, which rendered his limbs almost powerless. I think it well to mention these facts; having of late read and heard of some of the extraordinary theories whereby persons ignorant of the subject seek to show the world how the wonderful things occurring in Mr. Home's presence are accomplished. Mr. Home could not have moved a down pillow with his feet, and the large table at which we sat—and which, I may add, rose entirely from the ground more than once in the course of the evening—was an exceedingly heavy one. We all looked under the table when it became suspended in the air, and nothing whatever earthly was in contact with it. As to the hand all present saw being a stuffed glove, I shall believe that when I have become convinced that the hand I now write with is a stuffed glove also.

"I went home a happy woman. My prayers that night were the overflowings of a heart filled with gratitude to heaven, and the intensest joy. Sleep was banished from my eyelids; and the hours passed in a waking dream of delight. Ever and again my thoughts turned to the new proof of her presence that my darling had promised, and I busied myself with wondering speculations as to what that proof would be. I asked nothing more; for already my soul was satisfied beyond the possibility of doubt; but I felt, and rejoiced to feel, that some fresh token would be granted me; and so I tried to conquer my impatience, and to await the revelation with the calmness of assured hope.

"In the early morning I wrote a few words to a dearly-valued friend, asking her to come to me at once. She arrived; and as soon as we were together I began a recital of the marvels I had seen and heard. The half was not told when my friend pointed to the bureau, and said, 'Did you not hear rappings on that piece of furniture?' Instantly they were repeated. 'It is the signal,' I exclaimed, 'and it is there the box is hidden.' The key of that drawer of the bureau which contained my treasures was in my dressing-room. I ran to get it, and, unlocking the drawer, took out the box, which also was locked. With trembling fingers I turned the second key, and lifted the lid. The little boots—they are light summer ones—lay there, with the white silk elastic uppermost. *On the elastic of one boot was imprinted a perfect star, and in the centre of the star an eye.* The substance with which it is drawn is black. It has since faded slightly, but remains still thoroughly distinct. So mathematically perfect is the drawing that great skill and precision are necessary for an accurate copy to be taken. I have had an engraving made of it, which Mr. Home will give." (See below.) "It is an exact *facsimile* of that cherished token. At each of the six points there is, as will be seen, a letter. United, they form the name of my darling.

"I ordered my carriage at once, and drove to the hotel where Mr. Home was staying. Let me here state that not only had he never been within my house, but that up to the time of compiling this account—more than two years later—from my memoranda taken at that time, he has not even seen the house to my knowledge or his own. While I was showing him my little treasure—now doubly dear—manifestations again took place. Naturally I hoped and expected that they would proceed from the one whose life and love had now become so glorious a certainty tome. Instead, a singular medical receipt was given, and I was told to use it for my eyes. I had been long a sufferer through an inflammation of the eyelids, and was at that very time under medical treatment. I made use of the remedy thus strangely provided, and with most beneficial result; inasmuch as I experienced within only a few days a relief which celebrated oculists had failed to procure me during a long course of advice. Thus, apart from that inestimable and never-to-be-forgotten consolation which God, in His mercy, granted to my soul, I was physically benefited.

"I have decided to give these facts to the world from a deep sense of duty, and from that alone. They will answer, I hope, the 'Cui bono?' I have heard of. My darling's visit has come to me as a ray of the glory of that kingdom where there is neither parting nor sorrow, where all tears are wiped away, and God alone gives light. I have not belief, but certitude. The shadows of earth may gather darkly, but through them all pierces the clear splendour of that star which gleams where He who doeth all things well has in His love placed it, and lifting my eyes to the bright messenger I can say with a rejoicing heart—

"I THANK THEE, O LORD!"

APPENDIX

"OUR FATHER"

Between two and three years ago I read in a Spiritualist publication, *Medium and Daybreak*, a short poem said to have been dictated by the spirit of Chatterton. There was true poetry in the composition, and memories were awakened in its perusal. It seemed a waif from the great ocean of thought, that had drifted down, and found a resting place. I knew nothing of the medium, or his position in life, but I felt an irresistible desire to write to him. I reasoned thus:— If he is in reality a medium, my friendly counsels may be of use to him—at least, in teaching him to avoid certain quicksands where fond hopes have, before now, been engulfed. I also thought that, if he were not a medium, and himself possessed the talent of writing such a production as the one alluded to, it would be only doing right to encourage him in continuing to develop so beautiful a gift. A correspondence ensued, which terminated in his becoming a member of my household in the capacity of secretary. I have had most ample opportunity of studying the young man, and without hesitancy I affirm that I fully believe his poetic talent to be a direct inspiration. His gift is not under his control, and whether it be Chatterton who guides—and I can see no reason why it should not be the spirit it claims—I am well convinced the poetry is not the production of the medium.

The poem from which I am now about to make extracts was partly written when he came to me, and it is only very lately that the completion has been given. It purports, as will be seen, to be dictated by Chatterton through the medium, J. V____

I

"One shadow still upon my life is cast,
One fragment of the sorrows of the past
The hated chain of memory links me yet
With days whose deeds I've striven to forget.
Wan from the gulf of Time they rise again—
The dead years: heavy with that weight of pain
Whose presence galled me to such bitter mirth,
When, in my misery, I walked the earth.

II

"My birth in England was, and England gave
My hapless clay the shelter of the grave:
Would pity guide a pilgrim to that tomb?
By time effaced, it shares the common doom;
But Tully's skull was reared the Forum o'er,
And Cromwell's mould'ring frame a gibbet bore:—

If earth thus fail her mightiest dust to keep,
A pauper's bones could scarce in safety sleep;
And branded so, 'twould seem, did worms receive
The all I, dying, to man's care could leave.

III

"The deadliest stab it was that Fate could deal;
The single wound my soul was formed to feel.
Secure I moved from every dart beside
In harness fashioned of despair and pride;
And careless where my clay in death should dwell
As is the eaglet of his broken shell.
Had it been laid where birds their carols sing,
And fair flow'rs leap to greet the fairer spring;
Or, on some field that slaughtered thousands saw,
The wild dog gorged, and filled the vulture's maw;
Or journeyed slow the solemn aisle along
To where repose the happier sons of song;—
Had it, where highways met, endured, unfelt,
Such shame as never was on Nero dealt;
Had each bleached bone—proud fate!—beneath the surge
Mixed with the dust for which the sea makes dirge,
The rites assigned nor blame nor praise had won—
Earth had her earth, and I my life lived on.
Enough,—the Furies found a loathly tomb,
And left me leprous with the pauper's doom.

IV

"O Soul! and can these trifles gall thee yet?
Thy broken shackles wherefore not forget?
Beneath the turf is laid now all the clay
That moved above it in my fleshly day;
Empires since then have ended—mighty thrones
Are crumbled utterly as those few bones
That once a spirit and its woes locked fast,
And now are atoms o'er the earth's face cast:
The dust is utterly as Pander's gone,
The soul, undying as the stars, burns on;
And longings, quenchless as itself, doth nurse,
To pierce the mysteries of the universe."

A little further on the poem passes from the particular to the general, and sketches as follows the obstructers of progress in the Past:—

"Such were the bigots whose fierce rage, of old,
Burdened the earth with horrors manifold—
Spending in slaughter half their fleshly day,
And seeming devils clothed awhile with clay.
'Tidings of love and peace' they preached, and came
Upon such mission armed with steel and flame:
A city razing for a dogma's sake

And answering reason with the ready stake.
In all lands bled their victims; yet they still
Affirmed such slaughter as their Master's will;
That—deep though flowed the sea of human blood,
Christ smiled applause, and Heaven their works held good;
And louder, livelier, rang each seraph's lyre
When chain's limbs writhed in the consuming fire.
Nor ceased with death the bigot's hate—he gave
The soul to other flames beyond the grave;
Made hell of heretics the certain doom
And showed eternity a fiery tomb,
Where prisoner souls should endless horrors know,
While, pitiless, the Father watched their woe.
A fable 'twas by every Church received,—
A lie the holiest bosoms half believed;
Till even the martyr, dying, smiled to think
His foes, departing, needs to woe must sink,
And hoped from heaven to watch by quenchless fire
The hands enwrapped that lit the funeral pyre.
Alas!—if bitter to mankind it prove
To vex with punishment the things they love,
How deep the woe that Deity would own
To list unceasing to His children's moan!—
To mark, still jarring with the seraph's strain,
The cry of spirits fixed in fiery pain,
And, glancing downward on their torment fell,
See Heaven grow tarnished with the smoke of Hell!
'Forgive them, Father,' Christ,—if Christ again
Could shine serene among the sons of men—
'Forgive them Lord,' would Jesus plead, 'who see
But passions—evil as their own—in Thee;
They that, misguided, think the falsehood true
Thou, foe to sin, must loathe the sinner too;
Who, when Truth beams the brightest, hold it night,
And, blind themselves, would give their fellows sight;
Forgive them, Father, if they have not known
Thy children's joys and sorrows are Thine own;
That, wild as sweeps Eternity's wide sea,
Thy love, eclipseless, points a path to Thee;
And every chastisement to error given
A balsam is that heals some soul for Heaven.'"

After various spirited and beautiful passages which I am reluctantly compelled to omit, the creeds of humanity are considered in their relation to the actual facts of spirit-life, and the view that opens on man at his passing from this world to the next is thus described:—

"And what is't Constantines or Cæsars find?
A judge relentless, or a father kind?
They find with every action wrought below

Is linked some fragment of man's bliss or woe;
That perfect in a moment none can be,
Nor hopeless any for eternity;
They learn that of the thousand creeds of earth
Was none that all in error had its birth.
For, cheerful aye through Superstition's night
The glories break of Truth's undying light,
And ethics fair may through foul dogmas show
Like golden threads that in the dull rock glow.
The veriest bigot who a text can make
Pretence for all the torment of the stake,
From the same scripture draws command more pure
To clothe and aid the naked and the poor;
The Turk, whose Koran's with uncleanness fraught,
That law yet rescues from the drunkard's fault;
The Black, the Mongol, each could pick at need
True jewels from the dunghill of his creed—
Pearls radiant with a purity divine,
And cherished somewhat e'en by Vice's swine.
'Tis thus the various faiths of earth live on,
When far from earth their pioneers are gone;
Though many an error mars the picture's grace
Some faint show hath it of the Father's face,
Some happy trait, by intuition caught,
Outweighs the lines with priestly falsehood fraught;
Obscured and slight, that beauty still we view,
And half forget the worthless in the true."

There follows now what is assuredly the best portion of the whole poem. In many lines of great force and interest the beliefs and actions of the Israelites are described and criticized. I have read these stanzas to various authors and divines of my acquaintance—including a bishop of the Church—and even those who dissent most strongly from the views unfolded agree that they have seldom heard a finer composition. I confess that I myself incline rather to the soft beauty of the concluding part of the poem than to the tragic power here displayed, but the excellence of the lines is past question. The description, however, occupies such space as quite to preclude my quoting it here; and it seems a pity to mutilate it by extracts. I content myself, therefore, with quoting a few lines which may serve as specimens of the many omitted. They are from an apostrophe to the Deity regarding the actions of the Jews on their entrance into Palestine.

The cities wherein heathens had enjoyed
Thy gifts, went down, and e'en the sites were void;
Their masters' clay was cast in bloody graves,
Their mistresses remained the murd'rers' slaves;
From Dan to Gibeah the work was done,

And Israel rested in the vineyards won.
Of nations who their masters late had reigned
The maids alone, to worse than death, remained.
Their lust on these the people of the Lord
Wreaked, when each male was smitten with the sword.
For crimes thus vile were Hebrew pæans sung,
For such have blissful shouts through Jewry rung:
Her prophets praised Thee as a Sire who joyed
To see Thy sons by other sons destroyed—
Who grateful from Thy throne in Heaven looked down
As rose the smoke from many a heathen town,
And held that servant at the highest worth
Whose sword most fearfully had scourged the earth.
Such faith the wand'rers had—their scriptures still
Bear record that Thy mandate was to kill;
In solemn fashion is the story told
Of murder to Thy glory done of old,
And bright as Orient gems the verses glow
That sing of Israel's triumphs o'er the foe.
Skilled was each poet-prophet to impart
The light that dwells within the minstrel's heart,
But yet the glory to those pages given
Was scarce a gleam that had its source in heaven."

The first part of "Our Father" ends by describing how the conceptions regarding the attributes of the Deity which the Hebrew has formed on earth are gradually abandoned by him on his entrance to a higher life. The "change that comes o'er the spirit of his dream" is summed up as follows:—

"He finds, with each advance his soul may show,
A brighter glory round the Godhead flow;
In spirit turns he to that heavenly ray
And basks in all the splendour of the day,
Then cries, enraptured, to the Sire above,
'No more I fear Thee, Lord, for Thou art Love!'"

The second part of the poem wants the tragic elevation of the first; but this is amply compensated by its beauty, and depth of thought. Here is how the obscurement of Christianity by priestcraft is dealt with:—

"The mightiest sceptre conqueror ever grasped
That hand now wields which to the Cross was clasped;
With lordly diadems doth Earth adorn
The brow that knew the piercing of the thorn;
And when in prayer her children's voices blend,

Thy name, O Christ! the loudest doth ascend:
To Thee the incense floats of many a shrine,
And nations hail Thee as a Prince divine.

 *   *   *   *   *

Yet scarce the purple flung Thy form around
Can hide the rankling of a secret wound,
And though Earth's diadem doth weight it now
Judæa's thorns were easier to Thy brow,
Nor all the incense darkling in Thy praise
May veil from man the sadness of Thy gaze.
He knows Thee not, and sects with sects unite
In anxious strife to shut Thee from his sight;
And souls who plead to see Thee as thou art
Are shown some monster of the priestly heart—
Christ that never on the earth's face trod,
A hybrid shape, with naught of man or God."

The mission of Christ then comes under consideration, and he is made to define it as follows:—

"'I come,' of old thou saidst, 'to give earth light,
To guide the stumbling steps of man aright,
And whilst this joy o'er others' years I cast
In unshared sorrow must my own be pass'd:
Weary the path, and, when that path be trod,
'Tis mine in agony to pass to God:
O, bitter portion!—but my pity still
Can whisper blessings on the blind who kill;
The love that stays me through the woe of death
Shall find expression with my parting breath,
And plead, as Hatred's roar my spirit stuns,
"Father, forgive, for they too are Thy sons!"'
Such stooped on Palestine the Heavenly Dove:
His portion, poverty—his weapon, Love:
The olive branch of peace to man He bore,
And stretched that sceptre every nation o'er:
His parting smile was joy, his dying prayer
Breathed hope his murderers that joy might share.
If oft, whilst adding weary year to year,
Big from his eye would roll the burning tear,
His own woe never did such drops betray;
'Twas that he yearned all tears to wipe away,
And bore—and gladly bore—the pangs of earth
That others' joy might from his pain have birth;
His starry life a bright example, given
To point the erring to the peace of heaven."

Next we have a review of the corruptions which gradually crept into the Church. It concludes with the following fine lines:—

"'I bid ye love,' said Christ,—His Church's way
To read such Scripture was, 'He bids Me slay.'
Her dogmas shaped she human doubts to test,
And butchered rebels with a holy zest;
And, lest the Hell she preached in myths had birth,
For ages strove to make a hell of earth:
The hideous stake she reared, and bleared the sun
With smoke from pyres where devilry was done;
And still an unreal Satan cursed, nor knew
Herself was fouler than the Shape she drew.
The Heaven she promised was an arbour, blest
With all the languor of eternal rest,
Where lazy saints some droning psalm might suit
To match the thrillings of a golden lute;
Or, journeying slow through never-ending spheres,
In blissful idlesse spend their wealth of years:
Their single task in concert palms to flaunt,
And, gathered round God's throne, Hosannas chant,
Prompt, should Hell's mouths send forth too weird a groan,
With anthems loud to hide the horrid tone.
Alas, that Hell!—the terrors round it set
Were such as ne'er in older Tophets met:
Clasped to one burning bosom, son and sire
Writhe hopelessly in never—slack'ning fire;
The air is flame,—the only language, cries
Of tortured spirits howling blasphemies;
And, mingling with these sounds, the serpent's hiss
Or demon's laugh floats wild from the abyss,
And deathless fire is wrapped each heart around,
And every brow with knotted snakes is bound;
Whilst livid Furies hang the sufferers o'er,
And cry—'This torment is for evermore.'
No tears are known—for how may tears be shed
Whilst brow and brain seem charged with molten lead?
No tears are seen; but each pale wretch his eye
May lift despairing to a distant sky,
And view, enthroned 'mid Paradise's glow,
An unmoved Sire who coldly scans his woe;
And catch, as zephyrs bear them from above,
The echoings of the anthem 'God is love.'"

"And Love Thou truly art!" proceeds the poet:

"And Love Thou truly art!—nor ever gave
As limit of that boundless love the Grave.
I bow, and thank Thee, Father, that no sea
Of flame and darkness shuts my soul from Thee:
Wide are the heavens that of Thy glory tell,
Yet all too narrow for the bigot's hell;
And still the chastisements Thou shapest prove

Thy justice tempered with exceeding love;
A love that shall at length be understood
When all of ill hath blossomed into good."

Here my extracts must cease. The conclusion is at least equal to anything given by me, but I can accord no more space; and I trust, besides, that some brother spiritualists who can discern nobler things in spiritualism than dark *séances*, puppet-shows, and third-rate jugglery, will unite to find means whereby so beautiful a composition, and one that cannot fail to reflect honour on our cause, may be given to the world in its entirety. The fragments I have printed here will serve to indicate what the poem is as a whole, and I trust there remains enough elevation of sentiment amongst spiritualists to prevent that poem being lost.

The Recorded Mediumship of D. D. Home

Mental Mediumship:
- Clairvoyance
- Healing
- Second-sight (Precognition)
- Trance communication
- Trance healing
- Trance impersonation
- Trance prescription
- Trance speaking in foreign languages

Physical Mediumship:
- Apports
- Direct writing
- Electrical sparks from fingers, able to light a gas jet
- Elongation and shrinking of body
- Fire/flames coming from body
- Images from a sitters mind displayed in a crystal placed on head
- Independent voice
- Innocuous contact with fire
- Levitation of himself
- Levitation of objects
- Materialisation of hands
- Materialisation, full
- Movement of objects
- Playing of musical instruments whilst being touched
- Playing of musical instruments without being touched
- Raps (percussion)
- Removal and restoring the smell and taste of a lemon
- Removal of heat from burning object
- Spirit lights
- Spirit music
- Spirit perfumes
- Transfiguration

Unknown Phenomena:
'Phenomenon of a gradual change from darkness to no earthly dawn.'
"There occurred a gradual illumination of the apartment. It appeared like the twilight half an hour after the dawn. The light continued to increase for about fifteen minutes, and then it gradually diminished."

SDU PUBLICATIONS
PIONEER SERIES

J. J. Morse	Practical Occultism and a Spirit Interviewed
Nettie Colburn Maynard	Was Abraham Lincoln a Spiritualist?
Emma Hardinge	Questions Answered Extempore
Margery Crandon	"Margery" The Medium
Helen Hughes	The Mediumship of Helen Hughes
Estelle Roberts	Fifty Years a Medium

For more information visit our website www.sdu3.com or contact me:

MINISTER STEVEN UPTON
Tel: 01909 489828
Email: steven@s-upton.com